The WPA Guide to 1930s

New Jersey

The WPA Guide to 1930s New Jersey

Compiled and Written by the Federal Writers' Project of the
Works Progress Administration for the State of New Jersey

Sponsored by The Public Library of Newark
and The New Jersey Guild Associates

AMERICAN GUIDE SERIES

RUTGERS UNIVERSITY PRESS
New Brunswick, New Jersey

FIRST PUBLISHED IN JUNE 1939 by The Viking Press
Reprinted in 1986 by Rutgers University Press

Library of Congress Cataloging-in-Publication Data

New Jersey, a guide to its present and past.
The WPA guide to 1930s New Jersey.

Reprint. Originally published: New Jersey, a guide
to its present and past. New York : Viking Press, 1939.
(American guide series)
Bibliography: p.
Includes index.
1. New Jersey—Description and travel—Guide-books.
I. Federal Writers' Project (N.J.)   II. Newark Public
Library.   III. New Jersey Guild Associates.   IV. Title.
V. Series: American guide series.
F132.3.N46   1986   917.49'0443   85–25599
ISBN 0–8135–1152–6

NEW JERSEY GUILD ASSOCIATES, INC.

Louis Adamic	Dr. Paul F. Lazarsfeld
Prof. John E. Bebout	Dr. Eduard C. Lindeman
Franklin Conklin, 3rd.	Mrs. William Milwitzky
Alexander L. Crosby	Charles A. Philhower
Mrs. Arne Fisher	Joseph Reilly
Louis Ginsberg	Sylvia Smith
Dr. Milton R. Konvitz	Michael A. Stavitzky
Dr. William Carlos Williams	

Contents

LIST OF ILLUSTRATIONS ix

LIST OF MAPS xv

PUBLISHER'S NOTE TO 1986 EDITION xvii

SPONSORS' FOREWORDS xviii

SPONSOR AND PUBLISHERS' NOTES TO SECOND 1939 EDITION xix

PREFACE xxi

GENERAL INFORMATION xxiv

CALENDAR OF EVENTS xxx

TOUR KEY MAP xxxiv—xxxv

I. New Jersey: The General View

A NEW JERSEY SILHOUETTE 3

NATURAL SETTING: 7

Geography, Topography, and Climate; Geology and Paleontology; Plant and Animal Life; Conservation and Natural Resources

ARCHEOLOGY AND INDIANS 28

HISTORY 35

GOVERNMENT 55

INDUSTRY AND COMMERCE 69

LABOR 79

AGRICULTURE 89

TRANSPORTATION AND COMMUNICATION 96

THE PRESS 110

RACIAL AND NATIONAL GROUPS 118

FOLKLORE AND FOLKWAYS 126

EDUCATION 134

RELIGION 142

THE ARTS: 151

Literature; Theater; Music; Architecture; Painting, Sculpture, and Crafts

II. Cities and Towns

ATLANTIC CITY 189

BAYONNE 201

BORDENTOWN 207

BURLINGTON 216

CAMDEN 225

ELIZABETH 238

FREEHOLD   250
HACKENSACK   256
HOBOKEN   262
JERSEY CITY   270
MORRISTOWN   283
MOUNT HOLLY   292
NEW BRUNSWICK   298
NEWARK   312
THE ORANGES AND MAPLEWOOD   339
PASSAIC   345
PATERSON   349
PERTH AMBOY   361
PRINCETON   370
SALEM   390
TRENTON   398

III. Tours

TOUR 1.   (New York, N. Y.)–Jersey City–Elizabeth–
Trenton–(Morrisville, Pa.). US 1   417

TOUR 2.   Newark–Hillside–Clinton–Phillipsburg–
(Easton, Pa.). US 22   428

TOUR 3.   (Piermont, N. Y.)–Alpine–Fort Lee. US 9W   435

TOUR 4.   (Suffern, N. Y.)–Pompton–Morristown–Lambertville–
(New Hope, Pa.). US 202   439

TOUR 5.   (Unionville, N. Y.)–Sussex–Newton–Columbia–
(Portland, Pa.). STATE 8N, unnumbered road,
STATE 8   452

TOUR 6.   (Milford, Pa.)–Montague–Newton–Trenton–
Junction with US 30. US 206   459

TOUR 6A.   Montague–Walpack Center–Flatbrookville–
Rosencrans Ferry. Old Mine Rd.   472

TOUR 7.   Morsemere–Dover–Hackettstown–(Portland, Pa.).
US 46   475

TOUR 8.   Elizabeth–New Brunswick–Princeton. STATE 27   484

TOUR 9.   Newark–Montclair–Franklin–High Point Park–
(Port Jervis, N. Y.). STATE 23   490

TOUR 9A.   Junction with STATE 23–Ringwood–Greenwood Lake–
Junction with STATE 23. unnumbered roads   499

Tour 10.   Elizabeth–Morristown–Washington–Phillipsburg–
                        (Easton, Pa.). STATE S24, STATE 24   508

Tour 11.   Lambertville–Washington Crossing–Trenton. STATE 29   519

Tour 12.   Junction with STATE 30–Flemington–Frenchtown–
                        (Uhlerstown, Pa.). STATE 12   523

Tour 13.   Middlesex–New Brunswick–Old Bridge–
                                    Matawan. STATE S28   527

Tour 14.   West Orange–Whippany–Ledgewood. STATE 10   529

Tour 15.   Buttzville–Ringoes–Trenton. STATE 30   533

Tour 16.   (Hillburn, N. Y.)–North Arlington–Newark–
                        Junction with US 22. STATE 2, STATE 21   538

Tour 17.   (Staten Island, N. Y.)–Elizabeth–Plainfield–
                        Somerville–Junction with US 22 and US 206.
                                    STATE 28   546

Tour 18.   Junction with US 1–Perth Amboy–Toms River–
                                    Cape May. US 9   551

Tour 18A. Freehold–Tennent–Monmouth Battlefield.
                                    COUNTY 22 and 3   565

Tour 19.   Junction with US 1–Hightstown–Camden–Pennsville–
                        (New Castle, Del.). US 130   569

Tour 20.   Ocean Grove–Freehold–Hightstown–Trenton. STATE 33   579

Tour 20A. Junction with STATE 33–Imlaystown–Fillmore.
                                    unnumbered roads   583

Tour 21.   Matawan–Colt's Neck–Junction with STATE 35.
                                    STATE 34   588

Tour 22.   South Amboy–Red Bank–Point Pleasant–
                                    Lakewood. STATE 35   591

Tour 23.   Atlantic City–Berlin–Camden–(Philadelphia, Pa.).
                                    US 30   596

Tour 23A. Egg Harbor City–Batsto–Pleasant Mills.
                                    unnumbered roads   602

Tour 24.   Atlantic City–Malaga–Pennsville–
                        (New Castle, Del.). US 40   607

Tour 25.   McKee City–Williamstown–Glassboro–Bridgeport–
                        (Chester, Pa.). US 322   611

Tour 26.   Lakewood–Wrightstown–Camden. unnumbered roads,
                                    STATE 38   615

TOUR 27. Laurelton–Lakehurst–Medford–
Junction with STATE 38. STATE 40   622

TOUR 28. Junction with US 130–Woodbury–Mullica Hill–
Salem. STATE 45   628

TOUR 29. Pennsville–Salem–Millville–Clermont. Pennsville–
Salem Rd., STATE 49   631

TOUR 29A. Salem–Oakwood Beach–Elsinboro Point. Tilbury Rd.,
Fort Elfsborg–Salem Rd.   641

TOUR 29B. Shiloh–Roadstown–Greenwich. unnumbered roads   643

TOUR 29C. South Dennis–Rio Grande–Wildwood. STATE S49   645

TOUR 30. Point Pleasant–Seaside Heights–Lakehurst. STATE 37   647

TOUR 31. (Philadelphia, Pa.)–Camden–Mount Ephraim–
Junction with US 322. STATE 42   649

TOUR 32. Mullica Hill–Pittsgrove–Bridgeton. STATE 46   654

TOUR 33. Brooklawn–Malaga–Millville–Tuckahoe. STATE 47   657

TOUR 34. Egg Harbor City–Tuckahoe–Seaville. STATE 50   663

TOUR 35. Ship Bottom–Manahawkin–Junction with STATE 40.
STATE S40   666

TOUR 35A. Ship Bottom–Harvey Cedars–Barnegat City.
unnumbered road   669

TOUR 35B. Ship Bottom–Beach Haven–Holgate. unnumbered road   672

TOUR 36. Mechanicsville–Long Branch–Asbury Park–Brielle.
STATE 36, COUNTY 9, STATE 4N   675

TOUR 37. (Philadelphia, Pa.)–Palmyra–Junction with US 30.
STATE S41   685

IV. Appendices

CHRONOLOGY   689

BIBLIOGRAPHY   697

INDEX   705

Illustrations

THE STATEHOUSE, TRENTON   Page   2
W. Lincoln Highton

THE PULASKI SKYWAY   4
N. J. State Highway Commission

PASSAIC RIVER FROM PULASKI SKYWAY   9
W. Lincoln Highton

SCHOOLEYS MOUNTAIN   15
W. Lincoln Highton

OYSTER FLEET ON COHANSEY RIVER   25
Charles W. Benson

THE OLD BARRACKS, TRENTON   43
W. Lincoln Highton

ROEBLING PLANT, TRENTON   73
Roebling Co.

CANNING TOMATOES, CAMDEN   77
Campbell Soup Co.

SILK MILL WORKER, PATERSON   83
Samuel Epstein

HARVESTING CRANBERRIES   91

RAILROAD YARDS, WEEHAWKEN   97
Samuel Epstein

THE "JOHN BULL"   101

UNLOADING LUMBER, PORT NEWARK   105
W. Lincoln Highton

STATE NORMAL SCHOOL, GLASSBORO   135
Charles W. Benson

TRINITY EPISCOPAL CHURCH, NEWARK   143
W. Lincoln Highton

WALT WHITMAN'S TOMB, CAMDEN   155
Nathaniel Rubel

THE DEMAREST HOUSE, RIVER EDGE   173
Nathaniel Rubel

COLONIAL APARTMENTS, BORDENTOWN   177
Samuel Epstein

STATUE OF LINCOLN, NEWARK 183
W. Lincoln Highton

BEACH FRONT, ATLANTIC CITY 191
Fairchild Aerial Surveys, Inc.

MUNICIPAL AUDITORIUM ATLANTIC CITY 199
Fred Hess and Son

BAYONNE BRIDGE 205
Samuel Epstein

CLARA BARTON SCHOOL. BORDENTOWN 214
Nathaniel Rubel

HISTORICAL SOCIETY BUILDING, BURLINGTON 223
Charles W. Benson

VIEW OF CAMDEN FROM PHILADELPHIA 227
Fairchild Aerial Surveys, Inc.

WALT WHITMAN HOME, CAMDEN 233
Charles W. Benson

SHIPBUILDING, CAMDEN 236
N. Y. Shipbuilding Co.

FIRST PRESBYTERIAN CHURCH, ELIZABETH 241
W. Lincoln Highton

RUG WEAVING, FREEHOLD 251
W. Lincoln Highton

BERGEN COUNTY COURTHOUSE 257
Samuel Epstein

S.S. LEVIATHAN AT HOBOKEN 265
W. Lincoln Highton

HOLLAND TUNNEL 273
Port of N. Y. Authority

THE MEDICAL CENTER, JERSEY CITY 281
W. Lincoln Highton

THE FORD MANSION, MORRISTOWN 290
W. Lincoln Highton

BURLINGTON CO. COURTHOUSE, MT. HOLLY 295
W. Lincoln Highton

QUEEN'S BUILDING, RUTGERS UNIVERSITY 307
W. Lincoln Highton

VOORHEES CHAPEL 310
N. J. College for Women

DOWNTOWN NEWARK 315
Fairchild Aerial Surveys, Inc.

AMERICAN INSURANCE CO. BUILDING, NEWARK 321
W. Lincoln Highton

PENNSYLVANIA R.R. LIFT BRIDGE   333
   Samuel Epstein

NEWARK AIRPORT   337
   W. Lincoln Highton

PASSAIC FALLS, PATERSON   350
   Samuel Epstein

THE WESTMINSTER, PERTH AMBOY   366
   Nathaniel Rubel

NASSAU HALL, PRINCETON UNIVERSITY   373
   W. Lincoln Highton

PRINCETON UNIVERSITY CHAPEL   377
   Nathaniel Rubel

PRINCETON GRADUATE COLLEGE   387
   Nathaniel Rubel

SALEM OAK   395
   W. Lincoln Highton

BATTLE MONUMENT, TRENTON   411
   W. Lincoln Highton

GEORGE WASHINGTON MEMORIAL BRIDGE   416
   Samuel Epstein

HAMILTON-BURR DUEL MARKER   420
   Samuel Epstein

GENERAL MOTORS ASSEMBLY LINE   425
   General Motors Corp.

STANDARD OIL REFINERY, BAYWAY   427
   Esso Marketers

WASHINGTON BRIDGE, APPROACHES   436
   Fairchild Aerial Surveys, Inc.

OAKLAND   443
   Nathaniel Rubel

DAIRY PLANT, POMPTON PLAINS   447
   Nathaniel Rubel

SMITH'S STORE, WATERLOO   465
   Nathaniel Rubel

MUSCONETCONG RIVER   469
   Samuel Epstein

PICATINNY ARSENAL   479
   N. Y. Journal-American

HIGH POINT MONUMENT   491
   Fairchild Aerial Surveys, Inc.

RINGWOOD MANOR   503
   Nathaniel Rubel

Post Office, Ralston 515
Samuel Epstein

Covered Bridge, Stockton 521
Samuel Epstein

Chick Hatchery 526
W. Lincoln Highton

Harvesting Wheat 537
Samuel Epstein

The Steuben House, River Edge 541
W. Lincoln Highton

Newark Waterfront 545
W. Lincoln Highton

Raritan River 553
Fairchild Aerial Surveys, Inc.

Duck Shooting, South Jersey 558
Fred Hess and Son

Beach at Ocean City 561
Atlantic Studios

Surf Casting, Cape May 564
Atlantic Studios

Old Tennent Church 567
Samuel Epstein

Chesterfield Friends Meeting House 573
W. Lincoln Highton

Lincoln Forge, Fillmore 585
Nathaniel Rubel

Pine Barrens 603
W. Lincoln Highton

Swedesboro 614
Samuel Epstein

Pottery Worker, Haddonfield 619

U. S. Naval Hangar, Lakehurst 625
Nathaniel Rubel

Hancock House, Hancock's Bridge 633
W. Lincoln Highton

Unloading Oysters, Bivalve 636
Samuel Epstein

Oystermen's Community Center 639
Samuel Epstein

AUCTION AT GREENWICH 644
W. Lincoln Highton

HORSE BREEDING FARM, BELLMAWR 653
Charles W. Benson

PARVIN STATE PARK 659
N. J. State Dept. of Conservation and Development

KIMBLE GLASS WORKS, VINELAND 661
Nijholm

SPEEDBOATS, GREAT EGG HARBOR 665
Atlantic Studios

BARNEGAT LIGHTHOUSE 671
W. Lincoln Highton

SANDY HOOK LIGHTHOUSE 677
Nathaniel Rubel

GUGGENHEIM MANSION, LONG BRANCH 681
Samuel Epstein

BURNING MORRO CASTLE 684
Fairchild Aerial Surveys, Inc.

Maps

TOUR KEY MAP	Page xxxiv–xxxv
ATLANTIC CITY	196
BORDENTOWN	211
BURLINGTON	219
CAMDEN	231
ELIZABETH	243
HOBOKEN	267
JERSEY CITY	278
MORRISTOWN	287
NEW BRUNSWICK	302
NEWARK	326
NEWARK BUSINESS DISTRICT	327
PATERSON	356
PERTH AMBOY	365
PRINCETON	382
TRENTON	406

Publisher's Note
to 1986 Edition

During the 1930s the Federal Writers' Project of the New Deal Works Progress Administration employed thousands of people in need of work to write a set of travel books known as the American Guide Series. A guide was written for each of the forty-eight states and for Alaska, as well as for selected cities and towns. Many of the guides have been reprinted since the thirties. We are pleased to be able to reprint the guide to New Jersey, originally titled *New Jersey: A Guide to its Present and Past*. The authors and consultants who worked on this book included well-known literary figures such as William Carlos Williams and Louis Adamic as well as aspiring authors with no literary reputation then or now.

We have photoreproduced our edition from the original 1939 edition. The second printing of that edition included a correction inserted over the Neptune City entry on page 594. We have retained the original version, but have reproduced the corrected version on page 595, in place of a photograph, "Sailing on the Atlantic." In addition, we have omitted an oversize map of New Jersey that was placed in a pocket glued into the binding at the back of the book, and we have moved the Tour Key Map, originally printed as endpapers, to pages xxxiv–xxxv.

There is one other detail worthy of note in the publishing history of this volume. The authors of the guide, represented by the New Jersey Guild Associates, and the publisher of the second printing, Hastings House, had a dispute over politically sensitive material that had been stricken from the manuscript and never restored. A record of that dispute was included in the second printing. We have reprinted that record on page xix.

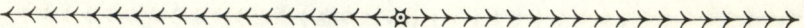

Sponsors' Forewords

This story of New Jersey is cause for pride to those who love the State, but must also give pause to those who can be critical at the same time.

Its beauty and romance, its ugliness and the commonplace have been preserved in an unusual balance by the collaborators in the evaluation of the State.

The Editors are to be heartily congratulated upon an achievement of note, as this Guide is a distinct contribution to a knowledge of the history of New Jersey.

BEATRICE WINSER, *Librarian*
Newark Public Library

The New Jersey Guild Associates as co-sponsors with the Newark Public Library have a deep sense of satisfaction in bringing before the public the *New Jersey Guide.* Here at last is an authentic story of our State that will warm the hearts of the old residents and prove interesting reading for anyone who may happen upon it.

Highways and wayside taverns are adequately described, but this new kind of guide leads to strange and remote places. It undertakes excursions into history and economics and the arts. Afield, it detours from the main traveled roads for unexpected forays to spots that scarcely one tourist in a thousand would find unaided—places that are unknown even to the motor-minded residents of New Jersey. In a very real sense the book lifts up familiar, sun-baked stones to reveal the quiet life beneath.

Our hope is that publication of new and revised editions of the Guide may become a New Jersey custom.

THE NEW JERSEY GUILD ASSOCIATES

Sponsor and Publishers' Notes
to Second 1939 Edition

The New Jersey Guild Associates is glad to present a reprint of the *New Jersey Guide*. The 5,000 copies printed in 1939 have been sold—a solid testimonial to the work of the WPA writers, research workers, and editors who wrote the book. Hastings House, the new publisher, plans to maintain a permanent staff for the later revision of this and other state guides.

We regret that some facts in New Jersey labor history, which were stricken from the original manuscript in 1938 at the instigation of the Dies Committee Investigating Un-American Activities, have not been restored in this reprint. The deleted references concerned the use of teargas in a strike of agricultural workers at Seabrook Farms in 1934; the activities of 300 guards which Radio Corporation of America Manufacturing Company hired through a detective agency during a strike at its Camden plant in 1936, and the use of detective agencies by corporations such as Campbell Soup Company, Phelps-Dodge Copper Products Corporation, Congoleum-Nairn Inc., and New York Ship Building Corporation.

The details are part of the printed record of the La Follette Committee's investigation. Since they were published by the daily newspapers and other periodicals, there seems to be no good reason to fear that publication in the *Guide* would result in libel suits.

Despite these omissions, the book as a whole gives an honest portrait of the State—a portrait that is unusual because the writers detoured from the main roads to explore lonely spots that few tourists would ever find.

THE NEW JERSEY GUILD ASSOCIATES

Publishers' Note

The Publishers regret the difference that has arisen between them and the New Jersey Guild Associates, sponsor of the New Jersey State Guide, as to inclusion in the present edition of certain material concerning the history of labor in New Jersey, omitted from the first edition of the *Guide*. The Publishers are reliably informed that the material referred to in the Associates' statement printed herewith, was not originally omitted because of political pressure, but for the same reason that it is omitted now. The Publishers' agreement with the Associates provides that new material to be offered by the Associates would be included in the new edition, provided it was not libelous. Such material was received in due course by the Publishers and submitted by the Publishers to competent counsel, who advised that it might be held libelous if untrue and accordingly might well expose the Publishers to claims for damages by the parties alleging that they had been libelled. Hastings House, therefore, availed itself of its right under the terms of the agreement with the Associates, to reject the new material. This new edition of the admirable New Jersey State Guide, written by the Federal Writers Project of New Jersey, is reprinted without any change of text whatever.

WORKS PROGRESS ADMINISTRATION

F. C. Harrington, *Administrator*

Florence S. Kerr, *Assistant Administrator*

Henry G. Alsberg, *Director of the Federal Writers' Project*

Preface

NEW JERSEY: *A Guide to Its Present and Past* is an attempt to present not only the background and development of old New Jersey, but also the rapidly changing scene of the State today. If the book achieves its purpose it will serve a contemporary need, and in addition it will preserve the flavor of present-day New Jersey for scholars of the future.

The guide is a cooperative product, the work of field workers and research workers, of writers and editors, and of competent authorities in every department of New Jersey life. Newspaper files, libraries, and many other sources have been searched for information; mechanics and farmers, scholars and policemen, artists and aviators have been interviewed. Most of the material, however, has been gathered first-hand: every major city in the State has been studied by reporters, and field workers have traveled every foot of the main highways from High Point Park to Cape May. Checking and rechecking of these thousands of items have produced, it is hoped, a minimum of error. We ask readers who find mistakes to write to the publisher, so that future editions may be corrected.

In order to keep this one-volume guide within practical book length, it has been necessary to abridge drastically the voluminous data assembled in the course of the project. Much of this material, however, will be made available in detailed studies or in encyclopedic form at a later time.

It would be an endless task to list all the consultants whose aid has made the book possible. Special thanks are due, however, to Miss Beatrice Winser for making available the facilities of the Newark Public Library and for her valuable assistance; and to Dr. Milton R. Konvitz, who acted as general consultant. Specialists in various fields have contributed materially in the preparation of several of the introductory essays. Professor John E. Bebout of the University of Newark directed the work on the *History* essay and, in collaboration with Professor Fred Killian, also of the University of Newark, contributed the section entitled *Government*. Professor Herbert Woodward of the University of Newark contributed the section on *Geology,* and together with Dr. Horace G. Richards of the State Museum provided the material on *Paleontology*. Professor Carl Woodward of Rutgers University wrote most of the essay on

Agriculture. The chapter entitled *Archeology and Indians* is the work of Dr. Dorothy Cross of the Indian Sites Survey.

Among others who gave valuable criticism are: Sarah B. Askew, secretary and librarian of the State Public Library Commission; Professor Robert G. Albion of Princeton University; Theodosia Bates, director of the New Jersey Gallery of Kresge department store, Newark; Mary Boggan, Hackensack librarian; Henry Reed Bowen, general secretary of the New Jersey Council of Religious Education; Van Wyck Brooks; Professor J. Douglas Brown of Princeton University; Professor L. H. Buckingham of Newark University; the Reverend Ellis B. Burgess of the United Lutheran Synod of New York; Elizabeth V. Colville, editor of *Musical New Jersey;* J. Hallam Conover of Freehold; Royal Cortissoz, art editor of the New York *Herald Tribune;* Elbert Cox, superintendent of Morristown National Historical Park; Phoebe Crosby of Philadelphia; Kenneth W. Dalzell of the American Institute of Architects; George de Cou of Moorestown; Professor Frank de Vyver of Duke University; Professor Norman Foerster, director of the School of Letters at the University of Iowa; the Reverend William Hiram Foulkes, of Old First Presbyterian Church of Newark; Lewis Gannett of the New York *Herald Tribune;* the Reverend L. Hamilton Garner of Newark; Marguerite L. Gates, assistant librarian, Newark; C. A. George, Elizabeth librarian; Louis Ginsberg of Paterson; Nathan L. Goldberg, assistant editor of the *Guild Reporter;* Abe J. Greene, city editor of the Paterson *Evening News;* the Reverend R. D. Gribbon, Archdeacon of the New Jersey Diocese of the Protestant Episcopal Church; Stephen Haff Jr., trustee of the Jersey City Museum Association; Edward Sothern Hipp, dramatic editor of the Newark *Sunday Call;* William S. Hunt, publisher of the Newark *Sunday Call;* Edward Alden Jewell, art editor of the New York *Times;* Laurence B. Johnson, managing editor of the *New Jersey Educational Review;* Professor Wheaton J. Lane of Princeton University; Frank Jewett Mather, director of the Princeton Museum of Historic Art; Nell L. Meyers, Freehold librarian; George Miller, regional director of the Historical Records Survey; William Milwitzky of Newark; Professor Sherley Morgan, director of Princeton University School of Architecture; Lewis Mumford; Grace D. McKinney, religion editor of the Newark *Evening News;* Howard D. McKinney, director of Rutgers University School of Music; Maurice F. Neufeld, acting secretary of the New Jersey State Planning Board; George A. Osborne, Rutgers University librarian; Frederick S. Osborne, director of public information at Princeton University; William J. Pickersgill of Perth Amboy; Charles A. Philhower, superintendent of Westfield Junior High School; Corliss Fitz Randolph, president and librarian of the Seventh Day Baptist Historical Society; Vergil D. Reed, assistant director of the Bureau of the Census; Leonard H. Robbins of the New York *Times;* Grace D. Rose, Morristown librarian; Joseph S. Sickler, postmaster of Salem, New Jersey; Samuel Slaff of Passaic; Professor James G. Smith of Princeton University; Mary Cook Swartwout, director of the Montclair Art Museum; Cornelia B. Thompson, principal of Asbury Park High School; Professor Willard Thorp of Princeton University; Norman F. Titus, secretary of the State Chamber of Commerce; Lydia Weston, Burlington librarian; A. Edmund Williamson, executive secretary of the Chamber of Commerce of the Oranges and Maplewood; and Edmund Wilson.

This book was prepared under the supervision of Mrs. Irene Fuhlbruegge, State Director, and Alexander L. Crosby, State Editor, both of whom resigned before publication.

VIOLA L. HUTCHINSON
SAMUEL EPSTEIN } *Assistant State Directors*

JOSEPH SUGARMAN, JR.
IRVING D. SÜSS
BENJAMIN GOLDENBERG
FRED EPPELSHEIMER } *Editors*

General Information

Railroads: Pennsylvania (Pennsy); Delaware, Lackawanna and Western (Lackawanna); Central Railroad of New Jersey (Jersey Central); Erie; Lehigh Valley; West Shore; Baltimore and Ohio (B & O); and Reading serve important points. Hudson and Manhattan R.R. (the Tubes) between Newark, Jersey City, Hoboken, and New York.

Bus Lines: Interstate: Greyhound, Public Service, Pan-American, Martz, Safeway Trailways, Golden Arrow, Champlain, Edwards, De Camp, Garden State, Jersey Central-Reading Transportation, and others. Intrastate: Public Service and many small independent lines connecting principal towns and cities.

Steamship Lines: Jersey City: Dollar Line, "Round the World"; American Export, to Mediterranean ports; American-Scantic Lines, to Scandinavia, Poland, Russia; Moormack, to South America. Hoboken: Gdynia-American, to Poland, Denmark, West Indies, Bermuda; Holland-America, to Europe, Cuba, Mexico; Cosulich, to Mediterranean and Adriatic ports; Red Star, to Belgium; Lamport and Holt, to South America.

Airlines: Newark: terminal of Transcontinental & Western Air, United Airlines, Eastern Airlines, and American Airlines. Camden: airport for Philadelphia, terminal of United Airlines (western route), Transcontinental & Western Air, Eastern Airlines, and American Airlines.

Highways: Ten Federal highways, including US 1 from Canada to Miami and US 30 from Atlantic City to Astoria, Ore. All State and U. S. routes patrolled by State police. Gasoline tax 4¢.

Traffic Regulations: Speed Limits: 40 m.p.h. on open highway, 15 approaching intersections; 20 in residential and business districts; unless posted otherwise, 15 in town and city districts *not* controlled by lights or traffic officers; 10 in all school or other restricted districts. General Rules of the Road: Driver approaching intersection from right has right-of-way.

No turn may be made at a red light, unless indicated by a green arrow or sign. Vehicles must stop at least 10 ft. in rear of streetcars stopped for receiving or discharging passengers except at established safety zone. Trolley cars may be passed on R. only, except on one-way streets. Vehicles operating on roads with clearly marked lanes must keep R., using center lanes for passing only. No passing at intersections, on hills, curves, or other places where view is obstructed for minimum of 500 ft. Ambulances, fire engines, and police cars have right-of-way at all times. Two braking systems, each operating on two wheels, required. Headlights and taillights must be lit from one-half hour after sunset to one-half hour before sunrise. Nonresident may operate car without permit within the State for period reciprocally agreed upon by State of residence and New Jersey. Motorist involved in accident must wait until police appear, and report to them; or report to State police. Telephone operator will give direct connection. Trailers subject to restriction by local ordinances. *Prohibited:* Parking on paved portion of highway or on any part of road unless a 15-ft. passage is left for other vehicles, with view of 200 ft. each way. Parking within 25 ft. of intersection, or within 50 ft. of stop sign, or within 10 ft. of fire hydrant.

State Police Substations:

Absecon	Newton
Berlin	Penn's Neck
Cape May Court House	Pompton Lakes
Columbus	Port Norris
Farmingdale	Scotch Plains
Flemington	Somerville
Hightstown	Teaneck
Keyport	Toms River
Malaga	Washington
Mantua	Woodbridge
Milltown	Woodstown
Netcong	

Accommodations: Good hotels in larger cities. Many fine hotels at coast and lake resorts, open in season. Tourist homes, small hotels, and dining accommodations in nearly all towns.

Liquor Laws: Hours and days of sale and other regulations fixed by cities and towns. Package goods sold in saloons, grocery stores, drug stores, delicatessens, and similar places.

Climate and Equipment: Topcoats or wraps should supplement summer wardrobe at seashore, mountain, and lake resorts. Otherwise, seasonable wardrobe will suffice. Occasional fogs in spring and fall along the shore and lowlands. Moderate snowfall usually, but main highways are always kept open.

Poisonous Reptiles and Plants: Rattlesnakes and copperheads, while not common, are found in the northern mountains and in the pinelands of the south and central areas. Poison ivy and poison sumac are common.

Information: The State department of conservation and development, Trenton, N. J., provides leaflets and other information on State parks and forests. Excellent maps are sold by the department at nominal prices (write for list); of especial value are the atlas sheets, 27 by 37 in., covering the State with 37 maps on a scale of 1 m. to the in. (50¢ each). Bureaus of information on New Jersey travel and vacation resorts are maintained by the Newark *Evening News* and Newark *Sunday Call.*

Recreational Areas: New Jersey has 120 miles of ocean front along the Atlantic Coast and, behind it, many inlets and bays with ideal conditions for yachting and fishing. There are more than 40 beaches, patrolled by lifeguards. In most of the larger resorts the beach front is controlled by the municipality, private individuals, clubs, or hotels. Free bathing is permitted in some of the less populous sections. The northern lake region includes nearly 100 bodies of water in the woodlands and hills of Morris, Sussex, Passaic, and Warren Counties, with large summer colonies. In addition to Palisades Interstate Park, 1,700 acres held jointly with New York, the State maintains the following 14 parks: Ringwood Manor, Hacklebarney, Voorhees, Swartswood, Washington Crossing, Washington Rock, Parvin, Mount Laurel, Musconetcong, Cranberry, Hopatcong, High Point, Stephens and Cheesequake. There are eight forests operated by the State and most of the State parks and forests have free facilities for picnics; lakes for bathing and boating; well-stocked streams for fishing, subject to State laws; trails for hiking and horseback riding. Parvin and Swartswood offer free supervised swimming. The Appalachian Trail, Maine to Georgia, runs for 2 miles along the Kittatinny Ridge from Delaware Water Gap to High Point Park, the highest section of the State. Various counties have extensive park systems. The South Mountain and Eagle Rock Reservations in Essex County enclose 2,500 acres of natural forest, bridle paths, trails, camp sites, picnic grounds, and drives. The most important Federal reservation is Morristown National Historical Park. Many municipalities have recreational centers and playgrounds with wading and swimming pools and other recreational facilities for adults and children.

General Rules: Written permit required for fires in a State reservation. Many fireplaces are provided. Smokers should use extreme care; causing a fire in any forest reserve is a misdemeanor. State laws provide penalties for cutting, injury, or removal of trees, shrubs, plants, or flowers by any person without the consent of the owner of the property.

Fishing: Practically every species of salt-water fish natural to temperate waters of North America is found in the coastal waters. All the larger seashore resorts maintain fishing piers, and powerboats for deep-sea fishing. Surf casting, free on most beaches, is practiced at many spots. Among the choice trout streams are the Musconetcong, Pequest, and South Branch of the Raritan, in the northern section, and Wading River in the southern section. In addition large-mouthed and small-mouthed bass, pickerel, perch, and sunfish are plentiful throughout river and lake waters. The State distributes annually 130,000,000 fish from the Hackettstown hatchery and maintains five public fishing and hunting grounds. *License:* Resident fishing, $2.10; nonresident, $5.50. Resident hunting and fishing, $3.10; nonresident, $10.50. Note: Hunting and fishing laws are changed frequently; tourists are advised to obtain up-to-date information. Licenses are issued by the State fish and game commission, Trenton, N. J., through agents including city and county clerks and other local officials.

Fishing Laws: Game fish are defined as bass, trout, pike, perch, and pickerel. *Open Seasons* (dates inclusive): Broad, brown, rainbow trout, and salmon, Apr. 15–July 15 and Sept 1-30; bass and crappie, June 15–Nov. 30, except from Delaware River. Pike, pickerel and pike-perch, May 20–Nov. 30 and Jan. 1-20, except from Delaware River. From Delaware River and Bay tributaries: bass, crappie, pike-perch, pickerel, pike, and trout, June 15–Dec. 1. From Delaware River and tributaries between Trenton Falls and Birch Creek; bass, crappie, pike-perch, pickerel, pike, June 15–Dec. 1; trout, Apr. 15–July 31. *Daily Limit:* Trout and salmon, 10 (trout 7 in.); black and Oswego bass, 20 in all (9 in.); rock bass, 20; calico bass and crappie, 20 in all (6 in.). Pike, pickerel, and pike-perch, no daily limit from open water; 10 when fishing through ice (14 in.); 10 from Delaware River (12 in.). Trout, 10 (6 in.), from Delaware River, Bay and tributaries.

Prohibited: Sale or purchase of black or Oswego bass, except for propagating; sale of pike-perch, pike or pickerel caught through the ice; fishing for trout, bass, pike-perch, pike, or pickerel after 9 p.m.

Hunting: Deer, the largest game in the State, are found chiefly in the State forests set aside for their conservation, but many roam the mountains of the northern counties and the pine forests of the southern plain. The State game farms breed and release yearly about 70,000 head of small game, including rabbits, quail, and partridge. The coastal salt marshes and inlets abound in waterfowl. The northern lakes, rivers, and mountains attract quail, partridge, pheasants, etc. There is some fox hunting in Somerset and Morris Counties, and raccoon hunting with trained dogs in the country southwest of New Brunswick.

License: Same fee as fishing (see above).

Open Seasons (dates inclusive): Quail, rabbit, gray hare, black or fox squirrel, male English or ringneck pheasant, ruffed grouse, prairie chicken, wild turkey, Hungarian partridge, Nov. 10–Dec. 15. Geese, ducks, coot (crow ducks), and Wilson snipe or jacksnipe, Nov. 26–Dec. 25; sora, clapper, and king rail (marsh hen or mudhen), other rails and gallinules (except coot), Sept. 1–Nov. 30. Woodcock, Oct. 15–Nov. 14. Skunk, mink, muskrat, otter (may only be trapped), Nov. 15–Mar. 15. (No open season on wood, ruddy, bufflehead, canvasback, or redhead duck, brant, snow goose, Ross's goose, or swan.) Special State license required for woodcock. Deer (only those having horns at least 3 in. long), Dec. 17–Dec. 21. Raccoon, Nov. 1–Dec. 31, excepting deer season. *Daily Bag Limits:* 10 quail, 6 rabbits, 6 gray squirrels, 3 ruffed grouse, 2 male pheasants (30 in season), 3 Hungarian partridge; ducks (except wood, ruddy, canvasback, redhead and bufflehead), total of 10 of all kinds; geese (except snow goose, Ross's goose, and brant), total of 4 of all kinds; 15 coot, 15 Wilson's snipe or jacksnipe.

Possession Limits: One day's bag: sora, 25; other rails and gallinules (except sora and coot), total of 15 of all kinds; woodcock, 4; deer, one buck a year ($100 penalty for exceeding limit); raccoon, no daily limit, but 15 during season.

Prohibited: Use of any snare, snood, net, trap, or any device for catching or trapping game birds or game animals; shooting at any game bird or game animal from power boat, airplane, hydroplane, or automobile; use of ferrets or poisons.

Yachting and Boating: Inlets and bays along the coast are lined with summer yacht clubs. Important events yearly on Navesink, Shrewsbury, and Toms Rivers, Absecon and Barnegat Bays. For motorboats, National Sweepstakes Regatta yearly at Red Bank on the Navesink, others on the

Passaic. Speedboat races every summer at Hopatcong and other northern lakes, and on Raritan, Manasquan, and other rivers and bays. Canoeing on many rivers and lakes.

Golf: There are more than 100 golf courses in the State owned by private, semiprivate, and public clubs. The best known course is Baltusrol, at Springfield, scene of many major tournaments.

Tennis: Many municipalities provide public tennis courts, and county parks have increased tennis facilities in recent years. The Seabright Lawn Tennis Cricket Club and the Orange Lawn Tennis Club hold annual championship matches.

Other Games and Sports: Important intercollegiate football matches are held at Princeton and Rutgers. Other colleges, and high schools and private preparatory schools have scheduled games; Newark, Paterson, and Trenton have professional teams. Baseball is played informally on sandlots all over the State. Most high schools and colleges have teams, and Newark, Jersey City, and Trenton have professional teams. Outdoor polo is played at Rumson and Burnt Mills. There is bicycle racing at Nutley; automobile racing at Woodbridge; boxing and wrestling in Newark, Jersey City, and many other centers.

Winter Sports: An Erie R.R. snow train runs to High Point Park, where there are miles of ski trails and a recently completed ski jump. There are other ski jumps in county parks, closer to urban centers. All natural lakes and those in parks are used for ice skating. Tobogganing and snowshoeing are popular in many State and county parks. The North Branch of Shrewsbury River at Red Bank has been an iceboating center for 50 years. Lakewood, Morristown, and Atlantic City have ice carnivals, and Elizabeth has dog-sled races. Indoor sports include polo at Newark, East Orange, Westfield, Red Bank, and Trenton; ice hockey in the new municipal stadium at Atlantic City; track meets and basketball in armories and halls throughout the State.

Calendar of Events

(nfd means no fixed date; locations subject to change have been left blank.)

Jan.	2nd wk	Morristown	Eastern States Skeet Championship
	nfd	Morristown	Ice Carnival
	nfd	Atlantic City	Men's Championship Squash Tournaments
	nfd	Trenton	Agricultural Show
	nfd	Elizabeth	Dog-sled Races
	nfd	Watchung Reservation Union County	Cross-Country Ski Meet
	nfd	Salem	Muskrat Skinning Contest
	nfd	Newark	Metropolitan Opera
Jan.	& Feb. } nfd	Red Bank	Ice Boat Races
Jan.	or Feb. } nfd	{ Lakewood	Winter Sports Carnival
		{ Atlantic City	Ice Carnival
Feb.	14	New Brunswick	Twilight Concert
	2nd wk	Newark	Dog Show
	nfd	Atlantic City	Atlantic Coast Women's Squash Championship
	nfd	Lake Mohawk	Winter Carnival
Mar.	20	Plainfield	Union County Badminton Tournament
	4th wk	Newark	Indoor Polo Championship
	nfd	Newark	Contemporary Club, Grand Opera
	Lenten Season	Union City	Passion Play, *Veronica's Veil*
Apr.	10	Burlington (Cor. High and Broad Sts.)	Election of Officers of Council of W. Jersey Proprietors
	2nd Fri.	Statewide	Arbor Day
	26	Finns Point	Confederate Memorial Pilgrimage
	Sat. before } Palm Sun.	Atlantic City	Dog Show
	Palm Sun.	Atlantic City	Style Parade
	Easter Sun.	Atlantic City	Easter Parade
		Palmyra	Sunrise Service
		Elizabeth	Sunrise Service

nfd	Cape May	Mackerel Fleet Race from Gloucester, Mass.
May 1	Paterson	May Day Parade
15-30	Glassboro	Blossom Festival
	Pitman	Blossom Festival
31	Camden	Walt Whitman's Birthday Celebration
1st wk	Newark	Horse Show
2nd wk	Newark	Flower Show
1st & 2nd wk	South Jersey	Blossom Time in Fruit Belts
last wk	Madison	Dog Show
Decoration Day & every Sat. until Columbus Day	}Newark	Amateur Trotting Races
nfd	Atlantic City	Horse Show
nfd	Jersey City	Hudson County Progress Exposition
nfd	New Brunswick	Pageant and Horse Show
nfd	Summit	Horse Show
nfd	South Orange	Dog Show
June 5-6	Atlantic City	Flower Mart
13	Princeton	Track Meet
last wk	Rumson	Dog Show
nfd	Swedesboro	Service at Old Trinity Church
nfd	North Bergen	German Day Exercises
nfd	Camden	Outdoor Mass, American Legion
nfd	Paterson	Festival of Nations
nfd	Atlantic City	National Headliners Frolic
nfd	Newark	Open-air Symphony Concerts
nfd	Maplewood	Golf Tournament
nfd	Princeton	Westminster Choir
nfd	West Orange	Rock Spring Horse Show
July 4	New Brunswick	Outboard Motorboat Races
	Westfield	Sunrise Service
	Newark	Amateur Trotting Races
4-10	Wildwood	"Mibs" (Marbles) National Championship
16	Hammonton	Festival of Our Lady of Mt. Carmel
30-31 & Aug. 1	}Rumson	Horse Show
nfd	New Brunswick	Poultrymen's Field Day
nfd	Barnegat Bay	International Star Race
nfd	Rumson	Polo Meet

nfd	Spring Lake	Tennis Tournament
nfd	Seabright	Tennis Tournament
nfd	Deal	Women's Golf Tournament
nfd	Livingston	Golf Tournament
nfd	Rumson	Golf Tournament
Aug. 4	Elizabeth	Italian Night Program
2nd Sat.	Keyport	Salt Water Day
1st wk	Pitman	Pitman Grove Camp Meeting
2nd wk	Atlantic City	Moth Boat Races
3rd wk	Atlantic City	Life Guards Races
3rd or 4th wk	Red Bank	National Sweepstakes Regatta
4th wk	Ocean Grove	Methodist Camp Meeting
nfd	Ventnor	Middle Atlantic Coast Tennis Tournament
nfd	Pitman	Grange Day
nfd	North Bergen	Plattdeutsches Volksfest
nfd	Clementon	Drum and Bugle Corps Competition
nfd	Sea Girt	Governor Day
nfd	Asbury Park	Carnival and Baby Parade
nfd	Belvidere	Farmers' Picnic
nfd	Lake Hopatcong	Motorboat Races
Sept. 1	Port Norris	Sailing of 300 Oyster Vessels
20-25	New Brunswick	Horse Show
1st wk	Atlantic City	Showmen's Variety Jubilee (Includes Beauty Pageant)
1st wk	Newark	Trotting Meet at Weequahic Park
last wk	Trenton	State Fair
Sat. & Sun. before Labor Day	Atlantic City	Power Boat Regatta
Labor Day	Ocean City	Yacht Club Regatta
	Hohokus	Trotting Races
	Camden	Labor Day Services
	Lake Hopatcong	Yacht Races
nfd	Hohokus	Automobile Races
nfd	Hoboken	Drum and Bugle Corps Competition
nfd	Trenton	Feast of Lights (Italian)
nfd	Far Hills	Fox Hunt
nfd	Rumson	Horse Show
Oct. 11	Camden	Pulaski Day
nfd	New Brunswick	Florists' Day
nfd	New Brunswick	Chrysanthemum Field Day
nfd	Three Mile Run	Coon Dog Championship

		Newark	Electrical Show
	nfd	Newark	Electrical Show
	nfd	Paterson	Egg-laying Contest
	nfd	Camden	Food Show
	nfd	Elizabeth	"Own a Home" Show
Nov.	3rd wk	Newark	Automobile Show
	nfd	Newark	Stamp Exhibition
Dec.	24	Burlington	Singing by the Waits
	3rd wk	Newark	Horse Show
	nfd	Atlantic City	Eisteddfod (Welsh Festival)

KEY TO TOURS

TOUR	TERMINAL	PAGE
1	† Fort Lee—Trenton *	417
2	Newark—Phillipsburg *	428
3	† Alpine—Fort Lee	435
4	† Pompton—Lambertville *	439
5	† Sussex—Columbia *	452
6	* Montague—Hammonton	459
6A	Montague—Rosencrans Ferry	472
7	Morsemere—Hackettstown *	475
8	Elizabeth—Princeton	484
9	Newark—High Pt. Park †	490
9A	Jct. State 23—New Foundland	499
10	Elizabeth—Phillipsburg *	508
11	Lambertville—Trenton	519
12	Flemington—Frenchtown *	523
13	Middlesex—Matawan	527
14	West Orange—Ledgewood	529
15	Buttzville—Trenton	533
16	† Saddle River—Newark	538
17	† Elizabeth—Somerville	546
18	Woodbridge—Cape May	551
18A	Freehold—Monmouth Battlefield	565
19	Jct. US 1—Pennsville §	569
20	Ocean Grove—Trenton	579
20A	Jct. State 33—Fillmore	583
21	Matawan—Laurelton	588
22	South Amboy—Lakewood	591
23	Atlantic City—Camden *	596
23A	Egg Harbor City—Pleasant Mills	602
24	Atlantic City—Pennsville §	607
25	McKee City—Bridgeport *	611
26	Lakewood—Camden	615
27	Laurelton—Camden	622
28	Jct. US 130—Salem	628
29	Pennsville—Clermont	631
29A	Salem—Elsinboro Point	641
29B	Shiloh—Greenwich	643
29C	South Dennis—Wildwood	645
30	Point Pleasant—Lakehurst	647
31	* Camden—Williamstown	649
32	Mullica Hill—Bridgeton	654
33	Brooklawn—Tuckahoe	657
34	Egg Harbor City—Seaville	663
35	Ship Bottom—Jct. State 40	666
35A	Ship Bottom—Barnegat City	669
35B	Ship Bottom—Holgate	672
36	Mechanicsville—Brielle	675
37	* Palmyra—Jct. US 30	685

† New York line
* Pennsylvania line
§ Delaware line

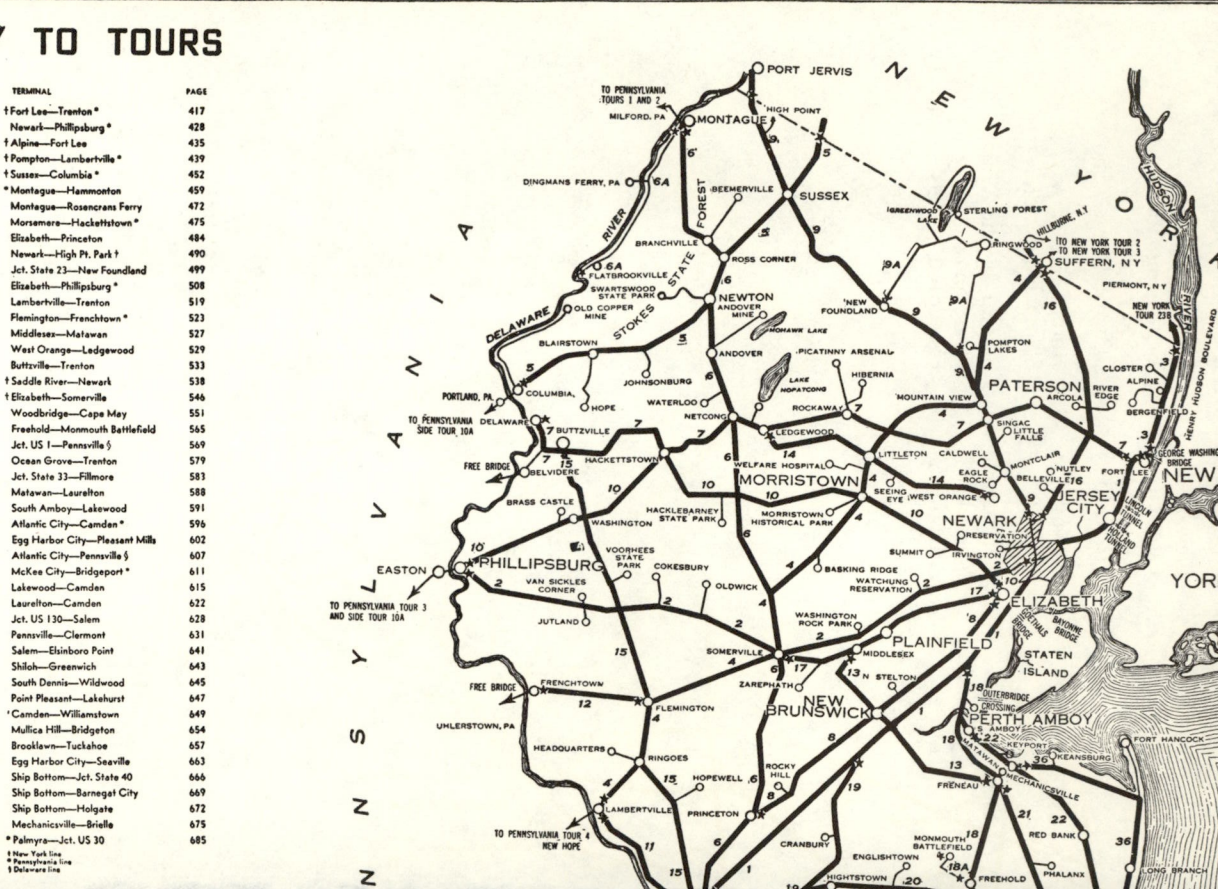

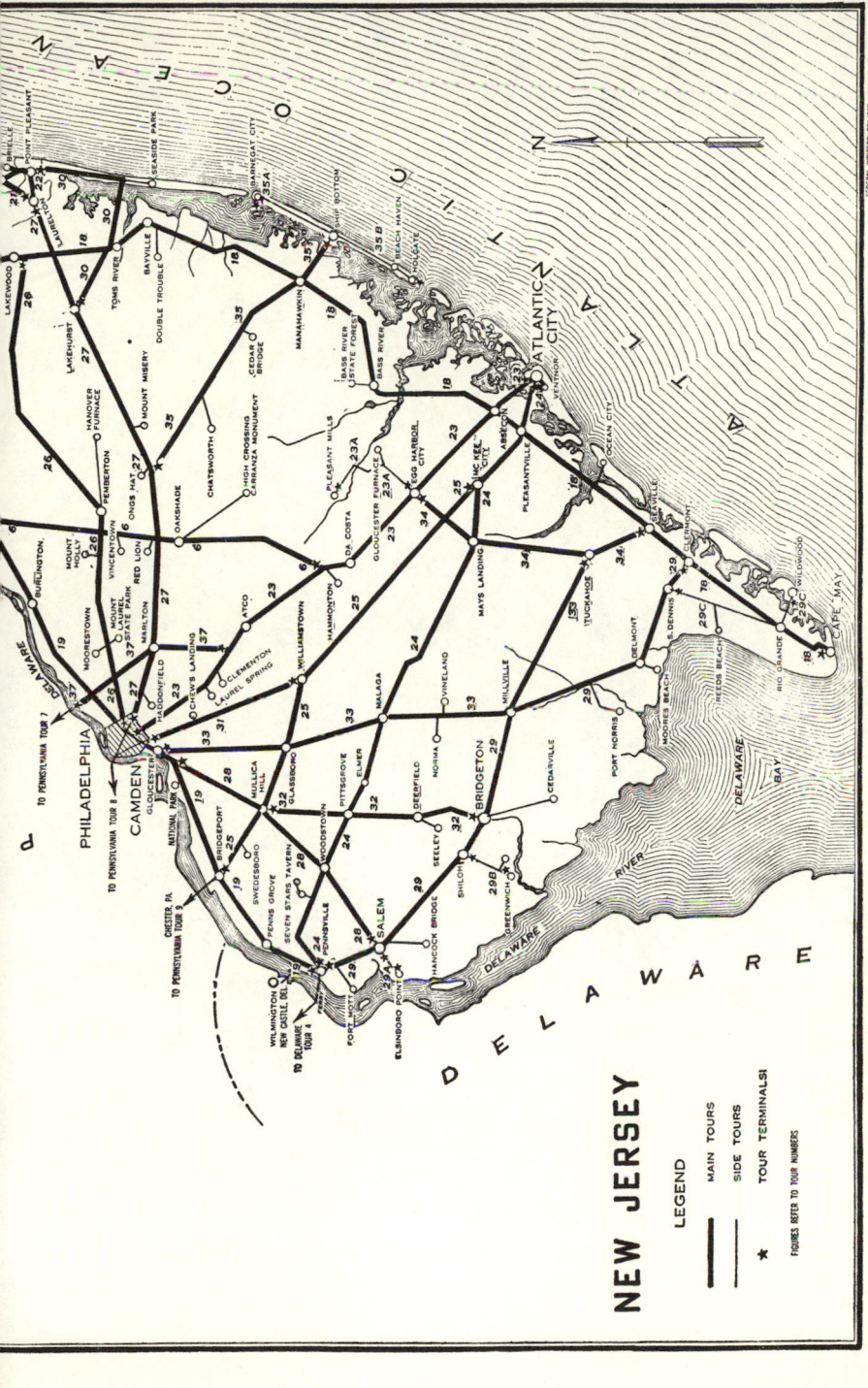

NEW JERSEY

LEGEND

— MAIN TOURS

-- SIDE TOURS

★ TOUR TERMINALS

FIGURES REFER TO TOUR NUMBERS

ATLANTIC OCEAN

DELAWARE RIVER

DELAWARE BAY

FEDERAL WRITERS PROJECT W.P.A. NEW YORK CITY.

PART I

New Jersey: The General View

THE STATE HOUSE, TRENTON

A New Jersey Silhouette

NO PHRASE or nickname can supply an index to New Jersey, for in physical and sociological composition the State is fundamentally diverse. It is often called the Garden State; with equal reason it might be labeled the Factory State, or the Commuter State.

Geographically, New Jersey offers rugged hills, and a long stretch of ocean shore attracting millions of visitors each summer; fertile soil for orchards and truck gardens, and miles of sandy waste covered by ferns and stunted pines. Industrially, the State produces an amazing variety of goods. It maintains a full quota of reasonably paid mechanics, and at the same time numerous sweatshops paying wages of $4 and $5 a week. For generations Paterson and Passaic have been national battlefields for organized labor. Yet within walking distance of these cities are other communities where picketing is considered a crime.

Politically, New Jersey is noted for one of the strongest Democratic machines of the Nation and a hardly less virile Republican organization. It is also a testing ground for the Labor Party movement. Culturally, the State is enriched by Princeton and Rutgers Universities, Stevens Institute, an excellent school system, the fine Newark Public Library, and several noted museums. Yet within an hour's ride from the most densely populated sections are mountain people who have lived for 150 years in ignorance and poverty akin to that of Southern hill folk.

Since the time when New York and Philadelphia were villages, New Jersey has been the corridor between them. Colonial post roads have evolved into the strikingly designed concrete highways and bridges that signify a motor-minded population. Fittingly, it was New Jersey that pioneered with the cloverleaf intersection to sort unceasing streams of traffic. Roads have been laid so straight and broad that the long-distance autoist speeds across the State, seeing little except a landscape of reinforced concrete and billboards, although many pleasant villages and quiet country lie a little way off the main highways.

New Jersey's characteristic disunity extends back to the years of early settlement, when the separate provinces of East Jersey and West Jersey

3

THE PULASKI SKYWAY, BETWEEN NEWARK AND JERSEY CITY

were created. The civil government and Puritanism of New England were stamped upon the eastern province, which was to become the urban manufacturing area, while the western province (now "South Jersey") concentrated on agriculture and adhered largely to the Quaker faith. Although the two provinces were united under a single government in 1702, fusion has never been completed. Residents of southern New Jersey still look askance at products of the northern half, especially when the product is political oratory. The term "North Jersey" is used as a geographical designation with little sentiment, but "South Jersey" is spoken of by fishermen and farmers almost as a Virginian speaks of the Old Dominion.

In more recent years the State has become the home of tens of thousands of people who work in New York or Philadelphia. The commuter reads newspapers from those cities on his way to work; he rides on railroads that, except for the Jersey Central, bear names taken from other States; and when he has money to spend for a good time at night, his pleasure often falls into the category of interstate commerce. The legitimate theater is practically non-existent within New Jersey. Night life is decentralized by hundreds of neon-signed roadhouses, many of them large enough for a thousand patrons.

But the State does not belong to the commuters. Of more significance are the oystermen and fishing captains of the coast; the truck farmers and dairymen; and the merchants, professional workers, and industrial workers of towns and cities. The greatest share of New Jersey's working life is in the factories, whose output of refined copper, petroleum products, textiles, electrical equipment, machinery and other goods gives the State sixth rank in the Nation for value of manufactures, although it is only ninth in population.

Off the arterial roads are hundreds of small villages where the tempo of life is in keeping with the general stores, white frame churches, and schoolhouses; where a good corn crop is more interesting news than the murder of a Manhattan artist's model, and where the county's chief horse trader is more representative of the community culture than the automobile dealer. People in these villages are independent of cities. They are as firmly rooted to their homesteads as the stone walls and rail fences that mark their lands.

Equal to the rural Jerseyman's apparent contempt for the neighboring metropolises (whose residents buy most of his produce) is the simulated scorn of New Yorkers for that unexplored portion of the United States lying between the Hudson River and Hollywood. New Yorkers in general know little of New Jersey. Although Newark is much closer to New York's City Hall than are many sections of the greater city, it is sometimes assumed to be a remote station on the Pennsylvania Railroad. Relatively few New Yorkers ever have penetrated the miles upon miles of pine barrens on the coastal plain; they have never seen Bordentown, where the early nineteenth century is alive on every street, nor the small villages resting solidly in the pockets of northern mountains.

Like China, New Jersey absorbs the invader. On summer week ends, when city asphalt is soft enough to take heel prints, the State's highways are thronged with the cars of New Yorkers and Pennsylvanians bound for the coast resorts. And it is to "Jersey" that apartment-worn residents of Manhattan and Philadelphia move by thousands when the desire for space, grass, clean air, better schools, and lower rents can no longer be denied.

Millionaires have joined the exodus across the Hudson and Delaware. They have crowned the low-lying hills with their mansions and greenhouses, converted the fields into golf courses, decorated the roadsides with spring-blooming forsythia, and imported dogs and horses by the hundreds.

The State inherited a large foreign population from the years of wholesale immigration, and received many additional immigrants who moved from other States between 1920 and 1930. Lying at the back door of Ellis Island, the industries of New Jersey absorbed so many shiploads of Europeans that the foreign-born population in some manufacturing centers is still as high as one-third. Negroes came also to work on farms or in factories, and racial discrimination followed, particularly in southern New Jersey—a section that lies partly below the Mason-Dixon Line. According to the report of the Interracial Committee of New Jersey Conference of Social Work (1932), "Although civil rights are guaranteed by law to Negroes in New Jersey, their personal privileges are increasingly more limited."

Holding to the older traditions are the members of local historical societies, the Daughters of the American Revolution and similar organizations. Washington fought much of the Revolution on New Jersey soil, and the places associated with his name have been marked and preserved. Tales of Indian raids and Indian-killing are still being told, although the Indian population has decreased to some two hundred. Monuments to vanished industry and commerce are the ruins of bog-iron furnaces throughout southern New Jersey, the weed-grown ditches of the two canals that crossed the State from the Delaware River, and hundreds of small streams that once provided power for mills on almost every pond.

Toryism was rampant in New Jersey at the time of the Republic's birth, and the State is still a seething mixture of liberal and reactionary forces. Today the dominant corporation is Public Service, the vast utility concern that sells electricity, gas, and transportation to most inhabitants of the State. Consumers have won an initial fight for lower rates, and Camden is the scene of what amounts to a civic crusade for public ownership.

But the average resident, particularly in the commuting belts, is perhaps less concerned about the destiny of New Jersey than are the editorial writers of the great New York dailies. The voter looks to Washington or to his borough hall, and scarcely knows when the legislature is sitting at Trenton. The commuter has no time to read the editorials as he sprints alternately from train to ferry and from ferry to train. The industrial worker's chief concern now seems to be the future of national labor organizations. As for the farmer, he finds the soil good and usually votes Republican.

Natural Setting

Geography, Topography, and Climate

NEW JERSEY is the fourth smallest State in the Union; only Connecticut, Delaware, and Rhode Island are smaller. It has an area of 8,224 square miles, of which 710 square miles are water surface. The State has an extreme length north and south of 166 miles, and an extreme width east and west of 57 miles.

With the exception of the 50-mile northern boundary from Hudson River to Delaware River, separating it from New York, the State is entirely surrounded by water, 300 miles of which are navigable. It is bounded west and south by the Delaware River and Delaware Bay, dividing it from Pennsylvania and Delaware. On the east it is bounded by the Atlantic Ocean, the Hudson River, Arthur Kill, Kill van Kull, and New York Bay, which separate it from New York.

The State falls naturally into three physical divisions of sharply differentiated scenery. In the north is the mountainous, lake-studded region known as the Appalachian Highlands; in the central, or Triassic section, are gently rolling hills, supporting most of the State's urban and industrial development; and in the large southern Coastal Plain are fruit orchards and market gardens, swamps and pine wastes, miles of beaches and shallow bays.

The Appalachian Highlands section, which extends northwest of a line that might be drawn through Pompton, Morristown, Lebanon and Clinton to Delaware River, includes slightly less than two-fifths of the State's area. Along the northwest border are the level-topped narrow Kittatinny Mountains, which achieve the highest elevation in the State—1,805 feet above sea level at High Point. These mountains are part of the Appalachians. Bisecting them is the famous Delaware Water Gap, 900 feet wide at the base and 4,500 feet wide at the top, with sides rising to a height of 1,200 feet or more.

The thickly wooded ridges of this area form a natural park. In Sussex

County, more than 12,000 acres along the Kittatinny range have been set aside as Stokes State Forest to preserve at least a portion of the State's woodland in its pristine beauty. Winding roads and trails penetrate the dense forest growth, and rock-strewn streams invite the fisherman.

Shut in between the Kittatinny Mountains on the west and the Highlands on the southeast is Kittatinny Valley, largest of the many fertile valleys in this section that are used for farming and dairying.

Several parallel ridges, remarkably uniform in height, and some of the oldest rocks in America, form the lesser elevations. Among the best-known are the Green Pond, Schooley, Hopatcong, and Jenny Jump; between them, lakes, swamps, brooks and narrow valleys are frequent. Summer resorts and large country estates are situated throughout this region. To the south lies cleared land used for agriculture. The Highlands do not end at the State line but stretch northeasterly to West Point, where they become the Highlands of the Hudson, and southwestward into Pennsylvania. Elevations in this area average about 800 feet.

Lake Hopatcong, in the south central section of the Appalachian Highlands district, is the largest inland body of water wholly within the State. It has an area of 2,443 acres and a shoreline of more than 40 miles. Greenwood Lake, with 1,290 acres, is divided between New Jersey and New York. Nearby is Wanaque Reservoir, the State's largest artificial lake. Scores of smaller lakes, many of glacial origin, are found in this region.

One-fifth of the State, a long strip barely 20 miles wide, the city belt of New Jersey, lies within the Triassic Lowland division, which extends from Delaware River to Hudson River, and north from US 1 (the straight-line highway between Newark and Trenton) to the base of the Ramapo Mountains.

Manufacturing and commerce have centered in this area, with the result that it includes Paterson, Passaic, Jersey City, Newark, Elizabeth, New Brunswick and Trenton—every large urban center in the State with the exceptions of Camden and Atlantic City. West and north of Newark is a string of closely built-up residential towns: Maplewood, the Oranges, Bloomfield, Nutley, Clifton, and suburbs of Paterson.

The red soils of the weak Triassic sandstone and shales are not utilized extensively for agricultural development. However, the section running southwest along the Piedmont belt, just above US 1, is one of the oldest farming districts in the State.

Rising abruptly from the sandstone plain generally characteristic of the district are the traprock formations known as the Palisades, Sourland, Watchung, and Cushetunk. They are forested and rise from 400 to 500

feet above sea level. The Palisades, the most important of these, extend as far as Weehawken from a point north of the New York boundary, gradually decreasing in height. The traprock formation continues to the Kill van Kull channel and into the Watchung Mountains west of the group of suburbs known as the Oranges, but south of Weehawken has little scenic appeal.

The State's three principal rivers, the Passaic, Hackensack, and Raritan, all drain this section and are partly navigable. The Passaic, the most important commercially, rises in the southern part of Morris County and runs northeast to Little Falls, where it descends 40 feet by a cascade and rapids. In Paterson the river drops 70 feet into a vertically-walled gorge to form Passaic Falls, a spectacular sight when high water causes an overflow. Usually the river's entire volume is diverted for electricity production. From the falls, the river turns southward and empties into Newark Bay.

The Hackensack enters the State about five miles west of the Hudson, flows parallel with that river and empties into Newark Bay, around which are thousands of acres of marshland. The Raritan, largest river wholly within the State, rises in Morris County, runs eastward and empties into Raritan Bay. It drains an area of 1,105 square miles. Some of the streams provide water power, as may be seen at Paterson, High Bridge, Pottersville, and Raritan.

The Coastal Plain division, comprising about 4,400 square miles, or more than half of the State's area, sweeps inland and northward from the ocean up to the general course of US 1. One-third of the plain is less than 50 feet above sea level; two-fifths are between 50 and 100 feet; and one-fourth is 100 feet above sea level. One-eighth of the plain consists of tidal marsh.

Fringed though it is with these tidal marshes and containing many inland swamps, the plain in certain areas is highly productive. The clay beds and greensand marls of the northern section provide good farm land, producing melons, potatoes, corn, and other standard market crops. Westward in Burlington County is one of the most important fruit-growing districts of eastern United States.

The southern and central part of the plain is covered largely with stunted pine woods—the famous pine barrens. Throughout this area are cranberry bogs. The swamp land yields in addition large quantities of sphagnum moss (used by nurserymen for potting) and medicinal herbs. Early settlers quickly discovered the value of the Great Cedar Swamp in Cape May County, on Tuckahoe River. Buried at shallow depths and perfectly preserved were the trunks of giant cedars, which were hauled from the swamp and converted into shingles and other building material.

Beaches and tidal marshes extending from Raritan Bay to Cape May on the Atlantic Ocean, and from the Cape to Camden on Delaware River, almost encircle the area. Sand bars along the coast have always been a hazard to mariners and fishermen. Capped by sand dunes, the bars are slowly becoming part of the mainland because of the accumulation of sediment washed into the basins from the shore. Rivers with swampy banks, the large extent of unproductive land, and a lack of good harbors have generally retarded the development of the Coastal Plain.

From Manasquan south the coast is a succession of shallow inlets, river mouths and long sandy beaches. Barnegat, Little Egg Harbor, and Great Egg Harbor are the most important harbors on the southern coast. The Delaware River is navigable up to Camden.

Principal rivers, none of which runs for more than 36 miles, are the Pequest, Great Egg Harbor, and Maurice. The drainage pattern is dendritic, or treelike.

The sole important elevation in this section is the Navesink Highlands on Lower New York Bay, highest point on the open Atlantic Coast between Maine and Florida.

An ocean to the south and mountains in the north account in part for New Jersey's strikingly varied climate. The southern tip of the State, at Cape May, has a uniform summer coolness, but escapes hard winters because it is out of the northern storm path and protected by the nearness of the Gulf Stream. The northern highlands have the coldest winter weather of any section in the State.

The mean temperatures range from 49.2° F. at Dover in the north to 55.4° at Bridgeton in the south. The highest recorded temperature in the State was 109° at Somerville on September 21, 1895. At Riverdale in Bergen County, a record low of 34° below zero was reported on January 5, 1904. Seacoast temperatures have never fallen to more than 10° below zero.

Consistently mild weather has contributed to making Atlantic City an important health and resort city. Its average winter temperature is 34°, while the summer mean is 70°.

Annual rainfall throughout the State averages 48 inches, with less precipitation along the southern shore and slightly more in the northern district. The State escaped the worst of the drought in 1930, receiving 19 inches of its normal 35-inch rainfall in the growing season.

Snow falls in the period from November to April. The growing season, between killing frosts of spring and autumn, varies in length from 155 days in the Kittatinny Mountain region to 203 days along the coast.

Geology and Paleontology

Geologists divide New Jersey as it is today into three provinces. The first, known as the Appalachian Highlands Province, contains the highest ground in the State and extends northwest from a line connecting Suffern, Morristown, and Milford. Extending 20 miles south of the Ramapos to US 1 (the Newark to Trenton highway) and lying between the Delaware and Hudson Rivers, is the Triassic Lowland, a less elevated section. South of US 1 is the lowest land in the State, comprising the Coastal Plain Province.

Each section has been shaped by the interplay of sub-crustal forces and external agencies such as erosion by surface water and invading ice. And the character of each has exercised physical control over man's cultural history within its boundaries. Cities, farms, and factories are placed today largely where the results of geological processes—not man—suggested.

The Appalachian mountain ridge, on the northwestern boundary, resulted from tilted-up layers of hard rock that have withstood erosion while the less durable rocks were gradually worn away to form the Kittatinny Valley. The lower Highlands ridges are largely composed of hard rocks of granite, gneiss, limestone, slate, sandstone, and siliceous conglomerates.

These rocks are the oldest in the State, consisting largely of pre-Cambrian and Paleozoic types. Along the Ramapo Mountains on the southern border of this region is a great fault, or fracture, dating back many millions of years to the time when a vast block of rock-crust broke away and settled. Although the hard sandstone ridges carry a soil sufficiently hospitable for forest growth, the only productive soil is found on the soft shales and limestones of the well-settled valleys.

The Triassic Lowland, a long strip barely 20 miles wide, is the urban and industrial center of New Jersey. The underlying rocks of this section are chiefly red sandstones and shales, which through decay have given their color to the soil. Although not conducive to extensive farming, this formation has provided excellent sandstone for building and roadmaking.

Several ridges in this province, notably the Watchung Mountains, have successfully resisted erosion because of their hard volcanic rock. The Watchungs may owe their origin to one of New Jersey's geologic oddities, Snake Hill, which is probably the eroded stump of an ancient volcano. This rough rock-pile has a lonely site in the Hackensack meadows, just north of the Pennsylvania Railroad main line, where it is one of the first things seen by outbound travelers from New York as the train leaves the Hudson tunnel.

The most spectacular sight in this area is, of course, the Palisades of the Hudson. Rising in places to more than 500 feet, these great stone columns are the edge of what was once a thick sheet of molten rock that, forced upward from great depths in the earth's interior, spread out horizontally between layers of sedimentary sandstone and red shale—like the chocolate filling in a layer cake. Cooling slowly far beneath the surface, this layer acquired its perpendicular columns through shrinkage and cracking. Over a long period of time, erosion removed several thousand feet of sediment in the layer above, finally exposing the Palisades. Because of greater hardness they have survived countless centuries of erosion.

For 17 miles within the State this rock wall parallels the Hudson, disappearing from sight near Weehawken. But the formation can be traced under the waters of Kill van Kull to Staten Island, where it makes a farewell appearance as an unimposing little heap of rocks in an open field. Soundings have shown that the canyon of the Hudson extends 400 miles to sea—a natural marvel easily comparable with the Grand Canyon of the Colorado.

The broad Coastal Plain region is the center of New Jersey's market gardens, pine forests, and beach playgrounds. Along the Atlantic coast south of Point Pleasant, a long broken row of sand ridges rises above sea level. These ridges have been built up offshore by the action of waves and ocean currents. Similarly, tidal marshes and beaches extend around the State from Raritan Bay on the east coast to Camden on the western boundary.

Fertile soils are found upon the inner coastal plain. An inner belt of Cretaceous greensands and marls, valuable as fertilizer, extends across the State from the Raritan to the Delaware. As a whole, the area is one of sedimentary rocks. Contrasting with the fertility of the farming district is the great pine forest that covers more than 3,000 square miles in the southeast.

Age of Invertebrates. Tests involving radioactive minerals indicate that crystalline rocks in the Highlands region are at least one billion years old. Geologists have pieced together a story of New Jersey that antedates the dinosaur by many millions of years. At the earliest time in geological records, the northwestern section of the State was the floor of a long and narrow inland sea. This gulf was separated from the open Atlantic by a mountainous barrier on the site of the present continental shelf. Erosion gradually wore down the mountains, the soil and debris being distributed on the floor of the sea. Ultimately this sediment converted an arm of the sea into dry land.

The animals of this inland sea were all invertebrates; shellfish and trilobites were dominant. The shellfish superficially resembled those of our present sea, while the trilobites were peculiar animals, smaller but otherwise not unlike the king crab or horseshoe crab of the New Jersey coast today. Fossils of these animals are occasionally found in quartzite and limestone which in the form of sand and limey ooze formed the sea-floor during this period. Perfect trilobites are very rare in New Jersey. Quarries near Blairstown and Columbia have yielded fragments.

During the Ordovician period, which followed the Cambrian, limestones and shales were being deposited. The animals of the Ordovician sea were more numerous than those of the Cambrian, but again they were all spineless. Sponges, corals, shellfish, and trilobites are occasionally found in the rocks deposited in this sea, for instance near Jacksonburg, Newton, and Branchville.

Age of Reptiles. Millions of years later, during the Triassic period, came the Appalachian revolution, when the earth's crust shivered and made mountains. The eroded mountains near the sea were pushed bodily northwest, wrinkling the layers of sediment that had filled this ancient trough. These huge wrinkles were the ancestral Appalachian Mountains. A long period of erosion followed; the newly formed mountains were slowly worn down, their waste being spread upon an eastern piedmont that lay, in Triassic time, between the new mountains and the relics of the old barrier. The weight of these new deposits was too much for the earth's crust. A large block split off and sank, squeezing upward enormous quantities of black lava that spread over the floor of this valley. (The line of fracture is known today as the Ramapo fault.)

The elevation of the Appalachian Mountains left a valley between them and the older mountains of Appalachia. Several fresh-water lakes must have existed in this valley, for today there are remains of many fish in the deposits that eventually filled the lakes. A great many of these fossil fish have been found in the vicinity of Boonton.

More sediment from the bordering mountains on the east and west covered the lava. Finally, earth movements tilted the entire strata to a gentle northwestward slope; a series of fractures enabled the crustal blocks to slip downward as they became tilted.

The irresistible forces of erosion—forces that have carved New Jersey as the State exists today—continued their assault on the mountains. The ancestral Appalachians were slowly leveled off. Another series of sediments, now known as the Cretaceous, was built up along the coast, spreading inland over part of the Triassic rocks. This encroaching sea deposited beds of gravel, sand, clay, and greensand marl that are important units of the Coastal Plain today. Ancestors of the modern shellfish inhabited these waters and built great shell beds covering many square miles; dinosaurs waded in the coastal marshes, leaving footprints on the muds of geologic time; sea serpents, sharks, crocodiles, and huge turtles disported nearby. Their habitat was probably the dense vegetation or marshes near the sea. Great forests of palmlike trees grew along the shores of these estuaries, and tangles of huge ferns and slender branchless trees, not unlike our present horse-tail rushes, choked the marshes. The finding of a fossil cycad at Woodbridge has suggested that the climate was much warmer than it is today.

The dinosaurs and some of the other reptiles of this period were numerous, and their remains have occasionally been found in southern New Jersey. A model of the large dinosaur (Hadrasaurus) found many years ago near Haddonfield can be seen in the State Museum at Trenton. Shark

SCHOOLEYS MOUNTAIN, NEAR HACKETTSTOWN

teeth and bones of crocodiles and turtles are often found in deposits of Cretaceous age.

During construction of the George Washington Memorial Bridge, excavations made in Triassic rock of the Palisades revealed tracks of dinosaurs. Traces and skeletons of dinosaurs and other fossil animals have been uncovered also at Fort Lee and near Princeton.

Cretaceous marine fossils deposited by the sea that covered most of southern New Jersey are even more numerous than the terrestrial ones. The shells of large clams and snails and the pens of a squidlike animal *(belemnite)* are often found in the Cretaceous deposits at such places as New Egypt, Marlton, Crosswicks, Mullica Hill, and Lenola.

Age of Mammals. Once more the earth's crust moved. This time, however, it was not a convulsion, but a rather gentle upward push that elevated the whole Atlantic coastal belt. Streams etched out new valleys, with the hardest rock surfaces resisting erosion longest. The Delaware River came to grips with the ancient bulk of Kittatinny Mountains––a grandfather in a range of patriarchs. Whereas the eroded remains of Kittatinny once stood scarcely higher than the river's crest, its hard rock was now rising anew as part of the general onward and upward movement. But the mountain's uplift was slow enough to give the river a chance to use its cutting tools. The Delaware did not need to carve through a mountain wall, nor did it find a ready-made gap. It merely held its course as the mountain rose, sawing downward through both hard and soft rock. The result of that successful operation is the Delaware Water Gap.

Most of the ancient plane surfaces disappeared at this time, except for the table top of the Palisades and the flat summits of venerable Schooley's and Kittatinny Mountains. The Schooley peneplane, as it is designated by geologists, is a conspicuous but little known souvenir of a long stage in erosional history.

It was at the beginning of this period, the Tertiary, that the dinosaurs and other large reptiles suddenly and rather mysteriously disappeared. Their place was taken by the mammals. Although many kinds of mammals were living throughout the country during this period, and New Jersey probably had its quota, Tertiary fossils are not common.

The northern part of New Jersey was much as it is today, while the southern part was covered several times by a warm shallow sea. Many of the shellfish were similar to those of the Cretaceous seas, but others were more like those of our present oceans. There are various deposits of Tertiary fossils in New Jersey, but probably the best known is near Shiloh in Cumberland County, where a large fauna of Miocene fossils has been found in the marl pits.

The Ice Age. The surface of New Jersey was geologically ready for man something less than a million years ago. Then the climate gradually became colder. Down the valleys of Lake Champlain, the Connecticut and St. Lawrence Rivers, long fingers of ice from Canada crept southward. Finally these fingers merged into a solid sheet of ice that swept all resistance before it.

Vast quantities of rock, soil, and debris were pushed across country for many miles. Remnants of this material, known as the terminal moraine, still mark the former edge of the ice from Perth Amboy northward through Plainfield, Summit, and Madison to Denville; and from Denville due west through Netcong, Hackettstown, and Belvidere to the Delaware River. A line through these towns marks the southern limit of the glacier's advance.

Mammoths and mastodons roamed the country at this time. One of the finest specimens of mastodon found in the State is in the museum of Rutgers University. The skeleton, remarkably complete, was excavated in 1869 from a bed of gray marl in Mannington Township, Salem County. It is 22 feet long and 9 feet 8 inches high. Six other mastodon skeletons were found between Vienna and Hackettstown, and several teeth were recently dredged off the coast.

Although this period, the Quaternary or Pleistocene, is called the Ice Age, there were periods between advances of the ice when the climate was probably milder than today. Water from melted ice flooded much of the land adjoining the present shore line. Fossils from this warm, interglacial sea include species that are now restricted to warmer waters off the Carolinas and Florida. Many specimens were recently found when sand was pumped from the bottom of the marshes in Cape May and Atlantic Counties to convert the lowlands into real estate developments. In addition to shells, a few larger fossils were found, including bones of the deer, whale, and numerous fishes.

Drainage systems were, of course, seriously disturbed by the arrival of the glacier, by the newly formed deposits, and by the great amounts of water released when the ice melted. Many of the lakes and swamps of Sussex County are of glacial origin. The Passaic River, which formerly pursued a short route seaward through the Watchung Mountains at Summit, was blocked by morainal material. A large lake was formed behind the mountains and temporarily overflowed near Bernardsville. As the ice edge receded, perhaps no longer than 20,000 years ago, the river found lower outlets for this Lake Passaic, finally adopting a hairpin course through Paterson—a 20-mile detour. The river is still making that detour today, the change being responsible for the spectacular Passaic Falls within the city of Paterson. The last of Lake Passaic may be seen in the Great Swamp near Myersville in Morris County.

Plant and Animal Life

Because of a topography that ranges from mountainous highland to sandy plain, with marked differences in soil and climate, New Jersey has a variety of wild life surprising in so small an area.

The greater part of the Coastal Plain, covered with deposits of loose sand and gravel and a growth of stunted oak and pine, with some white cedar survivors, is only the "Pine Barrens" to most residents of New Jersey. But for more than a century botanists have considered this region one of the most interesting in the United States. Swamps, drained by brownish cedar-tinged streams, are veritable marine gardens.

On damp sandy spots near cedar swamps at 30 known places throughout the pine barrens is found the little fern, *schizaea pusilla* (curly grass), the outstanding rarity of the State. Since its discovery in 1805 at Quaker Bridge it has attracted naturalists from Europe and elsewhere. The fronds, seldom more than five inches in length, are identified readily only by those who know that the plant bears little resemblance to a fern.

Known to but a few is a sandy pocket, on an old wagon road in southern New Jersey, where the passionflower blooms profusely. It is perhaps the only sight of its kind in the State. Vast stretches beneath the pine trees are covered with the trailing pyxie plant, smallest evergreen shrub in the world, growing only one-half inch high and putting forth white star-shaped blossoms in April. Woods of the Coastal Plain are green at all seasons with swamp magnolia, laurel, and holly, in addition to the pines and cedars.

The northern forest growth is in general similar to that of New England. Almost 20 varieties of oaks are common in the State, and the maple, beech, locust, and birch are found in large numbers. Chestnut and hickory trees, once abundant, are practically all gone. Old elms to match those of Connecticut towns are found along village streets. In the northern swamps the red maple and pin oak are typical. Ferns grow in greater profusion northward.

Spring comes in New Jersey when the snowy wreaths of the shadbush —so named because it blooms when the shad are running—appear on the hillsides and in the dry open woods, along with trillium, hepatica, and the eggshell-white blossoms of bloodroot. In the pine barrens a rare April flower is that of the sand myrtle, a little plant with dark leaves somewhat like those of box, and a smother of white blooms lasting many weeks. Arbutus is found in the woodlands and on sunny slopes as well. In late March and early April the pale yellow blossoms of the spice bush, and in autumn its scarlet berries and brilliant gold leaves, add color to the wet woods and marshes.

The staggerbush, with delicate, pinkish-white, nodding flower clusters, blossoms from April to June. Wild azalea grows almost anywhere, scenting the air with its bright pink flowers. The plant is known also as the pinxterbloom because it is seen on Whitsunday, for which the Dutch word is *Pinkster.* On dry soil exposed to the sun is the birdfoot violet. The showy Virginia cowslip, with pink buds opening sky-blue, takes root in low meadows and on stream banks, blossoming throughout the summer.

Along roadsides near the shore the beach plum puts forth pure white blossoms in May. The deep red or purple fruit of this low straggling tree is much used for preserves; the Indians prized it. Throughout the State the spring green of most woodland is beautified by the delicate white of the flowering dogwood. Woods and highways in nearly all parts of New Jersey are graced by the mountain laurel, with pinkish-white blooms and evergreen leaves. On the borders of swamps and moist woods the fragrant creamy-white flowers of sweetbay, or magnolia, are seen early in May. Also found commonly on damp ground is the mayflower, or mayapple, with umbrella-shaped leaves.

In late June and early July the partridgeberry, with delicate pinkish-white blossoms, brightens the oak and hemlock woodlands of the northern counties. Neighbors of this plant are the wintergreen, with drooping white bells; the pipsissewa and pyrola, with waxen blossoms touched with red; the dainty yellow ladyslipper, of the orchid family; and the rattlesnake plantain, also an orchid, with a short spike of tiny white florets rising from a rosette of mottled leaves.

Sunny swamps are the wild-flower strongholds of mid-July, with turkscap lilies, the meadowrue, and pitcherplants; tiny, glistening sundews, unrolling white spikes; the rose-pink orchid; and the fringed orchises in purple, yellow, and white. A patch of brilliant orange milkwort will be seen on a sandy dike; near it bladderwort raises yellow blossoms above the shallow water where its fringelike leaves float. Turkeysbeard, the odd plant of the southern swamps, abounds in sandy bogs. Its short stiff leaves curve upward, almost exactly like a turkey's beard, and there is a golden gleam from its yellow spikes. Seed capsules are reddish-brown; the stalks and bracts, buff.

Handsomest wild flower of its color is the rich orange butterflyweed, seen in sandy fields and along roadsides throughout the summer. Blossoming in July also are the false indigo, with violet-blue flowers; the yellow indigo; Jersey-tea, a shrub with plumy white flowers seen in dry open woodlands and along gravel banks (used by Colonial housewives as a substitute during the British boycott); the fringed bleedingheart; the pink turtlehead; the brilliant blue closed gentian of the pine barrens; the blue cornflower of the northern fields; and of course the daisy, which turns some northern pastures into an almost solid white. Constant companions of the daisy are the buttercup, red and white clover, and yellow mustard.

In August, roadside fences and waste places are covered with matrimony-vine and its purple blossoms. The vine is a runaway, having escaped from New England gardens. Honeysuckle scents the air in many places from the northern counties to Cape May. Another fragrant plant is the sweet pepperbush, with snowy spikes, seen on stream banks. The sweetspire has spikes of bell-shaped white blossoms in summer, and brilliant crimson foliage in autumn. In low moist ground grows the cardinal flower, brightening the woods with its deep red torchlike spikes.

A roadside favorite during August and early September is joe-pye-weed, its tall stalks crowned with dull pink clusters. Often seen near it are the deep purple blooms of ironweed, and the familiar goldenrod. Queen Anne's lace with its clusters of tiny white blossoms faintly tinged with green, black-eyed-susan, and sunflowers, are also common along highways. In swampy sections the marshmallow, a shrub with large pale-pink flowers, mingles with reeds and cattails. Damp roadside ditches are preferred by the handsome tiger lily, whose spotted orange blossoms add bright color throughout the State.

Colder weather brings out the bright hues of berries of vines and shrubs. Perhaps the most generally admired is the bittersweet, with orange-red berries, seen in thickets or against stone walls. Sumacs are a rich red with foliage and fruit. In a few swamps and woods the rare witch hazel puts forth clusters of golden blooms among its dying leaves, making a weird but astonishingly beautiful effect after the first frost.

Vandals and Christmas peddlers have placed the native holly in danger of extinction. The tree is still found in many sections of the Coastal Plain (a grove of fine old trees is in the Sandy Hook military reservation), dwarfed and misshapen by repeated stripping of its branches. Last and brightest color display of the year is made by the black alder, whose scarlet berries, densely crowding the branches, light up swamps and thickets long after the surrounding foliage has turned brown.

The State has many varieties of both shore and land birds. The long line of coast with its series of indenting bays and rivers invites a variety of species. Most familiar is the herring gull, found in great numbers. This bird picks up clams along the salt river banks and drops them from a height on rocks or hard-packed sand to break them open. Sandpipers flit along the beach, skillfully evading the incoming waves. They take flight suddenly in a body and catch the sunlight on silver wings.

In the shallows of inlets and marshy lakes the great blue herons stand as if on stilts, patiently waiting for a catch. The little green heron is common; the night heron and the least bittern are also found. In stunted trees along shore roads are seen the crude nests of the American osprey or fishhawk, poorly built structures of sticks to which the birds return year after year. The osprey circles over the waves until it sights a fish; then it plummets downward with closed wings, and carries the flapping prize off to its nest. The Barnegat Bay region is famous for ducks, which give good sport to hunters every season. In southern New Jersey, bald-headed eagles select the tops of tall trees for their vast and weighty nests. These birds live as long as 125 years.

The Delaware River provides a route for migratory birds, and favorable homesites along its wooded banks. Up and down its length the bobolinks pass. The males, in shining black and white, arrive first. When the females join them, nests are made in upland meadows and the male pours forth the maddest and merriest of all bird songs. Summer over, their bright colors change to dull brown and the song becomes a sharp "chink." Many southern species follow the river north. Among them are the mockingbird and the summer tanager, the first with its rare song, the second with its splotch of brilliant color.

Birds of the Allegheny zone cross the northern border of the State to nest in the hills. These include the blue-headed vireo; the hermit thrush, one of the best singers; and the veery, or Wilson's thrush. Some of the rarer warblers, such as the hooded and the brilliant Blackburnian, are also summer residents. Thousands of wood warblers cross New Jersey each spring and fall, on their long journey between Alaska and Patagonia. It is a great moment for a bird lover when he glimpses these tiny birds of passage, beautiful in color, courageous in flight.

In New Jersey orchards bluebirds sing, and purple finches dance on apple-tree boughs. Goldfinches match their colors with the yellow thistle. Wood thrushes by the roadside "sing each song twice over" in the evening; quail answer one another from the fence rails, while a brown thrasher in a tree-top sings alone.

Urban areas are dominated by the ubiquitous English sparrow; starlings are also numerous. Robins, common in suburban regions, roost together in the country in flocks of as many as 2,500 for protection against owls. Flickers and other woodpeckers, wrens, catbirds, song sparrows, orioles, brown thrashers, flycatchers, swallows and brilliant blue jays nest on the fringes of cities, as well as in the country. The ruby-throated hummingbird is a frequent visitor to flower gardens, and the night-flying whippoorwill is often heard.

Foe of other birds as well as of small rodents is the shrike, which kills for pleasure. The great northern shrike has been known to kill robins. Captured mice are jammed onto thorns, or wedged tightly into crotches. The barn owl is frequently seen, and the screech owl is commonly heard; occasionally the white Arctic owl is found in New Jersey. At Mountainville in Hunterdon County is a buzzard's roost where from 75 to 100 buzzards gather every summer.

Rose-breasted grosbeaks, which feed on potato bugs, were numerous in New Jersey in 1907; since then, for reasons unknown to ornithologists, they have been comparatively scarce. Evening grosbeaks were seen at Belvidere in 1916, and have been reported at other times.

Largest of New Jersey mammals is the deer, found in both northern and southern woods. Virginia deer are stocked by the State fish and game commission. Bears are occasionally reported in the northern woods, and a few wildcats are left. Foxes have become so numerous in the southwestern marsh area that marine hunts have been organized to check their depredations on the valuable muskrat population. A few mink remain at large; others are raised for their fur. Raccoons are still common, and so are woodchucks and opossums. The porcupine is gradually becoming extinct, and the beaver has all but vanished.

The skunk, perhaps the most dignified and fearless of all animals, has withstood the march of urbanization and, along with the weasel, is a source of annoyance to poultrymen. Squirrels, chipmunks, and rabbits are seen even in suburban areas; the flying squirrel is common in the northern counties.

The rattlesnake and copperhead, both relatively common in northern parts of the State, are the only poisonous reptiles. The great mountain blacksnake, entirely harmless, attains a length of eleven feet. Among the handsomest of New Jersey snakes are the yellow and brown-banded kingsnake, and the pine snake, with a whitish body marked with brown black-margined blotches. As the name implies, it is a native of the pine barrens.

There are many types of turtles, including the giant sea turtle, the snapping turtle (chief ingredient of a prized New Jersey dish, snapper soup), and the mud turtle (stinkpot) of wood and marsh. Hell Mountain near Mountainville is a terrapins' retreat, where many hibernate in the marshes beside a natural spring.

Conservation and Natural Resources

Nature has endowed New Jersey with splendid physical resources that support the vast industrial system built by man. To preserve, develop, and stimulate the utilization of these natural benefits is the task of the New Jersey State Department of Conservation and Development, the State Planning Board, the State Fish and Game Commission, and other public and private agencies.

The land problem involves soil conservation, forestry work, and the selection of areas for recreational uses or watershed purposes. Water policy includes provision for an adequate drinking and industrial supply, maintenance of streams and lakes for recreation and power development, pollution abatement, and flood control. The classification of minerals and determination of the extent and location of the supply are the work of the State geologist. Wild life resources are conserved by fish stocking, the establishment of game preserves, and the limitation of hunting and fishing.

Nearly one-half the total land area of the State is forest or "wild land," unsuited to farming because of inferior or depleted soil. Some of these 2,000,000 acres can be reclaimed for agriculture by improved methods of soil treatment, but the greater portion is most easily adapted to public uses such as recreation, development of timber and water supplies, and the preservation of wild life.

Although the pine lands of southern New Jersey are of small agricultural use, they have been found suitable for chicken farming and the cultivation of cranberries, blueberries, and timber. Similarly, dairying has flourished in the northern part of the State, where excessive slope has limited farming.

The principal soil conservation work in New Jersey is carried on by the Federal and State Departments of Agriculture on demonstration projects totaling 37,000 acres. In 1937 the legislature created the New Jersey Soil Conservation Committee, to have general control of all soil conservation activities and programs in the State. Crop rotation and strip cropping are two important techniques in the effort to avoid depletion and to protect the soil from erosion by water and wind.

For forest development as well as recreation the State maintains 8 forests, with a total acreage of 54,374, and 14 parks. The State forests range in size from 21,555 acres (Lebanon) to 43 acres (Jackson). Between these limits are the Bass River, Belleplain, Green Bank, Jenny Jump, Penn, and Stokes Forests. Forestry work includes investigation and experimentation, reforestation, cooperation with private landowners in forest problems, and —most important of all—the prevention and fighting of forest fires.

Valuable timber in the State is largely confined to hardwoods in the north, and yellow pine and cedar in the south. The relative percentages of trees available are: oak, 47 percent; pine, 22 percent; maple, 7 percent; cedar, 6 percent; hemlock, 5 percent; all others, 13 percent.

The famous Pine Barrens of southern New Jersey consist of hundreds of square miles of stunted pine trees, swamps, and scrub growth. This area's history is an object lesson for conservationists. The original pine, cedar, and oak growth was recklessly cut for shipbuilding and charcoal burning until about 1860, when it was virtually exhausted. The second growth proved to be of poor quality, and the region has remained barren except for small sections where the State has treated the soil in an attempt to produce another healthy crop of pine or to develop transplanted species.

To bolster the diminishing lumber trade within the next 75 years and to demonstrate the timber-growing possibilities of the State, the Department of Conservation and Development has purchased 35,000 acres of idle land, and these are being improved by scientific cutting and planting. The State also maintains two forest nurseries where several million seedlings are grown annually for planting in State forests and for sale to landowners. In recent years the Civilian Conservation Corps has cooperated with the State forester by planting 40,000,000 trees and collecting between 7,000 and 8,000 pounds of tree seeds.

Reforestation consists of providing for immediate new growth of the tree species best suited to a particular locality, as mature timber is cut or destroyed. Reproduction may be effected by seedlings or sprouts from the original stand, or by artificial reforestation where natural reproduction is insufficient or where new tree species are desired.

The entire forest area from Port Jervis and Suffern to Cape May is under observation from 19 lookout and auxiliary tower stations. Fires are fought by crews with shovels, brooms, and other equipment, including pumps capable of forcing a stream of water through a mile of hose. Airplanes, for use in large fires, are now being equipped with two-way short wave radio apparatus. In the past 12 years there has been, in the face of a 35 percent increase in the number of fires, a 26 percent reduction in the total area burned and a 46 per cent decrease in the size of the average fire.

The problems of adequate domestic water supply, stream pollution, and water for power and recreation are handled by six State agencies and two interstate committees. The most important of these are the State Water Policy Commission and the North Jersey District Water Supply Commission, which provide for an adequate water supply. The total daily domestic and industrial consumption of water in New Jersey is estimated at between 400 and 500 million gallons. The total water resources of the State have been placed at from 3,595 to 3,870 million gallons daily, the exact amount depending upon the extent to which the Delaware River ultimately can be utilized.

Important flood-control work is now in progress in the Passaic Valley, last flooded in 1936. The program includes creation of permanent lakes or

OYSTER FLEET ON COHANSEY RIVER, GREENWICH

reservoirs in the tributary areas of the river, and widening, deepening, and diking the river at strategic points. A flood problem that has not yet been solved is the further reclamation of the Passaic Meadows in the Newark area, where valuable land is now constantly under water.

According to the State Planning Board, New Jersey is weak in stream sanitation. The $3,500,000 shellfish industry has been driven to the Maurice River and the lower Delaware section by stream pollution in the Raritan and Shrewsbury Rivers areas. Similarly, in waters along the Atlantic coast, contamination by sewage and industrial waste threatens the deep-sea fishing industry. Oyster culture, centered in the Maurice River Cove, which contains the largest continuous oyster acreage in the world, is under the supervision of the Board of Shell Fisheries.

To safeguard these enterprises and to protect streams important to future water supply, the State Planning Board recommends the formation of joint sanitary districts to be administered by properly related committees. The gravest situation is in the New York Bay section, where pollution threatens the State's beaches; this danger is being met by the work of the Interstate Committee on New York Bay Pollution, of which New Jersey is a member.

Although the amount of power derived from water in New Jersey is small compared to that of many other States, its annual value is estimated in excess of $800,000.

Probably all of the State's important mineral deposits have been located accurately by Federal and State surveys, so that now the major problem is to control the rate of extraction. The leading minerals are greensand marl, zinc, clay, potash, iron, talc, and quartz.

The zinc mines at Franklin are among the world's largest deposits of this mineral, and in total production rank second only to those of the Mississippi Valley. Ore from this locality is conspicuous because of the three colored minerals it contains—red zincite, black franklinite, and green willemite.

The tremendous marl deposits, estimated at almost four billion tons, are important for fertilizer, water softening, and sand stiffening in the glass industry. The greensands take their coloring from glauconite, which contains potash. Although commercial production from this source has not been tried, it is estimated that a thousand-year supply of potash for the Nation is available, should the expense of processing be justified.

The clay resources are used for fire bricks, high grade plastic pottery, stoneware, and terra cotta. Iron mining, as late as 1880 chief among the State's industries, has been reduced to insignificant proportions by competition from Lake Superior ores.

In the stone industries, the State ranks first as a producer of trap-rock. There are also extensive white and blue limestone deposits. Sand and gravel, important for road construction, are found in the Woodbridge and South Amboy area. Talc, the base for talcum powder, is abundant in serpentine rock near Phillipsburg. Large amounts of nearly pure quartz sand, valuable for glassmaking, are in the southern section.

The conservation of fish and game has been a cardinal point in the general conservation program of the State. Through its game management program, it maintains ten public shooting and fishing grounds and numerous game preserves, many of them in the State parks and forests. These are stocked from the State's wild life sanctuary, the State Fish Hatchery at Hackettstown, and three State game farms. The Fish and Game Commission also stocks private streams and lands.

The New Jersey State Planning Board, set up by the legislature in 1934, is preparing a master plan for the State. The board coordinates the activities of several State departments in order to attain a better distribution of public works expenditures in urban, agricultural, and undeveloped areas. In its *First Annual Report of Progress* (1935) the board stressed the importance of conservation and development, showing by reports and surveys the need for long-term planning in utilizing and protecting the State's natural resources.

Archeology and Indians

ARCHEOLOGISTS concerned with New Jersey usually center their interest on two main problems: (1) remains of the Lenni Lenape Indians and their ancestors or predecessors, and (2) traces of an ancient, possibly glacial age, man. About the Indians there is much conclusive information, but evidence of ancient man has been the crux of New Jersey's major archeological dispute.

The theory of an ancient man in New Jersey was first advanced with evidence by Dr. Charles C. Abbott, a Trenton physician, who discovered crude argillite blades, which he assigned to the glacial period. The spot where these remains were found in gravel along the Delaware River bluff, one mile south of Trenton, consequently became one of the most important archeological sites in the eastern United States. An article concerning his finds, written by Dr. Abbott in 1872, raised a storm of argument.

Late in 1887 Henry C. Mercer, curator of the Museum of American and Prehistoric Archeology at the University of Pennsylvania, investigated the site. He reported that "No token of an antecedent race was discovered." Beginning in 1894 and continuing for nearly twenty years, the Abbott farm was excavated by Ernest Volk, under the direction of F. W. Putnam of Harvard University. Volk, agreeing with Dr. Abbott, wrote that "the conclusive evidence . . . asserts the antiquity of man on this continent at least as far back as the time of these glacial deposits in the Delaware Valley." Dr. Leslie Spier dug several trenches on the Abbott farm in 1914 and 1915. He found large stone blades, arrowheads, and other artifacts of a simple culture differing widely from that of the historic Lenni Lenape Indians, but he did not attempt to answer the question of its being a possible Paleolithic, or Stone Age, culture.

In April 1936 the Indian Site Survey, a Works Progress Administration project sponsored by the State Museum and directed by Dr. Dorothy Cross, began excavations at the Abbott farm and later at other sites. Nothing has been discovered yet that may be attributed to an ancient or glacial man. On the contrary, what evidence has been uncovered tends to disprove Dr. Abbott's interpretation of his findings; as an instance, designs on recently unearthed pottery indicate that the earlier people responsible for them were not of the glacial age, but lived shortly before the Lenape.

The scantiness of evidence of these earlier people is in direct contrast to the great number and variety of Indian artifacts found by members of the Survey and by other investigators. From the tools, implements, decorative or ceremonial items, weapons, skeletons, and household units discovered, much progress has been made in determining the life and customs of these aborigines. Of importance are the remains of their homes, mere darkened spots in the ground. The sunken posts around which the bark and grass houses of the Indians were built have left their marks; and these, when plotted out, serve as a basis for reconstructing the actual living quarters.

The tools and agricultural and household implements afford an especially good indication of the cultural level. Made primarily of stone and clay, they demonstrate an appreciable ingenuity. Knives, drills, scrapers, hoes, and spades were chipped into shape from the harder stones. Some of the uses to which the tools were put can be determined. For example, the edges of the knives sometimes have one or more notches where they have been used for shaping rounded objects, such as reeds for arrow shafts. Some hoes and spades show signs of having been fitted into handles. Another method of shaping tools was by grinding and polishing. Most of the cutting implements—axes, hatchets, adzes, and gouges—were made in this way.

Mortars and pestles show one method for preparing food. Clay pots and stone hearths also tell the story of cooking methods. (Pots and baskets were frequently sunk in the ground, and the food cooked by placing hot stones in the vessels.) Food was sometimes stored in large pots of thin clay, buried so that the rim was flush with the surface of the house floor. Some of these pots, most of them cracked, have been recently excavated. They are decorated with impressions of fiber or bark.

Other smaller pieces of pottery and fragments that can be reconstructed bear elaborate incised designs extremely important in tracing tribal distribution. Each group of Indians used definite patterns in decorating its pottery, and, where given designs are found, the work is almost certainly that of some particular group. Certain mixtures of designs show relations between the tribes.

Among the most interesting items are ornaments made of the rarer stones—banded slate, rose quartz, steatite, serpentine, mica, schist, and clay marl—highly polished. These include pendants, beads of tubular and disk shapes, gorgets more elaborately designed than pendants and with more than one perforation, and banner stones. There has been much speculation about the banner stones—usually highly polished stones in the shape of butterfly wings, which were centrally drilled or notched. Early historical accounts suggest that they were mounted on shafts and carried as scepters, but there is disagreement on this point. Among the rarest ornaments are the bird stones, shaped like birds; these were made only from the finer stones, such as slate, steatite, and serpentine. Boat stones, resembling canoes and sometimes perforated to be worn as pendants, are also among the rare items.

More than 15,000 implements have been found to date (1939) in various excavations made by the Indian Site Survey. Judging by the artifacts found, the Abbott farm site must have been a favorite place for hunting, fishing, and farming. Numerous arrowheads, spearheads, and other implements of the chase have been found here, together with sinew stones, used for making animal gut pliable, and semi-lunar knives, used for scraping flesh from hides or for chopping meat.

The innumerable net sinkers, usually mere notched pebbles, show that fishing was popular. Hoes, mortars, and pestles, found in surprising quantities, indicate that the land was cultivated even more extensively than was formerly supposed. Axes and gouges prove that the felling of trees and wood-working were common practices.

Indians

The Indians who inhabited New Jersey when the white man came called their country Scheyechbi and themselves Lenni Lenape, meaning "Original People." The Colonists named them Delawares because most of them lived along the Delaware River.

The Lenni Lenape belonged to the general group of Algonkian Indians in northeastern United States and eastern Canada. The larger tribe was divided into three sub-tribes. Each sub-tribe was further divided into family groups, each having an individual totem or guardian spirit. The Minsi (or Munsee) sub-tribe lived in the north, and used the wolf as a totem; the Unami, in the central part of the State, adopted the turtle; and the Unalachtigo, in the south, were known by the wild turkey.

Where the Lenape came from is uncertain. According to their own legend they originated in the north country, probably southern Canada. Famine and war forced them southward through western New York, into Ohio, and then eastward to the shores of the "salt sea" or Atlantic Ocean. A remarkable record of this migration was painted in picture writing on strips of bark and called the *Walum-Olum,* or "Red Score." A copy is reputed to have been discovered in Kentucky by Constantine Samuel Rafinesque-Schmaltz, who interpreted the pictures in 1833.

The Lenape arrived in New Jersey not many centuries before the first white men. Possibly there were not more than 10,000 tribesmen here when European colonization began. They were a healthy group, slightly above average height, but it was not long before their number was decreased considerably by small migrations, the white man's diseases, and liquor.

Large villages were built by the Lenape. During the proper seasons they camped near their favorite hunting and fishing grounds and quarries. The entire State was honeycombed with well-defined trails that led to these haunts and connected the larger villages. Since Colonial roads largely followed the earlier trails, it is possible to trace many of these today. For water travel the Lenni Lenape made extensive use of dugout canoes.

One of the most important routes was the Minisink Trail, which connected Shrewsbury Inlet on the Atlantic Coast with Minisink Island in the Delaware River four miles south of Milford, Pennsylvania. On the New Jersey mainland opposite the island was the largest Minsi village. Innumerable trails crossed the State from the Delaware to the ocean, where the Indians went to catch shellfish, which they dried before carrying home. The numerous shell heaps along the coast, principally in the salt marshes near Tuckerton and Barnegat, are evidence of this practice.

Villages were composed of round and oval houses. The round structures were usually occupied by a single family, while the more spacious oval ones occasionally supported several households. Chiefs had large houses, and the council houses were also roomy.

Groups of houses were sometimes provided with a stockade, a device borrowed from the Colonists. The houses were made by placing saplings in the ground at regular intervals around the circumference of a circle or oval, and tying their tops together. This skeleton was covered with strips of bark or overlapping bundles of grass, securely lashed to the framework. A hole was left in the roof for smoke from an inside fire.

The inside furnishings were simple. Pine boughs were used for beds. Household utensils were made of stone or wood. Occasionally wooden benches served as seats and beds.

Skins of the deer, elk, wolf, bear, and raccoon were used in making the Indians' scanty clothing. The men wore a small loin cloth, with a blanket thrown over the shoulder. Leggings and moccasins of skin completed the wearing apparel, except for necklaces and armbands of sharks' teeth, shells, wooden and stone beads, and pendants. With mussel shells they pulled out their beards and hair, leaving a scalp lock down the center of the head to which painted feathers were frequently fastened. Chieftains sometimes affected two locks. Faces and exposed parts of the body were painted and tattooed with designs of snakes, eagles, turkeys, and imaginary beings.

Women wore short skirts, with a loose tunic fastened on one shoulder. Turkey feathers were dyed and made into skirts for dress occasions. Their hair, worn either loose or in two braids, was held in place by painted bands of deerskin. Before marriage their faces were brilliantly painted to attract the attention of prospective husbands. Children wore no clothing until they were three years old, and thereafter simply a loin cloth.

Most of the food supply was secured from hunting and fishing. In certain sections of the State, however, agriculture flourished. The ground was cultivated with crooked sticks or crudely chipped hoes mounted on shafts. For fertilizer, a dead fish was buried at the base of the growing plant.

Corn, squash, and beans were the chief products, all grown in the same field. Corn was usually ground into meal, from which bread and a kind of porridge called samp (adapted by the early settlers as mush) was made. Occasionally the meal was mixed with water, rolled up in leaves, and baked in ashes. For winter use, corn meal was charred and placed in storage pots sunk in the ground. Such storage pots have been found on the Abbott farm at Trenton.

Meat and fish were boiled or broiled. Shellfish were dried, smoked, and used as seasoning for meats or mixed with corn and beans. Broiling was done over an open hearth fire. Heated stones were dropped into clay pots containing food and water for boiling.

Trade was generally conducted by barter, although the Indians had a medium of exchange in the form of small tubular shells or painted wooden beads called wampum. Black and white beads were used, the black being twice as valuable as the white. Wampum was used either by the piece or by strings, usually a foot long.

The white settlers took advantage of this cheap currency, and manufactured it from conch and periwinkle shells in regular factories on Long Island, at Pascack near Hackensack, and at Egg Harbor, New Jersey. This was considered legal currency for purchasing products from the Indians until it was outlawed toward the end of the seventeenth century.

The religion of the Lenni Lenape was very simple. They believed in one supreme god or Manitou, who was supported by lesser beings having charge of various parts of everyday life. Elaborate ceremonies were presented in honor of the various deities, but individuals seldom prayed to them. Each Indian had a guardian spirit, who was supposed to have his particular interest at heart and to whom he turned in time of need. At the time of puberty the male child was turned out into the forest, where he remained without food or drink until some object, animate or inanimate, feeling sorry for him, presented itself in a dream; this object then became his guardian spirit.

From the time the first white explorer Verrazano anchored off the shores of New Jersey in 1524 until the last group of Indians left the State in 1802, the relationship between aborigines and whites was, on the whole, peaceful and friendly.

Numerous treaties were formulated, the Indian interests being taken care of by brilliant native chieftains and sympathetic white statesmen. Perhaps the most notable chief of the Delawares was Teedyuscung, who represented his people at the five councils of Easton between 1756 and 1761. In treaty making, the Indians of New Jersey were usually affiliated with their kinsmen on the western shores of Delaware River because they "drank the same water." Teedyuscung represented the entire group. He had a remarkable career as a bold warrior, opportunist Christian, eloquent speaker, and able counselor for his tribe. Born near Trenton shortly after the turn of the century, he became chief in 1754, and continued to rule until 1763, when he died in his burning house.

Teedyuscung was mainly interested in restoring the prestige lost by the Delawares in 1725, when they became subservient to the Iroquois after refusing to fight against the English. During this association, the Iroquois addressed the Delawares as "women," because the women in the Iroquois council were the ones who had the right to ask for peace, and the Delawares had often shown peace-loving tendencies. They were frequently called upon as mediators during the Colonial period.

Another great leader was Oratam, chief of the Hackensacks during the middle part of the seventeenth century, who represented his people at numerous peace treaties and land transfers in the northern part of the State.

The rapid decline of the Indian population after the coming of the white men was due principally to sale of their lands, to disease, and to liquor. By 1758 there were but a few hundred scattered over the entire Colony. In that year the Colony purchased 3,000 acres of land for a reservation at the present village of Indian Mills in Burlington County. Here were collected almost 100 Indians, mainly Unamis, who agreed to surrender their title to all unsold lands, and attempted to form a self-supporting community. Governor Bernard appropriately named the community Brotherton. The Colony erected private homes, a meeting house, a general store, and a sawmill. The Indians kept their rights to unrestricted hunting and fishing. Stephen Calvin, a native interpreter, was the local schoolmaster. This Utopia did not last long, and in 1762 the group petitioned the assembly to pay bills for provisions, clothing, and nails.

In 1801 the Indians living at New Stockbridge, New York, invited their kinsmen at Brotherton to join them. The Lenape petitioned the legislature again, and a law was passed in that year appointing three commissioners to dispose of the Brotherton tract at public sale. The land brought from $2 to $5 an acre, enough to pay the Indians' fare to their new home, allow a donation to the New Stockbridge treasury, and leave a remainder that was invested in United States securities.

In 1822 the Stockbridge group moved to Green Bay, Wisconsin. Ten years later the New Jersey contingent appealed to Bartholomew Calvin, son of their old schoolmaster, for further monetary aid in exchange for the relinquishment of hunting and fishing rights not mentioned in the 1801 settlement. Calvin obtained a legislative grant of $2,000. In a stirring speech of acceptance he said:

"Not a drop of our blood have you spilled in battle; not an acre of our land have you taken but by our consent. These facts speak for themselves, and need no comment. They place the character of New Jersey in bold relief and bright example to those States within whose territorial limits our brethren still remain. Nothing save benisons can fall upon her from the lips of a Lenni Lenape."

History

NEW JERSEY'S position as a main corridor of eastern United States has broadly affected her political, social, economic, and cultural history. Lying between two metropolises, New York and Philadelphia, the State from early times has been the highway and often the stopping place for hordes of people of many races, religions, and cultures.

This location has brought both embarrassment and blessing. Governor Woodrow Wilson, who thought of New Jersey as "a sort of laboratory in which the best blood is prepared for other communities to thrive upon," gave the key to the State's history when he remarked in 1911 that "we have always been inconvenienced by New York on the one hand and Philadelphia on the other . . ." He called the State "the fighting center of the most important social questions of our time" and explained that "the whole suburban question . . . the whole question of the regulation of corporations and the right attitude of all trades, their formation and conduct . . . center in New Jersey more than any other single State of the Union."

The first white man to see, and possibly to land on, the New Jersey shore is believed to have been the Florentine navigator, Giovanni da Verrazano, sailing in the employ of the French Crown. In 1524 he is said to have anchored his vessel off Sandy Hook and with a small boat explored upper New York Bay as far as, or almost as far as, the New Jersey shore.

Almost a century later, in 1609, Henry Hudson, employed by Holland, sailed the *Half Moon* into New York Bay, dispatched a sounding party as far as Newark Bay and then sailed up the Hudson River. Within a few years the Dutch sent out trading expeditions and established a post at Manhattan, the base for the invasion of New Jersey. The first known outpost west of the Hudson River was the trading station of Bergen, founded in 1618 by colonists from the island. Five years later Captain Cornelius Jacobsen Mey, who had sailed into the Delaware River in 1614, set up Fort Nassau on the east bank of the river, near the present site of Gloucester. Mey's name survives in Cape May.

Actual settlement of the unnamed New Jersey section of New Netherland was slow. Accordingly, the West India Company offered the feudal title of patroon and a grant of land to any member who would establish a specific number of settlers. In 1629 the company granted to the Burgomaster of Amsterdam, Michael Pauw (Pauuw), a tract on the shore opposite Manhattan where his agent, Cornelius Van Vorst, began to develop an estate called Pavonia. At the same time two other patroons, Godyn and Blommaert, shared a grant on both sides of Delaware Bay. Both attempts were futile, and Indian raids in 1643 drove all whites across to Manhattan from the Jersey side. By 1645 the only Dutch survival was the Van Vorst estate in Pavonia which had become the farm of the West India Company.

The Swedes came to New Jersey shortly after the New Sweden Company had built a fort and trading post in 1638 on the western shore of Delaware River. A vast tract of land between Cape May and Raccoon Creek was purchased from the Indians in 1640; small trading posts were peopled mostly with Flemings, Walloons, and Finns. The enterprise was poorly managed, however, and failed to attract many settlers.

The Dutch, who had reoccupied Fort Nassau after the Swedish arrival, were for a time friendly enough with the Swedes on the Delaware to unite with them against the encroaching English, whose claim was based upon John Cabot's discovery of North America in 1497. However, the Dutch unwisely considered Swedish competition in furs more dangerous than England's territorial ambitions. During the autumn of 1655 Peter Stuyvesant, Governor of New Netherland, peacefully took over the Swedish forts on the Delaware basin, thus ending the Swedish phase of the Colony's history.

With the problems of its Rebellion and stormy Protectorate behind it, England seriously went into the business of colonization. In 1664, Charles II granted to his brother James, Duke of York, the Dutch domain, which included the area now New Jersey. In the same year the English took over New Netherland with a naval expedition. Having been treated by the mother country as less important than the fur-bearing animals they trapped, the few hundred Dutch and Swedish colonials in the New Jersey section of the grant indifferently took the oath of allegiance to England.

The change in sovereigns was far more significant than the inhabitants of Bergen, the largest settlement, could have sensed. From its experience in Virginia and Massachusetts Bay, England was learning that permanent settlements were commercially sounder than the trading posts established by the Dutch and Swedes as a short-cut to riches. As an indication that colonization was to be the English policy, the Duke of York's Deputy Governor in New York, Richard Nicolls, immediately issued the so-called

Elizabethtown and Monmouth patents, providing for the founding of New Jersey towns on the New England model.

While Nicolls was still at sea, the Duke of York in June 1664 created New Jersey with a stroke of his quill. He granted the area between the Hudson and Delaware Rivers to two of his favorites, John, Lord Berkeley and Sir George Carteret. The area was to be known as *Nova Caesarea* or New Jersey in memory of the island where in 1650 Carteret as Governor had sheltered the Duke from Puritan England. The new proprietors commissioned 26-year-old Philip Carteret, a cousin of Sir George, as New Jersey's first English Governor.

York's simple act not only created New Jersey but also perplexities for the Colony for the next 40 years. Unaware of the Duke's grant, Governor Nicolls in New York encouraged settlements at the sites of contemporary Elizabeth, Shrewsbury, and Middletown. These settlements, as well as that of Newark in 1666, were made chiefly by religious dissenters from New England and by adventurous Long Islanders. Confusion began when Philip Carteret arrived at Elizabethtown in 1665 and was surprised to find four families under the Nicolls grant. Some of the colonists brought by Nicolls compromised temporarily by taking the oath of allegiance required by Berkeley and Carteret.

When the Governor's first assembly met at Elizabethtown in 1668 with delegates from that village and from Bergen, Newark, Middletown, and Shrewsbury, it became clear that New England Puritanism was dominant in the settled part of the Colony. Swearing, drunkenness, and fornication were made penal offenses and the child over 16 who cursed or smote at parents might incur the death penalty. The government operated under "The Concessions and Agreements of the Lords Proprietors," which Carteret had brought from England in 1665. This document, which may be termed New Jersey's first constitution, contained a particularly emphatic guarantee of religious liberty, no doubt motivated by the Proprietors' desire to promote rapid settlement.

The smoldering controversy over the dual land grants broke out in the assembly. Many settlers held that their grants from Nicolls and deeds of purchase from the Indians gave valid titles to their land, and that the Proprietors did not have the right of government. Barred from the assembly for this stand, a number of delegates formed the basis of an Anti-Proprietary party which in 1670 refused to pay quitrents to the Proprietors. The revolt spread and in 1672 five of the seven settlements—Newark, Elizabethtown, Woodbridge, Piscataqua, and Bergen—held a revolutionary assembly at Elizabethtown. They deposed Philip Carteret as

Governor and elected as "president" James Carteret, dissolute son of Sir George. With the settlers insisting that the Duke's lease to the Proprietors did not convey governing power, Philip Carteret hastened to England to lay the matter before the Proprietors, that they might be able to present their case. The King upheld the rights of Berkeley and Carteret against the grants of Nicolls.

A sudden attack by Holland temporarily swept aside these technical wrangles. In 1673 a Dutch fleet arrived at Staten Island and regained a portion of Holland's New World holdings, including New Jersey—but only until 1674, when the territory was restored to England by the Treaty of Westminster. Legally the province had thus reverted to the Crown, and Charles II regranted it to the Duke of York who in turn reconveyed the eastern part to Sir George Carteret. Philip Carteret returned as Governor in November 1674; four counties (Bergen, Essex, Middlesex and Monmouth) were created, and a system of courts and grand juries was established.

If eastern New Jersey seemed on the point of extricating itself from the snarls of conflicting claims, western New Jersey was just beginning an even more confused career. Before the King issued the charter of renewal to York, Berkeley in 1674 turned over his proprietary rights to John Fenwick in trust for Edward Byllynge. Immediately these two Quakers quarreled over their shares, and in 1676 William Penn arbitrated the case by awarding nine-tenths to Byllynge and one-tenth to Fenwick. Byllynge, however, became insolvent, and Penn, Gawen Lawrie, and Nicholas Lucas were appointed trustees for his creditors. Because this action involved New Jersey lands, it happened indirectly that William Penn's first Quaker colony was West Jersey.

In 1675 Fenwick settled Salem with his family and a few friends. Like Byllynge, he was soon in financial trouble; ultimately Penn and the other trustees acquired control of part of his land. On July 1, 1676, Byllynge and the three trustees entered into a "quintipartite deed" with Sir George Carteret. This agreement officially clarified the previous haphazard division of the province into West and East Jersey by drawing a line northwest from Little Egg Harbor to a point on Delaware River just north of Delaware Water Gap, Carteret retaining East Jersey, and West Jersey passing into the hands of the Quakers.

The choice of the boundary itself represented more logic than almost any previous act in the management of the Colony. The line cut through what is still the least populous part of the State. Across that wasteland there was neither commercial, political, nor religious unity. East Jersey, the section northeast of the boundary line, has always been dependent upon New York, while West Jersey has been linked to Pennsylvania and Delaware. Not even modern super-highways nor radio have been able entirely to controvert the astuteness of the men who divided the Colony.

The "Concessions and Agreements" for the government of West Jersey, adopted in 1677 and largely devised by Penn himself, provided a liberal and surprisingly modern frame of government, although the constitution was never put into full effect and it was not until 1681 that the first assembly met. Meanwhile, the present town of Burlington had been settled by Quakers in 1677 and other colonists were arriving in considerable numbers.

New Jersey was faced with a struggle for independence in 1674 when the Duke of York sent Edmund Andros to New York with authority to govern New Jersey as well, even though Governor Philip Carteret had returned on the same boat with Andros. No man to waste a prerogative, Andros in 1676 dispatched soldiers to the Salem district and jailed Fenwick as a usurper, although he (Fenwick) was shortly released. The death of Sir George Carteret in 1679 gave Andros an opportunity to employ high-handed methods in East Jersey. Philip Carteret was warned to relinquish the governorship; when he refused, Andros jailed him. Insisting that all New Jersey trade should clear through New York, Andros aroused so much popular disapproval that he was summoned to England to answer charges, leaving Carteret master of East Jersey. A strongly worded remonstrance, probably the work of Penn and his Quaker associates, induced the Duke of York to accept New Jersey's independence of New York.

The elimination of Andros failed to bring harmony to East Jersey and in 1682 the province was put up at public auction. For the sum of £3,400 Penn and 11 associates obtained the land; their shares were divided into innumerable fragments, many of which were purchased by Scots and other non-Quakers. Perth Amboy, which had already attained the dignity of port of East Jersey, was selected as the capital in 1686.

While the population of the two Jerseys grew to an estimated 15,000 in 1702, the Proprietors became, as one historian phrases it, "mere rent-chargers." Their position was no happier than the traditional one of any landlord. Finally, after riots and interference with government dignified by the name of "revolution," the Proprietors of both East Jersey and West Jersey surrendered their governing power to the Crown in 1702 and New Jersey became a united Royal Colony under the administration of Lord Cornbury, the Governor of New York.

Despite the merging of the two Jerseys, separate capitals were maintained at Perth Amboy and Burlington, the legislature meeting alternately in the two cities until after the Revolution. And although New Jersey was to remain under New York's Governor until 1738, the Governor held a separate commission that recognized the political independence of the Colony.

The Proprietors, it must be noted, relinquished only their civil authority. Their land rights were retained and proved a troublesome influence on political affairs in the Colony. To this day the successors of Penn and his associates maintain small offices in Perth Amboy and Burlington, where they meet regularly and exercise jurisdiction over any unlocated or new land, such as fluvial islands.

Lord Cornbury's instructions provided for a council and an assembly, guaranteed some personal rights, and in effect formed a constitution for the united province. New Jersey retained its own legislature and officials, who found many causes for disagreement with the new Governor.

Cornbury was removed after five years. His successors encountered Proprietary disputes and continual complaints against absentee government from New York. Finally Lewis Morris of Monmouth County was named in 1738 as the first Governor of New Jersey alone.

Morris had frequently complained against previous Governors; but now, as legal representative of the King, he faced the same difficulties that formerly he had fostered. He found it hard to get troops for King George's War, and there was frequent trouble in managing the currency. When Morris died in 1746 his salary had been unpaid for two years, and was never collected by his widow.

Increased population on many small farms developing throughout the Province resulted in new rebellion against the territorial claims of the Proprietors. Disputes over the old Nicolls grants were kept alive, and squatters in the western part of the Colony stood their ground. The doctrine of man's natural right to land frequently appeared. Riots against the Proprietors broke out at Newark in 1745 and soon spread to other sections, continuing under Governor Belcher until the outbreak of the French and Indian War in 1754.

As a Royal Province New Jersey made notable economic progress, although it did not rank as one of the most valuable Crown possessions. The farms yielded a variety of fruit, vegetables, poultry, and cattle, and the grain crop was important enough to make New Jersey one of the "bread colonies." Hunterdon County was known as the "bread basket," producing more wheat than any other county in the Colonies. Cider and apple brandy were then, as now, well known products. By 1775 the Colony was an important source for iron, leather, and lumber, while some glass and paper were produced. On the whole, however, economic development suffered from the proximity of New York and Philadelphia.

Despite the late start in settlement, population grew with fair rapidity. By 1726 the total was 32,442 (including 2,550 slaves); 47,402 (3,981 slaves) by 1737; 61,383 (4,605 slaves) in 1745. At the outbreak of the Revolution the population was estimated at 138,000.

Several important cultural contributions were made by the Colony. In architecture some of the finest examples of the Dutch Colonial were built in New Jersey—comfortable stone houses, modest in scale and design, and in harmony with their surroundings. From the early Swedish settlements came the pattern for the typical log cabin of the American frontier. The founding of the College of New Jersey (later Princeton University) and of Queen's College (later Rutgers University) made this the only Colony with more than one college. New Jersey was the center of the humanistic work of John Woolman, the Quaker preacher of Mount Holly. Other sects developed notable strength, the Baptists having been established at Middletown in 1668, and the Presbyterians at Freehold in 1692.

Continual disagreements between the royally appointed Governors and the popularly elected assemblies, combined with unwise commercial restrictions put in force by the British Government, ranged New Jersey in 1774 on the side of Massachusetts against the British. In February of that year the assembly had already followed the lead of Virginia by appointing nine men as a Committee of Correspondence; similar township and county committees sprang up during the summer. On July 21, county committees met at New Brunswick as the First Provincial Congress and chose Stephen Crane, John de Hart, James Kinsey, William Livingston, and Richard Smith as delegates to the proposed Continental Congress at Philadelphia.

In spite of strong Tory sentiment—later proved by the organization of six battalions of Loyalists—anti-British feeling swept New Jersey. In November 1774, at Greenwich on Cohansey River, a band of young men disguised themselves as Indians and burned a shipload of tea. Indignant citizens of Newark branded a New York printer "a vile ministerial hireling" and boycotted his paper. Rejection of other Loyalist papers from New York and Philadelphia later resulted in the founding of a local and patriotic press. As the Royal agents desperately tried to stem the tide of the Revolution, volunteers began drilling on village greens in the summer of 1775, and official after official yielded his authority to the aroused Colonists. Finally, in June 1776, the Provincial Congress arrested Governor

William Franklin, natural son of Benjamin, when he attempted to revive the defunct assembly.

The strategy of the Revolutionary generals showed that New Jersey's position on the Hudson and Delaware Rivers rendered the State dependent upon the fortunes of New York and Philadelphia in war as well as in peace. To the discomfort of the patriots of 1776 and the delight of local patriots ever after, Washington spent one-quarter of his career as Commander in Chief in New Jersey, moving his army across the State four times. Within its boundaries were fought 4 major battles and at least 90 minor engagements.

Toward the close of 1776 Washington retreated across the northern part of the State and into Pennsylvania, seizing every boat for miles along the Delaware to prevent British pursuit. On Christmas night he recrossed the river and captured the Hessian garrison at Trenton in a surprise attack that did much to rebuild the waning morale of the Revolutionaries. A few days later, after outwitting Cornwallis at Trenton, he marched by night to Princeton and there on January 3, 1777, defeated three British regiments. The exhausted American Army then went into winter quarters at Morristown.

Coming by water route from New York, the British seized Philadelphia in September 1777; but in June 1778, they evacuated Philadelphia and retreated across the State, harassed by Jersey troops. Washington hurried with his main army to intercept the British Army of General Howe in the indecisive Battle of Monmouth on June 28. That winter, parts of the Continental Army encamped at Somerville, and in the winter of 1779–80 Washington again made his headquarters at Morristown. From New Brunswick in 1781 the American Army started its march southward to the final victory at Yorktown. In 1783 Washington delivered his farewell address to part of the Army at Rocky Hill, near Princeton.

The war proved a stimulus to agriculture, industry, and commerce in New Jersey. The State's farmers, sometimes involuntarily but mostly with the shrewdness of non-combatants, turned a handsome profit supplying provisions to both sides. Ironworks, gristmills, sawmills, fulling mills, tanyards, and salt works operated at capacity. Goods brought in by privateers and smugglers were advertised in the newspapers, indicating the luxury possible to those who could afford it. Prices rose and labor was scarce. In the rapid shift of values, due partly to monetary inflation, fortunes were made and lost. The end of the war found the debtor a problem for the first time since 1776. The lure of the West was soon to prove an attraction too strong for tax-burdened farmers on worn-out lands to resist.

THE OLD BARRACKS, TRENTON

In June 1776 the fourth Provincial Congress of New Jersey had transformed itself into a constitutional convention and on July 2 adopted a combined declaration of independence and constitution. The hastily drawn document provided for its nullification "if a reconciliation between Great Britain and these colonies should take place. . . ." Nevertheless, this constitution was retained for 68 years. The Colony's long struggle with Proprietary and Royal Governors inspired a provision for annual election of the Governor by the legislature. This arrangement, at first adopted by several other States, obviously violated the prevailing theory of separation of powers (executive, legislative, and judicial) in a free government. New Jersey's first State Governor, William Livingston, was elected August 27, 1776, for one year.

In the two-house legislature, the upper chamber (the council) was composed of one representative from each county, a precedent for equal county representation in the senate under the present constitution. The lower house (the assembly) was apportioned among the counties roughly by population.

The franchise was limited to "all inhabitants of this colony, of full age, who are worth £50 proclamation money . . ." Under laws passed in 1790 and 1797, women were permitted to vote. In 1807, however, the women were disfranchised by a statute justified as "highly necessary to the safety, quiet, good order and dignity of the State." This harsh stricture came from a legislature beset with charges of fraudulent voting by women, notably in an exciting referendum on the location of the Essex County Courthouse. Another 1807 statute reduced voting qualifications by giving the franchise to any taxpayer.

For brief periods, two New Jersey towns had the honor of being the National Capital—at least the temporary capital. When, in June 1783, Congress in session at Philadelphia was confronted by mutinous troops, demanding what it could not give, the session was adjourned to meet again on June 30, at Princeton. There, in somewhat cramped quarters, the National Government remained seated until November 4. A year later, November 1, 1784, Congress convened at Trenton. It was even thought that a "Federal town"—a permanent National Capital—would be built near Trenton. The plan however never materialized—New York and Philadelphia were too powerful—and the Congressional session at Trenton was very brief. Congress adjourned on Christmas Eve of 1784 to meet again a fortnight later in New York City.

New Jersey in the days after the Revolution was grimly compared to a keg tapped at both ends. The State's economy was seriously hampered by commercial restrictions imposed by New York, through which most of the State's goods had to pass. Her representatives demanded that Congress be given power over interstate commerce and the exclusive right to lay duties on imports. When New York and other States failed to meet their fiscal obligations to the weak Congress, New Jersey also withheld payments to the Federal Treasury, hoping to force more co-operative action. Finally, New Jersey was one of the five States that participated in the Annapolis Conference of 1786, which led to the Constitutional Convention at Philadelphia in 1787.

At the Philadelphia convention New Jersey, long conditioned to fear New York and Pennsylvania, became the chief spokesman for the small States in their struggle against the Virginia or "large-State" plan for a powerful national government with a Congress based on population. Although the Virginia plan was adopted for the House of Representatives, the New Jersey plan of equal representation matured into the provision for the balancing Senate. The small States' victory was the greater one, since Congress could not act without the consent of a majority of the States, regardless of population.

A further New Jersey contribution to the Constitution was the all-important clause which declares that the Constitution, laws, and treaties of the United States shall be the supreme law of the land. From this clause, together with the provision for a national judiciary empowered to determine all legal questions involving the Constitution, the United States Supreme Court later derived the power to harmonize Federal and State laws with the Constitution by the process called judicial review.

Satisfaction with the document itself and with the opportunity for protection against New York and other neighboring States resulted in prompt ratification. On December 18, 1787, New Jersey became the third State to approve the Constitution.

Between 1790 and 1840 the foundations of the State's present industrial system were laid. In 1791 Alexander Hamilton founded the Society for Establishing Useful Manufactures, selecting the Great Falls of Passaic River as the site for an industrial city, Paterson. The first factory built at Paterson began to operate in 1794, printing calico goods. As Newark's leather and Trenton's pottery industries grew, businessmen developed important branches of commerce. Banks were chartered at Newark, Trenton, and New Brunswick during the first decade of the nineteenth century, and insurance began in the same period.

At Trenton, which had become the State capital in 1790. the legislature sensed the power of trade. Many turnpike companies were chartered even before the need for good roads was emphasized by the War of 1812. Scientists and inventors—John Fitch and Colonel John Stevens with their steamboats and, later, Seth Boyden with malleable iron and patent leather —accelerated the trend toward industrialization.

On this groundwork there rose, following the short depression at the end of the Napoleonic Wars in 1815, a 20-year prosperity. By 1828 the State had about 550 miles of gravel and dirt roads under 54 charters. Between 1810 and 1840 New Jersey ranked third as an iron producer in the Nation. The value of iron products in 1830 was about $657,000; glass and pottery, $490,000; and cotton products, $1,733,000. Encouraged by the protective tariff of 1816, investors developed water power and mill sites for textiles and flour. By 1830 Paterson had fulfilled its early promise and had become a busy mill town, rich with profits and scarred with labor exploitation.

To weld the expanding sections of the State as well as to modernize the New York-Philadelphia highway, the industrial barons of the day hurried across-State transportation lines. Colonel John Stevens of Hoboken had proved in 1824 that his "steam waggon" could run 12 miles an hour. Six years later his son Robert got a charter for the Camden and Amboy Railroad, and by 1834 the line was finished. The railroad soon absorbed the new Delaware and Raritan Canal, which it paralleled. In 1831 the Morris Canal between Newark and Phillipsburg opened a water route to a rich mining district. Newark, because of its key position on the canal and rail routes and on Passaic River, strengthened its grip as the leading city of the State. With the stage set for even greater economic progress, the speculative bubble of industrial prosperity burst in the panic of 1837.

During the 1830's New Jersey was affected by the spirit of reform that was sweeping the country, partly as a result of the industrial revolution. The legislature began to allot money for public schools; hospitals were built; and a start was made toward guarding the public health. In 1844 Dorothea Dix presented to the legislature a memorial describing the disgraceful conditions in jails and poorhouses and the medieval treatment of the feebleminded, epileptics, and the insane. Public indignation resulted in prison reform and the establishment of an insane asylum. Reform was a leading topic in public meetings and in newspaper columns. With an increase of almost 200,000 in population since 1790, the citizens of the State were demanding democratization of their political structure.

It came in 1844. A constitutional convention swept away property qualifications for voters, provided for separation of powers among the three governmental departments, and included a formal bill of rights and a clause permitting amendment (the latter had been omitted from the 1776 document). The 1844 constitution has been amended only three times.

When the business cycle swung toward good times in 1845, the Camden and Amboy Railroad emerged as a monopoly, since the charter, after merger with two terminal roads, prohibited any other line between New York and Philadelphia. So complete was the railroad's grasp of the State's economic and political life that New Jersey was for a generation bitterly referred to as "the State of Camden and Amboy."

Rising anti-slavery feeling together with pro-tariff and anti-immigrant sentiment turned the State Republican in 1857, at its first opportunity to elect a Republican Governor. But, in the crucial election of 1860, the conflict between industrial and agricultural interests and anti-slavery men and unionists-at-any-cost split New Jersey's electoral vote for the only time. Lincoln received four votes and Douglas three.

In 1863 copperhead opposition to the Civil War, partly created by the New York bankers' mistrust of Lincoln, caused New Jersey to revert to political type and elect Joel Parker, a Democrat, as Governor. Yet New Jersey provided 88,000 troops and $23,000,000 for the war.

After 1865 profits from war supplies and a favorable location as the nexus of the most populous and prosperous sections of the Nation contributed to an intense industrial activity. Paterson was processing two-thirds of the country's silk imports; Newark could proudly hold an impressive trade exhibition of its varied manufactures in 1872; kerosene and other oil products were being refined in Bayonne; and agriculture was passing into its present form of lucrative truck farming. While real estate companies plotted chimerical developments, the legislature recklessly issued charters for any kind of money-making enterprise. The great economic spree which lasted until the panic of 1873 fastened New York's hold upon New Jersey more securely than ever.

The hold that the Camden and Amboy had upon the State had been considerably weakened by 1867. In that year its opponents, seeking a charter for a competing line across the State, had turned the legislature into a roundhouse battleground. When the Camden and Amboy sensed that public opinion would ultimately spell defeat, the company prudently leased its lines to the Pennsylvania Railroad. The Pennsylvania took up in 1871 where its predecessors had left off and brought about a Republican victory in the legislature. The railroad retained a majority in 1873, but this time it was the legislators who felt the popular wrath. They passed a bill opening the State to all lines.

Although the Pennsylvania lost the battle, the State's history shows that it won the war. The act giving any company the right to put down rails in New Jersey was much less objectionable to the Pennsylvania than the alternative of a special charter to a single competing line. Like its predecessor, the new company succeeded during the next generation in maintaining a powerful hold on the State government.

As far back as 1871, however, public opinion had caused the legislature to attempt checks on railroad domination. In that year the railroads were denied free loading space along the Hudson. In 1883 Leon Abbett was elected Governor on a platform calling for railroad franchise taxes. Although the subservient legislature compromised on a plan for assessment and taxation of railroad property, this action resulted in investigation of the Lackawanna Railroad. A State audit of the company's books yielded New Jersey several hundred thousand dollars.

Nevertheless, for more than a quarter of a century the railroads generally enjoyed an extraordinary privilege to profiteer. This license illustrates the beginning of a gradual blurring of party labels between 1870 and 1900, for even on the few occasions when the Democrats won complete control of the State government, their efforts to curb the railroads were feeble. Shut out of the Governorship since 1869, the Republicans had to bid for power by such trivial stratagems as seeking the Prohibition vote through the passing of a county option law in 1888. Such schemes failed to elect a Governor, but the Democrats' own corruption finally lost them the legislature in 1893. Even then the Republican victory was delayed while eight hold-over Democratic senators attempted to steal the senate back from the Republicans simply by organizing themselves into a rump senate, which prevented the seating of any new members. This bold bid was thwarted by the courts.

Except for the electoral split in 1860 and a shift to Grant in 1872, New Jersey gave a majority to every Democratic Presidential candidate between 1852 and 1896. In the latter year Mark Hanna himself was astounded when New Jersey gave McKinley a plurality of 87,692 over Bryan, and elected John W. Griggs as its first Republican Governor in 30 years.

Several factors were responsible for the Republican ascendancy. As the pseudo-agricultural party, the Democrats lost relative strength because the number of farms decreased after 1880. At the same time, the commuter vote, composed largely of Republicans from New York and Philadelphia, increased. Finally, the economic eye of the State was becoming more and more sensitive to the high-tariff button eternally pinned on the Republican lapel.

In that era of seemingly limitless national expansion—when the value of manufactured products in New Jersey rose from $169,237,000 in 1870 to $611,748,000 in 1900—the State began to assume its present leadership in industry. To man the prospering factories and mills, thousands of immigrants, chiefly from southern and eastern Europe, poured into the industrial cities where they quickly established lasting foreign quarters. In the brick and terra cotta works around Perth Amboy, in the heavy industries of Newark, in the woolen mills of Passaic, in the shipyards of Camden, and in the ceramic plants of Trenton, European skills joined with native enterprise to further New Jersey industry.

The State, which had grown from a population of 373,306 in 1840 to 1,883,669 in 1900, was becoming a more integral part of the economic and cultural life of the Atlantic seaboard. Much of the spirit of speed and efficiency of New York and Philadelphia business life flowed across the Hudson and Delaware, quickening the tempo of New Jersey's cities and suburbs. In the same way, important cultural threads of the two metropolises were spun across, drawing up New Jersey in the weave.

The State's educational facilities were strengthened by the founding of Rutgers Scientific School in 1863 and by the opening of Stevens Institute of Technology in 1871. In the latter year a free school system was established and in 1874 a compulsory education law was passed. To Princeton College many of the well-to-do families of New York and Philadelphia sent their sons.

As early as the 1840's Cape May was a summer social capital, and after the Civil War Long Branch became the vacation choice of Presidents—as well as the playground for the Astors and Fishes of New York, the Biddles and Drexels of Philadelphia. A quarter of a century later Atlantic City and Asbury Park were performing the same service for many thousands of Philadelphia and New York vacationers. New Jersey's oyster and cranberry industries catered to the national appetite, while its truck gardens and dairy farms supplied a large portion of the produce sold in metropolitan markets.

For New York and Pennsylvania financiers and for corporation builders generally New Jersey offered a special attraction. From the 1870's on, the State's lax incorporation laws invited the formation of trusts and monopolies in hastily rented offices in Newark or Jersey City. When Lincoln Steffens and the other "muckrakers" began to investigate "big business" they contemptuously labeled New Jersey "The Mother of Trusts."

New Jersey's role as a green pasture for foaling corporations illustrates several important characteristics of the State at the turn of the century. Mark Sullivan, in *Our Times*, has raised the question of why New Jersey "voluntarily assumed a role which made it a subject of jeering for twenty years," after New York and Ohio court decisions had killed the trusts in those States. He cites the theory of Steffens that New Jersey's position as the terminal of many great railroad systems made the State responsive to corporate influence, and he suggests that nearness to Wall Street may also have been a factor.

Another probable reason, Sullivan points out, was the fact that many of the ablest New Jersey citizens were commuters who took little interest in the State in which they merely slept. "In such a community," he concludes, "it would be easy for politicians and lawyers representing financial interests to take possession of the machinery of the State and to use it to the advantage of the interests they represented. The revenue accruing to the State from the fees it received for providing a home for outside corporations lightened the burden of taxes on New Jersey voters and their property. Many New Jersey people frankly and publicly justified the laws favoring the trusts on that ground."

The nineteenth century revolt against railroad domination was soon paralleled by an early twentieth century attack on the trusts and machine politics. George L. Record, who had broken with the Hudson County Democratic machine, was the leader of the "New Idea" movement that carried the assault. Closely associated with him were Mark Fagan, who repudiated his boss after being elected the first Republican mayor of Jersey City in many years; Austin Colgate, Frank Sommer, Everett Colby and others. Their program called for election reforms, equal taxation of railroads and utilities, and regulation of public utilities. Although the New Idea men accomplished little during the terms of Governors Stokes and Fort, they had their chance with Governor Woodrow Wilson.

Paradoxically, Wilson was nominated in 1910 by the Democratic leaders against the opposition of the young progressives in his party. Colonel George Harvey was looking for a 1912 Presidential candidate. He induced James Smith Jr., titular Democratic chief, to select Wilson as a man who would impart a respectable tone to the gubernatorial campaign. When the "safe" professor from Princeton University repudiated the bosses during the campaign, they did not take him seriously. When, however, after election, Wilson successfully supported James E. Martine against Smith for United States Senator, the machine politicians realized that they had unwittingly elected a champion of the progressives.

Upon the strength of this victory, Wilson was able to push through his bewildered legislature bills for direct primaries, regulation of public utilities, employers' liability, and other reforms, which were in part inspired and supported by some of the New Idea Republicans, notably George L. Record. Thus Wilson sought to justify his belief in the mission of New Jersey as a "mediating" State, destined to inspire and lead her neighbors into better ways. His courageous and successful fight for reform made him President in 1912, in spite of the bitter opposition of the very men who had deliberately started him on the road to that office.

Wilson held his post in Trenton until March 1, 1913, completing his program by passage of the "Seven Sisters" acts. With these laws he hoped to restrain monopolies and to impose penalties against individual officers of offending corporations. Other States promptly invited the business which New Jersey turned away; while New Jersey "mediated," they would take the cash. With Wilson safely in Washington, the "Seven Sisters" acts were gradually repealed until by 1920 there was hardly a vestige left, but New Jersey never recaptured her former pre-eminence as the favorite home for new corporations.

Ironically, at the time when the State was first perceiving the danger of corporation control, there arose a new industrial power. In 1903 the Public Service Corporation was formed and started on its way toward virtual control of gas and electric power, trolley and bus transportation.

Under Governor Fielder the reform movement continued at a slower pace until it was interrupted by the World War. New Jersey's geography and its industrial resources gave it a strategic part in the conflict. Camp Dix at Wrightstown was an important training center, and Camp Merritt (near Dumont) and Hoboken became known to a majority of the men who went overseas as their last points of contact with the homeland. New Jersey shipyards were unceasingly busy and New Jersey factories supplied a large proportion of the Nation's chemicals and munitions. Governor Walter E. Edge declared, however, that the outstanding features of his wartime term were "the inauguration of the State highway system, the Delaware River Bridge, and the Hudson River Tunnels," and the establishment of the State department of institutions and agencies.

The State's post-war improvement of transportation facilities attests Edge's perspicacity. When the automobile required another modernization of the New York-Philadelphia highways, New Jersey responded with a splendid and expensive highway system, a proud bid for the praise of millions of travelers who annually cross its borders. Another post-war development was a widespread popular campaign against the utilities, featured by attacks on the gas and electric rates and a spreading though scattered demand for public ownership.

To understand New Jersey in the twentieth century, it is necessary to visualize the progressive transformation of the State from an agricultural to a primarily industrial and urban region. In 1890 the urban population was about 60 percent; by 1900 it was about 70 percent, and by 1930 it was 82.6 percent.

While wealth and industry continued to increase, agriculture declined in relative importance. The amount of improved farming land dropped from 1,977,042 acres in 1899 to 1,305,528 acres in 1924, although the total value of farm produce showed a gain, largely because of the concentrated poultry and dairy industries. On the other hand the value of industrial output multiplied sixfold from $611,748,000 in 1900 to $3,937,-157,00 in 1930, and the number of wage earners rose from 241,582 to 442,328.

The total population more than doubled between 1900 and 1930, rising from 1,883,669 to 4,041,334. The most spectacular growth was in the five counties of the New York metropolitan area which reached a total of 2,496,558, about three-fifths of the State's population.

A large volume of immigration helped to push census figures upward and to increase the diversification of population that began in Colonial times. To the Colonial settlers—Dutch, English, Scotch and smaller numbers of French, Germans, Swedes, Negroes and others—thousands of Irish and Germans had been added by the middle of the nineteenth century. In the latter part of the century large numbers of immigrants from southern and eastern Europe poured into New Jersey via New York.

The State's immigrant population was further increased between 1920 and 1930 (after the influx from Europe had been stemmed by Federal legislation) through migration from other States. Although the foreign-born white population of the entire Nation increased by only 111,013 in that decade and most States showed a decline, the figure for New Jersey rose by 106,014 to a total of 844,442—almost double the number of foreign-born whites in 1900.

The most rapid increase in the Negro population occurred in the large cities, beginning when World War industries mustered man power. Many hundreds of Negroes were also imported for work as servants in the homes of wealthy residents of Montclair and other suburban communities. By 1930 the Negro population was 208,828, almost treble the figure in 1900.

The twentieth century politics of New Jersey has continued to be dominated—after the interruption of Woodrow Wilson's term as Governor—by the natural conservatism of the industrial and business interests. The conservative forces have helped to defeat movements toward municipal ownership of utilities, to hamper organization of labor, and to del[...] ernization of the archaic property tax system.

In the political field, the blurring of party labels in the 1880's became almost a total effacement by the 1920's. Although New Jersey remained Republican in national politics from 1896 to 1932, except when Wilson won in 1912, it has been much more inclined to elect Democratic Governors. Since Wilson's term, the Republicans have elected only three Governors, Walter Edge in 1916, Morgan Larson in 1928, and Harold G. Hoffman in 1934. The former two derived great strength from concurrent Presidential tickets; while Hoffman's stormy administration demonstrated the candor with which Frank Hague, Mayor of Jersey City and the State's most powerful Democrat, harmonized the theoretical differences of the two major parties to obtain quick unchallenged action for his conservative supporters. This unusual cooperation between Democratic and Republican chieftains moved the New York *Times* to exclaim editorially, "If most politics is queer, New Jersey politics is queerer."

Both Hoffman and Hague have made official efforts to check the growth of the Congress of Industrial Organizations in mass industries. Although locally the Democratic Party had for years advocated legislation to curb injunctions in labor disputes, it reversed its position in 1937. Mayor Hague explained that he felt the shift was necessary to avoid frightening employers or prospective employers from the State.

The responsibility for piloting the State through the depression fell on both the Democratic and Republican Parties. The administration of relief was handled by the State until 1936, when the legislature turned it back to the municipalities. Although the change was hailed by some as a step toward economy and common sense, searching and severe criticism soon came from experts of the State and Federal Governments. In 1937, a study for the Social Science Research Council showed that the average New Jersey family on relief lived 40 percent below the minimum subsistence standard, and that it was practically impossible for many of the smaller communities to give adequate aid.

In the 1937 gubernatorial campaign the Democratic candidate, Senator A. Harry Moore, defeated the Reverend Lester H. Clee by the slender margin of 43,600 votes, as compared with a Moore plurality of 230,053 in the 1931 election. Dissatisfied with the results of the election of 1937, representatives of a large portion of the 425,000 New Jersey members of the Committee for Industrial Organization and the American Federation of Labor held a preliminary convention in the fall of 1937, looking toward the formation of an independent Labor Party in New Jersey.

Despite population growth and industrial changes undreamed of in Colonial days, the essential pattern of New Jersey history remains inseparable from that of her neighbors across the Hudson and Delaware Rivers. Concrete highways, steel rails and air lanes have made New Jersey more than ever the corridor between New York and Philadelphia. The State's factories and farms help to sustain the economy of the neighboring metropolises; its homes and apartment houses shelter many thousands of New York and Pennsylvania workers; its industrial and labor policies, its corporation laws and its tax system are determined always with an eye to their effect upon competition with the neighboring States.

Government

ALTHOUGH government in New Jersey is essentially the same in general pattern as in each of the other 47 States, there is an amazing number of important differences. In this treatment of the constitutional and political structure of the State, emphasis is placed on these differences as well as on the antiquities and the innovations of which New Jersey citizens are especially proud.

At the outset of the Revolution the fourth Provincial Congress of New Jersey transformed itself into a constitutional convention and on July 2, 1776, adopted a constitution which contained a declaration of independence. New Jersey was the fourth Colony to take this step; and although the work was done hastily and was not intended to be permanent, the constitution was retained for 68 years.

Reflecting the antagonism of its framers to executive interference with the legislature, the constitution was a strange document in that it violated the "separation of powers" principle in a great variety of ways. The Governor was to be elected by the legislature every year; yet he was granted both judicial and legislative powers. At the same time the legislature reserved a large measure of executive and judicial power for itself.

In the case of Holmes v. Walton in 1779, New Jersey set the first precedent after the Revolution for exercise of the power of judicial review—the right of courts to declare legislative acts invalid.

The Constitution of 1844: Despite obvious inefficiencies and inequalities in the original constitution and bitter attacks on it, it continued in force until 1844. Then popular sentiment, stirred by democratic Jacksonian tendencies, demanded further revision. Lacking any machinery for revising the original constitution, the legislature of 1844 simply went ahead and called a convention. The work of the convention was ratified at a special election on August 13. The new constitution abolished property qualifications for voters and legislators, recognized the principle of separation of powers among the three departments of government, and (unlike the document of 1776) included a formal bill of rights and provision for amendment.

Only three times (1875, 1897, and 1927) in the period of nearly 100 years since its adoption has the New Jersey Constitution been amended—not because few amendments have been proposed but because the process is extremely difficult. Amendments must be passed by two successive legislatures and then approved by the people, with the restriction that amendments may not be submitted to popular vote more often than once in five years.

For more than 60 years attempts have been made to revise the document as a whole. But the legislature has never consented to a constitutional convention, largely because the senate, which is based upon equal representation of the counties, has feared that a convention might revise this system, thus shifting the balance of power from the less populous counties. Industrial New Jersey therefore continues to live under a constitution designed for an essentially agricultural population.

Aside from its age and inflexibility, the New Jersey Constitution is distinguished as one of the briefest in the country, containing only the bare outlines of a frame of government. It embodies little regulatory law, and the legislature is left with full responsibility for setting up administrative departments, most of the courts, and practically the entire system of local government. This situation somewhat compensates for the difficult amending process.

The Legislature: Like every other State except Nebraska, New Jersey has a two-house legislature. But in other important respects the State's legislative machine is distinctive. One of the seven smallest in size, it is composed of a senate of 21 members (one for each county) and an assembly of 60. It is one of only five State legislatures that hold annual sessions. New Jersey is now the only State that has annual elections for members of the lower house, and no other State has a three-year term for senators. Equal representation of the counties in the State senate, giving the balance of power to the less populous counties, is another unusual feature, inherited from the constitution of 1776.

Members of the assembly are apportioned among the counties according to population. For more than 40 years assemblymen were elected by districts within the counties, but in 1893 the State Supreme Court declared this method unconstitutional, thus requiring the election of each county delegation at large. The matter would doubtless never have reached the courts if both parties had not been scandalously gerrymandering the assembly districts.

The overwhelming advantage of the smaller counties in the upper house is shown by the fact that the four largest counties, with 54 percent of the

State's population in 1930, have only 19 percent of the voting strength in the senate. In the assembly the "Big Four"—Essex, Hudson, Bergen, and Union Counties—have 52 percent of the voting power. Although much may be said for finely balancing the legislature between the rural and metropolitan areas, the system has been bitterly criticized. As far back as 1873 the Newark *Daily Advertiser* lamented editorially:

> The pine-barrens have beaten the populace. Ten gentlemen, representing the wealth, power, honor and good sense of the State of New Jersey, representing also the bulk of its population and its true will and purpose, yesterday voted for a competing railroad between New York and Philadelphia. Eleven other men, whose title is Senator, representing an innumerable host of stunted pines, growing on sand-barrens, voted the bill down . . . You can't make pine trees vote nor endow them with a conscience.

Because of the small size of the State, the legislature can conduct its sessions on an unusual plan, meeting only every Monday night during the greater part of the session. Any legislator can travel by rail or motor from his home to Trenton in not more than three hours. This makes it possible for members to live at home and conduct their regular professional or business activities while the legislature is in session. It is important that they do so, since senators and assemblymen are paid only $500 a year.

The Governor: New Jersey is the only State with a three-year term for Governor, matching that for State senators. The Governor's salary of $20,000 is the highest paid by any State except New York. As in a dozen other States, the Governor may not succeed himself, but this restriction operates more severely in New Jersey than in these other States, in each of which the Governor enjoys a four-year term. Since 1844 only three men have been elected twice to the Governorship: Joel Parker and Leon Abbett each served two terms, and A. Harry Moore is now in his third term. Another peculiarity is that in New Jersey, as in only three other States, the Governor is the only official chosen by State-wide election. There is no Lieutenant Governor, the next in line being the president of the senate.

In the number and variety of offices filled by gubernatorial appointment the Governor of New Jersey has a decided advantage over those of most other States. For example, he appoints all State judges and county prosecutors—positions filled in many other States by election. Nevertheless his position is not so powerful as one might suppose. Some administrative officials are chosen by the legislature, and most of the others either have terms longer than that of the Governor or administer departments headed by boards whose members have overlapping terms.

As in only six other States, a bare majority of the legislature can override the Governor's veto; the veto power is therefore of little value. Another serious handicap to the Governor is his incapacity to succeed himself. Woodrow Wilson bitterly denounced this constitutional limitation in 1913, pointing out that the politicians "smile at the coming and going of Governors as some men in Washington have smiled at the coming and going of Presidents, as upon things ephemeral, which passed and were soon enough rid of if you but sat tight and waited."

It naturally follows that no Governor except one with the most unusual qualities or remarkable good luck can make and keep himself the dominant factor in State government. Woodrow Wilson did it because he rode into office on a wave of reform sentiment that transcended party lines, and he developed an effective technique of appealing to the people through newspaper interviews and public addresses. Perhaps the greatest of his assets was his inflexible obstinacy in holding to a position, no matter how terrifying the opposition.

New Jersey follows an acknowledged pattern in American politics, according to which the legislature and the Governor act largely in consultation with party leaders. Legislative policy is frequently determined through informal councils of legislative and party leaders.

The State is one of 18 in which the Governor does not have full power of pardon. A strange feature is that the Board of Pardons includes, in addition to the Governor, the chancellor and the six lay judges of the Court of Errors and Appeals, thus injecting the highest court of the State into what always has been considered an executive prerogative designed to correct miscarriages of justice for which there was no judicial remedy.

Executive Departments: When the constitution was adopted in 1844, the State administration consisted of little more than the Governor, six constitutional departments, and a single State institution, the prison at Trenton. Since that time the number of State departments and agencies has increased steadily. The movement has been checked, but never stopped, by occasional consolidations involving a few related departments.

Today there are more than 80 separate administrative departments in the State government; and if the semi-independent boards heading the several institutions and agencies are included, the total is approximately 100 distinct administrative agencies.

A rough classification shows that there are approximately a dozen departments or agencies dealing primarily with the State's fiscal affairs; about half a dozen primarily engaged in maintaining law and order; 8, not counting the 17 separate institutions and agencies under the department of institutions and agencies, responsible for protecting public health and welfare; more than 20, counting some 15 examining boards, engaged in economic regulation and promotion; 16 or more responsible for public works, conservation, and recreation; and about 2 primarily devoted to education and research. A few of these departments or agencies are at present languishing for lack of appropriations, but they may always be revived by new funds.

The State pay roll is the best index of the phenomenal increase in governmental operations during the past few years. From the fiscal year 1916–17 to the fiscal year 1936–37 the number of employees as reported by the Civil Service Commission jumped from 2,900 to about 11,800; and the pay roll climbed even more sharply from $3,600,000 to about $18,-500,000.

The number and variety of the State departments and commissions long have constituted an obvious argument for reorganization and simplification. For nearly 40 years such a movement has been under way, but progress has been slow. In 1925 the legislature received a plan for merging 78 permanent departments into 14 large units; nothing at all was done about this report. Four years later the National Institute of Public Administration made similar recommendations. Nearly all of these were likewise ignored, but some fiscal reforms were made.

Princeton University was the next institution to play doctor to the State government. Dr. Harold W. Dodds prescribed some of the same medicine recommended by the Institute of Public Administration, including consolidation of all fiscal functions under one commissioner responsible to the Governor. But the legislature showed its characteristic distrust of the Governor and instead of unifying the financial structure added one more department.

Most of the State departments are administered by boards appointed by the Governor. Board members generally are not paid, although necessary expenses are customarily granted and some very adequate salaries are given to a few—such as the three public utility commissioners, who draw $12,-000 annually. Each board usually selects the active department head, although the Governor appoints both the boards and the commissioners of education and aviation. Thirteen other department heads are appointed by the Governor subject to senatorial confirmation and in most cases with terms longer than the Governor's. Only two department heads are appointed by the Governor to hold office at his pleasure. The heads of five important departments are elected by the two houses of the legislature in joint session.

Confirmation of appointments by the senate is anything but an empty form in New Jersey. Gubernatorial recommendations have not infrequently been turned down, often under the principle of senatorial courtesy which requires that the nominee be acceptable to the senator from his home county. Political horse trading becomes almost imperative when the Governor must bargain with a hostile senate, a common situation in New Jersey.

One of the most important executive departments has developed from the old State prison and the first hospital for the insane, which opened in 1848. This, the department of institutions and agencies, administers 17 institutions for the insane, feebleminded, tubercular, delinquent, and epileptic, and for old soldiers; and two agencies: the commission for the blind and the board of children's guardians. Mental hygiene clinics operated under this department provide the services of expert psychiatrists for the ordinary citizen who cannot afford to pay private practitioners. New Jersey's work in this field has placed it well ahead of most other States.

An administrative curiosity in New Jersey is the department of agriculture. The State board of agriculture consists of eight members chosen by a convention of delegates from the chief farm organizations of the State, an unusual example of functional representation.

An obvious result of New Jersey's location between New York and Philadelphia has been the necessity for working agreements with her neighboring States on interstate construction projects and port development, the management of water supply and garbage disposal. New Jersey operates, jointly with New York, the Palisades Interstate Park, and is also a partner in the Port of New York Authority, builder of four great bridges and two vehicular tunnels linking the two States, and a model for similar publicly owned corporations throughout the country. At Camden the State joined with Pennsylvania in building the Delaware River bridge to Philadelphia. It was thus natural that New Jersey took the lead in 1935 in a step for permanent commissions on interstate cooperation, to operate both regionally and nationally.

One of nine States with civil service systems, New Jersey shares with Massachusetts the distinction of being one of the two States in which jurisdiction of the commission has been extended to all county and local units operating under civil service. Only 10 of the 21 New Jersey counties and only 22 municipalities have adopted the civil service system, but these include the largest population areas and well over half of the full-time employees in local units of the State.

Local Government: According to a 1937 Princeton University bulletin there are 1,137 separate self-governing units within the State classified as follows:

Counties	21
Cities	52
Boroughs	254
Towns	23
Townships	233
Villages	3
School Districts	551
Total	1,137

In addition, the survey found about 225 special intra-municipal districts and about a score of regional and inter-municipal districts and commissions. "This is the New Jersey patchwork . . . ," says the Princeton report.

The terms "city," "town," "borough" and "township" are entirely meaningless as far as classification by size or area is concerned. The largest city is Newark, with nearly half a million residents; the smallest is Corbin City, with a population of 256. The largest township is North Bergen, population 40,714; the smallest is Pahaquarry, population 80. North Cape May and South Cape May, with populations of 5 and 6, are the smallest boroughs.

Patchwork government is expensive, the Princeton survey declares. Citing the police organization, a 1936 bulletin says:

There are 350 separate and independent police departments in New Jersey, of which 127 are in the five counties covering a scant 700 square miles of northeastern New Jersey. Nowhere else in the United States is there such a concentration of separate police agencies in so small an area.

This goes far to explain the fact that costs of New Jersey police protection are not only the highest in the United States for cities of the corresponding size groups, but in some cases *they are nearly twice as high.*

At the entrance to the Holland tunnel a citizen can be arrested by at least five different sets of police officers, for violation of several sets of traffic laws.

Six municipalities have the city manager form of government, the largest being Trenton, a city of more than 125,000. Cape May City in 1937 abandoned the manager plan for the commission form, which is so generally preferred by the larger municipalities that the Princeton experts have labeled New Jersey "the most commission-ridden State in the Union." Fifty-three of the 565 municipalities in the State are now operating under the commission form authorized by the so-called Walsh Act of 1911. In these municipalities, which include Newark, Jersey City and many other large cities, all legislative and administrative functions of local government are vested in a single commission, usually of five persons, elected at large every four years.

The system originally was lauded as simple, responsible, and easy for the public to control. In practice, however, the lack of centralized responsibility in a single executive, the failure to distinguish between policy formation and administration, the designation of politically elected commissioners to head departments requiring able technical direction, and especially the lack of centralized financial administration—all have run counter to the high hopes of the municipal reformers of the early part of the century.

Under the general municipalities act the 233 New Jersey townships have the same powers and functions as all other local units. Township government is substantially of the commission form, the principal difference being that the township committeemen are elected for overlapping terms, so that the whole committee is never voted in or out at the same time. Township government, therefore, displays the same weaknesses as the pure commission form.

The other types of local government—city, borough, town—vary widely. A relatively small number vest substantial authority in the mayor as a real chief executive, but much more numerous are those in which administrative responsibility is largely taken by the council, or by committees or boards not effectively controlled by the mayor. Thus, even these units display weaknesses similar to those of townships and commission municipalities, especially the lack of centralized financial control. This doubtless accounts in large measure for the gloomy situation described by the Princeton survey in June 1936 when it reported that the course of municipal government in New Jersey had resulted in a gross debt of almost 20 percent of net taxable valuation, $121,479,000 in uncollected property taxes, 1 out of every 8 municipalities in default on notes or bonds, and 12 municipalities in virtual bankruptcy and under State supervision.

For counties, the governing body is a "Board of Chosen Freeholders" of three, five, or nine members, which is in reality the familiar commission plan again. But these boards are by no means overworked since judges, prosecutors and some other officers are appointed by the Governor, while the sheriff, county clerk, and surrogate are elected by the people. All of these officials and others besides are wholly or largely beyond control of the freeholders. Chief functions of the county boards are the building and maintenance of roads and bridges, and the management of county institutions other than the jail. Salaries of the freeholders are as high as $6,000 in the two largest counties.

Parties and Elections: Governor Woodrow Wilson advocated the direct primary as a means of taking the nomination of candidates and the selection of party committee members away from the bosses and giving the parties back to the people. Although the old-line politicians fought for retention of the convention system, Wilson won. It is a tribute to the ingenuity and the steadfastness of purpose of the political leaders of both parties that the direct primary appears to have had little effect upon control of the parties.

In the Democratic Party, the result perhaps has been to strengthen the State organization led by Jersey City's present (1939) mayor, Frank Hague. His Hudson County organization is held by students of practical politics to be probably the most smoothly running machine in the country. Substantially one-third of all the votes cast in the State Democratic primary come from his county.

Republican leadership is more scattered, and the party's primaries often present lively contests in striking contrast to the peaceful balloting of the Democrats. Usually the party is controlled by a semi-permanent coalition of leaders from Republican strongholds.

The overwhelming Democratic vote in Hudson and Middlesex Counties, and considerable Democratic strength elsewhere, make it relatively easy for the Democrats to elect a Governor. But apportionment in the legislature based on counties seriously handicaps their efforts to win a majority in either house. Since 1910 the Democrats have elected their gubernatorial candidate six times out of nine, whereas they have controlled both the assembly and senate in only two years—1913 and 1914. This constant division of State machinery between the two major parties has been cited as justification for the system (roundly attacked by Woodrow Wilson) under which leaders of the two parties unite in political action. This system, it is said, tends to prevent a deadlock on appointments and legislation.

Minor parties have played practically no part in New Jersey politics. Great efficiency of the two major party organizations, and the support of organized labor for candidates of one or the other party, have prevented the Socialists and other groups from showing any considerable strength.

Annual conventions for preparing party platforms are held after the primary elections. An interesting law names as delegates the members of the State committee of the party, the candidates for the legislature, governorship and Congress, as well as hold-over members of the legislature.

The Administration of Justice: New Jersey courts have changed relatively little since the time of George III, and the intricate judicial system is puzzling to the lawyer as well as to the layman. There are about twenty different courts created by the constitution or by legislative enactment; several have overlapping jurisdictions, and two or three are practically without parallel in other States.

Charles H. Hartshorne's characterization of the New Jersey judicial system, written in 1905, is as accurate today as when it was penned: ". . . our system is the most antiquated and intricate that exists in any considerable community of English-speaking people . . . Both courts and procedure were brought here from England by our colonial forefathers and were worked into shape fitted to the needs of a rural community of eighteenth century colonists. They are fundamentally in that shape today." Although procedure has been greatly simplified since 1905, the court structure itself has become more rather than less involved.

The State has three distinctive judicial hierarchies: the law courts, for the trial of criminal and civil actions under statutory law; the eqity courts, for giving legal relief not afforded by the law courts; and the prerogative or probate courts, for wills and estates.

The Court of Errors and Appeals is the highest tribunal in each of these three hierarchies. As the name implies, it handles nothing except appeals from the lower courts. It is unique in name and structure. Six of its sixteen members are laymen (or at least need not be lawyers), while the other ten comprise the chancellor of the State, the chief justice and the eight associate justices of the Supreme Court. The chancellor is the presiding judge. The provision for lay members, who are appointed for six-year terms, stems from Colonial times; indeed, until 1844 the Governor and his council constituted the court of last resort.

In the law courts the second highest body is the Supreme Court, which handles both criminal and civil cases, although the latter are limited to suits involving $3,000 or more. It is authorized to superintend or review the conduct of all inferior courts and public officers. The chief justice receives $19,000 a year and the eight associate justices get $18,000. The term is seven years.

The Circuit Courts enjoy common law jurisdiction in civil cases concurrent with the Supreme Court within the counties in which they are held, and statutory jurisdiction in a number of specific matters. The Common Pleas Court, consisting of from one to five judges in each county, also deals with civil matters, but its judges hear criminal cases when they sit in the courts of Quarter Sessions, Special Sessions, and Oyer and Terminer.

Civil actions involving less than $500 are tried in county or city district courts. In some counties there are also criminal district courts to relieve the common pleas judges of lesser criminal trials. At the very bottom of the system are the recorders' courts, the police courts and local justices of the peace.

New Jersey is one of a half dozen States in which the equity or chancery courts are still separated from the common law courts. The chief equity judge is the chancellor, appointed by the Governor for a seven-year term at a salary of $19,000 a year. The chancellor, in turn, appoints ten vice chancellors for seven-year terms at salaries of $18,000 each. The vice chancellors, acting theoretically for the chancellor, sit individually at strategic points throughout the State. As mentioned above, the chancellor is also the presiding judge of the Court of Errors and Appeals. The Chancery Court is assisted by numerous masters in chancery appointed by the chancellor.

The Court of Chancery has been vigorously attacked and defended in connection with its issuance of injunctions in labor disputes. Trade unionists and liberals have for years unsuccessfully sought an amendment to the State constitution that would curtail the court's power. Mortgage foreclosures, divorces, insolvencies, and guardianships are other matters that come before this court.

In the third judicial hierarchy the chancellor and his ten vice chancellors constitute the Prerogative or High Probate Court. As the chief probate judge, the chancellor is known as the Surrogate General or Ordinary; and a vice chancellor sitting on probate matters is termed a Vice Ordinary. Appeals to the Prerogative Court lie from the Orphans' Court, held by a common pleas judge—another example of the crisscrossing of the New Jersey judicial system.

The prerogative courts have jurisdiction over matters relating to wills, administrators and executors of estates, guardianship, and the recovery of legacies. Uncontested wills are admitted for probate before the surrogate of each county. The surrogate, although he is sometimes thought of as the lowest probate judge, is in reality nothing more than an administrative officer.

Attached to the common law system is the important Juvenile and Domestic Relations Court, which does not logically belong in any of the three hierarchies. This court is held by separate judges in the four largest counties—Essex, Hudson, Bergen and Union. In all other counties, a common pleas judge adds this to his multifarious duties.

Under New Jersey's juvenile court act no person under 16 is deemed capable of committing a crime, although the Court of Errors and Appeals has twice held that the constitutional guarantee of trial by jury renders the Juvenile Court (which does not use a jury) incompetent to hear cases involving "the malicious killing of a human being." The act, one of the most progressive in the United States, allows wide authority to the judge. At least in the four counties with separate judges, these courts are sharing with those in only a few other jurisdictions in the country the distinction of blazing a trail toward a new conception of juvenile delinquency and perhaps of crime in general.

Unusual is the fact that all State judges, from the members of the Court of Errors and Appeals to the civil and criminal district court judges, are appointed by the Governor with the consent of the senate. In most other States all or nearly all judges are elected. In spite of the allegation that politics plays a part in these appointments, New Jersey courts have attained a high standing. One recent study of the prestige of the highest State courts gave a better rating to the courts only of New York, Massachusetts, and Illinois. Moreover, there is a seldom broken custom of reappointing justices of the higher courts regardless of politics.

Attempts to simplify the judicial machinery have been defeated for many years. Since 1930 the Judicial Council, consisting of the attorney general and representatives of the courts, the bar association and the legislature, has been making recommendations for changes in the constitution, the statutes, and the rules and procedures of the courts. Some real progress has been made; but so far the council has been unsuccessful in securing the adoption of its constitutional amendments, the most important of which would create a separate high court of appeals in place of the present Court of Errors and Appeals. This would have the result of ending the dual role played by Supreme Court justices and the chancellor as both trial judges in their respective courts and appellate justices in the Court of Errors and Appeals. The Judicial Council proposals would also eliminate lay judges, and would create a separate court of pardons.

Penal Institutions: In contrast to its archaic legal machinery, the State's penal institutions are as progressive as any in the land. One of the best features is the system of segregation, classification and individual treatment of inmates. Criminals are classified and put in separate institutions for men, women and youths, as well as for the feebleminded, epileptic, tubercular and insane.

Each institution has a classification committee consisting of the superintendent and other officers, including a physician, a psychiatrist, a psychologist, a chaplain and the director of education. This committee studies each inmate upon admission, prescribes a course of personal treatment, and reports periodically on progress. The advisory committee on penal institutions, probation and parole of the Wickersham Commission on Law Observance and Enforcement in 1931, after describing this system in detail, commented: "It is clear that there is a plan of institutional treatment, carried on by a whole State, quite unusual in the United States."

Work is an essential part of the program. The prison industries in New Jersey are conducted under what is called the "State use system." This means that goods produced are sold only to State departments or agencies, and thus do not find their way to the open market in competition with the products of free labor.

The State has an unusually liberal probation law, under which sentence can be suspended for practically any crime if circumstances indicate that imprisonment would destroy the convict's usefulness without giving additional protection to society. Parole is supervised by the State department of institutions and agencies, while probation is handled by the counties. As a result, the probation system is highly developed in some of the larger counties, but is still in a rudimentary stage in others.

Paying for Government: What does this remarkable system of government, this bewildering aggregation of State departments and local units, cost the people of New Jersey, and how do they pay for it? Dogmatic answers cannot be given to these questions because of the inadequacy of the records and because of theoretical differences in opinion as to just what should be included in the term "cost of government." The following statements dealing primarily with the revenue system will give, however, a rough sketch of the problem.

According to *Local Government Bulletin No. 2* of the Princeton Local Government Survey, the total State and local taxes levied in New Jersey for the year ending December 31, 1935, were $320,477,621. A little more than a quarter of this amount was in State taxes, the rest in local taxes. Since the State returns a considerable amount of its revenues to local units, the Princeton survey points out that the total tax bill was earmarked for expenditure by the several units of government in the following proportions:

State	$ 58,134,259
Municipalities	133,340,732
School Districts	80,470,796
Counties	48,531,834

The Princeton report concludes, therefore, that "local government in New Jersey, including the counties, spends over four-fifths of the State and local tax dollar."

It must be borne in mind that the above figures do not represent actual total expenditures or costs of government. Something less than a third of the money used in government in New Jersey is derived from nontax revenues in the form of a great variety of fees, permits, grants, earnings, etc. In addition, a considerable amount of borrowed money is spent each year, but such money must be repaid out of receipts from taxes and other sources.

The general property tax—that is, the tax on real estate and personal property both tangible and intangible, including the tax on railroads—is the backbone of the New Jersey tax system. In 1935, according to the Princeton survey, "the property tax provided 76 percent of the total State and local tax revenue and 89 percent of all local tax revenues." As a result of the incompleteness of the assessment of personal property, about nine-tenths of the general property tax revenue is derived from real estate.

The United States Census Bureau reported that in 1932 only four States —Indiana, Illinois, Michigan, and Arizona—obtained as large a proportion of their State and local taxes from real and personal property as New Jersey. This is especially remarkable in view of the fact that New Jersey is one of the most highly industrialized States; and the assumption would be that financial and commercial enterprise would yield a higher proportion of revenue.

About 96 percent of the taxes on property goes to the counties, municipalities and school districts. The State derives the bulk of its revenue from other taxes; notably more than $18,500,000 from the gasoline tax, almost as much from motor vehicle registration and license fees, and varying but substantial amounts from transfer inheritance taxes. Corporation taxes, including taxes on foreign insurance companies, annually yield several million dollars, as do beverage licenses and taxes. For four months in 1935 a consumers' sales tax produced good revenues, but the tax proved so unpopular that it was repealed at a special session of the legislature.

Aside from property taxes, the principal local tax revenue is derived from public utilities. Local units also collect the poll tax, dog taxes and miscellaneous license taxes, while the State government collects small sums from a variety of minor taxes and licenses. The fish and game commission collects about one-third of a million dollars from sportsmen's licenses. All told, State and local units in New Jersey collect about 30 different kinds of taxes. Nevertheless, New Jersey is one of 18 States with no income tax.

Industry and Commerce

AGRICULTURAL development was the chief economic interest of New Jersey during the early period of its existence as a Colony. Small farms were intensively cultivated in the eastern section and large plantations, operated mainly by Negro slaves, flourished in the west. Although the isolation of farm people contributed to the establishment of home industry, it likewise stunted commercial manufacturing.

The self-supporting farm was the standard unit of the Colony's economy for the two earliest generations at least. Even the small towns clustered at the head of tidewater regions on the eastern shore or along the Delaware were largely devoted to agriculture. Soap, candles, textiles, even tools were manufactured in the home by the pioneer women and children.

Trade, however, began to flourish almost as soon as the Colonists sighted the Indians. Furs, skins, and tobacco found a ready market in England; oil and fish in Spain, Portugal, and the Canary Islands; and agricultural products in neighboring Colonies and the West Indies.

Gradually manufacture spread from the home to the community. The miller, almost invariably first on the scene, was soon joined by the weaver, fuller, tanner, shoemaker, and carpenter. Newark had a commercial gristmill in 1671, and the earliest sawmill was established in Woodbridge in 1682. Tanning, which had been started as a business in Elizabeth in 1664 by the Ogden family, quickly led to saddlery and harness making.

The fine forests in southern New Jersey yielded their lumber to ship carpenters of Burlington, Salem, Newton, and Cape May, where shipbuilding became a leading industry. Equally significant was the development of whaling from Cape May and Tuckerton; in many respects these towns rivaled the more celebrated New England ports of the Colonial period. Tar and turpentine were also important exports from the southern part of the Colony.

Toward the close of the seventeenth and opening of the eighteenth centuries, several industries were founded in New Jersey that were destined to become not only leading sources of wealth but traditional occupations as well. An abundant supply of beaver, raccoon, and sheep furnished the materials for hat manufacturing, which attained its greatest strength in the southern area. At the same time, the Colony was rapidly becoming distinguished for its brewing skill. Hoboken, still identified with beer drinking, had the first brewery in 1642. Beer was a major interest in Burlington in 1698. Two years later, Newark made more than 1,000 barrels of cider, and Jersey applejack seems to have been as renowned among the Colonies as it was throughout the East during the recent prohibition era.

In several spurs of the Appalachian range, running through the northern and central sections of the State, lay mineral deposits unusual for their richness and variety. The State's earliest iron works were established at Shrewsbury in 1676 by Colonel Lewis Morris, a merchant of the Barbadoes. Forges, furnaces, and bloomeries began to appear all over the northern part of the State, with a concentration at Boonton, the center of seven rich mines in Morris County which supplied most of the Nation's iron. These mines were a mainstay to Washington's army during the Revolution.

At the same time, swamps throughout southern New Jersey were utilized as an important source of iron deposits. Iron-laden water impregnated the marshy soil; the Indians had long used this ore, mixed with bear grease, to make an excellent war paint. The ore was hauled to charcoal-heated furnaces built on the banks of streams, which provided power for the bellows and an easy means of shipping the finished product. Weymouth, Batsto, and Atsion were typical iron centers—thriving little communities a century or more ago but ghost towns today. The bog-iron industry lasted until the middle of the nineteenth century, when competition from the iron mines and coal-burning smelters gradually smothered it.

Copper mines were worked in New Brunswick, and in 1768 the discovery that the marl of Monmouth County could be used as fertilizer led to the establishment of another new industry. Steel manufacture at this time was concentrated principally in Trenton.

Another famous early industry in New Jersey was glass making. The first glass factory was founded at Allowaystown in 1740 by Caspar Wistar, a German immigrant. The sand of the southern part of the State proved especially suitable for the manufacture of glass, and within a few decades Salem County was a leading producer of bottles, jugs, pitchers, and other glassware.

The selection of the Falls of Passaic (now Paterson) for the site of a gigantic manufacturing enterprise marked New Jersey's emergence as an important industrial State. Sponsored by Alexander Hamilton in 1791, this undertaking to utilize abundant water power was part of a scheme to make the new Nation independent of foreign industrial products. Although this grandiose aim was not realized, the Society for Establishing Useful Manufactures did succeed in attracting a large part of the textile industry to Paterson.

The first census of manufactures taken in New Jersey in 1810 placed the total industrial wealth at $4,816,288, listing textiles, hides, leather, iron products, and liquor as the most important goods. Cotton manufacture and cotton machinery so completely dominated Paterson at this time that it earned the title of "The Cotton City." Twenty-five forges indicated the growth of mining, while items like 36,000 packs of playing cards and 300,000 pounds of chocolate candy illustrated the diversity of industry.

The invention of new processes in the manufacture of iron, notably Seth Boyden's discovery of a method for making malleable iron in Newark in 1826, brought increased prosperity to this flourishing business. In 1830 the East Jersey Iron Manufacturing Company established a $283,000 plant at Boonton, capable of producing 1,000 tons of malleable iron annually.

Boyden also contributed to the growth of the leather industry with his process for making patent leather. Moses Combs had earlier founded the shoe industry in Newark, and by the end of the eighteenth century a majority of the city's industrial population was engaged in the leather trade. Combs was also famous as the first slave owner in local history to teach his slaves a trade in order to raise their economic and social level.

Shortly after the rise of leather Newark developed another manufacture which has remained one of its leaders. In 1801 Epaphras Hinsdale opened on Broad Street a jewelry factory which soon became a fashionable gathering place for the ladies of the town. By 1836 the industry numbered four establishments, with an annual output valued at $225,000 and 800 workers employed. Many years, however, had to pass before the general public would accept articles known to have been made in America. Believed to be products of Paris or London, Newark jewelry, remarkable for its workmanship, found a market in the largest cities here and abroad.

The influx of European immigrants in the 1840's supplied needed man power to the State's growing factories. Paterson gradually shifted from cotton to silk manufacture after 1840, when John Ryle devised a way of winding silk on a spool. A decade later New Jersey ranked second only to Connecticut in the national production of spool silk, and Paterson was already known as "The Silk City."

In the same period, potteries were founded at Trenton, brick works expanded enormously at Perth Amboy, and in 1852 Edward Balback established America's first smelting and refining plant, on the Passaic River near Newark, where he refined the floor sweepings from local jewelry factories. Woolen mills, formerly situated chiefly in the south at Mount Holly and Bridgeton, began to move north to Passaic.

Old industries yielded to this amazing variety of new occupations. Between 1840 and 1850 Newark alone had been producing more than 2,000,000 pairs of shoes annually. On the eve of the Civil War, however, the industry there as well as in Orange and Burlington revealed the strain of New England competition. Similarly the discovery of rich iron deposits in Michigan and Minnesota began to reduce the State's mining importance.

During the next 20 years the State rode the waves of prosperity born of the Civil War. Although the conflict severely cut trade with the agricultural South, compensations were found in Union Army orders, and improved transportation facilities opened new world markets.

Textiles, locomotives (the first in the State had been built at the Rogers Works in Paterson in 1837), carriages, and machinery achieved wide domestic and foreign sale. Although iron mining was headed downward, the manufacture of heavy machinery in Newark, Jersey City, and Paterson (the latter a center for railroad construction) appeared to make up the loss. Railroads spread all over the State and linked New Jersey more firmly with the rest of the Nation.

Following the panic of 1873, the State entered another period of expansion in which the gains began to fit into New Jersey's industrial pattern as it appears today. Bayonne started on its way to becoming one of the great oil refining centers of the world in 1875 when the Prentice Refining Company established a still there. John D. Rockefeller came next, and within a decade three other companies followed Standard Oil to the site so close to the huge oil and kerosene market in New York City. The steel cable industry was established in Trenton by the Roebling family, and that city became known as a center of supply for suspension bridge construction after the Roeblings built Brooklyn Bridge.

The work of Thomas A. Edison at Menlo Park and Edward Weston at Newark established in New Jersey a vast electrical industry, especially in light bulbs and phonograph records, dynamos, and power plant supplies. John Wesley Hyatt's invention of the roller bearing and celluloid and Hannibal Goodwin's perfection of photographic film introduced important new manufacturing activities into Newark and its environs. As electricity replaced steam in industry, the State's manufacturing strength continued to grow even in the face of depressions. The tremendous rise in immigration from southern and eastern Europe after 1880 brought abundant cheap labor to factories, mills, and foundries.

WIRE MAKING IN THE ROEBLING PLANT, TRENTON

The manufacture of paper and paper boxes, slaughtering and meat packing, and the canning of fruit and vegetables rose in importance after the turn of the century. The hat industry, which in 1892 had produced more than 4,000,000 hats, including a $250 sombrero, was beginning to decline as was the production of ceramics, cast-iron piping, glass, and jewelry. Paterson, where in the 1880's more than one-third of the Nation's silk factories were situated, began to feel the effects of the industrial drift southward to cheaper labor. The dyeing and finishing of textiles, however, increased.

At the outbreak of the World War, New Jersey, along with the rest of the country, faced a period of industrial uncertainty, despite which economists hoped that the feverish gains and losses of the two previous decades might balance into some kind of stability. Abuse of the State's easy incorporation laws had made it a legal dumping ground for young and ruthless corporations, seriously in need of industrial discipline.

The guns of Europe, however, shattered the opportunity for normal growth by plunging the State into the most intense industrialization in its history. The production of high explosives, textiles, steel, and ships rocketed to new heights. The Bureau of Statistics reported that expansion in manufacturing was 400 percent greater in 1916 than in any preceding year. Chief among the cities that benefited from the industrial resurgence were Newark, Perth Amboy, Jersey City, and New Brunswick. The chemical industry in New Jersey sprang up almost overnight. Six factories for the production of aniline, formerly imported from Germany, were set up within the State, the most important at Kearny. Other towns that became chemical centers were Carteret, Chrome, Maywood, and Perth Amboy.

The success of aircraft in the war made aeronautical manufacture in New Jersey a leading industry, chiefly represented by the Wright Aeronautical Corporation of Paterson, one of the world's largest airplane engine factories.

The tide of war prosperity, except for recurrent dips such as that of 1921, continued to rise until 1929. The value of manufactures from 1919 to 1929 increased $165,091,000, whereas workers' wages for the same period rose only $10,000,000, and in the same decade, through technological improvements, there was a decrease of 60,000 workers. Production in chemical factories was 450 percent greater in 1929 than in 1914. Electrical supplies multiplied by 700 percent in the same period, foundry products by 300 percent, and petroleum products by 300 percent.

Building in the middle 1920's prospered to such an extent that the appearance of many New Jersey cities was transformed by the construction of new skyscrapers, factories, apartment houses, small-home developments, and public parks.

In New Jersey as elsewhere this prosperity vanished with the crash in 1929. The State, which had been increasing its industrialization at a terrific rate since 1900, suddenly halted and backslid, so that by 1932 its formerly busy industrial sections became silent witnesses of reckless spending and general lack of planning. Shantytowns built of galvanized iron, packing boxes, and other materials salvaged from dumps sprang up in front of idle factories, and relief became the real industrial problem of the State.

The situation gradually improved. By 1934 recovery slowly began to make itself felt throughout the paralyzed industrial structure. Production in 1937 reached pre-depression levels in some fields, greatest gains being made in the electrical, iron, steel, and aircraft industries. Widespread layoffs in the latter part of the year, characterized as a "recession," interrupted the period of the "little prosperity."

Latest available figures (the 1935 Census of Manufactures) report 377,-078 wage earners in New Jersey, receiving $397,170,661 in 7,468 establishments, the total value of manufactures being listed at $2,439,426,000. These figures represent an increase of 21.3 percent in number of wage earners and 43.6 percent in value of manufactures over 1933. The State has ranked sixth in the Union for industrial production since 1850.

The most important New Jersey industries ranked according to the value of annual output by the 1935 Census of Manufactures are petroleum refining, copper smelting and refining, chemicals, electrical supplies, dyeing and finishing, paints and varnishes, clothing, rubber goods, and foundry products. On the basis of the number of workers employed, dyeing and finishing of textiles holds first place with 16,961 employees.

The State ranks first in the Nation in smelting and refining of copper, dyeing and finishing of textiles, and the production of rubber goods (other than tires). It is second in the manufacture of silk and rayon and chemicals.

The greatest concentration of industry is in Newark and the surrounding area, including Jersey City, Paterson, Passaic, Elizabeth, and Bayonne. Centers of industry outside the metropolitan area include Camden and Trenton on the Delaware River and Perth Amboy on Raritan Bay. Although the "company town" as such is rare in the State, many small communities surrounding the large cities depend solely upon two or three factories or plants for their economic existence.

Petroleum refining, with a yearly output valued at $157,000,000, is centered in Bayonne, where four large companies maintain huge plants to which oil is piped from the Middle West. Three enormous copper and lead smelting firms and a score of smaller gold, silver, and platinum plants constitute the rich refining industry, with annual production valued at $182,000,000. About one-sixth of the zinc in the United States is mined at the New Jersey Zinc Company's plant at Franklin.

Electrical supplies, a comparatively new industry in New Jersey, are manufactured principally in the Newark sector, where appliances, dynamos, and incandescent lamps are produced; while Camden leads the country in the manufacture of radios. The annual output of the electrical industry is valued at $91,000,000.

Paterson and Passaic are the traditional homes of the textile industry. Although the manufacture of silk, rayon, and cotton goods has been steadily declining in this area for the last three decades, it remains—together with finishing and dyeing of textiles—the major occupation. High tax rates, excessive power costs, and destructive price-cutting by some operators have combined to weaken the textile industry in New Jersey. Many of the silk and cotton manufactures have moved their machinery into New England, Pennsylvania, and the South. In 1933, when production throughout the Nation was beginning to rise from the low point of 1932, the output of silk and rayon in New Jersey was 60 percent lower than in pre-war years. Since textiles, however, still employ a greater number of the State's workers than any other one industry (approximately 30 percent in the many branches), the decline constitutes one of New Jersey's most pressing industrial problems.

Other industries that contribute significantly to the State's wealth are cigar and cigarette manufacturing; slaughtering and meat-packing; printing and publishing; canning, in Camden; rubber goods manufacturing, in Trenton and Passaic; shipbuilding, in Kearny and Camden; jewelry-making, in Newark; and soap-making, in Jersey City.

New Jersey houses many industries, not included in the leading group, which nevertheless by virtue of location or individuality are of great importance in the State economy. Trenton is the center of clay-products manufacturing for the entire Nation. Lenox, Incorporated, produces a chinaware known the world over. Trenton is also headquarters for the three plants of the John A. Roebling Son's Company, the world's leading manufacturers of wire cable and rope.

A number of unusual manufacturing concerns have developed in New Jersey. In North Plainfield is one of the Nation's five telescope factories. At Burlington is the only company in the United States which makes artificial human hair and horse hair, and here also is a birch carriage factory that manufactures jinrikshas for Japan, one-wheeled carts for Korea, and big-wheeled trekking wagons for use on South American plantations. Red Bank has three shops exclusively devoted to the hand-hammering of gold leaf.

The smooth functioning of New Jersey's industrial structure depends in large measure upon power, light, and transportation facilities, supplied in almost monopolistic fashion by the Public Service Corporation. Formed in 1903, this corporation acts as a holding company for Public Service Gas and Electric Company, and Public Service Coordinated Transport, both operating companies.

A rapid process of absorbing smaller utilities has brought Public Service to a position where it supplies about 80 percent of all electricity generated throughout New Jersey and about 86 percent of all gas. There still exist 14 independent gas companies and 10 electric companies which serve smaller communities; about half of these are municipally owned. The efforts of the city of Camden in 1934 to build a municipal power plant were thwarted by the State legislature, which voted against the city's issuing bonds to finance the venture.

CANNING TOMATOES, CAMDEN

This threat of municipal ownership, as well as formation of citizens' committees all over the State, has caused Public Service to reduce its rates slightly in recent years. Rates for the residential consumer are now, for example, $2.20 for 24 kilowatt-hours and $5.41 for 100 kilowatt-hours. Thirty-six other States, according to a Federal Power Commission report in 1936, have lower average rates than those in New Jersey.

Public Service also holds a commanding position in local streetcar and bus operation and in intercity transportation. In 1936 this corporation, generally considered the largest single employer in the State, listed 19,674 workers.

Banking and Insurance: Banking in the Colonies originated in New Jersey, when in 1682 Mark Newbie, a Quaker, persuaded the General Assembly that his souvenir Irish copper coins ("Patrick's pence") could be put into circulation in the neighborhood of Camden *(see Tour 31)*. This was the first authorized use of currency in the Colonies, and Newbie became in effect the first American banker.

Out of this modest but shrewd beginning grew the complicated banking structure of present-day New Jersey. Banking did not develop into a large commercial undertaking until about 60 years ago when industry began to demand a unified currency, sources of credit, and a generally stable financial structure to stand back of the post-Civil War expansion. Notable early banks in the State were the Newark Banking and Insurance Company, which in 1804 received the first bank charter in the State, and the Trenton Banking Company. The latter, also founded in 1804, is the oldest bank in the State. The oldest bank in Newark is the National State Bank, founded in 1812. A State department of banking and insurance, with jurisdiction over private banks as well as State banks, building and loan associations, and remitters of funds abroad, was established in 1891.

The national banking system in 1936 included 266 New Jersey establishments out of a total of 417 banks in the State. Total resources of the banks were listed at $2,349,705,942. Since 1900, trust companies have increased rapidly and today dominate New Jersey banking. At present 142 such institutions have combined resources exceeding $1,000,000,000. Savings banks showed a corresponding rise, the number of depositors increasing from slightly less than 75,000 in 1900 to 574,667 in 1936. The Federal Deposit Insurance Corporation in March 1934 insured 400 New Jersey banks with 3,153,601 accounts and deposits of $869,981,197.

The Fidelity Union Trust Co. of Newark is the State's largest and most important banking organization. It is the 36th largest bank in the United States and has resources exceeding $150,000,000. Second is the Trust Company of New Jersey, in Jersey City, with resources of about $86,-000,000. The Howard Savings Institution of Newark is the largest savings bank in the State with 95,000 depositors and $50,000,000 resources.

Newark is the fourth largest insurance city of the Nation, outranked only by New York City, Hartford, and Boston. Insurance in New Jersey began in 1810, when a group of Newark business men organized a mutual fire insurance company as a measure of public welfare, without thought of deriving profit. This company still survives as one of the groups within the Royal Insurance Company of London.

In 1846 the American Mutual Insurance Company was founded in Newark. A year earlier, life and casualty insurance had been founded in Newark with the organization of the Mutual Benefit Life Insurance Company. In 1877 the Prudential Insurance Company was established and quickly became the dominant company in the State. Its success has been due mainly to its emphasis on industrial insurance, providing for small weekly premiums that place a $1,000 policy within the average worker's reach, although at a comparatively high annual rate.

Labor

THE course of the workingman's struggle for higher wages and better working conditions in New Jersey has followed generally the pattern of that struggle throughout the country. Periods of prosperity usually brought militant, stubbornly fought strikes, while depression frequently retarded the growth of unionism and the advance toward more equitable social and economic adjustments. The decline in union membership during the boom years 1923–1929 was an exception to this general pattern; and, in the opposite direction, the less prosperous years 1933–1938 have brought progressive labor legislation and increase in union membership, though largely through the action of forces and leadership Nation-wide in influence. The State has seldom been a leader in trade union activities, but it has served, in many cases, as something of a proving ground for trade union theories. On the whole, labor has traveled a rough road, for local and State governments have been consistently conservative.

The lodging of mass production industries such as steel, textiles, oil, chemicals, and electrical supplies in the northeastern section of the State made New Jersey for some time an open-shop stronghold. On the other hand, the large number of cities with more than 25,000 population provided fertile territory for craft unions. Over the years, the embattled textile workers of Paterson and Passaic have become the State's symbol of resistance to exploitation.

Throughout the Colonial period rigid stratification of classes in both agriculture and industry prevailed. Industrially the old guild system of master, journeyman, and apprentice without actual guild organization was firmly entrenched, and in agriculture, slaves and indentured servants formed the main classes of laborers. For every slave imported each settler received 175 acres of land, and in 1737 slaves comprised 8.4 percent of the population. Slave riots were sufficiently violent and frequent to cause a citizen in 1772 to urge parliament to pass a law "obliging owners of the slaves to send them all back to Africa at their own expense." The most serious insurrections occurred probably in connection with other political events, as at Raritan in 1734, at Hackensack in 1741, and, some years later, at

Elizabethtown. As the Revolution approached, free labor began to displace slaves and indentured servants.

The industrial revolution, which closely followed the political revolution against England, created a favorable opportunity for labor organization as it replaced home manufacture with the factory system. Despite this and the growth of many other natural fields for unionism, notably railroad and canal construction, iron and glass making, and pottery production, organization until 1850 was almost wholly confined to the older individual crafts. The extremely harsh conditions of the Paterson textile factories made them an exception. Here, women and children, who formed the majority of the employees, were required to be at work at 4.30 a.m.; the whip was frequently used to obtain speedier production, and the work day lasted up to 16 hours.

One of the earliest recorded strikes and the first recorded sympathy strike in America occurred in these Paterson mills in 1828. The employees, including a large number of children, walked out, demanding restoration of the noon lunch hour (which the company had changed arbitrarily to one o'clock) and reduction of the work day from $13\frac{1}{2}$ hours to 12 hours. Carpenters, masons, and mechanics struck in sympathy with the millhands. The strike was lost, although later the owners conceded the 12 o'clock lunch.

Trade unions organized by journeymen in several crafts caused the first real wave of strikes in New Jersey. Rising costs of living unaccompanied by increased wages during the prosperous period 1830–1836 resulted in at least a dozen important strikes. In 1835 or 1836 shoemakers in Newark, Paterson, and New Brunswick; hatters in Newark; textile workers in Paterson; harness makers and curriers in Newark; and building trades workers in Trenton, Paterson, New Brunswick, and Newark—all battled for high wages, and in some cases for the 10-hour day. A majority of the strikes was won by organized trade societies that closely resembled the present-day "locals" of international unions. Early cooperation among such societies was evidenced by a $203 contribution from the Newark workingmen to striking textile workers in Paterson.

Recognition of the value of such mutual aid led 16 trade societies to form a Newark Trades Union, which today would be called a city federation or central labor council. Although this body sanctioned strikes and lent moral and financial assistance, the individual trade societies shouldered the brunt of strike action. The Newark group played an important part in 1836 in the formation of the National Trades Union; New Brunswick also had a trades union, but it did not participate in the national movement. Paterson's organization, grandiloquently styled "The Paterson Association for the Protection of Laboring Classes, Operatives of Cotton Mills, Etc.," joined with the Newark Trades Union.

Workers' cooperation coupled with the burgeoning of radical thought paved the way for labor's entry into politics during the turbulent thirties. In September 1830 a group of farmers, mechanics, and workingmen from Essex County met in Newark to form a Workingmen's Party. Although the outcome is unknown, records show that the meeting demanded the removal of property qualifications for voting, the taxation of bonds and mortgages, and free schools. In 1834 and 1836 attempts were again made to establish a labor party in Newark. Their failure may be traced to the founders' apparent aim to build a patchwork political party rather than a strictly labor party, as demonstrated by their nomination of a coach lace manufacturer for mayor.

The panic of 1837 temporarily halted the remarkable progress of the previous decade. Along with most other trades unions, the Newark group expired during the long depression, and in 1840 labor sacrificed its tiny political independence to the Whig onslaught against the "panic-making" Democrats. The following quarter of a century was marked by the growth of reform movements rather than militant trade unionism. Labor neglected organization for Fourierism, land reform and the struggle for the 10-hour day. Perth Amboy and Trenton were centers of the reform movements; workingmen in the latter city were mainly responsible for the passage in 1851 of the 10-hour working day law which also prohibited labor of children under 10 years of age.

Out of this law, which characteristically carried no provisions for its enforcement, developed the Paterson textile strike of 1851. This struggle lacked the united front of the 1835 strike, and, although there was some attempt to form a union to sustain the law, most of the strikers lost their demands or agreed to work the 10-hour day at a reduction of wages.

Three years later a spectacular dispute arose between the directors and the engineers of the Erie Railroad. The engineers objected to a company rule which made them solely responsible for the safety of the trains. They tied up the railroad's traffic, and were charged with violence against strike-breakers. The difficulties were compromised, but in 1856 a new strike occurred when the company discharged 10 members of a negotiating committee which was seeking to revise the objectionable rules. The Erie employed a strong police force to guard the nonstrikers; contemporary journals warned readers against traveling on the road during the strike. Although the struggle was won by the company, the engineers were prepared for participation in the national railroad organization that grew up after 1852.

Despite an epidemic of strikes in the late fifties, organization activities fell off during the Civil War. When they were resumed after 1865 it was on a broader, more nearly national basis. New Jersey contributed to this widening through the work of Uriah Smith Stevens, a native of Cape May, who founded the Knights of Labor in Philadelphia in 1869. This organization (whose sessions were secret until after 1878) sought to form a national alliance of skilled and unskilled workers, women as well as men, but its progress was impeded for almost a decade by the results of the panic of 1873. One of the earliest New Jersey groups to join was that of the ship carpenters and caulkers of Camden, organized in 1873 as Local 31. Other State locals were formed by Trenton printers, Jersey City mechanics, and Newark brewery and leather workers.

During this period the State was the scene of two important events that indicated labor's rising strength. In 1877 the Socialist Labor Party, the oldest labor party in the country, was founded at Newark at the second convention of the so-called Working Men's Party of the United States. This early organization had grown from a union of various socialist groups (1874–76). In 1882 Peter McGuire of Camden and Matthew Maguire of Jersey City started to campaign for the establishment of an official Labor Day. Despite these significant trends, it was said in 1882 that the window glass workers of New Jersey constituted the only large body of workers in the State that had steadily maintained a trade organization throughout the previous 15 years.

Improved conditions after 1882 swelled the membership of the Knights of Labor, which more and more showed itself a forerunner of industrial unionism. It made rapid strides in railroads, textiles, hats, cigars, leather, machinery, and pottery. The organization reached its peak in the State in 1887 with an enrollment of 30,000 out of a total of 50,000 organized workers; 11,000 of these were in Newark alone.

A combination of causes brought about the sudden and swift downfall of the Knights. The looseness and latitude of the organization made strike operations difficult, and its leaders tended toward conciliation rather than militancy. More serious, however, were the external obstacles and internal wrangles arising from the invasion of mass production industries employing unskilled labor. In these fields the Knights lacked the strength to cope with the employers, who could easily dissuade immigrant labor from unionism and could use the new arrivals as strikebreakers. Finally, the

SILK MILL WORKER. PATERSON

advocates of the old craft union system bitterly and constantly fought the national policy.

These dissenting factions gradually made their way into the new American Federation of Labor which completed the local disintegration of the Knights by a vigorous push into the State shortly after 1890. The organization, set up on a craft union basis, was successful in unionizing the theatrical, printing, metal and building trades, although brewing and textile operatives were organized industrially. The federation concentrated on skilled workers and, although it became the official voice of labor in New Jersey, it generally neglected the mass production industries which dominated the State after 1900.

The most important struggles in New Jersey labor history have been the Paterson silk strike in 1912–13, under the leadership of the Industrial Workers of the World; the Passaic woolen and worsted strike of 1926, the first strike in the country in which acknowledged communists played a vital part in organization; and the Paterson silk and dye strikes of 1933 and 1934. Only the 1933 strike was notably successful. Both the silk workers' and dyers' unions won recognition, with pay increased from $12 and $13 weekly to $18 and $22 in the silk mills, and wages as low as 20 cents an hour in the dye houses raised to 66 cents.

Perhaps the most ruthless labor massacre in New Jersey occurred early in 1915 when "deputy sheriffs" hired from a Newark detective agency fired on an unarmed group of pickets standing outside of the Williams and Clark fertilizer factory at Carteret. A member of the local police force testified later to the peacefulness of the strikers, whose losses were 6 dead and 28 wounded. Twenty-two deputies were arrested on charges of manslaughter but were later released. The following year guards of the Standard Oil Company at Bayonne killed 8 and severely wounded 17 men. As with the Carteret killings, this assault outraged even the conservative press.

For about half a century the efforts of workers in New Jersey, as elsewhere in the United States, to form unions have been handicapped or crippled by the activities of industrial spies. The La Follette committee's report (1938) on violations of the rights of labor showed that 11 New Jersey corporations alone spent 12 percent of a $9,440,132 national total for espionage, strikebreaking, munitioning, and similar activities in 1933–37.

At least 31 other New Jersey concerns were listed as clients of detective agencies that provided spy service. All of the widely known detective agencies had contracted with one or more New Jersey corporations to provide lists of union members or workers interested in unionization; or reports on union meetings; or armed guards for strikebreaking—or all of these services. In every important manufacturing city spies worked side by side with the employees, often taking a prominent part in union activities, and turning in daily reports that resulted in the sudden dismissal and blacklisting of an unestimated number of workers.

At present the New Jersey State Federation of Labor claims approximately 250,000 dues-paying members, organized in about 1,000 local unions. There are 21 central labor bodies in the State, which include most of the A. F. of L. local unions in the respective county districts. Strongholds of organized labor are Newark, Passaic, Elizabeth, Trenton, Paterson and Camden.

Of recent origin is the work of the Committee for Industrial Organization, which established a special North Jersey Council early in 1937, later supplanted by the Greater Newark Industrial Council. Similar councils have been set up in Trenton and Camden. The C.I.O., with a State-wide membership estimated (1939) at 175,000, is attempting to organize on an industry-wide basis thousands of workers who have been neglected by craft unions. The committee's immediate objectives in the State are the textile, steel, heavy machinery, and electrical industries.

Although Governor Harold Hoffman warned early in 1937 that he would tolerate no sit-down strikes involving the C.I.O., a number of such strikes, as well as ordinary walk-outs, have been called successfully. The organization's drive continued virtually unimpeded until December 1937 when it launched an offensive against the open-shop refuge of Jersey City. Police of that city seized distributors of literature, prevented mass meetings, and jailed organizers. However, in April 1938 the ban against the distribution of literature was lifted.

The American Newspaper Guild's successful strike in 1934–35 against the Newark *Ledger* (the Nation's first large-scale strike of newspapermen) not only established the Guild as a labor power but also broke ground for the subsequent C.I.O. drive to organize white-collar workers. Including the Guild, C.I.O. affiliates in this field late in 1937 numbered approximately 2,700 members. Among these were office, professional and insurance workers, architects, engineers, chemists and technicians, State and municipal employees, retail clerks and professional medical workers. The A. F. of L. has also organized teachers and has retained a portion of the unionized office workers. An independent white-collar union is the State chapter of the National Lawyers' Guild.

Because New Jersey remains "The Garden State," the unionization of agricultural and allied workers constitutes an important labor objective. The first farm labor organization in the State developed in 1934 from a strike at Seabrook Farms in Cumberland County. Although the A. F. of L. subsequently chartered agricultural locals in three other counties, in 1937 the New Jersey membership of 1,500 helped to organize the international union of United Cannery, Agricultural, Packing and Allied Workers, which immediately affiliated with the C.I.O.

To one other class of workers the C.I.O. opened wide the door to full-fledged unionism. In line with its drive for industrial unionism, the C.I.O. offered Negroes equal membership with whites and established locals in fields where Negro employees predominate. Organizers have been conspicuously successful with junk yard, novelty and felt, and domestic workers. The A. F. of L. responded by increasing the Negro membership of the International Union of Hod Carriers, Building and Common Laborers and by organizing building service workers. The great mass of Negro labor, spread over light industry and mercantile establishments, still remains unorganized.

Union labor in New Jersey keeps vigilant watch on the entrance of "runaway shops." According to the State Federation of Labor, of 250 factories that moved to the State in 1936 approximately 200 were "fugitives" from trade union activities. Most of these shops were in the needle trades; a few manufactured cosmetics, hats or textiles. They have invaded Essex, Passaic, Union, Hudson, Morris and Monmouth Counties. In 1937 a runaway umbrella shop from New York was established at Boonton; union organizers signed up a majority of the underpaid girls, and a strike was called. The manufacturer moved to Pennsylvania, and again was harried by the union. He returned to Boonton, and finally went back to New York. There are many other instances of sweatshop operators being pursued across State lines.

Not so progressive as the labor legislation of New York, Massachusetts or Wisconsin, New Jersey laws protective and favorable to labor have slowly increased since the impetus given 25 years ago by Woodrow Wilson. In 1932 the Consumers' League of New Jersey established a labor standards committee which unites the efforts for labor legislation of a score of progressive organizations. In 1937 the State Federation of Labor cooperated with the Consumers' League, the New Jersey League of Women Voters and the New Jersey Federation of Women's Clubs to secure an appropriation for the enforcement of the minimum wage statute and maximum hour law for women passed in 1933. A somewhat similar coalition succeeded in 1935 in having the legislature ratify the Federal Child Labor Amendment.

Progressive labor continues to struggle against the power of the Court of Chancery to grant injunctions in labor disputes. An anti-injunction bill was passed by the assembly in 1936 but was defeated in the senate. A major factor in the defeat, it is alleged, was the withdrawal of the traditional Democratic support for the bill on the ground that its passage would frighten industry from the State.

In common with other industrial States, New Jersey is faced with the problem of regulating industrial home work. The State department of labor licenses these operators, but it has not had sufficient funds to enforce even the meager health restrictions. The latest census shows that 5,000 operators have been licensed but since each family works under a single license, the total number of home workers may well be 15,000 or even 20,000. The median wage for this type of work is figured to be 9 cents per hour and the average family income $2.60 weekly. Major home work products are dolls' clothing, knitted goods, and powder puffs. The legislature has to date failed to pass the industrial home work bill sponsored by the Consumers' League, which would drastically reduce health hazards and raise wage levels to those paid for similar employment in factories.

Undoubtedly this menace to legitimate industry and to the preservation of minimum wage standards accounts for a large number of New Jersey workers who earn a sub-subsistence wage. According to a survey completed in 1937 by the minimum wage division of the State labor department, 34,000 women and children receive less than $5 weekly and 292,000 less than $17.

After a generation of allying itself with either the Republican or Democratic parties, New Jersey labor took a step toward political independence in 1935 when Labor Party tickets entered the field in Essex and Passaic Counties. Although none of the nominees was elected, the action led to the formation of the State-wide Labor's Nonpartisan League the following year. Thus far the organization has endorsed two successful candidates in the Newark city election of 1937 (one of them Vincent J. Murphy, secretary of the State Federation of Labor), and held the balance of power in the last gubernatorial contest. The estimated 150,000 members of the league are expected to form the nucleus of the proposed State Labor Party.

Along with its quest for political independence, labor is seeking economic independence by joining professional and white-collar workers in cooperative enterprises. Cooperative leaders look to such economic activity to provide consumers with a means of controlling prices and the cost of living. Fifty years of effort in New Jersey resulted in the establishment by December 1936 of 240 consumer-producer cooperatives. Of these, 120 were credit unions; 42, agricultural purchasing organizations; and 26, urban food stores.

Consumer cooperatives, which chiefly sell groceries and fuel supplies, are strongest in the northern and central urban areas; producer cooperatives naturally center in the agricultural south. Jersey Homesteads, organized by the Resettlement Administration in 1935, is considered one of the most modern cooperative experiments in the United States. With a garment factory, gardens and homes, it represents a fusion of the industrial, agricultural and consumer interests of cooperative enterprise. This fusion typifies on a small scale the social goal of the cooperative movement.

Agriculture

NEW JERSEY is rightly called "The Garden State." Its truck-farms, extending from the northern mountains to the southern plain, are mere garden patches when compared with the western prairies or southern plantations. But these gardens produce a large proportion of the fruits and vegetables consumed in New York and Philadelphia. For these millions as well as for its own, New Jersey has developed exceptionally prosperous small farms and some of the highest types of agricultural specialization.

The State has three main soil and topographical farm belts. Underlain largely with limestone and other glacial rock, the northern counties are hilly and in some places even mountainous. Here dairying and the raising of grains and other field crops predominate, with scattered centers for market gardening. Although found in all sections of the State, commercial poultry farms are concentrated in the northern and central areas.

In the middle counties are fertile loam lands, level or rolling, with a rich subsoil of greensand marl. Of first rank in this section are truck crops and potatoes. Grain, hay, fruits, and milk are secondary.

The southern counties of the level sandy coastal area contain, in addition to a broad expanse of pine barrens, large fertile areas that yield excellent apples, peaches, cranberries, and other small fruits and vegetables. Peach blossoms in Burlington and Cumberland Counties make this section the agricultural show-place of the State in spring.

When the early settlers arrived they found the Indians growing corn, pumpkins, gourds, tobacco, and beans. Taking a lesson from the natives, they cleared the lands, and with the help of seeds and livestock imported from the old country, soon made New Jersey an important agricultural colony.

Although its large wheat yield ranked New Jersey as one of the "bread colonies" before the Revolution, the farmers were already anticipating the present-day variety in products. Large farms had been established in the south on which Negro slaves performed most of the work. This system was readily adapted to flax-raising, a major pre-Revolutionary crop. Although white labor predominated in the north, Negroes were commonly seen in the small fields and large orchards, which produced fruits, vegetables, and cider. The hill country specialized in grazing, and about 1750 New Jersey was reckoned the leading sheep-raising Colony. By the time the armies of Washington and the British were criss-crossing the State, New Jersey offered a ready supply of horses and pork from the north, flour and grain from the central part, and fruits and thread materials from the south.

After the Revolution a period of serious depression was intensified on New Jersey farms by the ravages of the Hessian fly in the wheat fields. This was followed by a gradual upward trend in agriculture that reached fruition in the middle of the nineteenth century. During the next half century agricutural societies were formed in the several counties. Worn-out soils were restored by the use of marl, lime, and fertilizer, and crop yields soared.

The horse replaced the ox, and constant improvements in machinery increased the output of the individual farmer. A New Jerseyman, Charles Newbold of Burlington County, had patented in 1797 the first cast-iron plow. Newbold is said to have spent $30,000 in perfecting and introducing his plow, but farmers at first refused to use it through fear that it might poison the soil. Other improved plows were made by Peacock, Deats and Stevens. New Jerseymen also contributed to the development of reaping and tillage machinery and the improvement of livestock breeds. The famous Jersey Red breed of hogs originated in the State.

With the growth of the urban population in adjoining States and the opening up of the West in the last half of the nineteenth century, general farming gradually gave way to specialization. The production of field crops, hogs, and sheep declined as the cultivation of berries, fruits, and vegetables increased. Dairying became paramount in the north, and the rich central loam lands were given over largely to Irish potatoes, sweet potatoes, and tomatoes. By 1900 New Jersey had truly become "The Garden State."

During the nineteenth century New Jersey dairymen turned from the production of butter and cheese to the production of milk for the nearby city markets. A number of world's record cows emerged from the State's Holstein, Guernsey, and Jersey herds. In 1898 the world-famous Walker-Gordon farm was established at Plainsboro, where in 1930 was built the "Rotolactor," the most advanced of mechanical milking devices. A New

HARVESTING CRANBERRIES, OCEAN COUNTY

Jersey farm in 1904 produced the first quart of certified milk in America.

The baby chick industry originated in Hunterdon County in 1892. New Jersey hatcheries now annually distribute millions of baby chicks, and the State is one of the leaders in commercial egg production. The Jersey Black Giant breed of poultry, as suggested by the name, was developed within the State.

Two wild fruits found by the early settlers, the cranberry and the blueberry, were domesticated largely through the intelligent and progressive efforts of New Jersey farmers. New Jersey now ranks second among the States in the production of cranberries and first in the production of cultivated blueberries. In the 1820's Seth Boyden developed an improved variety of strawberry, so large that 15 of them weighed a pound.

Specialization in farming has reached a remarkable peak on Seabrook Farms, Incorporated, just north of Bridgeton. Here, on 5,000 acres owned or leased by the corporation, industrial technique and efficiency engineering have been applied to agriculture. Lands once worked by small farmers living in perennial semi-starvation have been absorbed by the company and converted into profitable acreage. The similarity to industrial method extends into the financial set-up, for here is a farm with a holding company, and a subsidiary company to handle canning and packing operations. To illustrate the intense agricultural specialization: Peas are planted in patches covering as many as 200 acres, with rows so close together that the usual method of cultivation is impossible. Aphis and other pests are controlled by dust sprayed from the farm's two airplanes; and, instead of being picked by hand, the vines are harvested whole by reapers and the peas separated by specially built viners.

The farm has its own reservoirs, railroad sidings, and concrete highways, plus a trucking fleet with special refrigerating apparatus for hauling frozen foods to market. Farm hands as well as factory girls punch time clocks, and company police patrol the land. Two bitterly fought strikes in 1934 for higher wages and union recognition carried the industrial parallel even further. The first strike brought a wage increase, but the second resulted in withdrawal of union recognition, although wages were not altered.

Nurseries represent an even more intense type of specialization. Trees and shrubs, vegetable and flower seeds are raised for an international market. At Bound Brook is the largest orchid-growing plant in the country, and Camden County has the largest dahlia farm in the State. Rose growing is centered in Morris County; the extensive greenhouses of Madison have given that community the nickname of the "Rose City." Nursery and greenhouse products total nearly $10,000,000 in value annually.

The State pioneered in agricultural education and research. In 1864 the legislature designated the Rutgers Scientific School as the Land Grant College. In 1880 the State set up an agricultural experiment station at New Brunswick—the fifth of such State stations to be founded in this country. The State board of agriculture was established in 1875 and reorganized in 1916 to provide for the present department of agriculture.

Other agencies that have contributed significantly toward the progress of New Jersey agriculture include the various State and local agricultural societies and associations, the high school departments of agriculture, the State Grange with its local branches scattered throughout the State, and the State Farm Bureau Federation.

These public and semi-public agencies have taken the leadership in developing New Jersey's farms. They have provided scientific training in agriculture for young men and women and kept farmers abreast of new discoveries in management of soils and crops, as well as in control of destructive insects and diseases. Farmers, manufacturers, and tradesmen have all received protection against fraud in handling farm produce and supplies.

The agricultural experiment station conducts experiments in dairy science at Beemerville in Sussex County, a cranberry-blueberry laboratory in Burlington County, a poultry pathology laboratory in Cumberland County, an oyster laboratory in Cape May County; also poultry contests in Passaic, Hunterdon, and Cumberland Counties, and a pigeon contest in Cumberland County.

Among the many contributions the experiment station has made to agricultural progress are new varieties of peaches, such as the Golden Jubilee and the Cumberland, the new Rutgers tomato, the discovery of vaccine for poultry bronchitis, improved fertilizers, control of potato diseases, the reduction of the mosquito pest, improved methods of sewage disposal, growth of greenhouse vegetables and flowers with nutrient solutions in sand, new dairy rations, and improved strains of field crops. New facts about human and animal nutrition have been revealed. Discoveries in soil science and other departments have won world-wide recognition. Since 1914 the New Brunswick station has conducted the largest peach-breeding experiment in the world, pollenizing by hand as many as 30,000 blossoms in one season. The orchards attract thousands of visitors to the college farm.

Through the extension service of the New Jersey College of Agriculture and the agricultural experiment station, scientific information is made readily available throughout the State. The college, in cooperation with the United States Department of Agriculture, maintains an office in every county but one. Expert agents assigned to these offices give free service to the local residents and to groups of persons who seek advice on questions relating to agriculture and home economics. Also, thousands of boys and girls are members of the 4-H Clubs directed through the county offices.

New Jersey farmers have suffered severely from two notorious pests. The older and more destructive is the Japanese beetle, first discovered in 1916 at Cinnaminson. This bright metallic-green native of Japan, three-eighths of an inch in length and about the same in width, has blazed a destructive trail over most of the State and adjoining sections of Pennsylvania and Delaware. Control methods have been devised, but the beetles are still responsible for a vast amount of damage to the business of nurserymen and to deciduous foliage—from peach trees to roses—in the New Jersey area. The second pest is the Mexican bean beetle, a native of Central America, which was reported by bean growers in 1927 as doing some damage in Cape May County. Spraying and dusting have proved effective in controlling the spread of this prolific insect, which kills bean plants by feeding on the leaves until only a lacy shell remains. About one-quarter of an inch in length, the Mexican bean beetle has yellow or copper-colored wings with sixteen small black spots.

In recent years there has been decided progress in methods of marketing farm produce. Through the leadership of the State department of agriculture, standard grades have been established and ways and means provided for marketing much produce cooperatively. Motor trucks have largely displaced the railroads as carriers of produce, and New Jersey farm products are now marketed at roadside stands in large quantities.

New Jersey farmers obtain many services from their marketing and purchasing organizations. There are 57 different associations, one or more serving every county in the State. Twenty-three of these, serving approximately 6,500 members, are concerned only with purchasing various farm supplies. Twenty associations devote themselves entirely to marketing farm produce for their 6,000 members. Twelve combine both marketing and purchasing and serve about 5,500 farmers. The largest purchasing organization is the South Jersey Farmers' Exchange in Woodstown, which buys for 2,500 members in Salem, Gloucester, and Cumberland Counties. Another important purchasing association is the Grange League Federation Exchange, Incorporated, of Ithaca, New York, which serves 1,600 members in seven New Jersey branches.

The marketing organizations specialize in certain products such as blueberries, peaches, potatoes, and poultry, or deal in general farm products. Their fruit and vegetable auction markets are situated to serve the nine counties in which the great fruit and vegetable supplies are grown. Largest of the marketing associations is the Flemington Auction Market Cooperative Association, serving 1,300 farmers. Two other large organizations are the Monmouth Farmers' Exchange in Freehold and the Gloucester County Agricultural Association in Glassboro.

In 1935 the Federal Census showed 1,914,110 acres of farms in New Jersey, occupying about 40 percent of the total land area. Dairy products are preeminent in money value, followed by vegetables, eggs, and grain. The State leads all others in production for market of lima beans, cucumbers, and eggplants; and it holds second place in asparagus, string beans, spinach, and green peppers. Other important vegetable crops are tomatoes, beets, cabbage, cantaloupes, cauliflower, celery, sweet corn, lettuce, onions, and peas.

The money value of all crops in 1935 was $87,054,275, but a more typical figure would probably be that of 1929: $106,055,000. Values of principal agricultural products in 1936 were:

Grain	$10,219,000
Hay	4,756,000
Vegetables	15,774,000
Fruit	4,739,000
Berries	2,128,000
Potatoes	9,586,000
Sweet potatoes	2,520,000
Milk	25,500,000 *
Eggs	13,000,000 *
Baby chicks	2,200,000 *

* 1935 estimate.

‹‹‹‹‹‹‹‹‹‹‹‹‹‹‹‹‹‹ ✸ ›››››››››››››››››››››

Transportation and Communication

AS ONE of the great natural terminals of the country, New Jersey has developed with considerable profit to itself a transportation system in line with the shipping and travel needs of the Nation. Its historic role as a highway between New York and Philadelphia has made it the transport broker of the Middle Atlantic States.

Eight trunk railroads cross the State to converge on the west bank of the Hudson River, where an elaborate transfer service for passengers and freight to New York has been created. Transoceanic shipping is handled largely by the ports of Newark, Jersey City, Hoboken, and Perth Amboy on the east, and on the west by Camden. The State has constructed an inland waterway along the Atlantic Coast and has dredged its navigable streams to develop inland ports. Newark has the most important transcontinental airport in the country.

Highway traffic within New Jersey has generally assumed a cross-State diagonal course, with the north central part dominated by US 1 from Jersey City to Trenton, and the south depending chiefly on the Camden-Atlantic City roads. The excellence of the highway system has made possible a general use of busses, which are steadily eliminating the once important trolleys.

Colonial transportation in New Jersey began with the Dutch settlers' cautious use of the footpaths already worn through the forests on the west bank of the Hudson River by the Lenni Lenape Indians. The colonists gradually widened these narrow trails, first by walking double file for added safety, then by driving their cattle and carts over them. When wagons and stagecoaches came into use, the trails began to assume the appearance of roads. Many eventually developed into the broad highspeed thoroughfares of the present highway system.

The need for communication with their countrymen across the Hudson led the early Dutch to operate the first ferries between what are now New

RAILROAD YARDS, WEEHAWKEN

York and Hoboken. These were rough-hewn rowboats or flat-bottomed rafts, which passengers were called to man whenever a squall came up. At the same time, the colonists ventured with small skiffs on the northern lakes and down the streams.

As settlements spread southward and trading centers developed, the need for swifter transport became urgent. New Jersey, lying between New York and Philadelphia, two rapidly growing cities that afforded good markets for its products, was the birthplace of the American stage wagon. Freight transportation, which preceded passenger conveyance, was started shortly before 1700 between South Amboy and Burlington. Soon afterward passengers began to ride the hard uncomfortable wagons, first advertised in 1723. Regular routes were established by the middle of the next decade between South Amboy and Burlington and between New Brunswick and Trenton. From these points travelers were transferred to sloops to complete the journey to New York or Philadelphia.

Intense rivalry between the through lines caused operators to improve their service with changes of horses, stronger wagons, and more direct routes. They filled the public prints with advertisements accusing one another of deceiving and defrauding their customers, but the public profited from the competition by quicker travel. In 1752 Joseph Borden, inaugurating a new line out of Bordentown, proudly advertised a trip from New York to Philadelphia requiring only 30 to 40 hours. This was actual driving time. Allowance for stopovers, delays and breakdowns commonly ran the total to 72 hours—still a vast improvement over the original five-day trip. Fast electric trains now cover the distance in 1 hour and 35 minutes.

Four, six, and sometimes eight horses were needed to haul the wagons over the miserable dust heaps or mud bogs that served as roads. Passengers not only had to endure the jouncing and tossing of the wagon but also were forced often to walk up steep rises in the road or help rescue horses stalled in a slough. The vehicles were brightly painted but hardly easy-riding; a strip of leather nailed across the back of a seat was luxurious. Washouts on the roads were frequent, and passengers were constantly in danger of falling from the wagons. The only comfort on the trip was provided by the roadside inns or the stage boats, which advertised "fine commodious cabins, fitted with tea tables and sundry other articles of convenience to add to the comfort of the ladies."

In 1764 a new company speeded the trip by starting a wagon in Philadelphia and sending it over the ferry at Trenton. The same year Sovereign Sybrandt came near to establishing an all-land route between New York and Philadelphia by running his stage overland from New Brunswick to Elizabethtown, thence to Paulus Hook (Jersey City) by post road. He avoided the perils of the bays, but still required five ferryings. The time of the trip was cut to two days in 1771 by Joseph Mercereau's "Flying Machine," and within a few years thereafter heavy coaches were introduced that greatly reduced the dangers of the journey.

A direct result of the rise of coaches was the improvement of the roads. At the beginning of the nineteenth century, an inadequate road system was sending most of the products from the farms and mines of the Delaware Valley down that river to the Philadelphia market. Partly to bring this trade to the east, the State began chartering turnpikes to supplant the dirt and corduroy roads. The first of these improved highways linked the Morris County iron mines with the infant industrial center of Newark; others followed from Trenton to New Brunswick, Jersey City to Hackensack, and Newark to New Brunswick. By 1828 the legislature had granted 54 turnpike charters. Like the old Indian trails, these turnpikes have formed the basis for some of the best roads in the State.

Steamboats: While land routes were being speeded by simple expansion and construction, water travel was improved by the inventive skill and courage of men who saw the possibility of applying the principle of James Watt's stationary steam engine to sailing vessels. John Fitch, a poor clock-mender from Connecticut who lived for a time in Trenton, and Colonel John Stevens, a rich Hoboken engineer, labored to make the steamboat a reality on New Jersey waters.

In 1786 the State legislature granted to Fitch all rights to operate steam-propelled craft on the waters of the State. In the summer of that year, Fitch made his first trial on the Delaware with a queer looking boat, having a row of paddles on each side. While no great success, it warranted the construction of two more boats in 1787–8. Fitch's best work was his commercial steamboat of 1790. Although it carried passengers and freight between various points along the Delaware and the Schuylkill on a regular schedule, it received so little patronage that it was abandoned. This was, however, 17 years before Robert Fulton prospered with his larger *Clermont* on the Hudson.

In 1791 Stevens obtained a patent on an engine for running a boat with paddles, and seven years later he tested his own steamboat on a run down the Passaic from Belleville to New York and back. In 1804 he tried again with a steamboat, the *Little Juliana,* having the first screw propeller. Finally in 1808 he applied for a license to run the *Phoenix,* his best boat, as a steam ferry between Hoboken and New York. This was the first steam ferry in the world, but its career was curtailed by the Hudson River monopoly that Robert Fulton had obtained. Stevens then took his boat around to the Delaware, and the *Phoenix* became the first steamboat to sail the open sea.

To circumvent Fulton's hold on the Hudson, Stevens and others used the ingenious "teamboat" ferry, twin boats with a wheel between the two hulls. Power was furnished by eight horses walking in a circle on deck and turning a crank. It required no royalty payment to Fulton and operated successfully for some time.

Canals: Increased activity in the northwestern mining district and the south central agricultural area led to the construction of two canals to hasten shipments and enlarge the State's share of the Pennsylvania trade. The Morris Canal, chartered in 1824, passed through the iron-mining and in-dustrial district from Jersey City to Phillipsburg, connecting the Delaware and Lehigh Rivers with the Passaic and the sea at Newark Bay. It was completed in 1831 at a cost of $2,850,000, but never realized the hopes of its backers. Hampered by a channel that was never large enough to handle the heavy traffic, it paid so poorly that in 10 years it was closed. Reopened in 1841, it closed again, and later was leased in perpetuity to the Lehigh Valley Railroad. Recently both the railroad and the canal owners surrendered their rights to the State, but kept the Jersey City terminal of "the ditch." In Newark the city has constructed a subway for trolley lines in the canal bed.

The Delaware and Raritan Canal, extending from New Brunswick to Bordentown, was in its heyday one of the three most important canals in the United States. Chartered in 1830, it began inauspiciously, for in the same year the legislature permitted the Camden and Amboy Railroad to parallel it from South Amboy to Bordentown. To avoid being overcome by the railroad, the canal owners joined their stock with the Camden and Amboy but maintained separate operation. The combination thus obtained a monopoly on traffic between New York and Philadelphia, all passengers being allotted to the railroad and all freight to the canal.

The Delaware and Raritan's prosperity rested largely on coal from the Schuylkill Navigation System, the first link in the transport of coal from the Schuylkill section to the sea. But association with the Schuylkill later proved disastrous, for floods, mismanagement, and railroad competition after the Civil War crippled its trade. In 1871 the Pennsylvania Railroad leased the Camden and Amboy and with it the ailing canal. The new owner refused to permit coal from the Schuylkill mines, now controlled by the rival Reading line, to pass through. This loss of 1,000,000 tons of freight a year eliminated the Delaware and Raritan as an important waterway. It limped along doing a little business, until recently, when the Pennsylvania surrendered the title to the State. At present the Federal and State Governments are considering a plan to build a ship canal through the same territory.

The Railroads: Success with the steamboat inspired Colonel John Stevens to work on the idea of a steam railroad. He petitioned his own State legislature and Governor De Witt Clinton of New York to consider his proposal for a railroad which would run trains at 18 miles an hour. This suggestion won as little attention as his plan to connect New York and New Jersey by a tunnel on the bed of the Hudson. In 1824, however, when he was 75 years old, he demonstrated an experimental "steam waggon" which ran 12 miles an hour on a circular track at his Hoboken estate. This was the first locomotive built and operated in this country.

His son, Robert L. Stevens, carried on to complete the task of building New Jersey's first railroad. Confidence abounded at a meeting in Mount Holly in 1828 to promote the project; the success of the elder Stevens and of British railway ventures swept aside the opposition of stagecoach operators, who prophetically attacked the plan as a scheme for monopoly.

"JOHN BULL," NEW JERSEY'S FIRST LOCOMOTIVE

In 1830 the company obtained a charter for the Camden and Amboy Railroad, first to be operated in the State, and sent Robert Stevens to England to buy equipment. This included all-iron rails, instead of the wooden rails that had been tried on tramways.

After a favorable demonstration of the locomotive *John Bull* at Bordentown in 1831, the Camden and Amboy speeded construction and in 1834 completed the route from Camden to South Amboy. It acquired control of the Philadelphia and Trenton Railway Company, which had built a line from Philadelphia to Morrisville (opposite Trenton) and owned the rights to constructing a railroad between Trenton and New Brunswick. By making a traffic agreement with the New Jersey Railroad and Transportation Company, which ran a line from Jersey City to New Brunswick, the Camden and Amboy in 1840 consolidated its holdings and opened the first through all-rail line from New York to Philadelphia.

Other important lines chartered and constructed in this period were the Elizabeth and Somerville, the Morris and Essex, and the Paterson and Hudson, all of which knitted together the growing cities of the north and the surrounding mining and agricultural sections.

Favored by the State legislature with the necessity of paying only an insignificant "transit fee" and with an ironclad monopoly concession on rail transportation between New York and Philadelphia, the Camden and Amboy rapidly grew into a powerful corporation. In return for valuable favors received, the railroad turned over to the State 1,000 shares of stock. The ultimate result was that the railroad entrenched itself so strongly in the State's political field that New Jersey acquired the sobriquet of the "State of Camden and Amboy."

Others eyed the rich monopoly with envy. The New Jersey Central Railroad, then a small line operating across the northern part of the State, built a line southward as far as Bound Brook. Meanwhile a railway, later to become the Philadelphia and Reading, was laid to a point opposite Trenton. Completion of the link between Trenton and Bound Brook would form the competing road from New York to Philadelphia.

For five years the question of a franchise was fought in the legislature between the backers of the new line and the Camden and Amboy. When public opinion crystallized against the domination of the corporation, the Camden and Amboy skillfully shifted responsibility by leasing its lines to the Pennsylvania. The struggle became more furious as the Pennsylvania was attacked as an "alien" interest. Bribery, violence, and subsidized newspapers were common weapons on both sides. At length the public sickened of the battle and demanded a general law opening the State to all railroads, with prudent restrictions. The act was passed promptly, and the link between Trenton and Bound Brook was assured at last.

But when the construction crews began work, the Pennsylvania applied for injunction after injunction against the New York and Bound Brook Railroad, as the new road was called. The fight became so acute at Pennington, where the two roads crossed, that the Governor had to call out the militia. By the time the troops restored order, the crossing had been achieved and the grip of the railroads had been loosened, if not broken.

New Jersey has today more railroad track per square mile than any other State. The system features concentration of terminals on the west bank of the Hudson, feeders for ocean traffic, and eight great trunk lines across the central and northern parts of the State. In all, 2,179 miles of track within the State are being operated by 27 railroads, of which 15 are first class.

Railroad construction has been concentrated in the central industrial region of the State where travelers and shippers are offered a wide choice of routes and schedules. In the northern and southern sections, however, coverage and service are generally inadequate.

Across the mountains and into the valleys of the northern part of the

State run the Pennsylvania, the Erie, the Lackawanna, and the Jersey Central, hauling mine, forest, and farm products eastward to New York. They also carry thousands of commuters and vacationers between the many resorts and suburban communities in this area. The Pennsylvania, Lehigh Valley, Reading, and Jersey Central bear the major burden of traffic in the manufacturing belts, in which lies the New York-Philadelphia route, one of the richest runs in the world. The large cities in this area are all linked with their surrounding suburbs and each other by a network of minor lines.

Agricultural south New Jersey depends chiefly upon the Pennsylvania and the Reading for cross-State shipments of its produce to Philadelphia, while it uses the Jersey Central for travel within the district. The State's long seashore playground is served by the Pennsylvania, Jersey Central, and Reading. Newark, with six trunk line stations, is the busiest railroad center in the State. Camden, Hoboken, and Jersey City are also major terminals.

Electrification of the Pennsylvania and the Lackawanna Lines has considerably increased the value of nearby real estate and has tempted thousands of new commuters into the State. The Hudson and Manhattan tunnels from Newark and Jersey City to New York, constructed in 1911, daily carry thousands of commuters over one of the busiest short runs in the country.

Highways: New Jersey's State highway system is largely a war product. When a vast output of munitions and war supplies was rushed to the Atlantic coast, trunk line railroads were overloaded, and motor trucks were drafted. Railroad freight was dumped beside the rails and reshipped by truck.

Although in 1890 New Jersey became the first State to provide State aid in construction of highways, the roads were not sufficiently developed to meet the wartime need. All through the State, businessmen patronized the motor express lines that sprang up by hundreds. The old county and town roads nearly went to pieces under the pressure of the new freight traffic. The slogan of "Win the War with Transportation" brought the State into long-delayed action. The legislature in 1917 voted to build a State system of 15 roads connecting the principal industrial and shipping centers.

Post-war use of the motor truck demanded speed and expansion in this program. In 1926 a special road commission recommended an expenditure of $300,000,000 for the highway network, half of which has been spent on road construction and maintenance to date.

New Jersey's present highway system is generally considered to be surpassed only by that of California. It is 26,767 miles in extent, of which 17,315 miles are "improved." The State-controlled portion totals 1,877 miles; the remainder is administered by local communities or by counties. The Federal Government has given important aid in the improvement and development of the State's highways. In addition to previous extensive projects carried through under the Works Progress Administration, twenty new county-wide projects have been approved for New Jersey (April 1938), averaging approximately one million dollars expenditure in each county. These projects provide for improvement of principal and secondary roads of the present system, construction of new roads, widening of highways, and building of bridges and culverts. Up to March 23, 1938, grants made to the State of New Jersey under the Public Works Administration totaled $2,817,655. These grants were made for the construction of bridges and viaducts and for the elimination of various grade crossings, the total cost of which is estimated at $6,693,221. The Civilian Conservation Corps also has done valuable work in the improvement of public properties in the State.

The excellence of the system, however, has not prevented an appalling record of death and accident on the highways. One of the most dangerous roads in the State is US 1, the superhighway from George Washington Bridge to Trenton. Efforts to reduce hazards on the roads include the gradual elimination of the three-lane highway, considered among the most treacherous of road designs; increased use of divided highways, and the institution of the cloverleaf crossing. This latter device, introduced in New Jersey, cuts down the risk of collision at congested intersections by sorting the traffic into one-way streams without crossings. The State is also experimenting with daylight illumination (sodium vapor lighting) to reduce the dangers of night driving.

Three troops of State police patrol the State highways. Numerous stations connected by telephone and teletype enable rapid concentration of a force in any locality where it is needed. Headquarters are in Trenton, where contact is maintained with the State administration and with the commanding officer and staff of the National Guard.

Outstanding among State highways is the Pulaski Skyway over the Newark meadows, part of US 1. Three and one-half miles long, it steps across two rivers on high cantilever bridges. No toll is charged.

Completing the highway system are bridges, tunnels, and ferries connecting the State with its neighbors. The major links with New York City

UNLOADING LUMBER, PORT NEWARK

are three Port of New York Authority enterprises: the $60,000,000 George Washington Memorial Bridge, running from 181st Street in Manhattan to Fort Lee on the New Jersey side; the Holland Tunnel, extending from Jersey City to Canal Street, Manhattan; and the new Lincoln Tunnel, linking midtown Manhattan with Weehawken. Hudson River ferries have survived the competition of the tunnels and the bridge by reducing their rates.

Three Port of New York Authority toll bridges join New Jersey with Staten Island. They are Bayonne Bridge between Bayonne and Port Richmond, with the longest steel arch span in the world (1,675 feet); Goethals Bridge from Elizabeth to Howland Hook, and the Outerbridge Crossing from Perth Amboy to Tottenville. The Delaware River Bridge, between Camden and Philadelphia, and 10 other toll and 15 free bridges span the Delaware.

One result of the construction of bridges and tunnels across the Hudson has been the shift from congested Manhattan of a part of its population into New Jersey. The trend began with the construction of the Hudson tubes, and between 1910 and 1930 Manhattan lost almost half a million residents while New Jersey's four counties of the northern metropolitan area increased in population by 690,000.

Similarly, the rise of the motor bus since the World War has caused amazing growth in the suburban zones of New Jersey's large cities. Rural districts have almost overnight become modern towns with most of the conveniences and few of the disadvantages of the urban centers nearby. The Public Service Coordinated Transport, largest local bus operator in the country, covers most of the State with lines that carried 292,398,000 passengers in 1936. The same company's trolley lines carried 118,075,000 passengers in that year. Like its neighboring States, New Jersey once had an extensive network of interurban trolley lines, but streetcars have been steadily displaced by busses. Some of the busses are equipped with trolleys for electric operation as well. Interstate bus lines cross the State in generally the same directions as did the Colonial stages, and have been particularly conspicuous in competing with rail service to Philadelphia and shore points.

Water Travel: New Jersey shares navigation of the Delaware River with Pennsylvania and Delaware for sea-going vessels as far as Trenton, and for small craft to Port Jervis, New York. The State's other important navigable streams are the Passaic, Hackensack, and Raritan, all of which afford ready access to inland ports in the industrial area. The Hudson

River, Kill van Kull, and Arthur Kill are shared with New York for river trade and ocean transport.

A plan for an important inland waterway has been suggested by the Board of Commerce and Navigation of New Jersey. According to this plan the old Delaware and Raritan Canal and the Delaware River, from Trenton southward, would become links in the Intracoastal Waterway from Boston, Massachusetts, to the Rio Grande, Texas. The project would involve the Federal Government's making navigable this part of the Delaware; and opening and restoring to use the old canal, or constructing a new one. The State maintains all inland waterways and operates State inland waterway terminals.

The principal deepwater ports on the northwest border of the State for overseas and coastwise transportation are Newark and Elizabethport on Newark Bay, Perth Amboy on Raritan Bay, Jersey City and Bayonne on New York Bay, and Hoboken, Weehawken and Edgewater on the Hudson. On the Hudson County waterfront 100,000 passengers yearly arrive or depart by regular transoceanic steamship lines, which also handle freight in quantity. At Hoboken a modern feature is the seatrain steamship service that carries 101 loaded freight cars on each boat to Havana and New Orleans. Camden, with regular steamship lines operating to Baltimore and Hawaii, dominates ocean transport on the Delaware side.

A continuous inland waterway extends along the Atlantic Coast for 115 miles from the head of Barnegat Bay to Cape May. It is used chiefly for pleasure sailing and the shipping of sea products, petroleum, and lumber.

Air Travel: Newark Airport is the busiest in the United States and one of the busiest in the world. Established in 1929 as the eastern terminus of the Nation's air mail service, it registers 125 take-offs and landings of transport planes daily. Four of the great transcontinental systems operating passenger lines use it as their terminal. As such, Newark has become virtually synonymous in the public mind with long-distance air travel.

The Newark meadows were selected for the metropolitan terminal because their situation affords excellent landing facilities and quick transfer to New York City. Access to Manhattan is greatly facilitated by the Pulaski Skyway and the Holland Tunnel. The first regular passenger line was established in 1929 between Newark and Boston by American Air Lines. While most of the other large cities in the State operate busy commercial airports, Camden, serving Philadelphia, is the only other regular transport stop in New Jersey. It has recently become a transcontinental terminus.

Transatlantic Zeppelins have since 1924 used the United States Naval Air Station at Lakehurst as their American terminal.

Wire Systems and Radio: Telegraph service, now extended to even the smaller towns in the State, had its experimental origin in New Jersey. In 1838, six years before his celebrated success over a longer distance, Samuel F. B. Morse tested the electromagnetic telegraph at the Speedwell Iron Works near Morristown. At Princeton University, a few years before Morse began his work, Joseph Henry, professor of natural philosophy, constructed an electric apparatus that carried signals sounded on a bell from his home on the campus to the Hall of Philosophy.

An important innovation in telegraph service was the introduction of wireless newspaper bulletins at Atlantic Highlands lighthouse in 1899 during the America's Cup yacht races. Messages were transmitted from a steamboat to the lighthouse, where they were relayed to New York City.

The telephone has quickly become an indispensable social and commercial instrument in the State, and perhaps more than any other modern invention has welded it into one large community. The New Jersey Bell Telephone Company has created a State-wide system including approximately 685,000 telephones in 1937. With 204 phones per 1,000 population reported in 1936, New Jersey ranked second only to California in the extent of telephone service.

Conversations between all parts of the United States and Europe, Central and South America over shortwave radio telephone are transmitted from the Bell station at Lawrenceville, and received from abroad at Netcong. The Radio-Marine Corporation maintains a transoceanic wireless telegraph station at Tuckerton.

New Jersey, and specifically the city of Newark, was closely identified with early experiments in radio broadcasting. WJZ broadcast a world series baseball game on October 7, 1921, from the Westinghouse plant at Orange and Plane Streets, Newark. This was the world's second station, the first having been KDKA in Pittsburgh. The station was later sold to become part of the National Broadcasting Company. The transmitter remained in Newark for a time, but was later moved to Bound Brook.

WOR, Newark's second station, started broadcasting February 22, 1922. Built by L. Bamberger and Company and housed in its department store building, the station has pioneered in many phases of radio. In the fall of 1922 it communicated with Selfridge's store in London, and a year later reached Tokio. In 1924 the station asked all listeners to try to locate the dirigible *Shenandoah,* which had slipped its moorings and become lost. Soon telephone calls began to come in, and the ship's position was relayed to the crew. WOR has pioneered in spot news and symphony orchestra broadcasts, and developed many technical improvements. It is now the home station of the Mutual Broadcasting Company.

The 1920's saw the establishment of several other stations, some of which still survive, usually under different call letters. The State now has 13 broadcasting stations and a number of experimental laboratories.

The Press

NEW JERSEY editors put "first things first" and hoe their own row. Their determination to emphasize local news and features against the national and international content of New York and Philadelphia dailies has produced in an essentially urban State a prevailingly suburban type of journalism. Almost without exception, the New Jersey press daily declares its independence from its metropolitan rivals.

The majority follow the lead of the Newark *Evening News* in reporting not only the minutiae of their own cities but also social, political, and cultural activities of hamlets within a 50-mile radius. An example of the strong New Jersey sense of local importance was a *News* headline on November 2, 1937: "NEW YORK ALSO VOTES TODAY." The necessity for this provincialism, however, becomes apparent when circulation figures of New Jersey and out-of-State papers are compared.

Neighboring newspapers have made greatest inroads in the heavily populated suburban areas. One New York paper alone, a tabloid, has a weekday circulation of 199,000 and a Sunday circulation of more than 400,000 in New Jersey. Likewise, one Philadelphia daily sends to New Jersey 65,000 copies, an eighth of its total circulation.

In comparison, the 36 English-language dailies in the State, of which only a very few print Sunday editions, have a circulation of approximately 800,000 on weekdays and 218,700 on Sundays (including that of the Sunday weeklies). Improved delivery facilities are increasing the circulation of metropolitan papers in the State without causing a corresponding decline in that of New Jersey's own papers. Readers of out-of-State journals usually buy a local paper also.

This same influence of neighboring cities caused early New Jersey journalism to limp decades behind that of other Colonies. At the outbreak of the Revolution, the population of the Colony still looked to the nine Pennsylvania papers—three of which were printed in German—and to their four contemporaries in New York for information on the Old World and the New. James Parker's effort to establish a local publication,

The American Magazine, at Woodbridge in 1758, brought him at the end of two years only fines and imprisonment.

The first cry of a newsboy hawking his wares in New Jersey was heard in the fall of 1776, when Hugh Gaine temporarily moved his New York *Gazette and Weekly Mercury* across the river to Newark. His innovation in salesmanship had been preceded, a year earlier, by the appearance of a wall newspaper at Matthew Potter's inn at Bridgeton. Three or four hand-written sheets, every Thursday morning, attracted a swarming chattering crowd of farmers, teamsters, and townspeople to the walls of the old tavern. This lively sheet, called the *Plain Dealer,* came to an abrupt end after it had dealt a bit too plainly with the practice of bundling.

The heat of partisanship during the Revolution led to the rise of a local press. The *New Jersey Gazette,* the State's first real paper, was produced by Isaac Collins, former "Printer to the King," from the identical plant in Burlington where, several decades earlier, Benjamin Franklin had printed the first currency for the Province. Backed by Governor William Livingston and members of the State legislature, this weekly appeared as a single folio sheet, 9 by 14 inches, four columns to a page, on December 5, 1777. Typical of Revolutionary papers, it was pledged to support the "Interests of Religion and Liberty" and opened its columns with "pleasure and alacrity" to "Essays useful or entertaining, or schemes for advancement of Trade, Arts and Manufactures."

Only three contemporary New Jersey papers date back to the eighteenth century, and only one of these, the Elizabeth *Daily Journal,* was founded early enough to participate in the Revolution. Washington and Hamilton lent "friendly assistance" to Shepard Kollock, a Chatham printer, for the establishment of his *New Jersey Journal,* forerunner of the present Elizabeth daily.

Collins' *Gazette* waned after the peace of 1783 and finally expired in 1786. The same year brought the *New Jersey Magazine and Monthly Advertiser* to New Brunswick and the *Mercury and Weekly Advertiser* to Trenton—short-lived, ponderous, pedantic sheets that catered mainly to the property-holding class. For years Kollock's *Journal* remained the only publication in the State with an appeal to the common man.

The passionate controversy between Hamilton's Federalism and Jefferson's Republicanism gave rise to new partisan papers. The present Trenton *State Gazette* and the New Brunswick *Sunday Times* were both founded in 1792 to champion political movements. In Newark, John Woods, a former apprentice of Kollock, began, on May 13, 1791, weekly publication of Woods' *Newark Gazette.* This ardent Federalist advocate was soon opposed by one equally vehement for States' rights, the *Sentinel of Freedom,* founded in 1796.

The Newark *Daily Advertiser,* established in 1832 as a daily edition of the *Sentinel,* absorbed the parent organization in the following year. It survived until 1906 on legal advertisements thrown to it by politicans, although it had no circulation. Today's Newark *Star-Eagle,* the result of a merger of the *Daily Advertiser,* the Newark *Evening Star,* and the *Morning Eagle* thus lays claim to the title of the city's oldest daily.

The *Sentinel* (originally spelled "Centinel") was typical of that intense personal journalism which frequently led opposing editors to the dueling grounds. The paper built up Jefferson's political machine in Essex County and drove the *Gazette* out of business. A vituperative editorial in the *Sentinel* of January 1, 1805 commented:

> The Newark Gazette expired on Tuesday of a decline which it bore with Christian fortitude. This legitimate child of federalism was generated by corruption, progressed in infamy, and finally died in disgrace. . . . Let the people say Amen! Amen!

Undoubtedly the fiercest anti-Federalist, however, was Philip Freneau, sailor, scholar, and poet of the Revolution. His *New Jersey Chronicle,* founded in 1795 at Mount Pleasant (now Freneau), assailed the aristocratic theories of Adams and Hamilton and charged that they were heading the Nation toward monarchy. Jefferson later made Freneau editor of his *National Gazette.*

But the readers' interest extended beyond politics. The new century saw the inception of a large number of country weeklies, which generally held with the Camden *Mail* "that exclusive devotion to any one party does not afford the widest field of usefulness for a newspaper." Some of New Jersey's prominent weeklies date back to this demand for a respite from politics: the Sussex *Register* (1813) of Newton, the Monmouth *Inquirer* (1820) of Freehold, the *New Jersey Herald* (1829) of Newton, and the Salem *Sunbeam* (1844). These papers were trail-breakers for suburban types that have remained characteristic of the State.

These old sheets did not know the meaning of "local color." Neither the city editor nor the society reporter had appeared. Though churches existed in abundance, there are no records left of their harvest dances or clam bakes. The advertisements alone permit a few glimpses into the late stagecoach and early railroad days. Exceptions were items like the following, which were widely reprinted: "A sturgeon, seven feet long, leaped through the cabin window of a sloop moored at Bridgeton while the crew was asleep, and did considerable damage to the cabin."

The story of a "panther hunt" near Blackwoodstown in 1819 found equal credulity among the rural readers. One editor explained that "the panther is of the feline species, a sort of first cousin to the tiger, and ranges the depth of the remotest American forests."

Payment in kind was a common occurrence: Editor Barber of Woodbury announced in a front page notice that his woodpile was running low and that a few loads from his debtors would be acceptable. The editor of the *Columbian Herald* once informed his subscribers that he was willing to take "cats and grain" for the $2 yearly subscription price. The value of cats can only be surmised.

The State's first daily paper was the Newark *Daily Advertiser,* founded in 1832 as a daily edition of the *Sentinel of Freedom.* The *Advertiser,* which ultimately became the present *Star-Eagle,* backed the Whigs and the candidacy of Henry Clay. The *Advertiser* remained alone in the field for more than a decade before its success inspired in rapid succession papers in Newark, Jersey City, and Paterson. Most of these, however, were ephemeral. The Trenton *State Gazette,* an old post-Revolutionary weekly that was converted into a daily in 1847, is the only survivor.

The *State Gazette* inaugurated the first telegraphic news service in New Jersey. On January 13, 1847, the publishers announced with "the greatest satisfaction" that, "simultaneously with the morning daily papers of Washington, Baltimore, Philadelphia and New York," they were publishing that day "the proceedings of Congress yesterday, transmitted by the Magnetic Telegraph . . . a feat never before accomplished or thought of in New Jersey." The Newark *Advertiser* shortly followed suit. The old Associated Press—founded in 1848 and dissolved in 1899—was used by Thomas T. Kinney, the *Advertiser's* editor and publisher, as early as 1851.

At the end of the Civil War the manufacture of newsprint from wood pulp increased the possibilities of profitable publishing. The Jersey *Journal* of Jersey City appeared in 1867, and in the next 12 years 10 of the existing daily papers began publication. In the same period the Newark *Sunday Call* (1872) was established. Though it issues no daily edition, it has become the most important Sunday paper in the State. Its policy of treating New Jersey as one large community in which weddings and politics vie for the reader's interest has made it as much a part of Sunday morning in New Jersey as toast and coffee. The *Call* has been particularly energetic in vivifying the history and folklore of the State.

Under the management of the Kinneys, father and son, the Newark *Advertiser* became the best-equipped paper in New Jersey. They introduced steam power, cylinder presses, and other advanced mechanical equipment. A worthy contemporary until its cessation in 1894 was the Newark *Evening Journal,* whose militant editor, William Fuller, opposed the Civil War and the draft, and urged fair treatment of the defeated South.

After Richard Watson Gilder had lent a distinctive literary tone to the *Advertiser,* Wallace Scudder in 1883 established the Newark *Evening News* which within two decades ranked with such vigorous publications as the Springfield *Republican* and the Hartford *Courant.* Comprehensive presentation of New Jersey and a consistently progressive technical policy make it one of the Nation's foremost six-day newspapers. Like the *Call* on Sundays, the *News* on weekdays throws the searchlight on a wide arc of its own dooryard. Its earliest editions, which often resemble abridgements of several country weeklies, justify its claim to the title, "New Jersey's Great Home Newspaper." In April 1938 the *News* received the Francis Wayland Ayer Cup, offered annually by N. W. Ayer & Son, Inc., to the daily newspaper chosen as the most outstanding for typographical excellence.

More than half of New Jersey's daily and Sunday papers have been founded since the invention of the linotype machine by Ottmar Mergenthaler in 1885. Activity was particularly strong in the northern section, where papers were started in Paterson, Hoboken, Plainfield, and Hackensack. Expansion after 1900 gradually filled journalistic gaps in the south. The most recent dailies in the State are the Atlantic City *World* and the Ocean City *Sentinel-Ledger,* both founded in 1935.

Weekly newspapers have continued to spring up over the State, many of them in saucy defiance of established dailies. Bergen County, with 70 weeklies in 71 municipalities, is now said to lead the Nation in this journalistic abundance. Practically every one of these journals follows a pattern—possessing an incipient Walter Winchell and relieving the boiler-plate material with descriptions of the actions of a small-town mayor, or the social coup of a debutante. Legal advertising forms a large portion of their revenue. The State has no weekly as salty and indigenous as *Crawford's Weekly* in Virginia, but Carl Wittman's Fair Lawn and Paramus *Clarion* strangely enough holds its conservative readers by attacks on fascism, irresponsible government and big business.

As a whole, country weeklies still have a precarious existence, and not all unsuccessful present-day publishers display the sardonic humor illustrated long ago in the Camden *City Directory* by a picture of a tombstone with the inscription: "Here Lies the Camden *Local News*—Died April 1882—For Lack of Nourishment—H. R. Caulfield, Ex-Publisher."

The contemporary personality of the press in New Jersey is distinctly native. The large newspaper chains are represented in the State only by Paul Block's Newark *Star-Eagle* and Frank Gannett's Plainfield *Courier-News*. The metropolitan tabloids are imitated in a modified form only by the Newark *Ledger* and a brace of Sunday weeklies. Most of the dailies are limited to two or three editions; and only a few, including the Atlantic City *Press* and the Trenton *Times,* have a Sunday edition. The Newark *Evening News* is perhaps the only State paper which devotes appreciable editorial or reportorial space to international affairs and national questions, not directly involving New Jersey.

In style, content, and appearance New Jersey newspapers pursue a leisurely course, mainly uninfluenced by towering headlines, colored sheets, or adventurous type experiments. Columns and features have a decidedly local flavor; sports writing covers even the activities of grammar schools; and syndicated material has firmly entrenched itself. Among the New Jersey journalists who have had their products syndicated was the late Howard Freeman, cartoonist of the Newark *Evening News.*

The general tone of the editorial pages is conservative. For a long time, it was strongly marked by a tendency to support the National administration, irrespective of political badge. Not more than half a dozen dailies list their politics; most of them adopt the opaque classification "Independent." In general the papers of Newark and Jersey City have spoken for Democratic policies, while those in the southern part of the State advocate Republican policies. There have been few hard-fought newspaper crusades against economic and political ills. The most notable campaigns in recent years have been those of the Newark *Star-Eagle* for reduction of Public Service Corporation electric rates and the Camden *Courier* and *Post* for a municipal power plant.

New Jersey publishers have displayed marked ability in developing the business side of publishing. For thirteen consecutive years the Newark *Evening News* has led the six-day papers of the country in classified advertising. Brisk advertising managers have corraled enough space to make the average price of a New Jersey daily three cents, and to keep the number of pages well above sixteen.

Newspaper owners have united in the New Jersey State Press Association, which cooperates with the department of journalism at Rutgers University in placing young writers. Devoted chiefly to an annual survey of the newspaper scene, the publishers' organization has generally followed the American Newspaper Publishers' Association in formulating both editorial and labor policies.

The American Newspaper Guild, now numbering 245 members in the

State, has a wide appeal in New Jersey, for the Guild won its first important victory in the Newark *Ledger* strike of 1935. The organization extends over the State, but is strongest in Newark and Camden, and in Hudson County. In these areas the Guild has made the most significant advance toward securing for editorial workers salaries and wages equal to those long established by typographical unions.

New Jersey's large immigrant groups have developed a vigorous and colorful press. Concerned equally with events at home and in the fatherland, the foreign-language papers perhaps represent the most definite political opinion and the most cosmopolitan spirit in the State press. Although reduced in scope of influence by the growing Americanization of their readers, the papers still figure prominently in the politics and culture of New Jersey.

Between 1850 and 1900 the Germans composed the largest group of foreign-born. In 1852 the New Jersey *Freie Zeitung,* the best-known and most influential of all the State's German newspapers, was founded in Newark by Benedict Prieth, a liberal who had fled his native Austria after the abortive revolution of 1848. It flourished as a daily for more than seven decades, and only lately has been reduced to a weekly. Other German publications followed, until Hudson County—called "the most German county in the Nation"—had nine, including two dailies. Another historic German publication is the New Jersey *Staats Journal,* started in Trenton in 1867.

Only the Ukrainians have a daily paper in New Jersey today. Their *Svoboda* of Jersey City, founded in 1893, has maintained a steady circulation of 14,000. Other groups, like their English-speaking neighbors, look largely to New York and Philadelphia for their daily reading. A number of weeklies, such as the *Italian Tribune* and the *Polish Kronika* of Newark, the *Magyar Herald* of New Brunswick, the *Nowiny* of Trenton and the *Polak-Amerykanki* of Perth Amboy, serve their respective language readers. Several papers published in English stress the interests of English-speaking Jews. Among them are the *Jewish Chronicle,* Newark; the *Jewish Ledger,* Atlantic City, and the *Jewish Standard* and the Hudson *Jewish News,* both of Jersey City. The last named paper and the *Morgen-Stern* of Newark also publish Yiddish editions.

General labor news is presented mainly by a northern New Jersey edition of the weekly *People's Press* and the monthly *Union Labor Advocate,* of Elizabeth. In December 1935 the Paterson *Press* was launched as the State's first cooperatively owned newspaper, financed largely by Paterson workers and by members of printing trades unions of New Jersey and adjoining States. The paper, an outgrowth of a successful open shop campaign by the two Paterson dailies, succumbed in September 1936 from a shortage of funds. Although the *Press* did not get beyond the weekly stage, it distinguished itself by a campaign, the most outspoken in New Jersey press history, against too high electric rates.

Racial and National Groups

ALTHOUGH the farmlands of New Jersey have attracted immigrants during three centuries, the greatest influx of foreign-born has been to the industrial centers developed within the last hundred years. Close by New York City and the Ellis Island immigrant station, New Jersey absorbed wave after wave of Europeans until today it ranks fifth among the States in its percentage of foreign-born residents.

According to the United States census for 1930, the State had 844,442 foreign-born whites, plus 1,413,239 native whites of foreign or "mixed" parentage, constituting together about 57 percent of the total population. Negroes numbered 208,828, about 5 percent of the total. Native whites of native parentage were about 38 percent of the State's population, compared with an average of about 57 percent for the Nation.

Leading nationalities represented in the foreign-born white population, as recorded by the 1930 census, are shown below:

Nationalities	Number	Percent of Total Population
Italian	190,858	4.7
German	112,753	2.8
Polish	102,573	2.5
Irish	63,236	1.5
Russian	62,152	1.5
English	51,629	1.3
Scotch	34,721	.9
Czecho-Slovakian	32,358	.8
Hungarian	32,332	.8
Scandinavian	27,895	.7
Swedish	13,360	.4
Norwegian	7,870	.2
Danish	6,665	.1
Austrian	24,010	.6
Dutch	14,762	.4

Englishmen, Swedes, and Hollanders were first among the white newcomers to penetrate the wilderness that was to become New Jersey. Together they appropriated the property of the Lenni Lenape Indians, a friendly pastoral people. In 1930 the State had an Indian population of 213, although no Indian reservation remains.

The Swedes moved into the Delaware Bay region in 1638, and thereafter remained apart from the main stream of New Jersey history. Swedesboro, a village of some 2,000 inhabitants on Raccoon Creek, near Camden, is a present-day reminder of these earliest settlers. A few Scandinavian settlements along the seacoast, of which Barnegat City is the best known, are sustained by the fishing trade.

The Hollanders, frugal and industrious, formed a substantial and lasting element in the population. Numerous Dutch Reformed congregations scattered through Bergen and adjoining counties testify to the stubborn Dutch zeal for religious authority that figured so prominently in European and early American events. Some of the most genial customs of American life, including sleighing and ice-skating, Christmas festivities and other ceremonies, were introduced by the Dutch. Most of the more recent immigrants live in Bergen and Passaic Counties, in communities such as Prospect Park.

But the dominant factor throughout New Jersey in Colonial days was the English. With the Scotch they founded the old towns of Elizabeth, Perth Amboy, Middletown, and Shrewsbury. The military seizure of the Colony from the Dutch in 1664 decided the future Anglo-Saxon rule of New Jersey.

By 1790 the English numbered 98,000, in a total population of 170,000. All the political, economic and cultural principles by which the Colonists ordered their affairs had been transplanted from Great Britain. Long after the Revolution had broken the power of London, these principles retained their influence. Although the British were at first mainly an agricultural and official element in New Jersey, the 86,000 foreign-born English and Scottish residents of today are chiefly employed in industry and commerce.

By the middle of the nineteenth century the English, Dutch, Scotch, Germans, and Irish had fused into a relatively stable society. On the outskirts of the social structure, though not definitely segregated, were the Negroes. Aided by State emancipation laws, they had passed from slavery into wage labor as gardeners, tannery workers, house servants, coachmen, and building trades workers. Their barber shops and laundries, catering establishments, and orchestras were patronized by both races. Some owned stores on Broad Street in Newark.

Hard times following the industrial revolution and political persecution in Europe produced the second great wave of immigration. Between 1844 and 1850 the Irish population in New Jersey more than tripled, largely because of the severe potato famine in the homeland. Despite their traditional hostility to the Anglo-Saxon race, the Irish speedily adapted themselves to their new environment, and rose swiftly to economic equality with other nationalities. In Newark, Jersey City, Hoboken, and Paterson they began as a laboring element in the factories, but before long had acquired control of the building trades. To New Jersey they brought a volatility unknown to the established nationalities. The Irish participated significantly in trade unions and also formed the backbone of political organizations that seldom supported measures of vital concern to the workingman. The Irish have been the great fraternalists of the State, responsible perhaps for the founding of more societies and orders than any other group.

It was not, however, until the coming of the German "Forty-eighters" —political refugees from the reaction raging in Germany following the attempt of the people to exterminate feudalism—that any appreciable change was made in certain long-established social customs in New Jersey.

For more than 200 years English Puritanism had kept watch over the public morals of society. The "Forty-eighters," fresh from battlefields where the great questions of economic and political liberty were being decided, held a liberal attitude toward religion and the Sabbath. They developed community singing, occasionally neglected business for intellectual pleasures, and enjoyed outdoor life to the fullest. In addition, they became a progressive element in American politics and a force in building the trade union movement.

The Germans applied their technical knowledge and energy to the development of the country's resources. They became skilled workers in many industries, particularly in the electrical field, and were mainly responsible for the rise of the brewing industry.

More significantly, the Germans were pioneers in the movement for free public education. Their love of music was reflected in the Sängerfest, an annual singing festival of the Germans in the northeastern part of the United States which began in New Jersey in 1891. Largest of German organizations in the State today is the German-American League.

In the middle decades of the nineteenth century, both Germans and Irish were persecuted by the Know-Nothing Party, a secret society that in some respects resembled the modern Ku Klux Klan and Black Legion. The dour and bigoted Americans comprising this group objected to the Catholicism of the Irish and the political liberalism of the Germans. Although they organized thug onslaughts to drive the immigrants out of the country, and even carried their alien-baiting to the polls, they failed to make an appreciable reduction in the growing number of refugees and pioneers from the Old World.

The immigrants of the late nineteenth and early twentieth centuries were motivated more by economic than political considerations. Leaving their homelands, where life had been hard and crude, they converged on the growing commercial and industrial cities of Newark, Jersey City, Paterson, Passaic, New Brunswick, Trenton, and Camden. They established communities bordering on the very shadows of the factories, much as their peasant ancestors clustered beneath the walls of the feudal manor. Their economic position was modestly secure, but reports of their prosperity were fantastically exaggerated by steamship agents in order to bring thousands more from the Old World.

Poles began to come to New Jersey in large numbers in 1870. In Hudson County alone they now number 23,000, most of them being employed at heavy labor in the factories and oil refineries of Jersey City and Bayonne. More than 5,000 Polish immigrants live in Newark, where they are distributed among a variety of industries.

Polish women assume a large part of their families' economic burden. In Jersey City a large laundry employs nearly 1,000 Polish women, and in the woolen mills of Passaic they number at least 5,000. Bad housing, fatigue, and poverty have caused a certain physical deterioration among these women, who in their native land are exceptionally handsome. The Poles are deeply religious, and in the Greek and Roman Catholic churches they find their chief opportunity for artistic expression. Like the Germans, the Poles are a musical people, and singing societies and orchestras are usually a feature of their many fraternal and national organizations.

Residents of Italian stock in New Jersey constitute more than 10 percent of the total of Italian stock in the United States. Late nineteenth century arrivals for the most part, the Italians are found in every county and in every industrial center. Some have entered agriculture, notably in settlements near Vineland and Hammonton and generally throughout south New Jersey. The cultivation of peppers, artichokes, and eggplants is an Italian importation. In Chatham and Madison many Italians are employed in greenhouses.

But the majority of Italians are found in factory and construction work. In Paterson, national center of the silk-dyeing industry, more than 10,000 work in the dye houses. They are also numerous in the silk mills. Shrewd in business and real estate investments, the Italians are also among the most substantial members of the trade union movement. In Passaic County they are the backbone of one of the Nation's largest local unions, Dyers' Local 1733.

Czecho-Slovakians are numerous in the Passaic County textile region. Elizabeth has a number of Lithuanians. Hungarians, concentrated in and around New Brunswick and Perth Amboy, account for more than 12 percent of all Hungarians in the United States. They were the nucleus for the town of Roebling, one of the few company towns in New Jersey. Turks, Syrians, and Armenians are also employed in the textile mills of Paterson and Passaic.

One of the most prominent groups in New Jersey is that of the Jews, chiefly immigrants from Poland and Russia. The earliest sizable Jewish community grew up in Newark about 1844. This was a time of large Jewish immigration, when thousands fled from Western and Central Europe to escape enforced military duty and to live under more democratic conditions. At first mainly pack peddlers, they later opened butcher shops, drygoods stores and cigar factories, and within a generation had become significant factors in the commercial and financial life of the State. During the 1880's, religious persecution in Russia and Poland brought an even larger number of Jews to New Jersey. Less readily adaptable to new conditions than the earlier immigrants, they have nevertheless become important as small merchants in the larger cities and, like their German predecessors, have made a valuable contribution in the professional fields.

Today New Jersey, with 225,306 Jews (1927), is fifth in the United States in Jewish population, and is exceeded only by New York in its proportion of Jewish residents. The cultural and philanthropic institutions of the Jews form a network serving the entire State. In Newark, where the Jewish population is approximately 75,000, they maintain 30 congregations and more than 250 charitable, social, fraternal, and communal bodies.

Of the 1,738 Chinese recorded in the 1930 census, the majority are laundrymen and restaurant workers, although a few are engaged in other forms of commerce. Only 439 Japanese were listed as residents in 1930.

The 208,828 Negroes of New Jersey (1930) are distributed mainly in the industrial areas of Newark, Jersey City, Paterson, and Elizabeth, though a few live in practically every rural district and small town. They are also numerous in such residential towns as Montclair and Morristown, and in the resorts of Atlantic City and Asbury Park.

Large scale immigration during the nineteenth century squeezed Negro artisans and laborers out of industry, forcing them more and more into menial and unorganized jobs at substandard wages. A growing poverty pushed them into the worst sections of the cities, where disease and apathy spread among them.

Negroes suffer serious exploitation and discrimination. In Jersey City, for example, squalid houses in the most run-down sections cost Negro families from $30 to $50 a month. Residential discrimination is common throughout the State. Practically all public school systems south of Princeton have separate buildings or classes for Negroes (*see Education*).

Although Negroes constitute less than 5 percent of the State population, Negro deaths are 8 percent of the total; infant mortality, 12 percent; deaths from tuberculosis, 20 percent; unemployment, twice the percentage for whites. Of all juvenile delinquents convicted, 24 percent are Negroes. Having important bearing on these facts is the statement of Egerton Elliot Hall, Rutgers University (1933):

> No situation more clearly reflects the low economic status of New Jersey's Negro population than its housing and neighborhood facilities. The President's Conference on Home Building and Home Ownership reported: "At least three types of social pathology have been observed to have a high and inescapable correlation with the character of Negro residence areas. These are: (1) a high rate of delinquency, (2) a high rate of mortality, and (3) a distorted standard of living."

In spite of these handicaps, the Negroes have registered a number of positive advances. Illiteracy among Negroes in New Jersey was reduced from 30 percent in 1880 to 7 percent in 1930. There are more than 500 Negro school teachers and as many professional workers in the State. Despite discrimination, the Negro has played an important part in the silk, rubber, steel and cigar-making industries and in agriculture.

In southern New Jersey is Gouldtown, a small village peopled chiefly by descendants of four mulatto families who have intermarried for more than 175 years, with only an occasional infiltration of other blood stocks. Although situated in a poor and timber-exhausted land, the people of Gouldtown have preserved a dignity that is reflected in the number of teachers, ministers, and scientists who have come from the town. Lawnside, near Camden, the only borough in New Jersey governed entirely by Negroes, began as a station on the Underground Railroad. The tract of land was purchased in 1840 by Quaker abolitionists who divided it into lots, which they sold to Negroes at low prices. From simple farmers the inhabitants of Lawnside have grown into a group whose achievements in self-government and in economic and social advancement have made them interesting to Negro students and research workers from many parts of the country (*see Tour 23*).

In the wild rugged country of the Ramapo Mountains in the north live the so-called Jackson Whites, some 5,000 mountaineers as far removed from the urban life a score of miles away as those in eastern Tennessee. The basis of the group was 3,500 white and black women imported from England and the West Indies by the British military authority in New York during the Revolution. After the war the women found refuge in the New Jersey hills with exiled Indians from North Carolina and they were soon joined by Hessians. Later Italians, Dutch, and more Negroes added to the mixture.

Long isolation as economic outcasts in their hovels and at their miserable jobs has made the Jackson Whites suspicious of city folk and apparently resigned to their fate as a racial oddity. They now constitute a genuine social problem in a State that for the most part knows them only as the subject of sensational newspaper stories *(see Side Tour 9A)*.

Many of the European groups, especially the Italians, Poles, and Hungarians, have settled in particular quarters of the larger cities or have founded separate towns and villages, where they keep alive the customs, languages, and in some cases the modes of thought of their fatherlands. The extremely large number of Italians in the State has made the study of Italian a regular foreign language course in many of the larger high schools.

The absorption of foreign groups is proceeding with varying degrees of rapidity. In general, however, the Europeans wear American clothes, talk "American," and in many cases have exchanged their own traditions for those of their adopted country. The process has cost New Jersey many colorful ceremonies and practices formerly common among immigrants. The rousing German singing societies in Newark and Hoboken have virtually disappeared; Poles and Russians are gradually abandoning their own Christmas and New Year's celebrations for the Santa Claus and horntooting of Americans; and Italians no longer repair to the countryside to celebrate religious festivals.

This drift is exemplified, perhaps, by the change of foreign names to Americanized forms. Italians have been conspicuous in resisting American nomenclature, holding to names such as "Salvatore" and "Mauriello" that have a musical quality in contrast to the more usual clipped Anglo-Saxon names.

Relations between the various races and nationalities, on the whole, have been amicable in New Jersey. There have been occasional cases of racial clash. Riots between Italians and Negroes were common during the Italo-Ethiopian crisis, and several years ago the civil war in China had its repercussions in violent strife in Newark's Chinatown. Similarly, adherents of the present regimes in Germany and Italy have indulged in anti-Semitic activities and have in turn been subject to boycott.

The native-born American's natural curiosity to examine foreign customs at first-hand has done much toward breaking down barriers. Those who try "real" Italian spaghetti or "genuine" Hungarian goulash, or who attend a Polish wedding or a Greek service as a spectacle, usually come away with a more enlightened view of the minority groups. Schools and churches have developed extensive programs both to promote Americanization and to explain foreign backgrounds to the Americans themselves.

In the large cities economic necessity has called forth considerable cooperation among the once-isolated groups. The depression itself proved in most cases an important uniting force. Strong prejudices weakened before common economic distress and the need for joint action, as in hunger demonstrations in Newark in 1932 and the march of the unemployed to Trenton in 1936. The revelation of deplorable living conditions among industrial workers has brought community action for better housing and improved facilities for recreation.

Folklore and Folkways

BY DEFAULT, the title of official State demon has rested for nearly a century with the Leeds Devil, a friendly native of Atlantic County who has traveled extensively throughout southern New Jersey. Although the exact date of his birth is not known, there is no doubt as to his maternal parentage. A Mrs. Leeds of Estelville, a small community near the Great Egg Harbor River, found that she was an expectant mother. The expectations of Mrs. Leeds were neither great nor enthusiastic, and in a petulant moment she cried out that she hoped the stork would bring a devil.

In due time the long-billed bird made a perfect three-point landing in either the Leeds cabbage patch or rose garden, depending on which school of obstetrical thought the reader accepts. The sequence of events from this point is somewhat confused. One version is that Mrs. Leeds told the stork to take the baby back where it came from, and a few minutes later the accommodating bird returned with a red-faced little devil tied up in a napkin. The other story is that the human baby promptly assumed the form of a demon and flew out of the window. At any rate, Mrs. Leeds was surprised and perhaps regretted her hasty wish.

The young devil is believed to have spent his adolescence in the swampland, beyond the reach of truant officers and child guidance clinics. Soon after attaining his majority he started going out nights and made himself widely known to the population of southern New Jersey.

Cloven-hoofed, long-tailed, and white; with the head of a collie dog, the face of a horse, the body of a kangaroo, the wings of a bat, and the disposition of a lamb—that is the Leeds Devil. He has never harmed a soul, nor violated even a local ordinance. There is every reason to believe that his nocturnal ramblings have been actuated by a sympathetic curiosity about the affairs of man. One report is that he is writing a thesis, *A Plutonian Critique of Some Awful Aspects of the Terrestrial Life,* in preparation for a doctor's degree from the University of Hell. The more scientifically minded people of the State therefore consider it unfortunate that the devil's field work has been hampered by door-slammings and curtain-drawings. Only old Judge French showed any kindness to the demon scholar. Every morning for years, it is said, the judge and the devil engaged in lively discussions of Republican politics, while breakfasting together on South Jersey ham and eggs.

Practically everyone in southern New Jersey knows of one or more persons who have seen the devil, but very few will acknowledge personal acquaintance. Councilman E. P. Weeden of Trenton was aroused on a cold January night in 1909 by the sound of someone's trying to enter the door. Thinking that one of his seventh ward constituents might need help in a domestic crisis, the councilman jumped from his bed. He was amazed to hear the flapping of wings; and from the second-floor window, he could see impressions of a cloven hoof deep in the snow on the roof of the porch. On the same night the devil visited the State arsenal, leaving his characteristic hoofprints around the chicken house but not disturbing a fowl. Although the Negro settlement at Pitman Grove was omitted from the devil's itinerary, report of his travels was believed responsible for a remarkable spurt in church attendance and a decline in beer drinking that lasted for months.

A reward of $500 for the devil's capture was once offered by J. F. Hope, a Philadelphian. Mr. Hope said that the devil was his own, and that it was not a devil at all but a rare Australian vampire—one of the only two ever captured. The reward has never been claimed.

There is a tradition that each reappearance of the devil is an omen of war. It was no surprise to residents of Atlantic County when the Italo-Ethiopian conflict broke out just a few months after William Bozarth saw the devil in the pine country at Batsto. Another person who vouches for a view of the devil is Philip Smith, a Negro slaughterhouse worker in Woodstown. Smith, whose reputation for honesty and sobriety is unimpeachable, was looking out the window just before midnight on an evening in 1935 when he saw the devil walking down the sidewalk across the street. "Looked to me something like a giant police dog, kind of high in the back," Smith related. "He walked past the grocery store and disappeared."

Most of the State's ghosts seem to prefer haunting one particular spot. Seven Stars Tavern, built in 1762 near Woodstown, is headquarters for a number of ghosts, and has been called the champion haunted house of New Jersey. The specter of the builder has been seen digging in a nearby field, presumably for treasure hidden during the Revolution; two sisters named Stevens said a woman's ghost visited their bedroom; and Bluebeard, a reputedly blasphemous pirate, had his neck twisted by the devil.

There was also a band of fighting ghosts, one of whom was called Beelzebub; and a number of apparitions whose names alone survive—the Indian, the Peeping Woman, the Horse and Rider, the Hessian, and others.

Absecon Island, near Atlantic City, is the wellspring of a group of semi-supernatural tales centering around Lafitte, Kidd, Teach, and other buccaneers. During violent storms the islanders are said to have lured ships onto the dangerous Brigantine shoals in order to plunder them. The decoy was a lantern hanging from a pole lashed to a jackass, which was led back and forth. To a ship in the outer waters, the light would seem that of a vessel peacefully riding out the storm in a harbor. The shoals completed the work. The inhabitants then put off in boats and salvaged the cargo of the wrecked boat, taking care to murder any surviving members of the crew. Being deeply religious, the islanders taught their children to pray that a ship would run aground.

In 1717 pirates were supposed to be "fifteen hundred strong at least" along the coast, and one ship flying the skull and crossbones off Sandy Hook was captured by a man-o'-war out of Perth Amboy. Legendary treasure has been sought in the region, but none has ever been found. Blackbeard, who roamed along the Delaware, is said to have buried a treasure at the base of a black walnut tree on Wood Street, in Burlington. The hoard was guarded by a reckless Spaniard, who let himself be shot with a charmed bullet and was buried upright. The ghost of a large black dog that was buried with the man is sometimes seen on the street.

A different sort of treasure is reputed to be buried in the sand pits near Downer, Gloucester County. Presumably brought there by runaway slaves as a fund for trips on the Underground Railroad, it will be found only by the direct descendant of such a slave, at a time when the Negro race is again in dire need. The treasure is guarded by a giant rabbit, who digs new hiding places faster than a brace of steam shovels whenever the hoard is threatened.

Many stories center around a character who actually lived, Jonas Cattell—scout, guide, soldier, and sportsman extraordinary. He was born near Woodbury in 1758, and during his 91 years he became southern New Jersey's most eminent personality. Jonas first won renown early in the Revolution, when he lured Count Donop's Hessians into a trap at Red Bank. For 15 years after the war he was known as an unequaled hunter and fisherman, and for 40 years thereafter he was whipper-in for the Gloucester County Fox-Hunting Club. Even at an advanced age he once covered 120 miles on foot in a little more than 24 hours.

During the last decade of his life the sturgeon episode occurred, and it has never been doubted, because Jonas had a well-founded reputation for strict integrity. One day his line jerked so hard that it nearly pulled him overboard. Towed by a sturgeon whose tremendous size momentarily dazed even this intrepid sportsman, his boat dashed madly upstream. Recovering, Jonas shortened his line and finally jumped into the water, grappled with his catch, and succeeded in heaving it into the boat. The fish was so large that its tail drooped over the edge. It continued to struggle and the gyrations of the tail, acting as a propeller, drove the boat forward at an unprecedented speed. Jonas finally had to release the monster, since by then he was far from home.

Although no one else ever saw the fish, Jonas continued to lure it with fresh joints of meat, and the two soon became friends. One time the sturgeon took him for another ride. As they flew upstream, Jonas saw that they were going to strike a low bridge, over which a herd of cattle was passing. He cut the line, but the fish went on and crashed into the bridge, from which a cow and her calf fell into the water. The sturgeon gorged himself on the fresh beef. Soon thereafter cattle began to disappear from pastures bordering on streams, but no trace of the thief was left behind. Angry farmers set a careful watch. One finally saw the sturgeon crawl from a stream, using his tail for propulsion, and carry off a cow. The cattle owners, however, could never capture the marauder. They blamed Jonas as the patron of the fish, and he was kept in poverty the rest of his life, doling out sums from his meager pension to pay the huge meat claims.

A fishy odor also permeates the stories told about "Stretch" Garrison, who had a farm on the Maurice River near Delaware Bay. One day he happened to catch a shark. He slipped the anchor rope and let the fish tow him for a while. The creature headed up the river at such a rate that he ripped out the oyster beds for 50 yards on each side. There wasn't much water in the river, but the shark kept right on and dug a new channel for five miles up to Stretch's landing. By that time he was too worn out to go any farther, so Stretch tied him up, and fetched a bridle, saddle, and spade bit. After several months he finally trained the shark to gee and haw. Stretch made a lot of money riding the shark up and down the river every day delivering the United States mail.

Stretch was a scientific agrarian. He had trained a couple of cows to plow, so he didn't need any horses. At night he would milk the cows and pour the milk into a churn. The churn was rigged up to a treadmill on which the cows stood. Before he left the barn, Stretch would put a forkful of alfalfa hay in the rack in front of the cows, just out of reach. The cows stood there pawing the treadmill all night trying to reach the hay, and next morning the milk would be churned to butter. Continuous reaching made the cows grow bigger every day, and this gave Stretch an idea. He had a young rooster named Big Boy, which he started to feed off the top of a box. Next week he put the feed on top of a sugar barrel. Big Boy did nothing all day long but jump up and down, stretching every muscle. After a while he got big enough and strong enough to pull a truck. Stretch had to feed him from the roof of the porch, and had to use a concrete mixer to prepare his feed.

One day Stretch mixed up a batch of concrete, colored it green, flavored it with corn liquor, and fed it to Big Boy. The rooster ate up every bit of it, and when it hardened he turned to stone. Stretch gave him to the city fathers, who put him on top of the power plant and wired him for light and sound; he made a fine fire siren. But they finally had to take him down, because all the roosters in the vicinity were so jealous that they crowed at him night and day.

New Jersey, as might be expected, has several tales about mosquitoes. The first settlers of Bergen County found the district overrun with mosquitoes, some of which were as large as sparrows. The Indians had trained them to inoculate game with a secret preparation that paralyzed the animal until the hunter came within arrow range. When it was found that insects which had been fed on white blood made better hunters, the Indians encouraged them to bite the settlers. The settlers retaliated by killing the chief's most valuable thoroughbred. He immediately mustered his warriors and attacked. During the height of the conflict the Indians brought up their mosquito fleet, and the Dutch had to sue for peace.

Another legend tells of a group of men working all night in the salt works at the Manasquan River Inlet who were besieged by mosquitoes. The workmen crawled under a large iron kettle. The mosquitoes immediately began drilling into the metal; and as each proboscis appeared on the inside, the workmen would strike it with their hammers, riveting it fast. Finally, when a number had been hammered to the kettle, the mosquitoes simply flew away with it—after which the rest of the swarm made short work of the men.

The large Negro colony in Atlantic City has invented a mythical character, Darby Hicks. A new arrival from the South is terrified by being told that Hicks is looking for him with a razor and two guns. Trying to find this person and explain matters, he is sent from one place to another and frightened by repeated warnings. Some high-strung men have been known to quit their jobs, buy guns and knives, and walk the Northside for months looking for their unknown enemy.

A compound of medieval and ancient American lore survives among the "yarb folk" of southern New Jersey. From native herbs and plants they have developed a pharmacopoeia of simple vegetable cures. The percentage of coincidental success has been large enough to justify a survival of faith in their superstitions. Some of the remedies are:

Consumption: Boil two handfuls of sorrel in a pint of whey; strain and drink twice a day.

Corns: Apply bruised ivy leaves, and in 15 days corns will drop off.

Measles: Place a cut onion in the room of the sick child.

Warts: Rub with a radish; or rub with half a raw potato and then throw potato over left shoulder.

To make hair grow: Wash every night with a strong concoction of rosemary.

The old custom of growing a balsam apple into a bottle continues in many rural places. This was done immediately after the flowering by carefully tying the bottle on the arbor that supported the balsam vine. When the apple was deep orange and almost ripe, presenting a beautiful appearance inside the glass, the stem was cut. The bottle was then filled with whiskey and corked airtight. The contents were used for stomach disorders, swellings, and muscular pains.

Weather forecasts are based upon a variety of signs, some of them reliable and others fantastic. Rain is believed due when a cat washes its face, when birds fly close to the ground, when there is no dew in the morning, when many snails come out, and when fish jump from the water. The town of Washington is a center for predicting the character of the coming winter; local sages prognosticate on the basis of the arrival of katydids and the behavior of caterpillars. A long or bad winter may be expected when squirrels store an unusual quantity of nuts, or bees gather a large store of honey or when moss is thick on the north side of a tree.

To the fishermen of south New Jersey, the sea gull is the outstanding symbol of good luck, and to kill one is considered equivalent to committing suicide. An injured gull that alights on a ship is royally treated; when the bird recovers it is set free, always over the starboard side.

For the most part, the customs of the agricultural areas trace back to the eighteenth century immigration from northern Europe, while those of the industrial cities are derived from central and southern Europeans and Negroes.

In south New Jersey, folk customs center mainly around annual farm events and such social functions as weddings, births, and funerals. One practice, said to be dying out rapidly, is that of a community gathering at hog killing time, usually beginning on New Year's Day. The fattened hogs are thrown on their backs, stuck with a long knife, and allowed to bleed. After they are dipped into boiling water and scraped, estimates and wagers are made on the weight. The carcass is cut up, the lard rendered, and scrapple and sausage ground. After a plentiful supper the rooms are cleared, fiddles and accordion are produced, and the guests take part in a "hoedown" consisting of square and other country dances.

Berrying picnics are also popular. Quoits, charades, baseball games, and bathing are among the recreations for which the plentitude of huckleberries provides an excuse. Oyster suppers are an old custom in Gloucester County, often begetting romance and marriage. Harvest home suppers are a standby of many rural churches throughout the State; some, served in the open, attract more than a thousand guests, among whom invariably will be local politicians. In many towns the volunteer fire department holds an annual fair, the main attraction being a chance on anything from a basket of groceries to a new automobile. Salt Water Day, still observed annually at Keyport, had its origin more than a hundred years ago, when farmers made a yearly holiday visit to the seashore.

Among the Easter sunrise services, the one at Lakeview Memorial Park, Burlington County, is especially impressive. This is conducted by the Palmyra Moravian Church from a hillside altar overlooking a lake. To the right of the altar stands a "singing tower" of chimes, and in the rear is an immense cross brilliantly illuminated by lights of changing colors. At the break of dawn, chorals are sung by a group attired in white surplices, accompanied by an ensemble of trumpets and trombones. The historic liturgy, which begins around 5 a.m., is attended by thousands.

In December at Atlantic City occurs the Eisteddfod, a six-day Festival of Song that perpetuates an ancient Welsh custom derived from the triennial assembly of the Welsh bards and minstrels.

Hallowe'en, aside from State-wide jollification, still produces two unusual observances in Bergen County. The Welsh make a fire, and each member of the gathering throws into it a white stone marked with his name. He then retires for the night and looks for his stone in the morning. If he does not find it, he is marked for the grave within the year— a superstition that may survive from ancient Druid beliefs. The Irish of the same section have a much more cheery custom. Each family prepares for the holiday supper a dish known as "callcannon," a conglomerate of onions, potatoes, and parsnips. Placed in the mass are a gold ring and a key. Whoever finds in his portion the ring, signifying early marriage, or the key, meaning departure on a journey, will be the recipient of good luck. On Thanksgiving Day, masked and costumed children parade the streets in Jersey City and its environs begging for pennies.

The German-American societies of northern New Jersey hold an annual Plattdeutsches (low-German) Volksfest in North Bergen, usually attended by from 12,000 to 15,000 persons. The program includes old costume dances, skits, and athletic events.

Hammonton is transformed into an Italian town every July 16. From 20,000 to 25,000 persons flock there from four States to observe the Feast of Our Lady of Mount Carmel. Beginning early in the morning, mass is celebrated each hour. The highlight of the festival is a religious procession in which statues of favorite saints are carried through the streets.

In the early development of North Bergen, an area of farms and woods beyond the boundary of the township was known as "the Jungles." This territory, long since surrounded, now occupies three blocks near the center of town, and here arose the annual custom of crowning a "King of the Jungle." The first authentically recorded coronation was in 1910.

On a specified day in summer, contestants strove with each other in wrestling and in drinking ale, the winner being enthroned on a gaily bedecked barber chair. The defeated candidate then fanned the champion's brow with brooms as he downed two more tankards to justify his exalted position. In recent years the wrestling has been foregone for the brew now supplied by enterprising politicians.

Education

PUBLIC education in New Jersey developed somewhat slowly during the first two centuries of the State's history. The progress achieved in converting the Colonial log schoolhouse into the post-Revolutionary academy was limited by the persistent idea that only those who could pay were entitled to an education. In the last 70 years the united resources of the State have replaced the academy with the present free school system.

The most important single advance in education was the legislative act of 1871 which abolished all fees for instruction in public schools. Opportunities for rich and poor were thus placed on a common level. The hickory stick and the lash gradually went the way of the one-room building. Even the kindergarten system, founded by enterprising women as a means of making a living, was taken over by the State.

Cornerstone accomplishments in building an educational program were the creation of a State-controlled system of training teachers in normal schools, the consolidation of small, weak rural schools into larger and stronger units, the development of a State-wide system of high schools, and the founding of a State college with free scholarships. Federal funds have made possible many additions to public school buildings in the past five years. In the broadening field of adult education Perth Amboy and the South Orange-Maplewood union have established notable lecture and training courses that are being imitated throughout the State.

For the school year of 1936–37, the school system had an enrollment of 779,713 pupils, of whom 192,757 were in high schools. The complete educational program of that year cost $103,425,026 and employed 28,256 teachers. The average annual salary of day school teachers was $1,898—a decrease of $245 since 1931. Publicly owned school buildings numbered 2,171, besides 31 rented structures. Value of buildings, land and equipment was listed at $341,111,987, and the net State school debt was about $198,000,000.

Such has been the rise of what its opponents of a century ago bitterly opposed as "a pauper system."

Once the early Dutch, Swedish, and English settlers had successfully

STATE NORMAL SCHOOL, GLASSBORO

pushed the Indians away from the coasts, they turned to providing education for their young. Ministers held services in the log cabins and then gave religious instruction to the children. On their insistence schoolmasters were brought from abroad to aid them.

The early log schoolhouse was about 16 feet square. Windows cut into the log walls were covered in winter with sheepskin or oiled paper. There was a huge fireplace at one end, and near the windows a rough desk for the older children, who were learning arithmetic.

Frontier education was primitive. Reading was the main course, supplemented at times by writing, spelling, and arithmetic. The stern Dutch and Puritan schoolmasters excelled in discipline, literally requiring their pupils to toe the chalk line drawn across the schoolhouse floor. Slab benches hardened the younger children against the usual punishment for failing to toe the mark.

In the towns, the apprenticeship system in the crafts and trades aided the progress of education. By contract the master was bound to teach his apprentice not only his occupation but also "to read, wryte and cypher." This led Moses Combs, an early Newark shoe manufacturer, to found a night school for his apprentices; later the privilege was extended to others. In Woodbridge as early as 1691 the town schoolmaster was engaged to teach until 9 o'clock on winter nights, presumably for the benefit of apprentices and other workers.

Although these crude schools continued well into the last century, more advanced institutions were founded in the older settlements for those able to pay the cost. Newark Academy was opened in 1774, and the Trenton Academy three years later. Princeton University had been established in 1746 by the Presbyterians at Elizabeth, and Rutgers was founded as Queen's College by the Dutch Reformed Church in 1766. A Princeton graduate opened a grammar school at Elizabethtown in the same year and other college men followed his example.

The first move toward a free public school system in New Jersey was made in 1813, when friends of education tried to obtain $40,000 from the State for a school fund. After three years' effort, the fund was started with $15,000. Four years later the legislature authorized inhabitants of townships to raise money for education of children unable to pay fees. The State augmented its financial support in 1828 by allocating to education taxes from banks and insurance companies. In the same year, a convention of welfare associations at Trenton appointed a committee to publicize the need for better schools. Nearly 12,000 children were reported devoid of education and one-fifth of the voters illiterate.

Although many citizens were moved by such findings, education was still considered a luxury. It is related that the first school principal in Newark was named primarily to curtail what the superintendent considered waste of fuel. Incidental to his duties as janitor, he was to supervise the course of study.

Clara Barton, later founder of the American Red Cross, was a pioneer builder of the free school system in New Jersey during the middle of the last century. Having obtained a teacher's certificate at the age of 15 in her native Massachusetts, she offered her services without charge for three months to aid the free school at Bordentown, a center of opposition to "free schools for paupers." Her faith in the system was more than justified by the quick growth of the school, which had an enrollment of 600 pupils in its second year.

Spurred by organizations and individuals, the State gradually assumed its mounting obligation. New Jersey's first high school was founded at Newark in 1838, the third oldest in the country. In 1841 the State board of education was given general supervision over education, and in 1855 the first State normal school was founded at Trenton. Finally, 16 years later, the legislature passed a bill declaring all public schools free. To education was allotted the proceeds of sales from State lands under water.

Shortly after 1870 a rapid expansion of high schools began in the northern and central counties. Much of the success of the movement was due to the influence of President James McCosh of Princeton.

Since the Civil War, higher living standards for the wage earner have fortified higher ambition for the schooling of his children. A ceaseless demand has produced high schools in every town of importance, while smaller neighboring districts have combined their resources to establish high schools or have paid for tuition in nearby towns.

Through high expenditures and well-conceived planning New Jersey has broadened the scope of its school system beyond that of many other States. The State's educational expense per pupil is exceeded only by California, Nevada, and New York. The average cost for each student in average daily attendance in 1932 was $126.39, against a national average of $81.36. The outlay fell in 1936–37 to $113.99, a decrease of nearly 10 percent. As a result of the State's liberal educational program, the proportion of illiterates declined from 5.1 to 3.8 percent in the period of 1920–30.

Expansion of schoolhouses and teaching staffs has been matched by efforts to develop courses of study suitable to the special groups arising from an industrialized civilization. The foreign-born white population of New Jersey is now above 840,000 or about 22 percent of the whole, and there are more than 1,400,000 white residents of foreign or "mixed" parentage. Americanization courses have been installed in the regular schools for the children and adult evening classes have been established.

In the central and southern parts of the State a separate elementary school system is maintained for Negro children. This is not a State policy, but depends rather upon the county and community, many small municipalities in which there are few Negro residents being unable to afford the double expense of a biracial system. Negroes attend all the institutions of higher learning in the State, with the exception of Princeton University. Despite the State's democratic educational program, Negroes often may not teach in their own localities after graduation from the State Teachers' Colleges. Paterson, Newark, and Jersey City are among the noteworthy exceptions to this practice. The State maintains the Manual and Industrial School for Colored Youth at Bordentown, where 32 teachers give more than 400 pupils occupational education and regular academic training.

For more than half a century school attendance has been required of all children between the ages of 7 and 16. To this law has been added a statute forbidding the employment of children under 14 years of age and requiring those over 14 to be certified in fundamental schooling before they may work. Continuation schools have been provided for part-time workers; manual training, vocational, and agricultural schools have been created in the farming and industrial areas to meet the demand for technical and scientific training. An extensive program has been designed for backward children, defectives, and cripples, as well as for the blind, deaf and dumb.

The State has been a leader in attempting to give individual attention to pupils, as opposed to the mass instruction of the past. Newark and other large cities have been particularly quick to modify the old curriculum, to adopt modern methods of instruction, and to experiment boldly in an effort to prepare their pupils for contemporary living.

Much remains to be done before equality of opportunity for every child in the State is achieved. Although at present the wealthier cities and towns are able to enlist the most qualified educators, many communities lack funds to provide adequate teachers, buildings, and equipment.

Most school districts employ nurses who keep close watch on the pupils to prevent epidemics and to safeguard general health. For 25 years school districts have been required to engage physicians as medical inspectors to ascertain physical defects of pupils. Dental clinics are being established in increasing numbers, and health education has been incorporated into the curriculum by State law.

The motor bus and the consolidated school have in the last 20 years aided in overcoming some rural handicaps. Towns have pooled resources to build consolidated schools and to obtain better instructors and equipment. The State has accelerated the consolidation of the rural free schools and the extension of high school privileges by assuming three-fourths of the cost of transporting children to school centers. There are still, however, 320 one-room schools and 255 of two rooms each, housing more than 10,000 children.

A commission named in 1932 by Governor A. Harry Moore to survey school conditions recommended that the State should guarantee at least $57 annually for every child of school age. Total cost to the State to supplement the funds of economically weak towns was estimated at $21,-000,000 a year. Action on an equable distribution of State aid has been delayed by the depression.

After making deductions for State institutions and losses through failure of tax collection, property value decline and litigation, officers of the New Jersey State Teachers' Association estimate that in recent years State aid to public schools has actually totaled not more than $5,500,000. This is 6 percent of the cost of public education in New Jersey, compared with

89 percent provided by Delaware, 66 percent by North Carolina and 33 percent by New York.

In recent years, the school tax system has failed to provide funds promptly, causing a reduction of teaching facilities in weaker communities. In 1934 the State had 485 fewer teachers than in 1931 although the number of pupils had increased by 18,700. Salaries were delayed, courses curtailed, and the average teacher's salary fell from $2,143 to $1,821. In one city 70 percent of the elementary pupils have been on part time. Cities were forced to close summer schools and vocational evening schools, while rural schools, hardest hit of all, were using textbooks published before the World War, including geographies of pre-war Europe.

Much of the difficulty has been ascribed to the system of deriving school funds almost exclusively from property taxes. Leading educators urge that at least 20 percent of the burden be shifted to sources less likely to dry up at the first indication of hard times.

Critics also object to State aid on the basis of the total daily attendance of pupils in the public schools. Under this plan, by which each county gets back a substantial portion of the money it raises for the State school tax, the counties and communities least able to support public schools receive the least assistance from the State.

New Jersey is one of five States with a State-wide tenure of office law. A teacher cannot be removed nor his salary decreased after three years of consecutive service, except on charges and after a hearing. However, teachers from some communities assert that they have signed waivers relinquishing the right to protest such dismissal or decrease in salary. Under a law approved in 1919, pensions are provided for in the form of annuities from the teachers' own contributions. Payment is made after the age of 62 or following retirement, which is compulsory at 70.

The State board of education is a bipartisan body of ten, not more than five of whom may be members of the same political party. The board approves selection of county superintendents, can withhold funds from any local board for failure to comply with State school laws, and issues teachers' certificates, which are valid in any part of the State. Teachers cannot be employed without certificates, and (with the exception of foreign language instructors) they are required to be citizens of the United States. A teacher's oath of allegiance to the Constitution of the United States is required under a law passed in 1935. No test case has resulted, and there is no record of a teacher's refusing to comply with the law.

The State conducts six normal or training schools for teachers, situated in Trenton, Montclair, Newark, Glassboro, Paterson, and Jersey City.

These are all four-year schools with authority to confer academic degrees, and since 1913 all six have maintained summer schools.

New Jersey has two outstanding universities, Princeton and Rutgers. A land-grant college since 1864, Rutgers was designated the State university of New Jersey in 1917, and receives direct State aid and funds for free scholarships. It ranks favorably with most State universities east of the Mississippi and has made significant scientific and governmental contributions to State progress. Its College of Agriculture maintains experimental stations throughout the State. Established in 1918 as part of the State university is the New Jersey College for Women, which has developed rapidly into one of the most progressive women's schools in the Nation.

Princeton, along with Yale and Harvard, is traditionally one of the country's "Big Three." It has sent forth from its beautiful Gothic buildings many men prominent in public affairs. Princeton has recently begun to emphasize the social sciences and has undergone a campus democratization, largely inspired by Woodrow Wilson. The university curriculum is particularly strong in architecture, politics, mathematics, and the classics.

Also at Princeton, although not part of the university, is the Institute for Advanced Study, a small center for experiment and research in science and the humanities conducted by some of the world's leading scholars. Albert Einstein is a member of this group.

Stevens Institute of Technology at Hoboken (opened in 1871) holds a distinguished place among the technical and engineering schools of the country. It was the first college in the United States to grant the degree of mechanical engineer. It has become a tradition to give only that degree, but the M.E. carries with it training in civil, electrical, and chemical engineering, as well as the economics of engineering.

Organized in 1935, the University of Newark provides higher educational opportunities for those in the lower income brackets in the crowded northern New Jersey area. It represents a consolidation of New Jersey Law School, Dana College, Mercer Beasley Law School, Newark Institute of Arts and Sciences, and the Seth Boyden School of Business. In four years it has achieved an acknowledged reputation as a leading liberal university. The South Jersey Law School at Camden, Upsala College at East Orange, and Newark College of Engineering are other well-known institutions.

New Jersey has many private schools of long-established reputation. Among the outstanding religious schools are the College of St. Elizabeth at Convent Station, Drew University at Madison, Seton Hall College at South Orange, and Centenary Collegiate Institute at Hackettstown. More than 70 schools in the State prepare students for colleges and universities.

Among the better known preparatory schools are the Hun School at Princeton, Lawrenceville Academy at Lawrenceville, Bordentown Military Institute at Bordentown, and the Peddie School at Hightstown.

A widespread parochial school system under the direction of the clergy covers the two Roman Catholic dioceses in the State. There were 263 of these schools in 1935, with an enrollment of nearly 116,000 pupils.

New Jersey's libraries are an important adjunct to its educational system, aided by a law permitting taxes to be levied for their establishment in any community. There are 337 municipal libraries and 11 county libraries. The Newark Library, founded in 1888, achieved an exceptionally prominent position under the leadership of John Cotton Dana. Only four towns of more than 2,000 population are without library service. There are 4,000,000 books in use, and many city libraries have provided outlying rural sections with reading matter by means of the library truck. The New Jersey Public Library Commission was established in 1900 to encourage and aid library service throughout the State. It has headquarters at Trenton, where it acts as a clearing house for book requests, aids in establishing new libraries, and gives advice on all questions and problems that affect libraries in New Jersey.

Several New Jersey museums contribute a broadening influence to education. Largest and widest in its service is the Newark Museum, one of the first of such institutions in the country to specialize in science and industry. It also has important art and historical collections. Noteworthy in the historical field are the New Jersey State Museum at Trenton, the Historical Museum at Morristown, and the Museum of the New Jersey Historical Society in Newark. The Montclair Art Museum's collection consists chiefly of paintings and sculpture, and the Paterson Museum features natural science. Among the museums developed by State colleges and universities, the most important are the Stevens Institute of Technology Museum at Hoboken, largely devoted to mechanics and science, the Museum of Historic Art and various scientific collections at Princeton University, and the geological and agricultural museums at Rutgers University.

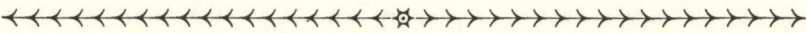

Religion

WORSHIP in New Jersey is as various as the population itself, ranging from the guttural chants of the Greek Orthodoxy to the carefully accented English of the Episcopalians; from the enthusiastic disorder of revival meetings to the heavy dignity of urban churches; from crossroads houses of God to massive cathedrals.

In the city areas religious interest has become mainly a matter of Sunday observance; seemingly the church exerts a diminishing influence over its members' private lives. To attract the individual's time and support, a number of denominations in New Jersey, as elsewhere, have developed forums, athletics, and entertainments similar to those of civic, fraternal and labor organizations.

In smaller communities, especially those of the rural south and the residential north, the church has preserved an important measure of prestige and control. It remains strong enough in many small towns to enforce local Blue Laws; ministers in certain communities may reprove publicly women who smoke and men who drink. Frequently the churches continue to be the principal charitable and social welfare agencies.

Historically New Jersey has a reputation for ecclesiastical tolerance and liberalism. It was one of the four original Colonies that successfully resisted attempts of the Church of England to create an established church. The several individual churches, however, achieved a local hegemony no less stringent than that of an official church. Despite the brave statement entered into the records of West New Jersey in 1676 that "No men, nor number of men upon earth, hath power or authority to rule over men's consciences in religious matters," the separate churches remained until well after the Civil War jealous institutions that would brook no other loyalties.

Early Dutch immigrants established in 1662 at Bergen (now Jersey City Heights) the first duly instituted church in the Colony, the Bergen Reformed Church of the Dutch Reformed denomination under the jurisdiction of the Classis of Amsterdam. This denomination, however, was ham-

TRINITY EPISCOPAL CHURCH, NEWARK

pered in its growth after 1664, when the English conquest of New Jersey carried with it the adoption of English forms of faith.

The English settlements in New Jersey, following the fall of the Dutch, were largely made by Puritans from New England and Long Island, who quickly thwarted the Catholic hopes of James, Duke of York, and the Proprietors' plans to establish the Church of England in the Colony. Connecticut Congregationalists founded Newark in 1666 as a theocracy, where voting privilege necessitated membership in the church. While the foundation for two centuries of Calvinist domination was being laid in northern New Jersey, Baptists pushed down from Rhode Island in 1668 to establish the first Baptist church south of that State at Middletown.

The Colony's spirited wrangles with the Crown brought disfavor upon the proponents of the Church of England. The church was finally founded at Perth Amboy in 1698, but was almost immediately made the scapegoat in continued disputes with royal authority. It soon disappeared as the official church and was later re-established as the Episcopal Church.

In 1675 Quakers began to settle West New Jersey and established there the oldest Friends' colony in America. Adopting the southern plantation way of life, the Quakers practiced the tolerance they preached. They opposed war, argued against slavery (although their wealth depended upon the continuance of the system), and set other Colonials an example by keeping their treaties with the Indians.

New Jersey's tolerance did not extend to Roman Catholics. The Colony legislated in 1700 against priests, instructing that they be "deemed incendiary and disturbers of the public peace and safety, enemies of the true Christian religion, and adjudged to suffer perpetual imprisonment." Under determined missionaries such as Father Ferdinand Farmer and Theodore Schneider, Catholicism stubbornly grew, but as late as 1785 probably no more than 1,000 Roman Catholics were in the State. Not until 1814 was the State's first parish established in Trenton.

The Lutherans did not become an important group until 1732 when church members from the Palatinate in Germany settled in the Mahwah district of northern New Jersey, Oldwick, Long Valley and New Brunswick. In 1750 the northern Palatine Lutherans united their forces and built the present stone church in Oldwick.

By the middle of the eighteenth century the Colony was geographically divided into four religious units. The Dutch Reformed members were predominant along the Hudson River; heirs of the Puritan tradition ruled Newark and its environs; Perth Amboy and the central section harbored the greatest mixture of creeds; and south and west, with the exceptions of small groups of Baptists and Presbyterians, the land was controlled by Quakers.

Among the minor sects that developed in New Jersey during the Colonial period were the Seventh Day Baptists and the Universalists. The former sect was founded in 1707 at Piscataway by dissenters from the local Baptist congregation. Although the sect was weakened in 1789 when the Shrewsbury church as a body moved to Salem, West Virginia (then part of Virginia), its national headquarters are still in Plainfield.

In 1770 the Reverend John Murray established the Universalist Church of America. Murray, it is said, was wandering through the woods of southern New Jersey after a shipwreck, when he came upon a lonely church in the woods. Instructed by one Thomas Potter, who had built the church with his own hands in order to expound the universal fatherhood of God, Murray forthwith preached the first Universalist sermon in America. At about the same time Moravians emigrated from Bethlehem, Pennsylvania, to Hope, but according to historians, "by trusting too much to the honesty of those with whom they had business, suffered in their pecuniary affairs. In 1808 they returned to Pennsylvania."

Methodism started later than most of the other major sects. Although George Whitefield had held evangelistic meetings in New Brunswick in 1740, there was no real impetus toward that faith until 1770 when Captain Thomas Webb of the English Army set up an active group at Burlington. The following year a society was organized in Trenton, where in 1773 the first Methodist church was built. The most important force in the early period of the church was Bishop Francis Asbury, who toured the southern part of the State with remarkable success in organizing congregations.

The Revolution found Roman Catholics incensed by Crown persecutions; Quakers, Baptists, and Presbyterians opposed to England; while the Episcopalians, a good proportion of the noncombatant members of the Society of Friends, and some east New Jersey Calvinists remained loyal. The revolutionary clergy apparently played an important part in the war, for Royal agents' reports frequently contained reference to "rascally ministers" and "perfidious preachers."

The constitution of 1776 was accounted a liberal document by its framers. In guaranteeing freedom of religious worship, it stated, however, that *no Protestant* should be denied either civil rights or trial by jury on account of his religion. It was not until the adoption of a new State constitution in 1844 that laws excluding Roman Catholics from public office were repealed.

The membership of Christian denominations increased rapidly between the Revolution and the Civil War. Methodists inaugurated their celebrated camp meetings which by 1820 were common affairs; these culminated in the establishment of Ocean Grove in 1869, a religious resort where even now on the Sabbath the gates are closed and bathing and automobile traffic are prohibited on this day. The Episcopal and Baptist Churches enjoyed corresponding growth, and Roman Catholic membership was greatly increased by immigration following the Irish famine of 1845.

An idealistic, Utopian spirit swept over the State in the 1830's and 1840's, giving rise to a variety of sects and schisms. In 1837 Mormons settled at South Toms River where they carried on evangelical efforts for a decade and a half before joining their brethren in Utah. The liberal Hicksite teachings shortly afterward caused a lively row among the usually peaceful Quakers. Similarly, exceptionally fervent and frequent evangelism and unauthorized public prayer meetings interrupted the peaceful progress of the long-established churches.

Although Jews first settled in Monmouth County in the eighteenth century and Benjamin Levy, prominent London Jew, served as a Proprietor of West New Jersey, it was not until the middle of the following century that they were of sufficient number to found a temple. Sixty Jewish families in Newark organized Congregation B'nai Jeshurun in 1848, the first in the State, and the next year a congregation by the same name was founded in Paterson. Until 1880 most Jewish immigrants were orthodox believers from Western Europe, principally Germany. Quick to be integrated with modern America, they naturally formed the nucleus of the reformed Jewish movement in this country. Orthodox Jews began to outnumber the reformed in the late nineteenth century when Russian and Polish persecution drove thousands out of European ghettos into the industrial regions of America and New Jersey.

European immigration after 1880 altered considerably the prevailingly English character of the Christian church throughout the State. Roman Catholicism expanded with the sizable increase in Italian population, and the Greek Orthodox Catholic Church made considerable gains. The German Lutheran Church, although founded in Colonial times, was significantly enlarged by political and military refugees from Germany. Negroes from the South after the Civil War also increased the membership of the Baptists and Methodists.

The last major denomination to be founded in New Jersey was the Christian Science Church, which first held informal meetings at Long Branch in 1893. The First Church of Christ, Scientist, of Jersey City, formed in 1896, was soon followed by others in Newark, Camden, and Orange.

The United States Religious Census of 1926 (the latest available) counted 101 denominations in New Jersey, of which 65 are named and the remainder listed as "all others." In that year there were 3,497 churches and 1,983,781 members. Church property was valued at $162,654,034. Sunday schools numbered 3,064, with 489,651 students and 49,980 teachers.

The Roman Catholic Church has the largest membership in the State with a total of 1,055,998. (U. S. Census of 1926.) A Papal decree of December 1937, creating the Archdiocese of Newark to include the entire State, attested official recognition of the size and importance of the Catholic Church in New Jersey. Archbishop Thomas J. Walsh was placed in charge. The Catholics' principal sectarian activity is an elaborate parochial school system augmented by Seton Hall College for men in South Orange, St. Elizabeth's College for women at Convent Station, and Georgian Court College, also for women, at Lakewood, as well as smaller institutions of higher learning.

Roman Catholics have perhaps the most spectacular public demonstrations of faith of any group in the State. Especially notable is the production of *Veronica's Veil*, a Passion Play staged annually since 1914 during Lent under the direction of Rev. Joseph N. Grieff at St. Joseph's Parish in Union City. The cast requires 300 members. The Holy Name Society of the Roman Catholic Church holds annual parades in all large communities. In Newark as many as 50,000 march.

Protestant membership totals about 900,000. More than two-thirds of this membership is divided among the denominations (figures from 1936 denominational reports):

Presbyterian	175,134
Methodist Episcopal	149,204
Protestant Episcopal	91,557
Baptist	62,998
Dutch Reformed Church in America	38,375
United Lutheran	37,458
Christian-Congregationalist	17,036

The Protestants do not subsidize an elaborate educational system. They have, however, several important theological centers, notably the Presbyterian schools at Princeton and Bloomfield; the Dutch Reformed seminary, one of two in this country, at New Brunswick; and the Methodist institution at Drew University, Madison. Several small schools are supported by the Episcopal Church. The Baptists support the International Baptist Seminary in East Orange where foreign-born students are trained and ordained as missionaries to their native countries. The scope and intensity of the struggle between modernist and fundamentalist in the schools appears to have intensified the generally conservative trend of Protestantism in the State.

The Jewish population of 225,306 is served by 188 houses of worship (membership figures not available). Each synagogue or temple is an independent organization and its government is congregational. Divided into Reformed, Conservative, and Orthodox sects, Jews differ more upon questions of custom, ceremonial and theology than upon tenets of faith. Orthodox Jews, the largest group, stem chiefly from Russia and Poland; while conservatives, usually representing the second generation, come also from Eastern Europe and from Central Europe. The reform movement is confined mainly to Jews of German descent, with an accretion drawn from Jews of Middle and Eastern European origin or descent.

Both the reformed temples and the orthodox synagogues engage in considerable philanthropic work, much of it nonsectarian. Jewish religious instruction centers in the reformed Sunday Schools and the orthodox and conservative in the Talmud Torahs, schools where thousands of youths study the Hebrew language and Jewish ceremonies and customs.

Among the Negro population (208,828) the church is the most important and the financially strongest institution. Since 1812, when the free Negroes organized the First Baptist Church at Trenton, the number of Negro churches has increased to 412, with a membership of 71,221 representing 19 denominations. The Baptist is the largest group with 159 churches and a membership of 41,129. The group next in importance, the Methodist, established the Mount Pisgah A. M. E. Church at Free Haven (now Lawnside) in 1813. St. Philips Church, another historic body, was organized at Newark in 1856. The Negro church is becoming more of a social center, and its ministers more and more interested in social and political affairs. The rapid influx of Negroes from the South has caused a large increase in the number of meeting places. In urban centers this sudden increase in membership has been largely responsible for the "storefront" churches, buildings formerly used as stores.

In addition to the larger denominations there are many religious sects of varying strength. In the south, the Quakers, with 3,546 orthodox and Hicksite members and 29 meeting houses, still hold a prominent position. The Greek Orthodox Church with 9 churches and 5,424 members and the Russian Orthodox with 12 churches and 9,783 members are strongest in the industrial cities of Newark, Bayonne, and Passaic. The last-named city is the scene of a struggle for control of the Russian Church between members sympathetic to the Union of Soviet Socialist Republics and Russians opposed to this regime.

New Jersey has been fertile territory for strange religious offshoots. The Pillar of Fire Movement, organized in 1901 at Denver, has had its national headquarters since 1908 at Zarephath near Bound Brook. The Pillar of Fire doctrine is described as Methodistic in character, dedicated to "true scientific research as against false speculation of modernism and higher criticism destructive to orthodox Christian faith." Disciples practice their faith with such unrestrained vigor and enthusiasm that they are known locally as "The Holy Jumpers."

The sensational cult headed by the Negro, Father Divine, maintains a number of "Heavens" throughout the State, principally in the metropolitan area. The funds for the original "Heaven" in Sayville, Long Island, are said to have been furnished by a resident of Newark, one Pinninah, who is now called Mother Divine. From apparently inexhaustible funds Divine provides free banquets to the destitute, purchases blocks of real estate, and finances his $1.50 a week lodging houses. "He's God! Peace, it's wonderful! Thank you, Father!" is the chant of his thousands of Negro and white followers. Sometimes frenzies in New Jersey "Heavens" have terminated in clashes with the police.

Another unusual sect is that of Jehovah's Witnesses, scattered about the State but strongest in the northern section. Its members object to the vaccination of school children and condemn as idolatrous the practice of saluting the flag. Opposition to the flag salute has been taken to the courts as a test of civil liberties, and the Witnesses have won their point in an appeal to the United States District Court.

The ramifications of "Jersey Justice" have on occasion interpreted in a narrow fashion the religious liberties apparently granted by the State Constitution, which ranks high for its liberality. In the celebrated case of Eaton v. Eaton in 1936, despite constitutional guarantees to the contrary, the Court of Chancery denied a mother the custody of her children on the ground that her communistic and atheistic views were contrary to public policy of the State. The decree was upheld by the Court of Errors and Appeals, although the latter body, in its opinion, did refer to her beliefs as "irrelevant."

Organized religion, as such, exerts practically no State-wide political influence, although the Catholic Church successfully opposed legislation for the sterilization of defectives. Affected by their neighboring metropolitan areas, churches in the northern part of the State show a general trend toward liberalism, while those in the southern section are more conservative. The clergy as a whole has limited its support chiefly to the more widely accepted labor reforms, the peace movement, and good government drives.

Attempts to make concrete this type of liberalism have cost several New Jersey ministers their churches. The Reverend L. Hamilton Garner, an outspoken liberal, was forced from his Newark pastorate at the Universalist Church in 1937 after he had sponsored a community forum in which left-wing speakers participated. For similar reasons the Reverend Archey Ball was obliged to leave his Methodist pulpit in Ridgewood.

Two of the best-known New Jersey clergymen have won secular and civil prominence, respectively, as exponents of a more conservative type of religion. The Reverend William Hiram Foulkes, pastor of Old First Presbyterian Church of Newark, was in 1937 elected Moderator of the Presbyterian Church in the United States. In the same year the Reverend Lester H. Clee, pastor of Newark's Second Presbyterian Church, became titular head of the New Jersey Republican Party after losing a close race as its gubernatorial nominee. Clee became known first for his enormously successful Bible classes and then, while a State legislator, as the spokesman for the Clean Government faction from Essex County.

Interchurch cooperation has made considerable progress throughout the State. The New Jersey Council for Religious Education, successor to the New Jersey Sunday School Association, founded in 1858, operates as a unifying force among Protestant denominations. New Jersey is the only State in which the national and State units of the religious groups have set up such a cooperative staff plan. In several communities Protestant denominations have accepted either the John D. Rockefeller or Federal Council of Churches plan for union and have pooled their material, as well as spiritual, interests.

Thanksgiving and other national holidays are occasions for joint Jewish and Christian services; seminars and institutes on marriage, crime, and other sociological questions usually invite a complete clerical representation. In Newark and the larger cities there has been a marked advance in cooperation between Negro and white religious organizations. The cause of world peace, however, has accounted for the greatest measure of religious unity; no peace meeting in New Jersey is complete without the benediction of priest, rabbi, and minister. Pacificism not only has welded the churches together but also has been the strongest force for uniting religious and lay groups on a program of common action.

The Arts

Literature

FROM the time of Philip Freneau and Francis Hopkinson in the late eighteenth century, New Jersey has often shared in the leadership of American letters. In much the same manner that these Revolutionary poets led the way to the great poetic flowering of New England, Stephen Crane a century later influenced the modern American novel. More recently, the Humanism of Paul Elmer More at Princeton inspired the growth of a definite and influential school of American criticism. Between these peaks in New Jersey literature lies a chain of plateaus which represents a consistently solid contribution to American literature.

Those who, in the pre-Revolutionary era, looked to the printed word for inspiration and enlightenment were fed, for the most part, upon a native diet of theological dissertations, moral tracts, and political polemics. Against this dreary mass of what Charles Lamb termed *biblia-a-biblia,* or books that are not books, only the writings of the gentle Quaker preacher, John Woolman (1720–72), shine out conspicuously with the glow of creative literature.

Woolman, born at Ancocas (later Rancocas) in the province of West Jersey, served as a tailor's apprentice in his youth and then for a time had his own shop in Mount Holly. At the age of twenty-three he joined the Quaker ministry, spending the rest of his life as an itinerant crusader against the social evils of his time—chiefly the evil of slavery. His *Journal* embodies a remarkable picture of Colonial society. "Get the writings of John Woolman by heart" was Lamb's counsel, and Ellery Channing spoke of the *Journal* as "the sweetest and purest autobiography in the language."

The Revolutionary War produced Jonathan Odell (1737–1818), a native of Newark, whose rampant Toryism caused him to be driven from Burlington to New York in 1776. There he wrote three verse satires in which he characterized the Revolution as "a hideous hell-broth made up of lies and hallucinations." Prime objects of Odell's vicious attacks were two able patriot pamphleteers: William Livingston (1723–90), a vigorous

Elizabethtown Whig and the State's first Governor, and John Wither-spoon (1723–94), president of the College of New Jersey (Princeton), and a signer of the Declaration of Independence. Witherspoon also wrote widely on religious topics.

Although Philip Freneau (1752–1832) was a master of vitriolic political writing and a notable influence in shaping the course of post-Revolutionary democracy, it is as the first significant American poet that his fame endures. A few years after his birth in New York City, his family purchased a summer residence known as "Mount Pleasant," near Middletown Point, New Jersey. This became the poet's permanent home in later life, and near it he perished in a blizzard. Notable among his poems, in addition to some excellent patriotic verse and songs of the sea, are *The Wild Honey-suckle*, which has been termed "the first stammer of nature poetry in America," and *The Indian Burying Ground*, the earliest treatment of an Indian theme by an American poet.

A contemporary pamphleteering rival of the man whom George Washington is said to have characterized as "that rascal Freneau," and also a musician and poet of more than ordinary talent for his time, was Francis Hopkinson (1737–91), who married a daughter of Colonel Joseph Borden of Bordentown and after about 1773 made his home in that city. Hopkinson's satiric masterpiece was the ballad, *The Battle of the Kegs*, which described the launching of an early ancestor of the torpedo against British ships during the Revolutionary War.

In Washington's army during its retreat across New Jersey after the disaster at Fort Lee in 1776 was the Englishman who has been called "the pen of the American Revolution"; and at Newark this man began to write the first of his *Crisis* pamphlets, with its famous opening sentence, "These are the times that try men's souls." In this and a dozen or more later issues of *The Crisis*, Thomas Paine (1737–1809) did a splendid service in revivifying the flagging spirit of the Revolution. When he lived in Bordentown, from 1781 to 1787, he was chiefly occupied with writing on finance and economics. Paine returned there for a brief period in 1802, momentarily forgotten in the political quarrels of a Nation which he had helped to found.

Among the earliest of playwrights and novelists to make use of American material, as well as the first historian of the theater and of the arts of design in the United States, was William Dunlap (1766–1839), a native of Perth Amboy. Here the first eleven years of his life were spent, and here he was buried after his death in New York City. Briefer still was the residence in his native State of a far more famous literary figure, James

Fenimore Cooper, born at Burlington in 1789. Though his family moved to Cooperstown, New York, soon thereafter, the novelist made use of his native locale in *The Water Witch,* a tale of the New Jersey coast.

A frequent visitor who journeyed down from his home on the Hudson River was Washington Irving (1783–1859). He began his serious literary work in Newark during 1806–7 as a participant in roistering and bacchanalian dinners at the Gouverneur Kemble mansion, Cockloft Hall. The conviviality of his companions, known significantly as "The Nine Worthies" and "The Lads of Kilkenny," inspired the satiric *Salmagundi* papers, the success of which set the pattern for Irving's career. He also wrote poetry describing the Passaic River and the surrounding countryside.

As in the other arts, New Jersey's progress in literature slowed down between 1830 and 1860. Almost the sole original spark in the mass of indifferent writing of this period came from the Englishman, Henry William Herbert (1807–1858). From his cottage on the Passaic River near Newark, where he lived from 1845 until his death, he issued under the pseudonym of "Frank Forester" a large number of stories and sketches having to do with life and sport in the open. He also wrote several historical novels, less sententious and romantic than the prevailing mode.

With the Civil War a new literary leadership rose out of a profound change in the writers' point of view. The young critics, novelists and poets, who were to influence American taste for a generation, were acutely sensitive to the problems of a Nation passing from agricultural infancy to industrial youth. Beginning with Richard Watson Gilder's inquiry—now considered mild—and culminating in the harsh portraits by Stephen Crane, the theme of social exploration dominates the period up to 1900.

In certain respects Richard Watson Gilder (1844–1909) may be considered the first of the moderns, typifying in breadth of artistic and literary appreciation and in the solid virtues of conscientious citizenship two streams of American impulse toward a more civilized life. Born in Bordentown, he left the State while still a child and did not return until the Civil War period. After some reporting experience on the Newark *Daily Advertiser,* he engaged with Newton Crane in the founding of the Newark *Morning Register.* In 1870 he was appointed assistant editor of *Scribner's Magazine,* under J. G. Holland; and eleven years later, at the death of Holland, the magazine became the *Century* and Gilder its editor in chief.

In this position, which he held until his death, Gilder brought his creed of citizenship to bear upon the problems of late Victorian America. He was an early advocate of rapprochement between North and South, a stern opponent of Tammany corruption and an active participant in an early slum-clearance campaign in New York City. Gilder was an unfailing champion of high standards and "good taste," and his editorial attitude had a marked influence on the literary scene in America. Of his numerous volumes of verse, two of the best were tributes to his wife—*The New Day,* a series of love sonnets, and its sequel, *The Celestial Passion.* Though New Jersey saw little of him after the 1880's, the State may justly claim him as a distinguished native.

Edmund Clarence Stedman (1833–1908) combined shrewd business ability with considerable talent as poet and critic. His charming worldliness manifested itself in his conversational powers, shown at their best in literary gatherings at his homes in Newark, Elizabeth, and Irvington, where he lived from 1860 to 1870. Hither came Gilder and his sister Jeannette, a pioneer in the writing of literary news; Mary Mapes Dodge, excited by her plans for children's literature; Richard Henry Stoddard, at the start of his career as poet and critic; and the translator-poet, Bayard Taylor, who was then completing his notable translation of Goethe's *Faust.* Stedman's Victorianism, on the one hand, and his grasp of sound literary principles, on the other, greatly influenced these youthful "squires of poesy," as they romantically styled themselves. His gift of graceful lyricism is expressed in such poems as "Pan in Wall Street" and "Creole Lover's Song"; his anthologies of American and British poets are comprehensive; and with George E. Woodberry he edited the standard edition of Edgar Allan Poe.

Through the accident of illness, a little house on Mickle Street in Camden became one of those literary havens that recompense aging poets for their early struggles. Walt Whitman (1819–92), after ten years in Washington as a newspaper correspondent, a war hospital nurse, and a Government clerk, in 1873 suffered a paralytic stroke and retired to Camden, where his brother lived. He spent eleven years in his brother's house in Stevens Street, and the last eight years of his life in his own home at No. 330 Mickle Street.

During much of this time he was able to get about, going down to Timber Creek, a stream some ten miles below Camden, and enjoying walks and talks with intimates. Whitman's Camden period was not, however, merely the passive twilight of a creative life. Here he wrote some of his best prose in *Specimen Days and Collect* (1882–83), and prepared five new editions of *Leaves of Grass* (1876–92) to three of which were added new groups of poems—*Two Rivulets* (1876), *November Boughs* (1888), and *Goodbye, My Fancy* (1891). Artists, writers, and others who had felt

WALT WHITMAN'S TOMB, CAMDEN

the refreshing catharsis of Whitman's work frequented the house in Mickle Street; he was hailed by the literary elect of many foreign countries. Possibly no literary man ever lived to see a greater transformation of opinion regarding his own writings.

The Camden days marked the turning point of Whitman's career in two other respects. Now, for the first time, his writings earned him a measure of freedom from financial worries. An article, too, published in the West Jersey *Press* in 1876 which described him as "poor . . . old . . . and paralyzed" brought a prompt influx of gifts and money from friends and sympathizers all over the world. Both the reading public and the critics began to see fundamental decency in Whitman's honest naturalism. A last attempt in 1882 by sanctimonious editors to bowdlerize *Leaves of Grass* aroused a courageous and successful defense of the poet by many leading critics and editors. The "deathbed edition" of *Leaves of Grass* closed Whitman's Camden period.

Whitman's years in Camden became the theme of a vast body of writing, including *Visits to Walt Whitman in 1890–1891,* by J. Johnson and

J. W. Wallace, *Walt Whitman in Mickle Street,* by Elizabeth Leavitt Keller and *With Walt Whitman in Camden,* by Horace Traubel. Traubel's work is one of the most scrupulous and most minute records of an author in action since Boswell's *Johnson.* He (1858–1919) was a native of Camden, editor of a journal of liberal opinion, *The Conservator,* which he founded in 1890 in Philadelphia.

Stephen Crane (1871–1900), perhaps the State's outstanding native literary figure, represents chiefly a revolt against formalism and smugness in fiction, but his gifts are too varied and individual to be easily classified. At the age of twenty-five he published *The Red Badge of Courage,* a novel of the Civil War that attracted Nation-wide attention. Then, setting out to learn of war at first hand, he joined a Cuban filibustering expedition, and suffered experiences that were later epitomized in *The Open Boat,* which H. G. Wells called the finest short story in the English language.

Meanwhile, his reputation as a writer on war brought him commissions as war correspondent in the Greco-Turkish and Spanish-American Wars. The private publication of *Maggie: A Girl of the Streets* aroused a storm of criticism similar to that later evoked by Dreiser's *Sister Carrie.* Wholly different was the reception accorded his *Whilomville Stories,* an authentic record of New Jersey village life. In his two volumes of free verse, *Black Riders* and *War Is Kind,* Crane proved himself a master of epigrammatic compression. The last period of his life was spent in England, where he became the intimate friend of Joseph Conrad. He died of consumption, and was buried at Elizabeth, New Jersey. The Stephen Crane Association was formed to acquire his birthplace at No. 14 Mulberry Street, Newark.

Lean, tall, slow-speaking, and hollow-eyed, Stephen Crane challenged the mores of his day with a sometimes grim, sometimes half-smiling, integrity. It is his honesty of viewpoint and method, together with his interest in the effects of environment on character, that earned for him the title of "father of the American psychological novel," though actually his work barely preceded that of Dreiser.

Since the Revolution, New Jersey as a theme had been neglected by its authors. In the late seventies and eighties, however, many writers, both of New Jersey and elsewhere, began once more to use its historic and regional possibilities. Frank R. Stockton (1834–1902), who lived a large part of his life in many New Jersey towns, principally Morristown, vivified in *Stories of New Jersey* the discovery and settlement of the State and its part in the Barbary War and the War of 1812. He is best known for the short story *The Lady or the Tiger?* and for *Rudder Grange* and other novels which experimented with folk material. While Bret Harte (1836–1902) was in Morristown from 1873 to 1876 he wrote the rousing Revolutionary poem "Caldwell at Springfield," celebrating the parson who furnished the soldiers with Watts' hymnals for gun wadding and created the battle-cry, "Give 'em Watts, boys!" *(see Tour 10)*.

The Revolution and the military exploits of General Philip Kearny attracted the poet, Thomas Dunn English (1819–1902), who lived in Newark from 1878 until his death. His most popular work, however, is the sentimental lyric, "Ben Bolt," which was blared at him so often as a song that he wished he had never composed the verse.

The salty Swedish fishing and ocean lore of Barnegat City formed the basis for F. Hopkinson Smith's *The Tides of Barnegat*. This novel, written by a Pennsylvanian, is generally regarded as a highly successful treatment of New Jersey folk material. Among other out-of-State writers who dipped into the State's history and personality were Joaquin Miller, author of a ballad on Washington's crossing of the Delaware, and Mark Twain, whose travel notes leave something to be desired in the way of compliment toward New Jersey.

Mary Mapes Dodge (1838–1905) played literary fairy godmother to thousands of American children. She began as one of the pioneers in juvenile writing with *Hans Brinker: or, The Silver Skates* during her two decades in Newark and continued as the editor of the children's periodical, *St. Nicholas*. For three generations her books and magazine were as indispensable to a well-rounded childhood as a Fauntleroy suit or a Buster Brown haircut. Equally essential to the experience of youths were the hundreds of "seventy-five centers," especially the *Rover Boys* series by Edward L. Stratemeyer (1862–1930) of Newark. Edith Bishop Sherman of South Orange later expanded the juvenile field by using events in the growth of the State for background in her stories.

Besides exercising a notable influence upon American literary standards as editor of *Harper's Magazine* for fifty years, Henry Mills Alden (1836–1919) of Metuchen gave ample evidence of his own ability as a writer in three published volumes—*God in His World, A Study of Death,* and *Magazine Writing and the New Literature.* Henry Cuyler Bunner (1855–96) of Nutley was also a magazine editor who achieved success in authorship, his output comprising a quantity of graceful *vers de société,* two novels, and several volumes of short stories.

Hamilton Wright Mabie (1845–1916), who lived in Summit after 1888, wrote graceful critical essays and charming myths for children. He was one of the earliest scholars to popularize Shakespeare.

New Jersey claims a literary naturalist and scientific archeologist of some prominence in Charles Conrad Abbott (1843–1919). Trenton was his birthplace, and its adjacent countryside his hunting grounds. A few miles south of the city on the banks of the Delaware was the old Abbott homestead, "Three Beeches," which he occupied after 1874 and until the time of his death. His delightful essays on outdoor life found a host of readers.

Many Princeton men have been in the vanguard of the quest for principles that would govern both critical and popular writing in the twentieth century. Two particularly influential essayists were Henry van Dyke (1852–1933) and Paul Elmer More (1864–1936). Van Dyke typified the accomplished man of letters in his roles as essayist, minor poet, short-story writer, lecturer, and religious author. More's several volumes of *Shelburne Essays* gave him rank as one of America's foremost critics, and made him the lawgiver and spokesman of the Humanists. His insistence upon a grounding in the classics and a classical approach to literature, however, more deeply affected critical than creative writers.

The political influence of Woodrow Wilson (1856–1924) has overshadowed his very real contribution to literature. During his Princeton period, first as professor and later as president, he wrote six books on literary, historical and political subjects, including the five-volume *History of the American People*. While Governor of New Jersey, Wilson wrote the highly significant *The New Freedom*. This most explicit statement of his theories of government, intended to foreshadow his own administration, became the bible of pre-war liberals and is yet an important source for progressive thought; its tenets were incorporated in the platform of the Nonpartisan League. The clarity and deliberateness of Wilson's writing profoundly affected subsequent political literature.

The *Princeton Stories* of Jesse Lynch Williams (1871–1929) represent a high-water mark in collegiate fiction. Published in 1895, they marked the first public appearance of a talented young author who had been active in the university's literary and dramatic life. In 1900 he returned to his alma mater to edit for three years the *Princeton Alumni Weekly*. His later works—plays and stories—were written chiefly in New York.

Joyce Kilmer (1886–1918) of New Brunswick, through his death on a French battlefield and one short poem, *Trees,* achieved a posthumous recognition seldom accorded a minor poet. His life, after he had graduated from Columbia University and had taught Latin for a year in a Morristown high school, was chiefly that of a hard-working literary critic. In 1913 he became a Catholic, a conversion that influenced his writing in prose and poetry and led to one important literary work, *Dreams and Images: an Anthology of Catholic Poets.*

Randolph Bourne, whose life-span covered the same years as Kilmer's, was a native of Bloomfield. In the foreword to the posthumously published *Untimely Papers* (1919), James Oppenheim writes of Bourne, "He was a flaming rebel against our crippled life, as if he had taken the cue from the long struggle with his own body." Most of these papers are articles first published in *The Seven Arts,* of which Bourne was contributing editor. A group including Van Wyck Brooks, also a native of New Jersey, began publishing this journal advocating an American cultural life transcending nationalism. Randolph Bourne, already a contributor to other new liberal periodicals—the *Dial, New Republic,* and *Freeman*—became a leader. His earlier books, *The Gary Schools* and *Education and Life,* had shown him a disciple of John Dewey, but the collapse of liberal pragmatism in face of the national crisis convinced him that a new and more creative program was necessary. With courage, sensitivity, and intelligence he opposed the growing war sentiment in America, criticizing particularly those intellectuals "whom the crisis has crystallized into acceptance of war." *The Seven Arts* suspended publication in September 1917, the subsidy withdrawn because of the editor's anti-war position. In 1918, the last year of his life, he began *The State,* fragments of which are included in *Untimely Papers.* This, with *The History of a Literary Radical* (edited by Van Wyck Brooks, 1920), gives some indication of what Bourne's later work might have been. Unfinished though it is, *The State* seems now to many critics a prophetic indictment of the institution when it becomes a symbol of force rather than an expression of a people's life.

The magnet of New York began to draw writers away from New Jersey as far back as the days of Gilder and Stedman. Dorothy Parker, Alexander Woollcott, Robert Hillyer, and Edmund Wilson are associated with New Jersey only by the accident of birth. Conversely, others, such as Mary Wilkins Freeman, Joseph C. Lincoln, and Honoré Willsie Morrow, have made their homes here but have continued to write of other locales.

Contemporary literature in New Jersey reflects the diverse elements of American writing rather than any specific qualities inherent in the State. Princeton is the nearest approach to a literary center and there the flavor of a more sedate period lingers in the essays of George McLean Harper, the novels and essays of Katherine Fullerton Gerould, the travel books and biographies of James Barnes, the historical works of William Starr Myers, and the educational writing of Christian Gauss—to mention only a few diverse authors.

New Jersey novelists did not follow the lead of F. Scott Fitzgerald, who based *This Side of Paradise* on his student experiences at Princeton. They eschewed interpreting the spirit of the "jazz age" a decade ago, as they now for the most part avoid the problems of industrial and social conflict. Josephine Lawrence of Newark has come closest to current issues with a few novels that examine the domestic and business pattern of the middle class. Before he devoted himself exclusively to writing on dogs and travel, Albert Payson Terhune of Pompton Plains wrote several novels with a background of pre-war liberalism.

Greater diversity of temperament and interest characterizes the present-day poets of the State. Amelia Josephine Burr and Mrs. Dwight W. Morrow, of Englewood, representing the older tradition in both form and subject matter, have produced several volumes of charming and graceful verse.

William Carlos Williams, physician and author of Rutherford, has published *The Great American Novel, A Voyage to Pagany, Life Along the Passaic River,* some translations from the French, and a considerable amount of rather distinctive poetry. In 1926 he was awarded the *Dial* prize of $2,000 for services to American literature, and in 1931 he won a prize in poetry. His verse, free in form, is generally marked by social implications.

A liberal in politics and poetry, Louis Ginzberg of Paterson often embodies a touch of mysticism in his delicately constructed lyrics. The Revolutionary tradition of recording the State's history and development in verse is revived in the *Jersey Jingles* by Leonard H. Robbins of Montclair, as well as in the work of Joseph Folsom of Newark.

Preoccupation with the national scene has tended to blind New Jersey writers to the regional characteristics of their own State. No one has yet done for New Jersey what, for instance, William Faulkner has done for Mississippi or Robert Frost for New Hampshire. Appreciation of the local scene has been left, as a rule, to the journalists. No poet has yet written a ballad on the Pineys or the Jackson Whites. An outstanding story of mill life in Passaic or Paterson remains to be written, and, save for *The Tides of Barnegat,* the fishermen and oystermen of the coast are material left unused by creative writers. This virtually unexplored field requires only the touch of skillful authors to demonstrate its value as a source of American literature.

Theater

New Jersey's theatrical history is for the most part a tale told by yellowed programs, dog-eared newspapers, and fading recollections. As elsewhere, the brightest glory of the local stage is that of its yesterdays. Today the poor professional player seldom ventures into New Jersey but follows the way to Manhattan, and the amateur is the hope for tomorrow and tomorrow.

No brief candle, however, has the theater been in the State. It has flickered and glowed for more than a century and a half and still sheds a beam that lights good deeds in the theatrical world. As the theater is always dying elsewhere, so is it always dying in New Jersey. And as it never quite dies elsewhere, so it never quite dies in New Jersey.

Death by ecclesiastical edict was almost the fate of the Colonial theater in New Jersey. Until the post-Revolutionary relaxing of official and self-appointed censorship, traveling English companies, vaudeville troupes, animal acts and jugglers waged an uneven battle against the church. The puritanical fathers injudiciously permitted church presentations of Biblical dramatizations, which whetted the congregation's taste for the few Shakespearean companies that appeared in the State. The first professional production on record was that of a Shakespearean play by the Hallams, an English touring company, in Perth Amboy in 1752. The meager professional theater that did exist before the Revolution was limited to the few large towns, and was virtually in thrall to the British stage.

Apparently the Revolutionary veterans were confronted after the war with an earlier-day "jazz age." Peace brought a feverish quest for the types of amusement that previously had been banned. It is possible that British soldiers contributed to the upheaval, for according to legend Newark's earliest theatrical performance was a production of *Hamlet* enacted by British officers at Gifford's Tavern.

The earliest recorded play of American origin to be produced in Newark, and probably in New Jersey, was an untitled piece concerning a miserly character named Gripus, written in 1792 by Captain Jabez Parkhurst and acted by his students at the South Street School. Although more or less permanent companies acted in Newark, Perth Amboy, Trenton, and other cities between 1790 and 1810, plays continued to be produced only in taverns, schools, and churches.

The career of William Dunlap (1766–1839) of Perth Amboy foreshadowed with prophetic accuracy the future power of the major influences on the New Jersey theater, namely the church and the Manhattan stage. Dunlap, who lived in New Jersey until 1777, was one of the earliest American playwrights to handle native material and the country's first professional playwright. His best known play is *The Life of Major André,* one of the first uses of a native theme by a native dramatist.

The novelty and high quality of this tragedy gave Dunlap a commanding position in the growing theatrical world. He introduced the plays of the German Kotzebue in translation and pioneered in applying the Gothic "terror spirit" to American subjects, which led to the development of the conventional mystery play. He was a more skillful writer than manager, however, and when the Puritans attacked the theater in 1805 Dunlap's unstable company was among the first to succumb. He nevertheless continued to write plays, and in 1832 he climaxed his career with *A History of the American Theater,* the first documented story of the growth of the stage in America.

The religious reaction against the "new freedom" that had helped to ruin Dunlap gradually brought to an end the first flowering of the native stage. From about 1820 to 1845 the wrath of the pastors and deacons virtually swept bare the stages of the State. In place of Shakespeare, Sheridan, and Lessing, Newark and other cities subsisted on wandering troupes of minstrels, bell ringers, and circus performers.

It required the combination of the Mexican War, the religious wavering of the 1840's, and the arrival of less inhibited German and Irish immigrants to create a theatrical Renaissance. The opening of the Concert Hall in Newark in 1847 with *The Youthful Queen, or Christine of Sweden,* ushered in the smoky, romantic Opera House period. Until shortly after 1880 the local stage largely forsook classic British plays for Continental European melodramas that culminated in the corrupt American imitations known as thrillers and tear jerkers.

Despite the many towns on the New Jersey "road" between 1850 and 1870, the erection of theaters progressed slowly. Greer's Hall in New Brunswick first resounded to the snarls of the bloodhounds in *Uncle Tom's Cabin* in 1854, and in Hoboken Niblo's Garden had a respectable stage for German and American melodramas and romances. Perth Amboy had no theater before 1860, and road companies had to wait until 1867 before they could play Trenton's plush-and-gilt Taylor Opera House instead of the wooden-benched Temperance Hall.

Temperance and puritanism persisted in the face of such increasing luxury and freedom. The Trenton *Gazette* grudgingly welcomed the city's new theater with the following: "The influence of the theater is generally pernicious, socially and morally. Nevertheless, we think a place of dramatic amusement can be maintained in this community without detriment if it can be carefully supervised." The bluenoses were not only vigilant about the "new drama" but also powerful enough to make performances of *Pilgrim's Progress* and *The Curse of Intemperance* as frequent as those of the thrillers *After Dark* and *The Streets of New York*.

The emotionalism of the puritanical propaganda plays overflowed into the romances and contributed to their debasement into cheap and sentimental or hair-raising melodramas. Such plays as *Under the Gaslight*, *East Lynne*, and *In the Nick of Time* formed the repertory of the stock companies that developed after the Civil War and brought the theater to previously ignored places such as Bordentown, Paterson, Elizabeth, and Orange.

Occasionally in Newark, where the stock company tradition dated back to the less swashbuckling days of 1847, a troupe rose successfully to the requirements of Shakespeare, Otway, or Boucicault. Mrs. Emma Waller played so great a Lady Macbeth and Lady Teazle there in 1867 that she quickly became a New York and national sensation. While not usually productive of such players as these, the local stock companies were at least responsible for the building of theaters that afterward housed greater actors.

The first shower of stars burst upon the State's playhouses in the mid 1880's. Booth and Barrett in Shakespeare, Joseph Jefferson in *Rip Van Winkle*, and the Salvinis in Greek tragedy all played Newark, Trenton, Hoboken, and other towns later scorned by touring companies. This galaxy simultaneously dignified the one-night stand and broke the cold grip of social disapproval of the theater. After mayor, minister, and banker had received Edwin Booth as an artist, it was a little more difficult on general principles to run Mrs. Jarley and her "celebrated galvanic, man-unmotive, non-suspension wax works" out of New Brunswick as a menace to public decency.

Actors of smaller stature followed in the wake of these great names of the American theater. Annually eight horses galloped down the main streets of Bordentown and Burlington to announce the arrival of *Uncle Tom's Cabin;* pictures of chorus ladies in tights revealed that the boyhood musical delight, *The Black Crook,* had come back to Perth Amboy; and posters flamed from every wall in Paterson to rekindle the town's interest in *The Still Alarm.*

As serious American playwrights gradually developed, more and more troupes turned after 1890 to the work of Augustus Thomas, Charles

Klein, Clyde Fitch, and William Gillette for respite from the earlier blood-curdling histrionics. Companies in New Brunswick, Morristown, Newark, Passaic, and Trenton used their new problem plays to train actors for the greater stock companies in New York.

A new group of American stars accompanied the maturing of the American drama. Minnie Maddern Fiske, Maude Adams, Otis Skinner, and Walker Whiteside gave Newark and other large towns their first real opportunity to see excellent native actors in native plays. To these greatest days of the road, the State contributed Robert B. Mantell (1854–1928) of Atlantic Highlands, one of the hardiest and most traveled Shakespeareans of the century. For more than 50 years Mantell not only played the large stands but also carried Shakespeare to high schools, churches, and other groups unable to afford Henry Irving and Ellen Terry. Often he was the only important actor playing the classics outside New York.

While the road still lived New Jersey became a genuinely important factor in the American theater as a try-out center. The gay resort life of Atlantic City seemed to Belasco, Frohman, and Brady an ideal setting for testing shows prior to Broadway first nights. After Ziegfeld had succeeded there with the world premiere of his first *Follies* in 1907, Atlantic City built three theaters to appease the squabbling Broadway managers. Shortly afterward, Newark joined the "subway circuit," giving New Jersey many more genuine "first nights" than those enjoyed across the Hudson. Producers later booked Asbury Park and Long Branch for summer openings.

In those days of rich theatrical glory there was born in New Jersey the modern struggle between stage and screen. The Fort Lee bluffs anticipated Hollywood by raiding Broadway for its stars and thus became the first motion picture production center in the world. Between 1907 and 1916, 21 companies and 7 studios here laid the foundation for the present-day cinema industry. Primitive in method and naive in conception, the Fort Lee producers nevertheless developed Mary Pickford, John Bunny, and Broncho Billy Anderson, as well as the comedies of "Fatty" Arbuckle and Mabel Normand, the adventures of Pearl White and the romances of Theda Bara and Clara Kimball Young.

Oblivious to the motion picture threat, the stage soon yielded to the pressure of a more immediate foe. Once again the roll of war shaped the course of the theater in New Jersey; the road began to crumble, stock companies disintegrated, and the upstart "flickers" invaded the old opera houses. The muster of men, however, contained the seeds of birth as well as those of death for the theater. Although amateur or little theaters had been in sporadic operation in the State since before 1900, they first became important when they furnished the cluster of New Jersey training camps with entertainment and diversion. After the war, little theaters became as necessary to the well-bred community as plans for a soldiers' and sailors' monument. At the same time, under the leadership of Jesse Lynch Williams' *Theatre Intime* at Princeton, the State's colleges elevated the theater from a career to a profession by instituting extensive dramatic training courses and workshops. Even before this development in the college, the Thalians of Barringer High School in Newark had offered musical and dramatic productions of such unusual finish that between 1912 and 1918 they were recognized as one of the Nation's outstanding little theater groups.

By the time the old opera houses had been wired for sound pictures, the growth of little theaters in New Jersey was recognized as the virtual savior of "live entertainment." Moreover, the movement converted the emphasis on theater from the passive playgoing of thousands to the active contact of hundreds with dramatic production and its problems. In the last decade the groups have continued to increase so that their aggregate audiences challenge the size of those of the professional theater.

There are now approximately 100 amateur and little theater groups in the State. Their presentations range in interest and taste from the smart drawing room comedies of the Montclair Dramatic Club and the Green Door Players of Madison to *Bury the Dead* and other plays of social protest presented by the Newark Collective Theater. Many of the more important groups (such as the Chatham Community Players, the Monmouth Players of Deal, the Group Players at Trenton, and the Playhouse Association of Summit) specialize in recent Broadway successes. The university theaters, notable the New Jersey College for Women Theater Workshop and the Stevens Theater of the Stevens Institute of Technology, have led the way in experimenting with less well known plays and unorthodox stage techniques. At Millburn the Paper Mill Playhouse promises to develop into an art center with proved theatrical productions as its nucleus. A particularly valuable offshoot of the little theater movement is the New Jersey Junior League Children's Theater, which presents juvenile productions in Newark, Elizabeth, Orange, Englewood, and Plainfield.

While this new theater was spreading over the State, the old theater suddenly staged a spectacular last stand in Hoboken. There in the winter of 1928–29 Christopher Morley and Cleon Throckmorton added a chapter to American theatrical history by reviving the thriller of the 1860's, *After Dark,* and the musical comedy, *The Black Crook.* The novelty of

these productions to a new generation and the lure of Hoboken's celebrated beer came near to overshadowing the New York stage for the entire season. The beer continued to run the following year but not the
plays. Theatrically, however, the work of Morley and Throckmorton created a fresh interest in mid-Victorian entertainment.

Theatergoing in New Jersey today is chiefly a matter of buying two sets
of tickets—one for the play, and one for the train to New York. The
"road" has been reduced to Newark, Atlantic City, and occasional events
in Montclair, Trenton, and Princeton. In recent years the New England
practice of converting barns into summer playhouses has penetrated into
New Jersey mountain and shore resorts, with particular success in Maplewood and Deal. Because of their inherent impermanence, however, these
ventures cannot be expected to "save the theater" in New Jersey.

That never-ending task first assumed by the little theaters has recently
been undertaken by the Federal Theater Project of the Works Progress
Administration. During 1936, 1937, and 1938 the project has presented
its varied repertoire of more than a dozen plays to thousands, many of
whom were seeing their first professional performance. As the amateur
groups continue to convert playgoers into participants, the Federal Theater
widens the potential theatrical audience. Individually realizing a greater
measure of dramatic appreciation for the State, jointly they seek to lay a
new foundation for the rehabilitation of the professional theater.

Music

The story of music in New Jersey is primarily a story of the growth of
public interest and appreciation. The musical habits of the population
have progressed from the community psalm singing of Colonial times,
through bleak periods of Victorian disapproval and disinterest, to the late
nineteenth and early twentieth century movements for widespread enjoyment
and participation. To this growth the men of music themselves—composers, interpreters, and critics—have contributed in an unusually high
degree.

The number of important New Jersey musicians has perhaps been limited by the historic location of the great conservatories and concert halls
in New York, Boston, and Philadelphia. The State's proximity to these
centers has, however, provided an exceptional opportunity for hearing
fine music. Similarly, New Jersey has attracted from the nearby music
capitals many of the Nation's inspired and farsighted musical educators.
Lowell Mason, Dudley Buck, and William Batchelder Bradbury estab-

lished a lasting New Jersey tradition of leadership in the popularization of music. The State's geographical advantage may also partially explain its having many influential musical historians and critics. Their work extends from the incidental comments of William Dunlap and the singing texts of James Lyon before 1800 to the monumental critical histories by Oscar G. Sonneck and John Tasker Howard.

Music in New Jersey almost literally began between the leaves of the Colonists' prayer books. And for a century and a half there it remained. Gradually psalm singing expanded into oratorios and concerts of sacred music. Chinks in the religious armor were timidly filled by itinerant musical companies who volunteered, to the displeasure of the church, ballad operas and "variety entertainments" in noisy taverns. No such opposition inhibited the growth in aristocratic homes of spinet concerts and vocal performances accompanied by the flute, which later developed into society choral groups. Despite this inroad as well as the use of gay traditional music for dances, the direction of music in New Jersey up to the Revolution was almost unswervingly celestial.

From the unsorted mass of Colonial folk tunes, ballads, and instrumental imitations of European music emerged two New Jersey claimants to the title of "first American composer." Characteristic of their own period, Francis Hopkinson (1737–1791) and James Lyon (1735–1794) wrote occasional and patriotic music. Neither was an innovator or a national influence.

The year 1759 was the *annus mirabilis* specifically of New Jersey music, generally of American music. For in that year Lyon composed an ode for his commencement at the College of New Jersey (Princeton) and Hopkinson copied his own song, "My Days Have Been So Wondrous Free," into a notebook containing his favorite songs. Unable to discover the exact date of Hopkinson's composition, musical historians have differed on the question of his priority over Lyon as the composer of the first American song.

Hopkinson, who lived in Bordentown from 1773 until his death, was a musical amateur, especially able on the harpsichord and therefore interested in chamber music. In November 1788 he published *Seven Songs for Harpsichord or Forte-Piano,* said to be the first book of music published by an American composer. The songs, which were dedicated to George Washington, show a strong English influence. While appealing in their freshness they are important mainly as an indication of contemporary taste. Hopkinson also wrote the score for *The Temple of Minerva,* an allegorical-political masque or opera, privately presented in 1781.

Virtually unmentioned by musical historians until the twentieth century, Lyon was first in a long line of influential New Jersey music teachers. Six of this Newark minister's songs appeared in the collection of hymns and songs known as *Urania,* published in 1761. Among them was his adaptation of *Whitefield's Tune,* the first record of a native treatment of the tune which was to be used for *America.* In 1792 Lyon published *Directions for Singing, Keys in Music and Rules of Transposition,* one of the earliest American musical texts. His work as a teacher carried him as far north as Massachusetts.

The book for *The Archers,* the first commercially produced American opera, was written in 1796 by William Dunlap of Perth Amboy. Dunlap later sandwiched cursory musical criticism into his art and literary histories.

The earliest recorded concert in the State was in 1799, when permission had to be obtained from the local magistrate in Newark. Singing societies, recreational rather than commercial ventures, formed the backbone of musical enterprise until about 1850. There were half a dozen choral clubs in Newark by 1840, and others were scattered throughout the State. They sang the works of Handel, Bach, and Mozart, which also were the most popular program pieces for the few instrumental groups.

Such organizations aroused a lasting interest in music in the upper levels of society and created fertile ground for the mid-century drive for popular musical education. It was fortunate for New Jersey that in 1853 Lowell Mason (1792–1872), the dynamo of the movement to make music a part of the public school curriculum, chose to live in Orange. Fresh from his successful preachment of music for the masses in New England, Mason continued his educational work in New Jersey by lectures and concerts, and by training large choral groups. He was largely responsible not only for the spread of musical participation but also for the continuance of the religious influence. Known as "the father of American church music," Mason returned to the earliest New England traditions and composed many hymns that set the pattern for the stately hymnology of the American Protestant Church. Among his better-known works are "Nearer My God to Thee" and "From Greenland's Icy Mountains." In 1855 New York University awarded him the first honorary degree of doctor of music in America.

While Mason was broadening the audience for music, William Batchelder Bradbury (1816–1868) plunged into the equally necessary task of training music teachers. He organized the first convention of music teachers in Somerville in 1851, and later, as a resident of Bloomfield, he became an important adjunct to Mason's Nation-wide work. Also a force in the Sunday School music movement, Bradbury edited many song collections, among which *The Golden Chain* sold 2,000,000 copies.

Contemporaneous with the growth of American singing clubs and school music was the rise of the German singing societies. The Concordia, Germania, and Schwäbischer Sängerbund added a gay and lusty note to the rather formal and still churchified American singing. These groups, fed by large waves of immigration, became the workingman's chief contact with music in Newark, Trenton, Hoboken, Bayonne and Jersey City. National Sängerfeste attracted thousands of participants to northern New Jersey, long recognized as the American center for German music. Bands and small orchestras quickly followed the vocal groups and in 1855 a touring opera company played Weber's *Der Freischütz* in Newark. In the same year was founded the Newark Harmonic Society, the city's most famous singing group.

When this society was directed in 1865 by Leopold Damrosch, perhaps the greatest conductor of his day, and when five years later he selected a large number of singers from Newark and Jersey City for the first of his May Music Festivals, New Jersey music achieved maturity and national significance. Although Damrosch and Theodore Thomas later brought their symphony orchestras to the large cities, they did not inspire the development of instrumental groups comparable to the singing societies.

The impulse to popularize music gained new strength after the Civil War. George James Webb (1803–1887), who lived in Orange from 1871 until his death, used Mason's technique with large choral groups, particularly children, but concentrated on secular music. He introduced many patriotic and folk songs into the societies' repertoire and deliberately minimized the use of hymns and anthems. Nevertheless, Webb is remembered chiefly for his hymn, *Stand Up, Stand Up for Jesus.*

Dudley Buck (1839–1909) of West Orange attempted to do for instrumental music what Mason and his successors had accomplished for choral work. A celebrated organist and choral harmonist himself, he chose the lecture-recital as his medium of expression and later devoted himself to teaching. Buck was more than a popularizer, for his symphonic cantatas, *The Golden Legend* and *The Light of Asia,* are viewed as landmarks in the post-Civil War liberation of American music from the dominance of European models and influence.

New Jersey's contribution to this musical declaration of independence was enhanced by the work of Samuel A. Ward (1847–1903) of Newark and William Wallace Gilchrist (1846–1916) of Jersey City. Ward, a founder of the famous Orpheus Club of Newark, wrote the music for *America, the Beautiful,* recognized as the most esthetically satisfactory of American patriotic songs. Gilchrist, who was blessed with an almost unnatural gift for winning musical prizes, wrote symphonies that have been described as "facile, yet touched with originality."

While the German singing societies were yet in their heyday (1880–90) and native groups were in the ascendance in New Brunswick, Trenton and Perth Amboy, the arrival of other nationalities from Europe enriched the musical life of the State. Verdi and Rossini began to be heard in the gay Italian taverns of Newark and Paterson; more somber Slavic tones issued from the native instruments brought to Perth Amboy and Bayonne from Poland and Russia; and in many cities there mingled with the precise Protestant hymnology the majestic simplicity of Catholic music and the plaintive chants from Hebrew synagogues.

The twentieth century development of the phonograph and the radio has thus far retarded the desire and lessened the necessity for personal participation in music. The instruction of Mason, Buck, and Bradbury, which laid the foundation for intelligent listening, survived mainly in the schools of the State. The mechanization of music did, however, stimulate popular interest in the great artists who began to appear in New Jersey on concert tours. Newark led the way in 1912, under the leadership of C. Mortimer Fiske and Louis Arthur Russell, with a music festival featuring Metropolitan Opera stars. While choral groups declined, long years of piano, violin, and vocal instruction pressed upon reluctant children began to flower into small orchestras, string quartets, and amateur opera companies.

Pierre Key's *Music Year Book* for 1938 lists 59 private organizations actively devoted to the promotion and enjoyment of music in New Jersey. Among these are 15 orchestras, 12 music schools, 23 choral societies, and 2 opera companies. Musical and community organizations in the larger cities and wealthy suburbs regularly sponsor subscription concert series for half a dozen important musical events.

Among the more prominent vocal groups are the Bach Society of New Jersey, which annually in May presents Bach's *B Minor Mass* in Newark, the Essex County Opera Association, the Montclair Operetta Club, and the Opera Club of the Oranges. The Essex County Symphony Society annually holds a music festival in Newark, presenting leading singers and instrumentalists. The closest approach to a State-manned symphony orchestra is the New Jersey Orchestra, drawn principally from the Oranges, Montclair and Millburn. In December 1937 the Griffith Music Foundation was established by the Griffith Piano Company of Newark to coordinate and augment the existing musical activities of the State.

The activities of several educational institutions have enriched musical life in the central part of New Jersey. The Princeton University department of music, under the direction of Roy Dickinson Welch, has lately been enlarged and strengthened, notably by the addition of the well known composer-teacher, Roger Sessions. Rutgers' instruction and concerts comprise a major portion of musical affairs in New Brunswick. The Westminster Choir School at Princeton, where the noted composer, Roy Harris, is a member of the staff, has achieved national recognition for the excellence of its training, and the Princeton Theological Seminary is recognized as an innovator in ecclesiastical music. To the south, both Camden and Atlantic City support local groups and concert series.

In recent years the work of the Federal Government and of the State's churches has increased the scope of musical appreciation. By January 1939 the 27 orchestras and bands of the Federal Music Project of the Works Progress Administration had given 17,742 concerts to 10,884,690 people. Church music ranges from hymn singing in small towns to the production of Bach masses and Handel oratorios in urban centers. Particularly noteworthy in this field has been the revival of impressive performances of Gregorian chants under the auspices of the Roman Catholic Diocesan Institute of Sacred Music in Newark.

The Federal Government has also contributed to the discovery and codification of a considerable body of New Jersey folk songs. Herbert Halpert of the Federal Theater Project has recorded more than 500 songs, including indigenous American songs, sea chanties, children's game songs, fiddle tunes and a large number of ballads of British origin. He has concentrated on the songs of the Pineys, swamp dwellers of southern New Jersey. In the character of these recordings, Halpert believes he has evidence for the theory that southern New Jersey is the meeting place of the northern and southern American folk song tradition.

Never rich in composers since the Federal period, New Jersey today has a small number representing current differences in style and approach. Dean of the group is Henry Holden Huss (1862–) of Newark, renowned as teacher and pianist, composer of several concertos in the conservative romantic mold. George Antheil (1900–), who was born in Trenton, has been called the *enfant terrible* of modern American music. Although his *Ballet Mecanique* shows a vigorous and original talent, he has yet to surmount a reputation for the merely spectacular. Midway between these extremes are Philip James (1890–), a native of Jersey City, composer of several overtures; and Harriet Ware of Plainfield, whose songs, cantatas, and piano pieces have made her one of the Nation's leading women composers.

Other well known New Jersey musicians include Ernest Schelling (1876–   ), born in Belvidere, who holds high rank as both a composer and conductor, particularly of music for children; Paul Ambrose (1868–   ), organist and composer, of Trenton; Mark Andrews of Montclair, a talented and original director of choral groups throughout the State; and Jerome Kern (1885–   ) of Newark, whose gift for melodious composition, displayed in *Show Boat* and other popular operettas, suggests him as a latter-day Victor Herbert.

Among the State's prominent singers are Richard Crooks, Metropolitan Opera tenor, who was born in Trenton and now lives in Sea Girt, and Paul Robeson (1898–   ), the noted Negro concert singer and actor, a native of Princeton, who attended Rutgers College. Crooks made his professional debut at Asbury Park in 1910 with the late Mme. Ernestine Schumann-Heink.

When American music began to merit detailed record and interpretation, three New Jerseymen assumed the major share of that task. William J. Henderson (1855–1937), born in Newark and educated at Princeton, belonged to the notable group of musical critics in New York whose taste influenced music from Boston to San Francisco. In addition to his work on the New York *Sun,* he wrote a large number of books that popularized concert and operatic music. Perhaps the greatest of American music scholars was Oscar G. Sonneck (1873–1928) of Jersey City, whose most valuable work was his studies in early American musical history. He was later chief of the music division of the Library of Congress and also pioneered in the study of American Indian music. Yielding little to Sonneck in scholarship, John Tasker Howard (1890–   ) of Glen Ridge wrote *Our American Music* in 1930, the first full-length history of native music, with unusual consideration for the general reader. Howard's work, more essentially American in its critical attitude than Sonneck's, is unquestionably a vital chapter in the unassembled volume of American cultural history.

Architecture

New Jersey has produced two local styles of domestic architecture. First was the low sandstone Dutch Colonial house, a style developed in the Hackensack Valley, where it flourished until about 1800. During the

THE DEMAREST HOUSE, RIVER EDGE

same period, the brick and glass industries in the southern part of the State produced a second indigenous type of building best termed Swedish Colonial. Throughout the nineteenth century the State was affected by a succession of European influences, and it was not until the 1890's that New Jersey again began to work out architectural problems in terms of its own requirements. The result has been a new and refreshing approach in design, evident in suburban planning and resort development, but of late more particularly in industrial buildings.

Paradoxically, the Dutch style did not begin to develop in the north until after the English conquest of New Netherland in 1664. Introduction of slave labor in that year made the quarrying of brown sandstone practicable and was responsible for its use in the walls of the earlier homesteads. Cut from shallow quarries, it was laid in beds of clay mortar taken from the surrounding fields and mixed with straw, which became hard and weathertight when dry; when pointing-up was necessary in later years, it was done with lime mortar, leaving conspicuous white joints. Sometimes the builders used finished cut stone only on the front façade and for the corner quoins, filling in the remainder of the walls with coursed rubble, as in the Demarest house at River Edge, but generally the stonework was cut in regular coursed bond (as in bricklaying).

The predominant characteristics of the Dutch Colonial style are a long sweeping roof line, with deep overhanging eaves at front and rear, and close-cropped gable ends. Small houses were given a pitched roof; larger ones a gambrel roof with the upper pitch much shortened and flattened and the lower one lengthened and curved. In the later period the overhang was sometimes extended and developed into a porch at front and rear. The wall faces of the gable ends were shingled or covered with siding for protection. Often the bargeboard along the raked roof line was carved with ornament.

These houses nearly always faced south regardless of the direction of the highway, so that the eaves afforded day-long shade from the summer sun. As families outgrew their homes it was customary to add a wing larger than the original building. Thus the original structure of the Vreeland house (1818) in Leonia became the kitchen wing of a new and more pretentious dwelling. Frequently a second wing was added at the opposite end, forming a symmetrical composition, as in the Ackerman and Hopper houses on Polifly Road, Hackensack.

The charm and beauty of these houses have been enhanced by time, and the deep overhang of the eaves gives them an air of comfort and domestic security that is not often equaled in other types of American Colonial building.

Although the influence of the Swedes on the Dutch diminished after 1655, the architecture of the southern region of the State may be referred to as "Swedish." The predominant local building material was clay suitable for brick. The development of the glass industry, along with that of brick, resulted in the production of a glazed brick characteristic of the houses of West Jersey, and to this day a heritage in State industry. By 1700 William Bradway had built a house, still standing at Stowe Creek, in which a pattern of two-colored glazed brick was used, and by 1725 this practice had become quite common locally. Occasionally red and white bricks were used, but usually the body of the wall was red, bearing geometric patterns in dull blue. Often the owner's initials and the date of erection were worked into the gables in large letters and figures. This peculiarity appears to have culminated locally in 1754 with the ornate gable designs of the Dickinson house at Alloway.

These early brick houses are tall, narrow and rather urban in character. Dutch influence on the architecture of the Swedes first appeared in a small one-story house with gambrel roof, such as the William Penn house (1685) in Burlington. It became usual, however, to add a second story, leaving the projecting eaves along front and rear; this produced the "pent eaves" that became a fixed characteristic of the so-called Swedish style. Outstanding examples are the William Hancock house (1734) at Lower Alloways Creek and the Oakford house (1736) at Alloway.

The settlers of Salem, familiar with the English Renaissance style, introduced this tradition in the southern part of the State as early as 1675, and throughout the eighteenth century the tall narrow Dutch-Swedish houses tended to grow more nearly square. In 1804 the Morgan house was built in Pilesgrove, a fine example of Post Colonial brickwork. The Jacob Fox house in Washington (1813) continued the development still further, but its tallness recalls an earlier tendency. The William Johnson house at Lower Penns Neck (1815) marks the complete domination of the Georgian Colonial over the Dutch-Swedish style. One of the few surviving public buildings of this period is the Burlington County Courthouse in Mount Holly. Built in 1797 and 1808, the main courthouse is flanked by small one-story offices in separate buildings.

The influence of the English Renaissance appeared first at Elizabeth in 1664 with the arrival there of English settlers from Long Island and the mother country. They likewise applied the sturdy traditions of English building and the early forms of Georgian Renaissance to their local materials. By 1700 the development had been carried as far west as Morristown and it dominated the section until after the beginning of the nineteenth century. In homes, public buildings, and churches it produced forms which differed little from those of New England.

Queen's Building at Rutgers University (1825), designed by John McComb, architect of the New York City Hall, is striking by contrast for its austere simplicity and lack of French influence. Deep-set shuttered windows are spaced evenly across the smooth sandstone wall surfaces, and the slight break in the façade, which marks the central motif, is crowned with a low pitched eave pediment. The center of the roof is marked by a square Georgian lantern.

The old ecclesiastical architecture of New Jersey varied considerably with the character and background of the communities. The settlers from the north, although thoroughly imbued with the Georgian tradition, were seldom satisfied with that style for their churches after 1800. Although they erected fine churches in the Georgian manner, such as the First Presbyterian Church (1787) in Newark, they often succumbed to adorning them later with Gothic details. The Gothic windows of Old Trinity in Newark were substituted for Norman windows in 1809; and lancet windows were introduced about 1830 in St. James Church at Piscataway, a charming Colonial structure. Less pretentious Colonial churches are the

Presbyterian Church (1790) in Springfield, and Old Tennent Church (1751) near Freehold, both of frame construction. Not far removed from the feeling of Quaker meeting houses, their design is noteworthy for small fenestration and for the carved detail of cornices and doorways.

The Friends who settled widely throughout New Jersey developed a definite and rigid form of architecture, constructing their meeting houses with an eye to substantiality, economy and simplicity. Though the meeting houses vary in size, they have maintained a definite form for two centuries: generally plain rectangular brick structures, two stories high, with solid shutters on the first floor and louvered shutters on the second, two entrances on the front with a small porch, covered or uncovered. They are almost invariably set in a clearing behind sycamore trees. Good examples are the Chesterfield Friends Meeting House (1773) at Crosswicks and the one in Burlington (1764).

The State contains many examples of the Greek Revival style that began in Europe toward the end of the eighteenth century, and which attained national popularity under the leadership of Benjamin Latrobe, William Strickland, Robert Mills, and others. Architects copied ancient Greek details as closely as possible, and in numerous buildings sought to reproduce the lines of Greek temples. This severe style appears in several houses in Flemington, notably the Redding mansion, but its use was limited mostly to courthouses and churches. The Sussex County Courthouse (1847) in Newton and the Presbyterian Church (1851) in Pluckemin are typical examples.

From about 1850 to 1900 New Jersey suffered the ills of Victorian bad taste. The State has its share of fretwork, spindles, checkerboard panels and the mansard roofs of the period. Many a fine old house was ruined to conform with the taste of the time. Ringwood Manor, an old Colonial estate, was so changed and enlarged that all traces of the original design have been removed.

During this period the Victorian Gothic style developed. As in other States, architects of the so-called practical school began reproducing early English Gothic structures with questionable success and complete inaccuracy. Much of their work, the style of which has unfortunately set a precedent for church architecture, remains in the cities. Of brick or brown sandstone, or a combination of both, these buildings are gloomy reminders of an uninspired period. St. John's Episcopal Church in Elizabeth is a survival of this work.

Toward the end of the century the influence of H. H. Richardson and Louis Sullivan had sadly degenerated. Their followers indulged in bizarre

WROUGHT IRON BALCONY ON COLONIAL APARTMENTS, BORDENTOWN

reproductions of modified Romanesque and Byzantine types, whose bold mass and intricate detail appealed to the prosperous builders of the early twentieth century. For nearly a generation this heavy manner characterized residences, banks, churches, and other public buildings. Notable examples are the Peddie Memorial Baptist Church and the Prudential Insurance Company buildings in Newark, and W. A. Potter's Alexander Hall in Princeton.

"Collegiate Gothic" appeared in New Jersey in the buildings of Princeton University during the first decade of the twentieth century. Based upon the design of the university buildings at Cambridge and Oxford, the style is a modification of English Tudor. The use of local fieldstone with limestone trim instead of the usual combination of brick and stone of England gives the walls a very beautiful texture. The Commons at Princeton (Day and Klauder, architects) with traceried fenestration and delicate Tudor-Gothic finials and ornament is an excellent example of the style.

School architecture throughout the State is highly specialized. Rigid

State laws for heating, ventilation, and lighting offer little opportunity for variation on standard forms. Successful solutions to this problem are the Dwight Morrow School in Englewood by Lawrence L. Licht, architect, and the Hawthorne High School designed by Fanning and Shaw. Another is Licht's Trenton Central High. A combination of the Georgian Colonial and Classical Revival styles, it consists of a three-storied redbrick main building, with a Greek portico and an octagonal cupola, and two large wings repeating these motifs on a smaller scale.

Among the newer churches, two of the most interesting are the First Church of Christ, Scientist in Montclair and the Second Presbyterian Church in Newark. The former achieves dignity and charm by uniting a classic portico with a main building of Georgian Colonial design, while the latter is a fine example of modernized Gothic, exhibiting considerable grace despite an unconventional squatness.

Skyscrapers are not numerous. In Newark are the National Newark and Essex Bank Building, definitely neoclassic in form and treatment with modern detail on the plane surfaces; the Raymond-Commerce Building, treated in a pseudo-modern manner of Gothic ancestry, with much pointless ornamentation; and the American Insurance Company Building, of Colonial brick with limestone trim and Georgian Colonial detail. The New Jersey Bell Telephone Company Building (Voorhees, Gmelin and Walker, architects), while not strictly a skyscraper, is tall and massive; it is designed in a simplified modern style with strong accenting of vertical lines and strongly modeled ornamental relief.

Trenton's skyline is marked by moderately high but undistinguished buildings. Passaic, Perth Amboy, and other smaller cities each have raised one structure that citizens sheepishly refer to as "our local skyscraper." Elizabeth has a 15-story Courthouse Annex, labored and awkward in conception, while citizens of Camden have with much justice dubbed their 22-story nondescript City Hall and Courthouse Annex, "The Milk Bottle." On high ground in Jersey City is the Medical Center, one of the most impressive groups of tall buildings in the State. Of severe modern functional design, the cluster by John Rowland compares favorably with the Medical Center across the Hudson River.

Unique in the State are the fluttering towers and turrets of the boardwalk hotels in Atlantic City and other coast resorts, where rooms facing the water are at a premium and verticality in building perhaps is justified. Even more suggestive of New Jersey as a playground are the gay and ribald architectural grotesques of Deal and Elberon, summer resorts extraordinary. These immense barnlike castles of shingles or stucco, girdled by tiers of porches and sprouting myriad turrets, string along the water-front and nearby highways for miles.

Recent public buildings for the most part follow classical precedent, with many stylistic modifications. The tendency toward simplification of ornament and the adaptation of smooth plane surfaces in public buildings is evident in several new post offices. Housing facilities range from the two-room pine shack of the southern truck farmer to the baronial estates of the commuting stockbrokers in the north. The average urban home is the multiple dwelling, two-, three-, or four-family house, shingled and porched, and often with a tiny plot of grass. Thousands of city dwellers live in that peculiarly uncomfortable and unhomelike environment—an apartment above a business establishment, which may be anything from a fish market to a garage.

Newark, Trenton, and Jersey City have a large number of apartment houses, few of which attain a height sufficient to warrant elevators. Many are built around an inner court. Their romantic balconies, crenelated parapets, and random gargoyles attest the triumph of haste over taste in the building boom following the World War. East Orange has a row of luxurious apartment houses, conservative in design and mostly of red brick with white trim, suggesting a kind of suburban Park Avenue.

The problem of slum clearance has been attacked with varying success. In Newark the Prudential Life Insurance Company erected two sets of attractive tile-brick apartment houses, with recreation areas. One development is exclusively for Negroes. In 1937 the United States Housing Act established a fixed rental rate for all Government housing projects. The Stanley S. Holmes Village in Atlantic City, completed before this act had gone into effect, maintains a relatively high rental rate; but Westfield Acres, a series of small apartment buildings in Camden financed by the Public Works Administration, may prove to be a genuine step toward low-cost housing.

An interesting attempt at planned housing is the Radburn community (Henry Wright and Clarence Stein, architects) where streets are laid out for comfortable suburban living and the safety of children. The design of the dwellings is, however, discouragingly monotonous, and the scheme is cramped.

Jersey Homesteads, begun as a Resettlement Administration project, consists of two hundred small flat-roof houses of four to six rooms, built of cinder block and concrete with a judicious use of glass. They appear unattractive but are comfortable and are equipped with modern conveniences unknown in even the better class tenements. The cooperatively owned garment factory is a well designed one-story steel and glass structure. The school building is a low flat-roof brick and concrete structure, designed by Alfred Kastner in the modern "international" style. Vigorous treatment of mass, effective concentration of detail, and ample fenestration fulfill both aesthetic and functional requirements.

Industry until recently has contributed little to the New Jersey scene except the depressing warehouselike mills of Paterson and Passaic and the ugly red-brick factories scattered throughout Newark and other industrial centers. The five buildings of the CIBA Pharmaceutical Products Company at Summit (1937) designed by J. Floyd Yewell are an excellent example of attractive functional design. They are of light buff brick with purplish red brick facing on the window piers, suggesting continuous fenestration. The entrances are of glass brick and limestone, in pleasing harmony with the wall materials. An example of planning for industrial use is the imposing glass and steel one-story plant erected by General Motors at Linden (1937), and the fine sleek plant of the Coca-Cola bottling company in Harrison (1936).

In the last few years the so-called "modernistic" style has spread rapidly through Newark, Jersey City, and other cities, where store fronts in the business sections are fast assuming rainbow hues in glossy plate glass and gleaming chrome; neon light signs are integral parts of the design, their glowing tubes forming the names of the owners as well as panels and bands in the composition. The effect is neat, clean, and highly appropriate. The Newark Coca-Cola plant (1936) is a notable example of the modern trend. Its stuccoed walls are faced with black and ivory carrara, and the doors and windows trimmed with stainless steel.

A notable example of modern industrial design is the massive office building of the Kimble Glass Factory at Vineland. The building, designed by William Lescaze, is constructed of brick and structural glass with limestone slab facing. The highly functional plan provides a spacious main office chamber which serves as a central core around which are arranged various minor offices, conference rooms, and lounges. The simple masses of the building give outward expression to a well-organized plan. The furnishings of the interior were designed by the architect.

Transportation needs have provided the State with a number of impressive engineering projects, notably the Pulaski Skyway, a series of finely proportioned cantilever bridges, and Bayonne Bridge, longest steel arch span in the world and one of the most beautiful. Also worthy of mention are the Pennsylvania Railroad's stone arch bridge over the Raritan at New Brunswick, and the reinforced concrete arch bridge that carries US 1 across the same river. With New York and Pennsylvania, New Jersey shares two splendid suspension bridges, George Washington Memorial Bridge to New York and Delaware River Bridge to Philadelphia. The approaches to George Washington Bridge were designed by Cass Gilbert. The new hangar under construction (1939) at Newark Airport is expected to provide a setting more suggestive of the terminal's importance.

Of the State's railroad stations the Pennsylvania's in Newark is most important architecturally. Now a bus, trolley, and tube-train terminal for the city, the massive gray Indiana limestone building is of simple design, with a minimum of ornamentation and a maximum of intelligently planned space. The municipal bus terminal in Hackensack, a broad building of white brick and glass, is a good adaptation of the modern functional style.

Painting, Sculpture, and Crafts

Early art in New Jersey sprang from the industrial pattern of the Colony. Numerous Colonial craftsmen are honored anonymously today for their furniture making, tavern decorating, sign painting, and weaving. Their products are scattered through the homes of the State, particularly in the south, and in the countless antique shops that line highways and village main streets.

The deposits of pure quartz sand in southern New Jersey attracted European glass workers, and by 1750 the glass industry at Wistarburgh had become the Colony's most notable craft. It produced Wistar glass objects, delicately colored bottles and bowls and brilliantly surfaced glasses and globes. Remarkable for their purity of color and the originality of their wave and whorl designs, the broad-based Wistar products are among the most valued collectors' items. In 1775 another German family, the Stangers, founded a glass works at Glassboro which became equally famous for its wares.

Pottery began with the works established by Daniel Coxe at Burlington in 1688 and increased steadily in beauty and importance throughout the Colonial period, culminating in the founding of the Fulper Pottery Company in Flemington in 1805 and the American Pottery at Jersey City two decades later. Stoneware, crocks, flowerpots, and brown glazed ware from these potteries, as well as from those established later at Trenton, rank among the choicest in the Nation.

Representative of the minor crafts were Elias Boudinot's silversmithing, distinguished for its fine engraving; staidly colorful quilting of the Dutch housewives along the Hudson; dignified wrought-iron gates and fireplace pieces from the northern mine section; and accomplished cabinetmaking of the Egerton family in the Hepplewhite style in New Brunswick around 1790.

In formal art, the most notable Colonial figure of New Jersey was Patience Lovell Wright (1725–1786) of Bordentown, the first American to achieve fame as a sculptor. She won international recognition for her figures in wax, one of which, a full-length statue of William Pitt, was placed in Westminster Abbey, the first American work so honored.

As Americans gradually became interested in painting and sculpture New Jersey produced a number of artists whose work shows the prevalent influences of the first half of the last century. Typical of this group was Charles Parsons (1821–1910), a water-colorist and engraver for Currier and Ives. During this period William Dunlap of Perth Amboy, an unsuccessful historical painter, published *A History of the Rise and Progress of the Arts of Design in the United States,* which proved so valuable that he has been called "the American Vasari."

Asher B. Durand of South Orange throughout his long life from 1796 to 1886 earned the titles of "the Nation's most distinguished engraver" and "the father of American landscape painting." After a brilliant start at engraving copies of portraits, he turned in 1834 to landscape painting. The microscopic eye of the engraver working directly from nature fostered a passion for nicety of expression. This trend characterized his work and set the tone of the Hudson River school, which he helped to found.

The outstanding figure of the middle years of the last century was George Inness (1825–1894), who spent many years of his life in Montclair and some time in Perth Amboy. At first he was more or less in sympathy with the tradition of the Hudson River school and practiced a method akin to Durand's. But his art, as developed here and abroad, steadily broadened and deepened, becoming especially noteworthy for the richness of color. Under the influence of Corot he began to sacrifice detail to mass and to abandon the panoramic treatment in favor of accented composition.

Inness advanced the trend in landscape painting from the purely analytic form of Durand and his followers to a genuinely romantic stage. He sought to emphasize quality and force of emotion rather than scenic fidelity. Nature in all seasons and all aspects of the sky attracted him in his quest for harmony of form and mystical feeling. In his later years he passed into a genuinely mystical period, favoring canvases of eerie fogs

STATUE OF ABRAHAM LINCOLN, NEWARK

and strange lights instead of the earlier landscape and pastoral compositions.

Inness produced many masterpieces which rank him with the leaders of the Barbizon school; yet he remained essentially individual. In addition to his celebrated views of the Delaware Water Gap, he painted much of the New Jersey scene, particularly around Montclair. Six representative paintings now hang in the Montclair Art Museum. Contemporary critics are virtually agreed that Inness is one of the foremost American landscape painters.

By the middle of the nineteenth century cities were becoming sufficiently conscious of their past to install busts, shafts, and other memorials in parks and public buildings. Art schools began to develop in Newark and its suburbs; associations for the collection and exhibition of pictures were formed; and in several cities there was considerable sentiment for the erection of museums.

New crafts developed from changing industry. The looms of Paterson wove especially beautiful silk fabrics; terra cotta factories in Perth Amboy turned out decorative products of a high order. Leather workers in Newark produced fine hand-tooled work, and jewelry manufacture in that city was lifted above a commercial enterprise by skill in designing and unusually gifted workmanship. In the wake of these followed several other craft industries which included the world-renowned Lenox china of Trenton, the Edgewater tapestry looms, whose hand-woven products have been praised as "American Gobelins," and the fine stained glass and ecclesiastical brasses made by the J. and R. Lamb Studios in Tenafly.

Among those American artists who revolted against European conventions toward the end of the century was George Inness Jr. (1864–1926), also of Montclair. A landscape painter like his father, he was—like his father again—forward looking in his attitude toward painters' problems. Ralph Blakelock (1847–1919) of Orange was even more radical in his approach. His fantastic and imaginative art reached its height in his moonlight studies which have been termed "as individualistic as those of Albert Pinkham Ryder." Blakelock shared the elder Inness's interest in color and emotion but lacked the benefits of his original emphasis on detail.

Two New Jersey sculptors of the same period who helped break the bands of neoclassic traditions, which had so limited American work, were J. Scott Hartley (1845–1912) and Thomas Ball (1819–1911), both of Montclair. The latter is especially significant for his equestrian "Washington" and the "Emancipation" statue in Boston.

The outstanding sculpture in the State today is not, however, the work of New Jersey men. It includes the Newark figures of Gutzon Borglum, the Princeton Battle Monument by Frederick MacMonnies, and the Trenton Battle Monument by John Duncan.

As art has become liberated, first from the church and then from the whims of wealthy patrons, intelligent education has stimulated public interest. A trio of New Jersey men stands in the front ranks of the twentieth century drive for more general appreciation of art. John Cotton Dana (1856–1929) was the first museum director to promote the cause of contemporary American artists by purchasing and maintaining a representative collection in the Newark Museum. He was also an early exponent of the doctrine that industry affords scope for artistic accomplishment and appreciation. At Rutgers University John C. Van Dyke (1856–1932) for many years used his rank as one of the Nation's most respected art critics to awaken popular sentiment by lectures, prolific writing, and exhibits of his private collection. The sole survivor of the three is Frank Jewett Mather Jr. (1868–   ), whose creative attitude toward the history of art has earned him equal repute as art historian and director of the Museum of Historic Art at Princeton University.

The 1936 edition of *Who's Who in Art* lists 180 painters and sculptors in New Jersey and 14 art associations. The most active of the latter are the Newark Museum, the Art Center of the Oranges, and the Montclair Art Museum. Since 1936 the New Jersey State Art Committee has held regional and State-wide exhibits. In addition to most of the larger cities, many small towns such as Leonia, Westfield, and Hopewell periodically sponsor showings. The Modern Artists of New Jersey have expanded local conventional exhibitions by sponsoring travel exhibits, lectures, public forums, and demonstrations, and have secured gallery representation for the works of young and little known artists.

The Museum of Historic Art at Princeton University presents a panorama of the history of art from Egyptian and Chaldean times to about 1800. Notable are its collections of Italian Renaissance painting, medieval stained glass, ceramics, and seventeenth century prints. The chapel at Rutgers has an extensive collection of early and middle American portraits by Thomas Sully, John Vanderlyn, Henry Inman, and others. Among the many historical paintings of the New Jersey Historical Society in Newark are Gilbert Stuart portraits of Captain James Lawrence and Aaron Burr.

A worthy contemporary heir to the State's distinguished landscape tradition is John Marin (1890–   ) of Cliffside, who has been called by some critics "the outstanding water-colorist of his generation." Other resident artists representing many trends in current art movements include

Grant Reynard (1887–   ) of Leonia, a conservative water-colorist; John Grabach (1886–   ) of Irvington and Maxwell Simpson (1896–   ) of Elizabeth, modern experimentalists in many mediums; and Wanda Gag (1893–   ) of Milford, a noted illustrator. To these should be added the versatile and perceptive George (Pop) Hart (1868–1933), who chose Coytesville as his home but whose globetrotting resulted in an exceptionally varied body of water-color and charcoal work. Two painters who have done much to promote popular interest are F. Ballard Williams (1871–   ) of Glen Ridge, national chairman of the American Artists' Professional League, and Raymond O'Neill (1893–   ) of Roselle, chairman of the New Jersey State Art Committee in 1937.

New Jersey members of the National Academy of Design number seven. Of these Williams of Glen Ridge, Charles S. Chapman (1879–   ) of Leonia, Hayley Lever (1876–   ) of Caldwell, Van Dearing Perrine (1869–   ) of Maplewood, are painters. Ulric H. Ellerhusen (1879–   ) of Towaco and Frederick G. R. Roth (1872–   ) of Englewood are sculptors, and Allen Lewis (1873–   ) of Basking Ridge is a worker in the graphic arts.

Associate members of the Academy include five painters, Junius Allen (1898–   ) of Summit, William J. Baer (1860–   ) of East Orange, Harvey Dunn (1884–   ) of Tenafly, Henry Rankin Poore (1859–   ) of Orange, Harry M. Walcott (1870–   ) of Rutherford, and Howard McCormick (1875–   ) of Leonia in the graphic arts.

Atlantic City

Railroad Station: Union Station, Arkansas and Arctic Aves., for Jersey Central, Pennsylvania-Reading Seashore Lines, and West Jersey R.R.

Bus Stations: 9 N. Arkansas Ave. for Atlantic City Bus Co. Lines, Atlantic Coast Lines, Martz, Safeway Trailways, Lincoln Transit Co.; 1011 Atlantic Ave. for Quaker City, Capital Coach, National Trailways, Martz; Maine and Caspian Ave. for Atlantic and Shore Railroad Co., Shore Fast Line; Tennessee and Atlantic Aves. for Gray Line, Pennsylvania-Reading Motor Lines, Greyhound Lines, Public Service; 122 S. Maryland Ave. for White Way Tours, Sight-Seeing buses.

Taxis: 50¢ for any point in the city, two passengers; 10¢ for each additional passenger.

Streetcars: Fare 7¢.

Rolling Chairs: For rent along boardwalk; 75¢ an hour for two persons, $1 for three.

Traffic Regulations: Turns may be made in either direction at intersections of all streets except where traffic officers or signs direct otherwise. Watch street signs for parking limitations and one-way streets. Parking meters on Atlantic Ave. and all cross streets, and on Pacific Ave.

Accommodations: Approximately 1,200 hotels and boarding houses; many hotels open all year, others open June 15 to October 1. Rates higher in summer; complaints on overcharges should be sent to Chamber of Commerce.

Information Service: Atlantic City Information, Inc., 12 S. Arkansas Ave.; Atlantic City Press Bureau, 2327 Boardwalk; Chamber of Commerce, 2306 Pacific Ave.; Shore Motor Club of South Jersey, Hotel Ambassador, Pacific Ave.; Publicity Bureau, Boardwalk at Tennessee Ave.

Radio Station: WPG (1100 kc.).

Theaters and Motion Picture Houses: Three theaters; 15 motion picture houses.

Swimming: Beach front, free; Hygeia Pool, Rhode Island Ave. and Boardwalk; Ambassador Pool, Brighton Ave. and Boardwalk; President Pool, Albany Ave. and Boardwalk; $1.

Golf: Country Club of Atlantic City, Linwood and Ocean City Clubs, on US 9, reached by bus and streetcar from Virginia Ave., greens fee $2; Brigantine Golf Club on Brigantine Beach, green fees 75¢, Sat. and Sun. $1.

Crabbing and Fishing: Steeplechase Pier, Pennsylvania Ave. and Boardwalk; foot of Washington Ave. at Thoroughfare, Margate; 400 N. Massachusetts Ave.; N. Iowa Ave. and Thoroughfare; free. Boats from Trolley Terminal Wharves at Inlet, $2 per person, $5-$50 a day for chartered boats.

Baseball: Sovereign Ave. and Bader Field adjoining airport, four free diamonds.

Tennis: Albany Ave. Blvd. at airport, 12 courts, 25¢ per person; N. end of New Hampshire Ave., 10 courts, free, lockers 25¢; Drexel Ave. bet. Kentucky and New York Ave. for Negroes, 6 courts, free.

Riding: On beach October to May, $1.50 per hour; academies along shore road in Bargaintown, Northfield and Absecon, summer, $1 per hour.

Yachting and Speedboating: At Inlet, Longport Trolley Terminal, $1; Steeplechase Pier, 50¢.

Bicycling: On Boardwalk before 9 a.m.

Trapshooting: Westy Hogan's Shooting Lodge, Absecon Blvd., open all year.

Ice Skating: Convention Hall, November 15–April 15; adm. 25¢.

Skee-Ball Stadium: 2429 Boardwalk, 5¢ per game.

Annual Events: Horse show, May; Ice Carnival, Convention Hall rink, July–Sept.; Evening Star Yacht Club's Moth Boat Championship Regatta, August; Showmen's Variety Jubilee (modified beauty pageant), first week in September; Absecon Yacht Club's Margate-Longport Regatta, early September; Football, Convention Hall, November; Ice Hockey (Eastern Amateur League), Convention Hall, November 15–April 15.

ATLANTIC CITY (15 alt., 66,198 pop.) is many things to many people. To an estimated 16,250,000 persons annually it is the ideal vacation place; a carnival city as characteristic of this country's culture as Brighton or the Riviera are of Europe's. To some it represents the concentrated Babbitry of America on parade. To those of the city's 66,198 inhabitants who profit from the pleasure of the 16,250,000 it is simply a year-round business.

Atlantic City has developed neither as a super-resort of New Jersey nor as another Coney Island, but as a glittering monument to the national talent for wholesale amusement. As the pitchman who sells kitchen gadgets on the boardwalk says at the end of his spiel: "I don't coax anybody. If you want it, come up and get it!" And from all corners of the country the millions come—by bus, train, automobile, plane and yacht—throughout the year. Each season brings its characteristic crowd: honeymooners, teachers, elderly retired couples, vacationing white collar workers, ministers, businessmen and their families. Uncoaxed, they come and get it. Of the whole American population, only trailer-travelers who wish to bring their trailers into the city limits are prohibited by city ordinance. The hotels and rooming houses have no desire to see "The World's Health and Pleasure Resort" re-established on a freewheeling basis.

Except for the fact that the city fronts the Atlantic Ocean, Atlantic City's geography is unimportant to the visiting host. Yet it plays a vital part in their pleasure. The Philadelphians and Camdenites who come mostly for a day or a week-end's bathing seldom learn that the peculiar coast curve shields the section from devastating northeastern storms. Nor do the New Yorkers, who are more likely to spend a week or a fortnight, often realize that the Gulf Stream comes near enough Atlantic City to temper its winter climate. Finally, few of the visitors from all over the land notice that their mecca is actually an island: for the immense marshes crisscrossed by highways and railways, over which every visitor gets his first skyline glimpse of Atlantic City, hide deep channels that completely cut off this densely populated strip of beach from the mainland.

These natural considerations are subordinated to one of the most fascinating man-made shows playing to capacity audiences anywhere in the world. Here Madame Polaska reads your life like an open book; here Ruth Snyder and Judd Gray sit for eternity in horror-stricken suspense on an electric chair that fails to function; here an assortment of the World's Foremost Astrologers reveal the future at so much a glimpse; here hundreds sit and play Bingo; here the bright lights of Broadway burn through a sea haze; here Somebodies tumble over other Somebodies and over Nobodies as well.

Atlantic City is an amusement factory, operated on the straight-line,

AMUSEMENT PIERS AND BOARDWALK, ATLANTIC CITY

mass production pattern. The belt is the boardwalk along which each specialist adds his bit to assemble the finished product, the departing visitor, sated, tanned, and bedecked with souvenirs.

The boardwalk is unique. Sixty feet wide for much of its length, it is of steel and concrete construction overlaid with pine planking in herringbone pattern. Twenty miles of planks are used each year to keep it in repair. Along its four-mile length the city side is lined with huge hotels, broken by blocks of shops, restaurants, exhibit rooms, booths, auction houses, an occasional bank and even a private park. Architecturally the motifs are mixed, but functionally they unite in presenting a glittering, luxurious front.

The shops are a melange. Like the super-salesmen who operate them, they sell anything—Ming vases from China, maple furniture from Grand Rapids, laces from the Levant, jewelry from Newark, shawls from Persia, and ladies' ready-to-wear from New York. Confectionery shops, where one of Atlantic City's famous products, salt water taffy, is made and sold, radiate a sickly sweet fragrance among motion picture houses, circus side shows, frozen custard emporiums, shooting galleries, restaurants, and hot dog and hamburger stands. Commercially, the boardwalk achieves its greatest dignity in the permanent display shops of leading national advertisers and the smart shops studding the first floors of the large hotels.

The visitor may tire physically of the boardwalk, but he seldom leaves it. More than a dozen business firms and the city provide pavilions and benches where visitors may watch the passing show or gaze into the vastness of the ocean.

Thirsts are quenched at automatic soda fountains where a nickel in the slot sets in motion the mechanism that puts a paper cup abruptly under a spout that stops flowing when the fluid is exactly one-quarter of an inch from the top of the cup. The drinker has his choice of loganberry, chocolate, cherry, lemon and lime, fruit punch, La Pep, champagne ("nonalcoholic," the sign adds apologetically), root beer, ginger ale and grape.

Many continue the procession in rolling chairs, propelled mostly by Negroes, who are not paid for waiting time but only for every hour they push. Tips—the uppermost consideration of the 14,000 summer workers in Atlantic City—mean more to these men than to almost any other workers. Cryptically, they call a small tip "a thin one" and none at all "a flat."

The miles of fine white sand eventually draw the majority of visitors away from the miles of tough gray planks for a sun bath or a turn in the surf. The universal appeal of the sea, the tang and smell of salt water and sea air are probably the resort's most valuable possessions. The wide strip of white sandy beach is dotted with cabanas, umbrellas, beach chairs, and gaily togged bathers against the deep green of the Atlantic and the turquoise sky. The corps of 71 trained lifeguards is none too many when a Sunday crowd swells the beach population to more than 500,000.

The half dozen amusement piers extend well out into the ocean at wide intervals. "A vacation in itself" is the slogan of the largest pier; "six-ring circus" would describe the piers more accurately. One admission price admits the pleasure-seeker to any or all the goings-on: two moving picture houses with entirely different shows, a vaudeville house, science exhibits, a deep-sea diving horse, health talks, a chamber of horrors, a zoo devoted to baby animals, and a dozen or so other attractions. When eyes and legs grow weary, indoor rest rooms and outdoor solaria provide comfortable deck chairs.

Few visitors pass up the everlasting joy of selecting souvenirs and forget-Atlantic City-nots. First place among mementoes goes to various knickknacks made of suedelike yellow leather—purses, memorandum books, hanging receptacles for whisk brooms, moccasins, and handkerchief boxes. All, of course, are inscribed *Atlantic City;* each souvenir store is equipped with tools that can engrave Atlantic City on anything from the back of a turtle to a steel plate. Next in popularity are seashells ranging from common clams to exotic crenulated oddities.

Young honeymooners are the most lavish buyers of mementoes. They buy something for everyone back home and have each piece suitably inscribed: "To Mother, from Anna and Joe"; "To Grandma, from Anna and Joe"; "To Brother Pete, from Anna and Joe," and so on down the family tree. One favorite item is a gaudy pillow slip embroidered with a picture of a little cottage surrounded by flowers growing out of an orange lawn cut down the center by a green path. Beneath the cottage scene is an appropriate bit of verse:

To one who bears the sweetest name,
And adds a lustre to the same,
Who shares my joys—
Who cheers when sad—
The greatest friend I ever had.
Long life to her for there's no other
Can take the place of my dear

MOTHER
Atlantic City, N. J.

The summer millions dwindle to winter thousands, and the pace of Atlantic City perceptibly slows down after the annual September beauty pageant. It is then that the city wins its reputation as a health resort. To benefit from the mild climate and healthful sea air come elderly folk, who find respite from cold winters on the warm boardwalk and in the chatty living rooms of scores of rooming and boarding houses. The city becomes more sophisticated as a more urban group of business and professional people arrive to catch an off-season vacation. On the winter holidays and during the frequent conventions, however, there is a sharp, sudden return to the carnival summertime spirit, disconcerting indeed to the entrenched oldsters.

Backstage of the boardwalk, there is a gradual falling from the splendor of Atlantic City's front. Narrow side streets leading from the beach are crowded with phalanxes of small hotels, boarding houses, restaurants, and saloons. The majority are frame buildings and, unlike the boardwalk, recall that Atlantic City was founded in mid-Victorian times.

The first longitudinal street that parallels the boardwalk is Pacific Avenue, a heavy traffic thoroughfare. Here, among restaurants and small retail shops, stand many of Atlantic City's civic and religious buildings. A feature of this street is the jitney service, a steady stream of touring cars that pick up passengers at designated corners and carry them to any destination on Pacific Avenue for 10¢. For an additional 10¢ the driver will deviate into side streets.

Atlantic Avenue, second street from the boardwalk and paralleling it, is the city's chief business section. This is the one street where visitors can forget that they are in America's leading seashore resort, for it is much like the main streets of other cities of the same size. It is broad, and its many large buildings, including the city's one metropolitan department store, impart an air of mature solidity. Westward Atlantic Avenue abruptly becomes the Chelsea residential section, where large villas and attractive bungalows are fronted with well-tended lawns.

North of Atlantic Avenue the city deteriorates into a dingy section somewhat improved by recent slum clearance and street repairing. This is the Northside, home of Atlantic City's Negro inhabitants—23 percent of the total population and, next to that of Newark, the most important Negro population of the State. They form a reservoir of cheap labor for the hotels, amusement piers, restaurants, riding academies, and private homes.

In addition to the large group of unskilled workers there are many professional and business people. The colony supports 15 churches, a Y.M.C.A., a Y.W.C.A., a special playground, a public library branch, and *The Eagle,* a weekly newspaper. They have three elementary schools, and hold positions in the city and county governments. By tacit understanding the Negroes frequent certain portions of the beach at certain hours.

At the Inlet in the northeastern end of the city are several basins and harbors where pleasure craft and the fishing fleet tie up. The city's fishing industry, third largest of the State with approximately 3,000,000 pounds shipped annually, predates the amusement business. Every afternoon at about 4:30 the fleet of some two-score 50-foot boats brings in the catch. An even greater income, however, is obtained from the renting of boats and crew for pleasure fishing.

The history of Atlantic City is a fabulous success story of a city that knew what it wanted to be from its very infancy. Before 1852, when construction of the Camden and Atlantic Railroad began, Atlantic City was an island waste 5 miles off the mainland and separated from it by a series of bays, sounds, and salt meadows. It was known as Absecon (Ind., *place of swans*) Island or Absecon Beach where, historians say, "The frequency of shipwrecks and the undisturbed isolation of the island must have made it an attractive spot for refugees from war or justice." One historian repeats a story "that in the cupola of the first church . . . was stationed a look-out during the hour of service to acquaint the congregation of a vessel drifting in, in order that the Barnegat and Brigantine Beach people should not forestall them in reaching the scene of disaster and appropriating the best of what the waves would wash in."

Once the climate and beach of the Island were appraised, it was not long before a railroad from Camden was under construction. The railroad company assigned one of its engineers, Richard B. Osborne, to lay out the city. To the streets running across from the beach to the marshes he gave the names of the States; for those paralleling the beach he borrowed the names of seven seas: Atlantic, Pacific, Arctic, Baltic, Adriatic, Mediterranean, Caspian. Let Mr. Osborne give his own reasons: "Its proud name is for the nation; it has made her prominent, and will, every year of her existence, prove more and more appropriate as she reaches her manifest destiny—the first, most popular, most health-giving and most inviting watering-place . . ."

The year 1854 was a crowded one. The city was incorporated March 3. At the first election 18 of the 21 voters pushed their ballots through the slot of a cigar box, fastened with tape. In the same year the first train arrived from Camden, bringing 600 passengers. Many dined at a still uncompleted hotel. Other hotels were soon being built.

Meanwhile the Camden and Atlantic Land Company had bought land at $17.50 an acre and, as a contemporary newspaper reported, planned "to sell it some day for as high as $500 per lot." By 1877 the pressure of traffic was so great that a second railroad to Camden, 54 miles away, was built in the fast time of 98 days. This was known as the Narrow Gauge Railroad because of its 3½-foot gauge, 14 inches less than standard. The

West Jersey Railroad, known as the Electric, opened in 1906; it now maintains only a daily run to Newfield.

The boardwalk was the joint conception in 1870 of a local hotel man, Jacob Keim, and a conductor on the Camden and Atlantic, Alexander Boardman. They agreed that the beach was the principal attraction of Atlantic City and noticed that this attraction was nullified by cool or cloudy weather. They had their fellow citizens sign a petition to council, and on June 26, 1870, the first boardwalk was completed. It was set directly upon the sands, and was only 8 feet wide. The present structure, the fifth, dates from 1896.

The next milestone in the history of the resort was the invention of the rolling chair in 1884. M. D. Shill, a Philadelphia manufacturer of invalid chairs, gocarts and perambulators, came to Atlantic City and opened a store to rent out baby carriages to summer families. He also rented out invalid chairs for convalescents and cripples. Within a few years these invalid chairs evolved into the double chair with a pusher. Triple chairs followed, completing the fleet of comfortable sightseeing chairs of today.

In 1895 the picture postcard was naturalized in Atlantic City. In that year the wife of Carl M. Voelker, a local resident, visited Germany and returned with the idea. Mr. Voelker turned them out in his printing shop as an advertising medium for the beach front hotels, and the fad spread across the country.

During these late years of the nineteenth century the making of salt water taffy became a thriving industry. The name was derived from association rather than ingredients. The product is really a form of pulled taffy and is sold now by three large firms operating chains of stores along the boardwalk.

Atlantic City's showmanship achieved real individuality with the creation of the amusement pier, the first of which was built in 1882. The economic principle was the same as that of the skyscraper, except that it operated horizontally, the aim being to occupy little space on the boardwalk, yet to pack as much amusement behind the entrances as was physically possible. After the first of these ingenious structures dipped its spindly legs into the Atlantic's surf, others followed quickly. Their construction was facilitated, it is said, through the accidental discovery of a Negro laborer, who, while working in Delaware Bay, noticed the effect of water running swiftly from a hose upon the sand. His discovery of jetting was used in sinking foundation piles for the piers.

With the establishment of the amusement pier, Atlantic City's mold was almost unalterably shaped. Since the turn of the century the resort has largely devoted itself to improving and modernizing the basic amusement equipment and refining its technique of entertainment.

The city has shown itself determined to preserve an individuality, in spite of, or because of, its estimated 16,250,000 visitors. It retains the adopted metropolitan way of referring to streets as "blocks" instead of the South Jersey-Philadelphia "squares." It has capitalized on its latitudinal southern location to simulate a Dixie hospitality.

Politically and commercially it has become the vortex of eastern South

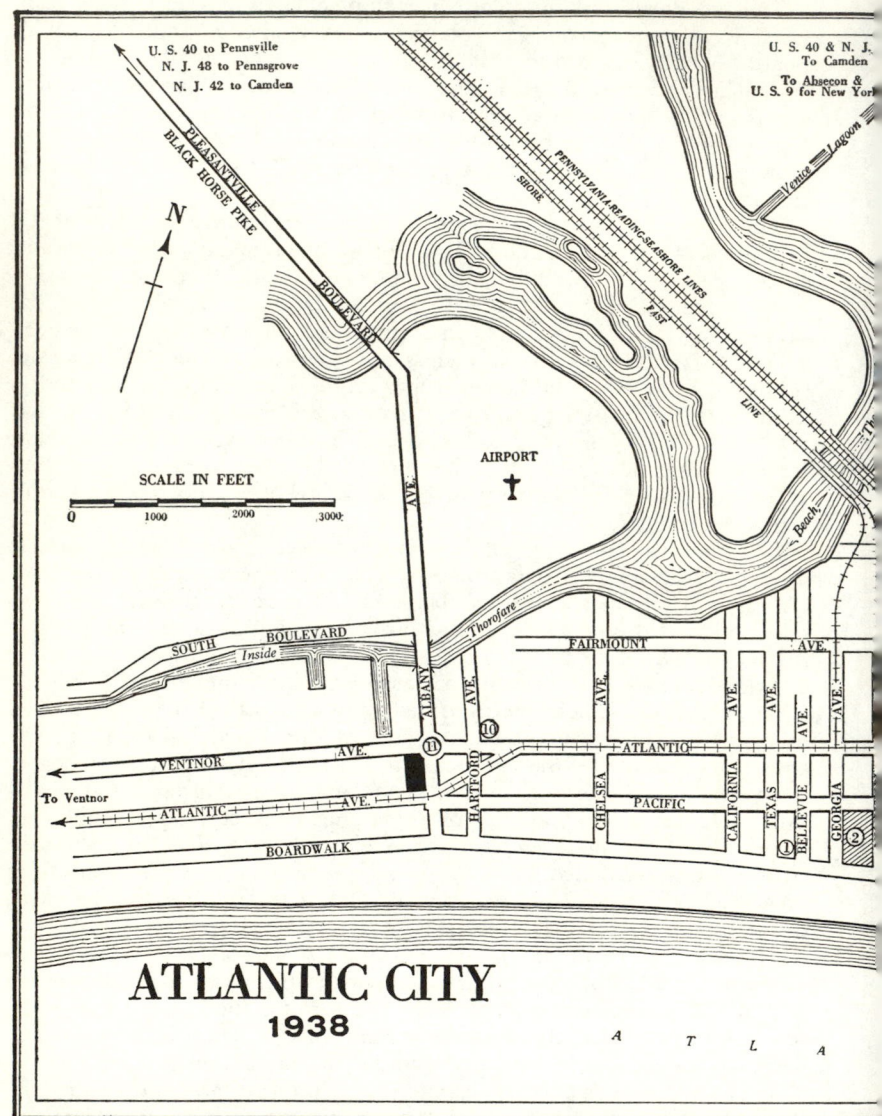

ATLANTIC CITY
1938

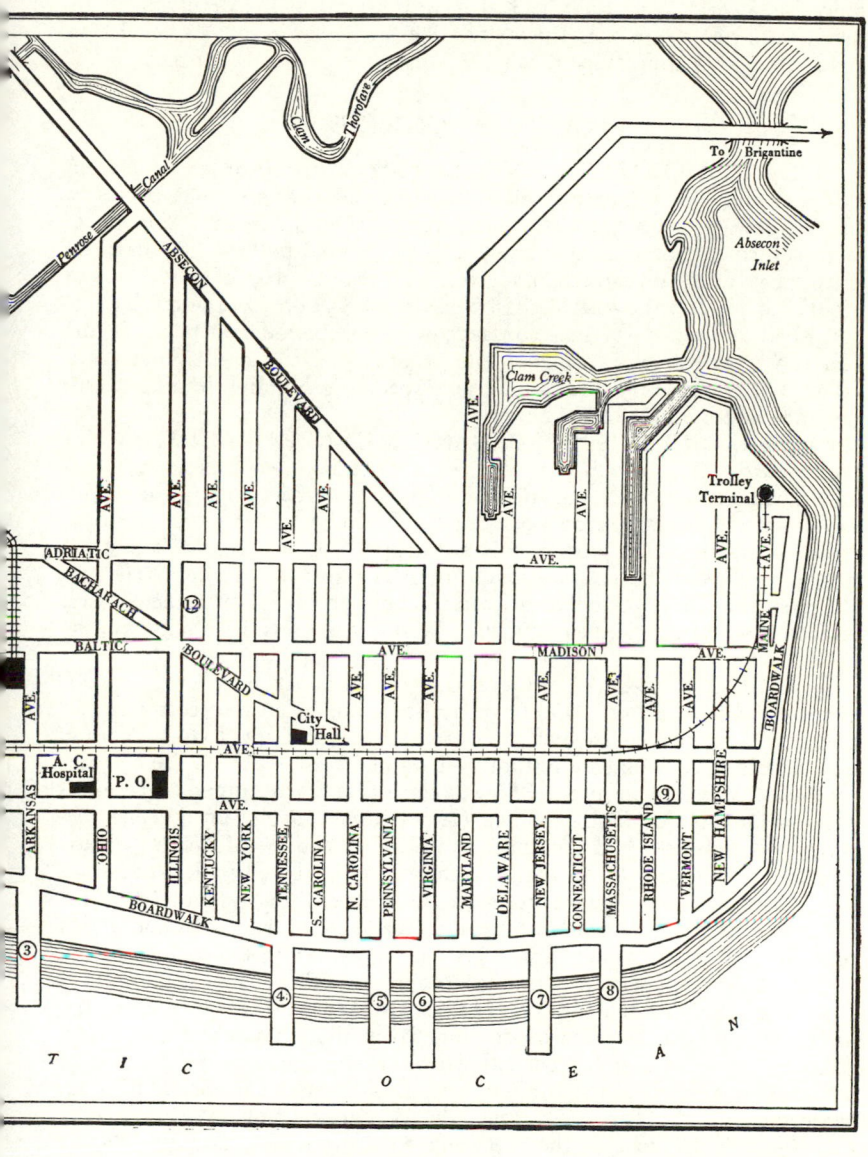

Jersey. Although Mays Landing is the county seat of Atlantic County, officials transact most of their business in branch offices at Atlantic City. Since the World War, civic leaders have encouraged the development of manufacturing, aware that their city, like any large resort, is subject to sudden loss of public favor through epidemics or natural disasters.

POINTS OF INTEREST

1. The MODEL AMERICAN VILLAGE, on the Boardwalk between Bellevue and Texas Aves., displays three houses, set at various angles to the "Highway," on a large semicircular lawn. One house is Tudor in design, constructed of masonry; another is a frame Cape Cod Colonial; the third is a frame and stucco modern type. The number of rooms varies from 7 to 12, and the cost of the houses from $5,000 to $15,000. Each is furnished and equipped in accordance with the period and price. In the rear is a town hall with stores on the ground floor and a village green in front. The exhibit is sponsored and equipped by a hundred leading manufacturers and builders of the country.

2. The CONVENTION HALL AND MUNICIPAL AUDITORIUM *(tours with official guides hourly, 25¢)*, on the Boardwalk between Georgia and Mississippi Aves., is said to be the largest of its kind in the world. Its auditorium seats 41,000 persons; the ballroom accommodates 5,000. An organ with 32,000 pipes, also a world's record, has been built into the structure. During the year the auditorium is transformed alternately into an ice-skating rink, a football gridiron, a polo and horse-show field and a steeplechase course. RADIO STATION WPG maintains its studio on the upper floor.

3. MILLION DOLLAR PIER, Boardwalk and Arkansas Ave. *(one admission price for all attractions)*, is 1,700 ft. long and the second largest pier in the city. It was named by its original owner, Capt. John L. Young, now deceased, as soon as a million dollars had been spent on the still uncompleted structure in 1906. In 1938 the name was changed to Hamid's Million Dollar Pier. The captain's former home *(open)* on the pier, beyond the beach line, had the unusual post office address of No. 1 Atlantic Ocean. The house is three stories high, and is equipped with a conservatory. Shrubbery and flowers grow in the surrounding garden. From the ocean end of the pier a fish net haul is made twice daily, at noon and 4 p.m. Species of fish which find their way into the big net include shark, tarpon, drumfish, barracuda, ray, sea robin, and others.

4. The CENTRAL PIER *(free)*, Boardwalk and Tennessee Ave., has in recent years concentrated on commercial exhibits. Once the city's longest pier (2,700 ft.), it has been destroyed three times by fire and is now less than one-third of its original length. The chief current exhibits include those of the Texas Company, the Beechnut Company, the Atlantic City Convention Bureau, the Encyclopaedia Britannica, and the Bicycle Trades Exhibit. There is also an arcade of small shops.

5. The STEEPLECHASE PIER *(free)*, Boardwalk and Pennsylvania Ave., caters to children with swings, merry-go-rounds, and other juvenile

THE MUNICIPAL AUDITORIUM, ATLANTIC CITY

amusement. It was built 800 ft. long in 1890, destroyed by fire in 1932, and rebuilt to 1,500 ft. to serve as a fishing and yachting center. It was originally George Tilyou's "Funny Place" where Coney Island oddities were burlesqued.

6. The STEEL PIER *(one admission price for all attractions)*, Boardwalk and Virginia Ave., is 2,000 ft. long, the largest of all. Among its novelties are three diving horses that, four times a day, gallop up a runway 45 ft. high and dive into a pool of water, a girl rider perched on each back. The late Dr. W. F. Carver, an Indian scout, originated this spectacular entertainment 50 years ago. His daughter now trains the horses. Other attractions are two movie houses and a zoo for baby animals.

7. The GARDEN PIER *(free)*, Boardwalk and New Jersey Ave., looks like the oldest but is actually the youngest pier on the boardwalk. It was built in 1915 and its incongruous Spanish architecture is somewhat atoned for by its fireproof construction. Garden Pier specializes in public entertainment; it provides bimonthly boxing and wrestling and semiprofessional basketball in the winter, and stage shows and occasionally opera in the summer.

8. The HEINZ PIER *(free)*, Boardwalk and Massachusetts Ave., is the highbrow of the boardwalk. Operated since 1898 by the canned-food producer, it features art exhibits, lectures, and educational-promotional displays. A series of eight model kitchens includes the little Dutch Kitchen,

the English, the Spanish of Don Quixote's time, the American of the time of Evangeline, the Civil War, and the modern dietary laboratory.

9. The ABSECON LIGHTHOUSE *(not open)*, Pacific and Rhode Island Aves., is the Eiffel Tower of Atlantic City—wherever the visitor looks he sees the 167-ft. structure, much like an oversize factory chimney with a glass cage perched on top. When erected in 1854 it stood 1,300 ft. from the water front. Within the next few years the Atlantic began to encroach on the shore line until the waves broke within 75 ft. of the lighthouse. Massive stone jetties were built to protect it, and as a result the ocean retreated until now it is two long blocks away. The light was abandoned in 1932.

10. The MASONIC TEMPLE, NE. corner Hartford and Ventnor Aves., is a square four-story building of Byzantine architecture, constructed of limestone and marble. The façade is adorned with six massive engaged columns. The cornerstone was cut from marble brought from the legendary quarries of King Solomon.

11. The WORLD WAR MEMORIAL, corner Albany and Ventnor Aves., is an open circular cella, with surrounding peristyle of Doric columns, designed by Carrere and Hastings. The marble walls are pierced with four doors; in the center is a heroic bronze monument, *Liberty in Distress*. The work of Frederick W. MacMonnies, it is a reproduction of the sculptor's work at Varredes, France, commemorating the first battle of the Marne. Liberty, naked but for knotted garments hanging from her elbows, her feet mired in writhen corpses, supports an inert male figure across her right thigh. Her distress is the one matter about which there is no question whatever.

12. STANLEY S. HOLMES VILLAGE *(open)*, Illinois and Baltic Aves., is the first slum clearance project attempted in New Jersey, and alleviates to a slight degree the housing conditions of Atlantic City's Negroes. Continuous structures of red brick, two and three stories high, contain 277 apartments and cover three square blocks. The buildings have large windows with steel frames, a central heating plant, and entrances that lead to the street and to spacious courts in the rear. The average rental (including gas, electricity, heat and janitor service) is $8.08 per month for each room. Tenants are selected from self-sustaining families only.

The village has been 100 percent occupied since one month after its opening on April 16, 1937. Considered one of the most successful projects in the country, it returned more than 10 percent over the cost of operation during its first 14½ months. Rental arrears amounting to $117.49 in June 1938 have since been paid up.

POINTS OF INTEREST IN ENVIRONS

Somers Mansion, *18.7 m. (see Tour 18)*; Batsto, *30 m.*, Pleasant Mills, *30.3 m. (see Side Tour 23A)*; pine and cedar swamps, *32.9 m. (see Tour 35)*.

Bayonne

Railroad Station: W. 8th St. and Ave. C. for Jersey Central R.R.
Buses: Fare 5¢.
Streetcars and Busses: Fare 5¢.
Taxis: Fare 35¢ within city limits.
Ferry: S. end of Ave. C for Electric Ferry to Staten Island; car and passengers 25¢, pedestrians 5¢.
Toll Bridge: Hudson County Blvd. and W. 7th St. for Staten Island; car and passengers 50¢, pedestrians 5¢.
Traffic Regulations: On Boulevard, stop on nearest corner on red or amber light; 1-hour parking in business district (Broadway) between 9 a.m. and 6 p.m.

Accommodations: Rooming houses.

Information Service: Chamber of Commerce, 51 E. 22nd St.

Motion Picture Houses: Six.
Swimming: Bayonne Y.M.C.A., W. 33rd St. between Ave. C and Boulevard; Industrial Y.M.C.A., 259 Ave. E; open-air pool, W. 63rd St. and Boulevard; Newark Bay at County Park, Ave. C and W. 40th St.
Tennis: City Park at W. 18th St.; County Park, Ave. C and W. 40th St.
Baseball: City Stadium, W. 14th St. and Ave. A.

BAYONNE (40 alt., 88,979 pop.) is the eastern end of the Nation's longest oil-pipe lines—the oil-refining center of the State. It is an isolated community of low, crowded buildings, lying on the tip of the peninsula that separates New York Bay from Newark Bay. Although it is closer to New York than are Newark or Elizabeth, it lags in reflecting the influence of the metropolis. Bayonne, in fact, at present has no hotel. Houses pack the streets so tightly that there is not even space for a cemetery.

On all sides but its northern boundary, where it merges into Jersey City, Bayonne is surrounded by water. On the map the city looks like a boot. The toe is Constable Hook and it juts into New York Bay where oil tankers rock at company wharves. The sole of the boot is Kill van Kull. The heel is Virgin Point, where Kill van Kull joins Newark Bay.

Physiographically the city strings its three-mile length along a ridge that follows closely the straight shore line of Newark Bay and then slopes easily to the low marshy shores of New York Bay. Hudson Boulevard, running along the ridge from Jersey City to Kill van Kull, borders the eastern edge of the better residential district, which stretches along the high ground above Newark Bay. Bisecting the industrial section built along the foot portion of the boot, the boulevard crosses Bayonne Bridge into Staten Island. The business center, paralleling the boulevard, is part way down the slope.

Outside the magnificent view across Newark Bay clear to Newark and Elizabeth, Bayonne has little of the unusual to offer the sightseeing visitor except the amazing oil-refinery section on Constable Hook. This is worth a visit if the sightseer has the patience and courage to thread its mazes, and the foresight to secure a pass that will admit him to the inner secrets of an oil refinery. The approach is by 22nd Street, which starts from Hudson Boulevard on the heights and descends across streets of retail stores, through a minor industrial and tenement district, and then loses itself in a thick forest of what appear to be gargantuan steel mushrooms. These are the oil tanks of America's major refineries, receiving crude petroleum pumped in unbroken streams from pipe lines that go through the Alleghanies to Pennsylvania, and Ohio, and under the Mississippi River as far west as Oklahoma and Texas. In Bayonne the crude oil is broken down or "cracked" into crude petroleum, gasoline, kerosene, naphtha, vaseline, various tars and pitches, and a host of minor products (such as chemicals and drugs) that emerge into common use under disguises that only scientists understand.

Most of the district is fenced off into carefully guarded areas owned and developed by the various refineries. A few of the smaller refineries are open to visitors on application at the gate. To enter the more spectacular major ones, however, one must obtain permits in advance, generally from headquarters in New York City. The New York offices are frequently willing to admit large parties under guides, but visitors are never allowed to wander at will. There are various causes for this intensive guarding. The nature of many refinery products is such that a careless sightseer with a cigarette could blow Bayonne into New York Bay; further, some of the processes are secret. The major refineries themselves are carefully planned miniature cities containing stores, community houses, first-aid hospitals, and restaurants for the use of the thousands of employees.

Other water-front factories produce chemicals, garments, cork, cables, yachts, and metal and food products. The business section stretches for twenty blocks along Broadway, a wide street packed with small food, clothing and accessory stores. Tall buildings and smart shops are lacking; Bayonne's merchants sell to workers. It is first of all a workingman's city, and its localized industries are attuned to this basic fact; so also are its recreations and its civic life, in which latter phase the labor question most naturally prevails. The city traditionally is open shop, but the bulk of the working population is organized either in company or in independent unions.

The homes in the better residential section consist of one- or two-family frame houses set well back from the sidewalk, with trees and close-cropped lawns. Most of them date from the building boom that followed the World War. On Newark Bay, adjoining a residential area, are city and county parks attractively landscaped with paths and drives, offering unexpected contrast to the industrial development close by.

The majority of the more than 22,500 foreign-born live on the eastern edge of the city in small frame structures, many with additions that obviously were home-made. Small truck gardens and grape vines in the backyards are a link to agricultural home countries. Poles predominate, with Italians, Russians, Irish, and Czechs following in that order. To many of the police and firemen English is a secondary language, spoken with a heavy foreign accent. Even the children speak with a distinctive inflection.

Prominent in the recreational life of the working population is the Industrial Y.M.C.A., erected with contributions from all the industries of Bayonne. It has a membership of 1,600. The "Y" sponsors, at a small cost to parents, a summer camp in Hunterdon County.

Bayonne is divided in its own estimate of itself. The difference may be illustrated by two examples: trucks of a furniture store carry huge signs which say that Bayonne has the "finest shops" and "the finest school teachers." On the other hand, a newspaper report of a 1936 meeting to protest high taxes and bonded indebtedness was headlined: "WHERE IS BAYONNE GOING? TO THE DOGS, SOME SAY."

Nothing remains in the city to recall its settlement. In March 1646, thirty-seven years after Henry Hudson stopped at the site of Bayonne before his sail up Hudson River, Jacob Jacobsen Roy, a gunner at New Amsterdam, received patent to a tract of land, called after him Konstapel's Hoeck (Dutch, *gunner's point*). Other grants were not issued until December 1654; a year later shelters were built as centers for Indian trading. Shortly after, the Indians, enraged at the Dutch trading tactics, drove out the settlers. Resettlement was made several years after the Dutch made a treaty with the tribesmen in 1658.

The peninsula was called Constable Hook when the British gained control of it in 1664, and later it became Bergen Neck. Trading shacks and forest gave way to homes and large estates. During the next century, the area became a pleasure center for the socialites of the New World.

Separated as it was from New Jersey's mainland and New York, Bayonne was the scene of only a few unimportant skirmishes during the Revolution. With the War of 1812 came the first industrial plant, the Hazard Powder House, which produced some powder for the Navy and for the forts in New York Bay.

To speed the movement of troops and munitions during the Civil War, the first railroad trestle was built across Newark Bay from Elizabethport, which until 1864 was the railhead.

In 1869 the township, which comprised Constable Hook, Bergen Point, Centerville, and Saltersville, was incorporated as the City of Bayonne with a population of 4,000.

The establishment of the Prentice refinery in 1875 marked the beginning of the city's change. The concern employed 20 men and produced 600 barrels of kerosene daily. The rural atmosphere gave way to increasing industrial clatter as in rapid succession the Standard Oil Company, the Tide Water Oil Company and other refineries, attracted by the natural advantages of the location, moved in. Four docks were constructed to take care of increasing tonnage; railroad tracks were laid; and pipe lines were built to bring crude oil directly from Oklahoma and from Illinois. Kerosene was the chief product of the cracking stills, with greases and lubricating oils as byproducts. Pollution from gasoline products, at first generally dumped into the bay, spoiled swimming and fishing.

Several times the Bayonne water front has blazed with spectacular oil fires, one of which (1900) lasted for three days. The last big fire was in 1930, when 18 tanks and dockage facilities of the Gulf Refining Company were destroyed by fire and a series of explosions with a $3,000,000 loss. Blazing barges drifted into New York Harbor, pursued by fireboats and tugs.

Twice the Standard Oil plant was the scene of strikes that left a heavy toll of dead and wounded among the employees. In 1915 one hundred still cleaners, striking for overtime pay, were joined by 5,000 other workers. At an expense of $250,000, the company called in a strikebreaking organization led by Pearl Bergoff. Five men were killed by police or imported strike guards. Sheriff Eugene F. Kinkead arrested the strike leader, J. J. Baly, and, when the strike was almost ended, he jailed 99 special company guards. The company finally yielded a small increase, but wages still remained below the prevailing level.

A year later the workers struck for a 30 percent wage increase for men earning less than $3 a day and a 20 percent rise for all others. The result was another series of battles that left eight workers dead and twenty-five seriously hurt. Strikers complained that their leaders were hampered in entering the city and that some of their local sympathizers were forced to leave their homes. The strike ended with nothing gained. Afterward Standard Oil became one of the pioneers in establishing a company union, or employees' representation system.

Although seven refining companies pay an estimated 41 percent to the city's property tax income, Bayonne residents bear a tax rate of $51.87 (1938). The bonded indebtedness is close to the statutory limit.

One of the strangest strikes in the history of the city began in the fall of 1937 when eight members of the American Newspaper Guild walked out of the Bayonne *Times* office after the publisher failed to put a wage and hour agreement into effect. Most of the leading Bayonne merchants and thousands of citizens gave their support to the small band of strikers, who finally won a sweeping victory despite a Chancery Court injunction that practically prohibited any strike activities.

POINTS OF INTEREST

1. BAYONNE BRIDGE *(toll: car and passengers 50¢, pedestrians 5¢)*, Hudson County Blvd. and W. 7th St., is the longest steel arch span in the world, exceeding a similar structure at Sydney, Australia, by 25 feet. Resting on the subsurface rock at the southern end of the Palisades, it sweeps across the Kill van Kull in a single span of 1,675 feet to Staten Island. The bridge deck is 150 feet above high water; beneath it passes a steady procession of tugs, lighters, oil tankers and freighters. For beauty of design its gray arch is rivaled in the metropolitan area only by the George Washington Bridge *(see Tour 1)*, a suspension span. Designed by Othman H. Ammann and Leon Moisseiff, the structure cost $16,000,000. Since its opening in 1931, traffic has not been great enough to take care of the carrying charges.

2. TRINITY EPISCOPAL CHURCH, Broadway and 5th St., was

BAYONNE BRIDGE OVER KILL VAN KULL

erected in 1881 after the burning of an earlier edifice. Built in the Victorian Gothic style from plans by E. J. N. Stent, the rough brownstone building was the scene in 1887 of the wedding of Nicholas Murray Butler, then a young tutor in philosophy at Columbia University, to Susanna Edwards Schuyler, daughter of the church's chief benefactor. Another prominent church member was Henry Meigs, first mayor of Bayonne and a president of the New York Stock Exchange. Early in 1938 the church attained new distinction when the rector, the Reverend William C. Kernan, opened the parish hall for a speech barred from practically every other hall in Hudson County: an address by Roger Baldwin, director of the American Civil Liberties Union, and a spearhead in the attack on Mayor Frank Hague of Jersey City for his campaign against trade union organizers.

3. ELCO WORKS *(open 9-5 weekdays)*, Ave. A and North St., is the oldest and largest builder of standardized cruisers in the United States. In the long, low building along Newark Bay are built small motorboats and 125-foot yachts with a complete series of intermediate sizes. During the World War, Elco built 722 submarine chasers. Organized in 1892, the company's first big job was the construction of 55 electric launches for the lagoons at the Chicago World's Fair in 1893.

Bordentown

Railroad Station: Pennsylvania Station, W. end Park St., for Pennsylvania R.R.
Bus Stations: 201 Main St., for Safeway Trailways; 200 Farnsworth Ave. for Public Service; Bordentown Grill for Martz Lines.
Accommodations: One hotel.
Motion Picture Houses: One.
Swimming: Delaware River, north of town.
Golf: Sunnybrae Golf Club, 3 m. NE. on State 39, 18 holes, greens fees 50¢; Sat., Sun. and holidays $1.

BORDENTOWN (65 alt., 4,400 pop.), a wind-swept village on a bluff rising sharply from the Delaware River, has a nineteenth century air, and a curious mingling of European and early American architecture. The tone of the village, set a century ago by exiled Bonapartist royalty, lingers in the town's half-secluded atmosphere.

The main community occupies its Revolutionary site and in some respects the appearance has changed but little. Houses are built flush with the red brick sidewalks, and often with no space between them. Where a narrow passage does permit a view of the rear, gardens of boxwood and evergreens are glimpsed. Many of the homes are of Colonial design, wooden or brick, with shuttered windows; others show Continental influence in their stucco exteriors and wrought-iron railings and trim. The colors of the town are pastel, as though faded by sun and wind; grays, yellows, creams, and browns predominate.

Conflicting with Bordentown's mellow charm is its small business center of conventional, suburban-type stores, in the very heart of which is a building with a perfect example of a Colonial doorway and delicately lined fanlight.

Along the bluff overlooking Delaware River the old houses are surrounded by gardens and fine trees: evergreens, sycamores, maples, willows and elms. The gardens, all extending to the edge of the bluff, have tiny summerhouses where the grandees of former days watched their own vessels and goods passing in the river and canal. Some of these houses on the bluff resemble the "pepper boxes" of the New England coast—two-storied square dwellings with flat roofs topped by a small watchtower. On a few of the most imposing, small signs read, "Apartments to let."

The tracks of a Pennsylvania Railroad branch lie in a deep and narrow cut through the center of the town; another track hugs the base of the bluff.

Settled in 1682 by Thomas Farnsworth, an English Quaker, the village was first known as Farnsworth's Landing. It became a busy shipping center, thanks to its location at the confluence of Delaware River and Crosswicks Creek. By 1734 the Landing had a stage line and packet service, making connections at Philadelphia and at Perth Amboy for the New York boat. This enterprise was established by Joseph Borden, for whom the town was soon named.

The pleasant site attracted the fashionables of Philadelphia as summer visitors. Among the Morrises, the Shippens, the Chews, the Norrises, and the Hopkinsons a gracious social life developed.

Patience Lovell (1725–1785), born in Bordentown of Quaker parentage, began as a child to model in bread crumbs and clay. As a young woman she went abroad to study art, but it was not until she was 47 and a widow with four children that her work received recognition. She won international attention for her figures in wax, notably one of Sir William Pitt which was placed in Westminster Abbey.

Bordentown was severely punished by the British for the famous "mechanical keg plot" of the Revolution. In January 1778 the British fleet was anchored in the Delaware at Philadelphia. One night the patriots upstream launched a flotilla of kegs filled with gunpowder, depending upon the river current to carry them to the fleet, which—unknown to the Colonials—had just been removed from its exposed position. Only one of the primitive mines exploded, but it killed four men and created a panic among the British. Thereafter every piece of flotsam was viewed with suspicion and orders were given to fire without warning upon any unidentified log, keg or barrel.

The mechanical kegs had been built in the cooperage of Col. Joseph Borden. It was his son-in-law, the talented Francis Hopkinson, who promptly wrote one of the best jingles of the Revolution, *The Battle of the Kegs,* 22 verses that were published throughout the Colonies and caused some British officers to wear countenances no less scarlet than their uniforms:

> Gallants, attend, and hear a friend
> Trill forth harmonious ditty:
> Strange things I'll tell, which late befell
> In Philadelphia city.
>
> 'Twas early day, as poets say,
> Just when the sun was rising,
> A soldier stood on log of wood,
> And saw a thing surprising.
>
>   *   *   *
>
> Sir William he, snug as a flea,
> Lay all this time a snoring;
> Nor dream'd of harm, as he lay warm
> In bed with Mrs. L——.
>
>   *   *   *
>
> Arise, arise! Sir Erskine cries;
> The rebels—more's the pity—
> Without a boat are all afloat,
> And rang'd before the city.
>
>   *   *   *
>
> The cannons roar from shore to shore;
> The small-arms loud did rattle;
> Since wars began, I'm sure no man
> E'er saw so strange a battle.

Angered no less by Hopkinson's verses than by the plot to blow up the fleet, the British sent 5 armed vessels and 24 flat-bottomed boats with about 800 soldiers to Bordentown in May 1778. At their approach, the townspeople destroyed more than 20 American vessels that had been lying at the White Hill. Disappointed, the British turned on the town and razed the home and store of Colonel Borden. As the colonel's wife sat in the middle of the street and watched the destruction, a British officer expressed his sympathy. The proud old lady retorted: ". . . This is the happiest day of my life. I know you have given up all hope of reconquering my country, or you would not thus wantonly devastate it." Before they left the British also burned two Continental galleys that had been moored up Crosswicks Creek.

Thomas Paine, the firebrand of the Revolution, made his home in Bordentown with Col. Joseph Kirkbride in 1783 before buying his own house. Here he received a cordial invitation from Washington to visit him at Rocky Hill. Paine had been virtually ignored, and Washington hoped thus to remind Congress of the value of his Revolutionary services.

After Paine had been rewarded by appointments to several responsible positions he was often visited at Bordentown by Benjamin Franklin, Gouverneur Morris, and other distinguished men. The gunsmith and dreamer, John Fitch, came with plans and a proposal of partnership in the building of a steamboat. Although Paine offered mechanical suggestions he was not further interested.

When Paine returned to Europe and became embroiled in the affairs of the French Revolution he still held an affectionate memory of Bordentown. In one letter he wrote: ". . . my heart and myself are three thousand miles apart; and I had rather see my horse, Button, eating the grass of Bordentown, than see all the show and pomp of Europe."

Following his escape from the guillotine and the publication of the *Age of Reason,* Paine again sought the comfort of the pleasant river town and, more particularly, of his friend, Colonel Kirkbride. His liberal religious views had outraged most of his former admirers, and there were few who cared or dared to greet him. But Colonel Kirkbride welcomed his old friend—only to flee with him from a mob of jeering pursuers who forced their way into the quiet garden and literally ran Paine out of town.

In the summer of 1790 the townspeople gathered on the bluff to cheer the first commercially operated steamboat in America. John Fitch, the ridiculed inventor, had at last succeeded in building a steam packet for a service along the Delaware, and Bordentown was a scheduled stop. Two years earlier Fitch had made an experimental trip from Philadelphia to Bordentown.

In 1816 Joseph Bonaparte, exiled King of Spain and brother of Napoleon, bought about 1,500 acres, which he developed into an elaborate estate on the outskirts of the town. No alien was then permitted to own property in the United States, and transference of title was delayed a year pending passage of a special act by the legislature. The little kingdom on the edge of the Delaware River earned for New Jersey the sobriquet of "New Spain."

Bordentown was the scene of a peacetime mechanical feat no less remarkable than the launching of the powder kegs. In 1831 there arrived from England a strange assortment of iron plates, pipes, bolts, nuts, rods, and other parts. These were the makings of the first locomotive to run on the new Camden and Amboy Railroad. To Isaac Dripps, a young mechanic of Bordentown who had never seen a locomotive, fell the task of assembling these parts without the aid of a shop drawing—the only item omitted by the British manufacturers. After 2 weeks of dogged effort, Dripps had the *John Bull* ready for service, and on November 12, 1831, at a point 1 mile northeast of Bordentown, the engine was successfully tested in a run with two coaches filled with distinguished passengers.

Shops employing hundreds of skilled mechanics were established in Bordentown for the construction and repair of locomotives and coaches. Meanwhile the Delaware and Raritan Canal was completed in 1834 from New Brunswick to Bordentown. For the succeeding 30 years the canal as a freight carrier made the town an important water transport center.

Bordentown was incorporated as a borough in 1825, and rechartered as a city in 1867. Population expanded to 6,000 with an influx of Irish and German immigrants, employed on the railroad and canal. As the town changed its character many of the aristocrats left their fine mansions.

In 1871 the Pennsylvania Railroad dealt a double blow to Bordentown. After it had leased both the railroad and the canal, it removed the railroad shops to its own locations in Altoona, Pa., and Newark, and stifled canal commerce by refusing to allow coal to be water-hauled in competition with the railroad. Bordentown has never recovered the commercial importance lost in those years after the Civil War.

In the last 50 years Bordentown's population has increased less than 14 percent and there are fewer inhabitants than during the railroad boom of the 1850's. Industry has hardly disturbed the rural quiet. Small factories produce trousers and overalls, ice cream, dyes, and bricks. The working population includes Negroes, Italians and Jews, many of whom live on the edge of town in nondescript houses, some of them quite old.

POINTS OF INTEREST

1. BONAPARTE PARK *(private)*, N. side of Park St., E. of 3rd St., is a 242-acre remnant of the 1,500-acre tract bought in 1816 by the exiled King Joseph of Spain. The only original building left of the luxurious estate is the GARDENER'S LODGE, near an entrance on Park Street. Vestiges of tunnels and grottoes today offer a contrast to the more modern country residence that has replaced Bonaparte's home.

For 23 years, as the Count de Survilliers, the exile lived here surrounded by a fortune in paintings and sculpture and other treasures, including Napoleon's crown jewels. At Point Breeze, as the estate was called, the ex-King was often host to such American statesmen as Daniel Webster, Henry Clay, and John Quincy Adams, and on Christmas he played Santa Claus for Bordentown's poor children.

Joseph's wife did not follow him to America, but the exile was com-

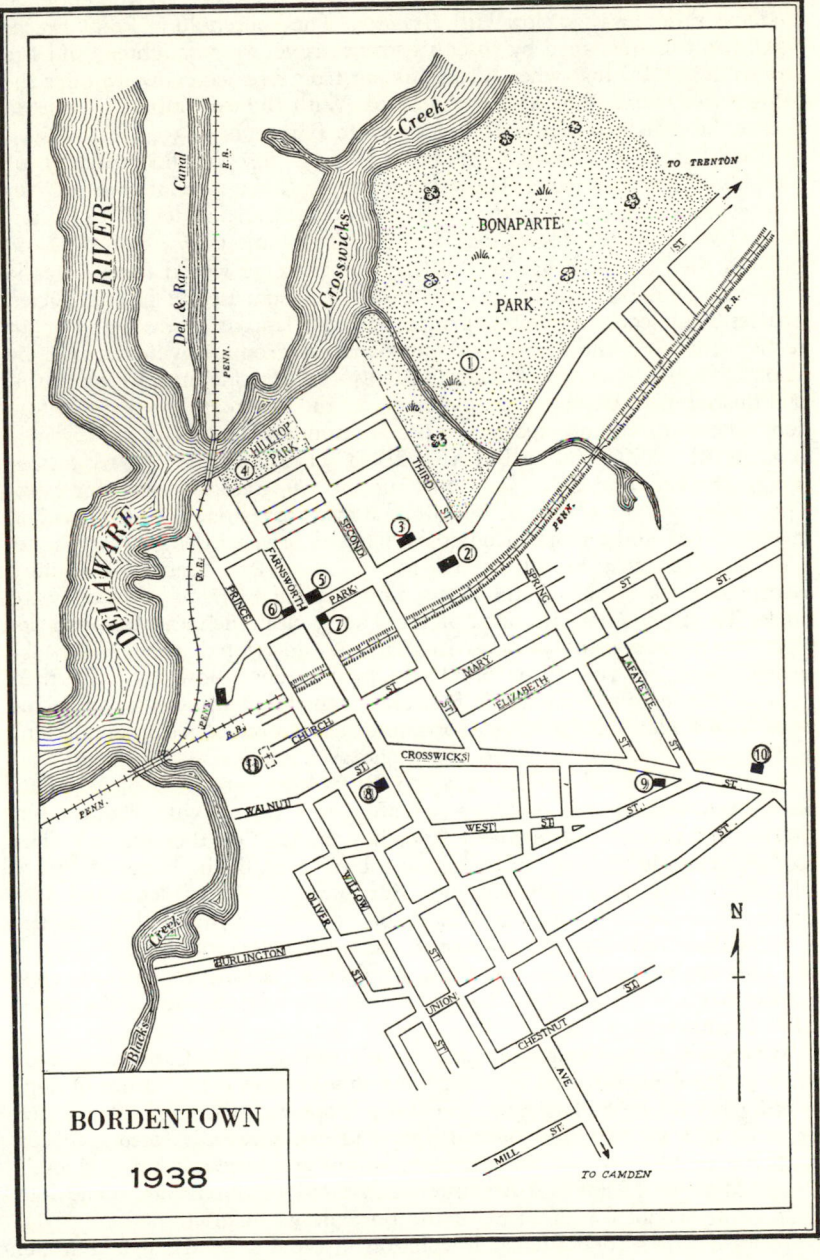

BORDENTOWN

1938

forted in his loneliness by the charming Annette Savage, whom he secluded 7 miles away at Bow Hill, Trenton. The household at Point Breeze was for a time managed by Joseph's vivacious younger daughter; and life was so delightful that when a commission from Mexico called to offer the throne, Bonaparte unhesitatingly refused. With the exception of a trip to France, he remained here until his return to Europe in 1839. Nearby lived Charles Lucien Bonaparte, nephew of King Joseph and husband of Joseph's daughter Zenaide. He was the author of the rare *American Ornithology* (4 vols.) that, together with the work of Alexander Wilson, constituted an important forerunner of Audubon's famous *Birds of America*.

The exiled monarch had hoped that Point Breeze would remain in the family forever. But when it passed to his grandson, Prince Joseph Lucien Charles Napoleon, the young prince sold the land in parcels and at an auction in 1847 the house and surrounding grounds were bought by Thomas Richards, who sold them to Henry Beckett, onetime British consul at Philadelphia. Beckett was nicknamed "the destroyer" when he tore down the mansion and erected the present nondescript dwelling.

2. BORDENTOWN MILITARY INSTITUTE, S. side of Park St. between 3rd and 2nd Sts., is an outstanding preparatory school for boys. The oldest part of the main building, a five-story stone structure with a mansard roof and small balconies over the doorway in the French style, was occupied by a French school for girls in 1837. Later a two-story Georgian brick addition and a two-story Colonial frame addition were made. The 15 smaller buildings of the school, of French and Colonial design, cover a campus of 55 acres. In 1870 a coeducational school was established which, in 1881, was purchased by President Bowen of the then existent Bordentown Female College and opened as a military institute for boys. The students are drilled according to United States Army regulations and prepared for college, West Point and Annapolis.

3. MURAT ROW *(private)*, 49-61 E. Park St., is a row of seven attached two-and-one-half-story houses of yellow stucco, with frame additions at the rear and little covered porches abutting on the sidewalk. The row was remodeled from what was once Linden Hall, the home of Prince Napoleon François Lucien Charles Murat, nephew of Joseph and Napoleon Bonaparte. The young prince, son of Joachim Murat, King of the Two Sicilies, and Caroline Bonaparte, came to America about seven years after his uncle, Joseph. He was a tall, handsome, dashing chap of 20 years, whose magnificent disregard for money cut a wide swathe in the social life of the town.

When his uncle heard of Lucien's elopement with Caroline Fraser, belle of Bordentown, he vowed that she should have the pleasure of supporting his nephew. This was, indeed, a prophetic vow; for after a few years of lavish living the young Prince had exhausted his fortune. Faced with the problem of supporting her children and meeting her husband's debts, Madame Murat and her sisters converted her luxurious home into a boarding school for sub-debs of the Bordentown district.

News of the second French Revolution in 1848 sent Murat to Europe. His cousin Louis Napoleon named him envoy to Turin, and he sent for his family. "Friends . . . had to pay their traveling expenses, and his two little boys were dressed in garments made from a coachman's livery . . ." Napoleon later made Murat a prince, and both his daughters married French noblemen.

4. HILLTOP PARK, N. end Farnsworth Ave., is a small municipal park offering a fine view of the broad Delaware, flowing between wooded banks and disappearing in the green distance. The park is on the bluff, just above Crosswicks Creek and the tracks of the Trenton division of the Pennsylvania Railroad. Parallel to the railroad is the old Delaware and Raritan Canal, sluggish and neglected, its banks overgrown with brush. At this spot were stables for as many as 200 mule teams, motive power for traffic that once numbered 115 barges in a single day. Between the canal and the river is Dike Island, formed by the dredging of the main channel to permit the passage of ocean steamers to Trenton.

5. COLONIAL APARTMENTS *(private)*, 1-3-5 E. Park St., occupy a reconstructed Revolutionary tavern, the American House, which was conducted by Col. Oakly Hoagland of the Continental Army. The original brick has been covered with stucco, but deterioration is evident. Around the second floor runs a decorative iron balcony with a gilded medallion of a woman holding a sheaf of wheat.

6. BORDEN HOUSE *(private)*, 32 Farnsworth Ave., is a stuccoed brick structure, painted a steel gray, with shutters and window trim in contrasting shades. Three chimneys rise from the slate roof. Tall trees cast their shadows on the red brick sidewalk and the three white marble steps with their graceful iron balustrades. Built flush with the sidewalk, the house is flanked on the north and east with a garden enclosed by an ornate iron railing. This is the only survival of the original building erected on this corner by the first Joseph Borden. The old house was demolished by the British in May 1778, and Borden's son erected the present building. From time to time its design has been modified.

7. HOPKINSON HOUSE *(private)*, 101 Farnsworth Ave., was the home of the statesman, Francis Hopkinson. The gable is dated 1750, and the old red brick is mellow with two centuries of weather. A dignified white doorway leads directly off the sidewalk; windows are large and white-shuttered.

Hopkinson married Ann Borden, daughter of Col. Joseph Borden, and in 1773 began the practice of law in Bordentown. He was 35 years old and already distinguished in his profession. At this time he began his career as a political satirist and statesman. After predicting the outbreak of the Revolution in *A Prophecy,* an essay published in 1774, he became a New Jersey representative to the Continental Congress and was one of the State's signers of the Declaration of Independence.

Although Hopkinson served for the first two years of the war as chairman of the Naval Board, he maintained his interest in science and art. Among his varied achievements were a military march in honor of Washington, and the design of the Great Seal of the United States. Recent evidence, consisting of bills approved by the Auditor General, but not passed by Congress, indicates that he was also a designer of the Stars and Stripes.

CLARA BARTON SCHOOL, BORDENTOWN

In one letter Hopkinson asked for a cask of wine for his services; later he raised his request to $7,200. It was rejected because the Treasury insisted that others had shared in the work. In November 1778 he published *Seven Songs,* his best lyric poetry and said to be the first book of music published by an American composer.

The Hopkinsons were not home during the British reprisal for the mechanical keg plot of 1778, but the invaders dined there. One unverified story is that they set fire to the house after removing Hopkinson's reflecting telescope, watchmaker's tools, and other possessions. But the officer in charge, Capt. James Ewald, impressed by the library, decided to overlook the rebel in honor of the scholar, and ordered the firebrands extinguished. After Hopkinson's death in 1791 the house went to his son, Joseph Hopkinson of Philadelphia, best known as the author of *Hail Columbia.*

8. FRIENDS MEETING HOUSE *(not open),* 302 Farnsworth Ave., is a plain brick structure covered with yellow stucco, hidden behind screening shrubbery and crowded between the Bordentown Banking Company building and a row of business places. It was constructed in 1740 as the first place of worship in Bordentown. The banking company has kept the property in good repair, but the church is no longer used.

9. CLARA BARTON SCHOOL *(key at nearby house),* 142 Crosswicks St., is a tiny brick building utilized by Clara Barton for her school. Before

the Revolution it was used as a school supported by fees paid by the parents of the pupils. Clara Barton, later to achieve fame as the founder of the American Red Cross, came to Bordentown in 1851 to teach. Aroused by the lack of schooling for children of the poor, she established in the one-room building a free public school, one of the first in New Jersey and in America. When the townspeople insisted that her work be supervised by a male principal, Miss Barton resigned. In 1921 the building was completely restored with funds given by New Jersey school children. It contains a few pieces of early schoolroom furniture.

10. The GILDER HOUSE *(resident custodian)*, Crosswicks St. opp. Union St., a two-and-one-half-story, white frame Colonial house, was the home in the 1880's of the Gilders—four brothers and a sister who achieved distinction in literature, the arts, and science: Richard Watson Gilder, author, poet and editor of *The Century;* Joseph and Jeannette, editors of *The Critic;* John Francis, composer; and William, geographer and explorer. The house was bequeathed to the city by Rodman Gilder, but a proposed museum has not yet been established.

11. The OLD BURIAL GROUNDS, W. end Church St., are on a hillside overlooking Black's Creek and Delaware River. One of these old cemeteries contains the bodies of early Quakers. Behind Christ Episcopal Church and circled by the other burial plots is the Borden lot, now known as the Hopkinson lot, surrounded by an ornamental fence. Here lie Joseph Borden, founder of the settlement; Joseph Hopkinson, son of Francis; his mother, Ann Borden Hopkinson; and Col. Joseph Kirkbride.

POINTS OF INTEREST IN ENVIRONS

John Bull Monument, *1 m.,* Prince Murat House, *5 m.,* John Woolston House (*c.* 1710), *10.5 m. (see Tour 6);* Jersey Homesteads, *21.1 m. (see Tour 19).*

Burlington

Railroad Station: Pennsylvania Station, Broad and High Sts., for Pennsylvania R.R.
Bus Stations: Broad and High Sts. for Safeway Trailways; 437 High St. for Public Service.
Taxis: 25¢ and up according to distance and number of passengers.
Pier: Town Wharf, N. end High St., ferry to Bristol, Pa., 10¢ for passengers, no automobiles.
Bridge: N. end Reed St. for pedestrians (10¢), N. end Keim Blvd. for automobiles (35¢) to Bristol, Pa.
Traffic Regulations: One-way traffic on Broad St. on each side of railroad track.

Accommodations: Small hotels and tourist houses.

Information Service: Post Office, SW. cor. Broad St. and Locust Ave.

Motion Picture Houses: One.
Swimming: Sylvan Lakes, 1.3 m. S. on Mount Holly Rd.; Delaware River, N. of city.

The identifying mark of BURLINGTON (20 alt., 10,844 pop.) is the single track of the Pennsylvania Railroad that runs through the center of the main street without benefit of curb or fence. In many other respects Burlington seems to have changed little from its eighteenth century character as capital of the Province of West New Jersey. A flourishing maritime center in the early years, Burlington has since been outstripped industrially and commercially by Trenton and Camden. But the town still serves as an outlet and marketing center for the rich agricultural region inland, and it has some industrial importance.

No entrance to Burlington reveals the sequestered charm that is part of the community. The State highway bypasses the town, but a number of roads from north, east, and south cross the adjacent flatlands and tap the business center on Broad Street. Another approach is from Pennsylvania, by way of Bristol Bridge across Delaware River. All of these roads lead past assorted factories and monotonously plain dwellings.

Broad Street deserves its name. There is plenty of room for the leisurely trains of the Pennsylvania and for the long narrow wooden station, like a corncrib, in the heart of the business district. Since 1834 locomotives and trains have operated on Broad Street and for the same length of time the citizens have complained about them. In 1926 the city council ordered removal of the track, but the only progress to date has been restriction of train speeds to 6 miles an hour and a regulation for blowing the whistle.

Many of the business buildings are the old homes of Quakers, modified for offices or stores. Much of their original simplicity of line and material has been retained.

The Colonial portion of Burlington, little changed during the last century, is west of High Street, lying between Broad Street and Delaware River. Back from the river, great trees cast flickering shadows over Colonial houses, patterned brick sidewalks, and narrow streets and alleys. Most of the houses are of red brick, or of brick painted gray or cream. Many are built flush with the sidewalk; stoops of two or three steps with delicate wrought-iron railings lead to graceful doorways with shining brass knockers. In the rear are English style gardens with formal paths, edged in low boxwood.

About 30 percent of the population is foreign-born. Industrial growth has brought in Poles, Italians, and Lithuanians. Southern Negroes, who came about 1900 for work in the iron foundries, comprise 10 percent of the population. Many Burlington people commute to work, some as far as New York. Hundreds are locally employed in a large silk mill, the two iron foundries and other factories.

Burlington still clings to its volunteer fire department. Another venerable civic organization is "The Friendly Institution," a benevolent society founded in 1790 by the Society of Friends for relief of "the worthy poor."

The town owes its existence to the Quakers, whose influence has persisted to the present. Two companies of Friends, one from London and one from Yorkshire, began the settlement in 1677. John Crips, one of the settlers, wrote in that year:

. . . the country and air seems to be very agreeable to our bodies, and we have very good stomachs to our victuals . . . The Indians are very loving to us, except here and there one, when they have gotten strong liquors in their heads, which they now greatly love . . .

During the following year Crips wrote:

. . . I do not remember that ever I tasted better water in any part of England, than the springs of this place do yield; of which is made very good beer and ale; and here is also wine and cyder . . . As for the musketto fly, we are not troubled with them in this place . . .

High Street was laid out with lots to the east for the Yorkshiremen and lots to the west for the men from London. The settlement, first called New Beverly, then Bridlington from the Yorkshire town, finally became Burlington. The land nurtured a steadily growing community and the new town soon took rank as one of the first permanent settlements in the western part of the Colony. The following year the ship *Shield* brought a second company of Quakers. A gristmill and a sawmill were built, and in 1681, after West New Jersey had become a separate province, the Colonial Assembly designated Burlington as the capital and port of entry. The Burlington yearly and quarterly meetings of Friends were established this year.

Burlington was one of the first settlements to provide for public education. In 1682 an act of the assembly gave Matinicunk Island in Delaware River to the town with the stipulation that the revenue be used for the education of youth. The money from farm tenants on the island is still spent for schools.

The first schoolhouse was a Quaker institution. Built in 1792 (now occupied by the Young Women's Christian Association), it was constructed partly with bricks from the meeting house erected 1683. Members of the Church of England who came to Burlington were antagonistic to the Quaker classes that existed long before the school was built. In 1714 the Episcopal Society appointed as schoolmaster Rowland Ellis, who complained that his efforts were "beset with Heathenism Paganism Quakerism and God knows what." Ironically, a majority of the 20 pupils enrolled under Ellis at that time were Quakers.

The Episcopalians were no more friendly toward the very few Presbyterian newcomers. Of them, John Talbot, rector of St. Mary's, said: "The Presbyterians here come a great way to lay hands one on another; but after all I think they had as good stay at home, for the good they do." Methodists and Baptists joined the settlement a good deal later. Burlington's fine old Colonial churches are its heritage from those first citizens.

The town was capital of the Province from 1681, alternating with Perth Amboy after the union of West and East Jersey in 1702. During this period Burlington was the residence of Deputy Governors Samuel Jennings and Thomas Olive, and of Governor Jonathan Belcher.

A dozen years after its founding the town had a large pottery, salt house, and other industries. Shipbuilding became increasingly important. By 1744 Burlington ranked with New York, Philadelphia, and Boston as one of the busiest ports in the country.

In 1776 the little city, then numbering 1,000, was chosen as the meeting place of the Provincial Congress, which there adopted the State Constitution. Secure in their prosperity, the citizens of Burlington did not take the Revolution too seriously. The invasion of the town by about 400 Hessians in December 1776, and the cannonading in the spring of 1778 by two British warships returning from an attack on American frigates farther up the Delaware, were accepted with equanimity. In fact British naval officers had to warn spectators from the Green Bank before the bombardment started.

Burlington's position on the main thoroughfare between New York and Philadelphia and the natural beauty of its site attracted many of the political and literary figures of the early days of the Republic. The town became a summer resort for the fashionables of Philadelphia.

An important contribution to agricultural methods was made by Charles Newbold of Burlington, who patented the cast-iron plow in 1797 *(see AGRICULTURE)*. Farmers first feared that it would poison the soil, but their prejudice was finally overcome.

About 1838 a silkworm industry was started with acres of mulberry trees, but the experiment failed. From the Civil War to the present Burlington's industries have developed substantially, but the once vital shipping trade has disappeared.

POINTS OF INTEREST

1. The JAMES LAWRENCE HOUSE *(private)*, 459 S. High St., gray stucco with white shutters, was the birthplace in 1781 of Capt. James Lawrence. At 16 Lawrence entered the navy as a midshipman on the *U.S.S. Ganges*. In the War of 1812 he distinguished himself as captain of the

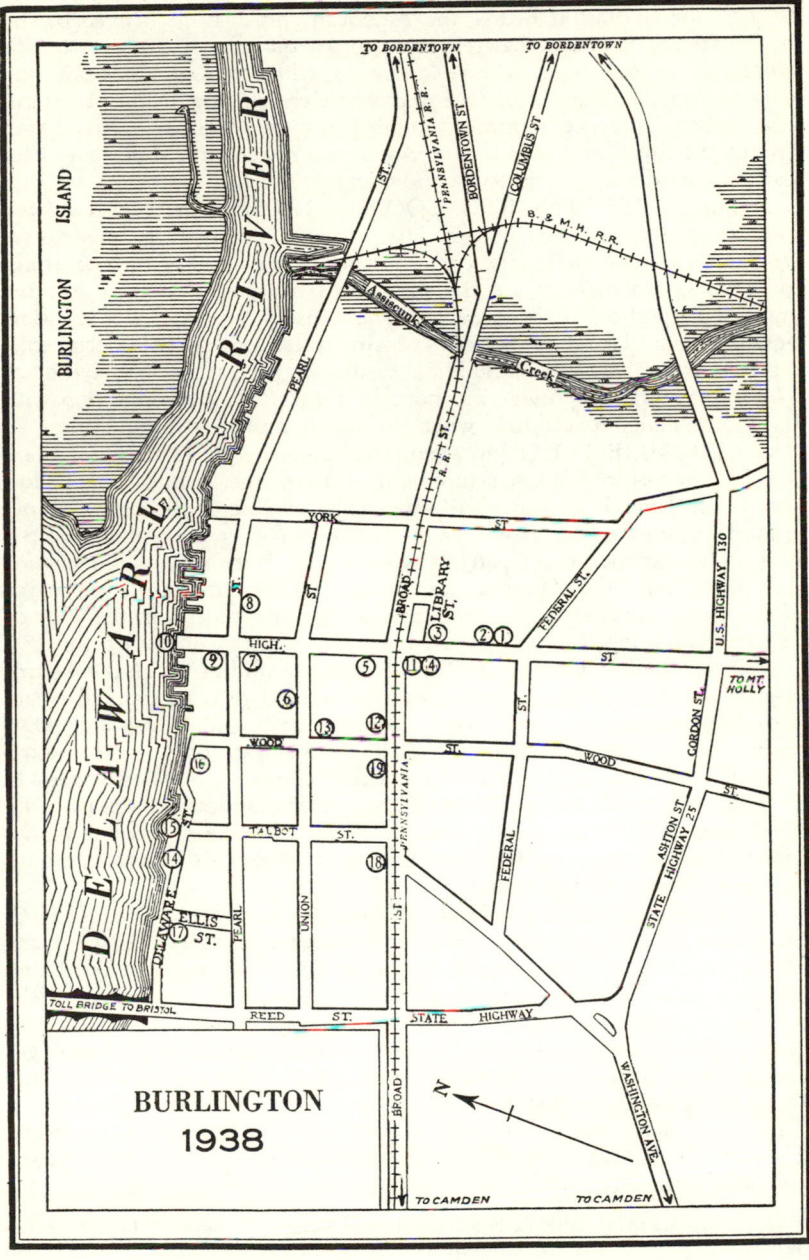

BURLINGTON
1938

sloop-of-war *Hornet* and was given command of the frigate *Chesapeake*. While lying in Boston Roads, the American ship was challenged by the British frigate *Shannon*. Lawrence put to sea on June 1, 1813. A terrific broadside was exchanged by the two frigates, with the *Chesapeake* suffering most severely. Boarders from the *Shannon* were already on the American vessel when Lawrence, mortally wounded, was carried below. His "Don't give up the ship!" was in vain; the Americans surrendered. Four days later Lawrence died and was buried with honors by the British.

2. The JAMES FENIMORE COOPER HOUSE *(open 3-6 Sun. and first Sat. of each month)*, 457 S. High St., has stucco walls lined to resemble stones, and shares the characteristics of many other early Burlington homes. Noteworthy are the fine detail of the wood trim and the graceful proportion of the windows. The house, headquarters of the Burlington County Historical Society, contains collections of early documents, pictures, and relics. In this building, rented by his parents, the author of *The Leather Stocking Tales* was born in 1789. Cooper's connection with Burlington ended a year later when the family moved to New York.

3. BLOOMFIELD HOUSE *(private)*, SE. corner S. High and Library Sts., is a three-story brick structure with mansard roof, painted pale yellow with white trim. It was originally the home of Joseph Bloomfield, Governor of New Jersey (1801–02, 1803–12). As a lawyer, Bloomfield successfully defended the young patriots who burned British tea at Greenwich *(see Side Tour 29B)*. He was a captain in the Revolutionary War, mayor of Burlington from 1795 to 1800, and a brigadier general in the War of 1812. He died in 1823 and was buried in St. Mary's Churchyard.

4. The HENRY CAREY HOUSE, the first building S. of the Metropolitan Inn on S. High St., is a three-story brick structure painted cream with brown trim, now used as a "Cocktail Grill and Restaurant" with rooms for rent upstairs. The structure contains part of a home erected *c.* 1678 by Thomas Olive, for a time acting Governor of West Jersey. In 1833 it was purchased by Henry Carey, early political economist, who lived here until 1854. At that time the Carey homestead was one of the most attractive spots of Burlington, with a garden extending south to where the City Hall now stands.

5. FRIENDS MEETING HOUSE *(open on meeting days)*, N. High St. between Broad and Union Sts., was erected 1784 adjacent to the site of the hexagonal structure built by the first settlers in 1683. Quiet and severe, it stands behind a great wall with heavy iron gates deep in the shadow of great trees, one of which, a giant sycamore, was standing in 1677. It is a typical example of the early meeting houses, with double entrances, great windows, and pitched roof. The BURIAL GROUND behind the meeting house, walled with brick, is the oldest cemetery in Burlington. Tall pines shade the graves which date from 1744. Under the broad branches of a sycamore is the GRAVESTONE OF THE INDIAN CHIEF OCKANICKON, inscribed:

Near this Spot Lies the Body of the Indian Chief Ockanickon, Friend of the White Man, Whose Last Words were "Be Plain and Fair to All, Both Indians and Christian, as I Have Been."

6. The LIBRARY *(open 3-6, 7-9 Tues., Thurs., and Sat.)*, Union St. between N. High and Wood Sts., one of the oldest in the country, is still operating under a 1757 charter from King George II. The present building, brownstone and severe in line, dates from 1864. The interior is a single high-ceilinged room encircled by a balcony. Portraits of respected citizens, together with one of King George II, are hung in every available niche.

7. The SITE OF SAMUEL JENNINGS' OFFICE is now a garden, a strip of green with a few shrubs between an apartment house at 206 N. High St. and the Synagogue at 212 N. High St. Jennings came to Burlington in 1680, a recommended minister of the Society of Friends, and served as first Deputy Governor from 1681 to 1684. In his office Benjamin Franklin set up the first copperplate press in America, and, as an assistant to Samuel Keimer, printed the first currency for the Province. In the same shop Isaac Collins, printer to the King, produced the first quarto Bible of American imprint, and New Jersey's first newspaper, the New Jersey *Gazette,* which came off the press December 5, 1777. This weekly paper, which measured 9 by 14 in., cost 25 shillings a year, and numbered among its paid up subscribers all the members of the State legislature.

8. The THOMAS REVEL HOUSE *(private)*, 8 E. Pearl St., is probably the oldest complete dwelling in Burlington. Erected 1685 by George Hutchinson, it was the office of Thomas Revel, registrar of the Proprietors of West New Jersey and clerk of the assembly from 1696 to 1699. The little house is hidden in one of the poorer sections of the town. It is two stories in height, of brick construction, with gambrel roof and two small dormer windows; one low-ceilinged room is downstairs and a very low-ceilinged bedroom is upstairs. Some old china cooking utensils and other odds and ends are kept here. The house is the headquarters of the Annis Stockton Chapter of the Daughters of the American Revolution.

9. OLD STEAMBOAT HOTEL *(private)*, 100 N. High St., was built in 1774 by Adam Sheppard and was known by his name until steamboat travel was established in 1808. The later addition of a porch and the generally run-down condition detract from what was once a fine three-story Colonial tavern.

10. The PUBLIC WHARF, N. end High St., is the municipally owned ferry slip. From this point passengers have crossed the river since 1680. Today a small launch leaves on the hour for Bristol, with room for a dozen or more passengers. The first ferry in 1713 was hauled by horses on shore, and once the steamboats from Philadelphia stopped here.

11. METROPOLITAN INN, SW. corner Broad and High Sts., is a cream stucco building, much altered since 1751 when it was known as the Blue Anchor Tavern. There are four stories in front, three in the rear. Its Georgian Colonial architecture is marred by a second-floor balcony enclosed with a wrought-iron railing. A coffee shop and a bar occupy the first floor; the rest is a hotel. For years the proprietors have met here when the weather did not permit outdoor voting. Since 1833 passengers listened here for the bell which announced the squeaking coaches of the Camden and Amboy Railroad, now the Pennsylvania.

12. The WEST NEW JERSEY PROPRIETORS OFFICE *(not open to public)*, Broad St. between High and Wood Sts., is a tiny, one-room, red brick building with white trim and a peaked roof. A yard and carriage shed enclosed by a red brick wall adjoin the office. In the gable of the roof is the shield or coat of arms of the Proprietors, a set of balanced scales upheld by a tree. The office contains original documents signed by William Penn.

The strange corporation known as the Proprietors of West New Jersey dates back to 1676, when William Penn and his associates divided the Province into two parts for colonization and government *(see HISTORY)*. The original agreement signed by the settlers, kept in the vault of the Mechanics National Bank in Burlington, is almost unsurpassed for beauty of diction and expresses the principles of civil and religious liberty more clearly than any other frame of government in Colonial history. Upon it rests much New Jersey law.

Still functioning under their charter from Charles II, the Proprietors of West New Jersey meet here every April 13 on the corner of High and Broad Streets to elect five members of the General Council. Four others are elected in Gloucester *(see Tour 19)*. No notice of the meeting is ever mailed, because the members, numbering thousands, are scattered over the world. The requirements for membership are ownership of 1/32 of a share and hereditary descent from one of the 151 original signers. Seldom does more than a handful attend the sidewalk meetings. The council meets at its tiny office in May; its only new business is exercise of its ancient right to dispose of any new land created in western New Jersey. Jurisdiction over the rest of the State is held by the Proprietors of East New Jersey *(see PERTH AMBOY)*.

13. The GENERAL GRANT HOUSE *(private)*, 309 Wood St., is a graceful, two-story shuttered home of yellow stucco with green trim. French windows are upstairs and down, and a delicate wrought-iron rail around the roof of the porch is overhung with wisteria. There is a hospitable expanse of lawn and great shade trees, all enclosed by a green picket fence. To this house General Grant sent his family during the Civil War. He is said to have been in residence there the night Lincoln was assassinated.

14. The GREEN BANK, narrow scallops of lawn at the edge of Delaware River, extends 3 blocks W. from Wood St. From this old-time promenade of Burlington residents is a view of Pennsylvania farm land—a mile across the river—and the finely proportioned, single steel arch of the BRISTOL BRIDGE. The view up the river is blocked by the jutting public dock and BURLINGTON *(or Matinicunk)* ISLAND.

15. SITE OF BARBARROUX WHARF, Green Bank at foot of Talbot St., is now merely a bit of lawn and a beacon light. As early as 1698 an important shipyard was established here where keels were laid for vessels that sailed to all parts of the world. In 1744 the privateer *Marlborough,* large enough for a crew of 150, was launched. Today the channel has been silted so heavily that no ship of any size could reach the site of the wharf.

BURLINGTON COUNTY HISTORICAL SOCIETY, BURLINGTON

16. GOVERNOR FRANKLIN ESTATE *(private)*, S. side of Delaware St. between Wood and Talbot Sts., is occupied by the GRUBB HOUSE, owned by the Veterans of Foreign Wars. It is a large dwelling of little architectural distinction. On these grounds once stood the home of the last Royal Governor of New Jersey, William Franklin, son of Benjamin. He was held here for a time as a prisoner of the Revolutionists.

On the lawn is a giant SYCAMORE TREE, one of the largest trees in the State. It measures 20 ft. 3 in. in girth. To its trunk, it is generally believed, the ship *Shield* was moored in 1678 when it arrived with early settlers.

17. ST. MARY'S HALL, S. side Delaware St., at Ellis St., is a private Protestant Episcopal School for girls founded in 1837 by Bishop George Washington Doane. There are five ivy-covered stone buildings and a chapel on the 18-acre campus, providing facilities for more than 100 students.

The BISHOP DOANE RESIDENCE *(private)* is on the school grounds almost beneath Bristol Bridge. It is the official home for the Bishop of the South New Jersey Diocese of the Protestant Episcopal Church. The house is a low, two-story building of tan stucco with brown wood trim and a hip roof. A square tower forms one end of the rambling structure; long windows on the first story, with small diamond-shaped panes typical of old England, extend almost to the floor.

18. The BRADFORD MANSION *(private)*, 207 and 209 W. Broad St., is an old brick house, divided for two families and painted tan on one side and gray on the other. Elias Boudinot, president of the Continental Congress *(see ELIZABETH)*, built the mansion about 1798. His daughter, Mrs. William Bradford, wife of the first Attorney General, lived here until the end, preserving the charm and formalities of that vanished era. The blue porcelain lions that once guarded the lawns were one of the sights of Burlington, and it is said that as late as 1850 old gentlemen in ruffled shirts, and ladies in stomachers of faded but lovely brocade were frequent visitors.

19. OLD ST. MARY'S CHURCH *(not open to public)*, NW. corner W. Broad and Wood Sts., built in 1703, is the oldest Episcopal Church building of the State. The congregation, although worshiping in a newer building, uses the communion service presented by Queen Anne. Old St. Mary's is an interesting example of early Georgian Colonial design. Of gray stucco with white trim, it has a slate roof crowned with a stubby, louvred lantern and strange little slotlike transom windows. Today the church is used for Sunday school and special meetings.

The newer ST. MARY'S CHURCH, adjoining, was completed in 1854 from the plans of Richard Upjohn, architect of Trinity Church in New York City. It is a fine, ivy-draped Gothic structure with a towering spire.

Behind the churches is the CEMETERY, originally called Christian burying ground to distinguish it from the burying ground of the Quakers. In the shadow of great trees between boxwood-lined paths lie many distinguished citizens.

A survival of the more closely knit communal life of early Burlington is St. Mary's Choral Society, organized in 1877 to perpetuate the old English custom of singing the *Waits* on Christmas Eve. As midnight is announced by the bell of Old St. Mary's the group leaves the guild house and walks through the town, singing before the home of each member. The ceremony ends with a hymn at the grave of George H. Allen, a tribute to his work in preserving the custom.

POINT OF INTEREST IN ENVIRONS

Roebling *(company town)*, 6.2 m. *(see Tour 19)*.

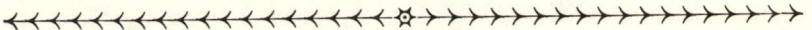

Camden

Railroad Stations: Pennsylvania Station, W. end Market St., for Pennsylvania R.R. and Pennsylvania-Reading Seashore Lines; Broadway between Carman and Mickle Sts., for Pennsylvania-Reading Seashore Lines; City Hall Plaza, Broadway and Carman St., for rapid transit line to Philadelphia.

Bus Stations: 209 N. Broadway for Quaker City line and Safeway Trailways; NW. corner Broadway and Market St. for Public Service and G. R. Wood interurban lines.

Airport: Central Airport, 2 m. SE. on Admiral Wilson Blvd., for Eastern Air Lines, United Air Lines, Transcontinental and Western Air, and American Airlines.

Taxis: 15¢ for first 1/5 m., 5¢ for each additional 1/5 m.

Trackless Trolleys and Busses: Fare 5¢.

Ferries: W. end of Federal and Market Sts. for ferries to Philadelphia; toll, 5¢ for pedestrians, 20¢ for automobile and passengers.

Bridge: N. end of Broadway for Delaware River Bridge to Philadelphia; toll, 20¢ for automobile and passengers; pedestrians free.

Traffic Regulations: Turns permitted in either direction except where signs direct otherwise. Traffic lights throughout city; no turns permitted on red light. Watch signs for parking limitations.

Accommodations: Hotels and boarding houses; no seasonal rates.

Information Service: Keystone Automobile Club, 631 Cooper St.; A.A.A., NW. cor. 7th and Market Sts.

Radio Station: WCAM (1280 kc.).

Motion Picture Houses: Thirteen.

Swimming: County Park Commission Pool, Farnham Park, locker fee 10¢; County Park Commission Pool, for Negroes, 9th St. and Ferry Ave., locker fee 10¢; Municipal Pool, Pyne Poynt Park, free to 2 p.m., locker fee 10¢ after 2.

Tennis: Pyne Poynt Park, Farnharm Park and Dudley Grange Park, 20¢ an hour per person.

Golf: Cooper River Country Club, Cooper River Parkway, 18 holes, greens fees 60¢, Sat., Sun. and holidays $1.

Annual Events: Yacht races, early summer, Delaware River; pilgrimage to grave of Peter J. McGuire, Labor Day.

CAMDEN (25 alt., 118,700 pop.) is utilitarian in architecture and arrangement of streets. The key to the city's early development was Philadelphia, which at the time of Camden's birth was the largest city on the continent. In fact, Camden grew out of the necessity for crossing the Delaware in order to get to Philadelphia; and the main east to west streets have always been long, broad thoroughfares leading to the ferries.

The heavy river traffic over bridge and ferries remains an important factor in the city's life, but Camden has acquired individual importance as the leading industrial, marketing, and transportation center of southern New Jersey.

Almost 300 factories, ranging from small shops to great plants occupying solid blocks, have been crowded into the city without control by any zoning plan. Industrial buildings line the water front in a phalanx and spread out into the residential sections.

Camden represents a job and a home. It might be called a two-story brick town, but there is beauty as well as naked utility in its brickwork. There are diagonally patterned brick sidewalks in the older residential districts—sidewalks with as many bumps and hollows as a path across a vacant lot. And there are simple, flat-roofed brick houses, relieved by white marble steps and lintels, shaded by sycamores, and possessed of all the graciousness of the Greenwich Village houses for which New Yorkers pay extravagant rents.

There are also rows upon rows of tight boxlike houses without space between—the typical home of the Camden worker. Of red or sometimes yellow brick, they differ little except as they may have large porches with heavy, round columns, or small porches with slender posts, or no porches at all. A utilitarian brown is the almost universal color for any style of porch.

Some variation is found in the occasional use of mansard roofs and bay windows and, more rarely, in the substitution of serpentine rock—distinguished by its peculiar yellow-green color—or brownstone for brick. Placed at regular intervals on many of the block-long cornices are wooden pinnacles that resemble helmet spikes of the old German army.

Camden's busy shopping center is in character with the working population. No large department stores and few smart shops here, but an abundance of smaller stores whose enterprising managers use every means to increase trade. It is not unusual to find the price of scrapple written in yellow paint on the sidewalk. On week-end nights several of the shopping streets resemble an oriental bazaar with flamboyant posters on store windows, multicolored neon signs flashing.

With a less than average quota of office buildings, Camden's lawyers, doctors, and other professional workers have followed the example of many merchants and established themselves in the first floors of old houses. Cooper Street, where front porches encroach upon the sidewalk in almost every block, summarizes the city's growth. Once lined with homes of the best people, it retains the houses along its eastern section, but sitting rooms have been converted into real estate offices and beauty parlors; westward toward the river, the façades of tall buildings that might pass for office structures are in reality the fronts of leading factories.

Camden is compact enough for neighbor to meet neighbor in the two subway stations. There are second-floor apartments above stores just across the street from the towering City Hall. Prevailing breezes carry to office workers in this fine edifice—which is locally known as the "Milk Bottle" —the odor of coffee beans roasting in a nearby factory, thus creating an atmosphere of *café au lait* for Camden's municipal government.

Side streets in some of the more congested sections barely manage to serve as passageways. It is not unusual to find brick houses fronting on little alleys no more than 6 or 8 feet from curb to curb. Unlike many other industrial cities, Camden seems to make a point of keeping streets and sidewalks neat and clean.

CAMDEN FROM PHILADELPHIA SIDE OF DELAWARE RIVER

Construction of the Delaware River Bridge cut into the heart of what was then the fine residential section and pushed many of the more prosperous citizens to new homesites in the suburbs. But although Camden is lacking in private show places, it is alive to the need for public parks. Noteworthy are Farnham Park on Cooper River, with extensive athletic facilities (Camden is so interested in sandlot baseball that the city officially sponsors a league); Dudley Park, in the eastern section of the city; and Pyne Poynt Park, now being developed on the shore of the Delaware River.

The civic stature of Camden may also be measured by the success of a model housing project and by a long campaign for a municipal power plant. As early as 1906 the voters approved a plan for building a plant, but action was postponed because of a shortage of money and a rate cut by the private utility. The proposition was again endorsed in 1933 by a vote of better than 2 to 1, and in 1935 by a vote of 5 to 1, but each time the citizens were blocked by legal actions instituted by Public Service Corporation.

Akin to the depression-born squatter communities is Line Ditch, lying at the west end of Jasper Street. It comprises about 150 one-story dwellings built of driftwood from the nearby rivers, scrap metal and other junkyard gleanings. No two homes are alike, except in their miniature reproduction of the Camden box design. The 500 inhabitants, including women and children, are served by a general store and a little church known as Line Ditch Chapel. There is no gas, electricity, or garbage collection, and the entire community gets water from a single tap. A Philadelphia real estate company owns the land and collects $2 a month rent from each family. The name Line Ditch, an old one, goes back to the time when Little Newton Creek, the city line, was known as the Ditch.

Camden is always aware of Philadelphia, and there is a custom—strictly confined to Camden—of referring to the "twin cities of the Delaware." Some years ago Philadelphians used to say vaguely, "Camden is over there in back of the Victor and Campbell's soup factories," and traveling Camdenites often said that they were from Philadelphia to forestall explanations. But an increasingly larger portion of the United States now knows that Camden is a city opposite Philadelphia. In particular, Philadelphians are aware of its location because the Camden airport serves as the terminal for Philadelphia traffic.

Despite the inducement offered by the only leather-upholstered subway cars in general use in the United States, so few Camden residents have ridden across the bridge to seek recreation after dark in Philadelphia that night train service has been canceled. Week-end parties in particular are longer and more enjoyable on the New Jersey side of the river, for Philadelphia taverns close at midnight on Saturday. The remark of Will Rogers at the dedication of the Delaware River Bridge, "Now we have a bridge we can get out of Camden when we want to," has proved something less than prophetic.

The ties with Philadelphia are deeply rooted in the history of the two cities. Both were permanently colonized by the Quakers, fleeing from religious persecution in England. The first Camden settler was probably William Cooper, who built a home in 1681 on the point of land below Cooper River and named the tract Pyne Poynt. In the same year scattered families of Friends set up a meeting, still in existence, the third established in New Jersey.

After Cooper took over a ferry to Philadelphia the settlement became known as Cooper's Ferries. Virtually all the rest of the present site of Camden was taken by John Kaighn, for whom the old village of Kaighntown was named, and by Archibald Mickle, upon whose farm Camden proper developed later. But the settlement grew slowly and by the beginning of the eighteenth century there were fewer than a dozen clearings in the wooded points on the Delaware. Philadelphia was more attractive to the newcomers.

A real estate boom began in 1773 when Jacob Cooper, Philadelphia merchant and descendant of William Cooper, laid out 40 acres as a townsite. He named the place Camden for the first Earl of Camden, the nobleman who had befriended the Colonies during their disputes with the mother country. Twenty-two communities in the United States have chosen the same name.

The Revolution checked development of the new village. During the British occupation of Philadelphia, Camden was held as an enemy outpost and a number of skirmishes occurred within the present city limits. Years after the end of the war Camden continued to be more a ferry terminal than a town.

About 1809 a small steamboat began operation as a ferry for passengers. Others followed, replacing the open boats that had double keels for use as runners when the river was frozen.

Originally part of Newton Township, Camden was incorporated as a city in 1828 and in 1844 was made the seat of Camden County. The city's real growth began in 1834 when it became the terminus of the Camden and Amboy Railroad, then the longest line in the country. All-iron rails, imported from England, were fastened to the ties with hook-headed spikes, the invention of Robert Stevens. The first locomotive, the *John Bull,* a duplicate of Stephenson's *Planet,* was also English-made.

For six years the line was the only through route between Philadelphia and New York. In 1840 the railroad company opened another line from Philadelphia via Trenton and New Brunswick direct to Jersey City, which reduced the importance of the Camden route but strengthened the transportation monopoly that gave New Jersey the name of the "State of Camden and Amboy."

On the night of March 15, 1856, the ferryboat *New Jersey* left its Philadelphia dock and caught fire in midstream. Ice floes made it impossible for the ferry to be beached, or for other craft to get to her aid. Sixty-one persons perished. This disaster, coupled with the financial panic of the following year, hindered the town's growth.

Following the Civil War, Camden was caught up in the tremendous industrial expansion that was the sequel to railroad building. Swiftly the water front was taken over by factories. When every site was filled, the shops and mills overran the town. Industry grew steadily, aided by an influx of foreign-born and Negro workers. The city's 11,340 Negroes are concentrated mainly in the district between Broadway and Mt. Ephraim Avenue, from Kaighn Avenue to Ferry Avenue. Five separate elementary schools, with Negro teachers, are maintained; graduates attend one of the city's two high schools. In the center of the Negro section is a public park and swimming pool.

Italians and Poles predominate among the foreign nationalities, with Englishmen and Russians next in order. The *Gazeta Dla Wszystkich,* a Polish weekly newspaper published in Camden, is the principal foreign-language journal of the city. Both the Poles and the Italians, who live in separate districts, are active in political affairs.

Camden's marine importance is indicated by a number of shipyards, one of which is the largest in the country. The well-equipped Camden Marine Terminals, operated by a State agency, have facilities for transferring cargoes directly from steamship holds to railroad cars.

POINTS OF INTEREST

1. The CITY HALL AND COURTHOUSE ANNEX, 5th St., between Market and Arch Sts., is a light gray granite structure of modified Grecian design, the work of Edwards and Green, Camden architects. Twenty-two

stories high, it is the tallest building in Camden. From the main building of five stories rises a 17-story tower, narrowing at the top into open work resembling the neck of a bottle. On the tower is a huge new clock in place of those that have ornamented Camden's city halls since 1876. The building houses county and city offices, making it often half Republican and half Democratic.

2. The COURTHOUSE, Broadway between Market and Federal Sts., is of Italian Renaissance style with a dome resembling that of the Capitol at Washington. Built in 1904, it was designed by Rankin, Kellogg and Crane of Philadelphia. Halls and columns are of white marble and ceilings are of Italian mosaic. In a second-floor courtroom, decorated in gold, a large oil painting by Nicola D'Ascenzo, *Justice and Her Scales,* hangs behind the bench.

After Camden won the hard-fought battle to create Camden County, the site for the courthouse caused a controversy between John W. Mickle, president of the Federal Street Ferry Company, who wanted it on his street, and Abraham Browning, operator of the Market Street ferry, who insisted that the building should be on his road. Under a compromise the courthouse was built on Broadway, equidistant from the two ferry approaches.

3. The FRIENDS SCHOOL *(open 9-3 schooldays),* 709 Market St., is a small and cheerful building of red brick, erected in 1794. Three stories high and barely wide enough for a row of three shuttered windows on each floor, it stands by itself behind a weathered picket fence, with a churchyard on one side and the schoolyard on the other. Except for a line of dentils in the molding of the cornice, the building is as plain as the one-story frame MEETING HOUSE, painted a dull gray, that stands at the rear of the yard. The school is operated as a private, progressive institution.

Near this spot a brisk skirmish took place in 1778 during the British occupation of Philadelphia. A regiment of the Queen's Rangers under Colonel Stirling directed heavy fire against General Wayne's foraging party in the woods along the Haddonfield road. The Americans were forced to retire, but the British failed to capture their supplies.

4. JOHNSON PARK, Cooper St. between 2nd and Front Sts., is an attractively landscaped block in the shadow of tall buildings of the RCA-Victor plant. In the center stands the COOPER BRANCH LIBRARY *(open 9-9 weekdays),* a neoclassic building erected 1919 from the plans of Karcher and Smith, Philadelphia architects. Behind a row of six Ionic columns is a mosaic frieze of opalescent glass, depicting *America Receiving the Gifts of the Nations.* Composed of 100,000 pieces, the mosaic was executed in the D'Ascenzo Studios, Philadelphia. The library has 22,000 volumes.

In front of the library is a wading pool and a bronze STATUE OF PETER PAN by George Frampton, with Peter standing on a tree stump. From the crevices of intertwining roots peer field mice, rabbits, squirrels, birds, and fairies. The park, library, pool, and statue were the gift of Eldridge R. Johnson, founder of the Victor Talking Machine Company.

5. The RCA-VICTOR MANUFACTURING PLANT *(open by ap-*

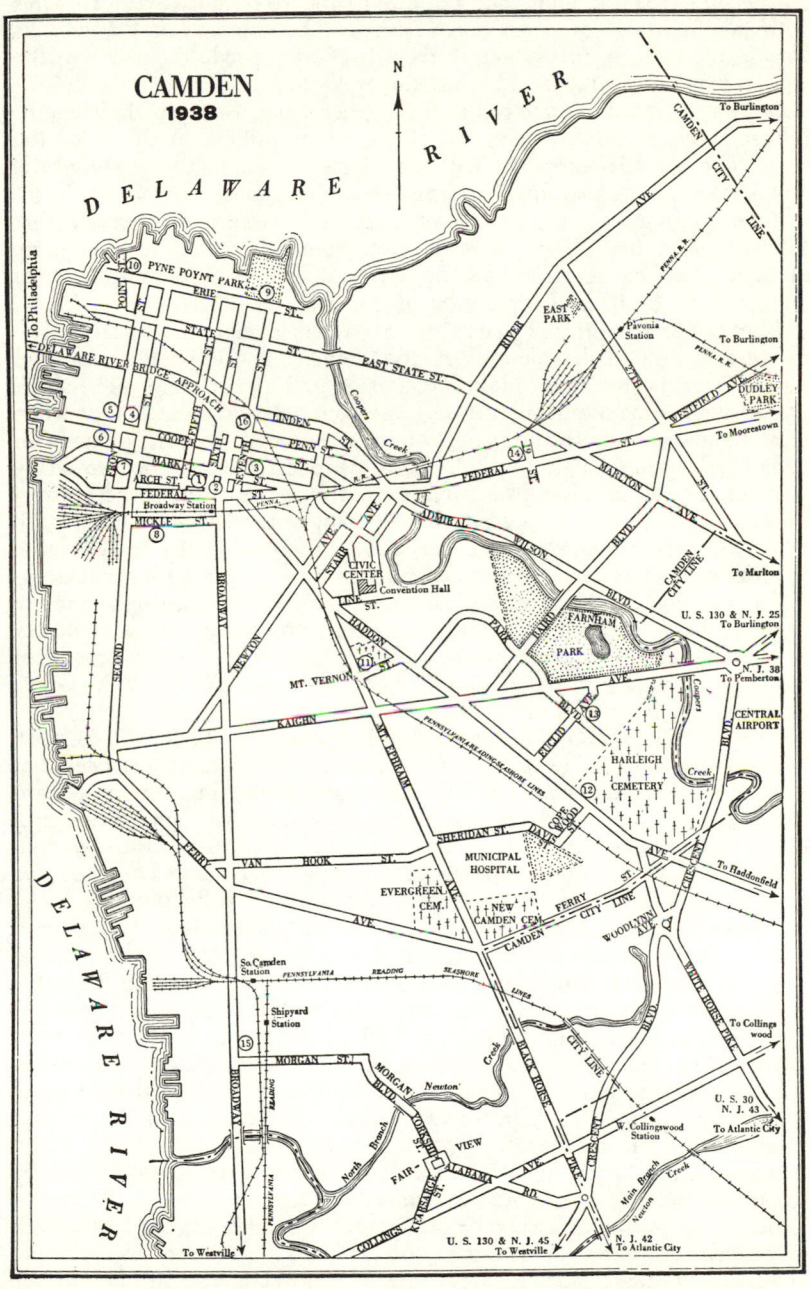

CAMDEN
1938

pointment), 201 N. Front St., extends to the river and covers 10 acres with tall buildings of concrete and brick. The company is the world's largest producer of phonograph records. Other products made by the 14,000 workers are radio and television equipment.

In 1894 a customer came to the little general repair shop of Eldridge R. Johnson, bringing for repair one of the crude talking machines of the time. Johnson repaired it, studied it, changed it, and finally produced the first Victor talking machine. Leading singers and musicians were brought to Camden from all parts of the world to make the flat disk records that Johnson substituted for cylinders. Johnson sold out in 1927 to a syndicate of New York bankers for $28,000,000 and retired. The company then merged with the Radio Corporation of America.

Blue-uniformed private guards in the streets around the factory recall turbulent scenes in the summer of 1936 when the United Electrical and Radio Workers struck for union recognition and higher wages. The strike gained wide attention as an issue of the courts vs. organized labor when local judges set bail totaling more than $1,000,000. Federal Judge William Clark reduced bail for individual prisoners from $5,000 to $100, commenting, "It is very unwise to attempt to use the courts in a labor dispute . . ." Settlement was made by agreement for an election, through which the union won exclusive bargaining rights. The La Follette civil liberties committee reported the expenditure of large sums for strikebreaking and espionage in the strike and pre-strike period. Since that time the company has signed with the union a contract providing for a scale of pay that is one of the highest in the industry and announced a new labor policy, employing former Assistant Secretary of Labor Edward F. McGrady as director of labor relations.

6. The ESTERBROOK STEEL PEN MANUFACTURING PLANT *(open 9-4 weekdays; guides)*, 8 Cooper St., is the oldest steel pen company in the United States. The company was founded in 1858 by Richard Esterbrook, an Englishman who brought 15 workers to Camden and produced 10,000 pens the first year. In the plant, a five-story structure of concrete and glass, are now employed 250 workers who make 200,000,000 pens annually. Fountains pens have also been added to the output.

7. The CAMPBELL SOUP PLANT *(open 9:30 and 1 weekdays; guides)*, S.W. corner 2nd and Market Sts., is the largest maker of canned soups in the world. The plant consists of 42 buildings covering 8 blocks; landmarks are the water tanks on the roof, built and painted as colossal replicas of red and white soup cans. Visitors are shown a $50,000 model kitchen, installed in 1936. The company buys large quantities of vegetables from New Jersey farmers, and on its own experimental land raises young plants which are distributed to growers. In the factory the number of employees varies seasonally from 2,500 to 8,000.

The industry began in 1869 as a small preserve factory conducted by Joseph Campbell and Abraham Anderson. In 1897 John T. Dorrance joined the company as a chemist at $7.50 a week. He developed the idea of condensing soups for canning, and in 1914 became president of the company. Dorrance amassed a fortune of $117,000,000; on his death in

THE WALT WHITMAN HOME, CAMDEN

1935 the State inheritance tax amounted to $15,000,000, which temporarily solved the problem of raising funds for relief.

8. The WALT WHITMAN HOME *(open 10-5 weekdays except Tues.; 1-5 Sun.)*, 330 Mickle St., is an unpretentious frame house set democratically in a solid row of dilapidated red brick houses occupied by Negroes and Italians. In Whitman's time the street was shaded by old trees; today the only tree in the block is an oriental plane before the poet's house. Built in 1848, the gray, flat-roofed dwelling was occupied by Whitman from 1884 to his death in 1892. In 1923 it was bought by the city and made into a museum for the foremost collection of Whitmaniana.

Among the exhibits are the cane used by the partially paralyzed poet; the rocking chair in which he sat by the upper story window after his legs became helpless; a great tin bathtub; a replica of the first edition of *Leaves of Grass;* furniture, books, papers, medals and even the poet's corkscrew.

When Whitman appeared in Camden in the spring of 1873, his most productive days were behind him, but although his body was stiffened by paralysis, his mind remained agile, and he constantly revised his poetry and even wrote several important prose works.

As his reputation grew, his home became the Mecca of literary friends and admirers from all over the world. There the poet modestly received their homage and delighted to entertain his dearest companions, John Burroughs, the naturalist, Horace Traubel, the Camden writer who was his Boswell, and Thomas Harned, one of his literary executors. No longer regarded as a dangerous libertine, Whitman sunned himself into old age in the rays of his great friendships.

He was singularly listed in the Camden directory of 1877: "Whitman, Walt, Poet, 431 Stevens Street." To most of the citizens, however, "Neighbor" might have been an even more appropriate designation. Ignoring the faint sniffs of "the best people," Whitman roamed the streets chatting with any and all who caught his fancy. He specially lingered in conversation with children and workingmen, whom he considered the clearest voices in "the human comedy." Now and then he would drop into a tavern for a short drink—or champagne on gala days—and a long talk. Strange-looking in his broad hat and unkempt beard, Whitman's desire to plumb the souls of his Camden neighbors was considered even stranger.

In the autumn of 1891 the Good Gray Poet began to build his gray stone tomb. Shortly afterward his right lung became affected; facing death with the same courage that had marked his life he spoke of himself as "a little spark of soul dragging a great lummox of corpse-body to and fro." With less fortitude than he himself had shown, Whitman's grieving friends saw the long struggle end in March of the following year.

9. In PYNE POYNT PARK, N. end 7th St., is the JOSEPH COOPER HOUSE *(open; resident custodian)*, erected before 1709 by a son of the pioneer William Cooper. It is perhaps the oldest dwelling in the city. Cooper's home apparently set the architectural style for Camden's row-houses. The original one-story structure, of rough stone with an irregular pattern of thick mortar, has a two-story red brick addition of Dutch Colo-

nial architecture. The two parts have no unity of design, color, texture, or shape. The interior of the older section is one large room, used as a community hall. Dusty and rather forlorn, it is furnished with a few camp chairs, park benches, and a battered upright piano. At one end is a huge brick fireplace with the original wrought-iron crane. The old bricks are painted a brilliant red, meticulously outlined in white; the walls are modernized by an application of green stucco and splotches of gilt. The park, situated at the confluence of the Delaware and Cooper Rivers, contains sports fields and other recreational facilities. Cooper River was the main highway to inland villages during the years of settlement, and it still bears a considerable traffic in towboats and barges serving industrial plants along its shores. The Cooper River Parkway, now under construction (1939) along the waterway, is to be the northernmost link in a series of parkways paralleling rivers and lakes between Camden and the ocean.

10. The BENJAMIN COOPER HOUSE *(open 9-4 weekdays),* NE. corner Erie and Point Sts., was built in 1734, and is excellently preserved. The rough-cut stone has weathered to a rich brown, blending with the gray woodwork. The mansard roof is a particularly graceful and well-proportioned example of the Dutch version of that style. Used now as an office for the John H. Mathis Shipbuilding Co., the tranquil old house has narrow lawns on each side of its stoop that merge abruptly with the gravel and cinders of the shipyard. During the Revolution the building, also known as the Old Yellow House and The Stone Jug, was the headquarters of Lieutenant Colonel Abercrombie, who commanded the British and Hessian outpost during the occupation of Philadelphia.

11. NEWTON FRIENDS MEETING HOUSE *(not open),* N. side Mt. Vernon St. between Mt. Ephraim Ave. and Camden Cemetery, built in 1801 on ground donated by Joseph Kaighn, was the first house of worship in Camden. It is a two-and-one-half-story rectangular building, of post-Colonial design, constructed of red brick with white trim. Quakers met here until 1915. In 1935 the building was restored with PWA funds under the direction of the Camden County Historical Society and is now used by the city for storage.

12. In HARLEIGH CEMETERY, Haddon Ave. and Vesper Blvd., is the TOMB OF WALT WHITMAN, a simple vault of rough-cut stone designed by Whitman "for that of me which is to die." Above the grilled door is a massive triangle of stone with the poet's name. The tomb is largely concealed by trees and shrubbery.

13. CHARLES S. BOYER MEMORIAL HALL *(open Mon., Wed., Fri., 1-4; other days by appointment),* NE. corner Euclid Ave. and Park Blvd., contains the Camden County Historical Society Museum. Erected in 1726 by Joseph Cooper, Jr., the tapestry brick structure of Georgian Colonial design is two and one-half stories in height, with a double chimney at each end. White trim contrasts with the dark brickwork; the lawns and trees of Farnham Park form a pleasant background.

On the first floor is a collection of Indian relics, Colonial kitchen utensils and Civil War mementoes. A library on the second floor contains hundreds of volumes on south New Jersey, maps and rare manuscripts; and

TANKER *MAGNOLIA* UNDER CONSTRUCTION, CAMDEN

on the same floor is a completely furnished Colonial bedroom. A large collection of newspapers is kept on the third floor.

14. HADDON CRAFTSMEN PRINTING PLANT *(open by arrangement)*, NW. corner 19th and Federal Sts., is a modern, office-type building of brick construction. Two wings with steel framework and glass sides are equipped to produce 15,000 books daily in addition to thousands of magazines and pamphlets. The plant is the only one in the United States that prints Gregorian music.

WESTFIELD ACRES, N. side of Westfield Ave. between Dudley and

32nd Sts., was financed with $3,000,000 of PWA funds. The model housing project covers 25 acres and includes 18 units with a total of 514 apartments of 3 to 5 rooms. The buildings are three-story brick structures of simple design, with many large, steel-framed windows. Spacious inner courts provide adequate sunlight and ventilation. Kitchens are equipped with electric ranges and mechanical refrigerators.

15. The NEW YORK SHIPBUILDING PLANT *(open by permission)*, 2448 S. Broadway, ranks first in size among privately owned shipbuilding plants in the Nation. Here were built the 888-foot Naval aircraft carrier *U.S.S. Saratoga* at a cost of $40,000,000, and the 668-foot transatlantic liners *Manhattan* and *Washington,* largest merchant vessels flying the American flag. The plant has facilities for simultaneous work on 28 vessels, ranging from tugs to warships. More than 5,000 workers are normally employed. A 5-month strike in 1935 won higher wages and the 36-hour week for members of the Industrial Union of Marine and Shipbuilding Workers of America.

16. The DELAWARE RIVER BRIDGE, N. end of Broadway, was the longest suspension bridge in the world when it was opened by President Coolidge in 1926. The main span of 1,750 feet was designed by Ralph Modjeski and built as a joint enterprise by the States of New Jersey and Pennsylvania. The bridge is noteworthy for the beauty of its lofty steel towers, sweeping cable lines and the decorations on the anchorages (large carved seals of New Jersey, Pennsylvania, Camden, and Philadelphia). The towers are 385 feet above high water; the piers extend 61 feet below sea level to bedrock on the Philadelphia side, and 85 feet on the Camden side. Twin cables 30 inches in diameter support the 57-foot roadway, two rapid transit tracks and foot walks with a clearance of 135 feet above the channel. The entire structure is 8,536 feet long; it took 4½ years to build and cost $40,000,000.

POINTS OF INTEREST IN ENVIRONS

Grave of Peter J. McGuire, Arlington Cemetery, *4.6 m.*, Central Airport, *2 m.*, Red Bank Battlefield National Park, *10 m. (see Tour 19);* Thackara House, erected 1754, *1.9 m. (see Tour 23);* Indian King Inn, Haddonfield, *8.3 m. (see Tour 27).*

Elizabeth

Railroad Stations: Pennsylvania Station, West Grand St., for Pennsylvania R.R.; Jersey Central Station, Morris Ave. and Julian Pl., for Jersey Central R.R., Baltimore and Ohio R.R., and Reading Co.; Jersey Central Station, 1st and Merritt Aves., for Perth Amboy and shore division of Jersey Central R.R.
Bus Stations: 287 N. Broad St. for Greyhound and Edwards; Spring and E. Grand Sts. for Safeway Trailways; Elizabeth Arch for Public Service.
Airport: 3 m. NE. on US 1 at Newark for Eastern Airlines, American Airlines, United Airlines, Transcontinental and Western Air.
Taxis: 40¢ within city limits.
Busses: 5¢ within city limits; no transfers.
Traffic Regulations: Turns may be made in either direction at intersections, except where traffic lights direct otherwise. Watch signs for parking limits.

Accommodations: Two modern hotels; many tourist homes.

Information Service: Chamber of Commerce at Winfield Scott Hotel, N. Broad St.

Motion Picture Houses: Eight.
Swimming: Dowd's Municipal Pool, Front and E. Jersey Sts., June 1 to Labor Day, 10¢ for children, 15¢ for adults.

Annual Events: Combined city and county sports events at Warinanco Park during summer.

ELIZABETH (70 alt., 114,589 pop.) is southernmost in a chain of old cities—now industrialized—that form continuous links along the Jersey shore in the metropolitan area. The city's northeastern boundary is a purely theoretical line marking the place where Newark begins. The centers of the two cities are only 5 miles apart, and the business and residential continuity between them is unbroken.

Elizabeth has seen its native American population augmented by an influx of workers from this country and Europe, and has watched old landmarks succumb to the demand for factories, apartment houses, and service stations. With a water front on Newark Bay and Staten Island Sound, the city was the natural terminus of the earliest highways and the first railroads. Although it is no longer an important terminal, Elizabeth has grown in stature as an industrial and residential area.

The better residential section has a handsome assortment of shade trees and gardens. Blue iris brightens many front yards in May; the somber leaves of the copper beech stand out against a cheerful background of blossoming horse chestnuts and catalpas, and the omnipresent maple. The colors of the town, with the exception of its greenery, are those of a manufacturing place; faded and stained reds, grays, yellows, and browns. The white clapboard dwellings that might be expected from Elizabeth's early American heritage are rarely found.

Houses range from the yellow brick flats and nondescript frame structures of the poorer sections to the commuters' and businessmen's compact, modern homes in the early American or English cottage style. Characteristic of the older residential district are the semi-mansions of the late nineteenth and early twentieth centuries: bulky structures, often with commodious corner towers and bay windows, built in combinations of brick and stone, shingle and clapboard, stucco and half-timber; decorated with a fantastic variety of porch columns and moldings.

Business buildings include a full quota of the heavy-corniced brick structures of 40 years ago. Others, of more recent construction, are simply and neatly designed. The city's one large office building is a 13-story structure modernly individualistic in design, its exterior richly decorated with aluminum panels and terra cotta ornaments. Red brick factories and a few modern industrial buildings fringe the city.

The northern end of the business district has a reminder of the days when Elizabeth was an important railroad terminal. This is "the Arch," where Broad Street dips to pass under a broad stone arch of the Jersey Central, and the viaduct of the Pennsylvania main line crosses over both the Jersey Central tracks and the street. Trolley cars no longer thump along Broad Street under the Arch; they have been replaced by trackless trolleys and busses. Above is an almost unending roar of freight and passenger trains on the two railroads. The decline of water transportation was followed by relocation of the city's industrial life; factories now are clustered mainly along the railroads more than a mile inland.

Elizabethans, because of the city's location on the metropolitan fringe, are a mingling of the urban with the suburban. Their culture is influenced by contact with New York's theaters, concert halls, and social movements. The city is well stocked with churches, some of them outstanding native specimens, others of European inspiration.

The labor movement is more advanced in Elizabeth than in the outlying communities. The textile workers maintain a local office, and the building trades have a central headquarters. For nearly 50 years the *Labor Advocate,* one of the State's very few labor newspapers, has been published monthly in Elizabeth.

The history of Elizabeth, oldest English settlement of the State, began in 1664, when the English ended Dutch control of New Netherland. In that year three Long Islanders, John Baily, Daniel Denton, and Luke Watson, received written license from the new English Deputy Governor of New York, Richard Nicolls, and bought from the Indians for the customary quantity of coats, gunpowder, and kettles a large tract extending from Raritan River to Newark Bay.

Farming operations were scarcely a year old when Philip Carteret arrived as the first English Governor of New Jersey. For his capital he picked a spot in the territory of the Long Island emigrants and named it Elizabethtown in honor of the wife of his cousin, Sir George Carteret. Sir George and Lord John Berkeley were at that time the sole Proprietors of all New Jersey.

In Elizabethtown Carteret compromised with the 80 Associates on division of the land. Houses were built by joint effort; so was a church, put up

on the Broad Street site now occupied by the graveyard of the First Presbyterian Church.

In 1668 Governor Carteret summoned the first general assembly to his
new capital. Two years later the Province was in turmoil over a dispute
that has not yet been settled. The original settlers had obtained license to
buy Indian lands from Colonel Nicolls, and they refused to pay annual
quitrents to Carteret. Carteret, unable to maintain authority, went to England
and returned with a compromise that kept peace for a time. Eventually
control of all lands passed to an organization known as the Proprietors of East New Jersey. When the Proprietors attempted to revive the collection of quitrents, the inhabitants promptly retorted that they had bought
their property from the Indians and owed not a cent to the Proprietors
or anyone else. In 1745 the controversy landed in Chancery Court; land
riots followed, and the suit, interrupted by the French and Indian Wars
and the Revolution, was never settled.

The Proprietors, with a flair for mismanagement, transferred the capital
to Perth Amboy in 1686, thinking that this village was destined for
greater things than Elizabethtown. But Elizabethtown withstood the shock
and in 1740 obtained from George II a charter as the "Free Borough and
town of Elizabeth," which called for a borough hall and a courthouse.
These were built on the site of the present Union County Courthouse. A
second charter was granted by the State legislature in 1789, and a city
charter was issued in 1855 and amended in 1863.

Elizabeth's industry developed along characteristic Colonial lines. By
1670 a merchant had established his shop; and six years later a brewer,
William Looker, began catering to the powerful thirsts aroused by day-
long work in the fields and woods. Mills were established for the production of lumber and meal. Good grazing promoted the raising of sheep,
swine, and cattle, which were shipped to New York. The tanning industry
received an early start and by 1687 Elizabethtown was shipping leather
to all of the Colonies. Ships of 30 and 40 tons sailed up the Elizabeth
River as far as Broad Street. Soon Elizabeth was building its own vessels
for pursuing whales, abundant off the Jersey coast.

The Revolution halted Elizabeth's development. The city was an important point in Washington's New Jersey maneuvers; it was, in fact, the
Achilles' heel in his defenses against the British in New York and Staten
Island across the Kill from Elizabeth. Time and again the British from
Staten Island made quick thrusts into the city, burning and pillaging. The
year 1780 was a particularly bad one for the village, marked by major en-
counters at nearby Connecticut Farms (now Union) and Springfield, and
a series of minor skirmishes through the countryside.

Impetus to industrialization came from New York in 1835 when a
group of New York businessmen, aware of what the new railroads would
mean to Elizabeth, bought a tract of land fronting for a half-mile on
Staten Island Sound. They laid it out in long rectangular plots and named
it "The New Manufacturing Town of Elizabeth Port."

During these years the water front was busy with fishermen and oystermen. It was called "downtown" as opposed to the "uptown" district

FIRST PRESBYTERIAN CHURCH, ELIZABETH

around Broad Street, and there was violent antagonism between the two sections. The downtown men were known as "salt water boys." At irregular intervals they declared a "salt water day" that was celebrated by throwing every available uptowner off the dock.

Formation of volunteer fire companies in 1837 made for further breaches of the peace. There was sharp competition between the fire companies, not because of anxiety over the burning building, but to obtain a hydrant for the water fight that followed every fire. Downtown Red Jacket Engine Co. No. 4 had the jump in early morning blazes on its rivals in the uptown Hibernia Engine No. 5, for the Red Jackets were up at 2 a.m. getting ready to sail for the Newark Bay oyster beds. Early evening fires provided the best competition; the Hibernians armed a man with a poker to prevent the Red Jackets from cutting their hose.

As a change from fighting with the uptowners, the oystermen used oars, oyster rakes, and boathooks in repelling Staten Island oystermen who ventured into Jersey waters. Every morning the fleets started up the bay, returning at 5 p.m. At daybreak oyster dealers from Prince Bay, Staten Island, would arrive with a large basket at the masthead, a signal that oysters were being bought, whereupon the men would flock out to sell.

There was one downtowner who was welcome all over the city—the clam vendor who drove his little horse cart slowly through the streets, singing hoarsely:

> Fine clams, fine clams,
> Fine clams, I say,
> They are good to stew,
> And good to fry;
> And are good to make
> A good clam pie.

In 1873 the first important industry, the Singer Sewing Machine Company, came to Elizabeth and "The New Manufacturing Town of Elizabeth Port" began to develop. Railroad extensions to the Pennsylvania coal fields resulted in the building of docks at the Elizabeth and Somerville Railroad Terminal, foot of Broadway, where freight and passengers were transferred to boats for New York. Coal was shipped to ports in New England and New York. The "Pig Iron Dock" was the center for pig iron brought in barges from northern New Jersey and New York and shipped by train to iron mills elsewhere in the country. The railroads stimulated the immigration of large numbers of Germans and Irish to the city. World War production brought thousands of Slavs and Italians to man Elizabeth factories.

Elizabeth now has 201 manufacturing plants. Products include Simmons beds, sewing machines, Kelly presses, refined petroleum, soap, chemicals, clothing, furniture, iron and steel machinery and other commodities to an annual value of more than $122,000,000.

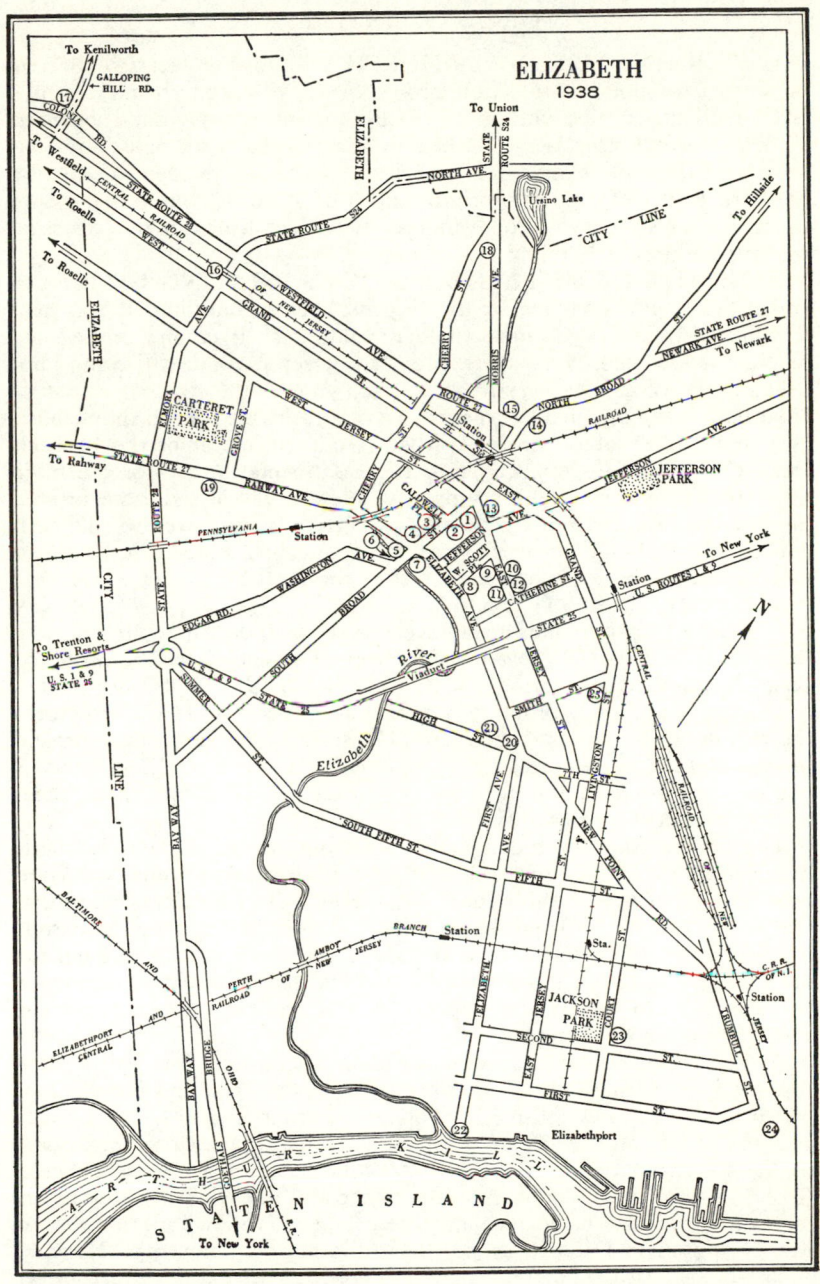

ELIZABETH
1938

POINTS OF INTEREST

1. ST. JOHN'S EPISCOPAL CHURCH, 61 Broad St., erected 1860, is of Victorian Gothic design, dull brown brick with stone trim. It stands on a small grassy plot with an adjoining ancient burial ground, between modern business structures. The heavily carved stonework of its 126-foot tower and the contrasting bands of brick and stone have been softened by the dark patina of age. The original church (of which there is a model in the warden's room) was built in 1706, and demolished in 1859 to make way for the present building.

2. The SITE OF SHEPARD KOLLOCK'S PRINTING OFFICE, 39 Broad St., is now occupied by the Regent Theater Building. It was here that Shepard Kollock, an ink-stained Revolutionist, lived and printed one of New Jersey's first newspapers, the New Jersey *Journal,* still being published as the Elizabeth *Daily Journal.*

Kollock was born in Delaware in 1751 and learned the printing business in the office of his uncle, William Goddard, editor of the Pennsylvania *Chronicle.* He resigned from the Continental Army for the more vital task of combating the Tory press of New York City. Kollock printed his first issues in 1779 in Chatham, N. J. In 1785 he moved to Elizabeth and built a combined home, printing office, and bookstore. When he died in 1839 he was buried across the street in the Presbyterian cemetery.

3. The FIRST PRESBYTERIAN CHURCH, Broad St., S. of Caldwell Pl., dedicated 1786, stands in a level grassy plot dotted with venerable tombstones and weather-beaten sarcophagi. The church is of soft-toned Jersey brick, trimmed sparingly with white wood; the unaltered windows in the façade are finely proportioned. A lean tapering spire rises to crown the well-developed tower at the front. The spire, blown down by a tornado in August 1899, was replaced in 1902. With peculiarly small brick corner quoins, this is one of the most pleasing examples of Georgian Colonial church architecture in the State.

The first building, a rough frame structure, served as church, courthouse, and meeting place for the first general assembly of 1668. A second church, built in 1724, was burned in 1780 by a British raiding party that crossed on January ice from Staten Island. The following year the pastor, the Rev. James Caldwell *(see Springfield, Tour 10),* was shot through the heart at Elizabethtown Point by a Continental sentry whose command he had been slow to obey. Upon evidence that he had been bribed to fire the shot, the soldier was hanged.

Another prominent pastor was Jonathan Dickinson, who became the first president of the College of New Jersey (now Princeton University), which he helped to establish. The college was chartered in October 1746, and classes met on the site of the present Sunday School building. Some of the students boarded at the minister's house on Pearl Street between Race Street and Washington Avenue. When the Rev. Aaron Burr (father of his more famous namesake) became president, following the death of Mr. Dickinson in October 1747, the institution was moved to Newark.

The PARISH HOUSE, of red brick, was erected 1917 on the Broad Street corner of the property. On this site an academy for young men was built in 1767. Among the students were Alexander Hamilton and Aaron Burr; Hamilton and his teacher left the school to fight in the Revolution. The academy, converted into a storehouse, was burned by the British in 1780.

4. The UNION COUNTY COURTHOUSE, NW. corner Broad St. and Rahway Ave., is of gray stone in the formal classical manner, designed by Ackerman and Ross. It was erected 1903 on the site of the old borough courthouse burned by the British in 1780. A broad sweep of stone steps leads up to the entrance door within a portico of fluted Corinthian columns, crowned with an entablature and pediment.

Behind the courthouse is the ANNEX, built 1925–31 from the plans of Oakley and Son. The annex is a square tower, 15 stories high, overornamented by numerous false window openings, Ionic pilasters, and stepped pyramidal roof. The UNION COUNTY HISTORICAL SOCIETY ROOM *(open 2-4:30 Wed.; 9:30-12 Sat.),* 4th floor, contains an interesting collection of portraits, books and historical relics.

5. PUBLIC LIBRARY *(open 9-9 daily),* SW. corner Broad St. and Rahway Ave., was built in 1912; a wing was added in 1929. It is a two-story stone structure of Italian Renaissance style, the work of E. L. Tilden. On this site was a series of famous Colonial and Revolutionary taverns: Nag's Head Tavern, The Marquis of Granby, Red Lion, and, after the Revolution, Indian Queen.

The New York *Gazette* of March 1760 reported that Elizabeth's library was founded in 1755, had upwards of 300 volumes and expected 70 more. In 1857 the Elizabeth Library Hall Association, incorporated the previous year by State charter, began a new building. The library was moved several times before it reached its present home.

6. The OLD MILL SITE, Broad St. at Elizabeth River, adjoins the library. The first mill in Elizabethtown was built here prior to 1669 by John Ogden, one of the city's founders. Before the Revolution the mill was owned by Barnaby Shute, an illiterate oysterman who unexpectedly came into possession of a fortune. The tradition is that Shute essayed the role of public benefactor by building, among other things, an elegant jail for his town. He became insolvent shortly thereafter and was sentenced as a debtor to be the first occupant of the new jail.

7. CARTERET ARMS *(open 10-4 weekdays),* 16 S. Broad St., is the home of the Woman's Club of Elizabeth. Erected *c.* 1795, it is a two-and-one-half-story building of local brick, with gambrel roof, dormers, and attractive entrance porch. It successively housed an orphan asylum, the public library, and the Elizabeth Historic and Civic Association.

8. CITY HALL, Elizabeth Ave. and W. Scott Pl., built in 1865 on the site of the first schoolhouse and of the old Adelphian Academy, and constructed of raspberry-painted brick, is designed in the baronial-industrial style of architecture so loved by the post-Civil War captains of American industry. It retains a measure of dignity. Half of the ground floor was originally occupied by a public market and the floor above served as drill room for the militia. The city has no deed for the land.

9. SCOTT PARK, E. Jersey St. between E. Scott Pl. and W. Scott Pl.,

preserves in the heart of Elizabeth some memory of old Elizabethtown. It was named in honor of Lieut. Gen. Winfield Scott of Mexican War fame. The Thomas Jefferson High School for boys faces the park on the east. Scott's house, razed in 1928, stood nearby at 1105 E. Jersey Street. Dr. William Barnet, a surgeon in the American Army, occupied the house from 1763 to 1790. When his home was plundered by the British in 1781, Dr. Barnet reported: "They emptied my feather beds in the streets, broke in windows, smashed my mirrors and left our pantry and storeroom department bare. I could forgive them all that, but the rascals stole from my kitchen wall the finest string of red peppers in all Elizabeth."

10. The BOUDINOT HOUSE (Boxwood Hall), 1073 E. Jersey St. *(private)*, a home for aged women, is an ample structure with mansard roof, tall chimneys and a massive door with a brass knocker. It was built by Samuel Woodruff, probably as early as 1752.

On the stone steps in 1781 Elias Boudinot gave a ringing address over the body of James Caldwell, slain pastor of the First Presbyterian Church. After the Revolution the house was owned by Jonathan Dayton, speaker of the House of Representatives and later U. S. Senator, for whom Dayton, Ohio, was named. Lafayette was entertained here in 1824, leaving a touch of Old World romanticism to color the dreams of young ladies who attended Miss Spaulding's fashionable school at the same spot 20 years later.

Boudinot, a distinguished Revolutionist, was president of the Continental Congress and a signer of the Treaty of Peace with Great Britain. In 1789, as a member of the House of Representatives, he introduced a resolution calling upon President Washington to proclaim a national day of thanksgiving. The President named Thursday, November 26, Thanksgiving Day.

11. BELCHER MANSION *(private)*, 1046 E. Jersey St., stands on the lot granted to John Ogden Jr., son of the early settler. The brick house, well cared for, is thought to have been built before 1742 and possibly before 1722; the Classical Revival porch was added a century later. The cove cornice is unusual. The dignified woodwork inside is richly carved. Jonathan Belcher, Royal Governor of the Province, lived here from 1751 until his death six years later. The Governor was a supporter of the plan for a College of New Jersey, and the house has been called the cradle of Princeton University. Washington, Lafayette, and Hamilton came here in 1778 to attend the wedding of William Peartree Smith's daughter "Caty" to Elisha Boudinot, brother of Elias.

Gov. Aaron Ogden later acquired the property and entertained Lafayette in 1824. The house was restored in 1899 by the then owner, Warren R. Dix, in time to entertain Lafayette's great-grandson in 1901.

12. NATHANIEL BONNELL HOUSE *(private)*, 1045 E. Jersey St., is believed to be the oldest house in the city. It was built prior to 1682 by Nathaniel Bonnell, who had been allotted 6 acres of land for a homestead in the late 1660's. The faded, two-story clapboard structure is in disrepair.

13. SITE OF THE ISAAC ARNETT HOUSE, 1155 E. Jersey St., is occupied by the Elizabeth Carteret Hotel. It was called the Isaac Arnett

House but it is remembered now for Isaac Arnett's wife Hannah, the Revolutionary Barbara Frietchie of Elizabeth. After Cornwallis had driven Washington from New York in 1776, he offered amnesty to all who would swear allegiance to the Crown within 60 days. The offer was tempting to some citizens of Elizabeth who shared the general despondency of the Colonists, and a group met at the Arnett house to discuss the proposition. In an adjoining room sat Hannah, knitting and listening. When she could stand it no longer, she flounced into the debate, ignoring her husband's efforts to keep his wife in her place. "We may be poor and weak and few," Hannah said. "England may have her limitless resources. But we have something that England has not. God is on our side. Every volley from our muskets is an echo of His voice. Shame upon you cowards!" The amnesty was refused.

14. The ELIZABETH DAILY JOURNAL PLANT *(open for group tours by appointment)*, 295 N. Broad St., is a modern red brick building. The newspaper, oldest in the State, was founded in 1779 by Shepard Kollock.

15. The WILLIAMSON HOUSE, 21 Westfield Ave., is now the Elks Home. Built in 1808 by Isaac H. Williamson (Governor 1817–29), it has a hand-carved stair rail and trim. The building was heightened one story when it was taken over by the Elks, and a large porch was added.

16. AMERICAN TYPE FOUNDERS PLANT *(open for group tours upon written application)*, 200 Elmora Ave., is the work of Day and Klauder, architects. In both plan and elevation the three-story red brick building is an admirable example of functional design. Kelly automatic printing presses are manufactured here as well as type, casts, and printing supplies and machinery of all kinds.

17. GALLOPING HILL MONUMENT, Galloping Hill and Colonia Rds., is a block of Barre granite with a bronze tablet, occupying a triangular plot. At this point the invading British army from Staten Island, marching through old Elizabethtown to Connecticut Farms and Springfield for the two battles of June 1780, turned into Galloping Hill Road. The invaders were constantly harried by militia under Major Generals Greene and Dickinson.

18. The CRANE HOUSE *(private)*, 556 Morris Ave., is of New England Colonial type, having white-painted siding, second-story dormer windows and half-windows below the eaves, as well as the customary one-and-one-half-story ell that served as the service wing. Built before the Revolution, the house has been continuously occupied by the Crane family; the first of the Cranes was Stephen, who settled in Elizabethtown in 1665. An old-fashioned garden around the original well has some of the oldest and finest red hollyhocks in Elizabeth. Seeds from these plants have produced blossoms almost black.

19. The OLD CHATEAU *(private)*, 408 Rahway Ave., is a large, grayish brick building with two wings; quoins and keystones over the windows are of brownstone. Erected *c.* 1760, the house, surrounded by trees, stands well back from the road on unkempt grounds. It was the main building on the estate of Cavalier Jouet, grandfather of the late Chancellor

Benjamin Williamson, and himself the grandson of Mayor Daniel Jouet of Angers, France. The Old Chateau and its lands were confiscated during the Revolution because the Cavalier remained loyal to King George III, who had allowed his forefathers to settle in England when they were exiled from France.

20. STATUE OF THE MINUTE MAN, 1st Ave. and High St., stands in Union Square. The sculptor, Carl Conrads, German-born Civil War veteran whose statue of Daniel Webster is in Washington, created a typical militiaman: shirt open at the neck, sleeves rolled up from brawny arms, one fist gripping the muzzle of his musket, and the head alert, as if straining for sight of invading British.

The statue commemorates Colonial resistance to British invaders in June 1780. On the night of June 7 Major General Knyphausen ferried 6,000 men across from Staten Island for a surprise attack. The troops marched up King's Highway (now Elizabeth Avenue) and met an outpost of 12 pickets at Union Square. After a first volley that mortally wounded General Stirling the pickets prudently gave way.

Continuing their march through Elizabeth, the British were halted by militia at Galloping Hill Road at Connecticut Farms (Union). During the night most of the British returned to Staten Island. A small force managed to hold the Elizabeth shore of Arthur Kill after a sharp encounter with the pursuing Colonials the following morning. About two weeks later Sir Henry Clinton resumed the attack with 5,000 troops. He proceeded to Springfield where he drove off an inferior force of militia and burned the town. Later the British retired to Staten Island.

21. CITY MARKET *(open 8-3 Tues., Thurs., Sat.)*, High St. W. of Elizabeth Ave., has authentic farm flavor. Truck gardeners and commission men back their trucks up to the curb in a solid row that extends around the corner on 2nd Avenue and display their produce on wooden tables, often under canvas shelters. The market is thronged with women shoppers who leisurely make their way through a gantlet of sales cries: "Feel those oranges—look at that juice—10 for a quarter!" "Lady, them are lovely berries. I'll show you the bottom. They're perfect!" Promptly at 3 o'clock a street-cleaning crew arrives and opens a fire hydrant to flush the littered street.

22. OLD FERRY SITE, SE. end Elizabeth Ave. on the Arthur Kill, is now merely a rotting municipal wharf with a railroad crane, an excellent view and 250 years of history. Beside it is the terminal of the Elizabeth-Staten Island Ferry, operating two single-deck, turtle-shaped boats that are the smallest and funniest vehicular ferries in New York Harbor. Almost a stone's throw across the channel is Staten Island, part of New York City, but desolate marshland here, except for the large Procter and Gamble soap factory in the background. Westward is a fine silhouette of the high cantilever span of Goethals Bridge *(see Tour 17)*; below is the small swing span of the Baltimore and Ohio R.R. bridge, little used, yet the only rail connection for freight traffic between New Jersey and New York City. Eastward, beyond the junction of Newark Bay with the Kill van Kull, is the graceful steel arch of Bayonne Bridge *(see BAYONNE)*. Along the

Elizabeth shore are several oil depots, lumberyards, coal-shipping docks, a shipyard, and sand and gravel yards.

At this point sailboat ferries to New York docked as early as 1679. Washington stepped aboard a gaily decorated barge here for his trip up the harbor to the inaugural in New York. Steam service was begun in 1808. When rail connections with Philadelphia were completed in 1834, Elizabeth was the transfer point for New York passengers; but construction of the New Jersey Central's bridge across Newark Bay, establishing through service to Jersey City, made the water route obsolete in the sixties. Today little breaks the stillness except the chug of passing towboats, the ferry company's mechanical turtles thumping their way across the channel, the blast of a siren as the Elizabeth River drawbridge is raised, and the drone of transport planes making for Newark Airport.

23. ST. PATRICK'S CATHEDRAL, 213 Court St., of Victorian Gothic design, is constructed of light gray stone. Its tall spires are conspicuous landmarks. The cathedral, erected 1887, is opposite Jackson Park, one of the half-dozen green squares in Elizabeth and reputedly the site of an Indian burying ground. Adjoining is St. Patrick's High School, oldest Catholic secondary school of the State.

24. SINGER SEWING MACHINE PLANT *(open for group tours upon written application)*, SE. end Trumbull St., is the largest industry of Elizabeth. Tall, many-windowed brick buildings are weathered and well covered with vines. In 1851 Isaac M. Singer placed on the market his first sewing machine, intended to be set up and operated on the packing case in which it was delivered, and propelled by a wooden treadle and pitman. By 1873 the demand for the machines was so great that the few small factories in New York were combined and moved to Elizabethport, where about 7,000 persons are now employed.

25. NEW JERSEY PRETZEL PLANT *(open weekdays)*, 816 Livingston St., employs deaf mutes hired through the State Department of Institutions and Agencies. The pretzel bending done by these workers is one of the few old handicrafts defying the machine age, since no one has succeeded in inventing a machine to put the twist in a pretzel.

POINTS OF INTEREST IN ENVIRONS

General Motors plant, Linden, *3.8 m. (see Tour 1)*; Edison Memorial Tower, Menlo Park, *9.7 m. (see Tour 8)*; Liberty Hall, former home of Governor Livingston, *1 m.*, Springfield Presbyterian Church, Revolutionary landmark, *6.1 m. (see Tour 10)*.

Freehold

Railroad Stations: Pennsylvania Station, Broad and Throckmorton Sts., for Pennsylvania R.R.; Jersey Central Station, Jackson and Mechanic Sts., for Jersey Central R.R.
Bus Station: Municipal Parking Lot for Lincoln Transit, Asbury Park and New York Transit; 23 W. Main St. for Gray Line; 6 E. Main St. opp. Courthouse for Public Service.
Traffic Regulations: Watch street signs for parking limitations.

Accommodations: One hotel, tourist homes.

Information Service: Municipal Bldg., W. Main St.; Public Library, E. Main St.

Motion Picture Houses: Two.
Trotting Races: Freehold Race Track, Park Ave. and W. Main St.

FREEHOLD (170 alt., 6,894 pop.) seen from the air is a dot among squares and oblongs of contrasting green fields edged with reddish clay. Up to the town's very doorstep spread the fields and woodlands of the gently rolling land of Monmouth County, the second richest agricultural county in the United States.

Without drawing too heavily on its storied past, Freehold has individuality produced by a fusion of rural, urban, and residential life. In an unobtrusive way it seems to embody America's growth from farm to factory. But country atmosphere dominates the town. Main Street is broad and tree-lined, and many stores in the small business section are in former private dwellings, but rarely is a horse tethered to the hitching posts along the curb.

Surrounding this provincial core is an industrial growth concentrated in a large rug factory that has blended with the community rather than altered it into a factory town.

Although Freehold has a full quota of industrial workers as well as business people and retired farmers, there is nothing that could be called a slum section. The town has an almost uniform degree of prosperous living equaled by few other New Jersey communities. Homes in the residential area range from Colonial through Victorian to contemporary American architecture, with a predominance of white-painted frame structures. There is plenty of room for lawns and trees—oaks, elms, maples, horse chestnuts, lindens, honey locusts, and copper beeches. Almost every house has a garden bright with such flowers as the oriental poppy, blue bachelor's button, lemon lily, and lavender iris.

Its position as county seat makes Freehold the center for the surrounding farm country. Traffic chokes the business section, especially when big farm trucks carry summer produce to the New York and Philadelphia markets. A steady stream of beach-bound motorists pours through the

RUG WEAVING, FREEHOLD

town on summer week ends, providing trade for several antique shops. Main Street, once the King's Highway and the old Burlington Trail, approximately follows a route once used by Indians, pioneer settlers, British and American soldiers, and early stagecoaches.

The first white settlement in the Freehold district was made about 1650. A permanent village was established here in 1715 by Scots from New Aberdeen (now Matawan), who had earlier left England because of persecution by Charles II. They chose the name of Monmouth Court House from Monmouthshire in England.

Coastal residents complained that politics was responsible for selection of a courthouse site in the inland wilderness, and the record shows that, at the very least, shrewd business sense was involved. In 1714, one year after passage of an assembly act designating Freehold Township as the site, John Reid bought an extensive tract of land. He sold part of his holdings to the county authorities for a courthouse site at the bargain price of 30 shillings, and immensely increased the value of the rest of his property.

Colonists gathered in the courthouse to protest the Boston Port Bill; later, in a more militant mood, they heard news of the battles of Lexington and Bunker Hill. In 1778 Freehold saw part of the Battle of Monmouth *(see Tour 18A)*. On June 27, the day before the fighting, Sir Henry Clinton and his army, retreating from Philadelphia to New York, occupied the town. The British commander and his staff established themselves in the present Moreau House.

The first of two early attacks occurred near the present high school on the northeastern edge of the town. On the slight rise of ground now known as Monument Park, behind the present courthouse, Col. Butler's detachment of Revolutionaries fired a heavy volley in the second skirmish, dispersing a body of the Queen's Rangers, the celebrated Tory corps.

During the hot Sunday on which Washington's troops tried to shatter the British forces, soldiers of both sides thronged in and out of the village. Lafayette led a party of horsemen down Main Street past the courthouse; various buildings were converted into military hospitals; and local residents fired on the escaping British from the shelter of trees and fences. The New Jersey *Gazette* later published a withering letter describing British outrages, and accusing General Clinton of conduct by no means to his credit.

The last important local episode of the Revolution was a public funeral in 1782 for Capt. Joshua Huddy, the Revolutionist who was summarily hanged by Tories as an act of vengeance *(see Tour 18)*.

By 1795 a post office was opened, under the shorter name of Monmouth. Six years later the name was changed to Freehold by postal authorities to avoid confusion with other Monmouths in the county. The first newspaper, the *Spirit of Washington,* appeared during the years 1814–15; and in 1834 the Monmouth *Democrat,* still in existence, was established. Several private schools were functioning at the middle of the century, one of which, the Freehold Institute, remains as the Freehold Military School, a preparatory institution.

A stage line with railroad connections at Hightstown enabled Freehold residents in 1836 to reach New York or Philadelphia in 7 hours. Plank roads were built to Howell and Keyport, speeding the transportation of marl and farm produce for shipment by water. The Freehold and Jamesburg Agricultural Railroad began service in 1853, and the marl pits at Farmingdale were later tapped by the Squankum Railroad. Both are now part of the Pennsylvania Railroad. A line paralleling the old plank road to Keyport was finally opened as the Freehold and New York Railway in 1880, and was later taken over by the Jersey Central.

A disastrous fire destroyed the courthouse and a number of buildings in 1873. The heat was so intense that no trace of the courthouse bell, placed in 1809, was ever found.

During the past half-century Freehold has progressed steadily as a center of agricultural enterprise, known chiefly for heavy shipments of potatoes. Modern concrete highways, some of them following the route of old toll roads, radiate from the town like the spokes of a wheel.

POINTS OF INTEREST

1. The COURTHOUSE, Main and Court Sts., stands in the center of Freehold, facing a maple-shaded lawn. Built in 1874 and remodeled after a fire in 1930, the stone structure is a conservative modern adaptation of Georgian Colonial design. There are two one-story porticoed entrances, and on the center of the roof ridge, a Georgian Colonial cupola with a clock. The building stands behind the site of the old courthouse, where General Clinton left more than 45 disabled men to be cared for by the Americans at the time of the Battle of Monmouth.

2. MONUMENT PARK, Court St., N. of the courthouse, a half-acre wedge of lawn, contains MONMOUTH BATTLE MONUMENT. The 94-foot shaft, capped with a statue of Liberty Triumphant, was designed by Emelin T. Littell and Douglas Smythe. Around the base are five bronze bas-reliefs by J. E. Kelly depicting battle scenes, including Molly Pitcher at her husband's gun (see Tour 18A). The cornerstone was laid in 1878 on the 100th anniversary of the battle; 6 years later the unveiling took place.

3. MONMOUTH COUNTY HISTORICAL ASSOCIATION BUILDING (open 11-5 daily except Mon.; 2-5 Sun.; adm. 25¢ on Thurs.), 70 Court St., is a graceful Georgian Colonial reproduction, a two-story brick building with pitched slate roof and white-painted woodwork. The entrance door is arched, with a well proportioned pediment above. Designed by J. Hallam Conover of Freehold, the building was opened in 1931. Housed in memorial rooms of authentic dignity are exhibits that include battle maps, the bell of the second courthouse, the writing desk of James Wilson, signer of the Declaration of Independence, mementoes of old racing days, and a fine collection of Colonial furniture. There is a LIBRARY (open 1-5 daily except Mon.; 2-5 Sun.) consisting of books, documents, church records, newspaper clippings, and paper money. In the unfinished attic is an assortment of household utensils, cradles and old chests.

4. ST. PETER'S EPISCOPAL CHURCH, 33 Throckmorton St., is considered the oldest church in use in New Jersey. Scottish and English Quakers built the original structure—consisting of four walls and a roof but no floor—in 1683 at Topanemus, 4 m. north of Freehold. Prominent in the meeting was George Keith, a Presbyterian Scot who came to America as a Quaker convert. A voyage to England changed Keith's mind and his faith once more; he returned as a Church of England missionary and converted all of the Topanemus Quakers. St. Peter's was moved south to Freehold, changing its denomination but not its congregation en route. The church was used as a hospital by the British at the Battle of Monmouth; at other times the Americans used it as a barracks and ammunition station. The white-shingled, two-story structure has a small, graceful belfry above the front gable. It has been extensively altered.

5. FREEHOLD RACE TRACK (*trotting races during summer; 1:30 Sat., adm. 50¢ for parking and grandstand; holidays, adm. 50¢ parking, 50¢ grandstand*), NW. corner Park Ave. and W. Main St., was reopened 1937 after a number of years of idleness. The track has changed little since 1873 when it first drew crowds from miles around. From the glaring red and yellow barns grinning Negro stable boys lead blanketed horses for exercise, trainers drive their sulkies around the course, and race track frequenters, many in the traditional checked suits, watch from the rail. The track was once the main attraction of the county fairs.

6. HANKINSON MANSION or Moreau House (*private*), 150 W. Main St., was built by a member of the Hankinson family in 1755 and is the oldest residence in Freehold. Great shade trees and a broad expanse of lawn add to the cool stateliness of the white shingled green shuttered mansion. The back of the structure faces the street. The house was built by the same workmen who erected Tennent Church (*see Tour 18A*) three years earlier, and repeats the detail of the exterior cornice and several interior features of the church. A hallway 11½ feet wide opens into spacious drawing rooms with fine mantels and paneled doors. A crude painting of a naval scene, above the fireplace in the great bedchamber, has been attributed to an unknown Hessian soldier. Clinton and his officers stayed here the night before the Battle of Monmouth, forcing the widow Conover to sleep in a chair in the milk-room, a lean-to still standing.

William Forman, sea captain and happy bachelor, bought the house and lived here with his brothers and sisters. Capt. James Lawrence was entertained by Forman, whose sisters strewed the hero's path with roses while the guests drank his health with opalescent wine. To Forman were addressed the lines of Philip Freneau's poem, *The Seafaring Bachelor:*

> In all your rounds 'tis wondrous strange
> No fair one tempts you to a change
> Madness it is, you must agree,
> To lodge alone 'till forty-three.

The captain died a bachelor.

7. A. AND H. KARAGHEUSIAN CARPET FACTORY (*open by permission*), Jackson and Center Sts., is the business that originated the

trade name "Gulistan" or "American Oriental." The factory covers several blocks and employs 1,500 persons; even larger plants are operated by the company in China and Persia.

In the designing department a dozen artists seek usable patterns, borrowing material from museums and libraries, copying old or new Oriental rugs, or executing original designs. The artists have their choice of 3,500 colors and shades, all combinations of the primary red, blue, and yellow. The jacquard weaving of Wilton rugs is done with a series of perforated cards that pass over perforated cylinders connecting with needles, which in turn guide the weaving of the design—somewhat in the manner of a player-piano. Strands not in use are raised to different levels and hidden in the bosom of the carpet until needed. At the same time a short, thin blade attached to a wire cuts the yarn, making the pile. A loom 15 feet wide, largest for Wilton rugs in this country, is here. For Axminster rugs, the design is transferred to a series of spools; each is one row in the rug, being used but once each time the pattern is made. To set up a loom for a 12-ft. rug, 8 girls must work 10 days on 4 setting machines. Large rugs were made here for the Radio City Music Hall in New York and for the new United States Supreme Court Building.

POINTS OF INTEREST IN ENVIRONS

Freneau Farm, *9.9 m. (see Tour 18)*; Molly Pitcher's Well, *1.4 m.,* Monmouth Battlefield and Tennent Church, *3.8 m. (see Tour 18A)*; Our House Tavern, *7.3 m. (see Tour 20)*.

Hackensack

Railroad Stations: Main St. Station, Mercer and Main Sts., for New York, Sus-quehanna and Western R.R.; Essex St. Station, Essex St. and Railroad Ave., for New Jersey and New York R.R. and Erie R.R.

Bus Stations: Municipal Bus Terminal, River St. opposite Demarest Place, for Public Service, Garden State Line, Flying Eagle Suburban Line, Westwood Trans-portation Co.; Public Service Terminal, State and Mercer Sts., for local busses; 352 Main St. for Greyhound.

Taxis: 35¢ within city limits.

Streetcars and Local Busses: 5¢; no transfers.

Accommodations: Boarding houses.

Information Service: Bergen County Chamber of Commerce, 210 Main St.

Motion Picture Houses: Three.

Swimming: Y.M.C.A., 360 Main St.; Y.M.H.A., 211 Essex St.; Hackensack Swim-ming Pool, River St. and Hackensack Ave.; Maple Springs Beach, Hackensack Ave. near Route 4; Garden Suburbs, Central Ave.

Tennis: High school field, First St. opp. Hackensack high school; Oritani Field Club, 18 E. Camden St.; Johnson Park, Main St. and Fairmont Ave.; Garden Suburbs, Central Ave.

Annual Events: Bergen County Salon of Photography, Fox Theater, March; Bergen County Electrical and Home Modernization Show, Hackensack Arena, April; Garden Federation Exhibit, Woman's Club, September.

HACKENSACK (134 alt., 24,568 pop.) is gaining in importance among the industrial cities encircling New York, because of its strategic position in the network of modern highways traversing northern New Jersey. The old city lies on the west bank of the Hackensack River, halfway between Paterson and the Hudson, and shows on its face the new blood pumped into it by the road development of the past decade.

Hackensack is built on the flatlands of a tidal river and like most such communities its local scene changes as its population growth stretches its boundaries. Most of the older section lies close to the river. The newer sections and many of the better residences are found on the higher ground that gradually rises to the west and north of the old business section. The civic center, where the courthouse and other public buildings are situated, is the focal point of several highways. Main Street, the principal thorough-fare, extends northward from this point.

The crush on Main Street makes unmistakable the suddenness of the city's recent change. The narrow, north-south street is jammed with traffic from all over Bergen County, and its sidewalks are closely packed with blocks of modern, neonized and black-glass store fronts which have already crowded out most of the leisurely older shops. Chain stores, in particular, have been erected so quickly and in such abundance that often their flash-ing signs are almost larger than their Main Street footage.

BERGEN COUNTY COURTHOUSE, HACKENSACK

The vista of Main Street, looking north, shows in addition to the jumble and squeeze of shops, a 10-story skyscraper, several impressive banks, and the latest in ornate motion picture houses, where again the size of the signs promises at least a Roxy or Radio City Music Hall. Shops have already spread to the adjoining side streets.

The many markets and bargain shops along Main Street attest Hackensack's position as the hub of Bergen County. Its daily paper is significantly called the Bergen *Evening Record,* and its publisher, John Borg, is a dominant figure in the city and county political life. Organizations such as the Young Men's Hebrew Association, the Young Men's Christian Association, the Child Welfare Association, and many others in Hackensack label themselves "of Bergen County." Despite this county-consciousness and a large percentage of commuters to New York and elsewhere in northern New Jersey, Hackensack has long been noted for its independence and individuality.

Oratory and litigation from 71 squabbling Bergen County municipalities are concentrated here at the county seat. To Hackensack come lawyers and politicians, drawn by pre-election maneuverings, and the editors of some 70 weekly newspapers that are nourished by legal advertising and enlivened by occasional investigations of municipal misconduct. Equally a part of civil life are the caravans of defendants and witnesses whose testimony makes talk for the town, and ammunition for editors and politicians alike.

Hackensack's industrial life is chiefly the manufacture of bricks, cement, slippers, and haberdashery. Low wages, especially for women workers, prevail in the clothing factories. Along the river, navigable only to Hackensack, is the sole industrial scene in the city; here are brickyards, a battery of oil tanks, a stone crusher plant, and warehouses with long lines of rumbling motor trucks and heavy barges. Southeast from the city spread the Hackensack meadows, a tidal flat covered with marsh grass. A crisscross of ditches has been dug by governmental agencies to check mosquito breeding.

In the residential sections the town has preserved an atmosphere of age and tradition. Streets here bear the names of New Jersey counties, Essex, Union, Passaic, etc., and those of pioneer families whose descendants are still active in the community, Zabriskie, Banta, and Hopper. Summit Avenue, a broad, tree-lined street, represents the long-established citizens with rows of large late-Victorian mansions surrounded by ample greenery. Gradually these homes yield to a newer section distinguished by a more frequent use of brick and granite and the styling of the 1920's. Down along the hill, upon which the better homes stand, sprinklings of modern adaptations of Colonial, English, and Norman styles mix with typical frame suburban dwellings and survivals of old Hackensack. Throughout the town at random points there are many authentic Dutch Colonial homes, sturdy reminders of the original citizenry. Hackensack is a genealogist's paradise where research flourishes.

The city's foreign-born population of 20.5 percent is largely concentrated in the area west of Hudson Street and south of Essex Street. It is almost a separate community, with a dominant population of Italians and a much smaller percentage of Poles. Most of the foreign-born work for public utilities, trucking firms, or contractors and live mainly in a typical Hackensack miscellany of old frame houses, recent bungalows, and an occasional brick structure.

The most sharply defined racial colony in Hackensack is the Negro section of about five blocks along First Street between Berry Street and Central Avenue. Although old wooden houses in varying states of repair give the area a more residential appearance than the average Negro urban section, dwellings are excessively crowded, with two and three families often living in a one-family house. The one school is attended almost exclusively by Negro children with teachers of both white and black races. Many of the 2,530 Negroes are active in the movement to better their economic position through political action, and have won recognition to the extent of three Negro appointments to the local police force.

The name Hackensack is supposed to be of Indian origin, but the exact derivation is vague. A favorite local pastime is the collection of different versions of the Indian spelling. These range from Achkinchesacky to Hockumdachgue, and new contributions are constantly being made. It has also been suggested that the town was named after an old tavern called the Hock and Sack, which sold hock, a popular Rhine wine, and sack, an appetizing sherry. This theory is more colorful than probable.

Hackensack dates back to 1647 when the Dutch from Manhattan established a trading post on the lands of Chief Oratam. Governed by the Council of New Netherland, the region was later known as New Barbadoes after the island whence came the original grantees. By 1700 the village was stamped with a Dutch imprint despite the English conquest. Until 1921, when the town received a city charter, its official name was still New Barbadoes.

The Revolutionary period was a turbulent one in Hackensack, with Tory and patriot intrigue. Foraging parties of Continentals and redcoats skirmished over the entire country. In 1780 Hessians and British plundered the village and set fire to the old courthouse on the Green.

After the war Hackensack continued to develop as a commercial and political center. In the early 1800's the Hackensack Turnpike was built, connecting the town with Hoboken, and making Hackensack the freight depot for northern New Jersey. The so-called "Windjammers of the Hackensack" plied the river and bay to New York City, further enhancing the community's shipping importance.

The conservatism of Hackensack's population was demonstrated when the Civil War broke out, popular sentiment favoring slavery to such an extent that an Abolitionist editor had his print shop raided, and the Union flag was publicly burned on the Green.

Construction of the New Jersey and New York Railroad station in 1869 accelerated Hackensack's growth as a residential community, the succeeding years being marked by large-scale real estate operations.

Incorporated as a separate governing unit in 1868, Hackensack, or New Barbadoes, had its affairs administered until 1933 by a group known as the Hackensack Improvement Commission, formed under an act of the State legislature in 1856. This body obtained mail delivery in 1858; introduced the gas street light in 1868; and the telephone exchange in 1882. The twentieth century brought an influx of a large commuting population. With the abandonment of the Improvement Commission, Hackensack's experiments with municipal government turned to the present city manager form, which has been conspicuously successful.

POINTS OF INTEREST

1. The GREEN, S. end Main St., was the Revolutionary camping ground for both American and British regiments. Encircled by a row of hedges and interspersed with flowers and shrubbery, the handkerchief-size square is a well-kept lawn traversed by concrete walks. The county's first courthouse, built on the Green in 1732, was burned to the ground by Hessian mercenaries in 1780. In Colonial days stocks and pillories for criminals stood here. Among the monuments are a bronze STATUE OF AN AMERICAN SOLDIER, erected as a war memorial in 1924, on a concrete and granite base with scenes representing all American wars, and a STATUE OF GENERAL ENOCH POOR, Revolutionary war hero.

2. The CHURCH ON THE GREEN (First Dutch Reformed) *(open weekdays on request)*, NE. corner of the Green, is one of the oldest churches in New Jersey. Built in 1696, rebuilt in 1728, and then enlarged at various intervals until 1869, the red sandstone structure is a fine example of Dutch Colonial church architecture, and the prototype of the other churches in Bergen County. Eleven members of the French Huguenot congregation three miles up the Hackensack River became communicants of the Dutch church. They brought from the French church stones bearing their names, some of which still form part of the present structure. Early in the nineteenth century a doctrinal controversy threatened to divide the congregation. In the midst of one bitter meeting, it is related, a bolt of lightning struck the keystone over the doorway, splitting it in two. Regarding this as a divine omen, the rival factions immediately settled the dispute. The adjacent cemetery contains the remains of many of Bergen County's pioneer settlers.

3. The MANSION HOUSE, NE. corner Main St. and Washington Pl., facing the Green, was built in 1751 by Peter Zabriskie and is still operated as a restaurant. A three-story, whitewashed sandstone building, it is of simple Dutch Colonial design, square and unadorned. A veranda which formerly ran along the front of the house was torn down many years ago. After the fall of Fort Lee in 1776, Washington was quartered here.

4. The BERGEN COUNTY COURTHOUSE, opp. the Green, constructed in 1912, architecturally is one of the most successful buildings in the State. This neo-classic structure designed by J. Riley Gordon was well conceived in proportion, detail and setting. The straightforward treatment of the entrance portico, with columns placed *in antis,* is strong and pleasing.

Directly east of the courthouse is the BERGEN COUNTY JAIL, a striking five-story building with modern lines and medieval battlements. The light brick surface is handsomely illumined at night by flood lights. Only the unobtrusive bars and screens on the windows indicate the building's use.

5. The BERGEN COUNTY ADMINISTRATIVE BUILDING, corner Main and Hudson Sts., designed by Tilton, Schwanewede and Githens, is neoclassic in style, excellent both in scale and detail. Completed in 1933, its four stories of Arkansas marble are well composed in a mass of great dignity. The building houses county agencies and administrative departments.

6. The JOHNSON FREE PUBLIC LIBRARY *(open 9-9 weekdays),* 274 Main St., also houses the HISTORICAL COLLECTIONS of the Bergen County Historical Society *(open 10-6 weekdays).* In addition to documents of various kinds the exhibit includes a large square stone used as a counterbalance in early hangings, a dugout canoe and other Indian relics. The building is of rock-faced Belleville stone in Victorian style, with a fancy bell tower and vine-covered walls.

7. The MUNICIPAL BUS TERMINAL, River St. opp. Demarest Pl., is a modern one-and-one-half-story structure of white-faced brick and glass. Designed by Spencer Newman and opened in 1937, it was financed jointly by the city and the Works Progress Administration. The severity

of the functional style is relieved by effective planting on the approaches. The terminal serves most busses operating in the Hackensack section.

8. The TERHUNE HOUSE *(private)*, 450 River St., near the Anderson Street bridge, is now shielded from the adjacent highway by a galvanized iron wire fence. Built in 1670 by John Terhune, a Hollander, it is the oldest building in Hackensack, and has the first known gambrel roof in New Jersey. The low porch, a later addition, faces the south, overlooking a broad expanse of the Hackensack River. It is shaded by a giant elm, said to be more than 600 years old. Few changes have been made in the Dutch Colonial house of whitewashed sandstone since it was built.

9. The HOPPER HOUSE, 249 Polifly Rd., now an inn, was built between 1816 and 1818 by slaves. It is an interesting example of how even the resolute Dutch succumbed to the Georgian influence in architecture. Although the original Dutch characteristics are reflected in the side and rear elevations, the front door is inconsistent with the general design.

POINT OF INTEREST IN ENVIRONS

Steuben House, *2.7 m. (see Tour 16)*.

Hoboken

Railroad Station: Hudson Pl. for Lackawanna R.R. and Hudson Tubes (connect with Pennsylvania R.R. and Erie R.R.).
Bus Station: D. L. & W. Station and Hudson Tubes for Public Service.
Taxis: 25¢ within city limits.
Piers: E. end 5th St., Holland-American, Cosulich Freight and Navigazione Libera Triestian Lines; E. end 8th St., Gdynia-American, Red Star and Pan-Atlantic Lines; E. end 7th St., Bristol City and Ellerman-Wilson Lines; E. end 14th St., Scandinavian-American Line; E. end 15th St., Lamport and Holt Line; Hudson Pl. and E. end 14th St., Lackawanna ferries.
Streetcars: Fare 5¢.
Traffic Regulations: Numbered streets, one-way, alternating (E. on odd-number streets). Parking limited on Washington St. and Willow St.

Accommodations: Hotels and rooming houses.

Information Service: Chamber of Commerce, 1 Newark St.; Lackawanna Terminal, Hudson Pl. (day and night).

Motion Picture Houses: One first-run; 3 others.
Athletic Fields: Columbus Park, Clinton and 9th Sts.; Oxford Oval, next to Lackawanna Terminal, S. of 9th St.
Swimming: Y.M.C.A., 13th and Washington Sts.
Tennis: Columbus Park, Clinton and 9th Sts.; Stevens Institute, 8th and Hudson Sts.; Hoboken Tennis Courts, Elysian Park.

HOBOKEN (10 alt., 59,261 pop.), incorrectly pronounced "Hobucken" by railroad conductors and a considerable part of the population, has three picturesque characteristics: a water front given over to commerce on a super-technicalized scale; a survival of the 'nineties, revealed in the staid solidity of the old-fashioned streets back of the water front; and a certain cosmopolitan atmosphere, due largely to the presence of restaurants and cafés where the European culture that started them still remains. Outstanding also is Stevens Institute, one of the first-rank engineering colleges of the country. The old residents and the Institute people do not apologize for Hoboken; they like it. Here they find much of the pleasurable life—however different in form—that marked the town 80 years ago when it was a resort for the first families of New York.

The city is cramped in a mile-square area between the Hudson River and the rump of the Palisades. Downtown Hoboken borders Jersey City; at Washington Street the workers in one factory can cross from one city to the other without leaving their room. On the northern boundary are Union City on the heights and Weehawken on the narrow strip of river front. There is hardly any empty space except for the little block-square parks and the Institute campus. Factories, stores, and out-of-date tenements are crowded together flush with the sidewalk. The most densely populated city in the United States, Hoboken has evenly laid-out streets in both directions, each packed with a mass of low, flat-roofed buildings.

The shopping district on Washington Street consists of three-, four-, and five-story painted brick or stucco buildings in an unbroken line on both sides of the wide street. Only a few of the stores show signs of recent renovation. Many of the entrances are raised a step above the street level in the style of the small town Main Street.

Near the college campus is a row of three- and four-story brownstone houses with high stoops, some of them with tiny patches of lawn protected by loose iron fences. On the northern slope of Castle Point are handsome, spacious homes with sloping terraces and broad lawns. Built of white stone or brick in the best style of the early 1900's, they stand on the highest ground in the city.

To seamen, as well as to visiting New Yorkers, River Street is the heart of Hoboken. An almost unbroken row of saloons, with cheap hotels and flats above, stretches along one side of this broad, paved street. On the other side are the entrances to the piers on Hudson River, protected by high wire fences. During the arrival and departure of great liners, River Street resounds to the rattle of innumerable trucks and taxis, the footsteps of excited, hurrying travelers and their friends. Between times the street is a Rialto of the seamen of all nations, interspersed with stevedores and longshoremen. The swinging doors of the many saloons admit tieless workmen in blue denim shirts, or loitering sailors looking for a berth. In larger backrooms the seafarers meet the local citizenry to dance at night to the music of small jazz bands, mechanical pianos or phonographs, or drink beer at small tables with checkered cloths.

Nothing more strikingly illustrates the post-war change in America's maritime life than the stories of River Street's yesterdays, and its life today. The River Street saloons, the sailors' boarding houses and resorts have been known the world over to sea-faring men for generations. The shop-talk of the seven seas was town gossip on River Street sidewalks. Strangers from inland could listen wide-eyed to casual stories of hardship and adventure, of hardboiled captains and wily owners, of nautical feats of sail and steam. Today the same saloons and sidewalks are still frequented by the jerseyed men of all nations who bear unmistakable stamp of their seafaring life. But the talk among these seamen is of unions and labor problems, of fabulous financing of steamship corporations as viewed from sailors' eyes, of horsepower and turbines and tonnage. The tang of the sea still permeates River Street, but the sailor has turned from a hardbitten adventurer into a trade unionist of a mechanized, technical craft.

Through this same area are taverns and dance halls of a different type where a respectable German clientele finds quiet entertainment reminiscent of Continental cafés, and excellent food, served in the best German tradition. There are larger places with old-fashioned fixtures, decorated mirrors, and cut-glass doorways outside swinging doors. Hoboken has been famous for its beer since 1642, though none is brewed here today.

Smoke-dirtied factories at the northern end of the city manufacture a variety of metal, chemical, food, leather, and foundry products, furniture and technical equipment. Ten steamship lines, three of them carrying passengers as well as freight, and five railroads, one of them serving only manufacturers in the city, make Hoboken a transportation center.

The majority of the population is of Italian extraction, although the German, Irish, and Polish nationalities are well represented. Most of the workers are employed in the factories, on the railroads, or on the docks that line the water front.

As early as 1640, the Lenni Lenape Indian territory of Hobocan Hackingh *(land of the tobacco pipe)* was settled by the Dutch of New Amsterdam. Shortly after, the Indians, aroused by a ruthless Dutch massacre in 1643, drove the settlers out and burned all the buildings with the exception of a brewery. The first in America, it had been built in 1642 by Aert T. van Putten, one of the earliest settlers. Peter Stuyvesant bought the land back from the Indians and later his relatives sold it to Samuel Bayard.

Very little occurred to differentiate Hoboken from other towns in New Jersey before the coming of Col. John Stevens, inventor and financier, who bought the whole area for $90,000 when the extensive land holdings of William Bayard, the Tory grandson of Samuel, were confiscated and ordered sold by the Bergen Court of Common Pleas. In 1804 Stevens mapped the territory into what he called the "New City of Hoboken" and auctioned the lots in New York.

Stevens put into service in 1811 the first regular steam ferry in the world, the *Juliana*. As early as 1808, however, he had operated the *Phoenix,* a steamship of his own design, as a ferry. He was forced to abandon the venture when Robert Fulton, who had secured sole rights to steam travel on the Hudson, objected. The *Phoenix,* sent south to Delaware River, was the first steamship to navigate at sea.

Colonel Stevens also devised the first iron floating fort, never completed although huge sums were spent on it; he drew plans for a vehicular tunnel on the bed of the Hudson, and for a bridge from Castle Point to Manhattan. In 1824, after arguing the feasibility of railroad transportation with doubting capitalists, Stevens built a locomotive and, on a circular track in Hoboken, conducted the first successful run in the United States.

Hoboken soon acquired world fame as a resort. Beer gardens, fireworks, mountebanks, and waxworks brought New York's citizens over in droves, and the beautiful country so close to the metropolis attracted society people and literary and artistic celebrities. John Jacob Astor built an extensive villa on the city's shores; Washington Irving, William Cullen·Bryant, Martin Van Buren, and other prominent people vacationed here. In Hoboken was founded the New York Yacht Club with John Cox Stevens, son of the colonel, as its first commodore. Organized baseball had its beginning in Hoboken. The first game was played in 1846 on the Elysian Fields by Hoboken's Knickerbocker Giants and New York.

The River Walk was soon packed hard and smooth by pleasure-seeking visitors, and Sybil's Cave became a lovers' rendezvous. The cave figured in one of Hoboken's early scandals when the body of Mary Rogers, a pretty young New York tobacco shop clerk, was found floating in the river

S. S. *LEVIATHAN* AT HOBOKEN TERMINAL

near the entrance. Edgar Allan Poe based his story, *The Mystery of Marie Roget,* on the newspaper accounts of the murder.

Hoboken's separation from North Bergen and its incorporation as a city in 1855 marked the beginning of a new development in its history. Industrialists were attracted by the ease of communication with New York and the advantages of the water front. An influx of labor, mainly Irish, came with the industries. Later the Hamburg-American Line made Hoboken its American terminus.

A $10,000,000 fire that resulted in 145 deaths broke out in the North German Lloyd line dock on the afternoon of June 30, 1900. Two blocks of the water front blazed, and several ships, including the *Main, Bremen,* and *Saale,* endangered shipping as they floated burning into the harbor. The fire probably started from a burning bale of cotton which, tossed overboard from a cargo ship, ignited a wooden pier.

When Hoboken was chosen as a major point of embarkation during the World War, strict military rule was imposed on the city. Anti-German feeling rose quickly and with disastrous effect on the German families who had made their homes here. The United States seized the larger portion of the steamship properties as a war measure and has held them ever since.

The labor required for the shipment of war supplies brought the population to an abnormal high. After the War, the exodus of many workers caused the failure of a number of businesses established during the boom.

During 1928 and 1929 Christopher Morley and his associates brought back the sophisticated New York crowds that once pressed into the two old theaters by presenting the melodramas of another generation. *After Dark* and *The Black Crook* kept the Rialto and Lyric alive with eager sightseers; "Seidel over to Hoboken" became a national phrase. But the competition from Harlem was too strong in 1929. The novelty-seeking crowd drifted away, and the theaters were closed, to reopen as third-run moving picture houses.

STEVENS INSTITUTE OF TECHNOLOGY

The buildings of Stevens Institute climb up the southern slope of Castle Point. With the single exception of the Castle, they are dark reddish brown structures, undistinguished architecturally, and for the most part clustered together off the campus lawns.

When Col. John Stevens was in the midst of his experimental work he conceived the idea for an "academy for the training of the young." But it was his son Edwin who carried out the plan after recouping much of the fortune lost by his inventive father. In 1867 the younger Stevens willed $150,000 for erection of a building and $500,000 as an endowment.

Four years later Stevens Institute was opened. Of the 21 students who enrolled the first year, one was graduted in 1873. The first faculty was headed by Dr. Henry Morton, formerly secretary of Philadelphia's Franklin Institute. With him were a group of outstanding scientists of the day.

In 1902, when Dr. Morton died, the presidency of the college was taken over by Alexander Crombie Humphreys. During the quarter-century of President Humphrey's tenure, Stevens experienced its greatest growth. Under the present administration of Dr. Harvey Nathaniel Davis, two new dormitories were constructed in 1937.

The only degree offered to the approximately 500 students, who may receive training in all branches of engineering, is that of Mechanical Engineer. Stevens is the only engineering school in the country with this system. The Institute maintains a summer engineering camp of 375 acres at Johnsonburg *(see Tour 5)*, where six weeks of actual field practice are given in the open country.

All campus buildings are open on weekdays, except as noted.

1. The ADMINISTRATION BUILDING, 5th St. between River and Hudson Sts., known to students and alumni as "The Old Stone Mill," is a three-story brownstone structure with a mansard roof. In the center of the building, a four-story square tower rises above the plain wooden doorway, flanked by small Corinthian columns. This was the original home of the Institute. Its ivy-covered walls distinguish it from the other buildings on the 30-acre campus. Formerly it housed all departments of instruction, but today it contains only the administration offices and the departments of physics, machine design and shop practice. The auditorium, scene of the

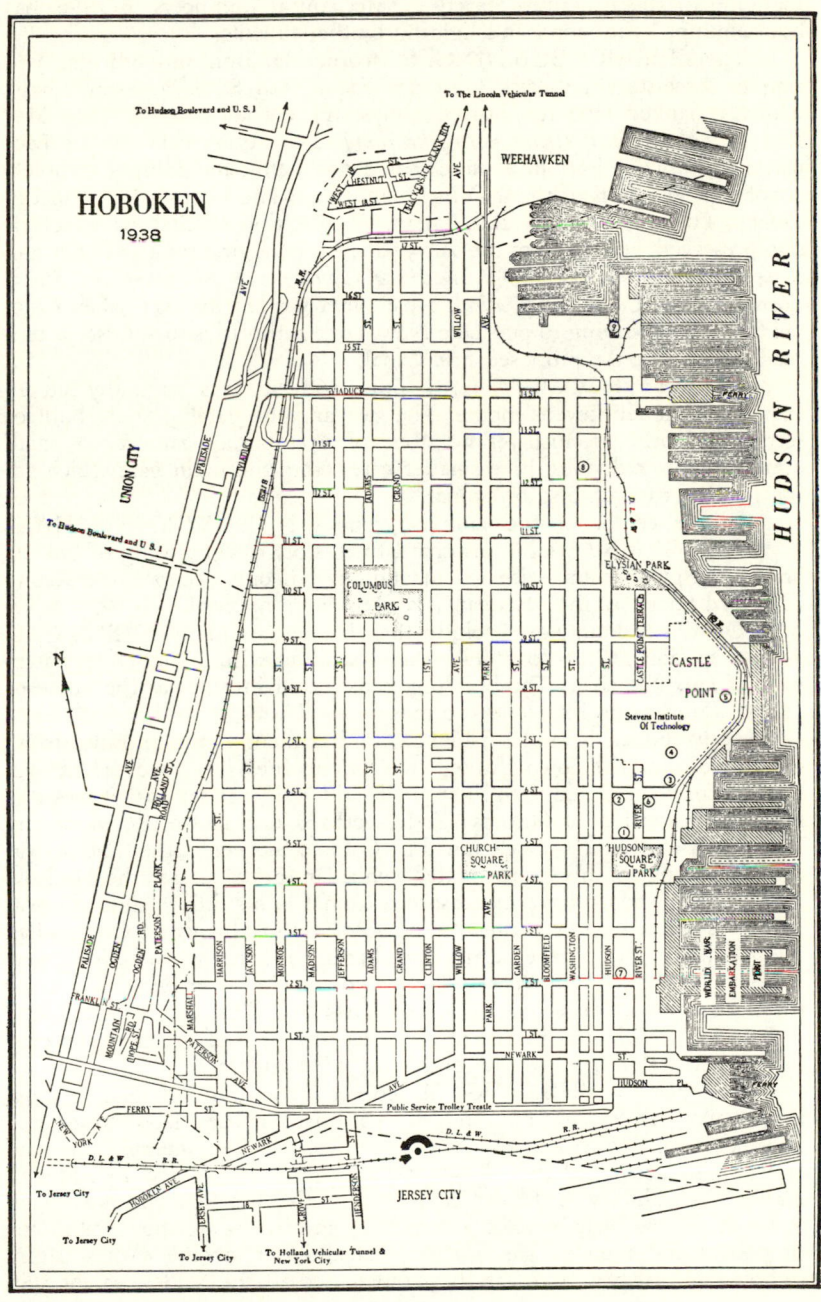

HOBOKEN
1938

HUDSON RIVER

founding of the American Society of Mechanical Engineers in 1880, has been equipped for sound and lighting by the students.

2. The LIBRARY BUILDING, SE. corner Hudson and 6th Sts., is a simple, three-story red-brick building. Facing 6th St. is a severe classic doorway flanked by wrought-iron lamps, the entrance to the LIEB MEMORIAL *(open on application to librarian)*. The library contains the Leonardo da Vinci collection of more than 1,000 items, including a complete set of reproductions of the da Vinci manuscripts and books on da Vinci in French, English, German, and Italian. A collection of Stevens papers is also preserved, among them the 1803 patent for the first tubular boiler and the prophetic *Documents to Prove the Advantages of Railways and Steam Carriages over Canal Navigation,* a pamphlet written in 1812 when Colonel Stevens was trying to persuade New York authorities to sponsor a railroad rather than the proposed Erie Canal.

3. The GATEHOUSE *(private),* E. end 6th St., was originally the entrance to Colonel Stevens' house. The gate and the gatehouse are built of serpentine rock, greenish-yellow stone of peculiar appearance. A small octagonal tower divides three smaller gates from the main gate which adjoins a larger tower, also octagonal.

4. In the center of the campus grounds is the WILLIAM HALL WALKER GYMNASIUM, an ornate, three-story oval building of old red brick. The gymnasium, with its surrounding balcony, occupies the second and third floors. In the basement is a tile swimming pool.

5. On Castle Point, overlooking the Hudson, stands STEVENS CASTLE, a spacious, three-story drab stucco building with a four-story watchtower facing the river. The building, constructed in 1853 as the home of John C. Stevens, is a students' dormitory.

Cleverly hidden behind a panel in the basement is the entrance to an old tunnel that led down through the cliff to the river road. There was much secrecy connected with the tunnel. Old residents say that it was dug before the erection of Stevens Castle, perhaps during the Revolutionary War. Or it may have been designed by Colonel Stevens at the time he was drawing plans for his contemplated vehicular tunnel under the Hudson. That Stevens should have made such a tunnel is not improbable; he was noted for extravagant experiments and absorption in his work. Once, when lying in bed with no paper at hand, he began to sketch the idea for a new machine on the back of his wife's nightgown. He asked her if she knew the figure he was drawing. "Yes," she answered, "the figure of a fool."

Fronting the river at the Point is the narrow strip of greenery comprising HUDSON PARK, a favorite rendezvous for strollers.

6. The NAVY BUILDING, SE. corner River and 6th Sts., a long, three-story, nondescript building of red brick, houses laboratories and classrooms for the departments of civil and electrical engineering, the general alumni office and the MUSEUM *(open 12-5 Wed. and by appointment).* The exhibits on the first floor indicate the development of mechanical locomotion. Early bicycles, automobiles and trucks are shown; airplane propellers and motors; gasoline engines and one of the earliest steam turbines. On display, too, are the motors used in the Selden patent suit,

when Henry Ford's claim as the inventor was contested; the first Ford car, built in 1899 and used as evidence of infringement in the litigation; and the "Selden Buggy," really a buggy with the shafts removed and an engine suspended over the front axle. Steam engines of various types, a section of the wooden water main of Aaron Burr's Manhattan Co. which was laid in 1799–1800, and many other mechanical and electrical devices are in the museum.

The building also houses the EXPERIMENTAL TOWING TANK, a long tank about three feet deep filled with water. Boat models are towed from one end to the other by motors in efficiency experiments.

OTHER POINTS OF INTEREST

7. The HOF BRAU HAUS, 42 2nd St., is the restaurant where Christopher Morley and his circle came for relaxation after the play. It is frequented by many New Yorkers who come for German food and German music, with diners and drinkers joining in the song—if not starting it.

8. An APARTMENT HOUSE (private), 1203 Washington St., is the former home of Hetty Green, once known as the world's richest woman. Recent additions of tiled lobbies and Venetian blinds give some semblance of modernity, though not much change has taken place in the five-story bright yellow brick building.

For Hetty Green, noisy, happy-go-lucky Hoboken held a particular charm: cheap rent and low taxes. Mrs. Green had no financial interests here when she rented a flat in the best apartment house in Hoboken in 1895. She was still close to her immense treasure in the Chemical National Bank on lower Broadway, and her rent was only $19 a month. Under various names she lived here until 1916, moving from flat to flat in the block of apartments. Just after she had lent $4,500,000 to the city of New York, a summons was issued for her because she had failed to pay the $2 dog tax in Hoboken. Swearing that she would never pay, she fled to Manhattan, returning only after her daughter had paid the tax. One of the reporters who dogged her constantly caught her fancy when he climbed into her apartment by way of the fire escape. She presented him with a bouquet of artificial flowers, commenting that she had paid $1.50 for it and that real flowers would have cost just as much and would have died within a day.

9. The SEATRAIN LINE, river front at E. end of Lipton Tea factory, is the only freight service of its kind in the world. Each Tuesday a ship docks and unloads full railroad freight cars; more cars are loaded Wednesday into the track-lined holds and the ship sails for New Orleans and Havana.

The two vessels of the company are specially constructed to accommodate their freight. Four different levels, each equipped with four lanes of railroad tracks, afford space for 101 freight cars. A huge well in the center of the ship, stretching across the whole width, is the entrance to the tracks on the different levels. The ship is docked beneath a 125-ton traveling crane that lifts movable sections of track on which the railroad cars are placed and lowers them to position in the central well or on the dock.

Jersey City

Railroad Stations: Exchange Place Station, Exchange Pl., for Pennsylvania R.R.; Pavonia Ave. and Hudson River for Erie R.R. and New York, Susquehanna & Western R.R.; Johnston Ave. and Hudson River for Jersey Central R.R., Baltimore & Ohio R.R., and Philadelphia & Reading Co.; Journal Square and Exchange Pl. for Lehigh Valley R.R.; Journal Square, Grove and Henderson Sts., Exchange Pl. and Erie for Hudson & Manhattan R.R.

Bus Station: Journal Square for Safeway Trailways, Greyhound, Martz, Golden Arrow, Public Service, Champlain, Edwards.

Taxis: 25¢ for 2 m.; 20¢ each additional mile.

Piers: Morgan St. and Hudson River for American Export Lines; 12th St. and Hudson River for Dollar Line; Exchange Pl. for Moore-McCormack Line; Pier B, E. end Grand St., for excursion boats; Pier C, E. end York St., for Pennsylvania R.R. commercial and excursion boats; Lackawanna Pier, E. end 16th St., for commercial boats; Pennsylvania Terminal, Exchange Pl., ferry to Cortlandt St., New York (all-night service), and to Desbrosses St. and Brooklyn; Jersey Central Terminal, E. end Johnston Ave., ferry to Liberty St. and W. 23rd St., New York (all-night service); Erie Terminal, E. end Pavonia Ave., ferry to Chambers St. and W. 23rd St.; S. end Washington St. for Gap ferry to Johnston Ave. section of Jersey City.

Streetcars and Busses: Fare 5¢ within city; Public Service busses from Exchange Pl. to Newark, making all local stops (10¢).

Traffic Regulations: Traffic lights at chief intersections; no turns on red light unless sign permits. One-hour parking limit in business section; parking restricted at Journal Square. Watch signs for one-way streets.

Accommodations: Hotels and boarding houses.

Information Service: Chamber of Commerce, 1 Newark Ave.; Auto Club of Hudson County, 3010 Hudson Blvd.

Radio Stations: WAAT (940 kc.); WHOM (1450 kc.).

Motion Picture Houses: Seventeen.

Swimming: Washington Park, North St. and Central Ave., 25¢ (15¢ for children); 35¢ Sat., Sun., holidays.

Tennis: Lincoln Park, W. end Belmont Ave., 40 courts, 25¢.

Annual Events: Lincoln Association annual dinner, Lincoln's birthday or nearest observable date; Holy Name Society parade, first Sunday after first Monday in October.

Millions of people carelessly regard JERSEY CITY (60 alt., 316,715 pop.) as a necessary rail and motor approach to Manhattan, but Jersey City advertises that it has "Everything for Industry." The daily commuters and motorists never see enough of the community to realize the accuracy of Jersey City's self-description. The propitious location of the city, close to the tremendous financial and consumer markets of New York City and metropolitan New Jersey, is an advantage equaled by its geographical position on upper New York Bay. This favorable situation has furnished Jersey City with shipping facilities which, in turn, have drawn motor routes and rail lines.

Hardly evident to autoists and bus passengers are hundreds of freight sidings and main line tracks, the wharfs and piers of the water front, the barges and the freighters that carry heavy cargoes from the factories.

The concrete and glass bulk of the American Can Company plant beside the ramp that descends from the Pulaski Skyway and the warehouses along the Holland Tunnel approach are the industrial samples that the city shows to the pounding stream of motor traffic that flows from the heights to the depths. The train passengers see equally little—fleeting glimpses from the windows of the Erie, Jersey Central, Lackawanna, or Pennsylvania coaches form a blurred and incomplete picture–while the commuters who use the Hudson Tubes view the city from its basement, hewn out of the tough rock of the Palisades.

Thus relatively few outsiders are familiar with the surface of this city, spread upon a peninsula between the Hudson and Hackensack Rivers, directly west of Manhattan.

Although many of the residents work in New York or in nearby communities, Jersey City is their home town as well as their home. Of primary interest is politics. In city and county employees and in their families has been instilled a political awareness that transcends interest in other civic and cultural problems. An elaborate framework of political clubs provides a social outlet for voters of all leading nationalities. Nonpolitical recreation is found in the motion picture houses and in sports, since dance halls and night clubs are prohibited. Nearby New York City provides other cultural and amusement channels.

Its site at the upper end of New York Bay has made Jersey City the terminal for nine trunk line railroads and steamship lines. Leading industrial products are soaps, pencils, cans, mouth wash, cigarettes, macaroni, meats, and steel. Other factories among the hundreds in the city produce a variety of goods ranging from electric elevators to pinless diapers.

The city's area, originally limited to Paulus Hook and Van Vorst Township, is partly the result of consolidations with neighboring communities— Bergen, Communipaw, Greenville, Claremont, Hudson City, Pamrapo, and Marion. Within living memory, parts of the city were swamps. Several sections still display characteristics of various stages in its spasmodic commercial and political growth. The downtown district, site of the original Paulus Hook settlement, is a rail and ship terminal with a large share of the city's factories. Many of the industrial plants consist of the first red brick structure surrounded by additions, some of them converted from old dwellings, stables or hotels.

Thoroughfares leading to the water front meet with a chaos of side streets that cross and interlace, forming odd-shaped islands upon which squat equally odd-shaped structures. Skeletons of abandoned buildings stand crumbling in the shadow of newer factories, humming with the roar of machinery. The residential streets are lined with tightly packed rows of two- and three-story brownstone or brick houses. Some are old and unoccupied, seemingly held erect only by the support of the neighboring structures.

The Newark Avenue shopping district, most important of half a dozen scattered business centers, consists of numerous small shops of variegated architecture and color. Nearness of the Manhattan retail section has deprived Jersey City of department stores commensurate with its size.

Hudson Boulevard, the principal north and south traffic artery of the county, cuts through the center of Jersey City at Journal Square, a broad plaza constructed in 1925. The square serves as a terminal for hundreds of busses of local and interurban lines. By night its three large motion picture houses and its brightly lit restaurants are crowded with patrons from up and down the peninsula.

South of the square, Hudson Boulevard penetrates the apartment house district, where tall and elaborate buildings are squeezing out the remaining private homes of wealthier citizens. Homes of undistinguished architecture lie farther south to the point where Jersey City imperceptibly merges with its neighbor, Bayonne. North of Journal Square the boulevard climbs the shoulder of the Palisades, with continuous urbanization into Union City.

The city has a foreign-born population of 70,313 (22 percent), including 16,097 Italians and 12,432 Poles. Germans are third in number, with 9,631; next in order are the Irish, 8,741; Russians, 4,415; and English, 2,807. There are 12,575 Negroes. The Polish residents have preserved to a notable degree many of their native customs, such as the large family gathering on Christmas Eve at which sacred wafers are eaten.

The site of Jersey City was first important as a North Jersey gateway for the Dutch traders who settled Manhattan. That relationship was expanded when the settlers began bringing their farm products to New York. Probably the first permanent settlement was made shortly after 1629, when Michael Pauw bought a tract from the Indians. Under the colonization plan of the Dutch West India Company he was required to settle fifty persons on the land. Cornelius Van Vorst, sent by Pauw to establish a plantation named Pavonia, enjoyed civil and judicial power, and enough prosperity to entertain the directors general of New Netherland. The house that he built in 1633 is supposed to have stood near the present corner of Fourth and Henderson Streets. Later Michael Paulez (or Paulusen), the company's overseer of trade with the Indians, occupied a house at Paulus Hook.

Dissatisfied with the feudal patroon system, the company bought out Pauw in 1634 for about $10,000 and built two houses at Pavonia; another was erected at Communipau (Pauw's community). After 1638 the company's officers obtained grants from Director General Kieft.

Unscrupulous trade practices against the Indians, plus Kieft's demand for tribute and his subsequent massacre of innocent Raritans, resulted in bloody reprisals by both sides. When peace was declared in 1645 only the Van Vorst manor had escaped destruction. Ten years later the Indians raided the settlement again after another provocative act. Governor Stuyvesant refused to permit settlement until 1660, when he granted a petition on condition that the colonists live in a fortified community. The first court was established in 1661.

The village of Bergen was laid out as an 800-foot square surrounded by a log palisade. Two streets, now Academy Street and Bergen Avenue,

HOLLAND TUNNEL UNDER HUDSON RIVER

intersected to form a public square, today known as Bergen Square. Within a year the settlement was large enough to require regular communication with New Amsterdam, and William Jansen began operating a rowboat ferry three times a week. For cattle and other cargo a flat-bottomed sloop was used. In 1662 the settlement hired a combination *voorleser* (sermon reader) and schoolmaster, being unable to afford an ordained minister.

The transition to English rule in 1664 took place smoothly, with thirty-three Dutch families later signing an oath of allegiance. At about that time a rough log church was built for the Dutch Reformed congregation; it was probably the first church erected in the Province. For many years the Dutch Reformed Church had an important role in the affairs of the growing community, which was chartered as a town in 1668 by Governor Philip Carteret.

During the next century the town was concerned with little besides farming. Establishment of improved ferry service in 1764 was followed several years later by the building of a race track at Paulus Hook. The opening of a new land route to Philadelphia made the Hook a vital link between New York and the south and west; formerly a monopoly had been enjoyed by Elizabethtown and Perth Amboy, which had better water connections with New York.

Close by the ferry was a tavern with stables, all under the same management. Schedules were carefully disarranged so that ferry passengers from New York arrived too late for the southbound stage in the morning, and had to stay overnight at the tavern.

An outpost of the British Army held a fort on Paulus Hook during the occupancy of New York. On the night of August 18, 1779, Major (Light Horse Harry) Lee led 300 men south from the American camp on upper Hudson River in a bold attack on the garrison. Crossing a moat at low tide, Lee's force stormed the fort at 3 o'clock in the morning and captured 159 men, about one-third of the defending force. The Americans lost only two killed and three wounded, and escaped northward before their retreat was cut off by other British detachments.

Speculative New Yorkers cast appraising eyes upon the site of Jersey City in 1804, immediately after Col. John Stevens' auction of lots in Hoboken. John B. Coles, a flour merchant, laid out city blocks in the Bergen area. Anthony Dey, a young New York lawyer, acquired land and ferry for a perpetual annuity of 6,000 Spanish milled dollars.

Dey's company was incorporated as the Associates of The Jersey Company under a charter that made the organization, in effect, the civil governing body. The real estate boom, however, was anything but resounding. Although a red brick tavern was built and a few small industries came, the political domination of the Associates hindered growth. Another obstacle was New York's claim to riparian rights up to the low-water line on the Jersey shore, which hindered the building of piers and wharves. The boundary dispute was unsettled for many years.

Steam ferry service began in 1812 with the *Jersey,* built by Robert Fulton. A passenger reported that the crossing was made in fourteen minutes as thousands watched from both shores, all "gratified at finding so large and so safe a machine going so well."

During this period, when the population consisted mainly of boatmen and transients and the town had neither jail nor policemen, the Hook became known for dog fights, bull baits, and drunken brawls. Efforts to obtain an autonomous government were balked by the Associates, who had great influence with the legislature. Finally the citizens succeeded in incorporating the City of Jersey in 1820, but the Associates retained special powers until 1838.

The year 1834 was a turning point in the city's growth. A treaty setting the line between New York and New Jersey in the middle of the Hudson River, while New York got Staten Island, gave the city access to its own water line. Terminals of the New Jersey Railroad (later the Pennsylvania) and the Paterson and Hudson Railroad (later the Erie) were established in Jersey City. Horse-car service to Newark, begun in September 1834, was replaced by steam in 1838. Meanwhile the Morris Canal, with its western terminal on Delaware River, had been extended from Newark to Jersey City in 1836.

Several important industries had already been established. As early as 1760 the Lorillard Tobacco Company had started a snuff factory. In 1884 the firm opened a night school for the 250 children then employed. Dummer's Jersey City Glass Company, later famous for its flint glass, began operations in 1824. The fireworks factory built by Isaac Edge Jr. became a training school for American pyrotechnists. Some of the foremost American potters learned their trade at the plant of the American Pottery Company, which was one of the first factories to compete successfully with leading English producers.

Other industries included Colgate soaps, Dixon pencils, steel, paper, beer and whisky. By 1860 the population was 29,000, an increase of almost 150 percent in nine years. Jersey City opened its first stockyards in 1866, and it was also for a time the western terminal of the Cunard Line, beginning in 1847.

The city was an important station on the Underground Railroad. Slaves were sent North hidden in the dead air space between cabins on Erie Canal boats. During the Civil War thousands of troops passed through the railroad stations and the city contributed full quotas of men.

Railroad and political battles colored the latter part of the nineteenth century. The monopolistic hold of the United Railroads (later the Pennsylvania) on the Jersey City water front was broken when the Jersey Central dumped New York refuse on tidal flats and built a terminal. Another terminal was established when the Erie Railroad blasted a tunnel through Bergen Hill.

The political struggles supplied such incidents as the Hudson County "Horseshoe," which gerrymandered nearly the whole Democratic vote into one assembly district, and an election in which ballots were printed on tissue paper so that more could be stuffed into each ballot box. Consolidations with neighboring communities were preceded by street and sewer contracts whose addition to the merged public debt caused an intolerable tax burden. The election of Mark Fagan, a New Idea Republican, as mayor in 1901 temporarily halted political scandals.

Construction of a railroad tunnel to Manhattan had been attempted as early as 1874. But it was not until William G. McAdoo, later Secretary of the Treasury, became interested in the project that it was completed (1909–10). The Hudson Tubes brought an increase in the number of factories and in the working population.

The Black Tom explosion on the Communipaw water front during the night of July 30, 1916, has been called the only successful German war plot in the country, although international litigation to fix responsibility and damages has not been concluded. Ammunition-laden railroad cars blew up with such violence that residents of Connecticut and Maryland felt the shock. The damage was estimated at $20,000,000, of which the greater part was in Jersey City. Loss in broken windows in the metropolitan area amounted to more than $1,000,000. Only seven lives were lost, although 75 mm. shells struck Ellis Island and other nearby places. After the United States entered the war, the city's factories were busy supplying materials to the Government.

St. Peter's College, chartered in 1872, closed during the war when more than half of its faculty and students enlisted. The college, conducted by the Society of Jesus, reopened in 1930 and now has more than 400 students.

Improvement of transportation facilities continued after the World War. Construction of the Holland Tunnel for vehicular traffic under the Hudson River was begun in 1920 by the Port of New York Authority and completed in 1927 at a cost of $48,400,000. The tunnel, used by an average of 32,500 vehicles daily, has been a money maker from the start. Twin tubes of two lanes each lie 72 feet below water level; the longer measures 8,557 feet (exceeding by 342 feet the length of the new Lincoln Tunnel at Weehawken). They are handsomely finished in white tile. Patrolmen are stationed at close intervals through the tubes. If a motorist has a flat tire, the nearest patrolman presses a button and within five minutes a tractor arrives. The tire is changed free or, if the driver has no spare, his car is towed from the tunnel without charge. Blowing of horns is prohibited because the loud echo might make the nervous driver swing over into the adjoining lane, thus breaking another rule. Air in the tunnel is changed every minute and a half by blower fans.

The city adopted the commission form of government in 1913. In that year Frank Hague, a Democrat who began his political career as a city hall janitor, was elected one of the commissioners. Four years later he became mayor, and he has since been continuously reelected by huge majorities. In addition to the mayoralty, Hague has held a vice chairmanship in the Democratic National Committee since 1924.

The per capita cost of government in Jersey City, listed as $65.80 in 1936, is the highest among the larger New Jersey cities. A well-publicized item in Jersey City's budget is the police force. Newark has 1,162 policemen, or 2.6 per 1,000 population, while Jersey City has an estimated force of 1,000, or 3.2 per 1,000.

Jersey City's police force, in addition to its usual duties, has prevented picketing and meetings for the purpose of union organization. Hague was once a close friend of labor leader Theodore Brandle. Brandle admittedly managed to become a union officer and officer of an employers' league so that he could "serve both sides" at the same time. While Brandle was becoming a millionaire labor leader with Hague's backing, Hague himself was not opposed to labor organization in Jersey City. But when Brandle refused to call off a strike of iron workers against the open shop contractors for the Pulaski Skyway in 1932, Hague charged that he was a "gorilla labor leader." Almost immediately after this denunciation Brandle's union agreed to accept his resignation by a vote of 359 to 1. Since that time Hague's attitude has been openly anti-union. During 1937–8, after seven trade unionists had been jailed without a jury trial for distributing handbills, national attention was drawn to the issue of civil rights in Jersey City. The American Civil Liberties Union, and the CIO, brought joint suit against Hague and others of the city administration to secure court orders permitting the exercise of civil liberties.

In October 1938 Federal Judge William Clark handed down a 15,000-word decision enjoining city officials from interfering with the plaintiffs' right to distribute leaflets and display placards similar to those exhibited at the time the suit was instituted. He upheld their right "to be and move freely in Jersey City," and "to address public meetings in the parks." The decision was hailed as a sweeping victory by the plaintiffs, while Hague pointed out that the ordinance requiring permits for public meetings had been upheld, and that the city would continue trying to keep "radicals and Reds" out.

The Medical Center, outstanding for size and equipment among New Jersey hospitals, is partly supported by Jersey City. The city also conducts the Special Service Bureau, a plan for the treatment of juvenile delinquency that has the approbation of social welfare workers throughout the country. The bureau coordinates the activities of the police and the board of education, saves young offenders from the stigma of a police record, and maintains a behavior clinic.

POINTS OF INTEREST

1. OLD BERGEN CHURCH, SW. corner Highland and Bergen Aves., is a dark brownstone and brick structure flanked by a lawn. Massive brownstone columns support a simple pediment, and the building is topped by a squat, square tower; the lack of a spire is distinctly felt. Cemented into the front wall between the two doorways are stones from the two previous churches, with the inscription: "1680 W-Day." "Kerk Gebouwt Het Yaer 1680. Bowt in Het Yaer 1773." The first structure was small and of octagonal design. For many years collections were in wampum, which was sold by the deacons to heads of families. The black velvet collection bags were attached to long poles and equipped with small bells to rouse the congregation at collection time. The present building was dedicated in 1842 with a Dutch sermon understood by many of the congregation. Church records were kept regularly in Dutch until 1793, and occasionally thereafter.

On the lawn of the church was an old CANNON, now relegated to the cellar because the carriage is broken. The firing of the gun each Fourth of July was the official city celebration of the holiday. An attempt to revive the custom, using an obsolete three-inch fieldpiece, proved unsuccessful because window panes in the vicinity did not survive the concussion.

2. The VAN WAGENEN HOUSE (*private*), 298 Academy St., shelters descendants of the Dutch family that in 1650 received a share of the land from Kill van Kull to Weehawken, deeded by the Indians to Peter Stuyvesant. Inside the late 19th century stone building hangs the original of this deed, together with documents bearing the seal of Philip Carteret and other pre-Revolutionary officials. The original building, which stood on the same spot, has contributed some of its doors, walls, and windows to the present structure. It is also known as the "Apple Tree House" because Lafayette, who made his headquarters here on a foraging expedition in 1779, entertained Washington at dinner under a large apple tree. From a portion of this tree, blown down in 1821, was made a very handsome gold-mounted cane, given to Lafayette, with this inscription: "Shaded the

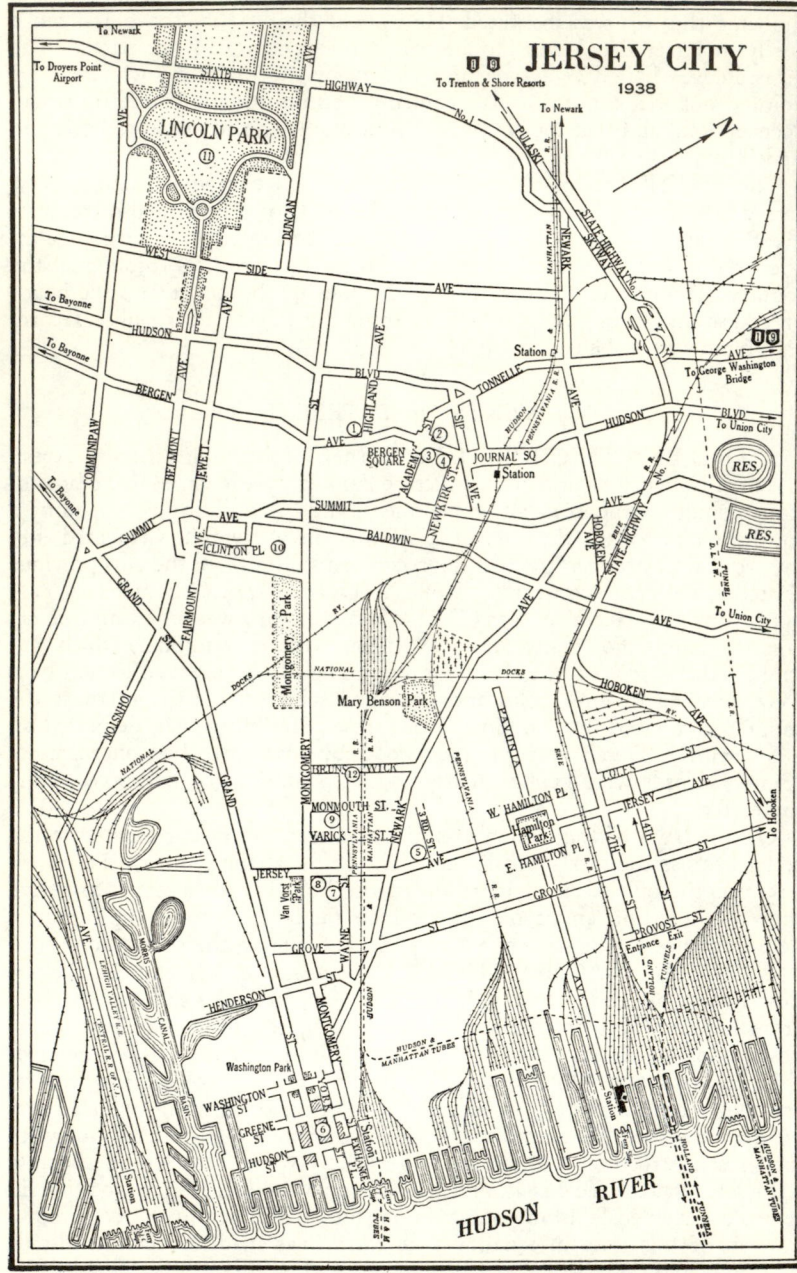

hero and his friend Washington in 1779: presented by the Corporation of Bergen in 1824."

3. The STATUE OF PETER STUYVESANT, NE. corner of Bergen Sq., stands in front of Public School 11. The figure of the irascible, wooden-legged last Dutch Governor was sculptured by Massey Rhind. An inscription notes the establishment in Bergen of the first organized church and the first school in New Jersey. The first teacher and *voorleser,* Engelbert Steenhuysen, was licensed in 1662 and allowed 250 gilders in wampum annually and "some other stipulations beside the school money . . ."

4. SITE OF THE SIP MANOR, SE. corner Newkirk St. and Bergen Ave., is now a business corner with only a tablet to mark its historic significance. The most recent account says that the house was built in 1664 by Nicholas Varleth and acquired in 1699 by Jan Arianse Sip. It was moved in 1928 to Wychwood, a real estate development in Westfield, N. J. The gardens were famous in old Bergen. It is said that Peter Stuyvesant often stopped to admire the flowers in the shade of a huge willow tree, the same tree from which Cornwallis is supposed to have hanged three spies.

5. The SAFETY MUSEUM *(open 9-4 weekdays),* 571 Jersey Ave., is housed in the top floors of the State Department of Labor offices. It is an exhibit of charts on occupational diseases and of safety devices on power presses, laundry and woodworking machines, and other equipment that employers must use to comply with State laws.

6. The COLGATE-PALMOLIVE-PEET PLANT *(not open to public),* 105 Hudson St., covers seven blocks with its 44 buildings, in which soaps, talcums, dentifrices and other products are made. The business began in 1806 when William Colgate set up his soap kettles in New York. In 1847 the factory was moved to Jersey City and in 1928, through merger with Palmolive-Peet Company, it became one of the world's foremost soap manufacturers.

The site is part of Old Paulus Hook. Up to the turn of the century the Hudson House, the tavern built by the Associates, was part of the plant, as was McCutcheon's Farmer's Hotel, a once famous hostelry.

The COLGATE CLOCK, facing the bay, has kept time for New York harbor over a generation. The present clock, 50 ft. in diameter with a minute hand weighing 2,200 lbs., was erected in 1924 to replace a smaller one; Colgate's advertising department says it is the largest clock in the world. Night workers in lower Manhattan office buildings can read the hour from the illuminated hands.

7. The IONIC HOUSE *(not open to public),* 83 Wayne St., was built by a Dr. Barrowe early in the 19th century. Five tall Ionic columns, two stories in height, stand in front of this great, boxlike, clapboard building, which is painted a dark green. Now used as a social center for members of the adjoining St. Matthew's Church, the house has been extensively changed. High-ceilinged rooms are trimmed with mahogany; silver handles are on the massive mahogany doors. Even the gas fixtures have something more than the basic ugliness of their kind; they are gilded figures of draped women—resembling the figureheads of sailing ships—holding torches

from which the jets project. Mr. August E. Kopp, resident sexton, has one of the few remaining glazed pitchers from the kilns of the American Pottery Co., a local pottery that won many international awards for its work.

8. PUBLIC LIBRARY *(open 9 a.m.-8:30 p.m. weekdays, reading room 9 a.m.-10 p.m.; reading room only, 2-9 p.m. Sun.)*, Jersey Ave. and Montgomery St., of Italian Renaissance design, is constructed of brick, trimmed with granite. It was designed by Brite and Bacon, and opened in 1901. In addition to 381,000 volumes, the library has three notable collections. On the museum floor is the OTTO GOETZKE GEM COLLECTION, probably the world's most complete exhibit of precious and semiprecious stones, representing the 30-year hobby of a Newark jeweler. One of the rarest of the 5,000 specimens is alexandrite, a variety of chrysoberyl found only in the Ural Mts. It is grass-green by day and columbine-red under artificial light. Another unusual specimen is olivine, a greenish pebble mined from Arizona soil by ants. The gems are in charge of the Jersey City Museum Association, which has other exhibits in the Bergen, Pavonia, and Greenville branches of the library. The ALLEN COLLECTION, consisting chiefly of household furnishings and wearing apparel of the 19th century, and the large JOHN D. MCGILL COIN COLLECTION are in the main library. The library has 13 branches.

9. JOSEPH DIXON CRUCIBLE PLANT *(not open to public)*, 167 Wayne St., is the only concern in the world handling a full line of graphite products including crucibles, paints, greases, and motor brushes in addition to millions of pencils. The business was started in 1827 in Salem, Mass., to manufacture graphite products, and shortly afterward moved to Jersey City. The production of pencils, now the main item, was an afterthought. Highly specialized machinery puts the graphite and the clay, components of the "lead," through a number of processes lasting several weeks. Other machines shape the lead, encase it between two pieces of grooved cedar, "cure" and shape the erasers, and turn out a finished pencil.

10. The MEDICAL CENTER, Baldwin Ave. at Montgomery St., is the largest hospital in the State, with beds for 1,800 patients. Four main buildings of light yellow brick and terra cotta, designed by John T. Rowland, rise 14 to 23 stories, forming the most imposing segment of the city's skyline. A 10-story structure houses the nationally known Margaret Hague Maternity Hospital, with accommodations for 400 mothers and their babies. More babies are born here probably than in any other hospital of the Nation; the total for 1936 was 5,088. Of the 6,096 mothers admitted that year, only 20 died, giving a maternal mortality of about one-third of 1 percent. The infant mortality was 2.5 percent. Both figures are well below the national average. The center is equipped to provide free care for all types of diseases.

11. LINCOLN PARK, W. end Belmont Ave., consists of 287 acres extending to Hackensack River. Almost half of the area has been developed—part on reclaimed marshland—with 11 baseball diamonds, 6 football fields, 18 tennis courts, a swimming pool, a quarter-mile track and other sports facilities. The park has a fine sunken garden and a fountain. The heroic STATUE OF LINCOLN, Belmont Ave. at Hudson Blvd.,

THE MEDICAL CENTER, JERSEY CITY

erected in 1929, was the work of J. E. Fraser; it is the third largest in the United States. A large lake is used for miniature yacht races and ice skating. The park is the largest unit of the Hudson County park system.

POINT OF INTEREST IN ENVIRONS

Newark Airport, *6.2 m. (see Tour 1).*

Morristown

Railroad Station: Lackawanna Station, Morris and Elm Sts., for Lackawanna R.R.
Bus Station: Park Pl. N. for De Camp, Public Service, and interurban lines.
Taxis: 35¢ for one passenger, 50¢ for two, 25¢ for each additional passenger within city limits.
Traffic Regulations: Traffic lights in business section. Watch signs for parking limitations and one-way streets. All traffic around the park is counter-clockwise.

Accommodations: Small hotels and tourist houses; no seasonal rates.

Information Service: Bus Terminal, 77 Park Pl.; Chamber of Commerce, 10 Park Pl.; Morristown Library, SW. corner Miller Rd. and South St.; information bureau on Park Pl. N., April through October.

Motion Picture Houses: Three.
Swimming: Municipal pool, Burnham Park, seasonal rates; 25¢ for children, 50¢ for adults, lockers free; health certificate by local physician required.

Annual Events: Water carnival and ice carnival at Burnham Park; Firemen's Parade, October.

It was once the boast of MORRISTOWN (400 alt., 15,197 pop.), a town with an extraordinary heritage from Revolutionary times, that within a radius of one mile from the Green lived more millionaires than in any other equal area in the world. It may not have been true. But this Colonial town is still marked by obvious signs of the extreme wealth brought here in the mauve decade and the years following.

Many of the millionaires long ago left for the more exclusive hills of nearby Bernardsville, Bedminster, Peapack, and Far Hills, where they could escape the annoyance of heavy automobile traffic. A number of the great houses were emptied during the depression, when the second generation was unable or unwilling to maintain them. Homes that cost hundreds of thousands were torn down to escape the burden of taxes, or sold at bargain prices (in one instance for less than the cost of the greenhouse) and remodeled on a smaller scale.

Today Morristown is being taken over by the well-to-do middle class. The change is welcomed by businessmen. As one banker commented, "It is better for Morristown to have 20 families in $15,000 or $20,000 homes than one millionaire on 20 acres."

Morristown spreads along both banks of the narrow Whippany River, partly occupying the shoulder of Mount Kemble, with a 597-foot peak, Fort Nonsense, in the city limits. Gillespie Hill is westward, Horse Hill to the north, and Normandy Heights to the east. From this snug setting roads radiate through the well-kept acres of gentlemen farmers to the surrounding communities.

Although only forty-fifth in size among the cities of New Jersey, Morristown, the Morris County seat, is something of a metropolis in miniature. Its banks serve residents of four counties, and from dusk to midnight a red neon glow is reflected above its embryonic skyline. These things are contemporary window dressing for Morristown's Revolutionary heart. The soil in this green basin has never lost the imprint of Washington and his army, visitors here for two critical winters.

There is an air of remote timelessness about the tree-bordered streets, blue flagstone sidewalks, and picket fences. Modern apartment buildings have sprung from the midst of old-fashioned houses, but the visitor still feels that the place is changeless. The park, formerly known as the Green, is at the very center of the community. From this Colonial green all important streets take their courses. Office buildings and two of the larger churches front on the park, with its winding pathways beneath great old trees. There is the same cumulative weather color that is found in old New England villages.

Through a bowery valley that divides the town, the winding Whippany River flows in a shallow bed. Once the center of the Colonial village, the vicinity of Spring and Water Streets on the riverside is now a typical slum section, housing a population largely Negro in an area known to its residents as Little Hollow.

Although Morristown is primarily residential, there are several small industrial enterprises, producing rubber goods, clothing, beach umbrellas, pharmaceuticals, and novelties. Wages, in many instances, are low and dictate a standard of living for the home-town workers that contrasts with the prosperity of the commuting residents.

When, about 1710, word came to the settlement at Newark that iron ore was plentiful beyond the Watchung Mountains, a small number of pioneers struck out on a wilderness road to engage in a new industry. One group selected a site at the foot of the present Water Street in Morristown, in the small valley (now known as The Hollow), and named their new village West Hanover. Newcomers spread to the tablelands above and formed a ring of improved properties around a central green which later became Morristown Green.

In 1739 a new county was laid out within the bounds of Hunterdon and named in honor of Lewis Morris, the first governor of New Jersey. The first session of the Morris County court was held in the tavern of Jacob Ford, the appointed justice. At this convening, the township of Morris was legally defined. Within two years the population was large enough to support a log church. A courthouse was built in 1755.

During the Revolution, when the demand for munitions tested the young industrial resources of the Colonies, no fewer than forty-five forges were operated in Morris County. In addition there were sawmills and gristmills on every sizable stream. The iron industry became the most important factor in the development of Morristown and neighboring communities.

No Briton or Hessian set foot in Morris County except as a prisoner, for the town was relentlessly defended as a key point in the theater of war. General Washington was aware of the natural advantage of Morristown's site on the frontier of the highlands. Good roads provided quick communication with Philadelphia and Congress, and made it easy to concentrate military supplies within striking distance of the British.

Washington led his exhausted army here in January 1777 for winter encampment in the Loantaka Valley after the victories at Trenton and Princeton. He returned with his troops to pass the winter of 1779–80. The men were quartered in crude huts in Jockey Hollow, while Washington made the Ford House his headquarters. With his army's condition even worse than it had been at Vallege Forge, the commander-in-chief established a quota system for levying supplies upon the various counties. He wrote to a friend that the men sometimes went "five or six days together without bread" and that at one time "the soldiers ate every kind of horse food but hay."

Count Pulaski helped to maintain morale by exercising his cavalry corps before the Ford House. His special stunt was to fire his pistol while at full gallop, toss it into the air, catch it, and hurl it at an imaginary enemy ahead. With one foot in the stirrup, and his horse still galloping, Pulaski would then swing to the ground and pick up the gun. Some of the best Virginia horsemen suffered bad falls in attempts to duplicate this feat.

During this winter occurred the court martial of Gen. Benedict Arnold, requested by the officer himself after the Supreme Executive Council of Pennsylvania had accused him of partiality to Tories and rudeness to American civil authorities when he was in command of Philadelphia. The trial was staged in the old Dickerson Tavern (no longer standing) with Maj. Gen. Robert Howe as presiding officer. The verdict was a recommendation for a reprimand by General Washington, a comparatively mild punishment, but one that stung the young officer. Arnold remained in the service only at the insistence of Washington, who placed him in command of West Point. There he entered into a plot with Major André's men to deliver the fortification to the British. It is said that Washington laughed heartily only once during his stay in Morristown—and that was when he was describing Arnold's ludicrous appearance as he galloped from the Robinson house near West Point to seek safety on a British vessel.

From 1780 until the fall of 1781 Continental troops were in and about the north New Jersey area. The Pennsylvania Line was quartered at Jockey Hollow in the winter of 1780–81 and from there went north to meet the troops that Washington was assembling at Newburgh for the final march to Yorktown.

When the iron industry diminished before Western competition during the nineteenth century, Morristown became largely a residential and shopping town. Thomas Nast, the cartoonist who created the Tammany tiger and pilloried Boss Tweed, made his home here. Bret Harte and Frank R. Stockton lived in Morristown for a time.

Rail connections between Morristown and Newark, over the tracks of the Morris and Essex Railroad, were established in January 1838. Today, approximately 1,200 persons commute daily to clerical jobs and executive positions in the cities of the metropolitan district, while a number of outsiders come to Morristown for work.

Tallyhos were characteristic of the recent decades when Morristown was peopled by millionaires and horse lovers. On any bright Sunday morning a walker along the tree-lined roads leading into the town might have been startled by the blast of a horn in the distance, then the fast beating of horses' hoofs, a flash of color from gaily liveried footmen—a cloud of dust and the bright equipage would be lost to sight. Famous were the annual parties given by the late Otto Kahn for his staff of servants and caretakers, numbering upwards of one hundred, on his forested estate in the Normandy Park section. The entire house was turned over to his employees, with continuous music and the best of refreshments provided.

POINTS OF INTEREST

MORRISTOWN NATIONAL HISTORICAL PARK, the first National Historical Park established and maintained by the Federal Government, lies partly within Morristown and partly in the city's environs. The park was created by an act of Congress in 1933 and was dedicated on July 4 of that year by Harold L. Ickes, Secretary of the Interior. The three units (Ford House, Fort Nonsense and Jockey Hollow), comprising more than 1,000 woodland acres of hill, glen and landmark, provide a fitting memorial to Washington's troops. *(Information available at superintendent's office in Historical Museum, rear of Ford House, 230 Morris Ave., daily except Sunday; and at field office in Jockey Hollow, daily except Christmas.)*

1. FORD HOUSE *(open 9-5 weekdays)*, 230 Morris Ave., ranks second only to Mount Vernon as a storehouse of Washington relics and associations, although it was looked upon for almost a century as just another place where Washington had slept. But in 1873 it was acquired by a group who organized the Washington Association of New Jersey and the house was transformed into a Revolutionary museum.

When in the winter of 1779–80 Morristown became again the military capital of the United States, Mrs. Theodosia Ford, widow of Col. Jacob Ford Jr., Revolutionary powdermaker, offered her home to General Washington, his wife and his staff.

Built by Ford in 1774 and quickly acknowledged as one of the finest residences in Morristown, the symmetrical façade of the house is designed in the Georgian style, with strong horizontal lines accentuated by a heavy cornice and hip roof. Wide boards placed horizontally simulate a surface of dressed stone. Especially notable is the entrance motif—the arched doorway and the window above. The entrance leads to a great central hall with authentic period furniture. In the mansion are household furnishings, and pieces of the china and silver used by Washington, Lafayette, and other Revolutionary generals.

THE HISTORICAL MUSEUM, a fireproof building directly behind the mansion, recently built by the National Park Service of the Department of the Interior, was opened February 22, 1938. Exhibits include valuable Washingtoniana, notably a number of the General's letters, a Gilbert Stuart portrait, the suit Washington wore on the evening of his inauguration, one of his swords, a cane, and his camp chest. Typical Kentucky rifles used by

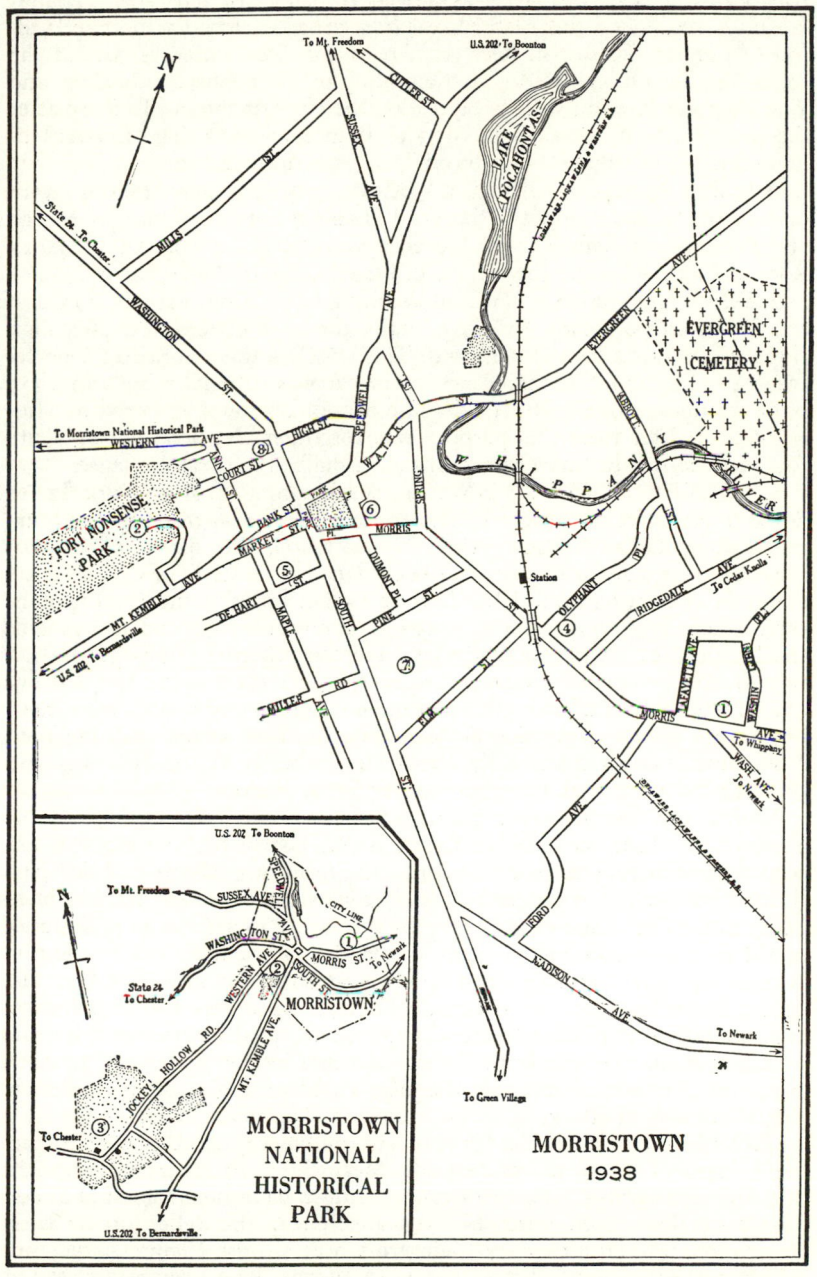

MORRISTOWN
1938

MORRISTOWN
NATIONAL
HISTORICAL
PARK

American troops are displayed, as well as British arms, and other accoutrements. A 104-pound link of the great iron chain, stretched across the Hudson to prevent the British fleet from reaching West Point, is part of the collection. Two dioramas depict the mutiny of the Pennsylvania Line, and Washington's meeting with Lafayette on the steps of the Ford House after the latter's return from his mission to France in 1780. The museum library has 2,000 volumes, chiefly on early American history.

A bronze STATUE OF GENERAL WASHINGTON on a giant stallion stands on a granite pedestal opposite the Ford House at the intersection of Morris and Washington Aves. Cast at Florence, Italy, it is the work of Frederick Roth of Englewood and the gift of E. Mabel Clark of Morristown.

2. FORT NONSENSE, NW. on Washington St. from Park Pl. to Court St., W. to end of road, 0.5 *m.*, occupies the northeastern end of a high ridge that projects into Morristown. This small earthen work has been reconstructed by the National Park Service. It was originally built in 1777 by Washington's orders for the defense of military supplies stored in Morristown. In later years this purpose was forgotten and people, coming to feel that the fort had never been of value, dubbed it Fort Nonsense.

3. JOCKEY HOLLOW, NW. on Washington St. from Park Pl. to Western Ave.; W. to Jockey Hollow Rd., 2.5 *m. (road well marked)*, extends along the early roads betwen New Vernon, Mendham and Morristown. A large amount of work has been done by the Civilian Conservation Corps in re-creating typical log huts and other units of the Continentals' camp grounds of 1779–80 and 1780–81. From old maps and war records the locations of trails and roadways have been charted. Signs guide visitors to sites occupied by various brigades, to a reconstructed hospital hut and to other points of interest. Lead bullets flattened by human teeth have been found on the camp site. Soldiers who had been caught stealing food from nearby farms customarily chewed on a bullet as the lash was laid on their bare backs as many as 100 times or more.

It was here that the grave mutiny of some 2,000 veteran troops of the Pennsylvania Line occurred on Jan. 1, 1781. Poorly fed and clothed, unpaid for twelve months, convinced that the recruiting officers had deceived them on the terms of enlistment, and angered because new recruits were being offered the handsome bounty of three half joes ($26.43), the men seized six field-pieces and prepared to march to Philadelphia for collective bargaining with Congress. In a brief skirmish the mutineers killed one officer, and several men were wounded before the leaders forced a dissenting minority to join them. General Wayne attempted to intervene, but the popular commander was warned that he would be put to death if he fired his pistols. He was assured that the men would willingly take his orders if the British should attack. With two colonels, Wayne accompanied the men as far as Princeton, where a form of arbitration was agreed upon that released most of the men from service. Meanwhile, Sir Henry Clinton had sent two emissaries to the revolters, offering a handsome sum if the men would lay down their arms. No less angered by this reflection on their Revolutionary loyalty than by their grievances against Congress, the mutineers turned over the British agents to Wayne, who promptly executed them. A small granite block under a great oak marks the GRAVE OF CAPTAIN ADAM BETTIN, who resisted the revolt.

THE JOCKEY HOLLOW WILD FLOWER TRAIL (entrance L. from Jockey Hollow Rd., 0.1 *m.* SW of junction with Camp Rd. and opposite parking area) is a loop of 1.3 *m.* through meadows, swamp and wooded hillsides bordering Primrose Brook. Along the footpath are native flora. Bridges and other structures are few and simply designed.

THE WICK HOUSE *(open 9-5 daily)*, NE. corner Mendham-New Vernon Rd. and Jockey Hollow Rd., was built in 1746 by settlers from Long Island. Its long sweeping roof line, single chimney, and low eaves are clearly the heritage of Southold and Southampton. Characteristic also is the use of hand-hewn shingle siding on the front of the house and clapboarding on the other three sides.

Capt. Henry Wick of the Colonial cavalry lived here, but it was his daughter who made history for the farmhouse. One winter day, so the story goes, Miss Temperance Wick was returning on horseback after summoning a physician for her mother. Colonial troopers tried to commandeer her favorite white horse. "Oh, surely," Tempe is said to have remonstrated, "you will let me ride him home first!" With that she brought down her whip on the horse's flanks and he took the hill at a gallop. At the farmhouse, the girl led the horse through the kitchen and into her bedroom. The soldiers came, searched the barn and nearby woods, and left. Another version is that Tempe rode her horse straight into the house without stopping to dismount. Conceding the liberal dimensions of Colonial door-frames and the delicate proportions of Miss Wick, the question remains: Who opened the door—Tempe, or the horse?

OTHER POINTS OF INTEREST

4. DR. JABEZ CAMPFIELD HOUSE *(open 10-5 Tues., Fri.)*, 5 Olyphant Pl., erected 1760, was the scene of Alexander Hamilton's successful courtship of Elizabeth Schuyler in the winter of 1779–80. The building is simply designed with flush eaves at the gable ends and a bracketed cornice. The entrance porch was added later. Owned by the Daughters of the American Revolution, the house contains a fine collection of Colonial furniture.

5. SANSAY MANSION *(private)*, 17 De Hart St., was built in 1807 by a man who was probably the most popular dancemaster of the State. It is a large, boxlike structure of modified Georgian Colonial design, with white-painted clapboards. Monsieur Sansay's origin was obscure, but he could teach the feather step and spring step far better than any of his nearby competitors. When Lafayette visited Morristown again in 1825, he was entertained at a dinner here.

6. FIRST PRESBYTERIAN CHURCH, 65 Park Pl., is a limestone structure with a large clock on the tower. Of a style that may be classified as Romanesque, the barrack-like structure does not compare with the fine Colonial church of classic Greek design that it replaced. The earlier building served as a hospital for Continental troops. Approximately 150 soldiers

THE FORD MANSION, MORRISTOWN

are buried in the old cemetery where stones date back to 1728. A plain marker indicates the GRAVE OF GENERAL JOHN DOUGHTY, who became the third commander in chief of the United States Army.

7. MUNICIPAL BUILDING, South St. between Pine and Elm Sts., is one of the most sumptuous city halls in the State, although hardly in keeping with Morristown's Colonial atmosphere. It was built in 1918 as the $400,000 home and private museum of Theodore N. Vail, former president of the American Telephone and Telegraph Co. He bequeathed it to the city with an endowment of $200,000 on condition that a duplicate amount be raised by the town. The civic response was less than hearty, some persons pointing out that the cost of maintaining the marble and granite mansion would be large. Finally an agreement was made which enabled the city to take possession without doubling the endowment although a sizable sum was spent for interior alterations. On the site of Mr. Vail's old house in front of the city hall, a lagoon and cenotaph were built as a war memorial. The mansion, designed by W. W. Bosworth, is finely executed in the Italian Renaissance style with light gray Italian marble. A wide veranda flanked by marble balustrades leads to the entrance; above is a colonnaded second-floor balcony. The entrance has two cast bronze doors with eight panels by Charles Kecht, depicting scenes in the history of Morristown. The original casting cost about $21,000, and two additional ones were made before the cast was satisfactory. Within, the double staircase of self-supporting masonry is a notable example of arch construction. Teakwood, oak and mahogany were used extensively for the floors and trim.

8. MORRIS COUNTY COURTHOUSE, Washington St. between Court St. and Western Ave., is an early 19th century building designed by architects Carter and Lindsey. The two-story structure of brick and sandstone is surmounted by a colonnaded and louvered belfry topped with a golden dome and weathervane. Four simulated Ionic columns divide the arched windows of the second story; in the pediment is a figure of Justice. The entrance, not unlike that of a private home, has a one-story portico with a pair of Ionic colonnettes on both sides. The courthouse is attractively painted in cream and white.

POINTS OF INTEREST IN ENVIRONS

Site of Speedwell Iron Works, *1.1 m.,* Alfred Vail House, *1.2 m.,* Kemble House, Revolutionary headquarters, *3.6 m.,* Van Doren Mill, *5.6 m. (see Tour 4);* The Seeing Eye, training school for dogs to lead blind, *4 m. (see Tour 14).*

Mount Holly

Railroad Station: Pennsylvania Station, 35 Madison Ave., for Pennsylvania R.R.
Bus Stations: Main and Washington Sts. for Public Service; 1 m. S. on State 38 for Quaker City Line.
Taxis: 20¢ and 25¢ to any part of town.
Traffic Regulations: R. and L. turns at all intersections; watch street signs for parking limitations.

Accommodations: Two hotels, many tourist homes.

Information Service: Post Office, Washington St.; traffic officer, Washington and Mill Sts.

Motion Picture Houses: One.
Swimming: Mill Dam Park, S. end Wall St.; Rancocas Creek, W. edge of town.

Annual Events: Horse show, variable date during spring, 5 m. S. on Medford Rd.

An old Quaker town and the Burlington County seat, MOUNT HOLLY (30 alt., 6,573 pop.) is named for a mountain that has everything except size. The holly-covered hill, a miniature Fuji cone, rises to an altitude of 183 feet from a level clearing in the northern part of the original 300-acre tract upon which the town was built. Rancocas Creek flows from the flatlands east of the hill. The stream crosses Main Street, the principal thoroughfare, near the center of the city and then turns eastward to the Delaware River, 12 miles distant.

Mount Holly is the center of an important agricultural area. Roads lead to it from all directions, traversing rolling country where fine fruit orchards are bright with blossoms in late April and early May.

Broad, shaded streets give the impression of a slow-moving country town. In the town's center modern stores adjoin old houses erected by early Quakers. Many of the homes are square structures of two and three stories, built flush with patterned brick sidewalks as in Burlington and Bordentown. Architecturally they are notable for their simplicity of line and detail, and distinguished by their solid wooden shutters, heavy hardware and wrought-iron railings and fences. Paint is used sparingly. The whiff of wood smoke, present even on a hot summer day, indicates the type of stove used in many of the old houses.

Along maple-lined High Street in the western part of the town live the wealthier citizens. Their houses, set in the midst of neatly clipped lawns and attractive gardens, shaded by fine trees, include typical examples of Victorian Gothic architecture as well as pretentious modern styles. In contrast to High Street is the collection of dilapidated dwellings and plain shacks on the southern edge of Mount Holly. This district is called Timbuctoo because, it is said, the first persons to live here were descendants of slaves from Timbuctoo.

In 1676 Thomas Rudyard and John Ridges purchased a share of land from Edward Byllynge and the trustees of West Jersey. In 1701 Edward Gaskill and Josiah Southwick bought Ridges' 871 acres, on part of which the town now stands. In 1723 the North Branch of Rancocas Creek was dammed for a sawmill and, later for a gristmill. An iron works was established about 1730 by Isaac Pearson, Mahlon Stacy and John Burr; British raiders later destroyed the works, which had been supplying cannon and shot for the Continental Army.

During the Revolution Mount Holly was occupied at times by British troops, who converted the old Friends Meeting House into a commissary. In 1779 the same building was used for sessions of the legislature when, during November and December, the town was the temporary capital of the State. Gov. William Livingston at that time named Thursday, December 9, 1779, as the first Thanksgiving Day to be officially observed in the State, in accordance with a Congressional resolution.

An act of the legislature transferred the county seat from Burlington to Mount Holly in 1796, and the courthouse was erected in that year. Construction of the Burlington and Mount Holly Railroad half a century later strengthened industrial enterprise. By then the town had five mills, a woolen factory, nine stores, a bank, two newspapers and a boarding school.

In 1865 the population of Mount Holly was 3,878, and the town enjoyed steady progress as a small manufacturing and trading center. Some years later Hezekiah Smith built his locally famous bicycle railway, a monorail line, to Mount Holly from nearby Smithville *(see Tour 26)*.

Since 1915 there has been little increase in industry or population. Most of the workers are employed in a score of small factories, chiefly knitting and weaving mills with leather goods manufacturing also important.

For many years Mount Holly has been publicized for the activities of Ellis Parker, former chief detective of Burlington County, who enjoyed a reputation as a suburban Sherlock Holmes. The bizarre climax of Parker's career was his conviction in 1937 on a charge of kidnaping Paul Wendel and obtaining by torture a confession of the Lindbergh murder. The false confession was used to delay the execution of Bruno Richard Hauptmann for the Lindbergh crime.

POINTS OF INTEREST

1. The COUNTY BUILDINGS, Main St. between Garden and Union Sts., are grouped as a unit with the large COURTHOUSE, erected 1796, in the center and the smaller SURROGATE'S OFFICE and ADMINISTRATION BUILDING, built 1807, on either side. The courthouse in particular is an outstanding example of Georgian Colonial design adapted to a public building. It is a two-story, yellow brick structure, with white trim, green shutters, and a well-proportioned tower. The entrance is lighted by a Colonial lantern; over the great oak door is the coat of arms of New Jersey in granite, and a graceful fanlight. The surrogate's office and the administration building are both one-story structures of brick, painted yellow, with green shutters and white trim.

2. The FRIENDS MEETING HOUSE *(not open to public)*, 77 Main St., is a red brick building of severely plain design, with white trim and a slate roof, erected 1775 and enlarged in 1850. The enlargement accurately follows the simplicity of the original style so that the new portion of the rectangular box is indistinguishable from the old. Two large sycamores and a growth of ivy soften the exterior. Within, the old benches show marks left by the butcher knives of the British commissary department at the time when enemy troops were quartered in the town.

3. The BRAINERD SCHOOL *(private)*, 35 Brainerd St., is a small, one-story brick building, brightly painted in yellow with solid shutters of green and white trim. Crowded between adjoining houses, the school is built flush with the red brick sidewalk and shaded by a large maple. In this building, erected 1759, the Rev. John Brainerd taught in 1767. From the nearby church the missionary made such fiery denunciations of British rule that the Hessians burned the structure before evacuating the town in 1778.

4. The STEPHEN GIRARD HOUSE *(private)*, 211 Mill St., is a two-story, gray clapboard structure with heavy green shutters. Additions, making up about two-thirds of the house, largely spoil the charm of the original two-room structure, which is marked by a wide end chimney. Girard, remembered for the fortune that helped to finance the War of 1812 and that established Girard College, a Philadelphia school for orphan boys, came to Mount Holly in 1777 from Philadelphia. He brought with him his young bride of a few months, Mary Lum, daughter of a ship's carpenter. In the basement of this house he opened a shop for tobacco, tea, rum, sugar, molasses and raisins. "He is said then to have been a little, unnoticed man, save that the beauty of his wife . . . worried and alienated his mind." Girard returned in 1778 to Philadelphia, where he entered foreign trade with a fleet of vessels named after his favorite philosophers and accumulated the fortune that made him a power in banking. It was the wife, not the financier, who ultimately died as a hospitalized mental case.

5. The MILL STREET HOTEL *(open)*, 67 Mill St., is the last remnant of the Three Tun Tavern of Colonial times. A "tun" was a hogshead or measure for liquor, and a tavern was known as a one-tun, two-tun or three-tun inn depending on its size. Erected 1720, it is one of the oldest buildings in Mount Holly. The original brick walls, revealed in places through a crumbling coat of stucco, were incorporated in the present structure which, altered many times, is still used as a hotel. A covered cobblestone driveway leads to the rear where stagecoaches once stopped in the carriage yard.

6. The JOHN WOOLMAN MEMORIAL BUILDING *(open daily except Tues., March-Oct.)*, 99 Branch St., was built in 1771 by the noted Quaker as a home for his daughter. Maintained as a tearoom by a memorial association, and attracting hundreds of pilgrims from the United States and abroad, the small red brick house of two stories with a white clapboard addition recaptures with startling realism the atmosphere of Colonial days. Beyond the white picket fence lies a fragment of old America, com-

BURLINGTON COUNTY COURTHOUSE, MOUNT HOLLY

plete with narrow brick walk, well with sweep, formal garden edged with boxwood, sundial and old trees. Indoors the smell of decades of wood fires permeates the house. From the hand-hewn beams of the low ceilings sage and gourds hang drying. A great corner fireplace has a blackened kettle hanging from the crane. Behind the dwelling is a small frame guest house, with limited overnight accommodations.

Born near Rancocas in 1720, John Woolman settled in Mount Holly at 20 "to tend a shop and keep the books" for a shopkeeper and tailor. He later became a successful merchant but gave up merchandising and confined himself to his tailoring trade because "Truth required me to live more free from outward cumbers." Woolman was also a conveyancer, but he refused to draw a will or write a bill of sale in which a slave was involved. He traveled extensively among wealthy slaveholding Quakers to urge the liberation of their slaves, and he was instrumental in awakening the Society of Friends to the evils of slavery. During a religious mission to England in 1772, he died at York.

Woolman is known today chiefly for the spiritual and literary beauty of his *Journal,* the second book selected by Dr. Charles W. Eliot for the Harvard Classics, and pronounced by Henry Crabb Robinson "a perfect gem!" Of Woolman, the English critic and diarist said: "His is a *schöne Seele,* a beautiful soul." In the world of religious thought, appreciation for Woolman has grown steadily. His religion was one of love for God and for his fellow men of all races and creeds. "To turn all the treasures we possess into channels of universal love," he wrote in his *Journal,* "becomes the business of our lives."

7. The RELIEF FIRE COMPANY HOUSE, 15 Pine St., is the headquarters of what is perhaps the oldest active volunteer company in the United States. The original company was organized July 9, 1752, as the Britannia; in 1787 the name was changed to Mount Holly Fire Company. In 1805 the firemen adopted the present name of their organization. The company has the original articles of agreement and a number of old leather buckets bearing the name "Britannia" and the date 1752. Behind the firehouse stands the original engine shelter, a small one-room building of hand-sawed boards, the inside blackened with age and the exterior painted a brilliant green.

8. MOUNT HOLLY PARK, N. end High St., surrounds MOUNT HOLLY *(good path to summit),* a distinctive bump in the low terrain. Barber and Howe observed almost a century ago that the hill was "said to be the highest land in the southern portion of New Jersey. From its summit an uninterrupted prospect is had, in every direction—where no Alps o'er Alps arise." Many other parts of southern New Jersey, however, have elevations exceeding that of Mount Holly.

On December 23, 1776, Count von Donop and a large force of Hessians engaged in an artillery duel here, directing their fire against some 500 American troops under Colonel Griffin on Iron Works Hill, S. Pine Street. Griffin lured the Hessian force from Bordentown to cut off support for Colonel Rall's garrison at nearby Trenton, which was overwhelmed by Washington's surprise attack 3 days later.

On the flatlands immediately to the west of the Mount stands the old grandstand of the Mount Holly race track, its huge ornate structure reminiscent of the pre-war decade when this race track figured importantly in turf events of central New Jersey. The race track has not been used in recent years except for occasional motor races.

POINTS OF INTEREST IN ENVIRONS

Mount Laurel State Park, *11.3 m.*, ruins of Hanover Furnace, *15.7 m.* (see *Tour 26).*

New Brunswick

Railroad Stations: Pennsylvania Station, junction of Albany and French Sts. and Easton Ave., for Pennsylvania R.R.; Sandford St. between Remsen and Throop Aves. for Raritan River R.R.

Bus Stations: Pennsylvania Station for Public Service and Greyhound; 22 French St. for Safeway Trailways.

Taxis: 35¢ within city limits.

Local Busses: Fare 5¢.

City Dock: Burnet St. near Commercial Ave.; excursion and fishing boats.

Traffic Regulations: Turns may be made in either direction at intersections of all streets, except where traffic officers direct otherwise; watch street signs for parking limitations and one-way streets.

Accommodations: Two modern hotels, several smaller hotels and boarding houses.

Information Service: Chamber of Commerce, Woodrow Wilson Hotel, George St. and Livingston Ave.

Motion Picture Houses: Six.

Swimming: The Natatorium, 507 Livingston Ave., 25¢ weekdays, 40¢ Sat. and Sun.; open only in summer.

Annual Events: Iris Field Day and Nurserymen's Field Day, New Jersey State College of Agriculture, May; Commencement exercises of Rutgers and New Jersey College for Women, June; Poultrymen's Field Day and Farm Crops Field Day, New Jersey State College of Agriculture, July; outboard motorboat races on Raritan River, July 4; Flower Show,· Horse Show, September; Rutgers University athletic contests, October through May.

NEW BRUNSWICK (125 alt., 34,555 pop.), situated on the south bank of Raritan River, combines the attributes of a manufacturing center, a college town, a market place and a county seat. It is far enough from other cities to live independently, even though the Pennsylvania Railroad designates it as the southwestern boundary of the New York commuting area.

A visitor in 1778 described New Brunswick as a "dismal town, but pleasantly situated." The riverside site is almost as pleasant as ever, but industrial development has converted the green shore into an area of brick-walled factories and old frame tenements.

The original green of the Colonial village is suggested by the tree-shaded square around which the municipal and Middlesex County buildings are grouped, and by the campuses of Rutgers University and its two affiliated schools: the New Jersey College for Women and the New Jersey State College of Agriculture. Half circling the city, these institutions occupy much of the high ground along Raritan River, which forms the northern and eastern boundaries of New Brunswick.

George Street, the main thoroughfare, is lined with modern shops. Glass-fronted first stories are topped with beauty parlors and offices of lawyers and dentists. Above the low skyline of two- and three-story brick and frame buildings rise the eight-story, white stone building of the First National Bank; the nine-story, red brick Hotel Woodrow Wilson; and the delicate white spire of the chapel at the New Jersey College for Women.

The automotive confusion at the business center, George and Albany Streets, brings together the main elements which constitute New Brunswick. Cars from the surrounding area outnumber local vehicles three to one, especially on Saturday nights when parking space is almost invisible. Out-of-town shoppers must thread their way through crowds of girls from New Jersey College for Women, young men from Rutgers, and a polyglot industrial population, emptying its pay envelopes. Albany Street lunchrooms, famous for hot dogs and hamburgers, serve the throng, while the students seek food and drink in a black and chromium cafe, cannily decorated with football murals. Many shoppers make a last stop for weekend supplies at the open fruit and vegetable stands in the Little Hungary section at the western end of Albany Street.

An embankment supporting the main line tracks of the Pennsylvania Railroad divides the city. The shabby yellow brick station has long been a favorite subject of complaint in letters to the New Brunswick *Home News,* but the arched stone bridge across the Raritan ranks as one of the finest of its kind in the State.

The city is known as a manufacturing center for surgical supplies and pharmaceuticals. The needle trades are gaining in importance, and the manufacture of cigars and cigar boxes absorbs another part of the 15,000 local workers. The foreign-born, comprising 27 percent of the population, are largely employed in New Brunswick's factories. Germans, Poles, Hungarians and Italians are the most numerous nationalities, in the order given.

The area around New Brunswick was occupied by the Lenni Lenape Indians and one or two white settlers when John Inian and 10 associates from Long Island bought about 10,000 acres in 1681. Inian and his associates were English. They established an English hegemony which was not threatened until 1730 when Dutch settlers from Albany began to change the national character of the community.

In 1686 Inian established a ferry, for which he received exclusive rights in 1697, and built a new road to Delaware Falls (Trenton). The locality, previously known as Prigmore's Swamp, was called Inian's Ferry in 1713. On the water front were built the first homes, and taverns for wayfarers.

For a time it seemed that the Landing, 1.5 miles upstream at the head of navigation, would eclipse Inian's Ferry as a townsite. But the fact that ships could reach the Landing only when the tide was favorable, while Inian's Ferry was accessible at all times, spoiled the Landing's chances. Now it is little more than a bridge with a background of meadow lands populated chiefly by cows.

The name Brunswick, in honor of King George I, also Duke of Brunswick, first appears in court records of 1724. In 1730, when the settlement consisted of 125 families, it received a charter from King George II. The

Dutch Reformed Church, which is known to have been in existence in New Brunswick as early as 1717, subsequently became a strong influence in civic life. Methodism made a start in 1740 when the evangelist, George Whitefield, preached to an immense crowd from the tail end of a wagon before the Reformed Church.

New Brunswick soon became one of the great agricultural depots of the Colony. Every stream that could turn a wheel had its mill. Warehouses and inns were erected, and the river front was lined with vessels.

Construction of the barracks in 1759 and their occupation by British troops after 1767 strengthened Tory sentiment among the wealthier citizens. Two years before, however, patriots had burned in effigy a delegate to the Stamp Act Congress for refusing to oppose the unpopular act. The crisis reached a head in 1774 when the Provincial Congress met here and chose delegates to the Continental Congress. Subsequent prohibition of trade with the enemy seriously injured commerce in New Brunswick, then a town of about 150 families.

Washington and his defeated army, retreating from New York, entered New Brunswick on November 28, 1776. Later, the general wrote, "In short, the conduct of the Jerseys has been most infamous. Instead of turning out to defend their country, and affording aid to our army, they are making their submissions as fast as they can. If the Jerseys had given us any support we might have made a good stand at Hackensac, and after that at Brunswick . . ." On December 1, Sir William Howe led the British into the city for a destructive occupation of seven months.

Compensating for the unsoldierly conduct of the local troops New Brunswick rivermen turned their whaleboats into fighting ships. They did so much damage in nightly raids upon British vessels around New York Bay that an expedition of 300 men was sent here to destroy the fleet of Capt. Adam Hyler, best known of the privateers. The burning of his boats and a skirmish with American militia was the last fight in or around the town.

Washington again brought his army to New Brunswick after the inconclusive battle at nearby Monmouth (Freehold) in the summer of 1778. And it was here that the Commander in Chief issued his unexpected order in 1781 for the march south that resulted in the British capitulation at Yorktown.

Trade revived after the war, and in 1784 the growing town was incorporated as a city. The first American railroad charter was granted in 1815 to John Stevens for a line from "near Trenton, to . . . near New Brunswick" but the road was never started. Rail service came with the building of the New Jersey Railroad, whose passengers were shuttled by stagecoach across Raritan River to the New York connection until 1838 when through service was made possible by a new railroad bridge.

The busy port attracted Cornelius Vanderbilt, who had begun to amass his fortune with the steamship *Bellona*. However, New Brunswick's importance as a shipping terminal began to wane in 1834 when the Delaware and Raritan Canal, 42-mile waterway to Bordentown, was opened. For a time, though, the city benefited from the through traffic. The canal boom was short-lived; railroad competition and domination put the canal boats out of business, although nominal operation continued to 1933.

By the middle of the nineteenth century the city had grown to 8,693. There were 120 stores, 1 bank, 8 churches, and 2 schools for girls. Rutgers College, after weathering financial crises and suspensions, was an established institution. In addition to a carriage factory, a cotton mill and several shipyards, New Brunswick had three units of the newly developed rubber industry, producing rubberized sheets, carriage tops and boots. Other products of the period were machinery, wallpaper, shoes and hosiery.

The manufacture of pharmaceuticals was begun in 1886 by Johnson and Johnson. In 1916 the pharmaceutical industry was augmented by the arrival of E. R. Squibb and Sons. The National Musical String Company, founded in 1897, produced the first harmonicas in America, and has since become the world's largest maker of steel strings.

After 1900 the city's industrial pattern changed. The promising rubber industry moved westward to get more room for expansion, but the empty factories were quickly occupied by the needle trades and other newcomers. The old carriage factories were succeeded by an automobile plant in 1910 when the Simplex Automobile Company began operations. During the World War the Wright-Martin Aircraft Corporation made Hispano-Suiza and Liberty motors in the Simplex factory, which is now used by the International Motor Company for the production of automotive parts.

Steady industrial growth has been the main stream of New Brunswick's history since 1850. But political controversies, revival movements, and a celebrated murder case have rippled the current. In the early nineties, when the city council was deadlocked on the choice of a president, a coin was tossed, it is said, to decide the vote. The Democrats charged that the Republicans had used a double-headed coin. The city's saloons once enjoyed such excellent patronage both downstairs and up that reformers declared, "It would be an injustice to the devil to condemn him to live in New Brunswick." Crusading evangelists moved in, set up their tents on Livingston Avenue and "converted" hundreds.

The Hall-Mills murder put New Brunswick on newspaper front pages in 1922 and again at the time of the trial in 1926. The Rev. Edward W. Hall, rector of the fashionable Protestant Episcopal Church of St. John the Evangelist, had been found shot to death under a crab apple tree in De Russey's Lane, near the city. Beside him lay the mutilated body of Eleanor Mills, a choir singer. Hall's widow, from the old and wealthy Stevens family, was tried for murder with two of her brothers; all were finally acquitted. The most important testimony for the State was given by the "Pig Woman," Mrs. Jane Gibson, who said that while she was riding her mule in nocturnal search for a pig thief she saw four persons at the scene of the killings.

At present (1939) the city has approximately 100 factories producing, in addition to the goods already named, chemicals, rugs and linoleum, fireworks, furniture, incubators, and clothing.

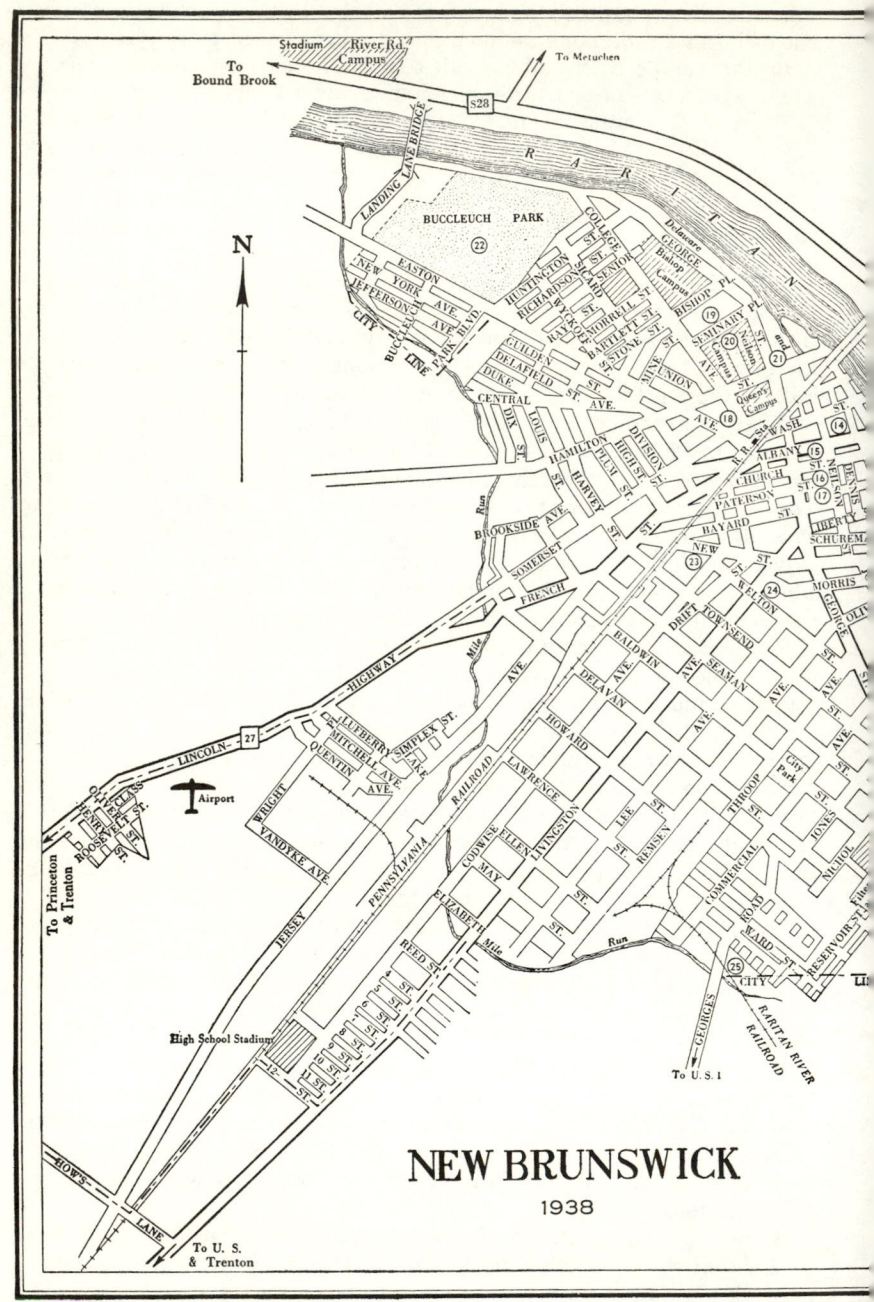

NEW BRUNSWICK

1938

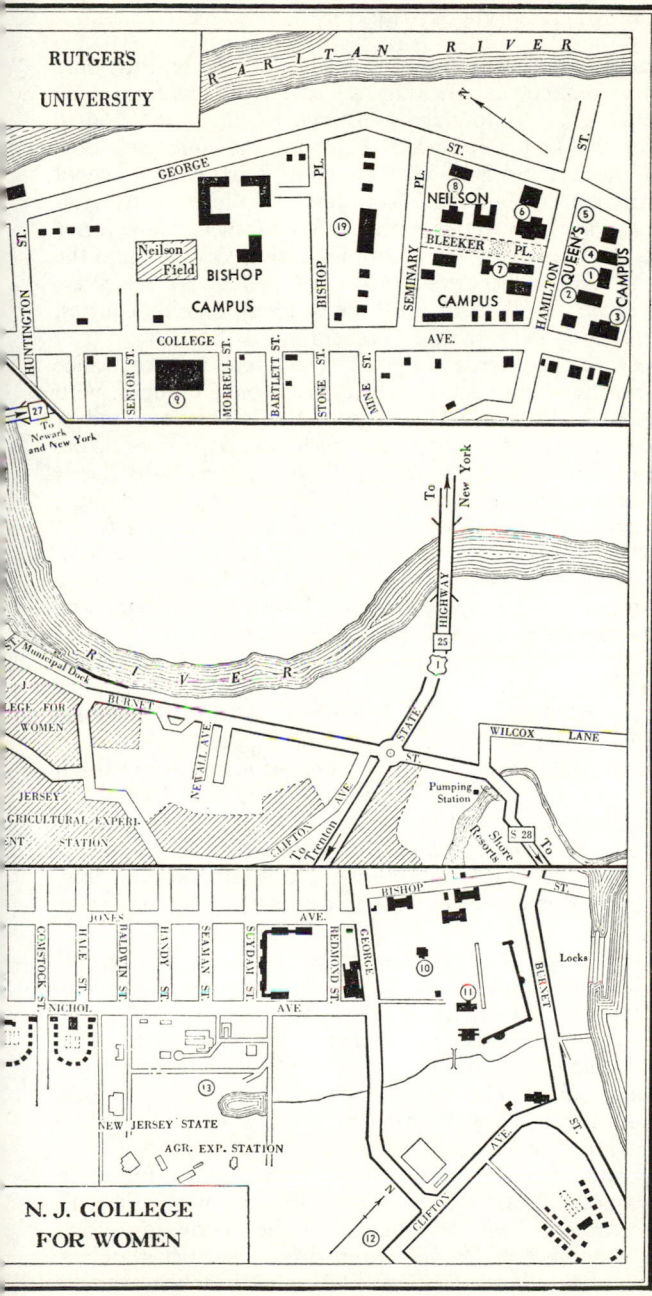

RUTGERS UNIVERSITY

Eighth oldest institution of higher learning in the country, and the only state university with a Colonial charter, Rutgers University *(buildings open unless otherwise indicated)* was founded as Queen's College in 1766 to prepare ministers for the Dutch Reformed Church. The university now includes the College of Arts and Sciences, College of Engineering, School of Chemistry, Department of Ceramics, New Jersey College of Agriculture, School of Education, New Jersey College for Women, New Jersey College of Pharmacy (at Newark), University Extension Division and the University College, which conducts evening courses in Newark and New Brunswick. The combined enrollment for all the colleges, evening courses, and special courses is 9,993. The faculty numbers 500.

The university has several scattered campuses, which tend to decentralize student life. In the northwestern part of the city is Queen's Campus, with the oldest buildings and fine trees. University activities are centered at Queens. Neilson Campus, with the library and technical departments, lies north of Queens. Still farther north is Bishop Campus, consisting chiefly of dormitories. The recently acquired River Road Campus, with a stadium, golf course and athletic fields, is on the opposite shore of Raritan River.

In the southeastern part of the city, separated from Queen's by the business district, is the campus of New Jersey College for Women. It is a colorful place in spring when the great cherry tree beside College Hall and the dogwood and crab apple near the chapel are in bloom.

Directly south of the women's campus is the college farm, a 750-acre tract with the six buildings and the greenhouses of the New Jersey College of Agriculture and the State Agricultural Experiment Station. The workmanlike aspect of this section is relieved by apple and peach orchards.

In contrast with nearby Princeton, many of whose students are from all parts of the country, the Rutgers undergraduates are chiefly from New Jersey's middle class. Most of the students are preoccupied with the serious business of getting an education and preparing themselves for earning a living after graduation. Nevertheless, several of the fraternity houses along College Avenue suggest an opulence in marked contrast to the democratic tone of the campus.

Although the college's charter was granted in 1766 by George III through Governor William Franklin, the school did not open until November 1771. Eighteen-year-old Frederick Frelinghuysen was hired as the entire faculty; there was one graduate at the first commencement in 1774. When the British occupied New Brunswick in 1776, Frelinghuysen left to serve as an artillery officer. The institution was moved from the old Red Lion Tavern building in New Brunswick to Millstone and then to North Branch, but returned at the end of the war.

Classes were suspended between 1795 and 1807 for lack of funds. In 1811 the college was established on its present campus when Queen's Building was first occupied. Two lotteries netted the young institution about $27,000, plus a number of lawsuits from dissatisfied ticketholders. The General Synod of the Dutch Reformed Church had taken over the college in an arrangement that lasted 57 years. When control of the college was returned to its trustees in 1864, the New Brunswick Theological Seminary became the separate institution that it is today.

During the period of church domination, the college officers anticipated the technique of obtaining large grants from wealthy individuals. Henry Rutgers, 80-year-old philanthropist, was a member of the Collegiate Church in New York whose pastor, the Rev. Dr. Philip Milledoler, had become president of Queen's College in 1825. Prudently the trustees renamed the college for Mr. Rutgers. Then they waited. After an anxious year, they received from Colonel Rutgers a draft for $200, to be spent for a bell. Later, Rutgers understandingly contributed a $5,000 bond.

When the college was designated in 1864 to receive $5,800 annually from the sale of government land, the work of the present State College of Agriculture began on a 90-acre farm.

Rutgers College became a State institution in 1917. A year later the New Jersey College for Women was opened as an affiliated institution. In 1924 the name "Rutgers College" was discarded for "Rutgers University." Since then the School of Education has been opened and the New Jersey College of Pharmacy, at Newark, has been absorbed.

Rutgers University is a State institution in a very real sense. Its educational work is by no means limited to the approximately 2,500 men and women undergraduates in the various colleges. County extension agents bring practical advice to housewives and farmers, answering questions on canning, poultry disease, and other problems of the home and farm. Campus buildings are thrown open for conventions; each year the university sponsors institutes on labor, banking and the press. Faculty members are constantly in service as speakers before women's clubs, civic groups and other organizations.

1. QUEEN'S BUILDING, Hamilton St. between George St. and College Ave., is the central building of Queen's Campus, and the home of the university's administrative offices. It is one of the best examples of Post-Colonial college architecture in the country. Designed by James McComb, architect of New York's City Hall, it was occupied as the first structure 14 years before the central section and cupola were completed in 1825. It is simple in mass and fenestration, relieved by a delicate cornice and low-pitched pediments, and crowned with a fine Georgian lantern. The somber brownstone walls are overgrown with ivy, which has mellowed the lines of the composition. Queen's represents the culmination of classic simplicity in the development of the architecture during the early Republican period. Offices open within from the broad center hall, from which a divided stairway leads to the second floor.

The CANNON on the lawn before the building was a gift from the Federal Government, marking the end of a campus war with Princeton College. In 1875 a group of Rutgers sophomores raided the Princeton campus and returned with a cannon, but not the one that Princeton men had boasted of stealing from Rutgers years earlier. After a reprisal by Princeton students, both sides returned stolen goods and Rutgers got a new cannon.

2. GEOLOGICAL HALL, W. of Queen's Bldg. *(open 9-5 weekdays),* another brownstone structure dedicated in 1873, has a collection of minerals, Indian relics and New Jersey fossils, including a mastodon from a marl pit near Salem in 1869.

3. WINANTS HALL, NE. corner College Ave. and Somerset St., houses the college postoffice, a cafeteria and dormitory rooms. The largest building on Queen's Campus, it has a columned porch, a brownstone first story and brick second and third stories. It was designed by Van Campen Taylor and erected in 1890.

4. SOPHIA ASTLEY KIRKPATRICK CHAPEL, E. of Queen's Bldg., a brownstone building erected in 1872, contains more than 90 portraits of university presidents, trustees and other notables. Among the painters were Thomas Sully and John Vanderlyn. Memorial windows presented by graduating classes are in keeping with the French Gothic architecture.

5. DANIEL S. SCHANCK OBSERVATORY *(not open),* SW. corner Hamilton and George Sts., was erected in 1865. Constructed of cream-painted brick and modeled after the Temple of the Winds in Athens, it has two octagonal towers linked by a short passageway.

6. The RALPH VOORHEES LIBRARY *(open 8 a.m.-11 p.m. Mon.-Fri.; 8-6 Sat.; 2-6 Sun.; 8-12 holidays),* Hamilton St. between George St. and College Ave., opposite Queen's Bldg., contains 261,469 volumes and 150,000 pamphlets, maps and manuscripts. It is known for its collections of original documents relating to New Jersey and New Brunswick history, among them the Joyce Kilmer manuscript collection, letters to George Washington, and the records of many of the State's oldest families. The library also has the Defoe collection of first and second edition pamphlets, the Henry Janeway Weston memorial collections of books and pictures dealing with Napoleon I, and the Thomas L. Janeway memorial collection of casts and photographs. Among the historical relics are a compass, chain and vernier that belonged to Washington; early prints, drawings and paintings; and a coin collection. Erected in 1902, the building is a squat structure of brownstone designed in the classic manner. The architect was Henry Rutgers Marshall.

7. NEW JERSEY HALL *(open upon application to Zoology Dept.),* Hamilton St. between College Ave. and George St., built in 1888, is of raspberry-red brick, three stories high, with corner towers. The building contains 25,000 specimens of seed plants and oysters.

8. CERAMICS BUILDING *(open on application to Ceramics Dept.),* 536 George St., is of red brick, in modified Georgian Colonial style. Various ceramic wares are manufactured on Thursdays, Fridays and Saturdays from 9 a.m. to 5 p.m. The department also maintains ceramics exhibits.

9. UNIVERSITY GYMNASIUM, College Ave. between Morrell and Senior Sts., is of modified Georgian Colonial architecture. It was built in 1931 on the grounds where the Nation's first intercollegiate football game was played by Rutgers and Princeton on Nov. 6, 1869. With 25 men on each team, Rutgers won, 6-4.

10. COLLEGE HALL, N. side of George St., E. of Bishop St., is the central unit of the campus of the New Jersey College for Women.

QUEEN'S BUILDING, RUTGERS UNIVERSITY, NEW BRUNSWICK

This converted brownstone residence, which was the entire college in 1918, now houses the administrative offices. Most of the other campus buildings were erected after 1918 and are largely of modified Georgian Colonial architecture.

11. ELIZABETH RODMAN VOORHEES CHAPEL, E. of College Hall, is designed in the Post-Colonial style. Built in 1926 from designs by Ludlow and Peabody, it is finely proportioned and noteworthy in the lack of over-ornamentation. The building has a slender white spire.

12. WOODLAWN *(not open)*, Clifton Ave S. of George St., was the home of James Neilson, trustee and benefactor of the university. The colonnaded white frame house, built early in the 19th century, faces a broad lawn, and resembles Mount Vernon in its architectural simplicity.

13. NEW JERSEY STATE COLLEGE OF AGRICULTURE and the AGRICULTURAL EXPERIMENT STATION, S. corner George St. and Nichol Ave., are housed in red brick buildings adjacent to tracts used for experimental farming. Here approximately 800 students obtain theoretical and practical training in scientific agriculture, for utilization in farming, teaching or in business associated with agriculture. The Experiment Station under the auspices of the Federal Government, established in 1880, seeks improved farming methods and new ways of fighting insect pests and plant diseases. The work of the station and the college has become widely known. A tablet marks the SITE OF THE JOHANNIS VOORHEES HOMESTEAD, built *c.* 1720 and partly burned by the British troops. The building was renovated and acquired by the trustees of the university in 1864. From this house scientific farm investigations concerned with tests of marl, manures and chemical fertilizers in the growing of corn, potatoes, wheat, clover and other crops were carried on as early as 1867. In 1872 the New Jersey Board of Agriculture was organized here.

OTHER POINTS OF INTEREST

14. SITE OF THE WHITE HART TAVERN, NE. corner Albany and Peace Sts., is occupied by a lunchroom that utilizes a few floorboards and beams from the old hostelry in which the Provincial Congress met in 1776. Washington was host to his staff in the White Hart on July 4, 1778, after the Battle of Monmouth. Benjamin Franklin, and Samuel and John Adams, were also entertained here.

Meetings of the New Jersey Medical Society, the State's first medical organization, were held in the tavern. The organization was formed in 1766 at the call of the Rev. Dr. Robert McKean, preacher, teacher and physician. A group of foremost doctors agreed to conduct their practice on the highest ethical standards. The legislature empowered the society to examine all candidates for the degree of M.D. and to confer diplomas. One of the founders was Dr. John Cochran, a member of Washington's staff who was referred to by the General in his lighter moments as "Dear Doctor Bones."

15. SITE OF COCHRANE'S TAVERN, SW. corner Albany and Neilson Sts., is occupied by the Public Service building. In the former tavern

General Charles Lee was imprisoned during his trial for insubordination after the Battle of Monmouth in 1778 *(see Tour 18A)*. Colonel Simcoe, the British raider, was also held here. One owner of the tavern was Bernardus Le Grange, most notorious Loyalist of New Brunswick, whose effigy was burned by angry Revolutionists and whose property suffered heavily at the hands of the commissioners of forfeited estates.

16. CHRIST P.E. CHURCH, SW. corner Church and Neilson Sts., a simply designed building of white-trimmed brownstone, stands on the site of the original 18th century English Church. The first church, erected 1743, with the exception of the tower, was taken down and rebuilt into the present structure in 1852, all the stone being utilized.

17. FIRST REFORMED CHURCH, Neilson St. between Bayard and Paterson Sts., was completed 1812 as the successor to two earlier structures. Of gray stone with brownstone quoins, the church has a white, three-tiered clock tower. In the graveyard are buried many Revolutionary soldiers and members of old New Brunswick families, some of them beneath stones dated as early as 1746. Under the pastoral care of Theodorus Jacobus Frelinghuysen (1720–1748) the church was a powerful influence in New Jersey.

18. RUTGERS PREPARATORY SCHOOL, NW. corner College Ave. and Somerset St., was founded as Queens College Grammar School when the college was established. A separate institution, it is one of the 12 oldest schools in the Nation. The recitation rooms are in a compact three-story structure of brick, painted dull yellow with brown trim. Dormitories and the gymnasium are several blocks N. on George St. An early advertisement informed parents that if their children were sent here, "the strictest Regard will be paid to their moral Conduct, (and in a word) to every Thing which may tend to render them a Pleasure to their Friends, and an Ornament to their Species."

19. NEW BRUNSWICK THEOLOGICAL SEMINARY, 17 Seminary Pl., consists of three buildings forming an open square known locally as Holy Hill. HERTZOG HALL, the massive, cream-colored central building, is used for classrooms and a dormitory. A tablet on a boulder at the entrance marks the SITE OF A BRITISH REDOUBT (1776–77). At the edge of the hill above the river an American battery under Capt. Alexander Hamilton covered the crossing, while Washington and his troops rested in the city for a few days during the retreat of 1776. SUYDAM HALL *(open 2-5 weekdays)*, of dark red brick, has a Biblical collection of relief maps and coins of the early Christian era, and a number of miniatures and larger figures of gods and goddesses in ivory. SAGE LIBRARY *(open 8:30-5:30 Mon.-Fri.; 8:30-1 Sat.; 7:30-10 Mon.-Thurs. eves.; 8-10 Fri. eve.)* contains rare books on religion and art.

20. A heroic STATUE OF WILLIAM THE SILENT, Seminary Pl. opposite the Seminary, was presented to the university in 1927 by the Holland Society of New York. The statue, considered the best piece of sculpture in the city, is a duplicate made by Toon Dupuis of The Hague from the original plaster model of Lodewyk Royer, 19th century Dutch sculptor.

VOORHEES MEMORIAL CHAPEL, NEW JERSEY COLLEGE FOR WOMEN

21. JOHNSON & JOHNSON PLANT *(not open to public)*, 500 George St., consists of 51 red brick buildings along the river, adjoining the Rutgers campus. Founded in 1886, the company has become one of the world's largest makers of surgical and medical supplies, and the city's chief employer of labor.

22. BUCCLEUCH PARK, N. end College Ave., is a landscaped tract of 73 acres on high ground overlooking Raritan River, just E. of Landing Lane Bridge. At the base of the slope, across the canal, a footpath (once a towpath) parallels the abandoned Delaware and Raritan Canal. The WHITE HOUSE *(open 3-5 Sun. and holidays, May 30 to Labor Day)*, in the park, near the intersection of College Ave. and George St., is a large clapboard and brick house painted white, of fine Georgian Colonial design. The entrances, doorways and both interior and exterior trim are typical of the excellent craftsmanship of the later Colonial period. It was built in 1729 by Anthony White, whose wife was the daughter of Lewis Morris, Colonial Governor. During Howe's occupation of New Brunswick the house was in British hands. Valuable hand-painted panels in the lower hallway, depicting scenes in India and landmarks of Paris, are said to have been imported from France early in the 19th century. The house has a collection of Colonial furnishings and apparel.

23. BIRTHPLACE OF JOYCE KILMER *(open 10-10 daily)*, 17 Codwise Ave., is a simple frame house, now the headquarters of Joyce Kilmer Post of the American Legion. The house contains memorabilia of the poet, who is best known for *Trees (see Literature)*.

24. GUEST HOUSE *(open on application at Public Library, adjoining)*, 60 Livingston Ave., was erected 1760 on another site by Henry Guest, a whaler and tanner. A good example of Colonial architecture, the house has ashlar stone walls and is remarkably free of ornament. Rare laces and shawls are exhibited in the building. Guest's son, Moses, a militia captain, helped capture the notorious British raider, Col. John Graves Simcoe. The most distinguished occupant of the building was Tom Paine, pamphleteer of the Revolution, who hid here from the British during the war.

25. E. R. SQUIBB & SONS PLANT *(not open to public)*, Georges Rd., manufactures pharmaceutical supplies, serums, vaccines, antitoxins and proprietaries. The company was established in 1858 by Dr. Edward R. Squibb, United States Navy Surgeon and one of the first experimenters with anesthetics.

POINTS OF INTEREST IN ENVIRONS

Grave of Abraham Clark, *12.7 m.*, Edison Memorial Tower, *7.8 m. (see Tour 8)*; Rutgers University Stadium, *2.4 m. (see Tour 13)*.

Newark

Railroad Stations: Pennsylvania Station, Raymond Blvd. and McCarter Highway, for Pennsylvania R.R., Lehigh Valley R.R. and Hudson and Manhattan R.R.; Jersey Central Station, 836 Broad St., for Jersey Central R.R., Baltimore and Ohio R.R. and Reading Co.; Lackawanna Station, Broad St. at Lackawanna Pl., for Lackawanna R.R.; Erie Station, E. end 4th Ave., for Erie R.R.
Bus Stations: Public Service Terminal, 80 Park Pl., for Public Service, Greyhound, All-American, Golden Arrow, Jersey Central-Reading, Safeway, Martz, Pan-American, Champlain, and Edwards. Pennsylvania Railroad Station also for Public Service, Greyhound, Champlain, and Jersey Central-Reading; 1190 Raymond Blvd. for De Camp.
Airport: 1.8 m. S. on McCarter Highway; 1 m. E. on US 1 to Newark Airport for Eastern Airlines, American Airlines, United Airlines, and Transcontinental and Western Air.
Taxis: Yellow Cabs, 15¢ first ¼ m., 5¢ each additional ¼ m.; all other cabs, 50¢ flat within city limits.
Streetcars and Busses: 5¢ within city limits; no transfers.
Traffic Regulations: No turns on red lights; no turns at Broad and Markets Sts. Watch street signs for parking limitations, one-way streets, and prohibited turns.

Accommodations: Hotels and boarding houses; no seasonal rates.

Information Service: Newark *Evening News,* 215 Market St.; Newark *Sunday Call,* 71 Halsey St.; Chamber of Commerce, 20 Branford Pl.; Public Service Terminal, 80 Park Pl.; Public Library, 5 Washington St.

Theaters and Motion Picture Houses: Shubert Theater, vaudeville and occasional road shows; Mosque Theater, concerts and occasional opera; 55 motion picture houses.
Golf: Weequahic Park, 9 holes, greens fees 25¢ per person Mon.-Fri., 50¢ Sat., Sun. and holidays. Hendricks field golf course, 18 holes, 50¢ per person Mon.-Fri., $1 Sat., Sun. and holidays.
Tennis: Weequahic and Branch Brook Parks, 10¢ per hour.
Boating: Weequahic and Branch Brook Parks, 30¢ per hour.
Fishing: Weequahic and Branch Brook Parks.
Riding: Weequahic and Branch Brook Parks.
Baseball: Ruppert Stadium, 258 Wilson Ave., International League.

Annual Events: Metropolitan Opera (one night), January; Dog Show, second week in February; Indoor Polo Championship, fourth week in March; Horse Show, first week in May, and third week in December; Flower Show, second week in May; Trotting Races, every Saturday from May 30 to October 12, also July 4 and first week in September; Symphony Concerts (open-air), variable dates during June; Electrical Show, October; Automobile Show, third week in November; Stamp Exhibition, November. Bach B Minor Mass, May.

NEWARK (33 alt., 442,337 pop.) occupies the western bank of the Passaic River where it joins Newark Bay. Westward, the wooded skyline of the Watchung Mountains overlooks the city and its suburbs. Eastward the city faces the gaunt flatlands of the Hackensack, with Jersey City and New York often visible from its taller buildings.

Newark is the metropolis of New Jersey, and the focus of the vast complex of industrial and suburban cities that modern machinery and transport has made of the northeastern corner of the State. From the days of sail and stagecoach, most of the great transportation routes from the south and west have concentrated here. Successively steam, automotive, and air transportation have followed the same trend for the same natural causes. The grouping of giant modern industries in this area is a logical consequence; so that today this two-century-old city presents the picture of a huge industrial beehive built over the staid old seaport and local market center that was once Newark. Since 1890 the city's population has doubled, and the variety of national admixtures that are always a part of this sort of expansion in America has given Newark a genuinely cosmopolitan tone.

Downtown Newark lies close to the remnants of the old seaport town. Broad Street, its richest and most striking thoroughfare, roughly parallels the Passaic River in this region, and then continues southward through the wilderness of thronging, busy streets, as the river recedes to the east. Market Street, an important business artery, crosses Broad Street at right angles, going eastward to the river front, now given over to railroad yards and giant factories.

The center of it all is the corner of Broad and Market Streets, known for decades as "The Four Corners." This point has been called the third busiest traffic center in the United States. A traffic control tower stands approximately on the site of the community water pump used in Colonial times when Broad and Market was the village square.

Market Street is the older business thoroughfare. As the shopping center of the city it has kept pace with the growth of the Newark area. It is not so spacious as its rival, Broad Street, but its building line on either side presents a façade of retail shops with variegated window displays, broken by an occasional motion picture theater. The city's largest department store is on Market Street.

The straight, spacious reach of Broad Street from Lincoln Park to Military Park where it bends to parallel the Passaic River, ranks among the attractive commercial thoroughfares of the country. On this mile of exceptionally wide street, with its landscaped restful parks at each end, are the city hall, many churches, banks, and the city's skyscrapers, housing insurance companies, banks and administrative offices of the area's industries. Broad Street serves also as a promenade for the office worker and the shopper. Its sidewalks are thronged all day, and when the big insurance companies and banks and offices dismiss their employees even its spaciousness becomes crowded to a degree unsurpassed in other metropolitan areas.

Architecturally Newark's important business buildings are functional structures, mostly free of excessive ornamentation. Cream and buff are the prevailing colors; brick and limestone the more usual materials. Largely the product of the prosperous 1920's, the newer structures are a cheering contrast to the Bank Street mass of grim, granite buildings erected by banks and insurance companies in the 1890's.

The business district of Newark is pierced by a number of narrow alleys

—relics of village years—that are used as shortcuts by pedestrians, as delivery routes by truck drivers and as atmospheric location by restaurateurs. Many of them record, perhaps, the indecisive courses of the settlers' cattle as they strayed home from grazing on the village green; one follows a dog-leg course, and has a motion picture theater at the joint. On warm summer days the shaded asphalt of the alleys is a refuge for store and office workers during lunch hours.

The majority of Newark's business and professional people work in the office buildings of this area. Three downtown institutions, Bamberger's department store, the Prudential Insurance Company and the Public Service Corporation (the State's foremost public utility), alone have almost 22,000 employees. For the youth of the city, in particular, this trio almost makes Newark a "company city." Most young Newarkers have worked at one time for "Bam's," "the Pru" or "the P.S."

Workers and shoppers travel to and from the outer residential districts mainly by bus. Most of the busses are orange-yellow vehicles with the red-triangle insignia of Public Service. The main streets of the city are continually crowded with busses, since downtown Newark is the terminal not only for local transport but also for a multitude of suburban bus lines. On several lines trackless trolleys have replaced streetcars and gasoline-run busses.

This endless stream of bus, trolley and automobile traffic away from the Broad and Market intersection divides into approximately 10 branches, each headed for a more or less residential district. These loosely defined population areas have developed as Newark has slowly crept up and out from the banks of the Passaic River. Some are almost as old as the Four Corners; others date back only 30 years or less. Two or three are highly nationalized; most are as much a population mélange as the city itself. A few wear the marks of wealth and beauty; the rest exhibit in row upon row the standard or substandard American home.

The old Forest Hill and Woodside sections in the north of the city still have the best homes, occupied largely by the group of citizenry that has the strongest historical feeling for Newark. Here the large frame and brick houses, comfortably spaced and attractively landscaped, reflect the character of their occupants. Alongside Victorian houses, early and late, have risen many apartment houses that tend to modernize the section, and sectional feeling is disappearing.

To the west is the contrasting Silver Lake area, with comparatively modern bungalows and six- and eight-family houses built within the last quarter of a century to house that section of the Italian population which first became economically able to move from the downtown slum area.

An apartment house belt follows the outer fringe of the business section. It is most heavily developed in the south along Clinton Avenue and the adjoining streets. Newark has not the number of apartment houses that might be expected for a city of its size, but the proportion of fairly modern buildings is evidence of new construction since the early 1920's. Brick is the prevailing material; often excess ornamentation reveals the preferences of the builders. Many of the buildings, however, are sober

DOWNTOWN NEWARK AND PASSAIC RIVER

brick structures around an inner court; most are only six or eight stories high.

The Weequahic section, on the southwestern boundary of the city, developed when a zoning ordinance that had forbidden apartment construction lapsed in 1925. This district has some of the most attractive newer homes in the city.

Southeast of the Pennsylvania Railroad main line, and limited on two other sides by the Central Railroad of New Jersey and the Pennsylvania freight line, is the Ironbound district, a triangular section of lowland solidly built with workers' frame houses, and blackened by the city's most important industrial plants. Because the shape of the land resembles the neck of a bottle it is also called Down Neck.

Once a most desirable residential section, it is now a strange mixture of century-old Newark families and European immigrants. The street names of Rome, Paris, Amsterdam and London attest World War changes from old German names rather than the rich variety of nationalities. Berlin Street was left unscathed because its two unfinished blocks had not been recorded on the books of the municipal bureau of streets.

The Ironbound district is even more a separate part of the city than its steel-railed boundaries would indicate. Scores of small independent retail shops serve a population which seldom visits the other portions of Newark. A lower middle-income area rather than a slum, Down Neck was chosen as the site of the Chellis-Austin apartments, built in 1931 by the Prudential

Insurance Company as an experiment in medium-cost housing for residents of moderate income. Few Newarkers from other sections see the district frequently except from the Pulaski Skyway along its eastern edge; many know only by hearsay of its existence.

A general monotony in housing, characterized by browns and grays, shows in that part of the Hill section to the west of the Four Corners. The bulk of the city's Negro population is concentrated here between Avon Avenue and South Orange Avenue, extending east almost to Broad Street. Their homes constitute the city's gravest housing problem, for they are mostly dilapidated tenements in roughly paved streets. In this section the poorly paid workmen buy three slices of bread for a penny, six cigarettes for a nickel and two soft drinks for six cents.

The remainder of the Hill section consists of Clinton Hill, composed mainly of one-family homes with an occasional apartment house; and a large area of tenements, partly occupied by a German colony.

In the northwestern part of the city are the Roseville and Vailsburg sections, which present old Newark with a suburban facing. Perhaps more than any other district, Roseville has a community sense, emphasized by homelike frame dwellings, strips of lawn and quiet streets. In Vailsburg, lying near Maplewood and Irvington, the prevalent housing unit is the two-family structure, set close to the curb and fronted with an iron rail.

The mortar that binds these bricks of the Newark social and economic structure is the city's impressive industrial development. Originally the major factor in its manufacturing growth was the city's situation on the Passaic River, which forms the eastern boundary. Now all the modern facilities of rail, motor transport, and air traffic are concentrated around or near this water front. The narrow channel, deep enough for ocean-going vessels, is spanned by a dozen highway and railroad drawbridges leading to the vast markets and sources of raw materials beyond. The winding water front, covered with docks, factories, lumberyards, railroad sidings and a sprinkling of dingy dwellings, shows how completely industry has conquered the city. Aside from the Ironbound district, which houses the breweries and paint and varnish plants, there is no well-defined industrial area. Small and large factories alike have penetrated into the residential and commercial sections, giving the impression that industrialization is virtually complete.

It has been said that every kind of product sold in the United States is manufactured in Newark. That is pardonable exaggeration; yet it is true that the city supports an amazing variety of factories, with an output ranging from jewelry to dynamos, from dentifrices to beer, from electric light bulbs to leather goods. Among the largest plants are those of General Electric, Weston, Westinghouse, the L. E. Waterman Company, the Celluloid Corporation, the Hoffman Beverage Company, the Wiss Cutlery Company and the Hollander Fur Dyeing Company.

Insurance dominates the city financially. Newark ranks as the fourth largest insurance center in the Nation and the second largest life insurance city in the country. The 19 Newark companies employ more than 30,000 office workers. The Prudential Insurance Company of America, chartered in 1877, is the titan organization. Other important companies are the Mutual Benefit Life Insurance Company, the American Insurance Company, the Firemen's Insurance Company and the Globe Indemnity Company.

The city's racial and economic diversity has been synthesized by a uniformly excellent school system. Newark has pioneered in education since 1794 when a local shoe manufacturer, Moses Combs, initiated classes for his apprentices. The city was one of the first in the United States to establish summer schools (1885), the second to set up all-year schools (1912), and the third (1838) to erect a high school building—forerunner of the present Barringer High School.

Newark was one of the first large cities to test many modern educational techniques, previously demonstrated only in small communities. Especially valuable experiments have been conducted with the platoon system or work-study-play plan. Under this system all activities—classrooms, auditoriums, gymnasiums, shops, and laboratories are in use every hour of the day. The school is divided into two parts. While one of the schools is in classrooms, the other is in special activities, auditorium, playgrounds, and gymnasiums. This means that only 15 classrooms are needed for a 30-class school, it is possible to supply a school seat for every child when he needs it, and the special facilities are available at no greater cost than it takes to supply classrooms only under the traditional plan. Local educators were among the earliest exponents of visual education as an aid to classroom teaching, and important work has been done in vocational instruction and in the use of motion pictures for English, history and science courses. More recently Newark has set a brilliant example for large cities in providing special training for physically and mentally handicapped children. Despite this imposing record, Newark, like its huge neighbor across the Hudson, suffers from overcrowded schools.

In the field of higher education are included the University of Newark; the State Normal School; the New Jersey College of Pharmacy, a division of Rutgers University; the Newark College of Engineering, and the Newark Technical School.

Newark has come a long way from the Anglo-Saxon stock of its founders. Close to Ellis Island, the growing industrial community has absorbed a large percentage of immigrants. In 1938 the foreign-born and children of foreign-born numbered approximately 295,000, slightly more than three-fifths of the total population. The Irish and Germans, totaling respectively 23,400 and 36,900, have since 1850 established themselves as integral elements in the community. The Irish helped to build the city and then assumed political control, while Germans founded the brewing industry and introduced singing societies and sports programs.

Since 1880 Italians have been numerically the dominant European nationality group. Although most of the 85,300 have been absorbed into manufacturing and construction, many have been successful in business and politics. Two decades after the arrival of Italians, Poles came in large numbers to work in heavy industry and construction; the Polish population is 35,600.

Jews were the only group drawn to Newark primarily by its trade possibilities. After a gradual influx of German Jews, there was a sharp rise between 1880 and 1900 in Jewish immigration from Russia and Poland. Most of the city's 65,000 Jews are now engaged in business or the professions. More recent arrivals are the 38,800 Negroes. The Negro population was small until they came by thousands to work in World War industries. Although many of the race live in poverty, others have succeeded in rising to at least middle income living standards and have been conspicuous in the State for leadership in Negro welfare.

In the inescapable process of Americanization, the city's races and nationalities are slowly losing their individuality. A strong reciprocal influence between them and the older American population shows itself in many spheres. Since the World War the native-born increasingly have frequented the foreign quarters. In turn, the foreign districts have been steadily diminishing, as the residents have moved into less nationalized sections.

The Urban League and the Interracial Committee promote direct cooperation between the white and black races. The European groups have united with each other and with the American population through the activities of such civic bodies as the Ironbound Community House, the Silver Lake House, the Welfare League and educational and church organizations. These tendencies foreshadow the cosmopolitan community in which the taste and experience of the Old World blend with the energy and optimism of the New.

Newark was settled in 1666 by Capt. Robert Treat and 30 families from New Haven and the vicinity. The village on the Passaic was the result of five years' search for a site where these former Connecticut citizens could obtain self-government and religious freedom.

In his haste to develop the territory, Governor Philip Carteret had promised to eliminate the Indian title to the settlement. His neglect in this detail brought the colonists face to face with angry Hackensack Indians almost as soon as they had disembarked. Complete peace was established in 1667 when the settlers purchased a tract extending from the Passaic River westward to the Watchung Mountains.

The source of the name Newark remains buried with the original settlers. It has recently been disproved that the inspiration came from Newark-on-Trent, the supposed English home of the Reverend Abraham Pierson, pastor of the first church. Scholars have therefore returned to the older interpretation that the name was originally the Biblical New Ark or New Work, meaning a new project.

Whatever the origin of its name, Newark was unmistakably founded as a theocracy with the Puritan Congregational Church securely in control of village affairs. The church quickly erected a barrier around the religious freedom won by emigrating from New Haven. Church membership was a prerequisite to owning land, holding public office and voting. The church maintained such strict supervision over personal and public life that early Newark was more Puritan than much of New England itself.

The severity of ecclesiastical rule discouraged new settlers. Like many other religious communities, Newark grew slowly within a narrow arc prescribed by its Puritan leaders. They established a school in 1676, laid out military training grounds and encouraged gristmills, tanneries and small shops which made the little community self-sustaining.

The Puritan hegemony was first openly challenged in 1687. The Rev. Abraham Pierson Jr., who succeeded his father as the town pastor, clashed with the conservatives. Five years later they coldly permitted him to retire and return to Connecticut, where he became the first president of Yale College.

It took another generation, however, in which more liberal Englishmen settled in Newark, to break the religious monopoly of Old First Church. About 1733 Col. Josiah Ogden, a pillar of this organization, which had become Presbyterian in 1719, gathered in his wheat on the Sabbath rather than let it be ruined by the rain. He stoutly defended himself before the outraged membership and finally withdrew from the church. Ogden then joined with the local Church of England missionaries and founded Trinity Church.

Despite this rupture, Newark moved through the eighteenth century as a Puritan town, with a Puritan interest in education and commerce and a Puritan horror of secular art and pleasure. In 1748 the College of New Jersey, afterward Princeton University, moved from Elizabethtown to Newark with the Rev. Aaron Burr Sr., pastor of Old First Church, as president. The college remained until 1756, when it was transferred to Princeton. In the same period forges and foundries began to work the products of nearby iron mines. Before the time of the Revolution, Newark was of sufficient commercial importance to warrant the building of roads connecting with ferries to New York.

The war itself divided Newark into Tories who gave ample aid to Lord Cornwallis and other British commanders who encamped here, and Revolutionaries whose cooperation won the praise of Colonial generals. Washington used Newark as a supply base on his retreat across the State in 1776. In addition to a number of raids and skirmishes in the center of the village, two battles and a skirmish were fought at Springfield, part of which was then Newark.

The value of trade and manufacture was one of the lessons learned by the city from the Revolution. Factories increased. In about 1790 Moses Combs founded the shoe industry and a few years later one-third of Newark's working population was engaged in some form of the leather trade. The impetus came from an abundant stand of hemlock trees on the nearby Orange Mountains, which provided bark for tanning.

Hand-in-hand with prosperity went an escape from religious scrutiny, and the town supported three of the finest taverns in the country. Possibly attracted by a carefree society group, the exiled Frenchman, Talleyrand, visited Newark in 1794 and stayed at what was later the David Alling House on the corner of Broad and Fair Streets. The length of his stay is uncertain but it is likely that while in Newark he devoted much time to study and writing. In the next decade Tom Moore, the Irish poet, was entertained by the Ogden family, and Washington Irving was inspired to

write the *Salmagundi* papers by many gay evenings at old Cockloft Hall,
the Kemble Mansion, which stood on the corner of Mt. Pleasant Avenue
and Gouverneur Street.

Finance, commerce and industry quickened the conversion of Newark
from a sprawling agricultural village into an important business center.
The first bank, the Newark Banking and Insurance Company, was organized in 1804, and six years later the Newark Fire Insurance Company
wrote the first of millions of Newark policies. One of the Newark companies established in this period has preserved from its earliest days a yarn
to the effect that when an Elizabeth woman, who was insured for $500,
fell critically ill, the officers became alarmed lest the company expire with
her. Accordingly, the president had the best local doctor attend her and sat
at her bedside himself until she recovered.

After the War of 1812, new industries pushed Newark into the position of New Jersey's leading city, which it has held ever since. In two decades the manufacture of jewelry, begun by Epaphras Hinsdale in 1801,
had become a leading occupation; Seth Boyden's work in patent leather
gave tremendous impetus to the leather trade; and by 1831 hat making
and brewing occupied large numbers of workmen.

Transportation developments began to link the growing city with the
rest of the eastern seaboard. One of the State's earliest railroads—the New
Jersey Railroad and Transportation Company—began operation in 1834
from Newark to Jersey City, while the Morris Canal, completed to Phillipsburg three years earlier, provided an outlet for Newark's products in
Pennsylvania and the west.

In 1836 Newark was incorporated as a city with William Halsey as its
first mayor. The population of nearly 20,000 was no longer exclusively of
Puritan gentry; the growth of industry had resulted in the formation of
16 trade societies, chiefly among plasterers, bricklayers, and corset makers.
By 1836 they were bidding for political power as labor organizations.

For two decades following the panic of 1837 economic progress was
slow, but this period witnessed an increased interest in social reform and
entertainment. Criminals were better treated and the mentally ill were regarded less as offenders against decent society. In 1848 a theater inaugurated a long history of romantic and tragic drama in Newark. By 1855
Germans had settled Newark in large numbers, and their Saengerfests
made the city one of the national centers of German music.

The outbreak of the Civil War seriously threatened a large intersec-
tional trade which Newark had established with the South. As an offset,
however, to the manufacturers' fears, the war boomed industry; hat and
shoe factories operated at full capacity to fill army orders and a general
prosperity was enjoyed. A visit from Abraham Lincoln en route to his
first Washington inaugural helped to solidify community sentiment. Newark sent 10,000 to the Union armies.

Modern Newark dates from the close of the Civil War. An industrial
exposition in 1872 showed that the city was becoming more and more
diversified in its manufacturing interests, although brewing, jewelry, and
leather still maintained the lead. But while these industries were at their

AMERICAN INSURANCE COMPANY BUILDING, NEWARK

peak, the scientific age was beginning to transform completely the city's industrial character. In 1869 John Wesley Hyatt invented celluloid and laid the basis for the important plastic industry. Eighteen years later the Rev. Hannibal Goodwin developed a process which later turned celluloid into film for photographic negatives. Thomas A. Edison's invention of the electric light bulb in nearby Menlo Park was responsible for the rise of a new industry in Newark. Later Edward Weston carried on the Edison tradition with many important electrical inventions.

The post-Civil War period was marked also by the city's finest literary flowering. Stephen Crane (1871–1900), the novelist, was its greatest literary figure. His contemporary, Mary Mapes Dodge (1838–1905), created the children's classic, *Hans Brinker or the Silver Skates,* and Edmund Clarence Stedman (1833–1908), banker-poet-editor, conducted literary salons in and around Newark for a decade. Richard Watson Gilder (1844–1909), editor of the *Century,* worked for a time after the Civil War on the old Newark *Advertiser* and with Newton Crane founded the Newark *Morning Register.* Noah Brooks (1830–1903), well known at the end of the last century as a journalist and author of books for boys, was editor of the Newark *Daily Advertiser* in 1884.

By the turn of the century the newer, electrified industries were crowding out the old steam crafts and preparing Newark for its future leadership in heavy, mass industrial enterprise. Municipal government under Mayor Joseph Haynes aided the upswing with improved water facilities, new buildings and sincere efforts to harmonize the interests of industry and the city. Similarly, the once independent unions contributed toward stabilization by consolidation into the American Federation of Labor.

The World War heightened Newark's position as an industrial center and laid the foundation for its future as a port. While factories worked on 24-hour schedules, the Federal Government developed struggling Port Newark into an army base and prepared it for major shipping operations. The citizenry invested nearly $200,000,000 in Liberty Bonds and sent more than 20,000 men into the fighting service.

Post-war prosperity made Newark more than ever the hub of northern New Jersey. Apartment houses in the residential districts and skyscrapers on Broad Street gave the city a metropolitan appearance. Airplanes replaced the earlier mosquitoes in flights over the old Newark meadows, and in 1929 the airport was designated the eastern air mail terminal. In 1935 a city subway, built in the bed of the Morris Canal, and a new Pennsylvania Railroad station were opened to modernize the city's transport system. By 1938 all trolley cars had been eliminated on downtown surface lines.

In recent years the influence of New York City has strongly colored Newark's social and industrial life. With the development of modern transportation after the Civil War, New York City overflowed into New Jersey. A network of automobile highways followed the railroads across the Hackensack meadows, with the result that Newark began increasingly to share New York City's suburban population with the New Jersey cities along the Hudson, without losing its identity as the market center for the west.

This overflow from New York was a basic cause of the sudden expansion in the 90's, noted above. Factories began crowding out the older residential districts along the river and along the main line of the Pennsylvania railroad between New York and New Jersey. The residents began moving to the higher ground farther up the river and along the base of the Watchung Mountains; then the wealthier commuting class from New York saw the advantages of the Watchungs as a residential haven, and soon the old villages which surrounded the city became prosperous—some of them very expensive—communities that reflect suburban New York life more than they do the quieter tempo of interior New Jersey.

The completion of the Hudson and Manhattan Railroad in 1911 between Newark, Jersey City, and New York under the direction of William Gibbs McAdoo greatly accelerated the intermingling of the population and speeded the development of the city. The new rapid transit attracted thousands from Manhattan to Newark and its suburbs, and in turn made "going to New York" for business or pleasure a Newark habit. Today, uncounted thousands commute daily to Manhattan offices and shops on the jerky red trains of the Hudson & Manhattan Railroad—known to everyone as "the Tubes." The same trains bring a substantial number of New Yorkers to jobs in Newark. Additional thousands of men and women who work in the banking, insurance and industrial offices of Newark have homes and interests in outlying suburbs. Like the New Yorkers they are only daytime Newark residents.

The city's newsstands offer further evidence of Newark's split personality. The logotypes of New York dailies outnumber those of Newark papers by a ratio of almost 3 to 1, and a large display of suburban and foreign language papers rivals the local publications. The patriarchal Newark *Evening News* is the most influential paper of the city and State. The *Sunday Call,* published only once a week, is as much a part of most Newark homes as the radio. Nevertheless, thousands of Newarkers daily supplement local papers with New York publications.

The result of these pulls to New York on the east and to suburbs on the west, is that modern Newark is very little a city of common interests. Yet between these sizable commuting groups exists a larger and less well defined mass that may be called the population proper of Newark. These citizens range from descendants of those who sailed from Connecticut in 1666 to those who sailed from Genoa, Odessa or Danzig in 1896. Bankers and machinists, jurists and janitors, teachers and night school pupils—they compose the aggregate, dynamic Newark.

Within the lifetime of a middle-aged Newarker, the city has altered its Puritan rhythm and outlook to conform with those of the power age. Its population of 246,000 in 1900 was resigned to a single high school; seven cannot accommodate the present demand. Important department stores have replaced a row of sleepy "emporiums." The century-old evil of pollution in the Passaic River has been largely curtailed by construction of a sewer serving several municipalities. Responsibility for these changes rests not only with the national spirit of progress but also with shrewd and careful planning by Newark leaders.

Notable among these was the late Mayor Thomas L. Raymond, who was responsible for many outstanding improvements, including Newark's deep-water port, airport, water supply system, well-lighted and well-paved streets, and its railroad and other transportation improvements. He had the gift of being able to visualize civic needs two or three decades ahead, and he had the energy to act upon his ideals.

While Mayor Raymond was busy transforming the physical and industrial scene, John Cotton Dana, Newark Librarian for 27 years, was equally active in broadening Newark's cultural life. Mr. Dana's creative energy has made the library and museum dynamic forces in Newark citizenship. In 1931 the city's first liberal arts college was named Dana College in honor of "Newark's first citizen." The city has for the most part genuinely striven to build the economic and cultural life which these two men envisioned. In the mind of the forward-looking Newarker, the preeminence of Newark Airport symbolizes the transformation of Newark into a twentieth century city.

The most impressive picture of Newark's civic growth is the night view of Newark from the Pulaski Skyway. Against the background of the gently sloping Watchung Mountains stands a cluster of modern skyscrapers. Before these towers gleam the red and white signs of nationally known factories. In the foreground an occasional barge or boat appears on the winding Passaic River. To the north, myriad street lamps and house lights dot the vast darkness, and to the south, the beacons of Newark Airport stream toward the stars.

POINTS OF INTEREST

(Points of Interest 1-10 and 15-24 are shown on Newark Business District map. Points 11-14, 22, and 25-32 are shown on the more inclusive Newark map.)

1. The FIRST PRESBYTERIAN CHURCH, 820 Broad St., stands aristocratic and serene at the Broad and Market bus stop, the busiest in Newark. The fine old building is the corporate successor of the original church of the Puritan Congregationalist founders of Newark. In 1719 the membership became Presbyterian. The present building was begun in 1787 and dedicated four years later. Until the middle of the following century, when town, school and church were no longer an indissoluble trinity, it was the center of the Presbyterian control of town affairs.

Known affectionately to people of all faiths as "Old First," the church today draws its membership from among the oldest and wealthiest families in the city, serves as an unofficial mentor in ecclesiastical affairs, and has not hesitated from time to time to champion the love of liberty which its founders sought to preserve. Its financial security rests partially on its title to the valuable land opposite on Broad Street where the church buildings originally stood.

The building is an excellent example of Georgian Colonial architecture. The freestone was quarried on Bloomfield Avenue and the mortar was made from piles of clam shells left by the Indians along the banks of Newark Bay. The gambrel roof behind the slender tower is a typical New Jersey touch.

2. NATIONAL NEWARK BUILDING, 744 Broad St., opened in 1931, is the tallest building in the State (472 ft.; 35 stories). Its design, by John H. and Wilson C. Ely, is a successful application of classical forms to the requirements of the skyscraper. Ten murals on the mezzanine by J. Monroe Hewlett and Charles Gulbrandsen depict symbolically the growth of trade and commerce in Newark.

3. MILITARY PARK, Broad St., Park Pl., Rector St. and Raymond Blvd., was laid out by the founders of Newark as a military training ground and was known for more than two centuries as the Lower Common. Today it preserves something of its original use as a community gathering spot, for it has the air of New York's Union Square. It is the popular forum for political soap-boxers, religious enthusiasts, and outdoor orators of every species. The Park has a statue of Frederick T. Frelinghuysen, American statesman.

Trinity Episcopal Church, NW. end of the park, is the only New Jersey church in a public park. Its origin is traced to about 1733. Then, according to legend, Col. Josiah Ogden broke with the older First Presbyterian Church over his right to gather wheat on the Sabbath. The first building was erected in 1743, destroyed by fire in 1804, and restored five years later. Only part of the tower of the original Colonial building remains. The Gothic Revival windows in the present structure date from rebuilding in 1809; the Norman entrance doors and porch are still later additions, though probably made before 1830. There is still a popular but groundless belief that Trinity Church would forfeit its site to the city if the steeple were painted any color except white.

The chief memorial in the park is a large bronze group, The Wars of America, by Gutzon Borglum, in memory of the land and naval forces in all national wars. It includes 42 human figures on a granite base, surrounded by a low fence of overlapping bronze swords. The outstanding sculpture represents soldiers of the conflicts of 1776, 1861, and 1917.

At the S. end of the park is the 112-foot Liberty Pole which resembles an electrical tower; it is on the spot where the original pole was erected in 1793.

A Statue of Maj. Gen. Philip Kearny, commander of the New Jersey volunteers in the Civil War, stands in the NE. corner of the park.

In DOANE PARK, a triangular plot immediately N. of Military Park, is a Bronze Statue of Msgr. George Hobart Doane, Civil War chaplain, rector of St. Patrick's Cathedral, and an outstanding citizen of the last century.

4. The UNIVERSITY OF NEWARK, 40 Rector St., is the result of a merger, effected in 1935, of five of Newark's older institutions of higher education—Dana College, Mercer Beasley Law School, Newark Institute of Art and Sciences, New Jersey Law School, and Seth Boyden School of Business. Under the new administration with Dr. Frank Kingdon as president, the university consists of the College of Arts and Sciences, the

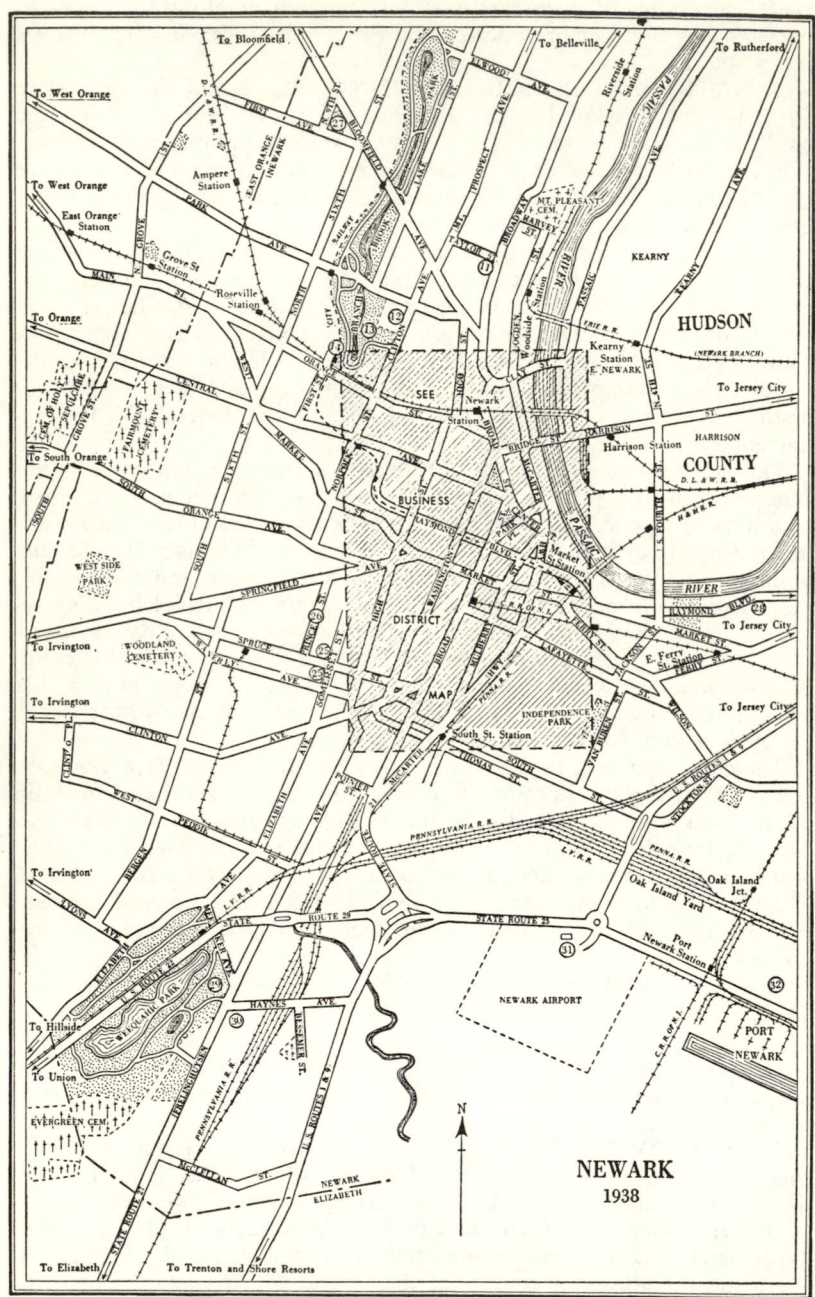

NEWARK
1938

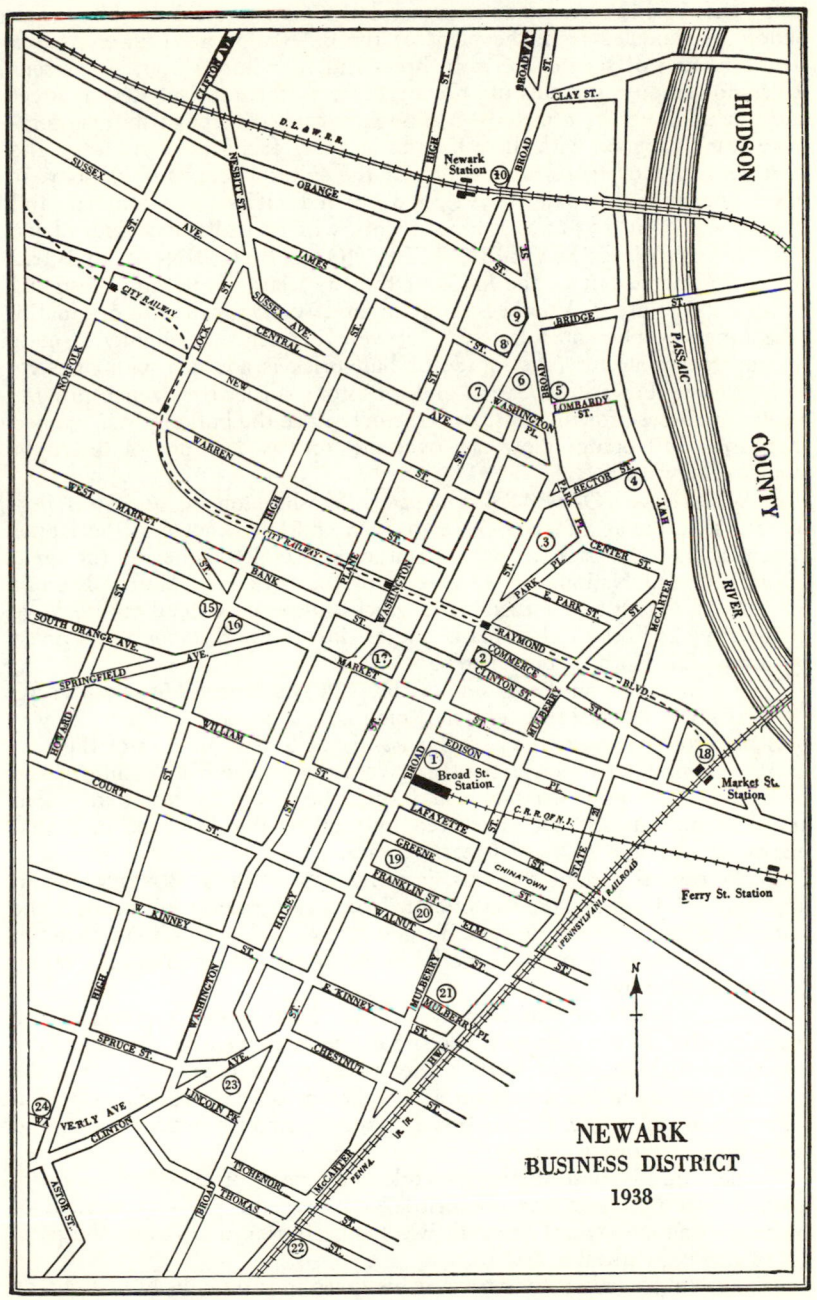

NEWARK
BUSINESS DISTRICT
1938

School of Business Administration, and the College of Law. The brick building remodeled from the plant of the old Ballantine Brewery, has a central section of six stories, with three- and four-story wings. At present it has no campus; students often congregate in the adjacent Rector Street and around a nearby cemetery. Although it carried through its first complete year's program with these limited building facilities in 1936–37, the institution already ranks high as one of the cultural centers of the city. It has a library of approximately 13,000 volumes. It is co-educational, and the registration in 1938 was 1,800 students, with a faculty of 125 members.

5. The NEW JERSEY BELL TELEPHONE BUILDING, 540 Broad St., is considered one of the finest of the city's large buildings. Designed in what its architects, Voorhees, Gmelin, and Walker, call with originality "the American perpendicular style," it well represents the dignity of mass in modern architecture. Its façade of buff brick is adorned with pilasters sculptured by Edward McCartan and sandstone corner bays which provide a substantial base for the 20-story structure. Since the building was opened in 1929, a soft orange glow cast over the top has been one of the night sights of Newark.

6. WASHINGTON PARK, Broad St., Washington Pl., and Washington St., set aside as a market place in 1667 and later known as the Upper Green, is now the background for statues and tablets honoring the great of the city and Nation. At the S. end of the park is J. Massey Rhind's STATUE OF GEORGE WASHINGTON, which shows the general taking leave of his army at Rocky Hill. This is one of three Newark monuments given by Amos Van Horn, a local merchant.

Facing Broad St. on the E. side of the park is a bronze MONUMENT TO CHRISTOPHER COLUMBUS, cast in Rome by Giuseppe Ciocchetti. It was presented to Newark in 1927 by the associated Italian societies of the city.

At a traffic intersection a few feet from the northern extremity of the park is the BRIDGE MEMORIAL, a shaft with the carved figures of an Indian and a Puritan at its base. Executed by Gutzon Borglum, the memorial marks the site of the Colonial market place.

In the central part of the park is a STATUE OF SETH BOYDEN, whom Thomas A. Edison regarded as one of "America's greatest inventors." The statue by Karl Gerhardt portrays Boyden at his anvil, shirt sleeves rolled to the elbow, a steam locomotive model in one hand and a book in the other. It was unveiled in 1890.

Boyden was attracted to Newark in 1815 by the city's reputation as a leather center. In his shop near the site of the monument he developed the process of making patent leather. Not being a promoter, he ignored the fortune that lay in his invention and went on to successful experimentation with zinc refining, the air brake, steam locomotive improvement, and the Hilton strawberry.

Boyden did his most important work in ten years of experimentation to produce cast iron that was not brittle and could be properly worked or hammered on an anvil. The result was his perfection in 1826 of the process of making malleable cast iron.

His uncommercial attitude toward his inventions brought him slight returns, and in later years he worked at a Hilton factory for $1.50 per day. He died in poverty at the age of 81.

7. NEWARK MUSEUM *(open 12-5 Tues.-Sat.; 7-9 Thurs.; 2-6 Sun.; summer schedule, 12-5 Tues.-Sat.)*, 49 Washington St., was founded in 1909 by John Cotton Dana to encourage the study of the arts and sciences and as a means of making graphic to Newarkers the history and value of their home industries. Originally situated on the fourth floor of the library building, the institution is now housed in a $750,000 limestone structure of severe classic design which Louis Bamberger, a local merchant, presented to the city in 1926. The handsome three-story building directly adjoins the Y.W.C.A. building which makes impossible a full appreciation of the museum. The architect was Jarvis Hunt.

Adjacent to the main museum building on the north and connected with it by an enclosed passageway is THE MUSEUM ADDITION BUILDING, opened in May 1938. This modern four-story brick structure houses the Junior Museum and lending department of the museum. Two-and-one-half floors are occupied by departments of the nearby Newark Public Library.

Directly in front of this building on Washington St. is the BALLANTINE HOUSE, built in 1878 by a prominent Newark brewing family. It is used for the museum's administrative offices and trustees' rooms.

John Cotton Dana was a pioneer in applying the theory of a "functional museum," an institution of immediate practical use to the citizens of its community. Frequently changing displays in the fields of fine and decorative arts, industrial design and processes, history and education, characterize its exhibition policy. Activities for adults include an arts workshop, a nature club, and a natural science program.

The museum is widely known for its work with children and for its place in the city's educational system. More than 5,000 children who have paid 10¢ for life membership in the Junior Museum, meet regularly in groups to draw, model, sew, and to study nature and Indian lore. Class visits to the museum's exhibits are a regular feature of the city school curriculum, and the lending collection of more than 10,000 objects is drawn heavily upon by teachers.

As early as 1914, Dana advocated the acquisition of the work of living American artists, and since that time, the museum has built up a noteworthy collection of American paintings and sculpture. It has also been conspicuous in encouraging New Jersey artists by exhibits and purchases of their work. Among other important possessions of the museum are the Crane collection of Tibetan art and religious objects, the Rockwell collection of Japanese prints, painting and sculpture and the Disbrow science collection.

The THOMAS L. RAYMOND WALLED GARDEN, behind the building, contains typical New Jersey flora, semitropical plants and trees, and a vegetable patch tended by the Junior Museum. A section is overlaid with historic street pavings of Newark, including cobblestone, flagstone, and Belgian block.

In the rear of the garden stands the OLD STONE SCHOOLHOUSE, Newark's oldest school building. This one-story brownstone structure with a miniature belfry was built in 1784 on Chancellor Ave., where it stood until 1938 when the Works Progress Administration moved it stone by stone to its present site. The building was visited by Washington in 1797.

8. The SECOND PRESBYTERIAN CHURCH, Washington and James Sts., is a fine example of modernized Gothic design composed of suitable plane surfaces relieved by carefully detailed, low-relief ornamental buttresses and stone traceried windows. In the auditorium are 26 stained-glass windows of various sizes that depict outstanding local citizens, spiritual leaders, and incidents in the life of Christ. The present building replaces one destroyed by fire in 1930. It is on the site of Newark's first foundry, erected in 1768.

9. NEWARK PUBLIC LIBRARY *(open 9 a.m.-9:30 p.m. Mon.-Fri.; 9-1 Sat.)*, 5 Washington St., is the dean and fountainhead of Newark's cultural institutions. Founded in 1888, it pioneered in civic responsibility and wove itself into the cultural and economic fabric of the city under John Cotton Dana, librarian from 1902 to 1929. He carried the library to the people, publicized it, and demonstrated its usefulness in developing citizenship. Mr. Dana made the library itself a force in civic improvement, whether the issue was as large as governmental reform or as small as efficient garbage collection. His desire to link the library with every phase of public life resulted in the establishment in 1904 of the business branch, the first of its kind, now a city-owned building, at 34 Commerce St.

The Main Library's four-story Renaissance building, faced with limestone, dates from 1901. The main building and the 8 branches contain more than 577,000 books, a collection of 723,335 photographs and prints, and 24,496 maps. There is also an information file of 139,500 clippings and pamphlets. Through its school department the library augments the work of every teacher in the city school system. It is one of the few large libraries in the country that admit the public to the stacks.

10. The JOHN PLUME HOUSE *(private)*, 407 Broad St., was probably standing in 1710 and is said to be the oldest dwelling in Newark. It is now the rectory of the adjoining House of Prayer, Protestant Episcopal Church built in 1849. Although both its exterior and interior show nineteenth century alterations, the two-story red sandstone house is the city's only pre-Revolutionary building. Genuinely in the Colonial tradition, its gambrel roof perhaps shows Dutch influence and the bracketed cornice is of special architectural interest.

During the Revolution the redoubtable Mistress Ann Van Wagenen Plume drove Hessian soldiers from the parlor where she found them chopping wood; later she locked a stray Hessian in her ice house. The knocker formerly on the door of the rectory is reputed to have been made from a piece of steel on the Hessian's hat, presented to Mistress Plume by the American soldiers as a reward for the capture.

More than a century later the Rev. Hannibal Goodwin developed in the rectory a flexible photographic film which made possible the motion picture. Handicapped by the continual breaking of the glass stereopticon plates that he used to illustrate Bible lectures, he sought a substitute.

In 1887 he applied for a patent on photographic films that could be wound on a spool and used in a camera. During the 11-year delay in granting the patent, a chemist in the employ of the Eastman Kodak Company applied for a similar patent and the company began to make a camera which embodied Goodwin's idea. Two years after receiving his patent Goodwin died, and only after years of litigation was his widow able to win a judgment (1914), shortly before her death.

11. NEW JERSEY HISTORICAL SOCIETY BUILDING *(open 10-4:30 Tues.-Sat.)*, 230 Broadway, is a handsome modernized Georgian-Colonial structure, modeled after the Old Philadelphia Hospital. Founded in 1845, the society became established in 1931 in its present home. In addition to various personal memorabilia, the society has a collection of valuable early manuscripts *(available on special request)*. These include the original copy of the Concessions of the Proprietors of the Colony, and various grants, patents, Indian deeds, and other documents of the seventeenth century. Among the paintings are Gilbert Stuart portraits of Capt. James Lawrence and Aaron Burr, and others of Gen. Peter Schuyler and Richard Stockton, Signer of the Declaration of Independence.

12. SACRED HEART CATHEDRAL, Clifton and 6th Aves., was begun in 1898 according to the plans of Jeremiah O'Rourke but the interior is still unfinished (1939). The final cost is estimated at $4,500,000. It was originally thought that a wealthy Catholic congregation would develop in the surrounding neighborhood, but the opposite has proved true. The cathedral is now used only for important church activities, such as the investiture of a bishop. Of medieval French Gothic design, the two towers, 232 feet high, are set obliquely to give an effect of depth. I. E. Ditmars was the second architect.

13. BRANCH BROOK PARK, W. of Clifton Ave. between Orange St. and city line (Belleville), is the largest of the Essex County parks. Almost 500 acres in area, it has extensive facilities for many sports including football, baseball and golf; there are also clay and grass tennis courts, two lakes for boating, fishing, and skating, facilities for open-air concerts, and a playground with equipment especially designed for crippled children. Japanese cherry trees have been planted by Mrs. Felix Fuld in the eastern end of the park.

14. NEWARK ACADEMY, 215 1st St., is the city's leading private school, and its oldest. Among its alumni today are many of the substantial leaders of industrial and civic life in Newark, and throughout the 19th century it was the focal point of education for the higher-income class of citizens, preparing students for the leading colleges of the United States and England, or fitting them for participation in local life according to the traditional standards of the city. The academy was founded in 1774. At various times during the Revolution it was a barracks for American troops, with the consequence that British raiders burned its one building in 1780, by way of retaliation. The school had a hard struggle for existence for some years afterward and in 1785 money for the school was raised by several lotteries including one of a slave who had been given to the academy. From 1802 to 1859 the academy was co-educational, but since the latter

date has received boys only. The three-story modernized Georgian Colonial style building with a two-story wing, erected in 1930, houses a preparatory school with accommodations for more than 300 boys. The academy has 250 students, with a staff of 25 masters.

15. ESSEX COUNTY HALL OF RECORDS, High St. and 13th Ave., a conventional neo-classic building, erected in 1927, Guilbert and Betelle, architects, strikes a brighter note in a section of small stores and brick and frame houses. About the entrance is a group of carved stone figures depicting the purchase of the site of Newark and its environs from the Lenni Lenape Indians.

16. ESSEX COUNTY COURTHOUSE, Springfield Ave. and Market St., is a modified Renaissance building with a granite base and marble structure. Built in 1906 the beautifully proportioned structure is the work of Cass Gilbert. More noteworthy than the seven murals in the main rooms and under the central dome is the historical painting by Frank D. Millet in the former grand jury room. It portrays the rebuke given in 1774 to the last Provincial Chief Justice of New Jersey by the foreman of the grand jury in reply to the jurist's charge that the grievances of the Colonists against Great Britain were imaginary. The *Landing of Philip Carteret,* the most celebrated painting of the illustrator, Howard Pyle, hangs in one of the civil court rooms.

In the plaza of the courthouse is the famous seated bronze STATUE OF ABRAHAM LINCOLN by Gutzon Borglum. In its grasp of the Lincoln spirit the statue is considered second only to that by Daniel Chester French in Washington. Since its unveiling in 1911, an integral part of a Newark child's experience has been to clamber up the legs, sit in the bronze lap or perch on the stovepipe hat alongside.

17. BAMBERGER'S DEPARTMENT STORE, 131 Market St., now owned by R. H. Macy and Company of New York, is the largest in New Jersey and ranks fourth in sales among the Nation's department stores. It is the home of the Bamberger Broadcasting Service, station WOR, a unit of the Mutual Broadcasting System. Beginning with the personal charity and civic contributions of Louis Bamberger and the late Felix Fuld, the store has shown unusual ability to combine cultural and business interests. It has sponsored symphony orchestras and opera performances, art and historical exhibits, symposia on public questions and educational activities. In February 1938 the store staged a "panorama," entitled "New Jersey, One of America's Great States," outlining the history and potentialities of New Jersey.

18. The PENNSYLVANIA R.R. STATION, Raymond Plaza West, Raymond Blvd. and Market St., is an imposing tribute to Newark's history as a transportation center. Jointly constructed by the railroad and the city and opened in 1935, it is used as a terminal for railroad trains, trolleys, busses, and tube trains.

The main building, of neo-classic design, has two massive arched entrances in a façade of limestone piers and glass. The architects, McKim, Mead, and White, have designed and executed the building on an appropriately monumental scale. Platforms to the north and south of the build-

PENNSYLVANIA RAILROAD LIFT BRIDGE, NEWARK

ing are sheathed with monotone brick walls, pierced by a design of modern fenestration and glass brick. Passengers reach the platforms by escalators and stairways.

The waiting room is spacious and high-ceilinged. Decorative plaques represent the advance of transportation from the canoe and horse to the railroad and airplane. A blue ceiling, walnut benches, and four large hanging globes of white bronze and flashed opal glass combine to make the atmosphere of the room unusually cheerful. Citizens expect that the increasing use of this terminal will show the necessity for improvement of its unimpressive surroundings.

Directly east of the Pennsylvania station is a LIFT BRIDGE spanning Passaic River over which run the railroad's tracks. Said to be an outstanding example of this type of bridge construction, it can be raised 111 feet in 85 seconds to give 135 feet of clearance above mean high water. The bridge measures 528 feet including approaches, and there are about 5,000 tons of steel in the superstructure.

CHINATOWN, Mulberry St. between Lafayette and Franklin Sts., was, until the post-War deportation of thousands of Chinese, one of the most exotic and dangerous places in Newark. Broken windows and rusted iron today in the once brightly illuminated Arcade, L. off Mulberry St., suggest little of the bazaars, jade shops, and tea houses that once attracted thousands of visitors. The present chop-suey restaurants occupy sites where gourmets once feasted on Chinese delicacies and where tong warfare and unrestrained gambling reached the point of a public menace. At one time Newark's Chinese population exceeded that of New York, and the section supported a self-styled "Mayor" whose "edicts" city politicians heeded. The number and importance of the Chinese is now insignificant.

19. CITY HALL, Broad St. between Greene and Franklin Sts., of late French Renaissance design, was erected in 1906. The four-story limestone structure, with its huge heavily ornamented dome, houses the city's administrative offices. The architects, Mowbray, Uffinger and Ely, have been criticized for sacrificing function and requirements to obtain an enormous interior. Cited examples of this are the immense rotunda with wide balconies, and the inadequate stairways. Decorations in rococo style harmonize with the monumental interior.

20. FEDERAL BUILDING, facing Federal Square between Franklin and Walnut Sts., is a ponderous neo-classical structure of conservative design; Lehman and Totten were the architects. Opened in 1936, it houses on the first floor the main post office and on the upper floors the United States District Court and the offices of various Federal agencies. Critics of the building hold that the interior hardly fulfills the promise of the dignified exterior. The walls are finished with salmon marble, and the ceiling is sky-blue over the entries.

21. The STEPHEN CRANE HOUSE, 14 Mulberry Pl., is an uninhabited, neglected building in squalid surroundings suggestive of the atmosphere of much of the author's writing. The Stephen Crane Association made every effort to preserve it as a museum, but without success. Crane was born November 1, 1871, in the staid, red brick house in what was

then a fashionable section of the city. Last of 14 children of a Methodist minister, he lived a life which clashed violently with his ecclesiastical New Jersey background. When he was about three, the family moved to Bloomington, then to Paterson, and then to Port Jervis, N. Y. At 16 he began gathering news for his brother's news bureau in Asbury Park. He left Syracuse University before completing his course and sought newspaper employment in New York.

At this period he wrote *Maggie: A Girl of the Streets,* a harshly realistic novel which publishers refused to handle. He published it himself, with no financial success. While discouraged at the penury of the literary trade, he wrote his masterpiece, *The Red Badge of Courage,* a Civil War story.

Following this success, he set out to learn of war at first hand by reporting the Greco-Turkish and Spanish-American wars. At the end of the latter he went to England, where he continued a friendship with Joseph Conrad. Long a victim of tuberculosis, Crane succumbed in Germany in 1900, leaving his friends to speculate on the greatness he might have achieved had he lived more than 30 years. He is buried in the family plot at Hillside, N. J.

22. The L. E. WATERMAN PLANT *(open by appointment),* 140 Thomas St., was opened in Newark in 1921. The four-story building is of red brick with cream trim. Within, 500 workers are employed chiefly in the manufacture of ink, pen points and metal accessories. Barrels are made elsewhere and shipped here for assembly. The most interesting sight in the plant is the assembling of a fountain pen. In the MUSEUM on the second floor an exhibit shows the development of the fountain pen. On display are a gold-mounted pen that belonged to President William McKinley, the pen used to sign the peace treaty of the Sino-Japanese War of 1894–95, and a desk set taken to Little America in 1929 by Admiral Richard E. Byrd.

23. LINCOLN PARK, Broad St., and CLINTON PARK, Washington St. and Clinton Ave., mark the end of the main downtown business area. In Clinton Park is J. Massey Rhind's excellent bronze reproduction of the Verrochio STATUE OF BARTOLOMEO COLEONO, fifteenth-century Venetian soldier. One of the few equestrian statues in the city, it was the gift of Christian Feigenspan, Newark brewer. Because of the reported decay of the original in Venice, this copy is considered of great value.

In Lincoln Park, opposite, neither statue nor tablet commemorates Lincoln. The MEMORIAL FLAG POLE was sculptured by Charles Niehaus and celebrates the World War victory.

24. TEMPLE B'NAI JESHURUN, 783 High St., houses the State's oldest Reformed Jewish congregation, organized in 1848. The present temple and school were dedicated in December 1915. Standing on a hill, the temple is of modified Moorish design, reminiscent of a mosque without minarets.

25. The DOUGLASS AND HARRISON APARTMENTS, 1-117 Somerset St., were designed as a slum clearance project exclusively for Negroes. Owned by the Prudential Insurance Co., and originally characterized as low-cost housing within the reach of the average Negro working family,

the project is in reality medium-cost housing with rentals ranging from $8.50 to $10 a room, close to the level of average apartment rents in Newark. The 12 brick buildings, 5 and 6 stories high, occupy 2 solid city blocks; there are 754 units of 2 to 5 rooms each.

The project was developed with the close cooperation of city authorities. After purchasing the land for $2,350,000, the insurance company resold about three-fifths of it to the city for $1,200,000 for development by the city for park purposes. Construction costs (approximately $1,800,000) were reduced through the help of the city and the Civil Works Administration in grading the entire site; the strip of land between the buildings is now maintained as a city park. The apartments, built in 1933 and 1935, were named for Frederick Douglass, former slave and distinguished abolitionist leader, and Richard B. Harrison, "De Lawd" of the Negro play, *The Green Pastures*.

26. PRINCE ST., between Spruce St. and Springfield Ave., resounds with Jewish accents from pushcart peddlers at the curb and vigorous bargaining in kosher food stores and retail dry goods shops. Despite the many synagogues along the six blocks, most of the Jewish merchants live elsewhere. The chief inhabitants of the flats above the stores are Baptist and Methodist Negroes. When the pushcarts are closed down for the day, the section changes from a little Ghetto to a little Harlem.

27. CITY SCHOOLS STADIUM, Bloomfield and Roseville Aves, is a municipally owned, open-air amphitheater, seating more than 14,000, used primarily for school athletics and educational programs. Band and orchestra concerts, pageants, operas and dramatic spectacles have been produced on the large shell stage.

28. In the FEIGENSPAN BREWERY *(open by appointment)*, 50 Freeman St., originated a genuine Newark commercial slogan, "P.O.N." Despite latter-day efforts to change its meaning to everything from "Pride of the Nation" to "PON My Honor," the founder, Christian Feigenspan, intended it to stand for "Pride of Newark." "P.O.N." achieved national repute during Prohibition when, for seven years, while the plant itself was closed, the illumined letters blazed from the building across the Newark meadows, indicating that hope burned eternal in the brewer's breast.

The brewery, founded in 1875, consists of two square blocks of 20 red brick buildings which give the impression of a single building. In addition to the brewing process, the plant affords a view of canning and bottling by gas compression. It employs 750 persons.

29. WEEQUAHIC (Ind., *head of creek*) PARK, between Meeker Ave. and city line (Hillside and Elizabeth), covers more than 300 acres and includes a 9-hole golf course, 12 clay tennis courts, bridle path, several large recreation fields for football, baseball and soccer, and an 85-acre, spring-fed lake stocked with game fish. Rowboats may be rented at the boathouse at the northern end of the lake.

The park has the oldest trotting track in the State, where every Saturday afternoon from May to October the Road Horse Association of New Jersey holds races *(free)*. A grandstand seating 5,000 adjoins the race

NEWARK AIRPORT

track. The southwestern side of the park is especially well landscaped and contains a beautiful rose garden.

On DIVIDENT HILL, the highest point in the park, is a tablet marking the scene of a meeting of 1668 at which the founders of Newark and Elizabethtown reached a boundary agreement.

30. The WESTON ELECTRICAL INSTRUMENT PLANT *(group tours by appointment)*, 614 Frelinghuysen Ave., was founded in 1888 by the Newark inventor and scientist, the late Dr. Edward Weston. As the manufacturer of electrical, radio and aircraft instruments, Weston typifies the power age in Newark industry.

In the half-dozen low, red brick buildings 1,200 workers make and exhibit a variety of products that quickly demonstrate the dominance of electricity in modern life. Outstanding perhaps is the "Photronic" photo-electric cell, developed by Doctor Weston in 1931. This cell can be made to actuate any of a number of devices by its response to varying light conditions. It was used at the Century of Progress Exposition in Chicago in 1933 to pick up rays from the star Arcturus to turn on the electric light which officially opened the exposition.

Among Doctor Weston's other inventions are the first reliable instrument for measuring direct current, and several devices for blind flying and landing in aviation.

31. NEWARK AIRPORT *(open day and night)*, on US 1, 3 m. SE. from Broad and Market Sts., brings more advertising to the city in a week than all the "Made in Newark" insignia achieve in a year. Busiest commercial airport in the world, it registers 125 scheduled take-offs and landings daily, and about 100 others. Passengers in 1937 totaled 270,000; so many of these were celebrities that two Newark newspapers run special airport columns. It is estimated that more than 30 percent of all air traffic (passenger, mail and express) throughout the United States is cleared through Newark airport, which serves as the terminal for New York City.

The flat fields and parking lots with their unkempt hangars are gradually being improved in better keeping with the precise operations which chart and guide the planes. Municipally owned, the field covers about 600 acres; its chief structures are the municipal administration building, built with CWA funds in 1935, and the waiting rooms of the four commercial air lines.

Although the port at present does not compare with Croydon in London or LeBourget in Paris in design and layout, it will be vastly benefited by the new hangar under construction (1939) by the Works Progress Administration. The four major lines will be housed in one mammoth hangar, 1,110 feet long and 150 feet wide, costing $3,900,000.

Opened in 1928 at a cost to date of $10,000,000, the airport was designated the following year as the eastern airmail terminal. It quickly became the eastern passenger travel center. Night landings and take-offs, requiring a galaxy of lights and precision of action, provide a striking spectacle. The heaviest traffic, however, is between 4:30 and 6:30 p.m.

32. PORT NEWARK, on Newark Bay adjoining the airport, has been transformed in 30 years from a desolate marsh to a seaport terminal representing a public and private investment of more than $90,000,000. It covers 2,200 acres, has 12,000 feet of marginal docks, including space for 20 freight steamers, and large warehouses.

POINTS OF INTEREST IN ENVIRONS

General Motors Plant, *8.9 m. (see Tour 1)*; Sip Manor House (1664), *13 m. (see Tour 2)*; Davis House (1676), *3.2 m.*, Eagle Rock Reservation, *7.2 m. (see Tour 9)*; Lionel Plant, *3.1 m. (see Tour 16)*.

The Oranges and Maplewood

Railroad Stations: East Orange—Lackawanna Stations, N. Grove St., N. Arlington Ave., Brick Church Plaza and Ampere Plaza, for Lackawanna R.R.; Erie Stations, Prospect St. and Brighton Ave., for Erie R.R.; *Orange*—Lackawanna Stations, Lackawanna Plaza and Highland Ave., for Lackawanna R.R.; Erie Station, Washington St., for Erie R.R.; *South Orange*—Lackawanna Stations, Sloane St. and Montrose Ave., for Lackawanna R.R.; *West Orange*—Erie Stations, Main St., Tory Cor., and Llewellyn Ave., for Erie R.R.; *Maplewood*—Lackawanna Station, Oakview Ave., for Lackawanna R.R.

Bus Station: Orange—Main and N. Essex Sts. for De Camp Lines.

Taxis: Rates vary from 35¢ to 50¢ per ride.

Traffic Regulations: Turns at intersections controlled by traffic lights. Watch signs and curb markings for parking restrictions.

Accommodations: Five hotels in East Orange, several smaller hotels and tourists' homes in East Orange, Orange and West Orange.

Information Service: East Orange—Chamber of Commerce and Civics, 19 S. Harrison St.; City Hall, Main St.

Motion Picture Houses: East Orange 4, Orange 4, South Orange 1, West Orange 2, Maplewood 1.

Golf: West Orange Public Golf Course, Prospect Ave. bet. Eagle Rock and Mt. Pleasant Aves., 18 holes, greens fees 50¢; Sat., Sun., holidays $1.50.

Annual Events: Orange—Founders' Day, February 9. *West Orange*—Horse Show, October. *East Orange*—Art Exhibition, spring and fall. *South Orange*—Dog Show, May; Orange Lawn Tennis Club Tournament, May; Horse Show, October.

MAPLEWOOD and the four ORANGES (Orange, East Orange, West Orange, and South Orange) are not governmentally a unified city, but all together they constitute a homogeneous community. Rising gradually from the lowlands around Newark upward along the slopes of the Watchungs to the west, the five municipalities pride themselves upon a mountain-plain relationship with the nearby metropolis. The large percentage of well-to-do residents among the 162,000 population gives this relationship a sociological as well as a geographical reality.

These municipalities do not resent their title of "typical American suburbs." It is grounded in civic independence, a high proportion of one- and two-family homes, and a paucity of grimy manufacturing plants. Residents, however, refine this distinction yet another stage by referring officially to the Oranges and Maplewood as "New York's most beautiful suburbs."

The justice of these two designations helps to define the Oranges and Maplewood. The typical achievements are the efforts largely of the older citizens, Jerseymen for several generations. This stock has combined with that of the 15,000 commuters of more recent origin to create a cultural atmosphere that has produced the Art Center of the Oranges, the South Orange-Maplewood Adult Education Center, homes which are show-places of the State, exceptional transportation facilities, and branches of smart Fifth Avenue shops.

Men of wealth and position from New York and Newark, among them many educational and religious leaders, have built handsome estates on the hills and in the valleys alongside those of financial and commercial tycoons. While the 442,337 people of Newark are represented in *Who's Who in America* by 77 names, 130 are listed from the 162,000 population of the Oranges and Maplewood.

Indicative also of the personality of the composite community is its politics. The Republican-Democratic division follows almost precisely the economic cleavage. Thus, wealthy and conservative South Orange annually returns a 5-2 Republican victory, while the large working-class population of Orange votes Democratic, 8-5. An almost even split usually results in West Orange, where fashionable Llewellyn Park elbows the Edison plant. Maplewood's slightly larger upper middle-class group explains its 2-1 Republicanism over East Orange's 5-3.

These non-Republican islands are in many senses the obstacle to complete homogeneity. In full view of the mountain castles lie rows of squalid homes in Orange and West Orange, and close by the superb East Orange apartment houses are Negro and poor-white tenements. The community has done handsomely in providing traditional public benefits, although it has not experimented far in economic reconstruction.

Bankers and brokers willingly support a splendid school system, to which most of them send their children in preference to private schools. Parks and playgrounds have been developed extensively for those who cannot stroll on their own greensward nor play on their own tennis courts. Health standards in most of the towns are high.

The Oranges and Maplewood have been markedly progressive in public consideration of family problems. A mock-trial in 1935 in which youth convicted its elders of neglect and mismanagement resulted in an Institute of Marriage and the Home, part of the Institute of Family Relations sponsored by the five towns' Council of Social Agencies and Welfare.

The desire to nurture these urban advantages without incurring the disadvantages of large urbanization perhaps best explains the community's faint disdain for Newark, the neighboring manufacturing center. This superiority is underlain with a constant fear of governmental absorption by the metropolis of Essex County. No less than the corporation executive on the hill, the Italian truck farmer in the valley glowers at the thought of union with Newark; to each, the suburban city represents the triumph of his individuality. Thus it follows that the Oranges and Maplewood agree wholeheartedly, even too wholeheartedly, with Mark Twain's roguish remark: "There's something nice about Newark. I think it's the suburbs."

East Orange

EAST ORANGE (170 alt., 68,020 pop.) is the largest of "The Oranges" and closest to the center of Newark, being less than two miles distant via

Orange Street. Two of its three main streets, Central Avenue and Main Street, are closely packed for blocks with shopping areas marked by specialty shops, good restaurants, and business establishments. These sections achieve a note of smartness with attractive branches of New York department stores.

Street after street of resolute late-Victorian frame houses characterize East Orange as a residential center. Except for an occasional bungalow, recent building has been limited to large apartment houses that tower above the city's spacious, landscaped one-family dwellings. An uneven glow from the gas street lamps and a vista of fine oaks and maples invariably warn the Newarker that he is "over the line."

Newarkers first "went over" to what is now East Orange in 1678. The community remained a part of Orange until the Civil War when its Republicanism forced it to break from the parent city and assume the independent status of a town, and the name of East Orange. For the balance of the century it grew slowly; its population was only 30,000 when it was incorporated as a city in 1899.

Although East Orange has never become a manufacturing center, since 1900 a number of industrial plants have been established throughout the city. Among the more important products are electric motors and generators and miscellaneous machinery.

Citizens take pride in their $1,000,000 MUNICIPAL CENTER, completed in 1929. The buildings are impressively designed in Italian Renaissance style, and they house one of the State's acknowledged exemplary governments. Outstanding achievements of the mayor and council government are the city's health and recreation programs. The public school system has a high ranking, and the library system includes the central building and three branches.

The city is the home of two institutions of higher education. UPSALA COLLEGE, Springdale Ave. and Prospect St., was founded in 1893 and is conducted by the Swedish Lutheran Church. Approximately one-third of its 400 students who take liberal arts courses are of Swedish extraction. All of the 14 college buildings, except a girls' dormitory and the chapel, are old frame mansions renovated for educational use. The PANZER COLLEGE OF PHYSICAL EDUCATION AND HYGIENE, 139 Glenwood Ave., has an enrollment of 150 students who prepare for teaching physical education. The plant consists of an administration building, a large gymnasium, a library, a fully equipped laboratory and several classrooms.

Orange

ORANGE (170 alt., 35,399 pop.) adjoins East Orange to the west and is the problem mother of all the other Oranges. As her offspring broke away they became so prosperous that Orange is now a poor relation whose behavior is sometimes a matter of family concern. Because its location in the valley of the Watchungs lacks the scenic beauty of the newer towns, the city has failed to achieve their social and financial eminence. Though often snubbed for teas and dinners, Orange sits in at all family conclaves—but not as matriarch.

Smallest in area of the five communities, Orange's inability to grow in any direction helps to explain its cultural and social lag. Its continued leadership in industry has earned it the largest Negro and foreign populations of any of the suburbs.

Orange was settled in 1678 with the aristocratic name of the Mountain Plantations. It is believed to have been afterward renamed in honor of William, Prince of Orange, who became William III of England. Up to the Revolution, Orange farmers were noted for their resistance to the Colonial government and were quick in 1776 to come down from the mountains to fight the British. After the war the governing Presbyterians characteristically turned to education, founding an academy in 1785 and a public library in 1793.

The industrial revolution brought the shoe industry to Orange, where it flourished as the leading manufacture until a decade after the Civil War. When it began to wane under competition from New England, it was replaced by hat manufacturing, for which the town was renowned until the turn of the century. Since that time Orange has been a center for electrical supplies, drugs and calculating machines.

Concentrated on Main Street, the business district of Orange has the air of a neighborhood shopping area of a large city. Stores are old and rather small and tend toward "bargain centers." Into them pour the factory workers from homes along the side streets. Like nearby Newark, Orange has the commission form of government, and its civic history under this form has been less happy than the administrations of the other Oranges and Maplewood.

West Orange

WEST ORANGE (190 alt., 24,327 pop.), immediately to the west of Orange, presents the sharpest contrasts within any one of the five communities. A small shopping district concentrated along Main Street separates age-worn workers' homes and several small factories from the elaborate mansions and magnificent landscape of Llewellyn Park.

The catalyzer between these extremes is the spirit of Thomas A. Edison. Rows of two-story frame houses, bordered by neatly kept lawns, are overshadowed by the steel-concrete buildings of the EDISON PLANT *(open on application)*, 51 Lakeside Ave. To this site the inventor moved in 1887 from Menlo Park and here he experimented with and perfected the moving picture machine, the phonograph and the alkaline storage battery. Today the plant occupies 29 acres and employs 2,100 workers in the manufacture of storage and primary batteries, portland cement, electrical controls, and the Ediphone for business dictation. Plans are under way to make a permanent museum of EDISON'S LABORATORY *(open 9-5 weekdays)*. In front of the building stand two four-wheeled car trucks, parts of the first and second commercial electric locomotives built by Edison in 1880 and 1882. Inside are a replica of the first phonograph, the actual kineto-phone of 1912 (a talking machine), and numerous Edison writings and awards. It was to this West Orange laboratory that reporters came on February 11, 1927, when Edison celebrated his 80th birthday. At that time the old scientist was asked, "Is there a God?" The answer, written on a slip of paper, was: "I do not know—do you?"

Before the arrival of Edison, West Orange was but a small town which had separated from Orange in 1862. Since the establishment of the plant, it has developed into a well-run, modernized community, distinguished for its own suburb of LLEWELLYN PARK *(gates open only to visitors of residents)*. Home of the Colgates, the Edisons, and of Maj. Gen. George B. McClellan, Governor of New Jersey after the Civil War, the area retains the unspoiled beauty of the mountains supplemented by skillful land-scaping. It was here that the first large-scale naturalization of such flowers as the crocus, narcissus and jonquil was undertaken in this country.

South Orange

SOUTH ORANGE (150 alt., 13,630 pop.) lies due south of Orange and West Orange. It is the smallest in population, most beautiful in natural setting, and richest in purse of the five communities. Its mountainous topography helps to maintain its social atmosphere.

With the exception of the shopping center on South Orange Avenue in the valley, the village is mostly a succession of vast, beautiful estates rising up the slopes of the First Watchung Mountains. On the East Orange boundary are a few small real estate developments where bungalows and two-family houses are adapted to more modest purses. The population includes 300 Negroes, 800 Italians, and several Japanese, the latter employed on the mountainside estates.

Known originally as the Orange Dale section of Orange, South Orange was established as a village in 1869. Governed by a non-salaried board of trustees and a president, it is one of the few incorporated villages in the State. Its few manufactures include toilet preparations, bituminous products, and cement blocks. The village has pooled its educational resources with those of Maplewood to achieve a first-class school system. It has been a leader in the crusade to exterminate the Jersey mosquito.

The village is the home of SETON HALL COLLEGE, South Orange Ave., founded in 1856 by the Catholic clergy of Newark Diocese. Since its separation from the religious seminary 10 years ago, the school has developed a cosmopolitan student body which now numbers 419. It has five buildings of stone quarried in nearby Belleville.

Maplewood

MAPLEWOOD (140 alt., 21,321 pop.) lies immediately south of South Orange and some four miles west of Newark's business center. Hence by no stretch of the compass could it properly be called "North Orange," as it so often is by Newarkers fond of rounding out the nomenclature of the Oranges. Incorporated in 1922, Maplewood is the youngest and in many ways the most progressive member of the Orange family.

Considerably less baronial than South Orange, with which it is closely associated, the town has a large percentage of owner-occupied one-family houses, smart and modern in appearance. There is a small shopping district on Springfield Avenue, similar to that in South Orange, another on Maplewood Avenue, and a few factories. Maplewood is especially proud of its recent growth, a 350 percent population increase in the 15 years following 1920.

Outstanding is COLUMBIA HIGH SCHOOL, 17 Parker Ave., used with two junior high schools and nine elementary grammar schools jointly by both Maplewood and South Orange. The high school houses the South Orange-Maplewood Adult Education Institute, a program of instruction and lectures, many of which are conducted by professors from Princeton University.

Maplewood's most historic spot is the TIMOTHY BALL HOUSE *(open)*, 425 Ridgewood Ave., built in 1743 and excellently preserved. At this two-and-one-half-story Colonial farmhouse of frame and stone, George Washington was a frequent visitor during the Revolution. The commander in chief was related on his mother's side to Timothy. The building was altered in 1772 and again in 1919 when it was opened as Washington Inn. Outside the old house still stands the historic walnut tree to which Washington used to tie his horse.

Passaic

Railroad Stations: Erie Station, Main Ave. and Jefferson St., for Erie R.R.; Van Houten and Passaic Aves. for Lackawanna R.R.
Bus Stations: 665 Main Ave. for Greyhound; 686 Main Ave. for Manhattan Transit; 707 Main Ave. for Public Service, Inter-State, Inter-City, New Jersey-New York Transit and local busses.
Local Busses: Fare 5¢.
Traffic Regulations: No turns on red light. Parking meters throughout business district at car-length intervals, 5¢ per hour.

Accommodations: Hotels, tourist homes.

Information Service: Traffic Bureau, Dept. of Public Safety, 336 Passaic St.

Motion Picture Houses: Five.
Swimming: Y.W.C.A. and Y.M.C.A.; Passaic Boys' Club, Pulaski Park (Passaic River).

PASSAIC (70 alt., 62,959 pop.) is a hustling textile town that, in spite of perennial complaints, has not yet rid itself of the double line of railroad tracks which run for about eight blocks through the center of the city. Bounded on one side by Passaic River, 15 miles upstream from Newark Bay, the city is bordered on the other three sides by the semicircular area of residential Clifton.

The long scar of the Erie Railroad main line across the face of the city is Passaic's identification mark. Each day more than 70 trains pass through the center of town, congesting traffic, blackening the streets and buildings with their smoke. At the crossings are darkened, two-story gateman's towers, each topped by a slanting roof and a stove-pipe chimney. On the curbs are silvered wooden booths for police who operate the traffic signals.

Main Avenue is the shopping center, lined by two- to four-story buildings with offices on the upper floors, and neon signs before tightly packed shops of modern appearance on the sidewalk level. Towering above these structures is an 11-story bank building, the local skyscraper.

Main Avenue also is Passaic's residential dividing line. From the ridge on the west, the broad, twisting streets of the residential district dip suddenly into the center of the town. One-family houses predominate; some are of modern architecture, while there are many imposing wood dwellings of the Georgian Colonial type, well spaced with deep well-kept lawns.

East of Main Avenue a progressively shabbier area stretches down to the river. Here the streets are narrow, with frame dwellings and congested tenements crowded beside huge factories. This is the "Dundee Section," where one-half the population is crammed into one-sixth of the city's area. Living in this section are most of the foreign-born who comprise about one-third the total population. Numerically the Poles are first, followed in turn by the Italians, Russians, Hungarians, Slovaks, Germans, Austrians, Dutch, Scotch, English, and Irish.

Through this area flows the sluggish Dundee Canal with its trash-laden bottom and oily scum. Almost everywhere are churches, some of them merely remodeled homes; others spread out over half a block or more.

Twenty years ago the "shawled woman of Passaic" symbolized the poverty of workers in the Dundee section. Today shawls are seen only on the older women; most of the others wear berets, or go hatless. The foreign-born cling to the language of their native countries, and many little stationery stores carry a full quota of foreign-language newspapers.

Many Old World customs and folkways are perpetuated in church ceremonials and lodge celebrations. The Russian bride and groom still eat from the same plate with the same fork at their wedding, and Italians still celebrate their saints' days with open-air, electrically lit pageantry, although these festivals are becoming increasingly commercialized.

Parochial schools have kept alive the mother tongues by teaching foreign languages. Lately this practice has been furthered by language schools formed by private organizations whose members are anticlerical. Cultural organizations such as the Polish National Home, the Slovak Catholic Sokol (*falcon* or *hero*), and the Matica Slovenska (*Slovak mother*) foster an appreciation of the old customs and new developments in the homelands. The Sokol, for example, publishes two national newspapers and sponsors a boys' organization comparable to the Boy Scouts; the Matica Slovenska is the chief Slovak cultural institute, with headquarters in Czechoslovakia.

Passaic is one of the centers of the Nation's woolen industry. One of its mills—the Botany Worsted Mills—claims to be the world's largest complete unit for the manufacture of woolens. Other important industries include handkerchief factories, with a daily output of 1,000,000 (almost two-thirds of the Nation's total), rubber manufacturing, and garment making.

Dutch traders were the first settlers of Passaic (Ind., *peaceful valley*). In 1678 Hartman Michielsen sailed up Passaic River from Manhattan, purchased Menehenicke Island, now Pulaski Park, from the Lenni Lenape Indians, and established a fur trading post. In 1685 Michielsen, together with his three brothers and ten others from Communipaw (Jersey City), acquired the extensive Acquackanonk Patent. Other Dutch adventurers followed the "Fourteen Farmers of the Acquackanonk."

During the Revolutionary War, Passaic, then known as Acquackanonk Bridge, was occupied by Washington's troops, retreating from the British. Lord Cornwallis and the British Army later entered the village. After the war Passaic continued its slow, steady growth as an important river port and agricultural center.

When the railroads began after 1830 to push their way through the Passaic valley, shipping and farming gradually gave way before industrial undertakings. The Dutch, Irish, and the few German families that had settled the area as farmers were followed by Slavic immigrants, attracted by the rising industry. In 1854 its name was changed to Passaic after the river around which its life centered. Six years after Passaic was chartered as a city (1873), the first trickle of immigrants from Central Europe began. George B. Waterhouse, head of a concern of manufacturers of shoddy, brought seven Hungarian immigrants to Passaic from Castle Garden, the Ellis Island of that day. In 1890, the year the Botany Worsted Mills were established, Polish families started to arrive in a steady stream that eventually made them the predominant national group in the city's population.

What newspapers called the first labor riot in the city's history took· place on May 5, 1906, during construction of the Passaic *Herald* building. The police and fire departments, aided by citizens, fought with striking members of an excavators' union. About one-third of the strikers were wounded, and many were arrested.

Organization of textile labor was long delayed by the Wool Council, official employment agency for the five largest manufacturers, and by a city ordinance that prohibited meetings without a permit. January 1926, however, saw the beginning of a textile workers' strike, destined to attain national importance because of the issue of civil liberties involved. It was precipitated by the discharge of a workers' committee that was asking the restoration of a 10 percent pay cut at the Botany Mills and spread to other mills until some 15,000 workers were out.

A year of strife followed, marked at times by police attempts to suppress public meetings as illegal. This brought liberal and radical leaders from all over the country to the scene to protest the restrictions on free speech. Several arrests followed. Norman Thomas, later Socialist candidate for President of the United States, was hauled down from the crotch of a tree from where he had attempted to address a meeting. He was arrested, but the case was never prosecuted. Ultimately the United Textile Workers took over the strike. The mill owners finally agreed to union recognition, and to arbitration. The union did not hold its strength during the ensuing decade, but under the Textile Workers Organizing Committee (formed 1936) a new unionization drive began.

During prohibition bootleggers and hijackers battled constantly for control of the Passaic area. So extensive were the operations that it was only mildly exciting to the citizenry when a pipe line was discovered under Passaic River conveying molasses from Wallington, on the opposite shore. In Passaic, the molasses was manufactured into alcohol and then pumped back to Wallington.

POINTS OF INTEREST

1. The VAN SCHOTT HOUSE, 125 Lexington Ave., in Revolutionary times, was the parsonage of the old Dutch Reformed Church. Although the building has lost many of its original Dutch lines, it retains a pitched roof bearing two cupolas and wide verandas with white columns. The house, now occupied as an undertaking establishment, received its name from Dr. Gerald J. Van Schott, who purchased and renovated it in 1899.

2. The TORNQVIST CORNICE, a curious piece of 19th century handwork, is perched on top of a garage, one of three pinkish brown buildings belonging to a sheet metal company, at 175 Washington Pl. The cornice,

about 25 feet long and painted a dirty buff, has an intricate floral design with decorative urns at each end. A sign tells that it was made by Peter Tornqvist for the Philadelphia Centennial in 1876.

3. In ARMORY PARK, between Gregory Ave. and Prospect St., is an old BURIAL VAULT, constructed as a morgue *c.* 1690. Built into a grass-covered mound, it has a brown sandstone front about 10 feet high; iron bars permit a free view of the interior. In 1921, during development of the park, several bodies were found in the vault. One was that of a fully uniformed Union soldier.

4. In CITY HALL PARK, Paulison Ave. S. of Passaic Ave., is the CITY HALL, a square brown sandstone structure, three stories in height, with towers at each corner. The building was planned in 1872 as a home by Charles McKnight Paulison, prominent citizen, but the panic of 1873 overtook Paulison before his mansion was completed. The unfinished house was bought and turned over to the city in 1891 by a group of interested citizens; the city then completed it. City Hall retains the name of Paulison's Castle. It stands on a steep hill called Tony's Nose; one Passaic historian explains that the name is derived from Gen. Anthony Howe, whose British troops drove the Continentals from the city. There is no record of Gen. Anthony Howe at Passaic. Anthony Wayne, however, encamped there Dec. 9, 1778.

5. SS. PETER AND PAUL'S RUSSIAN ORTHODOX GREEK-CATHOLIC CHURCH, NE. corner Monroe and 3rd Sts., is said to have been built with money donated by the Czar in 1911. The building is square, resembling churches in Moscow, with a huge dome and minarets at each corner. The congregation is sharply divided (1939) over whether the church shall be placed under the jurisdiction of a bishop sympathetic to the U.S.S.R. or one who, faithful to the Czar, fled during the Revolution. Litigation and even physical combat have marked the dispute.

6. The SITE OF ACQUACKANONK LANDING, 139-153 River Drive, shows little sign of its original activity. Early in the 18th century products from miles around were hauled here for shipment to New York. During its heyday, the Landing was a center of amusement; around it were grouped the stores and taverns that attracted farmers. Only a few bulkheads and pilings remain.

Paterson

Railroad Stations: Erie Station, Market St. and Railroad Ave., for Erie R.R.; Lackawanna Station, Lackawanna Plaza and Marshall St., for Lackawanna R.R.; Madison Ave. and Ellison St. for New York, Susquehanna and Western R.R.
Bus Stations: Market and Church Sts. for Public Service, Inter-City and Manhattan Lines; Ellison St. at City Hall for Public Service and independent lines.
Local Busses: Fare 5¢ each zone.
Taxis: 25¢ in city limits.
Traffic Regulations: Left turns may be made at nearly all intersections. No right turns on red lights. Watch street signs for parking restrictions and one-way streets. Parking meters in business section, 5¢ per hour.

Accommodations: One first-class and several other hotels in center of city.

Information Service: Alexander Hamilton Hotel, Market and Church Sts.; Traffic Department; Room 15, City Hall, Market and Washington Sts.

Motion Picture Houses: Ten, one with vaudeville.
Athletic Fields: Hinchliffe Stadium, Liberty and Maple Sts.; Eastside Park, E. end of Broadway at Passaic River; Westside Park, Totowa and Preakness Aves.; Sandy Hill Park, Market and Carroll Sts.; Pennington Park, McBride Ave. and Nagle St.
Swimming: Barbour's Pond, Garret Mountain Reservation, S. end of New St., free.
Tennis: Eastside and Westside Parks.
Golf: Passaic County Course, 27 holes, greens fee for county residents 75¢ weekdays, Sat. $1, Sun. and holidays $1.25; for nonresidents $1 weekdays, Sat., Sun., and holidays $2 (before noon), $1.50 (after noon); N. on W. Broadway to Union Ave., L. to Totowa Rd., R. 1½ m.

Annual Events: Industrial Exhibit, January 24; Easter Sunrise Service, Garret Mountain; Model Boat Regatta, May; Festival of Nations, June.

PATERSON (84 alt., 138,513 pop.) is one of the few American cities that have turned out almost exactly as they were planned. Alexander Hamilton envisaged a great industrial city at the Great Falls of the Passaic, and at the site he chose has developed the third largest city of the State and the manufacturing and commercial center for 500,000 people in northern New Jersey.

Built mainly on higher ground lying within the hairpin curve of Passaic River eighteen miles from its mouth at Newark Bay, Paterson is shadowed on the southeast by the rocky slope of Garret Mountain. The tightly built business center is separated from the chief residential area by the Erie Railroad tracks, elevated on an embankment and a series of bridges.

Above the rock-walled chasm of Passaic Falls the river's original beauty has been largely preserved in a well-landscaped park; downstream, at the opposite end of the city, another fine park stretches to the bank. Between the two parks the stony channel is hemmed by brick-walled factories or dull frame houses, and spanned by a number of bridges. Too shallow for navigation, the river serves only as a source for power at the Falls.

PASSAIC FALLS AND HYDROELECTRIC PLANT, PATERSON

The general appearance of the city bespeaks its industrial history. The greatest obstacle to order and symmetry is the random location within its 8.36 square miles of ubiquitous mill buildings. They are usually three- and four-story structures of dusty brick with rows of high windows running the length of each floor. Scores of manufacturers may occupy partitioned shops in a single building. Most of the mills are built flush with the sidewalk; the monotonous clatter of the looms echoes up and down the street. Tall water towers usually stand next to the buildings.

The millworkers' home often is a ramshackle tenement, or else a plain two-family house of frame construction. Crowded in the river section, sometimes braced against the old stone walls of the channel itself, or standing in lonely clusters on the outskirts of the city, these buildings generally lack the brightness of paint and flowers and grassplots. The impression is one of faded grays, browns and mustard yellows. Paterson's real color, usually missed by the visitor, is in the gay fabrics woven on the looms.

Artisans, small merchants, and others of the middle-income group have fairly modern homes, but the best residential area is the Eastside. Here are lawns and shrubbery in abundance and trim rows of maples on every street. The houses range from small and neatly designed structures of brick or frame to pretentious stucco dwellings in the Spanish style, equipped with tennis courts, and three-car garages. Some of these homes rest upon high ground overlooking the broad curve of Passaic River and offering a distant view of Manhattan's skyscrapers.

Lying between the Eastside and the shopping district is a section of modern apartment houses, churches and older houses, some with turrets and stone towers reminiscent of the period when a man demonstrated architecturally that his house was his castle.

The business life of the city is concentrated chiefly on three thorough-fares: Main Street, Broadway, between Main and Paterson Streets, and the section of Market Street that lies between the Erie Railroad Station and Main. An unusual number of banks of varying late Victorian architecture dominate the downtown district. Two up-to-date department stores, the one modern hotel, the leading motion picture house, and a miscellany of smaller shops and restaurants give the feeling of a shopping area. North-east of Market Street is Broadway, a conglomeration of drygoods stores, open-air markets, and bargain centers which serve the majority of the in-dustrial population.

Paterson residents are known as walkers. Taxicab drivers earn little, despite the attraction of exceedingly low rates. It is a common saying that to walk twice around the City Hall is to meet half of your friends. Local news and gossip often travel faster by word of mouth than by publication in the local newspapers.

For a century Paterson has been a nationally known proving ground in the struggle between employers and workers. Its industrial reputation as "The Silk City" has been balanced by its renown for hard-fought strikes, many resulting from technological improvements in the weaving industry elsewhere that have spelled meager wages and the stretchout for weavers operating Paterson's old-fashioned looms.

Since the city has 25,000 union members, much of the talk concerns labor conditions. So conscious is the average Paterson worker of the city's labor history that the dates of marriages, trips, and other personal events are commonly fixed by the year of an important strike. A Paterson strike converts the downtown district into a huge picket line and a mass meeting. In recent years the dyers' union has turned out as many as 5,000 members on a single picket line.

The city's reputation for labor disputes has for years distressed all the elements involved—the labor organizations, the chamber of commerce, and the city officials. In 1936 the city administration sought a solution by estab-lishing The Industrial Commission with an expert in industrial problems as consultant. The law provides representation on the seven-man commit-tee for mill owners, the bar, bankers, manufacturers, the chamber of com-merce, service organizations, labor, and the mayor, *ex officio*.

Although its main purpose is to strengthen Paterson's industries, the commission also aims to anticipate labor difficulties and to avoid strikes by conferences and arbitration. It played a conspicuous part in the silk settle-ment of June 1937, and intervened in a number of other disputes, but by its nature lacks the power to alter fundamental economic maladjustments. Business leaders incline to the belief that outside agitators are the cause of strikes. The millworkers retort that $10 weekly wages are the reason; and the larger manufacturers, who would prefer to pay better wages, declare that they are helpless in the face of Paterson's own brand of sweatshop competition, the family shop.

The proprietors of these shops are known as "cockroach bosses." The term, coined by a young girl organizer during the 1931 strike, has been accepted with self-contempt by the family shop bosses themselves, who believe in organization to protect themselves against the price-cutting converters (jobbers) but cannot stay organized.

These 400 manufacturers constitute the "curb exchange," a sidewalk trading place on Washington Street between Ellison and Market Streets. From early morning until late afternoon the manufacturers mill around, selling raw silk, buying finished silk, sight unseen; here family-shop operators contract to weave the converters' raw silk on a commission basis. Only acts of God and man, such as stormy weather or an Oriental war, clear the place. Even more than the large manufacturer, the cockroach boss is sensitive to the tide of Asiatic affairs.

Although scores of silk mills have moved from Paterson and few of the remaining shops have even as many as 100 employees, the industry still produces every kind of goods from fancy ribbons to coffin linings. The dominant industry is silk dyeing, whose 15,000 workers handle 75 percent of the Nation's textile output. Other important manufactures of Paterson are men's shirts, women's underwear, airplane motors, and other metal products.

The variety of Paterson's population equips it for an international outlook. More than 30 percent of the population is foreign born. Italians, Jews, Syrians, Poles, Germans, Russians, and Irish predominate. They form the backbone of the trade union movement and they have brought to Paterson a keen European interest in the arts and sports.

When the city is not talking labor problems, it is listening to concerts in music halls, participating in open forums at churches or "Y's," attending amateur theatricals, or using one of the city's many playgrounds. Paterson has drawn on its own character to attract cultural events and entertainments. This has been achieved, on the one hand, by capital's traditional patronage of the arts, and on the other by labor's quest for personal development.

Dutch settlers were early attracted to the great cataract on the Passaic which had been described to them by the Indians. In 1679 they obtained the first tract of land within the present bounds of Paterson. Many of the Dutch pioneers bore names still common in the city. For more than a century the Falls were merely an attraction for visitors, and the settlement remained small.

Then in 1791 Alexander Hamilton, Secretary of the Treasury, helped form the Society for Establishing Useful Manufactures (S.U.M.). The New Jersey Legislature voted the company perpetual exemption from county and township taxes and gave it the right to hold property, improve rivers, build canals, and raise $100,000 by lottery. The company selected, from a number of sites offered, the Great Falls of the Passaic River, which at that time had "no more than ten houses." Hamilton had favored this place, which he had seen during the Revolution, but he "did not make public this idea of his at the time, for fear that some of the men who did not live near the Passaic Falls might not contribute." Money was set aside by the S.U.M. for factories, and Major Pierre L'Enfant, designer of Washington, D. C., was hired to build a system of raceways.

Paterson grew out of the Society's 700 acres above and below the Passaic Falls and was named for William Paterson, then Governor of New Jersey. It was a company town, and its workers began to exhibit signs of dissatisfaction. S.U.M. records tells of "disorderly" calico printers as early as 1794. This resulted in the closing of the mill—the first lock-out in American history and the forerunner of a long string of industrial struggles.

The town continued to grow as an industrial center. When one industry failed, others replaced it. About 1825 Paterson became known as the "Cotton Town of the United States." Oxen are reputed to have provided power for the first cotton spinning here in a mill known as the Bull House.

In 1828 Paterson gave America its first factory strike when cotton workers quit their looms to protest a change in the lunch hour. The owners had asserted that the health and comfort of child workers would be improved by a 1 o'clock dinner instead of a meal at 12, making a more equal division of the day. The employees countered with a surprise demand for reduction of working hours from $13\frac{1}{2}$ to 12. Carpenters, masons and mechanics of Paterson also walked out, the first recorded instance of a sympathy strike in the United States. Although the strike was lost, it made a strong impression on the community, and the owners afterward restored the 12 o'clock lunch hour.

In 1831 the Morris Canal, penetrating the coal fields of Pennsylvania, was opened. The railroad came to town a year later when the tracks of the Paterson and Hudson River Railroad were laid. Both the canal and the railroad gave impetus to the town's development. In 1836 Samuel Colt established his mill, and the original Colt repeating revolvers were manufactured. In 1837 John Clark's modest machine shop produced one of the earliest American locomotives, the *Sandusky,* which was fashioned after an imported English model. Within 44 years 5,871 engines were made in Paterson and shipped to all parts of North and South America.

Silk manufacturing was permanently introduced to Paterson in 1840 when a plant under the supervision of John Ryle was established in the Old Gun Mill. By 1850 the new industry surpassed cotton and Paterson became known as the "Silk City." One year later the town was incorporated, and by 1860 its population reached approximately 19,600. Attracted by the rising silk industry, immigrants from Ireland, Germany, Italy, and Russia poured into Paterson, so that by 1870 the city had enough skilled workers to handle two-thirds of the raw silk imported into the United States.

Many of the foreign workers had been forced to flee Europe for championing various liberal causes. When, in 1886, conditions in local silk mills became unbearable, they led in calling a three-hour strike. The next important strike was a three-week walk-out in 1902, led by McQueen and Grossman, two Philosophic Anarchists.

That year brought a series of major disasters to the city. A fire started on February 8 and destroyed almost 500 buildings, including the City Hall and the entire business section. It was halted a mile from its starting point with the help of Jersey City and Hackensack firemen, who fought the blaze from roofs. Ruins of the fire had barely cooled when on March 2 the swollen Passaic River engulfed the lower portions of the city and swept away bridges, homes and buildings, causing damage of more than $1,000,000. Several months later a tornado struck the city, uprooting trees and houses and crippling vital services.

The silk industry reached its peak in 1910 when 25,000 workers in 350 large plants wove close to 30 percent of the silk manufactured in this country. Three years later all mills came to a standstill when workers, under the leadership of the Industrial Workers of the World, struck for the maintenance of the two-loom system (two looms for each worker to tend) against the owners' plans for an increased number.

The workers walked out on February 15; the employers raised the American flag on their empty mills and declared a lock-out. Carlo Tresca, Elizabeth Gurley Flynn, "Big Bill" Haywood, and John Reed, the young Harvard poet, came to lead the picket lines. When one picketer was killed, Haywood led 15,000 workers in the funeral procession. School children struck in sympathy with their parents, and gigantic mass meetings were held in the neighboring borough of Haledon, whose residents were largely sympathetic. Reed, who was jailed during the walk-out, staged the famous "Paterson Pageant" in Manhattan's Madison Square Garden for the benefit of the strikers. It was the greatest strike in Paterson history, but the workers went back to their looms in July, defeated.

In 1924, 20,000 workers waged an unsuccessful fight against the four-loom system. Manufacturers, blaming labor troubles, began hunting for sites with lower taxes, cheaper power, and more docile workers. By 1925 the exodus had begun. There were 700 plants then, but the factories were much smaller than formerly.

Although Paterson is still the largest single silk-producing center in the country, the industry has been seriously curtailed. Reasons for the decline are: antiquated plants that are unable to compete with newer mills of the South, Pennsylvania, and New England; the introduction of rayon; and the break-down of large units into small "cockroach" shops. Today 4,000 workers weave about 12 percent of the Nation's silk.

The growth of the dyeing industry in Paterson has offset the decline of silk manufacturing. Some of the largest plants in America, processing 70 percent of the Nation's silk and rayon, are here. Proximity to the New York market and the soft waters of the Passaic River led to the establishment of this industry. Its 15,000 workers emerged from the 1933 strike with the Dyers' Local 1733, the largest union in New Jersey. Inspired by the collective-bargaining clause of the National Industrial Recovery Act, the strike was the first successful one in many years.

POINTS OF INTEREST

1. GARRET MOUNTAIN RESERVATION, Valley Rd. at the Lackawanna R.R. bridge, is a 570-acre park and picnic ground on the rocky heights overlooking the city. Woodland trails, picnic groves, and broad lawns are maintained by the Passaic County Park Commission. Garret Mountain is said to have been named about a century ago for a secret society that met in garrets at the homes of its members.

LAMBERT CASTLE, on the mountain slope within the reservation, was built in 1891 by Catholina Lambert, an immigrant who became wealthy as a silk manufacturer. The building is a ponderous castellated structure of rough-surfaced red and gray stone, generously fenestrated, balconied and terraced. It now houses the administrative offices of the Passaic County Park Commission and the PASSAIC COUNTY HISTORICAL SOCIETY MUSEUM *(open 1-5 Wed., Thurs., Fri.; 10-5 Sat., Sun.)*. One room contains the furniture used by Garret A. Hobart of Paterson, who was Vice President in the first McKinley administration. Paintings and antiques are displayed in other rooms. The interior of the building is noted for scrollwork on the newelposts, stained glass windows, and elaborately decorated ceilings.

From the OBSERVATORY TOWER, near the castle and on the highest elevation of the mountain, stretches a fine view of the countryside for miles around and of the closely packed homes and mills of Paterson.

2. PATERSON MUSEUM *(open 1-5 Mon.-Fri.; 10-5 Sat.)*, 268 Summer St., contains one of the most complete mineral collections in the State. Other exhibits are Indian relics and curios, insects, reptiles, birds, fossils, and historical displays. The most interesting object is the 14-foot submarine built in 1878 by John P. Holland in the Old Gun Mill yard. This was Holland's first attempt at an under-water craft, and it promptly sank on its first trial in the Passaic River. Several other attempts were made, in one of which Holland kept the boat down for 24 hours, but he finally abandoned it to the river bank, where it sank into the mud. Almost 50 years later the hulk was located with a magnet and dug up by several Paterson youths who presented it to the museum.

3. DANFORTH MEMORIAL LIBRARY *(open 9-8 weekdays)*, SE. corner Broadway and Auburn St., is the main building of Paterson's public library system. The gray limestone structure, designed in straightforward formal Classic style, is the work of Henry Bacon. The dignified interior is finished in limestone and marble. It also houses an art gallery, featuring Paterson painters.

4. WASHINGTON MARKET, Washington St. between Fair St. and Hamilton Ave., is an open-air produce center consisting of open front stores and a few stalls along the sidewalk. It is not so large as it was 15 years ago, but it is still one of the noisiest and busiest spots of the city on afternoons and Saturday evenings.

5. The PASSAIC COUNTY ADMINISTRATION BUILDING, SE. corner Ward and Hamilton Sts., served as the postoffice until 1932. Built in 1898 in Flemish style, its prototype was the Haarlem Market in Hol-

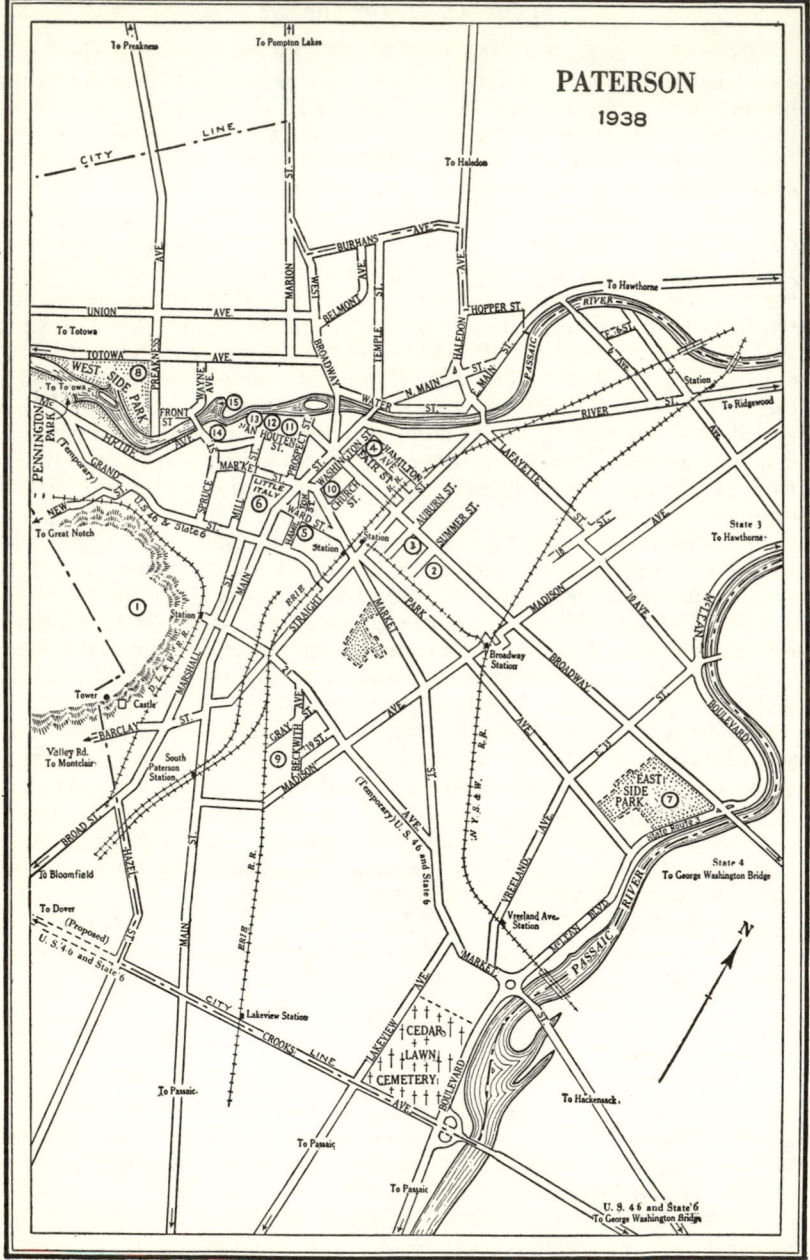

PATERSON
1938

land. Its red brick walls are generously banded, trimmed, keyed, and quoined with gray limestone. The style, selected as a tribute to the pioneer Dutch of the territory, is incongruous in its modern surroundings.

6. LITTLE ITALY, vicinity of Market, Cross and Mill Sts., is one of the sections inhabited almost exclusively by Italians. Frame houses, most of them lacking paint and many in disrepair, are built close together for the length of each block. The only substantial and modern buildings of the district are a school and St. MICHAEL'S CHURCH, a yellow brick structure of modified Gothic design. On March 19 Sicilians in this district honor St. Joseph, the patron saint of Sicily; specially baked delicacies are exhibited in unusual displays and afterward given to the poor. Feasting and dancing mark St. Michael's Feast Day, September 29. On October 12, Columbus Day, the Italian societies turn out in full uniform with bands and banners to parade through the business district. At LAZZARA'S MUSIC HALL, Cross and Ellison Sts., Italian opera companies make occasional appearances, and labor unions hold frequent meetings.

7. EASTSIDE PARK, Broadway and McLean Blvd., on high ground overlooking Passaic River, is a municipally owned recreation center. Noteworthy is the 2,000-foot floral embankment in the pattern of an English garden. In the central area are the GENERAL PULASKI MONUMENT and the SOLDIERS MONUMENT. The park has a deer paddock, and more squirrels at large than the park department wishes.

8. WESTSIDE PARK, Totowa and Preakness Aves., on Passaic River above the falls, also maintained by the city, has winding pathways over a gentle slope shaded by blue spruce and pine. There are terraces, flower gardens, lawns and shrubbery, and athletic fields. Canoes and rowboats are available.

In a small plaza is exhibited the FENIAN RAM, John P. Holland's first successful submarine. Launched in 1881, the 31-foot craft was financed largely by contributions from the Irish brotherhood known as the Fenian Society. A popular but erroneous belief was that the submarine was intended for use by the Irish against the British Navy. It was powered with a one-cylinder combustion engine and built for a crew of three. In a trial off Staten Island, the *Fenian Ram* dove 100 feet below the surface and remained submerged for an hour. The vessel lacked a periscope, however, and after Holland had startled a large number of ferry and tugboat captains around New York harbor by his sudden appearances, the submarine was sunk in collision with a ferry at Weehawken. Later it was salvaged.

The Government ignored the Irish schoolmaster's invention until 1893, when a contract was finally awarded. Seven years later the Navy Department accepted its first submarine, the *Holland*. The inventor, like Hudson Maxim, thought that his device would make war impracticable, but he lived to see the beginning of the World War.

9. WRIGHT AERONAUTICAL PLANT *(group tours arranged on application)*, 1120 E. 19th St., is the largest airplane engine factory in the United States. A subsidiary of the Curtiss-Wright Corporation, it occupies 25 acres of land and employs more than 3,500 persons, producing an-

nually more than 2,000 engines. The plant was established in Paterson in 1920 and since 1928 has expanded sixfold.

10. CITY HALL, Market St. between Washington and Colt Sts., is a three-story gray limestone building with a weathered copper dome surmounting a small tower. Erected in 1894 and rebuilt after the fire of 1902, it is the work of John M. Carrere, architect, and exemplifies his taste for the multi-plastered, arched, balustraded and heavily corniced work of the French Beaux Arts of that period. THREE BRONZE STATUES, portraying *Alexander Hamilton, Vice President Garret A. Hobart,* and *Nathan Barnert,* philanthropist and former mayor, stand in front of the building. Projections in the façade are a favorite gathering place of thousands of starlings, whose concerted chirping is easily heard above the noise of traffic. Toward nightfall the birds gradually settle down on narrow ledges, packed so closely that they resemble a mourning band across the building. A few years ago it was planned to drive the starlings away with Roman candles, but protests from bird lovers deprived the town of this spectacle.

11. The OLD RACEWAY, NW. corner Prospect and Van Houten Sts., is a sluggish stream 12 feet wide flowing between the sidewalk and the mills, and crossed at intervals by plank bridges. Originating in Passaic River above the falls, it has followed this course for almost a century, although its first value to the mills has long been outmoded by the development of electrical power. The waters of the raceway are used by adjoining dye plants. It does not follow the course of the first raceway built shortly after the founding of Paterson in 1792; rapid establishment of new factories made it necessary to alter the route.

12. FAMILY SHOPS, Grobart, Harmony, and Industry Mills *(open on application),* 11 Van Houten St., are crowded floors, partitioned off into units where entire families work 60 hours a week for about $12 each. Shafts fly up and down, shuttles weave in and out, and motors drone as father, mother, son and daughter scurry around four looms each, twisting and tying fine silk threads. A family shop consists of 8 to 20 looms, one quill-winding frame and odds and ends scattered over an oily, cage-like floor. Winding wooden stairs lead to electrically-lit factories where the smell is foul and the din is great. Most of the manufacturers show eyestrain and slight deafness from their work. These men—the "cockroach bosses" of Paterson—deny that they run the looms. "The looms run us," is their saying. Their overalls and shirts are tattered and grimy; their hands are oily and calloused.

In these buildings thousands of yards of silk are woven each week for dyeing. Most of the raw silk comes from Japan; small quantities are imported from China, Syria, and Italy. After the skeins are wound on bobbins, the threads of about 1,000 spools are wound around a beam by means of a warping frame resembling a large wheel.

The beam is placed on a loom after it is attached to a harness which moves up and down to allow the shuttles to be thrown back and forth, weaving the warp's threads into cloth. Each shuttle contains a quill of thrown silk or filling. Pieces of about 70 yards each are taken off each loom every three days, and are shipped to dye houses.

13. The OLD GUN MILL *(open on application)*, NW. corner Mill and Van Houten Sts., is a two-story brick structure occupied by the Arrow Textile Print Works. The building was erected 1836 by Samuel Colt, who here manufactured the first successful revolvers. Colt got his patent in 1835, and New York capitalists supplied money for the Patent Arms Company. The War Department, however, held that the revolver was impractical, and the enterprise was temporarily abandoned. After the Colt pistol had been tested in the Seminole War, large Government orders were awarded and the factory was busy until peace forced a shutdown in 1840. Shortly afterward Colt sold his last revolver to an Indian trader. Upon the outbreak of the Mexican War an order for 1,000 revolvers was given to the manufacturer; lacking a model, he had to pay a large price for one of his guns. This order was filled at Whitneyville, Connecticut.

In the same mill Christopher Colt, brother of the inventor, began in 1839 the first silk weaving in Paterson. After a few months he gave up the project.

14. A HYDROELECTRIC PLANT and a STEAM PLANT of the Society for Establishing Useful Manufactures (known throughout Paterson as S.U.M.) are in the gorge of Passaic River, just below the falls. From the sidewalk a steep, sodded embankment slopes to the level of the large brick buildings.

In 1791 Governor William Paterson of New Jersey signed the charter giving the tax-free Society for Establishing Useful Manufactures the right to organize and sell stock. Not until 1814, when a drastic reorganization of the S.U.M. took place and the Colt family became virtual dictators of the corporation's affairs, did a business boom start the society on the road to financial success. The history since then has been stormy, marked by numerous court cases and disputes with other organizations.

In 1824 the Morris Canal and Banking Company sued to gain rights to the Passaic River. The court ruled in 1829 that S.U.M. possessed title "to the flow of all the waters of the Passaic at the great falls, in their ancient channel without diminution or alteration."

Public opinion forced the society to relinquish its lottery rights in 1848, but the host of other charter privileges remained. When the hydroelectric plant was installed in 1912, the city of Paterson attempted to tax its operation, but the court again ruled in favor of S.U.M. Another suit was lost by the city in 1937. The municipal government contended that the society already had enjoyed 140 years of special rights and that by giving up manufacturing in 1796 and leasing the sites out to private concerns, it has forfeited its tax-exempt privileges.

15. PASSAIC FALLS, the best known scene of the Paterson area, plunges 70 feet from a rocky shelf into a vertically walled chasm just above the S.U.M. plants. Only during periods of melting snows or heavy rains does the waterfall exist; at other times the flow of Passaic River is entirely diverted by a S.U.M. dam just above the falls. In flood stage the yellow torrent throws up a fine mist that fills the gorge, and the roar can be heard for several blocks.

A steel footbridge spans the gorge but this is closed to the public by

S.U.M., owner of the falls. The adjacent shelfland, once a popular picnic ground, is accessible to sightseers. Had it not been for the action of the great glacier in blocking the old outlet of Passaic River some 20 miles southwest of Paterson, neither the falls nor the river would exist here today.

POINTS OF INTEREST IN ENVIRONS

Little Falls Laundry Plant, *9.4 m.,* Montclair Art Museum, *12.8 m.,* Grover Cleveland House, *14 m.,* Eagle Rock Reservation, *14.7 m. (see Tour 9).*

Perth Amboy

Railroad Station: Smith St. between Maple and Prospect Sts. for Pennsylvania R.R. and Jersey Central R.R.
Bus Stations: Smith and State Sts. and Smith and Water Sts. for Public Service and independent lines.
Taxis: 15¢ first ¼ mile, 5¢ each additional ¼ mile.
Ferry: Foot of Smith St. for Tottenville, Staten Island; 25¢ for pleasure car and passengers; Baltimore & Ohio R.R. connection to N. Y.
Bridges: Outerbridge Crossing to Staten Island, 50¢ for pleasure car and passengers; Victory Bridge to South Amboy and shore points, free.

Accommodations: Five hotels and several tourist houses.

Information Service: Public Library, 196 Jefferson St.

Motion Picture Houses: Five.
Swimming: Two beaches, Water St.; adm. 5¢.
Tennis: Hayes Park, foot of Brighton Ave.
Boating: Boat Basin, foot of Water St.

PERTH AMBOY (117 alt., 43,516 pop.) conceals beneath a rather unkempt modern industrial surface a Colonial seaport with a history that goes back to 1651. Scarcely one descendant of an original family remains in the city, but a few old homes and historic buildings are still in use—here as a rooming house or a roadside tavern, there as a private dwelling or a particularly decrepit unit of some slum area.

Highways from New Brunswick and the industrial cities of the north meet a network of roads from central New Jersey and the Atlantic coast that converge at Victory Bridge. To the east, narrow Arthur Kill separates the city from Tottenville, Staten Island.

To motorists bound to or from the Jersey shore, Perth Amboy consists of five traffic lights that sometimes tie up week-end traffic for miles. While cars creep along or come to a prolonged halt, drivers lean out to discuss with each other this red menace to the freedom of the road.

Passengers on the Tottenville Ferry from Staten Island get a more complete picture as the little red boat skirts the industrial water front, solid with wharves and factories, and eases into its slip at the foot of Smith Street. Beyond the slip, lining the bluff that fronts Arthur Kill and overlooks Raritan Bay, are some of the older homes, with occasional lookout towers patterned to the type of bygone architects and builders.

Leading from the labyrinth of picket-fenced corridors in the ferry house is Smith Street, rising sharply for two blocks. The rise effectively hides the city, isolating the ferry house and its environs like a quiet fishing village. There is no intimation of the industrial community just over the hill.

From this spot, where Perth Amboy itself began, Smith Street runs west as a traffic-burdened shopping center, flanked by two- and three-story brick buildings of indiscriminate architecture with stores on the street level and offices in the upper stories. The street takes on a momentary modernity as it passes Perth Amboy's lone skyscraper, the 10-story Perth Amboy National Bank at New Brunswick Avenue and State Street and finally disappears amid huge factories and blackened pitted fields beyond Convery Boulevard.

Smith Street is the backbone of Perth Amboy, creating a city out of the diverse national and economic groups that live here. Poles, Russians, Hungarians, and Czechs come out of their working class section known as "Budapest;" the Irish (and now Poles, too) leave behind the area called "Dublin;" Danes and Germans emerge from the bosoms of their nationalist groups, and meet in the anonymity of this street with the democratic name. Seventy-two percent of Perth Amboy's population consists of the foreign-born and their American-born children; Slavs predominate, with Danes and Italians next.

There are approximately 100 factories within the city, and their products range through cigars, vaseline, refined metals, neckties, lead pipe, asphalt, munitions, cables, lingerie, and auto parts, to the total value of about $274,000,000 annually. But Perth Amboy's basic industry is the manufacture of ceramic wares—tiles, bricks, terra cotta, and porcelain, made from rich local deposits of clay. Rows of kilns with tapering snouts pointing skyward are a characteristic feature of Perth Amboy and its environs.

The concentration of industry on this point of land is due to the presence of the fine natural harbor of Raritan Bay; the Raritan River, which flows into it; and Arthur Kill (or Staten Island Sound), one of the waterways serving New York City.

Perth Amboy is one of the few United States cities of its size with a volunteer fire department. Formed in 1880 after a tremendous blaze, the department quickly attracted members with a provision for lifetime exemption from taxes. The number of firemen and ex-firemen who pay no taxes has now become so great that any attempt to establish a paid department is resisted by a large bloc of non-taxpaying voters.

The site of Perth Amboy was part of a large tract purchased from the Indians in 1651 by Augustine Herman, a Staten Island Dutchman. After the English took possession of New Jersey, the charter to Woodbridge in 1669 stipulated "that Ambo Point be reserved . . . to be disposed of by the lords proprietors." Political difficulties during the next decade probably hindered settlement. In 1682 the twelve new proprietors described the point as "a sweet, wholesome, and delightful place," a view evidently long held by the Indians, who used it as a camp ground and for fishing excursions in the bay. The proprietors announced their "purpose by the help of Almighty God, with all convenient speed, to build a convenient town, for merchandise, trade and fishery, on Ambo Point." They contributed £1,200 to build a house for each, and by August 1683 three buildings had been completed.

Two years later the population took a sudden spurt when the Earl of

Perth permitted the immigration of nearly 200 oppressed Scots, many of whom were in prison as dissenters. These were soon joined by other Scots, English merchants, and French Huguenots. In 1686 the steadily growing commercial and shipping center was designated capital of East New Jersey. In 1718 Perth Amboy was granted the charter that makes it the oldest incorporated city in New Jersey. Five years later in Perth Amboy, William Bradford, official State printer, printed the Session Laws of 1723, the first printing in New Jersey.

The Indians had called this point of land Ompoge (large level piece of ground). Through a series of corruptions it became Ambo and then Ambo Point. This name persisted even though the community was dubbed New Perth in honor of the Earl; finally the two were blended into Perth Amboy. There is a story that the name arose when Indians, unfamiliar with Scottish kilts, referred to the Earl of Perth as a squaw. "No! Not squaw!" the Scot is supposed to have answered. "Perth am boy!" The nobleman, however, never crossed the Atlantic.

Tories were active in Perth Amboy at the outbreak of the Revolution, but several of the town's Royalist families fled when Revolutionists arrested Governor William Franklin and occupied the Governor's House in June 1776. Six months later the British jailed Richard Stockton, one of the five New Jersey signers of the Declaration of Independence.

During the war, Perth Amboy's tactical position at the mouth of Raritan River—highway for the whaleboat raids of Revolutionaries upstream—made it a goal for the contending armies. The town was occupied successively by the Americans under General Mercer and by the British under General Howe. Benjamin Franklin, Edward Rutledge, and John Adams stopped at Perth Amboy Inn in 1776 on their way to the conference on Staten Island, at which they refused Sir William Howe's offer of amnesty in exchange for surrender.

For twenty years after the Revolution, Perth Amboy was poor and barren, but from about the turn of the century until the Civil War the town enjoyed some vogue as a summer resort. The Governor's House was transformed into the Brighton House, a fashionable hotel, which became the social center for the hypochondriac rich utilizing the waters at the nearby spa. The city's industrial development began during the 1860's; its clay deposits were exploited, and steamboats replaced the sailing vessels. In 1832 South Amboy was made the terminal of the Camden and Amboy, the State's first railroad.

During this period, Eagleswood Military Academy was built as a school for young men. Eagleswood was also the home of Sarah Grimke, her sister Angelina Weld, and Angelina's husband, Theodore D. Weld, who were pioneers in the woman-suffrage movement and ardent Abolitionists. The school and home became the visiting place for many of the Abolitionists of the day, including William Lloyd Garrison and Wendell Phillips, and served as an important station of the Underground Railroad. One of the buildings is now part of a ceramics works.

Rebecca Spring, wife of the owner of Eagleswood, was also an Abolitionist. When John Brown and his companions were taken at Harper's Ferry and condemned to death, Mrs. Spring wrote to Aaron Dwight Stevens, one of the condemned men, and asked that she might bring his body for burial to Eagleswood. He replied that he was indifferent to what happened to his body after the spirit had left it, but agreed that she might bury him if his poverty-stricken father did not claim his body. Albert Hazlett, friend and conspirator with Stevens, also wrote to Mrs. Spring asking her to bury him by the side of his comrade. She visited the two men in the Baltimore jail and supplied them with food and clothing. After the execution the bodies were brought to Eagleswood and buried. In the 1890's the bodies were disinterred and sent to North Elba, N. Y., to lie with that of John Brown on his old farm.

The Lehigh Valley Railroad, which came to Perth Amboy in 1859, forecast the town's industrialization. After the Civil War, Perth Amboy gave itself wholeheartedly to the wave of industrial expansion that rolled over the land. With the establishment of new factories, foreign workers moved into the city, and the descendants of early residents gradually withdrew.

Among the factories that followed the already firmly established ceramic industry was the refinery of M. Guggenheim Sons, a most important link in the chain of mines and smelters that in 1900 acquired control of the American Smelting and Refining Company. In 1912 the workers at the refineries struck against the 12-hour shift. Armed guards and strikebreakers broke the strike after a number of bloody street battles that resulted in the death of four strikers.

POINTS OF INTEREST

1. The WESTMINSTER *(private),* 149 Kearny Ave., is the heart of Perth Amboy's history. But the rambling mass of weather-worn brick standing at the summit of Kearny Ave. hill contains little more than the foundation and the shell of the first two floors of the house, built on this site between 1768 and 1770 at the order of the Proprietors of East New Jersey. The original house was rented from the Proprietors in 1774 by William Franklin, last Royal Governor. Benjamin Franklin visited his son here before the outbreak of the Revolution but left when it was apparent that William would not change his allegiance. At midnight of June 17, 1776, Capt. Nathaniel Heard of Woodbridge and his Continental troops broke into the house and arrested Franklin. Mrs. Franklin remained for a time, but shortly afterwards the Colonials established Revolutionary headquarters here.

On July 2, 1776, Washington, anticipating that the British would attempt to sail up the Raritan and so drive a wedge between the American armies in New York and Philadelphia, installed General Mercer here to lead Perth Amboy troops in a counteroffensive. Mercer withdrew from Perth Amboy in December and joined Washington in the retreat from New York. Immediately after the American retreat, General Howe occupied Perth Amboy and used the Governor's House as headquarters.

After the Revolution the house was neglected; it was sold and resold and survived two fires. It was rebuilt as Brighton House in 1815. Matthias

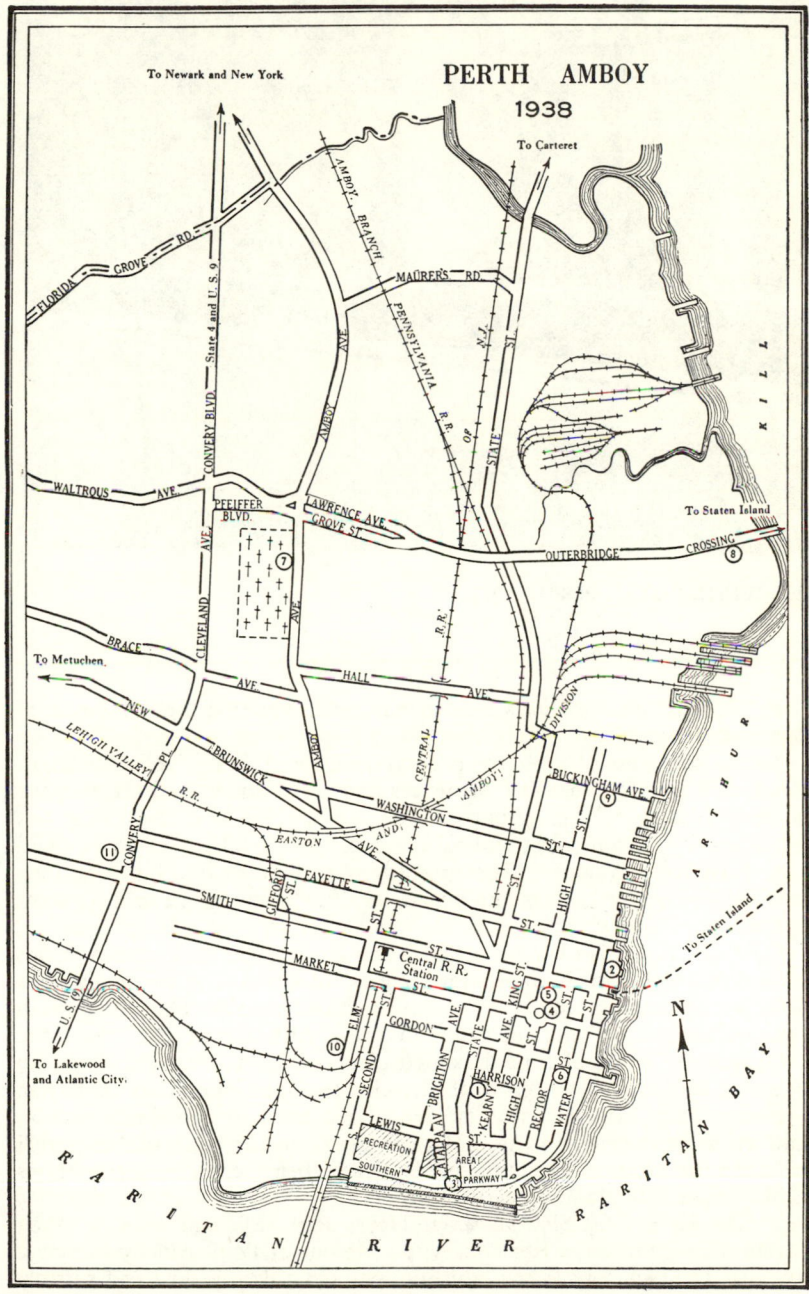

PERTH AMBOY
1938

THE WESTMINSTER, PERTH AMBOY

Bruen, at one time America's richest man, later acquired the hotel and re-named it Bruen House.

Bruen's son, who inherited the property, conveyed it to "The Presbyterian Board of Relief for Disabled Ministers and the Widows and Orphans of Deceased Ministers." This group called the place The Westminster. It was abandoned by them in 1903 and reverted to the Bruen heirs who then sold it to real estate developers. The grounds were divided into building lots, and The Westminster, after another series of sales, finally became a rooming house.

2. PARKER CASTLE *(private)*, Water St. one block N. of Smith St., is the oldest house in Perth Amboy. It was the home of many generations of the Parker family, prominent in local and State affairs. The rear portion was erected in 1723, and the front in 1789. At one time the site of the tall, gaunt old house of time-darkened clapboards was the most desirable in town. Standing at the crest of the rise that overlooks Raritan Bay, a three-story clapboarded section towers above the two-story brick section built on a lower level. In the midst of rusting debris and piles of gravel and sand the house is in imminent danger of being engulfed by factories inching their way along the water front.

3. KEARNY HOUSE *(private)*, Hayes Park, SE. end Catalpa Ave., was built in 1780 by the Kearnys, who were one of Perth Amboy's leading families. The two-story frame building, painted a dark yellow and scarcely

showing its age, was moved to the park from High Street when demolition was threatened. Repairs were begun in June 1938 to convert it into a museum.

Michael Kearny married Elizabeth Lawrence, Revolutionary poet and editor. This lady became known to the literary world of the day as "Madame Scribblerus," a pseudonym by no means a poor characterization of her verse. Of her half-brother, Capt. James Lawrence of "Don't give up the ship!" fame, Madame Scribblerus wrote:

> My brave, brave Jim's a sailor Jack
> Upon the treacherous sea—
> A sailor who loves poetry
> All taught to him by me.

4. CITY HALL, City Hall Square, a white brick building with green trim, is on the site of the Old Jail and Courthouse, ordered built in 1713. The courthouse, also rebuilt in 1767, served as a school, meeting place of the Colonial Assembly, and pulpit from which George Whitefield, the Billy Sunday of his day, preached some of his fire and brimstone sermons. The present mansard-roofed structure, erected in 1870, was built around part of the old courthouse.

In the square park in front of City Hall is a STATUE OF GEORGE WASHINGTON, done in terra cotta by Nils Nillson Alling, a local sculptor. The statue was commissioned and presented to the city by Scandinavian residents in 1896. In recent years this little park has been used for a picturesque demonstration of the progress of Americanization in the polyglot city. Local societies of expatriates of various European nations have taken to planting commemorative trees on the rim of the circle of the Washington Statue as a token of devotion to their new country.

5. SURVEYOR GENERAL'S OFFICE *(open Wed., adm. $1.50)*, City Hall Square, is a tiny, boxlike brick building of a dirty buff color, built just after the Civil War. Here are held the semiannual meetings of the General Proprietors of the Eastern Division of New Jersey, an amazing relic of the Colonial land-grant system. Whenever new land appears in New Jersey, the Proprietors of either the Eastern Division or the Western Division *(see BURLINGTON)* lay claim to it; and a quitclaim from the Proprietors is necessary for possession. For example, alluvial deposits from the Shrewsbury River created an island some years ago, which was duly sold. The corporation has valuable stock holdings. Any descendant of the original Proprietors who holds at least a 96th part of a share is entitled to a vote.

6. ST. PETER'S EPISCOPAL CHURCH, Rector and Gordon Sts., is the home of the oldest Episcopal Parish in New Jersey. In 1698 the Bishop of London, on the petition of several proprietors, appointed the Reverend Edward Perthuck to the parish. Services were held in one of the houses fitted out as a church. When the Society for the Propagation of the Gospel was organized in 1701, it sent to the Province the Reverend George Keith, who included Perth Amboy among his stops. A church was chartered in

1718 and completed in 1722. From its tower Perth Amboy patriots kept watch on the activities of Tory neighbors across the Kill. The present brick building of Gothic style was erected 1853 on the foundations of the earlier church. Within are the original pews, and a paten and chalice presented to the church in 1728. The adjoining CEMETERY contains the graves of Perth Amboy's earliest settlers. John Watson, the first portrait painter in America, and William Dunlap, the earliest American-born playwright to use native material, are buried here.

7. FIREMEN'S MONUMENT, Alpine Cemetery, 703 Amboy Ave., commemorates the death of nine firemen who were killed when their engine crashed into a locomotive June 15, 1921. The statue is of a walrus-moustached fireman in full regalia, holding the nozzle of a hose.

8. OUTERBRIDGE CROSSING *(toll: car and passengers 50¢),* approach E. end Grove St., is a cantilever span across Arthur Kill to Tottenville, Staten Island. The bridge was named for Eugenius H. Outerbridge, former chairman of the Port of New York Authority, which built it in 1928. From plaza to plaza the length is 10,200 feet, with truss spans of 2,100 feet and a clearance of 135 feet. A consistent money loser, the bridge has never enjoyed the traffic that was expected from the $10,000,-000 investment.

9. ATLANTIC TERRA COTTA PLANT *(open for group tours upon written application),* 59 Buckingham Ave., the first ceramic factory established in Perth Amboy, started operations in 1846 as A. Hall and Sons, manufacturers of porcelain household wares. It now specializes in terra cotta work from local clay. Products of its kilns were the pediment of the Philadelphia Museum of Art, and the roof of the new Supreme Court Building in Washington. The plant also supplied special variegated brick and gold tile with black glaze trim for the new Dutch Colonial Perth Amboy Post Office.

10. RARITAN COPPER WORKS of the International Smelting and Refining Co., a subsidiary of the Anaconda Copper Mining Co. *(open for student group tours upon written application),* S. end Elm St., is the foremost refining plant for copper, silver, and gold imported at Perth Amboy. Foreign nations send more than $1,000,000 a month in gold and silver into New Jersey through the port of Perth Amboy; a similar amount enters Perth Amboy via the port of New York, and an even greater quantity comes by rail from American mines. Much of this is refined here. All commercial forms of refined copper, such as wire bars and ingots, are produced here, in addition to by-products of refined silver and gold, platinum, palladium, selenium, tellurium, copper sulphate, and nickel sulphate. The plant is one of the largest in the world using the electrolytic process of refining.

11. OLD STONE HOUSE, Convery Pl. N. of Smith St., a one-and-one-half-story frame building with a new concrete front, was part of Eagleswood Military Academy and later served as a studio for George Inness, who lived in Perth Amboy for about three years—1865 to 1868. Everything but the foundations, walls and gambrel roof has been completely changed since Inness worked here. The building is now a roadhouse.

POINTS OF INTEREST IN ENVIRONS

General Motors·Assembly Plant, *13 m. (see Tour 1)*; Freneau Farm, *14.9 m. (see Tour 18)*; Marlpit Hall (museum), *17.9 m. (see Tour 22)*; Monmouth Battlefield, *28.4 m. (see Side Tour 18A)*.

Princeton

Railroad Station: Princeton Station, foot of University Pl., for Pennsylvania R.R.
Bus Station: 182 Nassau St. for Trenton Transit Co. and Greyhound; Bayard Lane and Stockton St. for Somerset Bus Co. (No local service.)
Taxis: One passenger within borough limits, 35¢; more than one passenger, 25¢ each.
Streetcars: Witherspoon and Spring Sts. for Trenton and Princeton Transit Co. (No local service.)
Accommodations: Two hotels; numerous inns, tourist homes, boarding houses.
Information Service: Princeton Travel Bureau, University Store, on campus W. of Nassau Hall; Borough Hall, Stockton St. opposite Princeton Battle Monument.
Theater and Motion Picture Houses: McCarter Theater; 3 motion picture houses.
Swimming: Brokaw Memorial Pool, open to townspeople during summer.
Skating: Hobart Baker Rink, open Tues. and Thurs. evenings, Sat. morning (adm. 40¢).
Boating: Carnegie Lake, Washington Rd., for crew racing and canoeing.
Golf: Springdale Golf Club, Stockton Pl. and College Rd.; greens fee, $2 week-days, $3 Sat., Sun. and holidays; $1.50 and $2 when accompanied by member.
Baseball: University Field, Olden St. and Prospect Ave.
Annual Events: All-Star Ice Carnival of Princeton Nursery School at Baker Rink in February; Talbott Music Festival of Westminster Choir School, Princeton Inter-scholastic Track Meet, both at Palmer Stadium during May; Princeton Interscholastic Tennis Championships, on university courts, May; Invitation Track Meet, Palmer Stadium, June; athletic contests at announced dates during collegiate year; Princeton Commencement Week, usually third week in June.

PRINCETON (200 alt., 6,992 pop.) lives for Princeton University. A division between town and campus cannot be made. The gates to the campus open on Nassau Street, the main thoroughfare, lined with shops that blazon the orange and black Tiger colors; the railroad station follows the collegiate Gothic style of the newer university buildings; stores, board-ing houses and hotels cater largely to Princeton men and their guests. Townspeople cheer Princeton football teams, attend commencements and gather for Princeton entertainments.

The aristocracy of the village, including resident Princeton graduates and trustees of the university, mingles freely with the faculty, forming a mature social group that serves as a stabilizing influence for the continuous flow of youth.

The old order is deeply rooted in the eighteenth century village, spread along a low ridge in one of the most pleasantly green sections of the State, but the bright scions of the twentieth century have been grafted onto the little town. Filling stations and lubritoriums elbow antique shops and old houses along Nassau Street where horns once sounded in the days of coach racing; and glistening store fronts yield abruptly at the second-floor level to age-darkened original clapboard.

Palmer Square, the $4,500,000 civic center intended to remake Princeton into a "square town," lies north of Nassau Street, along a 400-foot front between John and Baker Streets. The plot was partly occupied by Negro slums until 1936, when a corporation headed by Edgar Palmer, New Jersey zinc magnate, began reconstruction. Under the direction of Thomas Stapleton of New York, architect, it is expected that by 1941 Princeton's Colonial charm will be recaptured. Old Nassau Inn has gone; in its place stands a charming reproduction of a Colonial tavern, complete with gambrel roof, first floor overhang and low kitchen wing. But it is something of a shock to find the tavern firmly attached to a large, four-story, yellow brick structure which houses the guests.

The façade of the motion picture house, a native Colonial fieldstone gable flanked by little Colonial arcades attached to low wings, grows directly out of a massive brick wall—the body of a modern auditorium. Inside the theater, the walls of the foyer are finished in metal; the shell-shaped and serrated ceiling of the auditorium, based upon Dr. H. Lester Cooke's isophonic curve theory of the perfect reflection of sound, is called the first of its kind in the world. Rambling around the sides of the square is a series of smaller apartment units, each a reproduction of a particular Colonial prototype, each one highly pleasing, but in the mass giving the restless effect of a museum collection of architectural Americana.

The Pennsylvania Railroad and the university have combined to make Princeton a society center of New Jersey. Close enough to New York and Philadelphia for convenient commuting, the town is yet sufficiently secluded for businessmen, scholars, statesmen and scientists to retire to its retrospective and scholastic calm.

The business life of Princeton is largely sustained by the university. No manufacturing is permitted within the borough limits.

The advantages of the site, and the academic atmosphere generated by Princeton University have attracted other educational institutions. These include Princeton Theological Seminary, the Institute for Advanced Study, Rockefeller Institute for Medical Research, Hun Preparatory School, Westminster Choir School, St. Joseph's College, Mercer Junior College, Miss Fine's School and Country Day School.

The half-dozen Quaker families who settled in the Princeton area in 1696 were not the first in this region. Predating them by 15 years was Capt. Henry Greenland, that irascible insurgent who was instrumental in dissolving the Colonial legislature in 1681. His plantation, established the same year, occupied most of what is now the town. One of the Quaker settlers was Richard Stockton II, whose descendants played an important part in national affairs. At first the settlement was called Stony Brook after the small stream that borders two sides of Princeton, but in 1724 the residents chose the name of Prince's Town (later shortened to Princeton) supposedly because of the proximity to King's Town (Kingston). Princeton was an important coaching center then: sometimes as many as 15 coaches would start off each way on Nassau Street, part of the New York-Philadelphia highway.

The town was slow to build until the middle of the eighteenth century when Princeton University was moved here from Newark and a Presbyterian Church was formed. During the years prior to the Revolution both the students and townspeople were active in the cause for independence. The State government was organized in Princeton under the new constitution in 1776, and the Council of Safety, a wartime tribunal with official power, met in Princeton several times. The village became a target for Tory hatred; farms were plundered and families destroyed by the marauding British.

Toward sunrise of January 3, 1777, Washington and his main army of a scant 2,500 men approached Princeton after an all-night march over an ice-covered back road from Trenton, where Cornwallis and his superior main army slept in the belief that they would crush the Americans at sunrise. In Princeton were three British regiments under Colonel Mawhood, and three troops of dragoons.

Washington divided his troops at first, but then led the Pennsylvania militia to support the troops of General Mercer who had been bayonetted in an advance action. The British, in the face of the entire American Army, prepared for a heavy assault. Washington made several futile attempts to rally his tired troops. Finally he reined his horse facing the enemy and sat motionless. With Washington still between the lines, both sides leveled their rifles. A roar of musketry was followed by a shout from the Americans as the British lines gave way. When the smoke cleared, Washington—unharmed—urged his men on in pursuit.

The battle ended in Nassau Hall (where two of the British regiments had taken refuge) when a daring militia captain with a handful of men charged into the hall. About 100 of the enemy had been killed and nearly 300 were made prisoners. Although the American loss did not exceed 30, the brief fighting took a heavy toll of officers. General Mercer died of his wounds nine days later.

Washington led his tired men off on the Rocky Hill road, just in time to escape the pursuing forces of Cornwallis, and headed for winter encampment. The victory at Princeton, coming on the heels of the maneuver at Trenton a week earlier, went far toward establishing new confidence throughout the Colonies in Washington's tatterdemalion troops. Frederick the Great went so far as to characterize Washington's strategy as the most brilliant operation in all military history.

In the summer of 1777 the first State legislature met at Princeton, and was addressed by William Livingston, first Governor of the State. At these sessions the original State seal, first in the new Nation, was adopted.

From June to November of 1783 the town was the Nation's capital. Threatened in Philadelphia by unpaid soldiers who were imitating the Pennsylvania Line mutineers, the Continental Congress, "one by one, hurriedly in the night, fearing abduction by their threateners," left Pennsylvania and established offices at Princeton. To be close to the proceedings, Washington was summoned to Princeton. He moved with his family to Rocky Hill *(see Tour 8)*, where he lived for 3 months and wrote his historic farewell address to the army.

After the Revolution the quiet stability of Princeton was undisturbed

NASSAU HALL, PRINCETON

except by occasional student riots and, to a less extent, by the War of 1812, in which a number of Princeton men fought. In 1813 the borough of Princeton was reincorporated with added territory.

Princeton men were mainly responsible for drawing the town out of the stream of New York-Philadelphia traffic. It was largely their money that financed construction of the Camden and Amboy Railroad (1834) and the Delaware and Raritan Canal (1832), neither of which passed through the town.

Before and during the Civil War, Princeton was divided on the slave question. But when the many southern students did not return after their holidays in 1863, sympathy grew for the northern cause. Feeling was not unanimous, however, and even during the course of the war two pro-northern students were expelled for dousing a southern sympathizer under the town pump. More than 100 Princeton students served with commissions in the two armies.

After the Civil War the town had an abortive industrial boom. The New Jersey Iron Clad Roofing, Paint and Mastic Company, incorporated in 1868, evidently borrowed its name from Civil War naval vessels. Another company was formed in the same year to exploit a patented process for seasoning wood and preventing mold in fabrics, but the business was hampered by a series of fires and explosions.

The borough obtained a new 49-section charter in 1873, which drew the following comment from a contemporary historian: "It is like a garment cut much too large for the person who is to wear it, but the town may grow up to the dimensions of this charter in time." This cautious prophecy has been partly fulfilled; the 1880 population of 3,209 was increased by a scant 700 in the ensuing 20 years, but was finally doubled in the 1930 census.

The Spanish-American War had little effect upon the then rapidly expanding university, although many students volunteered for service. More than 5,000 Princeton men were in uniform during the World War, and a scholarship was founded in memory of each of the 151 who died in service.

Princeton University

Princeton University, mellowed by the traditions of two centuries of student life, is the product of a continued liberalization of the educational concept upon which it was founded. It was a wave of practical frontier students that first jolted the college from its narrow position as a Presbyterian school; it was a group of forward-looking educators who attracted other men of international distinction to Princeton's service; and it was the liberal spirit generated by both these forces that has directed the continued growth and widening influence of the Nation's fourth oldest university.

The 800-acre campus, separated only by Nassau Street from the town, slopes gradually to Lake Carnegie. With Nassau Hall as a nucleus, the campus reflects the varying architectural tastes and styles of the 180 years during which the buildings were erected. But the lawns, the trees and the spreading ivy give a feeling of harmony. Nassau Hall and the older dormitories nearby sound a frank note of the determined righteousness of the Presbyterian founders. Farther from Nassau Hall, the buildings are usually collegiate Gothic, a pleasing, refreshing and refined style based upon the collegiate architecture of Tudor England. Short flights of steps lead from one building level to another, following the contour of the land. The neatly trimmed, crisscrossing paths do not follow a formal plan; they were laid after students had marked out a trail by constant usage. Many students use bicycles in going to and from classes, but there is no feeling of crowding until the machines are stacked in piles in the entries of classrooms.

Princeton offers varied liberal arts and science subjects from which the student must elect 36 semester courses in his four years of study for the Bachelor of Arts degree. He completes his required credits with a comprehensive examination and a thesis in the field of his major. The program of humanities is designed to give a broad survey of contemporary life with a specialized course in a particular field. The School of Public and International Affairs, conducted principally for juniors and seniors preparing for a public career, comprises the departments of history, politics, economics and social institutions. Each student in the division is required to take "the conference on public affairs," an undergraduate seminar-type course concerned with contemporary problems. The two professional schools, engineering and architecture, and the School of Public and International Affairs have both undergraduate and graduate departments. The Graduate School offers courses leading to Master of Arts, Master of Fine Arts and Doctor of Philosophy degrees. Fellowships and scholarships are available to exceptional students.

In the sophomore, junior and senior years, class instruction in the reading departments (philosophy, languages, history, etc.) is augmented by informal conferences on the extra-class reading. This arrangement, known as the Preceptorial System, is "meant not only to stimulate interest in the subject-matter of the course, but also to bring students into more intimate contact with their teachers than is possible in the more formal exercises of the classroom." Six or seven men meet with the preceptor in informal conferences, aimed at discovering and correcting misconceptions or confusion in the student's mind and stimulating and enlightening him with regard to the study in hand.

The university has a faculty of 365. Undergraduate students (for the school year ending in 1938) numbered 2,388, and advanced students totaled 277. A Negro has never been admitted.

Princeton has always made an effort to prepare its students for public service. During its first 20 years the majority of graduates entered the Presbyterian ministry and were instrumental in founding many important schools and colleges. Under Witherspoon, the fighting parson, the trend turned toward political service. Among his graduates were a President, a Vice President, 10 Cabinet officers, 12 Governors, and scores of Congressmen and State legislators. Of the graduates from 1800 to 1850, 1 out of 12 became members of the executive, judicial or legislative branches of State governments. This tradition of public service led Woodrow Wilson to describe the Princeton of Witherspoon's day as "the seminary of statesmen."

Princeton men are required by college regulations to "conduct themselves in a manner becoming scholars and gentlemen." By way of clarification it is set forth that students may not bring liquor into their rooms, nor there entertain a woman alone at any time nor, when the woman is attended, after 6 p.m. After every examination the student signs a pledge on his "honor as a gentleman" that he has not cheated. Participation in a riot—considered almost a right by students of a century ago—is ground for dismissal. Unless exempted by the dean, freshmen and sophomores must attend at least one-half of the Sunday chapel services, and all undergraduates are forbidden to maintain or operate a motor vehicle in Princeton or vicinity. Marriage is also prohibited for undergraduates, except with the dean's approval.

Except for these and other minor regulations, the Princeton student is relatively free. A minority has participated actively in liberal factions of national student groups and peace movements. The Veterans of Future Wars, an organization formed to ridicule out of existence the soldier's bonus bill, did not accomplish this purpose, but when the group disbanded the officers pointed out that they had "awakened the people of the country to the absurdity of war." In a more frivolous manner, Princeton men temporarily set up a bureau to offer solace by mail to the lonely hearts of Vassar College.

Many students work their way through college, but the campus also has its counterpart of town society. This consists of the heirs of blue-book families, the cosmopolitan style-setters for the collegiate world. Between these two groups lies the great bulk of students. As upperclassmen, most Princeton men eat in one of several clubs, the Princeton substitute for the fraternity system. Fronting on Prospect Avenue, the clubs range in architectural style from English Tudor to Georgian Colonial. Wealthy students week-end in New York or Philadelphia, or sometimes take advantage of opportunities to visit friends at one of the eastern colleges for women. After the spring vacation, seniors are permitted to wear "beer suits," white canvas jackets and overalls that fit loosely as pajamas and wrinkle just as easily.

By choosing carefully a relatively small percentage of those who apply for admission, Princeton has maintained high standards. The faculty is distinguished by many scholars of international reputation.

The College of New Jersey (as Princeton was first called) was opened at Elizabeth in 1747 as the result of a movement, begun in 1739 by the Synod of Philadelphia, to meet a need for Presbyterian educators. The original faculty consisted of one man, President Jonathan Dickinson, who was assisted by a tutor in instructing the six students. Upon the death of Dickinson, the college was moved to the Newark parsonage of the new president, the Rev. Aaron Burr (father of the Vice President). There the first commencement was held November 9, 1748.

The account book of Samuel Livermore, class of 1752, preserved in the

UNIVERSITY CHAPEL, PRINCETON

library, gives a picture of student life. For his trip from Boston to New York, 19 days, he carried:

5 quarts of West Ind. Rum	£1	7s	6d
¼ ℔. Tea @ 48s		12s	
Canister		6s	
1 doz. Fowls	2	8s	
2 ℔. loaf sugar @ 8s		16s	
1 doz. & 8 lemons	1	9s	
3 ℔s. butter		12s	
box		5s	
	7	15s	6d

Mr. Livermore's wardrobe included, among other things, 13 shirts and 7 pairs of stockings, but only 1 pair of breeches. For his studies he carried a Bible, Latin and Greek testaments and grammars, a Latin dictionary and lexicon, Ward's *Introduction to Mathematics,* Gordon's *Geography,* and a copy each of Virgil and Cicero.

Seeking a new site, the trustees favored Princeton as the halfway point between New York and Philadelphia. The larger town of New Brunswick, however, was first given an opportunity to provide land and money; neither condition was met, and Princeton's grant was thereupon accepted in 1752. Four years later the college was moved to the newly completed Nassau Hall, "the largest stone building in the Colonies."

Money raising was a serious problem. The stern Presbyterian fathers saw nothing irregular, however, in obtaining funds from lotteries. Five of the seven authorized by the legislature brought not only money but also disputes with the winners, and the last two were abandoned.

A growing spirit of revolt against English authority crystallized when the Rev. John Witherspoon, who had been brought from his native Scotland in 1768 to direct the college, urged the Colonies to declare themselves free. "We are not only ripe [for independence]," he thundered, "but rotting." The students promptly organized a militia company, and for almost eight years the college existed precariously. Nassau Hall was alternately occupied by both armies, yet all commencements except that of 1777 took place on schedule.

Witherspoon accomplished the long, uphill task of reorganizing and rebuilding the college after the war. Upon his death in 1794 Dr. Samuel Stanhope Smith, his son-in-law, became president and the college passed into what has been called the "reign of terror." Although Presbyterian leaders criticized Dr. Smith for his "liberality," he established such strict rules for student conduct that the undergraduates beat their tutors and discharged huge cannon crackers. The burning of Nassau Hall in 1802 was laid to students; half a dozen young men were expelled.

Dr. Smith's successor, the Rev. Ashbel Green, devised an even more tyrannical discipline that led to the "rebellion of 1817." Shortly after midnight on a January morning the students locked up their tutors and set fire to the outbuildings. When townspeople came to the aid of the college authorities, the rebels barricaded themselves in Old North and held it for a day by virture of cutlasses and pistols. The disturbance was finally quelled, but until Dr. Green resigned in 1822 he continued to make rules and to put all of his remarkable powers at work to enforce them.

While these administrators were partly occupied in limiting student freedom, they were also instituting liberal educational reforms. The establishment of professorships in natural history and chemistry during Smith's administration was the first provision for regular study of these subjects in an American college, outside of medical curricula.

Under the relatively peaceful administrations of Presidents Carnahan and Maclean, an increased enrollment and sizable gifts made possible new buildings and curricular extensions. A law school, added for a short period during Dr. Carnahan's tenure, indicated that the College of New Jersey was outgrowing the limits of a classical educational institution.

Under Carnahan's administration the lightening of discipline was demonstrated in a curious way. The students adopted a coverall gown of brilliantly figured calico which hid any defects of hasty dressing. As John Jackson Haley of the class of 1842 wrote to his father: "In regard to a loose gown, I observe they are very fashionable here, made like overcoats with plain rolling collars much like the 'OLD fashioned open vest collar', & wadded skirts. The students wear them to Prayers, recitation & about college. They extend about half way between the knee & foot, in length, are made of fancy calicoes, to suit the taste."

During the term of the university's most loved president, Dr. James McCosh (1868–1888), the system of elective studies, now functioning in every major university, was adopted. The change upset the rigid theory of church-sponsored instruction, and paved the way for the graduate school of specialized study, opened in 1877.

Many anecdotes about McCosh are still told. Making the rounds one night, the president noticed that a light was burning after hours in a student's room. McCosh knocked sharply on the door and demanded admittance. "Who is it?" the student called. "It's me, Dr. McCosh," was the answer. "Go to!" came the prompt retort. "If you were Dr. McCosh, you would have said, 'It's I!'" The President, his reputation as a grammarian at stake, withdrew in silence and in later years told the story on himself. It was a Hallowe'en custom to take Dr. McCosh's old closed buggy from the carriage house and drag it miles into the country. In 1887 the students were successful in getting the buggy out quietly; they trotted and ran with it almost to Kingston, where they turned into a farmyard. At that moment, Dr. McCosh poked his head through the window and said, "Thanks so much for the ride, boys. Now, if you will, please drive me home again."

A fuller measure of personal freedom and responsibility for students was achieved in 1893 when the honor system of unsupervised examinations was instituted. During the 14-year term of President Francis L. Patton 17 new buildings were erected and on October 22, 1896—the 150th anniversary of the chartering of the College of New Jersey—the name was changed to Princeton University.

Woodrow Wilson, the first Princeton president who was not a clergyman, is remembered for three great reform fights. He won the first, for the institution of the preceptor system, an adaptation of the English tutorial system. Next he campaigned for the division of the school into colleges or "quads" in which the students would live and eat. This plan threatened the exclusive eating societies supported by wealthy students who fostered what William Allen White has called "the Junior Union League Club" attitude. Influential alumni aided the student opposition, and Wilson lost.

The loss of his third fight had much to do with Wilson's resignation and his entry into politics. The controversy concerned the location of the graduate school, but it was deeper than that. Wilson wished the school to be an integral and democratic part of Princeton, while a group of trustees led by Dean Andrew F. West insisted upon a secluded institution, associated with the university in name only. Carrying his fight to sympathetic alumni in the west, Wilson made a national issue of his thesis: "I cannot accede to the acceptance of gifts upon terms which take the educational policy of the university out of the hands of the trustees and faculty, and permit it to be determined by those who give money." He won the first engagement when he persuaded the trustees to decline a $1,000,000 gift. But when a second gift of $10,000,000 (which later shrank to $2,000,000) came from the Isaac C. Wyman estate, with Dean West named as executor, Wilson knew that refusal would be impossible. He was beaten.

Princeton has not yet raised a monument to its illustrious president. No granite shaft, however, will be a more fitting memorial than the development of Wilson's ideal for his university: "Princeton in the Nation's service." The culmination of this ideal educationally was the establishment of the School of Public and International Affairs in 1930.

John Grier Hibben, professor of philosophy, was elected to succeed Wilson in 1912; he served until a year before his death in an automobile accident in 1933. Under President Hibben the administrative reorganization of the university was virtually completed. Faculty autonomy was assured, and greater economic security for the teaching staff was provided. President Hibben introduced a pioneering plan of study designed to foster the individual initiative of the student. The university expanded both materially and scholastically, particularly bolstering its work in pure science. Since 1933 the president has been Dr. Harold Willis Dodds, formerly professor of politics at Princeton, and editor of *National Municipal Review*.

Important work has been done by two survey groups. The industrial relations section has made several revealing studies of working conditions, wage levels and capital-labor relationships; the Princeton Local Government Survey has published a series of graphic analyses of the financial and administrative organization of New Jersey municipalities. A number of its suggestions have been incorporated in State laws.

The Princeton University Press is doing distinguished work in typography. In addition to publishing noteworthy texts and theses, it produces books of verse and fiction. Although a separate institution, the press is under direction of the university trustees, faculty and alumni.

UNIVERSITY POINTS OF INTEREST

1. FITZ RANDOLPH GATEWAY, named for Nathaniel Fitz Randolph, who gave the land for the first building, is the main campus entrance. The gateway, with its great wrought-iron gates and stone piers crowned with eagles, is the work of McKim, Mead and White. The gates are opened only on special occasions. Students regularly use the small side entrances.

2. NASSAU HALL, the first campus building, is a three-story sandstone structure, with low pitched roof surmounted by a white wooden lantern. When Robert Smith of Philadelphia erected Nassau Hall in 1756, he produced all the building he could for the money and wasted very little on superfluous ornament. Stylistically it follows the later Renaissance of England. The entrance gable motif of arched doorway with stone balcony and arched window above is disproportionate, but age has lent the building a soft dignity, and ivy has relieved the Presbyterian severity of the rhyth-

mic rows of windows. Sleek bronze tigers, the work of A. Phimister Proctor, flank the entrance steps. The tiger, the Princeton symbol, is derived from the orange and black colors on the Princeton Heraldic device.

Each year another ivy vine is planted by the graduating class. Stones bearing the class numerals are set in the building after a custom begun in 1870.

To honor Princeton's war dead the entrance of the building was remodeled in 1920 as a MEMORIAL HALL. Beyond Memorial Hall is the FACULTY ROOM, originally used as the college chapel. In this room funeral services of the Aaron Burrs, father and son, were held, and here Washington received the thanks of the Congress at the end of the war. On the walls are portraits of Woodrow Wilson; William, Prince of Orange and Nassau, for whom the building was named; and Washington, by Charles Wilson Peale, in a frame once used for a portrait of George II. The portrait is said to have been decapitated by a shell when Alexander Hamilton bombarded the British troops barricaded in the building. It was at Nassau Hall that Congress, frightened out of Philadelphia, received the first official news of the Peace of Paris (1783) ending the Revolution, and two days later received the first accredited representative of a foreign power, the Minister of the Netherlands.

The entire building is used for administrative purposes, although until the beginning of the 19th century it housed the dormitory, refectory, classrooms and chapel.

3. The DEAN'S HOUSE, NW. of Nassau Hall, facing Nassau St., is now the official residence of the Dean of the Faculty. It was built at the same time as Nassau Hall for the president's house, and was used by all presidents from 1756 to 1879. John Adams, later President of the United States, wrote in his diary of a visit to the fiery Witherspoon in 1774. On a study window is an inscription scratched on the glass in 1804.

4. TWO GIANT SYCAMORES, each 90 feet high and 3 feet in diameter, are the only ones left of the row of STAMP ACT TREES which were planted before the Dean's House in 1765 at the order of the university Board of Trustees. Because they were planted the same year that England passed the Stamp Act, they have always been associated with that legislation.

5. FIRST PRESBYTERIAN CHURCH, Nassau St., is a Greek Revival structure with columns *in antis,* flanked by rectangular unembellished walls. Built in 1835, the church is the third on the site. Before erection of the first building in 1766, the congregation attended chapel services conducted by presidents of the college, who were then Presbyterian ministers. During the Revolution the original structure suffered at the hands of both the British and Colonial troops. From 1766 to 1896 college commencements were held in the successive churches.

6. MADISON HALL, SE. corner Nassau St. and University Pl., houses the university commons. Erected in 1916 and designed in the collegiate Gothic style by Day and Klauder, the walls are of local fieldstone with unusually delicate Gothic detail. The hall is composed of three units, each containing two refectories and connected to a central kitchen unit. Fresh-

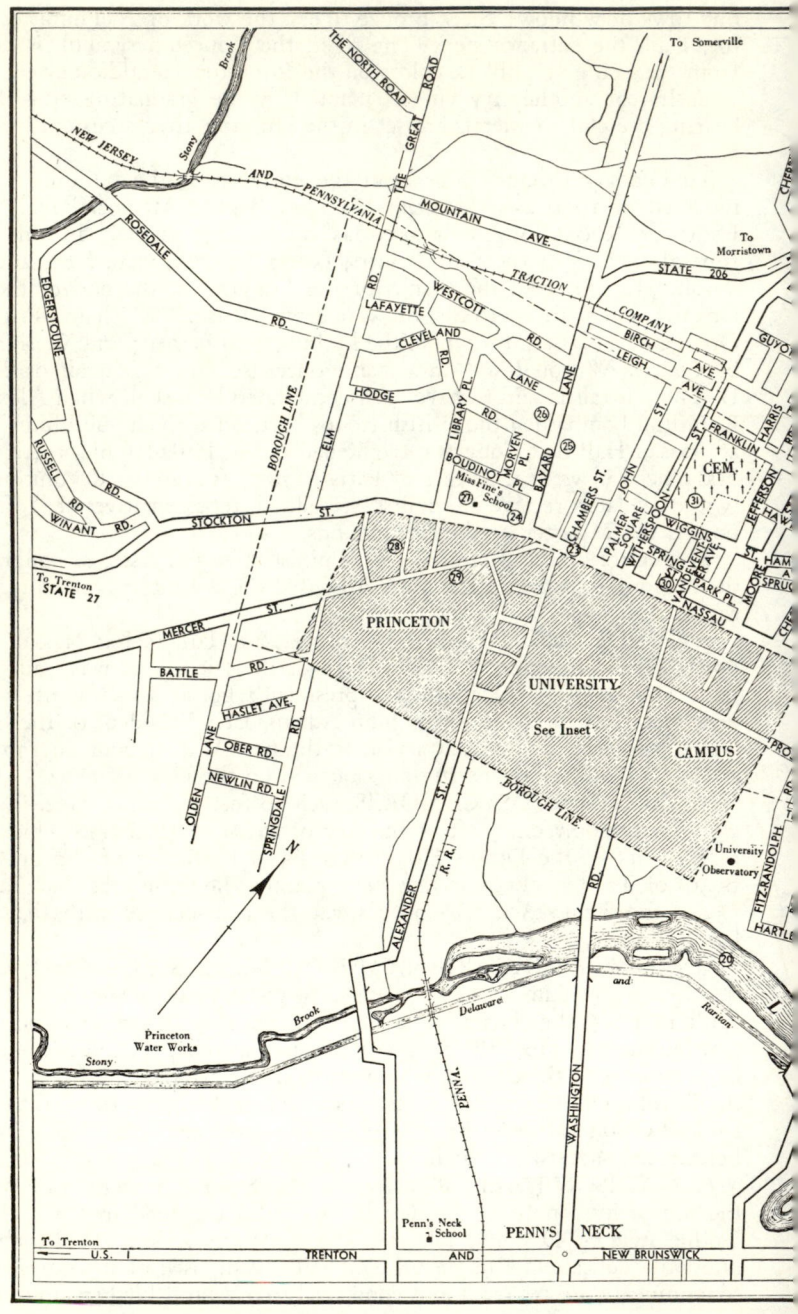

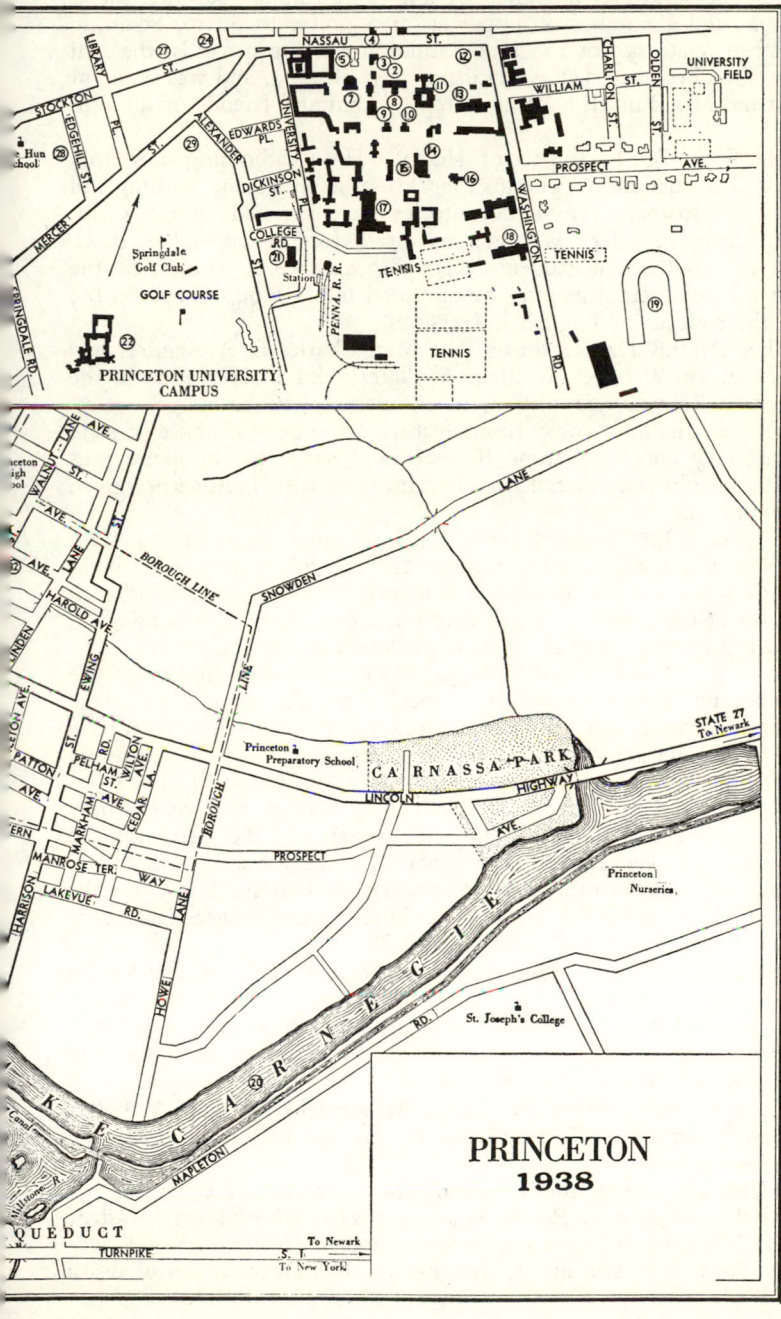

PRINCETON UNIVERSITY CAMPUS

PRINCETON
1938

men and sophomores are compelled by university rule to take their meals at Madison, and a number of upperclassmen prefer to do so. Standing on the approximate site of the Fitz Randolph burying grounds, the hall was named for President James Madison, class of 1771, and was paid for by gifts from Mrs. Russell Sage and from alumni and friends of the university.

RUSSELL SAGE TOWER is part of HOLDER HALL, adjoining dormitory on the east. The quadrangle contains the CLOISTER, with stone vaulting and lively Gothic ornament. These dormitories were planned on the quadrangle principle, President Wilson's substitute for the upperclass clubs. His thought was that the students occupying each court would—by the very proximity of their situation—be annealed into a group, much on the order of the colleges of English universities.

7. ALEXANDER HALL, the gift of Mrs. Charles E. Alexander, was built in 1892. The architect, William A. Potter, used an adaptation of the Richardsonian Romanesque without much success. The building is semicircular in plan; its most conspicuous feature is the great expanse of slate roof, broken by enormous stone dormers and supported on ponderous arches. The interior is decorated with Byzantine mosaics. Lectures are given in this auditorium.

8. A REVOLUTIONARY CANNON, in the main quadrangle behind Nassau Hall, with only the breech above the ground, is the center of an old tradition and the theme of the students' "Cannon Song." At each commencement the graduates break clay pipes over the "Big Cannon," as it is known, to indicate the severing of college ties.

9 and 10. CLIO HALL and WHIG HALL, the homes of two of the oldest collegiate literary societies in America, are the work of A. Page Brown. Identical in design, they are the epitome of the Greek Revival style —white marble reproductions of Grecian temples with Ionic hexastyle porticoes. Both were built as replacements in 1893. Originally the Cliosophic Society was known as the Well-Meaning Society, and what is now the Whig Society was the Plain Dealing Society. In the buildings are lecture rooms, libraries and recreation rooms for members.

A CANNON, sunk into the ground between the two buildings, was the object of a famous quarrel (the "Cannon War") with Rutgers University students in 1875 *(see NEW BRUNSWICK)*.

11. The UNIVERSITY LIBRARY *(open 8 a.m.-12 midnight; Sun. 2 p.m.-12 midnight; summer 8 a.m.-5 p.m.)* is formed by the architecturally unhappy union of the Chancellor Green and Pyne Library buildings. The two brown sandstone structures are connected by a room containing the delivery desk and the card catalog.

The CHANCELLOR GREEN BUILDING, designed by William A. Potter and erected in 1873, is of Tudor Gothic design. The building contains the general reading room.

PYNE LIBRARY, the southern half of the combined structure, erected 1897 and also designed by Potter, is a heavy Victorian building. Most of the library's 900,000 volumes and 116,000 unbound pamphlets and periodicals are kept here. The library also has the Hutton collection of death masks, the William Seymour theater collection, almost 300 papyri, a collection of cuneiform tablets, and a large number of documents and other special collections.

12. JOSEPH HENRY HOUSE *(private)*, SW. corner Nassau St. and Washington Rd., a severely simple, three-story yellow stone dwelling, is the residence of the Dean of the College. Designed by Professor Henry in the Classic Revival style and built in 1838, the house was moved to its present site in 1925. From 1832 to 1848 his benign features and vigorous frame were familiar on the campus and in Nassau Hall, where he taught classes in natural philosophy. Henry left the university to become the first director and secretary of the Smithsonian Institution, a position that he held until his death in 1878. His achievements in science, especially in electricity, and his activity in the organization of scientific groups, won broad recognition.

13. The UNIVERSITY CHAPEL, erected 1928, is of Gothic design. It is austere, reserved, and somewhat "cathedralesque" in its delicacy. Into the 72-foot-high arched nave and transept a deep blue light filters through stained glass windows. Seats for 2,000 persons make this one of the three largest college chapels in the world; the others are the University of Chicago chapel and the chapel of King's College, Cambridge University, England. On the heads of architects Cram and Ferguson have been poured both the vindictiveness of outraged stylists and the high praise of appreciative architectural authorities in a battle that began when the chapel was erected and has been vigorously continued.

14. The MUSEUM OF HISTORIC ART *(open 2-5; summer by appointment)* is a two-story structure of mottled yellow brick, designed by A. Page Brown in a modified Romanesque style, popular when the building was erected in 1889. In addition to the finest collection of Veronese art in the country, the museum contains exhibits of coins, medals, gems, marbles, plaster casts of ivory objects and representative art of the Far East, the Near East and Europe. Notable among the paintings is that of Aaron Burr, the younger, believed to be the work of Gilbert Stuart.

15. McCORMICK HALL, adjoining the art museum, was erected in 1922–26. The three-story building, designed by Cram and Ferguson in a free adaptation of several styles, is constructed of brown sandstone and yellow stucco. The structure houses the school of architecture, the art department, the Marquand Library of Art and some 340,000 architectural photographs.

16. PROSPECT, the large mansion set in spacious grounds S. of McCosh Walk, is the home of the president of the university. The house was built by John Notman in 1849 on the site of Col. George Morgan's home, and was acquired by the university in 1878.

17. The UNIVERSITY GYMNASIUM, erected 1903 from the plans of Cope and Stewardson, harmonizes with the collegiate Gothic style of architecture. The main entrance opens into a trophy hall where athletic prizes are displayed. Murals painted by William Yarrow show 13 kinds of college sports. The BROKAW MEMORIAL, built in 1892 and adjoining the gymnasium, contains the swimming pool.

18. GUYOT HALL, SE. corner of the campus on Washington Rd., a light red brick, four-story building topped by four towers, is the home of the departments of geology and biology. An ornate structure in Tudor-Gothic style, it was designed by Parrish and Schroeder and built in 1909. In the eastern section are zoological, anatomical, physiological and botanical laboratories. The GEOLOGICAL and BIOLOGICAL MUSEUMS have collections of fossil plants, vertebrates and minerals. More than 40,000 volumes are in the departmental libraries.

19. PALMER MEMORIAL STADIUM, built in 1914 from the design of H. J. Hardenbergh, is a U-shaped structure of reinforced concrete with seats for more than 50,000 persons. Until the fall of 1937, the excellently coached football teams of Herbert O. Crisler performed for the enrichment of the Princeton tradition and the more tangible enrichment of the athletic association. The association operates, however, under a standing deficit of $75,000. Although President Dodds attracted national attention in 1936 by his request that spectators keep liquor out of the stadium, the janitors still pick up empty bottles after every game. Invitation track meets annually attract large crowds.

20. LAKE CARNEGIE, on Washington Rd., formed by damming Stony Brook and Millstone Creek, is used for intercollegiate boat races in the spring, and for interclass contests in the autumn. The lake, 3.5 m. long and 800 ft. wide, was the gift of Andrew Carnegie in 1906.

21. McCARTER THEATER, University Place, designed by D. K. Este Fisher of the class of 1913, is a stone building with a small tower. Its rough-textured red stonework is in sharp contrast to the blue-gray tone of the other Gothic buildings. Thomas N. McCarter, of the class of 1888 and president of Public Service Corporation, joined with the Triangle Club in providing funds for erection of the theater in 1929. Broadway companies on tour use the well-equipped stage, but the most important production is the annual musical show of the Triangle Club, the Princeton dramatic organization. The show goes on tour each year; many of its original songs have become popular.

22. The GRADUATE COLLEGE, built in 1913, stands where part of the Battle of Princeton was fought. The collegiate Gothic buildings are grouped around a central quadrangle known as THOMSON COLLEGE, named for Senator John R. Thomson, whose widow gave the site. Adjoining the quadrangle is CLEVELAND TOWER *(open on special request)*, 173 feet high, a memorial to President Grover Cleveland, who was a Princeton resident and a university trustee. In a memorial chamber at the base of the tower a curious echo is heard. Unhampered by any necessity of harmonizing his work with previous buildings, Ralph Adams Cram has produced a beautifully proportioned cluster of Gothic dormitories that seem to grow easily from the base of the great tower, a masterpiece of Gothic form and detail, expressing—as the architect explained—the aspirations of higher learning.

PROCTER HALL, gift of the soap manufacturer, the late William Cooper Procter, member of the class of 1883, is the refectory and the chief public room. A memorial window, the work of Mr. and Mrs. William Willet,

GRADUATE SCHOOL AND CLEVELAND MEMORIAL TOWER, PRINCETON

who made the chancel window at West Point Military Academy, represents the Light of the World illuminating the seven liberal arts. The lower section shows Christ, as a child in the temple, under instruction by members of the Sanhedrin, the ancient Jewish council and tribunal. Seven lancet windows above contain the figures of the seven Liberal Arts. Pure and rather primitive colors are used in a treatment redolent of the 14th century. The Holy Grail window by Charles J. Connick illustrates the familiar legend. A great organ, intricate carving over the fireplace, and portraits about the hall make this one of the most impressive of the campus buildings.

OTHER POINTS OF INTEREST

23. INSTITUTE FOR ADVANCED STUDY, 20 Nassau St., has its administrative headquarters in a five-story, red brick office building, the tallest in Princeton. Academic work is carried on in Princeton University

buildings. The institute was organized in 1930 when Louis Bamberger, Newark merchant, and his sister, Mrs. Felix Fuld, contributed $5,000,000 to enable scholars to continue independent research beyond the Ph.D. level "under the guidance and stimulus of distinguished men." Actual work in mathematics began in 1933. In 1934 an anonymous gift of $1,000,000 made possible the organization of a school of economics and politics; a school of humanistic studies was added in 1935. Dr. Abraham Flexner is the institute director (1939); the best-known faculty member is Dr. Albert Einstein, naturalized German refugee. Einstein leads a quiet life in a small frame house with his daughter and secretary; he is seen occasionally at the motion picture houses and at McCarter Theater. The great physicist has been known to put aside his papers in order to solve a problem in simpler mathematics for a delegation of prep school boys who had failed to find the answer in an examination.

24. The PRINCETON BATTLE MONUMENT, intersection of Nassau, Mercer and Stockton Sts., is a 50-foot block of Indiana limestone with high relief figures of Washington leading his troops, urged on by a woman representing Liberty. General Mercer, who was mortally wounded in the battle, is distinguishable among the figures. The monument is the work of Frederick W. MacMonnies.

25. AVALON *(private)*, 59 Bayard Lane, so named by Dr. Henry van Dyke, writer and poet, is a three-story yellow stucco house with a spacious encircling veranda, an example of the southern influence. White wooden Corinthian columns rise two stories in front, and smaller Ionic columns are at the side entrance. It is believed that part of the house was built by Dr. Edmund Bainbridge in the 18th century. The widow and descendants of Dr. van Dyke still live there.

26. WESTLAND *(only garden open 9-5 weekdays)*, 58 Bayard Lane, a three-story dwelling built in 1854 by Commodore Stockton, stands in a large grove of old trees. The big yellow stucco house with white and green shutters was the home of ex-President Cleveland, who named it Westland in honor of his friend, Dean West of the Princeton Graduate School, and is still the residence of Cleveland's widow, now Mrs. Thomas Jex Preston Jr.

27. MORVEN *(private)*, Stockton St. and Library Pl., is the result of numerous additions to the home originally built in 1701 on land purchased from William Penn by Richard Stockton, grandfather of the Signer of the Declaration of Independence. The house, set behind a broad lawn and old trees, is of yellow-painted brick, three stories high with two-story wings. The Greek Revival porch has blotted out most of the dignity and grace of the original Colonial portion. When Cornwallis, pursuing Washington in 1776, made his headquarters here, the British dug up the garden and found two of three chests known to have been buried by the Stocktons. Washington, Lafayette, Rochambeau and other prominent Colonial figures were entertained at Morven.

28. The BARRACKS *(private)*, 32 Edgehill St., was a portion of the earliest Stockton Homestead, erected early in the 18th century. Two and one-half stories in height, the fieldstone house is a plain, rectangular struc-

ture with its side to the street and its entrance on a short lane. A high stone wall has a springhouse in one corner. British occupancy of the house in 1777 is said to have been the origin of its name, but historians agree that the Barracks was probably named during the French and Indian War.

29. PRINCETON THEOLOGICAL SEMINARY, Mercer St. between Library Pl. and Alexander St., is the oldest seminary of the Presbyterian Church in America. It was established as a graduate school for training clergymen in 1812. The buildings, spread out on almost two square blocks, are of brown stone or brick. Almost 200 students, including many from foreign countries, attend the seminary.

30. BAINBRIDGE HOUSE, 158 Nassau St., is the home of the Princeton Public Library *(open 10-9 daily, except Sun.; summer 10-11, 3-9; Sat. 10-1).* The little, two-story frame house of faded yellow with a painted brick veneer is noteworthy for the fine proportion of the windows and the graceful door. Commodore William Bainbridge, commander of the *Constitution,* was born here; during the Revolution the house was headquarters for General Howe. Students and faculty members, as well as townspeople, use the library's 14,075 volumes.

31. PRINCETON CEMETERY, NE. corner Witherspoon and Wiggins Sts., is the resting place of many distinguished Americans. At the southern edge are the graves of all dead presidents of Princeton except Finley, Dickinson and Wilson. Vice President Aaron Burr is also buried in this plot; the legend of a secret burial by night is untrue, for Burr was given full honors at the college chapel. Elsewhere are the graves of Grover Cleveland, Paul Tulane, founder of Tulane University; members of the Colonial Assembly and the Continental Congress, and many Presbyterian leaders. The oldest monument, dated 1761, marks the grave of a young college student.

32. WESTMINSTER CHOIR SCHOOL, Chestnut St. opposite Hamilton Ave., comprises four modernized Georgian Colonial buildings of red brick, with slender Ionic columns and well-spaced dormers, erected in 1934. The gracefully proportioned structures were designed by Sherley W. Morgan, head of the Princeton school of architecture. Dr. John Finley Williamson, president, organized the nonsectarian school in 1926 to train directors of church music. The 175 students follow a rigid course in physical training as an aid to voice culture and can often be seen jogging along the Princeton highways. Degrees of Bachelor and Master of Music are given.

POINTS OF INTEREST IN ENVIRONS

Drumthwacket, Pyne estate, *0.6 m.;* Tusculum, Witherspoon's home, *1.7 m.;* Lawrenceville School, *4.4 m. (see Tour 6);* Castle Howard Farm, *1.2 m.;* Berrien House, Washington's headquarters, *4.7 m. (see Tour 8).*

Salem

Railroad Station: Grant St. and Hubbell Ave. for Pennsylvania-Reading Seashore Lines.
Bus Station: E. Broadway and Market St. for Public Service.
Taxis: 15¢ and 25¢ within city limits.
Traffic Regulations: 2-hour parking on Broadway (business district).

Accommodations: 2 hotels; tourist homes.

Motion Picture Houses: Two.
Tennis: Johnson Park.

Annual Events: Muskrat skinning contest in February, County Courthouse, Broadway and Market St.

SALEM (16 alt., 8,048 pop.) is like an old, old sampler with a few bright spots; but it is time-worn and frayed. The old brick Georgian Colonial houses facing the brick-paved streets would stir envy in a Williamsburg reconstructionist, and the square, heavy, frame structures, typical of the Civil War era, are a living memorial to another historical period. Modern history, too, is represented by the semicircling rim of factories and faded workers' homes.

Because of its geographical position, 3 miles east of Delaware River and off main highways, Salem has developed as a relatively isolated community. The moorland quality of its surroundings adds to this sense of isolation. From the west the approach is over great tidal flats, partially submerged at spring tide and swampy always. The flats end abruptly with a small navigable stream known locally as Salem Creek, or Fenwick Creek, or oftener just "The Crick." This is Salem's western boundary, lined with wharves and modern factories that produce glassware, canned foods, linoleum and chemicals. Crossing a drawbridge the highway becomes a street that leads into West Broadway, the city's main thoroughfare. North, east and south the boundaries fade imperceptibly into miles of flat farm lands, across which modern highways reach Salem from Philadelphia and the Atlantic coast.

The streets are broad, shaded with venerable trees. Once they were muddy or covered with oyster shells, and traversed by feet bent on history-making errands. They are quiet streets seldom touched by the stream of traffic that cuts across the State.

The houses are built close to the sidewalk. Sometimes there is a tiny lawn, closely cropped, set off from the pavement by an intricately scrolled wrought-iron fence, or a row of iron staples about 3 feet high. Large, luxuriant gardens bloom at the rear of the homes.

It is the decorative system of its homes, however, that gives Salem a quality all its own. Some builders of a past generation seem to have been endowed with an extraordinary gift for lacy scrollwork, with which they adorned the exteriors of many of the old homes. Succeeding builders have carried the idea forward until now the visitor seems surrounded with wooden filigrees, delicate or unsightly but all original and distinctive to each house. Even the shabbier sections try to cover their defects with crude ornamental woodwork. Where this is not practical the householders paint doors and wood frames with startling colors.

In the center of the town are the stores of the business district, many the remodeled first stories of old buildings. Wood and metal awnings overhang the sidewalk and for the space of about half a block make a solid protective cover. Imperceptibly the business houses give place to homes fronted by unused hitching posts and carriage blocks.

Recent increases in population have changed the little Quaker town. However, there is still among the inhabitants a pride in the community's past history and traditions which are closely linked to the more than 50 existing Colonial houses of the early settlement. In dusty attics priceless antiques are stored, treasures handed down through generations. Many souvenirs of pre-Revolutionary vintage still occupy places of importance in the living rooms of the homes; others have been donated or lent to historical collections. Through the windows, ladder-backed chairs and ancestral portraits can be seen.

The Salem section has long been famous as a fur market for muskrat pelts. An outstanding community event is the muskrat skinning contest in February at the county courthouse. The 1937 champion set a record by skinning 10 "rats" in 3 minutes and 16 seconds; in the same contest a one-armed contestant outstripped several two-armed competitors. Fox hunting with hounds is also a popular sport, but within recent years farmers and chicken fanciers have almost exterminated the foxes.

Saturday is market day. Farmers from the surrounding area come to the county seat to lay in supplies for the following week; the streets lose their tranquillity and acquire a layer of banana and orange peels and apple cores. Children are sent to the movies, while basket-carrying parents walk up and down before the rows of stores. The custom is as old as the colony, and the advent of the automobile has rather strengthened than lessened it.

This small-town atmosphere gives no indication of the large glass, linoleum, canning, and chemical factories on the outskirts. A large percentage of the population is employed in them.

Many Salemites are lineal descendants of orginal or early settlers. A sizable Negro population lives on the outskirts, near the factories. There is a negligible number of foreign-born.

In 1675, just seven years before William Penn came to the opposite shore of the Delaware, John Fenwick and a group of English Quakers settled the region and founded the city of New Salem, the first permanent English-speaking settlement on the Delaware. Previous settlements had been made by both the Dutch and the Swedes, many of whom subsequently moved farther inland.

The settlers who came with Fenwick were imbued with ideals of religious freedom and self-government. Others of like mind were soon attracted. Within two years the land had been bought from the Indians and divided into lots. By Royal Commission in 1682 the city of New Salem became a port of entry for vessels. Trade and industry prospered in the 100 years before the Revolution and new towns sprang up about the original village.

The early Quaker settlement was swathed in litigation. For the sum of £1,000 the undivided half of New Jersey, later known as West Jersey, was conveyed to Fenwick by Lord Berkeley, who had received it as a grant from the Duke of York. Later, in a trial umpired by William Penn, Fenwick lost title to nine-tenths of the property on the ground that it had been purchased with funds advanced by Edward Byllynge. On the remaining one-tenth, which included the site of Salem, Fenwick had given a mortgage. The mortgagees and William Penn deprived Fenwick of his title to this land, too. The fact that Fenwick had been a major in Cromwell's army may have had something to do with his frequent troubles with Royal favorites.

The settlement was on the whole law-abiding, but the spirit of Quaker friendliness was not all-pervasive. The court record is illuminating:

. . . Eliza Windsor, with force and arms upon the body of Elizabeth Rumsey, . . . an assault did make, and her with a paddle over the head did strike, and also over the neck, and her collar bone did break, to the great damage of the said Elizabeth Rumsey. . . .

Early records name Thomas Lutherland as the only known Salemite tested by the medieval Ordeal of the Bier, by which a suspected murderer was judged guilty if the corpse flowed or spouted blood when the suspect's hand was extended toward the body. After a jury trial, Lutherland was hanged in Salem, February 23, 1691. More cruel was the execution of a Negro woman named Hager. She was burned at the stake in 1717 for the hatchet murder of her master, James Sherron, high sheriff. It was customary for the courtroom crowd to vote as to whether the death penalty should be invoked.

Salem saw fighting, plundering and murder during the Revolutionary War. In February 1778 Washington at Valley Forge sent a force of about 300 men under Anthony Wayne to obtain supplies from southern New Jersey. Wayne collected 150 head of cattle and brought them to Valley Forge. Salem beef saved the starving army. While Wayne was driving his bawling bulls, Howe, stationed in Philadelphia, sent Colonel Abercrombie with 2,000 men in a vain effort to stop him.

Another detachment of 1,000 British troops under Colonel Mawhood and about 500 Tories (the Queen's Rangers) under Maj. John Simcoe came to Salem the following month to forage. The Colonial troops formed a line of defense at Alloways Creek, 3 miles south. It was along this front that the ambushing of the Americans, the repulse of the British at Quinton's Bridge *(see Tour 29)*, and the Hancock House massacre *(see Tour 29)* occurred.

The Revolution started Salem's decline as a river port. British war vessels in the Delaware River throttled shipping, while the British occupation of Philadelphia drew attention to that city's superior advantages as a deep-water port.

At the end of the century the soil turned sour after 150 years of unscientific planting, and many Salemites moved west. Zadock Street left Salem in 1803, founded Salem, Ohio, and then Salem, Indiana, a few years later. His son, Aaron, established Salem, Iowa; the parade ended at the Pacific Ocean with Salem, Oregon. The exodus stopped with the discovery of marl, present in the region in unlimited quantities, as fertilizer.

By 1840 the general appearance of Salem was "thriving and pleasant," according to the contemporary historians, Barber and Howe. The town had a bank, a market, 8 churches, 2 fire engines, 2 libraries, a newspaper printing office, 3 hotels and about 250 homes.

During this period the office of high sheriff was still an important position. Salem County's sheriff was especially proud of his work in hanging Samuel T. Treadway, who had shot his estranged wife and was convicted in a much publicized trial. Shortly afterward the sheriff went to Philadelphia, it is said, and applied for a hotel room. The clerk informed him that all rooms were taken, whereupon the sheriff leaned over the desk and said: "I am the high sheriff of Salem County, I hung Treadway, and I want a room in this hotel."

"Sir," the clerk answered coolly, "if you were sheriff of hell and hung the devil it wouldn't make any difference to me. There are no rooms in this hotel."

The reputation of the Quakers as Abolitionists spread throughout the South by grapevine telegraph just before the Civil War, and many escaped Negro slaves made Salem a stop on the Underground Railroad.

Industry became more firmly established in 1863 when a railroad reached the city, which had lost its status as a village by incorporation in 1858. With industry came a steady increase in population, most recently an influx of Negroes.

POINTS OF INTEREST

1. SALEM COUNTY COURTHOUSE, NE. corner Broadway and Market St., is a square, two-story building, whose bricks have been repainted a dark red. A cupola rises from the center of the roof. The present structure, rebuilt in 1817 and in 1908, stands on the site of a brick courthouse erected 1735. On the lawn is an old BRASS CANNON of Italian manufacture, taken from the British in the Battle of Plattsburg, N. Y., in 1814. The cannon and its wooden carriage have been painted the same color as the courthouse.

2. OFFICES OF THE COUNTY CLERK AND SURROGATE, Market St. N. of the Courthouse, are in a high, one-story stucco building adorned with Corinthian columns and pilasters, built in 1851. On the curb is a FOUNTAIN, erected in 1901, which bears the legend: "Let him that is athirst come. W. C. T. U." The fountain is dry; the town is wet.

3. SALEM COUNTY JAIL *(open 2-5 Wed. and Sat.)*, Market St., between E. Broadway and Grant St., occupies a building which also houses

the offices of the mayor and sheriff. It is a two-story, red-brick, square structure with a wing at the left which contains the cells. Scrolled decorations above the window sashes match an ornate cornice.

Although the present jail was erected 1775 and rebuilt in 1866, Salem County prison records date back to 1709. The exact location of the earliest jail is not known, but there are several anecdotes about prisoners of long ago. Jailbreaks were frequent, and the sheriffs constantly advertised for the return of escaped prisoners.

The roof was a favorite medium of escape. In the very early days one John Mackentyre placed a candle on the end of a stick, thrust it through the window, and set the roof on fire. He failed, however, to escape. Schoolboys for years afterward chanted a ditty opening with the lines:

> Old John Mackentyre,
> He set the jail on fire . . .

In 1884 Jim Sullivan, a Negro sentenced to death for murder, tore a hole through the roof in order to watch a passing parade. The keepers, also among the spectators, did not see Sullivan on the roof. After the parade had passed, he returned to his cell. Three days later he was hanged, the last execution of this type by the county. The jail roof today is of slate. Near the jail stood the whipping post, where the backs of women as well as men were bared to the lash.

4. ALEXANDER GRANT HOUSE *(open by arrangement with pres. Salem Co. Hist. Soc.)*, 83 Market St., is a two-and-a-half-story brick structure, painted yellow. An extension reaches out about 6 feet toward the street. The windows, except two dormers in the worn shingle roof, are shuttered. The house was built in 1721 by Alexander Grant, whose descendants, Anna and Helena Hubbell, gave it to the Salem County Historical Society. For a time Robert Gibbon Johnson, one of Salem's earliest historians, lived here.

Exhibits on the main floor include Indian relics, Colonial kitchenware, farm implements, early deeds, manuscripts and books and a collection of pre-Revolutionary china and glass. A replica of a Colonial bedroom, old wearing apparel and other items are on display on the second floor. Also on the second floor is the Heinz collection of 300 canes, on display in the ELLEN MECUM MEMORIAL ROOM, meeting place of the Oak Tree Chapter of the Daughters of the American Revolution. The Sarah Bradway Harris collection of early kitchen utensils is on the attic floor.

5. GREEN'S HOTEL, 115 Market St., erected 1799, is a four-story greenish-yellow, mottled stucco building. From the second floor a veranda that stretches the length of the house overhangs the sidewalk. On the street level are stores with old-fashioned fronts painted a dingy dark green. The city's sporting element congregates here to listen to the stories of yesterday's baseball hero, "Whitey" Witt, the inn's host, and Salem County's Leon (Goose) Goslin, who returns each winter between seasons spent on the big-league diamonds to his home about 5 miles from the city.

6. MUNICIPAL BUILDING, 1 New Market St., a red brick structure

SALEM OAK

dating from 1889, was used by a bank until 1926. It has an ornately designed front with a round tower on one side, and a superimposed, slate-
covered dormer on the other. Across the front is a huge ribbon scroll with
a dark green border, inscribed, "City of Salem—Municipal Building."

7. An OLD LAW OFFICE *(private)*, directly behind the Municipal
Building, reputedly one of the earliest law offices in the country, was also
used as a medical office by Dr. Ebenezer Howell, Revolutionary patriot.
Built in 1732 for John Jones, the one-room octagonal structure of red
brick with a conical wood-shingle roof is now in poor condition.

8. FRIENDS BURIAL GROUND, W. Broadway between 4th and 5th
Sts., was set aside in 1676, a year after the town was founded. The plot
contains the remains of some of Salem's oldest settlers. Typical of Quaker
burial grounds the low white headstones, few of them more than 1 foot
high, have no inscription but the name and dates of birth and death.

The ancient SALEM OAK, the community's pride, stands within the
cemetery, near the main entrance. John Fenwick sat beneath its branches
when he bartered with the Indians for the Salem territory. Its age has been
variously estimated at from 500 to 900 years. Robert Burdette, the hu-
morist, judged that "Salem Oak is 4 years older than the Atlantic Ocean."
Cared for by the Society of Friends, the tree is in excellent condition, and
its acorns are collected each year to fill requests from all parts of the
world. When last measured the oak was 80 feet high with a maximum
circumference of more than 30 feet.

9. ORTHODOX FRIENDS MEETING HOUSE *(private)*, 107 W.
Broadway, is a replica of the Friends Meeting House on East Broadway.
It is a two-story, rectangular red brick building with a sloping tin roof,
and separate entrances for men and women. The tall shuttered doors and
window trim are painted yellow. At each end of the roof is a small red
brick chimney, one covered with cement. The structure was erected in
1852, 20 years after the Orthodox branch of Friends separated from the
Hicksite branch over a doctrinal argument. Only one family uses this
meeting house (1938).

10. BRADWAY HOUSE *(private)*, 32 W. Broadway, built in 1691,
is a rectangular, two-story brick building, the white paint now turned
gray. A red tin roof provides the only color. The house has been known
by a succession of names: "Governor's House," the "Light House," and
"Capital House." Royal Governors of New Jersey occupied the mansion,
notably Governor Cornbury, who arrived soon after the death of Edward
Bradway, said to have been the builder. Several times the provincial congress of West Jersey met here. The practice of placing a light in the gable
to guide mariners to the nearby wharf originated the name of "Light
House." Present-day Salemites refer to the building as the "Old Yellow
House," because of the paint once used. Surrounded now by cheap dwellings, the old house serves as an office for the Gaynor Glass Company,
whose plant extends to the rear.

11. FRIENDS MEETING HOUSE *(open meeting days)*, E. Broadway
opposite Walnut St., was erected in 1772 to replace an earlier brick building that stood within the Friends Burial Ground. Set behind a broad lawn

and picket-fence, it is a well-kept, two-story, red brick rectangular building, with two shuttered entrances on the street level. The entrances are protected by small overhanging roofs supported by slender columns. On one side is a porte cochere. These entrances, originally built for the men's and women's sections, are now used by both sexes. The early Quakers who founded the colony frequently met here for discussion of common problems. During the Revolution the building served as an overflow court for the trial of Tories.

POINTS OF INTEREST IN ENVIRONS

Pledger House, *1 m. (see Tour 28)*; William Hancock House, site of Revolutionary massacre, *4.1 m.*; Fort Mott, *8.4 m. (see Tour 29)*.

Trenton

Railroad Stations: Pennsylvania Station, S. Clinton Ave. near E. State St., for Pennsylvania R.R.; Reading Station, N. Warren and Tucker Sts., for Reading R.R.

Bus Stations: Central Bus Terminal, 21 W. State St., for Greyhound Line, National Trailways System, Royal Blue Coaches and Pan American Bus Lines; 38 W. Front St. for Trenton-Philadelphia Coach Co.; Trenton Transit Co. Terminal, 132 Perry St., for interurban lines; 21 N. Willow St. for Trenton and Lambertville line.

Taxis: 25¢ to 85¢ according to distance by zones.

Busses: 10¢.

Traffic Regulations: Traffic lights throughout city. Signs designate parking time limit. No turns permitted at Broad and State Sts.; turns in either direction permitted elsewhere. Watch signs for one-way streets. Out-of-town motorists who break minor traffic laws get warning tag, which must be turned in at police station or to traffic officer, penalty imposed with third tag.

Accommodations: Two large hotels, several smaller ones, many boarding houses and tourist homes; no seasonal rates.

Information Service: Chamber of Commerce, Hotel Stacy-Trent, 51 W. State St.; Hotel Hildebrecht, 27 W. State St.

Radio Station: WTNJ (1280 kc.).

Motion Picture Houses: Eleven.

Golf: Sunnybrae course, 4 m. SE. on US 130, 18 holes, greens fee 50¢; Sat., Sun. and holidays $1.

Baseball: Dunn Field, Brunswick Ave., home of the Trenton Senators, New York-Penn League.

Annual Events: Farm Show, January; State Fair, last week in September; Feast of Lights, religious festival in Italian colony, second Sat. and Sun. in September.

TRENTON (55 alt., 123,356 pop.), with a rich background as an early Quaker settlement and as the State capital, is primarily a manufacturing center. Residents are proud of its history, and there are plaques, monuments, and historic houses throughout the city. Nevertheless, Trenton chooses to identify itself by a sign almost as wide as Delaware River, fastened to the steel arches of the main highway bridge: "Trenton Makes —The World Takes."

The city lies on a low plateau at the head of navigation on Delaware River. Thanks to the rocky channel and rapids (known from earliest settlement as the Falls) that have made commercial development impractical along most of the shore, the river front is bordered by the trees and grass of an extensive park, making a green backyard for the State buildings and for the western residential section.

Assunpink Creek, site of a Revolutionary battle, bisects the city, closely paralleled by the depressed main line tracks of the Pennsylvania Railroad. Once this tributary of the Delaware was clear-flowing and tree-lined; it is now hemmed by retaining walls, spanned by many bridges, and burdened with the refuse of factories.

Trenton's skyline, dominated by the Capitol's golden dome, is marked by a few tall buildings, numerous church spires and the Battle Monument. Plane passengers see a slight haze of smoke from factories producing pottery, steel products, and rubber goods; a smudge that contrasts with the unobstructed greenness of the surrounding countryside of New Jersey and Pennsylvania.

Modern Trenton for the most part turns its back on the river and puts forward its best foot on State Street. Choked with traffic in the business center, this busy thoroughfare broadens for a short stretch before the Capitol buildings. The State's business is conducted in structures that vary from Italian Renaissance to modern classic design. Many departments have overflowed to quarters in nearby office buildings, and business houses have moved in close to the Capitol.

In the congested shopping district are a few large stores, with a miscellany of smaller shops along State Street and its principal intersecting thoroughfares, Warren and Broad Streets. Rows of two- and three-story structures are broken at intervals by taller buildings, or by a Georgian Colonial church that makes with its small green graveyard a quiet corner in the midst of pulsing commercial activity. With the click of the wrought-iron gate, one can step from today into Trenton's mellow past. Names on the old brown tombstones recall illustrious dames and burghers who once trod the flagstones to the church door.

In the western residential area, once a farming section with fences to protect the settlers' uneasy cattle, are comfortable homes, well shaded and adequately spaced with lawns. Some of these fine old houses date back a century or more. In sharp contrast is "Philadelphia Row," a block-long stretch of two-family brick houses, built as a unit, each porch or stoop identical, with nothing but a house number to distinguish one from another. The simple post-Colonial lines of some of the older brick houses, close by the business section, retain the dignity of the early 1800's.

The manufacturing districts lie chiefly to the south and east of the business center. The streets are cluttered with railroad spurs; miles of mesh fences, topped with barbed wire, some with a covering of ivy, enclose buildings of brick and stone. A few are modern structures, with a liberal display of glass against a framework of steel and concrete.

Bordering the factories is the slum section of Trenton, home of part of the Negro population. It is a typical district of ill-preserved houses, neither better nor worse than that of the average manufacturing city.

A complete city in itself, Trenton does not blossom and wilt with the coming and going of the legislators. The hotels are filled, of course, when the session opens each January; but in New Jersey the legislature holds sessions on Monday nights, rather than through each week. This arrangement makes it possible for the legislators to commute from their homes, and at the same time deprives the city of the opportunity of being the politico-social center of the State, as are some other State capitals.

In January of every year divisible by three Trenton is decked with flags and crowded with visitors for the inaugural ceremonies. The War Memorial Building, where the Governor takes the oath, is packed to the limit of its 2,000 seats. The ceremony is preceded by a procession of officers and is followed by a huge parade through the streets. An executive salute of 19 guns precedes the delivery of the Great Seal of the State to the Governor. An afternoon reception in the executive offices is followed by an elaborate ball in the evening. Formerly inaugurations took place in the Taylor Opera House with much less ceremony.

It is possible that Trenton's history dates back to Stone Age man. Dr. Charles C. Abbott made an exhaustive study of gravel deposits on his Trenton farm and reported in 1872 that crude implements he had discovered were of the glacial period. The weight of archeological opinion seems, however, to be against this theory *(see ARCHEOLOGY)*. In 1650 about 200 Sanhicans, a clan of the Unami subdivision of the Lenape, occupied part of this area. This agricultural group was noted for its skill in making lanceheads and arrowheads of quartz and jasper.

The first white settler was Mahlon Stacy, an English Quaker, who took up a grant of land in 1679 at "ye ffalles of ye De La Warr" and built a log mill and a clapboard house. The little hamlet that developed around this nucleus was called The Falls.

Recognizing the commercial possibilities of the site, William Trent, a Philadelphia merchant, in 1714 bought of Mahlon Stacy Jr. the remainder of his father's holdings of 800 acres on Assunpink Creek (Ind., *stone in the water*). Trent replaced the log mill with one of stone and *c.* 1719 built himself a fine house later called Bloomsbury Court, now the oldest in the city. In the same year court sessions of Hunterdon County were held in the village. Trent's energy and financial backing launched the settlement, which he called Trent's Town, into a period of steady growth. Its position at the head of sloop navigation made the town a shipping point for grain and other products of the area, and a depot for merchandise between New York and Philadelphia. Overland travelers found the village a convenient stopping place on King's Highway, while a ferry, chartered in 1727, afforded communication with Pennsylvania.

In 1745 the town received a royal charter of incorporation as a borough and town, although the charter was voluntarily surrendered five years later when it failed to bring any material benefits.

The townspeople hurried to the water front in 1746 and cheered the first raft of timber from the upper Delaware as it passed through the rapids on its way to Philadelphia. Many others followed during the next century; some carried from 500 to 600 bushels of wheat.

The first chief burgess, Dr. Thomas Cadwalader, ranked high in his profession. One of the first advocates of inoculation as a disease preventive, he is said to have introduced the practice in Trenton to combat smallpox. In 1750 Dr. Cadwalader gave £500 to found the Trenton Library Company, the first "public" library in New Jersey. It was almost wholly destroyed by British soldiers in December 1776 but revived in 1797 and lasted until 1855.

John Adams reported in 1774 that Trenton, as it soon became known, was "a pretty village. It appears to be the largest town we have seen in the Jerseys." Trenton resembled the shire towns of England, its hip or gable roofed dwellings facing the street, with gardens on both sides. The wharves were busy, and there were four churches, a courthouse, and a jail. In 1776 Trenton was a village of about 100 houses, mainly clustered along King and Queen Streets (now Warren and Broad Streets).

On the morning of December 26, 1776, Trenton was the scene of one of the most decisive battles of the Revolution. Washington, his prestige seriously reduced after his army had been harried across the State and into Pennsylvania by closely pursuing British, turned with about 2,500 troops upon his foe by executing the famous crossing of the ice-choked Delaware *(see Tour 11)*.

Washington had planned his surprise attack on the Hessians in Trenton for 5 a.m., expecting to find them asleep after a boisterous Christmas celebration. The difficult crossing of the river and the icy roads on the nine-mile march delayed until 8 o'clock the arrival of his two divisions, one marching by the lower road and one by the upper road, but apparently few of the Hessians were awake even then. The fighting was described by Washington in a report to Congress as follows:

> The upper division arrived at the enemy's advanced post exactly at 8 o'clock; and in 3 minutes after, I found, from the fire on the lower road, that that division had also got up. The out-guards made but a small opposition; though, for their numbers, they behaved very well,—keeping up a constant retreating fire from behind houses.
>
> We presently saw their main body formed; but, from their motions, they seemed undetermined how to act. Being hard pressed by our troops, who had already got possession of part of their artillery, they attempted to file off by a road on their right, leading to Princeton; but, perceiving their intention, I threw a body of troops in their way, which immediately checked them. Finding, from our disposition, that they were surrounded, and they must inevitably be cut to pieces if they made any further resistance, they agreed to lay down their arms . . .

The prisoners numbered 23 officers and 886 men. Colonel Rall, the Hessians' commander, was mortally wounded; Washington estimated the enemy's dead at "not above twenty or thirty," while the Americans' casualties were "only two officers and one or two privates wounded." One of the wounded officers was Lieut. James Monroe, later President, who helped to capture a Hessian battery. About one-third of the Hessian force escaped down the river road toward Bordentown.

After resting a few hours in Trenton, the American troops returned to the Pennsylvania shore. Two men died from the cold. Revolutionists throughout the Colonies were heartened by the unexpected success at Trenton and the British command was correspondingly alarmed. General Howe dispatched Cornwallis with 4,000 to 5,000 troops to intercept Washington should he attempt to recross New Jersey. The American Army, meanwhile, had recrossed to Trenton on the then frozen river.

Cornwallis arrived shortly before sunset on January 2 and found the Continental troops drawn up on higher ground on the farther side of Assunpink Creek. The engagement that followed, often confused with the

Battle of Princeton on the next day, is known locally as the second Battle of Trenton, or Battle of the Assunpink.

Three times the British charged up to the bridge and even onto it, but each time the assault was broken by a hail of Continental lead. An eyewitness wrote that when the first attack crumbled, ". . . our army raised a shout, and such a shout I have never since heard; by what signal or word of command, I know not. The line was more than a mile in length, and from the nature of the ground the extremes were not in sight of each other, yet they shouted as one man . . ."

A contemporary observer estimated that 150 enemy troops were killed. Washington knew, however, that a more determined assault would be made in the morning, which might overwhelm his poorly equipped army. Since a thaw had broken the ice sheet across the Delaware, an escape to the Pennsylvania shore was impossible. That night Washington and his officers conferred in the Douglass house to find a way out of the trap. It was General St. Clair, according to some historians, who suggested the retreat to Princeton by a little-used back road.

By good fortune the temperature dropped sufficiently to freeze this ordinarily bad road so that artillery wheels could be supported. The army marched off to whispered orders. To deaden the rumble of artillery wheels, rags were wrapped around the rims. "Rags were plentiful, but they were all on the backs of the soldiers," one historian commented. A skeleton force was left behind to keep the camp fires burning in sight of the British, who were singing around well-filled kettles only a short distance away. It is said that Washington even ordered dummy cannon mounted to aid the deception, a device used as recently as 1937 by Chinese defenders of Shanghai.

In the morning Cornwallis got hurried news of the Revolutionaries' success in overcoming the British garrison at Princeton (see PRINCETON). Fearing for the safety of a treasure chest of £70,000 and a large supply of military stores at New Brunswick, the British commander started his army in quick pursuit. But the American troops had turned off to find shelter in the Watchung Hills.

Trenton was chosen as the State capital in 1790 and two years later, still nothing more than a village, was incorporated as a city. The residents' earlier hopes of bringing the national capital to the bank of the Delaware, defeated by the opposition of southern States, were temporarily fulfilled when recurring epidemics of yellow fever caused the removal of national offices from Philadelphia. In 1794 and 1798 Trenton had several Federal offices, and in 1799 practically all of the departments were represented; even President Adams and his wife were temporary residents.

A covered bridge 1,100 feet long was built across Delaware River in 1806, described by the historians, Barber and Howe, as "one of the finest specimens of bridge architecture, of wood, in the world." Perpendicular iron rods, hung from arches, provided such sturdy support for the floor that the structure was used later by railroad trains.

Development of water power by the Delaware Falls Company, construction of the Delaware and Raritan Canal, and building of the Camden and

Amboy Railroad resulted in industrial activity that made Trenton a city in fact as well as in name. John A. Roebling moved his wire mill from Pennsylvania in 1848 and continued the manufacture of steel cable. The erection of Brooklyn Bridge a generation later publicized Roebling and Trenton throughout the world.

Pottery making, a Colonial industry, began to thrive after 1850. Craftsmen were imported from England and Ireland to teach local apprentices the art of producing wares that, by 1880, made Trenton known as the Staffordshire of America. The Ott and Brewer Company made in 1882 the first piece of American Beleek. Walter Lenox, one of the young apprentices, later laid the foundations for the Lenox Pottery. From Trenton potteries came, in 1873, the first porcelain sanitary ware in the United States. Trenton workers had formed trade unions as early as 1835, and in that year conducted a largely successful strike for a 10-hour day.

Growth of industry had by 1860 eliminated much of the city's quiet charm. Factories and houses for workers claimed terrain once dominated by Colonial dwellings. Down the center of North Broad Street (then Greene Street) ran the Street Market, two buildings stretching from State Street out to Academy Street.

In this period Trenton's most prolific writer—now largely forgotten—began his career. He was Edward S. Ellis, a school teacher who was one of the originators of the dime novel. At the age of 20 he wrote *Seth Jones, or The Captive of the Frontier,* which was published in 1860 by Beadle Brothers, New York, and sold 600,000 copies. Ellis produced about one hundred novels afterward.

In the early 1880's, the potters of Trenton were victimized by the blacklist. By agreement among the manufacturers, no worker could change employers without a written release from his last employer. The *Sunday Advertiser,* in an article headed "Local Fugitive Slave Law," reported in May 1883 the suit of Mary E. Slattery against the American Crockery Company for damages because of the girl's inability to get work elsewhere in Trenton. A judgment for $72 was finally given in 1884.

The city's greatest expansion occurred between 1880 and 1920, when the population increased by 90,379 as foreign labor poured in to man factories and mills. During this period the adjacent boroughs of Chambersburg and Wilbur, Millham Township, and parts of Ewing Township were annexed. Growth has perceptibly slowed since 1920. A number of industries have gone to other regions and many Trenton workers have moved to suburbs.

Both in population and in manufactures, the city ranks fourth in the State. The most important single industry is the making of wire rope and cables. Next in importance is the pottery industry. Several large cigar manufacturers have established factories here in recent years.

Deepening of the Delaware River channel to 20 feet made Trenton a port for seagoing vessels in 1932. The terminal is municipally operated.

As the State capital, Trenton has been the scene of important legal, as well as political, controversies. Perhaps the most famous trial was that of Charles Goodyear's suit against Horace Day for infringement of his patent on the rubber-vulcanizing process. Crowds gathered in March 1852 to hear Daniel Webster, then Secretary of State, successfully argue the case for Goodyear against Joseph Choate, another famous lawyer. Webster, reported the *True American,* "seems to be in ill health, although his massive brow is as bold and prominent as ever, and his large full eyes glow with intellectual fire." Webster had written his son that he was heavily in debt and welcomed the $10,000 fee. The audience was not disappointed when he summed up: "I believe that the man who sits at this table, Charles Goodyear, is to go down to posterity in the history of the arts of this country, in that great class of inventors at the head of which stands Robert Fulton; in which class stand the names of Whitney, and of Morse, and in which class will stand *non post longo intervallo* the humble name of Charles Goodyear."

The strangest spectacle ever seen in the Statehouse was occupation of the assembly chamber in the spring of 1936 by a delegation of unemployed, protesting the termination of State aid to the needy. The sit-down strike, starting with 25 persons and growing rapidly, lasted nine days and focused national interest on the capital. Seats and desks for legislators were converted into dining tables, beds, and card tables; corridors and the assembly chamber and gallery were jammed with strikers and curious onlookers. The legislature finally adjourned without taking any action except to refer the matter to a moneyless board and the weary groups of jobless marched quietly out of the Statehouse.

POINTS OF INTEREST

1. The STATE CAPITOL ANNEX *(open 9-5 weekdays),* W. State St. opposite Taylor's Place, is a four-story Indiana limestone building of neoclassic design, built in 1931. Designed by J. Osborne Hunt of Trenton and Col. Hugh A. Kelly of Jersey City, it is a well-planned H-shaped structure. Within the annex are a number of State departments and courts, plus the STATE LIBRARY of about 175,000 volumes, noted for its law, history and genealogy collections; and the STATE MUSEUM *(open 9-5 weekdays; 2-5 Sun.),* which contains exhibits of natural resources, archeology and fauna of New Jersey, as well as minerals, fossils and Indian relics. Schools throughout the State are provided with teaching aids from lending collections.

2. The STATEHOUSE *(open 9-5 weekdays; all night Mon. during legislative sessions),* 121 W. State St., is an unsatisfactory composite of additions and alterations, occupying a landscaped plot between State Street and Delaware River. What remains of the original structure, built *c.* 1792, is now a part of the present building, although exactly what part is uncertain. Subsequent growth has been without regard to any foresighted plan. After a fire in 1885, the present front portion and rotunda with gilded dome and lantern were erected in 1889 from the plans of L. H. Broome. The three-and-one-half-story facade is in the French Renaissance style, with a clumsy two-tier entrance porch supported on small scale polished granite columns. The ill-lighted main entrance corridor is hung with indistinguish-

able portraits of early Jersey statesmen and patriots; portraits of various Governors hang in the executive chambers. Against the walls of the cramped rotunda are musty cabinets of Civil War regimental flags. The second and third floors are labyrinths of gloomy corridors and passageways weaving in and out among erratically placed offices. In the basement, where a bar once provided convenient relief for hard-worked legislators, there is a lunchroom and lounge.

The assembly chamber, designed by James Moylan and built in 1891, is finished on the interior with Trenton tile, yellow oak, Italian marble, and iron. Individual desks, each with a spittoon, are arranged in the plan of an amphitheater. To the right and left of the speaker's desk are small pens flatteringly called press boxes. Suspended above on the sides and rear is the spectators' gallery, wholly inadequate for the accommodation of visitors who usually can neither see nor hear the speakers on the floor.

Similar to the assembly chamber but smaller is the marble senate chamber, planned by Arnold H. Moses and completed in 1904. At the rear of the capitol and between the two chambers is a massive, four-story stucco wing, built in 1907 from the drawings of George E. Poole, State architect.

3. The OLD BARRACKS *(open 10-5 weekdays, May to Aug.; 10-4, Sept. to April; adm. 10¢)*, S. Willow St. opposite W. Front St., is the only remaining unit of the five barracks erected in 1758–59 by the Colonial Assembly to house Colonial troops, previously billeted in private homes, during the French and Indian War. It is a pleasing example of the adaptation of early Georgian Colonial style to a military building. Of U-shaped design, the courtyard walls carry a two-story roofed porch, supported on thin wood columns that give a southern air. The masonry is of random fieldstone with white wood trim. British troops, Hessian jaegers and American soldiers were quartered here during the Revolution; afterward the structure was used for private dwellings. In 1813, Front Street was cut through the building, but the entire structure was restored about a century later. The original three long rooms have been divided into many small ones, some furnished with Colonial pieces, others used for exhibitions. One of the finest collections of Continental currency in the country is here. Some rooms are headquarters for various Colonial and Revolutionary societies. On the lawn is an elm grown from the root of the Cambridge tree under which General Washington assumed charge of the Continental Army. The property, restored by the State, is managed by the Old Barracks Association.

4. The OLD MASONIC LODGE HOUSE *(open 9-4 weekdays; 1-4 Sun.)*, NE. corner S. Willow and Lafayette Sts., is one of the oldest Masonic houses still standing north of the Mason and Dixon Line. It was built in 1793 by the local lodge, organized in 1787. The two-story Georgian Colonial building is of fieldstone, ivy-covered, with white trim and slate roof. The graceful doorway, deep set and arched, is lighted by an old lantern.

Much of American Masonic history appears to have had its beginnings in Trenton. In 1730 Masons in the Province of New York, New Jersey, and Pennsylvania requested of the Grand Lodge of England a deputation

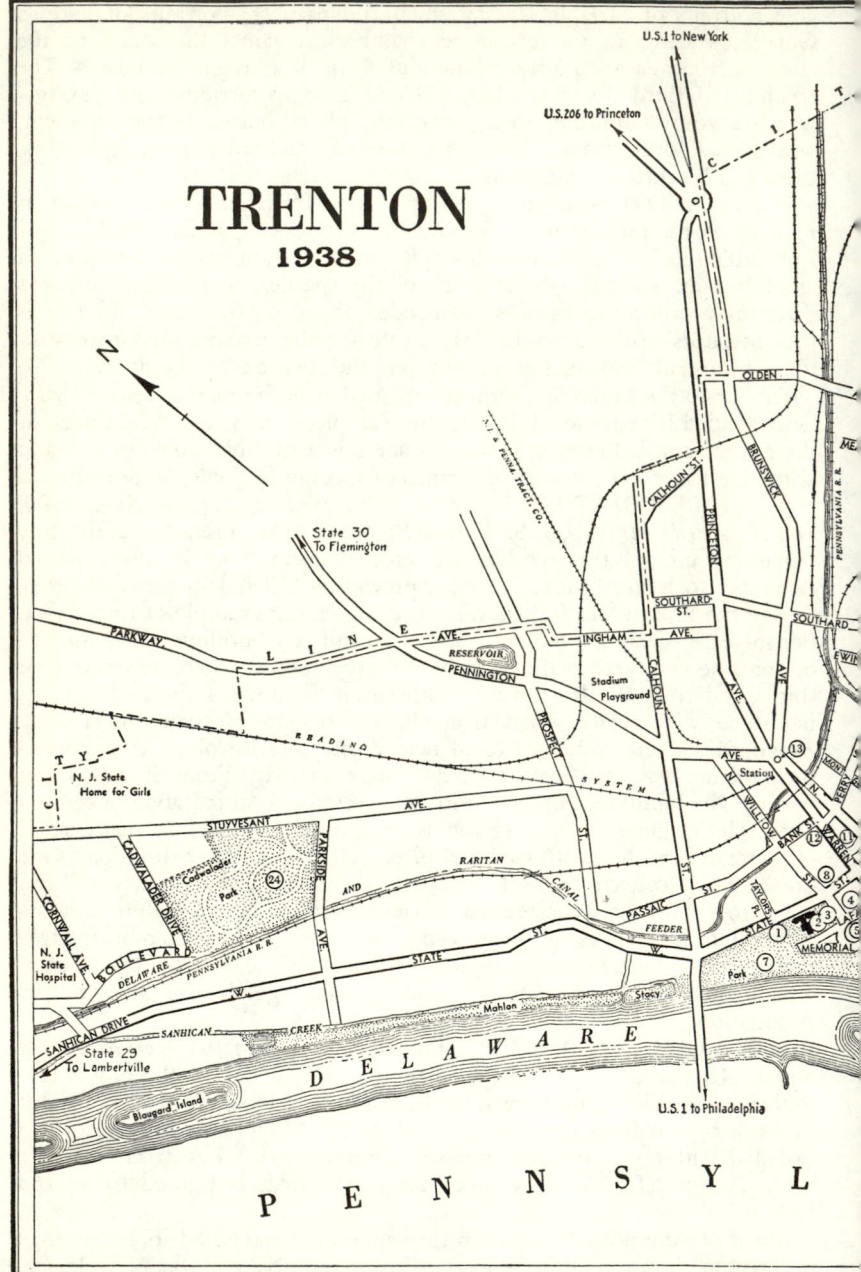

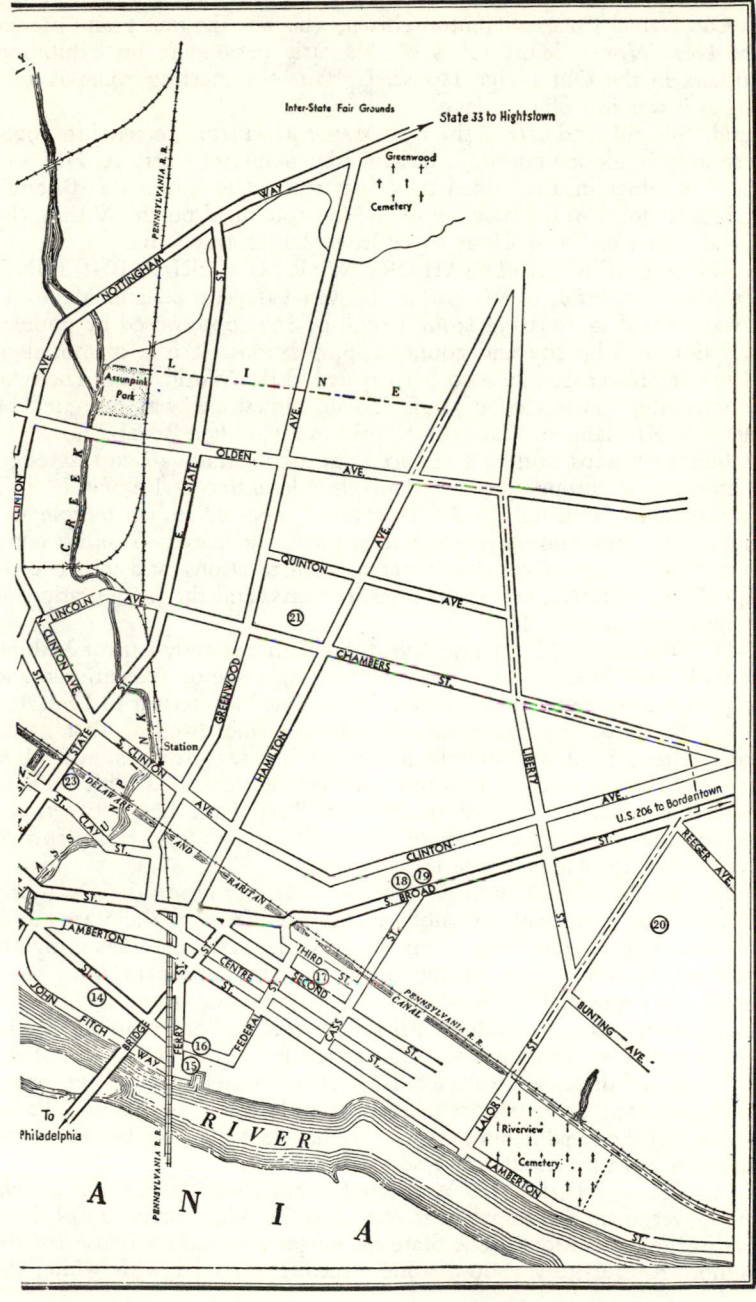

for the first provincial grand master in America. The honor was conferred upon Col. Daniel Coxe, a Trenton citizen, who was the first grand master in the New World. Many relics of this early period are on exhibition downstairs in the Old Lodge House. Upstairs the meeting room is furnished as it was in Colonial days.

Beside this old landmark is the new MASONIC TEMPLE, erected in 1928, a three-story limestone building, designed by architects Harry A. Hill and Ervin G. Gollner in a modified neoclassic style. The entrance is through three bronze doors in the base below the five-columned porch. Within, the wall and arches of the spacious foyer are of Italian travertine.

5. The SOLDIERS' AND SAILORS' WAR MEMORIAL BUILDING *(open 9-4 Mon.-Fri.)*, S. Willow St. betwen Lafayette St. and Memorial Dr., was erected in 1931–32 from a fund of $922,000, raised by popular subscription and by city and county appropriations. It is a memorial to residents of Mercer County who participated in the World War. The two-story structure, constructed of buff Indiana limestone, was designed by William A. Klemann and Louis S. Kaplan in a modified Renaissance style. Four flights of steps lead to a terrace with a balustrade around its edge. The entrance is through bronze doors in Florentine style; within is a Memorial Court, with floor and wall trim of imported Italian marble and ceiling of blue and gold polychrome terra cotta. There are two auditoriums, exhibit rooms, and offices for veterans' organizations and other civic groups. Important civic events, lectures, concerts, and the inauguration of the Governor take place here.

6. The DOUGLASS HOUSE *(private)*, extreme easterly part of Mahlon Stacy Park, near Memorial Dr., was the meeting place of Washington and his officers on January 2, 1777, when they planned the retreat to Princeton after the Battle of the Assunpink. The little frame dwelling then stood at 193 S. Broad St. It was brought to this site in 1923, its green and white Georgian Colonial exterior restored and the interior fitted with modern conveniences. The greensward of Mahlon Stacy Park lies between the house and the river; a picket fence surrounds the building, and a row of quivering poplars stands beside it.

7. MAHLON STACY PARK, Memorial Dr. bordering the Delaware, has 19 acres of lawn, paths, shrubbery and trees, framing the State buildings grouped at its edge. Seen from the park, the Statehouse has a dignity lacking in any other view. Bridges block the view upstream and down; the river flows rapidly here, its shallow waters tumbling over a rock-strewn bed with several small islands. Until a few years ago Sanhican Creek, the former water power canal of the Delaware Falls Co., ran the length of the park. Flocks of ducks were attracted by its still waters and by the open-handed generosity of legislators pausing from labor in the Capitol. Today the section of the canal behind the Capitol has been filled in, but its northern portion provides an attractive series of spillways.

8. HOTEL STERLING, 18 W. State St., has a section that was known as the Government House when it served as the official mansion of Governors in the early 1800's. The State no longer maintains a house for the Governor. A four-story yellow stone structure trimmed with white, the

hotel has been remodeled several times but retains some of its post-Colonial lines.

9. The FIRST PRESBYTERIAN CHURCH, 114 E. State St., has stood in dignified simplicity since 1841. Two township and two city churches, the first dating from 1712, preceded it. Two great fluted columns, surmounted by a pediment, frame the entrance doors, which are painted white and nail-studded in three oblong panels. A lofty, octagonal steeple crowns the stucco on brick building. Buried in the churchyard are many Revolutionists, among them Abraham Hunt, wealthy Trenton merchant. Hunt gave indirect assistance to Washington's victory at Trenton by pressing the Hessian commander to partake of the best in his cellar on the Christmas Night before the battle.

10. The OLD FRIENDS MEETING HOUSE, NW. corner E. Hanover and Montgomery Sts., is characterized by the customary modesty of a Quaker house of worship. Built in 1739, the simple gray stucco structure has a flat roof on one side and a peaked one on the other. The yard, like those of many other Quaker meeting houses, is shaded by a sycamore tree. George Clymer, a signer of the Declaration of Independence, and Gov. Richard Howell, who helped to burn British tea at Greenwich in 1774, are buried here along with such other prominent citizens as Dr. Thomas Cadwalader, Col. Lambert Cadwalader, and Gen. Philemon Dickinson.

11. ST. MICHAELS P. E. CHURCH, 140 N. Warren St., was erected 1819 and has been enlarged from time to time. It is an unusual example of post-Colonial design. Covered with tan stucco, it has mahogany-trimmed windows and entrance, and a crenellated roof that shows a Norman influence. An earlier church was standing on this site in 1748. In the small graveyard, resting place for many distinguished citizens, is buried Pauline Joseph Ann Holton, child of Joseph Bonaparte and the beautiful Annette Savage.

12. ST. MARY'S CATHEDRAL, 157 N. Warren St., was dedicated in 1871 and reflects the Victorian Gothic influence in line and detail. The cathedral stands on land where much of the fighting during the Battle of Trenton took place. A tablet on the adjoining OFFICE OF THE ROMAN CATHOLIC BISHOP of the Trenton diocese recalls that the Hessian commander, Col. Rall, died at his headquarters in the house that formerly stood here.

13. The BATTLE MONUMENT (*open 9-5 daily, adm. 10¢, children 5¢*), intersection of N. Warren St., N. Broad St., Brunswick, Pennington, and Princeton Aves., is a 155-foot shaft surmounted by a heroic statue of Washington. Designed by John Duncan and dedicated in 1893, it marks the spot where Washington's artillery opened fire in the early morning of December 26, 1776. Three bas-reliefs in bronze on the base of the shaft illustrate *The Crossing of the Delaware, The Opening of the Fight,* and *The Surrender of the Hessians.* Two bronze figures stand at the entrance. An elevator runs to the top, from which there is an excellent view of the city.

14. BLOOMSBURY COURT or The WILLIAM TRENT HOUSE (*temporarily closed*), 539 S. Warren St., erected *c.* 1719 by William

Trent, is the oldest house in the city. This fine example of early Georgian Colonial architecture was recently restored by emergency relief agencies. Of red brick with white trim, it is crowned by a hexagonal, copper-roofed cupola with a weather vane. The simplicity of straight lines with no ornamentation is accentuated by bare windows, the shutters being inside. The interior is little altered and retains the original stairway and floor boards. Nine fireplaces and a cellar kitchen fireplace, built by Colonel Trent, are still in good condition. Two upstairs rooms have the original plaster on the walls, and the hallways retain their first cornices. The main downstairs room has the original wall paneling. Well-shaped lawns, marked with boxwood, are enclosed by a brick and wrought-iron fence. There were lavish entertainments at Bloomsbury Court during the ownership of Lt. Col. John Cox, proprietor of the Batsto iron works that supplied the Continental Army. Cox had six daughters, all of whom made matches worthy of their not inconsequential personal charms. One admirer of the Cox girls was said to have been Count Jean de Fersen, who had come to America with Rochambeau because of gossip indicating that his attentions to Marie Antoinette were more than should be expected of a loyal subject of King Louis XVI.

15. The JOHN FITCH MEMORIAL, NE. corner John Fitch Way and Ferry St., is a boulder in honor of Fulton's forerunner in steam navigation. The site, as obscure as Fitch's name, overlooks the Delaware and an unkempt patch of grass and weeds adjoining the Pennsylvania R.R. embankment. Born in Connecticut, Fitch came to Trenton in 1769 as a gunmaker and metal worker. Here he learned the trade of a silversmith. He served as a lieutenant during the Revolution and later, fired by dreams of westward expansion of the new Nation, studied an idea for building a boat that could travel against the current of the great Mississippi and Ohio Rivers.

Fitch had heard of the stationary steam engine, although he had never seen one. He proceeded to build a boat propelled by a series of paddles on both sides that, in 1786, gave a successful demonstration before Benjamin Franklin and other noted men. Improvements made during the ensuing four years enabled Fitch's vessel to attain a speed of eight miles an hour against the Delaware current. Philadelphia newspapers in 1790, a full 17 years before Robert Fulton's *Clermont* was demonstrated on Hudson River, carried advertisements of Fitch's packet operating on a regular schedule between various points on the Delaware.

Although Fitch was granted exclusive rights to construct and operate steamboats by New Jersey and four other States, he was unable to win support of financiers and Congress. Discouraged, he retired to the backwoods of Kentucky and there committed suicide in 1798. He was buried in a pauper's grave at Bardstown, Ky. Later a memorial was erected in front of the Bardstown courthouse.

16. FARMERS' MARKET *(open 6 p.m.-11 p.m. weekdays during season)*, S. Warren St., S. of Ferry St., has two lanes of open sheds with the river and wharves for background. Every summer night except Sunday there is a line-up of trucks, pleasure cars and even wagons, all with dis-

BATTLE MONUMENT, TRENTON

plays of farm produce that attract a large number of buyers. The market has been operated by the city since 1918.

17. The NEW JERSEY STATE PRISON *(open upon identification Tues., Thurs.)*, 3rd St. between Federal and Cass Sts., encloses an entire block with its great red stone walls, studded with guard towers. Part of the present structure was erected in 1836. Numerous additions have been made, but the institution is still seriously overcrowded. Congestion has been relieved in part by the transfer of prisoners to farms at Leesburg and Bordentown, and by the removal of women inmates to a farm at Clinton.

Under the liberal management of the State department of institutions and agencies, a progressive program for handling prisoners has been developed in recent years. Striped suits were replaced with dark gray in 1917. Prior to that time, the State prison was known for a disciplinary system that was one of the most severe in the Nation. Operating today under a scientific classification plan and the honor system, the institution has more than one-fourth of its prisoners working on the farms as trusties. The escape record is one of the lowest in the country.

Inmates are taught elementary subjects up to the eighth grade and may, if they wish, continue their studies through correspondence courses. Instruction in trades is given in wood, tin, concrete, printing, and machine shops. Large numbers of shoes are manufactured and repaired.

A crowd of about one thousand persons gathered outside the prison walls on the night of April 3, 1936, to await word of the execution, after two reprieves, of Bruno Richard Hauptmann for the murder of Charles A. Lindbergh Jr. More than 100 city police, 50 State troopers, and a fire company, with hose connected, were on guard. Within, the stolid carpenter walked silently to the chair and was given three shocks of electricity while two ministers read the Bible in German. The convicted man, who had stoutly maintained his innocence, was pronounced dead at 8:47½ p.m. Two minutes later a guard walked to a window and nodded his head. A policeman outside said, "I guess that's all." The crowd dispersed quietly.

18. The JOHN A. ROEBLING SONS PLANT *(open by permission)*, 640 S. Broad St., produces wire rope and wire cable which not only support some of the world's largest bridges but are also used to strengthen and operate many airplanes. A modern, four-story, red brick building trimmed with Indiana limestone houses the administrative offices and technical departments. At the side and rear are the mills, also of red brick.

19. The SWITLIK PARACHUTE AND EQUIPMENT PLANT *(not open to public)*, 2nd floor of 649 S. Broad St., manufactures parachutes and other airplane equipment almost exclusively for the Federal Government. The company advertises the fastest-opening parachute in the world, and was the first to make the chair chute, a combination of chair and parachute.

20. BOW HILL *(private)*, 0.25 m. S. of Lalor St. between Bunting and Reeger Aves., was known as "Beau Hill" to wits of a century ago; for here the former King of Spain, Joseph Bonaparte, housed his lovely Quaker mistress, Annette Savage. The old red brick mansion stands back from

Lalor Street, lonely and neglected in the shadow of great trees, against a background of water towers and smokestacks of nearby factories.

Bonaparte is said to have met Annette when she sold him suspenders across the counter of her mother's store in Philadelphia. To shield her from the cold disapproval which his interest evoked in Philadelphia society, the Count de Survilliers (as he then called himself) took Annette to what he hoped would be friendly security in rural Trenton. But the good women of Trenton were no more hospitable to the ex-King's friend. It was a lonely life for Annette, with Bonaparte living several miles away at Bordentown; and the death of their young daughter, Pauline Joseph Ann Holton, added grief to loneliness. In 1824 Bonaparte took his mistress to New York State, where he built a house and laid out the town of Diana. The romance ended when the Revolution of 1830 sent Bonaparte back to his former queen. Annette maried a young Frenchman and eventually resumed storekeeping at Watertown, N. Y. Another daughter by Bonaparte, named Charlotte, grew to womanhood and so pleased Napoleon III that he legalized her parents' union and had Charlotte presented at court as his cousin.

Bow Hill was built *c.* 1785 by Barnt De Klyn, a French Huguenot who made a fortune selling cloth to the Continental Army and bought thousands of acres along the Delaware in the belief that Trenton would become the national capital. Since the death of the last of De Klyn's descendants to live in the house, it has been in charge of a caretaker.

21. CENTRAL HIGH SCHOOL, Chambers St. between Hamilton and Greenwood Aves., is considered one of the best equipped secondary schools of the country, with an enrollment of about 3,750 students. Built in 1932, the design adheres closely to the Georgian Colonial style. The central unit is of three stories, surmounted by a clock tower that unifies the entire composition; on each side is a wing in the form of a hollow square connected by enclosed cloisters. The architect was Lawrence L. Licht.

22. The LENOX POTTERIES *(open 9-5 weekdays),* 50 Meade St., manufacture internationally known pottery in a modern plant built largely of glass. Displayed in a Tudor style showroom are some of the best pieces produced, including service plates priced at $6,000 a dozen. Workmen execute with enthralling precision the successive steps in making china: mixing, pebble grinding, screening, ageing, shaping, drying, firing, inspecting, glazing, decorating, color firing and gold firing.

As a schoolboy in the late 1860's, Walter Lenox used to stand for hours before a little pottery that he passed daily, watching the transformation of dull clay into shapes of beauty. He learned the trade as an apprentice and resolved to set up his own pottery for making the finest china. But his backers were so skeptical that they stipulated that the building should be designed for use as a tenement in case the pottery failed. After many fruitless attempts, Lenox finally produced the creamy, richly glazed china for which his name is known.

Stricken blind and paralyzed in 1895, when his dream was all but realized, Lenox then had to depend on his friend and company secretary, Harry A. Brown, to solve the industry's money problems. When Brown paid off the last debt, a miniature kiln was built in the office and the canceled notes burned in it. Lenox stood by, tears running from his sightless eyes. He died in 1920.

23. The MUNICIPAL BUILDING *(open)*, 315 E. State St., is a three-story structure of neoclassic design erected in 1911 from the plans of Spencer Roberts. Twelve Doric columns above the broad steps form a colonnade along the second-story front. In the council chamber a fine mural by Everett Shinn depicts the pottery and iron industries of Trenton. Over the doorway is a painting of the original cruiser *Trenton*.

24. CADWALADER PARK, Parkside Ave., Stuyvesant Ave. and Cadwalader Dr., is the largest of the city's parks, with 208 acres. It is bordered in part by the Delaware and Raritan Canal feeder. Plays and concerts are given here in an outdoor theater. A small menagerie of wolves, monkeys, raccoons, rabbits, bears, and deer provides entertainment for Trenton youngsters.

POINTS OF INTEREST IN ENVIRONS

Walker-Gordon Farm with Rotolactor, *11.4 m. (see Tour 1);* Princeton University, *9.7 m. (see PRINCETON); John Bull* Monument to pioneer locomotive, *6.6 m. (see Tour 6);* Washington Crossing State Park, *8.3 m. (see Tour 11).*

PART III

Tours

GEORGE WASHINGTON MEMORIAL BRIDGE

Tour 1

(New York, N. Y.)—Fort Lee—Jersey City—Elizabeth—Trenton—(Morrisville, Pa.); US 1.
New York Line to Pennsylvania Line, 68.1 m.

The route is paralleled between Fort Lee and Jersey City by the Erie R.R.; between Newark and Trenton by the Pennsylvania R.R.
Meals and gasoline constantly available; first-class hotels in cities. Superhighway of four or six lanes throughout, paved almost entirely with concrete.

US 1, designed to speed the heavy traffic flow between New York and Philadelphia, avoids most urban congestion by by-passing every city. Because the road runs for miles without a turn and is the most heavily traveled State highway, many New Jersey residents avoid it. They choose the alternate route, State 27 *(see Tour 8)*, between Elizabeth and Trenton, which offers scenery and historic landmarks not found along US 1. Motorists who wish to test their skill on a modern highway should follow US 1. State police carefully patrol the route.

South of the George Washington Bridge, where the New York-New Jersey State Line is crossed, US 1 twists through a maze of underpasses and overpasses until it straightens out for a gradual descent along the western slope of the Palisades. Metropolitan residential and industrial development has claimed all of the land here, except for the marshy lowlands of Overpeck Creek. Westward are clusters of commuters' towns, and in the distance the hazy outline of the Ramapo Mountains. From Jersey City the road sweeps upward to Pulaski Skyway, giving a panorama of the New York hinterland, a region of smokestacks and marshes, of a few skyscrapers and many tenements, of patterns in steel rails and confusion in garbage dumps. Between Newark and Linden the industrial area thins out; southward the highway traverses New Jersey countryside, with farms, woodland, nurseries, and only an occasional factory until the outlying part of Trenton is reached. Hills are rare, and there is little in the landscape to divert the driver's attention from the long, straight path of concrete lying ahead.

US 1 crosses the New Jersey Line, 0 *m.*, on GEORGE WASHINGTON BRIDGE *(toll 50¢ for car and driver, pd. at Jersey end)*, 9.2 *m.* northwest of mid-town Manhattan (New York City).

The bridge, completed in 1931, is a dramatic gateway to New Jersey. Its steel towers rise 630 feet above the Hudson River and its main span is 3,500 feet long. The towers are twice the height of the Palisades at this point though the fact is not apparent to those on the structure. Four cables, each 47 inches in diameter and containing 26,474 wires, provide strength enough to support the present deck and another that can be added. The bridge cost $57,000,000 and 14 lives.

From the roadway, 250 feet above the river at the center, the view southward includes the tallest buildings of Manhattan, the high-perched tower of RIVERSIDE CHURCH at 122nd St., the unbroken line of apartment houses along Riverside Dr., the North River berths of the largest ocean liners, and the busy ferry traffic between the New York and New Jersey terminals. Northward is the path of summer excursion boats to Bear Mt., and of freight and passenger vessels between New York and Albany. Straight ahead, partly hidden by foliage in summer, is the sheer face of the PALISADES. This barricade of rock, given the form of columns when the molten mass cooled, shrank, and cracked beneath the earth's surface, was covered ages past by a layer of sediment several thousand feet deep, which was gradually worn away. Excavations for the New Jersey bridge approach revealed the tracks of dinosaurs in the Triassic rock.

At the end of the bridge approach in Jersey is a junction with US 9W (see Tour 3).

FORT LEE, 1.3 m. (280 alt., 8,759 pop.), appears chiefly as an assort-ment of roadhouses, oil stations, and small eating places. The residential and business district is off the highway (L). Little of the community is seen, however, because of the series of highway underpasses and over-passes designed for automatic sorting of the bridge traffic. (Watch care-fully for US 1 markers.)

During the Revolution this plateau at the crest of the Palisades was selected by Washington as the site of the fort for which the town is named. His plan was to prevent the British fleet from sailing up the Hud-son River to West Point. From the rocky bluff, Washington watched the attack and surrender of his garrison at Fort Washington, directly across the river, in November 1776. A few days later he was forced to abandon Fort Lee.

Early in the twentieth century Fort Lee became one of the cradles of the motion-picture industry. Before narrow, boxlike cameras, with reels on top like the ears of Mickey Mouse, cowboys and Indians exchanged fusillades and whoops as, respectively, they galloped madly to rescue the lovely maiden from a fate worse than death or to write another terrible chapter in frontier history. Serial thrillers are no longer made here, but a printing studio that normally employs several hundred persons still oper-ates. Some of the barnlike buildings used by the old studios are near the highway (L). A red dome and gilded cross (L) are on the CONVENT OF HOLY ANGELS.

Swinging south after its separation from the other bridge exits and approaches, US 1 crosses Main St., Fort Lee, down which Washington marched after evacuating the fort. For a short distance the highway runs on the western crest of the Palisades ridge. Here there is no rock wall, but elevation is sufficient to permit a broad view of Overpeck Creek in the valley below, and, beyond the next ridge, the slender line of the Hacken-sack River.

The road begins its descent to the valley on a long straight embankment. Below (R) lies the community of PALISADES PARK, with a cluster of apartment houses, small dwellings, and schools.

At 2.9 *m.* US 46 *(see Tour 7)* branches L. from US 1 and enters a depressed route through Morsemere.

MORSEMERE, 3 *m.,* a recent real-estate development, has a modern business district in the English Tudor style. US 1 is at street level, and turns L. on an overpass above the depressed route of US 46.

Entering the residential section of Ridgefield, US 1 is asphalt paved. A WORLD WAR MONUMENT stands in a small plot (L); just south of it at 3.4 *m.* is the old SAMUEL WRIGHT HOUSE (R), hugging the slope. Only the back is seen from the highway. Built in 1790, the structure is an excellent example of the Dutch Colonial style of architecture. Dormer windows and other additions and alterations have not spoiled the original charm. Other old houses are still standing along this part of the road.

RIDGEFIELD, 3.9 *m.* (30 alt., 4,671 pop.), has an unpretentious shopping center on the highway.

South of Ridgefield the highway is almost on the floor of the valley. On both sides of the road are drab homes and factories.

FAIRVIEW, 4.8 *m.* (20 alt., 9,067 pop.), is announced by the acrid smell from a bleachery. A few hundred yards from the highway (R) is a scattered group of 54 small gray buildings, the INTERNATIONAL FIRE-WORKS CO. PLANT, one of the largest manufacturers of display fireworks. Here were made the elaborate fireworks for the inaugurals of Presidents Wilson, Hoover, and Roosevelt. Routine business is the making of "True Lovers' Knots" and "Fountains of Youth" for use at conventions of fraternal orders and for civic celebrations.

Between Fairview and North Bergen the route passes a CEMETERY (L), and an adjacent MONUMENT WORKS that sells bird baths and bridge prizes as a side line. At 6.4 *m.* the twin towers of radio station WINS at Carlstadt are about 3 miles R.

On the upward slope (L) are rocky outcroppings of the underlying Palisades, upon which small houses and shacks barely find a foothold. Below, on the valley's edge (R), are a refrigerator terminal and a round-house of the N. Y. Central R.R.

At 7.9 *m.* is the junction with Bergen Pike, a concrete paved road.

Left on Bergen Pike, a well-posted road, to the junction with Hudson Blvd. East, 1.5 *m.*

1. Right on Hudson Blvd. East and R. down a ramp to the LINCOLN TUNNEL, 1.7 *m. (toll 50¢ for car and passengers),* opened December 22, 1937. Until a second tube is finished in 1940, the 8,215-foot tunnel will carry two-way traffic. Construction of the second half of the project, a 7,400-foot tube, will bring the total cost to $75,000,000. Built 60 feet under the low-water level of the Hudson River, Lincoln Tunnel was designed by Port of New York Authority engineers as a direct link with mid-town Manhattan.

2. Left on Hudson Blvd. East to (R) the SITE OF THE HAMILTON-BURR DUEL, 2.2 *m.,* near the bottom of the cliff at Hudson Blvd. East opposite Duer Pl., indicated by a marker in a small park on the brink of the Palisades. The residential section of Weehawken is on the cliff; 300 feet below, railroad tracks have been built on a narrow strip of land, bordered by the Hudson on the one side and the vertical escarpment on the other. Here, on the same spot where his son, Philip, had

HAMILTON-BURR DUEL MARKER, WEEHAWKEN

been killed in a duel 3 years earlier, Alexander Hamilton was mortally wounded by Aaron Burr, then Vice President of the United States, on the morning of July 11, 1804. For 15 years the two men had been political enemies, but it was not until Hamilton's libelous criticisms reached the press that Burr issued the challenge. Burr appeared on the grounds before Hamilton with his second and the surgeon. As the duellists were preparing, Hamilton stopped the proceedings to put on his spectacles. The two men fired in succession at the command, "Present!"; Hamilton's bullet passed through the limb of a cedar about 12 feet above the ground, while Burr's shot caught his opponent in the breast. Hamilton rose on his toes, twisted and fell to the ground. As Burr left the field, shielded by an umbrella to conform with the technicality of remaining unrecognized, he heard Hamilton exclaim: "This is a mortal wound, Doctor. I am a dead man!" Burr's comment was prophetic. "He may thank me," he said. "I made him a great man." Hamilton died on the afternoon of the following day. Inflamed by the press to view Burr as a murderer, both New York and New Jersey indicted him. Burr fled first to Pennsylvania, but threats of extradition and lynch mobs sent him to the aristocratic South, where the duelling code was respected. There he stayed until Congress reconvened and the temper of the country had cooled.

About 200 yards south, on Hamilton Ave., is the ALEXANDER HAMILTON MONUMENT, a stone base surmounted by a bronze bust of the first Secretary of the Treasury.

NORTH BERGEN, 8.3 *m.* (25 alt., 40,714 township pop.), has churches, stores, and two large gas tanks near the highway. The business section gives no indication of the extent of this residential township, and little indication of where the village begins or ends.

At 8.5 *m.* the route crosses the PATERSON PLANK ROAD, now paved. The original plank road, dating from 1816, was part of the Paterson-Hamburg Turnpike. The Hoboken-Paterson extension, laid in 1816, reduced the traveling time between Paterson and Jersey City from two days to one.

At 8.7 *m.* a traffic circle is the junction with State Highway 3 (R) which 1 mile west joins the Paterson Plank Road.

Entering the outlying northern section of Jersey City, US 1 follows Tonnelle Ave. The highway overpasses the main-line tracks of the Pennsylvania R.R., just W. of the only trunk-line tunnel from New Jersey into Manhattan. The gold-striped, streamlined electric locomotives operated between New York City and Washington use these tracks.

To the southwest is the irregular hump of LAUREL HILL, also called Snake Hill, lone break in the uniform flatness of the marshlands. Geologists say that it is probably the eroded stump of an ancient volcano that once cast up enough molten rock to form the Watchung Mts. 10 miles westward. The buildings of the Hudson County penal and welfare institutions are grouped on the hill.

The meadowlands have their own skyline. On the banks of the Hackensack River (R) stand the six great chimneys of a Public Service Electric and Gas Co. plant, and a gas and coke plant. Beyond are small hills of coke, several times the height of a freight car. The towers of railroad and highway drawbridges are grouped at the river close by.

At 11.5 *m.,* at a traffic circle, is the entrance to Pulaski Skyway.

Straight ahead from this circle on a concrete highway, to Newark Ave.; L. on Newark Ave. to Hudson Blvd.; R. on Hudson Blvd is JERSEY CITY, 0.7 *m.* (60 alt., 316,715 pop.) *(see JERSEY CITY).*

Points of Interest: Old Bergen Church, Van Wagenen House, Colgate-Palmolive-Peet Plant, Ionic House, Medical Center, Lincoln Park, and others.

Swinging R. from the traffic circle, US 1 enters PULASKI SKYWAY. This steel and concrete viaduct, named for the Polish nobleman who lost his life in the American Revolution, is 3.6 miles long, rises 145 feet above the Hackensack and Passaic Rivers, and cost $21,000,000. An average of more than 30,000 vehicles use it daily. This was a pioneer achievement in the solution of the problem of handling through traffic in one of the most congested traffic areas in the world; the situation here was aggravated by the marshy terrain, which has restricted the number of highways and bridges.

No towering office buildings dominate Jersey City's skyline (L), but rather the broad bulk of the Old Gold cigaret and the Listerine factories and, dominating all, the light gray units of the AMERICAN CAN CO. PLANT, close to the highway. The gray stone clock tower of ST. JOHN'S CATHOLIC CHURCH, near Journal Sq. in the heart of Jersey City, stands out.

The skyway rises to the cantilever span crossing the Hackensack River. Were it not for the heavy I-beam railing, there would be excellent views of the waterways adjacent to New York Harbor and of the Newark industrial area. Full views are possible only when the two high points of the skyway are crossed; from those points are seen the tall office buildings of Newark, almost hidden by the gas tanks of Harrison. To the L., seen by a right-angle glance through the railing, is one of the great garbage dumps for which the Newark meadows are famous. Next is the large WESTERN ELECTRIC CO. PLANT, at the head of Newark Bay where the Hackensack and the Passaic Rivers unite. The sun glints sharply from the roofs of hundreds of employees' cars, parked in neat formation next to the factory. To the rear (L) are the towers of midtown and then downtown Manhattan, then the slight elevation that is Brooklyn, the gap of The Narrows (entrance to New York Harbor) and finally the hilly outline of Staten Island, 8 miles south. The haze from factory smoke often obliterates part of the landscape, and the no-parking rule makes use of field glasses impracticable.

Two more large plants of Public Service, dominant power and local transportation company of the State, are R. of the skyway. The first of these is unusual because it boils mercury instead of water to operate its turbine for generating electricity.

The view farther R. is up the valleys of the Hackensack and the Passaic Rivers. The best picture of Newark, straight ahead, is from the cantilever span across the Passaic River. At the western end of the skyway US 1 enters the Newark city limits. Elevated on a fill, the road takes a straight course through a concentrated industrial area, with freight tracks of the Pennsylvania R.R. running parallel (R). Westward along the route is one of Newark's poorer residential districts.

Once more the highway climbs, bridging the main freight line of the Lehigh Valley R.R. It descends on a broad embankment, curving in a wide arc. On both sides are home-made huts and garden patches, occupying what was formerly a dumping ground. Built of materials salvaged from dumps, the huts have served for several years as daytime shelters for men, women, and children from needy families in Newark, who come here to raise vegetables for immediate consumption and for canning. The gardeners take almost belligerent pride in their work, competing for prizes for the best yields. In summer the huts are brightly decorated with flowers, flags, and latticework.

At 17.5 *m.*, at a traffic circle, is the junction with a paved road.

Left on this road to NEWARK AIRPORT, 0.2 *m.* *(see NEWARK)*.

At 18.5 *m.* is the junction with State 21 and US 22 *(see Tour 2)*, overpassed by westbound traffic on US 1.

Right on State 21 to the business center of NEWARK, 1.8 *m.* (33 alt., 442,337 pop.) *(see NEWARK)*.

Points of Interest: Newark Library, Plume House, First Presbyterian Church, Newark Museum, Weston Electric Plant, Sacred Heart Cathedral, Borglum's Statue of Abraham Lincoln, and others.

Between this junction and Elizabeth the road is a broad belt of asphalt, so crowded with trucks and pleasure cars that it is of more than usual danger. Concrete paving has not yet been laid because the earth fill is still settling into the marsh. On both sides of the low embankment the flats are covered with tall meadow grass and cattails, brightened with sunflowers in the summer months.

Several miles to the south is (L) the sweeping arch of BAYONNE BRIDGE, completed in 1928 and extending across Kill van Kull between Bayonne, N. J., and Staten Island, N. Y. With a span of 1,675 feet, it is the longest steel-arch bridge in the world. Almost straight ahead is the cantilever span of GOETHALS BRIDGE, finished in 1931, between Elizabeth, N. J., and Staten Island, N. Y.

Some of the large industrial plants of Newark are R. Next to the main line tracks of the Pennsylvania R.R. is ELIZABETH AIRWAY RADIO (L), a station maintained by the U. S. Department of Commerce to guide planes within a radius of 100 miles by means of the radio beam to Newark Airport.

At North Ave., Elizabeth, is the first traffic light west of Jersey City. The highway is safer here, with a grass strip dividing the street. Frame houses and some industrial and business establishments are on both sides of the road.

At 22.2 *m.* is the intersection with E. Jersey St.

Right on E. Jersey St. to the business center of ELIZABETH, 0.5 *m.* (70 alt., 114,589 pop.) *(see ELIZABETH)*.

Points of Interest: First Presbyterian Church, Union County Courthouse Annex (museum), Carteret Arms, Scott Park, Boudinot House, Singer Sewing Machine Plant, and others.

South of E. Jersey St. the highway is carried for a short distance on a concrete and steel viaduct, bridging cross streets near the center of Elizabeth. The elevation is enough to give a fine view of the city, accented by the needlelike spire of old FIRST PRESBYTERIAN CHURCH and the tall white tower of UNION COUNTY COURTHOUSE (R). The narrow channel of ELIZABETH RIVER, crossed by the viaduct, seems unbelievably small to have been an important waterway during Colonial and early republican years.

At 23.5 *m.,* at a traffic circle, is the junction with State 28 *(see Tour 17)*.

US 1 passes through the fringe of an extensive oil-refining district. Storage tanks of the Standard Oil Co. are illuminated nightly with colored lights. A familiar sight is the Standard Oil herd of goats, which keeps the grass around the tanks closely cropped; they are used instead of mechanical lawnmowers because of the risk of sparks. The road here enters the first open country west of George Washington Bridge.

LINDEN, 25.6 *m.* (25 alt., 21,206 pop.), has a business district to serve local people and the endless chain of motor traffic. A large part of the population works at local industrial plants. On the highway (R) is WHEELER PARK, an attractive recreational area maintained by the county. Just west of the park are (R) two of Linden's newest and most important industries, the neatly landscaped PLANT OF THE GORDON DRY GIN CO. and a GENERAL MOTORS ASSEMBLY PLANT *(open for group tours weekdays 10 a.m. and 2 p.m.)*. The Bayway refinery of the Standard Oil Co. of N. J. is within the municipality. Several miles from US 1 are (L) the twin masts of radio station WOR's transmitter at Carteret, each 485 feet high.

At 28 *m.* US 1 swings L., ascends an embankment, and crosses the RAHWAY RIVER. The big dome of the NEW JERSEY REFORMATORY *(open daily except Sunday by appointment; groups limited to 25 persons),* with its buttressed concrete wall and surrounding farm, is close to the highway (L). A school for juvenile offenders is conducted here with training in several industrial crafts.

The route traverses farming country in this section; red barns and an occasional dairy herd are reminders of the rural setting that was unbroken until construction of the speed highway several years ago spawned myriad Tip-Top Bars, Cozy Nooks, Servicenters, Klub Kalitas, and other accessories of highway culture.

At 30.3 *m.,* at the Rahway cloverleaf intersection, US 9 *(see Tour 18)* branches (L) from US 1.

Between this point and Trenton the highway is through woodlands and farm country. State police, wearing French blue coats and dark blue trousers with a broad gold stripe, patrol the road, using automobiles as well as motorcycles.

At 33.6 *m.* (R) is ROOSEVELT PARK, a tract of 192 acres that is the first unit of the Middlesex County park system. Men employed by the ERA and the WPA set to work on a small wilderness of marsh and underbrush and made a park, well landscaped and equipped with all facilities for picnickers. Over the hill is an artificial lake, and within the park are the new MIDDLESEX COUNTY TUBERCULOSIS HOSPITAL, a handsomely designed building erected with PWA funds *(see Tour 8),* and the KIDDIE KEEP-WELL CAMP, where undernourished children are given summer vacations.

The highway rolls with scarcely a curve through somewhat undulating country. For 5 miles the road was paralleled until 1937 by the rusty rails of what used to be a high-speed electric line between Elizabeth and New Brunswick. Electric cars gave way to a small motorbus, equipped with steel flanges on the tires, which made one trip as far as Bonhamtown Junction once a week. At this point the flanges were removed, the bus driven off the rails and turned around, and the flanges replaced. Weeks passed without any passengers being carried; the sole purpose of the run was to hold the franchise.

At 35.3 *m.* is the junction with a concrete and asphalt road.

Left on this road is BONHAMTOWN, 0.8 *m.* (80 alt., 800 pop.), a country village with two small churches, a school, and a general store, on a winding main street. The settlement dates far back into the Colonial period, and was the scene of skirmishes during the Revolutionary War. It is the site of the U. S. Army's RARITAN ARSENAL *(not open to public),* a large depot for the storage and distribution of ordnance material. In the magazine area can be stored enough ammunition to supply a field army for more than 30 days. The cost of plant and equipment on this 2,200-acre tract was $14,000,000; the value of material in storage is about $240,000,000.

PISCATAWAY, 3.5 *m.* (120 alt., 2,011 pop.), has a few modern business buildings scattered along its main thoroughfare. By far the most interesting and attractive structure in the community is ST. JAMES' EPISCOPAL CHURCH (L), a glistening white building, almost square, with four large pillars and a tiny steeple. This edi-

GENERAL MOTORS ASSEMBLY LINE, LINDEN

fice, the third built by a parish organized in 1714, was consecrated in 1837. It is a reproduction of the church destroyed by a tornado in 1835 that tossed the pulpit into the Raritan River, which carried it to the shore of Staten Island, 15 miles away. The original bell, brought from England in 1702, still hangs in the belfry. Curious inscriptions are found on the stones in the adjoining graveyard. One, dated 1693, tells of twin boys who skipped Sunday service to gather mushrooms in the woods. The mushrooms were, as the epitaph has it, "poyseond." Another tombstone is that of Harper, reputedly an atheist, who had obtained the deed to his new brick house on the day of the 1835 tornado. Celebrating his acquisition at the village tavern, he ran out into the road when the windstorm struck the town and defied God to kill him. Hardly had the blasphemous words left his lips, so the story goes, when the church roof blew off and a flying timber crushed him to death.

At **3.7** *m.* this side road rejoins US 1.

At 39 *m.* US 1 crosses the Raritan River on COLLEGE BRIDGE, a handsome structure of reinforced concrete arches, designed by Morris Goodkind of the State highway department and given an architectural award in 1930. Part of the campus of NEW JERSEY COLLEGE FOR WOMEN is R., spread out upon the bluff above the river. The spire is that of VOORHEES CHAPEL, on the campus. Beyond are some of the buildings of New Brunswick; and the view upstream is not unlike that at Stratford on Avon. The road passes the NEW BRUNSWICK WAR MEMORIAL (L) at 39.6 *m.*

At **39.8** *m.*, at a traffic circle, is the junction with State S28 *(see Tour 13).*

Right on State S28 is NEW BRUNSWICK, 2.5 *m.* (125 alt., 34,555 pop.) *(see NEW BRUNSWICK).*

Points of Interest: Rutgers University Campuses and Buildings, White House, Guest House, Joyce Kilmer Memorial (museum), and others.

South of New Brunswick are (R) the grounds of the NEW JERSEY STATE COLLEGE OF AGRICULTURE, 41.1 *m. (see NEW BRUNSWICK).*

At 44.8 *m.* is the junction with US 130 *(see Tour 19).*

The highway here closely follows the original route of stagecoach days, when it was an important land link between the water highways of the Raritan and Delaware Rivers. For almost 25 miles there is no perceptible curve, although there are two or three very slight deviations from a straight line. To prevent collision, the 11.9-mile stretch south of the railroad overpass has been divided by a center strip, and the work is to be continued toward Trenton. The concrete was forced apart by compressed air to make room for the strip and curbs; a new subgrade was prepared at the side, and as much as a 500-foot length was moved into position at one time.

Nurseries and well-kept farms are on both sides of the road. From a low-lying ridge at 54.3 *m.* is a view (R) of PRINCETON UNIVERSITY *(see PRINCETON)* across the meadowland of an intervening valley. The university buildings, largely hidden by oaks and elms, are dwarfed by the massive Grover Cleveland tower of the graduate school. In the foreground is the bulk of Palmer Stadium; through the trees is an occasional glimpse of Carnegie Lake.

At 54.7 *m.* is (L) the plant and animal pathology division of the ROCKEFELLER INSTITUTE FOR MEDICAL RESEARCH *(not open to public).* Founded in 1901, the organization has conducted investigations and instituted health reforms throughout the world. Of major significance has been the work of Dr. Wendell M. Stanley, who won the American Association for the Advancement of Science prize for his study of disease-producing viruses. Dr. Stanley announced in 1935 the isolation of the virus of a tobacco plant disease and the discovery that this virus was not a living animal organism (bacterium) but rather a gigantic protein molecule. In addition to its great size, this molecule differed from other protein molecules in a very important respect: it could reproduce itself. For years scientists had been looking for this missing link in evolutionary development—the bridge between the animate and the inanimate—a nonliving substance with the property of reproduction. Inanimate substances, such as proteins, were never before known to possess this property. Since the original discovery, other protein virus molecules, each different and each responsible for a specific virus disease in plants and animals, have been isolated. Dr. Stanley's work leads the way for the development of new methods in the prevention and treatment of human disease. It is possible that giant protein molecules, existing within the body in a harmless form, may change into a disease-producing virus, of the type that causes such diseases as infantile paralysis and the common cold. Further, discovery of the ability of some molecules to change may provide a key to the evolutionary process that has enabled Nature to create a multitude of different living species.

STANDARD OIL REFINERY, BAYWAY

At 55.6 *m.* is the junction with a dirt road, marked by a gatehouse.

Left on this road and visible from the highway is the WALKER-GORDON FARM *(open to public)*. Operated by the Borden Milk Co., the plant is known for its Rotolactor, a revolving platform that combines the method of an automobile assembly line with the mechanical features of a carousel, for the purpose of milking cows efficiently. The cows step on and off the platform and are milked and stripped in 12½ minutes, within one complete revolution of the wheel. The 1,400 cows are milked by the Rotolactor in less than 6 hours.

PENN'S NECK, 56.4 *m.* (100 alt.), is one of the most attractive hamlets on US 1. Here, just beyond the traffic circle, the road underpasses the Princeton branch of the Pennsylvania R.R. Beyond the cut of the hill are two Colonial mansions; a nursery rose field (L) provides several acres of color in season.

The road crosses the abandoned DELAWARE AND RARITAN CANAL at Bakers Basin, one of the few places where water still remains. Since the angle of intersection between highway and canal is 24 degrees, the construction of a drawbridge in 1931 presented an unusual problem in engineering. The fruit of many experimental designs, the bridge was first assembled at the mill and tested there before being put into place. Although the canal is only 28 feet wide here, the bridge required 110-foot girders, and its shape is that of an elongated lozenge instead of the usual rectangle. All of the machinery is R. of the road, and the bridge hinges at the end toward Trenton. Since the canal has been abandoned for a number of years, the bridge is no longer operated.

At 64.3 *m.* is (L) an artificial lake on Shabakunk Creek, a branch of historic Assunpink Creek. Herons often alight here, close by the highway.

At 64.8 *m.,* at a traffic circle, is the junction with US 206 *(see Tour 6).*

Left on US 206 to the center of TRENTON, 2.2 *m.* (55 alt., 123,356 pop.) *(see TRENTON).*

Points of Interest: State Buildings, Library and Museum, Old Barracks, Mahlon Stacy Park, First Presbyterian Church, Bloomsbury Court, Bow Hill, Lenox Potteries, and others.

Swinging R. from the traffic circle, US 1 runs past rows of typical brick houses on Princeton Ave., which continues as N. Warren St. and S. Warren St., to Bridge St.; R. on Bridge St. to the Delaware River Bridge.

At 68.1 *m.,* on the Delaware River Bridge *(free),* US 1 crosses the Pennsylvania Line 0.5 miles east of Morrisville, Pa.

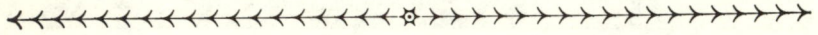

Tour 2

Newark—Hillside—Whitehouse—Clinton—Phillipsburg—(Easton, Pa.);
US 22.
Newark to Pennsylvania Line, 62.4 m.

Between Scotch Plains and Annandale the Jersey Central R.R., and between Perryville and Phillipsburg the Lehigh Valley R.R., parallel the route.
First-class hotels at both terminals; numerous restaurants and filling stations.
Concrete paved, two to six lanes.

Through the fringe of the Newark industrial area US 22 runs westward to the base of the wooded Watchung Mountains. Between Somerville and Annandale the route traverses an undulating plateau, with good views of farming country and the Appalachian foothills. Heavy truck and tourist traffic makes this narrow section dangerous, particularly at night. Musconetcong Mountain is crossed farther west, and the road slopes down to the Delaware Valley. Many fine examples of old stone Colonial houses stand within sight of the highway at various points. Good trout streams are found.

At a traffic circle, 0.5 miles west of the Newark Airport, US 22 forms a junction with US 1 *(see Tour 1).*

At 0.2 *m.* is the junction with State 21, here McCarter Highway.

Right on this road is the center of NEWARK, 1.8 *m.* (33 alt., 442,337 pop.) *(see NEWARK).*

Points of Interest: Newark Library, Plume House, First Presbyterian Church, Newark Museum, Western Electric Plant, Sacred Heart Cathedral, Borglum's Statue of Abraham Lincoln, and others.

WEEQUAHIC PARK, 0.9 *m.*, lies on both sides of the highway *(see NEWARK).*

HILLSIDE, 2.4 *m.* (50 alt., 18,000 pop.), hides its 37 industries behind a residential suburban atmosphere. Many of the commuters to Newark and New York offices do not know that they live in a town where almost everything from toothpaste to engines·is manufactured. Squeezed between residential sections of Newark and Elizabeth, the town reflects the personalities of the two larger cities. Among the nationally known concerns with plants here are the Gar Wood Industries, Inc., the Diesel Manufacturing Co., and the Neil and Spanger Lumber Co. Along the highway, at 2.9 *m.*, is (L) the BRISTOL-MEYERS CO. PLANT *(open upon application),* where toilet and drug products are made.

At 4.8 *m.* the highway bears L. at a junction with State S24 *(see Tour 10).*

UNION, 5.3 *m.* (100 alt., 16,472 pop.) *(see Tour 10).*

A recently developed residential area at 6.2 *m.* surrounds GALLOPING HILL GOLF COURSE, operated by the Union County Park Commission *(greens fees $1; $2 to $3 Sat., Sun., and holidays; lower rates for county residents).* The club occupies the low, rounded peak of Galloping Hill, so named because of the British military dispatch riders who galloped over the road here—an unusual sight for farmers who walked their horses on the steep hill.

At 6.6 *m.* is (L) DRIVE-IN THEATER *(adm. 35¢),* accommodating 400 cars on nine concentric, semicircular parking areas. Feature pictures are shown each night at 8:20 and 10:20, rain or shine, on a screen 55 feet wide and 45 feet high.

At 7 *m.* is (R) BATTLE HILL GOLF COURSE *(greens fees 50¢-75¢; $1-$1.50 Sat., Sun., and holidays)* and the UNION SPEEDWAY *(weekly or bimonthly races from early May until late Oct.; adm. $1.20-$2.25).*

Roadside stands along this part of the route specialize in cut flowers; in spring and summer there are acres of pansies and mountain pinks along the road. Honey, eggs, vegetables, and fruit are sold from the front steps of many residences.

Trout, bass, and perch fishing is excellent in the Rahway River at 7.7 *m.* *(no fishing Fri. when trout supply is replenished by State Fish and Game Commission).* Along both banks of the stream for 9 miles stretches the RAHWAY RIVER PARKWAY.

At MOUNTAINSIDE, 9.9 *m.* (140 alt.), a small residential community, is (L) ECHO LAKE PARK *(picnicking, fishing, and boating facilities)* in a valley surrounded by wooded hills and meadowlands. A stretch of untouched marsh provides a bird sanctuary.

At 10.5 *m.* is the junction with New Providence Rd., macadamized.

1. Left on this road, which becomes Woodland Ave., to SIP MANOR HOUSE (L), 0.9 *m. (private),* a two-story Dutch Colonial red-stone and shingle structure with a

peaked roof. The house, built in 1664 by Nicholas Varleth on the present site of Jersey City, was acquired in 1699 by Jan Arianse Sip. Former Gov. Peter Stuyvesant used to visit the house, and Lord Cornwallis was an occupant a century later during his march through New Jersey. Recently the dwelling was moved from Jersey City and reconstructed by the promoter of the real-estate development on which it stands.

2. Right on New Providence Rd. to WATCHUNG (Ind., *high hill*) RESERVATION, 1.6 *m. (picnic facilities; 25 m. of bridle trails; campsites including cots and tents $7 per week; open all year 7:30 a.m.-11 p.m.).* This reservation is the largest unit in the Union County Park System. Its 1,962 acres, white with dogwood in the spring, have been landscaped to retain their natural charm.

At 2.3 *m.* is LAKE SURPRISE *(rowboats $1.50 per day, 25¢ an hour; skating and fishing in season),* also called Silver Lake, Ackerman Lake, or Feltville Lake. It is stocked with pickerel, perch, largemouthed and smallmouthed bass, calico bass, sunfish, suckers, and catfish.

GLENSIDE PARK, 4.3 *m.* (300 alt.), known locally as The Deserted Village, is a community of a dozen summer and year-round homes. In 1845 David Felt, a New York merchant, built the dam that confines Lake Surprise, established a paper mill, and erected a company town, which he called Feltville. RUINS OF THE MILL are at the base of the hill at Blue Brook Gorge. At the close of the Civil War the property was purchased by a manufacturer of sarsaparilla; bankruptcy forced him to abandon it.

WATCHUNG RIDING STABLES, operated by the county, are across the lake at 4.6 *m. (horses $1.50 per hour).* A lighted ring permits riding in the early evening, and an outside jumping course is available.

SCOTCH PLAINS, 13 *m.* (150 alt., 11,186 pop.), is largely rural; most of its workers are employed in nearby towns. A group of Scottish Presbyterian and Quaker immigrants came here in 1684 after refusing to swear allegiance to the British Crown. At the corner of Park Ave. and Front St. is a tavern now operated as YE OLDE HISTORIC INN, built 1737, a two-story, yellow clapboarded building with two wings.

NORTH PLAINFIELD, 16.2 *m.* (100 alt., 9,760 pop.), on the Watchung slope, provides homes for many businessmen and workers in adjoining Plainfield.

The WILLIAM MOGEY & SONS, INC. PLANT, 46 Interhaven Ave. *(open weekdays 8:30-5:30),* is one of the five factories manufacturing telescopes in the United States. In a squat, two-story cement building, William Mogey (who founded the business in 1882), his sons, and seven other men each year turn out about 200 complete telescopes, a large quantity of optical parts for rifle sights, and lenses for other goods.

HYDEWOOD GOLF CLUB (R) is east of the main intersection with Watchung Ave. *(greens fees 35¢-50¢; 75¢ Sat., $1 Sun. and holidays).*

Along the North Plainfield section of the highway are roadhouses, restaurants, diners, and flower stands of exotic types from an open lean-to, or a Dutch windmill, to a much-gabled stucco structure. Darkness comes late to this highway; neon signs, tremulous bulbs, flares, and spotlights create an illuminated nightmare until the early-morning hours.

At 18.8 *m.* is the junction with a hard-surfaced road.

Right on this road, up a steep grade, to WASHINGTON ROCK STATE PARK, 0.9 *m.* Here, in the midst of stone fireplaces and other standard picnic facilities, including a tea house and hot-dog stand, is WASHINGTON ROCK, from which the General watched the movements of the British forces on the plain below during the months of May and June, 1777. A flag flies from a pole bedded in a stone column on which a tablet has been placed. On a clear day the view stretches for nearly 30 miles over northern New Jersey to Staten Island and Manhattan.

The transmitting mast of radio station WJZ is L., off the highway (*see Tour 13*).

At 22 *m.* the highway passes through the northern fringe of BOUND BROOK (50 alt., 7,372 pop.) (*see Tour 17*).

At 22.5 *m.* (L) are the REMAINS OF BREASTWORKS thrown up by Washington's men during June 1777 and the winter of 1778–79. These are slight hummocks on both sides of the road, well overgrown.

At 22.9 *m.* is the junction with a hard-surfaced road.

Right on this steeply upgraded road to the junction with a dirt road, 0.2 *m.*; R. on this road to the flagpole (L) on the SITE OF THE MIDDLEBROOK HEIGHTS CAMPGROUND, 0.3 *m.*, where the first Betsy Ross flag is believed to have been flown after its official adoption on June 14, 1777. Each June 14 a new 13-starred flag is hoisted and allowed to remain flying day and night for a year. This strong position in the hills was never attacked by the British while Washington's forces held it. In 1779, however, after the army had moved away, the British in New York staged a night raid into this area. They failed to burn the log huts because the timber was too damp.

At 23.9 *m.* is the junction with a hard-surfaced road.

Right on this road past a large stone quarry to a short but steep footpath that leads to CHIMNEY ROCK, 0.6 *m.* From this formation, similar to a chimney, Washington often watched troop movements in the plains to the east. The spectacular rock serves as a laboratory for geology students.

At 26.5 *m.*, SOMERVILLE (80 alt., 8,255 pop.) (*see Tour 17*) is by-passed.

At 27.1 *m.* are the junctions with US 202 (*see Tour 4*) and US 206 (*see Tour 6*). These highways are united with US 22 for 0.5 m.

At 27.7 *m.*, at a large traffic circle, US 22 bears R. US 202 and US 206 here separate (L) from US 22. At this circle is the junction with State 28 (*see Tour 17*), which is united with US 22 between here and Phillipsburg.

At the western side of the traffic circle on the ESTATE OF JOSEPH F. FRELINGHUYSEN (*private*) is (R) the large mansion in which President Warren G. Harding signed the Knox-Porter joint resolution on July 2, 1921, terminating the state of war between Germany and the United States, and between Austria-Hungary and the United States. A plate in the floor of one room of the spacious yellow brick and frame house commemorates the event. A painting by P. W. Muncy, hanging over the fireplace nearby, depicts the President in the act of signing. Harding, a week-end guest, is said to have been called in from a game of golf by the arrival of the papers from Washington. Without ceremony, he sat down before a sunny window and signed the treaty.

West of the traffic circle the highway has a two-lane concrete roadbed with frequent curves and grades. At 30.7 *m.*, across the checkered farm lands and rolling, evergreen-dotted hills in the foreground, is seen (R) the crescent end of the Watchung Mountains, with the tiny white spire of Pluckemin Church in the valley formed by the break.

The highway here follows the route of the former Easton or Brunswick

Turnpike, earlier an Indian trail, over which Lafayette drove while revisiting America in 1824.

The JAPANESE GOLDFISH HATCHERY (R), 30.4 m. *(open on application at office)*, maintains in pools and tanks from two to five million fish, many of them rare and unusual. They are shipped to many parts of the world.

NORTH BRANCH, 30.8 m. (70 alt., 300 pop.), on the North Branch of the Raritan River, was laid out in 1884. The village, with neat white houses and spreading trees, has changed little. There is still a blacksmith shop (L) by the highway, and the tiny POST OFFICE (R) is less than 10 feet square. Fine pastures and farm land surround the town.

At 30.9 m., in North Branch, is the junction with a dirt road.

Right on this road to the old JACOB TENEYCK HOUSE (L), 0.2 m. *(private)*, erected 1792 and standing among tall trees that almost conceal it from the road. The large, substantial stone house of two stories, a fine specimen in the Colonial style, was built by Jacob Teneyck. In the upper part of the massive front door are two large, oval-shaped panes of glass set diagonally and resembling, when lit up at night, huge almond eyes of an oriental giant. It is related that an old Negro, sent here one night with eggs from a neighboring farm, took one frightened glance at the weird sight, dropped the eggs, and ran home yelling with fright, "Ah seen de debbil!" Forty-eight blue and white tiles illustrating Scriptural passages are set in the long parlor fireplace.

The highway passes between varicolored fields rising to the hills (R) and a descending slope of farm lands toward Cushetunk Mountain (L). In the autumn, sumac and Virginia creeper add their scarlet tones to the more sober browns and yellows of the maples, beeches, poplars, and oaks.

WHITEHOUSE, 35.1 m. (180 alt.), consists of large, neat homes built along both sides of the highway for a mile. At 36.2 m. in WHITE-HOUSE MEMORIAL PARK (L) is the stone foundation of the white-plastered tavern for which the village was named. Two inns have kept the name.

At 36.2 m. is the junction with a macadam road.

Right on this road is OLDWICK, 3.5 m. (240 alt.), an old settlement known as Smithfield in Colonial days and, until recent years, as New Germantown. ZION LUTHERAN CHURCH, built 1750, is the oldest Lutheran church in continuous use in New Jersey. It has low walls, hip roof, and small square windows high above the ground. The interior has been considerably altered.

At 36.3 m. is the junction with a dirt road.

Left on this road through an open field to WHITEHOUSE or CUSHETUNK LAKE, 0.2 m., part of a real estate development that collapsed with the depression. The lake is fed by Rockaway Creek.

At 36.5 m. is CUSHETUNK MT. (L), a long, low hill with a sharp crest, named for an Indian chief. In the early days a German redemptioner, Balthasar Pickel, bought the mountain and gave his own name to it. Other Germans settled there, made the mountain a hog run, and called it Hog Mt. On the plains at its foot were great fields of cabbages for making the homeland dish of pork and sauerkraut.

POTTERSTOWN, 38.3 m. (260 alt.), is a farm village of half a dozen houses (R) on a left turn of the highway. Large dairies and several branches of Rockaway Creek almost encircle the town.

LEBANON, 40.4 *m.* (260 alt., 1,269 pop.), lying on a ridge, was founded in 1731 by German immigrants. Local historians relate that a group of Palatines bound for New York were greatly perturbed to find themselves in Philadelphia. They started overland with babes and baggage; when they came to this fertile, rolling country they decided to remain. Other Germans drifted down from New York State and soon the whole valley northward was known as German Valley *(see Long Valley, Tour 10)*.

Right from Lebanon on a macadamized road is COKESBURY, 3 *m.* (580 alt.), a quiet community of two churches, stores, and scattered houses.

Right from Cokesbury on a graveled road is MOUNTAINVILLE, 4.7 *m.* (400 alt.), a tiny settlement of white houses at the foot of HELL MT. or FOX HILL (957 alt.), a haven for buzzards and foxes. The surrounding area has attracted many wealthy New Yorkers and Philadelphians, including Thomas J. Watson, president of International Business Machines and one of the highest salaried men in the United States.

West of Lebanon a long uphill stretch takes the highway past the sprawling, gray stone buildings of ANNANDALE STATE FARM (R) at 41.7 *m.*, a State reformatory for boys. Until 1938 a large, black, four-story barn-like building stood high on the hill (R), its windows closed with white paper. It was a ghoulish reminder of the $500,000 investment of the Annandale Graphite Co. in 1925, abandoned in 1935. For 50 years one company after another failed to make a profit here, even though the hillsides for many miles northward contain large quantities of graphite.

ANNANDALE, 42.8 *m.* (270 alt., 500 pop.), is a shopping center for surrounding farms.

The STAGECOACH INN (R), 43.4 *m.*, now an antique shop, is said to have been built in 1770, but may be of earlier construction. In its cellar, once the taproom, are deep, 6-foot fireplaces. The wooden upper story was added later to the stone lower story. Millstones lie in the yard.

At 43.5 *m.* is the junction with State 30 *(see Tour 15)*.

CLINTON, 44.5 *m.* (190 alt., 932 pop.), has an old MILL on the banks of the South Branch of the Raritan River, a popular fishing stream. This is one of the few New Jersey gristmills still using water power. Its dim, heavy-raftered interior is cloudy with the dust of more than 100 years and its heavy stones turn as steadily today as ever. Rebuilt in 1836 from an older structure, it predates most of the Civil War architecture of the town. The CLINTON HOUSE (R), a two-story, rambling frame house with a square-columned porch, built about 200 years ago, was long a stopping place for the Easton stagecoaches. Even in the morning, cars with licenses of a dozen States stand before it, having brought patrons to the beamed Colonial dining room.

At 45.6 *m.* is the CLINTON STATE FARM (L), a corrective institution for women. Prisoners are employed in farm labor, and laundry and kitchen work.

PERRYVILLE, 47.5 *m.* (360 alt.), which consists of a single, large, red BRICK HOUSE (L), is for sale (1939). In 1812, when the building was being erected, news was brought of Commodore Perry's victory on Lake Erie and the owner raised an American flag, announcing that his house should always be called Perryville. After the opening of the Brunswick Pike the house became known as Brick Tavern, a name that is still used. Once a stopping place for drovers who came from the west with mules and horses for the eastern market, the building has been a private dwelling for 40 years.

1. Left from Perryville on a macadam road is JUTLAND (340 alt.), known mainly for the white frame farmhouse (L) at 0.9 *m.* where New Jersey's Battle of Jutland took place in 1926. Resisting service of a summons for cruelty to animals, Timothy Meany, a farmer, barricaded himself in his home. After Corp. M. Daly had been wounded in an attempt to serve the summons, State troopers stormed the house. During the all-night battle Beatrice Meany, Timothy's sister, was killed, and James Meany, a brother, and Trooper P. J. Smith were wounded. Three State troopers were later convicted of manslaughter.

2. Right from Perryville crossing Mulhockaway Creek to VAN SYCKLES CORNER, 1 *m.* (290 alt.), a crossroads settlement of three modern houses, the weatherbeaten frame of a former store, and the graceful stone and frame house that was, until 1860, VAN SYCKLES TAVERN. A cornerstone bears the date 1763. For many years the inn was a stopping place for Philadelphians enroute to Schooley's Mountain Springs *(see Tour 10);* Joseph Bonaparte, brother of Napoleon, stayed here on his frequent trips from Bordentown. The builder, who the present descendants of the Van Syckle family point out was no relative of theirs, was hanged at High Bridge for counterfeiting Continental money during the Revolutionary War.

At 48.8 *m.* is the junction with a dirt road.

Left on this road to a BAPTIST CHURCH, 0.1 *m.,* an ivy-covered stone building with green shutters, abandoned more than 40 years ago. The well-kept grass of the graveyard, the large oak trees, and the modern Van Syckle tombstones behind the church contribute to a deceptively prosperous appearance.

Westward the highway rises on a steady grade into the Musconetcong Mts. A crest at 50.4 *m.* offers an unusually fine view across the valley to the Pohatcong Mts. (R).

WEST PORTAL, 52.1 *m.* (420 alt.), named for the entrance to the 1,795-foot Lehigh Valley R.R. tunnel, is called "Little Switzerland" by its neighbors, because of its mountainous setting. A bold swindle was perpetrated here 40 years ago by two supposed contractors from New York, who arrived to construct a big "Government project." They imported 1,500 Italians from New York, charging each one $5 for his job, and hired local farmers to aid in building a large stone wall in the form of a square. At the end of the month, before anyone had been paid, the contractors disappeared. The owner of VAN'S SWIMMING POOL *(adm. 25¢)* used part of the stone for construction of his home.

The highway westward passes weather-worn old stone houses, and parallels the Musconetcong River.

BLOOMSBURY, 55.3 *m.* (300 alt., 639 pop.), built on both sides of the Musconetcong River, has houses so uniform in architectural design that they give the appearance of a prosperous company town. Many of the dwellings are tenantless. The graphite mill employs five men year in and year out, using imported raw materials.

At 56.8 *m.* is the OLD GREENWICH PRESBYTERIAN CHURCH (R) at the top of a small hill. Built in 1835, it has arched windows and stone walls covered with beige plaster. The congregation was established in 1740. A tablet on the wall is dedicated to the memory of 19 Revolutionary soldiers whose graves are in the shaded churchyard.

STILL VALLEY, 58.3 *m.* (350 alt.), has a farming population. The records of St. James Lutheran Church (L), Belvidere Rd., date back to 1750. The earlier building was of logs, thatched with straw, and the present structure (1854) is still known as The Straw Church, though constructed of red brick with slate roof and solid white shutters.

US 22 turns L., underpassing the Jersey Central R.R. and Lehigh R.R. A length of old houses, many of them crumbling stone and built flush with the road against a rocky hill, is the first sign of Phillipsburg.

PHILLIPSBURG, 62.1 *m.* (300 alt., 19,255 pop.) *(see Tour 10),* is at the junction with State 24 *(see Tour 10).*

US 22 turns L. at 62.3 *m.*

At 62.4 *m.,* on the free bridge over Delaware River, US 22 crosses the Pennsylvania Line, 0.3 miles east of Easton, Pa.

Tour 3

(Piermont, N. Y.)—Alpine—Fort Lee; US 9W.
New York Line to Fort Lee, 10.6 m.

Numerous gas stations, tourist homes.
Four- and three-lane concrete highway.

US 9W runs along the top of the Palisades, overlooking the Hudson River. Much of the route lies in woods, but the open sections afford fine views of the river several hundred feet below and of the opposite shore, covered thickly with the buildings of Yonkers and New York City.

US 9W crosses the New York State Line 2.6 miles south of Piermont, N. Y.

At 0.1 *m.* the road divides into a Y and becomes a one-way route (R). Much of the highway for a mile south of this point was built through dense woods across a seemingly bottomless swamp, believed by some geologists to have been the volcanic crater from which the Palisades erupted. Thousands of tons of mud were removed and trees, rubble, stone, and concrete were dumped into the pit. On this mattress the roadbed was laid.

At 1.5 *m.* is the junction with the one-way route for northbound traffic on US 9W.

APPROACHES TO GEORGE WASHINGTON MEMORIAL BRIDGE

Left on US 9W to POINT LOOKOUT, 0.5 *m.*, a parking place for observers on the sheer 500-foot cliff of the Palisades *(field glasses, 10¢)*. The black and silver expanse of the Hudson River, framed in the brown rock of the Palisades and the green fields and forests of the New York shore, stretches north and south as far as the eye can see. As the river broadens above Point Lookout, the shore line curves in a tremendous sweep. Far south the needle points of New York's skyscrapers, piercing through the closely woven texture of the huddled buildings, flash in the sun. Along its lower industrial end the Hudson becomes truly a New Jersey river. There the smooth current is broken by the swell of excursion boats, ferries, freighters, tugs, and garbage scows.

At 3.7 *m.* is the junction with Closter Dock Rd., now a hard-surfaced highway, which was laid out soon after Frederick Closter came here in the early seventeenth century under a grant from Holland. The FIELD HEADQUARTERS of the Palisades Interstate Park Commission is a vine-covered stone and log building (L) at the junction, on the northeast corner *(permission for use of campsites obtained here)*. The commission controls a series of parks, including this 13-mile strip along the Hudson River in New Jersey and large mountain areas in the adjoining part of New York. The first park commission was named jointly in 1900 by the Governors of the two States. Substantial gifts of property have been made by J. P. Morgan, the Rockefellers, Mrs. E. H. Harriman, and other wealthy persons.

Left on Closter Dock Rd., twisting down the face of the Palisades, to the junction with Henry Hudson Dr., a hard-surfaced road, 0.9 *m.*, running close by the river at the base of the Palisades—a more scenic route betwen Alpine and Englewood Cliffs than is US 9W on the plateau. At the junction with the drive is (L) the YONKERS-ALPINE FERRY, 0.3 *m. (40¢ to 50¢ for car and passengers)*. This is the approximate site of Closter's original ferry, which was operated with sloops in the seventeenth century. Later flat-bottomed bateaux, large enough to carry a wagon, were used.

1. Left from the ferry on a riverside trail to CORNWALLIS'S HEADQUARTERS, 0.25 *m. (not open)*. The little house, a two-story stone and wood structure with white paint and green shutters, was restored in 1934 by the Palisades Interstate Park Commission and furnished with Colonial pieces by the New Jersey State Federation of Women's Clubs. The stone section was built *c.* 1750. Lord Cornwallis made his headquarters here on Nov. 20, 1776, while his army of 5,000 was being ferried across the river to attack Fort Lee. Until about 30 years ago the house was a rendezvous for thirsty rivermen. When it was restored, removal of plaster showed smokeblackened beams, marked with chalk tallies of drinks taken on credit many generations ago.

2. Right on the foot trail to the HUYLER DOCK HOUSE, 1 *m. (usually open Sat., Sun. afternoons; free)*, a two-story stone structure with an attic, built by Byron Huyler more than 200 years ago. Huyler ran a ferry and used the house as a trading station and stage-line terminal. A Boy Scout troop has converted the building into an informal museum of flora, fauna, and relics from the park area. Picnic groves, parking areas *(15¢; Sun. and holidays, 35¢)*, and bathing facilities *(10¢)* are found along Henry Hudson Dr. Through lofty trees are fine views of the river and the New York skyline. At 5 *m.* is the junction with Palisade Ave., a brick-paved highway. L. on this road 0.4 *m.* to the DYCKMAN STREET (New York City) FERRY *(40¢ to 50¢ for car and passengers)*. R. on Palisade Ave., a steep, curving, brick-paved road, to ENGLEWOOD CLIFFS, 5.6 *m.*, at the junction with US 9W.

ALPINE, 4 *m.* (440 alt., 521 pop.), is a tiny village largely hidden among the rocks and trees of the Palisades. Hundreds of Sunday afternoon hikers from New York City come here to follow footpaths along the top of the Palisades or trails along the river bank.

Right from Alpine on a macadam road is CLOSTER, 2.7 *m.* (50 alt., 2,502 pop.), a village of frame buildings with new facings of brick or composition shingle. The town was the scene of a spontaneous strike in 1936 during the course of which a sympathizer was shot and eventually died The killing provoked a vigorous controversy over civil liberties, accentuated when the police forbade a memorial mass meeting, which, however, was finally held after an injunction had been obtained. The shop foreman was found guilty of the killing and was sentenced to serve from six to ten years in the State Penitentiary. The strikers were persuaded to return to work.

The TENAFLY WEAVERS, 61 Old Dock Rd., an industrial enterprise founded at Tenafly in 1916 by Miss Winifred Mitchell, is still under the direction of the founder. An outgrowth of a hobby, the factory has popularized its wide variety of woven products. The firm makes a practice of training young students in handcraft and absorbing them as operators.

Between Alpine and Englewood Cliffs, US 9W runs on the plateau immediately W. of the Palisades. Except for a few houses and roadstands, the highway is bordered by light forest growth. Occasional clearings afford glimpses of the Hudson River and the New York shore.

At 7.3 *m.* is the junction with E. Clinton Ave., a concrete-paved road.

Right on this road is TENAFLY, 2 *m.* (130 alt., 5,669 pop.), populated largely by prosperous New York businessmen. Dutch scholars say that Tenafly is from Thyne Vly or Garden Valley. Early Dutch and French Huguenot settlers first claimed lands here; farming days finally ended with the building of the Erie R.R. Elizabeth Cady Stanton, the feminist, was a Tenafly resident; so was Hetty Green, the capitalist *(see HOBOKEN)*, who established legal residence here to escape New York taxes. Fine elms and maples, set out by land developers who came with the railroad in the 1870's, shade the streets. The MARY FISHER HOME, NW. cor. Engle and Park Sts. *(open afternoons)*, is a Victorian stone house with rooms for 18 professional people. The home was founded by Miss Fisher, a school teacher who at first opened her own house to needy persons.

Continue on E. Clinton Ave. to Knickerbocker Rd., 2.7 *m.;* R. on Knickerbocker Rd. to the SOLDIERS MONUMENT, 3.9 *m.* (at Madison Ave.), on the site of Camp Merritt, World War cantonment where more than 1,000,000 troops were assembled before embarking. The monument, a 70-foot granite shaft, was the work of Capt. Robert Aitkins. Scrub and underbrush have claimed the deserted campsite; only the outlines of camp streets remain.

Left on Madison Ave. is DUMONT, 4.8 *m.* (80 alt., 6,500 pop.). The NORTH REFORMED CHURCH, SW. cor. Madison Ave. and Washington Ave., built in 1801, is the home of a congregation formed in 1748 by members of the older Dutch church at Schraalenburgh or Starvation Castle, now known as Bergenfield. The building has the tall, graceful spire characteristic of most Dutch Reformed Churches. The Georgian influence is shown in the details of the woodwork and in the unusual little oval panels of the spire.

Left on Washington Ave., formerly Schraalenburgh Rd., is BERGENFIELD, 5.7 *m.* (70 alt., 8,816 pop.). Right on Church St. to the OLD SOUTH PRESBYTERIAN CHURCH (R), erected in 1799. Many of the red sandstone blocks from a 1725 structure were used in this church. The building has straight, long lines, with the front façade broken by a square stone tower which rises to a wooden steeple. Above the center entrance is a fine rose window. All other windows are pointed Gothic.

ENGLEWOOD CLIFFS, 9.1 *m.* (320 alt., 809 pop.), is a small residential community in heavy woodland. Its sole industrial plant manufactures envelopes for money gifts at Christmas. A TOURIST CAMP with facilities for trailers is maintained by the Palisades Interstate Park Commission on Palisade Ave., one block east of US 9W. At the intersection is an especially gaudy example of the roadside pottery stands found on many New Jersey highways.

1. Left from Englewood Cliffs on Palisade Ave. to the DYCKMAN STREET (New York City) FERRY, 0.5 *m.,* and the junction with Henry Hudson Dr., an alternate route N. to Alpine *(see side tour above)*.

2. Right from Englewood Cliffs on Palisade Ave., a brick-paved road, is ENGLE-WOOD, 1.4 *m.* (30 alt., 17,800 pop.), a wealthy residential community on the slope of the Hackensack Valley. The main street, Palisade Ave., is broad and tree-less at the town's center, lined with one- and two-story stores. North of the business district, on shaded streets noted for autumn coloring, are costly homes on small estates, all but hidden by trees and shrubbery. The DWIGHT MORROW HIGH SCHOOL, in Dwight Morrow Park at Knickerbocker Rd. and Tryon Ave., is designed in the Tudor style and dominated by a tall central tower of open tracery, crowned with four finials. The ACTORS' FUND HOME, 155 Hudson Ave. *(open 9-5 daily)*, is a home for sick, disabled, and retired actors, founded by 248 prominent stage people, of whom Daniel Frohman is the lone survivor (1939). The home was first on Staten Island; it was moved to Englewood in 1928. Surmounting a finely landscaped knoll are the two white frame houses, each three stories high. The institution is supported by contributions and income from benefit performances arranged by Mr. Frohman. In its early years Englewood was known as "the English Neighborhood" because of English colonists in an area peopled mostly by Dutch and French Huguenots. Later the settlement became Liberty Pole, because of the pole that stood near the former Liberty Pole Tavern on the Common, Palisade Ave. and Tenafly Rd. A tall flagstaff marks the SITE OF THE LIBERTY POLE. The WORLD WAR MONUMENT, a soldier at ease before a granite shaft capped by a poised eagle, was done by Harry Lewis Raul of Orange.

South of Englewood Cliffs the highway enters a scattered residential section with remnants of woodland. Frequent openings frame vistas of the shining gray towers and web of George Washington Bridge.

COYTESVILLE, 10.4 *m.* (330 alt.), is an undisturbed little village that has been the home of many stars of screen and stage. Among them is Marjorie Rambeau, whose father still runs a hotel here.

FORT LEE, 10.6 *m.* (280 alt., 8,759 pop.) *(see Tour 1),* is at the junction with US 1 *(see Tour 1).*

Tour 4

(Suffern, N. Y.)—Pompton—Boonton—Morristown—Lambertville— (New Hope, Pa.) ; US 202.
New York Line to Pennsylvania Line, 81 m.

The road is paralleled at intervals in the northern section by the Lackawanna R.R., and between Copper Hill and Lambertville by the Pennsylvania R.R.
Frequent service stations and tourist homes; hotels in towns.
Well-paved roadbed, with stretches of four-lane concrete.

Northern New Jersey, which US 202 traverses in its southwesterly ramble between the New York Line and Delaware River, is a region of heights and rolling dips rising sharply from the generally flat land of the State. South of Suffern, with the green and purple-shadowed Ramapos to the north, the highway penetrates a country that has the clean, high look of the Berkshires. For miles around, the Ramapos rim minor hills and ridges between which narrow rivers twist their way into the cups of small mountain lakes. Old farm lands from Mahwah to Lambertville slope up to the foothills, rising and falling with the rocky core of the country; only at intervals do they give way to industrial encroachments. This route cuts open a cross-section of 200 years of America. Here are spots important in American history: the first sizable iron works built in the Colonies, which helped turn the tide of the Revolution; concrete-buried Indian paths followed by the Continental Army under Washington; and the house where Morse and Vail labored to bring forth the first practical magnetic telegraph.

The New York State Line is crossed 0.7 miles south of Suffern, N. Y. A few yards south of the State Line US 202 turns R. at the junction with a macadam road, the Franklin Turnpike.

Left here, on the Franklin Turnpike, past the SUFFERN BOYS' CAMP ACADEMY (L) and the AMERICAN BRAKEBLOK PLANT (R), to the WINTER HOUSE, 0.7 *m.*

(R), a two-story brown-shingled old Dutch dwelling believed by many local residents to be "the house with nobody in it" of which Joyce Kilmer wrote. If it is really the "tragic house, its shingles broken and black," Repeal has peopled it and put it in repair; today it is a wayside restaurant and bar. This 150-year-old place by the Erie tracks is a fine example of gambrel-roof Dutch Colonial architecture.

The Franklin Turnpike turns R. and at 0.8 m. is the business center of MAH-WAH (Ind., *beautiful*), consisting of several stores, a post office, and an Erie R.R. station. Mahwah residents assert that there is no such place as Mahwah; it has neither fixed limits nor a known population.

JOYCE KILMER'S WHITE COTTAGE *(private)* sits on top a steep hill in Mahwah, SW. cor. Airmount and Armour Rds. Flanked by birch and elm and surrounded by a rocky garden, the white-shingled, two-story house looks far down into the Ramapo valley. It is here, the local story runs, that Kilmer (1886–1918) wrote *Trees*, though other communities have also claimed the honor.

US 202 runs through an Erie R.R. underpass and crosses the Ramapo River at 0.4 m.

At 1 m. is the junction with State 2 *(see Tour 16)*.

US 202, known here as Old Valley Rd., runs straight ahead. Shaded with maple and shot through with the pungent odor of pine, this 3-mile stretch of macadam cuts into a district untouched by industry. Low, rambling, white-painted brick houses built by Dutch landbreakers are today the homes of Wall Street brokers and gentlemen farmers, their estates still enclosed by the winding stone fences with which the tidy Dutch marked their lands' limits.

The residents' feeling for the quiet countryside is not always expressed in a forbidding insistence on privacy. The RAMAPO WATER GARDEN, 1.4 m. (R), for example, is marked by a large sign that gives the impression of a commercial establishment; but inquiry reveals that its proprietor, a retired movie-theater owner from Brooklyn, has had the sign erected only to be hospitable, so that travelers will be encouraged to view his three fine lily ponds and tropical aquaria.

At 1.7 m. is (R) the JAMES CLINICAL LABORATORY *(private)*, where Dr. and Mrs. Robert F. James do general clinical work in a small white brick building that looks almost as old as their home but happens to be practically new. The blue-shuttered house, constructed of stone and mud with trimmed saplings for uprights and with a white clapboarded exterior, dates, in part, to Colonial times. It is one of three dwellings in this neighborhood that have been identified at various times as the original Hopper House, in which General Washington planned an attack on New York City.

At 2 m. is (R) a two-story, dormer-attic STONE HOUSE *(not open)*, its old white paint curling along its walls. During the Washington Bicentennial Celebration of 1932, when the New Jersey countryside was being ransacked for historic spots, this was declared by its present owner to be the original Hopper House. A marker was erected, but lasted only a couple of months because Henry O. Havemeyer, owner of the adjacent property, protested that a house standing on his estate was really the Hopper House. The ensuing dispute was settled when the New Jersey Historical Commission awarded the honor to the Havemeyer building and placed its marker there. But into the argument Mr. Havemeyer injects several last words, with a framed, typewritten statement attached to the marker. The closest Washington ever got to this present house, he says, was while warming his feet by the fireplace moved here from the old Havemeyer Inn, no longer standing. The Havemeyer HOPPER HOUSE is at 2.5 m. (R), a three-story square brick dwelling back of which is a tremendous gray barn once used as a carriage house. In an adjoining field is a small obelisk, carrying no inscription but marking the spot where Washington is said to have hoisted a diminutive Hopper maiden to his saddlebow.

At the ivy-covered CHURCH OF THE IMMACULATE CONCEPTION (L) and the DARLINGTON PUBLIC SCHOOL (R), 2.9 m., the road drops sharply. The red brick and limestone IMMACULATE CONCEPTION SEMINARY is atop the hill, well off the road (L) at 3.3 m.

North of Oakland there is a change in the character of the district; along with the old Dutch houses, their backs to the road, there is a sudden clump of "roadside rests." These have been the object of considerable acrimony on the part of some wealthier newcomers in Valley Rd. The beer and hamburger purveyors, however, find no harm in making their living out of a country in which they have spent all their lives.

OAKLAND, 8 m. (280 alt., 735 pop.), one of the oldest communities in Bergen County, is a cluster of frame buildings. It was known successively as Yawpaw (Ind., *wild plum*), The Ponds, Scrub Oaks, Bushville, and now Oakland. Its public edifices include a one-story brick borough hall and a brilliant red POST OFFICE (L), set in a two-story yellow frame building.

Hanging from a bracket in the public square is a SIGN announcing "Oakland, Bergen County, N. J. Established 1869." The legend is topped by a portrait of one Chief Iaopogh and the words, "Once There Was Indians All Over This Place." The sign was the donation of Robert T. Sheldon, a resident of Valley Rd.; Oakland people assert that the ungrammatical construction was insisted upon by Mr. Sheldon, who, they recall, said it was "a quotation from some author."

A SILK LABEL PLANT is the borough's sole factory. Its principal point of interest is the white stucco and stone BOROUGH HALL (R), constructed by WPA as a reproduction of the Church of the Ponds, built at Oakland in 1829. The hall, a Georgian edifice, is adjacent to the present brownshingled DUTCH REFORMED CHURCH (R), whose congregation celebrated its 225th anniversary in November 1935. A former pastor of the church, the Rev. Ilsley Boone, became the center of a local controversy some years back when he espoused nudism, of which he is today one of America's leading exponents.

South of Oakland, following the Ramapo River, US 202 swings R. at 9 m. through a district of bathing beaches (R), tourist camps, and hot-dog stands.

At 10.4 m. is the junction with a concrete bridge over POMPTON LAKES, leading into Pompton and the borough of Pompton Lakes.

Right across the bridge and immediately R. on Perrin Ave., a macadam road, to BIER'S TRAINING CAMP, 0.3 m., where top-rank professional boxers prepare for their matches. The camp makes "Pompton Lakes" a newspaper date-line known by fight fans throughout the country. It is jammed in spring and summer with tourists, sport lovers, and angle-men on hand to watch Louis, Canzoneri, or Berg go through their paces. Most of the Broadway visitors know the training camp only for its outdoor ring fronting the lake, its gymnasium, and its restaurant-bar. But the campsite has other historical associations than those of this year's greatest fighter of all time. The two-story white frame-and-stone house in which Dr. Bier and his family live is the 200-year-old SCHUYLER MANSION, in which General Washington and his staff attended the wedding of Peter Schuyler, Washington's aide.

Lakeside Ave. skirts the lake into the borough of POMPTON LAKES, 1 m. (200 alt., 3,500 pop.), where a DU PONT PLANT manufactures electric blasting batteries and metallic caps.

The ESTATE OF ALBERT PAYSON TERHUNE *(private)*, writer and dog fancier, stretches along both sides of US 202 at about 10.4 m. Terhune's house lies on the steep lake front, almost hidden by towering shade trees (R).

At 11.6 m., at the junction with the Paterson-Hamburg Turnpike, US 202 turns L.

The COLFAX SCHUYLER HOUSE (R), 11.8 m. *(private)*, has a warped and sagging roof, crumbled brick chimney, and great sloping cellar. It was built in 1697 by Arent Schuyler, whose descendants have occupied the house ever since it was built. The oldest part of the house is the right wing of the present main section, which is still in excellent repair and is in use today. Six slim, white Doric columns support the porch roof. The entrance has a cross-paneled "witch door" beyond which it was impossible for witches and evil spirits to penetrate.

US 202 turns R. at 12.3 m.

At 12.8 m. (R) are the FOX FARM *(free to patrons of roadstand)* and (L) CAPTAIN MACK'S WILD ANIMAL FARM *(adm. 10¢)*, competing zoos with animals that range from agoutis and kinkajous to peacocks and wildcats.

Three hundred broad acres along both sides of the macadam road at 13.2 m. are SHEFFIELD FARMS *(milking parlor open)*. Sweet timothy and alfalfa smells make up in bucolic atmosphere for the modern buildings where milk is drawn from cows by machine and pumped across the road for bottling. The luminous white milk houses are a cross between old Dutch mill buildings and the spare, trim twentieth-century industrial architecture.

At 13.9 m. is the junction with State 23 *(see Tour 9)*. Between this point and Mountain View, US 202 and State 23 are united.

At 15.6 m., at a traffic circle, US 202 becomes a dual concrete highway with an avenue separating the lanes.

MOUNTAIN VIEW, 17.3 m. (180 alt., 1,684 pop.), a residential and resort community, appears to the traveler as four corners of brick and frame buildings marking a right turn in US 202.

Left from Mountain View on Greenwood Ave., which turns R. and becomes Preakness Rd. at 0.6 m., to Mountain Ave., 1.3 m.; R. on Mountain Ave. to Totowa Rd., 1.5 m.; L. on Totowa Rd. to (L) the THEUNIS DEY MANSION, 2 m. *(open Tues., Wed., Fri. 12-5; Sat., Sun. 10-5; adm. 10¢)*, a red-brick boxlike structure with red-sandstone trim and a shingled gambrel roof. In the two-story house, built in 1740 for Col. Theunis Dey, Washington had his headquarters in 1780. At one time,

"ONCE THERE WAS INDIANS ALL OVER THIS PLACE."

many men and officers camped on the bare pine floor of its attic. The house has been preserved as a Revolutionary museum by the Passaic County Park Commission.

Turning R. on Greenwood Ave., US 202 separates from State 23 at 17.3 *m.* The highway crosses narrow Pequannock River onto the Boonton Turnpike (L). Lining the right bank of the river are the bungalows of summer visitors. Frame barricades separate the houses from the river edge and at frequent intervals steps lead down into the water.

A weed-grown ditch paralleling the road (R) is what remains of the old MORRIS CANAL, resting place for wind-blown newspapers and wax-paper sandwich wrappings.

A red brick SCHOOLHOUSE (L) identifies the community of LINCOLN PARK, 19.6 *m.* (182 alt., 1,831 pop.).

US 202 turns R. at 21.3 *m.,* crossing a Lackawanna R.R. overpass.

At 21.5 *m.,* across the railroad tracks, is (L) the WHITEHALL M. E. CHURCH. Built between 1860 and 1865 by farmers who gave their time and strength during winter afternoons, the church has been described as "the most beautiful country church in New Jersey." It is of Colonial design, with white clapboards and a spire; the pews within are also white. The building was renovated in 1929.

TOWACO, 21.8 *m.* (200 alt., 416 pop.), is a small suburban center that is a real-estate development; its Lackawanna R.R. station, with dull red roof and stucco walls, sets the architectural tone of the town. The community was formerly known as Whitehall. The land around Towaco is a rising plateau; high L. the deep cuts of sand quarries are seen in the hills.

MONTVILLE, 24 *m.* (350 alt., 900 pop.), is a collection of brown and gray frame buildings in the middle of which is, surprisingly, a three-story red-brick apartment house.

The right bend out of Montville is a long climb to the top of a high plateau. Broad peach acres (L) give way quickly to industry's smokestacks marking the entrance into Boonton.

BOONTON, 25.9 *m.* (400 alt., 6,866 pop.), built high into the ledge that overlooks precipitous Rockaway Gorge, has the alert look of a New England commercial center. Gray factory yards at the town's outskirts recede before the steep hill on which is the business district; Main Street thrives. If cities can be placed in time, Boonton fits most perfectly into the bustling, driving years of the eighties. An early iron works was established here and for about 50 years in the middle of the nineteenth century, when iron rails were demolishing the West's frontiers, the town was one of the largest iron centers in the country. Today its industrial plants comprise two nationally known hosiery mills, gunpowder, dynamite, and torpedo plants, a radio factory, several garment concerns, and two bakelite plants. Bakelite was first manufactured and commercialized in Boonton; a local man, Richard W. Seabury, opened an old rubber works to manufacture the new phenol product after large rubber companies had rejected the idea.

Boonton's steep, winding streets seem to have been hewn hurriedly out of the rock to keep step with industry's swift progress. Main St. itself, at a right angle to US 202 as it enters the city, winds up around the rim of the gorge's knife edge. From a wooden PAVILION *(open)* next to the bank building (R) is a view over the precipice into the Rockaway cut; below, the twisting river sluices its way through the sharp rocks and on the far bank the Lackawanna tracks gleam in the sun. Sheer crags rise above ROCKAWAY FALLS (R). One summit is known as THE TORN, from the Dutch word *toren,* or tower. Left, beyond the gorge, is the blue face of PARSIPPANY RESERVOIR. Once it was the good, dry community of Old Boone Town, busy with forges and iron works; in 1902 the town was flooded to provide a water supply for Jersey City. An underwater drama was enacted at the dam in 1904. When one of the pipe-line valves failed to close, Bill Hoar, a diver, went 90 feet below the surface to block the intake with a large wooden ball, weighted with lead. Hoar was trying to remove an obstruction when the torrent of water pouring through the open line snapped the 2-ton sphere forward, shattering the diver's leg and pinning him against the pipe. During the four days that Hoar was trapped newspaper extras detailed the progress of rescue attempts. Finally two other divers succeeded in partially closing the valve, but when Bill Hoar was hoisted to the surface, he was dead.

South of Boonton, the road crosses the Rockaway on a steel bridge and runs along the reservoir bank. The reservoir (L), 2,150 feet long, has a maximum depth of 110 feet.

At PARSIPPANY, 28.4 *m.* (300 alt., 210 pop.) *(see Tour 7),* is the junction with US 46 *(see Tour 7).*

At 28.8 *m.* is the junction with a macadamized road.

Left on this road to (R) the BENEDICT HOUSE, 0.1 *m.* *(private),* a three-story white clapboarded, gambrel-roofed structure with green shutters. To this house William Livingston, first Governor of New Jersey, brought his family to avoid the British who had put a price on his head and were continually raiding his Elizabeth home *(see Tour 10).*

West of Parsippany the landscape suddenly changes into the broad, spacious wooded lawns reminiscent of residential Long Island.

At 31.6 *m.* is the junction with State 10 *(see Tour 14).*

MORRIS PLAINS, 33 *m.* (400 alt., 1,730 pop.), an unobtrusive residential community, is the home of the G. Washington Coffee Co.

Right from the center of Morris Plains on a tar and graveled road, Glennbrook Pl., which turns L. to Central Ave.; R. on Central Ave. to GREYSTONE PARK, 1.5 *m.,* site of NEW JERSEY HOSPITAL for the mentally ill. Topping a high ridge in a rolling valley region, wide graveled driveways wind through its 400 gracefully landscaped acres, in the center of which the tremendous gray stone administration building looms as a dead end to Glennbrook Pl. Here, despite numerous building additions since 1871, when the hospital was founded, more than 5,000 patients receive treatment in space planned to provide for 3,080. The policy of this State instition is to restore all possible patients through active treatment. Individual attention from physicians and nurses, as well as from trained teachers of occupational therapy and physical education, has produced some excellent results in mental readjustment. A social-service bureau attached to the hospital investigates the history of patients admitted and assists in returning the recovered or improved person to a satisfactory place in society. Another extra-mural activity is the provision of psychiatric advice to neighboring communities.

At 33.9 *m.,* just north of Whippany River Bridge, on a private estate (L) is the small salmon-colored ALFRED VAIL HOUSE, a barnlike frame structure where Samuel F. B. Morse and Alfred Vail developed the magnetic telegraph in the fall of 1837. Three miles of wire were looped around the old building that day early in January 1838 when Vail ticked out "A patient waiter is no loser"—the first message officially recorded on Morse's instrument.

South of the bridge is the SITE OF THE SPEEDWELL IRON WORKS (R) where Stephen Vail, Alfred's father, supervised construction of the driving shaft for the *S. S. Savannah,* the first vessel to cross the Atlantic using steam as an auxiliary to sail (1819). The foundry has long since been abandoned. Crumbled sections of wall rise out of the ground here and there, and keen-eyed visitors can still find great, rusted, hand-wrought iron spikes. A nearby hollow, once a pond, has been reconstructed as a lake by the WPA. Adjacent to an old wall of the iron works is a large community fireplace built in 1918, providing the comfort of a roaring log fire in the open. The Whippany Bridge marks the northern entrance of Morristown.

At 34.6 *m.* is the junction with Sussex Ave., a tar road.

Right on Sussex Ave. to the MAGNETIC HILL, 3.3 *m.,* a puzzling refutation of the maxim that "seeing is believing." The spot can be picked out accurately by a wooden pike fence about 7 feet high (R). At a point where this fence forms an L, in what appears to be a shallow valley with a steep hill ahead and a gradual upward slope behind, the motorist should shut off his motor, release the brake and take the car out of gear. The car will coast slowly backward, *up* the gradual slope. The phenomenon is an optical illusion: the road here is really a slight downgrade; it appears uphill (in the wrong direction) merely because of its juxtaposition between two steeper hills.

MORRISTOWN, 35.1 *m.* (400 alt., 15,197 pop.) *(see MORRISTOWN).*

Points of Interest: Morristown National Historical Park (Ford Mansion, Museum, Fort Nonsense, Jockey Hollow), Dr. Jabez Campfield House, and others.

At 35.3 *m.* is the junction with State 24 *(see Tour 10).*

At 38.7 *m.* is (R) the KEMBLE HOUSE *(private),* built in 1750 by Peter Kemble, a noted Tory. It housed many leading figures of the Revolution and served as headquarters for General Wayne while his troops were stationed at Jockey Hollow. Much of the original character of the house has been lost by remodeling.

At 38.9 *m.* is the junction with a macadam road.

Right on this road to JOCKEY HOLLOW, 1 *m.,* a part of MORRISTOWN NATIONAL HISTORICAL PARK *(see MORRISTOWN).*

The section southwest of Morristown is known as the Mount Kemble district. Once covered by the great estates of the nineteenth century, it has largely been subdivided by real estate companies.

Two old buildings stand on each side of the road at the crossing of Passaic River, 40.7 *m.* They are the VAN DOREN MILL (R) and OLD MILL INN (L). Massive in its solid masonry, the mill has been owned and operated by the Van Doren family since 1842, when it was rebuilt to take the place of a smaller building erected in 1768. It was this mill, it is said, that ground the grist for Continental Army messes when Washington

A MODERN DAIRY PLANT, POMPTON PLAINS

was encamped at Jockey Hollow. The story runs that the present building's foundation was dug by a tramp in return for bed, board and tobacco; neighboring farmers and their sons cleared the ground of stones, and masons received 50¢ a day for their work. The $5,000 cost to the Van Dorens was cleared in the first year of operation. The mill still runs at a profit, providing flour for neighbors and visitors.

Old Mill Inn, across the road, is the reconstruction of a barn that stood close by the mill. It advertises itself as "quaint yet modern," and draws its tea-shop clientele from well-to-do tourists and residents of nearby towns.

At 40.8 *m.,* just south of Passaic River, is the junction with a macadam road.

Left on this road is BASKING RIDGE, 1.1 *m.* (360 alt., 1,500 pop.), which received its name from early 18th-century settlers who had seen wild animals come up from the lowlands to bask in the sun. It was at WHITE'S TAVERN here that Gen. Charles Lee, second only to Washington in the Revolutionary Army, was taken prisoner by the British after he had disobeyed Washington's order to rejoin the main body of the army 2 miles away. The village has a LOG CHURCH, built by Scotch Presbyterians in 1717, and the usual spot—in this instance under a great OAK, said to be 500 years old—where Washington stopped to eat lunch.

BERNARDSVILLE, 42.4 *m.* (420 alt., 3,336 pop.), is a village of one-story frame and brick buildings almost at the foot of MINE MT. Its shopping center, plump in the middle of US 202 as it enters town from the northeast, looks for all the world like a movie-set false front with the wooded mountain towering sharply behind. Originally known as Vealtown, it was given its present name by Roderick Mitchell, who settled here in 1840.

The winding, hilly road out of Bernardsville to the west commands a long rolling vista (L); sudden clumps of pine rise out of the slope (R).

FAR HILLS, 46.9 *m.* (150 alt., 560 pop.), shares a Lackawanna R.R. station with BEDMINSTER, 0.5 *m.* R. *(see Tour 6)*. Large estates of wealthy New Jersey families outlie both communities, which are separated by the North Branch of the Raritan River. Just W. of the river is the green stubble field (R) of the BURNT MILLS POLO CLUB. Far Hills is the scene of an annual horse and cattle show. Its twin village, Bedminster, is the center of a gentleman-farming area where manorial life is more important than crops. Hunting to hounds is a favorite sport of the proprietors and their friends.

At 48.3 *m.* is the junction with US 206 *(see Tour 6)*. US 202 and US 206 are united for 7.5 miles.

Just south of the junction is the old BEDMINSTER CHURCHYARD (R). The First Dutch Reformed Church, whose congregation the cemetery once accommodated, was built in 1759 on land granted by Jacob Vanderveer, a prominent banker. It no longer stands, but the graves of several early settlers are still visible. One of them reads: "Under this stone are deposited the remains of Julia Knox, an infant who died the 2nd day of July 1779. She was the daughter of Henry and Lucy Knox of Boston in New England." Henry Knox was General Knox of the Continental Army, then quartered at the Vanderveer house; and the simple inscription on the grave veils a story of rigid eighteenth-century religiosity. The story runs that Jacob Vanderveer had an insane daughter who was refused burial in the churchyard because she was "possessed of the devil." No man to flout his church elders, Vanderveer buried her in a little enclosure on his own land next the churchyard. When Knox's baby daughter died the performance was repeated; Julia was ruled ineligible for burial in the churchyard because her father was a Congregationalist. Mindful of his own experience, Vanderveer provided the Knoxes with a burial plot alongside his daughter's grave. Years later, the church accepted the land as part of its official graveyard. Till then, however, a narrow fence separated the graves of the two outcasts from the consecrated ground.

PLUCKEMIN, 50.2 *m.* (180 alt., 179 pop.), is another little village that ends just as its houses seem to be getting into the swing of being a community. A long-standing dispute revolves about the origin of its name. One school of stove-talk has it that the name is rooted in the custom of a local innkeeper who, anxious for trade, would stand in the road and simply "pluck 'em in." But other authority leans to the belief that Pluckemin is an Indian word meaning "persimmon." At any rate, local residents today pronounce the name Pl-kemin, with accent on the second syllable and the "kem" flattened out almost to "kam."

The village's most impressive building is the massive white plaster ST. PAUL'S PRESBYTERIAN CHURCH (R), standing on historic ground formerly occupied by St. Paul's Lutheran Church. The earlier building was erected about 1757 and its sandstone cornerstone, with a weather-dim Latin inscription, has been inserted in the portico of the present edifice. Predecessor of the old Lutheran church was a log building atop First Mt., about a mile east of the village. It was known as the Church on the Raritan, or the Church in the Hills; and it housed a meeting in August, 1735, that was the first Lutheran synod held in America. The meeting—"consistorium," the founders called it—was called to protest the conduct of the Rev. Johann Wolf who, it was said, had been charging exorbitant rates for sermons, baptisms, and funerals. His fee of 20 to 30 shillings for an adult's funeral was double the scale prevailing in Hackensack. Even after the synod, Mr. Wolf failed to mend his ways; he was subsequently replaced. The present Presbyterian Church, with its thick columns and attic porch, is a good example of the Grecian Revival style of the middle nineteenth century.

South of Pluckemin the road swings into the humped range of the FIRST WATCHUNG MTS. (L). At 50.5 *m.* is a point of considerable historic interest: a MINIATURE GOLF COURSE, still in operation (1939).

At 50.7 *m.* is the junction with a graveled road.

Left on this road to ECHO LAKE, 0.4 *m.,* lying in the cut of the First Watchungs. A good yell will rebound as many as seven times across certain parts of Echo Lake. There are numerous legends associated with it; about the best is that of Winona, daughter of the Raritan chief Camackanuck. It seems that Winona had displeased her father by falling in love with a minor Delaware chieftain called Thingerawso, and wily old Camackanuck, knowing that regular baths in Echo Lake were a sure remedy for mental disturbances, sent her down to the lake to take the cure. Whether Winona took the baths is not known; but she did use a big rock overlooking the lake as a trysting place to meet Thingerawso. Camackanuck finally imported a powerful Seneca chieftain named Connosota to marry his wayward daughter. That did not disturb Winona. She managed to lure the Seneca out to her rock on Echo Lake, where Thingerawso was set to kill him. Before Thingerawso could bring his tomahawk into action, however, Connosota drew a pistol and shot him. As he plunged down the cliff into the still water he cried, "Winona! Winona!" The Indian girl, arriving in time to see her lover sink, leaned over the ledge; Connosota, afraid she would fall, called out to her. The Seneca's cry mingled with the dying echo begun some time back by Thingerawso, and Winona, convinced her lover was calling her, jumped off the cliff to join him in death. The place was promptly called WINONA'S ROCK.

The legend is the source of another place name, BUTTERMILK FALLS, at Echo Lake. Thingerawso was to kill Connosota when, as a signal from Winona, he saw the falls turn white with milk the maiden would pour into the cascade.

At 55.4 *m.* is the junction with State 29-US 22 *(see Tour 2).* US 202 and State 29 are united between this point and Lambertville.

At 55.9 *m.,* at a traffic circle, US 22 joins State 28 *(see Tour 2).* US 206 separates (L) from US 202 at this point.

The road swings west away from the Watchung Mts. into a valley region of real farm land, well watered with vagrant brooks and streams. The two-lane concrete highway rises and dips in long straight stretches through rich corn and truck garden acres: the deep brown loam of plowed fields, paneled into green grazing meadows, levels out to the CUSHETUNK MTS. (R) and, off to the L., the SOURLANDS. Industry strides the land in a long line of high tension towers, like so many giant steel scarecrows.

THREE BRIDGES, 66 *m.* (120 alt.), is a small shopping center for farmers. Frame houses are along the road, and freight cars stand on sidings. Eighty-one-year-old Billie Griffith of the town remembers well the day when he ran away to become a "candy butcher" with a circus. But even better he remembers the time when the lady bareback rider hung her pink cotton tights on a line near his great bucket of lemonade. That day a strong breeze changed the drinking habits of a nation; the beautiful pink tights were blown into the lemonade. Billie Griffith was a good business man; having no time to make a new stock, he offered to a thirsty public its first drink of pink lemonade.

At 68.8 *m.* is the junction with State 12 *(see Tour 12).*

Right on this road is FLEMINGTON, 1.2 *m.* (180 alt., 2,729 pop.) *(see Tour 12).*

At 69.5 *m.* is the junction with State 30 *(see Tour 15).* Between this point and Ringoes US 202 and State 30 are united.

Two stands along the highway carry Flemington's imprint to the main route: a log cabin selling gay pottery products and a big shed offering eggs bought at the Flemington Auction (L).

At 69.8 *m.* is the junction with a paved road (R) to Flemington.

The highway crosses the Neshanic River three times between here and COPPER HILL, 70.9 *m.,* not quite a village, not quite a ghost town, reputed to have been once the center of a thriving copper-mining industry. It is said that the mine was sealed long ago during hard times; when industry revived the mouth of the mine had disappeared.

LARISON'S CORNER, 73.3 *m.,* is just that: a cornered junction of US 202 with two county roads (L). It is also known as Pleasant Corner. Here is the abandoned old brownstone AMWELL ACADEMY (R), founded in 1811 as a school appendage to St. Andrew's Church, discontinued in 1828 and reopened as a seminary in 1870 by Cornelius, Andrew, Katherine, and Mary Jane Larison. The tide of the nineteenth-century controversy between conservatism and science seems to have swirled to the doors of the little seminary at Larison's Corner and engulfed the family; in 1876 Cornelius and Mary Jane Larison, unable to convince Katherine of science's importance in the modern world, withdrew and set up their own school in the rear of their home. They called it the Ringoes Academy of Arts and Sciences.

The ROCKEFELLER FAMILY BURIAL GROUND is at Larison's Corner. About 50 feet from the highway (R), it is enclosed by a low stone wall set into the UNITED PRESBYTERIAN CHURCH CEMETERY. Some of the gravestones carry the name "Rockefellow." A granite monument, 10 feet square, is inscribed: "In memory of Johann Peter Rockefeller, who came from Germany about the year 1723. Died in 1763. He gave this land for a burial place for his family, its descendants, and his neighbors. This monument erected in the year 1906 by John Davison Rockefeller, a direct descendant." But according to George W. Tine, Rockefeller family historian, Johann was not buried here, but on a farm in the vicinity. In this county there are more living and dead Rockefellers than in any other locality in the country.

At 74 *m.* is the junction with a tar and graveled road.

Right on this road, which winds to HEADQUARTERS, 2.4 *m.,* a community of five or six stone and frame buildings. A sign on a store front (R) reads,

"Grover, N. J." This was the post office address of the village before the introduction of rural free delivery. Its present name derives from the local belief that Washington spent three nights here on his march to Trenton. An inclined dirt road (R) leads down to a greensward behind which are the two-story red sandstone UPDYCK MANSION and a stuccoed sandstone GRISTMILL and STOREHOUSE. The buildings were erected in the 1750's by "Rich John Updyck," a man who measured his money in half-bushel baskets. He quartered his many slaves in the basements of his buildings. It was at his house that Washington is said to have stayed.

RINGOES, 74.2 *m.* (220 alt., 250 pop.), claims the distinction of being the only village and post office of that name in the world. The community developed around Ringo's Old Tavern, established by John Ringo in 1720; the tavern burned down more than 100 years ago. The Amwell Valley Fire Co. (L) had quite a celebration in Ringoes in the summer of 1936. Royal blue and silver modernistic fair fittings, set up in papier mache to mark an emblazoned "Twelve Years of Progress," remained long after the event.

State 30 separates (L) from US 202 at Ringoes.

At the sharp dip of the road into Delaware Valley, about 79.5 *m.,* the high hills of Pennsylvania loom blue in the distance west of the rise of Lambertville's Delaware embankment. Tall clumps of trees rear up on opposite sides of the highway from time to time, showing how wooded ground was cut through to lay the straight road. In this approach to the Delaware there is an almost imperceptible change to the living habits of the State across the river; hayricks with red roofs, well-kept barns topped by glass cupolas and spires—small signs of solid establishment and pride in proprietorship associated with Pennsylvania's farming people.

LAMBERTVILLE, 80.7 *m.* (50 alt., 4,518 pop.), perches by the Delaware River on a narrow, hill-bound shelf opposite New Hope, Pa. US 202 turns L. then R. into the center of town, where MOOSE HALL stands in a sizable green. Beyond is CEMETERY HILL, its grassy slope studded with gravestones. Quiet, without the ingrown charm of Flemington, Lambertville nevertheless has the river town's air of potential excitement. Straight ahead is the free bridge to New Hope, and although Coryel's Ferry was discontinued years ago and the once busy feeder of the Delaware and Raritan Canal lies stagnant in its walls, the town's position on the Delaware provides its pulse with the quickening blood of outside traffic. At one time, early in the nineteenth century, Lambertville tussled for commercial supremacy with Trenton. The Belvidere Delaware R.R., built through Lambertville in 1851, gave it the lead over Phillipsburg and prodded its industries into activity: paper, rubber footwear, iron works, railroad machine shops. When the Pennsylvania R.R. took over the Belvidere, however, the machine shops were abandoned. Today, though no more than an industrial adjunct to Trenton, Lambertville has a crushed stone quarry, a small iron and steel plant, a paper mill, a pottery and a sausage factory. The town received a serious blow in 1938 when two of the most important plants manufacturing rubber goods moved away.

Known first as Coryel's Ferry and then as Georgetown, Lambertville received its present name when John Lambert opened the first post office shortly after the War of 1812. In 1732 Samuel Coryel had started his ferry service, establishing at the New Jersey end an inn of good repute. His ferries came into play in the Revolution when Cornwallis tried to capture the boats because they were providing a crossing for the Continental troops. Washington's men occupied the town at one time. The General himself was quartered in the JOHN HOLCOMB HOUSE on the north end of Main St. (R); a two-story, gray stone dwelling, it is still in use, and on Mondays large white things and little pink things flutter in the breeze from its porch.

The MARSHALL HOUSE, 60 Bridge St. *(private)*, a two-and-one-half-story tan brick structure with brown trim and a gabled roof, stands flush with the sidewalk. Erected in 1816 by Philip Marshall, descendant of John Hart, a signer of the Declaration of Independence, the house was for many years the home of his son, James Marshall. It was the younger Marshall, born in 1810, who started the greatest migration in American history when, in 1848, he discovered gold in California while superintending construction of Sutter's flour mill. Marshall died homeless and penniless in a county hospital at the age of 74.

The Lambertville Vigilante Society, still in existence, provides an insight into the life of the town in the early nineteenth century. The society was founded in 1837 for "the protection of the property of its members and the detection of thieves and other villians." Today little more than a dinner club, its officers retain titles that once meant business: telegraph pursuer, up-railroad pursuer, down-river pursuer, and so forth.

Near the river, R. of the bridge, are the really old streets of the town—narrow, humble, their houses almost flush with the curb.

The Delaware is smooth at Lambertville; down river about half a mile is Wells Rapids. Historians of a century ago record that "the passage of rafts at this place is an interesting sight; they shoot down with a great velocity, and as the stream is filled with rock, it requires the utmost care and skill in the raftsman to avoid foundering."

At Lambertville is the junction with State 29 *(see Tour 11)*.

At 81 *m.* on the wood-planked Delaware River Bridge *(free)* US 202 crosses the Pennsylvania Line, 0.5 miles east of New Hope, Pa. *(The authorities have established a 10-mile speed limit on the bridge. They mean it.)*

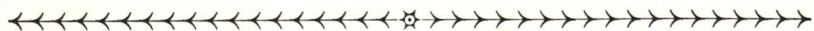

Tour 5

(Unionville, N. Y.)—Sussex—Newton—Columbia—(Portland, Pa.); State 8N, county road, State 8.
New York to Pennsylvania Line, 43.7 m.

The route is paralleled between the New York State Line and Sussex by the New York, Susquehanna and Western R.R.; between Sussex and Ross Corner by the Lehigh and New England R.R.; and between Marksboro and Columbia by the New York, Susquehanna and Western and Lackawanna R.Rs.
Hotels in larger towns; oil stations and tourist homes frequent.
Mostly concrete roadbed; some stretches of macadam.

The highway runs southwest, roughly paralleling the Kittatinny Mountains, highest range in the State. Running alternately along valley bottoms and the crests of ridges, it traverses a rich dairying and farming area. There are some exceptionally good views of mountains, streams, and country villages.

State 8N crosses the New York Line 0 *m.,* 0.6 miles south of Unionville, N. Y., and enters fine dairy country. Steep-sloped hills are crisscrossed with stone walls and studded with great red barns, each with one or two concrete silos.

At 2.1 *m.* the highway rises to the shoulder of a ridge. Across the valley of the Wallkill River (L) is the forested slope of Pochuck Mt. (994 alt.). Close to the highway are sturdy old frame farmhouses, many with half-windows on the second floor. Wells with windlasses are in the front yards.

Settlers came into the fertile Wallkill Valley in 1740. Most of them were of Dutch and French Huguenot extraction and had lived in the Dutch settlements around Albany. The Wallkill, flowing NE. to join the Hudson, offered a natural route for emigrants from the Hudson valley.

Largely unspoiled by signs, except those advertising such rural necessities as well drilling, State 8N has been chosen as a good medium for the small orange and black signs that describe, in doggerel spread over a series of five panels, the romantic conquests and other joys attained by users of a brushless shaving cream. One local resident, making the ultimate protest against these unscannable jingles, has nailed over a fifth sign (which revealed the brand name) a piece of cardboard bearing the neatly lettered word "NUTS."

At 6.3 *m.* the highway crosses a branch of the Erie R.R. at a grade and descends into the unimposing outskirts of Sussex. Nondescript frame houses perch on a hill slope, each with a small frame outhouse in the rear.

SUSSEX, 7.1 *m.* (450 alt., 1,415 pop.) *(see Tour 9),* is at the junction with State 23 *(see Tour 9).*

Between Sussex and Ross Corner the route is an unnumbered, but well-posted, county highway.

A crossroads at 8.6 *m.* is marked by black and white directional signs, below which is a smaller sign reading, "This is McCoy's Corner." Most of the farm population for miles around needs no guidance to the white FARMHOUSE (L) behind tall evergreens where William (Bill) Sharpe McCoy has lived for 50 years. During the last 40 years McCoy has been a horse dealer; he sells about 700 animals a year, not counting trades. He is a short, friendly man, with thin gray hair and a mustache; the trousers of his gray business suit are tucked into black puttees, and he wears overshoes around his stable and office behind the house. McCoy is his own banker in dealing with the farmers, keeping their notes and his other accounts in a green tin box that he carries out to his stable office every morning. If he needs cash, he can take a note on a horse to the Sussex bank and get it discounted. "But they wouldn't discount a note on an automobile," he says, "because there's too much depreciation." The best money he ever made was during the years that he ran a fertilizer factory. A relative, a veterinarian, kept him posted on mortally ill animals over a wide area. McCoy's follow-up system was successful, for he seldom hauled away a dead horse without selling a live one to the bereaved farmer. For six years McCoy was pianist for the Masons, and his violin has furnished many tunes for country dances. The violin bears a printed Stradivarius label along with the words, "Made in Germany"; a New York dealer once offered him $2,000 for it, but McCoy wouldn't sell.

South of McCoy's Corner the highway, here paved with macadam, swings through a valley, past occasional ponds and icehouses. Westward are the Kittatinny Mts., part of the Appalachian Range.

PELLETTOWN, 12.2 *m.* (420 alt.), is little more than a general store (R) and a railroad station at the crossing of the Lehigh and New England R.R. and Papakating Creek.

At 13.9 *m.* is (R) WINDING BROOK FARM, named for a tortuous stream that can water more cows per airline yard of length than any other brook in this part of the State.

In this area and elsewhere along the route, weathered, brownish slate formations are exposed in highway cuts. Known to geologists as the Martinsburg shale, the rock has hardened and become slate through metamorphism. Outcroppings continue into eastern Pennsylvania, where the rock is extensively quarried for commercial use.

ROSS CORNER, 15.9 *m.* (500 alt.) *(see Tour 6).*

The route is united with US 206 *(see Tour 6)* between Ross Corner and NEWTON, 20.8 *m.* (670 alt., 5,401 pop.) *(see Tour 6).*

Between Newton and Columbia the route is State 8. The road runs SW. from the center of Newton, up a steep hill past the old SUSSEX COUNTY COURTHOUSE (R) and through an attractive residential section. Climbing to a ridge, the concrete roadbed enters dairy-farming country.

At 21.7 *m.* (L) is a great pile of black stone against the slope of a hill about 200 yards from the highway. This is the remains of an old SLATE QUARRY, no longer worked.

At 24.3 *m.* is (L) the old FOUNTAIN HOUSE, a three-story red brick structure with peaked roof and scroll decorations on the eaves, in the middle-nineteenth-century style. A glassed-in porch and elaborate masonry have been added in front, but the old watering trough that gave the hotel its name is gone. For many years the Fountain House was the only place between Newton and Blairstown where stage passengers and farmers could get a drink; few farmers paused to refresh their horses without stopping at the bar. Prohibition crippled the hotel, but the place has now been modernized and reopened as the Forest Inn.

FREDON, 24.6 *m.* (720 alt.), is a highway junction and a small white SCHOOLHOUSE (L).

Right from Fredon on a macadamized road to SWARTSWOOD STATE PARK, 1.8 *m.* (*see Tour 6*).

At 26.2 *m.* is (R) the PINE RIDGE PAVILION, typical of many road-houses in this area. Here on a Saturday night the traditional country square-dance is kept alive by a crowd of millworkers from Newton and city dwellers from points as remote as Newark and New York. While the factory hand and his girl are shouting, "He's down, he's up!", the local farmer and his sons and daughters take their several ways to the street corners and movies of Newton.

YELLOW FRAME, 28.3 *m.* (889 alt.), consists of a church, a parson-age, and an old cemetery, crowning a hill with a fine view of the land-scape in all directions. YELLOW FRAME PRESBYTERIAN CHURCH (L), on the highest ground of any church in New Jersey, faces Dark Moon Rd., named for a long-vanished and once notorious tavern. The present church, like its predecessor of 1786 that gave a name to the district, is of frame construction, painted yellow with white trim. It has an open bell tower with a balcony, but none of the beauty that sprang from the fine lines of the early church. One member of the congregation explains that the old building was replaced in 1904 because of a gift of $1,000 toward con-struction of "a new-fangled church." So solidly was the 1786 edifice built that it was necessary to blast the old timbers apart. Still earlier, a log church stood on the hilltop, serving as a refuge against Indian raids. For-mer members of Yellow Frame Church, now living in various States, have formed a society to aid in the structure's maintenance. The society joins the congregation on the last Sunday in June each year for services in the morning and a midday dinner. In the old CEMETERY across Dark Moon Rd., are buried a number of Revolutionary soldiers, including Brig. Gen. Aaron Hankinson. Old tombstones bear verses warning the reader to "pre-pare for death," advice that seems out of keeping with the living beauty of green cornfields on the surrounding hillsides and sheep grazing in a pasture close by.

At 29.3 *m.* is the junction (L) with a macadam road.

Left on this road is JOHNSONBURG, 1.8 *m.* (580 alt., 162 pop.), a country village spread along a main street at the edge of a narrow valley. The town is hemmed by a rocky, wooded slope and, across the fields, by the high embankment of the Lackawanna R.R. From 1753 to 1765 the village was the seat of Sussex County. There were only a few log houses then; one of them, the jail, gave to the settlement its early name of Log Gaol. Standing back from the main street in the center of Johnsonburg and aloof from the frame dwellings is (R) the yellowish stone VAN NESS HOUSE (*private*), a plain and finely proportioned building of two stories. Built to square with the points of the compass, it served as a Protestant Episcopal Church from *c.* 1781 to *c.* 1850 when, as the incumbent postmaster puts it, "that denomination kinda got pinched out in this vicinity." In stagecoach days Johnson-burg was an important junction for travelers between Easton and Elizabeth; today it has only summertime significance because of the nearby camp for field work by civil engineering students of Stevens Institute of Technology. Two conferences, the Annual Economic Conference of Engineers and one for boys of high school age, are held at Johnsonburg annually. Left from Johnsonburg 0.1 *m.* on the Allamuchy road is the old CHRISTIAN CHURCH CEMETERY (R), enclosed by a stone wall. In the center a small, white marble obelisk marks the grave of Joseph Thomas, described as a "minister of the gospel in the Christian Church, known as the White Pilgrim by reason of wearing white raiment." Thomas, in whitewashed boots and astride a white horse with whitewashed trappings, rode into the Johnsonburg district in 1835. His mission ended after one sermon when he was stricken with smallpox and died at the age of 44. Leaders of the orthodox Christian Church did not want to bury him in their cemetery, lest his body contaminate those of the saints. The evangelist was therefore interred in the private burying ground of Dark Moon Inn, a plot maintained for those who lost arguments over cockfights and gambling. Eleven years later it was decided at a synod meeting that it would be safe to remove Thomas' body to its present resting place.

MARKSBORO, 31.2 *m.* (520 alt.), has freshly painted frame houses and a few stores on both sides of the highway. The village is well situated on the slope of a hill above Paulins Kill, where Col. Mark Thomson, Revolutionary soldier for whom the settlement was named, built a gristmill in 1783. The region still produces good corn, especially fine crops being noted by a few yellow ears hung beside the farmhouse door.

Between Marksboro and Paulina the highway gradually descends along the slope of a narrow valley, little more than a ravine, in which Paulins Kill runs swiftly toward the Delaware and in which the tracks of the New York, Susquehanna and Western R.R. find a footing. Beyond a low ridge to the northwest the bulky Kittatinny Mts. are outlined. Straight ahead is a view of Blairstown.

PAULINA, 33.1 *m.* (780 alt.), is marked by a dam across Paulins Kill, a few straggling houses and roadstands, and the only industry within a radius of some miles. This is a STEAM LAUNDRY (R), which washes the clothes and bedding of the students of Blair Academy.

At 34 *m.* is the junction (L) with a concrete road.

Left on this road is HOPE, 6 *m.* (470 alt., 200 pop.), a village with twisting streets that follow the contours of the hill on which it stands. Hope is stamped by the handiwork of Moravian colonists from Bethlehem, Pa., who settled here in 1774 after buying 1,000 acres from an earlier settler who lived in a log hut. Using native blue limestone, the Moravians built substantial houses, two mills, a brewery, a distillery, a tannery, a public inn, and a church—all that was needed for a self-sustaining community. Bachelors and unmarried women lived in separate houses. A peace-loving people, their conscientious refusal to fight in the Revolutionary War for a time labeled them as Tories; but they later won esteem by their devoted care of sick and wounded Revolutionists. A smallpox epidemic crippled the community in the early 1800's, and the colonists returned to Bethlehem in 1808, leaving many of their band in the village cemetery.

Many of the stone buildings are still standing, in restful contrast to newer structures of frame or concrete blocks. The MORAVIAN CHURCH (R) has been remodeled as a bank; the GIRLS' SCHOOL (L) enjoys summer trade as the American House, a hotel. Most interesting of all is the OLD MILL, with stone walls that have survived two fires since they were laid in 1768. Water power is used to grind grain for farmers, but the old wooden water wheel and the millstones have been replaced by an iron wheel and steel grinding machinery. A belt-drive system steps up the power from the great water wheel from 17 revolutions a minute to 2,000 revolutions at the grinder. Milton J. Vusler, the miller, is proud of the old raceway that the Moravians chiseled through solid slate to a maximum depth of 22 feet in order to straighten the course. He is also proud of the 1,200 bushels of corn that he harvested from his own 7 acres in 1937. The approach to the mill, down a hill from the center of Hope, crosses a stone viaduct built by the indefatigable Moravians.

BLAIRSTOWN, 34.4 *m.* (350 alt., 900 pop.), covers the northern slope of Paulins Kill valley and extends to the highway. Steeples of the Presbyterian and Methodist Churches and the silver cylinder of a tall water tank stand out above old trees. The town's chief industrial plant (factories are not permitted) is BLAIR ACADEMY, a preparatory school for boys, founded in 1848 by John I. Blair, the Lackawanna R.R. millionaire. Originally a co-educational school for the children of Presbyterian ministers in the Newton Presbytery, it was so popular that clergymen with 10 or 12 children eagerly sought the low-paying appointments to village churches in this area. The school is known today for its policy of demanding athletic competition from every student. The campus architectural style varies from the English Tudor to what might be termed a combination of the Richardsonian and Colonial.

The main street of Blairstown suggests an old western village, with second-floor porches over many of the stores. A one-floor department store displays leather boots and mackinaws on its porch, while the day's wash hangs from a clothesline on the porch above. Most of the buildings are frame; several are brightly trimmed in blue, green, and red, contrasting with mild gray and tan paint on the clapboards. The OLD MILL, on the main street has been remodeled in the Tudor style. With elaborate brick arches supporting humble stonework, the whole resembles a cinema designer's notion of the proper setting for "city boy meets country girl."

More than a century ago the town was known as Gravel Hill. It was aided in its growth as an educational center and as a shipping point for farm produce by John Blair, who earned his first dollar by selling 16 muskrat skins. He vastly increased his earning power by interesting himself in a pioneer chain store system, flour mills, iron mills, and railroads. As an established railroad builder, Blair found it inconsistent as well as irksome to ride by carriage from his Blairstown home to the station at Delaware, 12 miles distant, for a trip to New York. So, on July 4, 1876, he had his men start to build the Blairstown Railway between the two villages. The line was finished exactly one year later to the great delight of Blair and the townspeople, who were also permitted to ride by rail upon payment of the established tariff. The BLAIR HOMESTEAD *(private)*, a large, square, white frame house with a cupola, stands on high ground behind the mill. The lawn and walks are decorated and paved with a collection of millstones from miles around.

West of Blairstown the highway runs through the bottom of the Paulins Kill valley. Cedar-dotted grazing lands and farms are on both sides of the road.

HAINESBURG, 40.9 *m.* (340 alt.), was known more than a century ago as Sodom, for what specific sins the historians do not relate. It was customary, however, for traveling evangelists to confer that name on any settlement characterized by hardness of heart. The village apparently took a turn for the better when John Haines opened its first school. The most noticeable buildings in the small community are the yellow frame structures (L) of what was once a rich man's country estate. The LACKAWANNA R.R. BRIDGE (L) over Paulins Kill, 122 feet high, is a good example of reinforced concrete construction utilizing double arches.

COLUMBIA, 43.5 *m.* (320 alt., 287 pop.), a workaday town on Delaware River, has been nourished for more than 200 years by the water power of Paulins Kill. Early Dutch settlers, led by mining prospectors who made their way down Delaware valley, first built a mill dam here. A larger dam now supplies hydroelectric power. The population consists largely of railroad workers, retired farmers, and silk-mill workers employed in Portland, Pa., across the river.

Right from Columbia on an oiled road that parallels the river and crosses and recrosses a branch of the Erie R.R. to the DELAWARE WATER GAP, 3.2 m. Here the river cuts through the rocky, forested ridge of the Kittatinny Mts., affording a pass for a railroad and a highway on both shores. Geologists explain that the channel through the 1,635-foot mountain was carved many thousands of years ago during a period of crustal changes, when the rock mass of the mountain was being forced upward from a plain. As the mountain grew, the river kept pace by sawing a deeper channel. The commercial value of this scenic point has been exploited on the Pennsylvania shore where hotels were built many years ago; some of them have since burned. The New Jersey shore, more precipitous, and less accessible because of a narrow and rather rough road, has numerous summer cottages and camps in the woods.

(The route beyond this point is not recommended for motorists who wish to avoid rough mountain roads.)

Northward from Delaware Water Gap the dirt road climbs the mountain slope, past clumps of rhododendron and ferns, and then descends to the valley. Purplish-red shale is common here.

The MERCER COUNTY BOY SCOUT CAMP, 12 m. (R), marked by a small stone highway bridge, consists of a frame house and a three-story building finished in gray composition board, against the mountainside. This structure, now used as a mess hall and handicraft shop, was part of a copper-mine works.

Right from the stone bridge and up a good path along the stream about 500 feet to the OLD COPPER MINE (R), one of the "Mine Holes of Pahaquarry" whose origin has received much attention from historians but has never been completely explained. The drift is cut into solid siliceous shale, and is almost large enough to permit a person of average height to walk erect *(flashlight required)*. Old timbers are found about 50 feet from the entrance, making it inadvisable to go farther. It is possible that the mine was dug as early as 1664. C. G. Hine wrote after a visit in 1907: "No one knows who the original miners were, but the supposition is that they were some of the earliest Dutch explorers who disappeared long enough before the first actual settlers came to leave no memory or legend of themselves that is founded on anything more substantial than air. The surroundings are romantic and beautiful in the extreme, and it is a wonderful spot for a person with a well-trained imagination, provided he is careful not to sit down on a rattlesnake." The old mine was the southern terminus of the famous Old Mine Road to Kingston, N. Y., which has been called "the first good road of that extent ever made in any part of the United States." It played an important part in Washington's victory at Trenton when General Gates with seven regiments marched through here from Saratoga in December 1776. Gates chose this back route to avoid British forces in eastern New Jersey; four of his regiments reached Washington's depleted army only three days before the crossing of the Delaware.

The high price of copper in 1907 encouraged some entrepreneurs to open a new mine on top of the mountain. Ore was hauled by rail to machinery on the site of the Boy Scout camp. The venture soon failed. Part of the masonry work remains, next to the mess hall.

The road north to Millbrook follows the route of the original Mine Road. A graded road in fairly good condition leads over the mountains from Millbrook to Blairstown.

At 43.7 m., on a free, covered bridge over Delaware River, the highway crosses the Pennsylvania Line, 0.2 miles east of Portland, Pa.

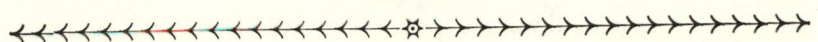

Tour 6

(Milford, Pa.)—Montague—Newton—Trenton—Junction with US 30;
US 206.
Pennsylvania Line to Junction with US 30, 131.7 m.

Between Branchville and Ross Corner and between Andover and Netcong the Lackawanna R.R., and between Princeton and Bordentown the Pennsylvania R.R., parallel
the highway.
Many tourist homes, camps, and filling stations; hotels in the larger towns.
Two- or three-lane concrete roadbed except for short stretches of macadam.

From the northern corner of the State US 206 runs almost directly
south. It cuts through the backbone of the Kittatinny range, a rugged region of forest, lake, and stream. The central section of the road runs
through rolling woodland and farming country, which includes the State's
most productive dairying region, and past the Revolutionary battlegrounds
of Princeton and Trenton. Southward US 206 traverses a picturesque dairy
country, until it reaches the pine woods, berry patches, orchards, and sandy
wastes of the Hammonton area.

US 206 crosses the Pennsylvania-New Jersey Line on the DELAWARE
RIVER FREE BRIDGE, 0.1 miles east of Milford, Pa. The river is smooth
flowing between rough banks of rock and pine. From the bridge the road
turns sharply R., climbing the rough face of the Kittatinny (Ind., *chief
town*) ridge.

MONTAGUE, 0.5 *m.* (520 alt., 40 pop.), is scattered along the two-
lane macadam highway with a few worn houses, a gas station before the
old country store, and (R) old BRICK HOUSE HOTEL *(open)*. Built in
1776 by Roger Clark with odd-size brick of local manufacture, the hotel
was afterward extended and graced with a double-deck porch that now
droops from the façade. Brick House is said to have given its name to the
locality in the Revolutionary period when it was a stop on the stagecoach
route between Buffalo and Hoboken. Montague and the entire upper Delaware frontier was frequently assailed by Indian raiding parties during the
wars with the French and during the Revolution. The ARMSTRONG
HOUSE, Old Mine Rd., long used as a hotel, was the stopping place for
raftsmen when lumber was floated down to Trenton and Philadelphia.
The frame part, two-and-one-half stories high with Dutch Colonial gambrel roof, is probably 50 years older than the one-and-one-half-story stone
annex built in 1843, with overhanging roof shading its low porch.

At 0.7 *m.* in Montague is the junction with Old Mine Rd. *(see
Tour 6A)*.

US 206 rises through one of the most picturesque sections of New Jersey. The land rolls away from the timbered mountains to a mass of little

hills and irregular small valleys. Much of the ground is cleared and fenced with fieldstone.

At 3 *m.* (L) are PUBLIC HUNTING AND FISHING GROUNDS in which grouse and game fish are numerous.

HAINESVILLE, 4.2 *m.* (640 alt., 311 pop.), a dairying center, lies about 100 yards (R) from the highway. A little town of mid-Victorian houses, a white steepled church, and an inn from stagecoach days, it thins out rapidly into scattered farms and barns along Beerskill River. This was once part of the hunting grounds of the Minisink or Munsee Indians *(people of the stony land)*. They called themselves Brothers of the Wolf, and wore wolfskins over their heads at ceremonies. Their descendants in Oklahoma have a legend that, like the brothers who founded Rome, two of their ancestors were nursed by a she-wolf. The babies' wails brought hunters to their rescue.

At Hainesville the highway takes the route of the Minisink Trail, which began on the Delaware River at Minisink Island and led to the seacoast near Perth Amboy. Western Indians passed over the trail, carrying furs to exchange for wampum and dried clams and fish from coastal tribes. One band of 700, carrying 70,000 pelts, was reported at Minisink in 1694. Arent Schuyler and other traders had posts on the trail. US 206 follows the trail route southeast to Branchville, touching it again at several points as far south as Stanhope. Heaps of shell, pottery, bones, and stone implements have been found along this route.

The highway, now two-lane concrete, rises steadily through hilly, rugged and thinly populated country. It follows, for 1.5 miles, the valley of Little Flat Brook, a trout stream.

At 7.3 *m.* is the confluence of Big Flat Brook, another popular trout stream, and Normanock Brook.

TUTTLES CORNER, 7.9 *m.,* is a hamlet of woodsmen.

At 8.1 *m.* the road crosses the northern boundary of Stokes State Forest.

The road is still uphill, most of the forest area being on the western slope of the Kittatinny Mts. The route follows a water-worn notch between peaks ranging in height from 900 to 1,100 feet.

NORMANOCK, 8.7 *m.* (L), is the office of the State Forest Warden and his aides, who are in charge of STOKES STATE FOREST *(hunting and fishing permitted; campsites 50¢ per night)*, largest New Jersey forest maintained for recreation, with an area of 12,428 acres. The forest was given to the State by Gov. Edward Stokes. Some of the campsites are in clearings on good roads; others are deep in the woods on rough, steep trails. They are equipped with stone fireplaces, tables, tent platforms, and some log cabins. Small game and birds are liberated in the area and the streams are stocked with fish annually.

KITTATINNY LAKE, 9.5 *m.* (R), is 1 mile long. A mountain, shaped like an inverted cap, rises boldly from the lake's farther shore.

At 9.6 *m.* is the summit of the pass (1,000 alt.). Here the road crosses the APPALACHIAN TRAIL, a footpath running through the mountains from Maine to Georgia.

Southward the descending highway enters CULVERS GAP, 9.7 *m.*

Through this stone portal Indians traveled centuries ago and later came trappers and Dutch traders. No railroad has penetrated the mountain wall stretching nearly 40 miles along the Delaware.

CULVERS LAKE, 10.3 *m.* (850 alt., 30 pop.), is one of the State's best-known lake resorts, but little of the lake is visible from the highway. Here the Sunday evening religious service has an unusual arena. About 7:15 p.m. a barge with enclosed platform, old-fashioned parlor organ, and a small choir is towed to the middle of the lake. Around it converge all manner of smaller craft, whose occupants join in hymns and hear a brief sermon. When the group breaks up, the myriad boats and canoes churning the water into white foam, sparkling with many lights, give the effect of beams radiating from the white barge.

The highway rolls southeast through grazing and dairying country with many Holstein and Guernsey herds.

BRANCHVILLE, 13.3 *m.* (550 alt., 685 pop.), is a thriving town with a few blocks of modest homes. Directly behind the bank (R) is the old PARK PLACE HOTEL, a group of odd houses bulked together into one building. It has a rambling, glassed-in porch topped with a series of globe-shaped lights along the balustrade. Opposite (L) are the FAIR GROUNDS where the annual Branchville Horse and Cattle Show is held in late August.

Branchville was laid out by surveyors as an eight-sided polygon resembling an Indian arrowhead.

Left from Branchville on an improved road, and L. at 1.2 *m.* through a country that leads other sections of the State in milk production. On the outskirts of BEEMERVILLE, 6.2 *m.* (760 alt.), is broad meadowland where the State maintains a large experimental MODEL DAIRY FARM *(open to public).* Foods and feeding methods are compared by experiments on nearly 300 Guernsey and Holstein cattle, and several varieties of cattle are being experimentally bred. Latest mechanical devices are used in the cultivation of cattle foods on the 1,200-acre farm. Near the center of Beemerville is a WILD ANIMAL FARM *(adm. 25¢).*

Southeast of Branchville, US 206 parallels Paulins Kill.

AUGUSTA, 15.2 *m.* (490 alt., 75 pop.), is a railroad junction and a small number of houses. The country is a broad, level plateau with gentle hills on both sides of it. In the vicinity have been found rock shelters and campsites of the Munsee Indians.

ROSS CORNER, 16.1 *m.* (500 alt.), consists of two large dairy plants on a branch of the Lackawanna R.R. and two modern service stations at the highway intersection.

US 206 is united with State 8 *(see Tour 5)* between Ross Corner and Newton.

US 206 turns sharply R., running southward through farm lands. Clumps of trees and domelike mounds dot the landscape. The mounds were left by the great North American glacier. Lakes of this region are attributed to the scooping out of the soil by the ice mass.

At 20.9 *m.* is the junction with a macadam road.

Right on this road, swinging through hilly farm country with some exceptional views, to PAULINS KILL LAKE, 3 *m.,* with boating facilities and scattered summer homes. Left at 4.4 *m.* at the junction with a macadam road to the junction with a graded road at 5.1 *m.* R. on this road to EMMANS GROVE, 5.5 *m.,* part of 536-acre SWARTSWOOD STATE PARK. Ample parking and picnicking accommodations are provided in a grove of evergreen and deciduous trees on a point jutting into SWARTSWOOD LAKE. Noteworthy is a large BED OF JAPANESE LOTUS, one of the few successful growths in this country. The plants are said to have been imported by a missionary.

The lake was named for Capt. Anthony Swartwout, British officer who had earned the hatred of the Indians by his active service in the French and Indian Wars. In 1756 a party of 13 Indians came from Pennsylvania to seize Swartwout and two of his neighbors in the thinly settled wilderness around the lake. The raiders captured a young man, Thomas Hunt, and a Negro servant. Stealing up to the Swartwout cabin, they shot Mrs. Swartwout as she went out to the milkhouse. Swartwout leaped for his rifle and musket; he killed two or three Indians and wounded others before he was taken. The Indians marched him a mile from his home, then slit his stomach and fastened one end of his entrails to a tree. Four of his children were slain at the spot before Swartwout, beaten and mutilated, was forced to end his life by winding his bowels on the tree as he walked around it. The Negro, Hunt, and two surviving children were carried away. The Negro escaped from Canada, and Hunt was exchanged after three years for some French captives. Swarthwout's little daughter grew up with the Indians and married a chief. The son learned of his parentage when he reached manhood. He returned for a visit to the settlement, and then went back to the forest to spend the rest of his life.

NEWTON, 21.1 *m.* (670 alt., 5,401 pop.), called by the Indians Chinchewunska *(side hill town),* is the county seat of Sussex County and largest dairy center of northern New Jersey. Most of its business section is grouped around the town square on the hill, known as CITY HALL PARK, a typical Civil War oasis, complete with monument and trees and flanked by three- and four-story brick blocks between the county buildings. The architecture is prevailingly Victorian. Newton was settled prior to 1761 by Henry Harelocker, a Dutch colonist and tavern keeper.

The old COURTHOUSE facing the square was built in 1847 and is a graceful example of late Classic Revival architecture with a severely plain pediment and Doric columns. The most famous building in Newton is the old COCHRAN HOUSE, also facing the square, at Main and Spring Sts. The inn has been rebuilt and modernized until now none of the original Colonial tavern of 1753 remains. General Washington and his staff were entertained here July 26, 1782, on their way to Newburgh, N. Y. Every spring the Sussex County Octogenarian Society, a playful group of 80-year-old boys, has its annual dinner at the Cochran House. Since 1929 men with white hair and men with no hair (or hardly any) have gamboled and cavorted and pirouetted and posed for a full page of pictures in the Sunday rotogravure section of the *New York Times.* They owe it all to the wonderful air of Sussex County, they say. The OLD ACADEMY *(private),* Academy St., is a Victorian landmark. Once known as Newton Academy, it is still a private school.

Southward on US 206 at 23.1 *m.* is (R) a handsome graystone building, the LITTLE FLOWER SHRINE, the home of Benedictine monks who operate a farm and gardens. The original structure, built 1840, was matched perfectly when the long central portion and the left wing were added in 1932. The land here is rocky, with outcroppings of scrub pine and bush and occasional bogs and swamps.

At 23.9 *m.* is the junction with a dirt road.

Right on this road to the CAREY FARMHOUSE, 0.6 *m.* (R), where directions will be given to MOODY'S ROCK *(accessible on foot),* the hiding place of James (Bonnel) Moody, leader of a Tory band that plundered the countryside during the Revolution. From a "plain, contented farmer" Moody rose by a series of bold exploits to a lieu-tenancy in the British army. Many of his ventures failed because of betrayal by his aides, but he did succeed in releasing several captured Tories from Newton jail, terrifying the inhabitants by simulating an Indian raid, and intercepting important dispatches to Washington. His failures included attempts to kidnap Governor Liv-ingston, rob the archives of Congress, and blow up the powder magazine at Succa-sunna. In 1783, while a guest of Sir Henry Clinton in London, Moody wrote the story of his adventures. The Tory chief's hiding place was beneath a huge ledge that hangs 25 feet out from the face of a low cliff to form an inverted L. The tip of the overhanging ledge is about 25 feet above the ground. Earlier visitors have painted their marks on the smooth rock or hacked their initials into it. Muckshaw Swamp, which offered additional protection to Moody, is now almost dry at this spot.

At 25.8 *m.* US 206 is macadamized.

At 26.4 *m.,* close to the road (L), are the ruins of a Revolutionary relic, the OLD FORT, built of local bluestone. The walls are crumbling, and what remains of the roof is a skeleton of sagging timbers. It was built in 1764, probably as a barn and storehouse for the iron from the Andover Furnace and Forge nearby. The Old Fort, however, served well as a de-fense against Moody's raids.

Opposite the fort a marker indicates the SITE OF ANDOVER FORGE, built in 1760 by William Turner and Joseph Allen of Philadelphia, both Loyalists. The Continental Board of War seized the forge in 1777 and placed it under the direction of Col. Thomas Maybury, who supplied much of the iron needed by Washington. An old GRISTMILL *(not open)* is 100 yards south of the fort and 100 yards L. of the road.

ANDOVER, 26.8 *m.* (620 alt., 479 pop.), is a small hill town of nineteenth-century atmosphere and cast, though its historic associations date back for two centuries. The town site and Andover Mine were parts of a tract of 11,000 acres obtained from William Penn's heirs by furnace builders.

In October 1932, Arthur Barry, the cultured criminal whose hauls reputedly reached the figure of $2,000,000, was captured on a nearby farm where he had lived 15 months. The tip of an Andover shopkeeper from whom Barry had purchased New York newspapers led to the arrest of the dapper, moustached second-story man who had fled to Andover after escaping from Auburn Prison in New York.

Left from Andover on a macadamized road to (R) the ANDOVER MINE, 0.7 *m.,* with the most extensive deposit of hematite ore known in the State. Along the road there is no indication of the mine except a 20-foot bank of shale. About 500 yards into the surrounding woods are huge piles of slag and a pit, 200 feet deep, from which ore to supply the Revolutionary armies was dug. Because the need for iron was great and the Andover iron produced the best steel in the Colonies, the mine was taken over by the State in 1778 at the suggestion of the Continental Congress. Supplying both the Andover and Waterloo forges, it was operated sporadically until the early part of the nineteenth century.

CAMP WAWAYANDA, 1.1 *m.,* on the shore of NEW WAWAYANDA LAKE which parallels the road (L), is conducted by the Y.M.C.A. It was named for an-other camp moved from a previous location because of the abundance of copper-heads.

Right at 2.7 *m.* to CAMP NORDLAND, 2.9 *m.,* at the tip of LAKE ILIFF, whose shores were the overnight camping ground of Indians on their trips to the coast. Signs indicate the *Einfahrt* (entrance) to the camp and the way *zu dem Jungendlager* (to the children's camp). Behind the long, single-story, yellow frame RECREATION HALL with its squat clock tower is the parade ground where disciplined uniformed troops, their arms outstretched in the Nazi salute, marched in review formation to celebrate the opening of the camp during the summer of 1937. In the recreation hall is a large picture of Hitler with a list of contributors to the camp fund below it and the slogan, *Auch dein Nagel hilft dem Bau* (Your nail, too, helps the building). Several of the larger New Jersey papers vigorously condemned the camp.

At 27.3 *m.* the highway passes under the embankment of the Lackawanna R.R. cut-off, 110 feet high and stretching for 3 miles across Pequest Valley. Built just prior to the World War, it helped to reduce the main line distance by 11 miles.

The road winds up into greater hills, rolling stony hummocks, heavily forested. "The largest hot dog in the world" barks from a typical roadside sign.

At 29.8 *m.* is (R) CRANBERRY STATE PARK, 42 acres of mountain country with a 1,000-foot frontage on CRANBERRY LAKE. When the State acquired the lake after abandonment of the Morris Canal, the shore property had already been privately developed. For this reason and because provision for access to the State property will be expensive, development of the public land has been delayed.

LOCKWOOD, 32 *m.,* is a few houses at the junction with a graveled and macadamized road.

Right on this road which is flanked by Lubber's Run and the Musconetcong River to the junction with a dirt road; L. on this dirt road is WATERLOO, 2.2 *m.* (660 alt.), a slumbering hamlet with few people in its old-fashioned houses. Long a deserted village, stranded when the iron industry went West, it lies on the north bank of the Musconetcong beside an old dam. Here was a port of the abandoned Morris Canal, which crosses the river at Waterloo. The towpath and lock remain in fair condition. Flush with the bank of the canal, so that no gangplank was needed from the deck of the boat to the floor of the shop, is the barn-like SMITH'S STORE, the only retail shop in Waterloo. Here, in the large trading-room, newly painted, and heated by a potbelly stove, in a place once given to mule trading and tall stories of adventure on the canal, are flour bins, counter, tea chests, shelves, and harness racks, with a meager stock of modern trade-marked package goods. A central pillar supporting the roof has been worn to a rounded base by the scuffing of numberless hobnailed boots that once trod the towpath beside the mule. The store has been in constant operation by one family since 1831, when the canal was opened.

Close by is an OLD STONE MILL of fine workmanship in dressed fieldstone. To this mill the canal boats brought as a backload from tidewater the famous Nova Scotia stone which was ground in the mill and used as a soil sweetener in cornfields. Water still stands in the old channel and pours over the sluiceways. The lock is ready to be swung; everything seems waiting for the shrill note of the skipper's tin horn, the cry of "Hey, lock!" and the bray of the mules. In the village are ruined walls of WATERLOO FOUNDRY, once supplied with iron brought by wagons from Andover Mines. This foundry, named for the victory of Wellington over Napoleon, is said to have given its name to the village.

Straight ahead on the road, which rejoins the macadam for 0.1 miles and then continues R. to FRENCH'S FOLLY, 2.9 *m.* (R), an industrial dream. In ruins beside a brook is an OLD MILL, built by James French, a native of Hoboken, who came to this vicinity in 1853 and left 50 years later. Some of the first Brussels carpet produced in America was made in the mill, which later manufactured fenders for canal barges. Its last use was as a drying and packing plant for medicinal herbs. Behind

SMITH'S STORE ON THE OLD MORRIS CANAL, WATERLOO

the mill, on a steep hill, are the ruins of STONE HOUSES, roofless shells with gaping holes.

At 32.9 *m.* US 206 passes a steep hillside (L). Beneath its surface the hill is a great mass of iron ore. High up on its slope are five shafts of STANHOPE IRON MINES, which served during the Revolution.

STANHOPE, 33.8 *m.* (800 alt., 1,089 pop.), is a compact cluster of modest little houses and stores. In Revolutionary years the village was the home of the Sussex Iron Co.; a few of the workers' one-story houses, resembling French peasant cottages, remain. The first anthracite furnace in the United States was built at Stanhope (*c.* 1841).

On the Morris Canal are RUINS OF AN INCLINED PLANE, where the boats were carried 75 feet up a railway run by water power to reach a higher level.

At 34 *m.* is (L) State-owned LAKE MUSCONETCONG.

NETCONG, 34.2 *m.* (920 alt., 2,097 pop.), the center of a large summer resort area, lies largely R. of the highway, a treeless thoroughfare lined with large homes. The town was first settled by workers in the nearby iron works and mines. Employment is now provided by the Lackawanna R.R. repair shops.

At 34.6 *m.* is the junction with US 46 *(see Tour 7).*

The road rises into the Morris County hills.

At 35.1 *m.* are (L) the tall RADIO RECEIVING TOWERS *(not open to public)* of the short-wave international telephone service of the American Telephone and Telegraph Co. Messages from Europe, Central America, and the West Indies are received here and amplified automatically for the telephone lines.

At 37.5 *m.* US 206 descends a steep slope into a long narrow valley between two ridges. The village of FLANDERS and an old millpond are L.

Fields in the valley are a checkerboard in green and brown, divided by a tree-lined branch of Raritan River.

The road rises again over a lesser ridge, uneven and rolling, with occasional farmhouses, and crosses Black River at 42.2 *m*.

On the road are (L) the outskirts of CHESTER, 44.1 *m*. (860 alt., 620 pop.) *(see Tour 10)*, at the junction with State 24 *(see Tour 10)*.

The route bears slightly R. into the deep valley of Middle Brook, through rolling farming and grazing country with the foothills of the Watchung Range (L) to the east.

BEDMINSTER, 51.3 *m*. (200 alt., 1,374 pop.) *(see Tour 4)*.

At 52.2 *m*. the highway unites with US 202 *(see Tour 4)*.

At 59.7 *m*., at a traffic circle, US 202 branches (R) from US 206, joining State 29. At this point US 22 *(see Tour 2)* branches from State 29 and is united westward with State 28 *(see Tour 17)*.

The highway passes the western edge of SOMERVILLE, 60.3 *m*. (82 alt., 8,255 pop.) *(see Tour 17)*. The route bears sharply R. and skirts a dairy farm area with a fine view of the Raritan Valley.

At 61.2 *m*. US 206 crosses Raritan River, winding sluggishly between low muddy banks.

Behind a mile-long stone wall backed by a dense screen of pine trees (R) is the DUKE ESTATE, 61.8 *m*. *(grounds open weekdays, only in absence of owners, on application at office)*, with 2,000 acres along the South Branch of the Raritan. The late tobacco manufacturer—whose fortune from Lucky Strike cigarettes changed old Trinity College in North Carolina to Duke University and made his daughter, Doris, the richest blonde on earth—spent lavish sums here to place woods, lawns, shrubs, formal gardens, artificial lakes, fountains, buildings, and works of art around his country home. The dwelling, now the home of Duke's daughter and her husband, James H. R. Cromwell, is a reconstruction in stone of the old farm homestead of the Colonial period that stood here.

The rolling countryside southward levels off into a great expanse of tree-fringed fields.

At 65.1 *m*. the road enters higher ground. Four miles west the wild Sourland Mts., scene of the Lindbergh kidnaping, form the horizon.

BELLE MEADE, 68.6 *m*. (100 alt., 51 pop.), is marked chiefly by a tavern and a few scattered musty houses near a candy factory—an industrial islet amid broad grassy meadows.

HARLINGEN, 69.9 *m*. (80 alt., 175 pop.), the center of a rich farming district, is a typical crossroads village with a great old DUTCH REFORMED CHURCH (R) built about 1842, a good sample of the ponderous Classic Revival architecture. The town takes its name from the Van Harlingens, one of whom, Johannis, was a founder of Rutgers University.

South of Harlingen the road pushes abruptly into rolling terrain, resembling sand dunes covered with sparse evergreen growth and tinged with the red of Jersey clay.

At 76.4 *m*. is the junction with a dirt road.

Right on this road to TUSCULUM, 0.5 *m*. *(open)*, home and estate of John Witherspoon, a signer of the Declaration of Independence and president of Princeton

(1768–1794), who erected the building in 1773. The Georgian Colonial house of rough-mortared local stone, apparently hand-cut, stands 50 feet from the road (L). British officers were quartered here in December 1776. Washington was a frequent visitor later.

The towers and spires of Princeton University appear (L) above the trees. US 206 swings L. in a great curve, following Bayard Lane.

PRINCETON, 77.5 m. (200 alt., 6,992 pop.) *(see PRINCETON).*

Points of Interest: Princeton University Campus and Buildings, Princeton Battle Monument, Morven, The Barracks, Bainbridge House, Westminster Choir School, Institute for Advanced Study, Princeton Theological Seminary, and others.

At Princeton is the junction (L) with State 27, here Stockton St. *(see Tour 8),* which is united with US 206 between Princeton and Trenton.

US 206 turns R., following Stockton St.

A few widespread houses line the road for some distance to DRUM-THWACKET (L), 78.2 m., the Moses Taylor Pyne estate *(grounds open).* The three-story Colonial mansion with five three-story columns across its front was built in 1832. Pyne, wealthy Princeton trustee, led the fight against Woodrow Wilson's plan for the establishment of a university commons.

On a 20-foot hill, 78.4 m., beside the road (L) stands the THOMAS OLDEN HOUSE, built 1696, the rickety home of a trapper. From its tiny porch Washington reviewed his troops on their march to Trenton in December 1776, and he twice used it in caring for both British and American wounded.

A MONUMENT (L), 78.5 m., marks the spot where on Jan. 3, 1777, Colonel Mawhood, leading the British from Princeton to join Cornwallis at Trenton, saw Washington's army marching on Princeton. He returned to intercept them, dividing his force here. The split assured the American victory in the Battle of Princeton *(see PRINCETON).*

At 78.9 m. the road crosses a brook on an old stone bridge. The crumbling walls of a STONE MILL are R.

COX'S CORNERS, 80 m. (170 alt.), is a small hamlet in the midst of rolling, half-forested land. The place was named for Dr. Daniel Coxe, Governor of West New Jersey, 1687–1692.

At 81.3 m. is (R) CHERRY GROVE *(private),* cor. Carter Rd. The house used by the British in December, 1776, when they held Trenton, is now occupied by descendants of Capt. George Green, owner during the Revolution. Two tall tulip poplars at the side of the old path to the entrance gate are known as "Bride and Groom trees" because a bridal pair planted two saplings in their first dooryard, according to the old custom.

LAWRENCEVILLE, 81.9 m. (130 alt., 750 pop.), was a post village incorporated in 1798 as Maidenhead, the name being changed in 1816 to honor Capt. James Lawrence ("Don't give up the ship!"). An iron fence with brick posts (L) marks the grounds of LAWRENCEVILLE SCHOOL, founded in 1810, an outstanding preparatory school for boys with an enrollment of 515. Thornton Wilder, the novelist, was a member of the faculty from 1921 to 1928. Main Street is a collection of stores, mixed with a few ancient and modern homesteads (R). These face the school buildings across the street, the older of which are of sturdy fieldstone, designed with Georgian righteousness.

At 82.6 m. is (L) the LAWRENCEVILLE PRESBYTERIAN CHURCH, built prior to 1716. Of red brick, it has arched windows and a tall, symmetrical spire. Hessians in 1776 compelled a captured American militiaman to preach a sermon here. In front of the church American pickets on January 2, 1777, killed one member of a Hessian patrol from Princeton. The body was buried opposite the church, behind the tavern, now the GOLDING HOUSE *(private)*, a two-and-one-half-story frame building. The tavern sheltered Lord Cornwallis on the night of December 8, 1776, when he followed Washington's retreating army on its way to Pennsylvania.

A group of high steel towers (R), which at night show red beacon lights, marks the TRANSOCEANIC RADIO STATION of the American Telephone and Telegraph Co., transmitting telephone messages from the United States and Canada to Europe.

Between Lawrenceville and Trenton the countryside is thickly populated.

At 84.4 m. the road crosses LITTLE SHABAKUNK CREEK, where Col. Edward Hand's riflemen repulsed Cornwallis's troops on their way to Trenton after Washington's victory.

At 86.6 m., at a traffic circle on the outskirts of Trenton, is the junction with US 1 *(see Tour 1)*.

South (straight ahead) on Brunswick Ave. to Broad St.; L. on Broad St. to State St., at the business center of Trenton.

TRENTON, 88.3 m. (55 alt., 123,356 pop.) *(see TRENTON)*.

Points of Interest: State Buildings, Library and Museum, Old Barracks, Mahlon Stacy Park, First Presbyterian Church, Bloomsbury Court, Bow Hill, Lenox Potteries, and others.

Left from Warren St. on State St. to Broad St.; R. on Broad St., crossing Assunpink Creek in the older section of the city.

WHITE HORSE, 92.7 m. (90 alt., 63 pop.), a small settlement on a high elevation, overlooks Crosswicks Creek. The village was named for the WHITE HORSE TAVERN (L), so called because General Washington passed here on a white horse. The innkeeper had a picture of the horse painted on his signboard, which hung from a buttonwood tree.

The highway turns R. and winds down to the arched concrete bridge crossing Crosswicks Creek. At the original wooden drawbridge, it is said, Colonial troops defeated a British detachment in June 1778. Crosswicks Creek took its name from the Indian village of Crossweeksung *(separation)*, so called because of the separation of the stream above it into two branches, and also because here stood a house of separation for Indian girls arriving at maturity.

Ascending to a higher level the highway underpasses the tracks of the Pennsylvania R.R., 94.9 m. About 200 feet L. on the railroad right-of-way stands the JOHN BULL MONUMENT. The *John Bull,* an English-made locomotive, was the first to travel this mile of New Jersey's first railroad, a part of the Camden and Amboy line *(see TRANSPORTATION)*. The base of the stone is encircled by a length of the first rails.

MUSCONETCONG RIVER AT WATERLOO

At 95.4 *m.* is the junction with US 130 *(see Tour 19)*.

BORDENTOWN, 95.9 *m.* (65 alt., 4,400 pop.) *(see BORDEN-TOWN)*.

Points of Interest: Bonaparte Park, Bordentown Military Institute, Hopkinson House, Clara Barton School, and others.

At 96 *m.* US 130 *(see Tour 19)* branches (R) from US 206.

US 206 descends into a wooded ravine with scattered laurel bushes and rises over a long hill.

MANSFIELD SQUARE, 97.8 *m.* (70 alt.), is a few houses at the intersection of Old York Rd., an early stage route that joined the West Jersey capital, Burlington, with East Jersey and New York.

MANSFIELD, 99.6 *m.* (100 alt.), is identified by an old FRIENDS MEETING HOUSE (R), a red brick building of plain design, standing behind great trees. For several years a $10,000 gift has been used to provide lectures and other cultural activities here. Culture is made more palatable by an abundant supply of free ice cream and cake, and residents from miles around assemble for the monthly entertainments.

COLUMBUS, 100.9 *m.* (80 alt., 535 pop.), is a delightfully old-fashioned village of frame houses, many of them dating to Colonial years. The town is busiest on Thursdays when farmers from a wide area participate in the weekly auction of horses, cows, produce, furniture, machinery and kitchen utensils.

The first settlers in this district were Thomas Scattergood and his wife, Elizabeth, who arrived from England *c.* 1676 and set up housekeeping in a cave on Craft Creek. Not the least of their contributions to growth of the Colony was the rearing of nine children.

For many years the village was known as Encroaching Corners because the building that now houses the POST OFFICE and STATE POLICE BARRACKS (L) projected upon the highway. Columbus also had distinction when it supported three competing hotels, each of them owned by a different Abner Page.

On the highway is (R) the COLUMBUS INN, a low, rambling brick structure with a wide covered porch, built in 1812. Mounted on a post is the bell once used to summon diners. The PRINCE MURAT HOUSE *(private)*, 32 Main St., a large, two-and-one-half-story brick dwelling with dormer windows projecting from the tin roof, was the home of Napoleon François Lucien Charles Murat in the early 1820's. The young prince, whose father Joachim, King of the Two Sicilies, had been executed in 1815, eloped with the handsome Caroline Frazer of Bordentown *(see BORDENTOWN)*. Two small Ionic columns support the porch roof, and above the double paneled doors is a fanlight.

At a crossroad, CHAMBERS CORNER, 104.8 *m.,* the roadbed becomes concrete.

At 106.3 *m.* is the junction with a dirt road.

Left on this road to the JOHN WOOLSTON HOUSE *(private)*, 0.1 *m.,* built for a son of the pioneer John Woolston, who bought land here from the Indians. The house, erected *c.* 1710, remained in the Woolston family until 1932. It is a two-and-one-half-story brick and frame structure of the Pennsylvania Colonial type with sections of the original pent roof, or overhang, intact. The east end was added *c.* 1800. The fine interior has been only slightly altered. The gable facing the highway has an arched tablet between the garret windows.

EWANSVILLE, 107.4 *m.* (50 alt.), a popular summer resort, is on the North Branch of Rancocas Creek, a Colonial winter highway (L). Along the banks are small cottages and bungalows shaded by great trees.

At 108.1 *m.* is the junction with State 38 *(see Tour 26)*.

At 110.3 *m.* is the junction with an improved road.

Right on this road is VINCENTOWN, 0.5 *m.* (40 alt., 1,865 pop.), a village on the banks of Stop-the-Jade Run. Along the winding main street are frame houses and stores, many of which are charming remnants of nineteenth-century architecture. The BANK (R) is worth noting for its entrance stoop and old-fashioned interior. Vincentown was known at one time as Quaky Town, because of a quivering of the soil at the edge of a millpond. Stop-the-Jade Run took its name from the troubles of Thomas Budd, an early settler, who founded Buddtown a few miles up the stream. When a young woman slave ran away, Budd posted notices in many villages offering a reward for her return. All closed with the appeal, "Stop the jade!"

Southward the highway cuts through wooded areas of pine and cedar, with holly, laurel, and fragrant magnolias. White birch trees stand out sharply.

HUCKLEBERRY HILL, 116.2 *m.,* is a slight elevation (R), noted for wild huckleberries.

At 116.9 *m.* is the junction with the hard-surfaced Tabernacle-Sandy Ridge Rd.

Left on this road is TABERNACLE, 1.4 *m.* (100 alt., 100 pop.), a hamlet in the wilderness where several roads meet. The tabernacle that gave its name to the place is believed to have sheltered David Brainerd, who worked among the Indians of the pines prior to the Revolution.

Southeast of Tabernacle on an improved road is HIGH CROSSING, 8 *m.*, summit of a low sandy ridge on the Jersey Central R.R. Immediately south of the crossing, about 50 feet (R) from the road, is the CARRANZA MONUMENT, a square, tapered shaft 10 feet high, in the center of a clearing. It was built through gifts of Mexican school children to the memory of Capt. Emilio Carranza, the pilot who fell to his death here in 1928. Carranza was returning to Mexico after a good-will flight to New York, repaying the similar visit of Charles A. Lindbergh.

Mile after mile US 206 cuts through stunted woods. Occasional clearings reveal a struggling effort at farming and a small unpainted house. Cranberry bogs provide employment for many of the residents here.

INDIAN MILLS, 120.4 *m.* (70 alt., 78 pop.), is the site of the first Indian reservation on the continent, established in 1758. Most of the old buildings are gone, and only a rusted wheel shows where a mill once stood. On the site of an old one-room SCHOOLHOUSE, today used for cranberry sorting, stood a church where the Indians worshiped; it burned in 1802. Behind it was the Indians' burying ground. Indian Mills today is a small settlement of cranberry pickers and a few farmers. The land is perhaps even more barren than when it was set aside for the survivors of the South Jersey or Turkey brotherhood of Indians, at a time when the Colonial government was striving to end the costly Indian war on its borders.

In August, 1758, an Indian delegation presented a formal request to the Colonial assembly for the allocation of this area. In three days the legislature complied, buying a 3,000-acre tract called Edge Pillock, or Edge-Pe-Lick, on which were built several cabins and a log meeting house. Friends of the Indians renamed the place Brotherton. Here the last tribesmen lived but did not prosper; in 1801 they sold their land and left to join kinsmen in the Lake Oneida Reservation, N. Y. A small remnant moved later to Wisconsin and then to Oklahoma and to Ontario, where their descendants still live *(see ARCHEOLOGY and INDIANS)*.

Several residents here remember Indian Ann, member of a half-breed family that remained when the others moved away. She had three husbands in turn, a Negro, an Irishman, and a mulatto, and sold Indian trinkets in many villages. Ann lived to be more than 100 years old, dying in 1890.

Between Indian Mills and Atsion the highway passes through a heavy wooded section, on nearly level ground.

ATSION, 124.2 *m.* (50 alt., 150 pop.), named for the Atsionk Indians, has a few worn buildings along the banks of Mullica River. A dam at the highway forms ATSION LAKE (R), the millpond of an early bog-iron works. Below its spillway are the ruins of the ATSION FURNACE, built in 1776, and a large stone and stucco MILL BUILDING that in turn manufactured iron, paper, and cotton. A large, deserted house of square design (L), with wide porticos and iron pillars embossed at the base with the furnace brand "A," is the SAMUEL RICHARDS MANSION, home of an eighteenth-century ironmaster. The GENERAL STORE is (L) close to the highway. A plain stuccoed building without an identifying signboard, it resembles a small chapel with its small belfry and austere architectural lines, although a haymow door on the second floor does not conform to church design.

Between Atsion and Hammonton the highway crosses a region of scrub oak and pine and cranberry bogs, and enters a sandy plain where berries and fruit orchards are extensive. Peach and apple blossoms in this area draw thousands of sightseers in late April and early May.

At 131.7 *m.,* on the outskirts of HAMMONTON (100 alt., 7,656 pop.) *(see Tour 23),* is the junction with US 30 *(see Tour 23).*

Tour 6A

Montague—Walpack Center—Flatbrookville—Rosencrans Ferry; Old Mine Rd.
Montague to Rosencrans Ferry, 19.8 m.

Few gas stations; occasional tourist homes.
Road graveled with small stretches macadamized; most parts unmarked, and though occasional signs point to "Old Delaware Road," the route is difficult to follow especially at junctions with other dirt roads. Rattlesnakes and copperheads abound in region; advisable to exercise caution when walking.

The southern part of Old Mine Road offers a glimpse into the history of New Jersey. Running southward at the foot of Kittatinny Mountains, close to the Delaware River, the route penetrates some of the State's most scenic country, popular with hunters, fishermen, and city-sated week-enders. Some of the farms are still owned by the descendants of the Dutch and French Huguenot settlers of the seventeenth century. Much of the route coincides with the traditional Old Mine Rd., which, it is believed, was built by the Dutch before 1650 in order to explore the mineral deposits described to them by the Indians. Nothing is known about these miners who laid the path from Kingston, N. Y., to Delaware Water Gap, but records of the Dutch West India Company indicate the existence of a rich iron mine here. In 1777 Robert Erskine, Surveyor General for General Washington, mapped the locality, placing the Old Mine Road exactly where it is today.

The whole countryside was frontier during the French and Indian wars.

The Old Mine Rd. branches R. from US 206 at MONTAGUE, 0 *m.* (520 alt., 40 pop.) *(see Tour 6).*

Almost invisible in a tiny weed-grown patch at 0.2 *m.* (R) are a few tombstones and a granite marker on the SITE OF MINISINK CHURCH. This was the second of four Dutch Reformed churches organized along the Delaware River in 1737 by the Rev. George Whilhelm Mancius of Kingston, N. Y. The first was at Port Jervis, N. Y.; others were at the mouth of Flat Brook and at Du Puy Ferry on the Pennsylvania side. The first pastor, the Rev. John Casparus Fryenmuth, served all four congregations.

At 1.1 *m.* is (L) a row of 10 tiny white cabins with green window trim, a modern note in the historic section. Each summer members of the North Bergen Patrolmen's Association vacation here.

At the entrance (R) to a private road, 2.4 *m.*, the Chinkchewunski Chapter of the D.A.R. has placed a large granite marker that points out the location of nearby historic spots.

Right on the private road to the BELL HOUSE *(private)*, 0.1 *m.* a small stone structure with a wooden gable and with windows only 1 foot above the ground. The ninth generation of the same family lives in the house. In the dark basement, early residents hid from the Indians.

Just behind the barns, and on the property of an adjacent farm, a hole in the ground and a few stones mark the SITE OF WESTBROOK FORT, one of a chain of seven forts along the Delaware constructed for defense against Indians. Today tall maples stand guard. Johannes Westbrook, an early settler, deeded land in 1731 to the people of the Minisink for a cemetery and a schoolhouse.

At 0.5 *m.*, through a gate and down a sandy lane to the Delaware River. Opposite this point is MINISINK ISLAND, the home of the Munsee or Wolf Clan of the Lenape Indians, and the starting place of the Minisink trail to the sea.

At 2.6 *m.* is (R) the ENNIS HOUSE (1734), in which lived William Ennis, the first school teacher of the region.

The RUINS OF FORT NORMANOCK, second in the chain of forts, are R. at 3.1 *m.* The fort was named for the island to the west in Delaware River.

At 5.8 *m.* is (R) the FISCHER or METTLER CEMETERY, about a block square, without benefit of fence, church, or trees. Many of the early settlers, including Evan Bevans, a Revolutionary soldier, were buried here.

At 6.7 *m.* is the junction of three dirt roads with a macadamized highway.

Right, down a sharp incline, to DINGMANS FERRY, 0.1 *m.*, and the only toll bridge *(pleasure cars 25¢)* north of Burlington. The bridge is high above the river, which flows clear and strong at this point. On the New Jersey side a smooth rocky ledge serves as front yards for summer cottages. Built 35 years ago, the wood and steel bridge earns up to $100 a day during the summer. The town and bridge were named for Judge David W. Dingman, who lived down the river and who, during Revolutionary times, frequently appeared in bare feet and nightshirt for court sessions in his home.

The road rises sharply away from the river and then descends to PETER'S VALLEY, 8.6 *m.* (520 alt.), or Bevans (pronounced Beevans). The first postmaster gave the latter name—his own—to the village, but failed to popularize it. To natives the place is known as Henfoot Corner because of the pattern made by four intersecting roads. The combined GENERAL STORE AND POST OFFICE (R), lit by kerosene lamps, has long been a forum for neighborhood discussions. Behind the old frame building is a handsome stone and frame house, more than a century old, with white columns two-and-one-half stories high. It is the home of the storekeeper.

The road twists through Flat Brook Valley, an extensive public hunting and fishing ground, along the right bank of Flat Brook. Occasional farms are spread along the foot of the mountains.

WALPACK CENTER, 11.9 *m*. (420 alt.), is a neat little village, modern to the extent of electric lighting and the bus that brings children from two other districts to school here. The WALPACK INN (R), 12.1 *m.,* probably built in 1750 by Isaac Van Campen, has been so much remodeled that little of the original except a stone shell remains.

At 13.1 *m*. is the entrance to the VALLEY DUDE and LAZY K RANCHES, New Jersey imitations of life in the mesa and mesquite country. Summer visitors, dressed in varying conceptions of western cowboy costumes, ride the trails that spread throughout the region.

At 14.3 *m*. (R) a WATERFALL shimmers 150 feet downward to a water wheel, generating electricity for a private home (L). Southward the valley is studded with small farms and hamlets.

As the road descends once more to the level of the brook, remains of an older road are visible at several points (L). These are supposedly the last traces of the original Old Mine Road.

A STEEL BRIDGE (L), 17.8 *m.,* was built by the county to provide access to two houses across the stream. Originally there was only one house, the large white one, whose occupants erected the small gray dwelling in order to take advantage of a county regulation that provides for bridge construction whenever two or more houses will be served.

FLATBROOKVILLE, 18 *m*. (400 alt., 102 pop.), hemmed on both sides by the mountains, has a few houses built close to the road. The only conceivable center of town is a one-story green frame building (R) that serves as the POST OFFICE as well as the home of the postmistress.

An abandoned DUTCH REFORMED CHURCH (R), 18.4 *m.,* removed from its original location in 1807, was used until 10 years ago. The neglected building is overgrown with poison ivy, its windows and doors gone. Beside it is the former FLATBROOKVILLE SCHOOL. The earlier SITE OF THE CHURCH (L), 19.2 *m.,* is hidden by low trees and underbrush. A flat granite marker indicates the position.

At 19.5 *m*. the route turns L. sharply to ROSENCRANS FERRY, 19.8 *m*. *(no service in winter)*, established a few miles S. in 1756 by Daniel Decker. In 1898 it was moved to the present site and taken over by the Rosencrans family. The ferry, little more than a raft carrying a single car, is propelled by a small gasoline motor and guided by a cable. Customers on the Pennsylvania shore ring a bell to get service.

Tour 7

Morsemere—Dover—Hackettstown—(Portland, Pa.); US 46.
Morsemere to Pennsylvania Line, 71.3 m.

The route is paralleled by the Lackawanna R.R. between Paterson and Denville and between Buttzville and the Pennsylvania Line; and by the Lehigh and Hudson R.R. between Vienna and Buttzville. Frequent service stations and tourist camps; hotels in cities and lake resorts.
Concrete roadbed for the most part, with stretches of improved macadam.

US 46 is the most direct route between George Washington Bridge and New Jersey's inland lake country. West of Troy Hills, where the low North Jersey meadowlands end, is a mountainous region studded with lakes that are rivaled only by the State's seacoast resorts in popularity with summer and winter visitors. The zigzag course at the western end of the route is lifted to heights unusual for New Jersey by rugged Schooleys Mountain, Pohatcong Mountain, and Jenny Jump; at the Delaware River is a long vista of Delaware Water Gap to the north.

US 46 is united with US 1 (see Tour 1) between George Washington Bridge and Morsemere.

At MORSEMERE, 0 m., US 46 branches (L) from US 1, dropping into an open cut through the business section of one of the sprightlier areas that mushroomed in boom times as metropolitan appendages. The highway emerges to overpass the Erie R.R. tracks and, at 0.8 m., broad Overpeck Creek, a branch of the Hackensack River. Tall marsh grass on each side of the road rises from the tidal swamp that forms the upper section of Jersey Meadows.

RIDGEFIELD PARK, 1.6 m. (60 alt., 10,473 pop.), is a commuters' borough. Frame houses pack Winant Ave., through which the highway runs. Like nearby communities the borough is keyed to real estate development: whitewashed blackboard signs advise visitors to "SNAP UP this BUY at $60 a month."

A concrete bridge at 1.8 m. crosses the New York, Susquehanna and Western R.R., the Ontario and West Shore R.R., and the Hackensack River. In the river valley (R), scattered with homes and factories, is the solid stone and steel of Hackensack. At a traffic circle, 2.1 m., the route is west across the floor of the valley, with scattered dwellings and small truck farms.

US 46 overpasses State 2 (see Tour 16) at 4.1 m., and climbs the western slope of Hackensack Valley. The slightly rolling open country is sparsely cultivated.

Passaic River is bridged at 8.1 m., and US 46 turns sharply R., continuing along the west bank.

At 9.1 m., at a traffic circle, the route becomes Temporary US 46.

Right at the traffic circle is EAST PATERSON, 0.3 *m*. (60 alt., 4,779 pop.), a town that has its own borough government, but is little more than an industrial adjunct to Paterson. A high wire fence separates the road from the tremendous plant of the NATIONAL PIECE DYE WORKS (L). On the bridge over Passaic River, from which green GARRET MT. (R) is seen rising sharply above the smoky industrial valley, a flying squadron of 500 dyers crossed from Paterson in a drenching rain during the great textile strike of October, 1933. They were met by East Paterson police, sheriff's deputies, and private guards. Two strikers were wounded by gunfire. After a 40-minute battle the dyers routed the police and joined the National Piece Dye workers of East Paterson in a mass picket line. Amicable relations between the company and its employees have obtained since 1934, when a union contract was signed.

Left along Market St. to 21st Ave.; L. on 21st Ave. to Jackson St.; R. on Jackson St. to Grand St.; L. on Grand St.

PATERSON, 11.5 *m*. (84 alt., 138,513 pop.) *(see PATERSON)*.

Points of Interest: Garret Mountain Reservation, Paterson Museum, Passaic Falls, Wright Aeronautical Corp. Plant, Family Shops (textile factories), and others.

The route turns L. at 13.3 *m*.

At 13.4 *m*. the highway crosses Passaic River by a wood bridge into Totowa Borough. Temporary US 46 ends at this point.

TOTOWA, 13.9 *m*. (160 alt., 5,000 pop.), is a residential extension of Paterson, in whose silk and dye mills a large part of the borough's adult population is employed. During the Revolution, Washington and his men were encamped at Totowa, where they drilled on a vacant field. One of the early settlers, Joshua Hott Smith, was involved in Benedict Arnold's plot. He escaped execution after a summary court martial delivered the rather remarkable judgment that he was undoubtedly guilty of every charge but that the evidence, unfortunately, was insufficient to convict him. Dutch scholars translate Totowa, or Totua as it appears in some early records, as *where you begin,* suggesting that it was once the frontier to the wild west.

The route turns L. at Totowa.

The highway, becoming concrete, traverses open country, unmarked by the populous industrial developments above Paterson. Clumped woods crowd the road in the relatively flat stretch west of Totowa.

At 16.4 *m*., at a traffic circle, is the junction with State 23 *(see Tour 9)*.

The road crosses Passaic River at 17.3 *m*.

The red stone FAIRFIELD REFORMED CHURCH at 18.3 *m*. (L) was built in 1804 by Aaron Vanderhoof for a Dutch congregation organized in 1720. A white frame steeple seems superimposed, built in pagoda style at a later date than the simple body of the edifice. The story runs that Vanderhoof agreed to build the church on condition that his family be given first pick of the pews. When it was almost finished, he learned that pews had already been allotted with only a second choice left for him. Outraged, he refused to erect the steeple, and left this scornful memento of the unfulfilled agreement:

Beautiful FAIRFIELD,
Proud people:
Elegant church
No steeple!

Poesy seems to be in Fairfield's tradition, if the Reformed Church graveyard is any indication; almost all of the epitaphs are rhymed. A good example is the one that glorifies the bones of Thomas Speer, who died in 1829 at the age of 76:

> Let worms devour my roasting flesh
> And crumble all my bones to dust:
> My GOD shall raise my frame anew
> At the revival of the just.

Low in altitude, with the Passaic River winding in and around it, this section is flooded much of the year. Still pools cover whole fields on both sides of the road; trees stand lonely in the water, as much as a foot or two of their trunks submerged. Left is LONG MEADOW, the northern end of Hatfield Swamp.

PINE BROOK, 21.2 m. (200 alt., 281 pop.), is on an island-like hill in the floodlands of the confluence of three rivers: Rockaway, Passaic, and Whippany. Subject to chronic inundation, Pine Brook is the central point of the Lake Whippanong Flood Control Survey Project, and is destined to become the dam site of the Passaic Valley Watershed. A large dairy farm is the borough's sole industrial plant.

The macadam road between Pine Brook and Parsippany is known as Death Highway because of numerous accidents. An AUTO COASTER at 24.6 m. (R) caters to tourists who want their thrills made to order: the sign advertising the long, rolling shoot-the-chute reads, "Miles of Smiles."

TROY MEADOWS, 24.7 m. (L), a wooded swamp with a high growth of marsh grass, is a natural bird refuge and breeding ground, reported by the Audubon Society to be second only to Cape May in New Jersey as a natural station for birds in seasonal migration. Some of these migrations extend over thousands of miles; the stubbled marsh W. of Pine Brook is a central point for flights to and from the Arctic Circle and the Argentine.

At TROY HILLS, 25 m., is the junction with a macadam road.

Left on this road to the TROY HILLS FAIR GROUNDS, 0.4 m. (R), where every September the Troy Hills Grange holds horse and cattle shows attended by breeders for miles around. BEVERWYCK INN, 0.8 m. (R), is an old, two-story white frame house now run as a restaurant and owned by Charles Edison, Assistant Secretary of the Navy and son of Thomas A. Edison, the inventor.

The highway west of Troy Hills climbs gradually to a summit at 26.2 m., where it dips down beneath the south wall of PARSIPPANY RESERVOIR (R), main storage lake of Jersey City's Rockaway River watershed.

At 26.9 m. (L), on a high hill crowned with a grove of oaks, stands the LITTLE WHITE CHURCH, where each Sunday the Rev. S. Trevena Jackson preaches streamlined sermons to a parish of strangers recruited from the motor traffic of US 46 and US 202.

PARSIPPANY, 27 m. (300 alt., 210 pop.), is at the junction with US 202 (see Tour 4). The village lies at the southern tip of Parsippany Reservoir. The vine-run red brick PRESBYTERIAN CHURCH (L) at the outskirts dates back to 1718, when John Richards, local schoolmaster, deeded 3½ acres to the township of Whippanong for a meeting house. The present building, with Gothic windows and Gothic panels in the doors near the pulpit, was erected 1828. Right from Cobb's Corners (local name for the junction of the two main highways) is a long vista of the reservoir to a horizon of blue hills beyond, with Boonton's busy streets framed in the rocky hill to the N. A bronze tablet at Cobb's Corners (R) records the fact that the pioneer village and forge of Old Boone Town lie submerged 60 feet in the valley inundated by metropolitan drinking water. At the opposite corner stands a remodeled TOWNSHIP HALL effectively screened by a service station and a grocery store on the first floor. In its chambers, each second and fourth Tuesday of the month, the gavel comes down at 8 p.m. to open the most dramatic sessions of township committee government in Morris County, where a lone but perennial Democratic chairman holds the fort against four equally inevitable Republicans.

A large, wire fence-enclosed estate at 27.6 *m.* (R) is where Mrs. Marcellus Hartley Dodge *(see MADISON, Tour 10),* the former Geraldine Rockefeller, plans to build dog kennels; it was once a circus winter quarters.

At 28.9 *m.,* on the crest of a stiff grade, is the junction with a tarred and graveled road.

Right on this road is MOUNTAIN LAKES, 1.1 *m.* (420 alt., 2,132 pop.), a late nineteenth-century real-estate development that really developed. Today it is a quiet, dignified community spread out in well-built homes around eight artificial lakes.

LAKE ARROWHEAD, 29.9 *m.* (R), is in a somewhat lower region. Perched on a hill W. of the entrance to the lake is (R) a WHITE FRAME HOUSE with green shutters, in an adaptation of a Colonial style of architecture. It was built in 1931 by Claude A. Miller, who wrote a book about his home, *An Early American House And The Fun We Had Building It.*

DENVILLE, 30.6 *m.* (540 alt., 2,120 pop.), a Lackawanna R.R. junction, is a thriving little community whose wide main street and busy commercial center give it the appearance of a larger town. At its southwestern tip is INDIAN LAKE, a popular summer resort, and in summer the village's population jumps to more than 10,000. Denville has a public works system that includes a municipally owned water works and nine lake playgrounds.

Far off US 46 and just west of Denville is BALD HILL (R)—not bald at all, but thick with trees and studded with a gleaming water tank.

The road mounts the lower shoulder of SNAKE HILL (L).

At 32.2 *m.* is the junction with an improved road.

Right on this road is ROCKAWAY, 1.1 *m.* (580 alt., 3,200 pop.), a sleepy mountain village cupped in the narrow valley of Rockaway River. A few of the inhabitants commute to Newark and New York, but most of them find employment in the three industrial plants—a piece dye works, a box-making factory, and a trucking machine plant. Once the center of a thriving iron-mining district, Rockaway today is the gateway to an almost abandoned sector of the State. The road climbs a steep hill leading through the stagnant shopping section of the town.

1. Right from Rockaway on Church St.; the road winds along the side of a hill overlooking the village and descends sharply to a broad valley, paralleling the tracks of an abandoned spur of the Jersey Central R.R.

16-INCH SHELLS AT PICATINNY ARSENAL

At the junction of the railroad tracks and Beach Glen Brook, 1.7 *m.*, is BEACH GLEN, where a sawmill produces rough-sawn boards from timber of the surrounding hills. A lumber shed and a log-cabin office are the only structures in sight, and the only sound is the loud buzz of the saw.

HIBERNIA, 2.8 *m.* (580 alt., 200 pop.), is an abandoned iron-mining town. There are a couple of dozen houses strung along the road and a like number against the steep hillside. Until about 1912 when the Warren Foundry and Pipe Co., last owner of the Hibernia Mine, ceased operations, Hibernia was a thriving town with a population that rose to 3,000 as the mine reached its peak production of 300,000 tons a year. The company is disposing of 15,000 acres to residents who have remained and to summer visitors who are attracted to the lake-studded country.

At 3.4 *m.* a millpond, almost hidden from sight in a hollow (R), marks the SITE OF HIBERNIA FURNACE, erected in 1763 and operated between 1767 and 1782 by William Alexander, son of the Surveyor General of New Jersey, a stanch supporter of the Colonial cause. Alexander called himself "Lord Stirling" even though the British House of Lords refused to recognize his right to the title. Like most of the furnaces throughout the Colony, Hibernia furnished iron for munitions for the Revolutionary army.

2. Straight ahead from Rockaway on Academy St. the road climbs a gentle grade through a woodland region broken here and there by modest homesteads.

MIDDLETOWN, 2.5 *m.* (820 alt., 100 pop.), is a cluster of well-kept frame houses lining the road and distributed through a hollow (R).

MOUNT HOPE, 3.5 *m.* (840 alt.), a sprawling mining town, reflects the dawn of better times along its main street where the houses have been well-kept and freshly painted since the Richards and Mount Hope mines reopened. But on the fringes of the town are rows of down-at-heel company houses in narrow, littered yards. Many of these, beyond repair because of age and neglect, are being vacated as mine workers buy the newer homes. The workers, mostly thrifty Hungarians, are encouraged by the mine operators to develop their own homesites, raise their own vegetables, chickens, and pigs. This has been an iron-producing area almost without interruption since Colonial times. In 1772, John Jacob Faesch, one of the outstanding ironmasters of his day, built the Mount Hope Furnace, which provided munitions for the Revolutionary army.

Beginning at 4.8 *m.* the woods on both sides of the road are fenced off with barbed wire, and trees are placarded "U.S. Government Reservation." This is PICATINNY ARSENAL, 5.8 *m. (open only by special permit),* a 1,400-acre reservation for the manufacture and storage of munitions for the Middle Atlantic Corps of the U. S. Army. Two brick and limestone three-story buildings and a number of smaller wooden structures set in a landscaped park give the atmosphere of a peaceful educational institution. A terrific explosion here on July 10, 1926, resulted in 19 deaths and $100,000,000 in damages. Bursting shells wrecked 200 buildings on the reservation and endangered surrounding towns; the glow of flames was visible from New York skyscrapers, more than 30 miles distant. The explosions made craters, still unfilled, each large enough to bury a building.

DOVER, 35.2 *m.* (560 alt., 10,031 pop.), sometimes called the "Pittsburgh of New Jersey," has its industrial heart placed well to the left of the highway. DOVER SPEEDWAY (L), a shooting gallery (R) and a roadside hot-dog stand built in the shape of a castle (L) introduce the town's eastern outskirts. Formerly an important port on the old Morris Canal, Dover is the shipping center of an iron-ore area that at one time made mining one of New Jersey's principal industries. The town has a MUNICIPAL FIELD (R) for athletics, and its MUNICIPAL PARK (L) is the scene of an annual North Jersey Fly Cast Meet, at which fishermen from all over the State gather on the grass to cast for the dry distance record. MEMORIAL PARK (L), a large greensward, serves as a front lawn for the mayor's house.

MINE HILL, 37.6 *m.* (860 alt., 1,100 pop.), is built along the slope of a steep hill. Most of its inhabitants work in the Scrub Oak mine *(see below).*

At 37.9 *m.* is the junction with a tarred and graveled road.

Right on this road to the Alan Wood Co.'s SCRUB OAK MINE, 0.6 *m.* One-story clapboarded company houses built on identical specifications, each in its allotted surveyed space, each fronted by a small square of lawn, line the single street leading to the mine. The Scrub Oak was founded in 1856 and today, after a period of inactivity ended by the threat of a new World War, is once more the largest operating iron mine in the State, with an estimated annual output of about 600,000 tons of low-grade ore. Byproducts—crushed stone, sand, and poultry grit— are sold locally and shipped throughout the State. The Scrub Oak employs about 400 workers of many nationalities.

KENVIL, 39.3 *m.* (720 alt., 1,000 pop.), formerly known as McCainville, advertises itself as the "Home of America's Oldest Continuously Operating Dynamite Plant"—the HERCULES POWDER CO. PLANT, founded 1871. Two major explosions brought the plant into the headlines in 1934. On March 8, four workers were killed in a packing-house blast that broke every pane of window glass in neighboring towns and shook a marine observation tower at Sandy Hook, 50 miles east. A sign was erected at the factory gate announcing that the accident was the first in 180 days, and that there had been no serious explosion on the grounds for 14 years. Five months later a detonation in the smokeless powder unit killed two men and injured three. The E. I. du Pont de Nemours Co. has had a large interest in Hercules.

At 40.5 *m.*, at a traffic circle, is the junction with State 10 *(see Tour 14).*

US 46 bears R. here with four lanes of concrete, east- and west-bound traffic being separated by a green avenue. Here, as in many other places in New Jersey, "Jesus Saves" is lettered on whitewashed rocks at odd intervals. The road is paralleled by the weed-sprung bed of the abandoned MORRIS CANAL.

At 41.6 *m.* is the junction with a concrete paved road.

Right on this road at LANDING, 1.3 *m.* (920 alt., 300 pop.), is the southern tip of LAKE HOPATCONG (Ind., *honey pond of the many coves),* largest inland body of water in New Jersey. Rugged hills hem in its 40-mile shoreline, reflected in the clear lake surface. Hopatcong is second only to New Jersey's seacoast resorts in popularity as a playground. BERTRAND'S ISLAND, near the eastern shore, was a Tory haven during the Revolution. Today it is an amusement park. On the lake front are a roller coaster, dance halls, many small cottages, and a five-story hotel.

A mile-long grade brings the road to a high point at 42.8 *m.* LAKE MUSCONETCONG is visible (R) half-way down the hill. The homes of STANHOPE are ahead at the foot of Roseville Mt.

At 43.7 *m.* is the junction with US 206 *(see Tour 6).*

NETCONG, 43.9 *m.* (940 alt., 2,097 pop.), is a hilly little village along Lake Musconetcong, peopled by workers in the Lackawanna R.R. shops, and nearby farms and mines.

West of Netcong is a long swing to the southwest through thick scrub woods. Far off (R) are the ALLAMUCHY MTS.

BUDD LAKE, 46.3 *m.* (940 alt., 750 pop.), is a summer resort on the broad, shallow lake of the same name. Frame cottages line the low lake front (R), many of them adorned with the rustic name-signs that haunt most lake pleasure resorts: Dew Drop Inn, Aw-Kum-On Inn, Blue Heaven. High wooded hills guard the northwestern rim of the lake. Budd Lake has been popular as a training-ground for prizefighters.

At 48 *m.*, where the road crosses the South Branch of the Raritan River, is the steep grade up SCHOOLEYS MT., sometimes known locally as Hackettstown Mt. Neatly partitioned farm lands rolling over the hills are reminiscent of New England. Gay pottery stands enliven the roadside. From the western slope of the mountain, the small homes and spires of Hackettstown are visible in the valley (R), over a ridge of bright green hemlocks.

MUSCONETCONG DAM, 51.9 *m.* (R), on Musconetcong River, creates the local swimming hole.

At 52.1 *m.* is the junction with State S 24 *(see Tour 10).*

At 52.3 *m.* is the junction with Plane St., a madacamized road.

Left on Plane St. to the junction with a tarred and graveled road, 0.5 *m.;* L. on this road and then R. to the NEW JERSEY STATE FISH HATCHERY, 0.8 *m.* *(open daily 8-4:30 except May 20–June 10; free).* Millions of brook, brown and rainbow trout, largemouthed and smallmouthed bass, yellow perch, and blue-gill sunfish are hatched every year in its 184 fresh-water ponds, and distributed to streams and lakes. Built in 1912, the hatchery has been self-supporting since 1915.

HACKETTSTOWN, 52.5 *m.* (560 alt., 3,038 pop.), a quiet, clean little town, is situated in the Musconetcong Valley between Schooleys and

Scotts Mts. Originally called Helm's Mills or Musconetcong, it became known as Hackettstown about the middle of the eighteenth century after Samuel Hackett, largest landowner in the district, leaped to popularity by setting up free and plentiful drinks at the christening of a new hotel.

On Church St. (L) is the CENTENARY COLLEGIATE INSTITUTE, a Methodist Episcopal school for girls. It was erected in 1869 and 1874 by the Newark M. E. Conference at a cost of $200,000, and, after a fire that destroyed the property in October, 1899, was rebuilt with an additional $300,000.

Mounting the shoulder of UPPER POHATCONG MT., the road rises and falls through a knobby region where the soil is jet black, glistening like soft, rich velvet. Onions, celery, and lettuce are grown here.

The descent into the Pequest Valley begins at 55.3 *m.* Straight ahead, over the long sweep of fields, is JENNY JUMP MT.

VIENNA, 56.3 *m.* (580 alt., 209 pop.), is a little maple-shaded village that was once a thriving industrial community. At the eastern end of town is (R) abandoned VIENNA FOUNDRY which, from 1860 to the end of the century, turned out double corn plows that made the reputation of the producer, Simon Cummins. Another abandoned plant, a sawmill north of the village, was owned by Fisher Stedman, inventor of wood-shaping machinery in use throughout the world today.

GREAT MEADOWS, 57.6 *m.* (580 alt., 250 pop.), is the center of the onion-celery-lettuce farms in this section of the State. It is situated on the tip of a fertile tract of lowland, once pure bog, reclaimed after a campaign begun single-handed in 1850 by Dr. J. Marshall Paul of Belvidere. Great Meadows was known as Denville before its principal interest became agricultural; then its main industrial plant was the Kishpaugh iron mine. A GREEK CATHOLIC CHURCH (L) offers a surprising architectural note: a silvered Byzantine cupola atop a severe wood frame.

Pequest River parallels the road between here and the Delaware. The swift, twisting Pequest is a haven for trout- and eel-fishermen; planked eel-runs rise out of the stream at high points like so many little riparian outhouses.

PEQUEST, 62.4 *m.* (450 alt.), appears as a single brown frame house (R) bravely marked with a street number, 1. The house is one of a series of dwellings that served as boarding houses for workers employed at a blast furnace nearby. The furnace has long since been abandoned; the other houses are well off the highway (L).

At 63.6 *m.* is the junction (L) with State 30 *(see Tour 15)*. A triple-arch stone bridge over the river here (L) bears a double burden: the Lehigh and Hudson R.R., which crosses the bridge, is itself crossed by the Lackawanna R.R.

BUTTZVILLE, 63.9 *m.* (430 alt., 500 pop.), seems to have had its appearance shaped by its name—with simple frame houses and stores, some of them unpainted. However, a grove within its limits—ISLAND PARK (L), a few hundred feet west of the junction with State 30—is known throughout the State as a fisherman's paradise. Surrounded by cool shade trees and offering rustic tables and benches for tourists, the grove is a special favorite with women anglers. Brown and rainbow trout abound in Pequest River at this point.

At 66.3 *m.* US 46 crosses Beaver Brook and turns north from Pequest River. The road here is a sharp cut through shale rocks on each side. To the west are the long, rolling hills of Pennsylvania.

At 66.5 *m.* is the junction with a concrete paved road.

Left on this road is BELVIDERE, 1.7 *m* (280 alt., 2,073 pop.), county seat of Warren County, a hilly town at the confluence of the Delaware and the Pequest Rivers. Worn one- and two-family frame houses are built on the narrow streets that lead to the prosperous-looking park that is the town square. Tall old trees in the park lend to the town an air of distinction, a rural atmosphere seldom found near the beaten track. Belvidere is restful by nature and design. The well-to-do farmers who come here to live have succeeded in welding together agricultural quietude and urban comforts. Known as Greenwich-on-the-Delaware before 1775, the present name was first used by Maj. Robert Hoops, who purchased land here from Robert Patterson, the first settler.

Under a Pennsylvania R.R. overpass at 67.2 *m.,* the highway turns R. to run parallel with the Delaware River alongside a high shale cliff in which is cut the Pennsylvania R.R. roadbed. The area at the foot of the cliff was covered to a depth of 7 feet during the Delaware flood of 1936. Clean against the sky about 12 miles to the north is the rugged crest of DELAWARE WATER GAP *(see Tour 5).*

At 68.1 *m.* is MANUNKA CHUNK JUNCTION (R), high on the Lackawanna R.R. embankment, one of the most euphoniously named railroad junctions in America and the point at which the Pennsylvania R.R. and Lackawanna R.R. meet to run along the same track.

DELAWARE, 70.6 *m.* (290 alt., 205 pop.), lies R. of US 46 at the bottom of the scarp on the bank of the Delaware. The town is a shopping center for the surrounding country and has several stores, a post office, a firehouse, and churches. Most of the buildings on the main street are brick, but the residences on the tree-lined streets are all frame. Its most noticeable buildings from the highway are the ROMAN CATHOLIC CHURCH and the METHODIST CHURCH—two white edifices with gold-tipped steeples, almost identical in architecture.

US 46 bears L. at 71 *m.*

At 71.3 *m.,* in the middle of a free bridge over the Delaware River, US 46 crosses the Pennsylvania Line, 1.9 miles southeast of Portland, Pa.

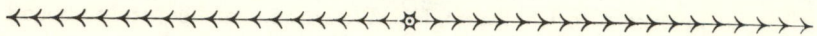

Tour 8

Elizabeth—New Brunswick—Princeton; State 27.
Elizabeth to Princeton, 33.7 m.

Paralleled by Pennsylvania R.R. throughout.
Adequate accommodations at close intervals.
Modern concrete roadbed, mostly three lanes wide.

State 27, part of the original Lincoln Highway, runs southwest across the State, through the fringe of the metropolitan industrial and residential area and touching the State's two great university centers. The southern part traverses somewhat rolling agricultural country, spotted with woods, streams, and an occasional lake or pond. Nearly 300 years ago the route was known as the Dutch Trail, the path of Dutch travelers from the Hudson to the Delaware. Later it became the Great Road and still later, the King's Highway.

ELIZABETH, 0 m. (70 alt., 114,589 pop.) (see ELIZABETH).

Points of Interest: First Presbyterian Church, Union County Courthouse Annex (museum), Carteret Arms, Scott Park, Boudinot House, Singer Sewing Machine Plant, and others.

State 27, following S. Elmora Ave., branches southwest from State 28 *(see Tour 17)* on Rahway Ave.

At 0.3 m. is WARINANCO PARK (R), part of the large Union County Park System, with green-bordered drives and broad, sunny lawns. The park was named for one of three chiefs of the Lenni Lenape Indians, who signed the original deed for what is now Union County. It has athletic fields, a concrete stadium, and a running track. A lake provides fishing, boating, skating, and ice hockey. On the picnic grounds are fireplaces. Dog-sled races take place annually when snowfall permits. A sunrise service is held in the park on Easter Sunday.

ROSELLE, 1.9 m. (70 alt., 13,021 pop.) *(see Tour 17)*, is skirted on its southern border (R).

LINDEN, 2.4 m. (25 alt., 21,206 pop.) *(see Tour 1)*, is L.

At 2.8 m. (R) is the SUNNYFIELD GOLF COURSE *(18 holes; greens fee 50¢; Sat., Sun., and holidays $1).*

The highway here retains most of its line of old elms and maples. Behind them are attractive homes.

RAHWAY, 3.5 m. (25 alt., 16,011 pop.), has at the northern edge an AIRPLANE RIDE, a miniature plane operating on a cable suspended between two high towers.

At 4 m. State 27 crosses the Rahway River. On both sides of the road extends the Rahway River Parkway, which has interested landscape artists because of vistas reminiscent of Italy, towering Lombardy poplars and shrubbery lining the slow-moving stream.

The business section of Rahway, 4.3 *m.,* is L. of the highway. Among the town's industrial firms are the Wheatena Co., the Three-in-One Oil Co., and the Merck Co., the latter operating one of the Nation's largest plants for the manufacture of drugs and chemicals.

Rahway's first newspaper, the New Jersey *Advocate,* was established in 1826 and has been continuously published.

The name of Rahway has been attributed to the Lenni Lenape phrase "na-wak-wa," meaning "in the middle of the forest." During the Revolution the settlement was known as Spanktown because a physician here had a habit of spanking his wife whenever he deemed it necessary, regardless of local opinion. The name Spanktown was used on Washington's military maps, but it acquired new significance when the Jersey militia gave a sound thrashing to British raiders here in January and June of 1777.

In the old PRESBYTERIAN CEMETERY (R), 4.2 *m.,* St. George Ave. near Westfield Ave., is the GRAVE OF ABRAHAM CLARK (1725–1794), a signer of the Declaration of Independence and a delegate to the Continental Congress. A monument marks his burial place.

Right from the center of Rahway on Lake Ave., a dirt road, to the BATTLE-FIELD OF ASH SWAMP, 3.8 *m.* Here, in the spring of 1777, Colonial troops surprised British infantry and light-horse feasting at the farm of Daniel Moore. The British countered and gave chase; unfamiliar with the ground, they fell into disorder when horses sank into the deep muck of the swamp toward which the Americans enticed them. British losses rose to 100 killed and many wounded. Only two Americans were killed.

The highway crosses Robinson's Branch, 4.7 *m.,* at another attractive park and playground and turns R. at 5.8 *m.* Several elaborate private estates (R) line the winding path of the old Colonial post road and the original Lincoln Highway—still marked by one small brown milestone. The tall, yellow grass that grows profusely here is called Indian grass.

COLONIA, 6.9 *m.* (40 alt., 506 pop.), a small residential town, is known to its neighbors as an "artistic" settlement. Writers and artists have tried several experiments in community operation of facilities, including a store, a nursery, and a social hall.

ISELIN, 8 *m.* (60 alt.), is a village of homes for the middle-class commuter and his family. The place was named for the Iselin family, prominent in New York financial and international yacht-racing circles.

MENLO PARK, 9.1 *m.* (100 alt., 355 pop.), is known for the SITE OF EDISON'S LABORATORY, marked by a rough-hewn granite boulder (R). In a hillside park behind the boulder stands the 129-foot MEMORIAL TOWER, topped by a huge electric light bulb about 14 feet high and 9 feet in diameter. The eight-sided tower is built of reinforced colored concrete. The great bulb is made of prismatic pyrex glass and illuminated by 12 lights inside. Bronze tablets to be placed on seven of the eight sides will tell of Edison's inventions. A bronze and glass door will give a view of the perpetual light at the base, burning since 1929. The tower stands on the spot where the first incandescent bulb was made. Edison's home is gone; his workshop and many relics have been removed by Henry Ford to his museum in Dearborn, Mich. Residents say that Edison also worked in the little WOODEN SHACK directly behind the highway memorial. For 10 years following 1876, Edison worked night and day at Menlo Park testing thousands of ideas and materials. He even tried the red whiskers of Mackenzie, the station agent, for a lamp filament—and rejected them. The laboratory was lighted by gas when he began work. When he moved his shop to West Orange in 1887, the incandescent lamp was being used in many cities. Edison here developed his system of electrical distribution, his commercial dynamo, the carbon transmitter for the telephone, the phonograph, the automatic telegraph, and other devices.

West of Menlo Park, Edison had a temporary right-of-way over the fields to Pumptown, 1.5 miles. On it he built the first electric railway line, an experimental affair later scrapped. The current was conveyed underground from two of Edison's electric-lighting dynamos at Menlo Park to one rail of the ungraded, hazardous track built of discarded horse-car rails. His first electric locomotive was a small, four-wheeled dump car on which was mounted a dynamo. This acted as a motor, receiving current through the wheels from one rail, and returning it to the other rails. Friction pulleys at first transmitted power to the driving wheels. The truck and wheels of the first cars are exhibited at the Edison plant in West Orange *(see WEST ORANGE);* out of it grew Edison's invention of the third-rail and trolley systems.

The glamor of great discovery has faded; Menlo Park now is simply a residential district, with a sawmill its only industrial plant.

At 9.4 *m.* is the junction with a dirt road.

Left 0.7 *m.* on this road under a stone railroad bridge to the NEW JERSEY HOME FOR DISABLED SOLDIERS *(open 9-7),* on the crest of a ridge (L). Established in 1866 at Kearny for veterans of the Civil War, the institution was transferred in 1932 to its present site of 150 acres. The home cares for veterans of all wars and in 1937 had one Civil War veteran on its roster. The building is a broad, two-and-one-half-story brick structure of Colonial design, with a white cupola.

Right on Parsonage Rd. from the entrance gate to Soldiers Home to the attractive new MIDDLESEX COUNTY TUBERCULOSIS HOSPITAL 0.9 *m. (open Tues., Thurs., and Sun.),* of Georgian style, built of brick with white trim. In the valley below the hospital is a small lake, part of ROOSEVELT PARK *(see Tour 1).*

METUCHEN, 11 *m.* (100 alt., 5,748 pop.), has long been known, half seriously, as the "Brainy Borough." Its residents, including many New York businessmen, take pride not only in fine dwellings and shaded streets but also in cultural pursuits. Outstanding literary and artistic figures have made their homes here. The AYRES or ALLAN HOUSE *(private)* is a one-story, cedar-shingled dwelling on Durham Ave. just off the intersection of Main St. and Middlesex Ave. Built in 1740, it is still in good condition. Beams are hand-hewn, pegged, and mortised. The original chimney remains, but the building never had a fireplace because it was designed to house servants.

The FIRST PRESBYTERIAN CHURCH, erected 1793, is on the northern side of Woodbridge Ave. adjoining Railroad Sq. The church is a large L-shaped frame building of a type common in the post-Colonial period, with hip roof and high windows. A square tower supports an octagonal belfry and a bell-shaped cupola covered with weather-stained copper. The FRANKLIN CIVIC HOUSE (L), on Middlesex Ave., a frame, peak-roofed structure with a bell tower, was an early New Jersey schoolhouse. It served as the town hall, and as the meeting-place of the Revolutionary Committee of Safety. Civic organizations, including a Little Theater group, now use the building.

Metuchen, known to the Indians as Matochshoning because of a former chief who lived here, was founded by Dutch and English settlers in the late seventeenth century. In 1777 and later, Metuchen was held by a strong outpost of Americans watching the British at New Brunswick. There were minor engagements in the vicinity.

At 11.2 m. State 27 turns L. in front of the FRANKLIN SCHOOL, making an S-turn under a bridge of the Pennsylvania R.R. and then over a bridge of the Lehigh Valley freight line to Perth Amboy, after which a sharp R. turn is made. On the latter railroad was made the first installation of automatic switch control, and it was on this line that Edison experimented with wireless telephony.

The highway runs through a flat and fertile farming country.

At 14.3 m. is the junction with an asphalted road.

Right on this road is STELTON, 0.5 m. (110 alt., 700 pop.), a residential community, formerly called Baptist Road. It was later named for the Stelle family, descendants of a French Huguenot who came to Staten Island about 1670. The Baptists in Stelton in 1689 organized the second Baptist congregation in New Jersey.

NORTH STELTON, 2 m., celebrated its 25th anniversary as a cooperative community in 1937. The origin of the colony was a series of advertisements in the old New York *Call* in the summer of 1912, urging heat-worn city dwellers to "get back to the land." By October a small group of German Socialists and other enthusiasts had, with the advice of George Littlefield, raised $8,000 and made plans for the purchase of a farm. The Letson farm and manor-house were selected upon the recommendation of the New Jersey State Agricultural Experiment Station, and a small band of settlers spent the winter on the tract. The group had formed the Fellowship Farm Cooperative Association, under which each member leased and individually farmed an acreage in proportion to the number of shares held; 11 years later deeds were granted. The farms were not successful on the whole, although poultry-raising became popular. Many of the colonists built bungalows on their plots and continued to commute to jobs in New York and other cities. Such community enterprises as a store and a bus line gradually passed into private control, largely because of the unwillingness of the democratically minded but inexperienced cooperators to delegate full authority to a competent management. During the depression, however, the colony established a cooperative garment factory that has operated successfully. An efficient volunteer fire company, housed in a building erected by the colonists, plays an important part in North Stelton's social life.

Established in about the same period was the adjoining Francisco Ferrar Colony, built around a progressive school with a philosophy that was predominantly anarchistic. Among the teachers in the Ferrar School were Manuel Komroff, Will Durant, and Rockwell Kent. The institution is still functioning as the Stelton Modern School.

HIGHLAND PARK, 15.8 m. (100 alt., 8,691 pop.), a suburb of New Brunswick, is divided by Raritan River from that city. At the NON-METALLIC STATION *(not open)* of the United States Bureau of Mines, SW. cor. Cleveland and Madison Aves., experiments are conducted in the origins of steel embrittlement, the chief cause of boiler explosions.

On the townsite was an Indian village in 1675, when the place was known as Raritan Falls from a small cascade.

At 16.5 *m.*, the eastern end of Albany St. Bridge across the Raritan River, is the junction (R) with State S 28 *(see Tour 13)*. State 27 and State S 28 are united for 0.4 miles.

NEW BRUNSWICK, 16.9 *m.* (125 alt., 34,555 pop.) *(see NEW BRUNSWICK)*.

Points of Interest: Rutgers University Campuses and Buildings, White House, Guest House, Joyce Kilmer Memorial (museum), and others.

State S 28 separates (L) from State 27 at the intersection of Albany and George Sts., New Brunswick. Straight ahead on Albany St. to French St.; straight ahead on French St.

Between New Brunswick and Franklin Park the highway runs through grassy fields, dotted with suburban homes, small chicken farms, and occasional roadside eating places.

At THREE MILE RUN, 21.6 *m.*, once stood a Dutch Reformed Church, built 1703, or earlier, by settlers from Inian's Ferry (New Brunswick). Coon dogs are brought here each year from the nearby country for the annual championship field trials.

At 23.3 *m.* (R) a bronze tablet marks the SITE OF THE FIRST COURT-HOUSE OF SOMERSET COUNTY, built 1716 and burned 1737.

FRANKLIN PARK, 23.5 *m.* (130 alt., 225 pop.), was an early Dutch community but is scarcely larger today than at its settlement. It has a dozen houses, a coon-hunting headquarters, a school, and an old DUTCH RE-FORMED CHURCH (R). The congregation was organized in 1710, and the Rev. Theodore Frelinghuysen, leader in the founding of Rutgers University, was pastor in 1720.

West of Franklin Park the land flattens out in a wide plateau spotted with forest islands, but mostly given over to cultivation. Well-kept farmhouses and barns are stamped with age.

The Sand Hill region (L) with its rugged growth of forest looks much as it did when Washington marched his troops through here.

KINGSTON, 30.2 *m.* (110 alt., 313 pop.), was settled about 1700 and bears today the unmistakable air of an old town, though the inns that catered to Washington and Provincial Governors are gone. White houses and rural stores line its main street and follow the somewhat haphazard roads that radiate from the central high point into the surrounding lowland. Joseph Hewes, a signer of the Declaration of Independence, was born here in 1730. The KINGSTON HOUSE *(open)*, on a bank beside Millstone River (R), stands on the site of Withington's Inn, where, during stagecoach days, as many as 400 guests were accommodated. It is a plain, two-story, stucco-covered roadhouse of the Victorian period with a high central dormer.

It was at Kingston that Washington and his army eluded the pursuing British under Cornwallis, Jan. 3, 1777, immediately after the Battle of Princeton *(see PRINCETON)*, by filing off to the north along the narrow road leading to Rocky Hill. The enemy, believing he had pushed on to New Brunswick to destroy the British army's winter stores, kept on the main road. Washington had actually planned to move as Cornwallis imagined against New Brunswick, but at a horseback conference with his aides as he approached Kingston it was decided that the men were too weary. The army rested two days at Rocky Hill and then marched to Morristown.

On the outskirts of the town at 30.4 *m.* the highway crosses the abandoned DELAWARE AND RARITAN CANAL. The old wooden locks are L.

At 30.5 *m.*, on the western side of Millstone River, is the junction with a macadam road.

Right on this road along the Millstone River is ROCKY HILL, 2 *m.* (100 alt., 512 pop.), in a small valley named for the large number of glacial boulders seen here. At the BERRIEN HOUSE *(open weekdays except Mon. 10-6, Sun. 2-4; adm. 10¢)* Washington made his headquarters from August to November, 1783, while Congress met in Princeton to draft peace terms with England. The house had been engaged by Congress for Washington's use, and here he wrote his farewell address to the army. It is a long farmhouse built in 1730 of white clapboard on a fieldstone foundation, with a plain peaked roof and gabled ends. Many pieces of furniture and other objects used by Washington and his wife in their stay of three months are displayed. When Thomas Paine, pamphleteer of the Revolution, visited here, Martha Washington greeted him as "another man who helped George win the war." Adjoining the house is the slave kitchen, a modern reproduction of a Colonial building. The property is maintained by the State.

At the junction is the old KINGSTON FLOUR MILL (L), an old frame building, where water power is still used in part. Behind the mill is the dam that forms CARNEGIE LAKE (L), a gift of Andrew Carnegie to Princeton University in 1906. The river has been dredged and widened for 3½ miles, providing a straight course for university crews. Across the lake are the gray stone buildings of ST. JOSEPH'S COLLEGE, a Roman Catholic institution.

At 31.8 *m.* is (L) the CASTLE HOWARD FARM *(garden open to visitors)*, dating back to 1685. One of its early owners, Captain Howard, a retired British army officer, was at the time of his death in 1776 sympathetic to the Revolution. His widow married another British officer and had to flee from the farm after the Battle of Princeton, leaving it in the care of President Witherspoon of Princeton College, to avoid confiscation. The family of Princeton's famous athlete, the late Hobart (Hoby) Baker, is now the owner.

At 32.1 *m.* are the grounds and buildings (R) of the former PRINCETON PREPARATORY SCHOOL for boys, closed in 1936 for lack of support.

State 27 follows Nassau St. to the Princeton Battle Monument at the intersection of Bayard St.

PRINCETON, 33.2 *m.* (200 alt., 6,992 pop.) *(see PRINCETON).*

Points of Interest: Princeton University Campus and Buildings, Princeton Battle Monument, Morven, The Barracks, Bainbridge House, Westminster Choir School, Institute for Advanced Study, Princeton Theological Seminary, and others.

At the Battle Monument, 33.7 *m.,* State 27 forms a junction with US 206 *(see Tour 6).*

Tour 9

Newark—Montclair—Franklin—Sussex—High Point Park—(Port Jervis, N. Y.); State 23.
Newark to High Point Park, 59.5 *m.*

The route is paralleled by the Lackawanna R.R. between Newark and Montclair; by the Erie R.R. between Little Falls and Pompton Plains; and by the New York, Susquehanna and Western R.R. between Butler and Beaver Lake and between Hamburg and Sussex.
Frequent tourist camps; hotels in towns.
Concrete roadbed for the most part, with stretches of macadam.

Northwest out of Newark's industrial environs, State 23 leaves urban pavements behind for high, rugged country. Mounting the rim of the old glacial continent to the north, the highway traverses a district of mountains, high valleys, and small lakes where farming is made difficult by the rocky character of the land. There are numerous summer resorts and camping grounds along the road. At the northern terminus is High Point Park, the highest elevation in New Jersey.

NEWARK, 0 *m.* (33 alt., 442,337 pop.) *(see NEWARK).*

Points of Interest: Newark Library, Plume House, First Presbyterian Church, Newark Museum, Weston Electric Plant, Sacred Heart Cathedral, Borglum's Statue of Abraham Lincoln, and others.

State 23, following Bloomfield Ave., branches west at its junction with Broadway in Newark. Bloomfield Ave. runs for 3 miles through an industrial and small retail section of Newark.

BLOOMFIELD, 3.2 *m.* (125 alt., 38,077 pop.), is an old settlement that has developed as a modern residential and industrial extension of Newark. Originally known as Wardsesson (Ind., *crooked place*), it got its present name when a town meeting decided in 1796 to honor Joseph Bloomfield, Revolutionary general and later Governor (1801–1812). The general contributed heavily in that year to the construction of the FIRST PRESBYTERIAN CHURCH, still standing on the green at Broad St. and Belleville Ave. It is a brownstone structure, with a brown wooden octagonal belfry, stained-glass windows, and bell-shaped cupola. A trace of the original name can be found in WATSESSING PARK (L), at the southern end of town, a unit of the Essex County Park System.

Montclair, Belleville, Glen Ridge, and Nutley have all been formed from the 20 square miles that was once Bloomfield. The city's factories, producing a wide variety of goods, have been built along its two railroad lines; among them are a Westinghouse plant and a General Motors parts unit.

BLOOMFIELD COLLEGE AND SEMINARY, facing the green at Broad,

WORLD WAR MONUMENT, HIGH POINT STATE PARK

Franklin and Liberty Sts., is a Presbyterian institution founded in 1810. The city was not always friendly to education and educators, however. Alexander Wilson (1766–1813), the great ornithologist, taught school in Bloomfield in 1801 for $160 a year. Wilson then described his neighbors as "canting and snivelling," and his work as "spirit-sinking and laborious." The DAVIS HOUSE *(private)*, 409 Franklin St., built 1676, is a vine-covered, two-story, sandstone structure with a peaked roof and with dormer windows on both sides of a gable over the double front door. With the exception of a slope-roofed wooden porch, the rear is the duplicate of the front. The Davis family came to this vicinity with Robert Treat's group. During the Revolution it was the home of Caleb Davis and his son, Joseph, both Continental soldiers. There is a story that Washington came here once for a night's lodging but left when he found Benedict Arnold had already established himself here. Historians, however, say that Washington came for entertainment and left when he found sick soldiers quartered in the home.

Bloomfield was the birthplace of Randolph Bourne, prominent pacifist, author of *Education and Living,* and philosopher of the American youth movement during the pre-World War literary renascence. Bourne died at the age of 32 in 1918, leaving an unfulfilled future but a decisive influence on his contemporaries.

GLEN RIDGE, 3.8 *m.* (200 alt., 7,365 pop.), is a commuters' borough with its own cultural life. The tone is set by its Women's Club, Men's Forum, Home and School Association, and a Civic Conference Committee that prides itself on the avoidance of politics by nominating a slate of Republicans and Democrats to the dollar-a-year town council and board of education. Based on the New England town-meeting idea, the committee plan was adopted in 1913 with little opposition. The committee's slate is invariably elected; the only opposition arose in 1923, when Sephas Shirley ran unsuccessfully for mayor on a rump ticket. Officers of the committee are, in turn, selected with the approval of the town council. Minor parties are ignored. Glen Ridge's three-block business center has aroused a good deal of interest as an example of town planning, and its most prominent landmarks are all community-owned—the large brick GLEN RIDGE SCHOOL (R), a fairly new MUNICIPAL BUILDING (R), an ATHLETIC FIELD (R), and a big brick building known as the COMMUNITY STORES (R).

MONTCLAIR, 5.3 m. (250 alt., 42,017 pop.), formerly a part of Bloomfield, broke off when the parent community refused to cooperate in building a railroad to run from Jersey City to the New York State Line. That was in 1868; today Montclair is larger than Bloomfield. Montclair has a sizable business center with impressive office and bank buildings; the community has been developed—and dwarfed—by its proximity to Newark. The township's history can be traced to 1666, year of a town meeting convened in Milford, Conn., to consider inducements proffered by Gov. Philip Carteret of New Jersey to establish a settlement on the banks of the Passaic River *(see NEWARK)*. It was at first divided into two parts, Cranetown and Speertown, for two early settlers; Stephen Crane (1871-1900), the writer *(see LITERATURE)*, was a descendant of the first Crane. None of Montclair's early buildings remains. The EGBERT HOUSE *(private)*, 128 N. Mountain Ave., a story-and-a-half brown sandstone dwelling with mansard roof and white-shuttered, small-paned windows, was built in 1786 by a Hessian ex-mercenary. A red-brick porch matches the chimneys at the ends of the house.

Another old building, at 369 Claremont Ave., is known as the GEORGE WASHINGTON WAYSIDE HOUSE *(private)* for no more apparent reason than that George Washington passed by it on his way from Totowa to support Lafayette's expedition against the British on Staten Island. Built more than 150 years ago, the little frame house was willed in 1831 to James Howe, an emancipated Negro slave. Washington did stay over in Montclair, at a house that stood at what is now Valley Rd. and Claremont Ave. The site is marked by a boulder on 6 square feet of green—a community-owned landmark that has attracted Robert L. Ripley's attention as the SMALLEST PARK IN THE WORLD.

Montclair is proud of its cultural life. The MONTCLAIR ART MUSEUM, L. at Bloomfield and South Mountain Aves., a large, two-and-a-half-story structure of cream brick fronted by four marble Ionic columns, is considered by Montclair residents an oasis in the art desert. The building was presented to the Montclair Art Association in 1918 by Florence Rand Lang. Its exhibits, most of them loaned, range from examples of modern art to ornaments excavated at Ur in Mesopotamia. Best-known artist resident of Montclair was George Inness (1825–1894), for whom the junior high school was named. The GARDEN THEATER, situated in a deep glen next to the MONTCLAIR HIGH SCHOOL (R), serves local theater-goers on summer nights. It is a natural amphitheater with rows of stone seats on the hillside and a brook at the bottom of the glen between audience and players. MONTCLAIR ACADEMY (L), a well-known school for boys founded 1887, is on the slope of the town's main street as it mounts the Watchung ridge.

Left from Montclair on South Mountain Ave. to Union St., a macadam road; R. on Union St. to Undercliff Rd., a macadam road; R. on Undercliff Rd., up a winding course of hairpin turns, to EAGLE ROCK RESERVATION, 1.9 *m*. From the 664-foot elevation, it is said, is seen a greater concentration of suburban dwellings than from anywhere else in the world. The panorama stretches east from the Passaic-Hackensack valleys to Newark, Jersey City and New York. Eagle Rock was used by Washington as one of a chain of observation posts that extended from Paterson to Summit. From here the countryside below was scanned for Tory raiders. A frequenter of Eagle Rock today (1939) is Carl J. Kress, the 32-year-old Orange bookbinder who holds a permit from the Essex Co. Park Commission to yodel in the reservation every morning between 8 and 8:45. Kress obtained the permit in 1936 after a policeman attempted to put an end to his Alpine habits on the ground that the park commission's rules prohibited singing or playing musical instruments on the reservation. At that, his unique grant allows him only "to yodel . . . subject to the rules and regulations of the park commission."

At 6.7 *m*. State 23 branches (R) from Bloomfield Ave.

Left (straight ahead) on Bloomfield Ave. through Verona *(see below)* to (R) the GROVER CLEVELAND HOUSE *(open 12-6 daily; also by appointment)*, 1 Bloomfield Ave., in CALDWELL, 2.6 *m*. The three-story white clapboarded house with a two-story extension has been a museum since it was presented to the State in 1934; it was restored and renovated by the WPA. The house contains many of the former President's personal papers and belongings. Grover Cleveland was born in this house on March 18, 1837, and lived here until he was four, when the family moved to Fayetteville, N. Y. At the death of his father the 16-year-old boy left for Ohio but stopped off in Buffalo to visit an uncle who found a position as law clerk for him. An early and active interest in politics soon led him to the forefront of public affairs. Through offices of increasing importance he finally rose to the Presidency in 1885. Cleveland was the only President to serve for two non-successive terms. After leaving the White House the second time, he retired to Princeton, where he took an active part in the affairs of Princeton University. He died at Princeton June 24, 1908.

State 23 skirts the eastern fringe of VERONA (360 alt., 7,160 pop.), in the valley between the First and Second Watchungs. Sparse thickets are clumped along the road (R); L. are the "model homes" of the borough —trim little white, green-shuttered, frame dwellings of the so-called Colonial style. The Verona area was owned by Caleb Hetfield, a Tory who took no chances on the outcome of the struggle and sold his holdings before the Revolutionaries had the opportunity to confiscate them. They later became the property of Christian Bone, a Hessian who deserted German George to fight for the American uprising.

Spread out at the foot of the wooded escarpment at 8.3 *m*. (L) are the buildings of OVERBROOK HOSPITAL, the Essex County institution for the care of the mentally diseased.

CEDAR GROVE, 8.1 *m*. (300 alt., 5,092 pop.), is a suburban village whose population includes the 2,500 patients and attendants at Overbrook Hospital.

State 23 underpasses the Erie R.R. tracks at 8.2 *m.*, through a scraggly cottage-scattered district dominated by the sharp brow of WATCHUNG MT. (L). A long vertical scar of brown earth streaked into the green-gray ridge at 8.5 *m.* is a MOTORCYCLE STUNT PATH, where cycling addicts risk their necks.

At 9.6 *m.*, where the road rises and the land R. falls sharply away, is the view of the southeastern edge of PASSAIC VALLEY studded with smokestacks and workers' homes, and the high hills of West Paterson to the E.

At 9.7 *m.* is the junction with a macadam road.

Right on this road is LITTLE FALLS, 1 *m.* (200 alt., 5,561 pop.), a prosperous town with 30 industries. Settled by eight Acquackanonk (Passaic) farmers who purchased a huge tract from the Indians in 1711, the community takes its name from nearby rapids of the Passaic River. The LITTLE FALLS LAUNDRY PLANT *(open daily 9-5 except Sun.)*, 101 Main St., housed in three red-brick factory buildings and a modernistic red-brick administration building, is the largest laundry in the world. Its 800 employees use 150,000 tons of soap annually to clean the clothes of 250,000 customers. The United Laundry Workers Union, an independent local organization with support from the Committee for Industrial Organization, struck in May, 1937, against union discrimination. When the township committee passed an ordinance to restrict the union's activities, the 450 strikers hired an airplane to tow a strike banner over northern New Jersey.

SINGAC, 12.5 *m.* (170 alt., 1,800 pop.), hibernates for three-quarters of the year; its bungalow-lined streets are as empty and quiet as those of any small village. But warm weather brings a spate of vacationing office-dwellers to swim and play handball on the banks of the murky Passaic; their pursuit of a two weeks' summer transforms the town with holiday magic, silk-trimmed shorts, Japanese lanterns, and ukuleles that can turn *Whose Sweet Baby Are You?* into a lyric promise of love to last even on the return to the city. The gray frame CHURCH OF OUR LADY OF HOLY ANGELS is L. Opposite it, on a vacant lot (R), is a recently constructed arched shrine of field stones with a life-size colored plaster image of Our Lady framed by a large neon aura.

State 23 crosses the Passaic River at 12.7 *m.*

At 13.2 *m.*, at a traffic circle, is the junction with US 46 *(see Tour 7)*.

The road levels out through a flat district of roadhouses and hot-dog stands, some designed with considerable ingenuity—rusticized shack-palaces, rambling Colonial Virginian manses, red and white doll houses—architectural apexes of a hamburger civilization.

MOUNTAIN VIEW, 14.4 *m.* (170 alt., 1,684 pop.), is an outspread little residential community and summer resort on the Pequannock River. The old brown frame MOUNTAIN VIEW HOTEL (R) does not hide its private business; at midday red pillows and pale blue mattresses are stuffed out on the window sills to air above the main highway. Rising on the town's outskirts (L) is a STEEL TOWER that looks very much like a diagram of heart action in the early stages of cardiac mitosis; it is a transmitter for WABC.

At 14.6 *m.* is the junction with US 202 *(see Tour 4)*. State 23 and US 202 are united for 2.3 miles north of Mountain View.

Cedars line the highway as it splits into two two-lane avenues and climbs to the north. At 16.6 *m.*, at the crest of a long rise in the road, is the sudden view of the hills above Packanack Lake and, far N., the foothills of the Ramapos.

At 17.3 *m.*, at a large traffic circle, State 23 branches (L) from US 202.

From the highway bridge above the Pequannock River, at 17.7 *m.*, is a glimpse of the turf-covered aqueduct running parallel to the river (R) from the Pequannock Reservoir to Newark.

POMPTON PLAINS, 18.9 *m.* (190 alt., 1,200 pop.), lies L. of the highway in the flat bed of a prehistoric lake. The faintly sloping tableland affords a low-flying bird's-eye view of the village, with small frame houses on the eastern fringe. Pompton Plains was for many years the home of Dan Voorhees, Tammany sachem, who continued his political activities until he was more than 100 years old.

The plain's northern rim is at 19.9 *m.*, where the road mounts to cross the Greenwood Lake division of the Erie R.R. The highway here cleaves almost in two a terrain that seems to have been made up by jamming two different kinds of land together: sudden high rocky ridges, scrubby with tree growth, one hill covered with conical pines (L); and a low, sand-pitted stretch of earth hollows (R). The sandy earth was deposited in the slow wake of the great glacier as it moved across New Jersey between 30 and 50 thousand years ago; the sharp rocks (L) are those of the pre-glacial continent.

At 20.7 *m.*, at a traffic circle, is the junction (R) with a paved county road *(see Side Tour 9A)*.

Jutting rock hills rise sheer above the highway as it begins a long, left-bending climb at 20.9 *m.* Farming in this country is an heroic job. Where the road bisects boulders to form a cut with sharp low cliffs on each side, the cross-section reveals no more than half a foot of crumbling topsoil on the rock's hard bed. Grazing lands in isolated soil pockets are blistered with strewn rocks.

A garbage dump at 23.8 *m.* (R) introduces the southeastern outskirts of BUTLER (580 alt., 3,420 pop.), itself an attractive little borough spread out (R) over rolling wooded country. The community was founded in 1695; among its residents are descendants of Hessians who quit King George's service to remain in America after the Revolution had succeeded. Butler has a Franciscan monastery at ST. ANTHONY'S R. C. CHURCH. A rubber factory employs many of the town's workers.

Hemlock glens drop away from the road at odd intervals. At 24.4 *m.* is a sign warning that the private property on a wooded embankment (R) is the YUNGBORN NUDIST CAMP conducted by Dr. B. Lust.

The road reaches a summit in the hilly country and for half a mile holds to a rolling plateau of rock-strewn pasture land partitioned by wood fences.

State 23 crosses the Pequannock River and the New York, Susquehanna and Western R.R. at 26.3 *m.*, narrowing to run between the parallel Pequannock (L) and a shale escarpment (R). This is a region of small lakes off the main highway, exploited by real-estate development companies as "The Idyl A While of the East."

At 27.9 *m.* is the INTAKE HOUSE (R), a yellow frame hotel whose name has nothing to do with its business. Standing at the southern entrance to the Pequannock watershed, it is named for the MACOPIN INTAKE at 28.2 *m.* (L). The intake, sometimes called the Newark or Pequannock Reservoir, serves the city of Newark; a wide metal-bound oaken pipeline, 50 years old, runs along the highway in the declivity to the L., spouting high, needle-thin streams of water from occasional leaks.

Bald rocks with a fuzzy overgrowth of trees and shrubbery—much like a two weeks' crop of hair on a shaved head—dominate the birch-lined highway. State 23 winds across the Pequannock River frequently between here and Stockholm. Down a long, right-winding bend are clumps of small Scotch pine, planted to hold back water for the reservoir.

CHARLOTTEBURG, 29.8 *m.* (750 alt., 22 pop.), requires keen eyes if the motorist's car is a fast one. It is a tiny settlement of scattered frame homes on the southern edge of the lake district. There was once an iron mine here, part of the Ringwood properties.

At 31.3 *m.* is the junction with a macadam road *(see Tour 9A).*

NEWFOUNDLAND, 32 *m.* (760 alt., 340 pop.), bases its principal claim to distinction on the local belief that it was the birthplace of William H. Seward, Secretary of State in President Lincoln's cabinet and a general thorn in Lincoln's side. Historians are agreed that Seward was born in Florida, N. Y. Few Newfoundlanders seem worried about the dispute; they simply have not changed their minds. The site of the alleged birthplace is not known. Newfoundland's most prominent building is the large frame NEWFOUNDLAND INN (R); its most interesting one is the POST OFFICE (L), a neatly constructed red brick building one story high, ranging in depth from 4 to 10 feet.

West of Newfoundland and past the upper finger of COPPERAS MOUNTAIN (L) is a surprising stretch of drab stubble country, and no hills. But at a crest in the road at 34.1 *m.* is the view westward of a long drop overtowered by the sharply rising mountains surrounding OAK RIDGE RESERVOIR which is at 35 *m.* (L), a big cup in the rocky, hemlock-thicketed hills. This might be Adirondack country; the Pequannock runs swiftly, forming roaring rapids at boulder-jammed bends.

STOCKTON, 37.4 *m.* (1,000 alt.), is a railroad station, a big REFRESHMENT STAND (R), and very little else. The village has, however, achieved considerable fame as the site of Dr. Herman Soshinsky's ROCK LODGE NUDIST CAMP *(private),* operated from May to September. Stockholm residents no longer grin when tourists ask about the camp.

The road is a straight upward ribbon W. of Stockholm, with pipe-thin silver birch on each side. A sign at 37.8 *m.* advertises LAKE STOCKHOLM (R), not visible from State 23, as "A Christian Community."

A frame shack of a post office at 40.8 *m.* is all that is visible of BEAVER LAKE, about a mile N. of the pond from which it takes its name.

The road drops until suddenly, at 42.2 *m.*, there is an end to the continuously rugged character of the district. The woods and the stubble-grown boulders drop away from a 100-yard strip of long, narrow pasture land extending across the road east to HAMBURG MT. (R). This is a sliver of farm country, the bottomland of the Wallkill River. Just off the road (L) is a big unpainted barn with a green hip roof—the first barn in many miles.

Gun-gray cuts in rock ledges at 42.7 *m.* (L) introduce the eastern outskirts of FRANKLIN (600 alt., 4,176 pop.), center of New Jersey's zinc-mining industry. Zinc dominates the land here; in the rocks, underground, and in row after row of gray shingled company houses. The highway itself is built over a maze of underground tunnels where 75 miles of electric railway connect mining operations *(visitors not admitted)*. Owned by the New Jersey Zinc Co., the region contains one of the largest supplies of zincite, franklinite, and oxide of zinc in the world; about 500,000 tons of zinc ores are extracted annually. Franklin was a mining town before the discovery of zinc. A hundred years ago it was a pig-iron center with two forges and a blast furnace. The town has only one old building, a brown, fieldstone CHURCH built in 1837. Originally a Baptist edifice, it has been used by Methodists and Presbyterians and is now a Jewish synagogue.

HARDISTONVILLE, 43.9 *m.* (600 alt.), is a suburb of Franklin. The company town's rim extends from Franklin into Hardistonville in the solid line of drab zinc-topped bungalows; the occasional white cottages with green shutters and painted roofs are the homes of company officials.

HAMBURG, 45.1 *m.* (440 alt., 1,160 pop.), is an outsprawled little village with concentrations of houses at its northern and southern ends and a Lackawanna R.R. overpass between. A yellow billboard at its southern tip introduces it as the home of Daniel Haines, Governor of New Jersey in 1843 and the "first to advocate a free school system." The HAINES MANSION, just N. of the railroad overpass at 46 *m.* (L), is a white, two-and-one-half-story dwelling with the gambrel roof and broad beams of Dutch Colonial architecture; it is now a tearoom. Hamburg has a BLACK-SMITH SHOP, operated for the last 50 years by the Woods brothers. Their principal job is turning out runners for the sleighs that are used to haul milk when deep drifts stop motor trucks.

Hamburg is at the junction with State 31.

Left on State 31 to (R) the THOMAS LAWRENCE HOUSE *(private)*, 0.7 *m.*, a two-story white frame dwelling with six square pillars, and with a cellar visible in its gray stone foundation. The house was built in 1841 on ground formerly occupied by the home built for Thomas Lawrence in 1794 by his father-in-law, Lewis Morris, a signer of the Declaration of Independence. Thomas Lawrence, a great-great-grandson of the original owner, lives here now. Family heirlooms include a white brocaded silk dress worn by a Lawrence lady at a ball celebrating Cornwallis' surrender at Yorktown, and taken out of the cedar chest to be worn again in 1853 at a social function in New York City given by the grandmother of the late President Theodore Roosevelt.

North of Hamburg the evidence of farming is more definite than those a few miles south. But the land is still sorry. Humpy, rockbound stubble fields roll E. for miles to POCHUCK MT. (R). At a ridge in the road at

49.8 *m.* is the view northward of the white homes of Sussex, built high among rolling hills.

SUSSEX, 50.9 *m.* (450 alt., 1,415 pop.), a vigorous little town, is one of the largest milk receiving stations in the State. It was originally known as Deckertown for Peter Decker, a Hollander who built himself a log cabin in 1734 and thereby provided latter-day historians with meat for a dispute over just where the cabin stood. The visitor is offered his choice of two sites: by a spring at Main and Spring Sts., where the grammar-school board has erected a marker; and the ground at 29 Hamburg Ave., where Fred W. Lawrence, owner of the property, recently found an oblong stone engraved, "P. D. 1749." Since there were no police department license plates at that time it is believed the stone came from above Decker's cabin door. Ralph Decker, a descendant of Peter, and president of the Sussex County Historical Society, favors the latter site. Sussex's FIRST BAPTIST CHURCH (R), Main and E. Main Sts., organized in 1756, is a frame structure with brownstone foundation.

At Sussex is the junction with State 8 N *(see Tour 5).*

Clove River crosses to the R. of the highway at 53 *m.* Far off (R) at this point the gleaming, silver-gray stone shaft of the monument at High Point is visible.

At 53.4 *m.* is an old, one-and-a-half story stone and frame HOUSE (R) guarded by a frightening totem pole. This structure was one of the Minisink forts, built as a dwelling at the turn of the eighteenth century by a man named Titsworth, son of the founder of Port Jervis and later killed by Indians. The place was 80 years old when Joseph Brant, the Indian chief from the Mohawk Valley, attacked it in 1781 with a band of Indians and British. It is known locally as Totem Pole; but the pole is probably not authentic. The old house is today a handicraft shop.

The Clove district is excellent farm land, a high region of uprolling pasture acres that fulfill in fertility the promise of the stubble fields at the southern end of the Wallkill Valley. As in most sections where farming has a long and satisfactory history, barns are solid and carefully built, often ornamented with silver-painted roofs or gilt weather vanes and ventilators. At 54.7 *m.* a large meadow (R) is the site of a projected High Point lake.

COLESVILLE, 56.9 *m.* (800 alt., 213 pop.), is a group of small frame houses—a dun-colored spot in high, bright country. A branch of Clove River runs through the village.

North of Colesville is a steady rise through intermittent forest and farm land. Stone walls take the place of frame fences, many of them shot through with the greenish shimmer of serpentine rock. This is apple country. At 58.2 *m.* (L) is a sod-covered STONE HUT well sunk into the ground—not an underground Revolutionary fort but an apple cellar built in 1891 by Jacob Slate, who liked his handiwork well enough to place an engraved stone tablet over the door. The unpainted BARN (R) is more than 100 years old.

The highway between Colesville and High Point is rough macadam; at 58.3 *m.* is the beginning of a stiff two-mile grade to the heart of High

Point Park. A sign at 58.6 *m.* warns of a $25 fine "for any person leaving a stone in the road."

The entrance to HIGH POINT PARK is at 59.5 *m.* *Large restaurant and cafeteria (L); campsites and open fireplaces free; hunting not permitted.* This is a 10,000-acre tract of wild forest land atop Kittatinny Mt., ranging in altitude from 900 to 1,800 feet, presented to New Jersey in 1922 by Col. and Mrs. A. K. Kuser of Bernardsville. Shaggy hemlocks, spruce, cedar, and Scotch pine guard its maze of graveled roads; swift brooks wind through the glens at greater altitudes than anywhere else in the State. The High Point Park Commission, headed by Albert Payson Terhune, has arranged tourists' attractions ranging from several ski runs to numerous comfort stations, all of them clearly marked by rustic signs. The park has reindeer paddocks (L) and a bear pit (R) at the southern tip of LAKE MARCIA *(swimming, free),* the highest natural spring lake in New Jersey.

Winding around the lake to the N., a steep graveled road leads to High Point itself. A sharp intake of breath usually accompanies the first snatched view through the forest (R) of the rolling miles to the N. and E.; and at 60.5 *m.,* at the 225-foot stone War Memorial, is the vista from the HIGH-EST POINT IN NEW JERSEY (1,827 alt.). The memorial obelisk stands on a great crag of a boulder directly overlooking Tri-State, the confluence of the Delaware and Neversink Rivers, where New Jersey, New York, and Pennsylvania meet. Just below is sizable Port Jervis, a toy town on the long bathtub of the Delaware, with the Neversink, a narrow snake, twisting along its eastern border. Far to the N. are the Catskill Mountains; to the E. is the Wantage Valley; to the W., Pennsylvania's Poconos; and beyond northern.New Jersey's rolling hills, on the clearest days, Delaware Water Gap, 80 miles south, is visible• Twenty-two towns and villages in three States can be seen from High Point, forming a mosaic with mountains, meadows, valleys, rivers, and lakes.

State 23 ends at the entrance to the park and a poor tar and gravel road twists down the side of the mountain through wild, wooded country.

At 64.3 *m.* the road crosses the New York State Line, 1.2 miles southeast of Port Jervis.

Tour 9A

Junction with State 23—Riverdale—Ringwood—Greenwood Lake—Junction with State 23; unnumbered roads.
Junction with State 23 to Junction with State 23, 27 m.

The road is paralleled by the Erie R.R. between Pompton Lakes and Hewitt.
Filling stations and lunchrooms at Pompton Lakes and Greenwood Lake.
Macadamized roads, most of them in good condition.

The route, forming a horseshoe around Wanaque Reservoir and the
west side of Kanouse Mountain, provides an excursion into New Jersey's
unwritten history. It penetrates a wild, rugged country, revealing traces
of currents forgotten in the life of the State: of the Jackson Whites, and
of the old, abandoned mines at Ringwood that helped to decide the fate of
the American Revolution.

The route branches north from State 23 *(see Tour 9)*, 0 *m.,* at a traffic
circle 1.8 miles north of Pompton Plains.

RIVERDALE, 0.9 *m.* (200 alt., 1,052 pop.), is a trim little village
built on a left bend in a hill-rimmed cup of flat land. The New Jersey
Historical Commmission has allotted to it a share in the State's Revolutionary history, and placed in a vacant lot (L) a marker asserting that "Washington quartered at the Schuyler House July 12, 1777, and visited Colonel
Van Cortlandt here March 28, 1782." But Riverdale's citizens claim nothing that is not their sure historical due. Miss Mary E. Mandeville, whose
grandfather was a Schuyler, knows of no Schuyler House in Riverdale. A
possible VAN CORTLANDT HOUSE *(private)* at which Washington may
have stayed is the two-and-a-half-story white frame dwelling with a first-
story body of gray fieldstone standing across the road from the marker.
Charles F. Mickens, who moved into it with his wife in 1886, thinks it
may be the place; Mr. Mickens built the frame second-story addition, putting plaster over the old beams—a renovation he has regretted, he says, for
50 years. The RIVERDALE WAR MEMORIAL (L) is a life-size statue of a
doughboy in a resolute stance, bayonet ready, fist clenched, his helmet
tossed beside him on the pedestal; the whole is neatly gilded.

The route turns R. at Riverdale.

Crossing Pequannock River on a concrete bridge at 1.3 *m.,* the road enters
the western outskirts of POMPTON LAKES (200 alt., 3,104 pop.) *(see
Tour 4)*. The POMPTOM REFORMED CHURCH and CEMETERY are L. The
church, a handsome white-painted structure of brick with a tall white
steeple and broad double doors, was built in 1814.

The route turns L. on Ringwood Ave.

HASKELL, 3.5 *m.* (250 alt.), is a drab community of flat frame bungalows. Its frame FULL GOSPEL ASSEMBLY (R) is almost opposite the
gaudy new building of simulated fieldstone that houses SILVER STAR TAV-
ERN, a popular local beer dispensary. On a big empty lot (R) are dilapidated REMAINS OF A DU PONT PLANT that was busy until 1913, when
operations were transferred to Pompton Lakes.

WANAQUE (Ind., *place of the sassafras*) RESERVOIR, 4.8 *m.* (300
alt.), is the largest in New Jersey. The lake, 6.5 miles long and 1 mile
wide, has a capacity of 27 billion gallons. It serves Newark, Paterson, Passaic, and several other cities. The 1,500-foot dam across Wanaque River
is an earth and rock fill, with a concrete core sunk to bedrock. On the
downstream slope is a series of reclining stone arches, designed chiefly for
ornament. When early spring floods choke the streams in the Passaic Val-

ley watershed, residents of down-river communities customarily hear rumors that cracks have appeared in Wanaque Dam. The newspapers investigate, reassurances are published, and nothing happens. Stone steps lead to the top of the dam, where the sweep of placid water hemmed in by wooded hills has the rangy appearance of an Adirondack lake. There are seven smaller dams in Wanaque Reservoir.

The word Wanaque has at least five accepted pronunciations in New Jersey: Wa-*nok*-kwee, *Wan*-a-kew, *Wan*-a-*kew*, Wa-*nok*-key and *Wan*-a-key. The fourth seems to be preferred.

At the foot of the dam are the SCHOOL and CHURCH OF ST. FRANCIS OF ASSISI, two flat buildings of simulated dressed stone standing directly behind the gray frame WANAQUE REFORMED CHURCH (L).

MIDVALE, in Wanaque Borough, can best be identified by the WANAQUE COMMUNITY HOUSE, 5.3 *m.* (L). The confusion in village boundaries should not disturb the visitor, for no one in Wanaque Borough seems to know where its component hamlets begin and end. The community house is a brown frame building of two stories with 12 large, homey rooms and the good smell of unpainted lumber. The ground-floor office of the borough clerk, adorned with flatwood benches for whoever cares to drop in for a chat, has a big stone fireplace. The top floor is given over to the police department. The building houses most of Wanaque's social events, from bingo parties to an occasional game of kelly-pool.

Outside the Community House is another WAR MEMORIAL, twin of the Riverdale statue. Habitués of the municipal offices are not sure which was erected first. The general opinion is that they were both bought at the same time, at a saving. The only dissimilarity is that the abandoned upturned hat of the Wanaque monument is open, whereas in Riverdale the crown has been covered over with a neatly fitted metal plate. This makes a difference to the birds.

Wanaque Borough's biggest industry is the HERCULES WOVEN LABEL MILL, occupying a long, low, gray frame building at 6.1 *m.* (L).

The road rises to cross the Erie R.R. tracks at 6.8 *m.*, where for a brief moment the mountain-rimmed reservoir is seen. At this point is the junction with a macadam road.

Left on this road, across and around the reservoir, to the junction with a dirt road, 2 *m.;* L. on this road and up a winding course through wildly beautiful mountain country to NATURE FRIENDS' CAMP *(open all year),* 3 *m.* It is run on a nonprofit basis by the Nature Friends' Society, a labor organization, and is modeled after the numerous country resorts conducted by trade unions in Germany up until several years ago. The camp has many rustic bungalows, tennis courts, and a 400-foot open swimming pool. Frequented by trade unionists of all nationalities from the nearby industrial towns of Paterson and Passaic, it is especially popular with Americans of German origin.

The road turns R. at the Erie R.R. tracks into a rural district where the reservoir is hidden from view by thick woods (L). Adjoining a refreshment stand and country store at 7.2 *m.* is a small frame ICE HOUSE (R) with a whitewashed advertisement on its brown front stating, simply, "Ice. Glory to Jesus." The proprietor of the establishment is a religious man who has seized the opportunity to broadcast his business and his faith at the same time. Seventy-two years old (1938), Mr. Rednor is also the driver of the school bus at Lake Erskine.

The reservoir reappears at 7.5 *m.* (L), where the Erie R.R. runs across it in a deep cove reminding visitors of the newsreel shot of a flood-imperiled trestle. Dominating the highway are steep rock embankments (R); green pine nurseries at their foot hold water for the big dam. Mountains, shaggy with pines, rise from behind the near hills, and small cedar-covered islands are reflected in the clear lake surface. Planted along the reservoir bank, within a wire fence, are clumps of young Norway spruce.

At 10.3 *m.,* at a junction, the route leads R. away from the main reservoir, but paralleling a northern arm.

At 12.2 *m.* is the junction (L) with a macadam road.

Right (straight ahead) on a macadamized road to RINGWOOD MANOR (L), 0.7 *m.* *(grounds open; 25¢ parking fee includes use of picnic tables),* owned by the State; it is being developed as the 100-acre Ringwood Manor State Park. Lying close to the mountain whose ore-laden veins supplied life blood to this community *(see RING-WOOD, below),* the great, rambling manor house of 78 rooms bespeaks the steady growth of the wealth and the changing taste of its owners. The original building *(c.* 1765) was a straight-forward mansion with a gambrel roof that is the only recognizable early feature left. From this have grown wings, massive and extensive; and in the modest Victorian era the whole was veiled by covering the original bare clapboards with a coat of white stucco, and trimming the structure with pseudo-Gothic bargeboards, bay windows, and Tudor cornices. The two-and-a-half-story mansion stands today on a knoll surrounded by great oaks and overlooking artificial pools fed by a cascade from a tile drain. In this big house the Erskines, Ryersons, Coopers, and Hewitts lived and married and had children.

Ringwood Manor *is* the American scene, representing an era when a man's wealth and prestige were measured by the size and elaborateness of his house. Here the knickknack and the whatnot broke away from the interior of the house and ran rampant over the lawns and gardens in the form of statuary, Civil War artillery, historic gateways, lamp-posts from New York, stone brackets from Rome, frogs from parts unknown, iron shafts from steamboats, and pig iron from the mountain. The curiosa amassed by Mrs. Abram Hewitt and other Hewitts includes (in part) statues depicting Africa and Europe, acquired from a bishop's palace in France; the former gate posts of Columbia College; a small lead fountain removed from a century-old New Jersey millstone; Indian grindstones; millstones from Padua, Italy; a pink marble well curb, iron ornaments, and lead bucket from Venice; stone columns from the New York Life Insurance Co. Building formerly at Madison Square, New York; a yew tree grown from a seed picked at the Abdul Hamud Palace, Constantinople; three entrance gates from the Middle Dutch Reformed Church in New York; a Chinese vase standing on a New Jersey millstone; a marble statue of Diana; another (French) of a small boy playing with a rabbit; and ornamental ironwork from the house of the British Governor-General of New York. The trees in front of the house were planted by Mrs. Martin Ryerson to mark the Peace of Ghent ending the War of 1812. Placed before the veranda are 25 links from the famous Hudson River barricade chain made in part at Ringwood, the anvil used to forge it, a *Constitution* cannon, and a Vicksburg mortar.

Washington was a frequent visitor at Ringwood. He was here during the Pompton mutiny of January 20, 1781, when between 200 and 300 rebellious soldiers were cowed by the shooting of two ringleaders after a brief court martial. General Howe's report of the mutiny and its suppression was written in the house. Later Washington returned with General Lincoln and others to celebrate the Declaration of Peace. It was a gay party, with guests from New York and no lack of spirits. Washington was so impressed by the Ringwood country that he is reported to have suggested that 150,000 acres be set aside as a national park and recreation ground, which he

RINGWOOD MANOR

held would be valuable if New York should become the largest city of the continent, if not in the world.

Part of the mansion was burned by the British during the Revolution. They came to destroy the forge, the story runs, but were sidetracked in the wine cellar. Revolutionary troops found them in their cups. Mrs. Erskine escaped from the burning building in her nightgown, her watch safely stowed away in her slipper.

Near the house on the sloping bank of a willow pond is the BRICK CRYPT containing Robert Erskine's body; his wife is not buried next to him. A SECOND CRYPT is the grave of Robert Monteith, Erskine's secretary. Erskine's ghost used to sit on top of the tomb with a blue lantern for a few years after a brick fell out early in the 19th century. The practice ended when Mrs. Hewitt had the brick replaced. Closer to the pond are three MARBLE VAULTS containing the bones of John Hewitt, his wife, Ann Gurnee Hewitt, and John Hewitt Jr. The elder Hewitt, born in 1711, is described as "a man without guile" and "one of the builders at Soho, New Jersey, of the first steam engine constructed in the United States." His son was less talented; all the stonecutter left for posterity to know about John Jr. was that he was "for many years trustee of the Public School of the 5th Ward in the City of New York."

Erskine was the last of his family to live in the now empty house. Locally, most renowned of the Hewitts were his sisters, the Misses S. C. and E. G. Hewitt. That is how they come down in official documents, and that is how they were known to the natives. Ringwood residents remember Miss S. C. as something of a caution. She rode all over the countryside on horseback at an advanced age, and the story is that she could not tolerate trespassers—ran them off the property herself. Miss E. G. was more the homebody, an excellent cook, whose crullers and doughnuts are still talked about.

On the main road L. at the junction with the Ringwood Manor road and across swift Ringwood Creek on a concrete bridge.

RINGWOOD, 12.3 *m*. (340 alt., 1,038 pop.), is more a company than a town, and more a tradition than a company. It appears as three old white buildings (R), neatly trimmed in blue—a two-and-a-half-story Victorian dwelling used as a BOROUGH HALL, a small frame structure housing the EPISCOPAL CHURCH, and the large brick COMPANY STORE, all clustered around the Erie R.R. siding to the old Ringwood mine. The story of Ringwood stretches back over 200 years of New Jersey history; the reputation of its iron mines, its forges, and the men who governed this 15,000-acre domain is unparalleled in a State that has known many forges and many large landowners. For miles around the influence of the old company is still felt, even though the mines have been closed for several years and the great house *(see side tour above)* is deserted. When a Ringwood resident speaks of The Company it is in capital letters; there are only two stores—both The Company's; and The Family can mean only the Hewitts, hereditary owners of the Ringwood Co. and all its works.

The company was founded as the American Iron Co. in 1763 when Baron Peter Hasenclever, a German, got wind of copper and iron ore discoveries in the Ramapos. The baron was a shrewd man. He bought up the land, went to London and set to work selling shares to the ladies of the court—even, it is said, to Queen Charlotte. The company made him manager of the property and sent him to Ringwood, where he opened an iron mine, lived in great style with a German brass band to serenade him on hot summer days, and made a great deal of money; very little of it went back to London. The baron was replaced by Robert Erskine, young Scottish mining engineer. It was Erskine who really made Ringwood. He developed the mine, opened new forges and rehabilitated the company's finances. Erskine was a good friend of George Washington's, and when the Revolution broke out the General appointed him geographer and surveyor-general of the Revolutionary armies. The Ringwood mine played a decisive part in the Revolutionary struggle. Its forges worked overtime turning out cannon and munitions, and much of the great iron chain, placed across the Hudson River below West Point to prevent the passage of British ships, was cast at Ringwood. Robert Erskine died in 1780 at the age of 45, but his forges made their mark on American life for a century and a half afterward. Here were cast cannon used on the main deck of the *Constitution* when she took the *Guerriere* in the War of 1812, and one of the two mortars fired at the capture of Vicksburg. The Ryersons operated the forges from about 1807 to 1853. They were succeeded by Peter Cooper, founder of Cooper Union in New York City; Cooper passed the job on to his son-in-law, Abram S. Hewitt, at one time mayor of New York, and the father of Erskine Hewitt who now is in charge of the family interests.

The mine, glory and driving force of Ringwood for 200 years, ceased operation in 1931 because of the competition from western ore close to the steel centers. Once a power in America's life struggles, the Ringwood Co.'s chief concern today is the promotion of Lake Erskine, a real estate development.

The real estate business office occupies a large part of the COMPANY STORE, which also houses the Ringwood post office and the Erie R.R. freight depot. This is one general store without a cracker barrel, without oratory, and without the friendly cluttered merchandise that has not seen an inventory in years. The real estate business office has cleaned all of that out. The only noise in the place is the clatter of typewriters and adding machines. Neatly stacked blue denim shirts and overalls line the shelves; bright glass cases exhibit nationally known brands of packed meat and groceries. There are no penny licorice twists here; only 5-cent packages of cellophane-wrapped candy advertised in every subway station in New York City. Ringwooders come in, make their purchases, and go out.

The road crosses the short spur of the Ringwood Branch of the Erie R.R. at 12.6 m., passing the sizable white RINGWOOD PUBLIC SCHOOL (R).

Behind the school, silent in the scrub woods scattered with unpainted, sagging shacks of former mine workers, is the entrance to the old RING-WOOD MINES—the Cannon, the Blue, the Bush, and the Hard. Peters and Hope, two of the biggest, are about a mile farther up. Boarded and locked, with only a caretaker in a tilted chair where once men worked to produce iron for America, the mines have not been operated since 1931. Peters Mine had a ghost in the days when production was steady and booming. At irregular intervals the miners would hear him knocking for company; the summons was nearly always followed by a serious accident. Now the miners are locked out, and the ghosts have the run of the water-filled shafts.

Upwards of 500 men were thrown out of work when the mines shut down; most of them were Jackson Whites. They came to the mines about half a century ago, attracted by the possibility of wages. Copper-colored, rather handsome with their angular features, and of normal intelligence, these people belie the weird tales that have been told about them.

Few isolated racial groups have had so tragic a history as the Jackson Whites. Hessian, English, West Indian, Dutch, Portuguese, Negro, Spanish, Italian, and American Indian by blood, their ancestry can be traced to 3,500 women shanghaied by the British authorities for the pleasure of their New York troops. In the crossing from England one boat-load was lost; and Jackson, the contractor, filled in his order with a substitute conscription from the West Indies. When the British evacuated New York City the women were released. But the authorities would have none of them, and they were forced to leave the city.

Ostracized wherever they went, half-starved, they struggled into the mountains of New Jersey and found refuge with a group of Tuscarora Indians banished from North Carolina. They were joined by another band of outcasts, Hessians stranded by the British government, which had brought them to America to fight the Revolutionaries. Runaway slaves and outlaw whites, unwanted men of all races, soon found their way to the haven in the Ramapos. Stray dogs, used for protection by the harried refugees, swelled the community. Many stories have been circulated concerning the alleged "savagery" of the Jackson Whites. None of them is true. Today they live in hovels that dot the forest bogs, haunted by poverty. There are a number of albinos among them, and some of these have been employed as freaks.

The road turns R. at 14.6 *m.*, through a district of woods and pasture land.

HEWITT, 15.5 *m.* (420 alt., 216 pop.), appears as a white frame Roman Catholic church (L), a small white school (R) and a store (R). The store, which also houses the post office, is the village's justification. It is a one-and-a-half-story white plaster structure with two wings and brown shutters, and it dates back to 1764. A sign outside advertises it as "Ye Olde Country Store;" the name is a misnomer. The old section of the building is the left wing, now in service as a wayside restaurant but never used in winter because of the lack of heat. The store and post office occupy the right wing, built no more than a decade ago. There is a more leisurely atmosphere here than in the other company store at Ringwood. Hill people drop by for their provender or for an occasional "bucket of light"— gallon of kerosene—and discussion can range from the Supreme Court to the time George Van Tassel had his ear cut off in a brawl over at Monksville.

Two ruined CONCRETE WALLS rise on each side of the road at 15.9 *m.* They are abutments of the old bridge of an abandoned Erie R.R. spur to Sterling Forest *(see below).* Interspersed with the shacks in the forest are old, solidly built stone houses; blue overalls hang from the clotheslines of both types of dwelling.

At 17.5 *m.* is the junction (R) with a hard-surfaced road.

Right on this road is BROWNS, 1.2 *m.* (630 alt.), a summer colony on the southern end of GREENWOOD LAKE, 7 miles long and extending north into New York State between steep, wooded mountains.

North from Browns on a concrete road that hugs the lake shore (R) and offers good views of the opposite shore; the New York Line is crossed at 4 *m.* Between this point and the village of Greenwood Lake the route is N. Y. State 210.

GREENWOOD LAKE, N. Y., 7.6 *m.* (630 alt.), is a collection of summer cottages, a few stores, and the homes of year-round residents spread around the head of the lake bearing the same name. For many years it has been rimmed with summer homes; elaborately ugly mansions of past generations still stand next to more gaudy creations of contemporary vacationists. The modern summer home may be nothing more pretentious than a brown shingled shack, or it may be covered with red, yellow, and aluminum paint and marked by a miniature lighthouse instead of the conventional signs, "Lakeside Rest" or "Oak Cottage." Steep mountains rise to 700 feet above the lake, leaving scant room for the cottages.

Left 1 block, then R. in Greenwood Lake; R. at 8.1 *m.*, and southward on a graded dirt road that cuts into the hillside along the eastern shore of the lake and then twists through rock-strewn woodland where groundhogs ignore passing automobiles. STERLING FOREST, 11.5 *m.*, is a quiet hamlet that has scarcely stirred since the great terra cotta ICE HOUSE (R) was abandoned and the Erie R.R. tore up the branch line that ran to the ice house. The little village lies on the shore of Greenwood Lake, almost straddling the New York-New Jersey Line. It broke into metropolitan newspapers in 1936 when experiments in carrying mail by rocket planes were made on the frozen lake. F. W. Kessler, a philatelist and member of the American Rocket Society, organized the Rocket Airplane Corporation of America for the trial flights. His aim was to fly more than 100 pounds of mail from New York into New Jersey, at a fee of 75 cents for each letter in addition to air-mail and special-delivery postage. Twin planes with a wingspread of 14 feet were built of duralumin at a cost of about $1,000 each; they resembled ordinary monoplanes without much streamlining. Motive power was provided by liquid oxygen and alcohol, injected under pressure into the compression chamber. On February 23 a detail of newsreel cameramen and a crowd of some 1,500 spectators gathered on the ice to watch the experiment. The first plane, named *Gloria,* was launched from a catapult, which, through an error in construction, sent the craft almost vertically into the air. As Nick Morin, who with his brother Mike owns the GREENWOOD LAKE LAUNCH WORKS (R) where the planes were assembled, described the flight: "She went up fast—then one wing went up and she came down—whang! She hit the ice, went up again, and came down—whang!" The mail cargo was then loaded into the second plane, also named *Gloria.* This craft was launched from the ice. After a slide of 400 feet it took to the air and sailed almost a quarter-mile before the power of the rocket tore the wings loose. The 6,000 letters and post cards did not pay for the experiment, and Mr. Kessler does not intend to try again. But the Morin brothers, who fought a losing fight to keep the railroad in Sterling Forest, think that rocket planes are a "good idea." One battered *Gloria* hangs from the roof of the launch works; Nick or Mike will gladly stop work on the mahogany hull of a cruiser to discuss the future of rocket craft. Other residents are skeptical. The foreman of a road gang remarked that "a husky man could have heaved that ship across the State line."

As the main road swings southwest from the Greenwood Lake junction, the country changes to rolling fields and pasture land, an agricultural district in a mountain area. Far off (R) are the rangy, flat-topped hills north of Bearfort Mt. Characteristic of this area is a water-worn purplish stone, flecked with white, known to geologists as the Green Pond conglomerate but more commonly called "pudding stone." It is often used for walls.

The main route turns R. at 19.6 *m.*

WEST MILFORD, 19.8 *m.* (700 alt., 350 pop.), is a tiny village on the east shore of PINE CLIFF LAKE. An old agricultural center once known as New Milford, it has developed as a small summer resort. Two churches set the tone of the community. One, the FULL GOSPEL CHURCH (L), at the northern end of town, is housed in a low green bungalow very much like the homes along the lake front. The other is the WEST MILFORD PRESBYTERIAN CHURCH (L), farther south, a handsome white frame structure with stone steps and a broad double door. It was built in 1807, rebuilt 1825. A sign outside announces: "This Church is open all day, every day, for Rest, Private worship or shelter from the Storm." The white frame BOROUGH HALL (R), built late in the nineteenth century on early American lines, was formerly a Methodist church.

Bear R. at 20.1 *m.*

South of West Milford the road begins the descent of the Kanouse Valley, a 7-mile stretch through wild, high wooded country dominated by BEARFORT MT. (R) and KANOUSE MT. (L). This is a district of apple orchards, of lone farmhouses in softly rolling fields at the foot of steep mountains, and of thin white fingers of birch along the road. It is good hunting country; the woods are full of pheasant, rabbit, partridge, and deer, plus a few foxes and bobcats. The occasional large black birds roosting somberly in the trees are not buzzards but turkeys, from nearby breeding farms.

IDYLEASE INN, a big three-story yellow frame building at 26.4 *m.* (L), is a sanitarium for tubercular patients. It was formerly a hotel.

At 27 *m.* is the junction with State 23, 0.7 miles south of Newfoundland *(see Tour 9)*.

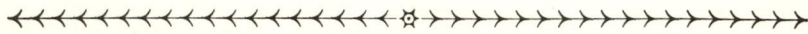

Tour 10

Elizabeth — Springfield — Morristown — Washington — Phillipsburg — (Easton, Pa.); State S24 and State 24.
Elizabeth to Pennsylvania Line, 64 m.

The road is paralleled by the Lackawanna R.R. between Chatham and Morristown and between Beattystown and Phillipsburg; by the Jersey Central R.R. between Chester and Long Valley.
Frequent service stations; hotels in towns.
Roadbed is concrete for the most part, with stretches of improved macadam.

State 24 offers a peaceful drive through exhilarating hill and mountain country. In the eastern section wealthy estates and the orderly homes of the commuting middle class cover ground once torn by the struggle for independence. West of Morristown is a high rolling farm region; tidy grazing lands and partitioned plowed fields are set into the hills at slants reminiscent of New England. The hill district reaches its peak at Schooleys Mountain. Except for the big cement and heavy machinery plants near Phillipsburg, the route avoids industrial developments.

State S24 branches northwest from State 28 *(see Tour 17)*, 0 *m.*, at Elmora and Westfield Aves. on the northern fringe of Elizabeth.

ELIZABETH, 0 *m.* (70 alt., 114,589 pop.) *(see ELIZABETH)*.

Points of Interest: First Presbyterian Church, Union County Courthouse Annex (museum), Carteret Arms, Scott Park, Boudinot House, Singer Sewing Machine Plant, and others.

Lawn-trimmed cottages line the highway in this suburban section. Well-ordered, unaspiring and pleasant, they are commuters' homes; by day the wide main street is almost bereft of a male population.

At 0.4 *m.* the roadbed becomes concrete, and Elizabeth peters out into the edge of Union with scarcely a noticeable change.

At 0.9 *m.* the route turns sharply L. into Morris Ave.

At 1 *m.* (R) is LIBERTY HALL *(private)*, screened from the road by tall trees and a green picket fence; it faces URSINO LAKE. Built in 1773 by William Livingston, first Governor of the State of New Jersey, the rectangular building now belongs to Capt. John Kean, son of former U. S. Senator Hamilton F. Kean. Tall spreading horse-chestnut trees, planted in 1772, shade the three-story white frame house where Sally Livingston, the Governor's daughter, married John Jay, first Chief Justice of the United States; where George and Martha Washington slept; and where Alexander Hamilton was once quartered. Erected on a solid brick foundation and surrounded by 300 green acres of maples, elms, and hilly meadowland, the place, now called Ursino, houses many relics of the Revolutionary period, including a bed in which both Washingtons slept.

A large estate opposite Liberty Hall is GREEN LAKE FARM (L), property of former Senator Kean. Fifty blooded Guernseys stabled in marble-paneled stalls share a barn with many valuable volumes and State records, the ex-Senator's private library. Running the place as a hobby, Mr. Kean delights in his library above the cow barn and in his chickens, which annually carry off blue ribbons at Manhattan's Madison Square Garden.

At 3.2 m. is the junction with US 22 (see Tour 2).

Sprawled over 10 acres of mud and scrub at 3.5 m. (L) are the unimposing remains of a once flourishing cooperative colony of reformed derelicts. SELF-MASTERS' COLONY, patterned after Elbert Hubbard's Roycrofters of East Aurora, N. Y., was founded in 1908 and led by Andress S. Floyd. Here, on 50 acres, approximately 40 hoboes, drunks, and dope fiends lived and worked, desperately trying to make good. During the boom years the men left for outside jobs; the camp failed in 1929, leaving the ruins of a print shop, a weaving place, and two dilapidated frame buildings. Michael Moore, a tall, 69-year-old, bewhiskered native, who speaks intelligently and says he's the last of the Mohicans, still holds the fort, weaving silk and cotton rugs and table covers on hand looms.

UNION, 3.6 m. (110 alt., 16,472 pop.), has a small business center in cream brick, limestone, and plate glass. The town was originally known as Connecticut Farms because of its first settlers, who came from Connecticut in 1749. The PRESBYTERIAN CHURCH on Chestnut St. was built in 1782, two years after British raiders burned the original church parsonage and most of the homes in the village before retreating to Staten Island. The stone church has one wall of brick and a wood siding on its gabled ends. Hessian soldiers who fell in the battle at Connecticut Farms are buried in the graveyard.

A bronze marker on the concrete bridge over the Rahway River at 5.6 m. bears witness that on June 23, 1780, the 2nd Rhode Island Infantry under Col. Israel Angell fought with "obstinate bravery" against the British. The phrase is George Washington's.

At 5.9 m. State S24 becomes State 24.

SPRINGFIELD, 6.1 m. (100 alt., 3,600 pop.), a quiet residential town, was the center of important Revolutionary fighting on June 23, 1780; a good part of the battle took place along the main street of the village. The white-shingled FIRST PRESBYTERIAN CHURCH (R) had an honorable part in it. When the Revolutionaries ran short of gun wadding the Rev. James Caldwell, Elizabeth pastor and chaplain of Colonel Dayton's New Jersey regiment, broke open the church doors and seized an armful of Watts' hymnbooks. The preacher threw them to the soldiers and shouted, "Give 'em Watts, boys—give 'em Watts!" Caldwell's wife, Hannah, had been killed two weeks before in the battle that razed Connecticut Farms. The Tories scornfully called him the "high priest of the Revolution," but to the patriots he was known as the "fighting parson." A marker commemorates Parson Caldwell's Revolutionary initiative. On the church lawn is the statue of a militiaman with the inscription: "Of what avail the plow or sail or land or life if Freedom fail!"

Right from Springfield on a paved road is MILLBURN, 1 m. (150 alt., 10,500 pop.), a one-talkie town pierced by several lakes and surrounded by many hills. Rich commuters live in impressive dwellings bordered by tall cedars and well-kept lawns. Settled by Elizabeth farmers and Upper Montclair Hollanders some 50 years before the Revolution, the town flourished along with its paper mills and hat factories. Both industries are gone, but a lone factory, employing about 25 girls in the manufacture of garments, now occupies the town's principal historical site, VAUX HALL, at 40 Main St. Here, in the simple two-story brick building, lived the Rev. James Caldwell (see above). At the HALL HOUSE (private), Parsonage Rd., Mayor A. Oakey Hall of New York found refuge from Tammany Hall and Boss Tweed. Old-timers recall how two white ponies hitched to a carriage used to carry the mayor for his daily mail. The PAPER MILL PLAYHOUSE, Brookside Dr. between Main St. and Glen Ave., at the entrance to South Mountain Reservation, is a center of Millburn's cultural life. It was established recently by the Newark Art Theater which, aided by wealthy patrons of the arts, transformed the 150-year-old Diamond Paper Mill into an ultra-modern headquarters for drama, art, and afternoon teas.

SOUTH MOUNTAIN RESERVATION, an all-year playground, spreads over the ridge immediately north of Millburn. More than 2,000 verdant acres, mostly in their natural state, stretch across hills and dales, woodland, and meadowland. Bridle paths wind through and around the park, and fishermen sink their bait in the East Branch of the Rahway River. In winter there is skiing, tobogganing, and sledding. In summer the curving trails attract hikers, and the grounds, with open fireplaces and fresh spring water, draw thousands of picnickers. Here also is the water supply of the City of Orange, crystal-clear water in a reservoir half a mile long and a quarter of a mile wide. From WASHINGTON ROCK (544 alt.) at the head of Crest Dr. there is an inspiring panorama of the vast metropolitan area to the east. Rocky steps and twisting paths lead to the valley below where Hemlock Falls sputters and drops some 40 feet down a crevice. At the rustic pavilion is an inscription reading: "Tradition places George Washington here in the summer of 1780 observing American troops thwart British efforts to reach Morristown, and destroy his base of supplies."

At 7 m. on State 24 is the forked junction with an asphalt paved road.

Left on this road is SUMMIT, 3.2 m. (447 alt., 14,556 pop.), a bright residential town that spreads out on the crest of FIRST WATCHUNG MT. The ridge served in Revolutionary days as a barrier to British penetration of the hill country in western New Jersey. A bronze tablet on a boulder on Hobart Ave., between Beacon Rd. and Morris Turnpike, marks the SITE OF OLD SOW, a small cannon now on the grounds of the Ford Mansion in Morristown, used as an alarm gun to notify Washington of the approach of raiding parties of British troops. The KENT PLACE SCHOOL for girls, with an enrollment of 300, occupies nine Tudor buildings spread across 23 acres of green at Morris Ave. and Kent Place Blvd.

At 9.2 m. (R) is the CANOE BROOK COUNTRY CLUB (private) with two 18-hole courses, scene of the women's national championship tournament in 1936.

Landscaped grounds at 8.5 m., where the roadbed becomes two lanes of concrete, are the beginning of a real-estate development.

In this section of more or less friendly homes, a grim, RED BRICK

CASTLE *(private)* rises out of a picket and wire-fenced estate at 9.8 *m.* (L). Turreted like an arsenal, the three-story building was built more than 50 years ago by George B. Vanderpool. The estate, a maze of wire fences, is patrolled by a uniformed guard; the wealthy Wall Street speculator gave full expression to his personality in the old towers and the sunken garden reached by marble steps.

At 10 *m.* the road crosses Passaic River on DAY'S BRIDGE, a concrete and steel structure at the place where the Revolutionaries crossed to give battle to the British at Springfield in June 1780.

CHATHAM, 10.6 *m.* (230 alt., 3,869 pop.), is a comfortable old town made new by the lawn-spaced homes of suburban commuters. Its principal industry is horticulture; the chimneys of two large greenhouses poke their heads over the hill west of the Passaic River. Chatham was at one time known as Bonnel Town. Its antiquarians are fond of boasting that no British troops ever entered the town. DAY'S TAVERN (R), a two-and-a-half-story frame building with wide front porch, just E. of the business center, was frequented a good deal by Washington and his officers. It is still doing business. Another old tavern (R) near the western edge of town, ELM TREE INN, was built in 1811.

Left from the center of Chatham on the Myersville road to the GREAT SWAMP, 2.6 *m.*, about 7 miles long and 3 miles wide. Here, in the Ice Age, was a lake caused by the North American glacier's choking the old outlet of Passaic River. The river was diverted by the debris thrust ahead of the ice mass into its present hairpin course about 30 miles to the north, before finding a new outlet at Passaic Falls, Paterson, on its way to the sea. The remnant of the ancient lake, stagnant and decrepit under the weight of its 20,000 years, lingers in the Great Swamp in black pools oozing up between clumps of moss and stunted trees. At some spots near the edges drainage has produced hay crops, but there is no human habitation. The swamp's most important citizens are wary, beady-eyed muskrats who have paid rent with their skins for centuries, first to the Indians and then to the white men.

BOTTLE HILL TAVERN (L), 12.6 *m.*, a white, two-story frame building with attic and porch, was built in 1812 on the site of an older inn of the same name. The story runs that the first proprietor, David Brant, lacking a sign for his hostelry, hung a bottle on a string and stretched it out over the road as a reminder to travelers. It was the post house for the Elizabeth-Morristown coach run, and in 1825 the Marquis de Lafayette was entertained here. The tavern has been preserved by the Madison Historical Society.

MADISON, 12.8 *m.* (250 alt., 7,481 pop.), a solidly built suburban town with a rich historical background, could pass for a New England village. It is enlivened by the presence of Drew University and Mrs. Marcellus Hartley Dodge. Madison's million-dollar MUNICIPAL BUILDING (L), on the other side of the Lackawanna R.R. embankment, is the gift of Mrs. Dodge, who is the former Geraldine Rockefeller, daughter of William Rockefeller and a niece of the late John D. Rockefeller. The building is a memorial to her son, Marcellus Hartley Dodge; its interior is finished in colored marbles and its rest rooms for policemen and firemen rival those of exclusive clubs. Madison is known as the "Rose City" because of its many greenhouses. Before 1834 it went by the plainer name of Bottle Hill. Some residents contend that the name was Battle Hill since the town site is said to have been the scene of two Indian skirmishes; but historians agree that the town took its first name from the nearby tavern.

The SAYRE HOUSE *(private)*, Ridgedale Ave., built *c.* 1745, was "Mad Anthony" Wayne's headquarters while his army encamped in the Loantaka Valley.

On the western outskirts of the town, at 13.4 *m.*, are the buildings of DREW UNIVERSITY (L). In 1929 its theological seminary received a real-estate endowment of $5,000,000 from the $40,000,000 fortune of Manhattan's Wendel sisters. The institution was founded by the Methodist Episcopal Church as a theological seminary in 1867, the centenary of American Methodism, on ground donated by Daniel Drew, stock-market speculator. The theological seminary now prepares men for the ministry and both men and women for teaching. Twenty buildings and two athletic fields are scattered across the 120-acre campus of flatland, oaks, and beeches, surrounded by a cut-stone fence. MEAD HALL, built as a private home in 1836, is a fine specimen of the late Southern Colonial type of architecture. The building stands behind a bronze equestrian STATUE OF FRANCIS ASBURY, first American Methodist bishop. ROSE MEMORIAL LIBRARY, built in 1938 to blend architecturally with Mead Hall, houses many valuable collections, including one of ancient manuscripts of the Greek New Testament and the Osborn and Tyerman Collections of Methodist publications. BROTHERS COLLEGE, housed in a modified Georgian Colonial style building of red brick with limestone trim, is an undergraduate school of liberal arts, opened in 1928.

Estates of the wealthy line the highway in the hills W. of Madison. At 13.9 *m.* (L) is the MRS. HARTLEY DODGE ESTATE *(private)*, enclosed in a stone, brick and wire fence. A dog show, one of the largest in America, is held on Mrs. Dodge's estate annually in May. Nearly 4,000 dogs from all over the country are housed in red and white tents on the greensward; as many as 40,000 visitors view the entries. The ESTATE OF HARTLEY DODGE is (R) opposite his wife's.

The COLLEGE OF ST. ELIZABETH is atop a high ridge at CONVENT STATION, 14.9 *m.* (R). Established in 1899 as an outgrowth of the Academy of St. Elizabeth, which dates back to 1859, it was the first Roman Catholic college in New Jersey to grant degrees to women. From the campus hilltop is a panorama of Passaic Valley 200 feet below, with the towns of Littleton, Boonton, Whippany, Parsippany, Hanover, and Pine Brook in view. The many gnarled, twisted trees on the college grounds are as sturdy today as when they were mentioned in deeds of a century ago as markers for boundary lines.

Large estates of the well-to-do introduce the eastern outskirts of Morristown. At 15.9 *m.* (L) is the MOUNT CARMEL CHAPEL AND MONASTERY of the Discalced Carmelite Nuns.

MORRISTOWN, 17.6 *m.* (400 alt., 15,197 pop.) *(see MORRISTOWN)*.

Points of Interest: Morristown National Historical Park (Ford Mansion, Museum, Fort Nonsense, Jockey Hollow), Dr. Jabez Campfield House, and others.

At 17.8 *m.* is the junction with US 202 *(see Tour 4)*.

At 18 *m.* is the junction with a macadam road.

Left on this road to JOCKEY HOLLOW, part of Morristown National Historical Park, 2.7 *m.* *(see MORRISTOWN)*.

At 18.5 *m.* (L) is BURNHAM PARK, where rolling green acres of woodland and meadows encircle the Morristown Municipal Swimming Pool. The site was occupied during the Revolution by Gen. Henry Knox and the artillery brigade.

West of Morristown the countryside fulfills the hint of New England that characterizes this part of New Jersey. Green, maize, and rust-colored fields fit into the rolling hills like pieces of a mosaic; neat wood fences separate the farm lands.

Hidden from the road by towering shade trees at 20.4 *m.* is ST. MARY'S MONASTERY (L), a Benedictine institution. AURORA INSTITUTE, a sanatorium, is high on the hill at 21.2 *m.* (L).

An overgrowth of tall trees and thickets at 23.5 *m.* (L) hides from the road the ESTATE OF GEORGE WASHINGTON *(private)*, coffee manufacturer.

The PRIVATE ZOO of the contemporary George Washington, enclosed in a wire fence adjoining the highway, occupies sloping meadow land (L) at 23.8 *m.*

MENDHAM, 24.9 *m.* (600 alt., 1,278 pop.), is a village of bay-windowed Victorian homes and great maples that arch over Main St. to shade the quiet walks. Two inns opposite each other at the town's cross-roads center dimly echo a rivalry that dates back to Colonial times: the BLACK HORSE INN (R) and the PHOENIX HOUSE (L). A sign outside the Black Horse fixes the date of its establishment at 1743. In the bar-room, however, is a framed card that advertises the birth year as 1735. According to those inhabitants who have wondered about the discrepancy themselves, 1735 was the estimate of a former proprietor. He had the card made, and then commissioned a local sign painter to emblazon the date outside. That sign painter seems to have been a man of considerable historiographic conscience. The true date, he said, was 1743. He thought the sign was a good idea; but it would go up right or not at all. The sign went up. The present owner is inclined to agree with his predecessor, but the sign still sways in the breeze.

A lone white frame building on sloping meadowland houses the BELL TELEPHONE AERONAUTICAL GROUND STATION *(not open to public)*, Kennedy Rd., established in 1930. It is the only experimental laboratory of its kind in the country. Aviators commonly call it the "central office of the skies" because it is in frequent contact with airliners in order to improve radio-telephoning between airships and the ground.

High on a hill at 25.7 *m.* is ST. JOHN BAPTIST SCHOOL FOR GIRLS, an Episcopal institution conducted by the Sisters of St. John the Baptist.

At 25.9 *m.* is (R) the WELL SWEEP ANTIQUE SHOP, housed in an old frame dwelling with the clutter of years on its porch. Rising majestically out of the jumble is its most startling exhibit, a life-sized wooden horse of the type once common in harness shops and now extensively collected by

Henry Ford. Beside the door is a slate for messages from callers when Mr. and Mrs. Edgar Fisher are not at home. In the summer of 1937, Mrs. Fisher found a note left by a motorist who contemplated buying the horse for two enraptured grandchildren. The signature was "Eleanor Roosevelt." The antique-shop owners have preserved the Roosevelt slate, but they wouldn't think of selling the horse. "Mrs. Roosevelt wouldn't know what to do with it if she got it," they say.

RALSTON, 26.2 m., is little more than a one-story POST OFFICE (R). That post office building, however, is the oldest in continuous use in the United States. It was erected in 1775 as a store by John Ralston, and ever since 1792 has served as a post office. Ralston built for permanence; the frame is made of hand-hewn oak, held together by mortised beams and wooden dowels, and the roof juts out a good yard past the front. Gray-brown color is the building's only sign of submission to time's slow fire. The post office has fourth-class rating, and people in its district have to come to it for their mail, though the regular route of the Mendham delivery service passes its very door. The government has paid rent for the use of the building only since 1931. Adjoining it is RALSTON'S HOME, built in 1771.

The LOUGHLIN MILL (open), 26.9 m. (L), famous for its Colonial applejack, is still making Jersey cider.

The road climbs steadily into a high farming region; L. is rugged MT. PAUL. Apple orchards and rolling pasture lands are front lawns for red barns and solidly built silos.

The scream of wind in wires and a sudden appearance of stunted telephone poles atop the embankment at 29.5 m. (R) call attention to an AMERICAN TELEPHONE AND TELEGRAPH CO. EXPERIMENTAL STATION (not open to public). Here, in a simple white shack that belies the imposing physics laboratory of its interior, the effects of weather on telephone equipment are studied.

At 29.9 m., on a L. bend, the roadbed changes to macadam.

CHESTER, 30.7 m. (860 alt., 620 pop.), is a leisurely little town with a wide, short Main St. and a few stores. The CHESTER HOUSE (R), now a hotel, was the first brick building erected in the town. It was built by Zephaniah Drake in 1812. Chester's first settlers, arriving in 1713, were attracted by the industrial possibilities offered by the waters of the Black River. They built sawmills, gristmills, and distilleries; later, woolen- and threshing-machine factories were established, and until 1890 iron mines operated in the midst of this peach-orchard area. They are all gone.

Chester is at the junction with US 206 (see Tour 6).

At 32.3 m., where the highway crosses the Black River, is the junction with a hard-surfaced road.

Left on this twisting road to HACKLEBARNEY STATE PARK, 1 m., 137 acres of hemlock, mature hardwood, dogwood, laurel, and azalea. The gorge of Black River, a good trout stream, runs through the park amid flowering shrubs and ferns. Although the park has no roads, it is well covered by trails for hikers and is equipped with fireplaces for picnicking. A parking area for automobiles is at the entrance. In early days the land was owned by an Irish settler named Barney Hackle.

The road takes a steep winding course uphill, and at 33.8 m. dips into

OLDEST NEW JERSEY POST OFFICE, RALSTON

Long Valley where the slopes are a patchwork quilt of fields and woodland. To the west are the white houses that make up the village of Long Valley, at the foot of Schooleys Mt.

LONG VALLEY, 35.5 *m.* (540 alt., 500 pop.), settled by Germans at the turn of the 18th century, was known as German Valley for more than 200 years; after the United States entered the World War, the name was changed. It is a tightly built little village in the center of a dairy- and truck-farming section. LONG VALLEY INN (L), built in 1787, has served liquor longer than any other tavern in the State N. of Trenton. The frame two-story building, remodeled in 1922, was known before the World War as the German Valley Hotel. Although lacking proof, the present proprietor is of the opinion that George Washington had a drink or two at the inn. Left is the OLD FORD HOUSE *(private),* built, according to an ancient tablet on the front, in 1774 by P. H. Wise, a German settler. It is a two-story frame structure of 12 rooms. Washington and his staff are said to have quartered here.

The road turns R. here, beginning, at 35.8 *m.,* the long, steep, winding pull up SCHOOLEYS MT. Halfway up the slope are clearings in the woods through which is the view (R) of the South Branch of the Raritan and of its watershed for many miles. Beyond the valley are lines of rolling hills. A sign on the summit at 36.9 *m.* (R) gives the elevation as 1,073 feet.

Along the grade are the old stone huts of German settlers; springhouses dot the roadside. Schooleys Mountain Springs, known to the Indians as a remedy for rheumatism and skin eruptions, have been famous as a health resort since 1770. The springs contain lime, iron, magnesia, soda and silica.

At 38 *m.* is the junction with a dirt road.

Left on this road to CAMP WO-CHI-CA, 4.5 *m.* The name is an abbreviation of "workers' children's camp"; it is conducted for underprivileged children. Here funds raised by the *Daily Worker* and other labor papers enable boys and girls to escape the cities' bubbling asphalt in the summer months to play in mountain surroundings once visited only by the Four Hundred.

Through wooded glens and along swift-running streams, the road begins the mile-long descent of Schooleys Mt. at 38.4 *m.* Where the forest breaks at 39.6 *m.* is the breath-taking view of MUSCONETCONG VALLEY (L). Cattle graze in the billowing green fields that rise and fall to white homesteads and the barns of dairy farms; the fertile green bottom lands roll west to SCOTTS MT. (L), a shoulder of the Upper Pohatcong.

At 40.7 *m.*, at the crossing of Musconetcong River, the road again becomes State S24.

Right (straight ahead) on State S24 to HACKETTSTOWN, 0.4 *m.* (560 alt., 3,038 pop.) *(see Tour 7),* where it forms a junction with US 46 *(see Tour 7).*

The route is abruptly L. to the southwest here on State S24 and runs along the bank of the Musconetcong (Ind., *rapidly running river*).

BEATTYSTOWN, 42.6 *m.* (500 alt., 90 pop.), is a small settlement through which General Burgoyne and his army marched on their way to Virginia after their surrender at Saratoga. The Musconetcong is well stocked here by the State fish and game commission.

At 43.3 *m.* is the junction with an improved road.

Right on this road is ROCKPORT, 1.5 *m.,* where the State maintains a GAME FARM that produces 10,000 pheasants a year.

Up a long grade at 46.9 *m.* the road swings (R) away from the Musconetcong. At 47.6 *m.* is an EMERGENCY RED CROSS POST housed in a service station (R).

PORT COLDEN, 49.8 *m.* (500 alt.), is a ghost town; its few homes and old yellow hotel are a faint echo of the days when the community was a port on the now abandoned Morris Canal. A weed-grown ditch marks the route of the canal.

At 50.1 *m.* is the junction with State 30 *(see Tour 15).* The route again becomes State 24.

WASHINGTON, 51.1 *m.* (460 alt., 4,410 pop.), is a quiet, sturdy town which, like Port Colden, was a stop on the old Morris Canal. Its position on the Lackawanna R.R. helped to save it from paralysis when the canal died. Once an important center for the manufacture of pianos and organs, it is now largely dependent on the hosiery industry. Washington was at one time called Mansfield Woodhouse, for a Presbyterian Church of the same name; the present name was taken from a tavern built in 1811 by Col. William McCullough, founder of the borough. The community has a Vigilante Society, founded in 1867 to combat horse thieves on the model of the Lambertville Vigilante Society; today its functions have extended to automobile thieves.

Right from the center of Washington on Belvidere Ave. to Bowerstown Rd., a loose stone road; L. on Bowerstown Rd. to (R) the CONSUMERS' RESEARCH PLANT *(open weekdays 9-4)*, 2 *m.*, a sturdy, barn-like two-story building of native stone with slate roof, designed by Robert Dunbar. Snugly placed at the foot of a wooded mountain with a fine view of the narrow valley in front, this is the seat of F. J. Schlink, director of an organization that advises consumers on what goods to buy and what goods to avoid, and known as co-author with Arthur Kallet of *100,000,000 Guinea Pigs*. Schlink has developed an individual reputation as an advocate of meat eating and as an enemy of patent medicines, big advertisers, raw fruit and vegetables, milk, and baker's bread. His caustic criticism of employers who showed hostility to organized labor was anticlimaxed in 1935 by the discharge of three of his employees who had helped to form a union. The resulting strike produced scenes that kept the normally quiet country town in an uproar. Armed guards patrolled the acreage about the main building and the outlying farm structures that are part of the property. On a fall day in 1935 a constable mounted on a farm horse rode into a crowd of several hundred strikers and sympathizers from local unions assembled on the road. His act provoked a riot that lasted for hours. The crowd surged through the ropes, showering the buildings with stones; automobiles were overturned and wrecked. By nightfall the guards were reinforced by hastily deputized farmers, armed with shotguns and rifles. Although the grounds at first were brightly illuminated from floodlights mounted on the building, the lamps were put out one by one with pellets fired by a methodical young hosiery worker, who hid in an adjoining cornfield and set a local record for bull's-eyes with an air rifle. Guns blazed as the deputized farmhands chased university graduates up and down the country lane west of the property. Strikebreakers barricaded within the building were evacuated in moving vans, with an escort of farmers. Miraculously, no one was killed or seriously injured. The strike ended a few months later when the union members and other technicians withdrew to New York City and established a rival organization, Consumers Union of United States, Inc.

At 51.6 *m.* on State 24 is the junction with an improved road.

Right on this road, at the foot of Scott Mt., is BRASS CASTLE, 1.4 *m.*, which offers some of the best trout-fishing in this well-stocked region. There is no architectural phenomenon at Brass Castle to match its name, which stems from an early settler, Jacob Brass. A cascade that crashes down several rock ledges at the Washington Water Co. reservoir is known as ROARING ROCKS. The macadam road up Scott Mt. is called Pleasant Dr. for the beauty of its views.

At 52.8 *m.*, for no apparent reason, is a staggering collection of lawn statuary (R): concrete nymphs, urns, and waterless fountains.

BROADWAY, 54.5 *m.* (350 alt., 150 pop.), is so called because of its wide main street which bears not the least resemblance to the parent thoroughfare of Manhattan. Broadway was at one time owned by the enterprising Col. William McCullough, who founded Washington, N. J., and had a good deal to do with the development of Asbury. Its most famous citizen was Peggy Warne, sister of Gen. Garret Vliet, who left her 10 children at home and served the Revolution by doctoring the local sick 50 years before Florence Nightingale was born. Mrs. Warne was not a physician, but she was a skilled obstetrician and practical nurse. While the few physicians in the county were away from home she rode all over the countryside, medicine in her saddlebags, to care for ailing citizens and convalescent soldiers.

Smokestacks draw attention at 56.2 *m.* (L) to the EDISON PORT-
LAND CEMENT PLANT founded in 1901 by Thomas Alva Edison. Pro-
digious crushers, invented by Edison and nowhere else in use, make little
ones out of 10-ton rocks quarried at the plant. Five miles of track join the
51 plant units and 3½ miles of conveyor belt are used to turn out 2,500,-
000 barrels of cement annually. Dust from the plant often blankets the
countryside for miles.

NEW VILLAGE, 56.6 *m.* (370 alt., 373 pop.), is an industrial frontier settled in 1899 to house workers at the then projected Edison Cement
plant. Left of the settlement is the plant quarry, a deep cut in the striated
brown-gray earth. Little dump cars burrow in and out of the pit on company trackage with limestone rocks for the big crushers.

A stretch of road at 57.6 *m.* is introduced by a sign announcing that
this was the first section of concrete highway built in New Jersey. The
construction dates back to 1912, and does not seem to have been repaired
much since. Cement dominates this neck of the Delaware country, only 12
miles south of Portland, Pa. At odd intervals mounds of earth along the
roadside reveal the grass-grown brick interiors of old limekilns.

With Scotts Mt. to the east the highway between here and Phillipsburg
is straight as a ruler, and the views north of the mountains are very
striking.

At 61.3 *m.* is the big INGERSOLL-RAND PLANT (L), manufacturing
jack-hammers and pneumatic tools. The plant, housed in 30 buildings
with 1,250,000 feet of floor space, employs 3,000 workers. Just ahead, over
a high ridge (L), are the workers' homes of INGERSOLL HEIGHTS, a
flat line of pillbox houses forming first notices of the nearness of Phillipsburg.

PHILLIPSBURG, 63.7 *m.* (300 alt., 19,255 pop.), long ago the site of
an Indian village called Chintewink, has all the smoke and grime of a little Pittsburgh. The city is built on a series of hills dropping down to the
Delaware River. From the ridge of Ingersoll Heights its dark rooftops
stretch to the L. in solid packs; scarcely a street intersection is visible from
the heights. The WARREN FOUNDRY AND PIPE CORPORATION SHOP is
five-eighths of a mile long; iron mines are on the premises, and its manufacturing process ranges vertically from the extraction of iron ore to the
production of finished pipes. The seven-foot pipe made here, used for
carrying telephone cable under the Harlem River, is constructed with a
passageway for repairmen.

The descent to the Delaware bridge is through a well-to-do residential
section of somber Victorian dwellings set back on terraced lawns (L) well
off the steep street. They overlook the industrial heart of the town on the
Delaware 100 feet below (R)—a sharp slice of cindered earth cluttered
with flatcars and smokestacks, intersected by the long gleam of the Pennsylvania R.R. tracks on the river's banks. Across the river are the crowded
buildings of Easton, Pa.

Phillipsburg is at the junction with US 22 *(see Tour 2).*

At 64 *m.*, on the DELAWARE RIVER BRIDGE *(free),* State 24 crosses the
Pennsylvania Line, 0.3 miles east of Easton, Pa.

Tour II

Lambertville—Washington Crossing—Trenton; State 29.
Lambertville to Trenton, 15.4 m.

Pennsylvania R.R. parallels the route throughout.
Usual accommodations; good concrete roadbed.

State 29, one of the few sections of well-paved road closely paralleling the Delaware River on the New Jersey shore, runs southeast almost at water level. This traffic lane between the river and the higher ground rising abruptly from the eastern bank offers scenery of more than average charm, including some fine views of the Pennsylvania countryside on the opposite shore. The road passes through Washington Crossing State Park, where Washington landed his army for a successful assault on the Hessians in Trenton.

State 29 branches south from US 202 *(see Tour 4)*, with which it is united halfway across the State, at LAMBERTVILLE, 0 *m.* (50 alt., 4,518 pop.) *(see Tour 4)*, 0.5 miles east of New Hope, Pa.

Right of the highway between Lambertville and Scudder's Falls is the wide ditch and towpath of the abandoned DELAWARE AND RARITAN CANAL FEEDER *(see TRANSPORTATION)*. A century ago it was the last link in the inland water route between the Pennsylvania coal fields and New York. The coal was carried in barges or scows pulled by mules.

Between the canal and the river are tracks of the Belvidere division of the Pennsylvania R.R. Construction of this line in 1851 doomed the canal.

Hills and woods shut off the view L. The Sourland Ridge, rising 450 feet, runs northeast for more than 15 miles. During the Revolution it served as a barrier to keep British and Hessian troops, quartered in Trenton, from raiding the rich Hunterdon County grain farms.

At 1 *m.* is WELLS FALLS of the Delaware, in reality nothing more than rapids. Old-time raftsmen guiding timber from the upper river to the cities below considered this the most dreaded point on the route.

At 1.4 *m.* the road makes a dangerous curve at the rocky shoulder of GOAT HILL (L). The hard trap rock of this ridge, volcanic in origin, has been extensively used in road building.

Across the river, which is here less than a quarter-mile wide, are the hills of Bucks County, Pa., in which Washington's battered army found refuge from British pursuers in December, 1776, after the disasters of Long Island and Fort Washington. The British were unable to continue the chase into Pennsylvania because the Americans had taken all of the boats for many miles. While an American outpost kept watch from Goat Hill, the troops across the river prepared for their counter-attack on Trenton.

At 3 *m.* the highway passes through MERCER COUNTY FARM, with workhouse and quarries where gray-clad prisoners work with sledge and hoe. A broad stretch of level ground lies between the highway and river. The hill (L) has been blasted for rock, leaving a precipice some 200 feet high.

Across the river is the stone OBSERVATION TOWER, on Bowman's Hill, erected by the Commonwealth of Pennsylvania on the site of a lookout used by American sentries watching the river ferries in 1776. Resembling a medieval castle, the memorial stands out boldly on the skyline.

The highway descends until it is 10 feet lower than the old canal feeder, with banks upheld by a retaining wall for half a mile.

At 5 *m.* the road bridges Fiddler's Creek, draining a green valley of rolling farm lands, neatly fenced and adequately supplied with farm buildings.

TITUSVILLE, 5.7 *m.* (70 alt., 300 pop.), is a sleepy little village with one narrow street along the riverbank lined by unpretentious homes and green lawns. Outstanding in the town's skyline is the steeple of the FIRST PRESBYTERIAN CHURCH. Cut off from the mainland by the old canal feeder, the community is almost an island. In its early days it was a shipping point for grain and produce.

Between Titusville and Washington Crossing the highway is through Washington Crossing State Park *(see below).*

WASHINGTON CROSSING, 6.9 *m.* (60 alt., 30 pop.), is a quiet hamlet that won a name and fame from 1776 sufficient to overshadow any future distinction the village may acquire. Its most interesting building is the small, white frame JOHNSON HOUSE *(open daily 9-5; free),* popularly known as the McKonkey House, which stands on a terrace (L) a few hundred feet north of the corner of State 29 and Pennington Rd. There is some evidence that this is not the original Johnson ferry house, but the Johnson Tavern; at any rate, it has been restored by the State. Here, more than 160 years ago, Washington is said to have found shelter on the Christmas night when his troops were crossing the Delaware for the surprise attack on Trenton. In rooms with low, beamed ceilings and great fireplaces are preserved interesting relics of Revolutionary times.

Along the riverbank is WASHINGTON CROSSING STATE PARK *(open all year),* where the Continental troops landed their big flat-bottomed boats, poled through the ice-choked river. Many of Washington's men, disheartened by the defeats of Long Island and New York, had deserted. The term of service for others had nearly ended. Only 2,400 to 2,700 remained, the British holding New Jersey with three times their number. "I fear the game is nearly up," Washington then wrote to his cousin, but as he wrote he planned the recrossing of the river and the blow at Trenton. A staff officer reported:

I am writing in the ferry house. The troops are all over, and the boats have gone back for the artillery. We are three hours behind the set time. Glover's men have had a hard time to force the boats through the floating ice with the snow drifting in their faces. I have never seen Washington so determined as he is now. The storm is changing to sleet and cuts like a knife. The last cannon is being landed.

OLD COVERED BRIDGE ACROSS DELAWARE RIVER AT STOCKTON

To carry his army across the river, Washington had gathered from upstream and downstream the so-called Durham boats, named for the designer, Robert Durham. These flat-bottomed, sharp-ended craft, some of them 66 feet long, were capable of holding 15 tons. They were propelled either by oars or by sails.

Washington wrote to Congress that his soldiers' march through the storm "did not in the least abate their ardor, and when they came to the charge each seemed to vie with the other in pressing forward." Many of the men crossed barefoot or with old rags wrapped around their feet in place of shoes, and thus they marched all night and fought and won in the bleak morning *(see TRENTON)*.

In the park are memorials to these events. Daughters of the Revolution have installed an old-fashioned flower garden in the rear of the ferry house. The rival Daughters of the American Revolution have erected a historic marker for the landing site on the riverbank. An old-fashioned Colonial pump on one of the public water-supply wells was given by the Sons of the American Revolution, and a tall flagpole displaying the colors came from their rivals, the Sons of the Revolution. The American Tree Association has planted 13 American elms, one for each of the 13 Colonies. In SULLIVAN GROVE and WASHINGTON GROVE tables and other picnicking facilities are available. A third grove at the east end of the park is being developed and will be named for Gen. Nathaniel Greene, a division commander in the battle.

In the old-fashioned garden is a fountain, erected by the Patriotic Order Sons of America in honor of John Honeyman, a spy who aided Washington with information before the battle. Learning of the Hessian plans for a drunken celebration, Honeyman left Trenton, allegedly to buy more cattle for the British. He allowed himself to be "captured," gave his information to Washington and was allowed to escape. At Griggstown, where he lived, Honeyman was first denounced by his neighbors. When Washington appeared there and told the people of Honeyman's great services, the spy became a hero.

Nearly half of the open land within the 293 acres of the park has been planted with seedling evergreens, enough to create a small forest. These were provided by a State Forest Nursery adjoining the park, where 2,500,-000 seedlings are grown annually.

At the rear of the ferry house is (L) CONTINENTAL LANE, a dirt road, the path that the army followed on the march to the battle.

Between Washington Crossing and Scudder's Falls the highway is at the base of low hills. Summer homes and estates are on the slopes, their lawns close to the road.

SOMERSET, 8.1 *m.* (60 alt.), once a Colonial village, is now a handful of suburban homes straggling along the highway. The JEDEDIAH SCUDDER HOUSE, built more than 200 years ago, stands L. of the highway. An old-fashioned rambling stone and frame structure, it is said to have sheltered several of Washington's soldiers who, fatigued or nearly frozen, were unable to march to Trenton.

Left from Somerset on a stone road to MERCER AIRPORT, 1.7 *m.*, owned by the

City of Trenton and equipped with three runways and plane-servicing facilities. The green rotating beacon is seen at night for long distances.

SCUDDER'S FALLS, 8.9 *m.* (50 alt.), a small residential community, was named for a pioneer landowning family. Amos Scudder was one of Washington's guides in the march on Trenton.

Swinging R. at 10.2 *m.,* the highway crosses the canal and railroad. Here the country flattens out into the broad plains typical of the lower end of Delaware River.

On spacious grounds at 10.7 *m.* is the VILLA VICTORIA ACADEMY (R), a school taught by Italian nuns, formerly the Harvey E. Fish home. It is a sturdy, simple, brownstone mansion.

The highway turns L., following Sanhican Dr. On the R. is Sanhican Creek.

BOXWOOD MANOR *(private),* an old yellow stone house, is on a tree-covered knoll at 11.8 *m.* (L). Built in 1775, it has the fine lines of the Colonial period.

At 11.9 *m.* the road passes under the attractively designed READING RAILROAD BRIDGE, with a series of arches spanning the highway, creek and river. The tracks carry main-line traffic between New York and Philadelphia.

State 29 (Sanhican Drive West), here W. State St., leads to Warren St. TRENTON, 15.4 *m.* (55 alt., 123,356 pop.) *(see TRENTON).*

Points of Interest: State Buildings, Library and Museum, Old Barracks, Mahlon Stacy Park, First Presbyterian Church, Bloomsbury Court, Bow Hill, Lenox Potteries, and others.

At Trenton State 29 forms a junction with US 1 *(see Tour 1).*

Tour 12

Junction with State 30—Flemington—Frenchtown—(Uhlerstown, Pa.); State 12.
Junction with State 30 to Pennsylvania Line, 12.8 m.

Accommodations in Flemington and Frenchtown; few roadstands.
Two-lane macadamized roadbed.

State 12 runs west through hilly country, a sparsely populated farming and poultry section. From the crest of hills on the dipping road, wide panoramas open with low mountains forming the horizon. The road slopes from the last rise sharply down to the Delaware River.

State 12 forms a junction with State 30 *(see Tour 15)* on the eastern edge of Flemington.

FLEMINGTON, 0.4 *m.* (180 alt., 2,729 pop.), is a quiet little village that was catapulted into the front pages of the world's newspapers in January, 1935, during the trial of Bruno Richard Hauptmann for the murder of Charles A. Lindbergh Jr. Press stories at the time recounted the angry bewilderment of the local citizenry at the spate of strange people the trial brought into the community. A walk through the town brings the feeling home. Here in a setting of white, green-shuttered houses, business makes haste slowly. There is still a general store where the latest sheet music dangles invitingly over silk hose, and penny candy fills a counter carrying a copy of Pearson and Allen's *Nine Old Men,* a testament to the existence of open minds in this conservative stronghold. The cars parked near the COUNTY COURTHOUSE, Main St., seldom bestir themselves the day long, and shady side streets are all but deserted. The courthouse is the center of life in the community. Built in 1828, the great Grecian Revival building was the seat of the law in Hunterdon County a century before newspapers learned how to string telegraph wires from their offices to the scene of a murder trial. Just opposite, the four-story UNION HOTEL—a lumbering, Hudson-River-Bracketed structure of nondescript date, sparrow-grass architecture, tall double-decker porches, and the genial vapidity of the nineties—serves the barristers who amble back and forth across the street to the courthouse.

Hunterdon County residents have recently benefited by the elasticity of New Jersey's tax laws. Since 1937 when the official headquarters of the Standard Oil Company of New Jersey were removed to Flemington, bringing in new tax revenue, Hunterdon County residents have paid 50 cents less per $100 valuation. When the company moved from Linden to Flemington, its taxes were reduced from $1,400,000 to $270,000. Standard Oil had previously saved $587,366 by moving from Newark to Linden.

The headquarters of this, one of the wealthiest corporations in the world, consist of a sign upon a lawyer's office at 117 Main St. and a safe that contains those records required by law to be kept here.

John Philip Kase is generally credited as being the town's first settler, although the community takes its name from Samuel Fleming. FLEMING CASTLE, 5 Bonnell St. *(private),* a little white plaster house two stories high, was built as a residence and inn by Fleming in 1756. The house was recently renovated by Mrs. Charles D. Foster, who presented it to the local chapter of the Daughters of the American Revolution. The rooms of the house are small, typically Colonial, and built on several different levels.

A short distance west of Fleming Castle on Bonnell St. is the old KASE CEMETERY (L), between two private homes. Most of the gravestones, bearing the name of Kase and dated from 1774 to 1856, are crumbled almost to illegibility. One stands straight and white in shafted marble, inscribed: "In memory of the Delaware Indian Chief Tuccamirgan, 1750." The marker was erected in 1925 in belated appreciation of the Indian's aid to the first settler. Tuccamirgan himself expressed the desire to be buried near his white friend.

The JASPER SMITH HOUSE *(private)*, 8 Main St., was a small single-story red brick building when it was built by Smith in 1768. A second story, built of pressed steel resembling brick, and the west wing were added much later. Each of the window frames in the older part is carved out of a single piece of wood.

The Flemington Vigilante Society for the Detection of Thieves was organized under a State law passed in 1780. The society still exists, ostensibly for social and sentimental reasons.

Flemington depends for its business mainly on a prosperous surrounding farm area. The FLEMINGTON EGG POULTRY AND LIVESTOCK AUCTION is the largest in the world. It was founded in 1930 as a cooperative to prevent the sharp dealing of commission men and wholesalers, and to provide fair prices for poultry and livestock farmers. In 1936 the auction sold $1,244,000 worth of eggs, poultry and cattle. Many of Flemington's business establishments are the first floors of old residences with scalloped shingles and ornamental woodwork.

Left at 0.6 *m.* on Main St., an asphalted road.

The highway traverses high, rolling farm country where acres of wheat and corn are planted on the hillsides.

Groves of trees and heavy thickets approach the road at intervals. The hills about 2 miles west of Flemington are remnants of a volcanic upheaval, and once were rich in argilite close to the surface. The Indians fashioned this mineral into tools and weapons. By building fires against the face of a cliff and dashing cold water against the heated sections they could chip off sizable pieces. The stone had to be worked soon after it was quarried because long exposure makes it too hard. Locally the mineral is called "blue jingler" because, when fresh, it rings if struck sharply.

CROTON, 5.3 *m.* (510 alt., 100 pop.), consists of an old barn, a general store, and half a dozen houses at the junction with a country road.

BAPTISTOWN, 9.6 *m.* (500 alt., 75 pop.), was so named because of two Baptist churches formed here for the early settlers. The blacksmith shop, drab frame houses, and a general store mark it as a meeting place for the farmers of the surrounding area.

From the crests of hills between Baptistown and Frenchtown wide panoramas of planted fields, blotched with the darker green of trees, spread out to the Sourland Mts. (east) and the hazy rises of the Pocono Mts. across the Delaware.

At 11.2 *m.* the road begins a sharp descent to the river.

FRENCHTOWN, 12.6 *m.* (130 alt., 704 pop.), is a polite little village crammed into a tiny space on the bank of the Delaware. A wooden sign at the outskirts of the town announces:

FRENCHTOWN
Speed Limit 20 miles per hour
THANK YOU

CHICK HATCHERY, FRENCHTOWN

The KERR CHICKEN HATCHERY *(not open)*, south end of Railroad Ave., has a daily output of 50,000 hatched chicks, which are shipped by parcel post or express. By means of mercury-vapor lamps the hens are induced to work long hours, resulting in more frequent sit-downs and increased production.

At 12.8 *m.*, on the Delaware River bridge, State 12 crosses the Pennsylvania State Line 0.3 miles east of Uhlerstown, Pa.

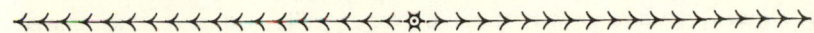

Tour 13

Middlesex—New Brunswick—Old Bridge—Matawan; State S28.
Middlesex to Matawan, 23.7 m.

Adequate accommodations.
Concrete roadbed, two to four lanes.

State S28 runs southeast from the Watchung Mountains, paralleling the Raritan River, water highway of early settlers. Crossing the river at the busy industrial town of New Brunswick, the highway traverses a plateau and then runs through low-lying farms and woodlands offering better than average rural scenery.

State S28 branches southwest from State 28 *(see Tour 17)* at the western edge of MIDDLESEX, 0 *m.* (40 alt., 3,504 pop.) *(see Tour 17)*.

The highway runs through the suburban residential section of East Bound Brook. During the Revolution the New Jersey militia in this section carried on guerilla warfare against the British and Hessian garrison of New Brunswick, to protect the flank of Washington's position in the Watchung Mountains to the west.

The highway runs close to the river, which in flood times often comes close to the roadbed.

At 1.5 *m.* on a gentle slope is (L) the 640-foot orange and white transmitting tower of RADIO STATION WJZ *(open to groups of not more than six persons)*, marked at night by 12 red lights. The triangular, open steel frame rests on a porcelain insulator 24 inches in diameter. Energized, the tower itself serves as a radiator of electric waves. Its ground system of 95,000 feet of 1-inch copper ribbon spreads over 20 acres.

At 3 *m.* is (L) the FIELD HOMESTEAD *(private)*, standing on a low knoll overlooking the Raritan. It is a low and rambling Colonial house built in 1743 by a grandson of the John Field who founded an extensive domain here in 1695. A colony of Negroes lives in the quarters once used by Negro slaves. East of the house 100 yards is an ancient INDIAN BURIAL GROUND, where hundreds of Indian weapons and utensils have been found.

At 4.3 *m.* the towers of the NEW BRUNSWICK RADIO STATION, Radio Corporation of America's second largest wireless station, are seen (R) across Raritan River. The station *(not open)* is used for transoceanic and transcontinental code transmission. The group includes 13 large tubular steel masts, each 428 feet high, and 20 smaller towers for short-wave transmission.

The new STADIUM OF RUTGERS UNIVERSITY, completed in 1938 largely with WPA labor and funds, is at 5.5 *m.* (L). A 260-acre tract here provides for future growth of the university. The stadium can accommodate 20,000 spectators. In adjoining fields are facilities for baseball, football, lacrosse, soccer, polo, and golf.

At 5.8 *m.* is (L) the LOW HOUSE *(not open)*, built by Cornelius Low in 1741. It was at the time the largest and most costly house in the once busy shipping community of The Landing; and it still ranks as one of the State's best examples of Georgian Colonial architecture, with a splendid entrance, sandstone walls, and hipped slate roof. Within are shell-head closets, and a paneled wainscot running along the hall and up the stairs.

THE LANDING, 5.8 *m.*, is marked also by LANDING BRIDGE (R), crossing the Raritan. Here was a thriving settlement of mills, warehouses, and stores that threatened to overshadow New Brunswick as a shipping center. The last of the structures at The Landing was razed in 1875 and today cattle graze in the meadows beside the river.

At 6.5 *m.* (L) is ROSS HALL *(private)*, almost hidden by trees and the surrounding shacks of a Syrian colony. Built in 1793 by Edward Antill, it once stood in the midst of a fine orchard and vineyard. Today the old mansion is run-down and neglected. Inside are hand-hewn beams, fine panel work, and carved shell-head closets.

At 7.3 *m.*, on a high knoll (L), is the white-painted MERCER HOUSE *(private)*. Erected about 1744 by Dr. William Mercer, brother of the Revolutionary General, it is basically of straight Colonial design, but has been so altered and enlarged from time to time that its original appearance is now all but lost under a festooning of porches and additions.

HIGHLAND PARK, 7.7 *m.* (100 alt., 8,691 pop.) *(see Tour 8)*, is L.

At Highland Park is the junction with State 27 *(see Tour 8)*. State S28 and State 27 are united for 0.4 miles.

State S28 turns R. at the junction and leads across Albany St. Bridge to the business center of New Brunswick.

The Pennsylvania R.R. Bridge across Raritan River is a fine example of arch construction in heavy stone, resembling the Roman aqueducts.

NEW BRUNSWICK, 8.1 *m.* (125 alt., 34,555 pop.) *(see NEW BRUNSWICK)*.

Points of Interest: Rutgers University Campuses and Buildings, White House, Guest House, Joyce Kilmer Memorial (museum), and others.

Left from Albany St. on George St.; L. on Clifton Ave. to Burnet St.; R. on Burnet St.

At 10.3 *m.*, at a traffic circle, is the junction with US 1 *(see Tour 1)*.

State S28 crosses an old millstream, Lawrence Brook, and runs through a stretch of grassy fields.

SOUTH RIVER, 13.7 *m.* (30 alt., 10,759 pop.), is passed (L) along its southern edge. This is a port for small craft on South River, a twisting arm of the Raritan. The town has an attractive residential section, modern stores, and a main street shaded by old trees. South River is in the heart of the New Jersey brick, clay and sand country. In the area are several Du Pont plants that have attracted a foreign working population.

South River's tax rate in 1937 was only 6 cents. The borough is supported mainly by the municipal power plant, one of the few in the State. Utilizing Diesel engines, the spotless station is regarded by South River residents as their foremost civic achievement. Rates for power and light, however, exceed those of the Public Service Corporation, private utility serving most of the State. The South River rate for 50 kw. hrs. is $4.20, compared with $2.94 charged by Public Service.

OLD BRIDGE, 16.2 *m.* (100 alt., 1,020 pop.), was a station stop on the old Camden and Amboy division of the Pennsylvania R.R., the first line built in the State. Anheuser-Busch, Inc., has a yeast plant here. The town is a small cluster of houses with a general store and a few other shops, lying in the small valley of Manalapan Brook.

Right from Old Bridge on an improved road is SPOTSWOOD, 2.1 *m.* (20 alt., 921 pop.). A charcoal iron furnace, forge, and flour mills here were seized by the New Jersey militia when their Tory owners fled in the Revolution. The RUINS OF THE IRON WORKS are found in part of its original dam, still standing on Matcha ponix Brook, which joins Manalapan Brook just northeast of Spotswood.

HELMETTA, 4.2 *m.* (40 alt., 801 pop.), is the home of one of the world's largest snuff factories, the GEORGE W. HELME CO. PLANT *(open only on permit from New York office).* This Jersey product no longer circulates in jeweled snuff-boxes as in Colonial days; but 40,000,000 pounds of it yearly leave here after fermenting, curing, scenting, sweetening, and flavoring processes, lasting from a year to 20 months. Most of the snuff goes to the South in tin boxes or containers made of skin. The snuff industry suffered little from the depression; recent years have been among its best. There are 375 employees. The original plant was built about 1825.

At 16.6 *m.,* at a traffic circle, State S28 leads L. into the northern portion of the sand belt. There is an unusual stand of white birch along the road. Some large areas are covered with scrub pine and oak.

BROWNTOWN, 19.6 *m.* (70 alt.), is merely a few scattered houses.

At 23 *m.* the highway crosses LAKE LEFFERTS, one of the twin lakes constructed as a community enterprise by the town of Matawan, which lies between them. Both bodies of water have been stocked with black bass and other fish.

At MATAWAN, 23.7 *m.* (60 alt., 2,246 pop.) *(see Tour 18),* State S28 forms a junction with US 9 *(see Tour 18).*

Tour 14

West Orange—Whippany—Ledgewood; State 10.
West Orange to Ledgewood, 26.9 m.

Tourist homes and roadhouses.
Concrete roadbed of three to four lanes, by-passing all towns.

The eastern section of State 10 runs through a thickly settled suburban area. The road climbs the ridges of the Orange Mountains and descends, only to roll up and down over a number of lesser hills in the manner of an elongated roller coaster. Farms and country estates are along the western section of the highway. There are fine views of broad valleys and higher mountains, typical of northern New Jersey.

State 10, following Condit St., forms a junction with Main St. in West Orange on the northern side of the new, Georgian style CITY HALL, a handsome brick structure.

WEST ORANGE, 0 *m.* (190 alt., 24,327 pop.) *(see WEST ORANGE).*

Point of Interest: Thomas A. Edison Plant.

State 10 runs west from West Orange on Mt. Pleasant Ave., up the steep grade of First Orange Mt. The ascent is made on sharp curves. Trees hide suburban homes L., but a fine view over the Oranges and Newark opens R. Beyond the ridge of the Palisades appear the projecting fingers of New York skyscrapers. In the early evening the city lights spread like a twinkling blanket on the plain below.

At 1.3 *m.* is the junction with Prospect Ave. on the top of the mountain.

Right on this concrete road to Eagle Rock Ave.; R. on Eagle Rock. Ave. to EAGLE ROCK RESERVATION, 1.6 *m.* *(see Tour 9).*

At Prospect Ave. is a SWEDISH RESTAURANT (R) that serves smörgåsbord.

State 10 descends the ridge, climbs Second Orange Mt. at the farthest fairways (L) of the ESSEX COUNTY COUNTRY CLUB *(private),* and slopes down into a valley only to climb again to the third and lowest ridge of the chain of hills. Here, over a broad expanse of meadows and pastures, are scattered farms and isolated dwellings.

LIVINGSTON, 4.7 *m.* (410 alt., 4,000 pop.), a lively business center with residential blocks of dwellings almost uniform in color and design, is named for William Livingston, New Jersey's Revolutionary Governor and one of the signers of the Constitution.

Its improved streets deaden into vacant lots as State 10 descends to the valley where the marshes of the Passaic River's backwaters lie north and south. In these slender troughs of wilderness, observers for the Audubon Society report, a great many kinds of birds nest in summer and rest during migrations. Beyond the hummocks and tules of the swamp extends a ridge identified as post-glacial, once having been an island in a great inland sea known geologically as Lake Passaic.

HANOVER, 8.8 *m.* (190 alt., 150 pop.), lies just L. of the highway. Of its dozen or so old-fashioned houses, six are used for the collection, restoration, and sale of antiques. The village was settled in 1710 by Germans who had sailed for New York but were driven by cross-winds to Delaware Bay. Moving northward, they found the fertile Passaic Valley lands to their liking and bought a tract. The HANOVER PRESBYTERIAN CHURCH, dating from 1835, was built largely with timber salvaged from an earlier church erected 1735. It has a low, square tower; the Gothic windows have diamond-shaped panes. Surplus lumber from the old church was sold by the congregation and some of the handsome white-pine paneling decorated a cow barn until it was resold for use in a Morristown mansion. The church cemetery contains the GRAVE OF DAVID YOUNG (1781–1852), the astronomer who is said to have charged the French Academy only $10 for making the decision that the Star of Bethlehem was not a comet.

The GREEN HOMESTEAD *(private)*, a low rambling, shingled structure painted white, built *c.* 1735 by Dr. Jacob Green, has five half-windows under the eaves. In addition to his duties as pastor, teacher, and physician, the doctor found time to operate gristmills and to produce a fine grade of rye whisky at a Troy Hills distillery. His son Ashbel limited himself to theology and, during the Revolution, soldiering. Ashbel was a favorite of Washington, who attended his wedding bringing a silver service, now preserved in the homestead, as a gift. As president of Princeton University (1813–1823), Ashbel Green became known as a theologian and scholar. The Hanover property is owned by his great-great-grandson, Ashbel III.

Whippany River, 11 *m.*, is crossed by a concrete bridge just below its confluence with Black Brook.

At 11.9 *m.* are (L) the high towers of the New Jersey BELL TELEPHONE CO. EXPERIMENTAL STATION, the proving ground for all radio developments made by the Bell Laboratories, the central research unit of the Nation-wide Bell System. The station was established in 1926 as an experimental broadcasting unit, and in 1927 the first wired television program in the world was successfully transmitted from it. As early as 1928 experiments were begun in airplane-to-ground radio telephony that have resulted in the widespread commercial and private use of this type of communication. Among other inventions perfected here is the single pole antenna used by many of the major broadcasting companies.

WHIPPANY, 12.2 *m.* (210 alt., 600 pop.), is a small industrial community. In four modern mills, cardboard is manufactured from wastepaper. Facing the main thoroughfare (R) is the old FIRST PRESBYTERIAN CHURCH, a modest weatherbeaten wooden structure, its windows and tower exactly like those of the one in Hanover *(see above)*.

At Whippany is the junction with a tar and graveled road.

Left on this road to (L) the SEEING EYE, 0.5 *m.*, a widely known institution for training German shepherd dogs to guide the blind. Many blind persons come here, lacking the confidence needed for a single step forward. When they leave, grasping the rigid U-shaped harness of the dog, they are ready to cross city streets. The training is efficient but expensive; philanthropic groups and persons make it possible to supply the dogs to the blind at a reasonable cost. It is only after rigid health and intelligence tests that the arduous three-month process of educating a dog begins. Bitches are preferred because they are gentler. The animal is taught to obey the commands, "Forward! Right! Left!"—and to ignore these commands when obedience might lead her master to serious injury or death. The blind also must be taught, and the broad grounds of the institution and busy streets of Morristown are the schoolrooms. The peak of the dual training comes when the dog learns to walk around obstacles high enough for her to pass under, but low enough to impede her master. A piece of string is stretched close to the ground. Little by little the barrier is raised until, instead of circling it, the dog can pass beneath it. When this occurs, she turns to see how her master is faring. Again and again this is repeated until the dog learns to judge her master's height and to circle obstacles that are too low.

The project was conceived by Mrs. Harrison Eustis when, on her travels through Europe, she was impressed by the extraordinary efficiency of the dogs used by the German and Swiss police and by the World War blind. Assisted by Elliot S. Humphries, a circus-animal trainer, Mrs. Eustis' experiments progressed until they came to the attention of a blind Southerner, Morris S. Franks. Franks' offer of his services was quickly accepted, and, after a period of training in Europe, he returned to America with only a dog to guide him. The journey was completely successful, and Franks prevailed upon Mrs. Eustis to continue her work here. He now directs the organization.

Alexander Woollcott broadcasts the story of the wife who returned a dog to the Seeing Eye with this note attached: "I am sending the dog back. My husband used to depend on me. Now he is independent, and I never know where he is."

West of Whippany the highway sweeps forward to the blue barrier of Watnong Ridge, an ancient continental seacoast that defines the entrance from the east to the north Jersey lakeland.

At 13.4 m. is (L) a GREEK CATHOLIC CHURCH, built 1921 by a congregation of Ukrainian emigrees who settled about Malapardis Creek. It is a one-story gray frame structure with a Greek cross surmounting its gilded, onion-shaped turret.

If a businessmen's association were formed in the small settlement, one man would constitute a quorum. Proprietor of the general store, he will swap stories over the bar in his tavern next door; or sell a plot of ground from his real-estate office just beyond; or fix a flat in his adjoining gas station.

Beginning at 14.2 m. both roadsides for 1.1 m. are fenced with high steel mesh, marking the domain of the McALPIN FARMS, with elaborate barns and well-kept dwellings. Developed as a country retreat for a tired Wall Street broker, the farm is locally famous for its milk.

LITTLETON, 15.3 m. (370 alt., 50 pop.), is at the junction with US 202 (see Tour 4). Here are a few cottages, a service station, and several roadside refreshment stands.

At 15.9 m. the road becomes the American Legion Memorial Highway, a four-lane concrete roadway with a landscaped center strip. The country is rougher here, with higher hills and distant views.

Reaching the final grade of Watnong Mt., the road passes at 16.6 m. CRAFTSMAN FARM (R), former country home of Gustave Stickley, designer of modern utilitarian furniture. Fieldstone and native timbers were used in the construction of house, silo, barns, stables, and sheds.

At 21.7 m. is the junction with an improved road.

Right on this road for 100 yards and R. up a long hill to (L) the RANDOLPH QUAKER MEETING HOUSE, 0.4 m. (key available at Cooper homestead, across the road). It stands on top of the appropriately named Mount Pleasant Hill, commanding a fine view of the surrounding hills and valleys, locus of many iron pits that once supplied the Dover furnaces. The church is a square structure, built in 1758 of hand-hewn timbers without nails; the door latches and blinds are also wooden. Within are the old time hanging partitions to separate men and women; a difficult stairway leads to a dark gallery in the front of which slaves were permitted to sit. Most of the settlers who attended services here moved westward in the 1820's. The church and cemetery are now in charge of a board of trustees.

State 10 climbs and descends a series of rounded hilltops until a sudden cut in the downward slope at 24.1 *m.* reveals the wide expanse of the Succasunna Plains, with the heights of Mt. Freedom (L) and the higher hills to the west bounding the valley of the South Branch of the Raritan. In the basin formed by the surrounding hills are deposits of decomposed vegetable matter, not yet peat but of high value for enriching soil. The land is dredged or pumped dry, then the product is harvested, dried, and sold as humus.

SUCCASUNNA, 25.3 *m.* (710 alt., 300 pop.), is an avenue of white Colonial houses paralleling the highway, with their barns and backyards along State 10. Elms shade fine dwellings that have been enlarged and re-modeled from the simple homes of "Old Suckysunny." The name in Lenape Indian language stands for *black stone,* or iron ore, which was once abundant here, and led to the discovery and exploitation of the vast magnetite and hematite deposits of the surrounding region.

At 26.9 *m.* State 10 forms a junction with US 46 *(see Tour 7)* in LEDGEWOOD (740 alt., 350 pop.), where the post office is in a single-story frame grocery store. The village surrounds a traffic circle.

Tour 15

Buttzville—Ringoes—Trenton; State 30.
Buttzville to Trenton 50.4 m.

The road is paralleled by the Lackawanna R.R. between Buttzville and Washington; the Jersey Central R.R. between Hampton and the junction with US 22; the Pennsylvania R.R. between the junction with State 12 and Ringoes; and the Reading between Marshall's Corner and Trenton.
Tourist homes and eating places along road.
Two-lane concrete roadbed throughout.

State 30 runs southward through the boulderous western part of the State, sloping downward gradually from the rolling mountain country where views of farm-dotted valleys open suddenly from the crests of hills. The road cuts through mountain passes and crosses swift streams to the tableland in the south where the trees are fewer, the brush more scraggly. Numerous antique shops and pottery exhibitions make up for the scarcity of roadstands.

State 30 branches S. from US 46 *(see Tour 7)* at BUTTZVILLE, 0 *m.* (430 alt., 500 pop.) *(see Tour 7).*

From both sides of the road the ground rises sharply or backs down to shallow valleys only to rise to new heights beyond. Open fields are blistered with huge rocks, deposited during the movement of the great glacier.

OXFORD, 2.1 *m.* (500 alt., 1,723 pop.), on the slope of Scotts Mt., is an iron-mining center. The village sprang up two centuries ago around Oxford Furnace, one of Washington's sources of military supplies. Most of the working population is employed in a dye factory in the valley of Musconetcong River (L). A drab Lackawanna R.R. station (L) and a squat water tank shadowing carloads of iron ore mark the entrance to the village. A tiny frame post office, painted brightly in black and white, contrasts with unpainted wooden shacks. Larger, better-kept houses are on the side streets.

Right from Oxford on a tarred gravel road to the OLD GRISTMILL, 0.2 *m.*, standing in a fork of the road. Built in 1750, it is a four-story stone building, its doors and shuttered windows set in paneled frames. At the top, where the pulley wheel to hoist the grain was formerly set, is a bell-gable resembling that of a Spanish mission; about 25 years ago the mill was converted into a Methodist church. Behind the mill are the RUINS OF OXFORD FURNACE, erected 1742 by Jonathan Robeson and operated until 1884. The stamping and rolling mill is a small, six-story building, the lower part of stone, the upper of red brick. At the base of a stone extension in the rear is the viaduct. Oxford residents tell of the ghost that appeared in 1877, eight months after Jerry Mack was found mysteriously dead near the furnace. Mack, an eccentric, wore ribbons streaming from his hat. His ghost, wearing the familiar long-tailed coat, appeared to a night shift of three men in the stack house. "Doomed to wander!" it said. Two of the men left by a window and ran 3 miles to their homes. The third fainted.

High on a hill R. of the fork is SHIPPEN MANSION *(private)*, a three-story, beautifully proportioned Georgian residence of local stone, its appearance marred by a frame glass-enclosed porch along the front. It was built in 1754 by Joseph Shippen and Dr. William Shippen, owners of the blast furnace.

The road climbs to a cut between Scotts Mt. and the Upper Pohatcongs, and slopes gently into a country of broad farming acreages and dairy farms that cover the valleys and make bald spots on the wooded hills.

WASHINGTON, 6.2 *m.* (460 alt., 4,410 pop.) *(see Tour 10)*, is at the junction with State 24 *(see Tour 10)*.

Between Washington and Glen Gardner the road is bordered by patterned fields that rise steeply to the tops of the low-lying Pohatcong Mts.

At 7.8 *m.* in an open field (L) is a large, stone LIMEKILN, set in the side of a hill. Used until about 1920, it is still in good condition. Fires were built in the two openings at the bottom, and the limestone, carted up the hill in wagons, was dumped in the brickline holes at the top.

At 12.1 *m.* is the junction with a macadam road.

Left on this road is GLEN GARDNER, 0.1 *m.* (540 alt., 554 pop.), little more than a single street intersecting the road. Fifty years ago the Clinton *Democrat* said of this street: "There are numerous snakes under the board foot-walks . . . Several persons have seen them stick their heads between the cracks and through the knot holes in the boards."

Straight ahead and up the mountainside above Glen Gardner is the NEW JERSEY STATE TUBERCULOSIS SANITARIUM, 1.8 *m.*, on the summit of Mount Kipp. The buildings are of yellow and gray stucco, two stories high with red metal roofs. Milk from a large herd of goats pastured on the mountainside is used for the 440 patients. The institution has a high reputation for its work.

Spruce Run, an old millstream, parallels State 30 through a high-walled ravine. The Jersey Central R.R. is on a rocky mountain ledge (L).

At 14.3 *m.* is the junction with a graveled road.

Right on this road across Spruce Run to (R) the SITE OF UNION IRON WORKS, 1.4 *m.*, a pile of stone overgrown with ivy in the shade of an apple orchard. The furnace was erected by William Allen, ex-mayor of Philadelphia, at about the time of his purchase of land here in 1742. Allen and his partner, Joseph Turner, were pro-British; their property was confiscated by Revolutionary authorities. The furnaces were working until the latter half of the 19th century.

At 15.2 *m.* is the junction with a macadamized road.

Left on this road is HIGH BRIDGE, 1.8 *m.* (350 alt., 1,860 pop.), where part of the Union Iron Works was situated. When the furnace was confiscated during the Revolution, Robert Taylor, one of the commissioners for the subsequent sale, bought part of the property and operated it as the Taylor Iron Works—predecessor of the contemporary Taylor-Wharton Iron and Steel Co. On the company's land is LAKE SOLITUDE *(swimming free on presentation of health certificate from High Bridge Health Dept.),* named for the home Taylor built here. John Penn, last Royal Governor of Pennsylvania and a descendant of William Penn, was held prisoner in Taylor's home for 6 months on the order of the Continental Congress in 1776. The town is small, its only modern note a cream-colored brick bank building.

The county road is scrub-lined, with masses of sumac bushes. It is paralleled (R) in spots by the South Branch of Raritan River. VOORHEES STATE PARK, 3.6 *m.*, on the summit of a steep rise on the southern slope of Musconetcong Mts., is being developed (1939) into a recreation center with smooth dirt roads, trails, and fireplaces and other picnic facilities.

State 30 passes through farm country that in the early part of the 20th century was planted with peach and apple orchards. So important was the peach crop then that the Lehigh Valley R.R. ran special "peach trains" between this area and the markets. When blight destroyed the fruit trees other kinds of crops were planted. The orchards are now reappearing.

At 17.2 *m.* is the junction with US 22 *(see Tour 2).*

The GOBEL ESTATE, 18.2 *m.*, is one of the largest farms in New Jersey. A tiny granite chapel and mausoleum in Gothic style is visible about a mile off the road (L). In the tomb is the body of the skinless-frankfurter tycoon.

For miles along the road are rolling pasture lands, woods, and planted fields, extending to the semicircular ridge of the Sourland Mts. to the southeast. Patches have been torn from the tree-covered sides of the Musconetcongs (R) and Cushetunks (L) to make room for expanding farm lands. Perched on the hills, breaking the even rows of crops, are tiny graveyards. Many farms in this area have modern outhouses built according to specifications of the State Health Department by the WPA privy project. Labor in constructing the sanitary pits was free, the property owner paying only for materials.

The FLEMINGTON FAIR GROUNDS, 25.8 *m.* (L), are used for county carnivals and fairs.

FLEMINGTON (R), 27.5 *m.* (180 alt., 2,729 pop.) *(see Tour 12),* is at the junction with State 12 *(see Tour 12).* The center of the village is by-passed by State 30.

US 202 *(see Tour 4)* forms a junction at 27.9 *m.*, uniting with State 30 to Ringoes.

RINGOES, 33.3 *m.* (220 alt., 330 pop.) *(see Tour 4).* Left here on State 30; US 202 *(see Tour 4)* branches R.

At 36.9 *m.* is the junction with a macadam road.

Left on this road is HOPEWELL, 3.2 m. (180 alt., 1,467 pop.), a quiet, sedate town that has settled back to normality since it was a newspaper date line in the Lindbergh kidnaping case. The town is much like a village Janet Gaynor might come from in any of her motion picture roles as a "small town" girl. Hopewell residents—who speak resentfully of those who arrived from the cities during the Lindbergh episode—live in homes set well back from broad, tree-lined streets. The OLD SCHOOL BAPTIST CHURCH, W. Broad St. (L), built in 1748, replaced an earlier structure erected 33 years before. It is a simple two-story brick building painted bright red, with heavy paneled doors and arched windows. The building was used as a hospital during the Revolution. A MONUMENT TO JOHN HART, a signer of the Declaration of Independence and donor of the church site, stands directly beside the church. The plain granite shaft was erected in 1865 by the State legislature. Hart died from hardships he endured when the British and Tories chased him from one hiding place to another for three years. Next to the monument is an old SPEAKING BLOCK, made of granite squares with a sandstone slab carrying an inscription set into the side. Joab Houghton stood on the block and inspired men to enlist in the Colonial militia when he brought the news of the battle of Lexington to Hopewell.

The ARTHUR KING HOUSE (private), W. Broad St. near the center of town (R), was built in 1756 for the Rev. Isaac Eaton, who was the head of a Latin school here. James Manning of Piscataway was Eaton's first pupil. Manning became a founder and the first president of Brown University. The house is a three-story, white frame, Colonial structure with blue-shuttered windows. It stands far back from the sidewalk, behind a terraced lawn dotted with giant sycamore trees. The HOPEWELL MUSEUM AND LIBRARY, W. Broad St. nr. Blackwell St. (open Mon. 2:30-5; Wed. and Sat. 2:30-5 and 7-9), is a three-story, brownstone, converted residence with a mansard roof and a wide veranda that runs across the front and curves around the side. The first two floors have narrow bay windows with brown shutters. The museum contains many Indian and Colonial relics.

Right from Hopewell on Princeton Ave. 1.1 m. to the place where the body of the Lindbergh baby was found. A footpath, marked by a grayish-white rail on two posts resembling a hitching bar, leads a few paces into a dense thicket (R). Here the body of Charles A. Lindbergh Jr. was accidentally discovered by a Negro truck driver, two months after the kidnaping in 1932. (The former Lindbergh home, 3 miles from Hopewell, is closed to visitors, and not visible from the highway. A Hearst photographer, who jumped on the running board of a Lindbergh car to snap a picture of his second son, young Jon, climaxed episodes of newspaper publicity so distasteful to the aviator and his family that the Lindberghs moved to England. Characteristically, Lindbergh announced the departure only to the dignified New York Times; the newspaper's executives locked every door and cut off all telephone service while an extra was rushed to press.)

The road winds through lowlands where once the waters of prehistoric Pensauken Sound flowed. Huge boulders, washed down from the northern part of the State in prehistoric times, make many of the fields fit only for grazing.

MARSHALL'S CORNER, 40.4 m., is only a gasoline station at an intersection with a county road. The tiny village that once stood here was named for William Marshall, whose son, James Marshall, discovered gold in California (see Tour 4).

At 41.6 m. is the junction with a macadam road.

Left on this road is PENNINGTON, 0 ' m. (210 alt., 1,335 pop.), a delightful old country village with a block or so of small stores and an unused trolley track on the main street. The town dates from 1697 when Johannes Lawrenson purchased the land. At first the village was called Queenstown, in honor of Queen Anne, but because of its insignificance people began to refer to it derisively as Penny Town. About 1747 it became permanently known as Pennington.

PENNINGTON SEMINARY, W. Delaware Ave. opp. Green Ave., is a leading boys'

HARVESTING WHEAT NEAR FLEMINGTON

school founded in 1843. The school is housed in a four-story building of red brick with white wooden pilasters and a mansard roof.

State 30 is level across the tableland near the Delaware River. Southward rise the smokestacks and water towers of Trenton's factories.

EWINGVILLE, 46.6 m. (140 alt.), a small suburb of Trenton, was once called Cross Keys because of a tavern by that name.

At 46.8 m. are (L) the recently completed red brick buildings of the STATE TEACHERS COLLEGE. Of modified Georgian Colonial design, they are set in a grove of trees about 300 yards from the road.

State 30, which follows Pennington Ave., leads to the Battle Monument, landmark near the center of Trenton.

TRENTON, 50.4 m. (55 alt., 123,356 pop.) (see TRENTON).

Points of Interest: State Buildings, Library and Museum, Old Barracks, Mahlon Stacy Park, First Presbyterian Church, Bloomsbury Court, Bow Hill, Lenox Potteries, and others.

At the Trenton Battle Monument is the junction with US 1 (see Tour 1).

◄◄◄◄◄◄◄◄◄◄◄◄◄◄◄◄◄◄◄◄◄◄❁►►►►►►►►►►►►►►►►►►►►►►

Tour 16

(Hillburn, N. Y.)—Saddle River—North Arlington—Newark—Junction
with US 22; State 2 and State 21.
New York Line to Junction with US 22, 29.1 m.

The Erie R.R. parallels the route between the New York Line and Hohokus.
Hotels in the larger towns. Lunchrooms and tourist accommodations at others.
Three- and four-lane concrete roadbed.

Crossing the New York State Line on the slope of the Ramapo Mountains, State 2 runs south, by-passing towns and traversing a dairying and
truck-farming section. Old houses and churches show the influence of early
Dutch settlers. The southern section of the route enters the industrial belt
of northern New Jersey.

State 2 crosses the New York State Line 0.7 miles south of Hillburn,
N. Y. The Ramapo Mts. shelter the sparsely distributed homes of the
Jackson Whites (see Tour 9A).

The road descends the ridge into the narrow Ramapo Valley with dwin-
dling Ramapo River at the nadir, and then rises on the foothills about 200
feet above the stream.

At 1.2 m. is the junction with US 202 (see Tour 4).

RAMSEY, 3.8 m. (340 alt., 3,258 pop.), is a shipping center for dairy
farmers and the residence of commuters to New York.

South of Ramsey the highway has four lanes of concrete with a center
parkway.

At 6.6 m. is the junction with a paved road.

Left here to SADDLE RIVER, 1 m. (150 alt., 657 pop.), a country town supporting a polo team in the Bergen County League. A tradition is that the settlement
was named by two Scottish land speculators, Captain Nichols and Richard Stillwell,
who bought several thousand acres from the Indians. Both saw the strong likeness
of the stream to Saddle Burn, a brook in Argyllshire.

Two recently developed areas of ultramodern cottages with cobalt shutters and scarlet roofs are R. at the northern entrance to Hohokus.

HOHOKUS (R), 8.9 m. (130 alt., 925 pop.), shows its more youthful
side to the highway, but its heart is on old Franklin Turnpike (R). The
ZABRISKIE HOUSE, E. Franklin Turnpike and Maple Ave., was built in
1790 by Caspar Zabriskie; it is a fine example of Georgian design in
stone, two and one-half stories high. The place is now called Hohokus Inn.

THE HERMITAGE (private), Franklin Turnpike on the Waldwick Borough line, was visited by George Washington in 1778. Capt. Philip De
Visne, known as The Hermit, built his house of cut red sandstone in English Gothic style with steep pitched roof, dormer windows of diamond-
shaped glass, and projecting wings. Here Aaron Burr courted Theodosia

Provost, a widow, who became his wife. Lafayette and Mrs. Benedict Arnold were also guests here.

In Colonial times Hohokus was known as Hoppertown, because of an early settler. The present name, from the Chihohokies Indians who had a chief town here, is still spelled Ho-Ho-Kus on the municipal building, but the post office, the U. S. Census Bureau, and the telephone company prefer the unhyphened form.

On the highway (R) at the southern end of Hohokus is the old TROT-TING TRACK, on which motorcycle and automobile races are now held from spring to fall.

At 10.1 m. is (R) Old PARAMUS CHURCH, a Dutch Colonial structure of red sandstone, erected c. 1800. In the earlier church that stood on this site, Aaron Burr and the Widow Provost were married in 1782; and here Gen. Charles Lee was court-martialed and dismissed for his retreat at the Battle of Monmouth *(see Tour 18A)*.

At 10.4 m. is the junction with Van Emburgh Ave., an improved road.

Left 50 yards on Van Emburgh Ave. to (R) the VAN EMBURGH HOUSE *(private)*, built in 1701, a one-and-one-half-story red sandstone structure with a gambrel roof. Small dormers and a modern extension destroy the typical Dutch lines. The stone, wood, and clay walls, nearly 2 feet thick, are well preserved. For 150 years the house dominated a farm of nearly 600 acres on which Ridgewood was later built.

PARAMUS, 11.5 m. (60 alt., 2,649 pop.), is an old Dutch farm community still growing vegetables for the city markets. A wide area on both sides of State 2 is covered with a black muck, especially suited to celery growing, giving Paramus the local name of Celery Town. Dutch colonists first settled here in 1666.

At 13.6 m. is the junction with State 4, a concrete paved road.

1. Right on State 4 to the ARCOLA MILL, 1.1 m., about 100 yards off the road (L), a square fieldstone and shingled tower on the bank of Saddle River. It was built in 1899 to mark the site of the Old Red Mill (erected 1745), which manufactured blankets for the Colonial troops.

2. Left on State 4 to Main St., RIVER EDGE, 1.8 m.; L. on Main St. to (L) the STEUBEN HOUSE, 2.3 m. *(open on application to caretaker)*, a long low Dutch Colonial house with a gambrel roof that forms an overhang sheltering the front porch. The rough-surfaced stone dwelling has two front doors that accommodated the families of John and Peter Zabriskie. In the western wall next to a low, thick, side door the Zabriskies placed a square stone plaque, carved with their initials, the date 1751, and a mill wheel, symbol of their trade. During the Revolution the Zabriskie brothers were Tories and their home was confiscated. In 1783 it was given as a reward for military services to Gen. von Steuben, who sold it back to the Zabriskies. The house has been presented by the State to the Bergen County Historical Society, who will maintain their headquarters there and also establish a museum.

At 15.4 m. is the junction with US 46 *(see Tour 7)*.

LODI, 17.3 m. (30 alt., 11,549 pop.), largely concealed by a low hill (R), is an industrial town. Behind the hill is the UNITED PIECE DYE WORKS, employing 800, and the scene of bitter labor disputes in recent years. Robert Rennie, a French dyer, named the town in 1825 for Napoleon's victory over the Austrians at the Bridge of Lodi.

HASBROUCK HEIGHTS, 18 m. (150 alt., 5,658 pop.), looks down on the highway from the brow of the hill (R). The town was founded by the Kip family in 1685, but the name was taken from another Dutch colonist. BENDIX AIRPORT is L., with flying field, aviation school, and hangars.

State 2 passes S. along the border of the vast area of the Hackensack Meadows, one of the channels through which the Great Glacier discharged its waters as it melted. Ahead (L) is a 10-mile view of tall grasses, yellow marsh marigolds, and cattails. The swamp, 50 square miles, is a breeding ground for marsh wrens, song sparrows, red-wings, bobolinks and a great variety of other birds. The minnows in the pools and small streams and the grasshoppers on the mud flats attract great flocks of shore birds during the migrating seasons. The tract has been well ditched to control mosquitoes. There have been many proposals by engineers to utilize these lowlands, but thus far the area has been used mainly for railroad tracks and smoking dump heaps.

WOOD RIDGE, 19.1 *m.* (190 alt., 5,159 pop.), is a mixture of postwar bungalows, gardens, small truck farms, gas stations and a few dingy frame houses. One of the few industries is the reclaiming of motion picture film. The first landowners here were the Brinkerhoffs, who came late in the seventeenth century.

MOONACHIE (L), 19.1 *m.* (10 alt., 1,465 pop.), is a fertile oasis in the marshland on a slight rise opposite Wood Ridge. The borough's name is that of an Iroquois who invaded this region from New York and col lected tribute long before pale-faced racketeers adopted his technique.

CARLSTADT, 19.4 *m.* (120 alt., 5,425 pop.), is a small bit of "Das Vaterland" planted in an American town on the rocky ridge between the Hackensack and Passaic valleys. Some of the streets are terraced, and steps lead from one level to another. The land was bought co-operatively from the original American owners by a group of German exiles, liberals and freethinkers who were seeking political liberty. The town, first called Tailor Town because many of the inhabitants worked for New York tailors, was later renamed Carlstadt *(Carl's town)* for Dr. Carl Klein, leader of the German group. On warm nights old folk songs, rhythmically punctuated by the tapping of beer steins, ring out from the popular Sommer Garten. New Yorkers come to the little town with its squat, dusky frame buildings, to participate in sports contests of the Turn Verein, or to take part in dramatic activities. The children study German in the public schools and even hear sermons in German at the German Evangelical Church.

On the Hackensack Meadows (L) the 430-foot transmitting tower of radio station WNEW dwarfs the distant towers of WINS and WFAB.

South of Carlstadt State 2 crosses a crooked section of the old Paterson Plank Rd., still bearing a name outmoded when the decayed planks were replaced by stone 50 years ago.

EAST RUTHERFORD, 19.9 *m.* (60 alt., 7,080 pop.), separated from Rutherford to the S. only by the tracks of the Erie R.R., is an industrial community that grew up around the Paterson Plank Rd. It was formerly called Boiling Springs Township because of a spring that bubbled from the earth.

RUTHERFORD, 20.8 *m.* (100 alt., 14,915 pop.), is a borough without a tavern. Its name was taken from John Rutherford, son of a retired Brit-

THE STEUBEN HOUSE, RIVER EDGE

ish officer but an active patriot and personal friend of Washington. The town was laid out on his land in 1862. Rutherford has a large commuting population, interested in musicales and amateur dramatics. The dilapidated KIP HOUSE *(private)*, 138 Union Ave., was built before 1720. It is a true Dutch Colonial structure of red sandstone blocks, a low and rambling house of several sections in poor condition. Washington once visited this home. The KETTELL HOUSE, 245 Union Ave. *(private)*, built prior to 1716, was the homestead of a 6-acre farm. This house, too, once sheltered Washington. It is a low, smooth-cut red sandstone dwelling, two stories high with a peaked roof that sweeps down to form the roofs of the front porch and the single-story rear extension. The side of the house faces the street.

State 2 turns L. at the entrance to LYNDHURST, 21.8 *m.* (60 alt., 17,362 pop.), an industrial town with a commuting population. Houses of monotonous uniformity are closely packed behind pocket handkerchief lawns. This section, first called New Barbadoes Neck by an early settler from Barbados, changed its name in honor of Lord Lyndhurst, a frequent visitor.

William R. Travers, wealthy New Yorker, built many of Lyndhurst's houses near the Passaic about 1880. He had a summer home and a race track here where August Belmont, banker and sportsman, "Boss" Tweed, the Tammany politician, and others were frequent visitors.

Right (straight ahead) from the entrance to Lyndhurst on Rutherford Ave. to the junction with Oak St., 1.3 *m.;* R. on Oak St., to the GIVAUDAN-DELAWANNA PLANT, 1.6 *m. (open by appointment),* the largest producer of synthetic aromatic compounds in the United States. In a dozen two-story cement buildings aromatics for odorizing perfumes, cosmetics, and toilet preparations are manufactured. Other compounds are used as deodorants in various products such as synthetic textiles and some rubber products, where natural odors are objectionable. Raw materials for the aromatics come from all over the world: civet from a gland of the civet-cat of Ethiopia, ambergris from the alimentary canal of the tropical sperm whale, musk from a pouch in the abdomen of the male musk-deer of central Asia, herbs, roots, resins, and grasses from lands ranging from Singapore to South America.

NORTH ARLINGTON, 24.5 *m.* (130 alt., 8,263 pop.), has a business section of one-story shops and nondescript one- and two-family frame houses. The first steam engine in America was brought here from England in 1753 by John Schuyler to pump water out of his copper mine, and was set up by Joshua Hornblower at a cost of about $15,000. The RUINS OF THE MINES are on Schuyler Ave. 0.2 m. N. of Belleville Turnpike, in the face of a cliff. Much loose earth has fallen into the two entrances and exploration is dangerous. A little farther down the cliff are the remains of a PUMP HOUSE used to work the mine.

The once profitable copper mine was discovered prior to 1719 by a Negro slave on the Schuyler plantation. While plowing he turned up an unusually heavy stone and took it to his master, a Dutch trader and Indian agent of the Province. An assay showed it was 80 per cent pure copper. When the slave was asked what reward he wanted he said: "A lot of tobacco." "What else?" asked the master. "More tobacco and a dressing gown like yours," was the answer. The slave refused freedom. Under British rule, the copper could not be smelted or manufactured in America and was shipped to Bristol in a crude state.

At North Arlington is the junction with Belleville Turnpike, built by Arent Schuyler about 1700.

Right on this road to BELLEVILLE, 0.9 *m.* (185 alt., 26,974 pop.), an old Dutch settlement on the steep bank of Passaic River. At first only the "Second River Section" of Newark, the town became a separate community in 1839. Some of the old houses are still standing along Passaic River, but the back yards of Newark's houses on the opposite shore have destroyed the beauty of the river scene. West of the broad, track-lined main street, which lies on a ledge overlooking the river, are monotonous streets with one-family frame houses of the type built by the thousands after the World War. Second River, the scene of a rear guard action in 1777, is the center of a new park being constructed by the Works Progress Administration. The first low-pressure steam engine made in America was manufactured at a plant in Belleville for John Stevens in 1798. The engine was installed in a boat that ran under steam power down the Passaic to New York. This was nine years before Fulton operated the *Clermont,* but eight years after John Fitch ran a steamboat on the Delaware.

The REFORMED DUTCH CHURCH, SE. cor. Main St. and Belleville Turnpike, built in 1725 and rebuilt twice thereafter, is of brown cut-sandstone. The simple lines of the structure are marred by a vine-covered uncut-sandstone extension. The graceful spire is peppered with Revolutionary bullet holes, hidden by the new layer of shingles.

The SPEAR MANSION *(private)*, 307 Main St., a square, three-story clapboarded building with a one-story extension, was built in 1710. In the stained-glass window above the door is the old street number, 360. Like many other old houses along this street, the dwelling has a glass-enclosed lookout tower.

Right from the center of Belleville to NUTLEY, 2.9 *m.* (238 alt., 20,572 pop.), which occupies part of the borderland of 1776—three low foothills of the Watchung Ridge that reach the Passaic River where "river guards" kept constant watch for enemy raiders during the Revolution. Its main business street still bears the name of William Franklin, last Royal Governor of New Jersey, though the town long ago dropped the name of Franklinville. The ENCLOSURE, a wooded tract set aside as a public park, was the center of a colony of writers and artists after the Civil War. Frank R. Stockton wrote *The Lady or the Tiger?* in his nearby home. Nutley's population more than doubled between 1920 and 1930 as the town became a popular residential suburb.

KINGSLAND HOMESTEAD *(private)*, cor. Kingsland Rd. and Lakeside Dr., was built in 1704 by Isaac Kingsland. In the cellar are a dungeon and chains used to subdue unruly slaves of the mill owner. One and one-half stories high with two one-story wings, it is built of native red sandstone. OLD NUTLEY MANOR *(private)*, north side of Chestnut St. next to Town Hall, was built by Jacob Vreeland in 1702. During the Revolution the owners of the house were British sympathizers, and the property was confiscated and sold to an American officer. The rectangular brownstone building is one and one-half stories high with a gabled roof.

Beneath the surface of the turnpike are the water-supply lines of Jersey City and Bayonne across the Hackensack meadows. There is a tradition that this highway, originally called Schuyler Rd., was built by sailors from the British fleet anchored in New York harbor during the Revolution in order to furnish an outlet for the copper needed in the manufacture of munitions.

The turnpike is the northern border of the ARLINGTON SECTION, a modern suburban residential neighborhood with detached homes and flowering gardens overlooking the Passaic River (R) from a ridge 140 feet high. Green moss on the red rocks is washed by tiny streams that trickle through seams in the ledge. Arlington residents often fail to mention that Arlington is under Kearny's town government Kearny, on the other hand, is proud of the Arlington development as evidence of its growth.

On the eastern slope of the Arlington ridge (L) is the large PYROXYLIN PLANT of the Du Pont Viscoloid Co. *(not open)*, which produces nitrocellulose plastic material for combs, brushes, radio sheeting, novelties, and many ornamental articles. The plant comprises many tiny shops placed at well-spaced intervals to reduce the fire hazard.

At Arlington State 2 follows Kearny Ave.

KEARNY, 25.7 *m.* (120 alt., 40,716 pop.), is known for a large proportion of Scottish residents and for its shipbuilding and other industries. Lying between the Passaic and Hackensack Rivers, the town is fortunately placed for commercial development. The 4-mile-wide meadow area along the Hackensack is being developed into a new industrial section. On higher ground along the highway are Kearny's homes, stores, and civic center.

The town's Scots, who came here originally to work in the mills, are active in the consumer cooperative movement; two retail stores are operated. The Scottish population also patronizes regularly the several fish-and-chips shops.

Kearny was named for Maj. Gen. Philip Kearny, brilliant cavalry officer who lived in the town when he was not fighting. He lost his left arm in the Mexican War, served with France against the Austrians in 1859, and returned to lead the first New Jersey troops into the Civil War. He was killed at Chantilly in 1862.

EAST NEWARK, 26.1 *m.* (20 alt., 2,686 pop.), is the dwarf among boroughs in this region with little room to grow except upward. Carved out in 1895, it is a wedge between Harrison and Kearny, only 2,000 feet long on the Passaic River front and 1,600 feet deep. The river divides the borough from Newark, where many of its industrial workers live.

State 2 follows N. 4th St. through Harrison.

HARRISON, 26.6 *m.* (130 alt., 15,600 pop.), an outgrowth of industrial Newark, is probably the only town of its size in the country that has no motion-picture theater. No ordinance prevents the establishment of a movie, but a $10,000 license fee does. A townsman reports that if any enterprising manager has $10,000 "he ain't came across yet."

Harrison is a machine shop. On the Passaic meadows to the east and south have been raised, among others, the gigantic plants of Crucible Steel, Otis Elevator, Worthington Pump, R.C.A. Radiotron, and Public Service Electric and Gas companies. Built for utilitarian purposes, Harrison has little decoration.

Right on Harrison Ave. (Newark Turnpike) and across Bridge St. bridge over the Passaic River to the junction with McCarter Highway (State 21), 27.2 *m.;* L. on McCarter Highway.

NEWARK, 27.4 *m.* (225 alt., 442,337 pop.) *(see NEWARK).*

Points of Interest: Newark Library, Plume House, Sacred Heart Cathedral, First Presbyterian Church, Newark Museum, Weston Electric Plant, Borglum's Statue of Abraham Lincoln, and others.

Right from Newark on Market St., bearing L. on Springfield Ave., both hard-surfaced highways, to IRVINGTON, 3.1 *m.* (212 alt., 56,733 pop.). In 1852 the town, originally known as Camptown, was named for Washington Irving, who was then at the height of his career. The people of Irvington are faithful sports fans who are as interested in Newark's International League baseball team as they are in their own semiprofessional teams, and in boxing and wrestling. The town was the center of sporting events even 60 years ago when the Irvington-Millburn road race was an annual event of great interest to cyclists. Both population and industry in this manufacturing suburb have a record of constant growth.

The LIONEL PLANT, 28 Sager Pl. *(open upon written application),* is the largest of three factories in the United States producing toy trains for a retail trade. Housed in a one-story red brick building, the company has made electric trains since 1900. In 1937 the output was 400,000 locomotives, 1,200,000 cars, and 568 miles of track. During the pre-Christmas peak up to 1,100 workers are employed. The company's most expensive locomotive is an $85 scale model of the New York Central R.R.'s Hudson type passenger engine, for which the preparatory work, including drafts-manship and the making of a brass model and dies, cost $60,000. This model was designed primarily for the 9,000 men in the United States who are scale-model rail-roaders, indulging in their hobby without the pretext of entertaining a child. Thanks to its manufacture of the Mickey Mouse handcar, the company enjoyed a good volume of business during the depression.

At 29.1 *m.* is the junction with US 1 and US 22 *(see Tours 1 and 2).*

WATER FRONT, PASSAIC RIVER, NEWARK

Tour 17

(Staten Island, N. Y.)—Elizabeth—Plainfield—Somerville—Junction with US 22 and US 206; State 28.
New York Line to Junction with US 22 and US 206, 26.5 m.

Central R.R. of New Jersey parallels the route throughout.
First-class accommodations in Elizabeth; tourist homes and small hotels elsewhere.
Three- and four-lane concrete roadbed.

State 28 runs west from the New Jersey water front through an industrial zone and a series of suburban towns, scenes of frequent clashes in the Revolution when the section was invaded by the British from Staten Island. Along the route at the base of the low-lying Watchung Mountains are many Colonial buildings, a few old mills, and picturesque old churches, though more recent development has largely obscured these survivors of the eighteenth and early nineteenth centuries.

On GOETHALS BRIDGE *(car and passengers 50¢)*, State 28 crosses the New York Line, 0.2 miles west of Staten Island. The route runs straight ahead from the Bridge Plaza over Bayway.

At 0.9 *m.,* at a traffic circle, is the junction with US 1 *(see Tour 1).* State 28 here follows Elmora Ave.

At 1.6 *m.* is the junction with State 27 *(see Tour 8).*

Right on Westfield Ave. to the business center of ELIZABETH, 2.1 *m.* (70 alt., 114,589 pop.) *(see ELIZABETH).*

Points of Interest: First Presbyterian Church, Union County Courthouse Annex (museum), Carteret Arms, Scott Park, Boudinot House, Singer Sewing Machine Plant, and others.

State 28 turns sharply L. on Westfield Ave. at the junction with State S24 *(see Tour 10)* and runs through a suburban section of small homes.

ROSELLE PARK, 3.9 *m.* (30 alt., 8,969 pop.), is largely a commuters' town. At its western end are (L) two BROADCASTING TOWERS used by the General Electric Co. for experiments. They were built in 1916 for testing the Marconi wireless telegraph instruments, made in a factory nearby. Industrial products of the borough are American oriental rugs, iron, and cement.

Left from Roselle Park on Locust St. is ROSELLE, 0.2 *m.* (70 alt., 13,021 pop.). Roselle also has a large commuting population and a few industrial plants. Its main highway, Chestnut St., is bordered by tall trees and modern homes. Opposition and rivalry have for years prevented a close link between the two communities. Thomas Edison for a time had a LABORATORY here in which he installed the first electric lighting plant in the world. Part of the building that housed the plant, Locust St. and First Ave., is still standing. It is a brown, one-story, T-shaped structure, with a low-pitched, tar-paper roof. The building is now an office for a lumber company. The PRESBYTERIAN CHURCH, Chestnut and Fifth Sts., has in its chapel the first electric chandelier that Edison made. Roselle was the first community in the world to have its streets lighted by incandescent bulbs. The SITE OF THE BIRTHPLACE OF ABRAHAM CLARK (1725–1794), one of the New Jersey signers of the Declaration of Independence, is indicated by a stone marker on Chestnut St. (R). The bathysphere used by Dr. William Beebe in his record descent into the ocean was built in Roselle at the plant of the Watson-Stillman Co.

CRANFORD, 6.2 m. (70 alt., 11,126 pop.), is an old residential town spread along the RAHWAY RIVER PARKWAY, a link of nearly 7 miles joining a series of county parks and playgrounds with the Essex County park system. There are facilities for summer and winter sports, a rifle range, and picnic grove. The Fourth of July canoe regatta is an anual affair. Gardens of fine old Victorian houses line the edge of the parkway on the riverbank. A broadening of the river parkway at the northern end of Cranford (R) is known as NOMAHEGAN PARK. The name Nomahegan is a variation of Noluns Mohegans, as the New Jersey Indians were called in the treaty ending the Indian troubles in 1758. It is translated as *women Mohegans* or she-wolves and was applied to them in scorn by the fighting Iroquois.

Opposite Nomahegan Park is 18-hole NOMAHEGAN GOLF CLUB *(greens fee 50¢).*

Westward on State 28 one suburban community merges with the next. Factories are spaced along the railroad (L), and the highway is well lined with dining cars and gas stations.

GARWOOD, 7.3 m. (90 alt., 3,344 pop.), manufactures rubber goods, aluminum products, oils, water heaters, asbestos packing, iron pipe novelties, electric motors, and pencil-vending machines. UNAMI PARK, equipped with picnic fireplaces, is at the southern end of the town. It is named for the Unami clan of Indians.

WESTFIELD, 8.6 m. (130 alt., 15,801 pop.), is a prosperous suburban town with substantial homes, and parks, playgrounds and other evidence of civic spirit. Many of its residents commute to jobs in nearby cities; others are employed in local industries. The PRESBYTERIAN CHURCH, Broad St. and Mountain Ave., is a white frame structure on the site of an earlier building that was the scene of the Revolutionary trial of James Morgan, who murdered the Rev. James Caldwell of Elizabeth *(see Tour 10).* Morgan was hanged on GALLOWS HILL, Broad St. at the northeast side of the town.

On Central and Mountain Aves. is (R) MINDOWASKIN PARK, named for one of three Indians who sold the site to Gawen Lawrie, Scottish deputy governor, in 1684. In an old INDIAN BURIAL GROUND, Broad St. and Springfield Ave., many relics have been recovered, and a few mounds remain. Some of the implements are in the Job Male Library, Plainfield.

The SCUDDER HOUSE *(private),* E. Broad St. opposite Gallows Hill Rd., was headquarters of the American General, William Alexander, during the Revolution. It is a one-and-one-half-story, green-shuttered structure of Georgian Colonial type, its broad side toward the street, with low roof, two dormers, and a small porch. There is a small wing at each end.

Up Mountain Ave. in December, 1776, came in triumph a company of Jersey militia, driving 400 cattle taken from British foragers at Woodbridge. This was the first occasion in this State, as officially reported, when British troops fled from the Americans. Through this hamlet in 1777 General Alexander's division of Washington's army fell back before an attack of the British army, which it had been harassing near Metuchen. Washington was attempting to lure the enemy against his strong position in the Watchung Mts. The British under Cornwallis entered Westfield, but could not be drawn farther.

FANWOOD, 10.7 *m.* (160 alt., 1,681 pop.), has a home-owning population protected by close restriction of business building. The town was named for Miss Fannie Wood, a writer, daughter of a Jersey Central R.R. official. The SPENCE HOUSE *(private),* Martine Ave., built in 1774, was used during the Revolution by American soldiers. A strong room in the cellar with the name "George Washington" carved on a beam is believed to have served as a prison cell. The building has two wings covered with white clapboards, green slat shutters, and a shingle roof. A large red brick chimney has the date 1774 in white brick.

1. Left from the center of Fanwood on Martine Ave. to the RUINS OF A CIDER MILL (L), 1 *m.,* on the grounds of Shackamaxon Country Club. Cider and applejack were produced here as early as 1740 by the builder, Simeon Lambert. A detachment of General Howe's British troops paused here on a June day in 1777, drank three barrels of applejack, and promptly forgot the orders for the day. All returned to Staten Island, leaving the countryside unharmed. The cider mill operated until 1908.

2. Left from Fanwood on Terrill Rd. to the FRAZEE HOUSE *(private),* 1.9 *m.* (R), at the junction with Raritan Rd. It is a low, white, shingled structure on a fieldstone foundation. In Revolutionary times Mrs. Elizabeth (Aunt Betty) Frazee lived here. Found baking bread for Continental soldiers by Lord Cornwallis, she handed him a loaf at his request, saying: "Your lordship will please understand that I give this bread in fear and not in love." Saluting, the British commander is said to have answered: "Not I, nor a man of my command, shall accept a single loaf."

PLAINFIELD, 13.2 *m.* (100 alt., 34,442 pop.), is a busy commuters' town with smart shops and substantial manufactures. Here are all types of dwellings from the huge, French-roofed, high-ceiled Victorian mansion of the 1870's to the most modern Cape Cod-type cottage. The QUAKER MEETING HOUSE (R), Watchung Ave. *(open daily by request on premises),* a plain brick structure with a small burial ground adjoining, was built in 1788. At the MARTINE HOMESTEAD *(private),* 950 Cedar Brook Rd., the banker-poet, Edmund Clarence Stedman (1833–1908), lived as a child. A large part of the white, clapboarded, two-winged house belongs to the original building erected on the same site in 1717.

WASHINGTON HEADQUARTERS *(open daily 10-5),* NW. cor. W. Front St. and Washington Ave., built 1746, was the dwelling of Deacon Nathaniel Drake, a staunch patriot. Washington stopped here while on reconnoitering expeditions into the plains E. of the town. The two-and-one-half-story, white, clapboarded Dutch Colonial building, oldest in the city, is occupied by the Plainfield and North Plainfield Historical Society.

GREEN BROOK PARK, entrance at Plainfield Ave. and W. Front St., extends 1.2 miles along both banks of Green Brook. It was the site of Blue Hills military post, a large earthworks fort guarding the paths to the American stronghold in the Watchung Mts. during the Revolution. CEDAR

BROOK PARK, Somerset Ave. at the southern end of Plainfield, features a SHAKESPEARE GARDEN: trees, flowers, and shrubs found in Stratford on Avon and mentioned in Shakespeare's works have been planted here and labeled. Opposite is the IRIS GARDEN with more than 5,000 plants of 1,200 varieties. Nearby is a large ORCHID GARDEN, and 60 flowering dogwood trees.

DUNELLEN, 16.5 m. (60 alt., 5,148 pop.), was conceived, planned and established (1868) by the Central R.R. of New Jersey. An independent corporation, directed by Jersey Central officials, laid out the streets and sold lots. The borough was incorporated in 1887. Though the derivation of the name is masked by countless theories and smoking-room jokes, the weight of authority rests with the simple solution of Mrs. Emily de Forest, daughter of the president of the railroad at that time. Mrs. de Forest says that her father took the first name of a friend, Ellen Betts, and prefixed the "dun" because he liked the sound of the combination. Mail from the Art Color Printing Co., which prints 10,000,000 copies of Macfadden magazines monthly, gives the small borough a first-class post office. The same concern prints the *World Almanac* and a large quantity of telephone directories.

Left from the center of Dunellen on Washington Ave. and R. on the Stelton Rd. is NEW MARKET, 1.1 m., known in Colonial times as Quibbletown. Baptist residents in 1707 began to disagree on whether the Sabbath should be observed on Saturday or Sunday and the controversy lasted for a century. American soldiers, camped here to watch the enemy, wrote of the place as "Squabbletown." The VAIL MANSION *(private)*, New Market Rd. (L), was built by Duncan Phyfe for Eliza Phyfe Vail, his daughter. Erected in 1814 on a Revolutionary campsite, it is noteworthy for its almost pure Classic Revival lines. The three-story, clapboarded building has four imposing Doric columns. South of New Market is HADLEY AIRPORT, 3.5 m., serving the New Brunswick area. In 1924 it became the first eastern air mail terminus; Newark Airport has succeeded it. Two planes of the Bell Telephone Co., used for experimental radiophone work, are kept here.

At 18.7 m. State 28 crosses Bound Brook or Boundary Brook, named by the Dutch prior to 1656 when they raised the flag of New Netherland here.

MIDDLESEX, 19.5 m. (50 alt., 3,504 pop.), has a number of greenhouses. Several are seen R. of the highway, which parallels Green Brook.

The YOUNG NURSERIES (R), 19.7 m., rank as one of the world's largest producers of orchids and gardenias. More than 500,000 orchids and between 50,000 and 100,000 bunches of a dozen gardenias each are sent out yearly from the 40-acre plant.

At 20.2 m. is the junction with State S28 *(see Tour 13)*.

BOUND BROOK, 20.6 m. (68 alt., 7,372 pop.), has important paint and chemical factories. Wide streets with old houses recall the town of Revolutionary times. To the north are Middlebrook Ridge and Washington's Chimney Rock lookout *(see Tour 2)*. Bound Brook lies along the Raritan River, pathway of early settlers prior to 1664. The river front is now occupied by three trunk railroads, all known as "anthracite roads," linking the Pennsylvania mines with the coast.

The SITE OF A BRITISH RAID is marked by a boulder at Main and East Sts. Near it stood a blockhouse garrisoned by 500 of Washington's troops.

On April 13, 1777, a British force of 4,000 under Cornwallis surprised the sleeping Continentals. Most of the garrison fled to the mountains but 100 were killed or captured.

Left from Bound Brook over the Raritan River bridge on an improved road to SOUTH BOUND BROOK, 0.5 *m.* (68 alt., 1,763 pop.), an industrial town that has grown from a village in which Baron von Steuben was stationed in 1778-9.

The road parallels the towpath of the deserted DELAWARE AND RARITAN CANAL (R), to ZAREPHATH, 3 *m.,* a small community founded by the Pillar of Fire, a religious sect. The society was formed in 1901 by Mrs. Alma White, a Methodist minister's wife, and named for the pillar of fire in Exodus that led the Israelites through the wilderness. The national headquarters and publishing plant were moved in 1908 from Denver to Zarephath, the name of the Biblical village where the widow fed Elijah. At 75, Mrs. White is the prophet of her faith, Bishop of her church and chief stockholder in a religious corporation having 43 temples from London to San Francisco.

The community is situated on an island between the river and the canal where workmen keep the attractively landscaped grounds in excellent condition. Drab three- and four-story structures cluster around the rambling Victorian ADMINISTRATION BUILDING. In a four-story cement-block building, 100 students attend classes of the preparatory school, the Bible Seminary, and the Alma White College. The people who walk the graveled paths do not suggest the "Holy Jumper" designation that nearby inhabitants have applied to their ecstatic worship. The men wear farmers' overalls, while the women are dressed in straight black dresses and the girls in blue ones, with white starched collars and cuffs.

Members of the colony farm the 1.5-mile stretch of land that lines the county road in return for a bed and meatless meals at a communal table. Supplemented by donations, the income from the farm supports the corporation's varied activities. Alma White makes inspirational talks over the corporation's private broadcasting station, WAWZ. She is the editor of *Pillar of Fire,* the society's weekly magazine, which advertises *Jerusalem,* by Alma White; *Looking Back from Beulah,* by Alma White; *Why I Do Not Eat Meat,* by Alma White; *Demons and Tongues,* by Alma White; and *The Story of My Life,* by Alma White.

West of Bound Brook State 28 runs through a peaceful dairying country. The Watchung Mts. recede in a broad curve to the northwest.

At 23 *m.* (L) is the SITE OF A CAMP where part of the Continental Army spent a wretched winter in log huts, with little fuel and food, during the winter of 1778-9. From the crossroad here Washington marched southward in August, 1781, on his way to Yorktown.

At the western end of the campsite State 28 follows Union Ave., then turns sharply L. to Main St. in Somerville.

SOMERVILLE, 25.5 *m.* (82 alt., 8,255 pop.), Somerset County seat, is a small, well-appointed modern town, trading center for a large farming area. The county buildings are at the town square. Its broad main street, now lined with stores and offices, was used nearly 300 years ago by Dutch traders, and, before that, by Indians. In 1846 the first telegraph line between New York and Philadelphia was built along this route.

Somerville was the western terminus of the Elizabethtown and Somerville R.R. In 1842 the first train was put into operation with much pomp and ceremony, including a luncheon of cake and lemonade for the distinguished passengers who hazarded the trip from faraway Elizabethtown at 4 miles an hour. This line later became part of the Jersey Central R.R.

The PARSONAGE of an old Dutch Reformed Church *(open daily 9-5; contributions),* Washington Pl. nr. Jersey Central R.R., a severe brick dwelling built in 1751, is known as the cradle of Rutgers University. The Rev. John Frelinghuysen here established the first Dutch Reformed theological seminary in America, which grew into Queen's College and later Rutgers *(see NEW BRUNSWICK)*. The parsonage was moved to this site from the banks of Raritan River. Opposite is the WALLACE HOUSE *(open weekdays 9-5, summer 9-6; contributions)*, occupied as headquarters by General and Mrs. Washington in 1778 and 1779. A fieldstone foundation supports a large main building and a smaller kitchen wing. The intense whiteness of the clapboards is accentuated by the solid, dark green shutters. The house has typical "witches' doors," with panels in the form of a double cross to keep out witches. The H-L wrought-iron hinges are variously supposed to stand for "Home and Love," "Heavenly Love" and "Holy Lord," but were probably functional in design. The larger wing contains all of the original woodwork and hardware; a fireplace in an upstairs room is framed by pictorial blue and white Dutch tiles. The kitchen wing has the original crane in the huge fireplace, and numerous utensils. What is said to be Washington's campaign trunk lies in the upper hall. Built of wood, it is about 10 feet long with a curved, sheet-iron top banded with iron straps and studded with rough-headed rivets.

The COURTHOUSE, Courthouse Sq., was the scene of the Hall-Mills murder trial *(see NEW BRUNSWICK)*. Opposite is the SOMERVILLE HOTEL, which includes the Tunison Tavern built 1770 by Cornelius Tunison.

At 26.5 *m.* is the junction with US 22 *(see Tour 2)* and with US 206 *(see Tour 6)*.

Tour 18

Junction with US 1—Woodbridge—Perth Amboy—Freehold—Lakewood—Toms River—Tuckerton—Cape May; US 9.
Junction with US 1 to Cape May, 139 m.

The route is paralleled by the Pennsylvania R.R. betwen the Rahway cloverleaf and South Amboy; the Jersey Central R.R. between Matawan and Freehold, and between Toms River and Barnegat; the Tuckerton R.R. between Barnegat and Tuckerton; and the Pennsylvania-Reading-Seashore Line between Pleasantville and Somers Point, and between Cape May Court House and Cape May City.
Adequate accommodations at short intervals.
Two- and three-lane concrete roadbed except for about 15 m. of macadam.

Running south from the metropolitan industrial area, US 9 crosses one of the most productive truck-garden districts in the State, and then enters the pine belt in which the countryside flattens, farms becoming scarcer as the road approaches the shore. The route touches several fishing villages and the gateways to the large seashore resorts. Though never more than a few miles from the series of sheltered bays that provide a channel for the Intracoastal Waterway, US 9 does not come to the ocean until it reaches Cape May City.

At RAHWAY CLOVERLEAF, 0 *m.*, US 9 branches south from US 1 *(see Tour 1)*. The design of this intersection without grade crossings, built as an experiment by the State highway commission in 1928, has been widely imitated.

WOODBRIDGE, 1.1 *m.* (30 alt., 8,331 pop.), a dormitory for hundreds of workmen in nearby factories of Perth Amboy and Carteret and for commuters to northern New Jersey cities and New York, has for almost 100 years been sustained by the clay deposits of the surrounding area. Local pay envelopes depend on the demand for terra cotta, firebrick, hollow tile, and ordinary brick.

The community was settled by 1665 by Puritans from Massachusetts Bay and New Hampshire. In 1751 James Parker established here the first press in New Jersey. His periodical, the *American Magazine,* on sale seven years later, succumbed after two years because of lack of patronage. Parker was fined and even jailed for exercising his right to run a free press.

Transatlantic sailing vessels once docked at Woodbridge, but silt from the claypits has converted Smith Creek into an inconsequential brook. Until the 1880's, Woodbridge was a fashionable watering place. The Arthur Kill is now so polluted by oil and sewage that even gulls avoid it.

South of Woodbridge the road swings past hills scarred by clay digging. The low-lying green hills of STATEN ISLAND are (L) beyond Arthur Kill.

At 2.2 *m.* US 9 bears R., following in turn Convery Blvd., Cleveland Ave., and Convery Pl.

At 3.2 *m.* is the junction with a paved road.

Left on this road to OUTERBRIDGE CROSSING, 1.7 *m. (toll: 50¢ car and passengers) (see PERTH AMBOY).*

At 4.5 *m.* on US 9 is the junction with Smith St.

Left on Smith St. to the business center of PERTH AMBOY, 3.8 *m.* (117 alt., 43,516 pop.) *(see PERTH AMBOY).*

Points of Interest: The Westminster, Parker Castle, St. Peter's Protestant Episcopal Church, Atlantic Terra Cotta Co., and others.

US 9 crosses Raritan River on Victory Bridge. Raritan Bay and Lower New York Bay are L. Beyond is the low-lying peninsula of Sandy Hook rising barely above water level at the foot of Atlantic Highlands; R. along the river banks are brick and ceramic factories.

At 5.9 *m.* the highway swings R. at a large traffic circle, uniting with State 35 *(see Tour 22)*, to by-pass the business district of South Amboy. The hills are bright in patches with the yellow pottery clay that underlies the region.

THE RARITAN RIVER AT PERTH AMBOY

SOUTH AMBOY (L), 6.8 *m*. (70 alt., 8,476 pop.), is also important in the clay industry. Claypits were dug here as early as 1807. The town has been one of the largest railroad terminals for shipment of Pennsylvania hard coal, which is dumped into barges to be towed to New York and New England.

At 7.3 *m*. US 9 separates from State 35 *(see Tour 22)*; R. on US 9.

The road swings south and east in well-engineered curves, crossing ravines and low-lying hills. The scrub woods, a mecca for huckleberry pickers, are broken occasionally by graded roads of yellow gravel and sand.

CHEESEQUAKE, 11.6 *m*. (100 alt., 205 pop.), takes its name from Cheesequake Creek, which, in turn drives its name from the "quaking bogs" along it; the creek, navigable from Raritan Bay, is a good fishing ground. During prohibition it was a favorite retreat for rumrunners whose speedboats, used for shuttling cases of liquor shoreward from the outlying mother ships, were low enough to clear railroad and highway drawbridges —an advantage lacking to the patrol boats, with their radio masts. Coast Guard skippers complained that bridge tenders were unduly slow in answering signals for open bridges.

Rolling eastward through fields of truck gardens and wild flowers and some woodland, the road dips at 14.6 *m.* to cross Lake Lefferts.

At 14.9 *m.* is the junction with a concrete street.

Left on this street is the business center of MATAWAN (Ind., *where two rivers come together*), 0.5 *m.* (60 alt., 2,264 pop.), a wealthy community lying between Lake Lefferts and Lake Matawan. Main St. is a modern thoroughfare, bordered by many houses more than 100 years old, and the FIRST PRESBYTERIAN CHURCH with a tower designed by Stanford White. Matawan's principal factory makes electro-plating supplies; others produce tiles and barrels. The New York and Long Branch R.R. curves sharply to include a station in Matawan because rich local residents bought heavily of stock when the line was planned. The less wealthy people of adjoining Keyport, deprived of the main line station that they had expected, have been sore for about 60 years. It is some consolation to Keyporters that the *Blue Comet* to Atlantic City and other fast trains do not stop at Matawan. The oldest house here is the HAWKINS HOUSE *(private),* Mill Rd., a remodeled Dutch Colonial frame dwelling of two stories, built *c.* 1700. The BURROWES MANSION *(restaurant),* 94 Main St., a three-story white frame house built in 1723, was the home of John Burrowes, the "Corn King," who was captured by the British during the Revolution. The defiance of Burrowes' daughter-in-law during the raid delayed the enemy long enough for her young husband to escape. There are bullet holes on the landing to the attic.

At Matawan on US 9 is the junction (straight ahead) with State 34 *(see Tour 21)* and (R) with State S28 *(see Tour 13).*

US 9 turns R. here and passes through FRENEAU, 15.6 *m.,* a residential and farming section of Matawan. It was named for Philip Freneau, Revolutionary poet and journalist. The FRENEAU FARM *(visitors admitted)* at 16.1 *m.* is easily recognized by two straight rows of maples flanking a driveway (L). The house at the end of the lane was burned and later replaced, but the tiny, clapboarded PRINTSHOP where Freneau published his New Jersey *Chronicle* has survived as an adjunct of the present building. Behind the house, on a knoll overlooking a quiet valley, is the GRAVE OF FRENEAU, marked by a marble shaft. Close by are the old locust trees under which Freneau composed poems and expressions of devotion to the beautiful Eleanor Forman, who was so moved by both that she became his wife. In the last years of his life Freneau lived about two miles from Freehold. Anything but a total abstainer, the 80-year-old poet left the village for his home one night during a blizzard. He fell into a ditch, broke his leg, and died in the snow. That was on December 19, 1832.

BEACON HILL (L), highest of the Mount Pleasant Hills, was one of a closely spaced chain of signal stations used to relay warnings when British vessels approached New York Harbor. The code system was elaborate.

MORGANVILLE, 17.2 *m.* (140 alt.), is a small village in the market garden belt. One 7-acre garden (R), under glass, produces cucumbers, lettuce, beets, and other products for sale in New York.

WICKATUNK (Ind., *place of an Indian house*), 19.1 *m.* (180 alt., 80 pop.), was named by the Jersey Central R.R. when its station was placed here, as a shipping point for a large area in which potatoes are grown.

The MARLBORO STATE HOSPITAL, 20.4 *m.*, a short distance L. of the highway, is one of three State institutions for the mentally ill. Fields on the 1,000-acre tract are worked chiefly by the patients.

MARLBORO, 21.7 *m.* (190 alt., 500 pop.), stands on a slight elevation, with large frame houses comfortably spaced along the highway. At this settlement marl was first used as fertilizer, following the discovery of its properties in 1768 by an Irish settler.

At 25.3 *m.* is the junction with an old dirt road (L) over which the British army under Gen. Sir Henry Clinton retreated to Sandy Hook after the Battle of Monmouth *(see Tour 18A)*.

FREEHOLD, 26 *m.* (170 alt., 6,894 pop.) *(see FREEHOLD)*.

Points of Interest: Monmouth County Historical Association Museum, St. Peter's Episcopal Church, Freehold Race Track, Karagheusian Carpet Factory, and others.

At Freehold are the junctions with State 33 *(see Tour 20)* and Throckmorton St. *(see Tour 18A)*.

Between Freehold and Lakewood is the northern end of the extensive pine belt. In this section there is but a scattering of pine woods with oaks, maples, and other trees of later growth.

LAKEWOOD, 38.2 *m.* (80 alt., 5,000 pop.), once a small settlement built around an iron works, is today dependent on a winter resort business promoted by the dry, temperate climate of the pine district. John D. Rockefeller Sr. had an estate here and there were other costly houses along the shores of Lake Carasaljo. US 9, running through the center of the town, is lined almost solidly with frame and stucco hotels, some of them reflecting in unkempt lawns the business lost in recent years when many wealthy patrons began to take their winter vacations in the South.

Establishment of a smelter in 1812, to utilize bog-iron deposits, gave the town the name of Washington Furnace. Later the community became known as Bergen Works and next as Bricksburg, in honor of James W. Brick, the ironmaster. Two New York Stock Exchange brokers bought 19,000 acres of pine woods in 1879 and built the Laurel House, which entertained Rudyard Kipling, Oliver Wendell Holmes, Mark Twain, William Faversham, Emma Calvé, and other celebrities. It was torn down several years ago.

Around LAKE CARASALJO, with its borders of pines, cedars, and laurel, elaborate cottages and grounds were built by the Astors, Vanderbilts, Goulds, Rockefellers, Tilfords, Kipps, Rhinelanders, and other socially prominent New Yorkers of the '90's. The name of the lake is a combination of Carrie, Sally, and Josephine, daughters of Brick.

GEORGIAN COURT COLLEGE *(visited only by permission)* occupies a 200-acre campus on the northern side of the lake. Originally a Catholic institution for girls in Plainfield, its collegiate division was moved in 1923 to the George J. Gould estate in Lakewood. The buildings are surrounded by sunken gardens, formal Italian gardens, Japanese gardens, and a golf course. Fountains and statuary are lavishly disposed about the grounds. The stables of the estate were so elegantly appointed that it was a simple matter to convert them into women's dormitories.

The NEWMAN SCHOOL FOR BOYS *(open daily 9-5)*, a Catholic institution, occupies two former estates on the lake. The lawn before LOCKE HALL, the central structure, slopes down to a pool surrounded by hundreds of daffodils and narcissi that make a brilliant spring display.

Lakewood is at the junction (L) with State 35 *(see Tour 22)*.

At 38.6 *m.* is the junction (R) with an unnumbered road *(see Tour 26)*.

At the southern end of Lakewood the SITE OF THE OLD BERGEN IRON WORKS (L) is recognizable from the highway.

Between Lakewood and Toms River the highway runs through pine country, though much of the growth is stunted. In the swampy ground by the road are cranberry bogs. Bracken and other common ferns thrive in ditches and beneath trees. The ground is uniformly flat and sandy, drained by sluggish little streams and creeks.

At 40.9 *m.* (R) is a relic of a vanished community, the remodeled inn known as SEVEN STARS TAVERN. The original tavern of that name, a stagecoach station on the Barnegat Bay-Freehold route, received its name after a guest, lying on his couch, was able to count seven stars through a hole in the roof; though the proprietor probably repaired the roof after further complaints, the nickname stuck.

At 47.5 *m.* is the junction with State 37 *(see Tour 30)*.

TOMS RIVER, 48.2 *m.* (20 alt., 3,290 pop.), county seat of Ocean County, is an attractive fishing community on the northern banks of Toms River, a waterway discovered in 1673 by the surveyor, Capt. William Tom. The town is widely known for its excellent clam chowder, always served with ship's biscuit.

The OCEAN HOUSE *(open)*, a large white frame tavern, has dominated the triangular town square since 1787. The earliest building is still in use in the rear. The old inn was a stagecoach stop on the Freehold to Tuckerton run. The OCEAN COUNTY COURTHOUSE *(open weekdays 9-5)*, Washington St., 3 blocks L. of the square built in 1850 as a modified copy of the Hudson County Courthouse, is a small red brick building with the tall classic columns and pediment of the Greek Revival style. It is attractively placed on a wide lawn under great trees. The COUNTY MUSEUM, in the offices of the publicity director, contains Currier and Ives prints, early newspapers, relics, and oddities.

During the Revolution the settlement was a starting point for patriots' raids and its residents were described by the British as "a piratical set of banditti." On March 24, 1782, a band of Tories led by British officers attacked the crude blockhouse, built on a knoll, approximately where the county courthouse stands today. Capt. Joshua Huddy, active in ridding Monmouth County of Tory refugees, was in command of the stockade with a few militiamen. Outnumbered and with ammunition spent, Huddy was forced to surrender. Without a trial, he was brought to Water Witch *(see Tour 36)* and hanged in retaliation for the killing of a Loyalist prisoner by patriots. The execution was directed by Capt. Richard Lippincott, a pre-war neighbor and friend of Huddy. General Washington, sharing the Colonists' wrath, ordered the death of an imprisoned British officer in reprisal, but an apology from Gen. Sir Guy Carleton, plus dissolution of the Loyalists' organization as the war drew near its end, closed the incident. The British burned the town after the attack. It became the county seat when it was later rebuilt.

The vanished Toms River salt works, most important of many plants along the New Jersey shore, were built in 1776 when the supply from England was cut off. Salt water was evaporated, and the thick residue strained and spread out to dry.

Right from the center of Toms River and then immediately L. across the old bridge to SOUTH TOMS RIVER, 1 m. This was in 1837 pioneer ground for the Mormons, who built without nails or other metal a small church that later served as the first Ocean County courthouse. It no longer exists, but there are several Mormon houses and the GRAVEYARD. Joseph Smith, founder of the Church of Jesus Christ of Latter Day Saints, visited the Toms River colony in 1840. Twelve years later his converts here joined their co-religionists at Salt Lake.

South of Toms River, US 9 crosses the river on a concrete and steel drawbridge. The shore (L) is crowded with small docks for fishing craft and pleasure cruisers.

In the pine trees (R) is BEACHWOOD, 49.3 m., a summer colony. A century ago it was the terminal of a mule-powered wooden railway that ran from charcoal-burning pits at Lakehurst to Toms River; stockholders and mules went back to the plow when the coal mines killed the charcoal trade. A few traces of the old railway remain.

At 54.7 m. is the junction with a graveled road.

Right on this road is DOUBLE TROUBLE, 3.5 m., (50 alt.), more a name than a community, in the pine and cranberry country. Nearly 100 years ago an old preacher and his wife lived near the dam that forms CEDAR CREEK LAKE. A colony of muskrats also resided there and about once a week burrowed through the dam. The parson and his closest neighbors repaired the dam time after time. Once the muskrats dug through twice in the same week, whereupon the preacher cried in despair, "Here's double trouble!" The community is active only when the Double Trouble Cranberry Co. brings in migratory workers during the berry season. Cedar Creek has the distinction of rising in the vicinity of Mount Misery, flowing through Double Trouble, and emptying into Barnegat Bay at Good Luck (now Lanoka Harbor).

LANOKA HARBOR, 55.5 m. (20 alt., 213 pop.), was originally Good Luck, then Cedar Creek, and next Lanes Oaks in honor of George Oaks, an old resident. Because the snug little port is hidden from the highway, the publicity-minded townspeople appended the word "Harbor" to the name. A final stage of evolution converted the jerky "Lanes Oaks Harbor" into streamlined "Lanoka Harbor."

At 56.5 m. a sign marks the entrance (L) to MURRAY GROVE (open), birthplace of the Universalist Church of America. Surrounded by oak trees, a small, white frame church still stands in a cemetery, near a brick church of later construction. The white church, rebuilt in 1841, dates from 1766 when Thomas Potter, an old settler, erected it to put an end to his wife's nagging. She resented his habit of inviting every itinerant clergy-

DUCK SHOOTING IN SOUTH JERSEY

man to hold services in the house. Potter's prayers for a minister with liberal views were answered in 1770 when a British vessel grounded on the peninsula across Barnegat Bay. One of the passengers who made their way to the mainland was John Murray, who happened upon Potter and his empty church. So strongly did the young man's beliefs appeal to him that Potter urged his visitor to remain as minister. Some time later Murray became the founder of the Universalist denomination, and the white church was willed to him by Potter. A rough boulder marks the approximate spot where the two men first met. In the church are boxed pews, a balcony, a potbellied stove, and thronelike chairs for those conducting services.

At 57.5 *m.* is (L) the STATE GAME FARM *(open by permission of warden)*. On this 550-acre tract about 15,000 pheasants are reared annually and distributed as game. A 100-acre breeding pond for wild ducks, adjacent to Barnegat Bay, is being built. The WARDEN'S HOME, of early American design, dates from 1784. A finely turned mahogany balustrade, imported from England, leads to the upper floor. The late George J. Gould once offered to pay $700 for the balustrade and supply a replica. The State declined his offer.

FORKED RIVER (pronounced For-ked), 57.8 *m.* (20 alt., 512 pop.), was the home of Gen. John Lacey of Revolutionary War fame. On the L. is the old FORKED RIVER HOUSE, which was the overnight stopping place of Capt. Joshua Huddy *(see above)* on his trips up and down the Jersey coast to inspect the Colonial militia. At Forked River is the RECEIVING STATION *(open 9-5)* of the Bell Telephone System's ship-to-shore service.

South of Forked River the highway crosses the first of three branches of the stream that gives the town its name. A State-maintained YACHT BASIN is close to the road (L). Fishing and sailing parties here find boats and skippers.

WARETOWN (L), 61 *m*. (14 alt., 511 pop.), is a quiet village, the home of retired sea captains and of many who earn their living from salt water. Waretown's most widely publicized resident is Barnegat Pete, a tame deer known to and claimed by every school child for miles around. Pete came into the district about three years ago and has remained to enjoy automobile riding and other pleasures of civilization. He wears a red and white blanket and an identification tag as a protection against hunters.

The place was named for Abraham Waeir, an early settler, who died in 1768. Waeir succeeded John Colver as the local leader of the Rogerenes, a sect founded by John Rogers. They came here in 1737, driven from Connecticut, where they had stirred a commotion by heckling preachers at Sunday meetings. The Rogerenes opposed any Sabbath day observance. During the Revolutionary period they disbanded, but later they appeared in Morris County.

BARNEGAT, 64.4 *m*. (35 alt., 1,100 pop.), has well-shaded old streets with a small shopping center R. of the highway, at the Jersey Central R.R. terminal. The town's name was originally, but never officially, Barendegat (Dutch, *breaker's inlet*). Often the place is confused with the smaller Barnegat City across the bay, where the famous Barnegat Light stands *(see Tour 35A)*.

For generations Barnegat's life has been linked to salt water. The Revolution brought a busy shipbuilding industry and a salt works to the place. The settlement had earlier produced pirates who in whaleboats preyed on grounded vessels lured from their course by false beacons.

MANAHAWKIN, 69 *m*. (25 alt., 825 pop.), is on the site of an Indian village of the same name (Ind., *good corn land*). MANAHAWKIN LAKE (R) is a cheerful foreground for this pleasant village, gateway to Long Beach Island on the ocean. The old BAPTIST CHURCH (R), built in 1758, has served many denominations; the small plain white wooden building has had Victorian additions of two narrow Gothic windows, a circular window in the gable, and a new wide vestibule with a narrow glass door, to belie its actual age. The small steeple is surrounded by a plain low balustrade. The village was the boyhood home of William Newell, Governor of New Jersey (1857–60) and of the Indian Territory (1880). Newell was also the originator of the U. S. Life Saving Service *(see Tour 36)*.

At Manahawkin is the junction with State S40 *(see Tour 35)*.

STAFFORDVILLE, 71.3 *m*. (30 alt.), takes its name from old Stafford Forge, built in 1797 about 2 miles west of the village. The hamlet is the home of farm laborers and a few baymen, who gain a living by clamming and oystering.

WEST CREEK, 74 *m*. (20 alt.), dates back to the Revolution and was a landing place later for supplies for Stafford Forge.

US 9 crosses several creeks draining cranberry bogs a short distance inland. During the summer laurel blooms in the woods on both sides of the road.

TUCKERTON, 76.8 m. (28 alt., 1,429 pop.), on Tuckerton River, is a shopping center for the Little Egg Harbor district. The highway follows the main street, which has a good quota of stores and one hotel. The town was founded about 1699 and by 1702 Friends had constructed a meeting house that was replaced in 1872 by the plain frame MEETING HOUSE in a grove (R), lying directly behind the business center.

In Colonial days Tuckerton was a notable port of entry; flax and molasses formed a large part of the trade. Silkworms were cultivated here and the town is still studded with mulberry trees. British raiders in 1778 burned 30 prize ships here taken by the Americans (see Chestnut Neck below).

US 9 crosses Tuckerton River on a bridge and embankment. A BOAT-YARD, reminder of Tuckerton's shipping history, is L.

At 77 m. is the junction with a graded dirt road.

Left on this road to the ELLEN LEEDS BARTLETT HOUSE (L), 0.1 m. (private). Two low-ceilinged rooms of this simple frame structure were built in 1699; they contain some fine Colonial furniture.

THE HUMMOCK, 2.3 m., is one of the largest shell piles left by the Indians along the Atlantic Coast. It lies in the marshland (R) about 100 yards from the road, and can be identified by several dead or dying cedars rooted in it. The long pile, over-grown with grass and rising some 8 or 10 feet above the flats, was built up over a long period by Indians who came here to get oysters and clams.

At 77.2 m. on US 9 is the junction with a graveled road.

Left on this road to TUCKERTON RADIO STATION, 3.3 m. (not open), transmitting station of Radio Corporation of America for marine messages. From a 600-foot tower umbrella antennae stretch to 10 encircling 300-foot towers, all visible for many miles along the coast. Transatlantic and coastwise marine messages are handled here. Built prior to the World War by German engineers, the station was taken over by the Federal Government before passing into private ownership.

At 83 m. on US 9 is the junction with a graveled road.

Right on this road into BASS RIVER STATE FOREST, 2.3 m., a 10,000-acre tract with excellent deer and duck hunting in season. In Bass River Forest is the remnant of a beaver colony that sought shelter in an abandoned cranberry bog where they found a broken dam once used to flood the bog. They replaced its ruined gate and made a lake of 7 acres.

The highway turns L. at NEW GRETNA, 83.7 m. (10 alt.), formerly known as Bass River. Tradition is that the place was called New Gretna Green prior to 1850 with the idea of making it a marriage center. New Jersey laws, however, proved unfavorable to marriage mills and the name was shortened to New Gretna.

At 85.9 m. US 9 crosses MULLICA RIVER, once famous for its oysters. It was named for Eric Mullica, who led a Swedish colony across the State from the Delaware in 1697.

At 88.3 m. in an unkempt clearing (L) is a tall MONUMENT to the patriots who participated in the Battle of Chestnut Neck, October 6, 1778. Because of highway rerouting the stone soldier on the shaft stands with his back to the new road. Chestnut Neck was an operating base for the

BEACH AT OCEAN CITY

privateers who used small boats for destructive raids on British merchantmen. To destroy the "Jersey pirates," Sir Henry Clinton sent an expedition here that pushed the patriots from their sand-dune fort, burned their village, and proceeded 15 miles up Mullica River to the mouth of Batsto River. Here 50 ironworkers gave such good account of themselves that the 1,500 British troops, believing that they were facing regular Colonial troops under Count Pulaski, retreated to their ships.

OCEANVILLE, 92.2 *m*. (30 alt., 313 pop.), is a country village spread along the highway.

Between Oceanville and Absecon there are occasional glimpses of Atlantic City, seen across Reed's Bay (L) between billboards and hotel signs. What appears to be an overgrown telephone pole just N. of the hotel towers is ABSECON LIGHTHOUSE.

At 95.1 *m*. US 9 swings diagonally R. to by-pass the business sections of Absecon, Pleasantville, Northville, and other communities on the mainland between Absecon and Great Egg Harbor.

At 96.1 *m*. is the junction with US 30 *(see Tour 23)*.

At 99 *m*. is the junction with US 40 *(see Tour 24)*.

At 106.3 *m*., just S. of the OCEAN CITY COUNTRY CLUB golf course *(18 holes; greens fees $2 daily, $1 after 4 p.m., $9 weekly)*, is the junction with a paved road.

Left on this road is SOMERS POINT, 0.7 *m*. The SOMERS MANSION *(private)* cor. May's Landing Rd. and Shore Rd., a wooden structure erected in the late 1700's, is in the Colonial style. A tablet on Shore Rd., north of the house, erected in 1932 by the Children of the Revolution, marks the site of the house in which Richard Somers was born. Master Commandant Richard Somers of the United States Navy, a brilliant young officer who commanded the *Intrepid*, a vessel loaded with explosives, was assigned to destroy the enemy fleet at Tripoli in 1804. Fired upon by the Turks, the *Intrepid* was blown to pieces; Somers and 12 others were killed. One theory is that Somers, fearing capture of his ship, deliberately carried a lighted lantern into the powder magazine. The mansion was recently deeded to the Atlantic County Historical Society as a museum. To Somers Point, known in the Revolution as Egg Harbor, American privateers brought many British prizes.

OCEAN CITY, 3.1 *m*. (5 alt., 5,525 pop.), is a bone-dry city by design of its founder. Since 1879 the community has catered to families from many States who return year after year. Situated on the northern end of one of the New Jersey shore islands, it has the double advantage of quiet inland waters and the ocean. Two inlets on the harbor side are the centers of beautiful residential sections. In the bay, close to the city, tradition says, is the sunken hulk of a Spanish galleon holding a treasure from the mines of Peru. Attempts to find the wreck have been futile.

At 107.1 *m*. GREAT EGG HARBOR is crossed by a long wooden toll bridge and embankment *(25¢ for car and passengers)*.

SEAVILLE, 115.4 *m*. (22 alt.), is a crossroads hamlet.

At Seaville is the junction with State 50 *(see Tour 34)*.

CLERMONT, 120.4 *m*. (20 alt., 309 pop.), was so named in 1886 by the first postmaster, Chester J. Todd, because his brother lived in Clermont, Fla.

At Clermont is the junction with State 49 *(see Tour 29)*.

SWAINTON, 122.5 *m*. (20 alt., 312 pop.), was once known as Townsend's Inlet. Confusion resulting from the development of a nearby community of the same name caused the local postmaster, Luther Swain, to circulate a petition for a new name.

In June, bright red roses are seen on trellises before many of the rather severe white houses on the highway. These structures bear a strong resemblance to the prim dwellings of Connecticut and other New England States that sent Colonists here, but the immaculate white paint and the green lawns of the Connecticut homestead are usually missing.

CAPE MAY COURT HOUSE, 126.5 *m*. (16 alt., 984 pop.), is the seat of Cape May County. The center of town (R) is dominated by the sparkling white nineteenth century COURTHOUSE, now used as a meeting hall. Next to it is the newly built brick COURTHOUSE, in the basement of which is a historical MUSEUM *(open weekdays 8-12, 1-4; Sat. 9-1; free)* with a large collection of miscellaneous relics, curios, weapons, and prints.

BURLEIGH, 129.5 *m*. (18 alt.), named for a Pennsylvania R.R. official, is one of the many communities of southern New Jersey whose residents can testify to one or more visits by the Leeds Devil *(see FOLKLORE)*. The creature is reported to have left his tracks here in snow on porch roofs.

WHITESBORO, 130.2 *m*. (21 alt., 300 pop.), a Negro settlement consisting of small frame houses straggling along the highway, was founded by Henry C. White, a former Negro Congressman from North Carolina.

RIO GRANDE, 132.1 m. (20 alt., 375 pop.), dating back to Colonial times, is at the junction with State S49 *(see Tour 29C).*

The road swings sharply L. and rolls across the flat, open country of the cape. Picturesque craft, sail and motor-driven, anchor in the crowded inlet on the northern outskirts of Cape May City.

CAPE MAY CITY, 139 m. (14 alt., 2,637 pop.), dean of the Jersey shore resorts, is resting after almost a century of catering to the most prominent figures in American public affairs and society. The city does not fret over its loss of patronage; it is content to call itself the Newport of ancient times and to remember the days when Presidents and society matrons talked small talk on the spacious verandas of its nineteenth-century hotels. The three- and four-story rambling frame hotels along the ocean boulevard are in good condition, but the general architecture is of the type seen in *Harper's Weekly* illustrations in post-Civil War years. Tall columns and high windows are characteristic.

Inland are smaller boarding houses, markets, and the gray- and white-painted homes of the all-year residents. On the roof peaks of some of the older houses are railed platforms, the "widow's walk," where the wives of the whalers once watched—sometimes vainly—for the return of the ships carrying their men.

The FIRST FORD AGENCY, 662 Washington Ave., got its first car from Henry Ford when he lost a beach race at Cape May in 1903 and had to sell his car for railroad fare back to Detroit. The car is exhibited.

Cape May's recorded history as a summer resort goes back to 1801 when Postmaster Ellis Hughes advertised in a Philadelphia newspaper: "The subscriber has prepared himself for entertaining company who use sea bathing, and he is accommodated with extensive house room, with fish, oysters and crabs and good liquors." The "extensive house room," according to Jefferson Williamson's *The American Hotel,* was a "great barnlike place said to have been composed of one large room, which was partitioned off with sheets into two rooms at night, the men sleeping on one side, the women on the other."

In their carpetbags guests brought their old clothes to wear as bathing suits. The modish "strip-tease" models were a thing of the future, and mixed bathing, though permitted, was carefully chaperoned. One set of debutantes came to the beach in the custody of an old Negro retainer lavishly bedecked in scarlet cloth and gilt lace, who ducked the girls and shooed off admirers.

Henry Clay, during the summer of 1847, was not so well protected. There was the time when frenzied women admirers of the "Mill Boy of the Slashes" chased him up and down the beach, finally caught him, and with their sewing scissors snipped locks of his hair for souvenirs.

To Cape May came Presidents Lincoln, Grant, Pierce, Buchanan, and Harrison. Horace Greeley, John Wanamaker, countless Congressmen, and wealthy society leaders vacationed here. Some of the descendants of these people still return annually.

The Cape, named for Cornelius Jacobsen Mey who sailed past in 1623

SURF CASTING, CAPE MAY

—14 years after Henry Hudson—was purchased in 1631 by Samuel Godyn and Samuel Blommaert. Into the waters surrounding the Cape came whaling boats, British men-o'-war, and pirates—all attracted mainly by the fresh water supply of LILLY POND, 0.8 *m.* S. on the Lighthouse Rd. to Cape May Pt., a 10-acre sheet of fresh water beautifully dotted with creamy white water lilies. Captain Kidd filled his water casks and supposedly cached part of his treasure near the pond. Col. William Quary unsuccessfully pursued Kidd to this region in 1699. During the War of 1812 British warships watered here until exasperated residents dug a ditch from the ocean to spoil the sweet water. The ditch was filled in after the war and the water gradually became fresh again.

Commodore Stephen Decatur, one of the resort's visitors, measured the rate at which the ocean was eating away the point. His survey indicates that 3 miles of land have been lost within historic time, including that holding two lighthouses. The present LIGHTHOUSE on the Point is a gray tower 170 feet high, with a 250,000-candlepower lantern visible for 19 miles.

Many vacationists carry away geological souvenirs, the "Cape May diamonds" found on the beach. These are bits of pure quartz, rounded by action of the water. They are samples of the vast deposits of glass sand underlying the district.

Tour 18A

Freehold—Tennent—Monmouth Battlefield; County 22 and 3.
Freehold to Monmouth Battlefield, 3.8 m.

Macadamized roads.

The road runs through fairly level farming country to the hillock upon which is Old Tennent Church, with a view over a large part of Monmouth Battlefield.

County 22 branches west from US 9 *(see Tour 18)* at FREEHOLD, 0 *m.* (170 alt., 6,894 pop.) *(see FREEHOLD)*, following Throckmorton St. to MOLLY PITCHER'S WELL (L), 1.4 *m.*, between the railroad and the road. The well is boarded over and shows few signs of care though it has a large historic marker. Three generations have venerated this boxed-in wellhead of wood and stone, though there is much dispute over the location of the original well; some historians say it was buried when the railroad was graded. There is no question, however, that Molly, 23-year-old wife of an artilleryman, carried water to men faint with thirst in the heat of the Battle of Monmouth. The soldiers, hearing her called "Molly" by her husband, called out: "Here comes Molly and her pitcher!" This they shortened to Molly Pitcher, and thus she has lived in history.

She had come here to see her husband and, finding some of the gunners near prostration from the 96-degree heat, had caught up one of the artillery buckets and carried water from a nearby well or spring. Finding her husband disabled and another of the gun crew slain, she seized the swab and worked the rest of the day sponging the gun, keeping up its fire, and giving courage to the entire battery. After the battle Molly was thanked by Gen. Nathanael Greene, speaking for the entire army. Next day, barefooted and in her powder-stained dress, she was presented to Washington. Molly's husband, John Caspar Haye, recovered, and his wife remained with the army until the end of the war. Afterward she lived in Carlisle, Pa.

TENNENT, 3.6 *m.* (131 alt., 150 pop.), is a hamlet of a few houses. It was along this route that Gen. Charles Lee advanced eastward in the Battle of Monmouth, only to fall back in confusion from the British attack *(see below)*.

The route turns R. from Tennent on Monmouth County 3.

At 3.8 *m.* is (R) the MONMOUTH BATTLEFIELD, which has its western boundary at the little hill, well covered with old trees and gravestones, that is crowned by OLD TENNENT CHURCH *(open daily 9 a.m. until sunset; apply to custodian on grounds)*. The plain white building, shingled with cedar, was built in 1751 to replace an earlier structure erected

1731. A small spire rises from the high gable in front, topped with an early Dutch weathercock. Within is an old-fashioned pulpit with overhanging sounding-board, high-backed, narrow pews, and a gallery that was reserved for slaves. From the time-worn communion table David Brainerd is said to have given the Sacrament to Indian converts. George II, in 1749, chartered the congregation, now oldest of the Scotch Presbyterian groups in this area. The church was first called Old Scots Meeting House and later the Old Freehold Church. In 1859 it was renamed in honor of one or both of its earlier ministers, the Rev. William Tennent and the Rev. John Tennent, his brother. William, a strong supporter of the Colonial cause early in the Revolution, died in 1777 and is buried beneath the center aisle.

Surrounding the church is the CEMETERY in which many of the men who fell in the Battle of Monmouth are buried. Among the graves is that of Lt. Col. Henry Monckton, a fine British officer. From the hill is a far view of the surrounding farms and woodlands. Down the southward slope and across the dirt road are the whitewashed buildings and pens where local farmers hold their annual harvest home festival in the last week of July. Sloping away to the southeast for nearly 3 miles is Monmouth Battlefield, extending to Freehold on both sides of the railroad.

Washington's army of about 15,000, marching to intercept Clinton's army of about equal strength, reached this point on a hot Sunday morning, June 28, 1778. The troops had emerged from the hills after a long period of inactivity following the winter at Valley Forge. The tide was then turning; France was sending a strong fleet to aid the Colonists, and the British government, alarmed, had ordered General Clinton to abandon Philadelphia and reinforce New York. For 10 days Clinton's army had been moving slowly across New Jersey with a 12-mile baggage train, heavy with plunder. To protect his supplies, Clinton had placed his main army behind the wagons and ordered the train to move on toward Sandy Hook, where British vessels were waiting.

Word of this maneuver reached Washington at Englishtown *(see Tour 20)* at 5 o'clock Sunday morning. He immediately ordered the advance guard under Gen. Charles Lee to attack, "unless there should be powerful reasons to the contrary." With 5,000 men Lee advanced to Briar Hill, about 1 mile north of Freehold, where the Americans saw the great baggage train fleeing with its escort along the Shrewsbury road. Finding the escort stronger than he had expected, Lee hesitated. Meanwhile the British picket guards repulsed an attack by Lafayette's cavalry; and when the horsemen fell back, the American infantrymen retreated in some confusion to the woods, most of them without firing a shot.

Turning on his pursuers, Clinton drew part of Knyphausen's men from the baggage train to his aid and advanced over the ground yielded by Lee's infantry and artillery. For almost 3 miles the Americans withdrew, reaching a point 0.7 miles southeast of Tennent Church, where they were met by Washington advancing with the main army. Rallying the retreating troops, Washington reformed the entire army into a long crescent, separated from the British by marshes.

OLD TENNENT CHURCH, NEAR FREEHOLD

Although biographers have represented the hot-tempered Washington as a man who abstained almost wholly from profanity, there are varying reports as to the General's exact words when he reprimanded the retreating Lee. General Knox, himself a hard-swearing soldier, was perhaps influenced by his own memory when, after the war, he said of Washington: ". . . Yes sir! He swore that day till the leaves shook on the trees. Charming! Delightful! Never have I enjoyed such swearing before or since. Sir, on that memorable day he swore like an angel from Heaven!"

Clinton first attacked the American left, but Lee's men with Stirling's artillery drove the British back. Then Clinton tried the American right, and was repulsed by General Greene's troops and Knox's artillery on Combs Hill. Finally the British grenadiers pushed toward the center into the deadly crescent. Here they were caught by the fire of "Mad Anthony" Wayne's riflemen, hidden by a barn, and by artillery fire from both flanks. Lieutenant Colonel Monckton, the grenadiers' commander, fell here with his men lying in heaps behind him.

A counter-attack was at once prepared by Washington, but darkness compelled a delay until morning. At midnight the British moved silently from their camp, leaving 44 of their wounded at Freehold. Their departure was not discovered until daybreak; Washington then decided that his men were too exhausted by the battle and by sweltering marches through sandy country to make pursuit practicable. He reported that the British left 249 dead on the field; the American dead he numbered at 69. Clinton made a smaller estimate of his dead. Undoubtedly the heat killed many on both sides.

To guard against another British effort to cut off New England from the other Colonies, Washington took his army north to the banks of the Hudson. Clinton reached Sandy Hook safely and embarked for New York. The Colonists everywhere were encouraged by the Americans' success in forcing the British regulars to retreat, yet the battle was not decisive.

General Washington, who for some time had been suspicious of Lee's loyalty to the Revolutionary cause, had Lee court martialed and dismissed from the army for his conduct in this battle. Lee's traitorous activities could not be proved, however, and many Americans felt that Washington had been unduly harsh. In 1855 a document was found that confirmed General Washington's suspicions. The document, in Lee's handwriting, was a plan for the conquest of the colonies, which had been prepared for Howe, the British commander in chief.

Tour 19

Junction with US 1—Hightstown—Camden—Pennsville—(New Castle, Del.); US 130.
Junction with US 1 to Pennsville Ferry, 87.9 m.

The Pennsylvania R.R. parallels the route between the junction with US 1 and Deans; the junction with State 33 and Burlington; and Paulsboro and Penns Grove. Usual accommodations throughout.
Two- and four-lane concrete or macadam roadbed in excellent condition; heavy freight traffic at night.

US 130, branching south from US 1 on the southern edge of New Brunswick, crosses the State northeast to southwest, avoids the congestion around Trenton and Philadelphia, and passes through more varied and attractive country than does the heavily traveled US 1. Small communities in the northern section retain much of the flavor of the days when the Dutch and the English made the first settlements here. Farms and woodlands lie all along the highway but, in the flatter countryside between Camden and Pennsville, corn shocks and trees alike are scarcer, and broad creeks and marshes are numerous. Between Bordentown and Pennsville, US 130 parallels the course of the Delaware River; tall chimneys of factories along the riverbanks are seen at intervals.

US 130 branches south from US 1 *(see Tour 1),* 0 *m.,* on the southeastern edge of New Brunswick. Several hundred feet R. stands the red and white steel tower of an airway beacon.

DEANS, 5.3 *m.* (85 alt., 200 pop.), in the center of farming country, still has pasture land on one of the corners at the intersection, with an old-fashioned red barn not far beyond.

DAYTON, 7.5 *m.* (117 alt., 390 pop.), was named for Jonathan Dayton of Washington's staff, who was later a delegate to the Constitutional Convention of 1787, a brigadier general in the United States Army, and one of the founders of Dayton, Ohio. The little village is an important shipping point for potato growers. A blacksmith shop and, in season, crowded corncribs and haystacks accent the rusticity. Many old houses are along the road in this region. Windmills have water tanks midway in their towers, an arrangement typical of the seacoast region.

At 11.1 *m.* is the junction with a concrete road.

Right on this road is CRANBURY, 1.4 *m.* (110 alt., 1,278 pop.), a center of a potato-growing district. It has early-American charm, plus such earmarks of more recent development as an apartment house and a Lions Club. The main street is lined with old frame houses, some of them converted into stores, others the homes of retired farmers. The post office is almost concealed within the bulky MASONIC HALL (L). Cranbury was settled in 1682 and here, 50 years later, David Brainerd, the young follower of George Whitefield, often preached to the Indians under one of the village elms. After his death of tuberculosis in 1747 at the age of 29, Brainerd's diary was an inspiration to many another "witness to the spirit."

On the northern edge of the town is (R) the L. P. CURTIN HOUSE, easily recognized by the white frame walls and the iron grillwork on the porch. Aaron Burr slept here in 1804 while fleeing from New York to Philadelphia after wounding Alexander Hamilton in the fatal duel. In summer the blossoms of the giant lotus on BRAINERD LAKE form one of the county's most beautiful spectacles. South of the lake is CRANBURY INN, a long, large, white frame house with a porch across the front. In 1780 the inn began to supply meat and drink to travelers on what was then the old York Road. Two of these wayfarers were Washington and Hamilton. The well-proportioned FIRST PRESBYTERIAN CHURCH, built in 1734, is painted an immaculate white; it has two fluted columns and a graceful lantern. In the well-kept cemetery behind the church, dates from 1758 are on the gravestones.

The highway by-passes Cranbury (R) through fields and across the eastern end of Brainerd Lake (R).

At 13.7 m., at a traffic circle, is the junction (R) with Cranbury's main street and a concrete road (L).

Left on this road is HIGHTSTOWN, 1.5 m. (100 alt., 3,012 pop.), a busy market place for the surrounding farm country with several small factories. The entrance to the town from the north is attractive, with grand old willow trees grouped on the shore of PEDDIE LAKE (L), and an ornate stone FIREHOUSE (R). Houses erected before 1800 are scattered about the village among buildings of later construction. Elaborate iron grillwork ornaments the porches of some of the old houses. The SARAH B. SMITH HOUSE *(private)*, 137 Stockton St., just behind the railroad station, was built in 1770, and in 1819 became the community's first post office. A modern touch is given Hightstown by the small concrete obelisks that serve as street markers.

Founded in 1721, the town was named for John Hight, an early landowner and miller. In 1834 it became a station on the Camden and Amboy R.R., the first railroad built in New Jersey. The PEDDIE SCHOOL is a private preparatory institution for boys, established in 1864. Eighteen buildings serve approximately 260 students, and the fine campus of 148 acres includes a private golf course.

Left from N. Main St. on Etra Rd. to JERSEY HOMESTEADS, 6.5 m., built as a project of the Resettlement Administration in 1935. Two hundred houses, built of cinder-concrete blocks, with flat overhanging roofs, and provided with air-conditioning, oil furnaces, and other modern equipment, are in horseshoe-shaped groups. Covering 1,200 acres in rolling, partly wooded country, Jersey Homesteads is a combined agricultural and industrial community, designed to move union needle-trades workers from the tenement districts of Philadelphia and New York. The colony is organized on a cooperative basis. Each family contributes $500 to a general fund to finance the equipment and operation of a women's clothing factory, and contracts to buy a home with a long-term mortgage. A 414-acre farm is part of the experiment. Net profits will be divided equally among all residents—factory workers, farm workers, and clerks in the cooperative stores. One purpose of the project is to show that an industry hitherto concentrated in the slum and sweatshop areas of large cities can be decentralized, and that its workers can improve their own living conditions by cooperative methods. It is expected that the school and other public property will be deeded over to the incorporated (1937) community. The well-designed modern factory will be purchased from the government. A notable feature is the COMMUNITY BUILDING, a low, flat-roofed, brick and concrete structure designed by Alfred Kastner in the modern International style. The design of the building is characterized by a vigorous treatment of the horizontal mass and an effective concentration of detail. There is ample fenestration and free use of structural glass brick.

Providing both recreational and educational facilities for the community, the building has a large community hall and gymnasium, a library, spacious classrooms, and a nursery. Of special interest are the hammered aluminum entrance doors, their low-relief figures modeled by Lenore Thomas and executed by Otto Wester, and the bright murals in the lobby executed by Ben Shahn. The murals picture a brief history of the Jewish people—their escape from Old World oppression and their toil to better working conditions in the New World. On the grounds are a wading pool and play areas.

South of the traffic circle US 130 by-passes Hightstown (L).

At 17 m. is the junction with State 33 *(see Tour 20)* which is united with US 130 between this point and Robbinsville.

WINDSOR, 18.9 m. (100 alt., 250 pop.), was named by the English who settled here about 1714. A row of old-time frame houses (L) lines the main street, but more conspicuous than those is the weathered brick GENERAL STORE (L) that for more than 100 years has served the large outlying farm district. Beyond the well-worn porch with iron posts is an interior redolent of rural life of a century ago. One display cabinet is filled with all kinds and colors of threads; another is stocked with spices. Both the cabinets and the wooden counters are even older than the potbellied stove in the center of the store.

Vineyards and nurseries thrive on the rich loam of the region, but potatoes are by far the most important crop. Prosperous farms show modern improvements and equipment, contrasting with weathered snake fences.

ROBBINSVILLE, 22.4 m., a small village off the highway (R), was once known as Hungry Hill because wayfarers found it hard to obtain food there. English Quakers settled the land in 1750; the village took its name from George Robbins, an early resident.

At Robbinsville State 33 *(see Tour 20)* separates (R) from US 130.

The business district of YARDVILLE, 25.4 m. (60 alt., 920 pop.), is a few hundred yards from the highway (R). A rubber mill and a floor-covering factory are the principal manufacturing establishments. The village, formerly called Sand Hill, was the point where passengers on the pioneer Camden and Amboy R.R. left the train to be shuttled by stagecoach to Trenton; in 1850 the name was changed to honor the first postmaster. Many inhabitants now commute between Yardville and Trenton.

At 25.6 m. is the junction with a macadamized road.

Left on this road is CROSSWICKS, 2 m. (85 alt., 275 pop.), a rural community "where every man joins the volunteer fire department when he reaches 21, and every woman joins the Ladies Auxiliary." Established by Quakers early in the 1680's, it is the only community with that name in the United States. Just as important to the inhabitants as the Fourth of July or Armistice Day are three annual dinners and fairs which everyone, no matter what his religious preference, attends. One is given by the Philanthropic Society of Friends in April, another is sponsored by the Crosswicks Community Association at the time of the grammar school graduation, and the third is given by the Methodist Congregation in October. The buildings supported by each of these organizations are grouped together in the town center. The METHODIST CHURCH, a tall, gray-painted frame structure, is directly across from the two-story, buff-colored frame COMMUNITY HOUSE, built in 1930. The CHESTERFIELD FRIENDS MEETING HOUSE, erected in 1773 partly with bricks from an older structure, is a two-story building of mellowed red brick set in the center of a huge yard, enclosed by a low cement-block wall. Wagon sheds, now painted white, and a red brick building, built in 1784 and used until recently as a school, are in the rear. Trim little double entrances and white shutters set off the easy grace of the building, that served as a barracks and hospital for Hessian soldiers who fought a battle with the Colonial troops at Crosswicks June 23, 1778. During the battle three cannonballs struck the church; one is still imbedded in the north wall. During the

Hicksite-Orthodox split in 1827, the meeting house was divided by sliding panels to accommodate both groups. The CROSSWICKS OAK, which measures more than 17 feet in circumference, shades most of the southwest corner of the yard. A plaque on the trunk states: "This tree was standing when William Penn arrived in America in 1682."

At 27.9 *m.* is the junction (R) with US 206 *(see Tour 6).* US 130 and US 206 are united for 0.6 miles.

At 28.3 *m.* is the junction with a marked, paved road.

Right on this road to BORDENTOWN, 0.5 *m.* (65 alt., 4,400 pop.) *(see BORDENTOWN).*

Points of Interest: Bonaparte Park, Bordentown Military Institute, Hopkinson House, Clara Barton School and others.

At 28.5 *m.* US 206 *(see Tour 6)* separates (L) from US 130.

The NEW JERSEY MANUAL TRAINING SCHOOL, 29.3 *m.* (R), is a State institution giving agricultural and industrial training to about three hundred Negro boys and girls. There is a small tuition fee. Part of the responsibility of the large teaching staff is to find employment for graduates of the school.

The Delaware River is visible (R) at 29.8 *m.* The land here is a low-lying plateau, slightly undulating, with ravines and shallow valleys cut by creeks on their way to the river.

At 32.7 *m.* is the junction with a concrete road.

Right on this road to ROEBLING, 1 *m.*, a company town established by John A. Roebling, founder of the large steel-cable factory known to engineers all over the world for its part in building Brooklyn Bridge and in supplying cables for George Washington Bridge, the Golden Gate Bridge and other big suspension bridges. Workers of Hungarian and other central European nationalities have long been employed in the plant. Viewed from US 130, the outlying fringe of company houses making up the town seems in keeping with the worst slum traditions. Closer examination partly disproves this, as some of the dwellings are of modern construction; all are of substantial brick, and the streets have been carefully planted with trees. Old-fashioned solid row construction has, however, made windows impossible except at front and back, and there is an atmosphere of somber monotony about the town that is in no wise lessened by the inherent ugliness of the mill buildings and the wasteland around them.

The highway here follows almost a straight line, avoiding the curves of the Delaware River, 2 to 3 miles R.

At 36.9 *m.,* where US 130 turns (L) to by-pass the city of Burlington, is the junction with a concrete road.

Right (straight ahead) on this road is BURLINGTON, 1 *m.* (10 alt., 10,844 pop.) *(see BURLINGTON).*

Points of Interest: James Lawrence House, James Fenimore Cooper House, West New Jersey Proprietors Office, Old St. Mary's Church and others.

At 41.5 *m.* is the junction (R) with a side road to Burlington. South of this point is the peach orchard section of Burlington County, where blossoms attract thousands of visitors each spring.

At 43.2 *m.* is Rancocas Creek, largest tributary of the Delaware River in this region. US 130 crosses the creek on a drawbridge now little used but suggestive of the busy traffic in lumber and charcoal that once passed here.

CHESTERFIELD FRIENDS MEETING HOUSE, CROSSWICKS

William Franklin, the ardent Tory son of Benjamin Franklin and last Royal Governor of New Jersey, had an estate on the banks of the creek.

BRIDGEBORO, 43.5 *m.* (20 alt., 500 pop.), lies on the south bank of Rancocas Creek, with a cluster of stores and frame houses L. of the highway.

CINNAMINSON, 47.2 *m.* (80 alt., 100 pop.), once had its provocative name on a postmark, but mail is now handled through the post office at nearby Riverton. To nurserymen and entomologists Cinnaminson is known as the initial port of entry of the Japanese beetle. In 1916 the first of these brightly colored beetles appeared in the community, unrecognized as the parent of countless billions of pests. The insect was probably imported as a grub, concealed in soil packed around the roots of Japanese iris. Only a year later the U. S. Department of Agriculture established the Japanese Beetle Laboratory, and ever since then Federal and State experts have waged continuous war on the destructive insect by quarantine rules, poison sprays, and the importation of parasitic enemies. Although the area of heavy infestation has a radius of scarcely 100 miles from Cinnaminson, stowaway beetles have traveled by automobile and train as far N. as Maine and as far W. as Missouri, settling new colonies there and at scores of way stations. Motorists should beware of hitchhiking beetles, especially during July and August when they are most numerous.

At the junction with a macadam road is the FRIENDS' MEETING HOUSE, a pleasant little red brick-building erected in 1859. It stands on a shaded knoll, back from the road (L).

At 48.6 *m.* is the junction with State S41 *(see Tour 37)*.

South of this junction the highway enters the Camden suburbs. The section is not very attractive, though Camden's backyard is better than the average outlying district of a manufacturing center.

At 51.6 *m.* is the junction with Cove Rd., a concrete highway.

Right on this road to ARLINGTON CEMETERY, 0.6 *m.*, with the GRAVE OF PETER J. McGUIRE, known as the "Father of Labor Day." The grave, marked by a 6-foot polished granite tombstone, is 225 yards north of the cemetery entrance. On Labor Day of each year it is visited by scores of workingmen and leaders of organized labor. During the 1870's McGuire carried on a one-man campaign for the 8-hour day and a national holiday for the workingman. In 1875 he made his home in Camden and later he organized several unions. With Samuel Gompers, he helped form the American Federation of Labor in 1881. Because of his success in settling strikes he became known as the "Great Arbitrator." Congress in 1894 finally declared Labor Day a national holiday and in succeeding years the Nation moved nearer to McGuire's goal of "8 hours for work, 8 hours for play and 8 hours for rest, and $1 an hour for skilled labor." McGuire died in 1906.

At 54.2 *m.,* Airport Traffic Circle, are the junctions with State 40 *(see Tour 27)* and State 38 *(see Tour 26)*.

US 30, States 42, 44, and 45 here unite with US 130 in the route south.

At Airport Traffic Circle is also the junction with Admiral Wilson Blvd.

Right on this boulevard to the business district of CAMDEN, 2 *m.* (25 alt., 118,-700 pop.) *(see CAMDEN)*.

Points of Interest: Friends School, Johnson Park, RCA-Victor Manufacturing Plant, Campbell Soup Plant, Walt Whitman House, Joseph Cooper House, Charles S. Boyer Memorial Hall (museum), and others.

By the traffic circle is (L) Camden's CENTRAL AIRPORT, a stop for four transcontinental lines and the terminal for Philadelphia traffic. Planes of Eastern Airlines, United Airlines, American Airlines, and Transcontinental and Western Air are scheduled (1939) for a total of 47 landings daily. The 220-acre field was established in 1929. The ADMINISTRATION BUILDING is a one-story, L-shaped structure of stucco, with a low roof. Two hangars are mostly of glass, with concrete columns. Philadelphia, no more pleased with the necessity of using a New Jersey airport than is New York by its dependence upon Newark Airport, plans to establish its own terminal.

South of the airport US 130 by-passes the business centers of suburban communities and twists through a succession of traffic circles.

At 55.1 *m.,* at a traffic circle, US 30 branches (L) from the route.

At 56.3 *m.* State 42 branches (L) from US 130.

At 58.7 *m.,* at a traffic circle, is the junction with State 47 *(see Tour 33).*

At 58.8 *m.* at another traffic circle, is the junction with a paved road.

Right on this road through Brooklawn to GLOUCESTER, 0.6 *m.* (10 alt., 13,796 pop.), a manufacturing city with a predominantly Irish population. Although most of the workers are employed in Camden and Philadelphia shipyards, others produce paper and cardboard, gas heaters, textiles, dairy products, and lumber in local plants. The well-paved streets run between rows of two-story houses, most of them frame structures needing the service of carpenter or painter, but a few standing out with all the freshness of new paint or recently laid brick. In Highland Park, the newer residential section, plain but attractive frame houses are set back on terraced lawns with abundant shrubbery.

Gloucester was the site of the first white settlement on the east bank of Delaware River. In 1623 Capt. Cornelius Jacobsen Mey, Dutch explorer, built Fort Nassau close by at the mouth of Big Timber Creek. Ten years later the colony of 24 men and women had vanished and the site was repossessed by the Indians. When the Swedes established a colony a short distance down the river, the Dutch restored the fort, only to abandon it once more. A permanent settlement got under way with the arrival of Irish Quakers in 1682. The vicinity of Gloucester was designated as the Irish Tenth when West Jersey was divided for the Proprietors *(see HISTORY).*

A Colonial courthouse and jail were erected in the growing village. During the Revolution several important skirmishes were fought in and around Gloucester. In subsequent years the town was outstripped in growth by its neighbors, although it enjoyed a brief renaissance in the late nineteenth century when Billy Thompson operated a race track, and a saloon was busy on every corner—and a number in between. Local ordinances now prevent Sunday sale of liquor until after the churches close; other and much older ordinances provide imprisonment and fine (half the fine to be paid to the informer) for playing baseball on Sunday, for reckless driving at 5 miles an hour, for wearing bathing clothes that do not cover the body from neck to knee, and for throwing dead cats and other animals into streets or alleys. Enforcement of these laws, however, is unheard of.

GLOUCESTER POINT PARK, New Jersey Ave. and King St., was occupied in November, 1777, by Lord Cornwallis and 5,000 British troops supported by the British fleet. The REMAINS OF THE AUGUSTA, a British frigate sunk after the Battle of Red Bank *(see below),* lie close to the retaining wall in the northwest corner of the park. Upon the retaining wall above is mounted a cannon from the ship. Under a sycamore tree near this spot a low marker of polished granite designates the MEETING PLACE, where the Proprietors of West Jersey have assembled annually since Colonial days to discuss their property interests. The SITE OF HUGG'S TAVERN, in the park where it stood for 179 years, is marked by a monument built of bricks from the old structure, razed in 1929. The tavern was the headquarters of the Revolutionary Committee of Correspondence of Gloucester County. Later, Cornwallis used it.

The U. S. IMMIGRANT STATION *(not open)*, S. King St. adjoining Gloucester Point Park, is headquarters for immigration and naturalization activities in southern New Jersey, Pennsylvania, Delaware, West Virginia, and eastern Ohio. Many criminal aliens are deported from this station upon their release from any of the 118 penitentiaries and jails in the area of jurisdiction, which is the largest in the United States. The ADMINISTRATION BUILDING is a white-painted clapboarded and shingled building of three stories with an irregular slate roof and two towers that do not match. This was the castle of William J. Thompson, who made a fortune out of shad-fishing, went into politics, built a race track, and became widely known as the Duke of Gloucester—a picturesque figure of the gay '90's, gone like the shad fishery. Planked shad, a local dish of excellent flavor and innumerable bones, is still served in season, however, at one local restaurant. The shad is attached to a short piece of board and roasted before an open fire.

The former WASHINGTON MILLS *(not open to public)* Ellis St. at the water front, cover two blocks with a four-story brick structure, divided at the center by a roadway to the river. There are four towers in front; a tall fifth tower at the center is ornately decorated. The textile mills were established in 1844 by David S. Bowen, a Philadelphia drygoods merchant. For many years the venture was successful, but competition from New England mills ultimately spelled failure. The machinery was sold to Japanese manufacturers and in 1924 the building was converted into a warehouse for cork.

At 59.4 *m.* State 45 branches (L) from the route *(see Tour 28)*. US 130 here branches (R) from the broad lanes of concrete to become an ordinary two-lane highway. There are frequent views of the Philadelphia skyline (R) along this section of the road. The countryside gradually loses its suburban spirit and once more becomes a region where the stubbly brown fields are in autumn spotted with bright pumpkins and yellow field corn.

A strange collection of concrete end-walls, sole remains of one-story buildings that formerly covered several acres, is standing on the pasture land (R) at 60 *m.* This was the SITE OF THE WOODBURY BAG LOADING PLANT, where gunpowder was packed for shipment overseas during the World War. Directly across the channel of the Delaware River are the tall cranes of the PHILADELPHIA NAVY YARD. When motors are being tested there, the wind carries their roaring to the Jersey shore.

At 62.2 *m.* is the junction with a concrete road.

Right on this road to RED BANK BATTLEFIELD NATIONAL PARK, 2 *m.* Here, on the high bank at the edge of Delaware River, stood Fort Mercer, hastily built in the fall of 1777 to prevent the British fleet from joining the land forces that had occupied Philadelphia. Before the earthworks had been completed by 400 Rhode Island volunteers, a surprise attack was made from the rear by 2,000 Hessian troops. Under Col. Christopher Green, Americans, many of them Negroes in rags, held their fire until the Hessian battalions swept up to the base of the ramparts; then they unleashed a hail of musketballs and grapeshot at such close range that wadding was driven into the faces and breasts of the attackers. With 400 dead and wounded, the Hessians fell back, reformed their lines and charged again. They were again repulsed and their commander, Count Donop, was captured, mortally wounded. As the "rented" soldier lay dying he said, "I die a victim of my ambition and the avarice of my sovereign." Meanwhile, American guns mounted on barges were hurling shots into the British fleet. Although the battle at Fort Mercer lasted barely half an hour, the naval engagement was continued the next day, October 23. Two British vessels, the 64-gun *Augusta* and the 18-gun *Merlin,* took fire and blew up. Fort Mifflin on the Pennsylvania side held out against the British fleet until

November 11, but it was finally pounded to pieces. Washington, unable to spare enough men for its defense, later abandoned Fort Mercer. Some of the old trenches have been reconstructed, and around a STATE MONUMENT are three cannon, long buried and finally discovered with a radio detector.

The only building nearby is the old stone and brick WHITALL HOUSE *(adm. 25¢; resident custodian)*, maintained by the Daughters of the American Revolution in honor of a Quaker dame whose nonchalance during the battle set an all-time record for even the calm folk of Gloucester County. Ann Whitall was busy with her spinning in an upstairs chamber when the battle began. Balls whistled past the gables; finally, one shot blasted its way through the wall and hurtled across the room into the opposite wall. The Quaker lady picked up her spinning wheel and went to the cellar, continuing her work until the battle ended and wounded men were brought to her house. While she bound up the wounds of Hessian soldiers, she scolded them for coming to America to butcher the Colonists. The house is excellently preserved, and in one of the two rooms containing Colonial furnishings is Mrs. Whitall's spinning wheel. Near the Whitall house is a PICNIC GROVE, with the usual accommodations.

The highway passes through level valley lands, utilized to a large extent for asparagus growing. Rows of cedar trees mark farm lanes and boundaries. Several tidal creeks are crossed.

PAULSBORO, 66.2 *m.* (15 alt., 7,121 pop.), lies west of Mantua Creek. A large oil refinery, a fertilizer works, a Du Pont paint factory, and some smaller industries make it a manufacturing center. The highway follows Broad St., along which are the stores and other business houses. Paulsboro has operated a MUNICIPAL GAS PLANT since 1909, apparently to the satisfaction of its voters since they have rejected a proposal to sell it. The plant is one of a scant dozen public-owned utilities in the State. In 1935 its receipts were $40,200, more than enough to defray all expenses and to cover $13,205 for interest charges and retirement of bonds.

The town dates back to 1681, when 250 colonists settled in the section. Philip Paul, for whom the settlement was named, arrived in 1685. His family Bible is kept in the BOROUGH HALL (L). In LINCOLN PARK on the water front (R) are the ruins of an old cellar. Shortly after the Revolution the house that stood here was occupied by a gang of counterfeiters, producing bonds and money worth even less than the Continentals then in circulation. When Government men raided the house, the ringleader stood at the top of the stairs and, hoping to gain time while his wife burned the counterfeits in an adjoining room, threatened to shoot the first man to come up. The Federal men saw through the ruse; there was no shooting.

GIBBSTOWN, 69.4 *m.* (10 alt., 208 pop.), is mostly a double row of frame houses, lacking the distinction of either Colonial or modern construction. Here live many of the workmen employed in one of the largest Du Pont high explosive plants, the town's main industry.

Du Pont pay envelopes are, in fact, the most important single source of income for residents of the entire section between Paulsboro and Pennsville. Although Wilmington is the capital of this industrial dynasty, operations have been extended across the Delaware River to an extent that affects the life of every town and hamlet in the river section. Many Pennsylvanians come by boat to work in the New Jersey factories making war materials, explosives, paints, dyes, and other Du Pont products.

At 73.1 *m.* is the junction (L) with US 322 *(see Tour 25)*. US 130 and US 322 are united for 0.7 miles.

BRIDGEPORT, 73.5 *m.* (20 alt., 850 pop.), has cornfields extending almost to the back door of a line of old and not unattractive houses on the main thoroughfare (R). The community is sufficiently large, however, to support an automobile sales agency and other business houses.

At 73.8 *m.* US 322 separates (R) from US 130.

Right on US 322 to the CHESTER (PA.) FERRY, 1.5 *m.* *(24-hour service May 30 to Oct. 1; 50¢ for car and driver, 5¢ for each passenger.)*

At 73.9 *m.* US 130 crosses Raccoon Creek, with dyked banks and broad marshlands. The earliest white settlers in this region, the Swedes, entered the territory by this creek about 1670 and founded the village of Swedesboro 5 miles upstream *(see Tour 25)*. During the Revolution, Cornwallis landed a force of 5,000 men here for a march north to attack the American fortifications at Billingsport and Red Bank.

Making few curves, the highway runs through a rather dreary section of lowlands. Farms and farmhouses are not numerous. The late afternoon sun glints more brightly on the shining aluminum paint of oil storage tanks across the river at Chester than on the still waters of the tidal marshes.

South of Oldman's Creek, the DELAWARE ORDNANCE DEPOT of the United States Army (R), a typical Army reservation in neatness and landscaping, borders US 130 for a mile. Established during the World War, the depot is still used for storing shells of both large and small caliber. One ordnance company numbering about 50 men is stationed here, and there are many civilian employees.

PENNSGROVE, 81.2 *m.* (12 alt., 5,895 pop.), is the southernmost town of consequence along the New Jersey shore of the Delaware River. The community has a motion-picture house, a bustling shopping district, and a large residential section. By situation and common industrial interests, Pennsgrove is closely linked with Wilmington, Del., across the river. *(All-year ferry service leaving Pennsgrove hourly 6 a.m. to midnight; car and driver 75¢, passengers 5¢ each. Messages received for patrons.)*

CARNEY'S POINT, 82.6 *m.* (10 alt., 3,050 pop.), is a southerly extension of Pennsgrove. A large colony of uniformly painted green and white frame houses (R) gives a key to the village's industrial life. These are Du Pont-owned dwellings, built as emergency shelters during the World War and since then improved for rental to employees. A Du Pont powder plant is situated nearby.

DEEPWATER, 85.1 *m.* (10 alt., 537 pop.), has two important plants, a Du Pont dye works and a power plant of the Atlantic City Electric Co.

At Deepwater is the junction (L) with US 40 *(see Tour 24)*.

PENNSVILLE, 87.6 *m.* (12 alt., 412 pop.), was once known as a center for sturgeon and shad fishermen, but pollution of the Delaware waters by waste from upstream industries has practically destroyed the fishing. Today the little village is chiefly a ferry terminal and another residential section for Du Pont workers. An amusement park, RIVERVIEW BEACH, is complete with roller coaster and swimming pool. The region around Pennsville was settled by Swedes after 1640.

Right from the center of Pennsville to the PENNSVILLE FERRY 87.9 *m.*, to New Castle, Del. *(24-hour service all year; car and driver 75¢, passengers 10¢; messages received and delivered for patrons.)* As the ferry moves from its Jersey landing, the low shore line of Delaware is seen ahead, scarcely broken by the roofs and spires of old New Castle. Wilmington, up the river (R), is indicated by a smudge of smoke from its many factories.

At Pennsville is the junction with a hard-surfaced unnumbered road *(see Tour 29).*

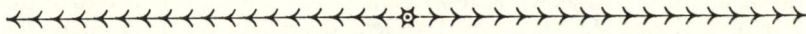

Tour 20

Ocean Grove—Freehold—Hightstown—Trenton; State 33.
Junction with State 4N to Trenton, 43.3 m.

The Pennsylvania R.R. parallels the road between Jerseyville and Freehold and between Hightstown and Yardville.
Good accommodations.
Modern 3-lane concrete roadbed.

State 33 runs west across the State between the ocean shore and Delaware River. It traverses a belt of sandy soil with scrub growth and thin settlement, then the rolling hill country and prosperous farmlands of Monmouth, the State's leading potato area, and scene of the Battle of Monmouth. At the western end are Trenton with its industrial and suburban district, and a number of small villages dating from the early Quaker settlements.

State 33 branches west from State 4N *(see Tour 36)* at OCEAN GROVE, 0 *m.* (20 alt., 1,182 pop.) *(see Tour 36).*

At 0.7 *m.* is the junction with State 35 *(see Tour 22)* at NEPTUNE CITY, 1.4 *m.* (30 alt., 2,258 pop.) *(see Tour 22).*

At the western end of Neptune City is the FITKIN MEMORIAL HOSPITAL (R), two imposing buildings in the dignified Georgian Colonial design of red brick and white decorations. Beyond is a group of stucco houses, kennels, nurseries, and (R) the ASBURY PARK GOLF AND COUNTRY CLUB *(18 holes; greens fee 75¢ to $1 weekdays, $2 Sat. and Sun.).* Jumping Brook, a tributary of Shark River, is crossed in an area where larger residences dot the rolling country.

HAMILTON, 4 *m.* (100 alt., 400 pop.), is a small, sunny old town on a hillside, almost entirely R. of the highway. Prior to the Civil War it was known as Greenville; during the Revolution it was called Trap because of the 200-year-old TRAP TAVERN *(private)* at the fork in the road (R). It is a large, plain, two-and-one-half-story weatherbeaten box with a patched clapboard front and shingled ends. Like many Colonial houses it was built exactly facing the four points of the compass and is not square with the road. Trap Tavern was so named because during the Revolution local men invited suspected British spies for a convivial evening here. They were plied with liquor, inveigled into the cellar, and locked up until the militia could take them prisoners. The tale is told of one patron named Slocum who had a rendezvous with death and kept the appointment. Slocum, a heavy drinker, was lifted into his wagon night after night, and his horses took him home. Suddenly, he stopped drinking, saying that in a dream the devil had told him he had just one year to live. The year passed in total abstinence. On the anniversary Slocum stopped at the Trap, had one drink, and drove off alone. A few minutes later several men arrived at the tavern, declaring they had heard violent quarreling on the road in the darkness. Next morning Slocum was missing. A searching party found the place where Slocum's horses had gone over an embankment into the mill-pond. The man's body was in the water, tangled in the reins. People still say that the devil did it.

West of Hamilton are many log tourist cabins in a flat country of sand and pines.

Shark River, crossed at 5.9 *m.,* is well known as an excellent crabbing spot, but no shark has been seen in recent years.

At 6.4 *m.,* at a traffic circle, is the junction with State 34 *(see Tour 21).* State 33 and State 34 are united for the next mile.

At a complicated overpass and underpass, 7.5 *m.,* State 34 *(see Tour 21)* separates (R) from State 33.

The highway runs through a sparsely settled country, with occasional picnic groves, to Marsh Bog Brook, 9.4 *m.,* where once flourishing cranberry bogs have been overgrown by weeds.

State 33 descends into a region of stunted oak and pine growth.

At SHACKS CORNER, 10.2 *m.,* is the junction with a graded dirt road.

Left on this road to a graveled highway; R. on this highway to OUR HOUSE TAVERN (R), 2.5 *m. (open),* an old inn said to have been built in 1684. It is a rambling structure built around a two-room section that was the original tavern. One step leads from the road to the broad porch, shaded by three great old trees. Wide lawns adjoin the building; flowering plants are in window boxes. Tradition is that a notorious leader of the pine robbers, named Fenton, was found at the inn by Monmouth County militiamen during the Revolution. Fenton, responsible for many killings, was promptly shot; his body was taken to Freehold and hung from a tree near the courthouse as a warning to outlaws. Another pine robber is said to have lived in a nearby dugout known as Fagin's Cave, which remains as a shallow depression in a dense thicket on the farm of George Patterson, 1 *m.* south of the tavern. Many treasure-hunting parties have combed this area, trying to find plunder supposed to have been buried by the outlaws. The tavern, once an important stage stop, has served as meeting place for courts, election boards, the township committee, and country dancers.

Scattered farms on a broad, flat area are encircled by woodland. A small stream seems appropriately named Killtime Brook.

JERSEYVILLE, 12 *m.* (50 alt., 40 pop.), a small hamlet known until 1854 as Green Grove, is in the midst of almost denuded timberland.

The sandy, flat country west of Jerseyville, where farmers raise good crops of corn and potatoes, is drained by many small streams flowing south to the Manasquan River. Ahead is the first view of the spires of Freehold, rising above the great trees of its wide streets. Farmhouses give way to suburban homes as the road crosses Debois Creek and the Pennsylvania R.R. tracks on a high bridge.

FREEHOLD, 15 *m.* (170 alt., 6,894 pop.) *(see FREEHOLD).*

Points of Interest: Monmouth County Historical Association Museum, St. Peter's Episcopal Church, Freehold Race Track, Karagheusian Carpet Factory, and others.

At Freehold is the junction with US 9 *(see Tour 18),* just S. of the business center.

At 16.2 *m.* the highway passes the southern edge of the MONMOUTH BATTLEFIELD *(see Tour 18A).* A marker relates that Washington established hospitals at Old Tennent Church, its parsonage, and Monmouth Courthouse. Recent research indicates that Tennent Church sheltered only one wounded soldier, while St. Peter's Church in Freehold was a hospital for both forces.

This is a district of apple and peach orchards, a cheerful sight for travelers in spring.

At 16.8 *m.* the road crosses a branch of Wemrock Brook. Right of State 33 and east of the brook the British artillery was placed, facing the American cannon west of the stream, both close to the site of the present road *(see Tour 18A).*

West of the brook State 33 rises on the slope of COMB'S HILL, about 80 feet above the stream. This hill (R) was the ground occupied by the American right wing under Gen. Nathanael Greene, supported by the artillery of Gen. Henry Knox.

At 17.5 *m.* is another branch of Wemrock Brook with an OLD MILL (R). The pond, popular with anglers, is the property of the Wemrock Fishing Club.

MILLHURST, 18.8 *m.* (120 alt., 125 pop.), is a hamlet of some half-dozen houses and a new brick schoolhouse in rolling open country. Close by is the MILLPOND (L) and the tumbled old MILL RUINS from which the place took its name.

Between Millhurst and Manalapan is excellent farming country, a rolling panorama of large farms, each house on its own shaded knoll overlooking fertile acres.

MANALAPAN (Ind., *good cultivation*), 22 *m.* (50 alt., 40 pop.), was the center of an area where the Unami, or Turtle clan of the Lenni Lenape had their homes when the white men arrived. There are few houses in Manalapan today. MANALAPAN INN *(private),* a drab old building at the crossroads (R), suggests by its small windows and good construction that it saw the Revolution and was a center of hospitality in stagecoach days.

Right from Manalapan on an improved road is ENGLISHTOWN, 4 *m.* (70 alt., 797 pop.), where Washington made his headquarters, June 27, 1778, the night before the Battle of Monmouth. The building he used for a council with his officers was the HULSE HOUSE, Main St., in the center of the village. Washington slept in the house, then the home of Dr. James English, the night before the battle. It is a low, two-story affair of severe Colonial design, with gables. The broad front has two doors and the gray tinge of age hides the original white. A great elm behind the house, under which the Commander in Chief is said to have sought seclusion, is known as the WASHINGTON ELM. The VILLAGE INN, west side of Main St. *(open)*, built in 1732, is long and narrow, with white clapboards and dark red shutters. An old pump set in the sidewalk is still in use. On the eve of the battle the American officers held a conference in the inn while their men passed the warm night sleeping in the surrounding fields. Here also Maj. Gen. Charles Lee, after the battle, wrote the letter which, together with his conduct on the field, led to his court martial and dismissal from the Army *(see Tour 18A)*. In the dining room Washington drew up the three charges on which Lee was tried. Relics of the battle are exhibited in two rooms of the inn. Three entrances lead from the long porch supported by square posts.

Englishtown was the home of Charles H. Sanford, nineteenth-century financier who was a pioneer in the development of Argentina. His gifts to his native village were a recreation field, a church, and the public library. He also provided the trust fund from which historic Tennent Church is maintained *(see Tour 18A)*. Englishtown is still the home of Harry Herbert, who began playing polo on the family farm many years ago and became the father of American polo.

At 24 *m.*, at a sign marking the Monmouth-Middlesex County line, is the junction (L) with a graded dirt road *(see Tour 20A)*.

Westward the highway passes old farms with broad potato fields and well-kept fences and buildings. Near Hightstown, church steeples and the buildings of Peddie Institute are seen ahead.

State 33 follows Franklin Ave. in Hightstown, passing florists' greenhouses and the plain residences of the town's outskirts.

HIGHTSTOWN, 28.7 *m.* (100 alt., 3,012 pop.) *(see Tour 19)*, is at the junction with the old Route US 130 *(see Tour 19)*.

At 30.6 *m.* State 33 forms a junction with the new route US 130 and unites with this route to Robbinsville.

At ROBBINSVILLE, 35.2 *m.* (130 alt., 125 pop.) *(see Tour 19)*, State 33 separates (R) from US 130.

Between Robbinsville and Trenton State 33 is lined with many roadstands and gas stations. The light soil is farmed to some extent, but the industrial and suburban belt of Trenton is steadily absorbing old farmlands.

HAMILTON SQUARE, 37.8 *m.* (100 alt., 1,558 pop.), was originally known as the Crossroads in Nottingham Township, and later was called Nottingham Square. The name was changed in 1842 to honor Alexander Hamilton. The town's industries include sanitary pottery, rubber goods, and radiators.

MERCERVILLE, 39 *m.* (90 alt., 164 pop.), clings to its rural character despite its proximity to Trenton. The settlement was once known as Sandtown and later as Five Roads. The present name honors Gen. Hugh Mercer, fatally wounded in the Battle of Princeton.

West of Mercerville, State 33 passes suburban homes whose residents are employed chiefly in Trenton industries.

At 40.8 *m.* (R) are the NEW JERSEY STATE FAIR GROUNDS with a long grandstand, race track, pens for displaying animals, and buildings for other exhibits of the State Fair, held annually during the last week in September.

At the fair grounds State 33 swings L. following Greenwood Ave. Right from Greenwood Ave. on Clay St. to Stockton St.; R. on Stockton St. to corner of E. State St. at the City Hall.

TRENTON, 43.8 *m.* (55 alt., 123,778 pop.) *(see TRENTON).*

Points of Interest: State Buildings, Library and Museum, Old Barracks, Mahlon Stacy Park, First Presbyterian Church, Bloomsbury Court, Bow Hill, Lenox Potteries, and others.

Tour 20A

Junction with State 33—Imlaystown—Fillmore; unnumbered roads. Junction with State 33 to Fillmore, 13.9 m.

Macadamized and graded dirt roads; latter soft and slippery in wet weather. Restaurant in Clarksburg.

This route, following a zigzag course southward through one of the best-ordered sections of New Jersey dairy country, is highly recommended for those who wish to see a part of the State untouched by tourists, with a few spots of more than ordinary historic interest that, unsung and unadvertised, will probably not survive many years. It is an area of millponds, but no factories; of dirt roads, but no railways; and of amazingly large barns and solid frame houses, but practically never a bungalow.

The junction of the dirt road with State 33, 0 *m. (see Tour 20),* is at the Monmouth-Middlesex County Line, identified by a metal sign on State 33, 9 miles west of Freehold and 4.7 miles east of Hightstown.

Through fairly level farming lands the narrow dirt road runs S. Lone cedars mark field boundaries; occasional clumps of silver birches lighten the woodland stretches in the leafless months.

At 2.2 *m.,* at the junction with a macadam road, stands a typically handsome farmhouse (R), a low frame building with white clapboards and with simple white posts supporting the porch roof.

The route continues L. on the macadam road.

PERRINEVILLE, 2.7 *m.* (150 alt., 175 pop.), named for an old family once prominent here, consists of two grocery stores, a synagogue, and an old red GRISTMILL (L), where the roadway forms the mill dam. The pond stretches back into wooded ravines. The road takes an S-shaped course through the handful of farmhouses, some offering accommodations for travelers, that comprise the rest of the village.

Howard Patterson, who is custodian of the schoolhouse, recalls the time when he tried to shake hands with the Jersey Devil. "It was a foggy night," he relates, "when I saw him all aglow, just a few feet off the road. I walked right up and put out my hand. Found an old tree trunk with two knotty arms, lit up with fox fire." The Jersey Devil, it should be noted, conventionally appears as a sort of winged creature with no more illumination than is provided by an occasional fiery snort *(see FOLKLORE)*.

At 3.4 *m.*, a crossroads, the route turns R. on a macadam road and over the hill to higher ground. This is poorer farming country, with wrecks of yesterday's automobiles and rusted farm machinery littering the yards; with iron bedframes serving as gates, and outhouses flaunting three or more varieties of roofing paper. A sky-blue mailbox and a daffodil-yellow house with blue trim offer examples of unregimented rural choice of pigments. Woods are thicker, with pines and patches of mountain laurel by the roadside.

At 6 *m.* is the junction with another macadam road.

Left on this road is CLARKSBURG, 0.3 *m.* (200 alt., 300 pop.), a small settlement in which the most imposing structure is BARNEY'S INN (R), advertising whisky and beer. This well-built and well-kept white, clapboarded hostelry has a row of squat, fluted concrete columns across the front, a regrettable afterthought. REDMEN'S HALL (L), unpainted for generations, is of enough local importance to be pictured on post cards sold at the adjoining GENERAL STORE AND POST OFFICE. The post-card rack is found well to the rear; at the entrance are piled rolls of roofing paper, galvanized iron buckets, axes, and a vast tray of arctics and hip boots. The most important customer of the post office is a local philatelist who gets scores of first-day covers and buys commemorative stamps by the sheet.

At 6.1 *m.*, high above the road level, is the rotting frame of WILLOW TREE TAVERN (R), built in 1781 and until recently used as a residence. Of rigidly plain lines with a recessed porch, the tavern was a stopping place in its early years for the four-horse coach between Philadelphia and Long Branch. The lower floor, then unpartitioned, served as a communal bedroom for men, women travelers being assigned to rooms upstairs. Joseph Bonaparte, with a retinue of French servants, was a guest. Old residents still relate that Bonaparte required his servants to taste every dish set before him, so afraid was he of being poisoned. Formerly on winter days farmers of the neighborhood hitched their fastest horses to sleighs and raced to Allentown, where the last man in paid for drinks. Then, fortified for a second heat, they raced back to the old Willow Tree, where the loser treated again. Thus the years passed until 1865, when the tavern was renamed the Temperance House. Shortly afterward it entered upon a decline that ended with its sale in 1878 for use as a private home. Handmade bricks laid between the studs are revealed where clapboards have been loosened. The interior, musty with the litter left by its last occupants, still has a corner cupboard, a boarded-over fireplace with a simply cut mantel, and a few hinges and other early hardware. Floors sag, and several layers of wallpaper are peeling away. Anyone who enters may play *Stealing,* the last record left, on a cabinet-size phonograph that stands by the fireplace where Benjamin Franklin once warmed his hands.

LINCOLN FORGE, FILLMORE

At 6.4 *m.* is the CLARKSBURG METHODIST CHURCH (R), a neat white frame building erected 1845.

Climbing gently, the road skirts a narrow valley (R), with a view of the tree-topped ridge to the N.

At 8.1 *m.* is the old LINCOLN HOUSE (R), advertised by its proprietor, Viktor Jadowski, as "a historical place, over 200 years old." Much of the historic flavor has been smothered by the dining-room extension built around the original dwelling. Mr. Jadowski, formerly chef of the Piping Rock Club on Long Island, has subordinated his interest in Lincolniana to the more vital business of feeding wayfarers; he has established no connection between the restaurant and Lincoln, and almost certainly there is none.

Two hundred yards directly up the hill behind the house, however, is COVEL HILL CEMETERY, accessible by a grass-grown lane. Seventy-five feet past the whitewashed gate, almost within the shade of a solitary hickory tree, is a small mound marked by a chunk of red fieldstone. The roughly carved legend reads: "Deborah Lincon, Aged 3 Y 4 M., May 15, 1720." Deborah was the child of Mordecai and Hannah Lincoln, great-great-grandparents of the President. Imbedded on the mound is a broken mayonnaise jar, one of the few signs of decoration in this weed-grown plot.

At 9.3 *m.* stands a rectangular brick building with a slate roof, adjoining a graveyard (R). This is the old EAST BRANCH MEETING HOUSE, dated 1816 on a marble block above the entrance but said to have been reconstructed in that year. Every door and window is securely locked or bolted; ivy has grown for many years over the boarded-up windows, and the stump of a sapling in the porch explains why one post is askew. The building, however, is in excellent condition, despite the unevenly baked bricks. An unusual architectural detail is the double door, with a single row of panels on the left door and a double row of panels on the right.

Banks along the road here are overgrown with honeysuckle. Neatness and prosperity stamp the large dairy farms standing at intervals of half a mile or so.

At 9.9 m. a milk platform and six houses comprise the settlement long known as COX'S CORNERS. A bronze tablet on a granite marker (L) relates that the Cox family dealt honorably with the Indians, fought in the Revolution, and constantly defended civil and religious liberties; the Coxes don't live here any more.

Left at Cox's Corners on the oiled side road.

Southward, the road takes an almost straight course to the edge of Imlaystown, where it turns L. to the main street.

IMLAYSTOWN, 11.2 m. (110 alt., 129 pop.), is a piece of the nineties—or even the sixties—preserved along one of the narrowest and crookedst main streets in New Jersey. Old residents say that the street follows the pattern of an Indian village that once stood here, on the banks of Doctor's Creek. The statement that local people can sit on their porches and shake hands with visitors who sit in their cars must, however, be discounted. Most of the houses are of plain gray or white frame construction; of special interest is the BARBER SHOP (R), an ordinary dwelling with the corner porch post neatly striped, and for good measure decorated with gold stars. The rest of the town's commercial life is handled by a garage, a poolroom, a gristmill, and the P. J. Malsbury GENERAL STORE AND POST OFFICE (R), at the triangle. The store has, outside, a hitching bar, little used, and an old pew from the Methodist Church that is frequently used as a resting place for observers of the Imlaystown scene, including five multi-hued cats.

From the bench is an excellent view of traffic at the triangle, of the bare exterior of TOWNSHIP HALL across the street, of barnyard geese on IMLAYSTOWN LAKE, and of business transactions at the adjoining mill, where cow and hog feed are ground by water power. The present building replaces one destroyed in the great fire of 1898. Prior to that time, Mr. Malsbury says, "the mill always operated ever since there were any mills." Modern improvements, such as furnace heat, have changed the character of the general store; but it is obviously the pulse of the community. Imlaystown has no justice of the peace and no policeman. "We could get a State trooper if we ever needed one," the residents explain.

Buck Hole Creek, an insignificant stream, joins Doctor's Creek at Imlaystown. Two thousand acres in the basins of these creeks were the manorial holding of Richard Salter in the early 1700's. It was Salter's only daughter, Hannah, who married Mordecai Lincoln.

Left from the Imlaystown triangle on County 26, a macadam road, to the junction with a graded dirt road at 2.4 m.; L. on this road to YE OLDE YELLOW MEETING

HOUSE, 3 *m.*, erected 1737 on land donated by Mordecai Lincoln's father-in-law, Richard Salter. The two-story frame building, well preserved and sheltered by veteran oaks, looks much like a plain farmhouse with front and back porches removed. A side door is kept unlatched so that anyone may try out the white box pews or climb to the large balcony in the rear. There are two other entrances, the doorstep for each being half of a millstone. It is still a yellow church—albeit a faded yellow—with blue shutters of varying designs. Descendants of the Baptist builders attend services in a newer church, more conveniently situated in Imlaystown. On the last Sunday in each July, however, members of the congregation and others of the neighborhood turn out for all-day preaching, interrupted only by a picnic lunch, at the old church. The large carriage shed has no tenants even on this day, for everybody comes in automobiles. A graveyard with an interesting variety of headstones and verses adjoins the building. Two black slate stones are dated in the early 1720's. Many of the graves have footstones shaped at the tops to match the curving pattern of the headstones.

Crossing the MILL DAM on Doctor's Creek, the dirt road runs S. through gently rolling farm lands. Signs for Cream Ridge should be followed.

Right at 12.2 *m.* at the junction with a dirt road.

Left at 12.8 *m.* at the junction with a dirt road.

Between this point and Fillmore the road takes an up-and-down course, almost in a straight line and usually between well-kept worm fences. Many of the old posts are capped with verdant bouquets of poison ivy. Crossing an iron bridge over Schoolhouse Brook, the road climbs slightly and ends at the junction with another dirt road.

FILLMORE, 13.9 *m.,* has one point of interest: the old LINCOLN FORGE at the junction (R). It is a small building, about the size of a two-car garage on a city lot, and it is, incidentally, used now for a garage by the tenant of the farmhouse next door. Three of the walls are of rough, red stone masonry, a full 18 inches thick; an end wall and the roof are of wood, recently built. Some two centuries ago the little stone shop housed the forge of Mordecai Lincoln (or Lincon), great-great-grandfather of Abraham. Mordecai was born in Massachusetts in 1686 and married Hannah Salter, a New Jersey girl. The young couple settled in this neighborhood early in the eighteenth century; the site of their dwelling has apparently been lost. A son, John, was born in 1716. He was the great-grandfather of the President.

A few of the old wooden-pegged beams remain, and there is an iron ring imbedded in the masonry that has been used to hitch horses by many generations of farmers. No tools of the blacksmith's trade are left, although the shop was maintained until about 40 years ago; Joseph Haley was the last proprietor. Inside is a sawhorse and a pile of stovewood. Bantam chickens feed from ears of field corn near the door. People who live in the half-dozen houses that comprise Fillmore know the story of the old shop, but a mile or so away the farmers and the farmers' wives have never heard of Lincoln's ancestor.

Fillmore was known in the early 1800's as Varmintown, probably because foxes and other small animals were plentiful in this area.

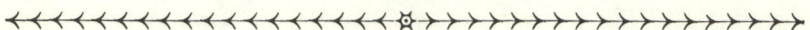

Tour 21

Matawan—Colt's Neck—Junction with State 35; State 34.
Matawan to Junction with State 35, 27.6 m.

Oil stations and lunchrooms plentiful.
Three-lane concrete roadbed of recent construction.

Designed as a short cut to the Jersey coast, State 34 avoids all but the smallest villages. The highway, running southeast, traverses a rolling agri‑ cultural region that once supplied much of the wheat for New York City's bread, and now yields chiefly potatoes, grapes, and other fruit. There are many apple orchards, as in Colonial days, supplying the cider and apple‑ jack industry for which New Jersey is well known.

State 34 branches southeast from US 9 *(see Tour 18)* at Main St., MATAWAN, 0 *m.* (62 alt., 2,264 pop.) *(see Tour 18)*, south of the business section.

The road shapes its course to the rolling farm country. With orchard‑ studded hills and broad fields and meadows drained by many brooks, the land has an air of assured prosperity. Farm homes and buildings are sub‑ stantial, even elaborate. Road stands offer produce raised nearby.

At 5 *m.* is the junction with a hard-surfaced road.

Left on this road is HOLMDEL, 0.7 *m.* (100 alt.), one of the oldest settlements in Monmouth County. The name is derived from the Holmes family, leading land‑ owners, and descendants of the Rev. Obadiah Holmes, who came from England in 1638 and became pastor of the Baptist Church at Newport, R. I. in 1676. This vil‑ lage, with its one main street lined with venerable elms and maples, was the original Freehold and bore that name probably 75 years before the present Freehold. The name was changed afterward to Baptistown. The old BAPTIST CHURCH, built in 1705, partly rebuilt in 1809, and remodeled in 1893, is on the right side of the short main street. A squat, faded buff building surmounted by a square belfry and a short spire, it is built close to the ground on a foundation scarcely visible. Each of its long, wide, shingled sides has three stained glass windows. At the BELL LABORATORIES STATION, Long Street Rd. *(not open to public),* radio reception is studied in conjunction with a station at Deal. Here sounds of mysterious origin are sometimes received; scientists trace their source to a point somewhere near the cen‑ ter of the Milky Way.

On the eastern edge of Holmdel (L), upon a commanding knoll, lie the exten‑ sive MACCAMPBELL VINEYARDS *(open daylight hours daily)* of former Assembly‑ man Theron MacCampbell. Wine and jelly grapes are shipped in carload lots. A table displays choice varieties of grapes. Back of the display area is a natural amphi‑ theater among tall oaks, known as The Forum, with a small platform and micro‑ phone. Benches seating 2,000 radiate in a huge semicircle. Audiences come from a wide area to hear public questions discussed on Sunday morning.

LINCROFT, 4.3 *m.* (60 alt.), is a village dating back to 1680. Here are the famous WHITNEY STABLES, with an indoor race track, where well-known race horses have been trained. Willegrodt Brothers, breeders of White Leghorn chick‑ ens that have won in many egg-laying contests, have an extensive POULTRY FARM in Lincroft.

VANDERBURG, 7.3 *m.* (115 alt.), once called Edinburg, is the center of a farming district. The well-known BIG BROOK GAME FARM here raises pheasants, ruffed grouse, and partridge for the New York market. A game preserve for hunting is provided. The hunter buys what game he wishes and releases it on the preserve; the birds not shot escape to freedom. Here is also a small fox farm.

At 8.5 *m.* is the junction with a hard-surfaced road.

Left on this road is PHALANX, 2.4 *m.* (120 alt., 27 pop.), site of a widely known attempt to form a more perfect social order. In September, 1843, half a dozen families arrived, advance guard of the North American Phalanx, which was the most enduring and successful of a series of such colonies established in the United States. The members pooled their resources, bought a farm, and built a communal barracks. They set aside Brisbane Hall as the future site of the Gothic Tower of Babel, the Phalanstery planned by Fourier, French philosopher whose writings had inspired the movement, as the proper form of housing. Fourierism had been promoted in America by Albert Brisbane, father of the late Arthur Brisbane, Hearst editor and columnist. The elder Brisbane had interested Horace Greeley in it and had persuaded him to turn over a daily column in the New York *Tribune* for the propagation of the doctrine. A group of people, farmers and businessmen, chiefly from up-state New York, and a certain number of perpetually hopeful people who had tried Shakerism, Owenism, vegetarianism, and other popular movements of the day, established the North American Phalanx here with Horace Greeley as vice president of the association. Because of the proximity of this place to New York City and the number of journalists who were interested in the association, the experiment received wide publicity, some favorable and some unfavorable. Those hostile to the attempt to establish a more satisfactory way of living emphasized the ideas of the more eccentric members of the community and raised a horrified shout over the discussions and trials of saner costumes for women, more practical methods of education, unusual wage standards, and equal rights for women. The community prospered for a time but many of the farmers and businessmen eventually became dissatisfied with sharing the fruits of their industry with those they believed were contributing less labor. A disastrous fire in 1854 destroyed the mills, and was largely responsible for the final dissolution of the colony. All that remains today is the old HOTEL *(private; visitors welcome)*, a weather-beaten, barn-like, two-story structure, standing well back from the highway in about the center of the hamlet. Alexander Woollcott, well-known raconteur, was born here.

COLT'S NECK, 9.2 *m.* (125 alt.), was originally named Caul's Neck for an early settler. The one-street village under great trees amid wide pastures is more than 200 years old. It became a famous breeding place for race horses, and a story persists that a colt of the renowned race horse, Old Fashioned, fell and broke its neck here.

COLT'S NECK INN, a few hundred feet R. of the highway at the crossroads at 9.2 *m.,* was built in 1717. George Washington is said to have stayed here at one time; Clinton's army marched past it after the Battle of Monmouth. The inn is an attractive, white-shingled public house, with a long, low stoop lined with flower boxes. It is the field headquarters of the Rumson Hunt Club founded by Peter Collier. Permission is granted to the hunters to ride over the surrounding farms during the hunt season, for which the club gives a big race meet and hunt supper to all the farmers every fall. Many of the Colt's Neck farms are luxurious estates.

One-time proprietor of the inn was Capt. Joshua Huddy, vigorous patriot who was executed by Tories. Huddy's house, which stood a few rods back from the highway, was once attacked by Colonel Tye and some

60 followers. The "colonel" was Titus, a mulatto slave who had escaped from his master in Shrewsbury and joined the Tories. Huddy and a young Negro servant girl, only occupants of the house, put up a strong defense for hours. When the attackers set fire to the house Huddy surrendered. The girl escaped. Crossing Shrewsbury River with his captors Huddy jumped overboard and won freedom. Colonial militia pursued the raiders and killed six; Tye died later of a wound.

South of Colt's Neck is an area of fine white sand and stunted pines. During the Revolution this region afforded shelter to several bands of outlaws, known as the Pine Robbers, led by British sympathizers. They lived in caves burrowed in the sand hills and hidden with brush.

The thin topsoil has closed this land to farming. There are stunted pines on both sides of State 34 and far ahead. The borders of the road are being planted with laurel.

Crossing a small range of tree-crowned hills, the highway opens upon a good view of the surrounding country. There is woodland and brush along the foot of the hills (L), covering Hockhockson Swamp. The HOMINY HILLS (R), a mile away, rise to a 308-foot peak on which stands a forest ranger's station. There were many gristmills a century ago on the streams flowing down from these hills. These have gone with the grain.

At 13.8 *m.* is the junction with State 33 *(see Tour 20)*, which here unites with State 34 for 1 mile. The highway passes southeast through an area of overnight cabins and tourists' rests.

At 14.9 *m.* State 33 *(see Tour 20)* separates (L) from State 34.

Swinging south, State 34 runs through miles of stunted pines and oaks and sandy wastes. There are few houses.

At 20.1 *m.* is the junction with a hard-surfaced road.

Right on this road is the DESERTED VILLAGE OF ALLAIRE, 2 *m. (open).* Today this is Camp Burton, a gift to the Boy Scouts of America by Arthur Brisbane, whose grave is on his former estate nearby. Old whitewashed brick buildings are scattered in a grove of magnificent sycamores, with woodland paths. There is an old millpond, a little white church, and one old iron furnace still intact, suggesting the busy community of a century ago. Allaire, or Monmouth Furnace as it was first called, was taken over by James Allaire, owner of the Allaire Works in New York City. The pipes for the first waterworks in New York City, the air chambers for Robert Fulton's *Clermont,* and large quantities of pots, kettles, and stoves were cast here. Allaire became a model town. Comfortable houses, some even elegant, were built for 500 employees and their families. A school was maintained at James Allaire's expense. A stagecoach was put in service to Red Bank, where steamboats were run by Allaire down the Shrewsbury to New York. He rebuilt the wooden town in brick, erecting kilns to make the brick. All the trees were planted by his orders. From 1834 to 1837 Allaire was at the height of its prosperity. It even had its own currency, used in the company stores. The discovery of Pennsylvania's coal and iron was the deathblow to Allaire. The works were moved to Pennsylvania so hurriedly that for years pianos and the larger pieces of furniture stood in the deserted houses.

At 20.9 *m.* is the junction with a hard-surfaced road.

Right on this road down a ramp to ALLENWOOD, 1 *m.* (122 alt.), in the valley of the Manasquan River. This small summer resort is the home of a modern COUNTY TUBERCULOSIS HOSPITAL, on Squankum Rd.

At 22.9 *m.,* at a traffic circle, is the junction with State 35 *(see Tour 22).*

At 23.8 *m.* (R) a granite marker with a bronze tablet marks the SITE OF THE EXECUTION OF SEVEN TORY BANDITS, including their chief. Capt. Samuel Allen, leader of the Minute Men of the New Jersey Coast, was the executioner.

At 24.4 *m.* the highway crosses Manasquan River on a fine concrete bridge and turns sharply R.

LAURELTON, 27.6 *m.* (10 alt., 350 pop.) *(see Tour 22)*, is at the junctions with State 35 *(see Tour 22)* and State 40 *(see Tour 27)*.

Tour 22

South Amboy—Red Bank—Point Pleasant—Lakewood; State 35.
South Amboy to Lakewood, 45.9 m.

Between South Amboy and Red Bank the New York and Long Branch R.R. parallels the route.
Good accommodations at close intervals; sea food served at most restaurants.
Fine concrete roadbed three lanes wide.

State 35 runs east and south, serving many of the northern New Jersey shore resorts. From the shore of Lower New York Bay the highway cuts inland, passing old villages in a rolling farm country. Between Neptune City and Manasquan Inlet the road is close to the ocean shore; it then swings inland to Lakewood in the pine lands.

State 35 branches south from US 9 *(see Tour 18)* on the southern edge of SOUTH AMBOY, 0 *m.* (70 alt., 8,476 pop.) *(see Tour 18)*.

The road crosses the higher levels of the clay banks, with a broad view (L) of Raritan and Lower New York Bays and the hills of Staten Island.

MORGAN, 2.1 *m.* (15 alt.), is the Pompeii of New Jersey. Here (R) are the RUINS OF A MUNITIONS PLANT destroyed during the World War by a Vesuvian upheaval of TNT. Its only archeologists are the junkmen who unearth bits of metal and building material from the debris. When the explosion occurred, shell fragments showered the country for miles, and windows were broken in Newark. Morgan's name has been kept alive by a railroad station and a concentration of boats and small docks at the inlet.

LAURENCE HARBOR, 3 *m.* (30 alt.), is a small resort. Twenty years ago it was a bleak section of shore line known chiefly to hunters and fishermen.

CLIFFWOOD, 4.7 *m.* (40 alt.), has a landmark known to all shore motorists, a colorful, imitation PIRATE SHIP (L), used as a real-estate office. This freebooting atmosphere ties up with local legend that Captain Kidd buried treasure at Cliffwood. Erosion has left the shore line of Kidd's time far out in the bay, thwarting search for his legendary cache. There is a small boardwalk and dancing casino on the beach.

At MECHANICSVILLE, 6.3 *m.* (35 alt.), mainly a few roadstands and service stations, is the junction with State 36 *(see Tour 36)*.

At the underpass is a junction with a macadam road.

Left on this road is KEYPORT, 1.1 *m.* (30 alt., 4,940 pop.). Its natural harbor, filled with fishing boats, has long been a boat-building center. The town annually celebrates Salt Water Day as a harvest festival in August. More than 100 years old, the custom is believed to have been inspired by Indian clambakes on the beach. Deeds made by Indians in 1665 show Keyport to have been one of the State's earliest white settlements. Chingarora was the Indian name for the place and Chingarora oysters became famous. As early as 1714 oysters were planted in Chingarora Creek.

At 10.7 *m.* is the junction with an improved road.

Right on this road is MIDDLETOWN, 0.6 *m.* (125 alt., 9,209 pop.), a village dating from the seventeenth century. Houses along the main street, mostly old and some with gardens of rare loveliness, stand well back, shaded by old elms and oaks. MARLPIT HALL *(open Tues., Sat., Sun. 11-5, adm. 10¢; Thurs. 11-5, free)*, King's Highway opp. the railroad bridge, is a museum maintained by the Monmouth County Historical Association. This long, wide-shingled Dutch type structure of a story and one-half was built *c.* 1684 by Edward Taylor. Its windows, including three tiny dormers, have heavy paneled shutters. Oval, bull's-eye glass is used in the top panels of the wide Dutch door. Furnished in Colonial style as a livable home, Marlpit Hall does not give the impression of a museum. Especially noteworthy are the pilastered fireplace and carved, shell-top corner cupboard in the dignified drawing room. The kitchen fireplace is large enough to roast an ox. CHRIST CHURCH, King's Highway at the SW. cor. of the first crossroad (R) about 100 yds. from Marlpit Hall was built in 1836 on the site of a 1744 church. It is a plain, white frame building with a square belfry on the gable directly above the doorway. The church is still supported by pirate gold—the income from "conscience money" left to this church and another in Shrewsbury by William Leeds, aide to Captain Kidd *(see SHREWSBURY, below)*. Middletown was originally a Baptist settlement, the first Baptist church in the State having been organized here in 1668. The present BAPTIST CHURCH, on King's Highway almost opposite Christ Church, was erected 1832. It is a small, severe white structure with two tall classic columns on the small recessed portico of its plain front. The RICHARD HARTSHORNE HOMESTEAD *(not open)*, cor. King's Highway and New Monmouth Rd., was built in 1670 by a London upholsterer and the owner of much land. The plain little dwelling is the oldest building in Middletown. William Penn and George Fox were entertained in it by Hartshorne, a devout Quaker.

At 12.1 *m.* is the junction with a dirt road.

Left on this road is CHAPEL HILL, 3 *m.* (200 alt.), a hamlet on a Colonial stagecoach route. About 13 houses, one a Revolutionary TAVERN *(private)*, make this a quiet relic of centuries past, with fine views over the bay. The tavern, now a residence, is at the NW. cor. of King's Highway and Leonardo Rd. It is a long structure, simple in its lines, with a Dutch split door. On the opposite side of King's Highway is a smaller building, where slaves or servants of travelers spent the night. On the north side of King's Highway, 0.5 *m.* east of the old tavern, set back in an overgrown clearing between trees, is CHAPEL HILL LIGHTHOUSE *(open 9-5)*, erected 1856. Its 1,000,000-candlepower light helps to guide ocean steamers into New York Harbor. The lighthouse is a small, severe one-and-a-half-story white house, with the light tower on the ridgepole.

Southward the land is rolling, with many farms and country estates.

RED BANK, 15.1 *m.* (35 alt., 11,622 pop.), owes its importance largely to its site on Navesink River, and its name to the river's clay banks. The town is brisk and up-to-date, with a narrow, treeless main street. Well-kept residences are set back from shaded side streets. For more than 50 years the river has been the ice-boating center of the New York area. In summer the town is the shopping center for outlying estates.

The largest factory is the SIGMUND EISNER CLOTHING PLANT, which specializes in Boy Scout and military uniforms. Gold beating is a small local industry, employing a few workers in shops at 31 Linden Pl., 139 Spring St., and 147 South St. The founder of the industry here was William Haddon, who 60 years ago taught his trade to two apprentices, one of whom passed it on to the present shop-owners. Here an ounce of gold is hammered by hand between successive layers of parchment into 2,500 sheets, 3⅜ inches square and 1/200,000 of an inch thick.

SHREWSBURY, 17.5 *m.* (45 alt., 857 pop.), is a restful interlude in the feverish life of nearby modern summer resorts. There has been little expansion here since the Congregationalists founded the place in 1664.

The ALLEN HOMESTEAD, NW. cor. of Broad St. and Sycamore Ave., a substantial two-story structure dating from 1667, is perhaps the oldest building in the county. The house is shingled and has a gambrel roof. Behind paneling close to an upstairs fireplace was found the skeleton of a youth who had hidden to escape service in the Continental Army. At the foot of the front stairs were bloodstains which, after a century of wear, were finally cut out. They came from the body of a British officer, slain by Continentals on whom he was spying. At another time a party of five Tories from Sandy Hook hid behind tombstones in the graveyard opposite and surprised a dozen unarmed Virginia Continentals in the house. Three of the Virginians were killed. The others, some wounded, were taken to the infamous Sugar House prison in New York.

CHRIST EPISCOPAL CHURCH, SE. cor. Broad St. (State 35) and Sycamore Ave. *(open daily),* is a severe, rectangular structure, erected 1769. It has high arched windows, an octagonal belfry and a Georgian Colonial tower in three sections. On the domed cap, supported by the belfry columns and arches, is a weather vane surmounted by an iron British crown that is pockmarked and perforated by patriot bullets. The parish history began October 20, 1702, with the baptism of 24 persons, including William Leeds, a reformed member of Captain Kidd's crew who later bequeathed his estate to the church. Among his belongings was a chest, a plain rectangular box 4 feet long and 2½ feet deep, which the church has exhibited at times. It has a hidden compartment—empty. The body of Leeds was moved here in 1906 and rests by the north side of the church tower. The present building, succeeding two others, was erected in 1769. In the church entry is displayed the original charter from King George II of England. There are carved canopies over pews formerly occupied by the Provincial Governor, Lewis Morris, and the rector's family. The chancel stairs are made from an old oak that long served as a belfry. On the lectern is one of the few known copies of the Vinegar Bible printed at Oxford, England, in 1717 by John Basket. A typographical error makes the heading over Chapter XX of Saint Matthew read, "The Parable of the Vinegar," instead of "Vineyard."

Several of the tombstones in the yard bear carved stone skulls with sweeping wings. Fourteen graves that date back nearly a century are those of Aaron Jones and his family, including small graves of 10 children, each of whom died within 10 days of birth.

The FRIENDS MEETING HOUSE *(not open)*, NE. cor. of the crossroads, is a plain, box-like structure built in 1816. There are separate entrances for men and women. The sliding partition that once kept the males and females out of each other's sight can still be raised and lowered, but its use has been abandoned. George Fox, the famous Quaker preacher, visited the meeting here in 1672. In his party was John Jay, a Barbados planter, who was thrown from his horse and picked up for dead. Fox felt the man's neck and found that it was dislocated, not broken. He snapped the vertebra back into place, and Jay's prompt recovery was hailed as a miracle.

EATONTOWN, 18.9 *m.* (25 alt., 1,938 pop.), was named for Thomas Eaton, who came here from Rhode Island before 1685. He constructed a gristmill that ran until 1920 and was later razed. Something of a local Paul Bunyan was Indian Will, who refused to emigrate with his tribe when their land was sold. Angered by his individualism, the tribe dispatched one messenger after another to kill Indian Will in single combat; but Will always won. In addition, he found time to drown his wife. Once, while eating supawn (mush) and milk at the Eaton house with a silver spoon, Will casually remarked that he knew where plenty of silver could be found. For a red coat and cocked hat he delivered a large amount of silverware to the Eatons, who shortly thereafter became affluent. Who cached the silver was never learned.

At 22.8 *m.* is the junction with Deal Rd., a graveled highway.

Right on this road to COLD INDIAN SPRING LAKE, 1.7 *m.* Chiefs of the Six Nations used to bathe here for the health-giving qualities then attributed to the water, which is now bottled and sold. The overflow forms a bathing pool in 100-acre PAMERICK PARK *(open; free)*, where picnic grounds and tourist cabins are available.

At 25.9 *m.* is the junction with State 33 *(see Tour 20)*. State 35 here becomes Neptune Highway.

NEPTUNE CITY, 26.5 *m.* (30 alt., 2,258 pop.), is an ocean resort town. Many of its residents, including a large proportion of Negroes, serve summer vacationers in the hotels and boarding houses of Asbury Park and Ocean Grove. There are tourist camps along the highway. Many houses lack paint, or have been painted in Joseph's-coat patterns as the owners found time to wield the brush. A number of dwellings stand on brick piers or wooden posts, since the ground is little above tide level. Fifty years ago the town became famous for its shore dinners and clambakes. It now maintains a pajama factory and an ice plant.

The City of Newark has a FRESH AIR CHILDREN'S CAMP at 82 Ridge Ave. *(open 7 a.m.-9 p.m. daily)*, with living quarters, playrooms, and playgrounds for a large number of children on brief vacations.

AVON BY THE SEA, 27.1 *m.* (10 alt., 1,200 pop.) *(see Tour 36)*.

Correction

NEPTUNE CITY, 26.5 *m.* (30 alt., 2,500 pop.), is a residential community bordering on Shark River. Established in 1881, the borough was the first to break away from Neptune Township. Sylvania Hall, once a community center, is now occupied by the U. S. Army for production of army training films. A famous Farmers' Market on Steiner and Railroad Aves. between Fourth and Fifth Aves. serves hotels, boarding houses, and retail stores along the entire coast as well as hundreds of Monmouth and Ocean County farmers. Fifty years ago the city was famous for its shore dinners and clambakes. Scotty's on Shark River Island held many famous political outings, including one given by Woodrow Wilson when governor of the state. Scotty's widow still conducts a boarding house there.

At 28.2 *m.* is the SHARK RIVER INLET, where deep-sea fishing boats, guides, and bait are available. Crabbing in the river is popular.

BELMAR, 28.5 *m.* (25 alt., 3,491 pop.) *(see Tour 36).*

South of the bridge State 35 bears R. along Shark River and, rounding Rhode Island Point, strikes inland again through rolling country and prosperous-looking farms. Here the State highway commission is elaborately landscaping the roadsides.

At 33.3 *m.*, at a traffic circle, is the junction with State 34 *(see Tour 21).* The highway turns sharply L. toward the coast.

BRIELLE, 34.2 *m.* (20 alt., 684 pop.), is at the mouth of Manasquan River where the stream joins the ocean. It has a large fishing fleet and boat yards.

At Brielle is the junction with State 4N *(see Tour 36).*

The route, swinging southeast, crosses Manasquan River over a new concrete bridge. This is an attractive place at high tide, with a shore fringe of trees shading pleasantly situated homes, and a number of small craft on the stream.

POINT PLEASANT, 35.4 *m.* (20 alt., 2,058 pop.), has a bungalow colony on its beach front.

At Point Pleasant is the junction with State 37 *(see Tour 30).* Here State 35 turns R. and runs inland.

At a lift bridge, 36.4 *m.,* the highway crosses a canal 1.5 miles long, connecting the Manasquan and Metedeconk Rivers. It is part of the Intracoastal Waterway, following the inside route to Cape May and thence to Florida.

LAURELTON, 40.8 *m.* (10 alt., 350 pop.), is at the traffic circle junction with State 34 *(see Tour 21)* and State 40 *(see Tour 27).* Once called Metedeconk (from "Mittig-conck," Ind., *good thrifty and living timber),* the town was later renamed Burrsville. It is a center for extensive poultry and egg farms.

Turning sharply R. from Laurelton the road winds northwest through evergreen forests and crosses the north branch of Metedeconk River. From this point, for 3 miles, are the grounds (L) of the LAKEWOOD ESTATE *(private)* of the late John D. Rockefeller. In places the estate borders the highway; at others a fringe of caretakers' and workmen's houses is outside the barbwire fence. There are two thickly wooded entrances in a tall hedge of fir trees.

LAKEWOOD, 45.9 *m.* (80 alt., 5,000 pop.) *(see Tour 18),* is at the junction with US 9 *(see Tour 18).*

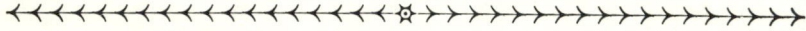

Tour 23

Atlantic City—Absecon—Egg Harbor City—Berlin—Camden—(Philadelphia, Pa.) ; US 30.
Atlantic City to Pennsylvania Line, 59.5 *m.*

Pennsylvania-Reading Seashore Lines parallel the route throughout.
Excellent accommodations at both terminals; gas stations and lunchrooms at frequent intervals.
Four- to six-lane concrete roadbed.

Northwest of Atlantic City US 30 runs through wide sandy wastes with stunted trees, then through a belt of rich fruit-growing land, important for wine grapes. In the western region are many orchards, and then a broad zone of suburban towns. Known as the White Horse Pike, the highway carries the bulk of the traffic to Atlantic City passing through Philadelphia.

US 30, following Virginia Ave., branches west from Atlantic Ave. in Atlantic City.

ATLANTIC CITY, 0 *m.* (15 alt., 66,198 pop.) *(see ATLANTIC CITY).*

Points of Interest: Model Home of America, Million Dollar Pier, Steel Pier, Heinz Pier, Stanley S. Holmes Village (low cost housing project), and others.

Left from Virginia Ave. on Absecon Blvd., which crosses the four inlets that separate Atlantic City from the mainland. Grassgrown marshes, occasionally glimpsed through an unending panorama of road signs, extend for miles, providing shelter and food for large flocks of water birds.

On the mainland, the road runs through several miles of salt marsh along Absecon Bay (R). The meadow grass here is used for bedding cattle and as a packing material.

ABSECON, 6.8 *m.* (30 alt., 5,158 pop.), is an old village named from Absegami (Ind., *place of the swans*). Many of the residents earn their living in Atlantic City, catering to the needs of its year-round influx of visitors. Fishermen, meadow farmers, and guides live in the community.

The village was a stopping point for travelers on horses and in stages long before the Revolution. It was a two-day stage trip from Absecon to Camden, at a tariff of three halfpence a mile.

In Absecon, at 7.4 *m.,* is the junction with US 9 *(see Tour 18).*

Northward the route traverses scrub-oak country, with few villages and scant population supported by the sandy soil.

POMONA, 12.3 *m.* (65 alt.), is little more than a railroad station. Small fruit farms cover the flat countryside. The Pomona district was settled by European peasants of many nationalities; its roads bear such names as Prague, Odessa, Mannheim, and Zurich.

GERMANIA, 15 *m.* (60 alt.), center of another section peopled by small fruit growers, is of German origin. Acreage for small orchards has been cleared in the scrub-oak and pine woodland. Dog breeding and chicken farming are other local enterprises.

EGG HARBOR CITY, 17.8 *m.* (63 alt., 3,478 pop.), a compact community of small homes and small industries, is a noted wine-making and grape-juice center surrounded by vineyards. There is a tantalizing odor when the wine presses are at work. John F. Wild in 1858 discovered that the soil and climate here were adapted to grape culture. The place had been founded eight years before by German immigrants who sought refuge from the Native American or Know-Nothing party; but its prosperity dates from Wild's experiments, which attracted many wine-grape growers from Germany. The industry experienced another boom after the Civil War with the influx of Italian growers. The vineyards, individually owned, are in most cases operated by the second and third generations of these families. American Renault wines, pressed from grapes of local growers and aged in old stone vaults, have become popular despite pressure from competing California districts.

Egg Harbor City was named in anticipation of a proposed canal to connect it with Gloucester Furnace and the Mullica River, 6 miles northeast. The canal was never dug, and the only maritime flavor of the community is its name. Near the center of the town are the buildings and FAIR GROUNDS of the Atlantic County Agricultural Society. The fair, with outstanding poultry exhibits, has long been an annual event in early September.

At 18.2 *m.* are the junctions with State 50 *(see Tour 34)* and an improved road *(see Tour 23A).*

Northwest of Egg Harbor City the highway runs through many fruit farms, including patches of raspberries and blackberries.

MAGNOLIA, 24.3 *m.* (80 alt., 1,522 pop.), an agricultural center, was known in Civil War days as Greenland, not from the climate but because of the greenish tinge of the soil. The town was renamed for the blossoms of magnolia trees in this area.

At 29.3 *m.* is the junction (R) with US 206 *(see Tour 6)*.

At 29.4 *m.* is the junction (L) with 12th St., a paved road.

Left on 12th St. is HAMMONTON, 1.2 *m.* (100 alt., 7,656 pop.), busy center of a fruit-farming area. It is a truck- and rail-shipping point with small industries and a flourishing cooperative farm-marketing organization. On West End Ave. is a wholesale FRUIT MARKET with cooperative auctions held twice a week under the big trees. Sales here have exceeded $1,000,000 a year.

Italians among the fruit farmers and shippers stage an annual street carnival on July 16 in honor of Our Lady of Mount Carmel, with a statue borne in a religious procession, gifts pinned to the garments. Fireworks, street dancing, feasting, and opening of homemade wine are parts of the celebration, which attracts thousands of visitors.

The town was named for John Hammond Coffin, who owned a glassworks here a century ago.

Northwest of the Hammonton junction US 30 passes farther into the rich fruit region. Peach orchards are plentiful here. Masses of pink and white blossoms are the center of Blossom Time festivities that draw thousands of spectators.

ELM, 32.1 *m.* (120 alt.), is a scattered village. On the southern outskirts (L) close to the road is a SILVER FOX FARM *(open 9-5, May to Dec.; free)*. More than 500 foxes, fed on a diet of cod liver oil, fresh meat, vegetables, and bone meal, are raised yearly. The best pelts bring from $500 to $1,000 each.

Pine woods replace the fruit farms along US 30 northwest of Elm. Inns and roadhouses, many of them colorful, are frequent.

ANCORA, 34 *m.* (90 alt.), is the site of the CAMDEN COUNTY PRISON. A well-kept farm worked by the prisoners provides practically all the vegetables, poultry, dairy products, and fruit used in the institution.

Orchards and vineyards line the highway NW. as the pines thin out. At the GRAPE EXCHANGE, 34.9 *m.*, large quantities of grapes are sold each autumn to wine manufacturers and to Italian residents who form temporary groups to buy grapes collectively for making home-pressed wines.

WATERFORD WORKS, 35.9 *m.* (125 alt., 326 pop.), was named for a glassworks founded in 1824. Near here three brothers, Sebastian, Ignatius, and Xavier Woos, settled in 1760 after fleeing their native Germany to escape military service. They built a log house with walls so well chinked and joints so tight that settlers came from miles around to inspect it. The Woos brothers, unable to speak English, said in German that their home was *schoen,* meaning "beautiful." Their American neighbors corrupted the word into "shane" and named the place Shane's Castle.

The brothers found bog iron in the swamps and sent to Germany for ironworkers who erected a furnace. Religious intolerance compelled the Catholic workers to meet secretly at Shane's Castle, where masses were said by traveling priests. The bog-iron venture failed; no trace remains of furnace or house.

CHESILHURST, 36.7 *m.* (120 alt., 298 pop.), a few houses along the road, is the center of a truck-farming district. On Wild Cat Branch is a modern cranberry bog.

DUNBARTON, 38.1 *m.* (120 alt.), has attracted Camden commuters by its well-kept houses and gardens. The woodland from all sides reaches up to the edge of lawns and tomato patches.

At 39.2 *m.* the road crosses Mechescatatauxin Creek. ATCO LAKE (L), a small pleasure resort, is formed from its waters.

At 39.7 *m.* is the junction with an improved road.

Right on this road is ATCO (Ind., *pure water*), 0.4 *m.* (150 alt.), once the site of a Lenape Indian village. Here are the rusty streaks of a primitive railway that once pushed nearly 10 miles east through the pines to Atsion, site of an early furnace. The old right-of-way is used as a road.

At 40.8 *m.* is the junction with State S41 *(see Tour 37)*.

At 40.9 *m.* is the junction with a macadam road.

Left on this road to the PEACOCK DAHLIA FARM, 1.5 *m.*, one of the State's largest producers of dahlia blossoms and bulbs.

BERLIN, 42.2 *m.* (160 alt., 1,955 pop.), owes its existence to the fact that it was just about here that passengers on the stagecoach from the coast to the Delaware River ferry began to be hungry. The stage, due at 3 p.m., was usually late. Hence the old name, Long-a-Coming, given to the town by impatient passengers. The change to Berlin came when a post office was established in 1867. The town has several small factories—metal, woodworking, fruit presses, hosiery, and brick—and a small flying field. Along a branch of Great Egg Harbor River, crossed here by US 30, a county park extends 2 miles.

At 45.7 *m.* is the junction with a macadam road.

Left on this road is CLEMENTON, 0.6 *m.* (50 alt., 2,605 pop.). Here is ROWAN'S CHARCOAL PIT, producing a charcoal used largely by metalsmiths in America and Europe for melting precious metals. The industry was founded in 1879 by John R. Rowan, who had discovered a new technique. It is said that the fires started in his original pit have never gone out. Rowan died at the age of 90 in 1931, and the plant is now operated by his son.

LINDENWOLD, 46.4 *m.* (85 alt., 2,523 pop.), is a town of commuters and workers in a nearby paint factory. It has a substantial Negro section with two churches.

At 46.5 *m.* is the junction with a hard-surfaced road.

Left on this road is LAUREL SPRINGS, 0.7 *m.* (85 alt., 1,343 pop.), founded in 1893, the year after Walt Whitman's death, when the few residents awoke to the probability that the place would become well known because the poet came here for his health. Whitman, during the spring of 1875, stayed with friends at the STAFFORD HOUSE *(private)*, Maple Ave. next to the firehouse. The two-and-one-half-story white frame farmhouse is the center of a celebration each May 31, the anniversary of the poet's birth.

STRATFORD, 47.6 *m.* (90 alt.), is the seat of the old WHITE HORSE HOTEL (L), former stage stop, post office, and town hall, which gave its name to the White Horse Pike. The original sign, a plain wooden piece depicting a white horse, still swings in the breeze. Since the white frame building was erected in the eighteenth century, it has been used continuously as a hotel, run by the same family. A spacious veranda runs across the front. Low ceilings, wide solid doors, small square windows with many panes, and part of the original floor remain, much as they were a century ago.

The highway runs through a fertile land of apple orchards, with an old-fashioned CIDER MILL (L) at 48.3 m.

SOMERDALE, 48.6 m. (85 alt.), has a NOAH'S ARK HOUSE on Warwick Rd., L. from the center. The structure was designed by an old sea captain who believed that the world would end in a flood. He built a home in the traditional shape of the Ark, inverted, with the roof forming the hull of the proposed vessel. The builder expected that the deluge would cause the house to topple and then reverse itself, floating away on its roof until it should land on some new Ararat.

LAWNSIDE, 50.5 m. (90 alt., 1,379 pop.), is the only Negro-owned and Negro-governed borough in New Jersey, and one of the few such towns in the United States. It was founded during the antislavery agitation of a century ago. Purchased for the Negroes in 1840, the tract was sold on long-term payments and appropriately named Free Haven. The place grew between 1850 and 1860, when neighboring Quakers were operating the New Jersey division of the Underground Railway. After the Emancipation Proclamation more Negroes arrived from Snow Hill, Md., and the community became known as Snow Hill. When the Philadelphia and Reading R.R. built a station, the town was renamed Lawnside.

Since incorporation in 1926, Lawnside has had Negro officials exclusively, from mayor to dog catcher. Its 155 white residents have left the town management entirely in the hands of their 1,224 Negro neighbors. Stores are mostly owned and operated by Negroes, but two chain groceries employ Negro clerks under white managers.

Although these conditions have existed nearly 100 years, intermarriage between the races is rare, and there is a surprisingly small number of mulattoes. Some of the dwellings are attractive in appearance, but modern comforts are lacking in most of them. Kerosene lamps and stoves are commonly used. There is a volunteer fire department and a police department with seven members who receive no salary and buy their own uniforms.

Heavily in debt, the borough holds tax title liens on 75 per cent of all properties. Foreclosures have not been executed because the municipal government cannot afford the expense. At one time 75 per cent of the town's population was aided by the ERA. Many home are shacks, unfit for habitation. Most of the men were laborers and the women domestic servants when the depression arrived, and almost the entire community found itself without work. Under the WPA the men have been employed in road building and the women in sewing.

The people are still able to support three beauty-culture parlors, licensed by the State, and there are many used cars in service. The town attracts Negro picnic parties from nearby states to its recreation center, LAWNSIDE

PARK. Negro students and research workers have been drawn to Lawnside from all parts of the Nation. Tourists stop for chicken dinners at the local inn.

The highway enters a district of suburban homes northwest of Lawnside.

BARRINGTON, 51.5 *m.* (75 alt., 2,252 pop.), is one of the newer towns on the outer edge of the Philadelphia-Camden metropolitan area.

HADDON HEIGHTS, 52 *m.* (85 alt., 5,394 pop.), is a residential community with wide, well-paved streets, fine old trees, and uncrowded lawns and gardens. The HADDON HEIGHTS NATURAL PARK AREA consists of 35 acres planted with many native trees, shrubs, and perennials. In the park is the GLOVER MANSION *(open daily 9-5)*, built *c.* 1705. Much of the structure's Colonial appearance has been lost by remodeling, but the old foundations and most of the walls remain. The house was built by John Glover, who came to America in 1703 after his discharge from impressment in the British navy. He sought and found Hannah Thorne, who had preceded him with her father to Pennsylvania; and in 1704 he brought her here, a bride. The old house is now an office of the Camden County Park Commission.

The town was named for John Haddon, an English Quaker, who acquired a large section of land in 1689 and sent his 20-year-old daughter, Elizabeth, alone to this country as his agent.

At 52.2 *m.* the road crosses old King's Highway.

AUDUBON, 52.8 *m.* (50 alt., 8,904 pop.), blazons its advantages in homes from a huge signboard at its entrance. The place was named for John James Audubon, the ornithologist, who studied birds in this section in 1829.

OAKLYN, 53.5 *m.* (40 alt., 3,843 pop.), on the south bank of Newton Creek, is a residential section for city workers. The region was settled by Quakers a few months before the founding of Philadelphia in 1682.

COLLINGSWOOD, 54.5 *m.* (20 alt., 12,733 pop.), a suburban town with many commuters, has wide lawns, tree-shaded walks, and three parks. KNIGHT PARK, in the center, was presented on condition that no saloon license be granted within its limits. Its Quaker settlers of 1682 named the place Newton. The only remaining landmark of the first settlement is the FRIENDS BURYING GROUND near the lake on Eldridge Ave. (L). A log meeting house, first in the county, stood beside it until 1737. The SLOAN BURIAL GROUND, of smaller size, adjoins the Friends cemetery. It was established in 1790 by James Sloan, after a disagreement among the Quakers. On the northern wall a marble tablet reads:

> Here is no distinction
> Rich and poor meet together
> The Lord is Maker of them all
> by James Sloan, 1791

Also on Eldridge Ave. is the THACKARA HOUSE *(open after 3:30 daily; free)*, oldest residence in Collingswood, erected 1754 by Isaac and Mary

Thackara and now used by Boy Scouts. The house bears the Thackaras' initials, built into the brickwork of the gable. Much of the interior is unchanged.

Some historians have placed the site of the land and log cabin of Mark Newbie on the shore of the creek west of the Friends Burying Ground. But nearby Woodlynne asserts that Newbie, who established the first American bank of issue, lived there *(see Tour 31)*.

At 55 *m.*, at a traffic circle, is the junction with US 130 *(see Tour 19)*. Here US 30 turns R. and is united with US 130 for 0.9 miles.

At 56.1 *m.*, at the Camden Airport traffic circle, is the junction with State 40 *(see Tour 27)*. US 130 here branches (R) from US 30.

Left at this point on Admiral Wilson Blvd., which leads through Camden to Delaware River Bridge Plaza *(bridge toll 20¢, car and passengers)*.

Left from the Bridge Plaza on Broadway 0.3 *m.* to the business center.
CAMDEN (25 alt., 118,700 pop.) *(see CAMDEN)*.

Points of Interest: Friends School, Johnson Park, RCA-Victor Manufacturing Plant, Campbell Soup Plant, Walt Whitman House, Joseph Cooper House, Charles S. Boyer Memorial Hall (museum), and others.

At 59.5 *m.* on the Delaware River Bridge, US 30 crosses the Pennsylvania Line 2.2 miles east of Philadelphia, Pa.

Tour 23A

Egg Harbor City—Batsto—Pleasant Mills; unnumbered roads.
Egg Harbor City to Pleasant Mills, 12.1 m.

Macadamized roadbed.
Garage service and restaurants at Egg Harbor City; a few filling stations along the route.

The route runs north to the smooth-flowing Mullica River and turns west to follow the course of the stream through the pines and cedars of Green Bank State Forest. Traversing a forgotten remnant of South Jersey's earlier days, the road passes several "forgotten villages," sites of Colonial industrial development.

North from US 30 *(see Tour 23)* at EGG HARBOR CITY, 0 *m.* (63 alt., 3,478 pop.) *(see Tour 23)*, on Green Bank Rd., a macadamized highway, to FRANKLIN D. ROOSEVELT PARK, 3 *m.* *(athletic fields, playgrounds, bathing beach)*. Much of the work on the 500-acre municipally owned park has been done by the WPA.

IN THE PINE BARRENS, CUMBERLAND COUNTY

The road passes between tree-bordered twin lakes fed by Indian Cabin Creek, where shaded pools attract many fishermen.

At 4.2 *m.* is the junction with Gloucester Rd., a dirt thoroughfare.

Right on this road through cedar swamplands to GLOUCESTER LAKE (R), 0.6 *m.*, which once supplied power to Gloucester Furnace.

Left at Gloucester Lake to (R) the SITE OF GLOUCESTER FURNACE, 1.6 *m.*, on Landing Creek. The remains of a dam and a pile of slag nearby are the only signs of the bog-iron furnace built in 1813 by John Richards, who was trained at Batsto Furnace under his uncle, Col. William Richards, one of Washington's officers. The old village, a stop on the Philadelphia stage route, has disappeared.

Green Bank Rd. turns L. through cut-over woodland.

WEEKSTOWN, 5.8 *m.* (20 alt.), is a community of a dozen houses, homes of forest workers.

The route turns R. at Weekstown, skirting the edge of GREEN BANK STATE FOREST *(open daylight hours; hunting permitted in season)*. The impenetrable growth of white cedar is so thick that the route resembles a darkened hall. The reservation covers 1,833 acres on both sides of the Mullica River, with giant trees, bathing beach, and picnic grounds. A 900-acre cedar swamp in the forest is one of the few surviving sources of New Jersey's early timber wealth.

In the forest are 65 trees that form part of the "Great Aspen Mystery." The species was first discovered on the eastern shore of Maryland by a tree expert, Fred C. Williamson, but it was not listed in the Yale Forestry School's catalog of 28,000 trees from all parts of the world. After microscopic examination of the leaves and wood, Professor Record of Yale identified it as a hybrid from the crossing of white poplar and aspen *(populus canescans)*. Professor Record could not explain to Williamson's satisfaction how these 100-year-old trees could have originated with the nearest trees of the parent species each almost 100 miles away. Nor could old residents or county records shed any light on the mystery.

GREEN BANK, 7.4 *m.* (10 alt.), one of the oldest settlements in South Jersey, is the site of a community of Swedes from the Delaware River settlement who arrived here in 1697, led by Eric Molica or Mullica. Mullica lived here for several years but later returned to Mullica Hill *(see Tour 28)*. The Swedes were absorbed by a later influx of English colonists whose descendants still hunt and fish along the banks of the stream.

Turning L. the route skirts the north bank of Mullica River, several hundred yards wide at this point. The opposite shore is a solid bank of white cedars, a beautiful background for the vistas of the river that appear at various points along the road. A few unkempt frame houses, scattered under the trees by the road and on the river bank, are weathered into harmony with the deep tangled forest surrounding them. The road winds through successive areas of white cedar and native pine, with some massive white oak trees along the roadside.

At 11.4 *m.* is (R) the RICHARDS MANSION *(private)*, an enormous stuccoed building on a small knoll about 100 yards from the road. A veranda runs along three sides of the square structure. A high tower, topping most of the surrounding trees, is utilized as a fire warden's lookout. In 1776 the mansion was the home of Col. William Richards, a friend of General Washington and manager of the Batsto Iron Works. It was restored in 1874 by Joseph Wharton, a Philadelphia business man, and is now owned by the Lippincotts, the publishing family.

BATSTO, 11.8 *m.* (30 alt.), a small community of frame houses almost exactly alike, is entirely surrounded by dense forest. Built originally to house workers on the Wharton estate, one of the largest in New Jersey, the homes are now occupied chiefly by wood-cutters and other members of South Jersey's forest people.

The town is situated at the foot of a millpond (R) formed by damming the Batsto River. The SITE OF BATSTO IRON WORKS, built in 1765 by Charles Read, is marked by a heap of slag near the dam. Munitions were made here for American forces during the Revolutionary War and the War of 1812. The forge also made the steam cylinder for John Fitch's steamboat, *Perseverance (see TRENTON)*, Dutch ovens, fish kettles, salt-evaporating pans, and other iron products.

Northwest of Batsto, in the area between Mullica River and its tributary, Batsto River, is the heart of the Jersey Pines, a deep scrub forest threaded by occasional trails and a few wretched roads, unmarked and not safe for automobile travel except in dry weather. The inhabitants are called the Pineys.

Conditions have changed somewhat in the 26 years that have passed since 1913, when Elizabeth S. Kite of the Vineland Training School startled people by her careful report in *The Survey* on the social problems created by the presence of this group of segregated, inbred people. The construction of roads through the Pines has broken down some of the barriers between the Pineys and the people around them. But no one knows how many tiny hovels built of cast-off cranberry boxes and miscellaneous lumber still remain in the recesses of the pine forest. And no one knows exactly how many Pineys still live in the squalor of these shacks, though it is believed that there are somewhat fewer than 5,000.

Though the origin of the group is a matter of speculation, Miss Kite said that some of the ancestors of these people deserted their Colonial villages for a forest life as a protest against rigid religious rules. This nucleus was augmented by Tory renegades and deserters from the British army during the Revolution. Further additions were the "Pine Robbers," outlaws whose "cruelty and lust" terrorized the countryside, according to Francis B. Lee's history of the State. From time to time young men of leisure, criminals and adventurers were attracted to the unsupervised wasteland. Revelers and members of hunting parties are said to have left nameless offspring here, and impoverished immigrants, driven from the towns by severe poor laws, added their seed to the heterogeneous stock.

Miss Kite reported that disease was rampant in the large families, and legal marriage was practically unknown. A woman kept house for a man, bore his children and was known as "John No. 1, John No. 2, or John No. 3," depending on whether she was the first, second, or third woman to live with John: she was free to leave and attach herself to another man when she chose.

The Pineys gain some income by cutting timber, and by gathering sphagnum moss, cranberries, and huckleberries. Many have vegetable gardens and some keep pigs, chickens, and a cow. While many of those cared for in the Vineland Training School, or brought under public supervision when they have wandered to the cities in search of work, are mentally subnormal, others have shown acute intelligence in their own limited world. Some people who have approached them with sympathy, asking their cooperation, refute the charges of widespread degeneracy and moronism and attribute the poor impression they make in part to shyness and to ignorance of the more complicated world around them.

Ellis H. Parker, the former Burlington County detective who came to know them in the course of his official duties, staunchly defends them and tells many delightful stories of his experiences among them. Parker once asked their help in discovering the body of a murdered man, which he believed had been buried in the sandy soil of the scrub forest. The searching party hiked deep into the barrens, their eyes scanning the branches of the trees overhead. They paid no attention to Parker's insistence that they examine the ground. Suddenly they stopped. "If the body is anywhere in this part of the woods," one said, "it is around this tree." The body was there. Questioned, the men explained to the detective that the leaves of a tree curl when the roots are disturbed.

Parker says that the Pineys are "the most law-abiding citizens of the State." But ignorance of the present-day world often leads them to action that seems to refute this. A staff correspondent of the *Newark Evening News* reported that U. S. Navy blimps must be careful in their flights over the area. The Piney bootleggers, suspecting that the low-flying blimps are seeking illicit stills, are quick on the trigger; frequently the small dirigibles return to Lakehurst from training flights with bullet holes in the fabric.

The establishment of Camp Dix nearby during the World War brought the modern world close to the Pineys for a time. Some of them for the first time learned the use of money when they worked as laborers at Camp Dix. These laborers and some of their friends were then attracted to urban centers, where they have intensified social problems. The shier and less competent and aggressive Pineys have withdrawn deeper into the forests.

At Batsto the route bears L., entering pine woods and crossing Mullica River.

At 12.1 *m.*, at a junction, is PLEASANT MILLS (10 alt.). The name of the scarcely distinguishable village, once Sweetwater, was changed in 1821 when William Lippincott of Philadelphia built the Pleasant Mills, a cotton textile factory.

The METHODIST CHURCH (R) is a plain wooden rectangular structure, built in 1808 on the site of Clark's Log Meeting House, which was erected in 1758 by Capt. Elijah Clark. Revolutionary soldiers and seamen are buried in the churchyard, with many of their graves marked by the iron tombstones peculiar to South Jersey. One of these soldiers, Joseph Johnson, often asserted that he had fired the first shot at Bunker Hill.

Left from the junction on a graded road a few hundred feet to (R) the KATE AYLESFORD HOUSE *(private)*, erected 1762, on the shore of a lake. Standing behind massive trees, the shingled mansion of two and one-half stories has simple, sturdy lines. There are dormer windows and broad end-chimneys. Here lived Honoré Read, daughter of the Colonial ironmaster, who is said to have been the heroine of Charles Peterson's novel, *Kate Aylesford.*

Much more exciting than the novel was an episode reported from the life of Miss Read. Joe Mulliner was the Atlantic County Robin Hood, who stole liberally and distributed his gain with equal open-handedness. When Honoré Read issued invitations for a party one day during the summer of 1781, Joe, whose desire for the handsome girl was legend, was omitted from the guest list. His record in shaking down the wealthy landowners and local tycoons was a more important social consideration with the high-born Honoré than his helpfulness to the poor. Turning to the methods of his pine woods forays, Joe made up for the snub by kidnaping the hostess on the day of the party.

Honoré was returned that night. Whether the ransom of whole-hearted affection demanded by Joe was paid, nobody knows. Joe never made any disclosure in the short span of life that remained before he was caught, tried and executed. Honoré wouldn't talk.

Across the road from the mansion, where the lake empties beneath a small highway bridge, are the RUINS OF PLEASANT MILLS. The old stone walls are mostly intact, and much of the iron machinery that utilized water power for a more recent paper mill remains. Powdered litter from dyeing operations has left bright colors on the rotting floor. Miles distant from any contemporary industrial plant, the old mill by the tree-swept stream would seem to merit the attention of a special kind of ghost.

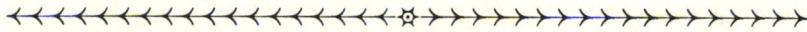

Tour 24

Atlantic City—Mays Landing—Malaga—Pennsville—(New Castle, Del.); US 40.
Atlantic City to Delaware Line, 67.8 m.

Pennsylvania-Reading Seashore Line parallels the route between Atlantic City and Malaga.
Small hotels and tourist homes in towns west of Atlantic City.
Concrete roadbed, three- and four-lane, except for a short macadam stretch. Motorists should exercise caution at the seven grade crossings on this route, several being in the path of seashore express trains.

US 40, part of the transcontinental Harding Highway, runs westward from coast marshlands, following an old Indian trail. The highway crosses the scrub-pine and cranberry-bog belt and rises to the truck farm and dairy country in the central section. Some of the villages and towns here are rich in Revolutionary history. The road descends gradually to the lowlands of the Delaware Valley, completing a bog-to-bog journey.

ATLANTIC CITY, 0 *m.* (15 alt., 66,198 pop.) *(see ATLANTIC CITY)*.

Points of Interest: Model Home of America, Million Dollar Pier, Steel Pier, Heinz Pier, Stanley S. Holmes Village (low cost housing project), and others.

US 40 follows Albany Ave., which branches northwest from Atlantic Ave. in the southern section of Atlantic City, at a traffic circle around the SOLDIERS MONUMENT.

Left (straight ahead) on Ventnor Ave. is VENTNOR, 1.2 *m.* (5 alt., 6,674 pop.), a part of Philadelphia moved to the New Jersey shore. But beside the long rows of Philadelphia houses and bungalows are the beautiful estates that enable

Ventnor to carry on the tradition of Cape May as the first blue blood of New Jersey resorts. The business section of the restricted area is the shopping center for the summer visitors; a second business district gets the trade of the majority of the all-year residents. Although it is suburban to Atlantic City, Ventnor has sufficient facilities to be a shore resort in its own right. Major events each summer are the casting tournaments held on the fishing pier extending from the MUNICIPAL CASINO on the boardwalk.

The route follows Pleasantville Blvd., crossing the tidal marshland and the quiet waters of GREAT THOROFARE, route here of the Inland Waterway, and passes at the R. the WPG TRANSMITTING STATION, Atlantic City AIRPORT, and BADER ATHLETIC FIELD. LAKE'S BAY is L.

PLEASANTVILLE, 5 m. (30 alt., 11,580 pop.), a residential suburb, is at the junction with US 9 (see Tour 18).

US 40 swings R. around a traffic circle at 5.1 m. and then L. around another circle at 7.5 m.

McKEE CITY, 12.7 m. (75 alt., 180 pop.), is hardly more than a traffic circle at this point, with almost as many billboards as inhabitants. At McKee City is the junction with US 322, the Black Horse Pike (see Tour 25), which here branches R. US 40 turns L. at the circle.

This is the center of a dense growth of Jersey pine extending for miles in every direction. It is an impressive panorama of vivid green treetops marred occasionally by gaunt wreckage of forest fires.

MAYS LANDING, 17.5 m. (20 alt., 1,868 pop.), is the seat of Atlantic County. It is also the national capital of the nudists, who in 1937 designated the community as their headquarters. Along the bank of Great Egg Harbor River, 2 miles south of the village, a 500-acre tract known as SUNSHINE PARK has been developed by this sun-loving cult. The park provides freedom, a reasonable degree of isolation, and plenty of mosquitoes and greenhead flies. Reporters for tabloid newspapers beat a path to the park entrance each summer when the national convention of nudists is held, but the cult's requirement that visitors disrobe is an obstacle to complete coverage of nudist news. Local residents interested in the nudist movement but as yet unwilling to affiliate make observations from rowboats in Great Egg Harbor River. Mays Landing was founded in 1760 by George May, a Philadelphian, who exchanged local bog iron and timber for salt, rice, and indigo from the Carolinas. A cotton mill is the only industrial plant in the town.

The ATLANTIC COUNTY ADMINISTRATION BUILDINGS, of red brick Colonial type of architecture, are appropriately set in a grove of old oak trees (R).

US 40 turns L. in Mays Landing, uniting briefly with State 50 (see Tour 34), and then turns R.

LAKE LENAPE, 17.8 m. (R), one of the largest in South Jersey, has recreational facilities and many summer homes along its shores. Fishing for wall-eyed pike, perch, and bass is excellent.

RICHLAND, 26.3 m. (100 alt., 500 pop.), is the central village for a colony of small farmers and poultrymen.

Between Richland and Buena the highway passes out of the Jersey pine belt, and cultivated fields become more extensive. Throughout southern

New Jersey wherever the original stand of pine has been cut a hardwood growth has replaced it. This new growth is noticeable west of Richland.

BUENA, 29.4 m. (100 alt., 150 pop.), is a center for Italian vegetable and fruit growers. In a sunny spot at the intersection of the highway is (L) a low, rambling tavern, THE MIDWAY, once a stage-coach station. Parts of the antique walls and floors remain. Washington is said to have had his horse shod across the road where a modern garage now stands.

LANDISVILLE, 30.6 m. (110 alt., 135 pop.), with its predominantly Italian population, was settled soon after the Civil War as a part of the colonizing efforts of Charles K. Landis. The village is a vegetable-producing and canning center. Many small stores are along the highway.

DOWNSTOWN, 31.7 m. (115 alt., 135 pop.), has taken the name applied to the whole area before 1800. The flat countryside is more thickly settled here, with many small truck and fruit farms. Most of the produce is sold to the canning factories whose water towers, chimneys, and buildings are seen R.

US 40 unites with State 47 (see Tour 33) at 36.9 m.

At MALAGA, 37.5 m. (90 alt., 410 pop.) (see Tour 33), US40 branches R.

IONA LAKE, 37.8 m. (R), is a popular fishing place formed by damming the Maurice River.

West of Malaga the countryside becomes slightly rolling with many wooded groves. At short intervals are deserted gravel pits, partly overgrown.

PORCHTOWN, 39.4 m. (100 alt., 125 pop.), is a tiny crossroads settlement on Little Ease Run. It consists of half a dozen houses clustered around a filling station. There are probably no more porches in Porchtown than in neighboring communities; the name was borrowed from Samuel Porch, an early settler.

ELMER, 44.4 m. (115 alt., 1,219 pop.), has substantial homes of retired farmers whose families have been established in the region for years. The borough is the shopping center and shipping point for the nearby farm country.

Between Elmer and Pittsgrove are larger farms, where dairying is an important industry. Grain, hay, and alfalfa are grown for stock feed.

The MAYHEW HOUSE (1792), 46.1 m. (L), lies beyond a wide pasture. Built of Colonial brick in simple square lines with a slightly sloping roof, the three-story house has the initials E. M. S. and the date 1792 worked into the east gable. It was built by Eliza and Selina Mayhew, great-grandparents of the present owner.

PITTSGROVE, 48 m. (135 alt., 212 pop.), is the center of the vast area of wasteland discovered by pre-Revolutionary settlers who soon learned the fertilizing value of marl. The entire section was barren until the dry, crumbling substance that lay near the earth's surface was spread over the land. Benjamin Franklin, in his Pennsylvania Gazette of April 23, 1787, related how a joyous gathering in this village witnessed the raising of an American flag with 13 stars and as many stripes, in front of the town tavern. A 13-gun salute followed.

A traffic circle in the center of the village is the SITE OF POLE TAVERN, named for the flagstaff, and burned in 1918. Even the town adopted the name of Pole Tavern; Pittsgrove is only the post-office designation. The old tavern, which had served as a pre-Revolutionary recruiting station, was the first regularly equipped military barracks with organization for defense in South Jersey.

Behind a cluster of evergreens on the tiny grass plot in front of the township hall is a BRONZE CANNON, bearing Latin inscriptions, the date 1763, and the Austrian coat of arms. It was captured from its original owners by the French; from the French by the British, and from them by local troops during the Revolution.

West of Pittsgrove vast fields stretch away to the horizon. Cattle graze in pastures enclosed by old rail fences. Sturdy barns, often in better condition of repair than are the farmhouses, top the rises in the fields.

At Pittsgrove is the junction with State 46 *(see Tour 32)*.

WOODSTOWN, 53.7 *m.* (30 alt., 1,832 pop.), has many old houses, including fine examples of Colonial architecture. Even the more modern buildings, such as the BOROUGH HALL (R) and some of the schools, show the Colonial influence. In sharp contrast to the older structures are the modern stores.

Woodstown has been a Quaker center since Jackanias Wood built the first house early in the 1700's. During the Revolution, American and British troops marched through Woodstown and foraging parties made their headquarters here. Close to the highway (R) is the QUAKER MEETING HOUSE, erected 1784, a large red-brick structure of simple lines with small, many-paned windows and a low sloping roof. The old carriage sheds still stand at the rear. Directly across the street is the FRIENDS INFIRMARY, still in use after more than a century of service. STONY HARRIS'S SALES CO. OFFICE, 158 N. Main St., identified by a brightly painted sign bearing the head of a bull, is a modern brick residence. Back of the house, spread over several acres, stand rows of stock and storage barns. Each Tuesday morning throughout the year long caravans arrive with everything from ancient household utensils to livestock, all to be sold at Stony's Auction. Everything is offered: fruit, battered furniture, the old cocked hat of some Revolutionary hero, hand-made needle work, livestock on the hoof, and modern refrigerators. The auctioneer wears a 5-gallon hat and high boots into which his trousers are tucked. He snaps a 20-foot whip over the heads of cattle to center the crowd's attention. Thousands attend the auction in the course of each year.

Woodstown is at the junction with State 45 *(see Tour 28)*.

At 56 *m.* US 40 crosses Salem Creek, used for navigation until the advent of the railroads. An occasional flat-bottomed boat still pushes its way upstream. The concrete ends at 61.3 *m.* and the road is macadamized for a short distance west.

Marshlands border the route. In the distance are the chimneys of riverfront factories at Wilmington, across the Delaware; closer are the stacks of industrial plants on the New Jersey shore. The shabby homes of factory workers appear in increasing numbers as the route nears the river.

The old SALEM CANAL, dug by hand in 1860, skirts the route at intervals. Formerly a drainage canal for Salem, it is now owned by the Du Pont Co., which uses it as an inland water reserve for a nearby dye plant.

SHARPTOWN, 56.2 *m.* (25 alt., 232 pop.), is a small community of half a dozen stores, a church, a single school, and a group of middle-class houses clustered in a triangle around an old oiled roadway. Up to the time of the Revolution the community was Blessington, the name of the Sharp family's plantation. Later Sharptown was a station on the Underground Railway.

Along the highway east and west of Sharptown are a number of marble milestones, some standing at a distance from the present road. How they got there no one knows.

Right from Sharptown on a narrow oiled road at the ice-cream plant to the SEVEN STARS TAVERN (L), 2 *m.*, built in 1762 by Peter and Elizabeth Louderback. The monogram and the date are woven into the brickwork of the south gable. Combining the old English and Dutch styles of architecture in checkered Colonial brick, the Seven Stars Tavern is a two-and-one-half-story, peak-roofed building with a slope-roofed two-story extension. Tradition has supplied it with a panorama of authentic ghosts; a pre-Revolutionary pirate—Bluebeard—who frequently visited the tavern for his nightly grog; and a Tory spy who was hanged from an attic window. At the western side of the main entrance is a small window, the sill about 6 feet high. This eighteenth-century counterpart of modern curb service was built to accommodate travelers on horseback. Right from the tavern to OLIPHANT'S MILL, 2.5 *m.*, where grist and feed have been dispensed to the surrounding countryside for more than a century. Practically every farmhouse in this section dates back at least to Revolutionary days.

Near the top of Oliphant's Hill is the MORAVIAN CHURCH (L), 3 *m.* A square, rather barn-like structure, it has perfectly plain lines in accordance with traditions of this sect. It was erected in 1786 on the site of a log structure built in 1747. The property was conveyed to the Protestant Episcopal Church in 1837 and is now used only for occasional memorial services.

The concrete ends as US 40 turns R. at 61.3 *m.*

At DEEPWATER, 65 *m.* (10 alt., 537 pop.) *(see Tour 19)*, is the junction with US 130 *(see Tour 19)*.

US 40 is united with US 130 between Deepwater and the Delaware Line, 67.8 *m. (see Tour 19)*.

Tour 25

McKee City—Williamstown—Glassboro—Bridgeport—(Chester, Pa.); US 322.
McKee City to Pennsylvania Line, 50 m.

The Pennsylvania-Reading Seashore Lines parallel the route between Williamstown and Mullica Hill.
Limited hotel service in larger towns; oil stations and lunchrooms at short intervals.
Roadbed nearly all concrete, two to four lanes wide.

US 322 runs northwest across the State, cutting through occasional dense pine and wide scrub-oak growth. The road passes an old bog-iron center of the early nineteenth century; farther north it touches fruit-growing country in which the glass industry once flourished. The route passes old Swedish farm villages, and crosses the Delaware River at Bridgeport.

US 322 forms a junction with US 40 *(see Tour 24)* at MC KEE CITY, 0 *m.* (75 alt., 180 pop.), which is chiefly a collection of large billboards at a traffic circle, advertising ferries of the Delaware River.

US 322 travels directly through the heart of the flat pine and bog country for mile after mile with no towns and few curves.

At 4.2 *m.*, at a cloverleaf intersection, is the junction with State 50 *(see Tour 34)*.

This section of the road, part of Black Horse Pike, carried passengers and freight between Philadelphia and the coast before railways were built.

At 8.9 *m.* is the junction with a graveled road.

Right on this road to the SITE OF THE WEYMOUTH IRON WORKS, 0.5 *m.*, and of a paper mill erected later on the same spot. Founded in 1800, the Weymouth furnace produced cannonballs, stove parts, and water pipes, employing about 200 workers. When the works burned during the Civil War they were replaced by a Manila-paper mill, also destroyed by fire. There remain gaunt walls 2 feet thick, with trees growing inside and out of the enclosure; piles of bog-iron ore and slag, and a tall, square brick chimney. Arches in the foundation span channels through which diverted waters of the Great Egg Harbor River still run. Across the river (R) are remnants of dams, bulkheads, and ditches, used to harness the stream. Sixty-two people still live here, facing the ruined factory buildings.

Northwest of this junction the deep forest crowds close to US 322. A few isolated summer cabins are among the trees.

At 25.1 *m.* State 42 *(see Tour 31)*, which is united with US 322 between McKee City and this point, branches (R) from US 322.

WILLIAMSTOWN, 25.6 *m.* (160 alt., 1,536 pop.), has a compact and active business area around the TOWN HALL (L), in the center of the community. Once a glass-making center, the town now depends largely on two canneries, which preserve fruit and vegetables.

Williamstown has gradually lived down its early name of Squankum (Ind., *place of the evil god*). The name was brought here in 1772 from Squankum, Monmouth County, by Deacon Israel Williams; 70 years later the town was named for the deacon himself. One historian recalls that in 1800 there were but four or five houses at Williamstown "within sound of the conch." This sea shell was brought to New Jersey in large quantities aboard sailing vessels trading with the West Indies and was used ashore as a dinner horn. At sea it served as a foghorn.

Macadam replaces concrete at the western end of Williamstown. The land takes on the appearance of a huge checkerboard, with large square fields of truck crops alternating with apple orchards.

GLASSBORO, 32 *m.* (145 alt., 4,799 pop.), is a business-like farm center displaying well-kept streets, neat one-family dwellings, and a prosperous-looking business center with bright store fronts. Although it owes its name to the once extensive glassworks here, that industry has completely vanished.

Development of fruit and poultry farms has led Glassboro to serve the region with a peach-basket factory, a dress factory, cold storage, and fruit and vegetable auctions held by the Gloucester County Agricultural Cooperative Association. In 1936 this market's sales reached $485,000. A plant on Delsea Dr. produces 2,000,000 gallons of apple cider annually, much of which becomes vinegar.

Glassboro dates back to 1775 when a German widow, Catherine Stanger, and her seven sons built a glass factory here. The cornerstone of the first plant is visible under the dining room of a building at 124 State St. Greensand and silica deposits boomed the glass industry, which reached its peak around 1840 when a bottle famous in the 1840 Presidential campaign was made here. Shaped like a log cabin, the flask was symbolic of candidate William Henry Harrison's supposed home. The bottles were filled by a Philadelphia distiller, E. C. Booz; soon known as "Booz bottles," they widely popularized the word "booze" or "boose," which as early as 1812 had been a potent noun in the vocabulary of Parson Weems, American evangelist.

With the adoption of modern machinery in the glass industry, the Gloucester factories succumbed to competition from other sections where a purer grade of glass sand was available.

On the highway (L) at 32.8 *m.* are the buildings of the GLASSBORO STATE NORMAL SCHOOL, one of six normal schools maintained by the State. The group of three large Georgian Colonial style buildings in red brick and white stone occupies a 55-acre tract. Part of the land produces vegetables for the 400 or more students.

At Glassboro is the junction with State 47 *(see Tour 33)*.

Westward along US 322 chicken farms replace the orchards, which reappear farther west on the low, rolling hills.

RICHWOOD, 35.7 *m.* (150 alt., 250 pop.), has a few modern homes and weathered houses. Built at the junction of five roads, the village was once known as Five Points.

MULLICA HILL, 38.8 *m.* (80 alt., 600 pop.) *(see Tour 28)*, is at the junction with State 45 *(see Tour 28)*.

Northwest of Mullica Hill the highway turns sharply R., then L., along low hills that slope down to Raccoon Creek (L), which twists through tomato-growing country, alive with activity during August and September, when the big crop is shipped by trucks to canneries. Gloucester County, through which the highway runs, produces 2,000,000 bushels of tomatoes annually, the third largest tomato crop from any county in the United States.

At 43.1 *m.* is the junction with old King's Highway, built in 1681 by order of the Provincial Legislature of West New Jersey.

Left on this road is SWEDESBORO, 1.2 *m.* (10 alt., 2,213 pop.), a large shipping station for farm produce. The main highway presents many contrasts. On it are important Colonial structures, poultry-dressing plants, and the offices of produce

"MAIN STREET," SWEDESBORO

shippers. One of the oldest Swedish settlements in the State, Swedesboro was known first as Raccoon. Until the Revolution it was the Swedish center of the region and an important point on the stage line between Salem and Camden. In 1778 the British and Tories from Billingsport burned the schoolhouse and other buildings.

TRINITY CHURCH, standing on a bluff at the intersection of the King's Highway and Raccoon Creek, and shaded by tall maple, buttonwood, and cedar trees, is a handsome Colonial structure. The graceful white spire, surmounted by a shining ball and vane, towers far above the ivy-covered brick walls with large Gothic windows. The church has recessed doors, fronted by heavily capped columns. Above the entrance, below the sloping eaves of the gabled roof, a circular slab set in the wall bears the simple inscription, "1784." Built in that year by the Swedish Lutheran congregation, Old Trinity was taken over by the Episcopalians five years later, upon the passing of the Swedish mission. The church still uses a silver communion service bought by the Swedish congregation in 1730 for £7.

The road descends into the bottom lands and turns sharply northward.

At 47.9 m., at the northern end of Bridgeport, is the junction with US 130 (see Tour 19). US 322 turns L. here and is united with US 130 through the village, for 0.7 miles.

BRIDGEPORT, 48.3 m. (20 alt., 850 pop.) (see Tour 19).

At 48.3 m. US 322 turns R., separating from US 130 (see Tour 19).

A stretch of concrete highway leads through a marsh, with dense growths of reeds, cattails, and coarse, sun-dried brown grass.

At 50 m., on the CHESTER (PA.) FERRY (24-hour service May 30 to Oct. 1; 50¢ car and driver; 5¢ for each passenger), US 322 crosses the Pennsylvania Line, 2 miles south of Chester, Pa.

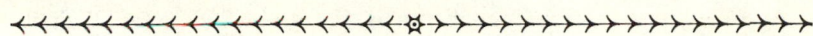

Tour 26

Lakewood—Wrightstown—Camden; unnumbered roads and State 38.
Lakewood to Camden, 52.2 m.

The Pennsylvania R.R. parallels the highway between New Egypt and Camden.
Good hotel accommodations at both ends of the route; service stations at frequent
intervals.
Paved roads in the eastern section; concrete, 3 lanes, at the western end.

West of Lakewood this unnumbered route runs through a sparsely settled pine-covered country. There are few hills; any elevation of more than
300 feet is considered a mountain. Cranberry bogs are numerous in the
lowlands drained by Toms River. The central section of the route traverses
first-rank dairying country, with patches of deciduous woods. Several small
communities are much more interesting than those found on main highways. The western part, between Pemberton and Camden, penetrates an
old suburban section, studded with many Revolutionary landmarks. Here
the road is State 38, a modern highway that skirts the edges of the most
thickly settled areas.

LAKEWOOD, 0 *m.* (80 alt., 5,000 pop.) *(see Tour 18)*.

West from US 9 *(see Tour 18)* in Lakewood on Central Ave., just
south of the business section.

WATERING RACE BROOK (L) has a name that has survived horse and
buggy days when this region sheltered the stables of many wealthy men
whose animals were exercised on the road.

Central Ave. becomes a county road that ascends with low hills on both
sides. The head of the ALLIGATOR, a ridge of reptilian form, rises 0.5
mile R. About 2.5 miles long, the ridge includes a menacing curved tail
apparently about to strike.

The road passes evergreen woods with an occasional hennery in a clearing of the pines. The few houses between Lakewood and Holmansville
are unimposing.

HOLMANSVILLE, 5.8 *m.* (110 alt., 98 pop.), is a small cluster of
houses. Left is the STATE QUAIL FARM of 128 acres. For many years it
was thought impossible to rear quail. Then the State established this farm
where nearly 10,000 fowl are raised annually for liberation throughout
New Jersey for hunters.

VAN HISEVILLE, 8.2 *m.* (100 alt., 85 pop.), is a small community
with a general store and a few old houses at the crossroads. It was named
for the Van Hise family, settlers of about 1750.

West of Van Hiseville the devastating results of forest fires are seen.
Deer in this region form a traffic hazard, particularly at night. It is estimated that there are 8,000 of the animals in the New Jersey pine country.

At 10 *m.*, just west of Toms River, is (L) JACKSON STATE FOR-
EST *(open; no picnic grounds)*, a tract of 43 acres where experiments in
pine culture are conducted by the State Department of Conservation and
Development, aided by Federal agencies. Forestry experts here are seeking
ways to reclaim New Jersey's 1,000,000 acres of pine barrens; to change
scrub oak to pine forest, which once covered most of south New Jersey
and in the Colonial period provided much income. White pines and two-
leaf pines are cultivated here.

CASSVILLE, 10.7 *m.* (120 alt., 205 pop.), a tiny old village once
known as Downsville, then as Goshen, was named Cassville for Gen.
Lewis Cass when a post office was opened in 1850. Cass, a veteran of the
War of 1812, was the Democratic presidential nominee defeated by Zach-
ary Taylor in 1848.

The southern part of Cassville is known as Webbville in memory of
John Webb, "old Peg-leg John," a schoolteacher who, about 1845, was
the first to cultivate the native wild cranberry. Watching the growth of the
small, vine-like bushes in a swamp that he had drained for meadow purposes gave him the idea of creating a cranberry bog. The first year he received about $50 a barrel for his crop, the berries being bought by Phila-
delphia ship chandlers who sold them to whalers as a preventive for
scurvy. Webb's innovation has brought bread to many people who cling to
the impoverished soil of the pine country. Since 1911 cultivation of the
swamp blueberry, as a result of experiments of the U. S. Department of
Agriculture, has been important. Blueberry growers around Cassville have
organized a cooperative association for marketing this crop, which has
yielded $600 an acre.

Right from Cassville on a macadam road is ROVA FARMS, 0.2 *m.*, a social experiment under the direction of the Russian Consolidated Mutual Aid Society of America. A group of Russian emigrees occupies 1,400 acres of woods and farm land with
an attractive pond and stream, and a large community hall, administration building, dormitories, and cabins. Founded primarily as an old-age annuity home, the
colony offers recreational facilities for transients and preserves Russian folklore,
songs, and dances.

In the wooded country west of Cassville the highway crosses large ponds
that are used to flood nearby cranberry bogs. Laurel, scrub oak, and pines
are abundant.

Houses are isolated and cheaply built. A brown carpet of pine needles
and cones covers the white, sandy soil in many places up to the edge of
the road, yielding a resinous, balmy odor. Often the whistling of the bob-
white and other quail, or the drumming of grouse, is heard.

ARCHERS CORNERS, 14.4 *m.* (160 alt., 88 pop.), was formerly
Davistown. Here are seen a few attempts at farming the poor, acid soil
enclosed by zigzag rail-fences.

Westward the road is on higher ground, the DIVIDE between the Delaware and coastal slopes. Scrub barrens are replaced by farming country.

On an old farm (L) at 15.7 *m.* is ZION METHODIST CHURCH, first of
that denomination in Ocean County. About 1789 Methodism was introduced in the log house of Job Horner, who lived on the farm that in-

cluded the present church site. The existing church replaced an earlier building that burned in 1837.

NEW EGYPT, 18.6 m. (75 alt., 500 pop.), a small agricultural village, straddles Crosswicks Creek. One-story shops and stores line both sides of the highway. Irregularly spaced along the graveled streets and surrounded by broad lawns and old trees are frame houses of Colonial and Victorian architecture, brightly painted in white and cream.

Crosswicks Creek here has been dammed to form OAKFORD LAKE (L), a vacation spot with woodlands on the shore. The creek was the route followed by the first Quaker colonists soon after their arrival on the Delaware in 1675.

At the time of the Revolution the village was known as Timmons Mills. After the victory at Trenton in December, 1776, Washington needed grain for his army. Benjamin Jones, one of the General's New Jersey advisors, had a large quantity of buckwheat flour and cornmeal stored at the mills; he sent his secretary, Joseph Curtis, to bring the milled grain to Trenton. Hailing the welcome arrival, Washington said: "Joseph has been in Egypt and gotten the corn." The village was Egypt until 1845, when the prefix "New" was added to avoid confusion with other Egypts. Center of a fine farm and dairy section, New Egypt still has a never failing corn crop.

The FORT HOMESTEAD (*private*), Main St. and Fort Ave., set in the ruins of vanished gardens, is flat-roofed, southern Colonial in style, with a three-story winding staircase, huge fireplaces and a large cauldron built into the kitchen wall, and even a "sweet potato hole" between floors. This was the home of former Gov. George F. Fort, and of his nephew, another Governor, Judge John F. Fort.

Left from the center of New Egypt on a graveled road is HOCKAMICK, 2 m., the remains of a lumbering village dating back to 1750. The name came from a peddler named Mick, widely known in the Pines as Hawker Mick, who lived here. In Hockamick are the RUINS OF A SAWMILL once run by the power of Jumping Brook. The old dam and the large millpond remain, water still running through the rotten spillway.

West of New Egypt the macadam road passes through an almost flat country, with broad fields enclosed by split-rail fences. Rambling, red brick farmhouses, some of them built more than 100 years ago, are half hidden in small groves of old trees. Chicken raising is extensive here.

COOKSTOWN, 21 m. (90 alt., 110 pop.), has a few small clapboarded houses huddled around an old dam holding back the water of North Run, once used to turn the wheels of Cook's Mill, which served the Colonists before the Revolution. A METHODIST CHURCH by the highway (L) was built in 1839; it stands within a graveyard that has served the neighborhood for nearly 200 years. Cookstown is large enough to maintain a garage and automobile sales depot, and 20 feet of sidewalk before the saloon at the bridge over Crosswicks Creek.

The HENDRICKSON MILL (R) dates back to 1732 and is still grinding flour and feed. From the timbers hang great cobwebs, formed not by spiders but by spray from the rush of water over the dripping wheel and by dust from the grain.

The COOKSTOWN HOUSE, SE. cor. Main St. and Brinteltown Rd., is a two-and-one-half-story building of whitewashed brick. It has a fanlight over the front door, a palladian window on the second floor, and fine arched dormers of leaded glass. A recent porch and a beer sign mar the old mansion, which is now a tavern.

MAHALALA, 21.7 *m.*, the Indian name of a section where the Boy Scouts of Burlington County have a camp, is close to a LAKE (R).

WRIGHTSTOWN, 23.3 *m.* (130 alt., 400 pop.), is a small community on the edge of an extensive military reservation, CAMP DIX. Thousands of ex-soldiers remember the little village with a few dingy old houses, many converted for the war period into stores and lunchrooms. A few scattered houses, a small group of one-story stores with squared fronts that hide the gables of their roofs, and a little used railroad station remain.

The highway cuts through the military reservation, covering 8,700 acres of low hills. Long rows of deserted barracks, huge parade grounds overgrown with grass, and an occasional concrete gun emplacement are left. There were once 1,600 buildings here, and 85,000 men were in training. CMTC and National Guard units still train here for three months each summer, and the camp has motor transport quarters and barracks of the 311th Infantry. An airport is used for military flights.

LEWISTOWN, 26.8 *m.* (80 alt., 120 pop.), at the southwestern edge of Camp Dix, is another hamlet that was lifted into temporary prosperity during the World War.

The road winds W. over a rolling terrain in dairying country.

At NORTH PEMBERTON STATION, 29.6 *m.*, the highway crosses the Pennsylvania R.R. at grade. This point has long been known as Comical Corner, apparently for no reason except that a county and a township road meet at the railroad.

PEMBERTON, 30 *m.* (75 alt., 783 pop.), is a quiet old farm center whose streets disclose the sturdy frame and brick residences of middle-class occupants. Old trees shade the streets and wide lawns. Time-stained houses attest the age of Pemberton, which largely escaped damage during the Revolution because it was a few miles off the line of marches and raids along the old King's Highway. Many of the residents, owners of large farms, now live in the town, while "renters" till the fields that have been owned by the same families for generations.

The business section consists of a number of small stores in a single block. Three well-filled cemeteries within grilled iron fences are on the main street.

The Pemberton district was settled by Quakers before 1690. Among the older buildings are the GRISTMILL (R) on Main St., still doing business, and the old PEMBERTON INN, SE. cor Hanover and Elizabeth Sts. The inn is a very long two-and-one-half-story brick building of strong Pennsylvania Dutch influence. It is flush with the sidewalk, with a narrow fanlighted door. Across part of the front is a one-story porch with an ornate wooden railing. The inn closed after the prohibition act was passed. The bar corner is unoccupied; an antique shop and three other stores occupy the rest of the ground floor.

POTTERY WORKER, HADDONFIELD

Pemberton was first called Hampton Hanover because it lay in both Northampton and Hanover Townships. Later the name was changed to New Mills, and in 1826 the present name was adopted in honor of James Pemberton, a Philadelphia shipping merchant.

CANNON RUN joins the Rancocas at Pemberton. A huge cannon is said to be buried deep in the mire here. The gun was built at Hanover Furnace, 10 miles east, to defend Marcus Hook on the Delaware River against British forces during the War of 1812. It was hauled as far as Pemberton by eight oxen. Here the wagon was mired and overturned, the gun going deep into the bog.

Left from Pemberton, on a hard-surfaced road, along the banks of the North Branch of Rancocas Creek, is BROWNS MILLS, 6 *m.* (60 alt., 255 pop.). It has been a health resort for many years, chiefly for tubercular persons, for whom the air of the pine forest is recommended. The mills, which gave the town its name, were operated by water from a lake 2 miles long, still here.

East from Browns Mills to the RUINS OF HANOVER FURNACE, 9.2 *m.,* at the western end of a lake. Between 1791 and 1864 iron was smelted here from nearby bogs. Cannon and balls were made for the Army and Navy in 1812, and Commodore Stephen Decatur is said to have served here as an inspector of munitions. Later the plant made much of the pipe that went into Philadelphia's early water system. Part of the great pile of slag that surrounded the old works remains, but much has been used to improve nearby roads.

The highway crosses Rancocas Creek at 30.1 *m.* Here stands an immense

PACKING SHED (L) in which cranberries are made ready for market. Berry pickers, brought from Philadelphia and Camden each year, live on the edges of the bogs in tents, cabins, and crude shelters.

Roadside stands with farm produce appear west of Pemberton, some built of boards, brightly painted white or pale blue, while others are of slabwood to give a rustic appearance.

Orchards of peach and apple trees edge up to the highway. Road signs warn pedestrians to walk facing traffic and to carry a light after dark, but well-lighted pedestrians are rarely encountered.

At 32.8 *m.* is the junction with US 206 *(see Tour 6).*

At 33.8 *m.* is the junction with a macadam road.

Right on this road is SMITHVILLE, 0.8 *m.* (30 alt., 100 pop.), consisting mainly of two-family houses of weathered clapboards. The village was founded in 1865 by the once famous Hezekiah Smith, whose high-wheel Star bicycle with a small wheel in back was a menace to life two generations ago. Here, on the country road that leads to the Newbold's Corners Road along the south bank of Rancocas Creek, is still the SMITH FACTORY that manufactured the bicycle about 1882, but now produces machinery. Smith sent the wheel to Washington, where his exhibition rider tried to pedal it down the steps of the Capitol and was arrested. Between Smithville and Mount Holly the inventor built his monorail bicycle railway to carry his employees to and from work. Bicycles resembling the present type hung from a rail laid on posts about 4 feet high. In 1879 Smith completed a steam wagon with kerosene firebox and boiler. It is said that the car made good speed but Smith decided that the people were not ready for such a vehicle, so he stored it in a barn. Later the citizens showed their appreciation by electing Smith to Congress and to the State senate. He campaigned in a carriage drawn by a trained moose from his native New England, driving about Burlington County and frightening every horse on the road. Workmen at the plant were organized into a widely known band which finally led Smith's funeral procession.

At 35.4 *m.* State 38 begins and continues to Camden.

At 35.4 *m.* is the junction with a paved road.

Right on this road is MOUNT HOLLY, 1.1 *m.* (30 alt., 6,573 pop.) *(see MOUNT HOLLY).*

Points of Interest: Courthouse (1796), Brainerd School, Stephen Girard House, John Woolman Memorial Building, Mount Holly, and others.

Westward the highway runs through a prosperous area of small farms, a region of egg production. The cooperative movement is strong in this section, the farm organizations maintaining regular egg auctions at Mount Holly.

At 37.6 *m.* is the junction with a macadam road.

Left on this road, which follows the twisting South Branch, is LUMBERTON, 1.4 *m.* (20 alt.), which has only one structure not built of wood. From a section of newer houses, the road enters the old treeless main street where stoops and front porches of the low, closely built houses are level with the sidewalk. The LUMBERTON HOTEL, Main St., is a three-story frame building, built c. 1790. The METHODIST CHURCH, on the same street, was erected in 1812 on Church St. and later moved to this spot. Bishop Francis Asbury, pioneer of Methodism, preached in the present church in 1813. Dimsdale Run or Bobby's Run, flowing into the Rancocas, was named for Dr. Robert Dimsdale, a learned Englishman who bought land here in 1684 from William Penn and built a sawmill. Large quantities of lumber, cordwood, and farm produce were shipped from Lumberton to Philadelphia. At the foot of Landing St., on the creek, is the BURLINGTON CO. IRON WORKS, which made the horse-head hitching posts once common in hundreds of cities.

At 37.7 *m.* State 38 crosses the South Branch of Rancocas Creek, water highway for nearly 200 years, now a favorite resort of canoeists. Tiny fir trees have been planted in cut-over tracts by CCC workers.

At 39.5 *m.* is the junction with an improved road.

Left on this road to the EDWIN CRISPIN FARM, 1 *m.*, where in 1916 scientists from the University of Pennsylvania uncovered Indian relics from a mound. Many banner stones and argillite implements of fine workmanship were obtained.

At 43.3 *m.* is the junction with an improved road.

1. Left on this road to MOUNT LAUREL STATE PARK, 2.3 *m.*, a 20-acre recreation area. The mountain rises 450 feet above sea level, highest point in this region, and offers views of spreading farm lands, streams, and old Quaker villages. Before the invention of the telegraph, Mount Laurel was one of a series of hills between New York and Philadelphia used by New York Stock Exchange brokers as signal towers from which were wigwagged reports and prices of stocks and bonds. Reports reached Philadelphia in 20 minutes. The apparatus was still in use in 1846.

2. Right from State 38 at the same junction is MOORESTOWN, 1 *m.* (70 alt., 6,500 pop.), laid out in 1722 by Thomas Moore. The most important building is the COMMUNITY HOUSE, Main St., a handsome stone structure of two stories in Tudor style that, with its old-fashioned garden, sets the pace for private homes and gardens in the community. It is a center for the town's social and civic activities. Main St. is a thoroughfare divided against itself. Most of the stores and other business offices are on one side of the street; directly across are dignified old residences and gardens. The FRIENDS SCHOOL and MEETING HOUSE, a group of red brick buildings of Georgian design, is the largest Friends' school in southern New Jersey. Classes are held for more than 350 pupils. The SMITH MANSION, 12 High St. *(private)*, was erected 1738. General Knyphausen and other Hessian officers stayed overnight here in 1778 during their retreat from Philadelphia. Some of the soldiers deserted in Moorestown, and their descendants are said to live in the neighborhood. The ZELLEY HOUSE *(private)*, on Stanwick Ave. 200 yds. east of Central Ave., has the date 1721 on its wall. It is built of red brick and has hand-hewn timbers. Around the house are the vineyards and orchards of its present owner, a fruit grower.

At 46.5 *m.,* at a traffic circle, is the junction with State S41 *(see Tour 37)*. Here State 38 is a part of the King's Highway of Colonial days, the route of Clinton's army on its retreat from Philadelphia in 1778.

The CAMDEN COUNTY PARK is on both sides of Rancocas Creek.

At 51.8 *m.* (L) is CENTRAL AIRPORT *(see Tour 19)*.

At the airport traffic circle is the junction with State 40 *(see Tour 27)*.

At 52.2 *m.,* at a traffic circle, State 38 forms a junction with US 130 *(see Tour 19)*.

Straight ahead on Admiral Wilson Blvd. to the Delaware River Bridge Plaza at the intersection of Broadway; L. from the Plaza on Broadway leads to the City Hall and Courthouse.

CAMDEN, 54.5 *m.* (25 alt., 118,700 pop.) *(see CAMDEN)*.

Points of Interest: Friends School, Johnson Park, RCA-Victor Manufacturing Plant, Campbell Soup Plant, Walt Whitman House, Joseph Cooper House, Charles S. Boyer Memorial Hall (museum), and others.

Tour 27

Laurelton—Lakehurst—Medford—Junction with State 38; State 40.
Laurelton to Junction with State 38, 55.4 m.

Hotel accommodations at terminals; few lunchrooms and filling stations in eastern
section.
Concrete roadbed of two to four lanes.

State 40 crosses the pine wastes, largely cut-over land with scrub growth,
much of which is now State-protected forest. In the western section the
highway enters a zone of small farms. The farms become increasingly fertile and the villages more numerous as the road nears the outskirts of industrial Camden.

LAURELTON, 0 *m.* (10 alt., 350 pop.) *(see Tour 22)*, is at the junction with State 35 *(see Tour 22)* and State 34 *(see Tour 21)*.

Bending R. on a slight downgrade, the road crosses the marshy, pine-
bordered waters of three branches of Metedeconk River, and then climbs
gently again.

At 0.9 *m.* another branch of the Metedeconk widens to form a LAKE
(L), in places choked with marsh grass.

The road runs straight over a flat area of new pines growing through a
burnt-over forest. Beyond the graveled shoulders is an expanse of white
sand, which offers poor nourishment to the skimpy vegetation. A few desolate chicken farms in a low grove of scrub oaks are the only habitations.

At 5.1 *m.* State 40 underpasses US 9 *(see Tour 18)*.

Swift streams, draining the sandy pine barrens, cut under the road at
intervals until a tall and slender water tank at Lakehurst is seen directly
ahead.

At 10.4 *m.* the roadbed is of tar and gravel and turns L. toward the
eastern end of Lakehurst.

At 10.5 *m.* is the junction with State 37 *(see Tour 30)*. Between this
point and Lakehurst, State 40 is united with State 37.

LAKEHURST, 10.9 *m.* (79 alt., 947 pop.), is a quiet little village that
has seen the iron furnaces prosper and fail, the charcoal industry rise and
fall, the railroad shops come and go, and the lighter-than-air craft hailed
and now seriously questioned. There are tall elms along the streets, planted
in the Civil War period when real estate men tried to put new life into
the old settlement of Manchester after the iron and charcoal industries
died. The town was almost wiped out, but in 1860 the "new railroad," the
Jersey Central, placed its repair shops here and Manchester again flourished. The shops have been closed since 1932; there is no industrial plant
in the village now and little farming around it.

Into a tavern here early in September, 1937, came a local blueberry picker, John Henry Titus, 91, with a kerosene-soaked rag in his shoe to ward off mosquitoes. According to *Time* magazine, "he sank to one knee, and, with gestures, once more recited his famous poem, *The Face on the Barroom Floor.*" Scholars, however, generally give H. H. D'Arcy credit for the poem.

Right from the center of Lakehurst on a macadam road to the UNITED STATES NAVAL AIR STATION, 1.2 *m.* *(open daily 8-6),* a wire-fenced reservation of 1,500 acres on a broad rise above the thick pines. Prior to the World War the tract was used first by private munitions makers and then by the Army chemical warfare branch as a munitions testing ground. After the armistice, Camp Kendrick, as it was called, was allocated to the Navy as a base for lighter-than-air craft. In 1923 the first American-built, rigid, lighter-than-air ship, the *Shenandoah,* made her initial flight from Lakehurst. The ZR-3 arrived from Germany on Oct. 15, 1924, and became the *Los Angeles,* now decommissioned. The *Akron* left this station and fell into the ocean off Barnegat in 1933. The *Macon,* which crashed in the Pacific, made test flights from here before proceeding to her base in California. Four small airships were stationed here in 1938: the K-1, the J-4, the G-1, and the ZMC-2, plus three airplanes for aerological observations. In 1936 and 1937 this station was used as the landing field for the commercial flights of the German airship *Hindenburg,* destroyed here by fire on May 6, 1937, in the space of 4 minutes with the loss of 36 lives. The tragedy occurred as the ship was 250 feet above the ground, maneuvering toward the mooring mast. The crowd, gathered to watch the landing, stood helplessly as travelers leaped flaming from the gondola or were burned alive. The cause of the spectacular airship disaster has never been completely determined. With the passing of the *Hindenburg,* Lakehurst lost its importance as a base for commercial lighter-than-air craft.

The station's many scattered buildings are dominated by gigantic hangars, the largest 961 feet long, 350 feet wide, and 200 feet high, which can house simultaneously all five airships assigned to the base and still have empty space. The steel frame of the hangar is encased in a silver-colored asbestos-composition material. The double doors are not attached to the building but are mounted on rollers. Each door weighs 2,700 tons and is operated by four 20-horsepower motors. Inside the large hangar on the south wall is a bronze memorial tablet dedicated to the 14 men lost with the *Shenandoah.*

A separate hangar for airplanes, a telescoping storage tank for helium gas, powerhouses, workshops, armory, administration building, and quarters make the station a small modern city.

In the SW. corner of the reservation is the CATHEDRAL OF THE AIR, a small Gothic-type chapel in gray stone, dedicated to those living and dead who have contributed to man's conquest of the air. Lakehurst is the only air station where the Navy raises and trains carrier pigeons.

The many small modern houses along the highway west of Lakehurst are rented to officers of the air station when quarters at the reservation are filled. Reduction of personnel has made this a deserted district.

The road passes a few patches of dense cedar woods, survivals of the time when large forests of pine and cedar covered much of this region. Huge white letters and arrows painted on the road are direction markers for airplane pilots. Long stretches of roadway with wide dirt shoulders edged with scattered pines present a desolate picture for miles ahead.

At Pole Bridge Brook (R), 22.1 *m.,* is WHITESBOG, one of the largest cranberry plantations of the State. The cultivated swamp blueberry, also produced here, was first developed commercially on this plantation. Burnt areas of the pines (L) and old sand pits filled with water break the monotony of the wooded waste.

UPTON, 24.3 *m.* (90 alt.), is a center for rattlesnake hunting. Some of the reptiles are sold to museums or zoos in the large cities, others go to tanners who prepare snakeskin for women's shoes and other leather goods. One well-known hunter here has caught thousands of reptiles, pine snakes as well as rattlers. Guides are available during the brief deer-hunting season.

At 25 *m.* is the junction with a dirt road.

Left on this road is the hamlet of MOUNT MISERY, 0.8 *m.* (120 alt.), with a long-deserted inn and a few decaying houses. The best explanation of the name is that it was shortened from Misericorde, or Mercy, which may have been bestowed by its first settler, Peter Bard, a Frenchman, who came here from Burlington in 1723. Residents now complain that the numerous protected deer leap over 6-foot fences to eat their garden produce, wild rabbits rob them, and rattlesnakes raid the hencoops.

UPPER MILL, 27.5 *m.,* has only two houses, the remains of a tiny mill settlement. On one, the date 1720 is carved on a log.

Westward the highway passes through LEBANON STATE FOREST, 27.8 *m.* *(see Tour 35).*

At 28.9 *m.,* at a traffic circle, is the junction with State S40 *(see Tour 35).*

At the traffic circle is the junction with a macadam road.

Right on this road is ONG'S HAT, 1.6 *m.* (100 alt.), a tiny village that hangs on the end of the pine country. The Ong family was among the first in this neighborhood. The tradition is that one young Ong slighted a woman who was so angered that she snatched the chimney-pot hat from his head and flung it into the branches of a pine tree. There the hat remained to give its name to the settlement.

West of Lebanon Forest the highway runs into the pine barrens. Straight walls of the wilderness flank the road, and signs of human habitation are lacking for miles. Narrow wagon trails lead to haunts of hunters and sportsmen in the forest. Laurel grows in abundance; its springtime bloom presents a brilliant spectacle. Small groves of silver birches occasionally break the dark green wall. The highway crosses many tiny creeks and streams of clear, cedar-tinged water.

At 29.8 *m.* (R) is a break in the forest wall, a new log cabin roadstand surrounded by tables and rustic chairs. Cranberry bogs, low sunken hollows resembling deserted excavations for immense buildings, overgrown with thick underbrush, edge up to the highway.

FRIENDSHIP CREEK, 34.9 *m.,* is joined farther south by Bread and Cheese Run.

Gradually the wooded region gives way to small farms with fruit orchards and planted fields. Hip-roofed barns and roomy old farmhouses stand under old trees a few hundred feet from the road.

At 36.8 *m.,* at a traffic circle, is the junction with US 206 *(see Tour 6).*

At 36.9 *m.* is the junction with a hard-surfaced road.

Right on this road is the odd little crossroads hamlet of RED LION, 0.2 *m.* (65 alt., 62 pop.). The village, eight weather-beaten frame dwellings, a dilapidated old barn, and a combination country store and filling station, clusters around a rambling hotel, RED LION INN. It is a three-story red brick structure of Colonial design, said to have been built in 1710. Only the outside lines of the old building remain unaltered; modern plumbing, electricity, and wallpaper have changed the interior.

Frank Peck, known as the "Water Wizard," is one of Red Lion's most popular residents, according to Henry C. Beck in *Forgotten Towns of Southern New Jersey*. With a divining rod, Peck stalks along a plot of ground, stops, moves on until the rod turns in his hand and points to the ground. "Here is the place to dig the well," Peck says. "Five dollars, please." The red lion that gave its name to the hotel and to the town is supposed to have been a mountain lion slain by an old resident, who, though badly clawed in the conflict, clubbed the animal until it was crimson with blood.

MEDFORD, 41.2 *m.* (60 alt., 550 pop.), founded by Quakers before 1759, is a quiet village on the edge of the pines, at the crossing of two old stage roads. On Union St. one block from Main St. is the brick Orthodox Friends Meeting House, built 1814, in a widespread grove of maples, elms, and sycamores.

The Medford Hotel, Main St. corner of Coates St., was built in 1842. The house interests antiquarians because of a row of plain iron pillars on its lower veranda, bearing the letter "B" near the base. This is the mark of Batsto Furnace, which made munitions in the Revolution. An earlier hotel building, burned in 1842, was rebuilt to make the present structure. Jesse Richards, ironmaster of Batsto, gave the posts to the innkeeper, Daniel Coates.

The South Branch of the Rancocas brought Quaker settlers here before 1759. The village was known by various names until Mark Reeve visited

Medford, Mass., and was so much impressed with the place that he induced his neighbors in 1828 to name their town for it.

At 41.4 m. is the junction with a macadam road.

Left on this road to PINE LAKE, 3.2 m., northernmost of a chain of five lakes known as TAUNTON LAKES, popular summer resorts. Pine Lake is now a favorite Sunday-school picnic site despite its earlier names of Whisky Hollow and Spirit Vale.

At 4.2 m. the route turns L. on a dirt road crossing a dam at the foot of Taunton Lake. Here (L), just below the dam, is the SITE OF TAUNTON FURNACE AND FORGE with a setting of stately old trees and old houses. The lake and dam gave power to the furnace, built in 1766 by Charles Read of Philadelphia.

West of Medford the route passes through rich, cultivated farm land. Venerable old brick farmhouses stand well back from the road. Lean-to kitchens or frame rooms seem to be temporary structures laid against the brick walls for support.

MARLTON, 46.7 m. (100 alt., 500 pop.), owes its name to an industry that has dwindled in late years—the mining of marl from pits in this area. This fertilizer added greatly to the produce of Burlington County farms in the last century. Marl is now used to soften water in industry and to mix with sand for molding steel. The town has changed little since its early days, and is well-kept despite its years. The BAPTIST CHURCH (R) was built in 1805. The GENERAL STORE at the Four Corners, a frame building, was erected in 1823.

At 47 m. is the junction with State S41 (see Tour 37).

A few turkey farms dot the countryside here, with huge flocks strutting within wire-enclosed fields or perching upon naked trees.

At 49.5 m. (R) stands the REEVE FURNACE, a brick stack bound with heavy iron hoops, built in 1875 in a futile attempt to revive bog-iron making here. The supply of bog ore was insufficient, so the furnace was converted to a lime kiln, burning oyster shells from the Delaware. In 1927 it closed because of the advancing price of fuel.

ELLISBURG, 51.7 m. (50 alt., 50 pop.), is a small group of houses and stores near a traffic circle. At the circle is the intersection with old King's Highway.

Left from the center of Ellisburg is HADDONFIELD, 1.9 m. (80 alt., 8,857 pop.), founded by a Quaker girl of 20, Elizabeth Haddon. Today mainly the home of commuters to Camden and Philadelphia, it retains a good deal of the country-like charm and simplicity of its early days. In 1710 Elizabeth was sent over from England by her father, who had no sons, to develop 400 acres of land. Within a year the young woman had started her colony, erected a home, and married John Estaugh, Quaker missionary, because she had the courage to propose to him. Longfellow tells the story of the romance with the "Theologian's Tale" in Tales of a Wayside Inn.

Later the "great road or King's Highway" was laid through the Haddon estate on its route from Burlington to Salem. At the time of the Revolution it was the most important thoroughfare in this region. Today the highway, shaded by old trees, is still the main street of Haddonfield, broad and leisurely even in its short business section. The center of town is the old section, the modern homes spreading out around it.

The SITE OF THE ELIZABETH HADDON HOUSE (private), NE. cor. Wood Lane and Marion Ave., is on a small hill rising unexpectedly from the midst of modern homes in the northeastern part of town. The grounds and buildings have retained their Colonial appearance, but the log home Elizabeth Haddon built burned in 1742. The sedate three-story brick house, built on the site in 1845, has a flat roof with great chimneys, solid white shutters, and a Classic Revival porch. Before the house are two English yew trees brought over in 1712 by Elizabeth, and on the door is her silver knocker. In the garden stands the original STILLHOUSE built by Elizabeth; it is probably the oldest structure in the community. The young woman won the lasting gratitude of neighboring Indians through the manufacture of medicinal whisky. From the very first the enterprise was so successful that the sick and ailing beat an almost constant tattoo on Elizabeth's silver knocker. Although the suffering tribesmen underwent treatment for prolonged periods, complete cures were rarely effected.

INDIAN KING INN *(open daily except Sun. 9-5; free)*, 233 King's Highway E., was built in 1750 by Mathias Aspden and has been a historic memorial since 1916. Several of the rooms are furnished with Colonial pieces; others have on display collections of Colonial relics. New Jersey's first legislature met here in 1777, when driven from Trenton by the British. It declared New Jersey a State, and in May of the same year adopted the first Great Seal of the State. The inn is a large three-story structure with pitch roof and white stucco walls. Pent eaves run across the street front, projecting far enough to give shelter to the low brick platform that forms a porch. A small hip roof with a dormer above the central second floor windows makes the design unusual.

The OLD GUARDHOUSE *(private)*, 258 King's Highway E., was connected with the Indian King Inn by an underground passage. Prisoners unfriendly to the American cause during the Revolution were tried by the Council of Safety at the inn and brought to the guardhouse through the tunnel. The house is an unpretentious, two-and-one-half-story structure of gray-painted brick.

ERLTON, 52.5 *m.* (45 alt., 856 pop.), its name not a New York version of "Oiltown," is a recently developed residential community. Red brick houses are scattered along the paved streets, with large fields between the dwellings.

At 52.9 *m.*, at a traffic circle, are the lawns and trees of CAMDEN COUNTY PARK (L), with Cooper Creek flowing through it, parallel to the highway.

The distant houses of Camden are L.—long rows of two-story brick buildings. The city chimneys are seen on the skyline.

A large grassy plot enclosed by a high wire fence is WARREN BUCK'S ZOO (R), 53.7 *m. (adm. 10¢)*, recently moved here from Camden. Wild animals, including monkeys, small felines, and birds, are exhibited.

The highway passes the COOPER RIVER GOLF CLUB (L) at 54.7 *m.* *(9 holes; greens fee 60¢, Sat., Sun. and holidays $1).*

At 55.4 *m.*, at a traffic circle, is the junction with State 38 *(see Tour 26)* and US 130 *(see Tour 19)* 2.7 miles east of Camden.

◄◄◄◄◄◄◄◄◄◄◄◄◄◄◄◄◄◄ ✿ ►►►►►►►►►►►►►►►►►►►

Tour 28

Junction with US 130—Woodbury—Mullica Hill—Woodstown—Salem;
State 45.
Junction with US 130 to Salem, 28.4 m.

Pennsylvania-Reading Seashore Lines parallel the route between Junction with
US 130 and Mantua.
Hotel accommodations in larger towns; meals, gasoline stations, and garage service
available.
Two- and four-lane concrete roadbed.

State 45 runs southwest through a row of Camden suburbs into rich
farming and dairying land. The country then changes to the typical pine
and scrub barrens, broken by an occasional farm. Farther south it climbs
low rolling hills on which grow the famous Gloucester County tomatoes.
The land flattens out again as the road approaches the industrial section
of Salem. There are many buildings with historic associations along the
route.

State 45 branches south from US 130 in Westville (see Tour 19).

The highway pursues a straight course between the tracks of the Pennsylvania-Reading Seashore Lines (L) and homes of commuters (R). An
occasional open field breaks the monotony of solid rows of brick dwellings
of Philadelphia pattern.

At 1.8 m. is the junction with a dirt road.

Right on this road to the MANOR HOUSE (private), 0.6 m., 1337 Colonial Ave.,
a two-story Dutch Colonial home built in 1688 by John Ladd Sr., surveyor and
court officer. The original Colonial lines have been almost wiped out by alterations.
Ladd was expelled by the Quakers because he married couples who did not belong
to meeting, and because it was determined that he could not be a good court officer
and a good Quaker.

WOODBURY, 2.8 m. (50 alt., 8,172 pop.), the seat of Gloucester
County, has an up-to-date business section and is the center of a prosperous
farming region.

State 45, here Broad St., follows a section of the King's Highway that
linked Burlington and Cape May. The QUAKER MEETING HOUSE (L),
built 1716, has had several additions. It is a plain, two-and-a-half-story
brick structure covered with ivy and shaded by large trees and a low porch
across the broad front. Inside are massive, hand-hewn timbers, wooden
benches, and an old wood stove, contrasting with the modern covering of
the wide board floors and the mosquito screens. The meeting house was
used as a hospital during the Revolutionary War.

Opposite the Meeting House is the PAUL HOTEL, built in 1720 from
surplus bricks ordered for the meeting house, and still in service. Confis-

cated from a Tory owner during the Revolution, the inn became known after the battle of Red Bank as The American Defeating the Hessian. Additions and changes have obliterated its early lines. At the town center on Broad St. are the GLOUCESTER COUNTY COURTHOUSE (R), a brownstone, steepled structure built in 1787 and modernized in 1885; the Ionic-columned HALL OF RECORDS, erected 1926; and the CIVIL WAR MONUMENT.

Opposite the courthouse is (L) the JOHN COOPER HOUSE *(private)*, a substantial red brick building. Cornwallis took over the house in November, 1777, as his headquarters. The owner, John Cooper, a member of the Continental Congress, was forced to flee, leaving his well-filled wine cellar to a foe with a raging thirst. The house has a large fireplace and fine, paneled woodwork. The door panels are in the "Holy Cross door" tradition of England, so designed to protect the house from evil spirits. Deep marks on doors and frames were made by British bayonets.

The LAWRENCE HOUSE (L), 58 N. Broad St. *(open Mon.-Fri., 9-5; free)*, was built in 1765 by the Rev. Andrew Hunter, celebrated clergyman who took part in the Greenwich Tea Party *(see Tour 29B)*. Of native brick, the structure follows the typical South Jersey style, combining various features of Tudor and Dutch Colonial architecture. The house later belonged to John Lawrence, brother of Capt. James Lawrence *(see BUR-LINGTON)*, who lived here while attending school in Woodbury. The Gloucester County Historical Society exhibits a well-ordered collection of Colonial relics and documents.

FRIENDSHIP FIRE HOUSE (R) has in its yard a HAND PUMP FIRE ENGINE bought in 1799, the year the company was formed.

The region south of Woodbury is rich farming land. The farms are as broad as they were in 1777 when Gen. "Mad Anthony" Wayne successfully foraged here for Washington's army.

At 5.6 m. is the junction with a dirt road.

Right on this road to the MANTUA OAK, 0.4 m., estimated to be more than 600 years old. The tree stands on the banks of old Mantua Creek. The topmost branches are 87 feet high, and the girth of the trunk is 19 feet 9 inches. The trunk is sound, but some of the branches have begun to wither.

MANTUA (Ind., *frog*), 5.8 m. (35 alt., 2,697 pop.), is a quiet old farm center with closely built houses set behind lawns shaded by stately trees. There is still a frog chorus on the creek *(March-Nov., 7 p.m-4 a.m.; free)*.

South of Mantua short, scrubby oak trees, puny pines, and cedars line the road.

JEFFERSON, 8.6 m. (140 alt.), has a double row of houses, many of them glistening white, along the highway.

MULLICA HILL, 10.9 m. (80 alt., 600 pop.), rising from the banks of Raccoon Creek, has a mile-long, tree-lined main street with neat homes, and business places serving the farm region. It is named for Eric Molica, or Mullica, who led Swedish colonists across the State to the Mullica River in Burlington County *(see Tour 23A)*.

The brick QUAKER MEETING HOUSE (R), built 1808, is typical of the plain structures of the sect. Hand-split shingles were used on the roof with wrought nails. During the Civil War, Mullica Hill formed a complete company of Quakers who saw active service.

At Mullica Hill is the junction with US 322 *(see Tour 25)* and with State 46 *(see Tour 32)*.

The highway runs over a series of long rolling hills and through wide fields of sweet potatoes, asparagus, and tomatoes.

At 13.3 *m.* is (R) a small, square, white building, the former TOLL-HOUSE for the turnpike. It is now the office of an agricultural agent.

Giant silos, windmills, and barns form an impressive agrarian scene between Mullica Hill and Woodstown. The land gradually flattens as the road crosses Oldman's Creek at 16 *m.* This rich land attracted the Quaker followers of John Fenwick in 1675. Many of their descendants remain, farming the same acres.

WOODSTOWN, 19.1 *m.* (50 alt., 1,832 pop.) *(see Tour 24),* is at the junction with US 40 *(see Tour 24).*

State 45 crosses the headwaters of Salem Creek southwest of Woodstown at 19.8 *m.* Herds of cattle browse in wide fields, near corncribs made by stretching small-meshed, ratproof wire over a frame of planks, roofed to keep out the rain.

At 19.9 *m.* is the junction with a dirt road.

Left on this road to Fenwick Rd., 1.4 *m.;* L. on Fenwick Rd. is PORTERTOWN, 1.6 *m.* (70 alt.), a Negro village of dingy frame houses. This is old Bushtown, scene of "June Meetings" that until about 20 years ago emptied three southern New Jersey counties of their Negro population for a period of religious revival in the summer. Here singing bands vied to stir religious fervor; Negro spirituals were sung and new lines inspired while standing in the spirit with Moses on Pisgah's height viewing the promised land. Relays of preachers of varying sects followed one another with appeals to the emotions in "gravy" sermons, as they were termed. Just outside the camp gamblers gathered, liquor flowed, and there were orgies of betting. Bootleggers in the bushes and black queens in bustles offered temptation to saints and penitents alike who wandered away from meetings. The automobile is chiefly responsible for the passing of the Bushtown "June Meetings."

The highway at 21.9 *m.* passes the SALEM COUNTY HOME (L), its huge farm fenced by whitewashed boards in striking contrast with the red brick buildings.

At a road fork at 22.2 *m.* is the Fenwick Monument (L), erected in 1929, indicating the GRAVE OF JOHN FENWICK, founder of the Salem Colony, at a spot not exactly determined.

At 24 *m.* is (R) the SMITHFIELD HOUSE *(private),* a fine example of early Colonial architecture. Two and one-half stories high, the brick house has small porches, and a hip roof with a railed platform or widow's walk. Tall trees flank its lawn. It was built in 1685 by John Smith, one of John Fenwick's executors, who purchased the land from Fenwick's son-in-law, Samuel Hedge.

Immediately across the road, and set back somewhat from it, is the HEDGEFIELD HOUSE *(private),* three stories high, practically square, built with native brick and white marble trim. It was erected in 1722 by Samuel Hedge, who had married Anna Fenwick, daughter of the Quaker leader. Despite modern alterations, the house's original charm remains.

King's Highway rejoins the route at the POINTERS, 26.6 *m.* The latter name comes from the junction of three old roads here pointing toward Salem. Southward, groups of modern homes contrast with the nearby rural region. Added to the normal smells of the countryside are odors of linoleum in the making, and of vegetables cooking in the Salem canneries.

At 26.8 *m.* the highway passes through CLAYVILLE, a community of Negroes, which was formerly called Gallows Hill. The big MANNINGTON LINOLEUM MILL is L.

At 28 *m.* is the junction with a private road.

Left on this road to the PLEDGER HOUSE, 0.6 *m.,* a notable example of early Colonial checkered brickwork, erected in 1727 by John Pledger, Jr. On March 17, 1778, the day before the Battle of Quinton's Bridge *(see Tour 29),* British soldiers seized the house and forced members of the Johnson family, then living there, into the cellar, where they were held captive until after the soldiers left. One prisoner was seven-year-old Robert Gibbon Johnson, who later became the Salem County historian. He left a highly valued record of his recollections.

At 28.1 *m.* State 45, here Market St., leads to the center of Salem. SALEM, 28.4 *m.* (16 alt., 8,047 pop.) *(see SALEM).*

Points of Interest: County Buildings, Alexander Grant House (museum), Old Law Office, Salem Oak, Bradway House, Friends Meeting House, and others.

At Broadway and Market St. State 45 forms a junction with State 49 *(see Tour 29).*

Tour 29

Pennsville—Salem—Bridgeton—Millville—Clermont; Pennsville-Salem Rd. and State 49.
Pennsville to Clermont, 60.8 m.

Meals and garage service at many places; hotels in the larger towns.
Two- and three-lane concrete and macadam roadbed.

State 49 affords an interesting, nearly water-level route across south New Jersey. The western section for the most part runs through rolling, fertile farm land and hardwood forests. East of the Maurice River at Millville, the highway crosses a tidewater area with sandy soil, scrub pine, and small fishing villages. In the district between Salem and Bridgeton are many brick Colonial houses. Most of them, in continuous use since they were built, are in good condition. The southern end of the route runs through fishing villages, summer resorts, and tidal marshland.

The Pennsville-Salem Rd. branches east from US 130 *(see Tour 19)* in PENNSVILLE, 0 *m.* (12 alt., 412 pop.) *(see Tour 19)*.

The highway's straight line lies like a long ruler across the lowlands. On the R. are the marshes where countless muskrats are trapped each season. Rice was grown on these meadows in such quantities in Colonial days that cargoes of it were shipped to all the coast ports. Wild rice now grows here, and millions of birds, protected by law, feed upon it. Rush reeds and their furry cattail spikes are seen in profusion; meadowland is L., too, but a few reclaimed spots support small farms. The meadows have a peculiar but not unpleasant odor.

At 1.1 *m.* is the junction with a hard-surfaced road.

Right on this road to (L) the excellent two-story brick WILLIAM MECUM HOUSE *(private)*, 1.4 *m.* The original unit was erected in the early 1700's; the new section, with its checkered brick design in front, was added in 1737. The gable of the newer end contains the date of its erection along with the initials of the builder, "W M."

The FORT MOTT RANGE LIGHT, 1.5 *m.* (L), raises its black head almost 100 feet to serve mariners on the Delaware. A tall, wire mesh fence encloses the reservation (R), part of which, at 2.7 *m.*, is a U. S. WILD FOWL SANCTUARY.

At 2.8 *m.* is (R) the entrance to FORT MOTT *(open daily, in summer 8-5, in winter 8-4)*, one of the defenses placed along the Delaware early in the Civil War. Mines were strung across the river from this point in the Spanish-American War. Today the fort, its masonry walls hidden by earth, is manned by a skeleton force. The landing pier at Fort Mott marks Finn's Point, the name of the locality for nearly 300 years. Here the Swedes built a fort about 1660, planting a colony believed to have included some of their Finnish subjects.

At 3.7 *m.* is (R) the FORT MOTT NATIONAL CEMETERY *(open daily, in summer 8-5, in winter 8-4)*, the only national cemetery in New Jersey in which Confederate soldiers are buried. More than 2,400 prisoners captured in the Battle of Gettysburg, and later victims of an epidemic, have been interred here; an obelisk 85 feet high honors the Confederate dead.

FORT DELAWARE *(accessible only by Federal boat; adm. only with written permission from War Dept.)*, 1.1 *m.* offshore on Pea Patch Island, is seen from the cemetery. The fort dates from 1859. There is a legend that a boat loaded with peas once sank in very shallow water on the site. The peas sprouted and drift material became enmeshed in the vines, forming an island that grew to its present size, 178 acres.

HARRISONVILLE, 3.9 *m.* (10 alt., 320 pop.), settled by Quakers at some time after 1673, was the site of a tavern popular in Civil War days. It was known as the Pig's Eye and for a time gave its name to the village and vicinity. Along the highway are homes of workers in nearby Salem.

Southeast of Harrisonville loom the chimneys of factories in Salem. The highway crosses Salem River, turns R. on Griffith St. to the intersection of W. Broadway; L. on W. Broadway to the Municipal and County Buildings at the corner of Market St.

SALEM, 6.7 *m.* (16 alt., 8,047 pop.) *(see SALEM)*.

Points of Interest: County Buildings, Alexander Grant House (museum), Old Law Office, Salem Oak, Bradway House, Friends Meeting House, and others.

At Salem is the junction (R) with Tilbury Rd. *(see Tour 29A)*.

From Market St. straight ahead on E. Broadway, which becomes Quinton Rd. at Keasbey St.; L. on Quinton Rd. (State 49).

HANCOCK HOUSE, HANCOCK'S BRIDGE

Right from Salem on an oiled gravel road is HANCOCK'S BRIDGE, 4 *m.* (5 alt.), a muskrat-trapping center. The WILLIAM HANCOCK HOUSE (R), 4.1 *m.* *(open daily; daylight hours; contribution),* was erected in 1734 by William Hancock and his wife Sarah, whose initials are woven into the gable. The house was the scene of a massacre on the night of March 20, 1778, a few days after the Battle of Quinton Bridge. About 90 American rebels were asleep in the dwelling when a detachment of 200 enemy troops—most of them green-coated Loyalists—under Maj. John Simcoe made a surprise attack. Bayoneting the sentries, the raiders entered the house and systematically began to exterminate the sleeping men. No quarter was given; militiamen were stabbed while pleading to be taken prisoner. Judge Hancock, a Tory, who had fled during American occupation of the area, had returned to his home earlier that night and been captured by the Revolutionists. By mistake, his Tory confederates killed him in the dark. The only survivors were a small number of militiamen who managed to get out of the house.

Owned by the State, the house is under the care of the Salem County Historical Society. Hundreds of Colonial relics are displayed. Two bedrooms, a reception room and the old kitchen have complete Colonial furnishings. The two-story farmhouse faces the bridge over Alloway Creek behind a row of massive maples. Both the checkerboard and zigzag patterns are worked into its walls with glazed brick.

Behind Hancock House is a CEDAR PLANK HOUSE *(open daily daylight hours; contribution),* a tiny one-story structure built of cedar taken from nearby swamps more than 200 years ago by Swedish settlers. The hand-hewn planks are dovetailed at the corners, making uprights and even the usual wooden pegs unnecessary. The house contains Colonial relics.

The FRIENDS MEETING HOUSE, 100 yds. R. from Hancock House, was erected in 1756; an addition dates from 1784.

At Broadway and Market St. in Salem is a junction with State 45 *(see Tour 28).*

Southeast of Salem, State 49 runs through rich bottomlands with level, well-fenced fields and large barns backed by silos and outbuildings. Sleek herds of dairy cattle graze in abundant pastures. The farms produce potatoes, corn, and oats.

At 8.8 *m.* is (L) the DANIEL SMITH HOUSE *(private),* built in 1752, a three-story brick structure standing back from the highway and surrounded by trees. It has been rebuilt and enlarged until only the original north gable, which bears the date of erection, remains. It was the scene of an ambush that cost American lives *(see below).*

At 10 *m.* the highway crosses Alloway Creek over Quinton Bridge, scene of the battle March 18, 1778, when Maj. John Simcoe and a British battalion marched here from Salem. The bridge was guarded by Colonial militia under Col. Benjamin Holmes. Concealing most of their troops in and around the Smith house, the British first led the Revolutionary militia into ambush, killing many. Then the invaders tried to cross the bridge, but Andrew Bacon seized an axe and, under fire, cut away the draw section, dropping it into the creek. Arrival of the Cumberland County militia with artillery compelled the British to retreat to Salem.

The ruins of the REVOLUTIONARY BRIDGE are merely a few piles showing a few inches above the water, L. of the present span. A granite monument commemorating the battle stands 200 feet south of the bridge (L).

QUINTON, 10.2 *m.* (20 alt., 525 pop.), was held by the county militia in the skirmish at Quinton Bridge. Modest homes line the roadway. Two small canning factories and the waterworks are its only industrial plants.

South of Salem the farms are larger. Tomatoes and other garden produce, and some fruit and berries are shipped from here to canneries.

MARLBORO, 16.3 *m.* (70 alt., 500 pop.), is on the banks of Horse Run. The SEVENTH-DAY BAPTIST CHURCH here, belongs to a congregation established in 1811.

At 17.8 *m.* is the junction with a graveled road.

Right on this road is JERICHO, 3 *m.* (30 alt., 350 pop.), established 1690 when Joshua Brick erected a tavern and gristmill.

Right from Jericho on the old Jericho Pike to IVY MANOR *(private),* 4.6 *m.,* built in 1800 by John Wood. It is in the Georgian style, of time-mellowed red brick, ivy-covered and surrounded by old trees and shrubbery. The three-story building contains 18 rooms, most of them with fireplaces, and mantelpieces of fine Italian marble. This was the "Bull Tavern" about which several of George Agnew Chamberlain's stories were centered. It is now a sanitarium.

The highway passes through the section cleared and still farmed by Seventh-Day Baptists, with well-kept buildings, cultivated fields, and close-cropped pastures.

SHILOH, 19 *m.* (120 alt., 401 pop.), founded by Seventh-Day Baptists fleeing from persecution in England in 1705, was first known as Cohansey, an extensive settlement along the Cohansey Creek, named for an Indian chief. In 1771, when the Baptists were moving an old frame church 2 miles to Cohansey, they reached Six Corners here at sundown on a Friday. Work ceased and religious services were begun. Their pastor used as his text, "The Ark of the Lord resteth at Shiloh," and by common consent the name of the community was changed to Shiloh.

Serving the needs of its surrounding farm country, Shiloh business converges at its six corners with a blacksmith shop, several stores, and a post office. All Shilohites keep Saturday as their Sabbath; on Sunday all business places from the post office to the blacksmith shop are active, and the weekday wash adorns lines in backyards.

At Shiloh is the junction with a graveled road *(see Tour 29B).*

Between Shiloh and Bridgeton are several large apple orchards. Farms, fertile and well-kept, are spotted with small islands of trees. Near Bridgeton the highway is bordered by groups of modern homes.

State 49 enters Bridgeton from the west on Broad St.

BRIDGETON, 23.3 *m.* (30 alt., 15,699 pop.), is an interesting small city, where past and present are mingled with a New England atmosphere. Shady, well-paved streets are lined by neat houses, mostly new, with an occasional old vine-covered brick residence. A large glass factory has replaced the 20 smaller glass factories whose interests were merged when automatic machinery came into use. All through the night, in the growing season, loaded wagons and trucks bring vegetables and fruit to the canneries, the town's main industrial concerns.

Quakers founded Bridgeton in 1686, though a few scattered settlers were here before them. A bridge built across Cohansey Creek about 1716 gave the hamlet the name of Cohansey Bridge. Later it was changed to Bridge Town and then Bridgeton.

BROAD STREET PRESBYTERIAN CHURCH, Broad St. and West Ave., was built in 1792 with funds obtained by a lottery authorized by the Legis-

UNLOADING OYSTERS AT BIVALVE

lature. It is an outstanding example of Georgian architecture, with tall Gothic windows, a broad portico pillared and pedimented, high-backed white pews, high pulpit, brick-paved aisles, brass lamps designed for whale oil, and long-handled collection boxes. In the adjoining churchyard are buried many Revolutionary veterans, including Gen. Joseph Bloomfield, Governor in 1801–02 and 1803–12. A Quaker donated the land for the church and cemetery.

At Commerce St. is the entrance to 1,000-acre TUMBLING DAM PARK, surrounding an old dam built in 1814 to mark a millpond, now SUNSET LAKE. Between the lake and the edge of the town is the raceway, about 1.5 miles long, which is said to have been built in one year by a man and his two sons on wages of 50¢ a day each. In the raceway are lotuses, grown from seeds supposedly brought from Egypt 100 years ago by a sailor. Dogwood, laurel, and holly grow in profusion in the park. There is a bathing beach near Tumbling Dam, and fishing is permitted on Sunset Lake.

The GEN. GILES MANOR HOUSE *(private)*, 143 Broad St., where Lafayette was entertained, was built in 1792 and is in excellent condition. The MASONIC HALL *(private)*, a two-story frame building at Bank and Cedar Sts., was built in 1797. Many Bridgeton residents occupy houses dating from Colonial years.

In the COURTHOUSE *(open Wed. 2-5)*, Broad St., the Cumberland County Historical Society displays many historical documents and relics. The collection includes a bell cast in 1763, now called a Liberty Bell because it was rung to celebrate the signing of the Declaration of Independence.

At Commerce and Pearl Sts. is the junction with State 46 *(see Tour 32)*.

Right from Bridgeton on South Ave. is NEW ENGLAND CROSSROADS, 5 *m.*, where several country roads radiate. Here is (R) the Presbyterian OLD STONE CHURCH *(open on application to sexton)*, built of sandstone in 1780. It is well preserved, with brick aisles, high-backed pews, and a high pulpit. In the gallery is a continuous bench fastened to the rear wall, built for the mulattoes from nearby Gouldtown.

Southeast on the same road is CEDARVILLE, 7.3 *m.* (30 alt., 1,472 pop.), settled about 1700 as part of New England Town. The comfortable homes along the route are owned chiefly by retired farmers. At the Jersey Central R.R. station is the CEDARVILLE AUCTION BLOCK, a co-operative produce and auction market established in 1928; the organization of the market was carried on under supervision of the State Department of Agriculture. It did a $500,000 business in 1936. Auctions are held daily at noon, except Sunday, beginning about May 1. Visitors, though welcome, are cautioned that business is conducted wholesale, and for cash. The auction sells for 500 farms in a 30-mile radius. Farmers' and buyers' trucks form long lines around the block. One sample of everything offered by the farmer is taken from his load and opened on the table, or "block," where it is inspected by buyers. After a sale the farmer delivers his load to the buyer's truck, then stops at the office to collect his money. Often a farmer will toss a few cantaloupes or even a watermelon to the buyers. Out come jackknives, and the fruit is eaten at once. Buyers, their mouths full of melon, make bids by nodding, winking, or raising fingers.

At 24.7 *m.* State 49 crosses Buckshutem Rd., a remnant of the Burlington-Cape May route laid out by Colonial surveyors in 1705.

GOULDTOWN, 26 *m.* (85 alt., 700 pop.), is a colony of mulattoes, the descendants of four mulatto families that have intermarried for more than 175 years with only an occasional infiltration of other blood. These four families were named Gould, Pierce, Murray, and Cuff. The Goulds are believed to be descendants of John Fenwick, Quaker proprietor of the "Salem Tenth" in West New Jersey, who colonized this region. Elizabeth Adams, a granddaughter of Fenwick, who inherited 500 acres of land and married a Negro named Gould, is considered the founder of Gouldtown. Richard and Anthony Pierce, West Indian mulattoes, also settled here about 1750. They paid the passage from Holland for white sisters, Maria and Hannah Van Vaca, and married them upon arrival. The Murrays are believed to be of Indian descent; and the original Cuff was a slave who married his former master's widow. The residents of Gouldtown are a hard-working, highly respected people.

The community stretches for several miles along the highway and nearby dirt roads. The houses, mostly small and weather-beaten, are set off in small farms. It has always been a problem for Gouldtown residents to wrest a living from their scanty acres, and the countryside bears evidence of the struggle. The general effect of Gouldtown is somewhat subdued in keeping with these people who refuse to accept a Negro status, but cannot be classed as whites.

Between Gouldtown and Millville State 49 passes through successive areas of farm land and forest, steadily becoming flatter as the highway approaches tidewater.

MILLVILLE, 34.2 *m.* (30 alt., 14,705 pop.), an industrial center in a truck-farming and poultry-raising district, is a town with practically no foreign-born residents. Much of the countryside is still undeveloped forest. The town is at the head of tidewater in the Maurice River, famous for its fishing and oyster industry. On the city's northwestern border is UNION LAKE, 3.5 miles long, the largest body of fresh water in south New Jersey, whose sandy shores, sheltered by tree-crowned bluffs, are used for recreation.

A study of technological unemployment in Millville traces the development of the problem from the time when the first glass machine was installed in 1910. By 1923, the displaced workers who had remained in Millville were being supported by wives employed in the needle trades industries at miserable wages.

Millville was originally Shingle Landing, later Maurice River Bridge and The Bridge. Settled as a shipping center in 1720, Millville's future was determined when German glassmakers learned of the vast deposits of silica that underlie most of south New Jersey and are near the surface here. This sand was the foundation of the glass industry in America *(see Glassboro, Tour 25).* Right is the WHITALL-TATUM GLASS FACTORY *(open by appointment),* part of which was built about 1806; it is believed to be the oldest in continuous operation in the United States. In past years it has turned out many pieces now widely sought by collectors. The original factory and others are now included in a modern plant making glass bottles.

At Millville is the junction with State 47 *(see Tour 33).*

At 35.7 *m.* the highway, here Delsea Dr. passes ROOSEVELT PARK, a recently completed old age colony, sponsored by the City of Millville in co-operation with the WPA to house recipients of old age pensions. There are 13 small homes of several types, with modern conveniences, grouped around a community building.

South of Roosevelt Park the highway passes through flat cut-over lands, covered chiefly with scrub pine. This is the homeland of "Stretch" Garrison, claimed by many of the nearby hamlets as a native son. Stretch is credited in various yarns with riding sharks and porpoises up the Maurice River; with training does to decoy buck deer into his corrals, where they were translated into venison; with raising a rooster that grew tall enough to eat from the porch roof, and so on. Stretch, a mighty hunter and fisherman, easily held all records for wood chopping. No matter what feat is performed in the region, Stretch could do it better—ask any old-time resident.

PORT ELIZABETH, 40.7 *m.* (10 alt., 365 pop.), a quiet village of shaded streets and small houses, was settled probably in the late 1600's. It was named for Elizabeth Bodely, who in 1790 purchased the property of the Swedish and English farming community.

Philanthropists assembled many freed New Jersey slaves in Port Elizabeth. A schooner carried them to Haiti as farm colonists, but most of them

OYSTERMEN'S COMMUNITY CENTER, PORT NORRIS

came back discouraged. The town's chief marine business now is the operation of a boat yard.

BRICKSBORO, 41.6 *m.* (5 alt., 150 pop.), founded by John Brick, is considered part of the Port Elizabeth settlement. The original JOHN BRICK HOUSE *(private),* on the bank of Maurice River (R), is built of native brick and covered with white cedar siding. The house shows no signs of decay though nearly 150 years old.

At 42.4 *m.* is the junction with a concrete road.

Right on this road is MAURICETOWN, 1.5 *m.* (15 alt.), one of the Maurice River fishing ports which, combined, form one of the largest centers of the oyster industry in the country. There have never been more than 75 homes in this hamlet; yet a recently compiled list names 89 Mauricetown residents who were captains of sailing vessels on the Atlantic between 1846 and 1915. The town, like the river, took its name from the *Prince Maurice,* a ship captured by Indians and burned at a bend in the stream known as No Man's Friend. Prosperous in sailing days, Mauricetown now has a quiet existence.

At 5.7 *m.* is the junction with an oystershell road.

Left on this road and then R. 0.7 *m.* is SHELL PILE, named for the great heaps of oyster shells stacked outside of the oyster-packing sheds. This is a community of Negroes living in wooden barracks erected on stilts over the salt marshes. The shell roads to the mainland are renewed each year as the mud swallows the latest layer. From 500 to 1,000 Negroes here live their own lives in their own way, and present a united and rather hostile front to the rest of the world. Some of the younger men work on the oyster boats; the rest of the men and most of the women are oyster shuckers who work all day during the oyster season, knives in hands. Most of their many arguments are started—and finished—within their own group, and if the results are not too serious, State police and Port Norris authorities are apt to overlook bandages and bruises. Strange whites are not welcomed in Shell Pile. In February 1934 the oyster boats were frozen in. There was no work, no money, no food. A welfare society in Philadelphia sent a truckload of food to Shell Pile and distributed it among 500 Negroes. Another truckload was announced. Some of Port Norris's white people were resentful because the Negro population of Shell Pile had about doubled in two days, anticipating free meals. The second truckload reached Port Norris and was stopped in the center of the town. The food was distributed to white families; and a receipt, thanking the donors for the food, was given to the driver.

PORT NORRIS, 6.1 *m.*, on the main side route, exists by and for oysters, grown and harvested in the adjacent Maurice River Cove. The value of the annual catch approximates $6,000,000. The most casual visitor realizes that this is an oyster town. A typical sign on a store in its short business block reads, "Garrison's Restaurant, an old bed newly stuck up." The terminology is that used to describe a plot under the waters of Maurice River Cove where oysters had formerly been raised, which had been again prepared and seeded with oyster "spat." In addition to oysters in any style, a favorite dish in south New Jersey is usually available in the Port Norris restaurants: snapper soup, made thick with blood-red meat of snapping turtles. Turtles caught in many fresh-water ponds by farm boys and Negroes are readily sold to restaurants in the section. They are usually kept alive in washtubs until used. Muskrat potpie, made from young muskrats trapped in the winter, and weakfish roe, available only in the early spring, are other local dishes highly prized by old time South Jerseyites.

At 45 *m.* is LEESBURG STATE PRISON FARM (L), which covers 1,000 acres. Vegetables and fruits are grown and canned here for use in State institutions. The farm employs about 250 prisoners transferred from the State prison at Trenton.

At 48.1 *m.* is the junction with an oiled gravel road.

Right on this road over marshlands is MOORE'S BEACH, 2 *m.*, popular fishing resort on Delaware Bay. Drumfish are plentiful here.

DELMONT, 48.3 *m.* (10 alt., 500 pop.), has among its residents many old fishermen who take out fishing parties, "catch" oysters, and trap muskrats. Farms in this section are small and marshy. The soil is naturally fertile, but usually too wet to produce bumper crops of anything except mosquitoes.

ELDORA, 50.7 *m.* (15 alt., 219 pop.), is a boating and fishing resort. PICKLE POND furnishes good fresh-water bass and pike fishing.

Southeast of Eldora, State 49 skirts the broad marshes extending (R) to Delaware Bay.

DENNISVILLE, 56 *m.* (10 alt., 400 pop.), adjoins the GREAT CEDAR SWAMP. Buried 4 to 6 feet below the surface are remains of giant prehistoric white cedars preserved by the mire. Hand-split cedar shingles made from the logs dug out of this lumber mine furnished work and profit for Dennisville during the 1800's. These shingles were used to replace the roof of Independence Hall in Philadelphia. Occasionally one of the logs is still unearthed, and cut up here.

SOUTH DENNIS, 57.1 *m.* (15 alt., 310 pop.), resembles a New England town in its century-old architecture and deep shade. A large graveyard around the small Methodist church contains more tenants than are now alive in the village.

At South Dennis is the junction with State S49 *(see Tour 29C).*

CLERMONT, 60.8 *m.* (25 alt., 309 pop.), is a crossroads hamlet at the junction with US 9 *(see Tour 18).*

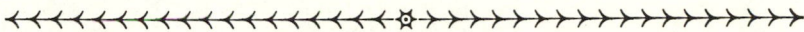

Tour 29A

Salem—Oakwood Beach—Elsinboro Point; Tilbury Rd., Fort Elfsborg-Salem Rd.
Salem to Elsinboro Point, 5.1 m.

Oiled gravel roadbed; footpath for final 0.5 m.

The road threads through a typical area of Delaware bottomlands, originally marshy but reclaimed long ago with drainage ditches by early colonists. The nearby Delaware River (R) borders many truck and dairy farms along the route. These fertile fields are the site of the earliest known Swedish colony in New Jersey. Some of the farm homes are survivors of the later Quaker and English settlements. This area, where there were Dutch traders and settlers in 1623, Swedes about 1643, and English at about the same time, did not have a permanent colony until 1675 when Fenwick and his Quaker associates arrived.

SALEM, 0 *m.* (16 alt., 8,047 pop.) *(see SALEM).*

Points of Interest: County Buildings, Alexander Grant House (museum), Old Law Office, Salem Oak, Bradway House, Friends Meeting House, and others.

Tilbury Rd. branches southwest from State 49 at Salem and follows Salem Creek.

At 1 *m.* the road turns L. past the DARKIN HOUSE *(private)* (R), a three-story brick structure erected 1720. It carries its years not lightly. In this vicinity Sir Edward Plowden, erstwhile founder of the Knights of Albion, unsuccessfully attempted to establish New Albion. Here, too, Thomas Lutherland, executed in 1693 after a jury trial following a test by the ancient Law of the Bier, is said to have committed a murder *(see SALEM).*

At 1.7 *m.* the road turns L. At the nearby bend (L) stands another DARKIN HOUSE *(private),* erected 1740. Like most South Jersey homes of this period, the Darkin house is essentially Swedish Colonial. The house is slowly falling into decay.

The road skirts plowed fields and pastures (L) where herds of fine cattle graze. To the R. are Salem Cove and many tidal creeks.

At 2.6 *m.* the route turns R. into the improved Fort Elfsborg-Salem Rd.

At 3.2 *m.* (R) is the SALEM COUNTRY CLUB *(private).* On the waterfront, 100 yds. south of the clubhouse, is the REDROE MORRIS HOUSE *(private),* a two-story brick and frame dwelling erected 1688. This is the earliest known example of the brick and frame combination so widely followed in farmhouse construction throughout the Salem district for more than a century. The massive oak beams supporting the first floor are 18 inches square; the walls are about 3 feet thick. The building is severely simple in outline, evidently constructed for permanence and utility.

OAKWOOD BEACH, 3.7 *m.,* a summer colony, faces the Delaware River. The beach was named for the many huge oaks that once stood here. Some of these were used at the Philadelphia Navy Yard to build wooden ships prior to the Civil War.

At 4 *m.* (R) is FORT ELSINBORO COUNTRY CLUB *(6-hole golf course; greens fee $1).*

At 4.1 *m.* is the junction with a graveled road.

Left on this road to (L) the COL. BENJAMIN HOLMES HOUSE *(private),* 0.4 *m.,* residence of the Salem County militia commander in 1778. The northern section, with a lower roof, was erected in 1750. British troops burned the interior in 1778 and destroyed the Holmes ferryhouse, which stood nearby.

The COCKED HAT SCHOOL (L), 1.2 *m.,* a tiny one-room structure, got its name from the defeat of a local politician whose ambitions were "knocked into a cocked hat" many years ago at an election in this building.

At 2.8 *m.* is the junction with a dirt road; R. here to the ABEL NICHOLSON HOUSE (R), 3.2 *m. (private),* built in 1722. One of the most massive of these early structures, the house has the rare diamond design and the date of erection woven into the side walls with glazed bluish brick.

On the northern bank of Alloway Creek is the GEORGE ABBOTT HOUSE *(private),* 3.8 *m.,* erected *c.* 1703. Members of the Abbott family were held captive in the two-and-one-half-story stuccoed brick house on the day of the massacre at Hancock House *(see Tour 29).* From a gable window, the family is said to have watched fugitives escaping across the marsh from Hancock House. On the day after the massacre, a Sunday, the Abbotts were stopped by the British on their way to the meeting in Salem. Extending crimsoned bayonets, the soldiers cried: "Behold the blood of your countrymen!"

The highway comes to a dead end at 4.6 *m.,* where cars may be parked. From this point a rough footpath, built upon a dike that holds back Delaware River tides, leads to ELSINBORO POINT, 5.1 *m.,* the site of the first Swedish settlement in.New Jersey. Swedish colonists built Fort Elfsborg here in 1643. The river narrows at this point and the Swedish guns were able to force Dutch trading ships to haul down their flags. So thick were the mosquitoes that the Swedes nicknamed the settlement Myggenborg, or Mosquito Castle.

There is neither monument nor sign of habitation on the site of the fort. In summer briars and honeysuckle are plentiful, and there are countless descendants of the original mosquitoes who were the victors in the Fort Elfsborg siege.

◄◄◄◄◄◄◄◄◄◄◄◄◄◄◄◄◄◄ ❀ ►►►►►►►►►►►►►►►►►►►►►

Tour 29B

Shiloh—Roadstown—Greenwich; unnumbered roads.
Shiloh to Greenwich, 6.8 m.

Partly graveled, partly oiled roadbed.

The road runs through undulating farm country toward the Delaware
River, penetrating an area where Quaker settlements were made by John
Fenwick in the 1680's. There are many eighteenth-century houses along
the route.

The Roadstown Rd. branches south from State 49 *(see Tour 29)* at
SHILOH, 0 *m.* (120 alt., 401 pop.) *(see Tour 29)* and winds past fertile
farm lands tilled by Seventh-Day Baptists. Houses are usually of brick,
sometimes coated with paint or stucco.

The HOWELL HOUSE *(private)*, 1.5 *m.* (R), was the rendezvous of the
young men of Cohansey who organized the Greenwich Tea Party to destroy a British cargo *(see below)*. This stone dwelling was occupied just
prior to the Revolution by the twin Howell brothers, later active in the
Continental Army. One of them, Richard, became Governor of New Jersey (1792–1801).

ROADSTOWN, 1.6 *m.* (110 alt., 220 pop.), is the home of the Ware
family whose hand-made chairs, widely known for more than a century,
are popular with collectors of old American furniture. The method of
weaving rush seats is a closely guarded secret. At the center of Roadstown
is the COHANSEY BAPTIST CHURCH, founded about 1737, a brick structure in a grove of sycamore trees. This structure replaced a former log
building erected near Sheppard's Mill *(see below)*.

SPRINGTOWN, 3.8 *m.* (30 alt.), together with the neighboring hamlet of OTHELLO (R), has been a Negro settlement for more than a century. Amateur architecture and carpentry prevail in the small, weather-
beaten, unpainted homes. The small wooden school and still smaller
church at the crossroads are the only buildings that bear evidence of continued use. Each house is surrounded by fields where farming is intermittently attempted. The residents are practically all workers on the nearby
farms. Springtown was established shortly after the Revolution to provide
living quarters for the Negro farm hands coming in from the South. It
was a station on the Underground Railroad during slave days.

Left from Springtown on a graded road is SHEPPARD'S MILL, 0.7 *m.*, where
a large, white MILL beneath old trees has been in continuous operation for more
than 125 years. It obtains power from a large millpond (L) and an overshot water
wheel.

At 6.4 *m.* the road turns L. becoming a wide, graveled highway, the

AUCTION AT GREENWICH

"Great Road" included in the original plans of Greenwich made by surveyors for John Fenwick in 1683. The road is about 2 miles long; for much of its length it is 100 feet wide.

GREENWICH, 6.8 *m*. (10 alt., 1,472 pop.), has at its northern end a small CANNING PLANT (R), occasionally operated; it is the only evidence of modern industrial activity. Old trees line the highway on both sides, flanked by delightful little old houses, set well apart. There are one or two boat landings on Cohansey Creek, ship chandlers' stores, and boat-gear establishments. Roadside stands and tourist homes are nonexistent. The cosmopolitan influences experienced by an early seaport and trading center is reflected in the variety of architecture, and in the materials used.

At 7 *m*. is (L) the STONE TAVERN *(private)*, built 1734, which looks much like the Dutch Colonial houses in northern New Jersey. It is believed that the cut stone of which it was built was brought to Greenwich as ballast in the hold of a trading vessel. The tavern originally dispensed hospitality and, on occasion, legal correction until the county seat was removed to Bridgeton. The building bears little evidence of its age. One hundred yards past the tavern is (L) the GIBBON HOUSE *(private)*, erected 1730, of local brick in the usual checkerboard pattern. It is three stories high, narrow, with two dormer windows. The interior, in splendid condition, is essentially as it was when the house was built.

At 7.2 *m.*, on the crest of a slight knoll, is (L) the QUAKER MEETING HOUSE *(apply for key at the Sheppard House just beyond)*, erected 1771. The SHEPPARD HOUSE *(private)*, facing Cohansey River, is a large brick farmhouse, almost square. A part of this pre-Revolutionary home is said to be the original building erected 1683. John Sheppard obtained a franchise in 1767 to operate a ferry across the Cohansey at this point for 999 years, but the ferry was abandoned in 1838.

In December 1774 the brig *Greyhound* unexpectedly put in at Greenwich with a cargo of tea owned by the East India Company. It was consigned to Philadelphia, but the skipper decided that the Greenwich cellar of Tory Van Bowen would be a safer storehouse. Local Whigs, angered by the arrival of the tea, met in Bridgeton to discuss action. Before any decision was reached, a group of younger men rounded up a band of 40 from Bridgeton, Fairfield, Shiloh, and Roadstown. Disguised as Indians, they marched on Greenwich, broke into the cellar and carried the chests to a bonfire on the square. The crackling flames and fragrant smoke aroused the whole town. Patriot exultation was not unmixed with regret at the loss of millions of good drinks; indeed, one of the tea burners, named Stacks, could not help stuffing handfuls of leaves into his close-fitting breeches. Before long his added bulk was noticed, and from then on to the end of his life he was known as "Tea" Stacks. Tory sympathizers complained bitterly about the tea burning, and the English shippers finally started a court action against half a dozen of the young Whigs. The early local historian, Johnson, relates that Chief Justice Frederick Smyth twice charged a grand jury on the tea burning, but each time the jurors reported no bills "for this plain reason—they were Whigs." On the SITE OF THE TEA PARTY in the market square the State erected a monument in 1908. Names of 23 of the tea burners are inscribed on the stone shaft.

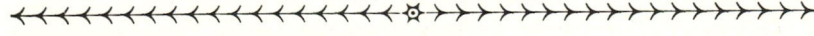

Tour 29C

South Dennis—Rio Grande—Wildwood: State S49.
South Dennis to Wildwood, 18.3 m.

Two-lane concrete roadbed.

Running southeast, the road skirts tidal marshes and travels through a sandy scrub-pine area. Signs of habitation are few except in the small farming and fishing villages. Numerous muskrat houses, rough piles of sticks and mud in marshy ground, are easily seen in autumn when the screening growth of summer vegetation dies.

State S49 branches south from State 49 *(see Tour 29)* at SOUTH DENNIS, 0 *m.* (15 alt., 310 pop.) *(see Tour 29)*.

GOSHEN, 3.5 *m.* (10 alt.), is a center for surrounding farmers and fishermen. Most of its homes are small and weather-beaten.

South of Goshen there are fewer houses. Swampy woodlands (L) and salt marshes (R) draw closer. Farms are narrow strips beside the roads, and most farmers gain some income from the bay. Tidal streams and marshes penetrate the upland (L).

At 6.1 *m.* is the junction with a dirt road.

Right on this road is REED'S BEACH, 1 *m.* (5 alt.), a fishing center for amateurs, with a few summer cottages.

At 6.6 *m.* (R) is C.C.C. Camp MC-73. The letters stand for "mosquito control"; the 300 youths here have been ditching and draining the marshes.

DIAS CREEK, 8.7 *m.* (15 alt., 126 pop.), is the site of an unusual industry—the king crab business. Locally called horseshoe crabs because of their shape, they are a survival of a distant geologic age. Near Dias Creek they are caught in large pounds or traps, brought to the shore, and boiled. The cooked meat is sold for chicken feed and the remnant is ground up for fertilizer. Originally known as Dyer's Creek, the community's name was changed many years ago when phonetic spelling was used in an application for a post office.

GREEN CREEK, 10.8 *m.* (15 alt.), serves summer guests. It is the gateway to several small vacation resorts on the bay shore.

Southward the highway turns from the bay shore and enters farming country.

At 13 *m.* is the junction with a dirt road.

Right on this road is NUMMYTOWN, 0.6 *m.* (15 alt.). It bears the name of the last local chief of the Unalachtigo Indians, King Nummy, who sold the remaining 16 miles of land along the bay shore prior to 1700. The Indians then moved to the less desirable Atlantic shore. Nummy spent the rest of his days on an island at the mouth of Hereford Inlet, that is still called Nummy's Island.

Opposite the junction in a field on the Locke farm 0.2 miles east of the road is (L) an unmarked INDIAN BURIAL GROUND. Bones are plowed up almost every spring; according to legend, King Nummy was buried here. A rude gravestone found years ago is in the museum at Cape May Court House *(see Tour 18)*, along with Indian implements and ornaments, most of them from Nummy's Island.

RIO GRANDE, 13.8 *m.* (20 alt., 375 pop.) *(see Tour 18)*, is at a junction with US 9 *(see Tour 18)*.

State S49 follows Rio Grande Ave. across the flat sand of Cape May and crosses the Intracoastal Waterway.

WILDWOOD, 18.3 *m.* (5 alt., 5,330 pop.), is a summer resort and port of call for the Atlantic fishing fleet. The shipments of cod, mackerel, and other fish are among the largest on the coast. Built around two small villages in 1912, the city shares a 5-mile ocean frontage with North Wildwood, West Wildwood, and Wildwood Crest, and embraces the business center for these towns. During the summer thousands of visitors walk the boardwalk or loll on the flat, black sand beach. Summer fishing parties are piloted by clammers and oystermen who live near the resort.

Tour 30

Point Pleasant—Seaside Heights—Lakehurst; State 37.
Point Pleasant to Lakehurst, 24.3 m.

The road is paralleled by the Pennsylvania R.R. between Bay Head and Seaside Heights, and by the Jersey Central R.R. between Pine View and Lakehurst.
Hotels in towns; tourist and trailer camps along route.
Two-lane concrete roadbed except for 1 m. of tar and gravel.

State 37 runs along a narrow peninsula that separates Barnegat Bay from Atlantic Ocean. Both the bay and the ocean are visible through breaks in the green-covered sand dunes. The peninsula forms an attractive summer-resort area, with excellent fishing and swimming facilities. Many yachts, launches, and sailboats are tied up at wharves and bulkheads, or anchored in Barnegat Bay. Turning west, State 37 crosses the bay on a causeway and loops back inland, penetrating the sandy, scrub pine belt that covers a large area along the coast.

State 37 forms a junction with State 35 *(see Tour 22)* at POINT PLEASANT, 0 *m.* (12 alt., 2,058 pop.) *(see Tour 22)*.

BAY HEAD, 1.1 *m.* (10 alt., 500 winter pop., 6,000 summer pop.), the northernmost and largest of a series of small summer resorts on the peninsula, lies at the head of Barnegat Bay. This is the starting point for the popular sailing and motorboat races that take place on the bay each Saturday and on Labor Day. Houses in the sand dunes on both sides of the road are of weather-beaten, brown-stained shingle for the most part. Along the ocean front are large and attractive modern homes built on the edge of a bulkhead, just above the wave-lashed beach. A narrow ocean-front boardwalk without rails stretches the whole length of the town. Facing the bay are large estates with private docks. The community was founded as a real estate development in 1879.

MANTOLOKING (Ind., *frog ground*), 3.5 *m.* (10 alt., 250 winter pop., 1,000 summer pop.), founded in 1878 by real estate promoters, has many wealthy summer residents. Along the lower edge of the town weathered shingle houses with varicolored shutters face the bay and ocean. Since no lawn will flourish in the sand, topsoil must be imported, or a rectangle of yellow gravel must be substituted for a lawn. Near a causeway crossing the bay (R) is a prosperous shipbuilding yard. The town has the largest fleet of 15-footers in the Barnegat Racing Association.

Every morning of the year at about 3 o'clock large fishing boats, manned chiefly by Scandinavians, set out for the nets about 1.5 miles offshore. The catch, which may contain everything from tuna and an occasional sword-fish to bluefish and weakfish, is brought in about five hours later. The boats are pulled out of the water by a block and tackle over an A-frame, with the aid of a team of horses.

CHADWICKS, 6.7 *m.* (10 alt.), the oldest community on the penin-sula (1830), consists of a scant half-dozen old houses. At an INN (R) boats and sailing instruction are available. The town bears the name of its founder, who built a large house to entertain his friends. Along the sand dunes on both sides of the highway the huge fishing nets of the Chad-wicks fisheries are stretched to dry before being mended.

Bayberry and sedge are everywhere. Where marshland lies close to the road on the bay side, tall cattails bend in the strong ocean breeze that keeps the peninsula cool on the hottest days. There is no long stretch of empty ground; old homes, dilapidated shacks, and even tents are used by sum-mer visitors.

LAVALLETTE, 8 *m.* (10 alt., 300 winter pop., 3,000 summer pop.), noted its 50th anniversary in 1937. This village, named for Admiral La-vallette of the U. S. Navy, has little to distinguish it from other peninsular resorts except a new tan brick BOROUGH HALL (R).

ORTLEY, 9 *m.* (10 alt.), named for Mitchell Ortley who settled here in 1818, has a few houses, hidden behind the sand dunes. Ortley spent much money on building an inlet here which would enable vessels to avoid the long trip south to Barnegat Inlet and would bring a good income from toll. After four years of digging, Ortley and his workmen celebrated the opening of the channel. When heads had cleared the next day, the canal had vanished. The running tide, instead of deepening the channel, had entirely filled it.

SEASIDE HEIGHTS, 10.3 *m.* (10 alt., 500 winter pop., 3,000 summer pop.), is differentiated from nearby towns by its block of stores and its Coney Island type of amusement concessions.

Along the boardwalk that runs S. of this point 4 miles to Seaside Park, the southernmost community on the peninsula, is every kind of amuse-ment and catchpenny device found in larger recreational centers.

At 10.3 *m.* is a junction, State 37 turning R. to cross Barnegat Bay.

Left (straight ahead) across the sand where CRANBERRY INLET flowed more than a century ago. During the Revolution this vanished channel was used by whaleboat men and small privateers who preyed upon the supply boats of the British forces in New York. Many prize ships were brought through Cranberry Inlet into Toms River, where their cargoes and even the ships themselves were sold. The inlet was named for the meadows on both sides, covered with wild cranberries that the sailors gathered for the prevention of scurvy.

BERKELEY, 0.9 *m.,* and SEASIDE PARK, 1.4 *m.,* are the residential districts of the more commercial Seaside Heights. Seaside Park has a few hotels and a yacht club with a well-appointed clubhouse. On the bay shore is the Pennsylvania R.R. bridge to the mainland.

South of Seaside Park there is no improved road through the sands of ISLAND

BEACH, 8 miles of perfect beach and grassy sand dunes extending to the north shore of Barnegat Inlet. During the Revolution, John Bacon and his notorious Barnegat pirates held this beach as their base. Bacon was shot by a band of patriots in a tavern near West Creek in 1783. Cranberry Inlet made this stretch of beach an island, which accounts for the name.

State 37 passes over part of Barnegat Bay and the Inland Waterway on a wooden bridge to PELICAN ISLAND, 10.9 *m.*, no more than a city block wide. From Pelican Island a fill, 1 mile long with a wooden draw-bridge, leads to the mainland. At the end of the bridge are many fish markets, clam bars, and overnight places for fishermen. A short distance L. of the bridge in the meadows on the shore where Toms River flows into Barnegat Bay were the first of the famous TOMS RIVER SALT WORKS *(see Tour 18)*.

BAYSHORE, 12.5 *m.*, is a community of a few houses, fishing headquarters, and sea food restaurants.

GILFORD PARK, 13.5 *m.*, was founded by Thomas Gilford, a wealthy New York broker. The first man to agitate for a bridge across Barnegat Bay, Gilford lived to see his idea realized.

At 15.3 *m.* a large, electrically lighted arrow marks a graveled road.

Left on this road is ISLAND HEIGHTS, 0.5 *m.* (40 alt., 453 pop.), a Barnegat Bay summer resort patronized chiefly by Philadelphia families. Unlike any other settlement in this region, it is built on a high bluff. The town is a survival of one of the many Methodist camp meeting settlements founded in New Jersey in the period following the Civil War. A summer camp of the Girls Friendly Society is here, as well as a camp for employees of the John Wanamaker department stores.

West of Gilford Park are small truck farms and several large poultry farms. The road rolls over low hills of the scrub-pine country, broken intermittently by patches of cultivated ground and frame farmhouses.

At 17.3 *m.* is the junction with US 9 *(see Tour 18)*.

Between the junction with US 9 and Lakehurst the dreary pine barrens, with clumps of tight brush, form dark green curtains on both sides of the road. Sometimes bright pink and white patches of laurel spot the otherwise solid stretch, or a small truck farm breaks the wall of stunted trees. Back from the road are wood swamps, with an occasional cranberry bog.

At 24.3 *m.* is the junction with State 40 *(see Tour 27)* at LAKEHURST (79 alt., 947 pop.) *(see Tour 27)*.

Tour 31

(Philadelphia, Pa.)—Camden—Mount Ephraim—Junction with US 322; State 42.
Pennsylvania Line to Junction with US 322, 19.2 m.

Pennsylvania-Reading Seashore Lines parallel the route between Camden and Grenloch.
Usual accommodations.
Three- and four-lane concrete roadbed, with boulevarded sections at intervals.

State 42, the Black Horse Pike, parallels White Horse Pike, US 30. The almost level country crossed by State 42 is one of the most productive fruit, berry, and garden-vegetable regions along the eastern seaboard. Centuries ago this route was used by Indians and later by the marching armies of British and American troops. It has borne heavily laden farm wagons transporting fruit and other produce to markets along Delaware River, and resounded to the echoes of six- and eight-horse stagecoaches. Week-end traffic is heavy.

On the DELAWARE RIVER BRIDGE *(toll 20¢ for car and passengers)* State 42 crosses the Pennsylvania Line, 0.5 mile east of Philadelphia, Pa. From the bridge deck, 135 feet above tidewater, is a good view of the water front and the industrial section of Camden. Directly below the bridge are rows of red brick houses with white doorsteps and window sills, homes of some of the oldest families in the community. PETTY'S ISLAND (L) is the last of three bits of land that once dotted the stream. Occupied today chiefly by the Sun Oil Co., it once brought disaster to the first steamboat regularly to ply the Delaware—John Fitch's *Perseverance,* which ran ashore on the southern tip of the island and sank, 17 years before Fulton steered his *Clermont* up the Hudson.

Right from the Bridge Plaza, Camden, on Broadway, to Federal St.; L. on Federal St. to Haddon Ave.; R. on Haddon Ave., leading to the CIVIC CENTER (L) at Line St.

CAMDEN, 0.9 *m.* (25 alt., 118,700 pop.) *(see CAMDEN).*

Points of Interest: Friends School, Johnson Park, RCA-Victor Manufacturing Plant, Campbell Soup Plant, Walt Whitman House, Joseph Cooper House, Charles S. Boyer Memorial Hall (museum), and others.

Right from the Civic Center at the junction of Line St., following Mt. Ephraim Ave. or the Black Horse Pike, which becomes State 42.

WOODLYNNE, 3 *m.* (20 alt., 2,878 pop.), is a dormitory for many Camden workers. The business center of the community is L. Only a block long, it is surrounded by tight rows of brick houses with small, fenced back yards. Woodlynne's BOROUGH HALL stands on the SITE OF MARK NEWBIE'S BANK, said to have been the first bank of issue in America. Newbie came here from Dublin in 1682 and in that year got a bank charter from the West Jersey Assembly. At a substantial discount he had purchased a quantity of farthings and halfpence struck in Ireland some 40 years earlier to commemorate the massacre of Protestants by Irish Catholics during a religious war. These coins, known as Patrick's Pence, were not legal tender in Ireland. Newbie was forbidden by the legislature to mint money, but an exception was made for the use of his Irish pence. The bank did a thriving business, but less than a year after its opening Newbie died and the coins were recalled for redemption. Coin collectors today value specimens at several dollars each.

The highway passes the CAMDEN FORGE CO. PLANT (R), where huge quantities of shells were made for American guns used in the World War.

The North Branch of Newton Creek, crossed S. of Woodlynne, is almost entirely covered with a blanket of creamy water lily blossoms during the late summer.

At 4 *m*. is the junction with Collings Ave., a wide paved street.

Right on Collings Ave. is FAIRVIEW, 0.5 *m*. (120 alt., 9,067 pop.), one of the few New Jersey communities with a planned pattern of streets. Diagonal roads lead from curving thoroughfares to Yorkship Square, the business section. Although part of the City of Camden, Fairview retains its identity, partly because of its position between forks of Newton Creek. The village sprang up to house employees of the New York Shipbuilding Co. during the World War. One- and two-family houses, built of red brick and white mortar along English and Colonial lines, are set on wide lawns along broad, well-paved, tree-shaded streets. Most of the inhabitants work in Camden and Philadelphia.

At 4.3 *m.*, at a traffic circle, is the junction with US 130 *(see Tour 19)*.

At 4.4 *m*. is the main branch of Newton Creek, here a slow-moving stream of clear, cedar-colored water. This branch was the route of the sailboat that brought the first Quaker settlers to Camden County from Salem, N. J., in 1682, to establish the settlement that has since become Woodlynne, Collingswood, and part of South Camden *(see Tour 23)*.

For a few miles southward the countryside is an unbroken strip of truck gardens with a distant background of pine, spruce, and scrub-oak trees. Rusted tin signs on roadside stores list the virtues of patent medicines, promising health for every live thing in the farmer's barn as well as for the members of his family.

MT. EPHRAIM, 6.1 *m*. (70 alt., 2,500 pop.), at the intersection of State 42 and the old King's Highway, was a Colonial settlement. Stagecoach companies operating between Camden, Philadelphia, and the coast chose Ephraim Albertson's tavern here as a station. Albertson supplied fresh horses for the stages, and maintained a large stable and carriage shed in addition to the inn. Modern business structures now stand on the site of the tavern.

The road climbs and descends low hills covered with dark green fir and pine trees. The sections cleared for farming grow larger, and the first orchards appear. Here, too, is the northern beginning of the "chicken pot pie" section. The fame of local housewives and their pies has spread far, attracting travelers with whetted appetites during the fall and winter months. Overnight guests in the region are introduced to fried scrapple, the inevitable breakfast dish of the countryside. Made from odd scraps of pork at winter "hog killings" and mixed with water-ground corn meal, scrapple is delicately flavored with a carefully compounded mixture of spices and herbs. It is sliced when cold and then fried.

BELLMAWR, 7 *m*. (50 alt., 1,123 pop.), is a comparatively new residential section on the site of the old Bell Farm, long famous for its fine draught horses. Originally known as Heddings for a church built here in 1865, the community changed its name when a post office was established.

Right from Bellmawr on Browning Lane Rd. to the BELL FARM, 0.5 *m.*, which is still producing Percheron horses under the management of a descendant of its Quaker founder. The animals bred here have won many blue ribbons.

RUNNEMEDE, 7.5 *m.* (60 alt., 2,436 pop.), is a suburban residential section that has had a succession of names during a history that dates back to 1683, when Quaker settlers named their community New Hope. They operated gristmills and other small industrial plants. The name was changed to Marlboro in honor of the British military leader over the objection of some residents opposed to England. In 1844 the name Runnemede was adapted from the meadow near London where King John signed the Magna Carta. Modern homes and stores are sprawled along the road with open fields between them.

GLENDORA, 8.6 *m.* (50 alt., 200 pop.), is largely a summer colony built around a small lake. During the winter an amusement park and the few cottages are empty.

CHEWS, 9.1 *m.* (50 alt., 856 pop.), on the South Branch of Newton Creek, was named for Col. Jeremiah Chew, Revolutionary officer. Around Chew's tavern the town and its adjoining settlement, Chew's Landing, grew. Chew owned small boats, which plied the creek until it became unnavigable.

Left from Chews on a paved road to 'the SITE OF CHEW'S LANDING, 0.3 *m.* The wharf is gone and the water in the creek is a mere trickle. On a small hill is CHEW'S LANDING HOTEL *(private),* built before the Revolution. It is now a weather-beaten, two-and-one-half-story frame building, with a peak roof, painted a dull olive drab. Old shutter hinges and other hardware are of hand-wrought iron. A later hotel stands almost directly opposite, constructed along similar architectural lines and painted white. WARWICK HOUSE or Jaggard House *(private),* on a hill at Chew's Landing overlooking North Branch of Timber Creek, was used as a hospital during the Revolution. It was built in 1756 by James Hillman. The Hessians crossed the creek on the old Haddonfield Road, close to the house, as they marched to the Battle of Red Bank. This crossing was known as Signy's Run for an Indian chief named Sigintas, who was buried nearby. The house is now used as an artist's studio.

BLENHEIM, 11.3 *m.* (80 alt., 71 pop.), consists of two stores and nine houses, supported chiefly by the operations of a small hosiery mill.

BLACKWOOD, 11.6 *m.* (75 alt., 1,500 pop.), the old site of Camden County institutions, stretches along both sides of the highway, presenting a sprightly picture that belies a history dating back to 1701. The population today is employed chiefly at industrial plants in Camden. The town was named for Capt. John Blackwood, a settler of 1741. Uriah Norcross, owner of several stage lines in the lower end of the State, lived here, and operated his transportation lines from an office near the crossroads. The deserted relics of a real estate boom form a ghost city along the southern outskirts of the town.

South of Blackwood the road turns L., presenting a view (R) at 12.5 *m.* of red brick buildings and tall chimneys, surrounded by a thick grove of dark green pines and spruces. The buildings belong to the CAMDEN COUNTY INSTITUTIONS, which care for indigent, tubercular, mentally sick, and other needy persons.

The highway dips into a more heavily wooded section, sweeping through a region where small tracts have been cleared for orchards and vineyards. The wooded section on both sides of the road is one of several State for-

HORSE BREEDING FARM, BELLMAWR

ests in this area. Frequent fires occur here, making blankets of smoke. The frames of tall fire towers rise above the trees.

Farms in this region supplied Washington's troops with grain and other foods, while the Army fought in and around Philadelphia. Raiding parties directed by British officers invaded the section.

GRENLOCH, 12.6 *m.* (60 alt., 750 pop.), is a small cluster of cottages erected along the shores of a spring-fed lake (L) with boating, fishing, and bathing facilities. Opposite the lake is WEBER'S BUFFALO FARM *(adults, 25¢; children, 10¢),* a 364-acre tract where five American bison graze. Here also are bears, elk, and other deer, monkeys, Philippine water buffalo, ostriches, and other birds. There are also collections of stuffed animals, old relics, minerals, and tropical plants.

Between Grenloch and Williamstown the highway is divided by a central parkway.

More vineyards, larger orchards, and wide fields under cultivation are southward on State 42. The fruit orchards resemble a colorful checkerboard during blossom time. Peaches, pears, apples, and cherries are raised.

Replacing the orchards farther south, the woodland comes close to the highway. Gnarled pines, stunted and twisted, scrub oaks, and an occasional magnolia tree, mingle in a thick undergrowth.

The southern end of the forest at 18.4 *m.* and more farms, devoted largely to the cultivation of grains, line the road.

At 19.2 *m.* is the junction with US 322 *(see Tour 25).*

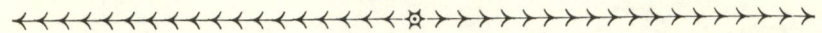

Tour 32

Mullica Hill—Pittsgrove—Bridgeton; State 46.
Mullica Hill to Bridgeton, 22.5 m.

The Jersey Central R.R. parallels the highway between Deerfield and Bridgeton.
Tourist homes and other accommodations.
Hard-surfaced roadbed throughout, partly concrete.

State 46 crosses sparsely settled, slightly rolling country dotted with scrub timber, orchards, and many well-kept farms, including the largest, most modern farm in the State. The few communities along the road date back to Colonial times. There are wooded and cut-over sections in which laurel grows profusely.

State 46 branches south from State 45 *(see Tour 28)* on the southern edge of MULLICA HILL, 0 *m.* (114 alt., 710 pop.) *(see Tour 28).*

Wide fields, producing a major part of the truck and vegetables grown in the region, border both sides of the road, and orchards grow to the edge of the winding highway. Small cemeteries are often encircled by ancient, red brick walls overgrown with ivy and other vines.

At 5 *m.* State 46 crosses Oldman's Creek. Swedish settlers lived here, when it was known as Alderman's Creek, before the English conquest in 1664. Fruit trees bloom here during late April and early May; Gloucester and Cumberland Counties arrange tours and post the highways for their Blossom Festival.

WHIG LANE, 6.6 *m.*, with a crossroads corner with one store, now closed, and two nearby houses, recalls the division of sentiment in south New Jersey during the Revolution. On the 2-mile road from which the settlement takes its name lived few people, but these were vigorous partisans of opposing causes, and each side strove to express and perpetuate its political faith in the naming of the road. One section was for a time called Tory Lane, but with Washington's increasing victories the Tories lost their name. The road has a few houses suggestive of Revolutionary times.

At PITTSGROVE, 8.5 *m.* (140 alt., 212 pop.) *(see Tour 24),* is the junction with US 40 *(see Tour 24).*

High tension lines of the Atlantic City Electric and Gas. Co. cross high over the road at 10.8 *m.* Just south (R) is the SAMUEL SWING HOUSE *(private),* built of local brick. The end of the house facing the road has the letters "SSS," the date "1775," and some decorative flourishes worked into the wall in white brick. The markings are for Samuel and Sarah Swing, who erected the house.

Throughout the countryside are many homes erected in the 1700's, all of Dutch and Swedish Colonial types of architecture, altered in varying degree by each builder.

SHIRLEY, 11.8 *m.* (143 alt.), consisting of a store and several houses, is the center of an important potato-growing district. Once known as Swing's Corners for the Swing family, early settlers, the town adopted its present name when a post office was established. Charlotte Brontë was at the peak of her popularity at the time, and the wife of the newly appointed postmaster suggested that Shirley, heroine of Miss Brontë's latest novel, be honored in naming the place. The post office was closed years ago.

Farms devoted to dairying, grain, and potatoes are spread on both sides of the highway. Beyond weather-worn snake fences of chestnut rails, modern tractors haul plows.

At 14.3 *m.* is the junction with a dirt road.

Left on this road to PALATINE LAKE, 3.5 *m.* *(private),* considered one of the best spots in south New Jersey for black-bass fishing. The lake and picnic grounds are popular for Sunday-school picnics.

At 14.5 *m.* is the junction with the Friesburg dirt road.

Right on this road to (R) the JOSEPH SNEATHEN HOUSE, 1.5 *m.* *(private),* a fine example of Colonial architecture. Built of brown Jersey sandstone interlaced with white lines of mortar, the two-and-one-half-story building has the initials of the builder and his wife, Rachel, and the date 1765 woven into the brickwork of the east gable. A few feet above the ground in the rear of the east wall is a cement-covered opening, once the outside door of an oven built within the fireplace in the kitchen. Tradition has it that the hole was walled up to prevent neighboring Indians from stealing bread and other food from the oven. The house stands on the banks of a stream, near a millrace that once provided power for a gristmill. Before Sneathen died he offered freedom to two of his slaves if they would dig a new raceway to the mill. The slaves dug the raceway but declined the offer of freedom.

DEERFIELD, 15.2 *m.* (120 alt., 717 pop.), shipping point for the summer potato crop, was once an important marketing center. The village was settled in 1732 by colonists from nearby Greenwich and Fairfield. According to local tradition, the original cost of 1,000 acres here was 10 shillings an acre. Settlers protested at the exorbitant price, and the community consequently acquired the name of Deerfield. The post office is called Deerfield Street.

Right from Deerfield on Deerfield Pike to the delightful DEERFIELD STONE CHURCH, 0.5 *m.,* erected 1771 of native sandstone. This Presbyterian structure has been used every Sunday since its erection. Although little changed outwardly, the interior has been modernized several times.

At 15.2 *m.* is the junction with a dirt road.

Right on this road is SEELEY, 2.7 *m.* On the shore of SEELEY LAKE (R) stood what is said to have been the largest gristmill and flourmill in south New Jersey. There are ruins of the undershot waterwheel and sections of old grinding stones at the dam and spillway. The SEELEY MANOR HOUSE *(private),* a two-story frame structure built in 1780, is a fine Georgian Colonial dwelling. A wing has been added on each end. The structure was the manor house of Josiah Seeley, who built his mill by the nearby lake. The property was acquired by Seabrook Farms *(see below)* when the corporation bought all of Seeley village to acquire water rights. It has recently been sold to a private owner. The house has its original walnut paneling, hand-made hardware, and wide, buttressed oak doors.

State 46 swings L. and runs through open farm country. At 15.8 *m.* is KOSTER'S NURSERY, which specializes in boxwood and rhododendron. Koster's blue spruce, a hardy, silvery-blue variety used extensively in landscape planting near salt water, was originated here. The nursery is a unit of Seabrook Farms *(see below)*.

At 15.9 *m.* is the junction with a dirt road.

Left on this road to the SEABROOK BULB GARDENS, 0.5 *m.,* with the largest planting of narcissus and tulip bulbs in New Jersey. When the flowers are in full bloom thousands of people are attracted to the several hundred brightly colored acres.

SEABROOK FARMS, 17 *m.,* is the largest single farm in the State, covering 9 square miles of fine soil on both sides of the highway. The annual crops of peas, beans, asparagus, and other vegetables are produced by modern industrial techniques applied to farming.

Seabrook Farms includes over 6,000 cultivated acres, 30 miles of improved roads, railroad facilities for the simultaneous loading of 30 cars, and a packing plant. Water for overhead irrigation of 250 acres is electrically pumped from three artificial lakes, making it possible to plant peas in rows only 7 inches apart.

The farm hands as well as the girls in the packing plant (more than 2,000 are employed during the busy season) punch a time clock; every item of cost and revenue is recorded and analyzed under the most up-to-date bookkeeping system; and an efficiency engineer is constantly at work on methods to improve production and reduce costs.

In April, 1934, Seabrook employees formed an independent union, which succeeded in having the 12½- or 15-cent hourly wages doubled. Later that summer the workers, led by Donald Henderson, a Columbia University instructor, again went on strike. The strikers lost their union recognition although wages were not reduced. The corporation has since abandoned its policy of employing migratory workers, who were housed in small frame shanties. Local residents are now preferred.

Diesel-engined caterpillar tractors plow, disc, and pulverize the rich soil. Instead of being picked by hand, the peas, one of the most important crops, are harvested, vines and all, with mowing machines. The vines are hauled by truck to large viners that separate and shell the peas. Afterward the vines are returned to the field as fertilizer.

The pea harvesting is completed before July 1, and the fields are promptly replanted with bush lima beans. The same culture and harvesting methods are followed.

In the packing plant the peas are graded by sizes with the aid of rotary sieves; then they are washed, steamed to a semicooked stage, packed in cardboard containers, and frozen solidly by refrigerating apparatus that maintains temperatures well below zero. A fleet of specially built trucks, also with refrigeration at the zero mark, carries the peas to market. Ninety per cent of the peas, lima beans, asparagus, and spinach grown at Seabrook Farms is frozen. The company also buys from neighboring farmers over a large area.

Orchards and farm crops are sprayed and dusted against insects and other pests. Airplanes flying near the ground scatter insecticides. The "dawn patrol" of six planes attracts many summer visitors.

An imposing feature of Seabrook Farms is the great array of greenhouses, each 300 by 60 feet. The soil is plowed by two-horse teams driven through the greenhouses. In the winter, roses, flowering bulbs, and radishes are grown. Tomato and pepper plants are started in the greenhouses and are later transplanted to open ground. Cucumber, squash, and lettuce are also grown under glass.

At 19.7 *m.* is CARLLS CORNER, the southern limit of Seabrook Farms. RADIO STATION WSNJ (L) tells its story in its call letters: it serves southern New Jersey.

BRIDGETON, 22.5 *m.* (50 alt., 15,699 pop.) *(see Tour 29)*, is at the junction with State 49 *(see Tour 29)*.

Tour 33

Brooklawn—Malaga—Millville—Tuckahoe; State 47.
Junction with US 130 to Junction with State 50, 51.8 m.

Pennsylvania-Reading Seashore Lines parallel the route between Brooklawn and Millville.
Hotels in larger towns; numerous oil stations and tourist homes, except between Millville and Tuckahoe.
Concrete roadbed of two to four lanes.

State 47 runs south through a suburban commuters' section to the fruit- and vegetable-growing area of Gloucester County. The road passes through the large Vineland agricultural colonies to Millville, an industrial city, and then cuts through 18 miles of forest to Tuckahoe, a Colonial seaport.

State 47 forms a junction with US 130 *(see Tour 19)* at BROOK-LAWN, 0 *m.* (20 alt., 1,753 pop.) a small suburb.

At 0.2 *m.*, on the southern edge of Brooklawn, the road crosses BIG TIMBER CREEK. An earlier bridge that carried the King's Highway (L) was destroyed by local militia during the Revolution to hinder the advance of Hessians to the Battle of Red Bank.

Just S. of the concrete bridge is the junction with a dirt road running along the southern bank of the creek.

Left on this road to the KAY HOUSE, or Hospital House, 0.2 *m. (private)*, near which Lafayette distinguished himself as a young volunteer during a skirmish in November 1778. With 300 men he defeated a British picket of equal strength posted here to guard the enemy's main body at Gloucester *(see Tour 19)*. Neighbors carried the wounded into the old brick house, the western part of which was built in 1685. The dwelling, badly damaged by fire in recent years, is a two-and-one-half-story brick structure, severely plain with narrow cornices, and chimneys at each gable and in the center. There are two narrow entrances on each of the longer sides.

WESTVILLE, 0.3 *m.* (20 alt., 3,462 pop.), is a commuters' suburb of middle-class homes banked by narrow lawns and shrubbery.

At 1.6 *m.* is old BUCKS TAVERN (L), now called Toppin's Inn. Much of the old tavern, built before 1755, remains. It is stucco-covered, with modern frame additions two and one-half stories high and has a wide glass porch across the front. The early interior is little changed.

The road rolls over low hills flanked by patches of thick woods, an occasional small farm clearing, tiny bungalows, and fruit orchards.

At 3.2 *m.* the highway passes through a vast piggery, where city garbage is used to fatten thousands of hogs. The sandy stretch is criss-crossed with high board fences.

At 5 *m.* State 47 curves slightly L. and widens to four lanes. Broad fields of tomatoes and other vegetables and large apple orchards line the road. There are pleasant odors of cider and vinegar in the fall.

HURFFVILLE, 8.2 *m.* (70 alt., 300 pop.), is a small community around a large canning factory. The most interesting local industry is the SPEAKER WAGON WORKS, for almost a century manufacturing vehicles that have hauled farm produce from this section.

South of Hurffville hen houses and long wire-enclosed runs filled with white and barred Rock poultry replace the orchards. Most of the farmhouses display neat little signs advertising "Day-Old Eggs," "Fresh Killed Chickens" and "Baby Chicks."

At 10 *m.* the highway crosses the main channel of Mantua Creek, named by the Mantua Indians for their brother and neighbor, the frog. An old MILLDAM (L) holds back the creek's waters.

At 10.1 *m.* is the junction with a hard-surfaced road.

Right on this road is PITMAN, 1 *m.* (130 alt., 5,411 pop.), whose population is almost tripled in summer by religious vacationists. One-story cottages for the visitors contrast with the solidly built homes of the residents of this prosperous town. ALCYON PARK, on the southern edge of Pitman, offers occasional horse racing, auto racing, and night baseball. ALCYON LAKE is popular for fishing, swimming, and rowing. The Gloucester County fair is held in Pitman every fall. Within a circular area of several acres enclosed by a paved road, known as Pitman Grove, is the TABERNACLE (R), in which the two-week meeting of the Pitman Grove Camp Meeting Association is held each summer beginning about August 1. Pitman Grove is a survivor of the camps established during the religious upheaval after the Civil War. From the tabernacle 12 streets radiate like the spokes of a wheel, following the plan of the holy city in the Book of Revelations. This summer path of earlier Methodists was carpeted with rustling leaves that blew into the tabernacle and were seized by the preacher as the likeness to fallen man, dead in sin.

At 11.9 *m.* is the junction with an improved road to Pitman.

GLASSBORO, 12.4 *m.* (130 alt., 4,799 pop.) *(see Tour 25)*, is at the junction with US 322 *(see Tour 25)*.

Orchards reappear south of Glassboro, with occasional patches of scrub pine and oak, common to the great waste area of southern New Jersey.

CLAYTON, 15.6 *m.* (130 alt., 2,351 pop.), is a bustling little com-

PARVIN STATE PARK, SALEM COUNTY

munity of freshly painted houses and well-kept lawns dependent on its several small industries. The town was settled before the Revolution.

FRANKLINVILLE, 18.6 *m.* (100 alt., 500 pop.), founded in 1800, is on the banks of Little Ease Run, which attracts many anglers. Practically all of the community depends on surrounding farms for a livelihood.

WILSON'S LAKE, 18.7 *m.* (L), is a fishing and bathing resort. A large factory here makes baskets for fruit and tomatoes.

Southward are broad acres of market gardens with overhead irrigation systems.

At 20.4 *m.* State 47 crosses Scotland Run, once a millstream, with several dams still standing near the highway. To the R. a broad cedar swamp lines the stream.

At 21.5 *m.* is IONA LAKE (R), 0.7 miles long, formed by damming the Maurice River. The lake once supplied power for early glassworks and gristmills. It now furnishes excellent boating and fishing; the State Fish and Game Commission stocks the lake each year with bass and perch.

At 21.8 *m.* is the junction with US 40 *(see Tour 24).* State 47 is united with US 40 for 0.6 mile.

MALAGA, 22.4 *m.* (90 alt., 410 pop.), is much the same kind of village that it was a century ago; but the window-glass works, founded in 1780, closed after 1840, when many of New Jersey's small glass factories were abandoned *(see GLASSBORO, Tour 25)*. The origin of the name has been ascribed both to early glassworkers from the Spanish city of Malaga and to the planting of Malaga grapes. There are many fruit farms in the surrounding country, and four local families bear the names of Peach, Apple, Pear, and Plum. The Malaga-Newfield Farm Producers' Association buys and sells for 70 farms.

At Malaga US 40 *(see Tour 24)* branches (R) from State 47.

A grove of tall oak trees (R) at 23.7 *m.* marks the WEST JERSEY CAMP-MEETING GROUND, founded 1873, better known as Malaga Camp. Methodists from many Jersey towns spend vacations in the more than 100 cottages set along winding, shaded drives. Religious services are held from August 1 to August 15 in an auditorium seating 800. Though many similar camp meetings that sprang up in South Jersey after the Civil War have disappeared, Malaga Camp has retained its popularity.

Small farms and poultry plants line State 47 in continuous panorama N. of Vineland. This is known as the Vineland Tract in Landis Township, a prosperous, slightly rolling farming region.

At 27.8 *m.* is the junction with Almond Rd., a graveled highway.

Right on this road is (R) a large yellow brick COLONY HOUSE for Negro patients of the New Jersey State Home for Feebleminded Females.

The banks of Maurice River, crossed at 1.6 *m.,* have recently been remodeled to provide a bathing beach and picnic grounds *(adm. free)*.

NORMA, 2.3 *m.* (90 alt., 1,000 pop.), and its neighboring Jewish communities of BROTMANVILLE and ALLIANCE to the north, and ROSENHAYN and CARMEL to the southwest, form essentially a single community with a common historical background. These communities represent a successful experiment in social service undertaken by the Hebrew Immigrant Society of New York City. In 1881 many Jewish refugees from Russia and Poland arrived in New York without funds, relatives, or friends in this country to provide for their immediate needs. The Hebrew Immigrant Society planned agricultural communities for the newcomers and founded the colony of Alliance. Settlers turned to garment making and handcrafts to supplement their income from farming and their aid from philanthropic sources. The soil, however, proved favorable for growing vegetables and berries, and second and third generation descendants of the original settlers are farming successfully. While few bearded elders with earlocks and long gabardines remain, many of the old Talmudic laws and Biblical customs are still retained, though some have been altered by the accelerated pace of modern living and the influx of other nationalities. A few modern homes stand out in sharp contrast to the small, weatherbeaten, architecturally diverse older houses. The synagogues and schoolhouses are attractive and well kept.

PARVIN STATE PARK, 4.8 *m. (open all year),* has been developed around PARVIN LAKE, 0.7 mile long. The lake was formed by damming Muddy Run, which once turned the wheels of sawmills and gristmills. Facilities for picnicking, swimming, and fishing are provided. The lake had been an excursion resort many years before its purchase by the State in 1931 together with 921 acres of land. Tall pines and dense swamp cedars tower above the slow-moving stream, and there is a fine growth of laurel and holly.

At 28.4 *m.,* at a traffic circle, is the junction with Landis Ave., a broad concrete-paved highway.

Left on Landis Ave. is VINELAND, 0.9 *m.* (110 alt., 7,556 pop.), business and industrial center for the surrounding farm region. Vineland is a small city, a promoter's dream, with the fingerprint of the engineer upon it. It is laid out in a square exactly 1 mile on each side. The streets cross at right angles with no short

KIMBLE GLASS WORKS, VINELAND

cuts or curves. The frame houses are close together, and the trees that line the streets were all placed at equal distances. It is the egg, fruit, and vegetable basket of the farmlands around it, as well as the home of a glassworks with 1,500 employees, and of lesser industrial plants. Charles K. Landis, who came here in 1861, spent 20 years building the colony. He drew farm settlers largely from the Middle Atlantic States and induced many Italian peasants to immigrate to his farms. Vineland was so named by its founder. Grapes were grown in large quantities during its first 25 years, but grape diseases compelled the growers to abandon most of the vineyards. For several years semi-weekly auctions of eggs at wholesale and daily auctions of fruit and vegetables have been held in Vineland by two cooperatives with nearly 1,200 farmer members. The VINELAND TRAINING SCHOOL, Landis Ave., the first institution to use the Binet intelligence scale in this country, celebrated its 50th anniversary in 1938. Under the direction of Dr. H. H. Goddard (author of *The Kallikaks,* one of the earliest studies of heredity as a factor in feeblemindedness), the institution built a reputation for clinical therapeutics and research which placed it among the foremost in the world. At the Wistar Laboratory research into the causes, prevention, and methods of training mental deficients is carried on. Dr. E. M. Doll is in charge of research, and Professor Edward R. Johnstone is the director of the school.

The NEW JERSEY HOME FOR FEEBLEMINDED FEMALES, Landis Ave. opp. the Training School, is a State institution with more than 1,000 patients.

The massive OFFICE BUILDING OF THE KIMBLE GLASS FACTORY is a notable example of modern industrial design. Designed by William Lescaze, the building serves a plant that manufactures bottles, vials, glass rods, and miscellaneous small items. The office is constructed of brick and structural glass with limestone slab facing. The highly functional plan provides a spacious main office that serves as a core around which are arranged various minor offices, conference rooms, and lounges. The office furnishings were designed by the architect.

Right from Vineland on Landis Ave. 0.5 *m.* to Mill Rd.; L. on Mill Rd. a few hundred yards to PALACE DEPRESSION *(open daily, adm. 10¢).* Its builder, George Daynor, purchased 4 acres of swamp in 1929. Using discarded material from an automobile junkyard, tin cans, and other flotsam and jetsam, he erected his palace. It is plastered with clay and resembles the gingerbread castle in *Fairy Tales by Grimm.*

At 20.5 *m.* State 47 crosses Tar Kiln Branch of Maurice River, where in Colonial times tar was obtained from pine trees. Destruction of forests killed the industry. The demand for wood fuel with the introduction of steam navigation was responsible for denuding the forests. In modern times Tar Kiln Branch has been reported as a haunt of the famous Jersey Devil, which frightened horses but ran from women, leaving cloven hoof-prints behind *(see FOLKLORE).*

MILLVILLE, 34.7 *m.* (30 alt., 14,705 pop.) *(see Tour 29),* is at the junction with State 49 *(see Tour 29).*

East of Millville the concrete highway unrolls for mile after mile through sparsely settled country, chiefly forest and cut-over lands. These are the Tuckahoe deer woods. During summer nights it is not unusual for the headlights of a car to outline a startled deer browsing at the roadside. Occasionally the deer, blinded by the lights, will stand motionless in the path of the car.

CUMBERLAND, 39.7 *m.* (30 alt.), a few scattered houses around CUMBERLAND LAKE, marks the site of a widely known bog-iron furnace and forge, Cumberland Iron Works, sometimes called Budd Iron Works, which produced iron from 1785 to 1840. On the L. at the lakeside is a marker erected by the State opposite the SITE OF THE FURNACE (R). Even the stone foundations are gone, but nearby are mounds of furnace slag. The lake was formed by damming Manumuskin Creek and using its power for the forge hammers and blowers. There is good fishing in the pond. At the foundry were made castings for the once famous 10-plate stoves and iron tombstones. In a small cemetery at Head of River *(see below)* some of these tombstones have withstood the weather more than 100 years without rusting; this resistance to rust is a property of bog iron.

At 45.3 *m.* a CRANBERRY BOG (L) edges the highway. On the bank of the bog, about 100 yards from State 47, is the HUNTER HOUSE *(private),* evidently never painted, marking the SITE OF HUNTER'S MILL. The house was built by the Hunter family, who operated a sawmill on Tuckahoe River (R) prior to 1800.

The highway runs through scrub, close to the marshland along Tuckahoe River. In summer flowering plants and grasses with feathery plumes 4 to 6 feet high crowd each other, and water-loving trees grow thickly. Cinnamon ferns flourish on dry ground, and the shallow ponds are decorated with white water lilies. There are many songbirds, hawks, and pinesnakes; occasionally rattlesnakes are killed near the marsh.

HEAD OF RIVER, 48 *m.* (L), the remains of a Colonial town, has a METHODIST CHURCH, built 1792, in the middle of a burial ground that has been in use for 150 years. It is a square, plain wooden structure, once painted white, with wide floor boards and narrow, high-backed pews. The pulpit is raised only two steps from the floor.

Head of River received its name as the head of navigation on the Tuckahoe in the days when a coastwise trade was carried on in sloops and schooners. The people here were lumbermen, charcoal burners, tar boilers, and turpentine makers. Only two houses, modern structures built along the highway, can be seen within a radius of several miles. The rest is forest.

Left from Head of River on a graveled road to the RUINS OF ETNA FURNACE (R), 0.3 *m.*, built in 1815 by John R. Coates of Philadelphia, land agent for William Penn's heirs, and Joshua and John Howell. The remains of the furnace are on a knoll 60 yards from the river. There are traces of a raceway, and the stack is still in fair condition. The furnace was filled at the top with charcoal, bog ore, and flux, wheeled up a ramp that has disappeared. Bar iron made here supplied blacksmiths at Tuckahoe and other small ports who made spikes 1 to 2 feet long for wooden ships, wharves, and buildings. The iron was worked into bars at Forge Pond, about 2 *m.* N. of the furnace.

MARSHALLVILLE, 51 *m.* (10 alt.), is largely a forgotten hamlet with a few farm-tenant houses and about half its surrounding fields abandoned and reverting to forest growth. The town was named for Dr. Randall Marshall, who built a window-glass factory here prior to 1840.

TUCKAHOE, 51.8 *m.* (20 alt.), lies on the south bank of Tuckahoe River. A white PRESBYTERIAN CHURCH (R), built 1851, is the center of a cluster of small homes; other houses spread along State 50. There are a few small stores, a large cannery, and gas stations. Nearly two centuries ago Tuckahoe was an important seaport, with busy shipyards. Quakers had settled this section prior to 1700 and had built a meeting house here, long vanished. Tuckahoe is the center of a fertile area raising early tomatoes, which are canned and shipped in large quantities.

The woods around Tuckahoe (Ind., *place where deer are shy*) are known for wild deer. Heavy undergrowth and marsh offer some protection against hunters. A PUBLIC HUNTING AND FISHING GROUND adjoins the village.

At Tuckahoe State 47 forms a junction with State 50 *(see Tour 34)*.

Tour 34

Egg Harbor City—Tuckahoe—Seaville; State 50.
Junction with US 30 to Junction with US 9, 26.1 m.

Pennsylvania-Reading Seashore Lines parallel the route between Buck Hill and Petersburg.
Accommodations scanty.
Concrete roadbed of two to four lanes.

State 50 runs through a flat, thinly populated country, depleted by forest fires. Between Mays Landing and Tuckahoe are relics of early activity in mining and lumbering. As the road bends away from the swamplands to the sea, it touches more fertile land where cultivated farms replace the barren scene.

State 50 branches south from US 30 *(see Tour 23)* at EGG HARBOR CITY, 0 *m.* (63 alt., 3,478 pop.) *(see Tour 23)*.

The highway runs through a pine forest, cut-over lands now covered with hardwood brush, and small farms settled largely by German families. There are a few gravel pits in this region where an occasional fossil fish or amphibious monster of ages past is dug up.

At 5.1 *m.*, at a cloverleaf intersection, is the junction with US 322, the Black Horse Pike *(see Tour 25)*.

To the R. are glimpses of a large cranberry bog yielding a poor living to workers in the neighborhood. Muskrats are a constant annoyance to the cranberry growers because of their tunnel-digging in the dikes and dams.

At MAYS LANDING, 7 *m.* (20 alt., 1,868 pop.) *(see Tour 24)*, State 50 is united briefly with US 40 *(see Tour 24)*. The highway crosses the Great Egg Harbor River and becomes a four-lane concrete road that swings R. This is a part of the by-pass recently constructed for through traffic.

BELCOVILLE, 8.3 *m.* (10 alt.), is a half-empty group of houses built by the Federal Government during the World War for workers at a nearby munitions storage ground. The highway is bordered (L) by a rusty wire fence surrounding the land used as a munitions dump.

ESTELVILLE, 11.5 *m.* (15 alt., 200 pop.), is one of the communities in the largest township of the State, Estell Manor. The name is derived from the D'Estail family, French Huguenots who settled here in 1671. A few houses, a church, and a school are all that is left of what was a prosperous glass-manufacturing center in the last century. Long forgotten by industry, the village is remembered as the birthplace of the Jersey, or Leeds Devil *(see FOLKLORE)*. Here in 1887 a devil is reputed to have been born to a Mrs. Leeds, who in a testy moment expressed the wish that the devil might take her undesired child. The young devil spent his early years in the swampland, but on reaching man's estate struck out to seek his fortune among the residents of southern New Jersey.

His visit at Trenton in 1909 honored Councilman E. P. Weeden among others. He was described as cloven-hoofed, long-tailed, and white; with the head of a collie, the face of a horse, the body of a kangaroo, and the wings of a bat. His calls, validated by the impression of a cloven-hoof, were reported in contemporary newspapers. All accounts indicate that he is possessed of a most amiable disposition. After successfully scaring the citizenry on many occasions, the Leeds Devil retired from active devilment until the Italo-Ethiopian war broke out in 1936, during which he was seen twice by the same man. The same year a posse of farmers armed with shotguns scoured forests and swamps of Woodstown in an effort to find the devil, who was accused of frightening women and children in the community.

South of Estelville State 50 crosses Stephen Creek and runs through well-drained wild country. On both sides of the road is the State-maintained, 2,000-acre ESTELVILLE GAME PRESERVE, chiefly for rabbits and deer. The highway swings L. at the southern end of the pine belt.

CORBIN CITY, 18.1 *m.* (20 alt., 256 pop.), though planned as a

SPEEDBOAT REGATTA, GREAT EGG HARBOR

commercial center by a real estate developer long ago, is a small village in a cranberry-growing section, built in a corner of the big city site. Most of the area once mapped into avenues and boulevards is marshland.

At TUCKAHOE, 19.2 *m.* (20 alt.) *(see Tour 33)*, is the junction with State 47 *(see Tour 33)*.

Much of the land formerly cultivated has reverted to forest and swamp growth; the chief products are now destined for sale at roadside markets and in the nearby shore resorts. The fields adjacent to the highway are usually tilled, but cultivation extends back from the road only a few hundred yards. The mild climate attracts many species of birds for the winter, notably the Canadian goose.

MIDDLETOWN, 20.9 *m.* (25 alt.), is a hamlet and railway station, close to a large deposit of brick clay.

The route here swings R. and crosses the railroad tracks on a ramp.

PETERSBURG, 22.5 *m.* (35 alt.), is a small farming town.

As the road runs southward ocean breezes come from the waters of inlets penetrating the land nearby. Land breezes carry the odor of pine, spruce, and hemlock.

SEAVILLE, 26.1 *m.* (20 alt.), the center of a farming region, is an old settlement made by English Quakers. The OLD CEDAR MEETING HOUSE (R), built in 1716, replaced a log building erected in 1700. Farmers gathered leaves, bark, roots, and seeds from the Great Cedar Swamp, west of the town, selling them for medicinal purposes. They also sell the swamp huckleberries to seashore hotels.

At Seaville State 50 forms a junction with US 9 *(see Tour 18).*

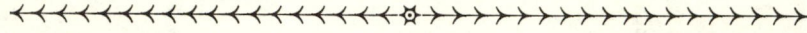

Tour 35

Ship Bottom—Manahawkin—Junction with State 40; State S40.
Ship Bottom to Junction with State 40, 29.3 m.

Limited accommodations.
Three-lane concrete roadbed throughout.

State S40 runs northwest across Manahawkin Bay from picturesque fishing scenes on Long Beach Island to the sandy mainland. It passes through the almost flat pine barrens where a small population makes a bare living from berries, moss, and other swamp products. The western section of the highway penetrates the State's largest reservation, Lebanon State Forest. Superficially, State S40 is an uninteresting highway, designed only for speed. The road offers rare opportunities, however, to any motorist with a feeling for swamp life akin to that of Thoreau, who preferred swamps to fine gardens. "Hope and the future for me are not in lawns and cultivated fields, not in towns and cities, but in the impervious and quaking swamps," he wrote. "My spirits infallibly rise in proportion to the outward dreariness. Give me the ocean, the desert, or the wilderness! . . . I enter a swamp as a sacred place,—a *sanctum sanctorum.* There is the strength, the marrow of Nature."

It is easy to find a good swamp on the mainland between Manahawkin and the junction with State 40. The motorist should watch for a sandy side road near any small stream and turn off for 100 yards or so. Shoes and stockings should be left in the car, and then there is nothing to do except wade in. A typical list of discoveries in one hour's exploration in midsummer is:

An old corduroy road formed of rotting logs and covered by 3 to 6 inches of water, leading on through cedar trees, highbush huckleberries *(loaded),* and fragrant clethra.

Pitcher plants, lying close to the ground, their leaves bright green and veined with red, or deep russet. The strange hollow leaves, half-filled with water, are lined with hairs that point downward. Insects crawl down the hairs—and never crawl back.

Round-leaved sundew, growing in the peat moss at the base of the cedar trunks. This is another carnivorous plant, whose tiny leaves lure insects with drops of a glutinous substance and then capture them with fine bristles.

Swamp grasses, 4 to 5 feet high, with furry brown heads soft as Angora kittens.

Several kinds of flowers, gold, pale lavender, starry white, that most amateurs have never seen.

Cranberries, with green fruit on tiny plants.

Dolomedes Tenebrosa, a dark brown spider with a 4-inch spread of legs and a very evident determination to guard her offspring, who are swarming, many hundreds of them, beside her in the web on a huckleberry bush.

An ancient turtle, 10 inches across, spending his last days in the sun on a mossy log.

SHIP BOTTOM, 0 *m.* (10 alt., 277 pop.), a treeless little town on the gray-white sand at the widest part of Long Beach Island, thrives on fishing and summer visitors. A new FISHING PIER *(adm. 25¢)* extends 584 feet into the ocean. At the foot of 14th St. lies the HULL OF THE FORTUNA, a three-masted Italian ship wrecked in the winter of 1909–10.

Ship Bottom's odd name is the center of controversy of date and detail rather than event. One tradition is that in 1817 Capt. Stephen Willits during a storm came upon a ship aground, bottom up. His men heard tapping inside and chopped a hole with an axe. Out stepped a beautiful young girl, whom they carried to shore, where she thanked them in a strange tongue, sank to her knees, and drew the sign of the cross on the sand. She was sent to New York and never heard of again.

The second version, dated 1846, duplicates the story of the capsized ship, the tapping, and the appearance of the beautiful young girl. Less adventurous, however, this maiden remained in the village, was properly wed, and ultimately became the ancestor of a Sandy Hook pilot.

At Ship Bottom is one of the six life-saving stations that guard this perilous coast. The wreck of the *Powhatan* in 1854 with a loss of 354 lives led to formation of a voluntary life-saving crew. One of the founders was Dr. William A. Newell, known as the father of the U. S. Life Saving Service, who had already obtained a Federal appropriation for this purpose *(see MANASQUAN, Tour 36).* On April 4, 1933, the *Akron,* U. S. Navy dirigible, was destroyed in a storm off this coast with the loss of 73 lives.

At Ship Bottom are the junctions with the unnumbered Long Beach Island roads *(see Tours 35A and 35B).*

At 0.6 *m.* a drawbridge crosses the channel of the Inland Waterway. Cedar stakes with a cross and triangle indicate the main channel. Stakes with discs and diamonds lead into side channels.

This short drawbridge leads to CEDAR BONNET ISLAND, a collection of tiny fishing islands whose shape resembles a sunbonnet. Close to the channel is a resort known to sportsmen as MOM'S PLACE (L). Skipper "Mom" traces her ancestry to a queen of the Lenape Indians. With one hand on the tiller and the other on the till, she keeps order while dispensing Barnegat hospitality and Jersey lightning.

Barnegat skiffs, molded cedar boats of broad beam with lapped strakes and engine aft, are frequently seen. They are open, for carrying big loads of fish; light enough to cross shallows in the bay, and sufficiently seaworthy to negotiate dangerous Barnegat Inlet.

Marshlands in the Barnegat Bay area are in the fall a favorite feeding ground for migratory waterfowl.

At 3.5 m. are PUBLIC HUNTING AND FISHING GROUNDS (R) bordering the bay, a 1,000-acre tract where food plants are raised to attract wild game.

MANAHAWKIN, 5.6 m. (25 alt., 825 pop.) (see Tour 18), is at the junction with US 9 (see Tour 18).

Close to the highway (R) on the northern outskirts is MANA-HAWKIN LAKE, made by damming old Mill Creek to flood nearby cranberry bogs.

State S40 runs in a northwesterly direction through a low and thinly populated area, well covered with stunted pines. At 5.8 m. the road turns slightly L. for its passage in a straight line for the next 17 miles to the northwest.

At 13.2 m., on a wooded ridge, is the junction with a dirt road.

Left on this road to CEDAR BRIDGE FIRE LOOKOUT, 0.8 m. (open), a 60-foot tower with men on 24-hour duty. From the observation platform is a sweeping view of the forest.
CEDAR BRIDGE, 1.2 m. (120 alt.), is a primitive settlement on a low hill where forgotten Jerseymen whose ancestors were Colonial settlers struggle for a living with poor soil and collect sphagnum moss for florists. The old CEDAR BRIDGE TAVERN (R) was used by the Philadelphia-Tuckerton stagecoach passengers for many years before the Civil War. It is now known as Clayton's Grove, a weatherbeaten, forgotten barroom.

State S40 drops down from the ridge with a view topping miles of wooded waste.

At 18.8 m., on a cleared knoll close to the road, is another FIRE LOOK-OUT (R). An excellent view of the long stretch of the Jersey pine belt is available from the platform, reached by steel stairs. Even from the road there is a broad vista of miles of wasteland, covered with scrub oaks and stunted pines barely waist-high. The stubby growth is like a coarse lawn as it sweeps away to become a distant blue-green sea. A few straggling trees rise above the mass, emphasizing the lonely scene.

At 21.9 m. is the junction with a graveled road.

Left on this road is CHATSWORTH, 3 m. (95 alt.), a haven for deer hunters, with a Jersey Central R.R. station and a few straggling houses on the edge of the scrub wilderness. In autumn the frost-touched leaves are tossed by the wind, appearing as leaping flames over the vast area—a land on fire. This illusion attracts tourists, and it has also caused many false fire alarms.

Along the highway the forests close in (R). The old macadamized road (L) that State S40 replaced serves as a shoulder.

At 22.3 *m.* the road enters LEBANON STATE FOREST, a tract of 34 square miles providing free camping, picnicking, bathing, fishing, and hunting. Largest of the State reservations, Lebanon is designed to improve the surrounding barrens. Its white cedar inspired the name Lebanon. Native cedar trees have been planted in the least injured cut-over areas. Elsewhere it is hoped to replace with pines the millions of stunted oaks that grow only about 4 feet high in the thin soil.

At 23.6 *m.* is the junction with a dirt road.

Left on this road to a CAMPSITE, 1 *m.*, in a small grove of silver birch and young pines. This is Butler Place, used as a hiding place for the settlers' cattle during the War of 1812 when the British were threatening this region. In 1830 an inn was erected here and the covered wagons, or "she-tops" as the traders called them, stopped en route to the shore towns. A footpath among the trees leads to tables, benches, and a pump that yields good drinking water. The grove was developed by the C.C.C. in 1936.

At FOUR-MILE CIRCLE, 27.6 *m.*, is the FOUR-MILE RANGER'S HOUSE *(campfire permits issued free)*. Opposite the house is the NEW JERSEY COLONY FOR THE FEEBLEMINDED, where specialists seek to reclaim the mentally undeveloped people who are a byproduct of the socially isolated group inhabiting the great pine area. More than 800 patients are in the long, low white buildings of the institution, founded 22 years ago. A large dairy and vegetable farm is operated. Hobbies are cultivated as an important part of the program; the boys here have nine thriving clubs, issue a weekly newspaper, and engage in handcrafts.

At 29.3 *m.*, at a traffic circle, State S40 forms a junction with State 40 *(see Tour 27)*, 7 miles east of Red Lion.

Tour 35A

Ship Bottom—Harvey Cedars—Barnegat City; unnumbered road.
Ship Bottom to Barnegat City, 8.5 m.

Two-lane macadamized roadbed.
Numerous boarding houses and small hotels, some open all year.

The road runs to the northern end of narrow Long Beach Island. Wave-worn timbers of wrecked sailing ships protrude from the sand of the lonely beach, which in the northern section is unsurpassed for beauty by any other part of the New Jersey Coast. During heavy winter storms much of the island is flooded.

The route branches N. from State S40 *(see Tour 35)* at SHIP BOTTOM, 0 *m.* (10 alt., 277 pop.) *(see Tour 35)*.

Northward at 0.8 *m.* is the widest part of Long Beach Island, nearly 1 mile broad, with the white sand beach (R) hidden from the road by a long chain of low dunes with a few patches of wiry grass, half buried by the shifting sand. The dunes shelter the villages from winter storms. In the poor soil holly trees, wild roses, and mallows have a root-hold.

SURF CITY, 1.1 *m.* (15 alt.), is a small village with a few blocks of boardwalk, some small hotels, and modern cottages. This resort was built in 1873 around the site of the former Mansion of Health, oldest of the island hotels.

Old-time sailing masters and pilots lived here when Surf City was a port and a lumbering center. The earliest settlers on the island were whalers, who came to this spot after obtaining a grant of land in 1690. Two hundred years ago a whale watch pole, a post about 15 feet high topped with a railed platform, stood on the beach. When a whale was sighted the boats put out to make the capture. The mammals were beached, stripped, and their blubber rendered on the sand.

HARVEY CEDARS, 3.7 *m.* (10 alt.), the island's oldest settlement, drew whalers from Long Island and New England soon after the war of 1812. The jaw bone of a whale and fragments of the spine serve here as a border for rose beds. Few of the old cedar trees are left. A large NURSERY (L), where gladiolus and other flowers are grown under the shelter of glass frames, is the brightest spot in town. For a quarter-century a group of Philadelphia artists has maintained a summer colony in Harvey Cedars. Their methods are business-like, yielding none of the arty atmosphere that characterizes similar colonies.

North of Harvey Cedars the route passes small clumps of stunted trees, bent by ocean winds.

HIGH POINT, 4.5 *m.* (24 alt.), is a small village clinging to the sheltered, sunset side of the low dunes. Gill nets are dried on stakes driven into the sand.

Along the road are a few chicken coops containing specimens of one of the peculiarities of Long Beach Island, the tailless rooster. The bitter experience of Long Beach housewives has taught them the need for scissors: many a good Sunday dinner has been blown out to sea on a gusty day when a vain cockerel, fancying himself an eagle in flight, has soared too high. Tailless, this aviator is grounded.

LOVELADY, 6.4 *m.* (10 alt.), is chiefly a Coast Guard station. The name, a source of discomfort to the Coast Guardsmen, derives from the original owner, Thomas Lovelady, a well-to-do Englishman of the early 18th century.

BARNEGAT CITY, 8.5 *m.* (10 alt., 144 pop.), is a salty, individualistic Scandinavian fishing village adjoining a famous old lighthouse. Norse names and features, blond, blue-eyed children, and leather-skinned seafarers, give the impression of a transplanted bit of Viking land. With medieval simplicity the village manages to do without drug store, doctor, police station, court, and motion-picture houses, centering its life around a small church, a school, and a few taverns. Unruffled bartenders reassure visitors during the fiercest gale, calling it "yoost a little blow."

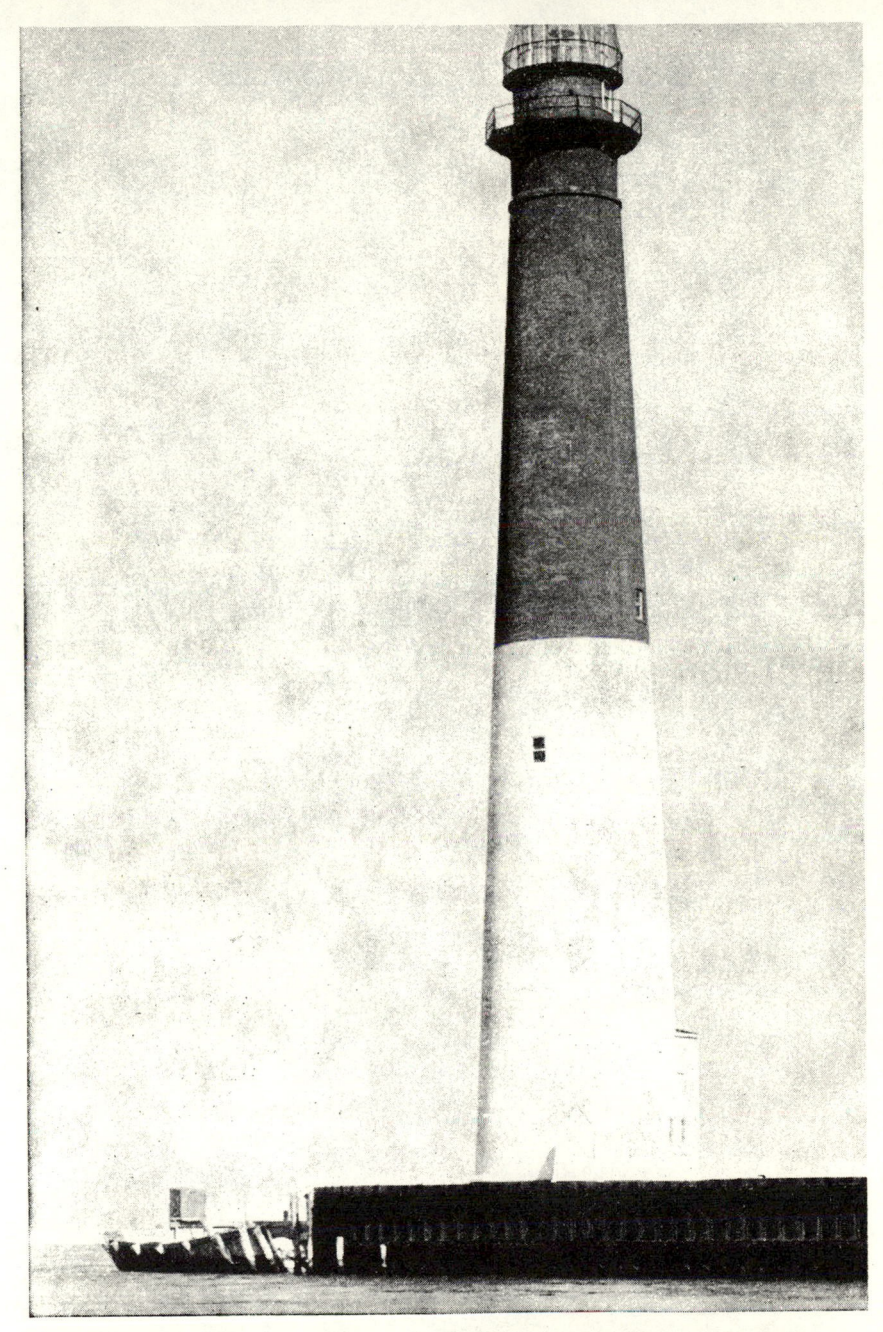

BARNEGAT LIGHT, LONG BEACH ISLAND

The painter, F. Hopkinson Smith, caught the charm and independence of these hardy people in his pictures and in his book, *The Tides of Barnegat*. Smith's father's firm built Barnegat Lighthouse *(see below)*, and the painter himself helped construct it. Annually hundreds of amateur deep-sea fishermen come here for the game tuna that swim in schools far off-shore. Neither they nor casual visitors can disturb the mild Scandinavian tenor of life, which includes the substitution of *spiritus frumenti* for coffee before the early morning trip across the dangerous bar to bring in the fish. The ocean sometimes conspires with the natives to preserve the atmosphere of the town. When some Philadelphia businessmen sought to convert it into a resort, the waves destroyed the hotel and the railroad.

Barnegat shelters a race of tailless sea-going cats that eat the surplus catch of the fishermen. The cats are descended from some Manx bob-tails shipped as ratters on a bark that went ashore near the Coast Guard Station.

BARNEGAT LIGHTHOUSE *(closed)*, 9.1 *m.* at the end of the road, was several hundred feet from the beach when built in 1855, but the inlet has cut a channel to its base. The 168-foot tower, painted red on the upper half and white below, marks the shoals where the lives of many Barnegat fishermen and of passengers on ocean vessels have been lost. Storms have so menaced the lighthouse's foundations that the Federal Government abandoned it in 1930, and replaced it with a lightship 8 miles off-shore. The State of New Jersey then took over the tower and has attempted to save it by a semi-circle of steel sheet piling. The townspeople have dumped old automobiles, brush, and other refuse into the channel, to check erosion of the sandy bank.

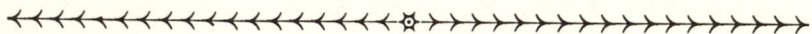

Tour 35B

Ship Bottom—Beach Haven—Holgate; unnumbered road.
Ship Bottom to Holgate, 9 m.

Concrete and graveled roadbed.
Summer hotels and tourist houses in the villages, a few open all year.

The road runs through the southern part of Long Beach Island, passing large sea fisheries and a succession of fishing and resort hamlets. A long line of rugged dunes shelters the fishermen's houses and the summer cottages.

The route branches south from State S40 *(see Tour 35)* at SHIP BOTTOM, 0 *m.* (10 alt., 277 pop.) *(see Tour 35)*.

The island narrows as the road leads southward. Sand dunes (L) block the view of the ocean; in the bay (R) the Intracoastal Waterway divides into two channels, marked by buoys and stakes.

BRANT BEACH, 2.3 *m.* (15 alt., 80 pop.), is a fishing resort within view of both the ocean and bay.

South of Brant Beach the road runs through white, sandy dune-land. The moving sands have often yielded human bones, reminders of bygone wrecks when sailors and passengers were buried wherever their bodies were found. The shifting of sand in the winter gales moves dunes from place to place, covering and uncovering these graves of unknown men and of wooden ships. Nowadays the unclaimed dead are taken to the Masonic plot at Barnegat or to Manahawkin for burial.

BEACH HAVEN CREST, 3.1 *m.* (20 alt., 111 pop.), is a small town with a permanent winter population. The Jersey Central Power and Light Station for the island is here. A long narrow arm of the bay reaches up almost to the highway.

BEACH HAVEN TERRACE, 5.4 *m.* (15 alt., 112 pop.), is a summer resort with year-round residents maintaining attractive frame houses. The old CLEAR VIEW HOTEL, a frame structure on the beach, became something of a local museum in the summer of 1937 when girls from a Philadelphia children's home occupied it and assembled a large collection of shells and botanical specimens from the beach and from swamps on the mainland.

South of this village the highway becomes a graveled road passing scattered summer bungalows. By the roadside are wax myrtle bushes, more commonly known as bayberries. From the purplish-white berries of these evergreens which are 3 to 4 feet high, wax candles are made every fall. Other myrtle bushes here, which do not produce wax, have small hard black berries; their aromatic leaves were, in antiquity, sacred to Venus.

SPRAY BEACH, 5.8 *m.* (15 alt., 50 pop.), presents Long Beach Island at its narrowest. On the bay side are the SPRAY BEACH YACHT CLUB and several houseboats.

The bay here is part of Little Egg Harbor, originally named Eyren Haven (Dutch, *harbor of eggs*) by the Dutch, who found eggs of sea birds in great abundance here. During the Revolution the harbor sheltered an American privateer fleet.

At 6.5 *m.* (L) on the beach is THE BREAKERS, a typical old frame hotel with red-carpeted floors and stairways. Most of the wall space is occupied by an amazing and wholly delightful accumulation of pictures, including such gems as a chromo of a seductive bathing girl—in a black suit reaching well below the knees—entitled, *A Chicken Sand Witch.*

BEACH HAVEN, 7.1 *m.* (7 alt., 760 pop.), with a number of hotels and a half mile of boardwalk, is popular among Philadelphia families and vacationers from other places, having achieved a reputation as a refuge from hay fever. The town has broad streets, busy markets, banking facilities, many handsome cottages, and several large hotels. The best known inn is the NEW HOTEL BALDWIN, a many-turreted frame structure on the beach (L); it was built by Matthias W. Baldwin, founder of the Baldwin Locomotive Works. The BEACH HAVEN TUNA CLUB *(open)*, a story-and-a-half building (R) facing the bay, was organized four years ago by a dozen skippers, writers, and rod experts, to promote tuna fishing.

Unique in Little Egg Harbor are the bait boats, a kind of marine market. They cruise in and out among the fishing boats, selling squid, moss bunkers, shedder crabs, and shrimp.

Beach Haven had a pirate thrill some 50 years ago. A little sloop anchored offshore and two men came into the Little Egg Harbor Life Saving Station, where they stayed for supper. Casually they inquired about two local landmarks, the Two Cedars and the old lighthouse nearby, and soon thereafter ostensibly turned in. At dawn the lookout man saw through his telescope two men digging furiously in the sand at a point between the Two Cedars and the old lighthouse. The guardsman aroused the crew; meanwhile the diggers were dragging a huge chest from the hole. When the Life Savers arrived the men were depositing the last gunny sacks on their yawl and were weighing anchor. The ancient iron-bound chest, an old rusty cutlass, a few Spanish coins, and a crumpled, yellow map lay on the ground. To the superintendent of Coast Guard stations at Asbury Park, the cutlass; to the treasure hunters—?

Bond's Hotel at Beach Haven, torn down 30 years ago, was one of the most noted shore places. Opened in 1851 by a Capt. Thomas Bond, a watchcase maker from Maiden Lane, New York, it was for half a century a luxury hotel for the elite from Pennsylvania and New York. The owner kept a flock of sheep to assure his guests of real spring lamb at all seasons. The dining-room door, covered with the carved names and initials of the "who's who" of its time, is now in the museum of the BEACH HAVEN LIBRARY. Captain Bond, a leader in life-saving, equipped a House of Refuge with the best paraphernalia obtainable for rescue work. On one occasion his men rescued some 400 famished immigrants from the ship *Georgia.* Guards were necessary to keep them under control while food was being prepared, but not one person was hungry when the passengers left for New York.

HOLGATE, 9 *m.* (20 alt.), is the southern-most town on the highway, a small group of houses dominated by a Coast Guard station on the bay side (R) and (L) a peculiar BARN *(private)* with a roof rising into a tall lookout tower. This is a man's playground, as suggested by the forthright name of one roadhouse, "The Liar's Rooster."

At 9.5 *m.* the pavement ends, with 1.5 miles of uninhabited beach beyond to Beach Haven Inlet at the island's tip.

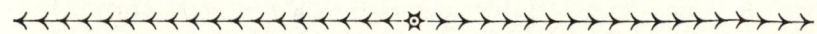

Tour 36

Mechanicsville—Long Branch—Asbury Park—Brielle; State 36, County 9, and State 4N.
Mechanicsville to Brielle, 34.8 m.

Route is paralleled between Mechanicsville and Long Branch by the Jersey Central R.R.; between Long Branch and Brielle by the New York and Long Branch R.R. Plentiful accommodations.
Concrete roadbed, two and three lanes wide.

State 36 runs along the southern shore of Raritan and Sandy Hook Bays through a series of small bathing and fishing resorts. At Highland Beach, the entrance to Sandy Hook, the route turns south over an ocean boulevard that passes through many of New Jersey's largest summer resorts. Almost every form of seaside dwelling is represented in the architecture of the homes along the way, from palatial mansion to tent.

State 36 branches east from State 35 *(see Tour 22)* in MECHANICS-VILLE, 0 *m.* (35 alt.) *(see Tour 22)*.

At 2.8 *m.* the highway runs between two small clear lakes, abandoned pits made by brickmakers digging clay. Cherry cider, apple cider, and quantities of smoked fish are sold at the numerous roadstands.

At 4.1 *m.* is the junction with a hard-surfaced road.

Left on this road is KEANSBURG, 1.1 *m.* (10 alt., 1,893 pop.), on Lower New York Bay, a resort and port of call for pleasure and fishing craft, with a summer population estimated at 50,000. A boardwalk almost 2 miles long, bordered by bathhouses and other concessions, runs along the beach, almost all of which is open to the public. At the foot of Maplewood Ave. is an open-air MARKET where sea food—just off the boat—is sold. The summer season ends with a carnival, a baby parade, and other events, under an elected king and queen. During prohibition, bootleggers' speedboats landed large shipments at a decaying steamboat pier, now used only by small boats. Keansburg was named in 1884 for Senator John Kean of Elizabeth.

BELFORD, 6.5 *m.* (20 alt.), is an old town of fishermen's houses, formerly called Shoal Harbor. In the salt meadows (L) small fishing boats, actually on narrow creeks, seem to be floating on the heavy grass.

A small elevation at 6.7 *m.* (R) is GARRETT'S HILL, where Lord Cornwallis encamped after the Battle of Monmouth. From this hill at the end of the Revolution horsemen started for Philadelphia with the news that the departing British had weighed anchor in New York Bay.

LEONARDO, 8.4 *m.* (20 alt.), covering several former farms of the Leonard family, consists of a group of cottages set in a large old orchard. Plans have been made for a larger lagoon for fishing boats, because of the proximity to the fishing banks off Sandy Hook.

At 9 *m.* (R), against the skyline of the hill, is a tall and narrow dwelling, the former OSCAR HAMMERSTEIN HOUSE *(private)*. After it had passed from the hands of the operatic and music-hall impresario it became an important headquarters for liquor smuggling, with a secret radio station, a murder story, and a small cement garage, said to be a freight elevator to hidden stores beneath.

During 1928 and 1929 the house contained one of the two most powerful radio stations in the United States, flashing messages from Maine to Florida. Airplanes were used by the smugglers to handle rush orders. In October, 1929, Federal agents raided the place, but all of the prisoners they captured were acquitted. Much later the man said to have been the ring boss, Al Lillien, was found shot to death in the garret here. He was reaching for a door to escape. Downstairs two empty coffee cups suggested that a friendly conference had preceded the killing. The murderer was never found.

ATLANTIC HIGHLANDS, 9.4 *m.* (40 alt., 2,000 pop.), founded in 1671 as Portland Poynt by Richard Hartshorne, a London Quaker, lies on the shore of Sandy Hook Bay within the sheltering arm of the Hook. The Jersey Central R.R. connects at its piers with fast steamboats that carry an army of summer commuters and tourists between this point and New York. The town has one main business street, bare of trees and crowded with small stores and shops. Atlantic Highlands, called Bay View in 1881, was the site of a Methodist camp meeting with a sylvan amphitheater and an octagonal tabernacle.

At 9.4 *m.* is the junction with First Ave., a paved road. This is an alternate route for about 3 miles between this point and Highland Beach. It is recommended for panoramic views not found on State 36.

Left on this road to Bay View Ave., 0.5 *m.;* R. on Bay View Ave., called the Scenic Drive, climbing sharply and passing old Victorian houses with the towers, turrets, bay windows, hidden porches, irregular contours, and baroque decoration popular in the late 19th century.

At 0.7 *m.,* around a sharp curve, is the junction (L) with a dirt road.

Left on this road, downhill, 0.1 *m.,* to HENRY HUDSON'S SPRING *(open),* also known as the Water Spout. That the explorer visited the spring is unconfirmed tradition. The Gloucester fishing fleet, sometimes numbering 300 schooners, used it regularly. In 1830 it was bought by Louis Desperaux, who built a cottage nearby, laid a pipe line, and charged shipmasters 5 cents a barrel for the fresh water. The spout house, "The Spout," and a flight of stone steps through a picturesque grotto leading from the house to the bay, have been restored. A man named Eldridge, once owner of the place, is believed to have been the first person in this country to gather clams with a long-handled rake. In 1863 he discovered that the entire bottom of the bay was covered with clams, but he kept this a secret until his heavy takes became common knowledge and his methods were exposed. Farmers deserted the soil and shell fishermen flocked to the spot in such numbers that the sheriff had to quell the ensuing riots.

HIGH POINT, 1.5 *m.* on Scenic Dr., has mounted binoculars *(10¢)* available for a sharp view of a panorama that embraces New York City, Long Island, and a broad sweep of Atlantic Ocean.

MOUNT MITCHELL, 2.5 *m.* (250 alt.), offers another fine view of land and sea, including the busy commerce of Ambrose Channel, entrance to New York Harbor. Mount Mitchell is the first land seen from incoming transatlantic liners.

With sharp hairpin curves, the road drops down the wooded slope behind the Highlands of Navesink, the collective name for all these headlands, and rejoins State 36 at 3.2 *m.*

SANDY HOOK LIGHTHOUSE

East of Atlantic Highlands, State 36 runs on Memorial Driveway for 0.5 *m.*, then on a six-lane route with a parkway. Tall pampas grass is planted on the wooded hills on each side of the highway.

At 11.5 *m.* is the junction (L) with the eastern end of the scenic alternate route *(see above)*.

At 12 *m.* is WATER WITCH, a section of Highlands, and scene of James Fenimore Cooper's novel of that name. The dwelling of 1762 in the story is gone, and its site lost. Near it stood the basswood tree from which the American patriot, Capt. Joshua Huddy, was hanged by Tories. The site, Waterwitch Ave. opposite Bayside Dr., is marked by a granite monument erected by the Sons of the American Revolution. A sign at the entrance to the business section advises: "Drive Carefully—Hospital, 7 miles."

HIGHLANDS, 12.5 *m.* (30 alt., 1,877 pop.), formerly Parkertown, is a fishing village and summer resort close by the ocean.

The fishing industry has declined greatly because of the competition with refrigerated cargoes from more distant points. On Monmouth Hills (R) the U. S. Navy in 1903 erected its first wireless station.

At 12.6 *m.* is the junction with an improved road.

Left on this road *(walk)* to Beacon Hill where are the twin towers of NAVESINK LIGHTHOUSE, 0.2 *m. (open 9-5)*. The original structure built here in 1828 was replaced in 1862 by the present brownstone, fortress-like building. In 1841 a Fresnel long-range lens, the first in this country, was brought from France for use in one of the towers. It is now on exhibition. Oil lamps in the south tower were replaced in 1898 by the first electric lighting unit installed in an American lighthouse. Today the tower has an incandescent light of 9,000,000 candlepower, visible for 22 miles, one of the most powerful on American shores. At the insistence of local residents, a blind was put on the tower to keep the revolving light from flashing into house windows. In front of the twin lights of a century ago, before the days of telegraph, were two windmill-like towers with large signal arms that reported the arrival of vessels. These signals were read on Staten Island by telescope and there relayed by another semaphore to a watcher on the roof of the Merchants' Exchange Building in New York.

State 36 ends in Highland Beach, at the eastern end of the Memorial Bridge crossing Navesink River. The route swings R. here on Monmouth County 9, or Ocean Blvd., a concrete-paved road of three lanes paralleling the ocean beach.

HIGHLAND BEACH, 13.1 *m.* (10 alt., 50 pop.), is a long line of old houses, many of which have been converted into roadhouses. There are also modern bungalows.

At 13.1 *m.* is the junction with a graveled road.

Left on this road is the entrance to SANDY HOOK, 0.1 *m. (adm. only on application to commanding officer of Fort Hancock)*, which juts 5 miles into the sea. The narrow sandy waste is overrun with poison ivy, huge holly trees, and many of the beach-plum bushes so cherished by the Indians that the first white owner was obliged to buy the bushes after paying for the land. The buildings of FORT HANCOCK, important unit in the fortifications around New York Harbor, are at the tip of Sandy Hook. It was to the Hook that Sir Henry Clinton took his army after the Battle of Monmouth, June 28, 1778. The lighthouse, 85 feet high and erected in 1763, is the oldest in service in the Western Hemisphere. American patriots sought to destroy it to mislead British shipping during the Revolution, but the light was too strongly held by the English. Smokeless powder, developed at nearby Farmingdale by Hudson Maxim, was first tried out by the Army at the Fort Hancock proving grounds in 1891. Heavy ordnance is still tested here. The fort has a garrison of 1,040 officers and men.

South of Highland Beach for 5 miles the road runs along a narrow neck of land, once a sand bar. The combination of hills, river, and sea is found nowhere else in the State. On the oceanside a long parapet of great boulders parallels the beach. Summer residents cross the railroad tracks to climb private steps to their own platforms on the wide stone wall, and then go down ladders to their strips of narrow beach.

At 15.2 *m.* is the junction (R) with Rumson Rd.

Right on this road across the Shrewsbury River and through the Rumson Hills is RUMSON, 1.5 *m.* (50 alt., 2,073 pop.), center of luxurious estates. The Navesink and Shrewsbury Rivers here are the scene of motorboat and sailboat racing in summer and skating contests and iceboat regattas in winter. Close to the river (R) is the SEA BRIGHT LAWN TENNIS AND CRICKET CLUB *(private)*, where invitation tennis championships are decided every summer, usually during the first week in August.

SEA BRIGHT, 15.4 *m.* (10 alt., 900 pop.), lies between the ocean and Shrewsbury River. In 1936 its area was doubled by dredging the river channel and filling the shallows along the river front. Sea Bright today has a short, wide, treeless main street, fenced from the railroad line, which goes through its center. It is one of the older shore resorts, originally a fishing village called Nauvoc, and later a busy landing on the riverside for New York excursion steamers.

South of Sea Bright, along both sides of Ocean Blvd., are expensive summer residences protected by enormous stone bulkheads. The highway has to be dug out of sand drifts at one place after every easterly gale; lawns and hedges are ruined. Many of the old mansions have been undermined, and several have been washed away.

At LOW MOOR, 16 *m.,* several islands in the Shrewsbury have been joined with the riverbank.

MONMOUTH BEACH, 17.3 *m.* (15 alt., 457 pop.), is another resort community. The borough leases to local members the spacious MONMOUTH BEACH CLUB (L), with its ballroom and open-air pool *(private)*. It is a white building with an emerald-green roof and bright awnings.

LONG BRANCH, 19.8 *m.* (25 alt., 18,399 pop.), second largest city on the New Jersey coast, is an all-year residential community as well as a summer resort of consequence. The town has also acquired a number of manufacturing establishments, among them garment mills that have been targets of a lively unionization campaign as runaway shops from higher wage districts.

The resort began in 1788 with a boarding house for Philadelphians who brought with them blue laws and religious meetings. By 1819 ocean bathing had become somewhat popularized but promiscuous bathing was taboo. When the white flag was run up, it was ladies' hour; the men had their turn when the red flag was hoisted. Later, in the 80's, however, a belle could not bathe without a male escort. The first gigolos in America were introduced at Long Branch, not as dancing partners but as bathing companions. Low-necked, spangled evening gowns were cut to knee length for the beach parade. The hotels were far back from the ocean and the beach was concealed by a high bluff and dunes. The only remains of the once famous bluff is the downgrade of Broadway, back from the shore front. Within the memory of old residents, there were cornfields on land now 600 feet offshore. The present Ocean Avenue is the third boulevard at the ocean front; each earlier one was destroyed by the sea.

Before 1839, New Yorkers arrived in search of seashore homes, and a boom came with them. Hotels and cottages were built, blue laws were displaced by dancing, drinking, gambling, and fast driving along the hard Blue Drive, now Ocean Avenue. In the 1850's another boom brought impressive hotels and the resort became a rival of Saratoga. A popular race track, Monmouth Park, was opened in 1870, and a railroad, connecting the town with New York in 1874, brought a peak of prosperity.

Long Branch, decked out in the cast-iron trimmings of the U. S. Grant era and the fretwork of early Pullman art, became the playground for all the vivid personalities of the flamboyant 80's and 90's. Phil Daly ran his gambling club in a blaze of glitter even on Sundays while his wife played hymns in her chapel in the Daly garden. When Daly died, his wife decided to carry on his clubhouse, but her hymns got the best of her. Dr. Helmbold, a patent-medicine millionaire, bought old hotels to tear down and a city block to rebuild as he strove to make Long Branch a fit place in which to drive his showy tallyho. He died a hopeless lunatic trying to sweep the sunshine from his front porch.

Here Lillie Langtry kept her private car for an entire summer on a railroad siding adjoining the home of her current protector; there Diamond Jim Brady drove Lillian Russell in an electric coupe brightly illuminated on the interior rather than with headlights, so that all might see and enjoy; and here Josie Mansfield and Ed Stokes admired Col. Jim Fisk and his regiment in their gold braid as they played at drilling on the Bluff Parade Grounds.

A wide boardwalk extends for 1.8 miles past amusement concessions, the fishing pier, and the summer hotels. The highway runs beside the boardwalk in full view of the ocean and beach. It widens to four lanes with a parkway in the center.

At Broadway is the former GREYHOUND RACE TRACK (R), now used for midget automobile races, a mechanical substitute for the horse racing that built the city's reputation. After the abolition of horse racing the resort declined. In recent years it has become popular as a vacation place for Italians of the Newark district.

In front of the track is a life-sized STATUE OF PRESIDENT GARFIELD, who died in Long Branch after he was shot in 1881. The dying President was brought from Washington to his summer cottage on a special train. To avoid a jolting ride by wagon, railroad laborers and townspeople worked all night laying half a mile of railroad track from the main line to the cottage, which stood on the grounds of the old Elberon Hotel, Ocean Ave. opposite Lincoln Ave. (Both cottage and hotel have been demolished.) The volunteer laborers were served by the hotels with coffee and sandwiches.

GUGGENHEIM MANSION, LONG BRANCH

President Grant for a time made Long Branch the Nation's summer capital. GRANT'S HOUSE *(private)*, 991 Ocean Ave., is a two-and-one-half-story, square, frame box with an enclosed octagonal porch extending from its southeastern corner. It has been redecorated in gray stucco, with white half-timber effect. Woodrow Wilson lived at SHADOW LAWN in West Long Branch. Presidents Hayes and Harrison stayed at the old Elberon Hotel.

At WEST END, 21.1 *m.*, a part of Long Branch, is the SAN ALFONSO RETREAT HOUSE of the Redemptorist Fathers (L), a week-end retreat for Catholic laymen. Here are two continuous rows of large estates and, at the southern extremity near Takanassees Bridge, a little gray EPISCOPAL CHURCH (R), known as the "Church of the Presidents." Wilson, Grant, Arthur, and Garfield attended services here.

At 21.7 *m.* the highway crosses Whale Creek and Whale Pond, recalling whaling days on this coast prior to 1860.

South of West End large summer dwellings of varied architecture, ranging, with occasional exceptions, from the merely gaudy to the noisily hideous, line both sides of the highway.

ELBERON, 22.6 *m.* (30 alt.), southernmost subdivision of Long Branch, had its beginning with the railroads. Despite many "To Let" and "For Sale" signs on extensive estates, the properties are well kept. Between them is an occasional fish house where fresh fish are landed every morning from the powerboats that tend the pound nets offshore.

DEAL, 24 *m.* (25 alt., 800 pop.), one of the newer and more fashionable resorts, was named for Deal, England. It has many elaborate homes, a borough-owned BATHING CASINO, tennis courts *(private)*, and a public beach *(nominal fees)*.

ALLENHURST, 24.7 *m.* (30 alt., 573 pop.), appears to be a continuation of Deal. Along the highway for a mile are large modern homes. Unlike most shore resorts, Allenhurst and its neighbors have shaded streets.

At the southern end of Allenhurst the highway skirts the eastern edge of DEAL LAKE (R), which reaches inland 2 miles with its five fingers. On its wooded shores are many attractive summer homes. At the southern end of the lake the highway swings sharply L., closely following the line of the boardwalk.

ASBURY PARK, 26 *m.* (15 alt., 14,981 pop.), is one of the best-known resorts in northern New Jersey. The streets are closely built with cottages, boarding houses, and hotels, some of them open all year.

In 1870, when this region was a wilderness, James A. Bradley, a New York businessman, visited the adjoining Ocean Grove camp meeting. He saw the possibilities of developing a large summer resort and bought 500 wooded acres, which he developed primarily as a summering place for temperance advocates so that no bad influences might encroach on the adjoining camp meeting. The city today reaches nearly 2 miles inland from the beach. The long boardwalk is lined with eating places, a fishing pier, recreational attractions, solariums, and shops where everything from imported Oriental rugs to souvenirs of the *Morro Castle* disaster are sold.

The city has erected on the oceanside a CONVENTION HALL and an AUDITORIUM. The entire boardwalk and its facilities have been leased to an operating company.

At the northwestern corner of the auditorium the steamship *Morro Castle* grounded in September, 1934, after a fire in which 122 lives were lost.

At the southern end of the boardwalk, swinging (R) past a PENNY ARCADE (L), the route passes WESLEY LAKE with its flotilla of bicycle-motored swan boats.

At 26.8 *m.* is the junction with State 4N.

Left on State 4N. The carefully guarded IRON GATES of Ocean Grove are L.

OCEAN GROVE, 26.8 *m.* (20 alt., 1,182 pop.), belongs to the Reconstruction Era and Queen Victoria. The resort was developed in the period of Eastlake architecture, with odd half-houses to which tent fronts are added, with fretwork villas, and with neo-Swiss chalets of the Centennial Exposition type, ornamented with tiers of narrow porches and turrets.

Founded in 1869 for Methodist camp meetings, Ocean Grove has always strictly observed the religious ideals of the founders. From the beginning, vehicular traffic has been forbidden from midnight Saturday until midnight Sunday. The city's gates are closed during that period and none but pedestrians may enter or leave; nor is bathing or any secular business permitted on the Sabbath.

At the head of Pilgrims' Pathway is the AUDITORIUM, which, like Solomon's Temple, was built without the use of nails. Here are held concerts by well-known singers and musicians. Near the auditorium is a fine, clay MODEL OF THE CITY OF JERUSALEM, in scale.

Each summer during the last week in August saints and sinners, penitents and probationers, evangelists, singers, and trombone players come from all parts of the country to hit the sawdust trail that leads to the Mourners' Bench before the vast platform in the auditorium. After hearing the call to repentance and new life, the pilgrims are joined by most of the population of the resort for the "march around Jerusalem," which closes the meeting. The tents, giving Ocean Grove the name of the Tent City and the authentic character of a camp meeting, are in the grove surrounding the auditorium.

On the boardwalk are the platform and choir seats for the famous beach meetings, for 60 years the scene of services during the summer on Sunday evening at 6 o'clock.

State 4N runs south along the edge of Ocean Grove.

At 27 m. is the junction with State 33 (see Tour 20).

BRADLEY BEACH, 27.8 m. (20 alt., 3,306 pop.), the first resort in the country to charge admission to fenced-in public beaches, is a strictly residential community begun by James A. Bradley, founder of Asbury Park. The plan of selling metal tags for admission to the beach has spread widely. The Woolley Fisheries have large pound nets offshore.

AVON BY THE SEA, 28.6 m. (15 alt., 1,200 pop.), is an old community of little more than half a square mile. Shark River adds to its water front and attracts many crabbing parties.

BELMAR, 29.5 m. (25 alt., 3,491 pop.), is a center for amateur anglers. Two 300-foot fishing piers extend into the ocean from the mile-and-a-half boardwalk. The BELMAR FISHING CLUB (private), on the land end of a roomy pier, is one of the largest surf angling clubs, with a membership of 585. Regattas and social events are sponsored by the Belmar Yacht Club. The summer population is estimated at 35,000.

SPRING LAKE, 31.2 m. (20 alt., 1,745 pop.), a fashionable resort on the ocean front, is built around a placid sheet of water from which it takes its name. Around the shore are mansions, cottages, and charming drives. The lake swarms with black bass, sunfish, pickerel, and trout. On the ocean are two miles of beach and a narrow boardwalk.

SEA GIRT, 32 m. (15 alt., 386 pop.), is New Jersey's summer capital. Units of the New Jersey National Guard train here each summer at the STATE MILITARY ENCAMPMENT (L), 32.8 m. (open from sunrise to sundown). The camp is on the shore of Stockton Lake, named for Commodore Stockton, a former resident who commanded the fleet that joined with General Frémont to take California from the Mexicans in 1846. The GOVERNOR'S RESIDENCE, known as the Little White House, is near the main entrance to the camp grounds. It is a simple frame building with wide

THE BURNING MORRO CASTLE, ASBURY PARK

porches. For three or four days each summer, set aside as "Governor's Day," delegations from every county in the State assemble here for speeches and band concerts.

MANASQUAN, 33.6 *m.* (15 alt., 2,320 pop.), is a summer community with Manasquan River offering facilities for sport. Along the beach near Manasquan the first successful American experiment in organized life-saving was made in 1850 when 201 persons were rescued from the *Ayrshire*. A dangerous sand bar running parallel to the shore caused many wrecks. Dr. William A. Newell, then Congressman and later Governor, started the movement for a government life-saving service in 1848. Through Dr. Newell's ingenuity was devised the crude apparatus that has developed into the Lyle life-line gun and the breeches buoy. Robert Louis Stevenson lived here for six weeks in 1888 while preparing for his migration to the South Seas, where he died of tuberculosis. He spent most of the time in bed; part of *The Master of Ballantrae* was written at the Union House, later burned. On bright days he went out with his stepson, Lloyd Osborne, walking along the river or sailing. Saint Gaudens, the sculptor, visited Stevenson here to make impressions of the author's hands for the medallion now hanging in the Metropolitan Museum of Art in New York.

The Indian name of the place means "an enclosure with a house," the braves parking their wives here for safety while they went hunting and fishing. Manasquan is today a year-round community with a large summer colony.

At BRIELLE, 34.8 *m.* (20 alt., 684 pop.) *(see Tour 22)*, State 4N forms a junction with State 35 *(see Tour 22)*.

Tour 37

(Philadelphia, Pa.)—Palmyra—Junction with US 30; State S41.
Pennsylvania Line to Junction with US 30, 19.4 m.

Tourist homes and roadstands.
Two-, three-, and four-lane concrete roadbed.

State S41 runs southeast through low, rolling sand and swamp country where a collection of half a dozen houses is called a town. Through truck farming and orchard land the road enters a region of better soil, more extensive farms, and more numerous roadstands.

State S41 crosses the Pennsylvania Line 10.8 miles east of Philadelphia, Pa. on the TACONY-PALMYRA BRIDGE *(passenger cars 30¢, pedestrians 5¢)*, a steel arch structure, almost a mile long, spanning the Delaware River. The bridge, owned by a private corporation, was opened in 1929. The main span is 525 feet long.

PALMYRA (10 alt., 4,968 pop.), is skirted at 0.5 *m.* Clustered houses are seen L.

Reddish, sandy earth along both sides of the road alternates with black, swampy ground, hidden by a thick growth of marsh plants. Narrow streams twist through the vegetation. Some of the sand hills are bare and perpendicular where the soil has been shaved away for use as fill.

At 2.5 *m.,* at an overpass, is the junction with US 130 *(see Tour 19)*.

At 3 *m.* is the northern end of the orchard region, with large groves of peach and apple trees. Rows of corn are often planted between the trees.

At 6.1 *m.,* at a traffic circle, is the junction with State 38 *(see Tour 26)*.

FELLOWSHIP, 7.4 *m.* (70 alt., 150 pop.), originally a Quaker settlement, is a small village of a half dozen fine old farmhouses and a few more in dilapidated condition.

At 10.6 *m.,* at a traffic circle, is the junction with State 40 *(see Tour 27)*.

Between Marlton and Kresson a scrub-oak forest borders the road.

KRESSON, 13.3 *m.* (90 alt., 100 pop.), was called Milford until 25 years ago when the name was changed to avoid confusion with another

Milford on the upper Delaware River. Road maps still carry the old name. At the western edge of the village is KRESSON LAKE *(adm. 10¢)*, with bathing facilities.

At 15.8 *m.* is the junction with a sandy road.

Right on this road to SUNSHINE LAKE, 0.3 *m. (adults, 25¢; children, 10¢)*, a natural body of water bordered on its eastern side by a large picnic grove. Swimming is permitted.

The outlying houses of Berlin *(see Tour 23)* straggle along the road (R).

At 19.4 *m.* State S41 overpasses US 30 *(see Tour 23)* and circles L. to form a junction.

PART IV

Appendices

PART E

Appendices

Chronology

1524   Giovanni da Verrazano, commissioned by Francis I, King of France, coasts along the New Jersey shore and possibly lands on the Jersey side of upper New York Bay.

1609   Henry Hudson sails along New Jersey coast, and ascends the Hudson River to the head of navigation.

c. 1618   Dutch trading post established at Bergen (Jersey City).

1623   Fort Nassau built by Dutch on Delaware River, near Gloucester, N. J.

1629   Michael Pauw obtains grant of present-day Jersey City, first recorded land transfer.

1636–37   Michael Pauw surrenders his grant.

1638   Swedish settlers enter Delaware Bay.

1640   Swedes purchase land from Cape May to Raccoon Creek from Indians.

1642   First brewery built at Hoboken.

1655   Dutch under Stuyvesant overthrow Swedish rule on the Delaware.

1661   Dutch court opened at Bergen.

1662   First school and church established at Bergen.

1664   Dutch surrender New Netherland (New York and New Jersey) to English. Col. Richard Nicolls takes possession for the Duke of York. Duke of York grants the New Jersey area to Lord Berkeley and Sir George Carteret.

1665   Gov. Philip Carteret makes Elizabethtown seat of first English government of New Jersey.

1666   Newark settled by 30 families from Connecticut.

1668   First meeting of assembly at Elizabethtown.
Bergen chartered. Grant of 276 acres is issued for Hoboken.

1672   First Quaker meeting house built at Shrewsbury.

1673–74   Dutch naval force reestablishes Dutch rule; but vacates in 1674.

1674   Berkeley sells his half of New Jersey to John Fenwick in trust for Edward Byllynge.

1675   John Fenwick founds Salem, first Quaker settlement in West Jersey.

1676   Byllynge interest placed in trust with William Penn and others.
Boundary between East and West Jersey defined by deed.
Earliest recorded iron works founded at Shrewsbury.

1677 Burlington settled by Quakers from Yorkshire and London; named West Jersey capital in 1681.

1679 First settlement in vicinity of Trenton.
Sir George Carteret dies.

1680–82 Richard Arnold and William Cooper settle at Cooper's Ferry (Camden).

1682 Governor Philip Carteret dies.
Mark Newbie opens Colonies' first bank of issue at Gloucester, distributing Irish halfpence.
William Penn, and 11 associates, buy East Jersey from the Carteret heirs.

1683 Perth Town (Perth Amboy) is platted, to become East Jersey's capital.
First tavern in the Jerseys is opened at Woodbridge.

1687 Edward Byllynge, chief proprietor of West Jersey, dies; his proprietary interest is acquired by Dr. Daniel Coxe, of London.

1688 First pottery established by Dr. Coxe at Burlington.

1690 Robert Barclay, a proprietor and life governor of East Jersey, dies.

1702 Proprietors of East and West Jersey surrender civil government to English Crown. East and West Jersey are merged. Lord Cornbury, Governor of New York, is separately commissioned as Governor of New Jersey also.

1737 Population 47,402.

1738 New Jersey separated from New York; Lewis Morris appointed Governor.

1739 Weekly mail route, by post boys, is established between New York and Philadelphia.

1740 First glass factory built by Caspar Wistar near Salem.
Rev. George Whitefield preaches at New Brunswick and Elizabethtown.

1743 First pig iron made in New Jersey—from a furnace at Oxford, Warren County.

1745 Population 61,383.

1746 May 21. Gov. Lewis Morris dies at Kingsbury, near Trenton.
College of New Jersey (Princeton University) chartered.

1750 Trenton Public Library is founded.

1753 First steam engine imported from England was delivered at Schuyler copper mine, in New Barbadoes Neck, now North Arlington, N. J., September 25. (First operated, March 12, 1755.)

1758 Brotherton, first Indian reservation in America, created at Indian Mills—3,000 acres in Burlington County.
October 18. At Easton, Pennsylvania, conference between Governors and Indian chiefs, Gov. Francis Bernard acquires from New Jersey tribes, for £1,000, a release of all Indian titles to New Jersey land.

1763   Sandy Hook Lighthouse (now oldest in America) erected. William Franklin becomes Governor.

1766   New Jersey Medical Society incorporated at New Brunswick. Queen's College (Rutgers University) chartered.

1774   July 21. First Provincial Congress assembles at New Brunswick. Nov. 22. Cargo of tea burned at Greenwich.

1775   May 23. Provincial Congress meets at Trenton. November–December. Provincial Assembly holds last session.

1776   William Franklin, last Crown Governor of New Jersey, arrested. July 2. Provincial Congress adopts State Constitution, proclaiming independence.
August 2. New Jersey's delegates to Continental Congress sign the national Declaration of Independence, adopted July 4.
August 31. First General Assembly at Princeton elects William Livingston first Governor.
November. General Washington skillfully retreats across New Jersey, after abandonment of Fort Lee.
December 8. Washington crosses Delaware River into Pennsylvania.
December 25-26. Washington recrosses Delaware, and defeats enemy forces at Trenton.

1777   January 3. Battle of Princeton; army retires to winter quarters at Morristown.
Washington and army quarter at Camp Middlebrook, Somerset County.
June. General Howe evacuates New Jersey. Goes by water to Delaware River. Occupies Philadelphia (September).
December 15. Isaac Collins publishes the *New Jersey Gazette*
Battle of Red Bank.

1778   June 28. Battle of Monmouth.

1779   Washington and army winter at Morristown (1779–80).
American forces, under Major Henry Lee, surprise British at Paulus Hook.
New Jersey Journal published at Chatham by Shepard Kollock to aid Revolutionists.

1783   June 30. Princeton becomes National Capital. Continental Congress holds session there.
Washington writes farewell address to army at Rocky Hill.

1784   New Brunswick incorporated as a city.

1787   Legislature gives 15-year steamboat monopoly to John Fitch, inventor.
December 18. New Jersey becomes third State to ratify United States Constitution.

1790   Population 184,139.
Trenton chosen as State Capital.

1791	Alexander Hamilton incorporates Society for Establishing Useful Manufactures and founds Paterson.
1794	First Paterson factory—calico prints—goes into operation. Moses Combs, Newark founder of shoe industry, opens first free vocational school.
1800	Population 211,149.
1801	Morris Turnpike—Elizabethtown to Delaware River—is chartered. Cape May becomes first summer resort to advertise for guests.
1804	February 15. Act passed making free all persons born in New Jersey after July 4, 1804. First bank chartered, the Newark Banking and Insurance Company. July 11. Aaron Burr kills Alexander Hamilton in duel at Weehawken.
1807	November 16. Franchise extended to every white male taxpayer.
1810	Population 245,562.
1811	First steam ferry operated between New York and Hoboken.
1817	Legislature permits townships to raise money for free schools.
1818	First patent leather produced at Newark by Seth Boyden. Vail Works at Speedwell (Morris County) builds machinery for *Savannah*, first steamship to cross the Atlantic.
1820	Population 277,575. Jersey City chartered.
1824	First steam locomotive in United States demonstrated by John Stevens on circular track at Hoboken.
1825	Excavation of Morris Canal, from Newark to Phillipsburg, begins.
1826	Seth Boyden produces first malleable cast iron in United States.
1828	Legislature first allocates taxes for support of education. Paterson mechanics join millworkers in first recorded sympathy strike.
1830	Population 320,823.
1831	Morris Canal opened from Phillipsburg to Newark.
1832	Legislature appropriates $2,000 to extinguish all Indian titles to land in New Jersey.
1833–34	New Jersey's first railroad, the Camden and Amboy, begins operation with English locomotive, the *John Bull*.
1834	Delaware and Raritan Canal between New Brunswick and Bordentown opened. Boundary dispute between New York and New Jersey settled.
1836	First Colt revolver made in Paterson by Samuel Colt.
1837	Locomotive industry of Paterson is founded.
1838	Samuel F. B. Morse demonstrates his magnetic telegraph at Morristown with Alfred Vail.

First high school opened at Newark.

1840   Population 373,306.
Silk winding on spools, devised by John Ryle, builds Paterson industry.

1844   New State Constitution abolishes property qualification for voters. Convention in session May 14 to June 29; Constitution ratified by people August 13.
Dorothea Dix stirs legislature to reform prison system and to build asylums.

1845   New Jersey Historical Society organized at Trenton.

1846   First professional baseball game in world played at Hoboken between Knickerbocker Giants and a New York team.

1848   Representative (later Governor) William A. Newell begins successful campaign for Federal aid to lifesaving service.
John Roebling moves his wire-rope factory to Trenton.

1850   Population 489,555.

1851   Clara Barton establishes free school at Bordentown.

1854   First wrought-iron beams for building rolled at Peter Cooper's Iron Works, Trenton.

1855   First New Jersey normal school (Trenton State Teachers College) established.

1858   First transatlantic cable message (sent to President Buchanan by Queen Victoria) forwarded from Newfoundland, received by John H. Wright at Trenton.
Steel-pen factory established at Camden by Richard Esterbrook.

1860   Population 672,035.

1861   April 30. State Legislature appropriates $2,000,000 for Civil War purposes.
May 3. Four regiments of New Jersey volunteers leave for Annapolis.
Maj. Gen. Philip Kearny, commanding New Jersey volunteers, slain in Battle of Chantilly.

1865   April. Civil War ends. New Jersey's contribution, according to Federal statistics, was 76,814 men, including re-enlistments; reduced to 3 years' standing, 57,908. (State records show up to 88,306 men.)
September. Rutgers Scientific School, at New Brunswick, opens.

1866   Legislature creates a State Board of Education.

1869   Celluloid patented by John Wesley Hyatt of Newark.
Rutgers defeats Princeton in first intercollegiate football game.

1870   Population 906,096.
First boardwalk completed in Atlantic City.

1871   Free public school system established throughout State.

Pennsylvania R.R. enters New Jersey with lease of Camden and Amboy lines.

Stevens Institute of Technology founded at Hoboken.

1872 Dr. Charles Abbott discovers important artifacts in Trenton gravels.

1873 Pennsylvania R.R. monopoly between New York and Philadelphia ends with law opening State to all railroads.

1874 Act making school attendance compulsory passed.

1875 Twenty-eight amendments to State Constitution ratified by the people.

1876 Standard Oil Co. establishes refinery at Bayonne.

1877 Socialist Labor Party of North America holds first national convention at Newark.

State Board of Health created.

Prudential Insurance Co. founded at Newark.

1878 Board of Labor Statistics is created.

1879 World's first practical incandescent lamp lit by Thomas Edison at Menlo Park.

1880 Population 1,131,116.

American Society of Mechanical Engineers founded at Hoboken.

1881 First successful submarine in world launched in Passaic River by John Holland.

1883 Agricultural Experiment Station established at New Brunswick.

Newark *Evening News* founded.

1884 Election of Grover Cleveland, only President born in New Jersey.

1885 Gen. George B. McClellan dies at Orange.

1887 Flexible photo-film invented by the Rev. Hannibal Goodwin, Newark.

State Board of Agriculture created.

1890 Population 1,444,933.

1890–91 Clark Thread Mills operatives strike (December-April, 3,000 workers).

1891 July 25. World's first smokeless powder, developed at Hudson Maxim's plant at Maxim, is first used in America at Sandy Hook in an 8-inch rifled gun.

1892 March 26. Walt Whitman dies at Camden.

1895 First woman (Miss Mary Philbrook) admitted to New Jersey Bar.

Highest temperature (109°) recorded at Somerville.

1896 Corporation laws revised to facilitate formation of trusts.

1897 State Constitution again amended.

1898 Three regiments of infantry mustered in at Sea Girt for Spanish-American War.

1900 Population 1,883,669.

June 30. Hoboken steamship and wharf fire; 145 lives lost.

1902   June 19. Paterson silk dyers strike.

1903   Public Service Corporation formed.

1904   Lowest temperature (34° below zero) recorded at Riverdale.

1908   Hudson and Manhattan R.R. Co. opens first tunnel under Hudson River between Jersey City and New York.

1910   Population 2,537,167.
Woodrow Wilson elected Governor.

1911   Legislature passes direct primaries act and other reforms urged by Governor Wilson.

1912   Woodrow Wilson elected President.

1913   John Reed and other radicals lead Paterson textile strike.

1915   Strike guards fire into pickets at Carteret fertilizer factory; 6 killed, 28 wounded.

1916   Black Tom explosion destroys large quantity of munitions on New York Bay.
Standard Oil workers in Bayonne strike; 8 killed, 17 wounded.

1917   Hoboken becomes World War embarkation port; Camps Dix and Merritt established for mobilization and training.

1920   Population 3,155,900.

1921   WJZ, world's second radio station, established at Newark.

1924   First transcontinental dirigible flight made by the *Shenandoah* from Lakehurst to San Diego in 4 days.

1926   Camden-Philadelphia suspension bridge opened.
15,000 Passaic textile workers on strike for a year.

1927   Holland vehicular tunnel between New York and Jersey City opened.
State Constitution amended.

1928   Goethals Bridge and Outerbridge Crossing, connecting New Jersey and Staten Island, opened.

1929   Air mail service begins at Newark airport.
Graf Zeppelin starts and finishes 21-day around-the-world trip at Lakehurst.

1930   Population 4,041,334.

1931   George Washington Bridge between Fort Lee and Manhattan opened.
Bayonne Bridge between Bayonne and Staten Island opened.

1932   Charles A. Lindbergh Jr., kidnaped at Hopewell.
Amelia Earhart flies from Los Angeles to Newark; first transcontinental nonstop flight by a woman.

1933   *Akron,* Navy dirigible, crashes off Barnegat; Admiral Moffett and 73 others lost.
Morristown National Historical Park established.
Pulaski Skyway between Jersey City and Newark dedicated.

1934   Ward Line steamship *Morro Castle* burns off Asbury Park; 134 die.

Dr. Harold C. Urey of Leonia receives Nobel Prize in physics.

1935   University of Newark organized.

Legislature ratifies national child labor amendment.

1936   Unemployed marchers occupy State Capitol for 9 days.

Bruno Richard Hauptmann executed at Trenton for murder of Lindbergh baby.

American Newspaper Guild members on Newark *Ledger* win Nation's first important strike of editorial workers.

1937   German dirigible *Hindenburg* destroyed by fire at Lakehurst; 36 die.

Perth Amboy pottery workers win first sit-down strike.

First tube of Lincoln Tunnel between Weehawken and New York opened.

1938   A. Harry Moore inaugurated as first third-term Governor under 1844 Constitution.

Swedes celebrate 300th anniversary of coming to Delaware Valley.

Voluntary census shows 287,530 totally unemployed in State; estimated maximum unemployed, 399,347.

Bibliography

This brief list, with a few exceptions, contains titles that deal specifically with New Jersey; it should be used as a supplement to standard histories, biographies, and reference works. Lack of space prevents listing more than a few of the many county, city, and church histories.

DESCRIPTION AND TRAVEL

Burnaby, Rev. Andrew. *Burnaby's Travels through North America.* Repr. from 3d ed. of 1798, with introduction and notes by Rufus Rockwell Wilson. New York, A. Wessels Co., 1904. 265 p. front., map. Burnaby visited America in 1759.

Kalm, Peter. *The America of 1750; Peter Kalm's Travels in North America.* The English version of 1770, rev. from the original Swedish and ed. by Adolph B. Benson. New York, Wilson-Erickson, 1937. 2 v. front., plates, maps, facsims. Experiences of distinguished Swedish botanist, who passed through South New Jersey. One of the best historical sources of the period.

Parsons, Floyd William, ed. *New Jersey; Life, Industries and Resources of a Great State.* Newark, State Chamber of Commerce, 1928. 404 p. col. front., illus. (incl. facsims.), col. plates, diagrs.

NATURAL SETTING

New Jersey. Geological Survey. *Final Report Series of the State Geologist.* Trenton, Murphy, MacCrellish & Quigley, 1888–1917. 8 v. in 9 parts. illus., maps, charts.

V. 1. *Topography, Magnetism, Climate.* 1888.

V. 2. *Mineralogy, Botany, Zoology.* 2 parts. 1890.

V. 3. *Water-Supply.* 1894.

V. 4. *Physical Geography.* 1898.

V. 5. *Glacial Geology.* 1902.

V. 6. *Report on Clays and Clay Industry.* 1904.

V. 7. *Iron Mines and Mining.* 1910.

V. 8. *The Quaternary Formations of Southern New Jersey.* 1917.

INDIANS

Nelson, William. *The Indians of New Jersey with Some Notice of Indian Place Names.* Paterson, Press Publishing Co., 1894. 168 p.

HISTORY

Andrews, Charles M. *The Colonial Period of American History.* New Haven, Yale University Press, 1934–37. 3 v. Vol. 3 devotes 43 pages to "Proprietary

Troubles in the Jersey's"; although even this experienced scholar cannot simplify a complicated and involved period (1664–1702), he gives the clearest record of the Colony's governmental development.

Baker, Ray Stannard. *Woodrow Wilson: Life and Letters: Princeton, 1890–1910.* Garden City, N. Y., Doubleday, Doran & Co., 1927. v. 2. 373 p. illus. *Governor, 1910–1913.* v. 3. 483 p. illus. Garden City, N. Y., Doubleday, Doran & Co., 1931. The most authoritative account of Wilson's New Jersey period.

Barber, John Warner, and Henry Howe. *Historical Collections of New Jersey.* Rev. ed. New Haven, J. W. Barber, 1868. 543 p. illus., plates, port., maps. Collection of interesting facts, traditions, biographical sketches, etc., relating to the history and antiquities of the State. Geographical descriptions of all important cities and towns. No other book has done so much to arouse interest in New Jersey history. Edition of 1868 contains State census (1865) reports.

Cooley, Henry Scofield. *A Study of Slavery in New Jersey.* Baltimore, Johns Hopkins Press, 1896. 60 p. (Johns Hopkins Univ. Studies in Historical and Political Science. Series 14, 9-10.) Documented, scholarly statement with bibliography. Discusses Indian as well as Negro slavery.

De Peyster, John Watts. *Philip Kearny.* Elizabeth, Palmer & Co., 1870. 512 p. illus. Personal and military history of the commander of the First New Jersey Brigade in the Civil War.

Documents Relating to the Colonial History of the State of New Jersey. Newark, 1880 to date. 39 v. Prepared and ed. by authority of the State of New Jersey at the request of the N. J. Historical Society. (Archives of the State of New Jersey. First series.)

Documents Relating to the Revolutionary History of the State of New Jersey. Trenton, J. L. Murphy Pub. Co., 1901–17. 5 v. Prepared and ed. by authority of the State of New Jersey at the request of the N. J. Historical Society. (Archives of the State of New Jersey. Second series.)

Duer, William Alexander. *The Life of William Alexander, Earl of Stirling; Major General in the Army of the United States during the Revolution.* New York, 1847. 272 p. (N. J. Historical Society Collections. v. 2.)

Fee, Walter R. *The Transition from Aristocracy to Democracy in New Jersey, 1789–1829.* Somerville, Somerset Press, 1933. 291 p. front., maps. Authoritative political history of 40 important years.

Fisher, Edgar Jacob. *New Jersey as a Royal Province, 1738–1776.* New York, Columbia University Press, 1911. 504 p. (Studies in History, Economics and Public Law. v. 16, whole no. 107.) The definitive history of the period.

Frothingham, Thomas Goddard. *Washington, Commander in Chief.* Boston, Houghton Mifflin, 1930. 404 p. illus., maps. Particularly valuable for a popular description of the New Jersey campaign.

Gordon, Thomas F. *Gazetteer of the State of New Jersey* and *History of New Jersey.* Trenton, D. Fenton, 1834. 2 v. in 1. Covers the history of the State from its discovery to the adoption of the Federal Constitution, plus "A General View of Its Physical and Moral Condition" in 1833. Despite imperfections, a useful book. Statistical tables.

Heston, Alfred M. *South Jersey: a History, 1664–1924.* New York, Lewis

Historical Publishing Co., 1924. 4 v. illus., maps. Colorful presentation, although marred by inaccuracies.

Heusser, Albert H. *The Forgotten General, Robert Erskine, F. R. S.* Paterson, Benjamin Franklin Press, 1928. 216 p. illus. An account of the manager of the Ringwood Iron Company, who drew the maps on which Washington's New Jersey campaigns were based. Thorough index.

Jones, E. Alfred. *The Loyalists of New Jersey.* Newark, N. J. Historical Society, 1927. 346 p. (N. J. Historical Society Collections. v. 10.) The incontrovertible evidence of Tory activity in the State during the Revolutionary period.

Knapp, C. M. *New Jersey Politics during the Period of the Civil War and Reconstruction.* Geneva, N. Y., W. F. Humphrey, 1924. 212 p. map.

Kull, Irving S., ed. *New Jersey: A History.* New York, American Historical Society, 1930. 5 v. illus. A cooperative work made up of signed articles by authorities. Excellent bibliographies.

Leaming, Aaron, and Jacob Spicer. *The Grants, Concessions and Original Constitutions of the Province of New Jersey.* Somerville, Somerset Gazette, 1881. 763 p. 2d ed. One of the great source books of New Jersey history.

Lee, Francis Bazley. *New Jersey as a Colony and as a State.* New York, Publishing Society of New Jersey, 1902. 5 v. illus. The best written and organized study of New Jersey history, though there is an occasional error.

Mellick, Andrew D., Jr, *The Story of an Old Farm,* or, Life in New Jersey in the Eighteenth Century. Somerville, Unionist-Gazette, 1889. 743 p. illus.

Mills, Weymer Jay. *Through the Gates of Old Romance.* Philadelphia, Lippincott, 1903. 282 p. illus. Includes a true picture of the last days of Aaron Burr and the courtship of Philip Freneau, the poet of the Revolution, and beautiful Eleanor Forman.

Monnette, Orra Eugene. *First Settlers of Ye Plantations of Piscataway and Woodbridge, Olde East New Jersey, 1664–1714.* Los Angeles, Leroy Carman Press, 1930–35. 7 v. illus., maps. Essentially a family genealogy, but incidentally a source book on the Huguenots in New Jersey.

New Jersey Historical Society. *Proceedings.* Published quarterly by the Society, Newark, 1845 to date. Invaluable source in the form of articles, notes, and reviews.

Sackett, William Edgar. *Modern Battles of Trenton.* v. 1: A History of Politics and Legislation, 1868–94. Trenton, John L. Murphy, 1895. 501 p. illus. v. 2: From Werts to Wilson. New York, Neale Publishing Co., 1914. 423 p. illus. Exciting and authentic, with an especially good account of the period of railroad domination. Topical indexes.

Smith, Samuel. *History of the Colony Nova-Caesaria, or New Jersey.* Trenton, State Reprint, William S. Sharp, 1890. 613 p. maps, index. First published 1765. 2d ed. 1877. A primary source book of New Jersey history to 1721.

Steffens, Lincoln. "New Jersey, a Traitor State." (In *The Struggle for Self-Government.* New York, McClure, Phillips & Co., 1906. p. 209-294.) The leading muckraker's analysis of New Jersey as the mother of trusts.

Stockton, F. R. *Stories of New Jersey.* New York, American Book Co., 1896. 254 p. Anecdotes of New Jersey history by a famous storyteller.

Tanner, Edwin P. *The Province of New Jersey, 1664–1738.* New York, Columbia University Press, 1908. 712 p. (Studies in History, Economics and Public Law. v. 30.) The most reliable study of this period.

Turnbull, Archibald Douglas. *John Stevens: An American Record.* New York, Century, 1928. 545 p. illus. Covers the achievements of five generations of the Stevens family.

Turner, Edward Raymond. "Woman's Suffrage in New Jersey, 1790–1807." (In Dept. of History of Smith College. *Smith College Studies in History.* Northampton, Mass., 1916. v. 1, no. 4. p. 165-187.)

Wilson, Edmund, Jr. "New Jersey, the Slave of Two Cities." (In Gruening, Ernest, ed. *These United States.* 1st series. New York, Boni & Liveright, 1923. p. 56-66.) This study by a native of New Jersey restates in modern terms the Colonial theme of New Jersey's subordination to New York and Philadelphia.

GOVERNMENT

Cline, Denzel C. *Executive Control over State Expenditures in New Jersey.* Princeton, University Press, 1934. 36 p. (Princeton University School of Public and International Affairs.) A scholarly pamphlet presenting the weaknesses in New Jersey's decentralized executive control.

Erdman, Charles R., Jr. *The New Jersey Constitution:* A Barrier to Governmental Efficiency and Economy. Princeton, University Press, 1934. 36 p. (Princeton University. School of Public and International Affairs.) A clear picture of the difficulty of attaining efficient government under a constitution almost 100 years old.

Everson, A. R., comp. *Facts about New Jersey and the Cost of Government.* Trenton, N. J. Taxpayers Association, 1935. 95 p.

New Jersey. State Planning Board. *First Annual Report of Progress.* Trenton, 1935. 147 p. maps.

———. *Second Annual Report of Progress.* Trenton, 1937. 124 p. maps.

Princeton. Local Government Survey. *Local Government Bulletins.* Princeton, University Press, 1936–37. A series of bulletins and pamphlets well illustrated with tables, charts, and extensive supporting memoranda.

Princeton University School of Public and International Affairs. *Report on a Survey of Administration and Expenditures of the State Government of New Jersey.* Princeton, University Press, 1932. 403 p. A significant study of State government, still applicable because so few of its recommendations were adopted.

Sedgwick, Theodore, Jr. *William Livingston:* A Memoir. New York, J. & J. Harper, 1833. 449 p. A valuable though inadequate book concerning New Jersey's first Governor.

AGRICULTURE

Woodward, Carl Raymond, and Ingrid Nelson Waller. *New Jersey's Agricultural Experiment Station, 1880–1930.* New Brunswick, N. J. Agricultural Experiment Station, 1932. 645 p. illus., maps.

INDUSTRY, COMMERCE, AND LABOR

Boyer, Charles S. *Early Forges and Furnaces of New Jersey.* Philadelphia, University of Pennsylvania Press, 1931. 287 p. illus., map. The best study of this important phase of New Jersey's economic life.

Brown, Norris W. *The Industrial Directory of New Jersey.* Trenton, 1934. 480 p. (New Jersey Department of Labor.)

Dyer, Frank Lewis, and Thomas Commerford Martin. *Edison, His Life and Inventions.* New York, Harper, 1929. 2 v. illus.

Port of New York Authority. *The Port of New York Authority: A Monograph.* New York, Port of New York Authority, 1936. 92 p. illus.

Stevens, James M. *New Jersey Manufactures, 1899–1927.* New Brunswick, Rutgers University Press, 1930. 61 p. (Bureau of Economic and Business Research. Bulletin 2.)

TRANSPORTATION

Boyd, Thomas Alexander. *Poor John Fitch, Inventor of the Steamboat.* New York, Putnam, 1935. 315 p. illus., map, bibliography. The first full-length biography of one of New Jersey's great inventors; derived largely from original Fitch manuscripts.

RACIAL ELEMENTS

Chambers, Theodore Frelinghuysen. *The Early Germans of New Jersey: Their History, Churches and Genealogies.* Dover, N. J., Dover Printing Co., 1895. 667 p. illus., maps.

Goldstein, Philip Reuben. *Social Aspects of the Jewish Colonies of South Jersey.* New York, League Printing Co., 1921. 74 p. map.

Johnson, Amandus. *Swedish Settlements on the Delaware; Their History and Relation to the Indians, Dutch and English, 1638–1664.* Philadelphia, University of Pennsylvania Press, 1911. 2 v. illus. A monumental and accurate work on early colonization, customs, and manners of settlers in West Jersey.

————. *The Journal and Biography of Nicholas Collin, 1746–1831.* Tr. from the original Swedish manuscript, with an introduction by Frank H. Stewart. Philadelphia, New Jersey Society of Pennsylvania, 1936. 368 p. illus. The Rev. Nicholas Collin was the last Swedish pastor in the old Swedes' churches on the New Jersey side of the Delaware.

Meade, Emily Fogg. *The Italian on the Land: A Study in Immigration.* Washington, Government Printing Office, 1907. 60 p. (U. S. Department of Labor. Bulletin 70.) Based on the Hammonton settlement.

Steward, William, and Theophilus G. Steward. *Gouldtown: A Very Remarkable Settlement of Ancient Date.* Philadelphia, Lippincott, 1913. 237 p. illus. Accepted as the authentic account of New Jersey's interesting colony of mulattoes.

Storms, J. C. *Origin of the Jackson-Whites of the Ramapo Mountains.* Park Ridge, The Author, 1936. 26 p. Describes a settlement in the Ramapos whose people have strains of Tuscarora Indian, Hessian German, English, Negro, and Italian blood.

EDUCATION

Collins, Varnum Lansing. *Princeton, Past and Present.* Princeton, University Press, 1931. 200 p. illus. The official and most authoritative history of the university.

Demarest, William Henry Steel. *History of Rutgers College, 1766–1924.* New Brunswick, Rutgers College, 1924. 570 p. The official history of the college.

Murray, David. *History of Education in New Jersey.* Washington, Government Printing Office, 1899. 344 p. (U. S. Bureau of Education. Circular of Information 1.)

New Jersey. Governor's School Survey Commission. *Report.* Trenton, 1933. 2 v. in 1. illus., charts, tables. v. 1: School costs and economies in the State of New Jersey. v. 2: Reconstruction of the system of public school support in the State of New Jersey. An objective and searching study of educational opportunities and school costs.

RELIGION

Gummere, Amelia Mott, ed. *The Journal and Essays of John Woolman.* New York, Macmillan, 1922. 643 p. illus. This edition of the original manuscripts is the most reliable work on the great Quaker teacher of Mount Holly.

PRISONS

Barnes, Harry Elmer. *A History of the Penal, Reformatory and Correctional Institutions of the State of New Jersey.* Trenton, MacCrellish & Quigley Co., 1918. 654 p. Vol. 2 of the New Jersey Prison Inquiry Commission Report; analytical and documentary.

MEDICINE

Wickes, Stephen. *History of Medicine in New Jersey and of Its Medical Men,* from the Settlement of the Province to A. D. 1800. Newark, M. R. Dennis & Co., 1879. 449 p.

LITERATURE

Austin, Mary S. *Philip Freneau, the Poet of the Revolution:* History of His Life and Times. Ed. by Helen Kearny Vreeland, great-granddaughter of the poet. New York, A. Wessels Co., 1901. 285 p. illus.

Beer, Thomas. *Stephen Crane, a Study in American Letters.* New York, Knopf, 1923. 248 p. The sole biography of New Jersey's most famous literary figure. More one author's appreciation of another than a complete record of Crane's life.

Irving, William, James Kirke Paulding, and Washington Irving. *Salmagundi:* or, The Whimwhams and Opinions of Launcelot Langstaff, Esq., and Others. New York, Putnam, 1902. 502 p. front. Printed from the original edition, with a preface and notes by Evert A. Duyckinck. 20 numbers, Jan. 1807–Jan. 1808. (Vol. 18 of *Irving's Works.*) Contains descriptions of social life at Cockloft Hall in Newark.

Traubel, Horace. *With Walt Whitman in Camden.* 3 v., illus., 1906–14. Vol. 1 has imprint: Boston, Small, Maynard & Co.; vol. 2: New York, D. Appleton & Co.; vol. 3: New York, Mitchell Kennerley. The three volumes report conversations with Walt Whitman during the years 1888 and 1889.

ART

Dana, John Cotton. *American Art:* How It Can Be Made to Flourish. Woodstock, Vt., Elm Tree Press, 1914. 31 p. Of all of Dana's writings this perhaps has had the most far reaching influence.

Newark Museum Association. *The Work of the Potteries of New Jersey from 1685 to 1876.* Newark, Museum Association, 1914. 34 p. illus. Extracts from authoritative works, presenting the best available information.

DRAMA

Morley, Christopher. *Seacoast of Bohemia.* Garden City, N. Y., Doubleday, Doran & Co., 1929. 68 p. illus. An amusing account of the author's attempt to revive old-time theatrical thrillers in Hoboken (1928–29).

SPORTS AND RECREATION

Hunt, William S. *Frank Forester* [Henry William Herbert]: A Tragedy in Exile. Newark, Carteret Book Club, 1933. 128 p. An evaluation of the Newark period of a noted 19th century writer on sports and outdoor life.

Torrey, Raymond H., Frank Place, Jr., and Robert L. Dickinson. *New York Walk Book:* Suggestions for Excursions Afoot within a Radius of 50 to 100 Miles of the City Including Forest Trails in Mountain Regions. New York, Dodd, Mead & Co., 1934. 332 p. Revised edition.

CITIES AND TOWNS

Beck, Henry Charlton. *Forgotten Towns of Southern New Jersey.* New York, Dutton, 1936. 278 p. illus.

————. *More Forgotten Towns of Southern New Jersey.* New York, Dutton, 1937. 338 p. illus. Two volumes of entertaining stories, written from the reportorial rather than the historical viewpoint. The second book contains an index.

Hatfield, Edwin Francis. *History of Elizabeth, New Jersey:* Including the Early History of Union County. New York, Carlton & Lanahan, 1868. 701 p. illus. Scope is broader than title indicates.

Nelson, William. *History of the City of Paterson and of the County of Passaic.* Paterson, Press Publishing Co., 1901. 448 p. First half devoted to genealogies; last half to customs, roads, bridges, and the Revolution.

Sherman, Andrew M. *Historic Morristown, New Jersey:* The Story of Its First Century. Morristown, Howard Publishing Co., 1905. 444 p. illus.

Trenton Historical Society. *A History of Trenton, 1679–1929.* Princeton, University Press, 1929. 2 v. illus. Authentic, colorful.

Urquhart, F. J. *History of the City of Newark, New Jersey, 1666–1913.* New

York, Lewis Historical Publishing Co., 1913. 3 v. illus. A minute study which emphasizes the rise of Newark industry.

Whitehead, William A. *Contributions to the Early History of Perth Amboy and Vicinity.* New York, Appleton, 1856. 428 p. illus. Contains accurate drawings of buildings and scenes as far back as 1832.

POINTS OF INTEREST

Ellis, Rowland C. *Colonial Dutch Houses in New Jersey.* Newark, Carteret Book Club, 1933. 61 p. illus.

Kelsey, Frederick Wallace. *The First County Park System:* A Complete History of the Essex County Parks. New York, J. S. Ogilvie, 1905. 300 p. illus., map.

Mills, Weymer Jay. *Historic Houses of New Jersey.* Philadelphia, Lippincott, 1902. 348 p. Only book of its kind, illustrated by drawings and photographs from old prints. Many anecdotes.

Society of Colonial Wars in the State of New Jersey. *Historic Roadsides.* Plainfield, N. J., 1928. 115 p. illus., map. Description of principal Colonial and Revolutionary landmarks in New Jersey; excellent historical map and bibliography. Tours arranged by counties.

Wallace, Philip B. *Colonial Churches and Meeting Houses.* New York, Agricultural Book Publishing Co., 1931. 291 p. illus. Covers Pennsylvania, New Jersey, and Delaware.

BIBLIOGRAPHY

Hasse, Adelaide R. *Index of Economic Material in Documents of the States of the United States.* Washington, Carnegie Institution of Washington, 1907–22. 13 v. in 16. New Jersey material appears in v. 13.

Index

Abbett, Gov. Leon, 48, 57
Abbott, Dr. Charles Conrad, 28, 158, 400
Abbott family, 642
Abolitionists, 259, 363, 393
Absecon, 597
Absecon Bay, 597
Accommodations, xxv
Achkinchesacky (see Indians)
Ackerman and Ross, 245
Acquackanonk Landing, site, 348
Acquackanonk Patent, 346
Actors' Fund Home, 438
Adams, Elizabeth, 637
Adams, Pres. John, 400, 402
Adams, Maude, 164
Adelphian Academy, 245
After Dark, 165
Age of Reason, The, 209
Agricultural Experiment Station, State, 92, 308
Agricultural products, value of, 94
Agriculture, 89-95, 253, 308, 422, 482, 535, 588, 656
Agriculture, State Board of, 60, 92, 308
Agriculture, State Dept. of, 23, 637
Agriculture, U.S. Dept. of, 23, 93, 574, 616
Airlines, xxiv
Airports: Atlantic City, 608; Bendix, 540; Camden Central, 107, 575; Hadley, 549; Mercer, 522-3; Newark, 107, 322, 338, 422, 549
Aitkins, Capt. Robert, 438
Akron, The, 623, 667
Albertson, Ephraim, 651
Alcyon Lake, 658
Alden, Henry Mills, 157
Alexander, Mrs. Charles E., 384
Alexander, Gen. William, 479
Allaire, 590
Allaire, James, 590
Allamuchy Mts., 481
Allen, George H., 224
Allen, Joseph, 463
Allen, Junius, 186
Allen, William, 535
Allenhurst, 682
Allenwood, 590
Alliance, 660
Alligator, the, 615
Alling, Nils Nillson, 367
Alpine, 437
Ambrose, Paul, 172
America, 168
America, the Beautiful, 170
American Airlines, 575
American Artists' Professional League, 186
American Brakeblok Co., 439
American Civil Liberties Union, 206, 276
American Crockery Co., 403

American Federation of Labor, 53, 84, 85, 86, 574
American Hotel, The, 563
American Insurance Co., 178, 317
American Iron Co., 504
American Legion, 311
American Magazine, The, 111, 552
American Mutual Insurance Co., 78
American Newspaper Guild, 85, 115-6, 204
American Newspaper Publishers Assn., 115
American Ornithology, 212
American Pottery, The, 181, 275, 280
American Red Cross, 215
American Smelting and Refining Co., 364
American Society of Mechanical Engineers, 268
American Telephone and Telegraph Co., 514
American Tree Assn., 522
American Type Founders, 247
Ammann, Othman H., 204
Amwell Academy, 450
Anaconda Copper Mining Co., 368
Anarchism, 487
Anarchists, 354
Ancora, 598
Anderson, Abraham, 232
Anderson, Broncho Billy, 164
Andover, 463
Andover Forge, site, 463
Andover mine, 463
Andrews, Mark, 172
Andros, Gov. Edmund, 39
Anheuser-Busch Inc., 529
Animals, 22, 559, 672
Annandale, 433
Annandale Graphite Co., 433
Annandale State Farm, 433
Annapolis Conference, 45
Antheil, George, 171
Antill, Edward, 528
Aphis, 92
Appalachian Highlands Province, 7, 11
Appalachian Mts., 7, 14
Appalachian Trail, 460
Arbuckle, "Fatty," 164
Archeology, 28-30
Archers, The, 168
Archers Corners, 616
Architecture, 172-81, 261, 478; Dutch Colonial, 173-4; "Swedish Colonial," 174-5; Georgian Colonial, 175; Greek Revival, 176; Victorian, 176-7; modern, 177-81
Arlington Cemetery, 574
Armenians, 122
Arnett, Hannah, 247
Arnett, Isaac, 247
Arnold, Gen. Benedict, 285

Arrow Textile Print Works, 359
Art Center of the Oranges, 185, 339
Art Color Printing Co., 549
Arthur Kill, 106, 362
Artifacts, 28-30
Asbury, Bishop Francis, 145, 512, 620
Asbury Park, 164, 682
Assembly, Colonial, 367, 405
Assembly, General, 77
Assembly, Provincial, 37, 396
Associated Press, 113
Associates of the Jersey Co., 274
Assunpink Creek, 398
Atco, 599
Atco Lake, 599
Atlantic City, 11, 130, 132, 164, 189-200,
    596, 607
Atlantic City *Press,* 115
Atlantic City *World,* 114
Atlantic County, 127
Atlantic County Historical Society, 562
Atlantic Highlands, 108, 676
Atlantic Ocean, 190
Atlantic Terra Cotta Co., 368
Atsion, 471
Atsion Lake, 471
Audubon, 601
Augusta, 461
Augusta, The, 575, 576
Aurora Institute, 513
Austrians, 118, 346
Avon by the Sea, 594, 683

B Minor Mass, 170
Bach Society of N. J., 170
Bacon, Andrew, 634
Bacon, Henry, 355
Bacon, John, 649
Baer, William J., 186
Bailey, John, 239
Bainbridge, Dr. Edmund, 388
Bainbridge, Commodore William, 389
Baker, Hobart, 489
Bakers Basin, 427
Balback, Edward, 71
Bald Hill, 478
Baldwin, Roger, 206
Ball, Rev. Archey, 150
Ball, Thomas, 184
Ballet Mécanique, 171
Baly, J. J., 204
Bamberger, Louis, 329, 332, 388
Bamberger Broadcasting Service, 332
Bamberger department store, 108, 314, 332
Banking, 45, 77-8, 320
Baptistown, 525
Baptists, 41, 144, 146, 148, 218, 487,
    592
Bara, Theda, 164
Barbarroux Wharf, site, 222
Barber and Howe, 296, 393, 402
Bard, Peter, 624
Barnegat, 559
Barnegat Bay, 647
Barnegat City, 157, 670
Barnegat Pete, 559
Barnert, Nathan, statue, 358
Barnes, James, 159

Barnet, Dr. William, 246
Barrett, Wilson, 163
Barringer High School, 165, 317
Barrington, 601
Barrowe, Dr., 279
Barry, Arthur, 463
Barton, Clara, 136, 214-5
Barton, Clara, School, 214-5
Baseball, xxix, 264, 280, 331, 336, 394
Basket, John, 593
Basketball, xxix, 199
Basking Ridge, 447
Bathysphere, 547
Batsto, 604
Batsto Iron Works, 410, 605
Battle of Assunpink, 402
Battle of Monmouth, 252, 265-8
Battle of Princeton, 42, 372, 467
Battle of Quinton Bridge, 634
Battle of Red Bank, 576
Battle of the Kegs, The, 152, 208
Battle of Trenton, 401
Battlefield of Ash Swamp, 485
Bay Head, 647
Bayard, Samuel, 264
Bayard, William, 264
Bayberries, 673
Bayonne, 201-6
Bayonne Bridge, 106, 201, 204, 423
Bayonne *Times,* 204
Bayshore, 649
Beach Glen, 479
Beach Haven, 673
Beach Haven Crest, 673
Beach Haven Terrace, 673
Beaches, 557, 562, 563, 595, 596, 607,
    642, 646, 647, 648, 669, 670,
    672, 673, 674, 675, 676, 678,
    679, 681, 682, 683, 684
Beachwood, 557
Beacon Hill, 554
Beadle Brothers, 403
Bearfort Mt., 507
Beattystown, 516
Beaver Lake, 496
Beck, Henry C., 625
Beckett, Henry, 212
Bedminster, 448, 466
Beebe, Dr. William, 547
Beemerville, 461
Belasco, David, 164
Belcher, Gov. Jonathan, 40, 218, 246
Belcoville, 664
Beleek, 403
Belford, 675
Bell Farm, 651
Belle Meade, 466
Belleville, 542-3
Bellmawr, 651
Bellona, The, 300
Belmar, 595, 683
Belvidere, 483
Ben Bolt, 157
Benedictines, 462, 513
Bergen, 35, 36, 37, 142, 271, 272
Bergen County, 114, 130, 132
Bergen County Administrative Building,
    260

Bergen County Historical Society, 260
Bergen *Evening Record,* 257
Bergen Hill, 275
Bergen Point, 203
Bergenfield, 438
Bergoff, Pearl, 204
Berkeley, 648
Berkeley, John Lord, 37, 38, 239, 392
Berlin, 599
Bernard, Gov. Francis, 33
Bernardsville, 447
Bertrand's Island, 481
Bettin, Capt. Adam, 289
Beverwyck Inn (Troy Hills), 477
Bier's Training Camp, 441-2
Big Brook Game Farm, 589
Birds, 20-1, 429, 477, 530, 540, 632, 662
Black Crook, The, 165
Black Horse Inn (Mendham), 513
Black Horse Pike, 612, 650
Black Legion, 120
Black Riders, 156
Black River, 514
Black Tom explosion, 275
Blacklist, 403
Blackwood, 652
Blackwood, Capt. John, 652
Blair, John I., 457
Blair Academy, 457
Blairstown, 456-7
Blakelock, Ralph, 184
Blenheim, 652
Block, Paul, 115
Blommaert, Samuel, 36, 564
Bloomfield, 490
Bloomfield, Gov. Joseph, 220, 490
Bloomfield College and Seminary, 490-1
Bloomsbury, 434
Blossom Festivals, 654
Blueberries, 91, 616, 623
Boardman, Alexander, 195
Boardwalk (Atlantic City), 191, 195
Boating, xxviii, 282, 331, 336, 386, 429,
      430, 461, 484, 506, 640, 647, 658,
      659, 675
Bodely, Elizabeth, 638
Bonaparte, Caroline, 212
Bonaparte, Charles Lucien, 212
Bonaparte, Joseph, 209, 210-2, 409, 412-
      413, 584
Bonaparte, Prince Joseph Lucien Charles
      Napoleon, 212
Bonaparte, Zenaide, 212
Bond, Capt. Thomas, 674
Bone, Christian, 493
Bonhamtown, 424
Bonnell, Nathaniel, 246
Boone, Rev. Ilsley, 441
Boonton, 70, 71, 86, 444
Booth, Edwin, 163
Bootleggers (*see Prohibition*)
Booz, E. C., 613
Borden, Ann, 213
Borden, Joseph, 98, 152, 208, 209, 213,
      215
Borden Milk Co., 427
Bordentown, 136, 207-15, 469, 572
Bordentown Female College, 212

Bordentown Military Institute, 141, 212
Borg, John, 257
Borglum, Gutzon, 185, 325, 328, 332
Bosworth, W. W., 291
Botany Worsted Mills, 346, 347
Bottle Hill Tavern, 511
Boudinot, Elias, 181, 224, 246
Bound Brook, 431, 549
Bourne, Randolph, 159, 491
Bowen, David S., 576
Boxing, xxix, 199, 441-2
Boy Scouts, 437, 458, 590, 618
Boyden, Seth, 46, 71, 91, 320; statue, 328
Bradbury, William Batchelder, 166, 168
Bradford, William, 363
Bradford, Mrs. William, 224
Bradley, James A., 682, 683
Bradley Beach, 683
Bradway, Edward, 396
Brady, "Diamond Jim," 680
Brady, William A., 164
Brainerd, Rev. David, 471, 566, 569-70
Brainerd, Rev. John, 294
Brainerd Lake, 570
Brainerd School, 294
Branchville, 461
Brandle, Theodore, 276
Brant, David, 511
Brant, Joseph, 498
Brant Beach, 673
Brass, Jacob, 517
Brass Castle, 517
Breakers, The (Spray Beach), 673
Brick, James W., 555
Brick, John, 639
Brick, Joshua, 635
Brick House Hotel (Montague), 459
Bricksboro, 639
Bridge Memorial, 328
Bridgeboro, 574
Bridgeport, 578, 614
Bridges, 106, 180, 402, 412
Bridgeton, 111, 112, 635, 657
Brielle, 595, 685
Brisbane, Albert, 589
Brisbane, Arthur, 590
Bristol Bridge, 222
Bristol-Meyers Co., 429
Brite and Bacon, 280
Broadway, 517
Brooklawn, 657
Brooklyn Bridge, 403, 572
Brooks, Noah, 322
Brooks, Van Wyck, 159
Broome, L. H., 404
Brothers College (*see Drew University*)
Brotherton, 33, 34
Brotmanville, 660
Brown, A. Page, 384, 385
Brown, Harry A., 413
Browns, 506
Browns Mills, 619
Browntown, 529
Bruen Matthias, 364-5
Bryan, William Jennings, 48
Buck, Dudley, 166, 169
Bucks Tavern, 658
Budd, Thomas, 470

Budd Lake, 481
Buena, 609
Bunner, Henry Cuyler, 157
Bunny, John, 164
Burleigh, 562
Burlington, 39, 40, 76, 181, 216-24, 572
Burlington County Historical Society, 220
Burlington County Iron Works, 620
Burlington Sycamore, 223
Burr, Aaron, 185, 245, 381, 389, 420, 538
Burr, Rev. Aaron, 244, 319, 376, 381
Burr, Amelia Josephine, 160
Burr, John, 293
Burroughs, John, 234
Burrowes, John, 554
Bury the Dead, 165
Bus Lines, list, xxiv
Busses, 106
Butler, 495
Butler, Dr. Nicholas Murray, 206
Butler Place, 669
Buttermilk Falls, 449
Buttzville, 482, 533
Byllynge, Edward, 38, 293, 392

CIBA Pharmaceutical Products Co., 180
Cabot, John, 36
Cadwalader, Dr. Thomas, 400
Caldwell, 493
Caldwell, Hannah, 510
Caldwell, Rev. James, 244, 246, 509, 510, 547
Caldwell at Springfield, 157
Calvin, Bartholomew, 34
Calvin, Stephen, 34
Calvinists, 144
Cambrian Period, 13
Camden, 82, 225-37, 574, 602, 621, 650
Camden, Earl of, 228
Camden and Atlantic Land Co., 194
Camden *City Directory,* 114
Camden City Hall, 178, 229-30
Camden County Park Commission, 601
Camden *Courier,* 115
Camden Forge Co., 651
Camden *Local News,* 114
Camden *Mail,* 112
Camden Marine Terminals, 229
Camden *Post,* 115
Camp Dix, 51, 606, 618
Camp Kendrick, 623
Camp Merritt, site, 51, 438
Camp Nordland, 463-4
Camp Wawayanda, 463
Camp Wo-Chi-Ca, 516
Campbell, Joseph, 232
Campbell Soup Co., 232
Camping, 430, 436, 438, 460, 499, 594, 669
Cannon Song, The, 384
"Cannon War," 305
Cape May City, 563
Cape May Court House, 562
Cape May Point, 564
Carey, Henry, 220
Carleton, Sir Guy, 557
Carlls Corner, 657

Carlstadt, 540
Carmel, 660
Carmelite Nuns, 512
Carnahan, Dr. James, 378
Carnegie, Andrew, 386
Carnegie Lake, 489
Carney's Point, 578
Carranza, Capt. Emilio, 471
Carrere, John M., 358
Carrere and Hastings, 200
Carrier pigeons, 623
Carter and Lindsey, 291
Carteret, 84
Carteret, Sir George, 37, 38, 39, 239
Carteret, James, 38
Carteret, Gov. Philip, 37, 38, 39, 239-40, 273, 318, 492
Carteret Arms (Elizabeth), 245
Carver, Dr. W. F., 199
Cassville, 616
Castle Howard Farm, 489
Castle Point, 266
Cathedral of the Air, 623
Cattell, Jonas, 128
Cedar Bonnet Island, 667
Cedar Bridge, 668
Cedar Bridge Tavern, 668
Cedar Creek Lake, 557
Cedar Grove, 493
Cedar mining, 640
Cedarville, 637
Celestial Passion, The, 154
Celluloid Corp., 316
Cemetery Hill, 451
Centenary Collegiate Institute, 140, 482
Centerville, 203
Central High School (Trenton), 413
Central Pier, 198
Century, The, 215, 322
Chadwicks, 648
Chambers Corner, 470
Chambersburg, 403
Channing, William Ellery, 589
Chapel Hill, 592
Chapman, Charles S., 186
Charles II, 36
Charlotteburg, 496
Chatham, 121, 511
Chatham Community Players, 165
Chatsworth, 668
Cheesequake, 553-4
Chesapeake, The, 220
Chesilhurst, 599
Chester, 466, 514
Chester House, 514
Chew, Col. Jeremiah, 652
Chews, 652
Chew's Landing, site, 652
Chew's Landing Hotel, 652
Chicago World's Fair, 206
Child labor amendment, Federal, 86
Chimney Rock, 431
Chinatown (Newark), 334
Chinese, 122, 334
Choate, Joseph, 404
Choral societies, 168
Christian Church cemetery, 455-6

Christian Scientists, 146
Church of England, 142
Churches
  Baptist:
    Holmdel, 588; Hopewell, Old School, 536; Manahawkin, 559; Marlton, 626; Middletown, 592; Newark, Peddie Memorial, 177; Roadstown, Cohansey, 643; Sussex, First, 498; Trenton, First, 148; Ye Olde Yellow Meeting House, 586-7
  Christ, Scientist:
    Montclair, First, 178
  Episcopal:
    Bayonne, Trinity, 204-5; Burlington, St. Mary's, 224; Elizabeth, St. John's, 176, 244; Freehold, St. Peter's, 254; Middletown, Christ, 592; New Brunswick, Christ, 309; Newark, House of Prayer, 330, Trinity, 175, 325; Perth Amboy, St. Peter's, 367; Piscataway, St. James', 175, 424; Ringwood, 504; Shrewsbury, Christ, 593; Swedesboro, Trinity, 614; Trenton, St. Michael's, 409; West End, 681
  Greek Catholic:
    Great Meadows, 482; Passaic, SS. Peter and Paul's Russian Orthodox, 348; Whippany, 532
  Hebrew:
    Newark, B'nai Jeshurun, 146, 335
  Lutheran:
    Carlstadt, 540; Oldwick, Zion, 432; Still Valley, St. James, 435
  Methodist:
    Archers Corners, Zion, 616; Clarksburg, 585; Cookstown, 617; Crosswicks, 571; Delaware, 483; Head of River, 662; Lumberton, 620; Pleasant Mills, 606; Whitehall, 444
  Moravian:
    Hope, 456; Palmyra, 132; Sharptown, 611
  Presbyterian:
    Basking Ridge, Log, 447; Bergenfield, Old South, 438; Bloomfield, First, 490; Bloomsbury, Old Greenwich, 434-5; Bridgeton, Broad Street, 635; Cranbury, First, 570; Deerfield, Stone, 655; Elizabeth, First, 240, 244; Hanover, 530; Lawrenceville, 468; Matawan, First, 554; Metuchen, First, 486; Milford, West Milford, 507; Morristown, First, 289; New England Crossroads, Old Stone, 637; Newark, First, 150, 319, 324, Second, 150, 178, 330; Parsippany, 477; Pluckemin, St. Paul's, 176, 448; Princeton, First, 381; Roselle, 546; Springfield, First, 176, 509; Tennent, 176, 254, 565-6, 581; Titusville, First, 520; Trenton, First, 409; Tuckahoe, 663; Union, 509; Westfield, 547; Whippany, First, 531; Yellow Frame, 455

  Quaker:
    Bordentown, 214; Burlington, 220; Camden, 230, 235; Cinnaminson, 574; Crosswicks, Chesterfield, 176, 571; East Branch, 585; Greenwich, 645; Hancock's Bridge, 634; Mansfield, 469; Medford, 625; Moorestown, 621; Mount Holly, 293, 294; Mullica Hill, 629; Plainfield, 548; Randolph, 532; Salem, 396; Seaville, Cedar, 666; Shrewsbury, 594; Trenton, 409; Tuckerton, 560; Woodbury, 628; Woodstown, 610
  Reformed:
    Belleville, 542; Dumont, North, 438; Fairfield, 476; Flatbrookville, 474; Franklin Park, 488; Hackensack, Church on the Green, 260; Harlingen, 466; Jersey City, Bergen, 143, 273, 277; Minisink, 473; New Brunswick, First, 309; Oakland, 441; Paramus, 539; Pompton Lakes, 500; Somerville, 550-1; Wanaque Borough, 501
  Roman Catholic:
    Butler, St. Anthony's, 495; Delaware, 483; Elizabeth, St. Patrick's, 249; Hewitt, 506; Immaculate Conception, 441; Newark, Sacred Heart, 331; Paterson, St. Michael's, 357; Singac, Our Lady of Holy Angels, 494; Trenton, St. Mary's, 409; Wanaque Borough, St. Francis of Assisi, 501
  Seventh Day Baptist:
    Marlboro, 635
  Universalist:
    Newark, Church of the Redeemer, 150
  Others:
    Haskell, Full Gospel Assembly, 500; Jersey City, St. Matthew's, 279; Newark, St. Philip's, 148; Parsippany, Little White Church, 477; West Milford, Full Gospel Assembly, 507
Cinnaminson, 574
Ciocchetti, Giuseppe, 328
Citizens' Military Training Camp, 618
City Market (Elizabeth), 248
City Schools Stadium (Newark), 336
Civil Liberties, 149, 206, 276, 347, 437
Civil Liberties Committee, U.S. Senate, 84, 232
Civil Service, 60
Civil War, 47, 82, 203, 259, 275, 320, 374, 544, 632
Civil Works Administration, 336, 338
Civilian Conservation Corps, 24, 104, 288, 646
Clams, 676
Claremont, 271
Clark, Abraham, 485, 547
Clark, E. Mabel, 288
Clark, Capt. Elijah, 606
Clark, John, 353
Clark, Roger, 459
Clark, Judge William, 232, 276
Clarksburg, 584

Classis of Holland, 142
Clay, 26
Clay, Henry, 563
Clayton, 658
Clayville, 631
Clear View Hotel (Beach Haven Terrace), 673
Clee, Rev. Lester H., 53, 150
Clementon, 599
Clermont, 562, 641
Clermont, The, 99
Cleveland, Pres. Grover, 386, 388, 389, 493
Cliffwood, 591
Climate, 11
Climate and Equipment, xxiv
Clinton, 433
Clinton, Gov. De Witt, 100
Clinton, Sir Henry, 252, 561, 566-8, 678
Clinton Democrat, 534
Clinton State Farm, 433
Closter, 437
Closter, Frederick, 436
Clymer, George, 409
Coast Guard, 670, 674
Coastal Plain, 7, 10, 11, 13
Coates, Daniel, 625
Coates, John R., 663
Coca-Cola Bottling Co., Harrison, 180; Newark, 180
Cochran, Dr. John, 308
Cochran House (Newton), 462
Cochrane's Tavern, site, 308
Cocked Hat School, 642
"Cockroach bosses," 352
Cokesbury, 433
Colby, Everett, 50
Cold Indian Spring Lake, 594
Coleono, Bartolomeo, statue, 335
Coles, John B., 274
Colesville, 498
Colgate, Austin, 50
Colgate, William, 279
Colgate-Palmolive Peet Co., 279
Colgate clock, 279
College Bridge, 425
College of Agriculture, State, 93, 308, 426 (see also Rutgers University)
College of New Jersey (see Princeton University)
College of Saint Elizabeth, 140, 512
Collingswood, 601
Collins, Isaac, 111, 221
Colonia, 485
Colonial Apartments (Bordentown), 213
Colt, Christopher, 359
Colt, Samuel, 353, 359
Colt family, 359
Colt's Neck, 589
Colt's Neck Inn, 589
Columbia, 457-8
Columbia High School (Maplewood), 344
Columbian Herald, 113
Columbus, 469-70
Columbus, Christopher, monument, 328
Columbus Inn, 470
Colver, John, 559
Combs, Moses, 71, 135, 317, 319

Comb's Hill, 581
Comical Corner, 618
Commerce, U.S. Dept. of, 423
Commerce and Navigation, State Board of, 107
Committee of Correspondence, 41
Communications, 108-9
Communipaw, 271, 272
Commuters, 4, 6, 48, 50
"Concessions and Agreements" (West Jersey), 39
"Concessions and Agreements of the Lords Proprietors," 37
Congregationalists, 144, 318
Congress, Continental, 41, 372, 381
Congress, Provincial, 41, 44, 55, 218, 300, 308
Congress, U.S., 44-5
Congress of Industrial Organizations, 53, 85-6, 276
Connick, Charles J., 387
Conover, J. Hallam, 253
Conrad, Joseph, 156
Conrads, Carl, 248
Conservation, 22-4
Conservation and Development, State Dept. of, 24, 616
Conservator, The, 156
Constable Hook, 203
Constitution, The, 389
Constitution, Federal, 45
Constitution of 1776, State, 44, 55, 145, 218
Constitution of 1844, State, 46-7, 55-6
Constitutional Convention, Federal, 45
Consumers' League of New Jersey, 86, 87
Consumers' Research, 517
Consumers Union of U.S., 517
Convent Station, 512
Convention Hall (Atlantic City), 198
Cooke, Dr. H. Lester, 371
Cookstown, 617
Cooper, Jacob, 228
Cooper, James Fenimore, 152, 678
Cooper, John, 629
Cooper, Joseph, Jr., 235
Cooper, Peter, 504
Cooper, William, 228, 234
Cooper family, 502
Cooper River Parkway, 235
Cooperatives, 87-8, 94, 116, 179, 525, 543, 570, 598, 613, 620, 637, 660, 661
Cope and Stewardson, 385
Copper Hill, 450
Copperas Mt., 496
Corbin City, 61, 664
Cornbury, Edward Lord, 39, 40, 396
Cornwallis, Charles Lord, 42, 247, 401, 402, 452, 548, 575, 675
Coryel, Samuel, 451-2
"Cotton Town of the U.S.," 353
Council of Safety, 372
Council of Social Agencies and Welfare, 340
Country Day School, 371
Court of Chancery, 87, 149, 204
Court of Errors and Appeals, 149

Courthouses: Bergen County, 260; Burlington County, 175, 293; Camden County, 230, annex, 178; Cape May County, 562; Cumberland County, 637; Essex County, 332; Gloucester County, 629; Hunterdon County, 524; Middlesex County, 551; Monmouth County, 253; Morris County, 291; Ocean County, 556; Passaic County, 355; Salem County, 393; Somerset County, site, 488; Sussex County, 176, 454, 462; Union County, 245, annex, 178
Cox, Lt. Col. John, 410
Coxe, Gov. Daniel, 181, 408, 467
Cox's Corners, 467, 586
Coytesville, 439
Crafts, 181, 184
Craftsman Farm, 532
Cram, Ralph Adams, 386
Cram and Ferguson, 385
Cranberries, 91, 472, 616, 620, 623, 662, 664
Cranberry Inlet, 648
Cranberry Lake, 464
Cranbury, 569-70
Cranbury Inn, 570
Crane, Newton, 153, 322
Crane, Stephen (1709–1780), 41, 247, 492
Crane, Stephen (1871–1900), 153, 156, 322, 334-5, 492
Cranford, 547
Creole Lover's Song, 154
Cretaceous Period, 14
Crime, 293, 301, 434, 463, 524, 536, 577, 580, 641
Crips, John, 217
Crisis, The, 152
Crisler, Herbert O., 386
Crispin, Edwin, Farm, 621
Critic, The, 215
Cromwell, Doris Duke, 466
Cromwell, James H. R., 466
Crooks, Richard, 172
Crop rotation, 23
Crosby, Alexander Lovelady, 426
Cross, Dr. Dorothy, 28
Crosswicks, 571
Crosswicks Oak, 572
Croton, 525
Crucible Steel, 544
Cuff family, 637
Culvers Gap, 460-1
Culvers Lake, 461
Cumberland, 662
Cumberland Furnace, site, 662
Cumberland Lake, 662
Cummins, Simon, 482
Cunard Line, 275
Currency, 221, 650
Curtis, Joseph, 617
Curtiss-Wright Corp., 357
Cushetunk Lake, 432
Cushetunk Mts., 432, 449
Czecho-Slovakians, 118, 122

Czechs, 202, 362

Dahlias, 599
Dairying, 89, 90, 94, 427, 442, 461, 477
Daly, M., 434
Daly, Phil, 680
Damrosch, Leopold, 169
Dana, John Cotton, 141, 185, 324, 329, 330
Dana College, 324, 325
Danes, 118, 362
Dark Moon Inn, 456
D'Ascenzo, Nicola, 230
Daughters of the American Revolution, 221, 289, 394, 522, 524, 577
Daughters of the Revolution, 522
da Verrazano, Giovanni, 35
Davis, Caleb, 491
Davis, Dr. Harvey Nathaniel, 266
Davis, Joseph, 491
Davis family, 491
Day, Horace, 403-4
Day and Klauder, 177, 247, 381
Day's Tavern, 511
Dayton, 569
Dayton, O., 246
Dayton, Sen. Jonathan, 246, 569
Deal, 682
Deal Lake, 682
Deans, 569
Decatur, Commodore Stephen, 564, 619
Decker, Daniel, 474
Decker, Peter, 498
Decker, Ralph, 498
Declaration of Independence, 152, 213, 363, 409, 452, 466, 485, 488, 497, 536, 547
Deepwater, 578, 611
Deerfield, 655
de Fersen, Count Jean, 410
De Forest, Emily, 549
De Klyn, Barnt, 413
Delaware, 483
Delaware and Raritan Canal, 46, 100, 107, 210, 213, 300, 374, 402, 427, 451, 489, 519, 550
Delaware Bay, 36
Delaware Falls Co., 402
Delaware Ordnance Depot, 578
Delaware River, 24, 35, 42, 106, 207, 398, 403, 452, 685
Delaware River Bridge, 106, 228, 237, 650
Delaware Water Gap, 7, 15, 184, 458, 483
Delawares (*see Indians*)
Delmont, 640
Democratic National Committee, 276
Democratic Party, 47, 48, 63, 81, 87
Dennisville, 640
Denton, Daniel, 239
Denville, 478
Desperaux, Louis, 676
D'Estail family, 664
de Survilliers, Count, 210, 413
De Visne, Capt. Philip, 538
Dewey, John, 159
Dey, Anthony, 274
Dey, Col. Theunis, 442

Dial, The, 160
Dias Creek, 646
Dickerson Tavern, 285
Dickinson, Rev. Jonathan, 244, 376
Diesel Manufacturing Co., 429
Dimsdale, Dr. Robert, 620
Dingman, Judge David W., 473
Dingmans Ferry, 473
Dinosaurs, 14
Directions for Singing, 168
Dirigibles, 623
Disease virus, isolation of, 426
Ditmars, I. E., 331
Divident Hill, 337
Diving horses, 199
Dix, Dorothea, 46
Dix, Warren R., 246
Dixon, Joseph, Crucible Co., 280
Doane, Msgr. George Hobart, statue, 325
Doane, Bishop George Washington, 223
Documents to Prove the Advantages of Railways and Steam Carriages over Canal Navigation, 268
Dodds, Dr. Harold Willis, 59, 380, 386
Dodge, Marcellus Hartley, 512
Dodge, Mrs. Marcellus Hartley, 478, 511, 512
Dodge, Mary Mapes, 154, 157, 322
Doll, Dr. E. M., 661
Dorrance, John T., 232
Double Trouble, 557
Double Trouble Cranberry Co., 557
Douglas and Harrison Apartments, 335-6
Douglas, Stephen A., 47
Doughty, Gen. John, 291
Dover, 480
Downstown, 609
Drake, Deacon Nathaniel, 548
Drake, Zephaniah, 514
Dreams and Images: An Anthology of Catholic Poets, 159
Drew, Daniel, 512
Drew University, 140, 512; Mead Hall, 512; Rose Memorial Library, 512
Dripps, Isaac, 210
Dummer's Jersey City Glass Co., 275
Dumont, 438
Dunbar, Robert, 517
Dunbarton, 599
Duncan, John, 185, 409
Dundee Canal, 346
Dunellen, 549
Dunlap, William, 152, 161, 167, 168, 182, 368
Dunn, Harvey, 186
Du Pont Co., 577, 578, 611
Du Pont Viscoloid Co., 543
Dupuis, Toon, 309
Durand, Asher B., 182
Durant, Will, 487
Durham, Robert, 522
Durham boats, 522
Dutch, 35, 36, 38, 118, 119, 174, 203, 239, 259, 264, 272, 299, 346, 352, 362, 391, 437, 438, 440, 453, 457, 476, 505, 575, 673
Dutch Reformed, 136, 142, 300, 304-5
Dutch West India Co., 35, 272

Dwight Morrow High School, 178, 438
Dyckman Street Ferry, 437
Dyers' Local 1773, 122

Eagle, The, 194
Eagleswood Military Academy, 363, 368
East Bound Brook, 527
East Jersey, 38, 39, 40, 363
East Jersey Iron Mfg. Co., 71
East Newark, 544
East Orange, 340-1
East Paterson, 476
East Rutherford, 540
Eastern Airlines, 575
Eastman Kodak Co., 331
Eaton, Rev. Isaac, 536
Eaton, Thomas, 594
Eaton vs. Eaton, 149
Eatontown, 594
Echo Lake, 449
Edge, Isaac, Jr., 275
Edge, Gov. Walter E., 51, 53
Edgewater Tapestries, 184
Ediphone, 342
Edison, Charles, 477
Edison, Thomas A., 72, 322, 342, 485, 486, 518, 546
Edison Memorial Tower, 485
Edison plant, 342
Edison Portland Cement Co., 518
Edison's Laboratory, 342, 485, 546
Education, 134-41, 217
Education, State Board of, 136, 139
Education and Life, 159
Edwards and Green, 229
Egerton family, 182
Egg Harbor City, 597, 602, 664
Eggs, 91
Einstein, Dr. Albert, 140, 388
Eisner, Sigmund, Clothing Co., 593
Eisteddfod, 132
Elberon, 681
Elco Works, 206
Eldora, 640
Electric light, 546
Electric rates, 77, 115, 117
Eliot, Dr. Charles W., 296
Elizabeth, 37, 69, 238-49, 423, 484, 508, 546
Elizabeth Airway Radio, 423
Elizabeth Carteret Hotel, 246
Elizabeth City Hall, 245
Elizabeth *Daily Journal,* 111, 244, 247
Elizabeth Historic and Civic Assn., 245
Elizabeth Library Hall Assn., 245
Elizabeth River, 423
Elizabeth-Staten Island Ferry, 248
Elizabethport, 203
Elizabethtown, 80
Elizabethtown Patent, 37
Elks Home (Elizabeth), 247
Ellerhusen, Ulric H., 186
Ellis, Edward S., 403
Ellis, Rowland, 218
Ellisburg, 626
Elm, 598
Elm Tree Inn (Chatham), 511
Elmer, 609

Elsinboro Point, 642
Ely, Wilson C., 325
Emergency Relief Administration, 424, 600
England, 36
Englewood, 438
Englewood Cliffs, 437, 438
English, 36-7, 118, 119, 229, 239, 272, 299, 346, 362, 505
English, Dr. James, 582
English, Thomas Dunn, 157
Englishtown, 581-2
Ennis, William, 473
Espiscopalians, 144, 218, 254
Erlton, 627
Erosion, 14
Erskine, Robert, 503, 504
Erskine family, 502
Essex County Opera Assn., 170
Essex County Symphony Society, 170
Estaugh, John, 626
Estell Manor, 664
Estelville, 664
Estelville game preserve, 664
Esterbrook, Richard, 232
Esterbrook Steel Pen Manufacturing Co., 232
Etna Furnace, ruins, 663
Eustis, Mrs. Harrison, 532
Ewansville, 470
Ewing, 403
Ewingville, 537

Faesch, John Jacob, 480
Fagan, Mark, 50, 275
Fagin's Cave, 580
Fairlawn and Paramus Clarion, 114
Fairs, 461, 477, 535, 582, 597, 658
Fairview, 419, 651
Family shops, 352, 358
Fanning and Shaw, 178
Fanwood, 548
Far Hills, 448
Farm Bureau Federation, State, 92
Farmer, Father Ferdinand, 144
Farmers' Market (Trenton), 410
Farnsworth, Thomas, 207
Father Divine, 149
Feast of Our Lady of Mt. Carmel, 133
Federal Building (Newark), 334
Federal Deposit Insurance Corp., 79
Federal Music Project, 171
Federal Theater Project, 166, 177
Feebleminded Colony, State, 609
Feebleminded Females, State Home, 661
Feigenspan, Christian, 335, 336
Feigenspan brewery, 336
Fellowship, 685
Fellowship Farm Cooperative Assn., 487
Felt, David, 430
Fenian Ram, The, 357
Fenian Society, 357
Fenton, 580
Fenwick, Anna, 630
Fenwick, John, 38, 39, 391, 396, 630
Fenwick Creek, 390
Ferries, 96, 99, 106, 221, 248, 249, 264, 273, 274, 361, 451-2, 578, 579, 614

Fidelity Union Trust Co., 78
Field, John, 527
Fielder, Gov. James F., 51
Fillmore, 587
Fine's School, 371
Finns, 36
Finn's Point, 632
Firemen's Insurance Co., 317
Firemen's Monument (Perth Amboy), 368
Fires, 204, 229, 253, 265, 354, 362
Fish and Game Commission, State, 659
Fish Hatchery, State, 26, 481
Fisher, D. K. Este, 386
Fisher, Mr. and Mrs. Edgar, 514
Fishing, 194, 198, 429, 430, 460, 474, 482, 484, 510, 514, 516, 517, 554, 581, 608, 609, 636, 640, 646, 655, 658, 659, 662, 663, 668, 669, 673 (see also Industry, fishing); laws, xxvii
Fisk, Col. James, 680
Fiske, C. Mortimer, 170
Fiske, Minnie Maddern, 164
Fitch, John, 46, 99, 209, 650; memorial, 410
Fitz Randolph, Nathaniel, 380
Fitzgerald, F. Scott, 160
Flag, American, 213-4, 431, 609
Flanders, 465
Flatbrookville, 474
Flax, 89
Fleming, Samuel, 524
Flemings, 36
Flemington, 181, 450, 524, 535
Flemington Auction Market Cooperative Assn., 94
Flemington Egg Poultry and Livestock Auction, 525
Flemington Vigilante Society, 525
Flexner, Dr. Abraham, 388
Flood control, 24-5, 477
Flowers, 18-20
Floyd, Andress S., 509
Fly casting contest, 480
Flynn, Elizabeth Gurley, 354
Folk music, 171
Folklore, 126-131
Folkways, 131-3
Folsom, Joseph, 160
Football, xxix (see also general information, cities)
Ford, Henry, 563
Ford, Jacob, 284
Ford, Col. Jacob, Jr., 286
Ford, Theodosia, 286
Ford agency, first, 563
Foreign born, 52, 118-25, 202, 217, 229, 242, 258, 264, 272, 299, 317, 342, 345, 352, 362, 391
Forest fires, 24
Forester, Frank (see Herbert, Henry William)
Forests, State: list, 23; Bass River, 560; Green Bank, 604; Jackson, 616; Lebanon, 624, 669; Stokes, 460
Forges (see Industry, iron)
Forgotten Towns of Southern New Jersey, 625

Forked River, 558
Forked River House, 558
Forman, Eleanor, 554
Forman, Capt. William, 254
Fort, Gov. George F., 617
Fort, Gov. John F., 50, 617
Fort Delaware, 632
Fort Elfsborg, 642
Fort Hancock, 678
Fort Lee, 164, 418, 439
Fort Mott, 632
Fort Nassau, 35, 36
Fort Nonsense, 283, 288
Fort Normanock, site, 473
Fortuna, hull of, 667
Fossils, 13, 14, 15, 17
Foster, Mrs. Charles D., 524
Foulkes, Rev. William Hiram, 150
4-H Clubs, 93
Four-Mile Circle, 669
Fourier, Charles, 589
Fourierism, 81
"Fourteen Farmers of the Acquackanonk," 346
Fox, Rev. George, 594
Fox Hill, 433
Fox hunting, 391
Frampton, George, 230
Franciscans, 495
Francisco Ferrar Colony, 487
Franklin, 497
Franklin, Benjamin, 42, 111, 221, 364, 609
Franklin, Gov. William, 41, 223, 363, 364; estate, 223
Franklin Park, 488
Franklinville, 659
Franks, Morris S., 532
Fraser, Caroline, 212
Fraser, J. E., 280
Frazee, Elizabeth, 548
Fredon, 454
Freehold, 41, 250-5, 555, 565, 581
Freehold Institute, 252
Freehold Military School, 252
Freehold Race Track, 254
Freeman, Howard, 115
Freeman, Mary Wilkins, 159
"Friendly Institution," 217
Friends Burial Ground, 396
Friends School, 230
Frelinghuysen, Frederick, 304
Frelinghuysen, Frederick T., statue, 325
Frelinghuysen, Rev. John, 551
Frelinghuysen, Joseph F., estate, 431
Frelinghuysen, Rev. Theodore, 488
Frelinghuysen, Rev. Theodorus Jacobus, 309
French, James, 464
French and Indian War, 40
French's Folly, 464-5
Frenchtown, 525
Freneau, 554
Freneau, Philip, 112, 152, 254, 554
Freneau farm, 554
Fresh Air Children's Camp, 594
Frog chorus, 629
Frohman, Charles, 164

Frohman, Daniel, 438
Fryenmuth, Rev. John Casparus, 473
Fuld, Felix, 332
Fuld, Mrs. Felix, 331, 388
Fuller, William, 114
Fulper Pottery Co., 181
Fulton, Robert, 99, 264, 274
Furnaces (*see Industry, iron*)

G-1, The, 623
Gag, Wanda, 186
Gaine, Hugh, 111
Galloping Hill, 429
Galloping Hill Monument, 247
Game Farm, State, 516, 558
Ganges, U.S.S., 218
Gannett, Frank, 115
Garden Pier, 199
Gardenias, 549
Garfield, Pres. James A., 680
Garner, Rev. L. Hamilton, 150
Garret Mt., 476
Garrett's Hill, 675
Garrison, "Stretch," 129, 638
Garwood, 547
Gary Schools, The, 159
Gaskill, Edward, 293
Gates, Gen. Horatio, 458
Gauss, Dean Christian, 159
Gaynor Glass Co., 396
Gazeta Dla Wszystkich, 229
General Electric Co., 316, 546
General Motors Corp., 180, 423, 490
General Pulaski Monument, 357
Geography, 7
Geology, 11-17, 418, 421, 454, 458, 495, 507, 511, 525, 564
George III, 41
George Washington Memorial Bridge, 106, 417, 572
Georgian Court College, 555-6
Gerhardt, Karl, 328
German-American League, 120
Germania, 597
Germans, 116, 118, 120, 162, 210, 242, 263, 264, 265, 272, 299, 317, 320, 346, 352, 353, 362, 433, 487, 505, 515, 540, 597
Gerould, Katherine Fullerton, 159
Gibbstown, 577
Gibson, Mrs. Jane, 301
Gigolos, 679
Gilbert, Cass, 181, 332
Gilchrist, William Wallace, 169
Gilder, Jeannette, 154, 215
Gilder, John Francis, 215
Gilder, Joseph, 215
Gilder, Richard Watson, 114, 153-4, 215, 322
Gilder, Rodman, 215
Gilder, William, 215
Gilford, Thomas, 649
Gilford Park, 649
Gillespie Hill, 283
Ginsberg, Louis, 160
Girard College, 294
Givaudan-Delawanna Co., 542
Glassboro, 612, 658

Glassboro State Normal School, 613
Glen Gardner, 534
Glen Ridge, 491-2
Glendora, 652
Glenside Park, 430
Globe Indemnity Co., 317
Gloucester, 575
Gloucester County Agricultural Assn., 94
Gloucester County Fox-Hunting Club, 128
Gloucester County Historical Society, 629
Gloucester Furnace, site, 603
Gloucester Lake, 603
Glover, John, 601
Goat Hill, 519
Gobel estate, 535
God in His World, 157
Goddard, Dr. H. H., 661
Godyn, Samuel, 36, 564
Goethals Bridge, 106, 423, 546
Gold rush, 452
Golden Chain, The, 169
Golden Gate Bridge, 572
Golden Legend, The, 169
Golf, xxix, 331, 336, 429, 430, 484, 510,
    530, 547, 561, 579, 627, 642
Gollner, Ervin G., 408
Gompers, Samuel, 574
Goodbye My Fancy, 154
Goodkind, Morris, 425
Goodwin, Rev. Hannibal, 72, 222, 330-1
Goodyear, Charles, 403-4
Gordon, J. Riley, 260
Gordon Dry Gin Co., 423
Goshen, 646
Goslin, Leon (Goose), 394
Gould family, 637
Gouldtown, 123, 637
Government, 55-68, 259, 276, 341, 342,
    343; Constitution of 1844, 55-6;
    legislature, 56-7; Governor, 57-8;
    executive departments, 58-60; local,
    60-3; county, 62; parties and elec-
    tions, 63; courts, 64-6; penal in-
    stitutions, 66-7; cost of, 59, 62, 628
Governor's residence, 683
Grabach, John, 186
Grange, State, 92
Grange League Federation Exchange, Inc.,
    94
Grant, Alexander, 394
Grant, Pres. Ulysses S., 48, 222, 681
Gravel, 26
Grazing, 90
Great American Novel, The, 160
"Great Aspen Mystery," 604
Great Cedar Swamp, 10, 640
Great Egg Harbor, 562
Great Egg Harbor River, 10
Great Meadows, 482
Great Seal of the U.S., 213
Great Swamp, 17, 511
Great Thorofare, 608
Greater Newark Industrial Council, 85
Greek Orthodox Catholics, 148
Greeley, Horace, 589
Green (Hackensack), 259
Green, Rev. Ashbel, 378, 531
Green, Col. Christopher, 576

Green, Capt. George, 467
Green, Hetty, 269, 437-8
Green, Dr. Jacob, 531
Green Bank, 222, 604
Green Creek, 646
Green Door Players, 165
Green Lake Farm, 509
Greene, Gen. Nathaniel, 565, 568
Greenland, Capt. Henry, 371
Green's Hotel (Salem), 394
Greenville, 271
Greenwich, 644
Greenwich Tea Party, 41, 220, 629, 643,
    645
Greenwood Lake, 506
Greenwood Lake, N. Y., 506
Greenwood Lake Launch Works, 507
Greer's Hall, 162
Grenloch, 653
Greyhound, The, 645
Greystone Park, 445
Grieff, Rev. Joseph N., 147
Griffith, Billie, 449-50
Griffith Music Foundation, 170
Griggs, Gov. John W., 48
Grimke, Sarah, 363
Grobart Mills, 358
Group Players, 165
Guest, Henry, 311
Guest, Moses, 311
Guggenheim, M., Sons, 364
Guilbert and Betelle, 332
Gulbrandsen, Charles, 325
Gulf Refining Co., 204
Gulf Stream, 190

Hackensack, 79, 256-61
Hackensack Improvement Commission, 259
Hackensack Meadows, 258, 540
Hackensack River, 9
Hackett, Samuel, 482
Hackettstown, 481, 516
Hackle, Barney, 514
Haddon, Elizabeth, 601, 626
Haddon, John, 601
Haddon Craftsmen, 236
Haddon Heights, 601
Haddonfield, 626
Hager, 392
Hague, Mayor Frank, 53, 63, 206, 276
Haines, Gov. Daniel, 497
Haines, John, 457
Hainesburg, 457
Hainesville, 460
Haley, John Jackson, 378
Half Moon, The, 35
Hall, A. Oakey, 510
Hall, Rev. Edward W., 301
Hall, Egerton Elliot, 123
Hall of Records, Essex County, 332
Hall-Mills Case, 551
Hallowe'en, 132
Halpert, Herbert, 171
Halsey, Mayor William, 320
Hamburg, 497
Hamburg Mt., 497
Hamburg-American Line, 265
Hamilton, 579

Hamilton, Alexander, 111, 245, 289, 352, 420; statue, 358
Hamilton Square, 582
Hammonton, 133, 472, 598
Hancock, Sarah and William, 634
Hancock's Bridge, 634
Hand, Col. Edward, 468
Hankinson, Gen. Aaron, 455
Hanna, Mark, 48
Hanover, 530-1
Hanover Furnace, site, 619
Hans Brinker: or, The Silver Skates, 157, 322
Hardenbergh, H. J., 386
Harding, Pres. Warren G., 431
Harding Highway, 607
Hardistonville, 497
Harelocker, Henry, 462
Harleigh Cemetery, 235
Harlingen, 466
Harmony Mills, 358
Harned, Thomas, 234
Harper, George McLean, 159
Harriman, Mrs. E. H., 436
Harris, Roy, 171
Harrison, 544
Harrison, Pres. Benjamin, 681
Harrison, Pres. William Henry, 613
Harrisonville, 632
Harris's, Stony, Sales Co., 610
Hart, George (Pop), 186
Hart, John, 41, 452, 536
Harte, Bret, 157, 285
Hartley, J. Scott, 184
Hartshorne, Charles H., 64
Hartshorne, Richard, 592, 676
Harvard Classics, The, 296
Harvest home suppers, 132
Harvey, Col. George, 50
Harvey Cedars, 670
Hasbrouck Heights, 539-40
Hasenclever, Baron Peter, 504
Haskell, 500
Hauptmann, Bruno Richard, 293, 412, 524
Havemeyer, Henry O., 440
Hawker Mick, 617
Hawthorne High School, 178
Haye, John Caspar, 565
Hayes, Pres. Rutherford B., 681
Haynes, Mayor Joseph, 322
Haywood, "Big Bill," 354
Hazard Powder House, 203
Hazlett, Albert, 364
Head of River, 662
Headquarters, 450-1
Hebrew Immigrant Society, 660
Hedge, Samuel, 630
Heinz Pier, 199
Hell Mt., 433
Helmbold, Dr. H. T., 680
Helme, George W., Co., 529
Helmetta, 529
Hemlock Falls, 510
Henderson, Donald, 656
Henderson, William J., 172
Henry, Joseph, 108, 385
Henry Hudson Drive, 437

Henry Hudson's Spring, 676
Herbert, Harry, 582
Herbert, Henry William, 153
Hercules Powder Co., 480
Hercules Woven Label Co., 501
Herman, Augustine, 362
Hertzog Hall, 309
Hessian fly, 90
Hetfield, Caleb, 493
Hewes, Joseph, 488
Hewitt, 506
Hewitt family, 502, 503, 504
Hewlett, J. Monroe, 325
Hibben, Dr. John Grier, 380
Hibernia, 479
Hicks, Darby, 130
Hicksites, 146, 148 (see also Quakers)
High Bridge, 535
High Crossing, 471
High Point (Monmouth County), 676
High Point (Ocean County), 670
High Point Park Commission, 499
High Point War Memorial, 499
Highland, 678
Highland Beach, 678
Highland Park, 487, 528
Highlands of Navesink, 676
Hight, John, 570
Hightstown, 570, 582
Highway construction, 426, 552
Highways, xxix, 3, 96, 98, 103-4
Hiking, 437, 460, 510
Hill, Harry A., 408
Hillman, James, 652
Hillside, 429
Hillyer, Robert, 159
Hilton strawberry, 328
Hindenburg, The, 623
Hine, C. G., 458
Hinsdale, Epaphras, 71, 320
Historic Sites Commission, State, 500, 539
History, 35-54; discovery and exploration, 35; early settlement, 35-8; English conquest, 36; as Proprietary Colony, 37-9; as Royal Colony, 39-41; during Revolution, 41-4; organization of State government, 44; foundation of industrial system, 45-6; transportation development, 46; railroad domination, 47; during Civil War, 47; machine age growth, 47; "Mother of Trusts," 49-50; Wilsonian reform, 50-1; during World War, 51; contemporary problems and politics, 51-4
History of a Literary Radical, The, 159
History of the American People, 158
History of the American Theater, A, 162
History of the Rise and Progress of the Arts of Design in the United States, A, 182
Hoagland, Col. Oakly, 213
Hoar, Bill, 445
Hobart, Vice Pres. Garret A., 355; statue, 358
Hobbie, Father Reeve, 148
Hoboken, 70, 97, 165, 262-9

Hockamick, 617
Hof Brau Haus, 269
Hoffman, Gov. Harold, 53, 85
Hoffman Beverage Co., 316
Hog Mt., 432
Hogs, 90
Hohokus, 538
Holgate, 674
Holland, 38
Holland, The, 357
Holland, John P., 355, 357
Holland Society of New York, 309
Holland Tunnel, 61, 106, 276
Hollander Fur Dyeing Co., 316
Holmansville, 615
Holmdel, 588
Holmes, Col. Benjamin, 634
Holmes, Rev. Obadiah, 588
Holmes family, 588
Holmes, Stanley S., Village, 179, 200
Holmes v. Walton, 55
Holton, Pauline Joseph Ann, 409, 413
Holy Hill, 309
Holy Name Society, 147
Hominy Hills, 590
Honeyman, John, 522
Hoops, Maj. Robert, 483
Hope, 456
Hopewell, 536
Hopkinson, Ann Borden, 215
Hopkinson, Francis, 152, 167, 208, 213-4
Hopkinson, Joseph, 214, 215
Hornblower, Joshua, 542
Horner, Job, 616
Hornet, The, 220
Horse Hill, 283
Hotel Sterling (Trenton), 408
Houghton, Joab, 536
Houses:
    Abbott, 642; Ackerman, 174; Allan,
    486; Allen, 593; Alling, 319; Arm-
    strong, 459; Avalon, 388; Ayles-
    ford, 606; Ayres, 486; Bainbridge,
    389; Ball, 344; Ballantine, 329;
    Barracks (Princeton), 388; Bart-
    lett, 560; Belcher, 246; Bell, 473;
    Benedict, 445; Berrien, 489; Blair,
    457; Bloomfield, 220; Bloomsbury,
    409; Bonnell, 246; Borden, 213;
    Boudinot, 246; Bow Hill, 412;
    Boxwood Hall, 246; Boxwood
    Manor, 523; Bradford, 224; Brad-
    way, 174, 396; Brick, 639; Brick
    Tavern, 433-4; Burrowes, 554;
    Campfield, 289; Carey, 220; Cedar
    Plank, 634; Cherry Grove, 467;
    Cleveland, 493; Clinton, 433; Cock-
    loft, 153, 320; Cookstown, 618;
    Cooper (Benjamin), 235; Cooper
    (James Fenimore), 220; Cooper
    (John), 629; Cooper (Joseph),
    234; Cornwallis's Headquarters,
    437; Crane, 247; Crane (Stephen),
    334; Curtin, 570; Darkin, 641;
    Davis, 491; Demarest, 173; Dey,
    442-4; Dickinson, 174; Doane, 223;
    Douglas, 408; Drumthwacket, 467;
    Egbert, 492; Emmis, 473; Field,
    527; Fleming, 524; Ford, 286;
    Fort, 617; Fountain, 454; Fox, 175;
    Franklin Civic, 487; Frazee, 548;
    Gibbon, 644; Gilder, 215; Giles,
    636; Girard, 294; Glover, 601;
    Golding, 468; Grant (Alexander),
    394; Grant (U.S.), 222, 681;
    Green, 531; Grubb, 223; Guest,
    310; Haddon, 626; Haines, 497;
    Hall, 510; Hammerstein, 676; Han-
    cock, 175, 634; Hankinson, 254;
    Hawkins, 554; Hedgefield, 630;
    Hermitage, 538; Holcomb, 452;
    Holmes, 642; Hopkinson, 213;
    Hopper, 440-1; Hopper (Hacken-
    sack), 174, 261; Howell, 643;
    Hudson, 279; Hulse, 582; Hunter,
    662; Ionic, 279; Johnson, 520;
    Johnson (William), 175; Kay, 657;
    Kearny, 366; Kemble, 446; Ket-
    tell, 541; Kilmer, 440; King, 536;
    Kingsland, 543; Kingston, 488;
    Kip, 541; Lambert, 355; Lawrence,
    629; Lawrence (James), 218-20;
    Lawrence (Thomas), 497; Liberty,
    508; Lincoln, 585; Low, 528;
    Manor, 628; Mansion, 260; Mar-
    shall, 452; Martine, 548; Mayhew,
    609; Mecum, 632; Mercer, 528;
    Morgan, 175; Morris, 642; Mor-
    ven, 388; Murat, 470; Nicholson,
    642; Oakford, 175; Old Ford, 515;
    Old Guardhouse, 627; Old Nutley,
    543; Old Stone, 368; Olden, 467;
    Parker, 366; Penn, 174; Pledger,
    631; Plume, 330; Ralston, 514;
    Redding, 176; Revel, 221; Rich-
    ards (Samuel), 472; Richards
    (William), 604; Ringwood, 176;
    Ross, 528; Sansay, 289; Sayre,
    512; Schuyler, 442; Scudder, 547;
    Scudder (Jedediah), 522; Seeley,
    655; Seven Stars, 127, 611;
    Shadow Lawn, 681; Sheppard, 645;
    Shippen, 534; Sip, 429-30; Smith,
    621; Smith (Daniel), 634; Smith
    (Jasper), 525; Smith (Sarah B.),
    570; Smithfield, 630; Sneathen,
    655; Somers, 562; Spear, 543;
    Spence, 548; Stafford, 599; Stage-
    coach Inn, 433; Steuben, 539;
    Stockton, 388; Stone Tavern, 644;
    Swing, 654; Teneyck, 432; Ter-
    hune, 261; Thackara, 601; Trent,
    409; Tusculum, 466-7; Updyck,
    451; Ursino, 509; Vail (Morris-
    town), 445; Vail (New Market),
    549; Van Cortlandt, 500; Van
    Emburgh, 539; Van Ness, 455;
    Van Schott, 347; Van Syckles, 434;
    Van Wagenen, 277; Vaux Hall,
    510; Vreeland, 174; Wallace, 551;
    Warwick, 652; Washington head-
    quarters (Plainfield), 548; Way-
    side, 492; Westland, 388; West-
    minster, 364; Whitall, 577; White,
    311; Whitman, 234, 289; Wick,
    289; Williamson, 247; Winter,

Houses (*Continued*)
439-40; Woodlawn, 308; Woolman, 294; Woolston, 470; Wright, 419; Zabriskie, 538; Zelley, 621
Housing, 123, 179, 200, 227, 237, 315-316, 335-6
Howard, Capt., 489
Howard, John Tasker, 167, 172
Howard Savings Institution, 78
Howe, Gen. Edward, 42
Howe, James, 492
Howe, Gen. Robert, 285, 502
Howe, Sir William, 300, 568
Howell, Dr. Ebenezer, 396
Howell, John, 663
Howell, Joshua, 663
Howell, Gov. Richard, 409, 643
Hubbell, Anna, 394
Hubbell, Helena, 394
Huckleberry Hill, 470
Huddy, Capt. Joshua, 252, 556-7, 589, 678
Hudson, Henry, 35, 203
Hudson City, 271
Hudson County, 116, 121
Hudson County "Horseshoe," 275
Hudson *Jewish News*, 116
Hudson River, 35, 42, 96, 99, 100, 102, 106, 182, 417, 419
Hudson Tubes (*see Railroads, Hudson and Manhattan*)
Hughes, Ellis, 563
Huguenots, 260, 363, 437, 438, 453, 664
Humanists, 158
Humphreys, Alexander Crombie, 266
Humphries, Elliot S., 532
Hun Preparatory School, 141, 371
Hungarians, 116, 122, 124, 299, 346, 347, 362
Hunt, Abraham, 409
Hunt, J. Osborne, 404
Hunt, Jarvis, 329
Hunt, Thomas, 462
Hunter, Rev. Andrew, 629
Hunter family, 662
Hunterdon County, 40
Hunting, xxviii, 448, 460, 474, 589, 663, 668, 669; laws, xxviii
Hurffville, 658
Huss, Henry Holden, 171
Hutchinson, George, 221
Hyatt, John Wesley, 72, 322
Hydroelectric plant (Paterson), 359
Hyler, Capt. Adam, 300

Ice Carnivals, xxix
Ice Hockey, xxix
Iceboating, xxix
Iceskating, xxix, 198, 282, 331, 430, 481, 484
Ickes, Harold L., 286
Illiteracy, 123, 137
Imlaystown, 586
Imlaystown Lake, 586
Immaculate Conception Seminary, 441
Immigrant Station, U.S., 576
Immigration, 49, 52, 119-22
Inaugurals, 400

Incorporation laws, 49
Indian Burying Ground, The, 152
Indian Lake, 478
Indian Mills, 33, 471
Indian Site Survey, 28
Indian Will, 594
Indians, 30-4, 96, 119, 130, 203, 217, 220, 239, 264, 272, 299, 318, 346, 400, 459, 460, 461, 462, 464, 471, 473, 498, 505, 527, 560, 581, 592, 594, 599, 621, 627, 646 (*see also Archeology*)
Industrial Commission, 351
Industrial home work, 87
Industrial Union of Marine and Shipbuilding Workers of America, 237
Industrial unionism, 82, 85-6
Industrial Workers of the World, 84, 354
Industry, 45, 47, 49, 69-76, 225-6, 229, 242, 265, 316, 319, 320, 363, 374, 403; air brakes, 328; airplane motors, 352, 357; alcoholic beverages, 70, 275, 320, 336, 423, 514, 597; artificial hair, 76; asphalt, 362; automobiles, 362, 423, 439; bicycles, 620; boats, 202, 206, 507; boxes, 299, 478; calculating machines, 342; canning, 73, 76, 232, 390, 612, 634, 644; cans, 271; carriages, 76, 301; cement, 258, 342, 343, 518, 546; ceramics, 46, 73, 181, 210, 218, 258, 362, 363, 368, 399, 403, 413, 451, 552, 553, 582, 599; charcoal, 599; chemicals, 74, 202, 210, 242, 263, 284, 299, 301, 311, 342, 343, 390, 542, 549, 577, 578; clothing, 70, 72, 73, 75, 202, 210, 242, 258, 284, 299, 301, 320, 342, 346, 352, 362, 444, 570, 593, 594, 599, 679; coke, 421; cork, 202; dyeing, 352, 354, 419, 478, 534, 539; electrical products, 72, 74, 75, 322, 337, 341, 342, 442, 486; elevators, 271; explosives, 74, 362, 444, 480, 577, 651; film, 322, 330; fireworks, 275, 301, 419; fishing, 69, 194, 198, 240, 640, 646, 648, 674; floor covering, 255, 301, 390, 546, 571, 631; food, 73, 76, 202, 210, 263, 271, 445, 451, 466, 485, 529, 575; fruit presses, 599; furniture, 242, 263, 301; gas, 421; gas heaters, 575; glass, 46, 70, 181, 184, 390, 396, 613, 635, 638, 661; gold beating, 593; graphite products, 280, 433, 434; handkerchiefs, 346; harmonicas, 301; incubators, 301; iron, 70, 71, 217, 284, 328, 444, 446, 451, 463, 464, 471, 479, 504, 518, 535, 546; jewelry, 71, 184, 320; labels, 441, 501; leather, 69, 71, 184, 240, 263, 319, 320, 328; locomotives, 342, 353; lumber, 575; machinery, 242, 249, 301, 341, 620; marl, 70; medical supplies, 299, 311, 485; metal prod-

Industry *(Continued)*
ucts, 70, 71, 74, 75, 184, 202, 263, 271, 275, 328, 352, 362, 368, 399, 451, 518, 582, 599; motion pictures, 418; paint, 75, 549, 577, 599; paper, 73, 275, 301, 438, 451, 575; parachutes, 412; pencils, 271, 275, 280; pens, 232, 335; petroleum, 72, 74, 75, 201, 202, 203-4, 242, 423, 485, 577; phonographs, 232, 342; plastics, 322, 444, 543; poultry, 91, 526; pretzel bending, 249; printing, 76, 221, 236, 242, 247, 363, 549; publishing, 76; radios, 232, 444; revolvers, 353, 359; rubber, 75, 76, 284, 301, 346, 399, 404, 495, 571, 582; salt, 218; shipbuilding, 69, 218, 222, 229, 237, 240, 301, 543; silkworms, 218; stone, 26, 419, 451; telescopes, 430; textiles, 45, 46, 71, 72, 75-6, 217, 301, 346, 353, 354, 358, 359, 476, 575; tobacco, 76, 271, 299, 362, 403, 529; toiletries, 242, 271, 275, 279, 343, 362; toy trains, 544; umbrellas, 284; wagons, 658; wire rope, 202, 362, 403, 412, 572; woodworking, 599
Industry Mills, 358
Ingersoll Heights, 518
Ingersoll-Rand Co., 518
Inian, John, 299
Inland Waterway, 649, 667
Inman, Henry, 185
Inness, George, 182-4, 368, 493
Inness, George, Jr., 184
Inoculation, 400
Institute for Advanced Study, 140, 387
Institute of Family Relations, 340
Institute of Marriage and the Home, 340
Institutions, Camden County, 598, 652
Institutions, Hudson County, 421
Institutions and Agencies, State Dept. of, 60, 249, 412
Insurance, 45, 78, 316, 320
Interior, U.S. Dept. of, 286
International Fireworks Co., 419
International Motor Co., 301
International Smelting and Refining Co., 368
International Union of Hod Carriers, Building and Common Laborers, 86
Interracial Committee, 318
Intracoastal Waterway, 107
Invertebrates, Age of, 13
Iona Lake, 609, 659
Irish, 118, 120, 162, 202, 210, 242, 264, 265, 272, 317, 346, 352, 353, 362
Iron floating fort, 264
Iroquois *(see Indians)*
Irving, Sir Henry, 164
Irving, Washington, 153, 319, 544
Irvington, 544
Iselin, 485
Island Beach, 648
Island Heights, 649

Italian Tribune, 116
Italians, 118, 121, 124, 202, 210, 217, 229, 242, 258, 264, 272, 299, 314, 317, 343, 346, 352, 353, 357, 362, 505, 598, 680
Ivy Manor, 635

J-4, The, 623
Jackson, Rev. S. Trevena, 477
Jackson Whites, 124, 160, 505
Jadowski, Viktor, 585
James, Duke of York, 36, 37, 38, 144
James, Philip, 171
James, Dr. and Mrs. Robert F., 440
James Clinical Laboratory, 440
Jansen, William, 273
Japanese, 122, 343
Japanese beetle, 93, 574
Japanese Goldfish Hatchery, 432
Jay, John, 509, 594
Jefferson, 629
Jefferson, Joseph, 163
Jefferson, Pres. Thomas, 111, 112
Jehovah's Witnesses, 149
Jennings, Gov. Samuel, 218, 221; office, site, 221
Jenny Jump Mt., 482
Jericho, 635
Jersey, The, 274
Jersey City, 82, 85, 134, 270-82, 421
Jersey City Museum Assn., 280
Jersey Devil, 126-7, 562, 584, 662, 664
Jersey Homesteads, 88, 179, 570
Jersey Jingles, 160
Jersey *Journal,* 113
"Jersey Justice," 149
Jersey Meadows, 475
Jerseyville, 581
Jetting, 195
Jewish Chronicle, 116
Jewish Ledger, 116
Jewish Standard, 116
Jews, 116, 122, 146, 148, 210, 317, 336, 352, 571, 660
Jockey Hollow, 288, 446, 513
Jockey Hollow Wild Flower Trail, 289
John Bull, 101, 210, 229
John Bull Monument, 468
Johnson, Eldridge R., 230-2
Johnson, J., 155
Johnson, Robert Gibbon, 394, 631
Johnson and Johnson Co., 311
Johnsonburg, 266, 455-6
Jones, Benjamin, 617
Jones, John, 396
Jouet, Cavalier, 247
Jouet, Daniel, 248
Judicial Council, 66
Juliana, The, 264
Jutland, 434
Juvenile delinquency, 277

K-1, The, 623
Kahn, Otto, 286
Kaighn, John, 228
Kaighn, Joseph, 235

Kallet, Arthur, 517
Kallikak family, 661
Kanouse Mt., 507
Kaplan, Louis S., 408
Karagheusian carpet factory, 254
Karcher and Smith, 230
Kase, John Philip, 524
Kastner, Alfred, 180, 570
Kate Aylesford, 606
Kean, Sen. Hamilton F., 509
Kean, Capt. John, 509
Keansburg, 675
Kearny, 543
Kearny, Michael, 367
Kearny, Gen. Philip, 157, 544; statue, 325
Kearny family, 366
Kecht, Charles, 291
Keim, Jacob, 195
Keimer, Samuel, 221
Keith, Rev. George, 254, 367,
Keller, Elizabeth Leavitt, 156
Kelly, Col. Hugh A., 404
Kelly, J. E., 253
Kemble, Peter, 446
Kent, Rockwell, 487
Kenvil, 480
Kern, Jerome, 172
Kernan, Rev. William C., 206
Kerr Chicken Hatchery, 526
Kessler, F. W., 507
Keyport, 132, 592
Kidd, Capt. William, 564
Kieft, Dir. Gen. William, 272
Kill van Kull, 106
Kilmer, Joyce, 158, 311, 440
Kimble glass factory, 180, 661
King George's War, 40
King Nummy, 646
"King of the Jungle," 133
Kingdon, Dr. Frank, 325
Kingsland, Isaac, 543
Kingston, 488
Kinkead, Eugene F., 204
Kinney, Thomas T., 113
Kinsey, James, 41
Kirkbride, Col. Joseph, 209, 215
Kitchens, model, 199, 232
Kite, Dr. Elizabeth S., 605
Kittatinny Lake, 460
Kittatinny Mts., 454, 456, 460
Kittatinny Valley, 12
Klein, Dr. Carl, 540
Klemann, William A., 408
Knickerbocker Giants, 264
Knights of Albion, 641
Knights of Labor, 82-3
Know-Nothing Party, 120
Knox, Gen. Henry, 448, 568
Knox, Julia, 448
Knox, Lucy, 448
Kollock, Shepard, 111, 244, 247; printing office, site, 244
Komroff, Manuel, 487
Kress, Carl J., 493
Kresson, 684
Kresson Lake, 686
Ku Klux Klan, 120
Kuser, Col. and Mrs. A. K., 499

Labor, 53, 74, 79-88, 120, 202, 204, 232, 239, 258, 265, 276, 284, 320, 347, 351, 353, 403
Labor, State Department of, 87, 279
Labor Advocate, The, 239
Labor Day, 82, 574
Labor legislation, 86-7
Labor Party, 3, 53, 81, 87
Labor riots, 79
Labor spies, 84
Labor's Nonpartisan League, 87
Lacey, Gen. John, 558
Ladd, John, Sr., 628
Lady or the Tiger?, The, 156, 543
Lafayette, Marquis de, 246, 277, 289, 566, 657
Lake Arrowhead, 478
Lake Carasaljo, 555
Lake Erskine, 505
Lake Hopatcong, 481
Lake Illiff, 463
Lake Lefferts, 529, 554
Lake Lenape, 608
Lake Marcia, 499
Lake Matawan, 554
Lake Musconetcong, 465
Lake Passaic, 17
Lake Solitude, 535
Lake Stockholm, 496
Lake Surprise, 430
Lakehurst, 622, 649
Lakes, 8
Lakewood, 555, 596, 615
Lamb Studios, J. and R., 184
Lambert, Catholina, 355
Lambert, John, 451
Lambert, Simeon, 548
Lambertville, 451, 519
Lambertville Vigilante Society, 452
Land disputes, 38
Land grants, 37, 38
Land riots, 40
Landing, 481
Landing, the, 299, 528
Landing of Philip Carteret, The, 332
Landis, Charles K., 609, 661
Landisville, 609
Lang, Florence Rand, 492
Langtry, Lillie, 680
Lanoka Harbor, 557
Larison family, 450
Larison's Corner, 450
Larson, Gov. Morgan, 53
Laurel Hill, 421
Laurel Springs, 599
Laurelton, 591, 596, 622
Laurence Harbor, 591
Lavallette, 648
Lawnside, 123, 600
Lawrence, Elizabeth, 367
Lawrence, Capt. James, 185, 218-20, 254, 367, 467
Lawrence, John, 629
Lawrence, Josephine, 160
Lawrence, Thomas, 497
Lawrenceville, 467
Lawrenceville Academy, 141, 467
Lawrie, Gov. Gawen, 38, 547

Lazzara's Music Hall, 357
Leather Stocking Tales, The, 220
Leaves of Grass, 154, 155, 234
Lebanon, 433
Ledgewood, 533
Lee, Gen. Charles, 309, 447, 539, 565, 566, 568, 582
Lee, Francis B., 605
Lee, Maj. (Light Horse Harry), 274
Leeds, William, 592, 593
Leeds Devil (*see Jersey Devil*)
Leesburg State Prison Farm, 640
Legends, 126-31, 425, 432, 447, 449, 450, 534, 542, 557, 562, 580, 584, 592, 594, 606, 611, 638, 662, 664, 667
Legislature, State, 56-7, 372, 399
Le Grange, Bernardus, 309
Lehman and Totten, 334
L'Enfant, Maj. Pierre, 353
Lenni Lenape (*see Indians*)
Lenox, Walter, 413
Lenox Potteries, 413
Leonardo, 675
Lescaze, William, 180
Lever, Hayley, 186
Levy, Benjamin, 146
Lewis, Allen, 186
Lewistown, 618
Lexington, U.S.S., 237
Liberty in Distress, 200
Liberty Pole (Newark), 325
Libraries, 141, 342; Beach Haven, 674; Burlington, 221; Camden (Cooper Branch), 230; East Orange, 341; Elizabeth, 245; Freehold, 253; Hackensack, 260; Hopewell, 536; Jersey City, 280; N. J. State, 404; Newark, 141, 330; Paterson, 355; Princeton, 389
Licht, Lawrence L., 178
Life Along the Passaic River, 160
Life of Major André, The, 162
Life Saving Service, U.S., 667, 684
Light of Asia, The, 169
Lighthouses:
    Absecon, 200, 561; Barnegat, 672; Cape May, 564; Chapel Hill, 592; Fort Mott, 632; Navesink, 678; Sandy Hook, 678
Lillien, Al, 676
Lilly Pond, 564
Limestone, 26
Lincoln, Pres. Abraham, 47, 320; statues, 280, 332
Lincoln, Joseph C., 159
Lincoln, Mordecai, 586
Lincoln family, 585, 587
Lincoln Forge, 587
Lincoln Park, 444
Lincoln Tunnel, 106, 588
Lincroft, 588
Lindbergh, Col. Charles A., 293, 412, 524, 536
Linden, 423, 484
Lindenwold, 599
Line Ditch, 227
Lionel Corp., 544

Lippincott, Capt. Richard, 557
Lippincott, William, 606
Lippincott family, 604
Liquor laws, xxv
Literature, 151-60, 322
Lithuanians, 122, 217
Littell, Emelin T., 253
Little Egg Harbor, 673
Little Falls, 494
Little Falls Laundry, 494
Little Flower Shrine, 462
Little Italy (Paterson), 357
Little Juliana, 99
Little theaters, 164-5
Littlefield, George, 487
Littleton, 532
Livermore, Samuel, 376-7
Livestock, 90
Livingston, 530
Livingston, Sally, 509
Livingston, Gov. William, 41, 44, 111, 151, 293, 372, 445, 508
Llewellyn Park, 343
Loantaka Valley, 285
Lock-out, first, 353
Lockwood, 464
Lodi, 539
Long Beach Island, 670
Long Branch, 146, 164, 679-80
Long Valley, 515
Long Valley Inn, 515
Longfellow, Henry W., 626
Looker, William, 240
Lorillard Tobacco Co., 274
Los Angeles, The, 623
Louderback, Elizabeth and Peter, 611
Loughlin Applejack Mill, 514
Lovelady, 670
Lovelady, Thomas, 670
Low, Cornelius, 528
Low Moor, 679
Lucas, Nicholas, 38
Ludlow and Peabody, 308
Lum, Mary, 294
Lumber, 24
Lumberton, 620
Lumberton Hotel, 620
Lust, Dr. B., 495
Lutherans, 144, 146, 341, 432, 449
Lutherland, Thomas, 392, 641
Lyndhurst, 541
Lyon, James, 167, 168

Mabie, Hamilton Wright, 157
MacCampbell, Theron, 588
MacCampbell Vineyards, 588
Macfadden publications, 549
Maclean, Dr. John, 378
Mack, Jerry, 534
Mackentyre, John, 394
MacMonnies, Frederick W., 185, 200, 388
Macon, The, 623
Madison, 121, 511
Madison Historical Society, 511
Magazine Writing and the New Literature, 157
Maggie: A Girl of the Street, 156, 335
Magnetic Hill, 446

Magnolia, 598
Maguire, Matthew, 82
Magyar Herald, 116
Mahalala, 618
Mahwah, 440
Malaga, 609, 659
Mammals, Age of, 15-6
Mammoths, 16
Manahawkin, 559, 668
Manahawkin Lake, 559, 668
Manalapan, 581
Manalapan Inn, 581
Manasquan, 684
Mancius, Rev. George Whilhelm, 473
Manhattan, 35, 418
Manhattan, U.S.S., 237
Manning, James, 536
Mannington Linoleum Mill, 631
Mansfield, 469
Mansfield, Josie, 680
Mansfield Square, 469
Mansion House, 260
Mantell, Robert B., 164
Mantoloking, 647
Mantua, 629
Mantua Oak, 629
Manual and Industrial School for Colored Youth, 137
Manual Training School, State, 572
Manufactures, Census of, 71, 74-5
Manunka Chunk Junction, 483
Maplewood, 339, 343-4
Margaret Hague Maternity Hospital, 280
Marin, John, 185
Marion, 271
Marksboro, 456
Marl, 13, 26, 393, 555, 609, 626
Marlboro, 555, 635
Marlboro State Hospital, 555
Marlborough, The, 222
Marlton, 626
Marshall, Henry Rutgers, 306
Marshall, James, 452
Marshall, Philip, 452
Marshall, Dr. Randall, 663
Marshall, William, 536
Marshall's Corner, 536
Marshallville, 663
Martine, Sen. James E., 50
Mary Fisher Home, 438
Mason, Lowell, 166, 168
Mason-Dixon Line, 6
Masonic Hall (Bridgeton), 636
Masonic Temple (Atlantic City), 200
Masonic Temple (Trenton), 408
Masons, Free and Accepted, 405
Master of Ballantrae, The, 684
Mastodons, 16
Matawan, 252, 529, 554, 588
Mather, Frank Jewett, Jr., 185
Mathis, John H., Shipbuilding Co., 235
Matica Slovenska, 346
Matinicunk Island, 217
Maurice River, 10, 639, 659, 660
Mauricetown, 639
Mawhood, Col., 392
Maxim, Hudson, 679
May, George, 608

Maybury, Col. Thomas, 463
Mayhew, Eliza and Selina, 609
Mays Landing, 198, 608, 664
McAdoo, Sen. William Gibbs, 275, 323
McAlpin Farms, 532
McCartan, Edward, 328
McCarter, Thomas N., 386
McComb, John, 175, 305
McCormick, Howard, 186
McCosh, Dr. James, 137, 379
McCoy, William (Bill) Sharpe, 453-4
"McCoy's Corner," 453
McCullough, Col. William, 516
McCutcheon's Farmers' Hotel, 279
McGrady, Edward F., 232
McGuire, Peter J., 82, 574
McKean, Rev. Robert, 308
McKee City, 608, 612
McKim, Mead and White, 332, 380
McKinley, Pres. William, 48
Meany family, 434
Mechanicsville, 592, 675
Medford, 625
Medford Hotel, 625
Medical Center (Jersey City), 178, 280
Meigs, Henry, 206
Mendham, 513
Menehenicke Island, 346
Menlo Park, 485
Mercer, Gen. Hugh, 372
Mercer, Dr. William, 528
Mercer Beasley Law School, 325
Mercer County Farm, 520
Mercer Junior College, 371
Mercereau, Joseph, 98
Mercerville, 582
Merck Co., 485
Mercury and Weekly Advertiser, 111
Methodists, 145, 146, 148, 218, 300, 512, 616, 620, 660
Metropolitan Inn (Burlington), 221
Metuchen, 486
Mexican bean beetle, 93
Mey, Capt. Cornelius Jacobsen, 35, 563, 575
Michielson, Hartman, 346
Mickens, Charles F., 500
Mickle, Archibald, 228
Mickle, John W., 230
Middle Brook Heights Campground, site, 431
Middlesex, 527, 549
Middlesex County Tuberculosis Hospital, 486
Middletown, 37, 41, 144, 479, 592, 665
Midvale, 501
Midvale War Memorial, 501
Military Encampment, State, 683
Mill Street Hotel (Mt. Holly), 294
Millburn, 510
Milledoler, Rev. Philip, 305
Miller, Claude A., 478
Miller, Joaquin, 157
Millet, Frank D., 332
Millham, 403
Millhurst, 581
Million Dollar Pier, 198

Mills, 69, 217, 284, 293, 430, 433, 446, 451, 456, 457, 463, 464, 467, 471, 479, 489, 534, 539, 581, 583, 586, 611, 617, 618, 643
Mills, Eleanor, 301
Millville, 638, 662
Mine Hill, 480
Mine Mt., 447
Minerals, list, 26
Mines, U.S. Bureau of, 487
Miniature golf course, 449
Mining, 26, 46, 70, 72, 450, 458, 463, 465, 472, 479, 480, 497, 504, 505, 533
Minisink (see Indians)
Minisink Island, 460, 473
Minisink Trail, 31, 460, 473
Minsi (see Indians)
Minute Man, statue (Elizabeth), 248
Mitchell, Roderick, 447
Mitchell, Winifred, 437
Model American Village, 198
Model Dairy Farm, 461
Modern Artists of N. J., the, 185
Modjeski, Ralph, 237
Mogey, William, and Sons Telescope Plant, 430
Mohicans (see Indians)
Moisseiff, Leon, 204
Molly Pitcher, 565
Molly Pitcher's Well, 565
Monckton, Lt. Col. Henry, 568
Monmouth Battle Monument, 253
Monmouth Battlefield, 565-8, 581
Monmouth Beach, 679
Monmouth County, 70
Monmouth County Historical Assn., 592
Monmouth County Tuberculosis Hospital, 590
Monmouth Democrat, 252
Monmouth Farmers' Exchange, 94
Monmouth Inquirer, 112
Monmouth Patent, 37
Monmouth Players, 165
Monroe, Pres. James, 401
Montague, 459
Montclair, 492
Montclair Art Assn., 492
Montclair Dramatic Club, 165
Montclair Operetta Club, 170
Monteith, Robert, 503
Montville, 444
Moody, James (Bonnel), 463
Moody's Rock, 463
Moonachie, 540
Moore, Gov. A. Harry, 53, 57
Moore, Daniel, 485
Moore, Michael, 509
Moore, Thomas, 621
Moore, Tom, 319
Moore's Beach, 640
Moorestown, 621
Moravians, 145, 456
More, Paul Elmer, 151, 158
Morgan, 591
Morgan, Col. George, 385
Morgan, J. P., 436
Morgan, James, 547

Morgan, Sherley W., 389
Morganville, 554
Morgen-Stern, 116
Morin, Mike, 507
Morin, Nick, 507
Morley, Christopher, 165, 266, 269
Mormons, 146, 557
Morning Eagle, 112
Morris, Lewis, 497
Morris, Col. Lewis, 70
Morris, Gov. Lewis, 40, 284
Morris Canal, 46, 99, 274, 320, 322, 353, 444, 464, 465, 481, 516
Morris Plains, 445
Morristown, 42, 283-90, 446, 512
Morristown Municipal Building, 291
Morro Castle, The, 682
Morrow, Mrs. Dwight W., 160
Morrow, Honoré Willsie, 159
Morse, Samuel F. B., 108, 446
Morsemere, 419, 475
Morton, Dr. Henry, 266
Moses, Arnold, H., 405
Mosquitoes, 130
Motion picture machine, invention of, 342
Motion pictures, 164
Mt. Ephraim, 657
Mt. Freedom, 533
Mt. Holly, 100, 292-7, 620
Mt. Hope, 479
Mt. Kemble, 283
Mt. Kipp, 534
Mt. Laurel, 621
Mt. Misery, 624
Mt. Mitchell, 676
Mt. Paul, 514
Mountain Lakes, 478
Mountain Plantations, 342
Mountain View, 442, 494
Mountain View Hotel, 494
Mountains, 8
Mountainside, 429
Mountainville, 433
Mowbray, Uffinger and Ely, 334
Moylan, James, 405
Muckshaw Swamp, 463
Mullica, Eric, 560, 604, 629
Mullica Hill, 613, 629, 654
Mullica River, 560
Mulliner, Joe, 606
Municipal Bus Terminal (Hackensack), 260-1
Munsee (see Indians)
Murat, Joachim, 212
Murat, Prince Napoleon François Lucien Charles, 212, 470
Murphy, Vincent J., 87
Murray, Rev. John, 145, 558
Murray family, 637
Murray Grove, 557
Musconetcong Mts., 434, 535
Musconetcong Valley, 516
Museums:
Beach Haven, 674; Bergen County Historical Society, 260; Berrien House, 489; Burlington, 220; Cape May Court House, 562; Camden County Historical Society, 235;

Museums *(Continued)*
Cumberland County Historical Society, 637; Historic Art, 141, 185, 385; Hopewell, 536; Huyler Dock House, 437; Indian King Inn, 627; Marlpit Hall, 592; Monmouth County Historical Assn., 253; Montclair, 141, 184, 185, 492; Morristown National Historical Park, 141, 286; N. J. Historical Society, 141, 331; N. J. State, 141, 404; Newark, 141, 185, 329; Ocean County, 556; Passaic County Historical Society, 355; Passaic County Park Commission, 442; Paterson, 141, 355; Safety, 279; Somers Mansion, 562; Stevens Institute of Technology, 141, 268; Union County Historical Society, 245; Waterman, L. E., 335
Music, 166-72
Music Year Book, 170
Muskrat skinning contest, 391
Mutual Benefit Life Insurance Co., 78, 317
Mutual Broadcasting Co., 109, 332
My Days Have Been so Wondrous Free, 167
Myers, William Starr, 159
Myggeborg, 642
Mystery of Marie Roget, The, 265

Nast, Thomas, 285
National Academy of Design, 186
National Broadcasting Co., 108
National *Gazette,* 112
National Guard, 104, 618, 683
National Industrial Recovery Act, 354
National Lawyers' Guild, 85
National Municipal Review, The, 380
National Musical String Co., 301
National Newark Building, 178, 325
National Park Service, 286, 288
National Piece Dye Works, 476
National State Bank, 78
National Trades Union, 80
Natural Resources, 23-6
Nature Friends' Camp, 501
Nature Friends' Society, 501
Navesink Highlands, 10
Nazis, 464
Negroes, 86, 90, 118, 119, 122-3, 130, 137, 148, 149, 193-4, 200, 210, 217, 229, 258, 272, 316, 318, 335, 336, 342, 343, 371, 391, 393, 399, 505, 562, 572, 600, 630, 637, 639-40, 643, 660
Neil and Spanger Lumber Co., 429
Neilson, James, 308
Neptune City, 579, 594
Netcong, 465, 481
New Brunswick, 42, 80, 298-310, 378, 426, 488, 528
New Brunswick *Home News,* 299
New Brunswick *Sunday Times,* 111
New Brunswick Theological Seminary, 309; Sage Library, 309; Suydam Hall, 309
New Brunswick War Memorial, 425

New Day, The, 153
New Egypt, 617
New England Crossroads, 637
New Freedom, The, 158
New Gretna, 560
New Hotel Baldwin (Beach Haven), 673
New Jersey, The, 229
N. J. *Advocate,* 485
N. J. Bell Telephone Co., 108, 513, 531, 588
N. J. Bell Telephone Building, 178, 328
N. J. *Chronicle,* 112, 554
N. J. College for Women, 140, 306-8; College Hall, 306; Elizabeth Rodman Voorhees Chapel, 308
N. J. College of Pharmacy, 317
N. J. Council for Religious Education, 150
N. J. *Freie Zeitung,* 116
N. J. *Gazette,* 111, 221
N. J. *Herald,* 112
N. J. Historical Society, 185, 331
N. J. Iron Clad Roofing Paint and Mastic Co., 374
N. J. *Journal,* 111, 244
N. J. Junior League Children's Theater, 165
N. J. Law School, 325
N. J. League of Women Voters, 86
N. J. *Magazine and Monthly Advertiser,* 111
N. J. Medical Society, 308
N. J. Orchestra, 170
"New Jersey Plan," 45
N. J. Pretzel Plant, 249
N. J. *Staats Journal,* 116
N. J. State Art Committee, 185, 186
N. J. State Federation of Labor, 85, 86
N. J. State Press Assn., 115
N. J. State Teachers' Assn., 138
N. J. Sunday School Assn., 150
N. J. Zinc Co., 497
New Market, 549
New Netherland, 35-6
New Sweden Co., 36
New Village, 518
New Wawayanda Lake, 463
New York, 42, 44, 45, 47, 49
New York Bay, 271
N. Y. *Gazette and Weekly Mercury,* 111
New York Harbor, 678
N. Y. Shipbuilding Co., 237
N. Y. Stock Exchange, 621
N. Y. *Times,* 536
N. Y. *Tribune,* 589
N. Y. Yacht Club, 264
Newark, 37, 41, 46, 80, 81, 87, 100, 108, 119, 136, 144, 161, 312-338, 422, 429, 490, 496, 544, 594
Newark Academy, 136, 331
Newark Banking and Insurance Co., 78, 320
Newark City Hall, 334
Newark Collective Theater, 165
Newark College of Engineering, 317
Newark *Daily Advertiser,* 57, 112, 113, 153, 322
Newark *Evening Journal,* 114
Newark *Evening News,* 110, 114, 115, 323, 606

Newark *Evening Star,* 112
Newark *Gazette,* 111, 112
Newark Harmonic Society, 169
Newark Institute of Art and Sciences, 325
Newark *Ledger,* 85, 115, 116
Newark Meadows, 422
Newark *Morning Register,* 153, 322
Newark *Star Eagle,* 112, 113, 115
Newark State Teachers College, 317
Newark *Sunday Call,* 112, 115, 323
Newark Technical School, 317
Newark Trades Union, 80
Newbie, Mark, 77, 602, 650
Newbie, Mark, bank, site, 650
Newbold, Charles, 90, 218
Newell, Gov. William A., 559, 667, 684
Newfoundland, 496
Newfoundland Inn, 496
Newman, Spencer, 260
Newman School, 556
Newspapers, 110-7, 257, 323, 346, 552;
    foreign language, 116; labor, 116
Newton, 454, 462
Niblo's Garden, 162
Nichols, Captain, 538
Nicolls, Col. Richard, 36-7, 239
Niehaus, Charles, 335
Night clubs, 271
Norcross, Uriah, 652
Norma, 660
Normal schools, 139
Normand, Mabel, 164
Normandy Heights, 283
Normanock, 460
North American Phalanx, 589
North Arlington, 542
North Bergen, 61, 133
North Branch, 432
North Cape May, 61
North German Lloyd, 265
North Jersey, 4
North Jersey District Water Supply Com-
    mission, 24
North Pemberton Station, 618
North Plainfield, 430
North Stelton, 487
North Wildwood, 646
Notman, John, 385
Nova Caesarea, 37
November Boughs, 154
Nowiny, 116
Nudism, 441, 495, 496, 608
Nummytown, 646
Nurseries, 92
Nutley, 543

Oakford Lake, 617
Oakland, 441
Oakley and Son, 245
Oaklyn, 601
Oakwood Beach, 642
Ocean City, 562
Ocean City *Sentinel-Ledger,* 114
Ocean Grove, 146, 579, 682
Ocean House (Toms River), 555
Oceanville, 561
Ockanickon, Chief, 220
Odell, Jonathan, 151

Ogden, Gov. Aaron, 246
Ogden, John, 245
Ogden, John, Jr., 246
Ogden, Col. Josiah, 319
Ogden family, 69
Old Academy (Newton), 462
Old Barracks (Trenton), 405
Old Barracks Assn., 405
Old Bergen Iron Works, site, 556
Old Bridge, 529
Old Burial Grounds (Bordentown), 215
Old Chateau, The, 247
Old Copper Mine, The, 458
Old Ferry Site (Elizabeth), 248
Old Fort (Andover), 463
Old Gun Mill (Paterson), 359
Old Masonic Lodge House (Trenton), 405
Old Mill Inn, 446-7
Old Mill Site (Elizabeth), 245
Old Mine Rd., 458, 472-4
Old Raceway (Paterson), 358
Old Steamboat Hotel (Burlington), 221
Old Stone Schoolhouse (Newark), 329
Oldwick, 432
Olive, Gov. Thomas, 218, 220
100,000,000 Guinea Pigs, 517
O'Neill, Raymond, 186
Ong family, 624
Ong's Hat, 624
Open Boat, The, 156
Oppenheim, James, 159
Opera, 170, 199
Opera Club of the Oranges, **170**
Orange, 341-2, 510
Oratam, Chief, 33, 259
Orchids, 549
Ordeal of the Bier, 392
Ordovician Period, 13
O'Rourke, Jeremiah, 331
Orpheus Club, 170
Ortley, 648
Ortley, Mitchell, 648
Osborne, Lloyd, 684
Osborne, Richard B., **194**
Othello, 643
Otis Elevator Co., 544
Ott and Brewer, 403
Our American Music, 172
Our House Tavern (Shacks Corner), 580
Our Times, 49
Outerbridge, Eugenius H., 368
Outerbridge Crossing, 106, 368, 552
Overbrook Hospital, 493
Oxford, 534
Oxford Furnace, site, 534
Oysters, 25, 242, 592, 639

Packanack Lake, 495
Page, Abner, 470
Pahaquarry, 61
Paine, Thomas, 152, 209, 311, 489
Painting, 182, 184. 185
Palatine Lake, 655
Palatine Lutherans, 144
Paleontology, 11-7
Palisades, 12, 262, 271, 272, 418, 419,
    436-7

Palisades Interstate Park Commission, 436, 438
Palisades Park, 419
Palmer, Edgar, 371
Palmolive-Peet Co., 279
Palmyra, 685
Pamrapo, 271
Pan in Wall Street, 154
Panzer College, 341
Paper Mill Playhouse, 165, 510
Paramus, 539
Pardons, State Board of, 58
Park, smallest in the world, 492
Park Place Hotel (Branchville), 461
Parker, Dorothy, 159
Parker, Ellis H., 293, 606
Parker, James, 110, 552
Parker, Gov. Joel, 47, 57
Parker family, 366
Parkhurst, Capt. Jabez, 161
Parks
    Municipal and County: Armory, 348; Bonaparte, 210; Branch Brook, 331; Buccleuch, 311; Cadwalader, 414; Camden County, 621, 627; City Hall, 348; Clinton, 335; Doane, 325; Eagle Rock Reservation, 493, 530; Eastside, 357; Echo Lake, 429; Elysian Fields, 264; Enclosure, The, 543; Garret Mt. Reservation, 355; Gloucester Point, 575; Hilltop, 213; Hudson, 268; Jackson, 249; Johnson, 230; Lakeview Memorial, 132; Lincoln (Jersey City), 280; Lincoln (Newark), 335; Mahlon Stacy, 408; Military, 325; Mindowaskin, 547; Monument, 253; Mt. Holly, 296; Nomahegan, 547; Pyne Poynt, 234; Rahway River Parkway, 429, 484, 547; Roosevelt, 424; Scott, 245; South Mountain Reservation, 510; Warinanco, 484; Washington, 328; Watchung Reservation, 430; Watsessing, 490; Weequahic, 336, 429; Westside, 357; Wheeler, 423; Whitehouse Memorial, 432
    State: list, xxvi; Cranberry, 464; Hacklebarney, 514; High Point, 499; Mt. Laurel, 621; Palisades Interstate, 436; Parvin, 660; Ringwood Manor, 502; Swartswood, 455, 462; Voorhees, 535; Washington Crossing, 520; Washington Rock, 430
    National: Morristown, 446; Red Bank Battlefield, 576
Parrish and Schroeder, 386
Parsippany, 445, 477
Parsons, Charles, 182
Parvin Lake, 660
Passaic, 79, 84, 345, 348
Passaic County, 122
Passaic County Park Commission, 355, 444
Passaic Falls, 17, 70, 352, 359
Passaic *Herald,* 347
Passaic Meadows, 25
Passaic River, 9, 153, 312, 345, 349, 549
Passaic Valley, 494, 530

Patent Arms Co., 359
Paterson, 71, 79, 80, 84, 349-60, 476
Paterson, Gov. William, 353, 359
Paterson City Hall, 358
"Paterson Pageant," 354
Paterson Plank Rd., 421
Paterson *Press,* 116
Patriotic Order Sons of America, 522
Patterson, George, 580
Patterson, Howard, 584
Patterson, Robert, 483
Patton, Dr. Francis L., 379
Paul, Dr. J. Marshall, 482
Paul, Philip, 577
Paul Hotel (Woodbury), 628
Paulez (Paulusen), Michael, 272
Paulina, 456
Paulins Kill Lake, 461
Paulison, Charles McKnight, 348
Paulsboro, 577
Paulus Hook, 271, 272, 273
Pauw, Michael, 36, 272
Pavonia, 36, 272
Pea Patch Island, 632
Peaches, 93, 572
Pearson, Isaac, 293
Peck, Frank, 625
Peddie Lake, 570
Peddie School, 141, 570
Pelican Island, 649
Pellettown, 454
Pemberton, 618
Pemberton Inn, 618
Penn, Gov. John, 535
Penn, William, 38, 39, 222, 388, 392
Pennington, 102, 536
Pennington Seminary, 536
Penn's Neck, 427
Pennsgrove, 578
Pennsville, 578, 632
Pennsylvania *Gazette,* 609
Pennsylvania Line mutiny, 285
Pennsylvania R.R. lift bridge, 334
Pennsylvania R.R. station (Newark), 332
People's Press, 116
Pequannock River, 444
Pequest, 482
Pequest River, 10, 482
Percheron horses, 651
Perrine, Van Dearing, 186
Perrineville, 583
Perryville, 433-4
Perseverance, The, 605
Perth, Earl of, 362, 363
Perth Amboy, 39, 134, 161, 240, 361-9, 552
Perth Amboy City Hall, 367
Perthuck, Rev. Edward, 367
Peter's Valley, 473
Petersburg, 665
Peterson, Charles, 606
Petty's Island, 650
Phalanx, 589
Philadelphia, 42, 44, 47, 49, 228
Phillipsburg, 46, 435, 518
Phoenix, The, 99, 264
Phoenix House (Mendham), 513
Phyfe, Duncan, 549

Picatinny Arsenal, 480
Pickel, Balthasar, 432
Pickford, Mary, 164
Pickle Pond, 640
Pierce family, 637
Pierson, Rev. Abraham, 318
Pierson, Rev. Abraham, Jr., 319
Piers, amusement, 192, 195, 198-9
Picnicking, 424, 429, 430, 437, 462, 482, 510, 514, 522, 547, 577, 594, 626, 655, 669, 686
Pillar of Fire, 149, 550
Pine Barrens, 23, 605-7, 608-9, 616, 624, 668
Pine Brook, 477
Pine Cliff Lake, 507
Pine Lake, 626
Pine Ridge Pavilion, 455
Pine Robbers, 590, 605
Pineys, the, 160, 171, 605-6
Pirates, 128, 649
Piscataqua, 37
Piscataway, 145, 424
Pitman, 658
Pitman Grove Camp Meeting Assn., 658
Pittsgrove, 609, 654
Plain Dealer, 111
Plain Dealing Society, 384
Plainfield, 145, 548
Plainfield and North Plainfield Historical Society, 548
Plainfield *Courier-News*, 115
Planning Board, State, 25, 26
Plants, 18-20; poisonous, xxvi
Plattdeutsches Volksfest, 133
Playhouse Assn., Summit, 165
Pleasant Mills, 606
Pleasant Mills, site, 607
Pleasantville, 608
Pleistocene Period, 17
Plow, cast-iron, 90
Plowden, Sir Edward, 641
Pluckemin, 448
Plume, Ann Van Wagenen, 330
Plutonian Critique of Some Awful Aspects of the Terrestrial Life, A, 126
Pochuck Mt., 453, 497
Poe, Edgar Allen, 265
Pohatcong Mts., 434, 535
Point Breeze, 210
Point Lookout, 436
Point Pleasant, 595, 647
Polak-Amerykanki, 116
Pole Tavern, site, 610
Poles, 116, 118, 121, 124, 202, 217, 229, 258, 264, 272, 299, 317, 345, 347, 352, 362
Police, State, 104, 424, 434, 470; substations, xxv
Polish Kronika, 116
Polish National Home, 346
Politics, 3, 47, 48, 50, 53, 60, 63, 81, 82, 87, 102, 111, 115, 275, 340
Pollution, 24, 25, 203, 323-4, 552, 578
Polo, xxix, 198, 448, 538, 582
Pompton Lakes, 441
Pompton Lakes (Borough), 442
Pompton Mutiny, 502

Pompton Plains, 495
Pomona, 597
Poole, George E., 405
Poor, Gen. Enoch, 259
Poore, Henry Rankin, 186
Population figures (*see chronology*)
Porch, Samuel, 609
Porchtown, 609
Port Colden, 516
Port Elizabeth, 638
Port Newark, 322, 338
Port Norris, 640
Port of New York Authority, 104, 106, 276, 368, 419
Portertown, 630
Ports, 107
Portuguese, 505
Potash, 26
Potatoes, 90, 253, 569, 655
Potter, Matthew, 111
Potter, Thomas, 145, 557
Potter, William A., 177, 384
Potterstown, 432
Poultry, 89, 91, 588, 658, 670
Powhatan, The, 667
Preceptorial System, the, 375
Prentice Refinery, 203
Presbyterian Board of Relief for Disabled Ministers and the Widows of Deceased Ministers, The, 366
Presbyterians, 41, 145, 147, 218, 342, 372, 376, 389, 566
Preston, Mrs. Thomas Jex, Jr., 388
Prieth, Benedict, 116
Prince Street (Newark), 336
Princeton, 370-89, 467, 489
Princeton Battle Monument, 185, 388
Princeton Cemetery, 389
Princeton Local Government Survey, 61, 67, 380
Princeton Stories, 158
Princeton Theological Seminary, 171, 389
Princeton University, 41, 136, 137, 140, 158, 159, 171, 177, 244, 246, 319, 370-87; Alexander Hall, 177, 384; Biological Museum, 386; Brokaw Memorial, 385; Chancellor Green Building, 384; Chapel, 385; Cleveland Tower, 386; Clio Hall, 384; Dean's House, 381; Fitz Randolph Gateway, 380; Geological Museum, 386; Gymnasium, 385; Graduate College, 386; Guyot Hall, 386; Henry House, 385; Holder Hall, 384; Lake Carnegie, 386; Madison Hall, 381; McCarter Theater, 386; McCormick Hall, 385; Museum of Historic Art, 385; Nassau Hall, 380-1; Palmer Memorial Stadium, 386; Procter Hall, 386; Prospect, 385; Pyne Library, 384; Revolutionary Cannon, 384; Russell Sage Tower, 384; Stamp Act Trees, 381; Thomson College, 386; Whig Hall, 384
Princeton University Press, 380
Printz, Gov. Johan, 614
Prison, State, 412

Privateers, 300
Probation laws, 67
Procter, William Cooper, 386
Proctor, A. Phimister, 381
Prohibition, 336, 347, 554, 606, 675, 676
Prophecy, A, 213
Proprietors of East New Jersey, 38, 39, 40, 222, 240, 362, 364
Proprietors of New Jersey, 37
Proprietors of West New Jersey, 38, 39, 40, 222, 575
Prospect Park, 119
Provost, Theodosia, 538
Prudential Insurance Co., 78, 177, 179 314, 316, 335
Public Hunting and Fishing Grounds, 460, 474, 663, 668
Public Library Commission, State, 141
Public Service Corp., 51, 76-7, 106, 115, 227, 314, 421, 544
Public utilities, 76, 108, 227, 529, 577
Public Works Administration, 104, 179
Pulaski, Count Casimir, 285
Pulaski Skyway, 104, 276, 421
Pumptown, 486
Puritans, 144, 318, 319
Putnam, F. W., 28
Pyle, Howard, 332
Pyne, Moses Taylor, 467

Quail Farm, State, 615
Quakers, 38, 39, 123, 144, 146, 148, 176, 217, 218, 228, 254, 296, 371, 391, 393, 396, 571, 575, 593, 601, 617, 618, 625, 628, 630, 632, 635, 651, 652, 666
Quartz, 26
Quaternary Period, 17
Queens College Grammar School, 309
Queen's Rangers, 392
"Quintipartite deed," 38
Quinton, 634

RCA Radiotron, 544
RCA-Victor Manufacturing Co., 230-2
Raccoon Creek, 36
Racing: automobile, xxix; bicycle, xxix; dog-sled, xxix; horse, 254, 297, 336
Radburn, 179
Radio, 108, 232, 423, 465, 468, 513, 527, 531, 546, 558, 560, 588 (*see also Industry, radios*)
Radio Corp. of America, 108, 232, 560
Radio stations: WABC, 494; WAWZ, 550; WINS, 419; WJZ, 108, 431, 527; WNEW, 540; WOR, 108, 332, 424; WPG, 198, 608; WSNJ, 657
Rafinesque, Constantine Samuel, 31
Rahway, 484
Rahway cloverleaf, 552
Rahway River, 424, 429
Railroads, xxix, 46, 47, 48, 96, 100-3, 194, 195, 203, 210, 216, 248, 249, 264, 269, 300, 346, 393; Belvidere Delaware, 451; Blairstown, 457; Burlington and Mount

Holly, 293; Camden and Amboy, 46, 47, 100-2, 210, 229, 363, 374, 402, 571; Camden and Atlantic, 194; Delaware, Lackawanna and Western, 48, 103; Electric, 195; Elizabeth and Somerville, 101, 242, 550; Erie, 81, 103, 274, 275, 345, 349; Freehold and Jamesburg Agricultural, 253; Freehold and New York, 253; Hudson and Manhattan, 103, 275, 323; Jersey Central, 102, 103, 239, 253, 275; Lehigh Valley, 100, 103, 364; Morris and Essex, 101, 285; Narrow Gauge, 194; New Jersey, 101, 274, 300, 320; New Jersey and New York, 259; New York Central, 419; New York and Long Branch, 554; Paterson and Hudson, 101, 274, 353; Pennsylvania, 47-8, 100, 103, 207, 239, 253, 274, 275, 299, 371, 398, 421; Philadelphia and Trenton, 101, 102; Reading, 100, 103; Squankum, 253; United, 275; West Jersey, 195
Rainfall, annual, 11
Rall, Col. Johann Gottlieb, 401, 409
Ralston, 514
Ralston, John, 514
Ramapo fault, 14
Ramapo Mts., 12, 504
Ramapo Water Garden, 440
Ramsey, 538
Rancocas Creek, 292
Rankin, Kellogg and Crane, 230
Raritan, 79
Raritan arsenal, 424
Raritan Bay, 362
Raritan Copper Works, 368
Raritan River, 9, 298, 362, 363, 425
Raul, Harry Lewis, 438
Raymond, Mayor Thomas L., 324
Raymond, Thomas L., Walled Garden, 329
Raymond-Commerce Building, 178
Read, Charles, 605, 626
Read, Honoré, 606
Record, George L., 50, 51
Recreation, xxvi
Red Badge of Courage, The, 156, 335
Red Bank, 593
Red Lion, 624
Red Lion Inn, 624
Redemptorists, 681
Reed, John, 354
Reed's Beach, 646
Reeve Furnace, 626
Reforestation, 24
Reform movements, 46, 50, 81
Reformatory, State, 424
Reid, John, 252
Relief, 53, 234, 404
Relief Fire Co. House, 296
Religion, 142-150
Rennie, Robert, 539
Reptiles, 22; Age of, 13-5; poisonous, xxvi, 458, 463, 472, 624
Republican Party, 47, 48, 63, 87
Republicans, New Idea, 50, 51, 275

Reservoirs: Macopin Intake, 496; Oak Ridge, 496; Parsippany, 445, 477; Pequannock, 495, 496; Roaring Rocks, 517; Wanaque, 500-1
Resettlement Administration, U.S., 88, 570
Revel, Thomas, 221
Revolution, American, 41-2, 151-2; Ash Swamp, 485; Bordentown, 208; Bound Brook, 550; Brooklawn, 657; Burlington, 218; Camden, 230; Chestnut Neck, 560-1; Colt's Neck, 589-90; Elizabeth, 240, 248; Fort Lee, 418; Freehold, 252; Gloucester, 575; Goat Hill, 519; Hackensack, 259; Hancock's Bridge, 634; Hopewell, 536; Jersey City, 274; Lambertville, 452; Lawrenceville, 468; Kingston, 488; Monmouth, 565-8; Morristown, 284-9; Mount Holly, 296; New Brunswick, 300; Newark, 319; Perth Amboy, 363, 364; Princeton, 372; Red Bank Battlefield, 576-7; Ringwood, 504; Salem, 392; Seaside Heights, 648; Shrewsbury, 593; Springfield, 509-10; Toms River, 556-7; Trenton, 401-2; Washington Crossing, 520-2; Westfield, 547-8
Reynard, Grant, 186
Rhind, J. Massey, 279, 328, 335
Richards, Jesse, 625
Richards, John, 477, 603
Richards, Thomas, 212
Richards, Col. William, 604
Richardson, H. H., 176
Richland, 608
Richwood, 613
Ridgefield, 419
Ridgefield Park, 475
Ridges, John, 293
Riding, 430 (see also general information, cities)
Ringo, John, 451
Ringoes, 451, 535
Ringoes Academy of Arts and Sciences, 450
Ringwood, 504
Ringwood Co., 496, 504, 505
Ringwood mines, 505
Rio Grande, 563, 646
Ripley, Rev. George, 589
Ripley, Robert L., 492
River Edge, 539
Riverdale, 500
Riverdale War Memorial, 500
Rivers, 9, 10
Road Horse Assn. of New Jersey, 336
Roadstown, 643
Robbins, Leonard H., 160
Robbinsville, 571, 582
Roberts, Spencer, 414
Robeson, Jonathan, 534
Robeson, Paul, 172
Robinson, Henry Crabb, 296
Rock Lodge Nudist Camp, 496
Rockaway, 478
Rockaway Falls, 445
Rockaway Gorge, 444

Rockefeller, Johann Peter, 450
Rockefeller, John D., 450, 555, 596
Rockefeller, John D., Jr., 72
Rockefeller family, 436, 450
Rockefeller Institute for Medical Research, 371, 426
Rocket Airplane Corp. of America, 507
Rockport, 516
Rocky Hill, 42, 488, 489
Roebling, 122, 572
Roebling, John A., 403, 572
Roebling family, 72
Roebling, John A., Sons, 412
Rogerenes, 559
Rogers, Mary, 264
Rogers, Will, 228
Rolling chairs, 195
Roman Catholic Diocesan Institute of Sacred Music, 171
Roman Catholics, 144, 147
Roosevelt, Eleanor, 514
Roselle, 484, 546
Rosencrans ferry, 474
Rosenhayn, 660
Ross Corner, 454, 461
Roth, Frederick G. R., 186, 288
Rotolactor, 90, 427
Rova Farms, 616
Rover Boys, The, 157
Rowan, John R., 599
Rowland, John T., 178, 280
Roy, Jacob Jacobsen, 203
Royal Insurance Co., 78
Rudder Grange, 156
Rudyard, Thomas, 293
Rumsey, Elizabeth, 392
Rumson, 679
"Runaway shops," 86
Runnemede, 652
Russell, Lillian, 680
Russell, Louis Arthur, 170
Russian Orthodox Catholics, 148
Russians, 118, 124, 202, 229, 272, 346, 352, 353, 362, 616
Rutgers, Henry, 305
Rutgers Preparatory School, 309
Rutgers University, 41, 49, 92, 115, 136, 140, 171, 185, 304-8, 551; Ceramics Building, 306; Geological Hall, 306; Gymnasium, 306; Kirkpatrick Chapel, 306; New Jersey Hall, 306; Queen's Building, 175, 305; Queen's Campus, 305; Schanck Observatory, 306; Stadium, 527; Voorhees Homestead, site, 308; Voorhees Library, 306; Winants Hall, 306
Rutherford, 540-1
Rutherford, John, 540
Ryerson, Mrs. Martin, 502
Ryerson family, 502, 504
Ryle, John, 71, 353

Saddle River, 538
Sage, Mrs. Russell, 384
St. Clair, Gen., 402
Saint Gaudens, Augustus, 684
St. Joseph's College, 371, 489

St. Mary's Choral Society, 224
St. Mary's Hall, 223
St. Patrick's High School, 249
St. Patrick's Pence, 650
St. Peter's College, 275-6
Salem, 38, 390-7, 631, 632, 641
Salem Canal, 611
Salem County, 70
Salem County Historical Society, 394, 634
Salem County Home, 630
Salem Creek, 390
Salem Municipal Building, 394
Salem Oak, 396
Salem *Sunbeam*, 112
Salmagundi, 153, 320
Salt Water Day, 132
Salt water taffy, 195
Salter, Richard and Hannah, 586
Saltersville, 203
Salvini, Tommaso, 163
San Alfonso Retreat, 681
Sand, 26
Sandusky, The, 353
Sandy Hook, 568, 678
Sanford, Charles H., 582
Sanhicans (*see Indians*)
Savage, Annette, 212, 409, 412-3
Savannah, The, 446
Scandinavians, 118, 648, 670
Scattergood, Thomas and Elizabeth, 470
Scenic Dr., 676
Schelling, Ernest, 172
Schlink, F. J., 517
Schneider, Father Theodore, 144
School of Public and International Affairs, 375
Schooleys Mt., 481, 515
Schooleys Mt. Springs, 516
Schooley peneplane, 16
Schuyler, Arent, 442, 460
Schuyler, Elizabeth, 289
Schuyler, John, 542
Schuyler, Susanna Edwards, 206
Schuyler mines, site, 542
Schuylkill Navigation System, 100
Scotch Plains, 430
Scots, 39, 118, 119, 252, 346, 363, 430, 543
Scott, Lieut. Gen. Winfield, 246
Scotts Mt., 516, 534
Scribblerus, Madame, 367
Scrub Oak Mine, 480
Scudder, Amos, 523
Scudder, Wallace, 114
Scudder's Falls, 523
Sculpture, 182, 184
Sea Bright, 679
Sea Girt, 683
Seabrook Bulb Gardens, 656
Seabrook Farms, 86, 91, 656
Seabury, Richard W., 444
Seafaring Bachelor, The, 254
Seaside Heights, 648
Seaside Park, 648
Seatrain Line, 269
Seaville, 562, 665
Seeing Eye, The, 531
Seeley, 655

Seeley, Josiah, 655
Seeley Lake, 655
Self-Masters' Colony, 509
Sentinel of Freedom, 112, 113
Sessions, Roger, 171
Seth Boyden School of Business, 325
Seth Jones, or The Captive of the Frontier, 403
Seton Hall College, 140, 343
Seven Arts, The, 159
"Seven Sisters" Acts, 51
Seven Songs for Harpsichord or Forte-Piano, 167, 214
Seven Stars Tavern (Ocean Co.), 556
Seventh Day Baptists, 145, 635, 643
Seward, William H., 496
Shacks Corner, 580
Shane's Castle, site, 598
Shannon, The, 220
Shantytowns, 74
Shark River, 580
Shark River Inlet, 595
Sharptown, 611
Sheffield Farms, 442
Shelburne Essays, 158
Sheldon, Robert T., 441
Shell Fisheries, State Board of, 25
Shell Pile, 639
Shenandoah, The, 108, 623
Sheppard, Adam, 221
Sheppard, John, 645
Sheppard's Mill, 643
Sherman, Edith Bishop, 157
Sherron, James, 392
Shield, The, 217, 223
Shill, M. D., 195
Shiloh, 635, 643
Shinn, Everett, 414
Ship Bottom, 667, 669, 672
Shippen, Joseph, 534
Shippen, Dr. William, 534
Shipping, 96, 107, 207, 218, 259, 269, 300, 322, 338, 348, 392, 401, 403
Shipwrecks, 194, 682
Shirley, 655
Shirley, Sephas, 492
Show Boat, 172
Shrewsbury, 37, 70, 593
Shute, Barnaby, 245
"Silk City," The, 351, 353
Simcoe, Maj. John, 392, 634
Simplex Automobile Co., 301
Simpson, Maxwell, 186
Singac, 494
Singer, Isaac M., 249
Singer Sewing Machine Co., 242, 249
Singing Societies, 169
Sip, Jan Arianse, 279
Sip Manor, site, 279
Skiing, xxix, 499, 510
Skinner, Otis, 164
Slate, Jacob, 498
Slattery, Mary E., 403
Slavery, 41, 79, 89
Slavs, 242, 346, 362
Slovak Catholic Sokol, 346
Slovaks, 346
Smith, F. Hopkinson, 157, 672

Smith, Hezekiah, 293, 620
Smith, Sen. James, Jr., 50
Smith, John, 630
Smith, Joseph, 557
Smith, Joshua Hott, 476
Smith, P. J., 434
Smith, Richard, 41
Smith, Robert, 380
Smith, Dr. Samuel Stanhope, 378
Smithville, 620
Smyth, Chief Justice Frederick, 645
Smythe, Douglas, 253
Snake Hill, 12, 478
Snowshoeing, xxix
Soccer, 336
Socialism, 487
Socialist Labor Party, 82
Society for Establishing Useful Manufactures, 71, 352, 359
Society for the Propagation of the Gospel, 367
Soil, 23, 89
Soil Conservation Committee, State; 23
Soldiers and Sailors War Memorial Building, 408
Soldiers Monument (Camp Merritt), 438
Soldiers Monument (Paterson), 357
Somerdale, 600
Somers, Commandant Richard, 562
Somers Point, 562
Somerset, 522
Somerville, 42, 431, 466, 550
Somerville Hotel, 551
Sommer, Frank, 50
Sonneck, Oscar G., 167, 172
Sons of the American Revolution, 522
Soshinsky, Dr. Herman, 496
Sourland Mts., 449, 519, 535
South Amboy, 553, 591
South Bound Brook, 550
South Cape May, 61
South Dennis, 640, 646
South Jersey, 4
South Jersey Farmers' Exchange, 94
South Jersey Law School, 140
South Orange, 343
South Orange-Maplewood Adult Education Institute, 339, 344
South River, 528
South Toms River, 146, 557
Southwick, Josiah, 293
Spaniards, 505
Speaker Wagon Works, 658
Specimen Days and Collect, 154
Speedwell Iron Works, site, 108, 446, 529
Speir, Dr. Leslie, 28
Sphagnum moss, 10
Spirit of Washington, The, 252
Spotswood, 529
Spray Beach, 673
Spring, Rebecca, 363
Spring Lake, 683
Springfield, 509
Springtown, 643
Squibb, Dr. Edward R., 311
Squibb, E. R., and Sons, 311
Stacy, Mahlon, 293, 400
Stacy, Mahlon, Jr., 400

Staffordville, 559
Stagecoaches, 96
Standard Oil Co. of N. J., 203, 204, 423, 524
Stanger, Catherine, 613
Stanhope, 465
Stanley, Dr. Wendell M., 426
Stanton, Elizabeth Cady, 437
Stapleton, Thomas, 371
State, The, 159
Statehouse, the, 404
Statehouse Annex, the, 404
Staten Island, 240, 248, 552
Steam engines, 542
Steamboats, 99, 229, 249, 264, 410
Steamship lines, list, xxix
Stedman, Edmund Clarence, 154, 322, 548
Stedman, Fisher, 482
Steel Pier, 199
Steenhuysen, Englebert, 279
Steeplechase Pier, 198-9
Steffens, Lincoln, 49
Stein, Clarence, 179
Stelle family, 487
Stelton, 487
Stelton Modern School, 487
Stent, E. J. N., 206
Stephen Crane Assn., 156, 334
Sterling Forest, 506
Stevens, Aaron Dwight, 364
Stevens, Col. John, 46, 99, 100, 264, 266, 268, 274, 300, 542
Stevens, John Cox, 264
Stevens, Robert L., 100, 229
Stevens, Uriah Smith, 82
Stevens Institute of Technology 140, 262, 266-9, 455; Administration Building, 266; Gatehouse, 268; Gymnasium, William Hall Walker, 268; Lieb Memorial, 268; Museum, 141, 268; Navy Building, 268; Stevens Castle, 268
Stevens Institute of Technology Theatre, 165
Stevenson, Robert Louis, 684
Still Valley, 435
Stillwell, Richard, 538
Stockton, 496
Stockton, Frank R., 156, 285, 543
Stockton, Richard, 363
Stockton, Richard II, 371, 388
Stockton Lake, 683
Stockyards, 275
Stoddard, Richard Henry, 154
Stokes, Ed, 680
Stokes, Gov. Edward, 50, 460
Stony Brook, 371
Stories of New Jersey, 156
Stratemeyer, Edward L., 157
Stratford, 599
Street, Aaron, 393
Street, Zadock, 392
Strikebreaking, 84, 204, 232
Strikes, 80, 81, 82, 84, 85, 86, 92, 116, 204, 232, 237, 347, 351, 353, 354, 364, 403, 437, 476, 494, 517, 539, 656
Stuart, Gilbert, 185

Study of Death, A, 157
Stuyvesant, Gov. Peter, 36, 264, 272, 277; statue, 279
Submarines, 355, 357
Succasunna, 463, 533
Suffern Boys' Camp Academy, 439
Suffrage, 46, 56
Sullivan, Jim, 394
Sullivan, Louis, 176
Sullivan, Mark, 49-50
Sully, Thomas, 185
Summit, 510
Sun Oil Co., 650
Sunset Lake, 636
Sunshine Lake, 686
Surf City, 670
Survey, The, 605
Surveyor General's Office (Perth Amboy), 367
Sussex, 453, 498
Sussex County Octogenarian Society, 462
Sussex *Register,* 112
Svoboda, 116
Swain, Luther, 562
Swainton, 562
Swamps, 666
Swartswood Lake, 462
Swartwout, Capt. Anthony, 462
Swedes, 36, 118, 157, 174, 391, 575, 578, 604, 613-4
Swedesboro, 613-4
Swimming, 280, 434, 481, 499, 501, 513, 535, 578, 594, 636, 658, 659, 669, 686
Swing, Samuel and Sarah, 654
Switlik Parachute and Equipment Plant, 412
Sybil's Cave, 264
Syrians, 122, 352, 528

Tabernacle, 471
Tacony-Palmyra Bridge, 685
Talbot, John, 218
Talc, 26
Talleyrand, Charles Maurice, 319
Taunton Furnace, site, 626
Taunton Lakes, 626
Taxes, 67-8, 139, 204, **276**
Taylor, Bayard, 154
Taylor, Edward, 592
Taylor, Robert, 535
Taylor, Van Campen, 306
Taylor Opera House, 162, 400
Taylor-Wharton Iron and Steel Co., 535
Teedyuscung, 33
Telegraph, 108, 446
Telephones, 108
Television, 531
Temple of Minerva, The, 167
Tenafly 437-8
Tenafly Weavers, 437
Teneyck, Jacob, 432
Tennent, 565
Tennent, Rev. John, 566
Tennent, Rev. William, 566
Tennis, xxix (*see also general information, cities*)

Terhune, Albert Payson, 160, 442, 499
Terhune, John, 261
Terminal moraine, 16
Terry, Ellen, 164
Tertiary Period, 16
Textile Workers Organizing Committee, 347
Thackara, Isaac and Mary, 601-602
Thalians, the, 165
Thanksgiving Day, 246, 293
Theater, 161-6, 266
Theater Workshop, New Jersey College for Women, 165
Theatre Intime, 165
This Side of Paradise, 160
Thomas, Joseph, 455-6
Thomas, Lenore, 570
Thomas, Norman, 347
Thomas, Theodore, 169
Thompson, William J., 575, 576
Thomson, Sen. John R., 386
Thoreau, Henry David, 666
Thorne, Hannah, 601
Three Bridges, 449
Three Mile Run, 488
Three-in-One Oil Co., 485
Throckmorton, Cleon, 165
Tide Water Oil Co., 203
Tides of Barnegat, The, 157, 160, 672
Tilden, E. L., 245
Tilton, Schwanewede and Githens, 260
Tilyou, George, 199
Time magazine, 623
Tine, George W., 450
Titus, John Henry, 623
Titusville, 520
Tobogganing, xxix, 510
Tom, Capt. William, 556
Tomatoes, 90, 93
Toms River, 556
Topography, 7-10
Tories, 41, 151, 252, 259, 300, 309, 319, 363, 372, 392, 397, 463, 543, 556-7, 589, 591, 634, 645
Torn, the, 445
Tornqvist, Peter, 348
Tornqvist cornice, 347
Totowa, 476
Towaco, 444
Track meets, xxix
Traffic regulations, xxix
Transcontinental and Western Air, 575
Transportation, 46, 51, 96-107; air travel, 107; canals, 99-100; highways, 103-6; railroads, 100-3; steam travel, 98-9; turnpikes and stages, 96-8; water travel, 106-7
Trap Tavern (Hamilton), 580
Traprock, 26
Traubel, Horace, 156, 234
Travers, William R., 542
Treadway, Samuel T., 393
Treat, Capt. Robert, 318
Treaty of Westminster, 38
Trees, 18, 23, 604
Trees, 158, 311
Trent, Col. William, 400, 409

Trenton, 42, 44, 72, 80, 82, 136, 141, 144, 145, 398-414, 428, 468, 523, 537, 583, 664
Trenton Banking Co., 78
Trenton Battle Monument, 185
Trenton Central High School, 178
Trenton Library Co., 400
Trenton Municipal Building, 414
Trenton *State Gazette,* 111, 113, 162
Trenton State Teachers College, 537
Trenton *Sunday Advertiser,* 403
Trenton *Times,* 115
Trenton *Times Advertiser,* 115
Trenton *True American,* 404
Tresca, Carlo, 354
Triangle Club, 386
Triassic Lowland, 8, 11
Triassic Period, 13
Trolleys, 106
Troy Hills, 477
Troy Meadows, 477
Trucks, 103
Trust Co. of N. J., 78
Trusts, 49-50
Tuberculosis Sanitarium, State, 534
"Tubes, the" (*see Huson and Manhattan R.R.*)
Tuckahoe, 663, 665
Tuckerton, 560
Tulane, Paul, 389
Tulane University, 389
Tunison, Cornelius, 551
Tunnels, 106, 264
Turks, 122
Turner, Joseph, 535
Turner, William, 463
Turnpikes, 98
Tuscarora (*see Indians*)
Tuttles Corner, 460
Twain, Mark, 157, 340
Two Rivulets, 154
Tye, Colonel, 589

Ukrainians, 116
Unalachtigo (*see Indians*)
Unami (*see Indians*)
Underground Railroad, 123, 128, 275, 363, 393, 600, 611, 643
Unemployed sit-in, 404
Union, 429, 509
Union City, 147
Union Hotel (Flemington), 524
Union Iron Works, site, 535
Union *Labor Advocate,* 116
Union Lake, 638
Unions, 276, 322, 351, 354, 679 (*see also Labor*)
United Airlines, 575
United Cannery, Agricultural, Packing and Allied Workers, 86
United Electrical and Radio Workers Union, 232
United Laundry Workers Union, 494
United Piece Dye Works, 539
United Presbyterian Church Cemetery, 450
U.S. Naval Air Station, 623
United Textile Workers Union, 347
Universalists, 145, 557-8

University of Hell, 126
University of Newark, 140, 317, 325
Untimely Papers, 159
Updyck, Rich John, 451
Upjohn, Richard, 224
Upper Mill, 624
Upper Pohatcong Mt., 482
Upsala College, 341
Upton, 624
Urania, 168
Urban League, The, 318
Ursino Lake, 508

Vail, Alfred, 446
Vail, Elizabeth Phyfe, 549
Vail, Stephen, 446
Vail, Theodore N., 291
Van Campen, Isaac, 474
Van Dyke, Henry, 158, 388
Van Dyke, John C., 185
Van Harlingens, Johannis, 466
Van Hise family, 615
Van Hiseville, 615
Van Horn, Amos, 328
Van Putten, Aert T., 264
Van Schott, Dr. Gerald J., 347
Van Syckles Corner, 434
Van Vaca, Maria and Hannah, 637
Van Vorst, Cornelius, 36, 271
Van Vorst Township, 271
Vanderbilt, Cornelius, 300
Vanderburg, 589
Vanderhoof, Aaron, 476
Vanderlyn, John, 185
Vanderpool, George B., 511
Vanderveer, Jacob, 448
Varleth, Nicholas, 279
Ventnor, 607
Verona, 493
Veronica's Veil, 147
Veterans of Foreign Wars, 223
Veterans of Future Wars, 376
Victor Talking Machine Co., 230
Victory Bridge, 361
Vienna, 482
Village Inn (Englishtown), 582
Vincentown, 470
"Vinegar Bible, The," 593
Vineland, 660-1
Vineland Training School, 605, 661
"Virginia Plan," 45
Visits to Walt Whitman, 155
Voelker, Carl M., 195
Volk, Ernest, 28
Von Donop, Count, 576
Von Steuben, Gen. Frederick William, 539, 550
Voorhees, Dan, 495
Voorhees, Gmelin and Walker, 178, 328
Voyage to Pagany, A, 160
Vreeland, Jacob, 543
Vusler, Milton J., 456

Waeir, Abraham, 559
Wages, 87
Waits, 224
Walcott, Harry M., 186
Walker Gordon Farm, 90, 427

Wallace, J. W., 156
Waller, Emma, 163
Wallkill River, 453
Walloons, 36
Walpack Center, 474
Walpack Inn, 474
Walsh, Archbishop Thomas J., 147
Walsh Act, 61
Walt Whitman in Mickle Street, 156
Walum-Olum, 31
Wampum, 32, 277
Wanamaker department store, 649
Wanaque Borough, 501
War Is Kind, 156
War of 1812, 46, 203, 218-20, 294, 669
Ward, Samuel A., 169
Ware, Harriet, 172
Ware family, 643
Waretown, 559
Warne, Peggy, 517
Warren Foundry and Pipe Co., 479, 518
Wars of America, The, 325
Washington, N. J., 131, 516, 534
Washington, Pres. George, 42, 111, 152,
    284-5, 286-8, 300, 344, 401-2,
    418, 440, 452, 489, 500, 502,
    520, 522, 531, 548, 557, 566-8,
    617; statues, 288, 328, 367, 409
Washington, George, 513
Washington, Martha, 489
Washington, U.S.S., 237
Washington Assn. of New Jersey, 286
Washington, G., Coffee Co., 445
Washington Crossing, 520
Washington Elm, 582
Washington Inn (Maplewood), 344
Washington Market (Paterson), 355
Washington Mills, 576
Washington Rock, 430, 510
Washington Vigilante Society, 517
Washington Water Co., 517
Watchung Mts., 12, 339, 421, 449, 494,
    510
Water, 24, 26
Water Policy Commission, State, 24
Water Witch, 678
Water Witch, The, 153
Waterford Works, 598
Waterhouse, George B., 347
Waterloo, 464
Waterman, L. E. Co., 316, 335
Watnong Ridge, 532
Watson, John, 368
Watson, Luke, 239
Watson, Thomas J., 433
Watson-Stillman Co., 547
Watt, James, 99
Wayne, Gen. Anthony, 230, 288, 348,
    392, 446, 512
Webb, George James, 169
Webb, John, 616
Webb, Capt. Thomas, 145
Webbville, 616
Webster, Daniel, 404
Weekstown, 604
Weems, Parson, 613
Welch, Roy Dickinson, 171
Weld, Angelina, 363

Weld, Theodore D., 363
Well-Meaning Society, 384
Wells Falls, 519
Wells Rapids, 452
Welsh, 132
Wendel, Paul, 293
Wendel family, 512
Wesley Lake, 682
West, Dean Andrew F., 379
West Creek, 559
West End, 681
West Indians, 505
West Jersey, 38, 39, 40, 174, 216, 217
West Jersey Camp-Meeting Ground, 660
West Jersey Press, 155
West Milford, 507
West New Jersey Proprietors' Office (Bur-
    lington), 222
West Orange, 342-3, 530
West Portal, 434
West Wildwood, 646
Westbrook, Johannes, 473
Westbrook Fort, site, 473
Wester, Otto, 570
Westfield, 547
Westfield Acres, 179, 236-7
Westinghouse Electric and Manufacturing
    Co., 316, 490
Westminster Choir School, 171, 389
Weston, Dr. Edward, 72, 337
Weston Electrical Instrument Co., 316, 337
Westville, 658
Weymouth Iron Works, site, 612
Whaling, 670
Wharton, Joseph, 604
Wheat, 89
Wheatena Co., 485
Whig Lane, 654
Whig Party, 81
Whilomville Stories, 156
Whippany, 531
Whippany River, 284
Whitall, Ann, 577
Whitall-Tatum Glass Co., 638
White, Bishop Alma, 550
White, Anthony, 311
White, Henry C., 562
White, Pearl, 164
White, Stanford, 554
White, Alma, College, 550
White Hart Tavern, site, 308
White Horse, 468
White Horse Hotel (Stratford), 599-600
White Horse Tavern, 468
Whitefield, Rev. George, 145, 300, 367
Whitefield's Tune, 168
Whitehouse, 432
Whitehouse Lake, 432
White's Tavern, 447
Whitesbog, 623
Whitesboro, 562
Whiteside, Walker, 164
Whitman, Walt, 154-6, 234, 599; tomb,
    235
Who's Who in America, 340
Who's Who in Art, 185
Wick, Capt. Henry, 289
Wick, Temperance, 289

Wickatunk, 555
Wickersham Commission, 67
"Widow's walk," 563
Wilbur, 403
Wild, John F., 597
Wild Honeysuckle, The, 152
Wilder, Thornton, 467
Wildwood, 646
Wildwood Crest, 646
Willet, Mr. and Mrs. William, 386
William the Silent, statue, 309
Williams, F. Ballard, 186
Williams, Deacon Israel, 612
Williams, Jesse Lynch, 158, 165
Williams, William Carlos, 160
Williams and Clark Fertilizer Co., 84
Williamson, Benjamin, 248
Williamson, Fred C., 604
Williamson, Gov. Isaac H., 247
Williamson, Jefferson, 563
Williamson, Dr. John Finley, 389
Williamstown, 612
Willits, Capt. Stephen, 667
Willow Tree Tavern, 584
Wilmington, Del., 578
Wilson, Alexander, 491
Wilson, Edmund, 159
Wilson, Pres. Woodrow, 35, 50-1, 58, 63,
    86, 140, 158, 376, 379, 384, 681
Wilsons Lake, 659
Winding Brook Farm, 454
Windsor, 571
Windsor, Eliza, 392
Winona's Rock, 449
Winter sports, xxix
Wise, P. H., 515
Wiss Cutlery Co., 316
Wistar, Caspar, 70, 181
"Witches' doors," 551
With Walt Whitman in Camden, 156
Witherspoon, Rev. John, 152, 375, 378,
    466, 489
Witt, "Whitey," 394
Wittman, Carl, 114
Wolf, Rev. Johann, 449
Woman suffrage, 44
Woman's Club of Elizabeth, 245
Women's Christian Temperance Union, 393
Women's Clubs, N. J. State Fed., 86, 437
Wood, Alan, Co., 480
Wood, Fannie, 548
Wood, Gar, Industries, Inc., 429
Wood, Jackanias, 610
Wood, John, 635

Woodbridge, 37, 111, 135, 547, 552
Woodbury, 628
Woodlynne, 650
Woodridge, 540
Woodruff, Samuel, 246
Woods, John, 111
Woodstown, 610, 630
Wool Council, 347
Woollcott, Alexander, 159, 532, 589
Woolley Fisheries, 683
Woolman, John, 41, 151, 296,
Woolston, John, 470
Woos family, 598
Workingmen's Party, 81
Working Men's Party of the United States,
    82
Works Progress Administration, 104, 260,
    330, 338, 424, 600
World Almanac, 549
World War, 51, 73, 103, 206, 265, 275,
    301, 322, 374, 431, 438, 664
World War Memorial (Atlantic City), 200
World War Monument (Englewood), 438
Worthington Pump, 544
Wrestling, xxix, 199
Wright, Henry, 179
Wright, Patience Lovell, 182, 208
Wright Aeronautical Co., 357
Wright-Martin Aircraft Corp., 301
Wrightstown, 618
Wyman, Isaac C., 380

Y.M.C.A., Industrial (Bayonne), 203
"Yarb folk," 131
Yardville, 571
Yarrow, William, 385
Ye Olde Historic Inn, 430
Yellow Frame, 455
Yewell, J. Floyd, 180
Yonkers-Alpine ferry, 437
Young, Clara Kimball, 164
Young, David, 531
Young, Capt. John L., 198
Young Nurseries, 549
Yungborn Nudist Camp, 495

ZMC-2, *The,* 623
ZR-3, *The,* 623
Zabriskie, Caspar, 538
Zabriskie, John, 539
Zabriskie, Peter, 260, 539
Zarephath, 550
Ziegfeld, Florenz, 164
Zoos, 199, 414, 442, 461, 513, 627, 653